W9-CTX-557

DATE DUE

			PRINTED IN U.S.A.

The **HUTCHINSON**

Concise
Dictionary
of
Music

The **HUTCHINSON**

Concise
Dictionary
of
Music

General Editor: Barrie Jones

FITZROY DEARBORN PUBLISHERS
CHICAGO · LONDON

any form or by any means,
ling, or by any information
ig from the Publisher.

The Hutchinson concise
  dictionary of music

FITZROY DEARBORN PUBLISHERS
919 North Michigan Avenue
Chicago, Illinois 60611
USA

or
FITZROY DEARBORN PUBLISHERS
310 Regent Street
London W1R 5AJ
England

Cataloging-in-Publication Data is available from the Library of Congress and the
British Library

ISBN 1–57958–178–1

First published in the US and UK 1999

Printed and bound in the United Kingdom by
The Bath Press Ltd, Bath, Somerset

Contents

Introduction

The English writer and publisher Hubert Foss differentiated between two kinds of reference book, contrasting 'those ponderous and almost complete tomes which one keeps on shelves and consults in quiet mood, and the pocket manuals which, ready at lathe or in taxi-driver's coat, offer the right amount of knowledge and understanding proper to the immediate situation'. Larger than most pockets yet kind to the purse, *The Hutchinson Concise Dictionary of Music* belongs to Foss's second category. Abridged from the acclaimed single-volume *Hutchinson Encyclopedia of Music* (1995), published in association with *BBC 'Music' Magazine*, and descended from the highly regarded *Everyman* (later *New Everyman*) *Dictionary of Music*, this new reference work draws directly on a long and distinguished line of musical expertise, in particular the accumulated scholarship of those who were involved in editing or revising its 'family' volumes (notably Eric Blom, Sir Jack Westrup, and David Fallows, and latterly David Cummings and Tallis Barker). However, every inherited entry has been thoroughly scrutinized, information has been updated in the light of recent research and about 100 new articles commensurate with the Dictionary's declared purpose have been commissioned.

The production of a more compact version of a large work that has already proved its usefulness requires a particular focus and a strict policy of selection. The chosen emphasis is the fundamentals of music, those technical and theoretical aspects which provide the foundation of any musical education. The volume thus comprises entries about the various musical genres, forms and the myriad instructions annotated in musical scores, biographies of composers (with lists of principal compositions), and information about significant works in the repertory, librettists, instruments and their mainstream repertory, instrument makers, theorists and musicologists, patrons, writers (on whose writings compositions are based), and some famous conductors in history. Excluded from its contents are biographies of instrumental performers and singers (apart from some performers who are also composers and some celebrated castrati), publishers, critics and writers on music, producers, directors, teachers and choreographers, as well as information about theatres and festivals.

With this sharp focus, *The Hutchinson Concise Dictionary of Music* addresses the needs of a wide range of users. Experienced and well-informed professional musicians, whatever many-volumed works of reference they may possess, occasionally have need also of one manageable book to which they can turn with the assurance that they will there be able to read a concise survey of some subject that interests them or find quickly some fact, name, date, musical term or opus number that has momentarily slipped their minds; avid concert-goers, enthusiastic CD collectors, and regular radio-listeners will equally welcome one which will inform without being beyond either the scope of their pockets or the depth of their understanding; and music students, whether as entrants for national examinations in the theory of music or candidates for more advanced qualifications such as GCSE, 'A' level, and some courses in higher education, will also find it an invaluable information resource on many counts. The Dictionary has been endorsed by the Open University as a recommended reference work for some of its music courses – it is a set text for *A214: Understanding Music: Elements, Techniques and Styles* – and it is fitting that two distinguished scholars of the Open University's Music Department, Professor Donald Burrows and Dr. Barrie Jones have been associated with the careful selection and editing of its contents.

The result of their labours is a balanced, coherent, and authoritative volume which provides an accurate and concise reference source for the core technical, biographical, organological, and other information vital to the comprehension and enjoyment of music. Remarkable for its high standards of scholarship, clarity of language, and the accessibility of its text, this Dictionary never makes formidable reading for the novice, pinpoints ample cross-references for the reader's further edification, and gives excellent value for money. Comprising approximately 7,500 entries and over 100 musical examples, it offers an indispensable storehouse of information to the layman and serves as a useful reminder to the expert as well as an invaluable research tool to the music student of all ages and in a wide variety of spheres.

ROBIN STOWELL
Professor of Music, Cardiff University

General Editor
Barrie Jones

Editorial Director
Hilary McGlynn

Managing Editor
Katie Emblen

Editors
Jane Anson
Eileen Auden
Małgorzata Nawrocka-Colquhoun
Peter Lewis

Technical Project Editor
Tracey Auden

Database Management
Nick Andrews

Production
Tony Ballsdon

Art and Design
Terence Caven

Stave Digitization
Tech Type, Abingdon

Typesetting
Mendip Communications Ltd,
Frome, Somerset

Acknowledgement
We are very grateful to Professor Burrows for his help and advice
in the early stages of compiling this book.

A

A the first note of the diatonic scale A–G, or A above middle C; orchestral ◊concert pitch.

The note A in the treble clef.

Aaron (Aron), Pietro (c. 1480–c. 1550) Italian monk and contrapuntist. He wrote on history and science of music; his *Toscanello* 1523 gives advice on musical practice. He worked in Imola and Venice, and entered the monastery of San Leonardo, Bergamo, in 1536.

ABA form in musical analysis, a compositional structure comprising three basic parts, in which the first section (A) is followed by a second, often contrasting section (B), before the original section (A) returns in the same or a varied state. It is a simple kind of ◊ternary form.

a battuta (Italian 'at the beat, with the beat') musical direction indicating that after a free passage the strict time is to be resumed.

Abbà-Cornaglia, Pietro (1851–1894) Italian composer. He studied at the Milan Conservatory and later became a teacher and music historian.

Works include: the operas *Isabella Spinola* (Milan, 1877), *Maria di Warden, Una partita di scacchi* (Pavia, 1892); Requiem; chamber music.

Abbado, Marcello (1926–) Italian composer and pianist, brother of Claudio Abbado. He studied with Ghedini at the Milan Conservatory, and since 1951 has held teaching posts in Venice, Piacenza, Pesaro,

and Milan; director of the Milan Conservatory 1972.

Works include: *Ciapo*, cantata (1945); *Costruziono* for five small orchestras (1964), concerto for violin, piano, and two chamber orchestras (1967), three string quartets (1947, 1953, 1969), concerto for piano, quartet, and orchestra (1969).

abbellimenti (Italian 'embellishments') ornaments, especially florid passages introduced into vocal music.

Abbey, John (1785–1859) English organ builder. He worked in Paris from 1826 and built many organs in France and South America.

Abe, Komei (1911–) Japanese composer and conductor. He studied in Tokyo and with Joseph Rosenstock in Germany. Professor of composition at Kyoto University 1969–74. His music is in a diatonic style.

Works include: two symphonies (1957, 1960), eleven string quartets (1935–82), serenade (1963), sinfonietta (1965), cello concerto (1942), piano concerto (1945), and piano sextet (1964).

Abegg Variations Schumann's op. 1, for piano, a set of variations on a theme constructed on the notes A Bb E G, and bearing the dedication 'à Mlle Pauline, Comtesse d'Abegg', who did not exist, though there was a family of that name. The existence of Meta Abegg has yet to be proved. The work was composed in 1830 and published in 1832.

Abel, Carl Friedrich (1723–1787) German musician and composer. He played the harpsichord and viola da gamba, and was a member of the court band at Dresden 1743–58. From 1759 he lived in London, where he was appointed chamber musician to Queen Charlotte.

Abel was joint promoter, with Johann Christian Bach, of the Bach-Abel Concerts (1765–81). He wrote a large quantity of instrumental music, of which the works for viola da gamba are perhaps the most notable. His 40 symphonies and overtures are notable for their advanced harmonic style.

Abélard, Pierre (1079–1142) French scholar and musician. He composed songs for his beloved, Héloïse, Latin Lamentations, planctus. He was castrated after secretly marrying Héloïse in 1118.

Abencérages, Les, ou L'Etendard de Grenade/The Abencerrages, or The Standard of Granada opera by Cherubini (libretto by V J E de Jouy, based on a novel by Jean-Pierre de Florian), produced Paris, Opéra, 6 April 1813. The story deals with Moorish adventures in Spain.

Abendmusik, or Abendmusiken (German 'evening music') evening performances of music of a semisacred character established by Tunder at Lübeck in the 1640s and becoming so famous there that they were imitated by other north German towns, especially Hamburg. They were held mainly during Advent.

Abert, Hermann (1871–1927) German musicologist of Czech descent. He was professor of music at Leipzig University in succession to Hugo Riemann from 1920 and at Berlin from 1923. He wrote many historical works, including a greatly enlarged edition of Jahn's *Mozart*.

Abgesang (German 'after-song') see ◊bar.

Abos, Girolamo (1715–1760) Maltese composer, especially of Italian opera and church music; several of his operas were also produced in London.

Abraham, Gerald (1904–1988) English musicologist, specialist in Russian music. He was professor of music at Liverpool University 1947–62, and Assistant Controller, Music, at the British Broadcasting Corporation (BBC) 1962–67. He edited volumes iv, vii, and ix of the *New Oxford History of Music* and coedited volume iii; he also wrote the *Concise Oxford History of Music*, 1979.

Abraham and Isaac Canticle II by Britten for alto, tenor, and piano. Composed 1952 for Ferrier and Pears and performed by them Nottingham, 21 January 1952.

Sacred ballad for baritone and chamber orchestra by Stravinsky (Hebrew text); composed 1962–64, first performed Jerusalem 23 August 1964.

Abramsky, Aleksandr (1898–1985) Russian composer. He studied at the Moscow Conservatory, and turned to Soviet ideology by writing an opera on the subject of life on a collective farm (*Laylikhon and Anarkhon*, 1943). His other works include a piano concerto (1941) and cantata, *Land of the Silent Lake* (1971).

Abreise, Die opera by d'Albert (libretto by F von Sporck, based on a play by August von Steigentesch), produced Frankfurt, 20 October 1898. The plot concerns a husband's early return from a journey to test his wife's fidelity.

Absil, Jean (1893–1974) Belgian composer. He studied at the Brussels Conservatory, where he became professor in 1931, after being appointed director of Etterbeek Music Academy in 1923. Among his influences were Hindemith, Milhaud, and Bartók.

Works include: the opera *Peau d'âne* (1937); ballet *Le Miracle de Pan*; radio opera *Ulysse et les Sirennes*; five symphonies (1920–70); four string quartets (1929–41); three string trios and other chamber music.

absolute music music that refers to nothing apart from itself. It is intended to be enjoyed purely for its sound, as opposed to ◊programme music, which is descriptive and has representational meaning.

absolute pitch, or perfect pitch in music, the ability to sing or to recognize by sound the pitch of a note, without any prior reference point with which to determine the particular note.

Abstrakte Oper no. 1 opera by Blacher (libretto by Werner Egk), first performed Frankfurt (concert), 28 June 1953; produced Mannheim, 17 October 1953. Text consists largely of nonsense words.

Abu Hassan Singspiel in one act by Weber (libretto by F C Hiemer), produced Munich, 4 June 1811. Abu and his wife attempt to feign death in order to gain a fortune.

Academic Festival Overture/Akademische Fest-Ouvertüre Brahms's op. 80, composed 1880 and first performed at Breslau (Wrocław in modern-day Poland), 4 January 1881, in acknowledgement of the honorary degree of doctor of philosophy, conferred on him by Breslau University in 1879. The thematic material is taken from German students' songs. The *Tragic Overture* was written as a companion piece.

Academie, or Akademie (German 'a little adagio') 18th-century German term for a concert.

Acante et Céphise *pastorale-héroïque* by Rameau (libretto by Marmontel), produced Paris, Opéra, 18 November 1751. Lovers are granted telepathic powers as protection against an evil bass.

a cappella (Italian 'in the style of the chapel') choral music sung without instrumental accompaniment. In modern music it is characteristic of gospel music, doo-wop, and the evangelical Christian church movement.

Accademia (Italian 'academy' from Plato's Academia) Italian society for the encouragement and furtherance of science and/or the arts. An 'Accademia di Platone' was founded, on Plato's model, at the Medici court of Florence in 1470. The earliest academy of any importance devoted primarily to music was the 'Accademia Filarmonica' of Verona (1543); later ones included the 'Accademia di Santa Cecilia' at Rome (1584) and the 'Accademia Filarmonica' at Bologna (1666). In France the movement began with the foundation of the 'Académie de poésie et de musique' by Baïf and Thibaut at Paris in 1570, with the aim of promoting the ideals of ◊*musique mesurée*.

accelerando (Italian 'quickening') in musical notation, indicating a gradual increase in tempo.

accent the distinctive articulation of individual notes or passages. Accents are dynamic, adding loudness; agogic, enlarging the beat (as in Viennese waltz rhythm); metrical, shifting the beat, as in syncopation; or timbre, as in melody accentuation using a wah-wah note.

Normally the main accent is on the first beat after the bar-line, and in any music divided into bars of more than three beats there is usually a secondary accent, less strongly stressed. Strong accents are marked by the sign > or by the abbreviations *sf* (*sforzando*) or *fz* (*forzando*).

An acciaccatura in Bach's Partita no. 3.

acciaccatura (Italian 'crushed') in music, an ornamental ◊grace note played simultaneously with, or just before, a normal note. It is released almost instantaneously. The notation is a ◊quaver in small type with a line through the stem.

accidental in music notation, a sharp (♯), flat (♭), or natural (♮) sign preceding a note which changes the pitch of the note by a semitone up (♯), down (♭), or back to normal (♮).

Music written in 'black-note' keys may require the rarer double sharp (𝄪) and double flat (♭♭) signs, indicating a change in pitch of a full tone.

accolade a brace used to join several staves.

accompaniment music and players providing a bass line, chord structure, and beat in support of a solo performer.

The accompaniment may provide harmonic support (as in the continuo playing of the 17th and 18th centuries), melodic imitation and continuation of the solo part (as in many 19th-century songs), atmospheric background (as in orchestral accompaniments to operatic arias), and so on. The art of the piano accompanist was raised to a high level in the 20th century by figures such as Gerald Moore.

Accompaniment to a Film Scene/Begleitungsmusik zu einer Lichtspielszene orchestral work by Schoenberg, op. 34. Composed 1929–30; first performed Berlin, 6 November 1930, conductor Klemperer. The three movements are for imaginary scenes.

accordatura (Italian 'at pleasure') the notes to which a string instrument is tuned.

accordion musical instrument of the free-reed organ type, comprising left and right wind chests connected by flexible, pleated bellows. The accordionist's right hand plays the melody on a piano-style keyboard of 26–34 keys, while the left hand has a system of push buttons for selecting single notes or chord harmonies.

It was patented under the name of Handäoline by Friedrich Buschmann (1805–1864) in Berlin in 1822, and by Cyrill Damien (1772–1847) under the name Akkordion (German 'harmony') in Vienna in 1829. The accordion spread throughout the world and can be heard in the popular music of Germany, France, China, Russia, and the USA.

Achille opera by Paer (libretto by G di Gamera), produced Vienna, Kärntnertortheater, 6 June 1801; Achilles and Agamemnon are allies in war but rivals during the siege of

Troy. Contains a funeral march said to have been admired by Beethoven.

Achille et Polyxène opera by Lully and Colasse (libretto by J G de Campistron), produced Paris, Opéra, 7 November 1687. Left unfinished at Lully's death and completed by his pupil Colasse.

Achille in Sciro/Achilles in Scyros opera by Caldara (libretto by Metastasio), produced Vienna, Burgtheater, 13 February 1739. Achilles delayed by love on his way to Troy. Also settings by Jommelli (Vienna, 1749), Hasse (Naples, 1759), Naumann (Palermo, 1767), Paisiello (St Petersburg, 1778), Pugnani (Turin, 1785).

Acide ◊festa teatrale by Haydn (librettist G A Migliavacca), produced Eisenstadt, 11 November 1763. Only fragments survive.

Aci, Galatea e Polifemo Italian serenata by Handel, composed Naples, 1708.

Acis and Galatea masque for soloists, chorus, and orchestra by G F Handel (libretto by John Gay, with additions by Hughes, Pop, and Dryden), composed c. 1718, performed Cannons, near Edgware; first public performance London, King's Theatre, 10 June 1732. A composite, bilingual version of this and Handel's Italian serenata (1708) received several performances in 1732. Galatea transforms Acis into a fountain, after he has been killed by the jealous Polyphemus.

Acis et Galatée/Acis and Galatea opera by Lully (libretto by J G de Campistron), produced at Anet at an entertainment given for the Dauphin by the Duke of Vendôme, 6 September 1686, first performed Paris, 17 September 1686.

acousmatic music music in which the composer uses electronic or computer-based means to shape sounds directly, without the use of notation or performers. The original sounds may be recorded or synthesized, or both. More or less synonymous with electro-acoustic music.

acoustic term describing a musical instrument played without electrical amplification or assistance, for example an acoustic guitar or acoustic piano. It is also a term used by musicians to characterize room response, an important factor in performance. A so-called 'bright' acoustic provides a lively reverberation while a 'dry' or 'muddy' acoustic is lacking in response; see ◊acoustics.

The Royal Festival Hall, London, designed with a neoclassical dry acoustic, had electrically assisted reverberation installed shortly after opening, in response to objections from musicians who performed there.

acoustics the science of sound generation and propagation, embracing psychoacoustics, a branch of communications science.

acronym any coded reference to a name using the letter-names of notes to form a motif. The most widely quoted is B-A-C-H, playing on the German note names B (B♭)-A-C-H (B♮); Schumann's *Abegg Variations* 1830 is dedicated to his friend Meta Abegg; Berg's *Chamber Concerto* 1923–25 includes motivic references to himself and Schoenberg.

D-S-C-H is the acronym for Dimitri SCHostakovich (German spelling, S being 'Es' or E♭), the basis of a monumental *Passacaglia on DSCH* 1961–62 by Ronald Stevenson. Boulez's tribute to Paul Sacher in *Messagesquisse* 1977 incorporates the French 'Re' for R.

action the internal mechanism of a keyboard instrument, such as the piano, harpsichord, or organ, which links the keys to the strings or pipes when the keys are depressed. On a string instrument, it refers to the space between the strings and the ◊fingerboard.

action musicale (French 'in two parts') a term used by Vincent d'Indy for some of his operas, evidently on the model of Wagner's 'Handlung für Musik'.

act tune term used in 17th-century England for a musical intermezzo or entr'acte performance between the acts of a play.

Actus Tragicus name often given to Bach's church cantata no. 106, *Gottes Zeit ist die allerbeste Zeit*. Composed c. 1707 for a funeral.

adagietto (Italian *a tempo*) direction indicating a pace slightly quicker than adagio. Best-known example is the fourth movement of Mahler's 5th symphony.

adagio (Italian 'at ease', 'leisurely') in musical notation, indicating a slow pace, slightly faster than or approximately the same as ◊lento, depending on the historical period in which the music was written. It is also used as the title of a piece of music, or as the distinguishing title of a single movement.

Adam, Adolphe Charles (1803–1856) French composer of light operas and founder of the Théâtre National, Paris, in 1847. His stage works include *Le Postillon de Lonjumeau/ The Coachman of Lonjumeau* (1836) and *Si j'étais roi/If I Were King* (1852), but he is best remembered for his ballet score for *Giselle* (1841). Around 80 of his works were staged.

He wrote about 20 vaudeville pieces for three Paris theatres, 1824–29, then an operetta, *Pierre et Catherine,* for the Opéra-Comique in 1829, and his first opera, *Danilowa,* in 1830. He was allowed to study at the Paris Conservatory only as an amateur, but eventually became professor of composition there in 1849. His autobiographical *Souvenirs d'un musicien/A Musician's Memories* and *Derniers souvenirs d'un musicien/Last Memories of a Musician* were published 1857–59.

Works include: OPERA *Le Châlet* (1834), *Le Postillon de Lonjumeau* (1836), *La Poupée de Nuremberg, Si j'étais roi* (1852), *Falstaff* (1856), *Richard en Palestine* (after Scott).

BALLET *Faust* (1833), *Giselle* (1841).

Adam de la Halle (c. 1240–c. 1290) French lyric poet, dramatist, and composer. His *Jeu de la feuillée* c. 1277 is one of the earliest French comedies. His *Le Jeu de Robin et Marion,* written in Italy c. 1282, is a theatrical work with dialogue and songs set to what were apparently popular tunes of the day. It is sometimes called the forerunner of comic opera.

Adams, John Coolidge (1947–   ) US composer and conductor. He was director of the New Music Ensemble 1972–81, and artistic adviser to the San Francisco Symphony Orchestra from 1978. His minimalist techniques are displayed in *Electric Wake* (1968), *Heavy Metal* (1971), *Light over Water* (1983), *Harmonielehre* (1984–85), and the operas *Nixon in China* (1987) and *The Death of Klinghoffer* (1991).

Adam und Eva opera by Theile (libretto by C Richter), produced Hamburg, at the opening of the first established German opera house, Theater beim Gänsemarkt, 12 January 1678.

Adam Zero ballet by Bliss (scenario by M Benthall, choreography by Robert Helpmann), produced London, Covent Garden, 8 April 1946.

adaptation (Latin *adaptare,* 'to fit to') in literature and music, term used to denote the modification of a particular art form to allow its suitable expression in another form, for example the adaptation of a play from a novel or the adaptation of a piece of music for a different type of instrument.

added sixth term invented by Rameau (*sixte ajoutée*) to describe the addition of a sixth

An added sixth in the key of C major.

from the bass to a subdominant chord when it is followed by the tonic chord.

additional accompaniments additional orchestral parts added to old oratorios and other works left by the composers in an incomplete state; to be played originally by the continuo player at the organ or harpsichord.

The most familiar examples are Mozart's additional accompaniments for Handel's *Messiah.*

'Adelaide' song by Beethoven to words by Friedrich von Matthisson, composed 1795–96 and dedicated to the poet.

'Adelaïde' Concerto violin concerto edited by Marius Casadesus in the early 1930s from a sketch supposedly written by Mozart and dedicated to Princess Adélaïde of France in 1766. It was in fact composed by Casadesus.

Adelson e Salvini opera by Bellini (his first) with libretto by A L Tottola. Produced Naples, San Sebastiano Conservatory, early 1825; revised 1826 with recitative replacing dialogue. Salvini, infatuated by Adelson's fiancée Nelly, recovers his senses after believing he has killed her.

Adieux, l'absence et le retour, Les/Farewell, Absence and Return title given by Beethoven's publisher for his piano sonata in Eb major, op. 81a, composed in 1809–10 and dedicated to the Archduke Rudolph to commemorate his absence from Vienna during the occupation by the French.

Adler, Guido (1855–1941) Czech–German musicologist and editor. He studied in Vienna, and was appointed professor of musicology at Prague University in 1885, becoming professor in Vienna, 1898, in succession to Eduard Hanslick. He wrote many books on music including studies of Wagner (1904) and Mahler (1916), and edited *Handbuch der Musikgeschichte* (1924).

Adler, Samuel (1928–   ) German-born US composer. He moved to the USA aged 11 and studied with Piston and Thompson at Harvard, and with Copland and Koussevitzky at Tanglewood. He was professor of composition at Eastman School, Rochester, from 1966.

Works include: the operas *The Outcasts of Poker Flat* (1962) and *The Wrestler* (1972); *The Disappointment,* reconstruction of an American ballad opera of 1767; six symphonies (1953–83); organ concerto (1970); concerto for orchestra (1977); flute concerto (1977); seven string quartets (1945–81); four violin sonatas (1948–65); *From out of Bondage,* cantata (1969);

The Vision of Isaiah for bass, chorus, and orchestra (1963); piano concerto (1983).

ad lib(itum) (Latin 'freely') musical direction indicating that a passage may be played freely according to the performer's invention. The term also applies to an instrumental part that may be added or omitted in the performance of a work.

Adlung, Jakob (1699–1762) German organist and scholar. He was organist at Erfurt from 1727, and professor at the Gymnasium there from 1741. He wrote important music treatises.

Admeto, rè di Tessaglia/Admetus, King of Thessaly opera by Handel (librettist N F Haym or P A Rolli), produced London, King's Theatre, Haymarket, 31 January 1727. Alcestis promises to sacrifice herself to save Admetus; a vehicle for the rival sopranos Cuzzoni and Faustina Bordoni.

Adorno, Theodor Wiesengrund (1903–1969) German philosopher, composer, and musicologist. Deeply influenced by the thought of Karl Marx, Adorno joined the influential Institute for Social Research in Frankfurt in 1931, becoming known as a member of the 'Frankfurt School' of sociologists. At the rise of Fascism he fled first to Oxford (1935–38) and then to the USA, eventually returning to Frankfurt as Professor of Philosophy in 1949.

As a young man, Adorno studied composition with Alban Berg, and he remained a great defender of the New Music of the Second Viennese School, which he saw as the 'authentic voice' of 20th-century music. He wrote prolifically on music, combining a practitioner's knowledge of compositional technique with his philosophical training, producing writings of forbidding intellectual complexity, but also of undoubted and profound insight. He is particularly known for his studies of individual composers, such as *Philosophy of Modern Music* (1948, on Schoenberg and Stravinsky), *In Search of Wagner* (1952), and *Mahler: A Musical Physiognomy* (1960).

Adrastus (lived 4th century BC) Greek philosopher. He was a pupil of Aristotle, and wrote a treatise on acoustics, *Harmonicon biblia tria*.

Adriana Lecouvreur opera by Cilea (libretto by A Colautti, based on the play *Adrienne Lecouvreur* by Scribe and E Legouvé), produced Milan, Teatro Lirico, 6 November 1902. Adriana meets a violent death from poisoned violets, given by a rival in love.

Adriano in Siria/Hadrian in Syria opera by Pergolesi (libretto by Metastasio), produced Naples, Teatro San Bartolommeo, with the intermezzi *Livietta e Tracollo*, 25 October 1734. Also settings by Caldara (Vienna, 1732), Galuppi (Turin, 1740), Hasse (Dresden, 1752), J C Bach (London, 1765), Holzbauer (Mannheim, 1768), Anfossi (Padua, 1777), Cherubini (Livorno, 1782), Mayr (Venice, 1798).

a due (Italian 'in two parts') generally written '*a 2*'. The term is also used in the opposite sense in orchestral scores where pairs of instruments are to play in unison.

Aegyptische Helena (Strauss). See ◊*Ägyptische Helena*.

Aenéas ballet with chorus by Roussel. Composed 1935, first performed Brussels 31 July 1935.

Aeneas i Carthago opera by J M Kraus (libretto by J H Kellgren), produced Stockholm, 18 November 1799; revived in concert form, Stockholm and New York 1980.

Aeolian harp wind-blown musical instrument consisting of a shallow soundbox supporting gut strings at low tension and tuned to the same pitch. It produces an eerie harmony that rises and falls with the changing pressure of the wind. It originated in India and China, becoming popular in parts of central Europe during the 19th century. The instrument is named after Aeolus, the god of the winds in Greek mythology.

Aeolian mode the mode or scale A–G, centred around and beginning on A, which uses only the notes of the C major scale.

aerophone one of the four main classes of musical instrument used in the original ◊Sachs-Hornbostel system, the others being ◊idiophone, ◊membranophone, and ◊chordophone. In instruments which are aerophones, the air itself is the primary vibrating agent. Subdivisions of aerophones distinguish between a wide range of types of instrument, but the class as a whole accommodates flutes and instruments of the orchestral brass family.

Aeschylus (525–456 BC) Greek dramatist. His tragedies, based on mythical history, inspired generations of composers. Amongst works based on Aeschylus' themes are: ◊**Fauré** (*Prométhée*), **Halévy** (*Prometheus*), **Hauer** (ditto), **Honegger** (*Prometheus* and *Les Suppliantes*), **Meyerbeer** (*Eumenides*), **Milhaud** (*Agamemnon*, *Choéphares*, and *Eumenides*), **Orff** (*Prometheus*), **Parry** (*Agamemnon*),

Pizzetti (ditto), **Taneiav** (*Oresteia*), **Weingart-ner** (*Orestes*).

aetherophone electrophonic musical instrument which produces notes from the air. The transitions between the notes produce a sliding wail like that of a siren. It was invented by Lev Theremin of Leningrad in 1924.

The pitch of the note is determined by the position of the player's hand, but skill and judgement are needed to find the notes of the chromatic scale. See also ◊theremin.

Affektenlehre (German 'doctrine of affections') 18th-century aesthetic theory, associated particularly with J J Quantz and C P E Bach, according to which music should be directly expressive of particular emotions. See ◊*Empfindsamer Stil.*

affettuoso (Italian 'affectionate, feeling') in musical direction, 'with tenderness'.

affrettando (Italian 'urging, hastening') in music, term often used to indicate emotional pressure as well as increase in speed.

Afranio Albonese (c. 1480–c. 1560) Italian priest. He was canon at Ferrara, and invented the phagotus.

Africaine, L'/The African Girl (original title *Vasco da Gama*), opera by Meyerbeer (libretto by Scribe), produced Paris, Opéra, 28 April 1865, after Meyerbeer's death. After sailing away from his native Portugal, explorer Vasco is rescued by tropic queen Sélika, whom he marries according to local custom. She later kills herself when he is seen with former love Inés.

African music generally, traditional music from the area of Africa south of the Sahara desert. The continent of Africa is the home of thousands of different musical styles, but these divide roughly into two regional traditions: North African music, which is strongly influenced by Islam and Arab music; and the music of sub-Saharan Africa (sometimes called 'Black Africa'), which many people consider to be 'true' African music. The music of western, central, and southern Africa is based on ◊rhythm much more than ◊melody or ◊harmony, and so ◊percussion instruments, especially drums, almost always play a prominent part.

The huge number of different musical traditions and styles in Africa makes generalization almost impossible, although there are certain predominant features that enable a very crude breakdown of the continent into two separate musical cultures: that of the sub-

Saharan peoples, and that of northern Africa. Broadly speaking, this division is one between the truly indigenous music of the South, and the Arab-influenced music of the North. Within these two categories there are naturally many subdivisions, and some African music falls outside either classification – such as that of Madagascar and parts of East Africa, which has been influenced by the music of South East Asia; and music in Egypt and Ethiopia, influenced by Coptic Christianity. Used loosely, however, the term 'African music' is generally taken to mean the traditional music of western, central, and southern Africa.

music in sub-Saharan Africa The main distinguishing feature of practically all traditional music south of the Sahara is its basis in rhythm, rather than melody or harmony, and its consequent predominance of percussion instruments. Music is almost always a group activity with an emphasis on polyphonic forms resulting from group improvisation on short, simple themes, and ◊cross rhythms formed by simultaneous performance of different rhythmic patterns. These rhythmic ◊ostinatos appear complex to the western ear, partly because of their juxtaposition with one another, but also because of their frequent use of irregular subdivisions of the beat – for example, grouping a sequence of twelve beats as $4 + 3 + 5$. The melodies in most African music are comparatively simple, being based on a ◊diatonic or ◊pentatonic scale, often only consisting of a few notes, with a static underlying harmony; because of this, tuned instruments have tended to remain few and simple, in contrast to the vast array of percussion instruments.

vocal music The same basic principles apply as much to vocal music as instrumental music: unlike the monodic folk music of many other cultures, traditional African music is primarily polyphonic and rhythmic. It is also very much a group activity, consequently there is much less evidence of solo song, except in areas with some Islamic influence, such as Nigeria, where the griot intones or sings traditional stories. The commonest form of vocal polyphony is the call-and-response pattern, with a soloist improvising a melody between choruses, but there are many other forms of group improvisation in as many as eight different voices. Much instrumental music also imitates the tone patterns of speech, and many musical instruments are able to 'talk': the so-called talking drums in particular are often used to communicate with one another, or to address the dancers, either praising them or giving instructions.

drums The drum is the most commonly found of all instruments in African music, and is also the most varied. It has been suggested that this ubiquity is due to the drum's use as a means of communication as well as being a musical instrument, and this is certainly the case with the talking drums of Nigeria, but it is more likely merely a consequence of the primarily rhythmic musical language. African drums take many forms, from the simple hollowed-out tree trunk to the hourglass-shaped, double-headed talking drums capable of varying pitch, but drummaking is a respected operation and the maker is usually a highly skilled artisan.

The simplest form is the slit drum, made from a hollowed log with a slit running lengthways, either side of which the wood is carved to give two distinct pitches, but the most variety is found in drums with membrane heads. Drumheads are made of a variety of animal skins, including goat, leopard, cowhide, sheepskin, and deer, and these are stretched over a resonant body, the most common forms of which are either cylindrical or bowl-shaped. Drums are made in a multiplicity of shapes and sizes: single-headed, either open or closed at the other end; or double-headed. Although drums are often played by hand, variously shaped sticks of hardwood are also employed. Talking drums are tuned and capable of producing a number of different notes – the 'language' they speak is not merely rhythmic, but depends also on the relative pitches of the notes.

other musical instruments It is not only the drums that are used to imitate language; almost all instruments in African music mimic speech patterns to a certain extent. Other percussion instruments include metallophones such as the **gong-gong**, a double bell, and various other gongs and bells; several versions of the xylophone, such as the **balafon**, which are made of a series of hard wooden strips arranged on a frame above gourd resonators; and the **mbira** or **sanza** (sometimes called the thumb piano or hand piano), made from a resonant board on which there is a set of metal tongues plucked with the thumb and fingers.

There are also a number of string instruments, the most common of which is the **musical bow** – similar to the hunting bow, but attached to any of a number of resonators such as gourds, or in the case of the Ugandan ground bow, a covered hole in the ground. Lute- and harp-like instruments are also found, particularly in central and western Africa, and include the ◊kora, a 21-string instrument from Mali. Less common in sub-Saharan countries are bowed string instruments, although varieties of fiddle are to be found in countries where there has been Islamic influence.

Wind instruments, although widespread, tend to be simple in comparison. There are rudimentary horns and trumpets, and many examples of flute or whistle, and in the north of the region forms of the Arab oboe, but the melodic range of these instruments is limited.

music in northern Africa Much of northern Africa has a basically Islamic culture, and the music of these countries is much more 'Arabic' than 'African'. Unlike sub-Saharan African music, it is primarily monophonic and melodic in structure, very often performed by solo performers or soloists with simple accompaniment, and there is much less emphasis on rhythm. As a consequence, it uses comparatively few percussion instruments in a secondary role to the many sophisticated string and wind instruments, which are usually Arabic in origin.

influence of African music African music and its rhythms have influenced much of the ethnic music of other continents, including the distinctive rhythms of much Latin American popular music, and have formed the principal component of jazz. The move towards more complex rhythmic structures, and indeed a rhythmic rather than harmonic basis, in western classical music has shown itself in an increased use of percussion instruments – many of them African in origin – and has prompted many composers to study traditional African music. This influence is most clearly seen in the work of the ◊minimalist composers such as Philip ◊Glass and Steve ◊Reich, but has had an effect on the whole spectrum of western art music.

modern African music Due to the colonization of Africa, and particularly as communication improves worldwide, the dissemination of western culture has increased: the process of influence now works both ways, as music from the west – especially pop and rock music – can be heard in all but the remotest parts of Africa. Although this has meant the virtual disappearance of traditional music in some urban areas, it has also given rise to hybrid forms: **highlife** was one of the first of these, appearing in the early 20th century in West Africa, followed by the now-familiar Southern African **kwela** in the 1950s, **juju** in Nigeria, and **congolese** in the Democratic Republic of Congo.

Age of Anxiety, The second symphony by Leonard Bernstein (after the poem by W H Auden), first performed Boston, 8 April 1949, conductor Koussevitzky.

Age of Gold, The/Zolotyi vek ballet by Shostakovich, op. 22. Produced Leningrad, 26 October 1930; choreography by E Kaplan and V Vaynonen; concerns activities of a Stalinist football team.

agitato (Italian 'agitated') in musical notation, indicating energetic, excited expression. If not part of the initial tempo designation (for example, *allegro agitato*), it implies a faster tempo than the preceding material.

Agnes von Hohenstaufen opera by Spontini (libretto by E Raupach), produced Berlin, Opera, 12 June 1829. Heinrich rescues Agnes from the evil King Philip of France; revived Florence 1954.

Agnus Dei (Latin 'Lamb of God') the fifth and last item of the Ordinary of the ◊Mass. Originally a part of the Litany, it was first introduced into the Roman Mass towards the end of the 7th century. It is not present in the Ambrosian rite. Its text is tripartite in structure, and its music in its simplest form consists of three statements of the same melody.

More complex plainsong settings exist and in the later Middle Ages numerous additional melodies were written. The Agnus Dei is naturally included in polyphonic settings of the Mass Ordinary, and in later settings of the same series of texts.

agogic a musical accent, affecting pulse and rhythm rather than dynamics, increasing the duration of a particular note. 'Agogic' also applies more broadly to all types of rhythm-related expression, such as ◊rubato and ◊rallentando.

Agon (Greek 'contest') ballet for 12 dancers by Stravinsky; composed 1953–57 first performed (concert) Los Angeles, 17 June 1957; produced New York, 1 December 1957,

choreographer Balanchine. Stravinsky's first music in serial idiom.

agréments ◊ornamentation of 17th-century French music, adopted as standard notation throughout Europe later in the Baroque period.

Agricola, Alexander (Alexander Ackerman) (1446–1506) Flemish composer. He is one of the most florid continental composers of the late 15th century, writing in a contrapuntal and decorative style. He served at the court of Galeazzo Maria Sforza, Duke of Milan, during the early 1470s, as well as with Lorenzo the Magnificent in Florence.

After a brief period at Mantua he returned to the Low Countries, and his name appears in the accounts of Cambrai Cathedral for 1475–76. After a second visit to Italy he entered in 1500 the service of Philip the Handsome, Duke of Austria (Philip I of Spain from 1504), whom he accompanied on journeys to Paris and Spain. During his second visit to Spain Philip died of fever, Agricola apparently dying at the same time. Agricola's epitaph (printed by Rhaw in 1538) states that he died at the age of 60, the date of death being established by his disappearance from Philip's court rolls.

Works include: 8 Masses, 2 Credos, 25 motets, and 93 secular pieces.

Agricola, Martin (Martin Sore) (1486–1556) German music theorist and composer. His most important treatise was a work in verse on musical instruments, *Musica instrumentalis deudsch* 1528 (based on Virdung's *Musica getutscht* 1511), and he contributed three pieces to Georg Rhaw's *Newe deudsche geistliche Gesenge* 1544.

Agrippina opera by Handel (libretto by V Grimani), produced Venice, Teatro San Giovanni Crisostomo, 26 December 1709. Wife of Roman emperor has Poppea as a rival in the promotion of her son, Nero.

Ägyptische Helena, Die/The Egyptian Helen opera by Richard Strauss (libretto by H von Hofmannsthal), produced Dresden, 6 June 1928. Errant Helen is forgiven by cuckolded husband.

1 A - gnus De - i, qui tol - lis pec - ca - ta mun-di: 1 mi - se - re - re no - bis
2   2
3   3 do - na no - bis pa - cem

A plainsong setting of the Agnus Dei.

Aho, Kalevi (1949–) Finnish composer. His music has developed from Russian symphonic influences, through atonality to postmodernism. He studied with Rautavaara in Helsinki and Boris Blacher in Berlin.

Works include: the opera *Insect Life* (1985–87), seven symphonies (1969–88), concertos for violin, cello, and piano (1981–89), three string quartets, oboe quintet (1973), solo violin sonata (1973), and accordion sonata (1984).

Aida opera by Verdi (libretto by A Ghislanzoni, based on a scenario by F A F Mariette and outlined in French by C Du Locle), produced Cairo, 24 December 1871; first performed in Italy, Milan, La Scala, 8 February 1872. Love triangle among (and eventually under) the pyramids.

Aiglon, L'/The Eaglet opera by Honegger and Ibert (libretto by H Cain, based on Rostand's play), produced Monte Carlo, 11 March 1937.

air see ◊ayre.

Airborne Symphony choral work by Marc Blitzstein in praise of the US Air Force Corps, in which the composer served during World War II; first performed New York, 23 March 1946.

Ajo nell'imbarazzo, L'/The Tutor in a Fix opera by Donizetti (libretto by J Ferretti), produced Rome, Teatro Valle, 4 February 1824.

Akeroyde, Samuel (lived 17th century) English composer. He was Musician in Ordinary to James II in 1687 and later to William and Mary. He contributed many songs to various collections and to the third part of Durfey's *Don Quixote* in 1696, the music to the first two of which had been written by Purcell the year before his death.

Akhnaten opera by Philip Glass (libretto by the composer with S Goldman, R Israel, and R Riddell), produced Stuttgart, 24 March 1984. The story is based on the hermaphrodite, monotheist Pharaoh of the 18th dynasty.

Akimenko, Feodor Stepanovich (1876–1945) Russian composer. He was a pupil of Balakirev and Rimsky-Korsakov in St Petersburg. He taught in the court choir, where he had been a chorister, but lived in France 1903–06 and settled there after the Russian Revolution. He was Stravinsky's first composition teacher.

Works include: the opera *The Queen of the Alps* (1914); orchestral and chamber music; sonatas; numerous piano works include *Sonate fantastique*.

Akutagawa, Yasushi (1925–1989) Japanese composer. He was active in Tokyo as a conductor and in promoting new music.

Works include: the opera *L'Orphée in Hiroshima* (1967), four ballets, including *Paradise Lost* (1951); *Ostinato Sinfonica* (1967), *Rhapsody* for orchestra (1971).

al (Italian 'at the, to the') in music, word used in various combinations with nouns, such as **al fine**.

Alain, Jehan (Ariste) (1911–1940) French composer. At the Paris Conservatory he studied organ with Marcel Dupré and composition with Paul Dukas and Roger-Ducasse. He became a church organist in Paris in 1935, but served in World War II and was killed in action.

Works include: numerous choral compositions, mainly sacred; three dances for orchestra; chamber music; piano and organ works; songs.

***à la manière de...* (French 'in the manner of...')** two sets of piano pieces by Casella and Ravel imitating the styles of Wagner, Fauré, Brahms, Debussy, Richard Strauss, Franck, Borodin, d'Indy, Chabrier, and Ravel.

alba type of troubadour-trouvère song, in which the singer watches for daybreak on behalf of two lovers (*Reis glorios*, by Guiraut de Bornelh). As used by the Minnesinger it was called *Tagelied*.

Albéniz, Isaac (1860–1909) Spanish nationalist composer and pianist. His works include numerous ◊zarzuelas and operas, the orchestral suites *Española* (1886) and *Catalonia* (1899–1908) (with the assistance of Paul Dukas), and 250 piano works including the *Iberia* suite (1906–09).

Born in Cataluña, Albéniz appeared in public as a pianist at the age of four.

Albéniz, Mateo Pérez de (c. 1755–1831) Spanish composer of church and keyboard music. He was maestro de capilla at Logroño and San Sebastian.

Albéniz, Pedro (1795–1855) Spanish pianist and composer, son of Mateo Pérez de Albéniz. He was organist at various towns from the age of 13 and in 1830 became professor of piano at Madrid Conservatory and first organist at the royal chapel in 1834. He was appointed piano teacher to Queen Isabella and the Infanta Maria Luisa in 1841. He wrote a method for piano, about 70 piano works, and some songs.

Albert, Eugen (Eugène Francis Charles) d' (1864–1932) French-English (later Germanized) composer and pianist, son of C L N d'Albert. He appeared with great success as a pianist, notably in Bach, Liszt, and Beethoven, and later went to Vienna for further study under Hans Richter, finishing with a course under Liszt. During World War I he repudiated his British birth, declaring himself to be entirely German. Of his 20 operas, only *Tiefland* (1903) has had any real success. The rest of his considerable output has largely fallen into neglect.

Although born in Scotland, he came from Newcastle upon Tyne, and after being taught by his father as a precociously gifted child, he went as Newcastle scholar to the National Training School in London (later the Royal College of Music). In 1892 he married Teresa Carreño, but they were divorced in 1895 (d'Albert married six times). In 1907 he succeeded Joseph Joachim as director of the Hochschule für Musik in Berlin.

Works include: OPERA *Der Rubin* (after Hebbel) (Karlsruhe, 1893), *Ghismonda, Gernot, Die Abreise* (Frankfurt, 1898), *Kain, Der Improvisator, Tiefland, Flauto solo, Tragaldabas (Der geborgte Ehemann), Izeÿl* (Hamburg, 1909), *Die verschenkte Frau, Liebesketten* (Vienna, 1912), *Die toten Augen* (Dresden, 1916), *Der Stier von Olivera* (Leipzig, 1918), *Revolutionshochzeit, Scirocco, Mareika von Nymwegen, Der Golem, Die schwarze Orchidee* (Leipzig, 1928), *Die Witwe von Ephesus, Mister Wu* (unfinished, completed by Blech).

OTHER *Der Mensch und das Leben*, choral work in six parts; symphony in F; overtures *Esther* and *Hyperion*; two string quartets; piano suite and sonata.

Albert, Heinrich (1604–1651) German poet, organist, and composer. He studied music at Dresden with Heinrich Schütz, who was his uncle. His parents, however, compelled him to read law at Leipzig University; but in 1626 he set out for Königsberg, was taken prisoner by the Swedes, and at last reached that city in 1628, resuming music studies with Stobäus. In 1631 he was appointed organist at the Old Church there, and became member of the Königsberg school of poets.

Works include: Te Deum, many hymns to words of his own, secular songs.

Albert, Stephen (1941–1992) US composer. His music embraces a variety of styles, including electronic. He won the Pulitzer Prize in 1985 for his symphony *Riverrun* (after James Joyce). A second symphony was posthumously premiered by the New York Philharmonic Orchestra in 1995.

He studied with Darius Milhaud, Roy Harris, and George Rochberg.

Works include: *Supernatural Songs* for soprano and chamber orchestra (1963); *Imitations* for string quartet (1964); *Winter Songs* for tenor and orchestra (1965); *Bacchae* for narrator, chorus, and orchestra (1968); *Cathedral Music* (1972); *Voices Within* for orchestra (1975); *Winterfire* for seven players (1979); *Into Eclipse* for tenor and orchestra (1981); *Riverrun* (1984); *Flower on the Mountain* for soprano and chamber orchestra (1985); *Processionals* for orchestra (1987); violin concerto (1988); cello concerto (1990); *Distant Hills Coming Nigh* for soprano, baritone, and chamber ensemble (1991); *Wind Canticle* for clarinet and ensemble (1992).

Albert Herring opera by Britten (libretto by E Crozier, based on Maupassant's story *Le Rosier de Madame Husson*), produced Glyndebourne, 20 June 1947. Much gaiety at a village fête.

Alberti, Domenico (c. 1710–1746) Italian singer, harpsichordist, and composer, a pupil of Antonio Lotti. The characteristic left-hand accompaniment figuration in his keyboard music has given his name to the Alberti bass.

Alberti, Gasparo (c. 1480–c. 1560) Italian composer, a singer at the church of Sta Maria Maggiore, Bergamo, from 1508. He was one of the earliest exponents of the compositional technique known as *cori spezzati* (Italian 'broken choir'), where a body of singers is divided into smaller groups performing alternately and all together.

Works include: five Masses, three Passions and other church music.

Alberti bass as used in the opening of Mozart's Sonata in C major, K.545.

Alberti bass a conventional broken-chord accompaniment common in 18th-century keyboard music, taking its name from Domenico Alberti, who made much use of it. Many familiar examples of the device can be found in the works of Haydn, Mozart, and Beethoven.

Albertus, Magister (lived early 12th century) French composer. A 'Benedicamus Domino' trope, *Congaudeant catholici*, is ascribed to him in the *Codex Calixtinus* of Compostela, around 1125, and is the earliest known three-part composition.

Albinoni, Tomaso (1671–1751) Italian Baroque composer and violinist. He wrote over 40 operas and numerous sonatas and *concerti à cinque* (concertos in five parts) for oboe, trumpet, bassoon, violin, organ, and strings, which helped to establish Baroque orchestral style. His work was studied and adapted by J S Bach.

He was wealthy and never held a musical appointment, but was a fully trained musician. His concertos were among the first to be in three movements, and the oboe concertos op. 7 were the first published in Italy. The popular *Adagio*, often described as being by Albinoni, was actually composed from a fragment of original manuscript by his biographer, the Italian musicologist Remo Giazotto (1910–).

Works include: 55 operas, including *Radamisto* (Venice, 1698), *Griselda* (Florence, 1703), *Pimpinone* (Venice, 1708), and *L'impresario delle Canarie* (Venice, 1725); 9 op. nos. for instrumental chamber combinations, including 5 sets of 12 concertos, 30 other concertos, 42 trio sonatas, and 29 violin sonatas.

Albion and Albanius opera by Grabu (libretto by Dryden), produced London, Duke's Theatre, 3 June 1685. An allegory of the Restoration of Charles II.

alborada (Spanish, from *alba*, 'dawn') 'morning song', in the same sense that a serenade is an evening song; *cf.* French *aubade*. Originally the alborada was a popular instrumental piece of northwest Spain, usually played on bagpipes.

Alborada del gracioso/The Jester's Morning Song a piano piece by Ravel, No. 4 of the set entitled *Miroirs*, composed 1905. Version for orchestra performed Paris, 17 May 1919.

Albrechtsberger, Johann Georg (1736–1809) Austrian music theorist, composer, and teacher. He was a prolific composer of church music and instrumental music, much of it in a contrapuntal style, and was for a

short time Beethoven's teacher. He held the post of court organist in Vienna and Kapellmeister of St Stephen's Cathedral, Vienna.

Albrici, Vincenzo (1631–1696) Italian composer and organist, brother of Bartolomeo Albrici. He was a pupil of Carissimi, and director of the Queen of Sweden's Italian musicians, 1652–53; Kapellmeister at Dresden from 1654; in the service of Charles II in London, 1664–67; he returned to Dresden in 1667, and was organist of St Thomas's, Leipzig, 1681–82; finally Kapellmeister at Prague, St Augustin.

Works include: Masses, psalms, concertos, and madrigals.

Albright, William (1944–) US composer, pianist, and organist. He studied at the Juilliard School and in Paris with Messiaen. He was a teacher of composition at Michigan University and director of the electronic music studio there.

Works include: multimedia and stage pieces (*Cross of Gold* 1975), orchestral music (*Bacchanal* 1981), chamber music and pieces for organ and piano, with jazz ensemble.

Albumblatt (German 'album leaf, page') in music, the title often given to a short piece, usually for piano, suggesting that the piece is one of many, forming a gathered album of unrelated pieces. Examples are by Schumann and Wagner.

Alceste opera by Gluck (libretto by R Calzabigi after Euripides), Italian version produced Vienna, Burgtheater, 26 December 1767. French version, revised by the composer (libretto by C L G L du Roullet after Calzabigi), produced Paris, Opéra, 23 April 1776. Alceste and husband Admète are saved from Hades by Hercules, as Alceste prepares to sacrifice herself for dying Admète.

Opera by Schweitzer (libretto by Wieland), produced Weimar, at court, 28 May 1773. The first German opera in the manner of Metastasio.

Opera by Strungk (libretto by P Thiemich, based on Aurelio Aureli's *Antigona delusa da Alceste*), produced Leipzig, 18 May 1693. Written for the opening of the Leipzig opera house.

Incidental music by Handel (later used for *The Choice of Hercules*) to a play by Tobias Smollett, composed for a production in London, Covent Garden, in 1750, which did not take place.

See also ◊*Alkestis*.

Alceste ou Le Triomphe d'Alcide opera by Lully (libretto by Quinault), produced Paris, Opéra, 19 January 1674.

Alchemist, The incidental music by G F Handel, partly adapted from *Rodrigo*, for a revival of Ben Jonson's play, produced London, Drury Lane Theatre, 7 March 1732.

Alchymist, Der opera by Spohr (libretto by K Pfeiffer, based on W A Irving's story *The Student of Salamanca*), produced Kassel, 28 July 1830. The alchemist Tarnow refuses to let his daughter Louise marry until he has discovered the philosopher's stone. He releases her áfter her lover impersonates the devil, demanding a young woman as payment.

Alcidor opera by Spontini (libretto by G M Théaulon de Lambert), produced Berlin, 23 May 1825. Designated a 'Zauber-Oper mit Ballet', it begins with a chorus of gnomes accompanied by anvils (anticipating Wagner's *Rheingold*).

Alcina opera by Handel (libretto by A Marchi), produced London, Covent Garden, 16 April 1735. Sorceress Alcina loses her magic powers on enchanted island, as Bradamante comes in search of the bewitched Ruggiero.

Alcione opera by Marais (libretto by A H de la Motte), produced Paris, Opéra, 18 February 1706. Neptune rescues young lovers after shipwreck.

Aldeburgh Festival annual festival of operas and other concerts, established 1948 at Aldeburgh, Suffolk. The events have centred on the works of Benjamin Britten, who lived at Aldeburgh, and take place at The Maltings, a concert hall at nearby Snape. First performances of Britten's works to be given here include the operas *A Midsummer Night's Dream* (1960) and *Death in Venice* (1973).

aleatoric composition music whose content is to some extent undetermined by the composer. Those who have used aleatory features in their works include John ◊Cage, Pierre ◊Boulez, and Cornelius ◊Cardew.

aleatory music (Latin *alea*, 'dice') method of composition practised by postwar avant-garde composers in which the performer or conductor chooses the order of succession of the composed pieces. Examples of aleatory music include Pierre Boulez's *Piano Sonata No 3* (1956–57), Earle Brown's *Available Forms I* (1961), and Stockhausen's *Momente/Moments* (1961–72). Another term for aleatory music is 'mobile form'.

Aleatory music is distantly related to the 18th-century 'musical dice game' and to the freely assembled music for silent movies using theme catalogues by Giuseppe Becce and others. The use by John ◊Cage of dice and the I Ching differs in that it intervenes in the actual process of composition.

Aleko opera by Rachmaninov (libretto by V I Nemirovich-Danchenko, based on Pushkin's poem *The Gypsies*), produced Moscow, 9 May 1893. Zemfira is killed by Aleko after she tries to join the gypsies.

Aleksandrov, Anatol Nikolaevich (1888–1982) Russian composer. He studied under A Taneiev and at the Moscow Conservatory, where he later became professor.

Works include: the operas *Two Worlds, The Forty-First, Bela* (Moscow, 1946), *The Wild Girl* (1957); incidental music for Maeterlinck's *Ariane et Barbe-bleue*, Scribe's *Adrienne Lecouvreur*; music for film *Thirteen*; overture on popular Russian themes and two suites for orchestra; four string quartets (1921–53); 14 piano sonatas, piano pieces; *Three Goblets*, for baritone and orchestra; songs, folksong arrangements.

Alembert, Jean Le Rond d' (1717–1783) French author, philosopher, and mathematician. His books included many studies of musical subjects, including acoustics, opera, and the theories of Rameau; as a musical author, he is best known for his articles to the *Encyclopédie*. He was one of the adherents of Gluck against Piccinni.

Alessandri, Felice (1747–1798) Italian conductor and composer. He studied at Naples and first worked at Turin and Paris; he produced his first opera at Venice in 1767, went to London the following year, and in 1786 to St Petersburg in search of a court appointment, which he failed to secure. From 1789 to 1792 he was second Kapellmeister at the Berlin Opera.

Works include: about 35 operas, including *Ezio* (Verona, 1767), *Alcina* (Turin, 1775), *Artaserse* (Naples, 1783), *Il ritorno d'Ulisse* (Potsdam, 1790), *Armida* (Padua, 1794), an oratorio, several symphonies, sonatas.

Alessandro opera by Handel (libretto by P A Rolli), produced London, King's Theatre, Haymarket, 5 May 1726. Alexander the Great in trouble with rival sopranos.

Alessandro della Viola (1530–after 1594) see Alessandro ◊Merlo.

Alessandro nell'Indie/Alexander in India opera by Johann Christian Bach (libretto by Metastasio), produced Naples, Teatro San

Carlo, 20 January 1762. Defeated by Alexander the Great, Indian King Porus resolves to rescue Queen Cleophis.

The first setting was by Vinci (Rome, 1729); others by Galuppi (Mantua, 1738), Pérez (Genoa, 1745), Sacchini (Venice, 1763), and Piccinni (Naples, 1774).

See ◊*Cleofide* and ◊*Poro, rè dell' Indie*.

Alessandro Stradella opera by Flotow (libretto, in German, by F W Riese, pseudonym 'W Friedrich'), produced Hamburg, 30 December 1844. It deals with doubtful incidents in the scandalous life of Stradella, and is based on a play with music, some by Flotow, P A A P de Forges, and P Dupert. Stradella deflects would-be assassins by singing to them of mercy and kindness.

Alessandro vincitor di se stesso/Alexander, Victor over Himself opera by Cavalli (libretto by F Sbarra), produced Venice, Teatro Santi Giovanni e Paolo, probably 20 January 1651.

Alexander Balus oratorio by Handel (libretto by T Morell), produced London, Covent Garden, 23 March 1748.

Alexander Nevsky, or Aleksandr Nevski film music by Sergey Prokofiev, composed 1938. Later arranged as Cantata, op. 78, for mezzo, chorus, and orchestra. First performance Moscow, 17 May 1939.

Alexander's Feast Dryden's ode set to music by Handel (words arranged and added to by Newburgh Hamilton), produced London, Covent Garden, 19 February 1736.

Alfano, Franco (1876–1954) Italian composer. He is best known for his 12 operas, including *Risurrezione/Resurrection* (1904), *The Shade of Don Juan* performed 1914, *Sakuntala* (1922), *The Last Lord* (1930), and *Cyrano de Bergerac* (1936). He completed Puccini's unfinished opera, *Turandot*.

He studied first at the Naples Conservatory and afterwards at that of Leipzig, under Salomon Jadassohn (1831–1902). He had some piano pieces published in Germany before the end of the century and in 1896 wrote his first opera, *Miranda*, on a subject from Fogazzaro. The ballet *Napoli*, produced in Paris in 1900, was his first big success, and was followed by the still greater success of his third opera, *Risurrezione/Resurrection*, a work in the *verismo* tradition. His most successful work was the colourful opera *La leggenda di Sakuntala* (1921). His first symphony was performed at San Remo in 1910. In 1919 he was appointed director of the Liceo Musicale Rossini at Bologna and in 1923 of the

Conservatory at Turin. After Puccini's death in 1924 he completed the unfinished *Turandot*, finishing the final scenes from Puccini's sketches; his work was not heard complete until 1982.

Works include: OPERA *Miranda, La fonte di Enschir* (Breslau, 1898), *Risurrezione/Resurrection* (based on Tolstoy) (Turin, 1904), *Il principe Zilah, L'ombra di Don Giovanni* (Naples, 1930), *Sakuntala* (after Kalidasa, 1922), *L'ultimo Lord, Cyrano de Bergerac* (Rome, 1936) (after Rostand), *Il dottor Antonio*.

OTHER ballet *Napoli*; two symphonies, *Suite romantica* for orchestra; piano quartet, three string quartets; sonata for cello and piano; songs include three settings of poems by Tagore and a cycle *Dormiveglia*.

al fine (Italian 'to the end') musical term used in cases where an earlier portion of a composition is to be repeated (*da capo*) and indicates that it is to be played over again to the end, not to some earlier place, which would otherwise be marked with a special sign, the appropriate direction being then *al segno*.

Alfonso X (1221–1284), known as *El Sabio*, 'the Wise' King of Castile and Leon. He assembled a collection of 400 songs in Galician-Portuguese, known as the *Cantigas de Santa Maria*, and founded a chair of music at Salamanca University, 1254.

Alfonso und Estrella opera by Schubert (libretto by F von Schober), composed 1821–22, but never performed in Schubert's lifetime; produced by Liszt at Weimar, 24 June 1854, with an overture by Anton Rubinstein. Schubert's original version was premiered at Graz, 28 September 1991. Alfonso gains the throne, marrying Estrella, the daughter of his father's enemy.

Alfred masque by Arne (words by J Thomson and D Mallet), performed at Cliveden, Bucks., the residence of Frederick, Prince of Wales, 1 August 1740. It contains 'Rule, Britannia'.

Opera by Dvořák, his first (libretto by K T Korner). Composed 1870; produced Olomouc, 10 December 1938. King Alfred defeats the Danes and frees his bride.

Alfred, König der Angelsachsen/Alfred, King of the Anglo-Saxons incidental music by J Haydn for a drama by J W Cowmeadow. First performed Eisenstadt, September 1796.

Algarotti, Francesco, Count (1712–1764) Italian scholar. His libretto *Iphigénie en Aulide* influenced the text set by Christoph Willibald von Gluck. Among many learned works he wrote a treatise on the reform of opera, *Saggio* *sopra l'opera in musica*, criticizing the practices of opera seria, published 1755.

Alghisi, Paris Francesco (1666–1743) Italian composer. He studied under Polarolo and was engaged for some time at the Polish court. Two operas were produced at Venice: *Amor di Curzio per la patria*, (1690), and *Il trionfo della continenza*, (1691). He also wrote several oratorios and other works.

Ali Baba, ou Les Quarante Voleurs/Ali Baba, or The Forty Thieves opera by Cherubini (libretto by Scribe and A H J Mélesville), produced Paris, Opéra, 22 July 1833. A new version of *Koukourgi*, composed 1793, but not performed.

Alina, Regina di Golconda opera by Donizetti (libretto by F Romani), produced Genoa, 12 May 1828. Courted by a tenor, Alina is eventually reunited with her lost husband.

aliquot parts (from Latin *aliquot*, 'some') parts contained by the whole, integral factors; in music, the parts of a fundamental note vibrating separately as overtones.

aliquot scaling, or aliquot strings additional strings introduced into the upper registers of pianos manufactured by the firm of Blüthner. These vibrate with those struck by the hammers, evidently on the old principle of the ◊sympathetic strings in bowed string instruments.

Alkan (1813–1888), pseudonym of Charles Valentin Morhange French piano virtuoso and composer. His formidably difficult piano pieces were neglected until the 1970s. Works include *Grande Sonate: les quatre âges* (1848) and 12 *Etudes* in every minor key (1857), of which numbers 4–7 constitute a symphony for piano solo and numbers 8–10 a concert for piano solo.

Born in Paris, he was so precocious as a player that he was admitted to the Paris Conservatory at the age of six. After a visit to London in 1833, he settled in Paris as teacher of the piano. In his works he cultivated an advanced, immensely difficult, and often very modern technique. As a performer he was ranked with Chopin (a close friend) and Liszt, but became a recluse after 1849. He is alleged to have met his death under a collapsing bookcase.

Works include: two piano concertos; piano trio; piano sonatas, numerous piano studies (including one for the right hand and one for the left), character pieces; four op. nos. of pieces for pedal piano.

Alkestis opera by Boughton (libretto taken from Gilbert Murray's English trans. of the tragedy by Euripides), produced Glastonbury, 26 August 1922.
Opera by Wellesz (libretto by H von Hofmannsthal, after Euripides), produced Mannheim, 20 March 1924.

alla (Italian 'at the, in the manner of'; French *à la*) word used in various ways in combination with nouns, for example *alla marcia* ('march-like'), *alla francese* ('in the French manner'). Also abbreviated *all'* with nouns beginning with a vowel.

alla breve, or cut time of musical tempo, indicating that the minim rather than the crotchet is the basic unit of the beat in a bar of two beats.

allargando (Italian 'broadening') in musical notation, indicating a gradual slowing down while still maintaining a full tone quality.

allegretto in musical notation, moderately quick, but not as fast as ◊allegro.

Allegri, Domenico (1585–1629) Italian composer. He was maestro di cappella at Santa Maria Maggiore in Rome 1610–29. His works include motets and music for voices and strings.

Allegri, Gregorio (1582–1652) Italian Baroque composer. He was maestro di cappella of the Sistine Chapel, Rome, 1610–29. His output of sacred music includes Magnificats, a cappella Masses, motets, and the celebrated *Miserere mei* (Psalm 51) for nine voices. This was reserved for performance by the chapel choir until Mozart, at the age of 14, wrote out the music from memory.

allegro (Italian 'merry, lively') in music, a lively or quick passage, movement, or composition.

Allegro Barbaro work for solo piano by Bartók, composed 1911 but not performed until 27 February 1921, in Budapest.

Allegro, il Penseroso ed il Moderato, L'/The Cheerful, the Thoughtful and the Moderate oratorio by Handel (libretto Parts i and ii by Milton, Part iii by Charles Jennens), produced London, Lincoln's Inn Fields Theatre, 27 February 1740.

Alleluia the third chant of the Proper of the Mass, sung immediately after the Gradual. The word is Hebrew ('praise ye Jehova'), and was sung in many contexts in Jewish life, but especially in connection with the singing of the Psalms. It was taken over unchanged by the Christian Church and sung both alone and as an addition to chants of various kinds, especially during the Easter season. As a Mass-chant of the Roman rite it was origin-

Alleluia. *The exact form as sung since the Middle Ages may be illustrated from the alleluia for the First Sunday of Advent.*

ally sung alone, at first during Eastertide only and, after the time of Gregory I, during the whole year except from Septuagesima to Easter. At some time before 750 one or more verses were added, in which form it became a responsorial chant, the choir singing the alleluia at the beginning and end, and the soloists the verse or verses in between.

The alleluia of the Ambrosian chant, possibly retaining more of its original oriental characteristics, is even more florid in character.

allemande medium-paced dance in four time, with an upbeat, in two symmetrical sections; the music forms part of a classical ◊suite.

Allen, Hugh Percy (1869–1946) English professor of music. He was conductor of the Bach Choir, London, 1901–20; professor of music, Oxford University, from 1918; and director of the Royal College of Music, London, until 1937. He was knighted 1920.

As professor of music at Oxford, Allen did valuable work in widening the scope and practicality of the courses there. He was a fine choral conductor.

Allison, Richard (lived 16th–17th century), or Alison, Alyson English composer. He first appeared as a contributor to East's *Whole Book of Psalms* in 1592 and published a collection of church melodies set for voices and instruments, *The Psalmes of David in Meter*, in 1599. Other works include lute music and 24 songs for voices and instruments, *An Howres Recreation ...*, published 1606.

all' ottava (Italian 'at the octave') in musical notation, a direction that a passage, so far as it is marked by a dotted line over it, is to be played an octave higher than it is written; it is usually represented by the symbol *8va*. If the dotted line is below, it means an octave lower.

Almahide opera by Giovanni Bononcini (libretto after Dryden's *Almanzor and Almahide*), produced London, Queen's Theatre, Haymarket, 10 January 1710. According to Burney, the first opera performed in England wholly in Italian.

alme, or almeh, al-mai ('the learned') name given by modern Egyptians and Arabs to the Egyptian singing girls who attend festivals, marriages, funerals, and other ceremonies. They are also found in Syria and other parts of the former Ottoman Empire.

almérie musical instrument, a kind of ◊lute. It was invented in the 18th century by Jean Lemaire, and its name is an anagram of his.

Almira opera by Handel (libretto by F C Feustking), produced Hamburg, Theater beim Gänse-markt, 8 January 1705. Handel's first opera; Almira loves Fernando but must marry Osman.

'Alpensinfonie, Eine'/An Alpine Symphony symphony by Richard Strauss, op. 64, first performed Berlin, 28 October 1915.

alphorn wind instrument consisting of a straight, usually wooden tube terminating in a conical endpiece with an upturned bell, sometimes up to 4 m/12 ft in length. It is used to summon cattle and serenade tourists in the highlands of central Europe.

The wood is split lengthways and hollowed out, then reunited and covered with bark or split cane to seal against leakage. In some areas the alphorn is made of metal.

al rovescio (Italian 'backwards') see ◊cancrizans.

Also sprach Zarathustra/Thus spake Zoroaster symphonic poem by Richard Strauss, op. 30, based on Nietzsche, composed 1896, first performed Frankfurt, 27 November 1896.

Altenberglieder five songs for voice and orchestra to picture-postcard texts by 'Peter Altenberg' (pseudonym of Richard Englander, 1862–1919), by Berg. At the first performance in Vienna of two of the songs, 1913, a riot caused the concert to be abandoned. First complete performance Rome, 24 January 1953, conductor Horenstein.

altered chord a chord in which one of the notes is raised or lowered by a semitone. The chord then includes augmented (enlarged) or diminished (contracted) intervals. Altered chords are often used to modulate keys (see ◊modulation).

alternatim a manner of performance in which singers or players are heard in alternation, as in between two sides of a choir or between choir and organ. It can also be applied to alternation between music styles, as in plainsong and polyphony.

alternativo a contrasting section, much the same as the trio in a minuet or scherzo, but often in a piece of a different character, and there may be more than one alternativo in a single piece. Familiar examples appear in Schumann.

alto (Italian 'high') voice or musical instrument between tenor and soprano, of approxi-

mate range G3–D5. As a prefix to the name of an instrument, for example alto saxophone, it denotes a size larger than soprano.

The traditional male alto voice of early opera, Anglican church choirs, male voice quartets, and choral societies, also known as **countertenor**. Trumpetlike and penetrating, it is an extension of the high (alto) male voice register, produced by falsetto. The term is also used as an abbreviation of **contralto**, the low-register ('contra-alto') female voice exemplified by English singer Kathleen Ferrier, which is rich and mellow in tone. Alto is also the French name for the ◊viola.

alto clef in musical notation, the C ◊clef in which middle C is represented by the 3rd line of a five-line stave. It was used by musicians and singers until the 18th century and is now used most commonly by viola players.

The alto clef.

alto recorder US term for the treble ◊recorder.

Alto Rhapsody (Brahms) see ◊Rhapsodie.

Alwyn, William (1905–1985) English composer. He was professor of composition at the Royal Academy of Music 1926–55; he wrote film music (*Desert Victory, The Way Ahead*), and composed symphonies and chamber music.

He was born in Northampton, and entered the Royal Academy of Music in London as a student of flute, piano, and composition, studying the last under John Blackwood McEwen (1868–1948) and obtaining the Costa Scholarship. He played the flute in the London Symphony Orchestra and his first work for orchestra, *Five Preludes*, was given at a 1927 Prom concert. His music includes an unperformed opera *The Libertine*. He also published *The Technique of Film Music* (1957).

Works include: the opera *Miss Julie* (1961–76), music for films, *Our Country, The Lost Illusion*, and many others; five preludes, concerto grosso, overture to a masque, and five symphonies for orchestra (1949–73); piano concerto, violin concerto, *Pastoral Fantasia* for viola and strings; two string quartets, Rhapsody for piano quartet; Sonata-Impromptu for violin and viola, sonatina for viola and piano; piano pieces; Divertimento for solo flute.

Alyabyev, Alexander Alexandrovich (1787–1851) Russian composer. He was an army officer who fought as a hussar against Napoleon, and cultivated music as an amateur from 1823.

Works include: two operas after Shakespeare: *Burya* (*The Tempest*, 1835) and *The Enchanted Night* (*A Midsummer Night's Dream*, 1839). His song 'The Nightingale' was used by Patti and Viardot for the letter scene in *Il Barbiere di Siviglia*.

Alypios (lived 4th century) Greek theorist to whom our knowledge of ancient Greek notation is due.

Alzira opera by Verdi (libretto by S Cammarano, based on Voltaire's play *Alzire*), produced Naples, Teatro San Carlo, 12 August 1845. Inca chief Zamoro stabs Gusmano, governor of Peru, as the Spaniard attempts to wed Zamoro's intended bride.

Amadigi di Gaula/Amadis of Gaul opera by Handel (libretto adapted from A H de la Motte's *Amadis de Grèce*, set by Destouches, 1699), produced London, King's Theatre, Haymarket, 25 May 1715. Amadigi and Oriana are united when the interfering infatuated sorceress Melissa abandons her deceptions.

Amadis opera by Lully (libretto by Quinault, based on the old Iberian romance *Amadis de Gaula*), produced Paris, Opéra, 18 January 1684. Amadis in adventures to win the doubting heart of Oriane.
Opera by Massenet (libretto by J Claretie), composed c. 1895 and performed posthumously in Monte Carlo, 1 April 1922.

Amadori, Giuseppe (c. 1670–after 1730) Italian composer. He was maestro di cappella in Rome, where his oratorio, *Il martirio di Sant' Adriano*, was produced in 1702. He also wrote Masses and other church music.

Amahl and the Night Visitors opera in one act by Menotti (libretto by the composer, after Bosch's painting *The Adoration of the Magi*), produced on NBC Television 24 December 1951. It is the first opera especially written for television.

Amarus lyric cantata by Janáček for soprano, tenor, baritone, chorus, and orchestra; composed c. 1897, revised 1901 and 1906. First performed Kroměříž, 2 December 1900.

Amat, Juan Carlos (1572–1642) Spanish scientist and author. He wrote the earliest-known treatise on playing the guitar, *Guitarra española* ..., published probably in 1586.

Amati Italian family of violinmakers working in Cremona about 1550–1700. **Nicolò Amati** (1596–1684) taught Andrea Guarneri and Antonio ◊Stradivari. Nicolò's grandfather **Andrea Amati** (c. 1511–c. 1580) brought the violin to its classic form.

Andrea Amati's earliest known violins were made with only three strings and it may have been he who first fitted the fourth string. He is known to have made small and large (the 'grand' model) violins and violas and to have made cellos, a set of which were commissioned by Charles IX of France after 1560 and some of which survive. The sound of his instruments is mellow and beautiful but less powerful than those of his successors of the Cremonese school, perhaps due to the highly arched belly which was a characteristic of his violins and violas.

Andrea was succeeded by two sons, **Antonio** (1550–1638) and **Girolamo (Hieronymus)** (1561–1630), who continued in the same tradition as their father, often signing their instruments jointly as 'the brothers Amati, sons of Andrea'. Nicolò Amati, the son of Girolamo, is the most illustrious member of the family. His violins produced a great intensity and richness of sound, which he achieved by using thicker wood and reducing the elevation of the belly. By this time Cremona violins had won the reputation, which they still hold today, of being the best in the world. The fame of Nicolò and of his pupils, Guarneri and Stradivari, has somewhat eclipsed the renown of Andrea and his sons, but they are remembered for their pioneer work in the introduction of a new craft into Italy.

Ambiela, Miguel (1666–1733) Spanish priest and composer. He was music director of the new cathedral at Saragossa, 1700–07, and maestro di cappella at Toledo, 1710–33.

Works include: Masses, *Stabat Mater*, and other church music.

Ambleto/Hamlet opera by Gasparini (libretto by A Zeno and P Pariati), produced Venice, Teatro San Cassiano, Carnival, 1705.
Opera by D Scarlatti (libretto ditto), produced Rome, Teatro Capranica, Carnival, 1715.

Ambros, August Wilhelm (1816–1876) Czech-born German musicologist. He studied at Prague University. His life's work was a history of music which at his death reached only the fourth volume and the early 17th century. He also composed a Czech opera, *Bratislav and Jitka*, and overtures to Shakespeare's *Othello* and Calderón's *Mágico prodigioso*.

Ambrosian chant in Christian church music, reformed chant introduced by St Ambrose in the 4th century. It retains many features of Middle Eastern religious chant.

The number of available modes (scales) was reduced to four; the interval of the fifth was established as the basis of tonal music, having a lower key note, from which the chant rose and to which it returned; and a higher dominant was established at the fifth, around which the chant was elaborated.

amener (French, probably from *mener*, 'to lead') a French dance of the 17th century in triple time and moderate pace, with characteristic six-bar phrases. It occurs in French instrumental suites and thence passed to some extent into German and Italian music.

America epic rhapsody by Bloch in three movements (1. 1620; 2. 1861–65; 3. 1926), composed 1926–27. First performed 20 December 1928 and then on 21 December 1928 simultaneously in seven US cities. It won the prize offered by *Musical America* for the best US symphonic work.

American musical terminology the main differences from British usage are nearly all direct translations from German. Whole note, half note, quarter note, (for semibreve, minim, crotchet) are used, as well as concert master for leader, and so on. The most potentially confusing is the word 'tone' meaning British 'pitch': hence Americans tend to use 'tone row' for British 'note row', 'neighbor tone' for 'auxiliary note', 'whole step' and 'half step' for British 'tone' and 'semitone'. Other details in which usage tends to cross the Atlantic in both directions include 'flutist' (flautist) and 'measure' (bar).

American organ keyboard reed organ similar to the ◊harmonium, differing from the latter in some details, particularly in sucking in the wind through its reeds instead of expelling it.

Its principle was discovered by a workman attached to Jacob Alexandre (1804–1876), an instrument maker in Paris, but he took it to America and the first important instruments of the kind were made by Mason & Hamlin of Boston around 1860.

Amériques work for orchestra by Varèse; instruments include sleighbells, steamboat whistle, and hand siren as used by New York Fire Department; composed 1918–22, first performed Philadelphia, 9 April 1926, conductor Stokowski.

Amfiparnaso, L'/The Amphi-Parnassus madrigal opera by Orazio Vecchi, produced Modena, 1594, and published Venice, 1597, described as a *commedia harmonica*. It consists of three acts and a prologue, and the characters are the stock figures of the *commedia dell' arte*, but the musical setting of their speech is in the form of madrigals for mixed voices. It has been supposed that the action was produced in dumb-show while the madrigals were sung behind the scenes, but a passage in the text which says that 'the spectacle is to enter by the ear, not by the eye' gives good reason to doubt this. The same subject was treated earlier in a smaller form by Lassus.

Amico Fritz, L' opera by Mascagni (libretto by P Suardon, based on Erckmann-Chatrian's novel *L'Ami Fritz*), produced Rome, Teatro Costanzi, 31 October 1891. Bachelor Fritz falls for Suzel after encouragement from the matchmaker Rabbi David.

Amid Nature, or In Nature's Realm concert overture by Dvořák, op. 91, composed 1891 and forming, with *Carnival* and *Othello*, a cycle with thematic connections, originally called *Nature, Life and Love*.

Amirov, Fikret Dzhamil (1922–1984) Azerbaijani composer. His music is influenced by local folk tunes.

Works include: the opera *Sevil* (1953); double concerto for violin, piano, and orchestra (1948); *The Pledge of the Korean Guerrilla Fighter* for voice and orchestra (1951); piano concerto (1957).

Amleto/Hamlet opera by Faccio (libretto by Boito, after Shakespeare), produced Genoa, Teatro Carlo Felice, 30 May 1865.
Opera by Mercadante (libretto by Romani, after Shakespeare), produced Milan, La Scala, 26 December 1822.

Ammerbach, Elias Nikolaus (1530–1597), or Amerbach German organist and composer. He was organist at St Thomas, Leipzig, from 1560 and published two books of music in organ tablature, containing important explanations of ornaments and modes of performance.

Amor brujo, El/Love, the Magician ballet by Falla, composed 1913–14, first performed Madrid, Teatro de Lara, 15 April 1915.

Amor coniugale, L' opera by Mayr (librettist G Rossi, after Bouilly), produced Padua, 26 July 1805 (four months before *Fidelio*, which is based on the same source). Condensed into one act, Leonore/Fidelio becomes Zeliska/ Malvino, Pizarro is Moroski, and Rocco is Peters.

Amore dei tre re, L'/The Love of the Three Kings opera by Montemezzi (libretto by S Benelli, from his play of the same title), produced Milan, La Scala, 10 April 1913. The king strangles his daughter-in-law and spreads poison on her lips; her lover and husband also die after kissing her.

amoroso (Italian 'amorous') musical direction indicating an emotional and tender manner of performance.

Amour médecin, L' comédie-ballet by Lully (libretto by Molière), produced Versailles, 16 September 1665.

Amours d'Antoine et de Cléopâtre, Les/The Loves of Antony and Cleopatra ballet by Rodolphe Kreutzer (choreography by J P Aumer, based on Shakespeare), produced Paris, Opéra, 8 March 1808.

Amram, David (1930–) US composer and horn player. He studied at the Manhattan School of Music and with Charles Mills. He has written incidental music for Shakespeare's plays, films, and jazz bands. He received a Commission from the Library of Congress in 1995.

Works include: the operas *The Final Ingredient* (ABC TV, 1965), *Twelfth Night* (1968); *Shakespearean Concerto* (1960), *King Lear Variations* for wind, percussion, and piano (1967), concertos for horn, jazz quintet, bassoon, and violin (1968–80); string quartet (1961), sonata for solo violin (1964), wind quintet (1968); cantatas *The American Bell*, *A Year in our Land*, and *Let us Remember* (1962–65).

Amy, Gilbert (1936–) French composer of advanced tendencies. His compositions show the influence of oriental music, total ◊serialism, and ◊aleatory techniques.

He studied with Darius Milhaud, Olivier Messiaen, and Pierre Boulez. He was director of the Concerts du Domaine Musical, specializing in new music.

Works include: *Messe* for soloists, chorus, and orchestra (1983); *Mouvements* for chamber orchestra (1958); *Adagio et Stretto* for orchestra (1978); *Alpha-Beth* for six wind instruments (1964); *Cycles* for percussion; *Epigrammes* for piano; *Chant pour orchestre* (1980); *La Variation ajoutée* for tape and instruments (1986); *Ecrits sur toile* for reciter and ensemble (1983); *Orchestral* (1987); *Choros* for male vocalists, chorus, and orchestra (1989); *Obliques* I–III for piano (1987–89); *Mémoire* for cello and piano (1989).

Ana, Francesco d' (1460–1503) Italian composer. His works include frottole (songs) and Lamentations. He is known to have been active at St Mark's, Venice, in 1490.

Anacréon *acte de ballet* by Rameau (libretto by P-J Bernard), produced Fontainebleau, 23 October 1754; revised and produced Paris, Opéra, 10 October 1758.

Anacréon, ou L'Amour fugitif opera-ballet by Cherubini (libretto by R Mendouze), produced Paris, Opéra, 4 October 1803. Poet Anacréon in love with protégée Chloë.

anacrusis alternative term for ◊upbeat.

Anakreontika Greek songs for mezzo and instrumental ensemble by Peter Maxwell Davies; first performed London, 17 September 1976.

analysis as recently as the 1950s, the analysis of music was widely understood to denote any kind of description with some technical component. But for more than a century there has been a growing academic discipline that attempts to explain musical phenomena by means as rigorous and logical as possible, to approach formal models of how music works, or to break down the organism of musical structures into smaller components. Pure musical analysis often eschews value judgement, which is more the province of the critic or aesthetician. See Hans ◊Keller, Leonard ◊Meyer, Jean-Jacques ◊Nattiez, Rudolf ◊Réti, and Heinrich ◊Schenker.

Ančerl, Karel (1908–1973) Czech conductor. Imprisoned during World War II, he resumed his career in 1945, becoming professor at the Academy of Musical Arts, Prague, in 1950. He conducted the Czech Philharmonic Orchestra 1950–68, and was music director of the Toronto Symphony Orchestra from 1969.

He studied with Jaroslav Křička and Alois Hába at the Prague Conservatory 1925–29, and was assistant to Scherchen in Berlin 1929–31. His public career began in 1931 as a theatre conductor and with Czech radio. He conducted at festivals of the International Society for Contemporary Music 1933–37.

Anda, Geza (1921–1976) Hungarian-born Swiss pianist and conductor. He excelled at Brahms, Bartók, and Mozart, whose piano concertos he conducted from the keyboard, inserting his own ◊cadenzas. His playing was noted for its clarity and subtle nuances.

andamento a fugue subject of more than usual length and often in two contrasted sections.

andante (Italian 'going', 'walking') in music, a passage or movement to be performed at a walking pace; that is, at a moderately slow tempo.

andantino in musical notation, a modification of ◊andante. Interpretation of the term has varied; it is not clear whether it denotes a faster or slower tempo than andante. Beethoven himself was unsure as to the meaning. Most recent composers intend a faster tempo.

Anderson, Beth (1950–) US composer and performance artist. Her compositions involve freedom of improvisation and employ a wide range of resources.

She studied with composers John Cage, Larry Austin, and Terry Riley at Mills College, Oakland, California; she also studied at the University of California.

Works include: the opera *Queen Christina* (1973) and text-sound piece *Riot Rot* (1984); oratorio *Joan* (1974), music theatre *Soap Tuning* (1976) and *Elizabeth Rex* (1983); *Revel* for orchestra (1985); *Music for Charlemagne Palestine* (1973); *Rosemary Swale* for string quartet (1986).

Anderson, Emily (1891–1962) English musicologist. Although employed in the Foreign Office, she edited and translated the complete letters of Mozart and his family (two volumes, 1938) and those of Beethoven (three volumes, 1962).

Anderson, Laurie (1947–) US composer and performance artist. She trained as a violinist and minimalist painter and in 1974 began making her own instruments, including a violin with an internal speaker. She has appeared widely in Europe and the USA, notably in multimedia, cyberpunk shows which employ a voice-activated synthesizer; contact microphones have turned her body into a percussion set. In 1973 she staged the 12-hour audiovisual show *The Life and Times of Josef Stalin* at Brooklyn Academy, USA.

Works include: *Americans on the Move* (1979, developed into *United States Live*, 1983); *New York Social Life*; *Time to Go* (portraying a museum attendant at closing time); *Empty Places* (1989); the autobiographical *Stories from the Nerve Bible* (1993); album *Bright Red* (1994).

An die ferne Geliebte/To the Distant Beloved song cycle by Beethoven (six songs), op. 98, to poems by A Jeitteles, composed 1816. It is the first German set of songs intended to form a connected cycle.

Andrea Chénier opera by Giordano (libretto by L Illica), produced Milan, La Scala, 28 March 1896. Chénier and Madeleine guillotined after the Revolution, after Chénier has been denounced by Gérard, a rival in love.

Andricu, Michel (1895–1974) Romanian composer. He studied at the Bucharest Conservatory and later became professor at the Royal Academy there, gaining the Enescu

Prize for composition in 1924. From 1926 to 1959 he was professor at the Bucharest Conservatory.

Works include: the ballet *Taina*; 11 symphonies (1944–70), 13 sinfoniettas (1945–73); nine orchestral suites (1924–58); serenade; three *Tableaux symphoniques*; *Suite pittoresque*; *Suite brève*; *Poem*, and other pieces for orchestra; string quartet (1931); *Novellettes* for piano quintet and other chamber music; sonatina; *Suite lyrique* and other piano works.

Andriessen, Hendrik (1892–1981) Dutch organist and composer. He studied under Zweers at the Amsterdam Conservatory, and later became director of the Utrecht Conservatory and choirmaster at the Roman Catholic cathedral there.

Works include: the operas *Philomela* (1950) and *The Mirror from Venice* (1964); eight Masses and *Te Deum*; four symphonies (1930–54), variations for orchestra; songs for voice and orchestra; chamber music; cello and piano sonata; organ works.

Andriessen, Louis (1939–) Dutch composer. His earlier work was influenced by John Cage, Charles Ives, and Igor Stravinsky; he later preferred the simplicities of minimalism.

He studied with his father, Hendrik Andriessen, and with Luciano Berio in Milan.

Works include: *Anachronie*, in memory of Ives, for orchestra (1966); *Reconstructie*, anti-imperialist theatre piece (1969); *What it's Like* for electronics and 52 strings (1970); *Uproar* for 16 wind, six percussion, and electronics (1970); *The Nine Symphonies of Beethoven* for ensemble and ice-cream bell (1970); *Il Principe*, after Machiavelli (1974); *Orpheus*, theatre piece (1977); *Matthew Passion* (1977); *George Sand*, theatre piece (1980); *Velocity* for orchestra (1983); *De Materie* theatre piece (1985–88); *Dances* for soprano and chamber orchestra (1991); *Facing Death* for four amplified strings (1991); *M is for Man, Music, Mozart* (TV show for the bicentenary); *Rosa* ('a horse drama', with Peter Greenaway, 1994).

Andrieu, F (lived late 14th century) French composer. He set a double *ballade* by Eustace Deschamps on the death of Guillaume de Machaut (1377).

Andromaque/Andromache opera by Grétry (libretto by L G Pitra, based on Racine's tragedy), produced Paris, Opéra, 6 June 1780.

Anerio, Felice (c. 1560–1614) Italian composer. He was a chorister in the papal chapel as a boy, later maestro di cappella at the English College in Rome, which he left for the service of Cardinal Aldobrandini. He was appointed composer to the papal chapel on the death of Palestrina in 1594, and commissioned to reform the Roman Gradual in 1611. **Works include:** masses, motets, hymns, and other church music; madrigals, canzonets.

Anerio, Giovanni Francesco (c. 1567–1630) Italian composer, brother of Felice Anerio. He was maestro di cappella at the cathedral of Verona in 1609, and 1613–20 was music instructor at the Seminario Romano and maestro di cappella of the church of the Madonna de' Monti in Rome. In the service of Sigismund III of Poland 1624–28. His secular music, including madrigals and canzonettas, is more progressive than that of many of his contemporaries. **Works include:** masses, requiem, Te Deum, and other church music; madrigals, canzonettas.

Anet, Jean-Jacques-Baptiste (1676–1755) French violinist and composer. He wrote sonatas and other works for violin. He travelled in France and Italy, studying with Corelli in Rome, and made a great reputation in Paris 1701–35, at the Concert Spirituel with the Violons du Roy. He retired to the court of the ex-king of Poland, Stanislas (Stanisław) Leszczyński, at Lunéville in 1738.

Anfossi, Pasquale (1727–1797) Italian composer, a pupil of Piccinni at Naples. He wrote operas from 1763, but had his first real success with *L'incognita perseguitata* (Rome, 1773). He later produced operas in Paris, London (a music director of the King's Theatre 1782–86), Berlin, and Prague. In 1762 he became maestro di cappella of St John Lateran in Rome. Mozart wrote insertion arias for two of his operas. **Works include:** OPERA *Armida* (Turin, 1770), *L'incognita perseguitata*, *La finta giardiniera*, *Il geloso in cimento*, *L'avaro* (Venice, 1775), *Gengis-Kan* (Turin, 1777), *La vera costanza*, *Il curioso indiscreto*, *I viaggiatori felici* (Venice, 1780), *Le gelosie fortunate*. OTHER church music.

Angélique opera in one act by Ibert (libretto by Nino), produced Paris, Théâtre Fémina, 28 January 1927.

Angiolina, ossia Il matrimonio per susurro/ Angiolina, or The Marriage by Noise opera by Antonio Salieri (libretto by C P Defranceschi, based on Ben Jonson's *Epicoene*), produced Vienna, Kärntnertortheater, 22 October 1800. See also ◊*Schweigsame Frau* (Strauss).

anglaise a dance form similar to that of the country dance, which in France became the *contredanse* in the 18th century, when the name of anglaise was sometimes given to it instead to show its English origin unmistakably.

Anglican chant a form of ◊plainsong used by the Anglican Church to set psalms, canticles (when they are not sung in a more elaborate setting), or other religious texts to music. It is usually sung in unison and with a free rhythm, based upon the inherent rhythm of the language. It may be accompanied by an organ, establishing a harmonic framework.

ängstlich (German 'anxiously, apprehensively') musical term used by Beethoven as a direction for the singing of the recitative in the 'Agnus Dei' section of his *Missa solemnis*.

Aniara opera by Blomdahl (libretto by E Lindegren, after H Martinson's epic poem 'Revue about men in time and space'), produced Stockholm, 31 May 1959. The action is set on board a spaceship.

anima (Italian 'soul') in musical notation, as in 'con anima', meaning that the music should be played 'with soul'. It is often confused with ◊animato, which is concerned primarily with a faster tempo.

Anima del filosofo ossia Orfeo ed Euridice/ The Philosopher's Stone, or Orpheus and Eurydice Haydn's last opera; composed 1791 in London but not performed. First known production Florence, 10 June 1951, conductor E Kleiber, with Callas and Christoff.

animando (Italian 'animating') in musical notation, indicating a gradual increase of tempo, in the manner of ◊accelerando.

animato (Italian 'animated') in musical notation, indicating an immediate increase of tempo, not a gradual one as in ◊animando.

Anna Bolena/Anne Boleyn opera by Donizetti (libretto by F Romani), produced Milan, Teatro Carcano, 26 December 1830. Anna goes to the block, accompanied by 'Home, Sweet Home'.

Anna Karenina opera by Hubay (libretto, in Hungarian, by S Góth, based on Tolstoy's novel), produced Budapest, 10 November 1923.
Opera by Iain Hamilton (libretto by composer) produced London, Coliseum, 7 May 1981.

Années de pèlerinage four sets of piano pieces by Liszt, mainly recording his travels in Switzerland and Italy:

1re Année: En Suisse, composed 1835–36, published 1855: 1. *Chapelle de Guillaume Tell.* 2. *Au Lac de Wallenstadt.* 3. *Pastorale.* 4. *Au Bord d'une source.* 5. *Orage.* 6. *Vallée d'Obermann* (inspired by Senancour's *Obermann*; the valley is an imaginary or unidentified one in the canton of Valais). 7. *Eglogue.* 8. *Le Mal du pays.* 9. *Les Cloches de Genève.* (Nos. 1, 2, 4, 6, and 9 originally formed part of an *Album d'un voyageur* for piano published in 1836: they were revised for the publication of the *Années de pèlerinage* in 1855.)

2me Année: En Italie, composed 1838–39, published 1846: 1. *Sposalizio* (after Raphael's picture in the Brera at Milan). 2. *Il pensieroso* (after Michelangelo's statue of Giuliano dei Medici in the Medici mausoleum at San Lorenzo, Florence). 3. *Canzonetta del Salvator Rosa.* 4. *Sonetto No. 47 del Petrarca.* 5. *Sonetto No. 104 del Petrarca.* 6. *Sonetto No. 123 del Petrarca* (Nos. 4–6 are transcriptions of settings of these Petrarch sonnets for voice and piano). 7. *Aprilès une lecture du Dante: Fantasia quasi Sonata* ('Dante Sonata').

3me Année, composed 1872–77, published 1883: 1. *Angelus: Prière aux anges gardiens.* 2. *Aux Cyprès de la Villa d'Este.* 3. ditto: *Thrénodie.* 4. *Les Jeux d'eau de la Villa d'Este.* 5. *Sunt lacrymae rerum en mode hongrois.* 6. *Marche funèbre* (in memory of the Emperor Maximilian I of Mexico, d. 19 June 1867). 7. *Sursum corda.*

Supplement to Vol. II: *Venezia e Napoli*, composed 1859, published 1861: 1. *Gondoliera* (on a canzona by Cavaliere Peruchini). 2. *Canzone* (on the gondolier's song in Rossini's *Otello*). 3. *Tarantella* (on some canzoni by Guillaume Louis Cottrau). (This set is partly a revision of an earlier one of the same title composed in 1840, but not published).

Ansermet, Ernest Alexandre (1883–1969) Swiss conductor. He worked with Diaghilev's Russian Ballet 1915–23. In 1918 he founded the Orchestre de la Suisse Romande, which he conducted until 1967. He was known for his accurate and well-balanced performances of Stravinsky's earlier music and gave the first performances of *The Soldier's Tale* (1918), *Pulcinella* (1920), and *Renard* (1922).

Originally a professor of mathematics 1906–10, he studied music with Ernest Bloch, Felix Mottl, and Arthur Nikisch. In 1961 he published a book criticizing certain aspects of modern, especially serial, music.

answer in fugue, the second entry of the subject, brought in while the first entry continues with a counterpoint to it.

Antar a programme symphony by Rimsky-Korsakov, op. 9, based on Senkovsky's oriental story of that name, composed 1868 as '2nd Symphony', revised 1875, first performed St Petersburg, Russian Music Society, January 1876, republished 1903 as 'symphonic suite'. The titles of the movements are I. Introduction; II. 'Joy of Revenge'; III. 'Joy of Power'; IV. 'Joy of Love'.

antecedent in musical analysis, a phrase or passage which is followed by a complementary ◊consequent phrase. Antecedent/consequent phrases are also known as 'question/answer' phrases. Compositions favouring this technique are associated most closely with the Classical period.

Antechrist work for chamber ensemble by Peter Maxwell Davies; composed 1967, first performed London, 30 May 1967.

Antegnati, Costanzo (1549–1624) Italian composer and member of a family of organ-builders famous in Northern Italy from 1470 to 1642. They built about 400 organs, including instruments used by Frescobaldi, the Gabrielis, and other Renaissance composers. He wrote Masses, motets and madrigals, and organ and other instrumental music.

Antheil, George (1900–1959) US composer and pianist. He is known for his *Ballet mécanique* (1923–25, first performed 1926, and revised 1952–53) scored for anvils, aeroplane propellers, electric bells, car horns, and pianos.

anthem a short, usually elaborate, religious choral composition, sometimes accompanied

Answer ———————————

Subject ———————————

An answer as found in the top voice of Bach's Fugue in C major, Well-tempered Clavier, Book 1, No. 1.

by the organ; also a song of loyalty and devotion.

Composers of anthems include Byrd, Gibbons, Purcell, Blow, and Handel.

anticipation the occurrence of a note or notes from a chord before the rest of the chord is sounded.

An example of 'anticipation' from Beethoven's Piano Sonata, Op. 27, No. 2.

Antico, Andrea de (c. 1480–after 1539) Italian composer and music publisher who worked mainly in Rome and then in Venice during the first half of the 16th century. His most important publication was probably *Frottole intabulate da sonar organi* (Rome, 1517), the earliest-known printed edition of keyboard music in Italy.

Antifone work for orchestra by Henze; composed 1960, first performed Berlin, 20 January 1962, conductor Karajan.

Antigonae play with music by Carl Orff (text by Hölderlin, after Sophocles), produced Salzburg, 9 August 1949.

Antigone incidental music to Sophocles' tragedy by Mendelssohn, produced at the New Palace, Potsdam, 28 October 1841, and repeated at the Berlin Opera, 13 April 1842. Daughter of Oedipus attempts to bury her brother, against the wishes of King Creon.
Opera by Honegger (libretto by Cocteau, after Sophocles), produced Brussels, Théâtre de la Monnaie, 28 December 1927.
Opera by Zingarelli (libretto by J F Marmontel), produced Paris, Opéra, 30 April 1790.

Antigono opera by Gluck (libretto by Metastasio), produced Rome, Teatro Argentina, 9 February 1756. Antigonus, king of Macedonia, is rivalled in love by his son.
Opera by Hasse (libretto ditto), produced Hubertusburg near Dresden, 10 October 1743.

antiphon (Greek *anti*, 'against'; *phone*, 'voice') choral music in Greek or Roman liturgy involving the exchange of responses between solo voice and choir, or between choral groups, hence antiphony.

antiphony music exploiting directional and canonic opposition of widely spaced choirs or groups of instruments to create perspectives in sound. It was developed in 17th-century Venice by Giovanni Gabrieli and in Germany by his pupil Heinrich Schütz and Roland de Lassus; an example is the double choir motet *Alma Redemptoris Mater* 1604. The practice was revived in the 20th century by Bartók, Stockhausen, and Berio.

Antiquis, Giovanni de (lived 16th century) Italian composer. He was music director at the church of San Niccolo at Bari; edited two books of *Villanelle alla napolitana* by musicians of Bari, including himself, published at Venice in 1574.

Antonio e Cleopatra opera by Malipiero (libretto by composer, based on Shakespeare), produced Florence, Teatro Comunale, 4 May 1938.

Antony and Cleopatra opera by Barber (libretto by composer, based on Shakespeare), performed on opening night of New York Metropolitan Opera in Lincoln Center, 16 September 1966; revised and produced at Juilliard School, New York, 6 February 1975.

anvil orchestral percussion instrument that imitates the sound of a blacksmith's anvil, but is constructed of small steel bars struck by a mallet of wood or metal. It can be so made as to produce notes of definite pitch, as in Wagner's opera *Das Rheingold*, but is usually indeterminate in pitch.

Apel, Nikolas (c. 1475–1537) German compiler of a large manuscript in choirbook form (Leipzig, University Bibliothek *D-LEu* 1494) containing sacred and secular music of the late 15th and early 16th centuries. It has been published in full by Rudolf Gerber and Ludwig Finscher in *Das Erbe deutscher Musik*, first series, *Der Mensuralkodex des Nikolas Apel* xxxii–xxxiv.

Apel, Willi (1893–1988) German-born US musicologist. He studied mathematics at Bonn, Munich, and Berlin Universities, and also piano under Edwin Fischer, Martienssen, and others. He settled in the USA in 1936, and taught at the Longy School of Music, Cambridge, Massachusetts, 1936–43, and Harvard University, 1938–42. He was professor at Indiana University 1950–63. His publications include *The Notation of Polyphonic Music* (fifth edition 1961), *Harvard Dictionary of Music* (revised edition, 1969), *Gregorian Chant* (1958), and *A History of Keyboard Music* (1972). Joint edition (with A T Davison) of

Historical Anthology of Music (2 volumes, 1946 and 1960).

aperto (Italian 'open, frank, straightforward') musical term used by Mozart in conjunction with *allegro* in some early works, such as the A major violin concerto, K219. The meaning is not clear, but may be taken to suggest an energetic delivery strictly in time.

a piacere (Italian 'at pleasure') musical direction indicating that a passage may be played or sung in any way the performer desires, especially in regard to tempo.

Aplvor, Denis (1916–) Irish composer of Welsh origin. He was chorister at Hereford Cathedral, later at Christ Church, Oxford, and studied composition with Patrick Hadley and Rawsthorne; later influences have included serialism.

Works include: the operas *She Stoops to Conquer* (libretto by composer after Goldsmith) (1947), *Yerma* (1959), *Ubu Roi* (1966); *The Hollow Men* (T S Eliot) for baritone, chorus, and orchestra (1939); piano concerto; two symphonies, two violin concertos; clarinet concertante (1981); Chaucer songs with string quartet (1936), sonata for clarinet, piano, and percussion, violin and piano sonata; clarinet quintet (1981); wind quintet (1981); songs with words by F García Lorca and others.

Apollo e Dafne Italian cantata by Handel, for soprano, baritone, and chamber ensemble; composed c. 1708.

Apollo et Hyacinthus Latin intermezzo by Mozart K38 (libretto by Rufinus Widl), produced Salzburg University, 13 May 1767. Hyacinthus murdered by jealous Zephyrus but Apollo transforms him into a flower.

Apollo Musagetes/Apollo, Leader of the Muses ballet for string orchestra by Stravinsky; composed 1927–28, produced Washington, DC, 27 April 1928 (choreography A Bolm).

apollonicon large organ playable both by hand and mechanically by barrels, built by Flight & Robson in London and exhibited by them in 1817.

Apostel, Hans Erich (1901–1972) German-born Austrian composer. He entered Karlsruhe Conservatory in 1916, and later studied with Schoenberg and Berg in Vienna, where he lived from 1921. In 1937 his *Requiem* won the Hertzka Prize.

Works include: *Requiem* (text by Rilke) for eight-part chorus and orchestra; *Variations on a theme of Haydn* for orchestra (1949); piano concerto; two string quartets; songs with

piano or orchestra on texts by Trakl and Hölderlin.

Apostles, The oratorio by Elgar, op. 49 (libretto compiled from the Bible by the composer), Part I of a trilogy of which II is *The Kingdom* and III was never completed. First performed Birmingham Festival, 14 October 1903.

Appalachia variations for orchestra with chorus by Delius, composed 1902, first performed Elberfeld, 15 October 1904, first London performance 22 November 1907. The title is the old Native American name for North America; the theme is an African-American folksong.

Appalachian Spring ballet by Copland (choreographer Martha Graham), produced Washington, DC, 30 October 1944. Orchestral suite from ballet performed New York, 4 October 1945, conductor Rodziński.

Appassionata (Italian 'impassioned') name commonly used for Beethoven's F minor piano sonata of 1804–05, op. 57, but not authorized by himself.

Appenzeller, Benedictus (c. 1485–after 1558) Flemish composer. A pupil of Josquin Desprez, he was in the service of Mary of Hungary, dowager regent of the Netherlands.

Works include: chansons, church music, a *Nenia* on the death of Josquin, and other pieces.

Applausus Latin allegorical oratorio by Haydn for soloists, chorus, and orchestra performed Zwettl, 17 April 1768.

Appleby, Thomas (1488–c. 1562) English organist and composer of church music. He was appointed organist of Lincoln Cathedral in 1538, and the next year organist at Magdalen College, Oxford. He returned to Lincoln in 1541, and Byrd succeeded him there in 1563.

appoggiatura, or leaning note in musical notation, a type of ◊grace note, of varying

Various symbols have been used in the past to indicate an appoggiatura, the commonest of which is a note in smaller type (top); beneath that is an approximation of how these are played.

length, occurring on a strong beat. It creates a ◊dissonance which is resolved by the melody moving a note lower. It was a form of ◊ornamentation used in the 17th and 18th centuries, and to a more limited extent in the 19th century.

Apprenti sorcier, L'/The Sorcerer's Apprentice scherzo for orchestra by Dukas on Goethe's ballad *Der Zauberlehrling*; first performed Paris, Société Nationale de Musique, 18 May 1897.

Arabella opera by Richard Strauss (libretto by H von Hofmannsthal, based on his story *Lucidor*), produced Dresden, 1 July 1933. Hofmannsthal's last libretto for Strauss.

Arabesk, An work by Delius for baritone, chorus, and orchestra (text by J P Jacobsen); composed 1911 and performed Newport, 1920. First London performance 18 October 1929.

arabesque a piece characterized by florid or ornamental melody. Debussy and Schumann wrote famous arabesques.

Aragonaise a Spanish dance of Aragon, known as the *Jota aragonesa*.

Araia, Francesco (1709–c. 1770), or Araja Italian composer. He produced his first opera in 1729. From 1735 he was for 24 years opera director to the Russian court in St Petersburg, where he produced several of his own works, *Il finto Nino* (1737), *Artaserse* (1738), *Scipione* (1745), *Mitridate* (1747), and *Bellerofonte* (1750). Another was *Cephalus and Procris* (1755), the first opera given in Russia known to have been sung in Russian and not in Italian.

Arbeau, Thoinot (1520–1595), anagram of real name Jehan Tabourot French priest and author. He wrote a book on dancing, *Orchésographie* 1589, which contains a large number of dance tunes current in 16th-century France.

Arbore di Diana, L'/Diana's Tree opera by Martín y Soler (libretto by da Ponte), produced Vienna, Burgtheater, 1 October 1787. Magic apple tree pleases the virtuous but the guilty are pelted.

Arbre enchanté, L', ou Le Tuteur dupé/The Enchanted Tree, or The Tutor Duped comic opera by Gluck (libretto by P L Moline, after J J Vadé), produced Vienna, Schönbrunn Palace, at court, 3 October 1759.

Arcadelt, Jacob (c. 1505–c. 1567) Dutch or French composer. He wrote masses and motets, but is particularly noted for his Italian madrigals.

He entered the papal chapel in Rome in 1540, and received prebends in 1545 at St Barthélemy and St Pierre, Liège, from Pope Paul III. In 1551 he left papal service to go to France and, in 1554, entered the service of Charles, Duke of Guise, who was eventually appointed Archbishop of Rheims. Arcadelt may also have been associated with the royal chapel of France for a time, for he is described as a musician of the king in 1557.

Arcadia in Brenta, L' opera by Galuppi (libretto by Goldoni), produced Venice, Teatro Sant' Angelo, 14 May 1749. The first comic opera by Galuppi written in collaboration with Goldoni. Fabrizio welcomes guests to his new villa by the river Brenta.

Arcana work for large orchestra by Varèse; composed 1925–27, first performed Philadelphia, 8 April 1927, conductor Stokowski.

'Archduke' Trio the name sometimes given to Beethoven's piano trio in B♭ major, op. 97, composed in 1811 and dedicated to the Archduke Rudolph of Austria.

archlute large lute, such as the ◊chitarrone or ◊theorbo, with two sets of strings, the pegs of which are set at different distances in the double neck; the longer bass strings have no fingerboard and can therefore not be altered in pitch during performance, but are used as the bass notes of the chords.

arco (Italian 'with the bow') in music, a direction to play with the bow, or to resume playing with the bow after playing pizzicato (plucked string).

Unusual instruments played with the bow include musical glasses, the suspended cymbal, and the musical saw.

Arden muss sterben/Arden must die opera by Alexander Goehr (libretto by E Fried, after the anonymous Elizabethan play *Arden of Faversham*), produced Hamburg, 5 March 1967.

Arensky, Anton Stepanovich (1861–1906) Russian composer. His works include the opera *Nal and Damayanti* (1904), the ballet *Egyptian Nights* (composed 1900, performed 1908), and the cantata *The Fountain of Bakhchisarai* (1899). He also composed church music, songs, symphonies, a set of variations for strings on a theme of Tchaikovsky, some chamber music, and many elegant piano works. His music is eclectic, but reflects the influence of Tchaikovsky.

Arensky was born in Novgorod, and studied under Karl Karlovich Zikke (1850–90) and, later (1879–82), under Julius Ivanovich Johannsen (1826–1904) and Rimsky-Korsakov at St Petersburg Conservatory. He was appointed professor at the Moscow Conservatory in 1882.

Works include: the operas *A Dream on the Volga* (on Ostrovsky's *Voyevoda*) (1891), *Raphael* (1894), *Nal and Damayanti* (1904); ballet, *Egyptian Nights* (1908); incidental music for Shakespeare's *Tempest*; two symphonies (1883 and 1889); piano concerto; chamber music, including piano trio in D minor; numerous piano pieces; choruses, songs, church music.

Argento, Dominick (1927–) US composer. He studied with Hovhaness and Hanson at the Eastman School and with Dallapiccola in Italy. His music is in an agreeably tonal idiom.

Works include: OPERA *Sicilian Limes* (1954), *The Boor* (1957), *Christopher Sly* (1963), *The Masque of Angels* (1964), *The Shoemaker's Holiday* (1967), *The Voyage of Edgar Allan Poe* (1976), *Miss Havisham's Fire* (1978), *Casanova's Homecoming* (1985), *The Aspern Papers* (1988), *The Dream of Valentino* (1993).

OTHER oratorio *Jonah and the Whale* (1973); *A Ring of Time*, for orchestra (1972); choral music and song-cycles, including *Six Elizabethan Songs* for voice and ensemble (1958); *In Praise of Music* (1977); *Five Variations* for orchestra (1982); *Casa Guidi*, five songs for mezzo and orchestra (1983); *Le Tombeau d'Edgar Poe* (1985); *Capriccio: Rossini in Paris*, for clarinet and orchestra (1985).

aria (Italian 'air') melodic solo song of reflective character, often with a contrasting middle section, expressing a moment of truth in the action of an opera or oratorio. Already to be found in Peri's *Euridice* (1600) and Monteverdi's *Orfeo* (1607), it reached its more elaborate form in the work of Alessandro Scarlatti and Handel, becoming a set piece for virtuoso opera singers. An example is Handel's 'Where'er you walk' from the secular oratorio *Semele* (1744) to words by William Congreve. As an instrumental character piece, an aria is melodious and imitative of a vocal line.

By the early 18th century an aria was a song in three sections, of which the third repeated the first, while the second introduced variety of subject matter, key, and mood. This is known more exactly as the 'da capo aria'.

After Handel's death (1759) and Mozart's youth (1760s) less rigid forms developed, sometimes based on sonata form (Mozart), and later shaped by the dramatic action of an opera (Beethoven, Weber) or oratorio (Mendelssohn).

Ariadne opera in one act by Martinů (libretto by composer after G Neveux), produced Gelsenkirchen, 2 March 1961.

Ariadne auf Naxos play with music (melodrama) by G Benda (text by J C Brandes), produced Gotha, 27 January 1775.
Opera by Richard Strauss (libretto by H von Hofmannsthal), originally a one-act opera played after a shortened version of Molière's *Le Bourgeois gentilhomme*, with incidental music by Strauss, produced Stuttgart, 25 October 1912; second version, with a new operatic first act, produced Vienna, Opera, 4 October 1916.

Ariane et Barbe-bleue/Ariane and Bluebeard opera by Dukas (libretto Maeterlinck's play with slight alterations), produced Paris, Opéra-Comique, 10 May 1907. Ariane releases Bluebeard's previous five wives from his castle.

Ariane, ou Le Mariage de Bacchus opera by Grabu (libretto by P Perrin, previously set by Cambert), produced London, Drury Lane Theatre, 30 March 1674.

Arianna opera by Marcello (libretto V Cassani), composed 1727, never performed in Marcello's lifetime; edited by O Chilesotti, 1885, produced Venice, Liceo Benedetto Marcello, 27 April 1913.
Opera by Handel (*Arianna in Creta*, libretto adapted from P Pariati's *Arianna e Teseo*), produced London, King's Theatre, Haymarket, 26 January 1734. Theseus and the Minotaur complicated by love subplot.

Arianna a Naxos/Ariadne on Naxos cantata by Haydn for soprano and keyboard; composed 1790.

Arianna e Teseo/Ariadne and Theseus opera by Porpora (libretto by P Pariati), produced Vienna, 1 October 1714.

Arianna, L' opera by Monteverdi (libretto by O Rinuccini), produced Mantua, at the ducal court, for the wedding of the Hereditary Prince Francesco Gonzaga with Margherita, Princess of Savoy, 28 May 1608. Most of the music is lost; only the *Lamento d'Arianna* (Ariadne's Lament) survives.

Aribo Scholasticus (lived 11th century) Flemish monk and music theorist. His treatise *De Musica* is important in the development of modal theory in the West, with its emphasis on melodic formulae as well as scales in the definition of mode.

arietta (diminutive of Italian *aria*, 'air') in music, a short, simple ◊aria.

ariette (French 'little aria or air') now the same as an *arietta*, but in early 18th-century French opera an elaborate aria (sometimes with Italian words) and in late 18th-century *opéra comique* a song introduced into a scene in dialogue. See ◊Debussy (*Ariettes oubliées*).

Ariodant opera by Méhul (libretto by F-B Hoffman, after Ariosto's poem *Orlando Furioso* 1516), produced Paris, Théâtre Favart, 11 October 1799. Othon attempts to make Ina leave her lover Ariodant.

Ariodante opera by Handel (libretto by A Salvi, based on Ariosto's *Orlando Furioso* 1516), produced London, Covent Garden, 8 January 1735. Lovers Ginevra and Ariodante threatened by the evil Polinesso, who would have Ginevra for himself.

Ariosi work by Henze for soprano, violin, and orchestra, to poems by Tasso; composed for Wolfgang Schneiderhan and Irmgard Seefried and performed by them Edinburgh, 23 August 1964.

arioso a type of ◊recitative (sung narration), of more lyrical than speechlike quality. Some composers use the arioso to initiate or conclude a recitative, such as Bach in his cantata *Ein feste Burg/A Safe Stronghold* (1724). It can also refer to a section or passage in an instrumental work, which imitates recitative, as in Beethoven's Piano Sonata No. 31 of 1821.

Ariosti, Attilo (1666–c. 1729) Italian composer. He produced his first opera at Venice in 1696, and was court composer in Berlin 1697–1703. Later, he visited Vienna, London, and Bologna, and wrote six operas for the Royal Academy of Music, London.

Works include: OPERA *La più gloriosa fatica d'Ercole* (Vienna, 1703), *Amor tra nemici*, *La fede ne' tradimenti* (Berlin, 1701), *Coriolano* (London, 1723), *Vespasiano* (London, 1724), *Artaserse*, *Dario*, *Lucio Vero*, and others.

OTHER oratorio *Nabucodonosor*, Passion oratorio and others, cantatas; lessons for viola d'amore.

Ariosto, Lodovico (1474–1533) Italian poet. His works inspired numerous musical settings, such as ◊Ariodant (*Orlando Furioso*, Méhul), Handel (◊Ariodante, ◊Orlando), ◊Holmès (*Orlando Furioso*), Roussel (*Enchantements d'Alcine, Les*), and Vivaldi (◊Orlando Furioso).

Aristoxenus of Tarentum (lived 4th century BC) Greek philosopher. His treatise *Harmonics* (on acoustics and music theory) is based on the music practice of his day rather than being purely speculative.

Arlecchino opera in one act by Busoni (libretto by the composer), produced Zurich, 11 May 1917. Adventures of Harlequin in Commedia dell'arte setting.

Arlesiana, L'/The Girl from Arles opera by Ciléa (libretto by L Marenco, based on Alphonse Daudet's play, *L'Arlésienne*), produced Milan, Teatro Lirico, 27 November 1897.

Arlésienne, L'/The Girl from Arles incidental music by G Bizet for Daudet's play, produced Paris, 1 October 1872. Bizet afterwards extracted an orchestral suite from it. (The second suite was arranged by Guiraud.)

Arme Heinrich, Der/Poor Heinrich opera by Pfitzner (libretto by J Grun), produced Mainz, 2 April 1895. Pfitzner's first opera. Singer and Knight can only be saved by the sacrifice of a virgin.

Armenian chant the music of the Church in Armenia from its establishment in 303. It pursued an independent path after the separation from the Greek Church in 536. Its original, alphabetical notation was replaced in the 12th century by a neumic system (in which the only manuscripts have survived), which cannot now be deciphered. The Church's collection of hymns (the *Sharakan*) is arranged according to the eight modes or *echoi*, apparently defined by melodic formulae rather than by scale.

Armida opera by Haydn (libretto by J Durandi), produced Eszterháza, 26 February 1784. Sorceress Armida attempts to seduce crusader knight Rinaldo.
Opera by Rossini (libretto by G Schmidt, after Tasso), produced Naples, Teatro San Carlo, 11 November 1817.
Opera by Dvořák (libretto by J Vrchlický, based on his Czech trans. of Tasso), produced Prague, Czech Theatre, 25 March 1904.
Also settings by Traetta (Vienna, 1761), Anfossi (Turin, 1770), Salieri (Vienna, 1771), and Sacchini (Milan, 1772).

Armida abbandonata Italian cantata by Handel for soprano, two violins, and continuo; composed 1707.

Armide opera by Gluck (libretto by Quinault, based on Tasso's *Gerusalemme liberata*), produced Paris, Opéra, 23 September 1777. Armide's intended victim is Renaud, but he escapes her traps.
Opera by Lully (libretto by Quinault), produced Paris, Opéra, 15 February 1686.

Arminio opera by Handel (libretto by A Salvi), produced London, Covent Garden, 12

January 1737. Rebel chieftain Arminius defeats the Romans in spite of a love subplot. Two operas by Hasse: I. (libretto by G C Pasquini), produced Dresden, at court, 7 October 1745; II. (libretto by Salvi), produced Milan, 28 August 1730.
Opera by Alessandro Scarlatti (libretto by Salvi), produced Villa Medici, Pratolino, September 1703.

armonica alternative name for the glass ◊harmonica, a musical instrument.

Armourer of Nantes, The opera by Balfe (libretto by G V Bridgeman, based on Victor Hugo's *Marie Tudor*), produced London, Covent Garden, 12 February 1863.

Arne, Michael (c. 1741–1786) English singer and composer, son of Thomas Augustine Arne (probably illegitimate). He made his first appearance as a singer in 1750, and a collection of songs, *The Flow'ret*, was published the same year. In 1761 he produced his first opera, *Edgar and Emmeline*. He also collaborated with other composers in the production of works for the stage, *A Midsummer Night's Dream* (with Burney and others, 1763) and *Almena* (with Battishill, 1764). He married the singer Elizabeth Wright in 1766, and the next year wrote the music for Garrick's *Cymon*, his most successful work. In 1771–72 he toured Germany, where he conducted the first German performance of *Messiah*. He was also interested in alchemy; his search for the 'philosophers' stone' twice ruined him. He is still known today for the song 'The lass with a delicate air'.

Arne, Thomas Augustine (1710–1778) English composer. He wrote incidental music for the theatre and introduced opera in the Italian manner to the London stage with works such as *Artaxerxes* (1762, revised 1777). He is remembered for the songs 'Where the bee sucks' from *The Tempest* (1746), 'Blow, blow thou winter wind' from *As You Like It* (1740), and 'Rule Britannia!' from the masque *Alfred* (1740).

Arne was educated at Eton and intended for the law, but practised secretly on a muffled harpsichord and learnt the violin from Michael Festing, until his father allowed him to make music his career. He also taught his sister Susanna singing, and she appeared in his first opera, a setting of Addison's *Rosamond*, in 1733. He wrote music for Henry Fielding's *Tom Thumb* (1733), William Congreve's *Judgement of Paris*, and John Milton's *Comus* (1738). He had married the singer Cecilia Young in 1736, and he and his wife worked successfully 1742–44 in Dublin,

which they twice revisited in the 1750s. The masque *Alfred* was produced in 1740, at the residence of Frederick, Prince of Wales, at Cliveden. In 1744 he was appointed composer to the Drury Lane Theatre, and in 1745 composer to the Vauxhall Gardens. In 1746 he supplied music for the masque *Neptune and Amphitrite* and the songs in *The Tempest*. He composed two oratorios, *The Death of Abel* (1744) and *Judith* (1761). In 1760, after a quarrel with Garrick, he gave up his post as composer to Drury Lane Theatre and became composer to the Covent Garden Theatre, where his popular dramatic pastoral *Thomas and Sally* was produced in 1760. In 1762 he produced his opera *Artaxerxes*, translated by himself from Metastasio and composed in the Italian manner. He was buried at St Paul's, Covent Garden. His son Michael (c. 1741–1786) was also a composer, mainly for the stage.

Works include: OPERAS AND PLAYS WITH MUSIC *Thomas and Sally* (1760), *Artaxerxes* (1762), *Love in a Village* (1762), *May Day*.

MASQUES *Comus* (Milton adapted by Dalton), *The Judgment of Paris*, *Alfred* (1740).

INCIDENTAL MUSIC Shakespeare's *As You Like It* (1740), *Twelfth Night*, *The Merchant of Venice*, *The Tempest*.

ORATORIOS *Judith* (1761); about 25 books of songs; eight overtures for orchestra.

Arnell, Richard (Anthony Sayer) (1917–) English composer. He studied with John Ireland at the Royal College of Music in London and took the Farra Prize in 1938. From 1939 to 1947 he lived in New York, where he was consultant to the British Broadcasting Corporation's (BBC) US service.

Works include: the operas *Love in Transit* (1958), *The Petrified Princess* (1959); ballets *Punch and the Child*, *Harlequin in April*, and *The Great Detective* (after Conan Doyle) (1953); film music; symphonies, symphonic poem *Lord Byron* and other orchestral music; violin concerto; five string quartets; piano and organ music.

Arnold, Malcolm Henry (1921–) English composer. His work is tonal and includes a large amount of orchestral, chamber, ballet, and vocal music. His overtures *Beckus the Dandipratt* (1948), *A Sussex Overture* (1951), and *Tam O'Shanter* (1955) are well known. His operas include *The Dancing Master* (1951), and he has written music for more than 80 films, including *The Bridge on the River Kwai* (1957), for which he won an Academy Award.

Arnold was born in Northampton and studied at the Royal College of Music in London. He began his career as a trumpeter, becoming principal trumpet in the London Philharmonic Orchestra in 1942. He later took up the career of a full-time composer, writing much orchestral and film music in an agreeably diatonic style. He soon became known for his witty, high-spirited, and well-designed compositions.

Works include: the ballets *Homage to the Queen* (1953), *Rinaldo and Armida* (1955), and *Solitaire*; more than 80 film scores, including *The Bridge on the River Kwai*; incidental music for Shakespeare's *Tempest*; overture *Beckus the Dandipratt* (1948) for orchestra; symphony for strings; nine symphonies (1951–87); concertos for horn, clarinet (2), flute (2), oboe, piano duet, and mouth organ; concertos for trumpet, recorder, and cello (1988–89); two string quartets (1951, 1975); violin and piano sonata, viola and piano sonata; piano works.

Arnold, Samuel (1740–1802) English composer. In 1765 he became composer to Covent Garden Theatre and produced the pasticcio *The Maid of the Mill* (1765). He was appointed organist of the Chapel Royal in 1783 and Westminster Abbey in 1793. He composed or arranged many works for the stage, including *The Spanish Barber* (1777), *Gretna Green* (1783), and *Turk and No Turk* (1784). He also wrote oratorios and church music.

Works include: OPERAS AND PLAYS WITH MUSIC *The Maid of the Mill* (1765), *The Portrait* (1770), *The Castle of Andalusia, Gretna Green* (1783), *Peeping Tom of Coventry* (1784), *Inkle and Yarica, The Enraged Musician* (on Hogarth's picture), *The Surrender of Calais* (1791), *Harlequin, Dr Faustus* (1766), *The Mountaineers, The Shipwreck, Obi, or Three-fingered Jack* and many others.

OTHER oratorios *Elisha, The Cure of Saul, The Resurrection* (1770), *The Prodigal Son* (1773); church music; overture for orchestra; odes for chorus; harpsichord music; songs.

Aroldo opera by Verdi (libretto by Piave), produced Rimini, Teatro Nuovo, 16 August 1857. A revision of *Stiffelio* (1850).

arpeggio (Italian 'like a harp') in music, the spreading of a chord to sound like a rapid succession of notes, usually from low to high. It is a technique of guitar playing, not of lute playing, where chords are played together on the beat.

The term 'arpeggio' is found in early keyboard music as an indication of style, for example in J S Bach's *Chromatic Fantasia and Fugue* (1720, revised 1730).

arpeggione six-stringed musical instrument invented by G Staufer of Vienna in 1823. A

The arpeggio sign indicates that the notes should be rolled upwards, starting from the lowest note.

hybrid between a cello and a guitar, it has a fretted fingerboard and is played with a bow.

Schubert wrote a sonata for it in 1824, which today is usually played in transcription for cello, viola, or clarinet.

arpicordo alternative and much rarer name for the ◊harpsichord.

arrangement, or transcription in music, the adaptation of a piece to an instrument or instruments other than those for which it was originally composed.

For example, orchestral compositions can be 'arranged' for the pianoforte (or vice versa). In some cases the 'recreation' of a work in a new instrumental medium virtually qualifies as original composition, as, for instance, in the pianoforte arrangements of Liszt and Busoni.

arranger a person who adapts or assists in orchestrating the music of another composer at the composer's request. The use of an arranger became established in Hollywood; Rachmaninov, George Gershwin, and Leonard Bernstein, among others, composed concert works employing such assistance.

Arrangers were also common in jazz: the more notable examples include Gil Evans (1912–1988), who arranged music for Miles Davis and others; and Billy Strayhorn (1915–1967) for Duke Ellington. Composers of unauthorized arrangements include J S Bach (Vivaldi), Mozart (Handel's *Messiah*), and Stravinsky (Tchaikovsky and Pergolesi).

Arrieta y Corera, (Pascual Juan) Emilio (1823–1894) Spanish composer. He studied under Nicola Vaccai at the Milan Conservatory and produced his first opera there in 1845, returning to Spain the following year. He was professor of composition at the Madrid Conservatory from 1857 and director from 1868.

Works include: the Italian operas *Ildegonda* (Milan, 1825), *La conquista di Granada* (1850, revised as *Isabella la Católica*, 1855); zarzuelas *El dómino azul, El grumete, La Estrella de Madrid, Marina*, and about 50 others.

ars antiqua (Latin 'old art') music of the Middle Ages, generally lacking ◊counterpoint. It includes ◊plainsong and ◊organum composed in France during the 12th and 13th centuries.

arsis (Greek 'lifting') in music, an alternative term, borrowed from Greek poetry, for ◊upbeat. It is the opposite of thesis (Greek 'lowering') or ◊downbeat. In German usage, however, 'arsis' and 'thesis' have opposite meanings to the original Greek and English words.

ars nova (Latin 'new art') music composed in France and Italy during the 14th century. Originally introduced by Philippe de ◊Vitry, it is distinguished by rhythmic and harmonic variety, and the increased importance of duple time (two beats in a bar) and independent voice parts. Guillaume de ◊Machaut mastered the style in France. In Italy the ◊madrigal grew out of ars nova.

ars subtilior (Latin 'the more refined art') term found in the writings of Philipottus de Caserta to describe a late 14th-century style of great notational and rhythmic complexity. Certain works by composers such as Philipottus, Senleches, Ciconia, and Asproys include cross-rhythms of a baffling complexity that has no parallels until the 20th century.

Artamene opera by Albinoni (libretto by B Vitturi), produced Venice, Teatro di Sant' Angelo, 26 December 1740.
Opera by Gluck (libretto ditto), produced London, King's Theatre, Haymarket, 4 March 1746. The second of Gluck's two operas for London; he performed an aria from it before Burney in 1770.

Artaserse/Artaxerxes opera by Abos (libretto by Metastasio), produced Venice, Teatro di San Giovanni Grisostomo, Carnival 1746. Attempt by Artabano to poison Artaserse is prevented by his own son.
Opera by Gluck (libretto ditto), produced Milan, Teatro Regio Ducal, 26 December 1741. Gluck's first opera. Other settings by Hasse (Venice, 1730); Graun (Berlin, 1743); and Jommelli (Rome, 1749).

Artaxerxes opera by Arne (libretto by composer, translated from Metastasio's *Artaserse*), produced London, Covent Garden, 2 February 1762. Revived London, 16 March 1995, in an edition by Peter Holman.

Arteaga, Esteban (1747–1799) Spanish scholar. He was a Jesuit priest, but after the suppression of the Order went to Italy, where he worked for many years with Padre Martini in Bologna. Five treatises on music survive,

the most important of them being that on opera, *Rivoluzioni del teatro musicale italiano*, published 1733–38.

Art of Fugue, The see ◊*Kunst der Fuge.*

arts festival programme of events and performances either promoting a single or a combination of art forms. Arts festivals vary in size, content, and duration, but all share the general objectives of staging and promoting artistic output within a clearly defined and structured programme. Examples include the Salzburg Festival in Austria (music), the Spoleto Festival in Italy (music, drama, art), and the Edinburgh International Festival in Scotland (performing arts).

Stemming from the traditional community-based festival, marking a time of celebration and rejuvenation, arts festivals became a prominent feature of European culture after 1945, and enjoyed huge popularity in the 1980s.

Over 500 arts festivals take place annually in the UK. These include the Notting Hill Carnival, which attracts an estimated 1.5 million visitors, and the ◊Glyndebourne opera festival.

Artusi, Giovanni Maria (c. 1540–1613) Italian composer and theorist. His four-part canzonets appeared in 1598, and his *L'Arte del Contrapunto* in 1586–89. Apart from his polemical works against Zarlino, Galilei, and Bottrigari, his *L'Artusi, overo delle Imperfettioni della musica moderna* (1600) singles out nine as yet unpublished madrigals by Monteverdi for special attack, to which the composer replied in the preface to his fifth book of madrigals (1605). Here he promised a treatise, never completed, to be entitled *Seconda Prattica overo delle perfettioni della moderna musica*, in contradistinction to the 'Prima prattica' of the conservatives. The controversy was continued in two more works by Artusi, published under a pseudonym (1606 and 1608), and by Monteverdi's brother Giulio Cesare in the preface to the *Scherzi musicali* of 1607.

Ascanio opera by Saint-Saëns (libretto by G Gallet, after P Meurice), produced Paris, Opéra, 21 March 1890. Character from Berlioz's opera *Benvenuto Cellini* resurfaces in episode from Cellini's life at court of Francis I at Fontainebleau.

Ascanio in Alba opera by Mozart (libretto by G Parini), produced Milan, Teatro Regio Ducal, 17 October 1771. Venus orders grandson Ascanius to marry the nymph Silvia.

Ascension, L' work for orchestra in four movements by Messiaen; composed 1933, version for organ 1934. Orchestral version performed Paris, February 1935.

Ashkenazy, Vladimir (1937–) Russian-born pianist and conductor. He was music director of the Royal Philharmonic, London, from 1987 and of the Berlin Radio Symphony Orchestra from 1989. He excels in Rachmaninov, Prokofiev, and Liszt.

After studying in Moscow, he toured the USA 1958. In 1962 he was joint winner of the Tchaikovsky Competition with John Ogdon. He settled in England 1963 and moved to Iceland 1968.

Ashley, Robert (1930–) US composer. He studied with Ross Lee Finney and Roberto Gerhard at the University of Michigan and was later influenced by Gordon Mumma and John Cage. With Mumma he cofounded the ONCE Festival for Experimental Music, 1961–68. He was also involved with the Sonic Arts Union, for the use of electronic music.

Works include: TV AND VIDEO OPERAS *In Memoriam ... Kit Carson* (1963), *That Morning Thing* (1967), *Music with Roots in Aether* (1976), *Perfect Lives* (1980), *The Lessons* (1981), *Atalanta, Acts of God* (1982), *Atalanta strategy* (1984), *Foreign Experiences* (1984), *El Aficionado* (1987), *My Brother Called* (1989).

OTHER electronic music theatre *Night Train* (1966), *The Wolfman Motorcity Revue* (1968), *What She Thinks* (1976), *Title Withdrawn* (1976); film music, chamber pieces and electronic works.

Ashwell, Thomas (c. 1478–after 1513), or Ashewell, Hashewell English composer. In 1508 he was *informator choristarum* (choirmaster) at Lincoln Cathedral, and in 1513 held the equivalent post in Durham. His surviving works include four Masses, two (*God save King Harry* and *Sancte Cuthberte*) in a fragmentary state and two (*Ave Maria* and *Jesu Christe*) complete.

Asioli, Bonifazio (1769–1832) Italian music scholar and composer. He worked in his native town at the beginning and end of his career, but in between was at Turin, Venice, Milan, and Paris. He wrote much church, stage, vocal, and instrumental music, and several theoretical treatises.

Asola, Giammateo (c. 1532–1609) Italian priest and composer. He was maestro di cappella successively at Treviso (from 1577) and Vincenza (from 1578). He wrote church music (including 12 books of Masses) and madrigals.

Aspern Papers, The opera in two acts by Dominick Argento (libretto by the composer, after Henry James); produced Dallas, 19 November 1988.

'Asrael' symphony by Josef Suk (his second); written in memory of his wife and of Dvořák, his father-in-law. First performed Prague, 3 February 1907.

Assafiev, Boris Vladimirovich (1884–1949) Russian composer and critic. He studied philosophy at St Petersburg University and music at the Conservatory, where he later became professor. He wrote numerous books on composers, including Glinka, Tchaikovsky, Skriabin, and Stravinsky, and on Russian and Czech music, under the pseudonym of Igor Glebov.

Works include: the operas *Cinderella* (1906), *The Bronze Horseman* (Pushkin, 1940); ballets, 27, including *The Fountain of Bakhchisserai* (after Pushkin, 1933), *Lost Illusions* (after Balzac, 1935); incidental music to plays by writers including Shakespeare, Tirso de Molina, Sophocles, and Schiller; five symphonies (1938–42), piano concerto; string quartet and other chamber works; many piano works, choruses, and songs.

assai (Italian 'much, very') adjective used in music terminology, for example *allegro assai*, 'very fast'.

Assassinio nella cattedrale, L'/Murder in the Cathedral opera by Pizzetti (libretto by composer after T S Eliot's dramatic poem), produced Milan, La Scala, 1 March 1958. Archbishop Beckett murdered at Canterbury.

Astaritta, Gennaro (c. 1745–after 1803) Italian composer of around 40 operas, 1765–93, including the popular *Circe ed Ulisse*, *L'isola disabitata* (Florence, 1773), *Armida* (Venice, 1777), and *Rinaldo d'Asti* (St Petersburg, 1796).

Aston, Hugh (c. 1480–1558) English composer. He completed his studies at Oxford in 1510, and was choirmaster at Newarke College, Leicester 1525–48. His works include six votive antiphons, two Masses, and a 'Hornepype' for keyboard. There are works on a ground bass of his by Whytbroke (for viols) and Byrd (for keyboard).

Astorga, Emanuele (Gioacchino Cesare Rincón) d' (1680–1757) Italian nobleman and composer of Spanish descent. His opera, *Dafni*, was produced in Genoa and Barcelona in 1709. His most famous work is a *Stabat Mater* (c. 1707). He also wrote a number of chamber cantatas in the manner of Alessandro Scarlatti. From around 1721 he seems to have lived mainly in Spain and Portugal.

An example of expressionist atonal music in which the composer avoids any clear key; from Schoenberg's 3 Piano Pieces, op. 11 (1909).

Astuzie femminili, Le/Women's Wiles opera by Cimarosa (libretto by G Palomba), produced Naples, Teatro del Fondo, 16 August 1794. Orphan Bellina wishes to marry Filandro, but there is competition from Don Lasagna.

Atalanta opera by Handel (libretto adapted from *La caccia in Etolia* by B Valeriani), produced London, Covent Garden, 12 May 1736. The nymph Atalanta is united with the shepherd king Meleager, in spite of her initial preference for the hunt and life in the woods.

Atem gibt das Leben/Breathing gives Life work for chorus by Stockhausen; performed Hamburg, 16 May 1975.

a tempo (Italian 'in time') in music, a direction to return to the original tempo. It is often found after ◊accelerando or ◊ritardando.

Athalia oratorio by Handel (words by S Humphreys), produced Oxford, 10 July 1733.

Athalie incidental music for Racine's tragedy by Fanny Mendelssohn, op. 74; choruses composed 1843, overture 1844–45, produced Charlottenburg, 1 December 1845.
The choruses were also set by Moreau (Saint-Cyr, 5 January 1691), Gossec (1785), Vogler (1786), J A P Schulz (1786), and Boieldieu (1836).

Atlantida, L' scenic oratorio by Falla (text by composer, after J Verdaguer); sketched 1926–46 and completed by E Halffter; produced Milan, La Scala, 18 June 1962. Spanish saga, from the flooding of Atlantis to Columbus and the New World.

Atmosphères work for orchestra by Ligeti; first performed Donaueschingen, 22 October 1961, conductor Rosbaud.

atonality music in which the sense of ◊tonality is distorted or obscured; music of no apparent key. It is used by film and television composers for situations of mystery or horror, exploiting dissonance for its power to disturb.

For Schoenberg, pioneer of atonal music from 1909, the intention was to liberate tonal expression and not primarily to disturb, and he rejected the term as misleading. Other exponents of atonality include Berg, Webern, Stockhausen, and Boulez.

attacca (Italian imperative 'attack, begin') musical direction placed at the end of a movement indicating that the next movement is to be started without a pause.

attacco (Italian 'attack') a short musical figure or phrase treated by imitation.

Atterberg, Kurt (Magnus) (1887–1974) Swedish composer and conductor. He composed in an undemanding style, and conducted much in Europe.

After training as a civil engineer, he studied music at the Royal Academy of Music in Stockholm under Hallén, and later at Munich, Berlin, and Stuttgart. He was music critic of the newspaper *Stockholms Tidningen* from 1919.

Works include: five operas; pantomime-ballets; incidental music for plays; Requiem (1914), *Järnbäraland/The Land of Iron-Carriers*, for chorus and orchestra (1919); nine symphonies (one in memory of Schubert), nine suites, *Swedish Rhapsody*, symphonic poem *Le Fleuve, Rondeau rétrospectif* and *The Song* for orchestra; symphonic poem for baritone and orchestra; concertos for violin, cello, piano, and horn; three string quartets; cello and piano sonata.

At the Boar's Head opera by Holst (libretto by composer, drawn from Shakespeare's *Henry IV*), produced Manchester, 3 April 1925.

Attila opera by Verdi (libretto by T Solera), produced Venice, Teatro La Fenice, 17 March 1846. Odabella avenges herself on Attila after her father has been murdered.

Attwood, Thomas (1765–1838) English organist and composer. Organist of St Paul's Cathedral and composer to the Chapel Royal from 1796 to his death, he was one of the original members of the Philharmonic Society in 1813, and a professor at the Royal Academy of Music on its foundation in 1823. He was also a friend of Mendelssohn, whose three Preludes and Fugues for organ, op. 37, were dedicated to him.

He was a chorister at the Chapel Royal; later studied in Naples and Vienna, where he was a pupil of Mozart 1785–87. His harmony and counterpoint exercises for Mozart still survive, with Mozart's corrections.

Works include: over 30 dramatic compositions; coronation anthems for George IV and William IV, service settings, anthems and other church music, and songs.

Atys opera by Lully (libretto by Quinault), produced at Saint-Germain, 10 January 1676 and first performed Paris, April 1676. Atys stabs himself for love and is transformed into a pine tree by Cybele.

Opera by Piccinni (libretto ditto, altered by J F Marmontel), produced Paris, Opéra, 22 February 1780.

Atzmon, Moshe (1931–) Israeli conductor. He won the Liverpool International Competition in 1964; conducted in Sydney and Hamburg 1969–76. He made his opera debut in Berlin in 1969. He was principal conductor Basle Symphony Orchestra from 1972, and became director of the Dortmund Opera in 1991.

aubade (French from *aube*, 'dawn') 'morning song', in the same sense that a serenade is an evening song; cf. Spanish *alborada*.

Choreographic concerto by Poulenc, for piano and 18 instruments; first performed Paris, 18 June 1929.

Auber, Daniel François Esprit (1782–1871) French operatic composer. He studied under the Italian composer and teacher Luigi Cherubini and wrote nearly 50 operas, including *La Muette de Portici/The Mute Girl of Portici* (1828) and the comic opera *Fra Diavolo* (1830). He wrote a *Manon Lescaut* in 1856, 37 years before Puccini.

Born at Caen in Normandy, he began to compose early, but as a young man was sent to London by his father, to follow a commercial career. His songs attracted attention, however, and on his return to Paris in 1804 he wrote cello concertos for the cellist Lamarre and a violin concerto for Mazas. In 1805 he appeared with a comic opera, *L'Erreur d'un moment*, the libretto of which had previously been set by Dezède, but he did not produce an opera in public until 1813 (*Le Séjour militaire*). It failed miserably, and he had no real success until his father's death in 1819 compelled him to make music his means of livelihood. *La Bergère châtelaine* (1820), was a brilliant success, and in 1822 he began his association with the librettist Scribe, and the two began a series of popular and successful productions, including *Fra Diavolo* (1830), *Le Cheval de bronze* (1835), *Le Domino noir* (1837), *Les Diamants de la couronne* (1841), and *Manon Lescaut* (after Prevost). *La Muette de Portici*

(1828), was a precursor of French Grand Opera. In 1842 he became director of the Paris Conservatory and in 1857 of the Imperial chapel.

Works include: OPERA nearly 50, including *Emma* (1821), *Leicester, Le Maçon, La Muette de Portici (Masaniello)* (1828), *La Fiancée, Fra Diavolo* (1830), *Le Dieu et la Bayadère, Le Philtre, Le Serment, Gustave III, Le Cheval de bronze* (two versions, 1835 and 1857), *Actéon, L'Ambassadrice, Le Domino noir* (1837), *Les Diamants de la couronne, La Part du diable, Haydée* (1847), *Marco Spada* (with a later ballet version), *Jenny Bell, Manon Lescaut* (1856), *La Circassienne.*

Aubert, Jacques (1689–1753) French violinist and composer. A pupil of Jean Baptiste Senaillé; he was a member of the king's 24 violins from 1727 and of the Paris Opéra orchestra from 1728. He wrote numerous violin concertos, concert suites, and other instrumental works.

Aubin, Tony (Louis Alexandre) (1907–1981) French composer. He studied at the Paris Conservatory, where Dukas was his composition master. He took the Prix de Rome in 1930; in 1939 he was appointed head of the music department of the Paris-Mondial radio station, and in 1946 professor at the Paris Conservatory.

Works include: the suite *Cressida* for solo voices, chorus, and orchestra (1935); cantata *Actéon* (1930); *Symphonie romantique* and *Le Sommeil d'Iskander* for orchestra; string quartet; sonata and *Prélude, Récitatif et Final* for piano; six Verlaine songs.

Aubry, Pierre (1874–1910) French musicologist and orientalist. He lectured on music history at the Ecole des Hautes Etudes Sociales in Paris, and did important research on French medieval music.

Aucassin et Nicolette 13th-century French narrative in prose and verse. Its verse sections show a technique similar to that employed in the *chanson de geste*, in that each pair of lines is sung to the same tune constantly repeated, each section being rounded off by a single line sung to a different tune. Its alternation between prose and verse, however, classifies it as a *chante-fable.*

Aucassin et Nicolette, ou Les Mœurs du bon vieux temps opera by Grétry (libretto by J M Sedaine, based on the French 13th-century tale), produced Versailles, at court, 30 December 1779, first Paris performance, Comédie-Italienne, 3 January 1780.

Auden, W(ystan) H(ugh) (1907–1973) English-born US poet and librettist. From 1935 he collaborated with Britten on *Paul Bunyan, Ode to St Cecilia,* and *Our Hunting Fathers.* His close relationship with Chester Kallman from 1948 resulted in librettos for Stravinsky's *Rake's Progress* (1953), Henze's *Elegy for Young Lovers* (1961), and *The Bassarids* (1966). Their work has been judged theatrically effective, but was also at times criticized as being somewhat contrived (the intermezzo in *The Bassarids*).

Audran, Edmond (1840–1901) French composer. He studied at Niedermeyer's school in Paris and first made his mark as a church organist and composer at Marseilles and Paris, producing a Mass, but later with operettas, the first of which, *L'Ours et le Pacha,* was produced at Marseilles in 1862. His first production in Paris (1879) was *Les Noces d'Olivette.* Others included *La Mascotte* (1880), *Gillette de Narbonne* (based on Boccaccio) (1882), *La Cigale et la Fourmi* (based on La Fontaine) (1886), *La Poupée,* and *Monsieur Lohengrin.*

Aufforderung zum Tanz/Invitation to the Dance piano piece by Weber, op. 65, which he calls a *rondeau brillant,* in waltz form with a slow introduction and epilogue, composed in 1819. Usually heard today in orchestral version by Berlioz.

Aufgesang (German 'fore-song') see ◊bar.

Aufstieg und Fall der Stadt Mahagonny/ Rise and Fall of the City of Mahagonny opera by Weill (libretto by Brecht), produced Leipzig, 9 March 1930. Jenny and Jim make out in the fat city but Jim can't pay the whisky bill.

Auftakt (German 'upbeat') see ◊upbeat.

Auftrittslied (German 'entry song') a song or air in a musical play or opera, especially a German *Singspiel,* by which a character introduces and describes himself to the audience, either directly or by addressing another character or characters, such as Papageno's first song in Mozart's *Die Zauberflöte.*

Augenarzt, Der/The Oculist opera by Gyrowetz (libretto by J E Veith), produced Vienna, Kärntnertortheater, 1 October 1811. Dr Berg restores sight to Wilhelmine, who turns out to be his long-lost sister.

Augenlicht, Das work for chorus and orchestra by Webern (text by H Jone); composed 1935, first performed London, 17 June 1938, conductor Scherchen.

1. Italian

2. German

3. French

4. 'Tristan 6th'

1. Italian; 2. German; 3. French; 4. 'Tristan 6th'. The earliest augmented 6th chord, occasionally found even in the 17th century, is the Italian 6th, a three-note chord (in C major). Since the structure of the German 6th (in equal temperament) is identical with that of the dominant 7th, it is extremely useful for modulation to distant keys. The famous opening chord of Wagner's Tristan und Isolde *may be interpreted as an augmented 6th like the French 6th but with the 3rd flattened, thus sometimes called the 'Tristan 6th' (here transposed from A minor to C minor for comparison).*

augmentation notation of a musical figure in larger time values, used in counterpoint in order to combine it with the same figure in smaller time values.

augmented 6th chords a group of chords that stand as the springboard for much of the more colourful harmonic style of the 19th century. They depend for their effect on the interval of an augmented 6th between the flattened 6th degree and the sharpened 4th degree of the diatonic scale. Almost invari-

Perfect 4th	Augmented 4th

Major 6th	Augmented 6th

Perfect and augmented intervals.

ably their logical progression is to the dominant (V) or to a second inversion triad on the dominant (I_4^6) which in turn leads to the dominant.

Of the four-note forms, the 'German 6th' first became a firm favourite at the end of the 18th century and was used with particular force by Beethoven. Less common is the 'French 6th', with its two middle notes a major 2nd apart. Finally, it may be noted that from the middle of the 19th century many other variants of the principle appear.

'Auld Lang Syne' song written by the Scottish poet Robert Burns about 1789, which is often sung at New Year's Eve gatherings. The title means 'old long since' or 'long ago'.

Auletta, Pietro (1698–1771) Italian composer. He made his debut as an opera composer at Naples in 1725 with *Il trionfo d'amore*, in which year he also received the title of maestro di cappella to the Prince of Belvedere. Several comic and then some serious operas followed. His most popular work, *Orazio* (1737), eventually became debased into a pasticcio by the addition of music by other composers, and was published in Paris as *Il maestro di musica* in 1753 under the name of Pergolesi.

aulos ancient Greek double-reed musical instrument, the equivalent of the Latin *tibia* and akin to the modern ◊oboe.

The double aulos often seen in pictures and sculpture would have enabled the melody to be accompanied by a drone, both sets of reeds being blown simultaneously by one player.

Aureliano in Palmira opera by Rossini (libretto by F Romani), produced Milan, La Scala, 26 December 1813. The overture was afterwards used for *Elisabetta regina d'Inghilterra*, and later for *Il barbiere di Siviglia*. Other parts of the music also appear in the latter work. Roman emperor Aurelianus allows Arsace and Zenobia to marry.

Auric, Georges (1899–1983) French composer. His works include a comic opera, several ballets, and incidental music to films including Jean Cocteau's *Orphée/Orpheus* (1950). He was one of the musical group called ◊Les Six, who were influenced by Erik ◊Satie.

Auric was born at Lodève, Hérault, and studied both at the Conservatoire and the Schola Cantorum in Paris. His first success was incidental music for Molière's *Les Fâcheux* (1923), which he turned into a ballet. After his music for René Clair's film *A nous la liberté* (1932) he was much sought after by both French and English film studios. He also wrote a few choral, orchestral, and chamber works, and numerous piano pieces and songs.

Works include: the comic opera *Sous le masque* (libretto by L Laloy, 1907), ballets *Les Noces de Gamache* (from *Don Quixote*), *Les Matelots*, *La Pastorale*, *La Concurrence*, *Les Imaginaires*; incidental music to *Les Fâcheux* (Molière), *The Birds* (Aristophanes, 1928), *Volpone* (Ben Jonson, 1927), *Le Mariage de Figaro* (Beaumarchais), *Le 14 Juillet* (Rolland, 1931), with nine others; film music *A nous la liberté* (René Clair), *Caesar and Cleopatra* (after Bernard Shaw); symphony, suite, overture, *Fox-trot* and *Nocturne* for orchestra; piano concerto; piano sonata and sonatina, *Three Pastorales* for piano; *Chandelles romaines* for piano duet; trio for oboe, clarinet, and bassoon; violin and piano sonata; several song cycles.

'Aus Italien' ('from Italy') symphony by Richard Strauss, op. 16, composed 1885–86

during and after a visit to Italy in March 1887. The four movements are entitled *On the Campagna*, *The Ruins of Rome*, *On the Shore of Sorrento*, and *Neapolitan Folk Life*; the last contains a quotation of Denza's *Funiculì funiculà*, which Strauss took for a folksong.

Aus meinem Leben/From my Life subtitle of Smetana's string quartet in E minor (1876). Slow movement depicts Smetana's love of his wife, and a sustained high note on the violin in the finale suggests his tinnitus.

Austin, Larry (1930–) US composer. He studied in California with Milhaud and Seymour Shifrin and taught at the University of South Florida and North Texas State University (from 1978). His works employ a full range of electronic effects and are cast for a variety of theatrical media.

Works include: *Improvisations*, for orchestra and jazz soloists, (1961); theatre pieces *The Maze* (1967), *Agape* (1970), *Walter* (1971); *Plastic Surgery* for tape and film (1970); *Phantasmagoria*, after Ives' unfinished *Universe* symphony (1982); *Sinfonia Concertante: A Mozartean Episode* (1986); *Concertante Cybernetica* (1987).

authentic cadence, or perfect cadence or full close in music, a harmonic progression or modulation ending with a ◊dominant harmony followed by the ◊tonic.

authenticity a trend initiated in Austria and the Netherlands in the 1950s and 1960s aiming to reproduce the original conditions of early music performance and instrumentation as a means of rediscovering aesthetic terms of reference. It was pioneered by performers like Nikolaus Harnoncourt and Gustav Leonhardt. Authenticity stimulated important practical research in manuscript editing and transcription, instrumentmaking, dance, architectural acoustics, and vocal techniques, and encouraged performance of vocal works in the original language. The interest in authenticity grew rapidly; there are a number of flourishing and highly regarded 'authentic' ensembles in the USA and in every major West European country as well as in certain Central European centres.

Notable exponents include conductors Christopher Hogwood, Andrew Parrott, Roger Norrington, John Eliot Gardiner, Trevor Pinnock, William Christie, Nicholas McGegan, Reinhardt Goebel, Frans Bruggen, and Ton Koopman, David Munrow (woodwind), Anthony Rooley (lute), Jaap Schröder (violin), Emma Kirkby (soprano), and Frans Brüggen (flute).

Avison, Charles (1709–1770) English organist and composer. A pupil of Geminiani and organist at St Nicholas' Church, Newcastle 1736–70. He is chiefly remembered for his treatise *An Essay on Musical Expression* 1752, but also wrote a quantity of instrumental music, including 48 concertos for chamber orchestra. He edited (with fellow composer John Garth, 1722–1810) 50 of Benedetto Marcello's Psalms in 1757. He is recognized as the foremost English concerto composer of his time.

Axman, Emil (1887–1949) Czech composer who studied at Prague University and was a composition student of Novák.

Works include: melodrama *Just Once*; cantatas and other choral works; six symphonies, symphonic poem *Sorrow and Hope*; suite, sinfonietta, suite *From the Beskides*, Moravian dances for orchestra; violin concerto; four string quartets (1924–46), piano trio, violin and piano sonata, cello and piano sonata; three piano sonatas, sonatina, and other piano works.

Axur, Salieri see ◊*Tarare*.

Aylward, Theodore (c. 1730–1801) English organist and composer. He was organist at several London churches. He received a doctorate in music from Oxford; he was appointed professor of music at Gresham College, London, in 1771.

Works include: incidental music for Shakespeare's *Cymbeline* and *Midsummer Night's Dream* (with M Arne, Battishill, and Burney) (1765); lessons for organ; canzonets for two voices; glees, catches, and songs.

ayre, or air 16th-century verse song with lute or guitar accompaniment, as in 'It was a lover and his lass' (1600) by Thomas Morley.

azione sacra (Italian 'sacred action') 17th–18th-century term for a sacred drama with music or acted oratorio, such as Mozart's *La Betulia Liberata*.

azione teatrale (Italian 'theatrical action') 17th-century term for an opera or musical festival play.

Azzaiolo, Filippo (lived 16th century) Italian composer of *villotte*, popular madrigal-like part songs. William Byrd wrote a keyboard piece on the bass of his popular 'Chi passa'.

B

B the seventh note, or leading note, of the scale of C major. In Germany B corresponds to B♭, and B♮ is represented by H.

Baal opera by Friedrich Cerha (libretto by the composer after Brecht), produced Salzburg, 7 August 1981. The poet Baal as a victim of society.

Baal Shem *Three Pictures of Chassidic Life*, for violin and piano, by Bloch (1923). Version for violin and orchestra, 1939; first performed New York, 19 October 1941, with Szigeti.

Baaren, Kees van (1906–1970) Dutch composer. He studied with Pijper, and was a leading Dutch exponent of serial music, exploiting both tonal and 12-note varieties of this kind of composition, and also very active as a teacher. From 1957 he was director of the Royal Conservatory in The Hague.

Works include: *The Hollow Men* (words by T S Eliot), cantata for chorus and orchestra (1948); *Variazioni per Orchestra* (1959); a string quartet and a wind quintet (*Sovraposizione I and II*) (1963).

Babbitt, Milton (1916–   ) US composer and theorist. He pioneered the application of information theory to music in the 1950s, introducing set theory to series manipulations and the term 'pitch class' to define every octave identity of a note name. His works include four string quartets, works for orchestra, *Philomel* for soprano and electronic tape 1963–64, and *Ensembles for Synthesizer* 1967, both composed using the 1960 RCA Princeton-Columbia Mark II Synthesizer, which he helped to design.

Babbitt was born in Philadelphia, Pennsylvania. He studied music and mathematics at New York University under Marion Bauer

(composer and writer, 1887–1955) and Philip James (composer and conductor, 1890–1975), and Princeton University, where one of his composition teachers was Roger ◊Sessions. From 1948 he taught at Princeton University.

Babi-Yar subtitle of symphony no. 13 in B♭ minor, for bass, male chorus, and orchestra by Shostakovich (text by Yevtushenko). Composed 1961, first performed Moscow, 18 December 1962. Babi-Yar is the site of a World War II massacre of Russian Jews by the Germans.

Bacchus et Ariane ballet in two acts by Roussel, scenario by A Hermant; produced Paris, Opéra, 22 May 1931. Suite no. 1 for orchestra, performed Paris, 2 April 1933, conductor Munch; Suite no. 2 performed Paris, 2 February 1934, conductor Monteux.

Bacewicz, Grażyna (1909–1969) Polish composer and violinist. She taught at Łódź Conservatory 1934–35, returning to Paris in 1945. Although most of her work has been described as neoclassical, her later music also uses avant-garde techniques.

She studied composition at the Warsaw Conservatory under Sikorski and later in Paris with Nadia Boulanger. Her fourth string quartet won first prize at the International Competition, Liège, in 1951.

Works include: four symphonies (1945–53); seven violin concertos (1937–65); cello concerto; piano concerto; concerto for string orchestra; seven string quartets; two piano quintets; six violin sonatas and various violin pieces.

B.A.C.H. a musical theme formed of the notes B♭, A, C, B♮ in German nomenclature and used by various composers as a reference to

Bach, who was himself the first to use it. Some examples are:

Albrechtsberger, Fugue for keyboard.

Bach, one of the subjects of the final fugue (unfinished) in *Die Kunst der Fugue* (four organ fugues are probably spurious).

Bach, J C, Fugue for clavier or organ.

Busoni, *Fantasia contrappuntistica* for piano and for two pianos.

Casella, *Ricercari sul nome di Bach* for piano.

Eisler, Trio on a 12-note row.

Honegger, *Prélude, ariso et Fughette* for piano.

D'Indy, *Beuron* in *Tableaux de voyage* for piano.

Karg-Elert, *Basso ostinato* in organ pieces *Sempre semplice*, op. 143; Passacaglia and Fugue, op. 150 for organ: Sonata, B♭ minor, op. 46, for Kunstharmonium.

Koechlin, *Offrande musicale* for organ (later orchestra).

Liszt, Fantasy, and Fugue for organ.

Nielsen (R), Ricercare, Chorale, and Toccata for piano.

Piston, Chromatic Study for organ.

Reger, Fantasy, and Fugue for organ.

Rimsky-Korsakov, Fugue in *Chopsticks* Variations for piano by various composers; six variations for piano, op. 10.

Schoenberg, Variations for orchestra, op. 31.

Schumann, Six Fugues for organ or pedal piano.

Bach, Carl Philip Emanuel (1714–1788) German composer. He was the third son of J S Bach. He introduced a new 'homophonic' style, light and easy to follow, which influenced Mozart, Haydn, and Beethoven.

In the service of Frederick the Great 1740–67, he left to become master of church music at Hamburg in 1768. He wrote over 200 pieces for keyboard instruments, and published a guide to playing the piano. Through his music and concert performances he helped to establish a leading solo role for the piano in Western music.

He was educated at St Thomas' School, Leipzig, and at the universities of Leipzig (1731–34) and Frankfurt an der Oder (1734–38), where he studied law. He claimed to have received his musical training entirely from his father. He was connected with the household of the Crown Prince of Prussia from 1738, and in 1740, on the latter's accession as King Frederick II, he was appointed harpsichordist to the court at Berlin and Potsdam. In 1744 he married Johanna Maria Dannemann, and in 1747 his father visited him at court. His most import-

ant works at this time were keyboard pieces, which contributed much to the development of a more homophonic style and modern formal procedures. His treatise on keyboard playing (*Versuch über die wahre Art das Clavier zu spielen* 1753 and 1762) is a valuable guide to contemporary practice. Bach found Berlin restricting, partly because his duties involved only harpsichord playing, and partly because of the king's conservatism, and in 1768 he moved to Hamburg as municipal director of music at the five principal churches. Charles Burney visited him there in 1772, and commented on his remarkable talent for improvising. In Hamburg Bach had wider scope, directing concerts with great success, and there he wrote most of his music for large forces, such as oratorios.

Works include: oratorios *Die Israeliten in der Wüste* (1769) and *Die Auferstehung und Himmelfahrt Jesu* (1780); Magnificat (1749), *Heilig/Sanctus* for double choir, Passions and other church music; 19 symphonies; 50 keyboard concertos; about 200 keyboard pieces (including sonatas, fantasias, and rondos), odes, and songs.

Bach, Jan (1937–) US composer. He studied with Copland and Donald Martino and has taught at Northern Illinois University from 1966. His works are based on traditional means.

Works include: the operas *The System* (1974) and *The Student from Salamanca* (1980); piano concerto (1975); *The Happy Prince* for narrator, violin, and orchestra (1978); horn concerto (1983); harp concerto (1986); chamber and vocal music.

Bach, Johann Ambrosius (1645–1695) German organist and composer. He was taught by his father, Christoph Bach. He was town musician at Erfurt from 1667, and at Eisenach from 1671.

He was the twin of Johann Christoph Bach. He married Elisabeth Lämmerhirt at Erfurt in 1668. In 1671 he was appointed town musician at Eisenach. His wife died in May 1694 and he married Barbara Margaretha Keul in November, but died himself three months later.

Bach, Johann Christian (1735–1782) German composer. The eleventh son of J S Bach, he became celebrated in Italy as a composer of operas. In 1762 he was invited to London, where he became music master to the royal family. He remained in England until his death; his great popularity both as a composer and a performer declined in his last years for political and medical reasons.

Bach, Johann Christoph (1642–1703) German organist and composer. He became organist at Eisenach in 1665 and remained there to the end of his life. He composed motets, church cantatas, chorale preludes for organ, and harpsichord music.

He was J S Bach's father's cousin.

Bach, Johann Christoph Friedrich (1732–1795) German composer. Among his most notable works are the oratorios on words by Johann Gottfried Herder (attached to the court at Bückeburg 1771–74), *Die Kindheit Jesu* and *Die Auferweckung Lazarus*; a third oratorio and an opera, *Brutus*, both on words by the same poet, are lost.

The ninth son of J S Bach, he was educated at St Thomas' School and Leipzig University, where he studied law. He received his music training from his father, and in 1750 was appointed chamber musician to Count Wilhelm of Schaumburg-Lippe in Bückeburg, where he remained for the rest of his life, becoming Konzertmeister in 1759. He married the court singer Elisabeth Münchhausen in 1755. In 1778 he visited his brother Johann Christian in London.

Other works include Passion oratorio *Der Tod Jesu* (words by Ramler); cantatas (some with Herder); 20 symphonies; keyboard concertos and sonatas; chamber music.

Bach, Johann Michael (1648–1694) German organist, instrument maker, and composer. Organist and parish clerk at Gehren from 1673, he composed motets, sacred arias, and other pieces.

Bach, Johann Sebastian (1685–1750) German composer. A master of ◊counterpoint, his music epitomizes the Baroque polyphonic style. His orchestral music includes the six *Brandenburg Concertos* (1721), other concertos for keyboard instrument and violin, four orchestral suites, sonatas for various instruments, three partitas and three sonatas for violin solo, and six unaccompanied cello suites. Bach's keyboard music, for clavier and organ, his fugues, and his choral music are of equal importance. He also wrote chamber music and songs.

His appointments included positions at the courts of Weimar and Anhalt-Cöthen, and from 1723 until his death he was musical director at St Thomas' choir school in Leipzig.

He married twice and had over 20 children (although several died in infancy). His second wife, Anna Magdalena Wülkens, was a soprano; she also worked for him when his sight failed in later years.

Although he was not always appreciated by his contemporaries, Bach's place in music history was aptly summed up by his first major biographer, Johann Nikolaus Forkel (1749–1818; *Über Johann Sebastian Bachs Leben, Kunst, und Kunstwerke*, 1802, English translation 1820 and 1920): 'He is the river, to which all other composers are tributaries'.

Born at Eisenach, Bach came from a distinguished musical family. After his father's death in 1695 he went to Ohrdruf and studied under his brother Johann Christoph. At 15 he became a chorister at Lüneburg, and at 19 he was appointed violinist in the court orchestra of the Duke of Weimar, but left the same year to become organist in Arnstadt. In 1705 he took leave to travel to Lübeck, to hear Dietrich Buxtehude play the organ.

In 1707 he moved to Mühlhausen, where he married his cousin Maria Barbara Bach; among their seven children were Wilhelm Friedemann and Carl Philip Emanuel. A year later he returned to Weimar as court organist, and remained there for nine years; during this time he wrote such famous cantatas as *Christ lag in Todesbanden, Weinen, Klagen, Sorgen, Zagen*, and *Ich hatte viel Bekümmernis*.

In 1717 Bach was appointed Kapellmeister to the court of Prince Leopold of Anhalt-Cöthen. His wife died in 1720, and he married Anna Magdalena Wülkens in 1721, fathering 13 more children. At Cöthen Bach had little opportunity for composing church music and there he wrote mainly instrumental works, including the *Brandenburg Concertos, Orchestral Suites*, and works for solo cello and violin. In these works instrumental music seems for the first time to emerge from private use into the public domain.

In 1723 he returned to church work when he succeeded Kühnau as Cantor of St Thomas' in Leipzig. He remained there for the rest of his life and wrote some of his greatest compositions there, including the B minor Mass, *St Matthew Passion*, and *Goldberg Variations*. In 1747, with his eldest son, Wilhelm Friedemann, he visited the court of Frederick the Great at Potsdam, where his second son, Carl Philip Emanuel, was court harpsichordist. Two years later his eyesight failed; an operation in 1750 was unsuccessful, and he spent his last months totally blind.

Although Bach is not credited with revolutionizing musical forms, he invested contemporary models with a unique brand of creative polyphony and intense spirituality: all his works were dedicated 'To the Greater Glory of God'.

Works include: CHURCH CANTATAS 200 are extant. Among those most frequently performed are no. 12 *Weinen, Klagen, Sorgen, Zagen* (1714), no. 20 *O Ewigkeit, du Donnerwort* (1724), no. 21 *Ich hatte viel Bekümmernis* (about 1714), no. 51 *Jauchzet Gott in allen Landen* (1730), no. 56 *Ich will den Kreuzstab gerne tragen* (1726), no. 61 *Nun komm der Heiden Heiland* (1714), no. 80 *Ein feste Burg ist unser Gott* (1724), no. 82 *Ich habe genug* (1727), no. 106 *Gottes Zeit ist die allerbeste Zeit* (about 1707), no. 140 *Wachet auf, ruft uns die Stimme* (1731), no. 147 *Herz und Mund und Tat und Leben* (1723).

SECULAR CANTATAS no. 202 *Weichet nur, betrübte Schatten* (about 1720), no. 211 *Schweigt stille, plaudert nicht* (*Coffee Cantata*, 1734).

OTHER CHURCH MUSIC Mass in B minor, BWV 232, assembled about 1748 from music previously composed by Bach; Magnificat in E flat BWV 243 (1723, including four Christmas texts; revised about 1730, in D, without Christmas texts); *St Matthew Passion* (11 April 1727 or 15 April 1729); *St John Passion* (7 April 1724, later revised); *Christmas Oratorio* BWV 248, six cantatas for Christmas to Epiphany (performed 1734–35); six motets BWV 225–30; *Easter Oratorio* (1 April 1725) BWV 249.

ORGAN 19 preludes and fugues, including E♭, ('St Anne', 1739) BWV 548; six trio sonatas BWV 525–530; Toccata and Fugue in D minor ('Dorian') BWV 538 and D minor BWV 565 (now doubtful); Fantasia and Fugue in C minor BWV 562 and G minor BWV 542; Toccata, Adagio, and Fugue in C BWV 564; Passacaglia in C minor BWV 582; *Pastorale* in F BWV 590 (about 1710); 134 chorale preludes BWV 599–768, some of the best known being *An Wasserflüssen Babylon* BWV 653, *Ein feste Burg* BWV 720, *In dulci jubilo* BWV 729, *Jesu, meine Freude* BWV 713, *Vom Himmel hoch* BWV 700, *Wachet auf* BWV 645.

OTHER KEYBOARD The Well-tempered Clavier, Books 1 (1722) and 2 (about 1740), 24 preludes and fugues in each, BWV 846–893; Capriccio in B♭, on the departure of a beloved brother BWV 992; Chromatic Fantasia and Fugue in D minor BWV 903 (1720); six English Suites BWV 806–811; six French Suites BWV 812–817; *Goldberg Variations* BWV 988; 15 Inventions BWV 772–786; 15 Sinfonias BWV 787–801; *Italian Concerto* BWV 971; six partitas BWV 825–830; seven toccatas BWV 910–916.

CHAMBER three Partitas for solo violin, in B minor, D minor, and E, and three Sonatas for solo violin, in G minor, A minor, and C BWV 1001–1006 (about 1720); six Sonatas for violin and harpsichord BWV 1014–1019; six Suites for solo cello BWV 1007–1012 (about 1720);

three Sonatas for viola da gamba and clavier BWV 1027–1029 (about 1720); Partita in A minor for solo flute BWV 1013 (early 1720s); *The Musical Offering* BWV 1079 (1747) for flute, violin, and continuo; *The Art of Fugue* BWV 1080 (about 1745–50), for keyboard.

ORCHESTRAL concertos, six Brandenburg, in F, F, G, G, D, and B♭ BWV 1046–1051 (1721), for violin in A minor and E, for two violins in D minor, for flute, violin, and harpsichord in A minor, seven for harpsichord and strings BWV 1052–1058, three for two harpsichords, two for three, and one for four; four orchestral suites in C, B minor, D, and D BWV 1066–1069.

Bach, Wilhelm Friedemann (1710–1784)
German composer. The eldest son of J S Bach, he was also an organist, improviser, and master of ♭counterpoint.

He was educated at St Thomas' School and Leipzig University, and received his musical training from his father. He was appointed organist of St Sophia's, Dresden, in 1723, and in 1746 succeeded Friedrich Zachau as organist of St Mary's, Halle. He married Dorothea Elisabeth Georgi in 1751. He resigned this post in 1764, and never held another permanent position, living an unsettled life and attempting to support his family mainly by teaching. In 1770 he moved to Brunswick, and in 1774 to Berlin. There his remarkable organ playing could still arouse astonishment, but his last years were spent in increasing poverty.

Works include: cantatas and other church music; 9 symphonies; keyboard concertos; 9 sonatas, 12 fantasias, and other works for keyboard; organ music.

Bachianas Brasileiras nine pieces for various instrumental combinations by Villa-Lobos, in which Brazilian rhythms are treated in the spirit of Bach's counterpoint (1930–44).

Bachofen, Johann Caspar (1695–1755)
Swiss composer. He was cantor of the grammar school in Zurich, 1720, and of the *Grossmünster*, 1742. He compiled and partly composed several books of hymns and sacred songs, collected in *Musikalisches Hallejulah* (1727), and in 1759 wrote a setting of the Passion oratorio by Brockes.

'Bach' trumpet special brass wind instrument of the trumpet type invented by Kosleck of Berlin and improved by Walter Morrow of London, so devised as to be capable of playing the high trumpet parts in the works of J S Bach and his contemporaries and forerunners. It was first heard at Eisenach in 1884.

backfall in musical terminology, taken from the note above. See ◊appoggiatura.

background see ◊structural level.

background music accompanying music for a stage or film production which serves to establish a mood or stimulate appropriate audience responses. It differs from ◊incidental music in not being part of the action, and in working on the listener subliminally.

The use of music as a media for psychological conditioning is prefigured in the 19th-century song without words, with Mendelssohn defending the view that music expressed a reality more definite than a poetic text. Magic lantern (early slide projector) entertainments accompanied by fragments of well-known works established a basis for the ◊film score. Today, the use of piped music in shopping malls extends the principle to real life.

badinerie (French 'teasing, frivolity, playfulness') a title given, sometimes as *badinage*, by French and German composers of the 18th century to light, playful pieces in quick 2–4 time (such as the final movement of Bach's B minor Orchestral Suite for flute and strings).

Badings, Henk (Hendrik Herman) (1907–1987) Dutch composer. Originally a mining engineer, he studied music with Willem Pijper and in 1935 abandoned science entirely for music. He was professor at the Music Lyceum, Amsterdam, and the Rotterdam Conservatory. In 1941 he was appointed director of the Royal Conservatory at The Hague.

Works include: the opera *The Night Watch* (after Rembrandt) (1942); ballets and incidental music for plays, including the electronic ballet *Kain* (1956); a cantata; 14 symphonies (1932–68); symphonic variations; *Heroic Overture*; violin concerto, cello concerto, concerto for two violins and orchestra; recitations with orchestra; four string quartets; violin and cello sonatas; piano pieces. From 1956 he composed electronic music, including two operas (*Salto mortale*, 1959).

bagatelle (French 'trifle') in music, a short character piece, often for piano.

bagpipes any of an ancient family of double-reed folk woodwind instruments employing a bladder, filled by the player through a mouthpiece, or bellows as an air reservoir to a 'chanter' or fingered melody pipe, and two or three optional drone pipes providing a continuous accompanying harmony.

Examples include the old French musette, Scottish and Irish pipes, smaller Northumbrian pipes, Breton *biniou*, Spanish *gaita*, and numerous variants in Eastern Europe, the Middle East, and North Africa. The Highland bagpipes are the national instrument of Scotland.

Bainbridge, Simon (1952–   ) English composer and conductor. He studied at the Royal College of Music and has taught there. He has conducted the BBC Symphony Orchestra and the Scottish Sinfonia.

Works include: *Music to Oedipus Rex* (1969); *Heterophony* for orchestra (1970); *Spirogyra* for chamber orchestra (1970); wind quintet (1971); string quartet; viola concerto (1977); *Landscape and Magic Words* for soprano and chamber ensemble (1981); *A cappella* for six voices (1985); *Metamorphosis* for ensemble (1988); *Cantus contra cantum* (1989); Double Concerto for oboe and clarinet (1990); *Caliban Fragments* for mezzo and ensemble (1991); clarinet quintet (1993).

Baird, Tadeusz (1928–1981) Polish composer. His music was influenced by ◊serialism, especially by Berg. He studied at Łódź Conservatory, and was imprisoned during World War II.

Works include: the opera *Jutro* (*Tomorrow*, after Conrad, 1966); three symphonies; *Cassation for Orchestra*; *Four Essays for Orchestra*; *Expressions* for violin and orchestra (1959); piano concerto; other orchestral music; *Goethe Letters*, for baritone, chorus, and orchestra (1970).

Bairstow, Edward C(uthbert) (1874–1946) English organist, conductor, and composer. After various organist's posts he took the DMus at Durham in 1901 and became organist and choirmaster at York Minster in 1913. He edited *The English Psalter* and wrote *The Evolution of Musical Form* and (with Plunket Greene) *Singing Learnt from Speech*. He was professor of music at Durham University 1929–46.

Works include: services, anthems; organ music; variations for two pianos.

Baiser de la fée, Le (Stravinsky). See ◊*Fairy's Kiss*.

Bakchantinnen, Die/The Bacchantes opera by Wellesz (libretto by the composer) based on Euripides; produced Vienna Staatsoper, 20 January 1931. Dionysus versus Pentheus in ancient Greece.

Baker, Theodore (1851–1934) US writer on music. He took his PhD at Leipzig with the first major study of US Indian music. He became literary editor of G Schirmer Inc., New York, in 1892, and published *A Dictionary of Musical Terms* (1895). His *Biographical Dictionary of Musicians* was issued 1900 and remains the leading US music reference book (fifth and sixth editions by Nicolas Slonimsky, 1978; seventh and eighth by Slonimsky and Dennis McIntire, 1984 and 1992).

Bakfark, Balint Valentin (1507–1576), also known as Greff-Bakfark Hungarian-born Polish lutenist and composer. He was a great virtuoso, as is reflected by the technical difficulty of his extant works. He published a lute book with Jacques Moderne of Lyon in 1552 (*Intabulatura ... transilvani coroniensis liber primus*) and a second with Andreae of Kraków (Andrzej z Krakowa) in 1565 (*Pannonii harmonicarum musicarum in usum testudinis factarum tomus primus*).

He learnt to play the lute while in royal service. He later lived in France, Vienna, and Padua, and was at the Polish court 1549–66.

Balakirev, Mily Alexeyevich (1837–1910) Russian composer. He wrote orchestral works including the fantasy *Islamey* (1869/1902), piano music, songs, and a symphonic poem *Tamara*, all imbued with the Russian national character and spirit. He was leader of the group known as 'The ◊Five' and taught its members, Mussorgsky, Cui, Rimsky-Korsakov, and Borodin.

Born in Nizhny-Novgorod, he was taught music by his mother, but learnt most of what he knew as a youth in the house of Alexander Ulíbishev, on whose estate he was able to use the music library and gain experience with the private orchestra. At 18 he went to St Petersburg, full of enthusiasm for national music, and won the approval of Glinka. In 1861 he began to form the group of nationalist musicians of which he became the leader. Cui became his first disciple; Mussorgsky, Rimsky-Korsakov, and Borodin followed later, and he even influenced Tchaikovsky to some extent at first. In 1862 he helped to establish the Free School of Music with the choral conductor Lomakin, and in connection with it conducted progressive symphonic concerts. In 1867 he became conductor of the Russian Musical Society.

In 1871 he had a grave nervous breakdown and withdrew from public life, feeling that he had been defeated by the 'official' musicians; he was forced to become a minor railway official to earn a modest living and turned to religious mysticism. Not until 1876 did he begin to take some interest in composition

again, and only in 1883, when he was appointed director of the Imperial Chapel, did he fully emerge once more. He retired in 1895 with a pension and took up composition anew, but again lived in seclusion and was almost wholly forgotten by his former friends. He died in St Petersburg.

As a composer, Balakirev is original, even though he reveals the influence not only of Glinka, but also of Chopin, Liszt, Schumann and, to a lesser degree, of Berlioz.

Works include: incidental music for Shakespeare's *King Lear* (1860); two symphonies, symphonic poems *Russia* and *Tamara*, overtures on a Spanish march, on three Russian themes, to *King Lear*, and on Czech themes; piano concerto (finished by Liapunov); many piano works, including sonata in B♭ minor, *Islamey* fantasy (1869), scherzos, mazurkas, nocturnes, waltzes, and other pieces; 43 songs; two books of folk songs; six anthems for unaccompanied chorus; cantata for the unveiling of the Glinka monument.

balalaika Russian musical instrument, resembling a guitar. It has a triangular soundbox, frets, and two, three, or four strings played by strumming with the fingers. A range of instruments is made, from treble to bass, and orchestras of balalaikas are popular in Russia.

Balfe, Michael William (1808–1870) Irish composer and singer. He was a violinist and baritone at Drury Lane, London, when only 16. In 1825 he went to Italy, where he sang in Palermo and at La Scala, and in 1846 he was appointed conductor at Her Majesty's Theatre, London. His operas include *The Bohemian Girl* (1843).

Balfe was the son of a dancing master. On the death of his father in 1823, he was sent to London as a pupil of Charles Edward Horn (1786–1849). He studied composition with Karl Friedrich Horn and appeared as a singer in Weber's *Der Freischütz* at Norwich. In 1825 Count Mazzara became his patron and took him to Italy, where he introduced him to Luigi Cherubini. He then went to Paris, met Rossini, and in 1827 appeared as Figaro in his opera *The Barber of Seville* at the Théâtre Italien.

Three years later he sang at Palermo and produced his first opera there, *I rivali di se stessi*. At Milan he sang with the soprano Maria Malibran and at Bergamo he met the Hungarian singer Lina Rosa, whom he married. Early in 1833 he returned to London and appeared in concerts. His first English opera, *The Siege of Rochelle*, was produced at

Drury Lane in 1835 and the next year Malibran sang in *The Maid of Artois*. In 1842 he went to live in Paris for some years and worked there with great success, though in 1843 he returned for a time to produce *The Bohemian Girl* in London, for which he is most famous today. Triumphant visits to Berlin in 1849 and St Petersburg in 1852 followed, and in 1854 he produced *Pittore e Duca* at Trieste. That year he finally returned to England, having bought property in Hertfordshire, where he took to farming.

Works include: OPERA 29, among which are *Un avvertimento ai gelosi* (Pavia, 1830), *The Siege of Rochelle* (1835), *The Maid of Artois, Joan of Arc* (1837), *Falstaff* (1838), *Le Puits d'amour, The Bohemian Girl, Les Quatre Fils Aymon* (Paris, 1844), *The Bondman, The Maid of Honour, The Sicilian Bride, The Rose of Castile, Satanella* (1858), *The Armourer of Nantes* (1863), *Il Talismano.*

OTHER operetta *The Sleeping Queen*; ballet *La Pérouse*; three cantatas, including *Mazeppa*; and many songs.

Ballabene, Gregorio (1720–c. 1803) Italian composer. One of the latest adherents of the *stile antico* 'old style', he wrote unaccompanied church music, often of considerable complexity, including a 48-part Mass.

ballabile (Italian 'in a dancing manner') term applicable to any piece in the form or character of a dance.

ballad originally a dancing song or the music for a dancing song. By the 14th century the term had lost its connection to dance and by the 16th century it designated a simple, narrative song. In the 19th century a ballad described a popular song, often of romantic nature.

ballade in literature, a poetic form developed in France in the later Middle Ages from the ballad, generally consisting of one or more groups of three stanzas of seven or eight lines each, followed by a shorter stanza or envoy, the last line being repeated as a chorus. In music, a ballade is an instrumental piece based on a story; a form used in piano works by Chopin and Liszt.

Ballad of Baby Doe, The opera in two acts by Douglas Moore (libretto by J Latouche), produced Central City, CO, 7 July 1956. Baby Doe and Tabor in trouble with their silver mine.

Ballad of Blanik, The/Balada blanická symphonic poem by Janáček after a poem by J Vrchický; performed Brno, 21 March 1920.

ballad opera an English light operatic entertainment, the fashion for which was set by John Gay's *The Beggar's Opera* in 1728 and continuing its vogue until the 1760s. The most distinctive feature of its music is that it consists mainly of short songs interspersed with dialogue and that they are not specially composed for the piece, but chosen from popular songs of the day.

Ballard (lived 16th–18th centuries) French family of music printers. The founders were Robert Ballard (c. 1525–1588) and Adrien Le Roy, who became music printers to Henry II in 1553, issuing chanson collections. The brothers Pierre and Robert ii (c. 1575–1650) continued the business, while Pierre's son Robert iii (c. 1610–1673) published orchestral scores; his son Christophe (1641–1715) published works by Campra, Charpentier, the Couperins, and Lully. The firm declined from 1722, when Rameau's *Traité* was published.

Ballard, Louis (1931–   ) Native American composer. He studied at Oklahoma University and had private lessons with Darius Milhaud and Carlos Surinach. He was program director of Indian Affairs at Washington, DC, 1971–79, and has published *Music of North American Indians* (1975). His works are indebted to the rhythms and tunes of his native music.

Works include: the ballets *Koshare* (1966) and *The Four Moons* (1967); *Incident at Wounded Knee* for orchestra (1974); *Ritmo Indio* for woodwind quintet and Sioux flute (1968); *Xactce'oyan/Companion of Talking God* for orchestra (1982); *Fantasy Aborigine* for orchestra (1984).

ballata a 14th-century verse form, often set to music, in which the refrain precedes and follows each stanza. The term implies an association with dancing.

ballet (Italian *balletto* 'a little dance') theatrical representation in dance form in which music also plays a major part in telling a story or conveying a mood. Some such form of entertainment existed in ancient Greece, but Western ballet as we know it today first appeared in Renaissance Italy, where it was a court entertainment. From there it was brought by Catherine de' Medici to France in the form of a spectacle combining singing, dancing, and declamation. During the 18th century, there were major developments in technique and ballet gradually became divorced from opera, emerging as an art form in its own right.

In the 20th century Russian ballet has had a vital influence on the classical tradition in the

West, and ballet developed further in the USA through the work of George Balanchine and the American Ballet Theater, and in the UK through the influence of Marie Rambert. Modern dance is a separate development.

history The first important dramatic ballet, the *Ballet comique de la reine*, was produced 1581 by the Italian Balthasar de Beaujoyeux at the French court and was performed by male courtiers, with ladies of the court forming the *corps de ballet*. In 1661 Louis XIV founded the Académie Royale de Danse, to which all subsequent ballet activities throughout the world can be traced. Long, flowing court dress was worn by the dancers until the 1720s when Marie-Anne Camargo, the first great ballerina, shortened her skirt to reveal her ankles, thus allowing greater movement *à terre* and the development of dancing *en l'air*.

During the 18th century ballet spread to virtually every major capital in Europe. Vienna became an important centre and was instrumental in developing the dramatic aspect of the art as opposed to the athletic qualities, which also evolved considerably during this century, particularly among male dancers. In the early 19th century a Paris costumier, Maillot, invented tights, which allowed complete muscular freedom. The first of the great ballet masters was Jean-Georges Noverre, and great contemporary dancers were Teresa Vestris (1726–1808), Anna Friedrike Heinel (1753–1808), Jean Dauberval (1742–1806), and Maximilien Gardel (1741–1787).

Carlo Blasis is regarded as the founder of classical ballet, since he defined the standard conventional steps and accompanying gestures.

Romantic ballet The great Romantic era of the dancers Marie Taglioni, Fanny Elssler, Carlotta Grisi, Lucile Grahn, and Fanny Cerrito began about 1830 but survives today only in the ballets *Giselle* (1841) and *Les Sylphides* (1832). Characteristics of this era were the new calf-length Romantic white dress and the introduction of dancing on the toes, *sur les pointes*. The technique of the female dancer was developed, but the role of the male dancer was reduced to that of being her partner. Important choreographers of the period were Jules Joseph Perrot (1810–1894), Arthur Saint-Léon (1821–1871), and August Bournonville. From 1860 ballet declined rapidly in popular favour in Europe, but its importance was maintained in St Petersburg under Marius Petipa (1818–1910).

Russian ballet Russian ballet was introduced to the West by Sergei Diaghilev, who

set out for Paris 1909 and founded the Ballets Russes (Russian Ballet), at about the same time that Isadora Duncan, a fervent opponent of classical ballet, was touring Europe. Associated with Diaghilev were Mikhail Fokine, Enrico Cecchetti (1850–1928), Vaslav Nijinsky, Anna Pavlova, Tamara Karsavina (1885–1978), Léonide Massine, Bronislava Nijinska, George Balanchine, and Serge Lifar. Ballets presented by his company, before its break-up after his death 1929, included *Les Sylphides*, *Schéhérazade*, *Petrouchka*, *Le Sacre du printemps/The Rite of Spring*, and *Les Noces*.

Diaghilev and Fokine pioneered a new and exciting combination of the perfect technique of imperial Russian dancers and the appealing naturalism favoured by Isadora Duncan. In Russia ballet continues to flourish, the two chief companies being the Kirov and the Bolshoi. Best-known ballerinas are Galina Ulanova and Maya Plisetskaya, and male dancers include Mikhail Baryshnikov, Irek Mukhamedov, and Alexander Godunov, now dancing in the West.

American ballet American ballet was firmly established by the founding of Balanchine's School of American Ballet 1934, and by de Basil and René Blum's (1878–1942) Ballets Russes de Monte Carlo and Massine's Ballets Russes de Monte Carlo, which also carried on the Diaghilev tradition. In 1939 dancer Lucia Chase (1897–1986) and ballet director Richard Pleasant (1906–1961) founded the American Ballet Theater. From 1948 the New York City Ballet, under the guiding influence of Balanchine, developed a genuine American Neo-Classic style.

British ballet Marie Rambert initiated in 1926 the company that developed into the Ballet Rambert, and launched the careers of choreographers such as Frederick Ashton and Anthony Tudor. The national company, the Royal Ballet (so named 1956), grew from foundations laid by Ninette de Valois and Frederick Ashton 1928. British dancers include Alicia Markova, Anton Dolin (1904–1983), Margot Fonteyn, Antoinette Sibley, Lynn Seymour, Beryl Grey, Anthony Dowell, David Wall, Merle Park, and Lesley Collier; choreographers include Kenneth MacMillan. Fonteyn's partners included Robert Helpmann and Rudolf Nureyev.

ballet music During the 16th and 17th centuries there was not always a clear distinction between opera and ballet, since ballet during this period often included singing, and operas often included dance. The influence of the court composer Jean Baptiste Lully on the development of ballet under

Louis XIV in France was significant (Lully was a dancer himself, as was the king). During this period many courtly dances originated, including the ◊gavotte, ◊passepied, ◊bourrée, and ◊minuet. In the 19th century, as public interest in ballet increased, Russia produced composers of international reputation such as Pyotr Il'yich Tchaikovsky, whose ballet scores include *Swan Lake* (1876), *Sleeping Beauty* (1890), and *The Nutcracker* (1892).

With the modern era of ballet which began in 1909 with the founding of the Ballets Russes, innovative choreography transformed the visual aspects of ballet and striking new compositions by Achille Claude Debussy, Maurice Ravel, and especially Igor Stravinsky (in, for example, *The Rite of Spring* 1913) left their mark not only on the ballet composers who followed, but on the course of music history itself. Later in the century, the formal tradition of ballet was upset by the influence of jazz, jazz rhythms, and modern dance originating in the USA, which introduced greater freedom of bodily expression.

Today there exists a wide range of musical and choreographic styles, ranging from the classical to the popular. Many full ballet scores have been reduced by composers to ballet ◊suites or purely orchestral works, which incorporate the essential musical elements, tending to omit musically nonthematic and transitional passages which may be, nevertheless, essential to the choreography and visual narration. Examples include Stravinsky's *The Firebird* (1910) and Ravel's *Boléro* (1928).

Ballet comique de la Reine stage entertainment performed in Paris, 15 October 1581, at the marriage of the Duc de Joyeux and Mlle de Vaudemont, under the supervision of Balthasar de Beaujoyeux. The verse was by the Sieur de la Chesnaye, the scenery by Patin, and the music by the bass singer Lambert de Beaulieu, Jacques Salmon, and others. It is in effect the first of the *ballets de cour*.

ballet de cour (French 'court dance') an entertainment combining music, spectacle, dancing, song, and drama, developed at the French court during the second half of the 16th century. Light-hearted allegories based on classical mythology, *ballets de cour* played an important role in the evolution of ballet. One of the best known is *Ballet comique de la Reine* (1581) commissioned by Catherine de' Medici.

It was the patronage of Catherine de' Medici, who would have seen similar entertainments at the Florentine court in her youth, that encouraged the development of lavish *ballets de cour*. As in a ◊masque, a closely related court entertainment, the parts were often played by members of the court – in the *Ballet comique de la Reine*, commissioned by Catherine de' Medici to celebrate the marriage of her daughter, Marguerite de Lorraine, both she and her daughter had roles.

The costume designs surviving from the early 17th century, especially those by Daniel Rabel (1578–1637), indicate the grotesque and humorous, as well as the opulent, aspects of these entertainments.

The fashion for hugely expensive and spectacular *ballets de cour* continued in the reigns of Henry IV and Louis XIII.

ballet-pantomime see ◊ballet.

ballett, or ballet a type of 16th–17th-century composition for several voices, resembling a madrigal, but in a lighter, more dance-like style.

balletti pieces of music intended for dancing, especially on the stage.

ballo (Italian 'dance') usually used in combination, for example *tempo di ballo*.

Ballo delle Ingrate, Il ballet-opera in one act by Monteverdi (libretto by O Rinuccini), produced Mantua, 1608. The work was published in *Madrigali guerrieri et amorosi*, 1638. The '*Ingrate*' of the title are ladies who have declined the attentions of their suitors. The ungrateful spirits are summoned from Hades and perform a melancholy dance.

Ballo in maschera, Un/A Masked Ball opera by Verdi (libretto by A Somma, based on Scribe's *Gustave III* set by Auber), produced Rome, Teatro Apollo, 17 February 1859. King Gustav stabbed by jealous husband of Amelia.

Bamert, Matthias (1942–) Swiss conductor and composer. He studied in Paris with Pierre Boulez and worked with the Cleveland Orchestra and the US Symphony Orchestra. He was music director of the Basel Radio Symphony Orchestra 1977–83, principal guest with the Scottish National Orchestra from 1985. He has also led the Ulster Orchestra (Sibelius and Saariaho), BBC Symphony Orchestra (first performance of Martin Butler's *O Rio!*, 1991), the National Youth Orchestra at the 1993 London Proms (*Gawain's Journey* by Birtwistle), and the London Mozart Players from 1993.

Banchieri, Adriano (1568–1634) Italian organist, theorist, and composer. He was a Benedictine monk, and helped to found the Accademia dei Floridi at Bologna in 1615. He wrote theoretical works, especially on ◊figured bass (*L'organo suonarino* 1605). *Cartella musicale* (1614) advises on vocal ornamentation. His sequence of madrigals *La pazzia senile* (1595) has been described as the first comic opera.

A pupil of Gioseffo Guami, in 1596 he became organist at the monastery of San Michele in Bosco (Monte Oliveto) near Bologna, to which he returned in 1609, remaining there until shortly before his death; from 1600 to 1604 he was organist at Santa Maria in Regola at Imola.

Works include: Masses; sacred symphonies and concertos; comic intermezzi for the stage; organ works.

band music group, usually falling into a special category: for example, **military**, comprising woodwind, brass, and percussion; **brass**, solely brass and percussion; **marching**, a variant of brass; **dance** and **swing**, often like a small orchestra; **jazz**, with no fixed instrumentation; **rock and pop**, generally electric guitar, bass, and drums, variously augmented; and **steel**, from the West Indies, in which percussion instruments made from oil drums sound like marimbas.

banda (Italian 'band') a military band, in particular a band used on the stage or behind the scene in an opera, as in Verdi's *Macbeth*.

bandurria, or pandora string instrument of the ◊cittern type, with six double strings which are plucked with the fingers or with a plectrum.

banjo resonant stringed musical instrument with a long fretted neck and circular drum-type soundbox covered on the topside only by stretched skin (now usually plastic). It is played with a plectrum. Modern banjos normally have five strings.

The banjo originated in the American South among black slaves (based on a similar instrument of African origin).

It was introduced to Britain in 1846.

Bánk-Bán opera by Erkel (libretto by B Egressy, based on a play by József Katona), produced Budapest, 9 March 1861. Bánk-Bán defends his wife in 12th-century Hungary, but both are dead at the end.

Banks, Don (1923–1980) Australian composer. After studying at Melbourne Conservatory he went to London in 1950, where he studied with Seiber. In 1953 he went on to study with Dallapiccola in Florence, and finally settled in London.

Works include: horn concerto (1960); divertimento for flute and string trio; duo for violin and cello; violin sonata; three studies for cello and piano; Three Episodes for flute and piano; film music.

Bantock, Granville Ransome (1868–1946) English composer and conductor; professor of music at the University of Birmingham 1908–34. He is chiefly known today for his colourful *Pierrot of the Minute* overture (1908). Also notable amongst his vast output in all genres, much of it inspired by the East, are the *Hebridean Symphony* (1915), the oratorio *Omar Khayyám* (1906–09), for chorus and orchestra, *Atalanta in Calydon* (1911), symphony for unaccompanied chorus and *Sappho*, an orchestral song cycle.

Born in London, the son of a doctor, he was educated for the civil service, but entered the Royal Academy of Music in 1889, where some of his earliest works were performed, and Lago produced the opera *Cœdmar* at the Olympic Theatre in 1892. After some experience in theatrical conducting, he gave a concert of modern English music in 1896. The next year he was appointed conductor at the Tower, New Brighton, where he introduced much contemporary music. In February 1900 he gave a concert of new English music at Antwerp and in September was appointed principal of the Birmingham and Midland Institute School of Music. He remained in Birmingham until 1933, where he succeeded Elgar as professor of music at the university in 1908.

Works include: STAGE operas, including *Sappho* (1906), *The Seal Woman* (1924).

ORCHESTRAL comedy overture *The Pierrot of the Minute* (1908), symphonic poem *Dante and Beatrice*, *Fifine at the Fair* (1901), *Hebridean Symphony* (1915), *A Pagan Symphony* (1926), Symphony no. 3 (*The Cyprian Goddess*); Celtic Symphony.

CHORUS AND ORCHESTRAL (with or without solo voices) *Omar Khayyám* (setting of Fitz-Gèrald's translation in three parts, 1909).

UNACCOMPANIED CHORUS choral symphony *Atalanta in Calydon* (Swinburne) (1911), and *Vanity of Vanities* (Ecclesiastes).

SONGS including cycles *Songs from the Chinese Poets* (eight sets).

CHAMBER Viola sonata (1919), three cello sonatas (1924, 1940, 1945), three violin sonatas (1929, 1932, 1940).

bar modular segment of music incorporating a fixed number of beats, as in the phrase 'two/three/four beats to the bar'. It is shown in notation by vertical 'barring' of the musical continuum. The US term is **measure**.

Barbé, Anton (died 1564) Flemish composer and first of a line of Antwerp musicians. He was Kapellmeister at Antwerp Cathedral 1527–62. He published Masses, motets, and chansons, and contributed a Dutch song to Tielman Susato's *Het ierste musyck boexken/The First Music Book* (1551), one of 11 volumes of pieces by composers of the time.

Barbe-bleue/Bluebeard operetta by Offenbach (libretto by H Meilhac and L Halévy), produced Paris, Théâtre des Variétés, 5 February 1866. Satirical version of the original 'Bluebeard' story.

Barber, Samuel (1910–1981) US composer. He worked in a Neo-Classical, astringent style. Compositions include *Adagio for Strings* (1936) and the opera *Vanessa* (1958), which won one of his two Pulitzer prizes. Another opera, *Antony and Cleopatra* (1966), was commissioned for the opening of the new Metropolitan Opera House at the Lincoln Center, New York City. Owing to an over-elaborate staging the opera was a failure at its premiere, although it has had some success in a revised version in 1974. Barber's music is lyrical and fastidiously worked. His later works include *The Lovers* (1971).

He entered the Curtis Institute of Music in 1924, winning a prize with a violin sonata in 1928. In the following years he won several more prizes, including the American Prix de Rome in 1935.

Works include: the operas *Vanessa* (1958) and *Antony and Cleopatra* (after Shakespeare, 1966, revised 1974); Two Essays, overture to Sheridan's *School for Scandal*, music for a scene from Shelley for orchestra; *Dover Beach* (Matthew Arnold) for baritone and string quartet (1933); *Knoxville, Summer of 1915* for soprano and orchestra; *Adagio for Strings* (from string quartet of 1936); violin concerto (1940), cello concerto (1945), piano concerto (1962), *Capricorn Concerto* for flute, oboe, trumpet, and strings; piano sonata; works for unaccompanied chorus; many songs.

Barber of Baghdad, The (Cornelius). See ◊*Barbier von Bagdad*.

Barber of Seville, The (Paisiello, Rossini). See ◊*Barbiere di Siviglia*.

barbershop a style of unaccompanied close-harmony singing of sentimental ballads, revived in the USA during the 19th century. Traditionally sung by four male voices, since the 1970s it has developed as a style of ◊a cappella choral singing for both male and female voices.

Barbershop originated in 17th-century European barbers' shops, which also offered dental and medical services; making music was encouraged among waiting customers.

Barbier, Jules see Michel ◊Carré.

Barbiere di Siviglia, Il, ossia La precauzione inutile/The Barber of Seville, or Vain Precaution (original title *Almaviva, ossia L'inutile precauzione*) opera by Rossini (libretto by C Sterbini, based on Beaumarchais' *Le Barbier de Séville*), produced Rome, Teatro Argentina, 20 February 1816. Rosina and Almaviva battle it out with Bartolo.

Barbiere di Siviglia, Il, ovvero La precauzione inutile/The Barber of Seville, or Vain Precaution opera by Paisiello (libretto by G Petrosellini, based on Beaumarchais' *Le Barbier de Séville*), produced St Petersburg, Hermitage, at court, 26 September 1782.

Barbier von Bagdad, Der/The Barber of Baghdad opera by Cornelius (libretto by composer), produced Weimar, 15 December 1858. Nureddin is helped by Abul Hassan in meeting Margiana.

Barbirolli, John (Giovanni Battista) (1899–1970) English conductor. Barbirolli excelled in the Romantic repertory, especially the symphonies of Elgar, Sibelius, Mahler, and Vaughan Williams. Trained as a cellist, he succeeded Toscanini as conductor of the New York Philharmonic Orchestra 1937–43 and was conductor of the Hallé Orchestra, Manchester, England, 1943–70.

Born in London, of French and Italian descent, he studied at Trinity College, London 1911–12 and at the Royal Academy of Music 1912–17. He made his debut as a cellist aged 11, and joined the Queen's Hall Orchestra in that capacity in 1915. He achieved recognition as a conductor in 1926, and later succeeded Toscanini as chief conductor of the New York Philharmonic Orchestra in 1937. He married the oboist Evelyn Rothwell in 1939. He returned to England in 1943, where he took over the Hallé Orchestra. In 1949 he was knighted and in 1950 received the Royal Philharmonic Society's gold medal. With the Hallé he gave the first performances of Vaughan Williams's seventh and eighth symphonies. He was guest conductor of the Berlin Philharmonic Orchestra, Boston Symphony Orchestra, and Chicago Symphony Orchestra.

Barcarola work for orchestra by Henze; it depicts a journey across the river Styx and quotes the Eton Boating Song. First performed Zurich, 22 April 1980, conductor Albrecht.

barcarole song of the type sung by Venetian gondoliers. The barcarole is always in moderate duple time (6/8 or 12/8), with a swaying rhythm. Instrumental barcaroles also exist, for example Chopin's *Barcarolle* (1846).

bard Celtic minstrel who, in addition to composing songs, usually at a court, often held important political posts. Originating in the pre-Christian era, bards were persecuted in Wales during the 13th century on political grounds. Since the 19th century annual meetings and competitions in Wales have attempted to revive the musical tradition of the bard.

Barenboim, Daniel (1942–) Israeli pianist and conductor. Pianist/conductor with the English Chamber Orchestra from 1964, he became conductor of the New York Philharmonic Orchestra 1970, musical director of the Orchestre de Paris 1975, and director of the Chicago Symphony Orchestra 1991. As a pianist he specialized in the German classic and romantic repertoire; as a conductor he has extended into 19th- and 20th-century French music, including Boulez. He was married to the cellist Jacqueline Du Pré.

Bärenhäuter, Der/The Bear Skinner opera by Siegfried Wagner (libretto by composer) produced Munich, 21 January 1899.

bariolage the alteration on a string instrument of the same note on an open string and a stopped string. Also the playing of high notes on a string instrument in high positions on the lower strings to obtain a different tonecolour or to facilitate the performance of rapid high passages without changing to lower positions.

baritone male voice pitched between bass and tenor, of approximate range G2–F4. As a prefix to the name of an instrument, for example baritone saxophone, it indicates that the instrument sounds in approximately the same range.

Dietrich Fischer-Dieskau (1925–) and Hermann Prey (1929–) are well-known German baritone singers. 'Baritone' is also the name of a valved brass instrument of the saxhorn family, similar in pitch to the euphonium.

Barkin, Elaine (1932–) US composer and writer on music. She studied with Leo Kraft, Irving Fine, and Boris Blacher; edited the journal *Perspectives of New Music* 1963–85, and is on the faculty of University of California in Los Angeles. Her music is influenced by serialism, graphic notation, and interactive performance techniques.

Works include: a string quartet (1969); *Inward and Outward Bound* for 13 instruments (1974); *Ebb Tide* for two vibraphones (1977); *De Amore*, chamber opera (1980); *Quilt Piece*, graphic score (1983); *Women's Voices* for four female reciters, tape, and slides (1983); *Encore* for gamelan ensemble (1989).

Barlow, David (1927–1975) English composer. He studied with Gordon Jacob at the Royal College of Music and with Nadia Boulanger in France. His early music was Romantic in style; from 1963 he adopted serial technique.

Works include: the church operas *David and Bathsheba* and *Judas Iscariot* (1969 and 1975); two symphonies (1950 and 1959), variations for cello and orchestra (1969), Sinfonietta concertante for clarinet and orchestra (1972); *The Lambton Worm* for narrator and orchestra (1969); string trio, string quartet (1969), brass quintet (1972); *Passion Music* for organ.

Barlow, Samuel (1892–1982) US composer. He studied at Harvard and in Paris and Rome, becoming active on behalf of liberal causes. His opera *Mon ami Pierrot* (1935) is based on the life of Lully and was the first by a US composer to be given at the Paris Opéra Comique. Other operas were *Amanda* (1936) and *Eugénie*. His symphonic concerto *Babar* (1935) uses slide projections but this, a piano concerto (1931), and *Biedermeier Waltzes* (1935) are in a conservative idiom.

Barlow, Wayne (Brewster) (1912–) US composer. He studied with Howard Hanson at the Eastman School and with Schoenberg at the University of Southern California in 1935. He was director of the electronic music studio at Eastman 1968–78.

Works include: *Zion in Exile*, cantata (1937), *Three Moods for Dancing*, ballet (1940), *Nocturne* for 18 instruments (1946), piano quintet (1951), *Images* for harp and orchestra (1961), *Vistas* for orchestra (1963), *Moonflight*, for tape (1970), *Soundprints in Concrete* (1972), *Voices of Faith*, cantata (1976), *Divertissement* for flute and chamber orchestra (1980); *Frontiers* for band (1982); *Sonatine for Four* (1984).

The approximate range of a baritone voice.

Barnby, Joseph (1838–1896) English conductor, organist and composer. He held various organist's posts in London; precentor at Eton College 1875–92, then principal of the Guildhall School of Music and Drama. Distinguished as a choral conductor, he gave oratorios by Johann Sebastian Bach and Antonín Dvořák and the first English performance of *Parsifal* (concert, 1884).

Baroque music music of the period following the Renaissance and preceding the Classical period, lasting from about 1600 to the deaths of Bach and Handel in the 1750s. Baroque music is characterized by contrapuntal independence of voices and instrumental parts, as epitomized by the ◊fugue, which flourished during these years; the development of ◊continuo writing, specifically the ◊figured bass, as an accompaniment to a melody line or orchestral parts; the ◊concertante style of contrasting effects, both instrumental (as in the ◊concerto grosso) and dynamic (for example, from forte (loud) to piano (soft), in the manner of an echo); the importance of melodic ◊ornamentation; the grounding of ◊tonic and ◊dominant as primary harmonies; and the establishment of four-bar phrases as a compositional norm. Baroque composers include Pachelbel, Bach, Handel, Vivaldi, Frescobaldi, and Monteverdi (in his later works).

Barraqué, Jean (1928–1973) French composer. His disciplined technique was well suited to ◊serialism, which formed a cornerstone of his composition. In 1955 he began work on his major composition, *La mort de Virgile*, based on the book by Hermann Broch, but never completed it.

He studied with Jean Langlais and Messiaen, later working in the experimental laboratories of the Radiodiffusion Française in Paris. His first compositions were a piano sonata, begun in 1950, and *Sequence for voice and ensemble*, revised 1955. In 1951 he wrote *Etude for electronic tape*. His last completed work was the clarinet concerto, 1962–68. He also wrote a short book on Debussy.

Works include: *Séquence* for soprano and chamber ensemble, (after Nietzsche, 1955); *Le Temps restitué* for voices and orchestra (1957); *Au delà du hasard* (based on Hermann Broch) for voices and instrumental groups (1959), *Chant après chant* for percussion (1966); piano sonata; *La mort de Virgile*, incomplete dramatic cycle.

Barraud, Henry (1900–) French composer. He studied first at Bordeaux and later at the Paris Conservatory with Caussade, Dukas,

and Aubert. He was expelled from the conservatory as a bad influence, but later in life turned to religion. In 1937 he was in charge of the music at the Paris World Fair; he then joined the radio service, where he rose to the post of head of the national programme in 1948.

Works include: the operas *La Farce de Maître Pathelin* (1938), *Numance* and *Lavinia* (1959); ballets *La Kermesse* (1943) and *L'Astrologue dans le puits*; film and radio music; oratorio *Les Mystères des Saints Innocents* (1947), cantatas and other choral works, including *La Divine Comédie*, after Dante, for five solo voices and orchestra (1972); three symphonies; piano concerto; woodwind trio, string trio, string quartet (1940), violin and piano sonata; piano music; songs.

barré (French 'barred') a chord on string instruments with fretted fingerboards, particularly the guitar, is said to be played barré when a finger is laid horizontally across the whole fingerboard, thus raising all the strings in pitch by the same interval's distance from the fundamental tuning.

barrel organ portable pipe organ, played by turning a handle, or occasionally by a clockwork mechanism. The handle works a pump and drives a replaceable cylinder upon which music is embossed as a pattern of ridges controlling the passage of air to the pipes. It is often confused with the barrel or street piano used by buskers, which employed a barrel-and-pin mechanism to control a piano hammer action.

The barrel organ was a common entertainment and parish church instrument in England during the 18th and 19th centuries.

Barry, Gerald (1952–) Irish composer. His major influences are the composers with whom he has studied: Peter Schat in the Netherlands, Stockhausen and Mauricio Kagel in Germany, and Friedrich Cerha in Austria. His *Cheveux-de-frises* caused a stir at the 1988 London Promenade Concerts.

Works include: the operas *The Intelligence Park* (1987) and *The Triumph of Beauty and Deceit* (1993); piano concerto (1977); *Handel's Favourite Song* for clarinet and ensemble (1981); *Cork* for string quartet (1985); *Sur les pointes* for chamber ensemble (1985); *What the Frog Said* for soprano, bass, and ensemble (1985); *Cheveux-de-frises* for orchestra (1988); *Reflections on Guinness* (1988); Sextet (1992); *Hard D* for orchestra (1992).

Barshai, Rudolf (1924–) Russian violist and conductor. He founded the Moscow Chamber Orchestra in 1956 and conducted it until he left Russia for Israel in 1976. Principal conductor of the Bournemouth Symphony Orchestra 1983–88; music director of the Vancouver Symphony Orchestra 1985–88. His transcriptions include Sergey Prokofiev's *Visions Fugitives*, for chamber orchestra, and Dmitri Shostakovich's string quartet no. 8, for string orchestra.

Bart, Lionel (1930–) English composer. He wrote both the words and music for many musicals including *Fings Ain't Wot They Us'd T'Be* (1959) and *Oliver!* (1960).

Bartered Bride, The/Prodaná Nevěsta opera by Smetana (libretto by K Sabina), produced, first version, Prague, Czech Theatre, 30 May 1866; revised version, 29 January 1869; final version (with recitatives), 25 September 1870. Marcenka and Jeník wish to marry, but must first overcome a previously arranged marriage and each other's subterfuges.

Barth, Hans (1897–1956) German-born US pianist and composer. A meeting with Ferruccio Busoni encouraged him to experiment with new scales, and in 1928 he invented a 1/4-tone piano, for which he composed a number of works. He also composed 1/4-tone chamber and instrumental music, as well as more conventional pieces.

Barthélémon, François Hippolyte (1741–1808) French violinist and composer. An exponent of the 'galant' style, he produced *Pelopida*, the first of several successful dramatic works, in 1766.

He settled in London 1765. A year later he married the singer Mary Young, daughter of Charles Young and niece of Mrs Arne and Mrs Lampe. He composed stage pieces for Garrick and visited France, Germany, and Italy with his wife, who sang there. He was a friend of Haydn during the latter's visits to London, and is said to have suggested the subject of *The Creation*.

Works include: the stage works *Pelopida* (1766), *The Judgement of Paris* (1768), *The Maid of the Oaks* (1774), *Belphegor* (1778); oratorio *Jefte in Masfa*; symphonies; concertos, sonatas, duets for violin.

Bartlet, John (lived 16th–17th centuries) English lutenist and composer. He published a *Booke of Ayres* for voices and instruments in 1606.

Bartók, Béla (1881–1945) Hungarian composer. His works combine folk elements with mathematical concepts of tonal and rhythmic proportion. His large output includes six string quartets, a *Divertimento* for string

orchestra (1939), concertos for piano, violin, and viola, the *Concerto for Orchestra* (1942–45), a one-act opera *Duke Bluebeard's Castle* (1918), and graded teaching pieces for piano.

A child prodigy, Bartók studied music at the Budapest Conservatory, later working with Zoltán Kodály in recording and transcribing the folk music of Hungary and adjoining countries. His ballet *The Miraculous Mandarin* (1919) was banned because of its subject matter (it was set in a brothel). Bartók died in the USA, having fled from Hungary in 1940.

Bartók's father was a director of agriculture; his mother, a schoolteacher, was a musician and taught him from an early age. He appeared in public as a pianist at the age of ten. He studied under László Erkel at Porzsony (now Bratislava) until 1899; he then went to the Budapest Conservatory, where he studied piano under István Thomán and composition under Hans Koessler (1853–1926).

Under the influence of Richard Strauss, Bartók wrote the symphonic poem *Kossuth* (1903), which was conducted by Hans Richter at Manchester in 1904. His first string quartet (1908) begins with echoes of late Beethoven but soon settles into a characteristic national idiom. About 1905 he began to collect folk tunes, often with Zoltán Kodály, and they discovered that the true Magyar music differed greatly from that of the Hungarian gypsies so far regarded as the only Hungarian folk music. Bartók was appointed professor of piano at Budapest Conservatory in 1907. The powerful opera *Duke Bluebeard's Castle* was composed in 1911 but not performed until 1918. After World War I he began to be known in Europe and the USA, and in 1922 was made an honorary member of the International Society for Contemporary Music. Some of his most demanding music was written in the years 1917–34: *The Miraculous Mandarin*, his first two piano concertos, string quartets nos. 2–5, and *Cantata Profana*. The lurid *Miraculous Mandarin* ballet was written under the influence of Stravinsky and the expressionist Schoenberg; it was banned after a single performance in Cologne.

Increasing political isolation in his homeland (Hungary became fascist before Germany) encouraged Bartók to pursue a career abroad. The first two piano concertos were premiered by him in Frankfurt, and exploit a full range of percussive effects. Bartók's own keyboard style was not appreciated by all – Percy Scholes reported that he had a touch 'like a paving stone'. Both concertos and the fourth and fifth quartets to some extent employ palindrome patterns, which with their formal repetition help to give coherence to chromatically complex music. A more easily accessible idiom, with longer melodic lines and less astringent harmony, was in evidence by 1938, with the *Music for Strings, Percussion and Celesta* and the second violin concerto. The sixth quartet (1939) was the last music he wrote in Budapest, and seems to find the composer in mourning for the world he was about to leave behind; each movement begins with a long, melancholy viola solo.

In 1940 Bartók emigrated to the USA, where he taught briefly at Columbia University and Harvard. He was already suffering from leukaemia and was not in demand as a pianist or, initially, as a composer. A 1943 commission from the Koussevitzky Foundation, for the *Concerto for Orchestra*, helped to alleviate his financial hardship. The third piano concerto was written when Bartók was mortally ill; the central adagio religioso pays direct tribute to Beethoven's 'Song of Thanksgiving' from the A minor quartet, although Bartók must have known that in his case there was to be no recovery from illness.

Bartók was one of the foremost composers of the 20th century. Much influenced by Hungarian folk music, he incorporated its rhythms and melodic characteristics into complex, subtle, and effective forms. Bartók's orchestral music has become relatively popular, although his genius is more fully revealed in his innovative approach to the keyboard and especially the string quartets, which are widely regarded as the best since Beethoven.

Works include: STAGE *Duke Bluebeard's Castle*, one-act opera (1911); *The Wooden Prince*, one-act ballet (1914–17); *The Miraculous Mandarin*, one-act pantomime (1918–23).

ORCHESTRAL *Dance Suite* (1923), piano concerto no. 1 (1926), piano concerto no. 2 (1930–31), *Music for Strings, Percussion and Celesta* (1936), violin concerto no. 2 (1937–38), *Divertimento* for strings (1939), *Concerto for Orchestra* (1943–44), piano concerto no. 3 (1945), viola concerto (completed by T Serly, 1945).

VOCAL *Cantata Profana* for tenor, baritone, chorus, and orchestra (1930), choruses on Hungarian and Slovak folk songs; many solo songs, including five to words by Endre Ady.

CHAMBER six string quartets (1908, 1917, 1927, 1928, 1934, 1939), two piano and violin sonatas (1921, 1922), sonata for two pianos and two percussion (1937, version with

orchestra 1940), *Contrasts* for violin, clarinet, and piano (1938), sonata for solo violin (1944).

PIANO *14 Bagatelles*, op. 6 (1908), Sonatina (1915), Suite, op. 14 (1916), sonata (1926), *Out of Doors* (1926), *Mikrokosmos*, 153 'progressive pieces' in six volumes (1926, 1932–39).

baryton complex, bowed, stringed musical instrument producing an intense singing tone. It is based on an 18th-century ◊viol and modified by the addition of sympathetic (freely vibrating) strings which are plucked by hand.

The baryton was a favourite instrument of Prince Nicholas Esterházy, patron of the Austrian composer Franz Joseph Haydn, who, to please him, wrote over 120 trios for violin, baryton, and cello, and many other works for the instrument.

Basili, Francesco (1767–1850), or Basily Italian singer and composer. He became director of the Milan Conservatory in 1827, and was maestro di cappella at St Peter's in Rome from 1837.

Works include: the operas *La locandiera* (1789), *Achille nell' assedio di Troia, Ritorno d'Ulisse* (1798), *Antigona* (1799), *Achille, L'orfana egiziana* (1818); oratorio *Sansone* (1824); Requiem for Jannaconi; several settings of *Miserere*; symphony.

Basilius, Der königliche Schäfer, oder Basilius in Arcadien/The Royal Shepherd, or Basil in Arcady opera by Keiser (libretto by F C Bressand), produced Brunswick, 1693. The first of more than 100 operas by Keiser.

bass the lowest male voice, of approximate range C2–D4. As the prefix to the name of an instrument, it indicates that the instrument sounds in approximately the same range.

Well-known bass singers include the Russians Fyodor Chaliapin and Boris Christoff. The term also covers the bass instrument of a consort or family, for example bass clarinet, bass tuba, and bassoon, having a similar range. An instrument an octave lower than bass is a contrabass.

The approximate range of a bass voice.

Bassani, Giovanni Battista (c. 1647–1716) Italian violinist and composer of the generation between Monteverdi and Vivaldi. He was organist at Ferrara from 1667 and was later in charge of the cathedral music at Bologna; he returned to Ferrara as maestro di cappella in 1683. He composed 12 oratorios, produced nine operas and brought out a large amount of church and instrumental music.

Bassano, Giovanni (c. 1558–c. 1617) Venetian composer and cornet player. He led the instrumental ensemble at St Mark's, Venice, and wrote instrumental music including ornamented transcriptions of vocal works by Gabrieli, Marenzio, and others.

Bassarids, The one-act opera with intermezzo by Henze (libretto by W H Auden and C Kallman after *The Bacchae* of Euripides), produced Salzburg, 6 August 1966; first British stage performance London, Coliseum, 10 October 1974, conductor Henze. Pentheus, in attempting to establish monotheism, incurs the wrath of Dionysus and his followers, who eventually kill him.

bass chantante (French 'singing-bass') bass voice especially suited to melodic delivery and lyrical parts.

bass clarinet ◊clarinet in B♭ with a range an octave lower than the ordinary instrument.

bass clef in musical notation, the F ◊clef in which the F below middle C is represented as the second line from the top of the five-line stave. Instruments with a range below middle C use the bass clef, including double bass, tuba, and piano (left hand).

The bass clef.

bass drum the largest drum of the orchestra or military band, with notes of indeterminate pitch, consisting of a cylindrical wooden body with two drumming surfaces (of hide or plastic). It is usually placed upright and drummed from one side.

In the military band, the bass drum is played together with the cymbals, one of which is placed on it, while the other is held in the player's non-drumming hand.

basse-contre low bass, whether a voice, an instrument, or an organ stop.

basse danse French dance of the 15th–16th century, so called because the feet were kept low, not thrown up in the air as in some other dances.

basset horn musical woodwind instrument, a wide-bore alto clarinet pitched in F, invented about 1765 and used by Mozart in his *Masonic Funeral Music* (1785), for example,

and by Richard Strauss. It was revived in 1981 by Karlheinz Stockhausen and features prominently as a solo in the opera cycle *Licht*. Performers include Alan Hacker and Suzanne Stephens.

Bassett, Leslie (1923–) US composer. He studied with Ross Lee Finney, Nadia Boulanger, and Mario Davidovsky (electronic music); from 1952 he has taught at the University of Michigan, as professor since 1977. His works are clearly constructed and convey a strong spiritual content.

Works include: variations for orchestra (Pulitzer Prize winner 1966); *Echoes from an Invisible World*, for the Bicentennial (1976); concerto for two pianos and orchestra (1976); trombone concerto (1983); *From a Source Evolving* for orchestra (1986); four string quartets (1951, 1957, 1962, 1978); Sextet (1979); *Duo-Inventions* for two cellos (1988); wind band music (Concerto grosso, 1982); choral works, songs, keyboard, and electronic music.

bass flute, or, more correctly, alto flute ◊flute in G with a range a fourth lower than that of the ordinary instrument.

basso cantante, or singing-bass, ◊bass voice especially suited to melodic delivery and lyrical parts.

basso continuo (Italian 'continuous bass') musical term, the original Italian term for ◊continuo.

bassoon double-reed woodwind instrument in C, the bass of the oboe family. It doubles back on itself in a tube about 2.5 m/7.5 ft long and has a rich and deep tone. The bassoon concert repertoire extends from the early Baroque via Vivaldi, Mozart, and Dukas to Stockhausen.

The bassoon was developed from the Renaissance ◊curtal about 1660 as a continuo instrument to provide bassline support. Further development in the 18th century led to the **double bassoon** or **contrabassoon**, an octave lower. Both instruments demonstrate an agility humorously at variance with their low pitch range and rich, glowing tone, but are also capable of dignified solos at high register, famously in the eerie opening bars of Stravinsky's ballet *The Rite of Spring* (1913).

The normal compass of a bassoon, though a few higher notes are possible.

basso ostinato (Italian 'obstinate bass', 'ground bass') a bass part in a composition continually tracing the same melodic outline.

bass trumpet ◊trumpet invented by Wagner, with a written compass an octave below that of the normal orchestral instrument.

Its range is more correctly described as tenor.

bass viol alternative name for the viola da gamba, a musical instrument.

Bastien und Bastienne *Singspiel* by Mozart, K50 (libretto by F W Weiskern and A Schachtner, based on Favart's parody of Rousseau's *Le Devin du Village*), produced Vienna, at the house of Anton Mesmer (the hypnotist) September 1768. Bastienne seeks the advice of a magician to win back the heart of inattentive Bastien.

Bataille, Gabriel (1575–1630) French lutenist and composer. He contributed music to ballets danced at the court of Louis XIII. Between 1608 and 1623 he published many lute pieces and songs.

Bateson, Thomas (c. 1570–1630) English organist and composer. He was probably organist at Chester Cathedral until 1609, when he became vicar-choral and organist at Christ Church Cathedral, Dublin. Two books of madrigals by him were published in 1604 and 1618.

Bathe, William (1564–1614) Irish priest and music scholar. In state service at first, he went to Spain and became a Jesuit priest in 1599. He wrote *Briefe Introductions to the True Art of Musick and the Skill of Song*, also *Janua linguarum*.

baton stick used by a conductor to control an orchestra. Typically, the baton is held in the right hand and is used in order to make the conductor's signals more apparent. Generally, conductors do not use a baton when working with choirs or small instrumental ensembles.

Earliest records of the baton date to the Sistine Chapel during the 15th century, when the conductor used a roll of paper to beat time. Lully used a large cane. During the 19th century the first violinist waved his bow to conduct. The modern baton seems to have originated in the early 19th century, with its use by Beethoven and Mendelssohn.

Battaglia di Legnano, La/The Battle of Legnano opera by Verdi (libretto by S Cammarano), produced Rome, Teatro Argentina, 27 January 1849. Rolando and Arrigo battle against the Germans, but Rolando must also fight when he discovers his wife Lida loves Arrigo. Later, the mortally wounded Arrigo proclaims Lida's innocence and the three are reconciled.

battement see ◊mordent.

Batten, Adrian (1591–1637) English organist and composer. He was a chorister at Winchester Cathedral as a boy. In 1614 he went to London as vicar-choral at Westminster Abbey and in 1626 became organist at St Paul's Cathedral. He was probably the copyist of the Batten Organbook.

Works include: 11 services, about 50 anthems, and other church music.

batterie an 18th-century term for rapid broken accompaniment figures. It is also a collective term for the group of percussion instruments in the orchestra.

Battishill, Jonathan (1738–1801) English harpsichordist, organist, and composer. He was a chorister at St Paul's Cathedral. In about 1762 he became harpsichordist to Covent Garden Theatre, where he produced in 1764 the opera *Almena*, written jointly with Michael Arne. About the same time he became organist of three city churches, and began to write church music. His best-known pieces are the anthems *Call to remembrance* and *O Lord, look down from heaven*. Other works include music for the stage, glees, catches, and songs.

Battle of Prague, The a descriptive piano piece with violin, cello, and drum *ad lib* by Franz Koczwara, composed 1788, of no musical value, but very popular in the early 19th century.

Battle of Vittoria, The Beethoven's 'Battle Symphony', op. 91, originally entitled *Wellingtons Sieg oder die Schlacht bei Vittoria*, first performed 8 December 1813. An extravagantly descriptive piece, originally intended for a mechanical instrument, it contains quotations from national songs, including *Rule, Britannia*.

battuta (Italian 'beat') musical term often used loosely in the plural (for example *ritmo di 3 battute*) to indicate a change in the metrical scheme of bars – not beats – grouped in unexpected numbers.

Baudo, Serge (1927–) French conductor. He made his debut in 1950 with the Concerts Lamoureux. He had engagements at the Paris Opéra from 1962, La Scala in Milan, and New York Metropolitan Opera, and was chief conductor of the Orchestre de Paris 1967–69. He gave the first performances of Olivier Messiaen's *Et exspecto resurrectionem mortuorum* (Chartres, 1965) and *La Transfiguration*

(Lisbon, 1969). He founded the Berlioz Festival, Lyon in 1979.

Baudrier, Yves (1906–1988) French composer. Originally a law student, in 1936 he formed the group La Jeune France with his fellow composers Jolivet, Leseur, and Messiaen.

Works include: Agnus Dei for soprano, chorus and orchestra; symphonies, symphonic poem *Le Grand Voilier* (1939); string quartet (1944); piano pieces.

Bauer, Marion (1887–1955) US composer and teacher. She studied with Nadia Boulanger in Paris and taught at New York University 1926–51. Her works are often in smaller forms and are neoclassical in spirit.

Works include: the piano pieces *New Hampshire Woods* (1921), *Sun Splendour* (1926, also for orchestra), and *Dance Sonata* (1932); string quartet (1928); viola sonata (1936); oboe sonata (1940); piano concerto 'American Youth' (1943); *China* for chorus and orchestra (1945). Her books include *20th-Century Music* (1933) and *How Opera Grew* (1955).

Bauldeweyn, Noel (died c. 1530) Flemish composer. Maître de chapelle of Notre Dame at Antwerp 1513–18, he composed sacred and secular music including the Mass *Da Pacem* formerly thought to be by Josquin Desprez.

Bavarian Highlands, Scenes from the six Choral Songs with piano, op. 27, by Elgar; composed 1895, first performed Worcester, 21 April 1896. Version with orchestra 1896. Nos. 1, 3, and 6 were arranged for orchestra alone as *Three Bavarian Dances*, performed Crystal Palace, 23 October 1897, conductor August Manns.

Bavicchi, John (1922–) US composer. He studied with Walter Piston at Harvard and after war service was active in Boston as a conductor and teacher (Arlington Philharmonic, 1968–82). His music often employs classical forms.

Works include: concertante for oboe, bassoon, and strings (1961); string quartet (1961); music for chamber orchestra (1981); *There is Sweet Music Here* for soprano and orchestra (1985); *Triptych* for horns (1987).

Bax, Arnold Edward Trevor (1883–1953) English composer. His works, often based on Celtic legends, include seven symphonies, *The Garden of Fand* 1913–16, and *Tintagel* 1917–19 (both tone poems).

He was Master of the King's Musick 1942–53. Knighted 1937.

Bayreuth town in Bavaria, south Germany, on the Red Main river, 65 km/40 mi northeast of Nürnberg; population (1995) 72,700. There are cotton textile, porcelain, cigarette, and optical industries. Bayreuth was the home of composer Richard Wagner, and the Wagner theatre was established in 1876 as a performing centre for his operas. Opera festivals are held here every summer.

The theatre introduced new concepts of opera house design, including provision of an enlarged orchestra pit extending below the stage and projecting the sound outwards and upwards. Bayreuth has a university (founded in 1975).

Bayreuth's Baroque buildings and Rococo palaces recall its former status as residence of the margraves of Brandenburg-Kulmbach. Wagner himself designed the theatre, the Festspielhaus. There is also a Baroque opera house (1748), as well as fine old churches, and a notable 18th-century castle (now a museum). The Eremitage, a Rococo castle, was often visited by Frederick the Great, whose sister was margravine of Bayreuth. Wagner is buried in the garden of his former villa.

Bazelon, Irwin (Allen) (1922–1995) US composer. He studied with Hindemith, Milhaud, and Bloch. Experienced in film music and incidental music for Shakespeare's plays.

Works include: seven symphonies (1963–80), *Chamber Symphony* for seven instruments (1957), *Symphonie Concertante* (1963), *Early American Suite* (1970), *Excursions* for orchestra (1966); *Spirits of the Night* for orchestra (1976), *Sound Dreams* for six instruments (1977), *Spires* for trumpet and orchestra (1981), *Trajectories* for piano and orchestra (1984); *Motivations* for trombone and orchestra (1985); *Legends and Love Letters* for soprano and chamber orchestra (1987); *Fourscore 2* for percussion quartet and orchestra (1988); two string quartets, three piano sonatas.

Beach, Amy Marcy (1867–1944), born Cheney US pianist and composer, also known as Mrs Henry Beach. She was one of the leading international composers of her day, influenced by Brahms, Debussy, and her US contemporaries writing in a romantic vein.

Works include: Mass in E; *Christ in the Universe* for chorus and orchestra (1931); *Gaelic Symphony* (1896, the first symphonic work by an American woman); piano concerto; string quartet, piano trio; numerous songs.

beak flute, German *Schnabelflöte* alternative name for the ◊recorder, a musical instrument.

Beamish, Sally (1956–) English composer and viola player. She studied at the Royal

Northern College of Music and with Lennox Berkeley. She played viola in various London ensembles. In 1989 she became resident in Scotland, cofounding the Chamber Group of Scotland.

Works include: music theatre *Ease* (1993); symphony (1992); *Tam Lin* oboe concerto (1992); Concerto Grosso for strings (1993); viola concerto (1995); *Magnificat* for soprano, mezzo, and ensemble (1992); chamber music.

Bearbeitung (German 'arrangement') in music, particularly the adaptation of a work for a different performing medium.

'Bear, The' nickname (*L'Ours*) of the first of Haydn's 'Paris' symphonies, no. 82 in C, composed 1786.

Opera by Walton (libretto by P Dehn and the composer, based on Chekhov), produced Aldeburgh, 3 June 1967. Widow Popova falls for husband's creditor.

beat a pulsation giving the tempo, for example a conductor's beat, or a unit of tempo, as in four beats to the bar. 'Beat music' is a general term for popular music having a strong and unvarying beat.

beat frequency in musical acoustics, fluctuation produced when two notes of nearly equal pitch or frequency are heard together. Beats result from the interference between the sound waves of the notes. The frequency of the beats equals the difference in frequency of the notes.

Musicians use the effect when tuning their instruments. A similar effect can occur in electrical circuits when two alternating currents are present, producing regular variations in the overall current.

Béatitudes, Les oratorio by Franck for solo voices, chorus, and orchestra (words from the Bible), composed 1869–79, first performed privately by Franck's pupils at his house, 20 February 1879 (piano accompaniment), and in public only after his death, Dijon, 15 June 1891.

Beatrice di Tenda opera by Bellini (libretto by F Romani), produced Venice, Teatro La Fenice, 16 March 1833. Beatrice is married to greedy Duke Filippo but loves Orombello. She is executed on account of infidelity and treason by the Duke, who loves only the power acquired through her lands and her lady-in-waiting, Agnese.

Béatrice et Bénédict/Beatrice and Benedick opera by Berlioz (libretto by composer, based on Shakespeare's *Much Ado about Nothing*), produced Baden-Baden, 9 August 1862. Shakespeare stripped to essentials.

Beatrix Cenci opera in two acts by Ginastera (libretto by W Shand and A Girri after Shelley's *The Cenci*, 1819, and Stendhal's *Chroniques Italiennes*, 1837), produced Washington, DC, 10 September 1971. Beatrix is executed after killing her incestuous father.

beats in acoustics, the clashing of soundwaves of slightly different frequencies produced, for example, by two piano strings for the same note not perfectly in tune with each other, or certain organ stops using two pipes for each note purposely kept slightly out of tune to produce that wavering effect. Sensitive ears perceive beats as slight periodical swellings of the tone on sustained notes, and piano tuners rely on beats to tell them whether the strings of any one note are in tune or not.

Beaulieu, Eustorg de (c. 1500–1552) French poet and musician. He wrote a few *chansons*, but is better known for his verse, including a collection of early Protestant song texts.

Beaumarchais, Pierre Augustin Caron de (1732–1799) French author and musician. He sang and played the flute and harp, teaching the latter to the daughters of Louis XV. His great trilogy of pre-revolutionary plays is perfectly structured for musical adaptation. *Le Barbier de Séville* (1775) was set by Paisiello in 1782 and performed all over Europe before Rossini's version of 1816. *La Folle Journée, ou Le Mariage de Figaro* (1784) had socially significant implications that are still present in Mozart's setting (1786). *La Mère Coupable* (1792) forms the basis of John Corigliano's *The Ghosts of Versailles*, successfully performed at the New York Metropolitan Opera in 1991 and featuring Beaumarchais himself as a kindly spirit who attempts to change history by writing a play that would save Marie Antoinette from the guillotine.

bebung (German 'trembling') musical vibrato achieved on the clavichord by a fluctuation of key pressure impinging on the metal tangent pressing on the string.

Bechstein, (Friedrich Wilhelm) Carl (1826–1900) German piano maker. He founded his own firm in 1856, after having worked as an employee of several other companies. It expanded rapidly, taking advantage of new technological developments, some of which were invented by ◊Steinway. The company was bankrupt 1993, but was saved by the intervention of the German government. Bechstein pianos are noted for their smooth but not particularly brilliant tone.

Beck, Conrad (1901–1989) Swiss composer. After studying engineering, he became a student at the Zurich Conservatory under Volkmar Andreae and others; later he studied in Berlin and Paris, where he lived 1923–32 and was closely in touch with Roussel and Honegger. He was awarded important prizes for composition in 1954, 1956, and 1964.

Works include: the opera *La Grande Ourse* (1936); incidental music for Goethe's *Pandora* (1945) and other plays; oratorios *Angelus Silesius* and *Der Tod zu Basel*; Requiem; *Der Tod des Oedipus* for chorus and orchestra; *Lyric Cantata* (Rilke) for female voices and orchestra; chamber cantata (sonnets by Louise Labé); five symphonies (1925–30), *Sinfonietta*, *Innominata*, and *Ostinato* for orchestra, concerto for string quartet and orchestra, *Konzertmusik* for oboe and strings, concerto, concertino, and rhapsody for piano and orchestra, cello concerto; five string quartets (1922–52).

Beck, Franz (1734–1809) German violinist and composer. He was a member of the Mannheim School of symphonists and a pupil of Johann Stamitz. He is said to have fled from Mannheim as the result of a duel; he went to Italy and later settled in France.

Works include: the operas *La belle jardinière* (Bordeaux, 1767) and *Pandore* (Paris, 1789); about 30 symphonies, *Stabat Mater*, keyboard music.

Becker, John (1886–1961) US composer. After studying at the Cincinnati Conservatory, he taught at Notre Dame 1917–27. From 1930 he was associated with Carl Ruggles, Wallingford Riegger, Henry Cowell, and other avant-garde US composers. His series of *Soundscapes* create novel effects of instrumentation, while his theatre pieces anticipate later mixed-media works.

Works include: stage pieces *A Marriage with Space* (1935), *Nostalgic Songs of Earth* (1938), *Rain Down Death* (1939), *When the Willow Nods* (1940), and *Faust: a Television Opera* (1951); seven symphonies (1912–54); two piano concertos and concertos for viola (1937) and violin (1948); *Moments from the Passion* (1945); film music and songs.

Bedford, David (1937–) English composer. He studied at the Royal Academy of Music with Lennox Berkeley and in Venice with Luigi Nono.

Works include: the school operas *The Rime of the Ancient Mariner* (1976) and *The Ragnarok* (1983); *The Camlann Game* (1987), *The Return of Odysseus* (1988) and *Anna* (1993); symphony for 12 players, *Sun Paints Rainbows on the Vast Waves* for orchestra (1982); *Star Clusters, Nebulae and Places in Devon* for chorus and brass (1971); *Seascapes* (1986), *The Transfiguration* (1988), *Frameworks* (1990), and *Plymouth Town* (1992), all for orchestra; *Toccata for Tristan* for brass (1989); *Allison's Concerto* for trumpet and strings (1993); *I am going home with thee* for six women's voices and strings (1993); many pieces for instrumental ensemble and voices and instruments, many of which reflect the fact that he is a teacher and a one-time member of the pop group The Whole World.

Bedyngham, John (died c. 1460) English composer. He wrote Masses, motets, and chansons, possibly including *O rosa bella*, often ascribed to John Dunstable. His music was widely known in continental Europe; one of his two Mass cycles is derived from a ballade by Binchois.

Beecham, Thomas (1879–1961) English conductor and impresario. He established the Royal Philharmonic Orchestra in 1946 and fostered the works of composers such as Delius, Sibelius, and Richard Strauss. He was knighted and succeeded to the baronetcy in 1916.

Beeson, Jack (Hamilton) (1921–) US composer. He studied with Howard Hanson at Rochester and with Bartók in New York in 1945, and was professor at Columbia University 1965–88.

Works include: the operas *Jonah* (1950), *Hello, Out There* (1954), *The Sweet Bye and Bye* (1957), *Lizzie Borden* (1965), *Dr Heidegger's Fountain of Youth* (after Hawthorne, 1978); also symphony in A (1959), *Transformations* for orchestra (1959), five piano sonatas, TV opera *My Heart's in the Highlands* (after Sorayan, 1970).

'Bee's Wedding, The' the English nickname of Mendelssohn's *Song without Words* in C major op. 67 no. 4, the German being *Spinnerlied* 'spinning-song'.

Beethoven, Ludwig van (1770–1827) German composer and pianist. His mastery of musical expression in every genre made him the dominant influence on 19th-century music. Beethoven's repertoire includes concert overtures; the opera *Fidelio* (1805, revised 1814); 5 piano concertos and 2 for violin (one unfinished); 32 piano sonatas, including the *Moonlight* (1801) and *Appassionata* (1804–05); 17 string quartets; the Mass in D (*Missa solemnis*) 1824; and 9 symphonies, as well as many youthful works. He usually played his own piano pieces and conducted his orchestral works until he was hampered by deafness in 1801; nevertheless he continued to compose.

Born in Bonn, the son and grandson of musicians in the service of the Elector of Cologne in Bonn, Beethoven became deputy organist at the court of the Elector of Cologne at Bonn before he was 12; later he studied under Haydn and possibly Mozart, whose influence dominated his early work. From 1808 he received a small allowance from aristocratic patrons.

Beethoven's career spanned the transition from Classicism to Romanticism. He was aware of the problems his music created for listeners and performers alike (part of the slow movement of the Choral Symphony had to be cut at its premiere), but although contemporary audiences found his visionary late music difficult, Beethoven's reputation was well established throughout Europe. Of his symphonies the best known are the Third (*Eroica*) (1803–04), originally intended to be dedicated to Napoleon, with whom Beethoven became disillusioned, the Fifth (1807–08), the Sixth (*Pastoral*) (1803–08), and the Ninth (*Choral*) (1815–24), which includes the passage from Schiller's 'Ode to Joy' chosen as the anthem of Europe.

Beethoven became a pupil of Christian Gottlob Neefe in 1781. In 1783 he was a harpsichordist in the court orchestra, and the same year published three piano sonatas. He was second organist at court in 1784, and in 1789 also a viola player. A visit to Vienna in 1787 to study with Mozart was cut short after only a few weeks by his mother's fatal illness, and he continued as a court musician in Bonn, meeting Count Waldstein in 1788. In 1792 he returned to Vienna to be a pupil of Haydn, whom he had met in Bonn. He remained in Vienna for the rest of his life, scarcely leaving the city or its suburbs. Tuition with Haydn was not a success (the impatient younger composer could not get on with his master, though his early music is full of Haydn's influence) and he took lessons from Johann Baptist Schenk, Johann Albrechtsberger, and Antonio Salieri. In 1795 he published his op. 1, three piano trios, and made his first public appearance in Vienna as a pianist and composer. He lived by playing and teaching, and later increasingly by the publication of his works.

The set of six string quartets op. 18, 1798–1800, though classical in form, are strongly expressive in content: the slow movement of the first work was said by Beethoven to portray the tomb scene in *Romeo and Juliet*. The first symphony, written in 1800, was easily understood in the context of recent works by Haydn and Mozart. The deafness which had threatened from as early as about 1795 increased, and his despair gave rise to the suicidal 'Heiligenstadt Testament' in 1802; Beethoven's musical response was the radiant and untroubled second symphony. His third symphony (*Eroica*) was dedicated to Napoleon, but Beethoven changed the dedication when Napoleon proclaimed himself Emperor. The symphony was highly influential in driving music towards the Romantic style asserted later in the century; symphonic form was also hugely extended. Beethoven conducted his only opera, *Fidelio*, in 1805; the difficulties he faced in reaching a final version are typical of his painstaking working methods. Beethoven's compositional process is summed up in *Fidelio's* development from old-fashioned Singspiel in the first scene to a convincing drama.

He refused to accept regular employment under the old system of patronage, but received support from the aristocracy: in 1808, for instance, Archduke Rudolph, Prince Kinsky, and Prince Lobkowitz agreed to pay him an unconditional annuity; the fifth symphony dates from the same year, and seems to proclaim the individual's sense of worth and identity. By 1806 he was forced to abandon public performance altogether. More time was now available for composition: there followed the fourth piano concerto, the Rasumovsky quartets, the violin concerto, sixth (*Pastoral*), seventh, and eighth symphonies and the *Emperor* concerto. By turns lyrical, expansive, serene, and dynamic, the music of this middle period gained Beethoven further public recognition as the leading composer of the day.

In 1815, after his brother's death, he temporarily became guardian to his nephew Karl, a task he took seriously and which caused him constant worry. The last five great piano works (four sonatas and the Diabelli Variations) were initiated in 1818 by the Hammerklavier sonata; these works pressed instrumental technique to new limits but at the same time combine intellectual depth with expressive power in a unique way not achieved by any other composer. By 1819 Beethoven was totally deaf, and communication with him was possible only in writing. He had begun work on the Choral symphony in 1817 and this was followed by the Missa Solemnis 1819–22 and the last five quartets 1822–26. In 1826 he caught an infection from which he never recovered, and his death the following year was due to dropsy.

Works include: STAGE opera, *Fidelio*, (1805, revised 1806 and 1814), incidental music for *Egmont* (Goethe, 1810), *The Creatures of Prometheus*, overture, introduction and 16 nos. for a ballet produced at the Burgtheater, Vienna, 1801.

CHORAL WITH ORCHESTRA Mass in C, op. 86 (1807), *Choral Fantasia*, for piano, chorus, and orchestra, op. 80 (1808), Mass in D, (*Missa Solemnis*), op. 123 (1819–22).

SYMPHONIES no. 1 in C, op. 21 (1800), no. 2 in D, op. 36 (1802), no. 3 in E♭ (*Eroica*), op. 55 (1803), no. 4 in B♭, op. 60 (1806), no. 5 in C minor, op. 67 (1808), no. 6 in F, (*Pastoral*), op. 68 (1808), no. 7 in A, op. 92 (1812), no. 8 in F, op. 93 (1812), no. 9 in D minor (*Choral*), op. 125 (1817–24).

CONCERTOS piano, no. 1 in C, op. 15 (1795), no. 2 in B♭, op. 19 (before 1793, revised 1794–95, 1798), no. 3 in C minor, op. 37 (?1800), no. 4 in G, op. 58 (1806), no. 5 in E♭, (*Emperor*), op. 73 (1809); violin concerto, op. 61 (1806), triple concerto for piano, violin, and cello, op. 56 (1804).

OVERTURES *Leonora* 1–3 (1805, 1806), *Coriolan*, op. 62 (1807).

CHAMBER Trio in B♭ for clarinet, cello, and piano op. 11 (1797); Variations for piano trio on *Ich bin der Schneider Kakadu* op. 121a (1798); Serenade for flute, violin, and viola in D, op. 25 (1800); Septet in E♭ op. 20 (1800); two quintets, for piano and wind in E♭ (1796), for strings in C, op. 29 (1801); 16 string quartets, op. 18 nos. 1–6, in F, G, D, C minor, A, and B♭ (1798–1800), op. 59 nos. 1–3, *Rasumovsky*, in F, E minor, and C (1806), op. 74 in E♭ *Harp*, (1809), op. 95 in F minor (1810), op. 127 in E♭ (1825), op. 130 in B♭ (1826; present rondo finale replaces original *Grosse Fuge*, op. 133), op. 131 in C♯ minor (1826), op. 132 in A minor (1825), op. 135 in F (1826); five string trios (1794–98); six piano trios, op. 1 nos. 1–3 (1794), op. 70 nos. 1 and 2, in D (*Ghost*), and E♭ (1808), op. 97 in B♭, (*Archduke*) (1811); ten violin sonatas (1798–1812); five cello sonatas (1796–1815).

PIANO 32 sonatas, op. 2 nos. 1–3, in F minor, A, and C (1795), op. 7 in E♭ (1796), op. 10 nos. 1–3, in C minor, F, and D (1798), op. 13 in C minor (*Pathétique*) (1799), op. 14 nos. 1 and 2 in E and G (1799), op. 22 in B♭ (1800), op. 26 in A♭ (1801), op. 27 nos. 1 and 2, in E♭ and C♯ minor (*Moonlight*) (1801), op. 28 in D (*Pastoral*) (1801), op. 31 nos. 1–3, in G, D minor, and E♭ (1802), op. 49 nos. 1 and 2, in G minor and G (1802), op. 53 in C (*Waldstein*) (1804), op. 54 in F (1804), op. 57 in F minor (*Appassionata*)

(1805), op. 78 in F♯ (1809), op. 79 in G (1809), op. 81a in E♭ (*Les Adieux*) (1801), op. 90 in E minor (1814), op. 101 in A (1816), op. 106 in B♭ (*Hammerklavier*) (1818), op. 109 in E (1820), op. 110 in A♭ (1821), op. 111 in C minor (1822); 15 Variations and Fugue on a theme from Prometheus, (*Eroica Variations*) in E♭ (1802); 33 *Variations on a Waltz by Diabelli*, op. 120 (1819–23).

SOLO VOICE Scena and aria *Ah! Perfido!* for soprano and orchestra (1796), *Adelaide* for tenor and piano (1795–96); *An die ferne Geliebte* for tenor and piano (1816).

Beffroy de Reigny, Louis Abel (1757–1811) French playwright and composer, known as 'Cousin Jacques'. Under this name he wrote satirical operettas popular during the Revolution, including *Nicodème dans la lune, Nicodème aux enfers*, and *La Petite Nanette*.

Beggar's Opera, The ballad opera, produced London, Theatre in Lincoln's Inn Fields, 29 January 1728, consisting of a play by John Gay interspersed with songs. The music, popular tunes of the day but for the most part not folksongs, was arranged by John Christopher Pepusch, who also composed the overture. There have been several modern realizations, including one by Britten (1948).

Beginning of a Romance, The/Počátek románu opera in one act by Janáček (libretto by J Tichý, after a story by G Preissová), composed 1891, produced Brno, 10 February 1894. Tonek romances the village beauty, Poluška.

Beglarian, Grant (1927–) Georgian-born US composer. He was influenced by Copland and Finney. He emigrated to the USA in 1947 and studied with Ross Lee Finney at the University of Michigan. He taught at the University of Southern California, Los Angeles, 1969–82.

Works include: string quartet (1948), *Symphony in Two Movements* (1950), *Divertimento* for orchestra (1957), woodwind quintet (1966), *Diversions* for viola, cello, and orchestra (1972), *Sinfonia* for strings (1974); *To Manitou* for soprano and orchestra (1976), *Partita for Orchestra* (1986).

Begleitungsmusik (Schoenberg). See ◊*Accompaniment to a Film Scene*.

Behrman, David (1937–) Austrian-born US composer of electronic music. He studied at Harvard and with Pousseur and Stockhausen in Europe. He worked with John Cage and David Tudor in the 1970s, notably for the Merce Cunningham Dance Company.

Works include: *Pools of Phase-Locked Loops* (1972); *Cloud Music* (1979); *Indoor Geyser* (1981); *Orchestral Construction Set* (1984); *Inter-Species Smalltalk* (1984); *Installation for La Villett* (1985); many albums of experimental music for CBS.

Being Beauteous cantata by Henze for soprano, harp, and four cellos (text from Rimbaud), performed Berlin, 12 April 1964.

Beinum, Eduard van (1901–1959) Dutch conductor. He was best known for his performances of Beethoven and was a champion of contemporary Dutch music. He toured Europe and America, and in 1956 became conductor of the Los Angeles Philharmonic Orchestra, but resigned and returned to Europe, where he died.

He studied with his brother and composition with Sem Dresden. After a post in Haarlem in 1926, he became second conductor of the Concertgebouw Orchestra of Amsterdam 1931–38, an associate to Willem Mengelberg in 1938, and his successor in 1945.

beklemmt (German 'oppressed') a term used by Beethoven in the Cavatina of the string quartet op. 130.

bel canto (Italian 'beautiful song') in music, an 18th-century Italian style of singing with emphasis on perfect technique and beautiful tone. The style reached its peak in the operas of Rossini, Donizetti, and Bellini.

Beldemandis, Prosdocimus de (c. 1375–1428) Italian music scholar. He wrote treatises on music, published between 1404 and 1413, and was professor of mathematics and astronomy at Padua in 1422.

Belfagor opera by Respighi (libretto by C Guastalla, based on a comedy by E L Morselli), produced Milan, La Scala, 26 April 1923. Candida is made to marry Belfagor, the Devil in disguise.

Belisario opera by Donizetti (libretto by S Cammarano), produced Venice, Teatro La Fenice, 4 February 1836. A Roman general blinded and exiled after being accused of his son's murder.

bell musical instrument, made in many sizes, comprising a suspended resonating vessel swung by a handle or from a pivoted frame to make contact with a beater which hangs inside the bell. Church bells are among the most massive structures to be cast in bronze in one piece; from high up in a steeple they can be heard for many miles. Their shape, a flared bowl with a thickened rim, is engineered to produce a clangorous mixture of tones. Miniature **handbells** are tuned to resonate harmoniously. Orchestral **tubular bells**, of brass or steel, are tuned to a chromatic scale of pitches and are played by striking with a wooden mallet. A set of steeple bells played from a keyboard is called a **carillon**.

The world's largest bell is the 'Tsar Kolokol' or 'King of Bells', cast in 1734, it weighs 220 tonnes, and stands on the ground at the Kremlin, Moscow, Russia, where it fell when being hung. The 'Peace Bell' at the United Nations headquarters, New York, USA, was cast in 1952 from coins presented by 64 countries.

bell in a wind instrument, the flat disc or flare at the opposite end of the tube from the mouthpiece.

In woodwind instruments, it acts as a shaped baffle controlling the expanding pressure wave emitted from the bell when all the finger holes are closed (at higher pitches pressure escapes from the highest open hole). In brass instruments, it also acts as a directional radiator, the thin metal vibrating with the variation between the escaping sound and atmospheric pressure.

'Bell Anthem' the name once given to Purcell's anthem *Rejoice in the Lord always*, composed c. 1682–85. The instrumental introduction contains descending scales resembling the ringing of church bells.

Belle Hélène, La/The Fair Helen operetta by Offenbach (libretto by H Meilhac and L Halévy), produced Paris, Théâtre des Variétés, 17 December 1864. A satirical version of the myth.

Bellérophon opera by Lully (libretto by T Corneille with B de Fontenelle and Boileau), produced Paris, Opéra, 31 January 1679. Bellérophon threatened by monster Chimaera after he rejects the wife of King Proteus.

Belli, Girolamo (1552–c. 1620) Italian composer. After studying with Luzzasco Luzzaschi, he was a singer at the Gonzaga court at Mantua, and was in Rome in 1582. He published several books of madrigals, of which six survive, as well as psalms, *Sacrae cantiones*, and other church music including masses.

Bellini, Vincenzo (1801–1835) Italian composer of operas. He collaborated with the tenor Giovanni Battista Rubini (1794–1854) to develop a new simplicity of melodic expression in romantic evocations of classic themes, as in *La Sonnambula/The Sleepwalker* and *Norma*, both 1831. In *I Puritani/The Puritans*

1835, his last work, he discovered a new boldness and vigour of orchestral effect.

His popularity after his death was enormous, but his operas later fell into neglect. Since World War II, however, singers including Maria Callas, Joan Sutherland, and Montserrat Caballé, have helped to restore their popularity.

Bellini was born at Catania, Sicily. His father, an organist, was enabled, with the help of a Sicilian nobleman, to send him to study with Niccolò Zingarelli at the Naples Conservatory, where he met Donizetti and Mercadante. His first opera, *Adelson e Salvini*, was produced in 1825, while he was still a student; it attracted the attention of Domenico Barbaia, who commissioned him to write a second, *Bianca e Gernando*, produced at the Teatro San Carlo in 1826. Its success induced Barbaia to ask for another opera (*Il pirata/The Pirate*) for La Scala, Milan; this was produced there in 1827 with Rubini in the cast. It was also successfully performed in Paris, and three other operas followed, at Milan, Parma, and Venice, before Bellini attained full maturity in *La sonnambula/The Sleepwalker*, brought out at Milan in 1831, with Maria Malibran as the heroine. *Norma* followed in December of the same year, with Giuditta Pasta in the title role. This opera marks the culmination of Bellini's style, with its long and elegiac melodic line and superbly crafted dramatic tension.

In 1833 Bellini went to London and Paris, where Rossini advised him to write a work for the Théâtre Italien. This was *I puritani/The Puritans*, produced there in 1835, with Giulia Grisi, Rubini, Antonio Tamburini, and Luigi Lablache in the cast; it was brought to London the same year for Grisi's benefit performance. Bellini went to stay with an English friend at Puteaux, at whose house he was taken ill and died.

Works include: the operas *Adelson e Salvini*, *Bianca e Gernando*, *Il pirata*, *La straniera* (1829), *Zaira*, *I Capuleti e i Montecchi* (1830, based on Shakespeare's sources for *Romeo and Juliet*), *La Sonnambula*, *Norma*, *Beatrice di Tenda* (1833), *I puritani* (1835); church music; songs; symphonies.

bell ringing, or campanology the art of ringing church bells individually or in sequence by rhythmically drawing on a rope fastened to a wheel rotating the bell, so that it falls back and strikes in time. **Change ringing** is an English art, dating from the 17th century, of ringing a patterned sequence of permutations of 5–12 church bells, using one player to each bell. See also ♭carillon.

'Bells of Zlonice, The' symphony no. 1 in C minor by Dvořák; composed 1865 as op. 3 but lost until 1923. First performed Prague, 4 October 1936.

Bells, The poem for orchestra, chorus, and soloists by Rachmaninov, op. 35 (text by Edgar Allan Poe, trans. by K Balmont); composed 1913, first performed St Petersburg, 30 November 1913. Revived 1936 and performed Sheffield, 21 October 1936, conductor Henry Wood.

belly the surface of string instruments, which lies directly beneath the strings; also sometimes the soundboard of the piano.

Belshazzar oratorio by Handel (words by Charles Jennens), produced London, King's Theatre, Haymarket, 27 March 1745.

Belshazzar's Feast cantata by William Walton (words from the Bible arranged by O Sitwell), produced Leeds Festival, 8 October 1931.

Incidental music by Sibelius for a play by H Procopé, first performed Helsinki, 7 November 1906. Orchestral Suite op. 51 in four movements first performed Helsinki, 25 September 1907.

bémol (French 'flat') in music, the sign for flat (♭).

Benedicite work by Vaughan Williams for soprano, chorus, and orchestra; composed 1929, first performed Dorking, 2 May 1930, conductor Vaughan Williams.

Benedict, Julius (1804–1885) German-born English conductor and composer. In 1835 he went to Paris and to London, where he remained for the rest of his life. He conducted a great deal in London, both opera and concerts.

He was a pupil of Hummel and Weber, and met Beethoven in Vienna in 1823, when he was appointed conductor at the Kärntnertortheater. Next he went to Naples, where he produced his first Italian opera in 1829. He was conductor of the Norwich Festival 1845–78, and of the Liverpool Philharmonic Society 1876–80.

Works include: OPERA *Giacinta ed Ernesto*, *I Portoghesi in Goa* (1830), *Un anno ed un giorno* (1836), *The Gypsy's Warning*, *The Brides of Venice* (1844), *The Crusaders*, *The Lily of Killarney*, *The Bride of Song* (1864).

OTHER two symphonies; two piano concertos; five cantatas, and other pieces.

Benevoli, Orazio (1605–1672) Italian composer. He held appointments at the churches of San Luigi de' Francesi and Santa Maria Maggiore in Rome, the former with an interruption 1644–46, when he was at the Austrian court in Vienna. In 1646 he became maestro di cappella at the Vatican.

Works include: Masses, motets, and other church music, much of it for several choirs in a large number of parts. The celebrated 53-part *Missa salisburgensis* formerly attributed to him, is probably by Biber.

Beni Mora Oriental Suite in E minor, op. 29 no. 1 for orchestra by Holst. Composed 1910 after a visit to Algeria: last of three movements is titled 'In the Street of the Ouled Naïls'; first performed London, 1 May 1912, conductor Holst.

Benjamin, Arthur (1893–1960) Australian pianist and composer. The influence of Latin American dance rhythms was important throughout his life. He was educated at Brisbane and studied at the Royal College of Music in London, where he later became professor. After fighting in World War I he returned to Australia to teach piano at the Sydney Conservatory 1919–20, but having developed as a composer, settled in London. He taught composition at the Royal College of Music in London from 1925, where Benjamin Britten was one of his pupils. From 1930 to 1936 he lived in Vancouver.

Works include: the operas *The Devil take her* (1931), *Prima Donna* (1933), *A Tale of Two Cities* (after Dickens) (1950), *Tartuffe*; film music including *An Ideal Husband* (after Oscar Wilde); symphonic suite *Light Music* and *Overture to an Italian Comedy* for orchestra; *Romantic Fantasy* for violin, viola, and orchestra, violin concerto (1932), concertino for piano and orchestra, chamber music, songs.

Benjamin, George William John (1960–) English composer, conductor, and pianist. He was a pupil of Messiaen, and his colourful and sonorous works include *Ringed by the Flat Horizon* (1980), *At First Light* (1982), *Antara* (1987), and *Cascade* (1990).

He studied with Messiaen and Yvonne Loriod in Paris from 1974, at the Paris Conservatory in 1977, and with Alexander Goehr at Cambridge. At the 1983 Aldeburgh Festival he gave the first performance of Britten's *Sonatina Romantica* (1940). Returning to France 1984–87 he worked at the electronic music studios at the Institut de Recherche et de Co-ordination Acoustique/Musique (IR-CAM).

Works include: *At First Light*, for chamber orchestra (1982); *A Mind of Winter*, for soprano and ensemble; violin sonata (1977), octet (1978), duo for cello and piano (1980); *Meditations on Haydn's Name*, for piano (1982); *Antara* for orchestra with electronics (1985–87), *Jubilation* for orchestra and groups of children (1985), *Cascade* for orchestra (1990), *Upon Silence* for mezzo and five viols (1990); *Helix* (1992) and *Sudden Time* for orchestra (1993).

Bennett, Richard Rodney (1936–) English composer of jazz, film music, symphonies, and operas. His film scores for *Far from the Madding Crowd* (1967), *Nicholas and Alexandra* (1971), and *Murder on the Orient Express* (1974) all received Oscar nominations. His operas include *The Mines of Sulphur* (1963) and *Victory* (1970).

He studied at the Royal Academy of Music with Lennox Berkeley and Howard Ferguson, and in Paris with Pierre Boulez. Influenced by Bartók, he has also used serial techniques but also writes in a lighter vein.

Works include: the operas *The Ledge* (1961), *The Mines of Sulphur* (1963), *A Penny for a Song* (1966), *Victory* (after Conrad, 1970); ballet *Isadora* (1981); symphonies; *Aubade* for orchestra; piano concerto (1968), oboe concerto, *Anniversaries* for orchestra (1982); *Love Songs* for tenor and orchestra (texts by e e cummings) (1985); four string quartets (1952–64); *Calendar* for chamber ensemble; three symphonies (1965, 1967, 1987); Sinfonietta (1984), *Dream Dancing* (1986), and *Celebration* (1992) for orchestra; *Memento* for flute and strings (1983); concertos for harpsichord (1980), clarinet (1987), saxophone (for Stan Getz, 1990) and for trumpet and wind band (1993); vocal music, and film, radio, and television music.

Bennett, William Sterndale (1816–1875) English pianist and composer. He was a chorister at King's College, Cambridge, and a student at the Royal Academy of Music in London. He then went to Leipzig, where he made friends with Mendelssohn. Schumann dedicated his *Etudes symphoniques* for piano to him. He conducted the first English performance of Bach's *St Matthew Passion* in 1854. He was professor of music at Cambridge University 1856–75, and principal of the Royal Academy of Music 1866–75.

Works include: incidental music to Sophocles' *Ajax* (1872); cantata *The May Queen* (1858), odes for the International Exhibition (Tennyson) and the Cambridge Installation of a Chancellor (Kingsley); anthems; six symphonies (1832–64), overtures *The Naiads* and *The Wood-Nymphs,* fantasy-overture on Moore's *Paradise and the Peri;* five piano concertos (1832–38); piano pieces, songs.

Benoit, Peter (Léonard Léopold) (1834–1901) Belgian composer. He was a pupil of Fétis at the Brussels Conservatory. He became conductor at a Flemish theatre and was keenly interested in Flemish national music as distinct from that influenced by French composers. He travelled in Germany and visited Paris, but tended more and more towards an indigenous type of music. His first opera was produced in 1857.

Works include: the French opera *Le Roi des aulnes* (on Goethe's *Erl King*) (1859); Flemish operas *The Mountain Village, Isa, Pompeja;* incidental music to Flemish plays; Te Deum, *Messe solennelle,* Requiem; oratorios *Lucifer* (1865) and *The Scheldt* (1868); *Petite Cantate de Noël* and many Flemish cantatas.

Bentzon, Nils Viggo (1919–   ) Danish composer. He studied piano with his mother and composition with Knud Christian Jeppesen (1892–1974).

Works include: four operas, including *Faust III* (after Goethe, Kafka, and Joyce, 1964); 15 symphonies (1942–80); eight piano concertos, four violin concertos, much chamber music, including chamber concerto, for 11 instruments, a chamber symphony, nine string quartets (1940–76), sonata for solo cello; 11 piano sonatas, *Propostae Novae* for two pianos; vocal music, including *Bonjour Max Ernst,* cantata for chorus and orchestra (1961).

Benvenuto Cellini opera by Berlioz (libretto by L de Wailly and A Barbier, based on Cellini's autobiography), produced Paris, Opéra, 10 September 1838. Boastful sculptor beats Pope's deadline.

berceuse lullaby, usually in the form of an instrumental piece in moderately relaxed duple time (6/8). The most famous example is Chopin's *Berceuse* (1844).

Berceuse élégiaque piano piece by Busoni, composed 1909 and added to the *Elegien* of 1907; orchestral version of 1909 is subtitled *Des Mannes Wiegenlied am Sarge seine Mutter/ The man's lullaby at his mother's coffin:* Busoni's mother died on 3 October 1909. First performed conducted by Mahler at his last concert, New York, 21 February 1911.

Berchem, Jachet de (c. 1505–c. 1565) Flemish composer, not to be confused with Jachet of Mantua. Probably organist to the ducal court at Ferrara in 1555, he wrote church music, madrigals for four and five voices, and French chansons. He is credited with being the first to compose a madrigal cycle, his *Capriccio* is a setting of stories from Ariosto's 'Orlando furioso'.

Berenice opera by Handel (libretto by A Salvi), produced London, Covent Garden, 18 May 1737. Egyptian queen in love problems before marriage to Alexander; a complex plot involving politics, jealousy, and anger resolves happily in the end.
Opera by Perti (libretto ditto), produced Villa Pratolino near Florence, September 1709.

Berenice, che fai? Italian cantata by Haydn for soprano and orchestra (text from Metastasio's *Antigono*), composed May 1795.

Berezovsky, Maksim Sosnovich (1745–1777) Russian composer. He was a pupil at the academy in Kiev, later a singer in the service of the court. In 1765 he went to Italy to study under Martini. On his return to Russia, unable to secure an appointment, he finally committed suicide. His most important contribution was to church music; he also wrote an opera, *Demofoonte* (1773, the first by a Russian to be given in Italy), and other works.

Berg, (Carl) Natanael (1879–1957) Swedish composer. He studied at the Stockholm Conservatory and in Paris and Vienna.
Works include: the operas *Leila* (after Byron's *Giaour*) (1910), *Engelbrekt* (1928), *Judith* (after Hebbel's drama) (1935), *Birgitta, Genoveva* (1946); five symphonies; symphonic poems; violin concerto; piano concerto; two string quartets, piano quintet.

Berg, Alban (1885–1935) Austrian composer. He studied under Arnold Schoenberg and developed a personal 12-tone idiom of great emotional and stylistic versatility. His relatively small output includes two operas: *Wozzeck* (1920), a grim story of working-class life, and the unfinished *Lulu* (1929–35), and chamber music incorporating coded references to friends and family.

His music is emotionally expressive, and sometimes anguished, but it can also be lyrical, as in the *Violin Concerto* (1935).

Berg was self-taught from the age of 15, and a pupil of Schoenberg 1904–10. Schoenberg's influence on him was profound, and may be measured as Berg passes from the extended tonality of his early works to atonality and, later, serialism. His use of serial technique is distinctive in that he does not avoid tonal references (as, for example, in the violin concerto). Accordingly, he remains the most accessible member of the Second Viennese School. In 1911 he married Helene

Nahowski. His first major work, the string quartet op. 3, dates from the same year.

His music was known only to a small circle until the 1925 production of *Wozzeck*. The Chamber Concerto and Lyric Suite, which followed shortly after, incorporate complex formal patterns, numerical puzzles, and autobiographical allusions. He was a friend of Alma Mahler and the death of her daughter, Manon, inspired his last completed work, the violin concerto. Dedicated 'To the Memory of an Angel', Berg wrote the concerto as a Requiem for Manon, yet in its poignant lyricism, quoting the Bach chorale *Es ist Genug/It is enough*, it is the composer's own last testament. His second opera, *Lulu*, was begun in 1929 but left unfinished after his death and not performed in the full, three-act version until 1979.

Works include: OPERA *Wozzeck* (after Büchner, 1917–22; produced Berlin, 1925) and *Lulu* (after Wedekind, 1929–35; two acts produced Zurich, 1937, act 3 realized by F Cerha, performance Paris, 1979).

SONGS, AND VOICE WITH ORCHESTRA 70 early Lieder; *Seven Early Songs* for voice and piano (1905–08, orchestral version 1928); *Five Altenberglieder* for voice and orchestra (1912, first performance Rome, 1953); *Lulu-Symphonie* for soprano and orchestra (1934).

ORCHESTRAL *Three Pieces*, op. 6 (1914–15, revised 1929; Chamber Concerto for piano, violin, and 13 wind instruments (1923–24; first performance Berlin, 1927); violin concerto (1935; first performance Barcelona, 1936).

CHAMBER piano sonata op. 1 (1907–08); *Four Pieces* for clarinet and piano (1913); *Lyric Suite* for string quartet (1925–26); adagio from Chamber Concerto arranged for violin, clarinet, and piano (1935).

bergamasca an Italian dance from Bergamo at least as old as the 16th century, called bergomask by Shakespeare.

Berger, Arthur (1912–) US composer. He studied with Piston at Harvard University, with Pirro, Pierre Lalo, and Paul Valéry at the Sorbonne in Paris, and composition with Nadia Boulanger; later influences included Babbitt and Webern. He became music editor of the New York *Sun*.

Works include: *Slow Dance* for strings; serenade for chamber orchestra (1944); three pieces for string quartet, wind quartet, two movements for violin and cello; ballet *Entertainment Piece* and other works for piano; *Words for Music Perhaps* (Yeats) and other songs.

Berger, Theodor (1905–1992) Austrian composer. He studied at the Vienna Academy, and was much influenced by his teachers, Korngold and Franz Schmidt.

Works include: *Malincolia* for strings (1938), *Homerische Symphonie* (1948), *La Parola* for orchestra (1955), *Symphonischer Triglyph* on themes by Schubert (1957), *Divertimento* for chorus, wind, and percussion (1968), violin concerto (1963); two string quartets (1930–31).

Bergknappen, Die/The Miners one-act Singspiel by Umlauf (libretto by P Weidmann), produced Vienna, Burgtheater, on the opening of its career as a national German opera, 17 February 1778. Old Walcher competes with young Fritz for the affections of Sophie; Walcher yields after Fritz rescues him in a mine.

Berglund, Paavo (1929–) Finnish conductor. After an early career as a violinist, he co-founded the Helsinki Chamber Orchestra in 1953; principal conductor of the Helsinki Radio Symphony Orchestra from 1962, and the Helsinki Philharmonic Orchestra 1975–79. He has conducted the Bournemouth Symphony Orchestra from 1964, music director 1972–79; associated with the revival of Jean Sibelius's early *Kullervo* Symphony. Principal guest conductor Scottish National Orchestra from 1981. Recordings include symphonies by Dmitri Shostakovich.

Bergonzi (lived 17th–18th centuries) Italian family of violin makers who worked in Cremona. **Carlo Bergonzi** (c. 1683–1747) began to work independently about 1716 and created his best instruments in the 1730s, rivalling Guarnieri and Stradivari. His son was **Michelangelo Bergonzi** (1722–1758).

Bergsma, William (1921–1994) US composer. He studied at Stanford University and the Eastman School of Music under Howard Hanson and Bernard Rogers, and after winning many awards he became a teacher of composition at the Juilliard School New York.

Works include: the opera *The Wife of Martin Guerre* (1956); ballets *Paul Bunyan* (1938) and *Gold and the Señor Commandante* (1941); choral symphony; choral works; symphony for chamber orchestra; four string quartets (1942–70); songs.

Berio, Luciano (1925–) Italian composer. His work combines serial techniques with commedia dell'arte and antiphonal practices, as in *Alleluiah II* (1958), for five instrumental groups. His prolific output includes nine *Sequenzas/Sequences* (1957–75) for various solo instruments or voice, *Sinfonia* (1969) for voices and orchestra, *Formazioni/Formations* (1987) for orchestra, and the opera *Un re in ascolto/A King Listens* (1984).

Berio was born at Oneglia. After studying with Ghedini in Milan and with Dallapiccola in the USA, he came into contact with members of the European avant garde such as Stockhausen, Boulez, and Bruno Maderna; with Maderna he founded an electronic studio, the Studio di Fonologia Musicale, at Milan Radio 1953–60. He lived in the USA 1963–72, teaching at the Juilliard School, New York , 1965–72.

Although Berio's compositional techniques are severe, the effect is softened by a pervasive wit and theatricality. He is one of the most active composers of electronic music and has worked with Boulez at the Institut de Recherche et de Co-ordination Acoustique/ Musique (IRCAM). He has also employed graphic notation; many of his works leave the performer a wide range of choices. He has been particularly concerned to explore the possibilities of language as developed in musical performance.

Works include: DRAMATIC *Laborintus II* (Paris, 1970), *Recital I (for Cathy)* (Lisbon, 1972), *La Vera Storia*, opera (Milan, 1982), *Un Re in ascolto*, opera (Salzburg, 1984).

ORCHESTRAL *Chemins I–IV*, after *Sequenze* for instruments (1965–75), Concerto for two pianos and orchestra (1973), *Points on the curve to find ...* for piano and 20 instruments (1974), *Concerto II (Echoing Curves)* for piano and ensemble (1988).

VOCAL *Chamber Music* (texts by Joyce) (1953), *Circles* for female voice, harp, and two percussion (texts by e e cummings) (1960), *Epifanie* for female voice and orchestra (texts by Proust, Joyce, Brecht, and others) (1961), *Sinfonia* for eight solo voices and orchestra (1968–69), *Ora* (text after Virgil) (1971), *Cries of London*, for eight solo voices (1973–75), *11 Folk Songs* for mezzo and orchestra (1975), *Coro* for 40 voices and orchestra (1976).

CHAMBER AND INSTRUMENTAL the important series of *Sequenze* (I–XI) for solo flute, harp, voice, piano, trombone, viola, oboe, violin, clarinet, trumpet, and guitar (1958–85), *Wasserklavier* for piano (1964), and a second string quartet (1986–90).

Berkeley, Lennox Randal Francis (1903–1989) English composer. His works for the voice include *The Hill of the Graces* (1975), verses from Spenser's *Faerie Queene* set for

eight-part unaccompanied chorus; and his operas *Nelson* (1954) and *Ruth* (1956).

Berkeley was born at Oxford, where he studied at Merton College until 1926. He then went to Paris until 1933 as a pupil of Nadia Boulanger. Much of his work is distinguished by a French elegance and neatness, but he also developed a more powerful style, especially in his opera *Nelson* (1954). Works of his were heard at the International Society for Contemporary Music festivals at Barcelona and London in 1936 and 1938, and at the Leeds and Worcester festivals 1937–38.

Works include: the operas *Nelson* (1954), *A Dinner Engagement*, and *Ruth* (1956); ballet *The Judgement of Paris* (1938); incidental music for Shakespeare's *Tempest*; music for film *Hotel Reserve*; oratorio *Jonah* (1935); psalm *Domini est terra* for chorus and orchestra; *Missa brevis*; four symphonies (1940–78); *Nocturne* and divertimento for orchestra; piano concerto (1947), violin concerto; three string quartets (1935–70); two violin and piano sonatas, sonata and pieces for piano; *Polka* for two pianos.

Berkeley, Michael (1948–) English composer, son of Lennox Berkeley. He studied at the Royal Academy of Music with his father, and with Richard Rodney Bennett. In 1982 his oratorio *Or shall we Die?* was performed in London: it contains a vivid protest at the threat of nuclear war. He was composer in residence at the London College of Music 1987–88.

Works include: the opera *Baa-baa Black Sheep* (after Kipling, 1993); *Meditations*, for strings (1976), oboe concerto (1977), *Fantasia Concertante*, for chamber orchestra; symphonies *Uprising* (1980), *Gregorian Variations*, for orchestra (1982), cello concerto (1982); *Elegy* for flute and strings (1993); *The Wild Winds*, for soprano and chamber orchestra (1978), *At the Round Earth's Imagin'd Corners* (text by Donne) for soloists, chorus and organ (1980); string trio (1978), violin sonata, string quartet (1981), clarinet quintet (1983).

Berlin, Irving (1888–1989), adopted name of Israel Baline Russian-born US songwriter. His songs include hits such as 'Alexander's Ragtime Band' (1911), 'Always' (1925), 'God Bless America' (1917, published 1939), and 'White Christmas' (1942), and the musicals *Top Hat* (1935), *Annie Get Your Gun* (1946), and *Call Me Madam* (1950). He also provided songs for films like *Blue Skies* (1946) and *Easter Parade* (1948).

Berlin grew up in New York and had his first song published in 1907. He began providing songs for vaudeville and revues and went on to own a theatre, the Music Box, where he appeared in his own revues in 1921 and 1923. Generally writing both lyrics and music, he was instrumental in the development of the popular song, taking it from jazz and ragtime to swing and romantic ballads.

Berlioz, (Louis) Hector (1803–1869) French Romantic composer. He is noted as the founder of modern orchestration. Much of his music was inspired by drama and literature and has a theatrical quality. He wrote symphonic works, such as *Symphonie fantastique* (1830–31) and *Roméo et Juliette* (1839); dramatic cantatas including *La Damnation de Faust* (1846) and *L'Enfance du Christ* (1854); sacred music; and three operas: *Benvenuto Cellini* (1838), *Les Troyens* (1856–58), and *Béatrice et Bénédict* (1862).

Berlioz studied music at the Paris Conservatoire. He won the Prix de Rome in 1830, and spent two years in Italy. In 1833 he married Harriet Smithson, an Irish actress playing Shakespearean parts in Paris, but they separated in 1842. After some years of poverty and public neglect, he went to Germany in 1842, where he conducted his own works. He subsequently visited Russia and England. In 1854 he married Marie Recio, a singer.

Berlioz was born at La Côte-Saint-André, Isère, the son of a doctor who taught him the flute, but wished him to study medicine. As a boy he also learnt the guitar and picked up theoretical knowledge from books. Sent to the Ecole de Médecine in Paris in 1821, he found the studies so distasteful that he decided to give them up for music. His parents made great difficulties, but Jean Lesueur accepted him as a pupil in 1823, when he at once set to work on an opera and an oratorio. The following year he wrote a Mass, which was lost for many years and was given its first modern performance in 1993. He entered the Conservatory in 1826, but failed several times to gain the Prix de Rome, winning it at last with the cantata *La mort de Sardanapale* (1830). In the meantime he had fallen in love with Harriet Smithson and expressed his feelings for her in the *Symphonie fantastique*. On the point of going to Rome, he became engaged to the pianist, Marie Moke, who during his absence married Camille Pleyel.

He wrote much in Rome, notably the overtures *King Lear* and *Rob Roy*, and returned to Paris in 1832, this time meeting Harriet and marrying her in October 1833. To supplement his income he became a music critic, writing witty and brilliant dissections of the idiocies of Parisian musical life. His *Messe des Morts*, commissioned by the French Government in 1836, was performed the following year at a memorial service for soldiers who had fallen in Algeria. In 1838 the violinist Niccolò Paganini sent him 20,000 francs to enable him to devote all his time to composition; the Paganini-inspired *Harold en Italie* had been written in 1834 and was followed by *Roméo et Juliette* and *Benvenuto Cellini*. He separated from Harriet in 1842 and started a liaison with Marie Recio. He travelled much with her during the next few years, and conducted in Germany, Vienna, Prague, Budapest, Russia, and London. His brilliant légende dramatique *La Damnation de Faust* was premiered in 1846 and the massive Te Deum in 1855, but Berlioz continued to suffer throughout his life from lack of public recognition, particularly in his own country. After Harriet's death he married Marie in 1854; meanwhile he had resumed his journalistic work. He composed his masterpiece, the vast opera *Les Troyens*, in the late 1850s. The practicalities of staging such a work in the Paris of his time were forgotten as he entered the world of Virgil's epic poem.

Berlioz completed his last opera, *Béatrice et Bénédict* in 1862, and Marie died the same year; he subsequently abandoned composition. He suffered much ill health during the 1860s and was greatly depressed by the death of his son Louis in 1867. After another visit to Russia he had a bad fall at Nice, where he had gone for his health in 1868, and he grew gradually more infirm.

For many years Berlioz's reputation rested on his *Symphonie fantastique*. It was not until his operas and other large-scale works were widely performed in the 1960s, that his true genius was fully revealed. He wrote seven books, including *Traité de l'instrumentation/Treatise on Orchestration* (1844) and his not always reliable *Mémoires*.

Works include: OPERA *Benvenuto Cellini* (1834–37), *Les Troyens* (two parts) (1856–58), and *Béatrice et Bénédict* (after Shakespeare's *Much Ado about Nothing*) (1860–62).

ORCHESTRAL *Symphonie fantastique* (1830), *Harold en Italie* (with solo viola) (1834), *Roméo et Juliette* (with voices) (1839), and *Symphonie funèbre et triomphale* (for military band, strings, and chorus) (1840), concert overtures *Carnaval Romain* (1844), *Le Corsaire* (1844).

CHORAL AND SONGS Mass (1824), *Messe des morts* (Requiem, 1837), *La Damnation de Faust* (1846), Te Deum (1849), and *L'Enfance du Christ* (1850–54); 6 smaller vocal works with orchestra or piano, including *La mort de Cléopâtre* (1829) and *La mort d'Ophélie* (1847); 28 songs including the cycle *Nuits d'été*.

Bermudo, Juan (c. 1510–c. 1565) Spanish friar and music theorist. He wrote three music treatises, published 1549–55, including the *Declaración* (1555), with the first organ music printed locally.

Bernard de Ventadour (lived late 12th century) Provençal ◊troubadour, probably born at the château of Ventadour. His father is said to have been a soldier and his mother a kitchen maid. He is known to have attended the coronation of Henry II of England and Eleanor of Aquitaine 1154. Some 40 of his poems remain, notable for their freshness and lack of artifice.

Bernardi, Steffano (c. 1585–1636) Italian priest and composer. Chaplain at Verona Cathedral, he studied in Rome later and became maestro di cappella of the church of the Madonna dei Monti. In 1611 he became maestro di cappella at Verona Cathedral, and in 1622 went into the service of the Archduke Karl Josef, Bishop of Breslau, and soon afterwards to Salzburg Cathedral, which he helped to consecrate in 1628. He wrote a Te Deum for 12 choirs (now lost), and many Masses, motets, psalms, madrigals, and instrumental works. His *Salmi concertati* deploy voices in different groups, as in the music of Schütz and Gabrieli.

Berners, Lord (Gerald Hugh Tyrwhitt-Wilson) (1883–1950) English composer, painter, and author. In the diplomatic service at first, he studied music at Dresden and Vienna, and also sought the advice of Stravinsky and Alfredo Casella. His operatic setting of Mérimée's comedy *Le Carrosse du Saint-Sacrement* was produced in Paris in 1924, and the ballet *The Triumph of Neptune* in London in 1926; another, with words by Gertrude Stein, *The Wedding Bouquet*, at Sadlers Wells in 1937 with settings designed by himself. He was famed for such eccentricities as dyeing the pigeons on his lawns different colours to match his moods.

Born at Arley Park, near Bridgnorth, Shropshire, and educated at Eton, he was in the diplomatic service 1909–24. His novels include *The Camel* (1936), *Far from the Madding War* (1941), and *The Romance of a Nose* (1942), and he also published two popular autobiographical works, *First Childhood* (1934) and *A Distant Prospect* (1945).

Works include: the opera *Le Carrosse du Saint-Sacrement*; ballets *The Triumph of Neptune*, *Luna Park* (1930), *The Wedding Bouquet*

(words by Gertrude Stein), *Cupid and Psyche* (1939); three pieces (*Chinoiserie*, *Valse sentimentale*, *Kasatchok*), *Fantaisie espagnole* (1920) and *Fugue* for orchestra (1928); *Variations*, *Adagio and Hornpipe* for string orchestra; *Le Poisson d'or*, *Trois Petites Marches funèbres* and *Fragments psychologiques* for piano; *Valses bourgeoises* for piano duet; songs including three sets in the German, French, and English manners.

Bernstein, Leonard (1918–1990) US composer, conductor, and pianist. He is one of the most energetic and versatile 20th-century US musicians. His works, which established a vogue for realistic, contemporary themes, include symphonies such as *The Age of Anxiety* (1949), ballets such as *Fancy Free* (1944), and scores for musicals, including *Wonderful Town* (1953), *West Side Story* (1957), and *Mass* (1971) in memory of President J F Kennedy.

Born in Lawrence, Massachusetts, he was educated at Harvard University and the Curtis Institute of Music. In 1943 he made his debut as a conductor, beginning a highly successful international career. From 1958 to 1970 he was musical director of the New York Philharmonic. Among his other works are *Jeremiah* (1944), *Facsimile* (1946), *Candide* (1956), and the *Chichester Psalms* (1965).

Bertoni, Ferdinando Giuseppe (1725–1813) Italian composer. A pupil of Martini at Bologna. Organist at St Mark's, Venice, from 1752 and choirmaster at the Conservatorio dei Mendicanti from 1757, he wrote many works for the female musicians there. He produced his first opera at Florence, 1745. In 1776 produced his *Orfeo*, on the libretto by Calzabigi already set by Gluck in 1762; it contains many echoes of Gluck's music. He visited London to produce operas in 1778–80 and 1781–83. In 1785 he succeeded Galuppi as maestro di cappella at St Mark's, Venice.

Works include: the operas *Cajetto* (1746), *Orazio Curiazo*, *Tancredi* (1766), *Orfeo ed Euridice*, *Quinto Fabio* (1778), and over 40 others; oratorios and Latin cantatas; string quartets; keyboard music.

Bertrand, Antoine de (c. 1535–c. 1581) French composer. In some of his settings of Ronsard's 'Amours' he experimented with quarter-tones. Altogether he published three volumes of chansons, and a volume of *Airs spirituels* appeared posthumously in 1582.

Berutti, Arturo (1862–1938) Argentine composer. He studied at the Leipzig Conservatory and in Paris and Milan, settling at Buenos Aires in 1896.

Works include: the operas *Vendetta* (1892), *Evangelina* (1893), *Taras Bulba* (after Gogol) (1895), *Pampa* (1892), *Yupanki, Khrysé, Horrida nox* (1908), and *Los heroes*.

Berwald, Franz Adolf (1796–1868) Swedish violinist and composer. His best-known music is in the four symphonies of the 1840s: the titles *Capricieuse* and *Singulière* suggest their originality. He also wrote operas, a piano concerto, symphonic poems, and some distinguished chamber music. His music is an individual product of the early Romantic period, and shows a fertile and unusual harmonic imagination as well as an original approach to questions of form, though much of it remained unplayed in his lifetime.

He was born in Stockholm, and composed several works before studying in Berlin. He twice visited Vienna, where he had more success at home, and was admired by Liszt and Schumann. His septet of 1828 was influenced by Spohr and Beethoven. Jenny Lind sang in his opera *A Rustic Betrothal in Sweden* (1847). Later stage works were less successful and *The Queen of Golconda* (1864) was not premiered until 1968. He settled at Stockholm in 1849 as director of music at the university and court *kapellmästare*; later he managed a sawmill and glassworks.

Works include: the operas *Leonida* (1829), *The Traitor, Estrella di Soria* (1848, revised 1862), *The Queen of Golconda* (1864, performed 1968); operettas *I Enter a Convent, The Milliner, A Rustic Betrothal in Sweden* (1847); incidental music to plays. Four symphonies, no. 1 *Sérieuse* (1842), no. 2 *Capricieuse* (1842), no. 3 *Singulière* (1845), no. 4 (1845); violin concerto (1820), piano concerto (1855); orchestral works include *Recollections of the Norwegian Alps*; Septet (1828); three string quartets, two piano quintets, and other chamber music; songs.

Besard (Besardus), Jean-Baptiste (c. 1567– after 1617) French lutenist and composer. He first studied law at the University of Dôle, then the lute with Lorenzini in Rome. Later, he lived at Cologne and Augsburg. He published theoretical works and collections of lute music including his own. His *Thesaurus harmonicus* of 1603 contains more than 400 pieces by various composers and includes a manual on lute playing.

Besseler, Heinrich (1900–1969) German musicologist. He studied at Freiburg im Breisgau, Vienna, and Göttingen, where later he became lecturer at the university. He was professor at Jena, 1949, and at Leipzig from 1956. He wrote on medieval and Renaissance music, notably in *Die Musik des Mittelalters und der Renaissance* (1951).

Besuch der Alten Dame, Der/The Visit of the Old Lady opera by Gottfried von Einem (libretto by F Dürrenmatt after his own drama), produced Vienna, Staatsoper, 23 May 1971. Long-jilted lady pays people of her home town for killing her lover.

Betrothal in a Monastery, The/Obruchenie v monastyre opera by Prokofiev (libretto by the composer and M Mendelssohn, after Sheridan's play *The Duenna*); composed 1940–41, first performed Leningrad, Kirov Theatre, 3 November 1946. After initial opposition from their father, Louisa and Ferdinando are allowed to choose their partners in marriage.

Betulia Liberata, La/Betulia Liberated oratorio in two acts by Mozart to a text by Metastasio, based on the story of Judith and Holofernes. The work was commissioned by a Paduan nobleman, Giuseppe Ximenes, Prince of Aragon, and composed 1771 in Italy and Salzburg but not performed in Mozart's lifetime. First British performance London, 6 November 1968, by Opera Viva. Metastasio's text was first set by Reutter (performed Vienna, 8 April 1734). Later settings by Jommelli (Venice, 1734), Holzbauer (Mannheim, 1760), Gassmann (Vienna, 1772), and Schuster (Dresden, 1796).

Bevis of Hampton, or Beves of Hamtoun, Anglo-Norman 13th-century romance. See ◊*Buovo d'Antona* (Traetta).

Bialas, Günter (1907–1995) German composer. He studied in Berlin 1927–33, and taught in Breslau, Weimar, and Munich. His music shows a wide range of influences, including neoclassicism, twelve-tone technique, and medieval polyphony.

Works include: three operas, *Hero und Leander* (1966), *Die Geschichte von Aucassin und Nicolette* (1969), *Der gestiefelte Kater* (1974); viola concerto (1940), violin concerto (1949), cello concerto (1962), *Sinfonia piccola*; sacred and secular choral music; three string quartets (1936, 1949, 1969); *Erwartung*, for organ (1972).

Bianca e Falliero, ossia Il consiglio di tre/ Bianca and Falliero, or The Council of Three opera by Rossini (libretto by F Romani, from Manzoni's tragedy *Il conte di Carmagnola*), produced Milan, La Scala, 26 December 1819. Bianca loves Falliero but is told to marry Capiello. Falliero is accused of treachery by the Council but is absolved in time to marry Bianca.

Bianca e Fernando opera by Bellini (libretto by D Gilardoni), produced Naples, Teatro San Carlo, 30 May 1826. Bellini's first opera heard in public. Fernando rescues father and sister Bianca from ducal usurper, Filippo.

Bianca und Giuseppe, oder Die Franzosen vor Nizza/Bianca and Giuseppe or The French before Nice opera by J F Kittl (libretto by Wagner), produced Prague, 19 February 1848. Wagner had written the libretto for himself in 1836; it is based on a novel by Heinrich König.

Bianchi, Francesco (c. 1752–1810) Italian composer. He was maestro al cembalo at the Comédie Italienne in Paris in 1775, where he worked under Piccinni and produced two operas. In 1778 he went to Florence, and in 1783 was appointed second maestro di cappella at Milan Cathedral. His most successful opera, *La villanella rapita*, was produced the same year in Venice. In 1795 he went to London as composer to the King's Theatre, and three years later to Dublin. He wrote popular opéras-comiques in Paris, 1802–07, but returned to London, where he remained until his death by suicide.

Works include: 60 operas, oratorios, church music, trio sonatas.

Biber, Heinrich Ignaz Franz von (1644–1704) Bohemian composer, virtuoso violinist, and Kapellmeister at the archbishop of Salzburg's court. His brilliant violin technique is best heard in the solo sonatas with continuo of 1681 and the 16 *Mystery* or *Rosary* sonatas of 1676. Spatial effects are created in the *Vesperae* (1693), the *Missa Sancti Henrici* (1701) and Mass in F minor. He also wrote an opera *Chi la dura, la vince* (1687), and the *Nightwatchman Serenade*.

Works include: the opera *Chi la dura, la vince* (1687), church music, several sets of violin sonatas, *Battalia* with violin, *Nightwatchman's Serenade*, partitas for three instruments; vespers for voices, strings, and trombones, and possibly the 53-part *Missa salisburgensis*, performed in Salzburg Cathedral in 1682 and formerly attributed to Benevoli.

Biches, Les/The Hinds ballet in one act with chorus by Poulenc; composed 1923, produced Monte Carlo, 6 January 1924, with choreography by Nijinska. Orchestral Suite in five movements (1939–40).

Billy Budd opera by Britten (libretto by E M Forster and E Crozier, on Herman Melville's story), produced London, Covent Garden, 1 December 1951. Revised 1960 and heard on BBC, 13 November 1960; produced Covent Garden, 9 January 1964. Accused of mutiny, Billy kills master-at-arms Claggart and is hanged by Captain Vere.

Billy the Kid ballet by Copland, produced New York, 24 May 1939.

binary form a composition in symmetrical halves, the first modulating to the ◊dominant key, the second modulating back to the starting ◊tonic key.

Binchois, Gilles de Bins (c. 1400–1460) Franco-Flemish composer. Along with the composers Guillaume Dufay (whom he knew) and John Dunstable, Binchois was a major figure in 15th-century music. He composed 28 Mass-movements, six Magnificats, and around 30 other liturgical works (motets and hymns) in a severely functional style. His most characteristic works, however, are his chansons.

Binchois was probably born in Binche, near Mons, and was organist at the church of Ste Waldetrude, Mons 1419–23. He was chaplain to Philip, Duke of Burgundy, from about 1430 until 1453, when he became provost of Saint-Vincent, Soignies.

He wrote around 55 chansons, mostly in three parts and in the form of *rondeaux* or *ballades*, with texts relating to courtly love. They are written in a more pleasing style than his sacred music; most are symmetrical and are set to graceful melodies for one voice and two instruments; they follow closely the form of the poetic text.

Binet, Jean (1893–1960) Swiss composer. He studied at the Jaques-Dalcroze Institute at Geneva and with Barblan, Templeton Strong, Bloch, and others. Lived in the USA and Brussels for a time. Several of his works were premiered by Ernest Ansermet.

Works include: three psalms for chorus and orchestra, *Cantate de Noël* for chorus and organ; ballets *L'Ile enchantée* and *Le Printemps* (1950); suites on Swiss and English themes and dances for orchestra; concertino for chamber orchestra; string quartet (1927) and other chamber music, songs, part songs.

Bingham, Judith (1952–) English composer. She studied at the Royal Academy of Music, London, and with Hans Keller, and has appeared as a singer with the Taverner Consort and Combattimento.

Works include: *A Divine Image*, for harpsichord (1976); songs for mezzo, baritone, and choruses (*A Hymn before Sunrise in the Vale of Chamonix*, 1982), Mass setting and *A Winter Walk at Noon* (1984); *Chartres* for orchestra

(1987), *The Uttermost* for tenor, chorus, and orchestra (1992).

Binkerd, Gordon (1916–) US composer. After study at the Eastman School and Harvard he was professor at the University of Illinois 1947–71. His music is tonally chromatic and contrapuntal in scope, and includes four symphonies (1955, 1957, 1961, 1963), two string quartets (1956, 1961), string trio (1979), four piano sonatas (1955–83), and choruses.

Birthday Odes works for solo, chorus, and orchestra written by English composers from the Restoration onwards to commemorate royal birthdays. Purcell wrote six for Queen Mary, consort of William III, as follows: 1. *Now does the glorious day appear* (1689), 2. *Arise my Muse* (1690), 3. *Welcome, welcome, glorious morn* (1691), 4. *Love's goddess sure was blind* (1692), 5. *Celebrate this festival* (1693), 6. *Come ye sons of art away* (1694).

Birtwistle, Harrison (1934–) English avant-garde composer. He has specialized in chamber music, for example, his chamber opera *Punch and Judy* (1967) and *Down by the Greenwood Side* (1969). Birtwistle's early music was influenced by US composer Igor Stravinsky and by the medieval and Renaissance masters, and for many years he worked alongside Peter Maxwell ◊Davies.

His operas include *The Mask of Orpheus* (1986) (with electronic music by Barry Anderson (1935–1987)) and *Gawain* (1991), a reworking of the medieval English poem 'Sir Gawain and the Green Knight', described as 'Birtwistle's *Parsifal*'. It was followed by *The Second Mrs Kong*, in which the composer returned to Orphic myth.

He was born at Accrington, and studied with Richard Hall at the Royal Manchester College of Music and later at the Royal Academy of Music, London.

The issue of large-scale form was resolved in his later works by the evolution of a more organic technique, in which the problems of a work find their solution in the musical material itself rather than relying on pre-existent formal models. Orchestral works include *The Triumph of Time* (1972) and *Silbury Air* (1977). His tape composition *Chronometer* 1972 (assisted by Peter Zinovieff (1934–)) is based on clock sounds.

Works include: STAGE *Punch and Judy*, opera in one act (1968), *Monodrama* for soprano, speaker, and instrumental ensemble (1967),

Down by the Greenwood Side, dramatic pastoral (1969), incidental music for National Theatre production of *Hamlet* (1975) and *The Oresteia* (1981), *Frames, Pulses and Interruptions*, ballet (1977), *Bow Down*, music-theatre (1977), *The Mask of Orpheus*, opera (1973–75, 1981–84; produced 1986), *Yan Tan Tethera*, TV opera (1986), *Gawain* (1991), *The Second Mrs Kong* (1994).

ORCHESTRAL *Chorales* (1960–63), *Three Movements with Fanfares* (1964), *Nomos* (1968), *An Imaginary Landscape* (1971), *The Triumph of Time* (1972), *Grimethorpe Aria* for brass band (1973), *Melencolia 1* (1976), *Silbury Air* for small orchestra (1977), *Still Movement* for 13 solo strings (1984), *Earth Dances* (1985), *Endless Parade* for trumpet and strings (1987), *Ritual Fragment* (1990), *Gawain's Journey* (1991), *Antiphonies* for piano and orchestra (1993), *The Cry of Anubis* (1995), *Panic* for saxophone, drums, and orchestra (1995).

VOCAL *Monody for Corpus Christi* for soprano and ensemble (1959), *Narration: a Description of the Passing Year* for chorus (1963), *Entr'actes and Sappho Fragments* for soprano and ensemble (1964), *Carmen paschale* for chorus and organ (1965), *Ring a Dumb Clarion* for soprano, clarinet, and percussion (1965), *Cantata* for soprano and ensemble (1969), *Nenia on the Death of Orpheus* for soprano and ensemble (1970), *The Fields of Sorrow* for two sopranos, chorus, and ensemble (1971–72), *Meridian* for mezzo, chorus, and ensemble (1970–71), *Epilogue: Full Fathom Five* for baritone and ensemble (1972), ... *agm* ..... for 16 solo voices and three instrumental ensembles (1979), *On the Sheer Threshold of the Night* for four solo voices and 12-part chorus (1980), *Songs by Myself* for soprano and ensemble (1984), *Words Overheard* for soprano, flute, oboe, and strings (1985), *Four Songs of Autumn* for soprano and string quartet (1987); *An die Musik* (1988), *White and Light* (1989), and *Four Poems by Jaan Kaplinski* (1991), all for soprano and ensemble.

INSTRUMENTAL *Refrains and Choruses* for wind quintet (1957), *The World is Discovered* for chamber ensemble (1960), *Tragoedia* for ensemble (1965), *Verses for Ensembles* (1969), *Ut heremita solus*, arrangement of Okeghem (1969), *Hoquetus David*, arrangement of Machaut (1969), *Medusa* for ensemble (1970, revised 1980), *Chronometer* for eight-track tape (1971), *Chorales from a Toyshop* (1967–74), *Carmen Arcadiae Mechanicae Perpetuum* for ensemble (1977), *For O for O, the Hobby Horse is Forgot* for six percussion (1976), clarinet quintet (1980), *Pulse sampler* for oboe and claves (1981), *Duets for Storab* for two flutes

(1983), *Secret Theatre* for string quartet and ensemble (1984), string quartet (1993).

Bishop, Henry (Rowley) (1786–1855) English conductor and composer. He produced *Angelina* (composed with Francesco Lanza, 1783–1862) at Margate in 1804 and the ballet *Tamerlan et Bajazet* at the King's Theatre in London, in 1806. From that time on he brought out one or more stage pieces almost each year until 1840.

Born in London, he studied under Francesco Bianchi. In 1813 he was one of the founders of the Philharmonic Society and became one of its conductors. He was appointed professor of music at Oxford in 1848. He was married twice; both his wives were singers: Sarah Lyon in 1809 and Anna Riviere in 1831.

Works include: over 100 pieces for the stage, including *The Corsair, The Circassian Bride* (1809), *Guy Mannering* (after Scott) (1816), *The Burgomaster of Saardam, The Heart of Midlothian* (after Scott) (1819), *Montrose* (after Scott), *The Law of Java, Maid Marian, Clari, Cortez, Faustus* (1825), *Aladdin, The Fortunate Isles* (1840); incidental music for three tragedies, for adaptations of Scott, Byron, and Shakespeare; oratorio *The Fallen Angel*; cantata *The Seventh Day*; three volumes of national melodies with words by Moore and other collections of arrangements.

bisser French verb from *bis*, 'twice', 'to encore'.

bitonality a combination of two parts in different keys, as in Stravinsky's *Duo Concertante* (1931–32) for violin and piano. Music of more than two simultaneous keys is called ◊polytonality.

Bizet, Georges (Alexandre César Léopold) (1838–1875) French composer of operas. Among his works are *Les Pêcheurs de perles/ The Pearl Fishers* (1863) and *La Jolie Fille de Perth/The Fair Maid of Perth* (1866). He also wrote the concert overture *Patrie* and inci-

dental music to Alphonse Daudet's play *L'Arlésienne* (1872), which has remained a standard work in the form of two suites for orchestra. His operatic masterpiece *Carmen* was produced a few months before his death in 1875. His Symphony in C, written when he was 17, is now frequently performed.

Bizet was born near Paris. His father, a teacher of singing, gave him his first instruction in music and at the age of nine, being exceptionally gifted, he was admitted to the Paris Conservatory, studying piano under Marmontel, organ under François Benoist (1794–1878), and composition under Pierre Joseph Guillaume Zimmermann (1785–1853). In 1853, when Zimmermann died, he became a pupil of his future father-in-law, Jacques Halévy, having already taken a first prize for piano. His Symphony in C of 1855 is the least known of his earlier works, and one of the finest pieces written by an adolescent; the score, however, was not performed until 1935. In 1857 he won the Prix de Rome, but before he went to Rome he had already gained a prize in a competition for an operetta, *Le Docteur Miracle* (1857), sponsored by Offenbach. He tied with Charles Lecocq, whose setting was produced alternately with his own at the Théâtre des Bouffes-Parisiens.

He wrote several works in Rome and on his return to Paris in 1860 he set out to capture the operatic stage; but although the Opéra-Comique accepted his one-act opera, *La Guzla de l'Emir*, he withdrew it, destroying it later. The Théâtre Lyrique produced his next work, *Les Pêcheurs de perles*, in 1863; *Ivan le Terrible*, written in 1865, said to have been burnt by him, was recovered in 1944 and performed at Mühringen Castle, Württemberg, Germany. In 1869 the conductor Jules Pasdeloup gave him his first chance to appear with an orchestral work, *Souvenirs de Rome*, which he later entitled *Roma*. In the same year Bizet married Geneviève Halévy.

F major and F sharp minor appear simultaneously in Ravel's bitonal passage from L'Enfant et les sortilèges.

In 1872 he was commissioned to write incidental music for Daudet's play, *L'Arlésienne*, produced at the Vaudeville in October. In 1874 Pasdeloup produced his overture *Patrie* (unconnected with Sardou's play), but Bizet had set to work before that on *Carmen*, which was premiered at the Opéra-Comique, with spoken dialogue, in March 1875. At first it scandalized audiences by its realism, and did not achieve its great popularity until after Bizet's death. It received 37 performances; but Bizet died after about 30 performances, before the work had won through prejudice to a decided success.

Bizet is clearly influenced by Gounod but far transcends his model. In a sense, his reputation has become hostage to his best-loved work; the passion and melody of *Carmen* should not obscure the same qualities to be found in the Symphony in C, *Les Pêcheurs de perles*, and even *La Jolie Fille de Perth*.

Works include: OPERA five, including *Les Pêcheurs de perles* (1863), *La Jolie Fille de Perth* (after Scott, 1866), and *Carmen* (after Mérimee, 1874); incidental music to Daudet's *L'Arlésienne* (1872).

ORCHESTRAL works include symphony in C major (1855, first performed under Weingartner, 1935), suite *Roma* (1868), *Petite Suite* (*Jeux d'enfants*).

OTHER numerous songs and piano pieces.

Blacher, Boris (1903–1975) German avant-garde composer. After studying in Berlin, he began his career under great difficulties during the Nazi regime, but later became successful as a composer, developing a system of variable metres following arithmetical progressions, upon which many of his works are based. In 1953 he became director of the Berlin Hochschule für Musik.

Works include: the operas *Fürstin Tarakanova* (1940), *Preussisches Märchen* (1949), *Abstrakte Oper no. 1* (1953), *200,000 Taler* (1969), *Das Geheimnis* (1975), chamber operas *Romeo und Julia* (1943, after Shakespeare) *Die Flut* (1946), *Die Nachtschwalbe* (1948); several ballets including *Harlekinade* (1939), *Lysistrate* (1950), *Hamlet* (1949), *Der Mohr von Venedig* (1955); scenic oratorio *Der Grossinquisitor* (after Dostoevsky 1947). Symphony, symphonic poem *Hamlet* (after Shakespeare), variations on theme by Paganini and other orchestral works; two piano concertos, viola concerto; five string quartets (1930–67) and other chamber music, piano music, songs.

'Black Key' Study Chopin's piano Study in G♭ major, op. 10 no. 5, written c. 1831–32 and published in 1833. It is so called because the right hand plays only on the black keys throughout.

Black Knight, The cantata for chorus and orchestra by Elgar, op. 25, a setting of Longfellow's translation of Uhland's ballad *Der schwarze Ritter*, first performed Worcester Festival, 1893.

bladder pipe musical instrument, an early ◊bagpipe with an animal's bladder used for the bag.

B-la-F Quartet a string quartet on the name of Belaiev by Rimsky-Korsakov, Liadov, Borodin, and Glazunov, performed on M P Belaiev's 50th birthday, 22 February 1886. It is constructed on the notes B♭, A, F.

Blaise le savetier/Blaise the Cobbler opera by Philidor (libretto by J M Sedaine, after La Fontaine), produced Paris, Opéra-Comique, 9 March 1759.

Blake, David (Leonard) (1936–) English composer. He studied at Cambridge, and with Hanns Eisler in Berlin; taught at York University from 1964. He uses serial technique, and is influenced by the music of the Far East.

Works include: the operas *Toussaint L'Ouverture* (1974–76, revised 1982) and *The Plumber's Gift* (1985–88); chamber symphony (1966), two violin concertos (1976 and 1983); three choruses to poems by Frost (1964), *Lumina*, cantata for soprano, baritone, chorus, and orchestra, to text by Pound (1969), *From the Mattress Grave*, 12 Heine poems for soprano and 11 instruments (1978); three string quartets (1962, 1973, 1982), Nonet for wind (1971), Capriccio, for wind, strings, and piano (1980); *The Spear* for mezzo, speaker, and ensemble (1982), *Rise, Dove* for baritone and orchestra (1982), *Scherzi ed Intermezzi* for orchestra (1984), *Seasonal Variants* for seven players (1985), *Pastoral Paraphrase* for baritone and orchestra (1986), cello concerto (1989–93).

Blake, William (1757–1827) English poet and artist. His works and thought inspired, among others, ◊Bolcom (*Songs of Innocence and Experience*), ◊Britten (*Songs and Proverbs*), ◊Connolly (*The Marriage of Heaven and Hell*), A ◊Goehr (*Five poems and an Epigram*), Job (Vaughan Williams), ◊Parry (*Jerusalem*), and ◊Tippett (*Song of Liberty*).

Blamont, François Colin de (1690–1760) French composer. He was a pupil of his father, who was in the royal band, and later of Michel-Richard Lalande. He became in 1719 superintendent of the royal music and, after

Lalande's death in 1726, master of the chamber music.

Works include: the stage pieces (mostly ballets and ballet-operas) *Les Festes grecques et romaines* (1723), *Le Retour des dieux sur la terre* (for the marriage of Louis XV, 1725), *Le Caprice d'Erato* (1730), *Endymion* (1731), *Les Caractères de l'Amour*, *Les Amours du printemps*, *Jupiter vainqueur des Titans* (1745), *Les Festes de Thétis* (1750); cantata *Circé* and three books of *Cantates françaises* for solo voice; motets with orchestral accompaniment.

Blaník (Smetana). See ◊*Má Vlast*.

Blas de Castro, Juan (c. 1560–1631) Spanish composer. In the 1590s he was private musician to the Duke of Alba at Salamanca and in 1605 musician and usher to Philip III. Lope de Vega and Tirso de Molina mentioned him in their works. Only 20 songs for three and four voices survive.

Blech (German 'brass') abbreviation often used in scores for *Blechinstrumente*.

Blessed Damozel, The (Debussy). See ◊*Damoiselle élue*.

Blind Man's Buff masque by Peter Maxwell Davies for high voice, mezzo, mime, and stage band (text by Davies from Büchner's *Leonce und Lena*, et al), first performed London, 29 May 1972, conductor P Boulez.

blind octaves a trick of piano writing: figures in octaves rapidly alternating between the two hands where the thumbs trace a continuous melodic line while the outer notes fly off at broken intervals.

Bliss, Arthur Edward Drummond (1891–1975) English composer and conductor. He became Master of the Queen's Musick in 1953. Among his works are *A Colour Symphony* (1922); music for the ballets *Checkmate* (1937), *Miracle in the Gorbals* (1944), and *Adam Zero* (1946); an opera *The Olympians* (1949); and dramatic film music, including *Things to Come* (1935). He conducted the first performance of US composer Igor Stravinsky's *Ragtime* for 11 instruments in 1918.

Bliss was educated at Rugby and Pembroke College, Cambridge, where he studied music under Charles Wood. He entered the Royal College of Music in London in 1913, studying with Stanford, Vaughan Williams, and Holst, but joined the army in 1914, serving until 1918. He was appointed professor of composition at the Royal College of Music in 1921, but took wholly to composing the next year, never holding any official post until he was appointed music director of the BBC in 1941, an appointment he resigned to Hely-Hutchinson in 1945. Early experiments with unusual musical media, as in a Concerto for tenor, piano, strings, and percussion and *Rout* for soprano and chamber orchestra to a text constructed of nonsense syllables, gained him a reputation as an *enfant terrible*. His early music was miniaturist in scope but he later embraced larger forms. With some success, Bliss sought to evoke comparisons with Elgar in his *Colour Symphony*, *Introduction and Allegro*, and violin concerto. He published his memoirs, *As I Remember*, in 1970.

Works include: DRAMATIC operas *The Olympians* (libretto by J B Priestley) (1949) and *Tobias and the Angel* (C Hassall) (1960); ballets *Checkmate*, *Miracle in the Gorbals*, and *Adam Zero*; incidental music for Shakespeare's *Tempest*; film music for *Things to Come* (H G Wells), *Conquest of the Air*, *Caesar and Cleopatra* (G B Shaw).

ORCHESTRAL *A Colour Symphony* (1922), *Introduction and Allegro* (1926), *Hymn to Apollo*, *Meditations on a Theme by John Blow* (1955); concertos for piano and two pianos; march *Phoenix* for the liberation of France; *Music for Strings*.

VOCAL *Morning Heroes* for orator, chorus, and orchestra (1930), *Pastoral* for mezzo, chorus, flute, strings, and drums, cantata *Mary of Magdala* for contralto, bass, chorus, and orchestra (1929), *Serenade* for baritone and orchestra (1929), concerto for piano, tenor, and chamber orchestra, *Rout* for voice and chamber orchestra, *Madam Noy* for voice and six instruments; several song cycles with various instruments or piano, including *Five American Songs* (Edna St Vincent Millay).

CHAMBER *Conversations* for flute, oboe, violin, viola, and cello; two string quartets (1941, 1950), oboe quintet, clarinet quintet; sonatas for violin and piano, and viola and piano.

Blitzstein, Marc (1905–1964) US composer. Born in Philadelphia, he was a child prodigy as a pianist at the age of six. He served with the US Army 8th Air Force 1942–45, for which he wrote *The Airborne* (1946), a choral symphony. His first great success was the opera *The Cradle Will Rock*, produced in New York in 1937 with piano accompaniment directed by Orson Welles, after a full performance was banned by the authorities. He was a political radical and was killed after an argument with American sailors.

Blitzstein appeared as solo pianist at the age of 15, and later studied composition with Scalero in New York, Nadia Boulanger in Paris, and Schoenberg in Vienna. He also studied piano with Siloti in the USA.

Works include: the operas *Triple Sec* (1929), *Parabola and Circula* (1929), *The Harpies, The Cradle Will Rock* (1937); ballet *Cain*; incidental music for Shakespeare's *Julius Caesar*; film music for *Surf and Seaweed, The Spanish Earth, No for an Answer* (1941), *Chesapeake Bay Retriever*; choral opera *The Condemned*; radio song-play *I've got the Tune*, Children's Cantata; *The Airborne* for orchestra, chorus, and narrator (1946); *Romantic Piece, Jigsaw* ballet suite, and variations for orchestra; piano concerto (1931), string quartet and serenade for string quartet; piano sonata and *Percussion Music* for piano (1929).

Bloch, Ernest (1880–1959) Swiss-born US composer. His music is highly coloured in its orchestration and rhythms, often drawing on elements of Jewish folk music. Among his works are the lyrical drama *Macbeth* (1910), *Schelomo* for cello and orchestra 1916, five string quartets, and *Suite Hébraïque* for viola and orchestra 1953. He often used themes based on Jewish liturgical music and folk song.

Born in Geneva, Switzerland, he was a pupil of Jaques-Dalcroze at first, then of Ysaÿe and Rasse at the Brussels Conservatory, and later at the Hoch Conservatory at Frankfurt, where Iwan Knorr was his composition master. His last teacher was Thuille at Munich, and he then went to live in Paris, where he began the opera *Macbeth* on a French libretto by Edmond Fleg. It was produced in Paris in 1910, but he had in the meantime returned to Switzerland to conduct subscription concerts at Lausanne and Neuchâtel. He was professor of music aesthetics at the Geneva Conservatory 1911–15. In 1916 he went to the USA and settled in New York as professor at the David Mannes School of Music. A second opera, *Jézabel*, begun there in 1918, was unfinished.

From 1920 to 1925 Bloch was founder-director of the Cleveland Institute of Music, and in 1925 he was appointed head of the San Francisco Conservatory. In 1930 he retired to Switzerland to live quietly in remote places. Some interest was shown in his work in England and a good deal in Italy, where his *Sacred Service* was produced at Turin and *Macbeth* was revived in an Italian translation at Naples 1938. But the anti-Semitic movement encouraged by the Fascists put an end to this appreciation. As a US citizen he could no longer remain absent from the USA without losing his adopted nationality, and he returned there to live in retirement at the end of 1938.

Works include: the opera *Macbeth* (1904–09), *Sacred Service* (*Avodath Hakodesh*) for baritone solo, chorus, and orchestra; violin concerto (1938); *Schelomo* for cello and orchestra (1916), *Concerto grosso* for piano and strings, *Voice in the Wilderness* for cello and orchestra (1926); two violin and piano sonatas, viola and piano suite, piano quintet, *Baal Shem* three pieces for violin and piano; *From Jewish Life* (three pieces) and *Méditation hébraïque* for cello and piano.

Blockflöte (German 'block flute') alternative name for the Ɵrecorder, a musical instrument of the fipple flute family.

block harmony a term used for a type of harmonic accompaniment, in which all the notes except the melody move together simultaneously in 'block' chords, without being made to depart from one another by means of figuration or counterpoint.

Blockx, Jan (1851–1912) Belgian composer. Most of his operas and all his cantatas for solo voices, chorus, and orchestra are set to Flemish words.

He learned music as a choirboy and went to the Antwerp School of Music, later to the Leipzig Conservatory. In 1886 he became professor and in 1901 director of the Antwerp Conservatory, succeeding Benoit, whom he followed as a Flemish music nationalist.

Works include: the operas *Jets vergeten* (1877), *Maître Martin* (1892), *Herbergprinses* (1896), *Thyl Uilenspiegel* (1900), *De Bruid der Zee, De Kapel* (1903), *Baldie*; ballet *Milenka* (1887); cantatas *Op den Stroom, Een Droom van 't Paradijs, Vredeszang, Klokke Roeland, De Scheldezang*; overture *Rubens*; Romance for violin and orchestra.

Blomdahl, Karl-Birger (1916–1968) Swedish composer. He wrote ballets and symphonies in Expressionist style. His opera *Aniara* (1957–59) incorporates electronic music and is set in a spaceship fleeing Earth after nuclear war.

Blomdahl studied at Stockholm under various teachers, including Hilding Rosenberg and Mogens Wöldike. In 1960 he was appointed professor at the Stockholm Conservatory.

Works include: the opera *Aniara* (a spaceship drama) (1957–59); incidental music; three symphonies (1943, 1947, 1950), symphonic dances, concert overture, *Concerto grosso* for orchestra; violin concerto (1946), viola concerto, chamber concerto for piano, wind, and percussion; two string quartets, string trio, woodwind trio, suites for cello and piano, and bassoon and piano; piano pieces; trios for women's voices.

Blow, John (1648–1708) English composer. He taught English composer Henry Purcell and wrote church music, for example the anthem 'I Was Glad When They Said Unto Me' (1697). His masque *Venus and Adonis* (1685) is sometimes called the first English opera.

He became one of the children in the Chapel Royal in London as soon as it was re-established after the Restoration in 1660, and was taught by Henry Cooke. He wrote three anthems in 1663 and took a share with Pelham Humfrey and William Turner in the 'Club Anthem' about 1664. About the same time, at Charles II's request, he set Robert Herrick's 'Go, perjur'd man' in the style of Giacomo Carissimi. John Hingston and Christopher Gibbons also had a share in Blow's musical education. In 1668 he succeeded Albert Bryne as organist at Westminster Abbey; in March 1674 he was sworn a Gentleman of the Chapel Royal, and the following July he succeeded Humfrey as Master of the Children. In November he married Elizabeth Braddock. In 1679 he was followed in the Westminster organist's post by Purcell, but returned as organist after Purcell's death in 1695. In 1687 he succeeded Michael Wise as almoner and choirmaster at St Paul's Cathedral (at that time unfinished). James II appointed him a member of the royal band and confirmed a previous appointment as Composer in Ordinary. Towards the end of the century he bought a property at Hampton, but still retained a house at Westminster, where he died.

Works include: about 12 services; over 100 English anthems, nine Latin anthems; masque *Venus and Adonis* (about 1685); Act Songs for Oxford University; at least 16 Welcome Songs, five for St Cecilia's Day, odes on the death of Queen Mary (1695) and of Purcell (1696); three coronation anthems for James II, one for William and Mary; anthem for the opening service at St Paul's Cathedral (1697); sonata for two violins and bass; harpsichord lessons, suites, and pieces; some organ pieces; song collection *Amphion Anglicus*, songs and catches, and other pieces.

Bluebeard see ◊*Ariane et Barbe-bleue*; ◊*Barbe-bleue*.

Bluebeard's Castle (Bartók). See ◊*Duke Bluebeard's Castle*.

blue notes a device in blues, the playing of certain notes, especially the third and seventh of the scale, deliberately out of tune, between major and minor.

blues African-American music that originated in the work songs and Negro spirituals of the rural American South in the late 19th century. It is characterized by a 12-bar, or occasionally 16-bar, construction and melancholy lyrics which relate tales of woe or unhappy love. The guitar has been the dominant instrument; harmonica and piano are also common. Blues guitar and vocal styles have played a vital part in the development of jazz, rock, and pop music in general.

1920s–1930s The **rural** or **delta blues** was usually performed solo with guitar or harmonica, by such artists as Robert Johnson and Bukka White (1906–77), but the earliest recorded style, **classic blues**, by such musicians as W C Handy (1873–1958) and Bessie Smith, was sung with a small band.

1940s–1950s The **urban blues**, using electric amplification, emerged in the northern cities, chiefly Chicago. As exemplified by Howlin' Wolf, Muddy Waters, and John Lee Hooker, urban blues became **rhythm and blues**.

1960s The jazz-influenced guitar style of B B King inspired many musicians of the **British blues boom**, including Eric Clapton.

1980s The 'blues *noir*' of Robert Cray (1953–) contrasted with the rock-driven blues playing of Stevie Ray Vaughan (1955–90).

In **classical music**, composers such as Ravel, Copland, and Michael Tippett have used the term loosely to refer to mood rather than a strict musical form.

Blume, Friedrich (1893–1975) German musicologist. He studied at Munich, Leipzig, and Berlin. He was a prisoner in England for three years during World War I. After teaching in Berlin from 1921 he became professor at Kiel University from 1934 to 1958. He was editor-in-chief of the complete works of Michael Praetorius and the series *Das Chorwerk*, and was editor of the encyclopedia *Die Musik in Geschichte und Gegenwart* (known as *MGG*). His books include a history of Protestant church music.

Blumenfeld, Harold (1923–) US composer. He studied composition at Harvard and with Hindemith at Yale; conducting with Bernstein. He directed the Opera Theater of St Louis 1962–66 and the Washington University Opera Studio 1960–71, presenting works outside the standard repertory.

Works include: the operas *Amphitryon* (1962), *Fritzi* (1979), *4-Score: An Opera of Opposites* (1985) and *Season in Hell: A Life of*

Rimbaud (1991–   ); *Eroscapes* for soprano and ensemble (1971); *Song of Innocence* for soloists, chorus, and orchestra (1973); *Voyages*, cantata after Hart Crane (1977); *La Face cendrée*, cantata after Rimbaud (1981); *Orchestral Evocations of Rimbaud* (1988).

Blumine original second movement of Mahler's first symphony, in D, and heard in the work's first performance, Budapest, 20 November 1889. The movement was discarded in 1894 and not performed again until 18 June 1976 at Aldeburgh, conductor Britten.

Blüthner, Julius Ferdinand (1824–1910) German piano manufacturer. He founded his firm at Leipzig in 1853.

Bluthochzeit opera by Fortner (libretto by E Beck after Lorca's *Bodas de Sangre*), composed for the opening of the new opera house, Cologne, and performed there 8 June 1957. Bride runs away with former fiancé on wedding day; bridegroom follows and both men are killed in the ensuing fight.
Opera by Szokolay (*Vérnász*, same source), produced Budapest, 30 October 1964.

B Minor Mass Bach's great setting of the Latin text begins in B minor, but as a whole centres on D major. The work was not composed in one piece, however, but in four sections, some of them intended for separate performance. The *Kyrie* and *Gloria* (constituting in themselves a complete Lutheran short Mass) were written in 1733, and used to support Bach's application for the title of Court Composer to the Elector of Saxony; the *Symbolum Nicenum* (Creed) c. 1748; *Sanctus* 1724; finally, the movements from *Osanna* to *Dona nobis pacem* c. 1748. Several of the movements were adapted from earlier works, such as church cantatas nos. 11, 12, 29, 46, 120, and 171 and the secular cantata *Preise dein Glücke*.

Boccherini, (Ridolfo) Luigi (1743–1805) Italian composer and cellist. He was a master of chamber music for string instruments, and was the most important Italian representative of the Viennese Classical style, writing in his own distinctive manner. He studied in Rome, made his mark in Paris in 1768, and was court composer in Prussia and Spain. He composed some 350 instrumental works, an opera, and oratorios.

Boccherini was born at Lucca. His father was a double-bass player, who began teaching his son himself, then sent him to Rome for further study in 1757. On his return to Lucca in 1761 he played cello in the theatre orchestra. With the violinist Manfredi he

travelled widely on concert tours in Austria and France. He was particularly successful in Paris 1767–68, where he published his first chamber music. In 1769 he went to Madrid and settled there, being first in the service of the king's brother, the Infante Don Luis, until 1785, when the latter died. In 1787 Boccherini was appointed court composer to Frederick William II of Prussia, who had the exclusive right to his works, but he seems to have maintained his residence in Madrid. After the king's death in 1797 he was apparently without a permanent post, for he spent his last years in increasing poverty, largely owing to inconsiderate treatment by his publishers. He died in Madrid.

Works include: the oratorios *Giuseppe riconosciuto* and *Gioas, rè di Giuda* (about 1765); *Stabat Mater* (1781), Mass (1800), cantatas, motets, and other pieces; zarzuela *La Clementina* (1780); concert arias; 26 symphonies; 11 cello concertos (including a pastiche by Grützmacher) and one each for flute, violin, and harpsichord; 91 string quartets, 48 string trios, 125 string quintets, 12 piano quintets, 18 quintets for wind and strings, 16 sextets, two octets; 27 violin sonatas, six cello sonatas.

Bockstriller (German 'goat's trill') a kind of vocal shake considered of no artistic value, produced by a rapid, bleating repetition of a single note. Wagner asks for this kind of shake from the tailors' chorus in the third act of *Die Meistersinger*.

Boehm, Theobald (1794–1881) German flautist and composer. He invented the **Boehm system** of improvements to the flute in 1832. Using metalworking skills, he applied a series of levers and keypads to the instrument which improved performance and enabled the pitch holes to be drilled at optimum acoustical positions instead of, as formerly, to suit the player's fingers. His system was later applied to other woodwind instruments.

Boëllmann, Léon (1862–1897) French organist and composer. His *Gothic Suite* is well known.

He was born in Alsace and trained as an organist under Eugène Gigout, a teacher of church music in Paris. He was appointed organist of the church of St Vincent de Paul.

Works include: symphony in F major; *Fantasie dialoguée* for organ and orchestra, *Variations symphoniques* for cello and orchestra (1893); piano quartet, piano trio; cello and piano sonata; church music, organ works include two suites (first *Gothique*, 1895).

Boesmans, Philippe (1936–) Belgian composer. He studied with Henri Pousseur at Liège and worked with him at the electronic music studios there from 1971. His music has also been influenced by the French and Italian avant garde.

Works include: the operas *La Passion de Gilles* (1983) and *Reigen*, after Schnitzler's play (1993); *Impromptu* for 23 instruments (1965); symphony for piano (1966); *Verticales* for orchestra (1969); *Intervalles* for orchestra (1973); *Multiples* for two pianos and orchestra (1974); *Attitudes* for soprano and ensemble (1977); piano and violin concertos (1978, 1979); *Conversions* for orchestra (1980); *Ricercar* for organ (1983); realization of Monteverdi's *Poppea* with an array of modern instruments (1989).

Boethius, Anicius Manlius Severinus (c. 480–524) Roman consul, senator, and philosopher. His most important work is the *De consolatione philosophiae* (some verses from which were set to music in Carolingian times), but he is also, in his *De institutione musica*, the interpreter of ancient musical theory to the Western world. In spite of some misconceptions, his work remained the fundamental basis of almost all medieval and Renaissance musical theory.

Boettcher, Wilfried (1929–1994) German conductor and cellist. He was conductor of the Hamburg Symphony Orchestra 1967–71 and guest conductor with other leading orchestras in Europe and the USA.

After studying in Hamburg and with Pierre Fournier in Paris, he founded the Vienna Soloists in 1959. He was principal guest conductor of the Northern Sinfonia, Newcastle, from 1986. He had opera engagements in Berlin, Vienna (State Opera), and Italy.

Bogatirev, Anatoly Vassilevich (1913–) Russian composer. He studied at the Minsk Conservatory under Zolotarev. Later he studied folksong and became deputy director of the Conservatory at Minsk.

Works include: the operas *The Two Foscari* (after Byron) and *In the Thick Woods of Polesye* (1939); incidental music for Romashev's *Stars Cannot be Dimmed*; *The Tale of a Bear* for solo voices, chorus, and orchestra; cantata *To the People of Leningrad*; string quartet, piano trio; *Manfred* suite (after Byron) and variations for piano; choruses, songs, folksong arrangements. In 1957 he made a performing version from the sketches of Tchaikovsky's seventh symphony.

Bohème, La/Bohemian Life opera by Leoncavallo (libretto by composer, based on Murger's novel *Scènes de la vie de Bohème*), produced Venice, Teatro La Fenice, 6 May 1897. Composed at the same time as Puccini's work.

Opera by Puccini (libretto by G Giacosa and L Illica, based on Murger), produced Turin, Teatro Regio, 1 February 1896. Rodolfo and Mimi face love and death in Paris.

Bohemian Girl, The opera by Balfe (libretto by A Bunn, based on a ballet-pantomime, *La Gypsy*, by J H V de Saint-Georges), produced London, Drury Lane Theatre, 27 November 1843.

Böhm, Georg (1661–1733) German composer. As a composer and organist he was an important forerunner of Bach. Before 1698 he was organist at Hamburg, then at St John's Church, Lüneburg. His works include a Passion, songs, and organ and harpsichord music.

Böhm, Karl (1894–1981) Austrian conductor. He is known for his stately interpretations of Beethoven, and of Mozart and Strauss operas.

Boieldieu, François Adrien (1775–1834) French composer. At 18 he composed his first opera, *La Fille coupable* (1793), which was produced at Rouen. In 1803 he occupied the post of maître de chapelle to Emperor Alexander at St Petersburg, but in 1811 returned to Paris to produce more operas, including the two most successful, *Jean de Paris* (1812), and *La Dame blanche* (1825).

Boieldieu was born at Rouen and studied under Broche, the organist of Rouen Cathedral. His first opera, *La Fille coupable*, was written to a libretto by his father, who was secretary to the archbishop. He also wrote many songs at that time, some of which were published in Paris. Having failed to establish a school of music at Rouen on the model of the Paris Conservatory, he left for the capital, where in 1797 he produced his first opera away from home, *La Famille Suisse*, which was so successful that he brought out four more within two years. He also became piano professor at the Conservatory in 1798. Being reproached by the composer Luigi Cherubini for having attained too easy a success on very slender gifts, he placed himself under that master for a course in counterpoint. In 1802 he married the dancer Clotilde Mafleuray, with disastrous results, and in 1803 he left for St Petersburg as conductor of the Imperial Opera. There he wrote nine operas 1804–10. In 1811 he returned to Paris, where he had greater success than previously; probably due to there being less competition and an improvement in his work.

He collaborated by turns with Cherubini, Charles Catel, Nicolò Isouard, Rodolphe Kreutzer, Ferdinand Hérold, Henri-Montan Berton, Ferdinando Paer, and Daniel Auber, also with some of these and Désiré Batton, Felice Blangini, and Michele Carafa in *La Marquise de Brinvilliers* of 1831; but his best works were composed alone. In *La Dame blanche*, to match the libretto from Scott, he used some Scottish folk songs. His last years were troubled by illness and poverty: he began to suffer from tuberculosis contracted in Russia, and his fortune declined until he was granted a state pension. In 1827 he was married for the second time, to the singer Jenny Philis-Bertin, with whom he had long been living and by whom in 1815 he had a son, Adrien Louis Victor, who also became a composer. Boieldieu lived at Geneva for a time not long before his death.

Works include: the operas *Le Calife de Bagdad* (1800), *Ma Tante Aurore* (1803), *Aline, Reine de Golconde* (1804), *La Jeune Femme colère, Télémaque* (1807), *Rien de trop, Jean de Paris* (1812), *La Fête du village voisin, Le Petit Chaperon rouge, La Dame blanche* (1825), *Les Deux Nuits*, and others; incidental music for Racine's *Athalie*; piano concerto (1792), harp concerto (1801), piano trio and other chamber music; duets for violin and piano, and harp and piano, six piano sonatas.

Boismortier, Joseph Bodin de (1689–1755) French composer. He is reputed to have written the first French concerto in 1729. He wrote three opera-ballets, *Les voyages de L'Amour* (1736), *Don Quichote* (1743), and *Daphnis et Chloé* (1747); eight cantatas, in two books (1724 and 1737), over 50 instrumental works including many for musette and vielle.

Boito, Arrigo (1842–1918) Italian poet and composer. He wrote libretti for several composers as well as for himself, including those of Verdi's *Otello* (1887) and *Falstaff* (1893). Boito is most often heard today as Verdi's late librettist, although his own opera *Mefistofele* (1868) is one of the finest musical settings of the Faust legend.

Boito was born at Padua and studied at the Milan Conservatory. At first he worked as a journalist in Milan and Paris, and served under Garibaldi in Austria. He travelled much in France, Germany, and Poland, and produced his Faust opera, *Mefistofele*, at La Scala, Milan. It proved a failure but was more successful when played in shorter form in 1875. His only other opera, *Nerone*, was not produced until 1924, six years after his death.

He also wrote the opera *Ero e Leandro*, but destroyed the music (the libretto was set by Bottesini and later by Mancinelli) and he wrote a libretto on *Hamlet* for Faccio. Boito published songs, novels, critiques, and dramas; of his verse the longest piece is *Re Orso*, a narrative poem describing the atrocities of the Minotaur.

Bolcom, William Elden (1938–) US composer and pianist. His works have been influenced by techniques of collage and microtonal electronics. As a pianist he has been heard in popular early American music, often with his wife, the mezzo Joan Morris.

Bolcom studied at Stanford University and the Paris Conservatory, and taught at the University of Michigan from 1973.

Works include: theatre pieces *Dynamite Tonite* (1963), *Greatshot* (1969), *Theatre of the Absurd* (1970), *The Beggar's Opera* (adaptation of Gay, 1978), and *McTeague* (1992); *Oracles*, symphony (1964), piano concerto (1976), symphony for chamber orchestra (1979), violin concerto (1983); octet for wind, strings, and piano (1962), *Session*, works for various instrumental groups, with drum play (1965–67), 14 piano rags (1967–70), piano quartet (1976), brass quintet (1980); *Songs of Innocence and Experience*, 48 Blake settings for solo voices and choruses (1958–81; version with orchestra performed Stuttgart 1984); Concertante for viola, cello, and orchestra (1985), clarinet concerto (1989), *Spring Concerto* for oboe and chamber orchestra (1989), *Fantasy Suite* for piano (1989).

bolero Spanish dance in moderate triple time (3/4), invented in the late 18th century. It is performed by a solo dancer or a couple, usually with castanet accompaniment, and is still a contemporary form of dance in Caribbean countries. In music, Ravel's one-act ballet score *Boléro* (1928) is the most famous example, consisting of a theme which is constantly repeated and varied instrumentally, building to a powerful climax. The ballet was choreographed by Nijinsky for Ida Rubinstein 1928.

Boléro an orchestral work by Ravel, commissioned as a ballet by Ida Rubinstein and first performed by her in Paris, 22 November 1928. It consists entirely of a single theme of Spanish character, repeated over and over again with different orchestration and in a gradual taut *crescendo*.

Bologna, Jacopo da (Jacobus de Bononia) (fl. 1340–60) Italian composer. He belongs to the earliest generation of 14th-century composers – all his known works are madrigals, and nearly all are for two voices. He also wrote a short treatise, *L'arte del biscanto misurato*.

Bolt, The ballet in three acts by Shostakovich (scenario by V Smirnov), performed Leningrad, 8 April 1931. Ballet suite (no. 5) op. 27a, performed 1933.

Bomarzo opera by Ginastera (libretto by M M Láinez, set in 16th-century Italy), performed Washington, DC, 19 May 1967; banned in Ginastera's own country, Argentina, owing to alleged obscenities in the ballet – Duke Francesco drinks a poisoned potion, believing it will bring immortality; as he dies, flashbacks of his tormented past and unfulfilled sexuality appear before him. Cantata *Bomarzo*, for baritone, speaker, chorus, and orchestra, performed Washington, 1 November 1964.

bombard double-reed wind instrument, the bass instrument of the ◊shawm family and a forerunner of the ◊bassoon.

bombardon, French, brass instrument of the ◊tuba variety. The name is derived from the bombard, and was previously applied to various instruments of the oboe and bassoon family. When used, the bombardon takes the lowest bass parts in military and brass bands. See ◊saxhorn.

bongos small Cuban drums played in pairs by the fingers and thumbs. They consist of hollowed-out pieces of wood with animal skin stretched over one end.

Bonini, Severo (1582–1663) Italian composer. He set Ottavio Rinuccini's poem 'Lamento d'Arianna' in recitative style in 1613, and wrote madrigals and spiritual canzonets for a single voice with ◊continuo accompaniment. He was organist at Forli. His *Discorsi e Regole*, published about 1650, contains important information on early opera.

Bonne Chanson, La cycle of nine songs by Fauré, set to poems from Verlaine's volume of that name, composed 1891–92, first performed Paris, 20 April 1895.
Symphonic poem by Loeffler, on the same source; composed 1901, first performed Boston, 11 April 1902.

Bononcini (or Buononcini) (lived 17th–18th centuries) Italian family of musicians. **Giovanni Maria Bononcini (1642–1678)** was a pupil of Bendinelli, and maestro di cappella of Modena Cathedral. He wrote a treatise, *Musico prattico*, also cantatas, sonatas, and suites.
His son, **Giovanni** (1670–1747), was a pupil of Colonna and of his father, and maestro di cappella at San Giovanni in Monte at Modena. He produced his first opera in Rome in 1692. Lived in Vienna, 1698–1711, in Italy 1711–20, in London, 1720–32 (where he had more success than Handel), later in France and Vienna. He wrote the operas *Tullo Ostilio* (1694), *Il trionfo di Camilla* (1696), *Xerse, Endimione* (1706), *Astarto* (1715), *Crispo, Erminia* (1719), *Farnace, Calfurnia* (1724), *Astianatte, Griselda* (1733), and many others, including an act in *Muzio Scevola* with Handel and Amadei; seven oratorios; funeral anthem for Marlborough; music for the Peace of Aix-la-Chapelle; Masses, Te Deum, psalms, *Laudate pueri*; and chamber cantatas and duets.
Antonio Maria (1677–1726) was the second son of Giovanni. He became maestro di cappella to the Duke of Modena in 1721. He wrote about 20 operas and oratorios.

Bonporti, Francesco Antonio (1672–1749) Italian composer. He trained for the priesthood in Rome from 1691 and studied music with the composers Giuseppe Pitoni and Arcangelo Corelli. On his ordination he returned to Trento, and spent the next 40 years in hope of a canonry. He retired disappointed to Padua in 1740.
Works include: motets; trio sonatas; concertos; 'Inventions' for solo violin, which may have influenced Bach's works in the same form.

Bontempi, Giovanni Andrea (c. 1624–1705) Italian castrato, theorist, and composer. He took the name of a patron, Cesare Bontempi, and sang in St Mark's, Venice, from 1643. At the end of the 1640s he went to Germany, where he became assistant conductor to Heinrich ◊Schütz in Dresden 1666, but devoted himself to science and architecture the next year. He returned to Italy in 1669 and after another visit to Dresden in 1671, settled down in his birthplace. He wrote three theoretical books.
Works include: the Italian operas *Paride* (1662), *Dafne* (1671), and *Jupiter and Io* (1673).

Boosey & Hawkes London music publishers and instrument makers. They were originally two companies: Boosey, founded in 1816 as British agents for Rossini, Hummel, Mercadante, and others, and also manufactured wind instruments from about 1850; Hawkes, founded in 1865, handling brass and military band music. They merged in 1930.
Their catalogue includes many 20th-century composers, for example Strauss, Prokofiev, Stravinsky, Bartók, Mahler, and Britten (1938–63). Contemporary composers include

Carter, Bernstein, Reich, Copland, Kurtág, Robin Holloway, and Peter Maxwell Davies.

bore the internal diameter of tubing of a brass or woodwind instrument. The diameter of the bore affects the character of the instrument's tone.

Boréades, Les tragédie-lyrique in five acts by Rameau (libretto by L de Cahusac), written for the court of Louis XV, 1763, but not performed. First full performance (concert) Paris, 16 September 1964; first stage performance Aix-en-Provence, 21 July 1982. Queen Alphise wants to wed Abaris, but must marry a descendant of Boreas, god of the north wind. After she gives up the throne and suffers the wrath of Boreas, Abaris is revealed to be related to the god, and the couple marry.

boree one of the old English names for the ◊bourrée, others being borea, bore, and borry.

Boretz, Benjamin (1934–) US composer and editor. He studied in New York with Foss, Milhaud, and Sessions. He has taught at Bard College from 1973 and was cofounder and editor of *Perspectives of New Music*, 1961–84.

Works include: string quartet (1958); *Group Variations I* for orchestra (1967) and *II* for computer (1971); *Liebeslied* for piano (1974); *Language, as a Music* for speaker, piano, and tape (1980); other pieces involving sound on tape.

Borgomastro di Saardam, Il/The Burgomaster of Saardam comic opera by Donizetti (libretto by D Gilardoni, based on a French play by A H J Mélesville, J T Merle, and E C de Boirie), produced Naples, Teatro del Fondo, 19 August 1827. The subject is that of Lortzing's *Zar und Zimmermann*.

Boris Godunov opera by Mussorgsky (libretto by composer, based on Pushkin's drama and N M Karamazin's *History of the Russian Empire*), composed 1868–69; enlarged and revised 1871–72; this later version cut and produced St Petersburg, Imperial Opera, 8 February 1874, the original having been rejected in 1870. Rimsky-Korsakov's edition produced St Petersburg, Imperial Opera, 10 December 1896. Further revised by Rimsky-Korsakov, 1908. The original produced Leningrad, 16 February 1928. Boris becomes tsar after having the heir to the throne murdered, but his guilt drives him insane and he eventually collapses and dies.

Borodin, Aleksandr Porfirevich (1833–1887) Russian composer. Born in St Petersburg, the illegitimate son of a Russian prince, he became by profession an expert in medical chemistry, but in his spare time devoted himself to writing music. His principal work is the opera *Prince Igor*, left unfinished; it was completed by Rimsky-Korsakov and Glazunov and includes the Polovtsian Dances. His other works include symphonies, songs, and chamber music, using traditional Russian themes.

His father, Prince Gedeanov, registered Borodin as the son of one of his serfs. Borodin displayed from childhood an equal liking for music and for science. He tried to compose at the age of nine and was given music lessons. In his studies at the Academy of Medicine he distinguished himself especially in chemistry, and while studying in Germany he met the pianist Ekaterina Protopopova, whom he married in 1863. The preceding year, having so far been self-taught in composition, he began to take lessons from Balakirev, who conducted his first symphony in 1869. In the same year, he began his opera *Prince Igor*, working on it at irregular intervals; the score, completed by Rimsky-Korsakov and Glazunov, contains some of his finest music. He lectured on chemistry at the School of Medicine for Women from 1872 to his death and wrote important treatises on his subject. In spite of being best known for such 'highlights' as the Polovtsian Dances and even *Kismet*, Borodin's music repays much closer attention; his best work is highly charged and colourful, without being lurid or melancholy in the manner of some of his contemporaries.

Works include: the opera *Prince Igor* (1869–87, unfinished); three symphonies (third unfinished); *In the Steppes of Central Asia* for orchestra (1880); two string quartets (1874–79, 1881); *Serenata alla spagnuola* for string quartet; *Serenade de quatre galants à une dame* for male voice quartet; *Petite Suite* for piano; songs.

borry English corruption of the French ◊bourrée found in 17th-century music, such as that of Purcell.

Bortkievich, Sergei Eduardovich (1877–1952) Russian composer. He wrote a book about Tchaikovsky and Nadezhda von Meck in 1938.

He studied law at St Petersburg and composition under Liadov, later at Leipzig. He lived in Berlin until 1914, when he joined the Russian army, and at Constantinople (now Istanbul) after World War I. From 1922 until his death he lived in Vienna.

Works include: the opera *Acrobats* (1938); two symphonies; symphonic poem *Othello*;

four piano concertos (one for the left hand), two violin concertos, cello concerto; piano sonatas and pieces; songs.

Bortniansky, Dimitri Stepanovich (1752–1825) Russian composer. He studied at Moscow and in St Petersburg under the Italian composer Baldassare Galuppi, whom he followed to Italy in 1768 with a grant from Catherine II. After further studies at Bologna, Rome, and Naples, he wrote motets and operas at Venice in 1776 and at Modena in 1778. In 1779 he returned to Russia and became director of the Imperial church choir, which he reformed and turned into the Imperial Chapel in 1796.

Works include: the operas *Le Faucon* (1786), *Le Fils rival* (1787), *Creonte*, and *Quinto Fabio* (1778); 35 sacred concertos, 10 concertos for double choir, Mass, chants.

Börtz, Daniel (1943–) Swedish composer. He studied with Rosenberg and Blomdahl; electronic music at Utrecht. His opera *Backanterna* (after Euripides) was premiered 1991 at the Stockholm Opera, directed by Ingmar Bergman. He has also written two church operas, *Landscape with a River* (chamber opera after Hesse, 1974), three string quartets (1966, 1971, 1987); *Josep K* for soloists, chorus, and orchestra (1969); eight symphonies (1973–88); two concerti grossi (1978, 1981); violin concerto (1985); oboe concerto (1986); *Parados* for orchestra (1987).

Böse, Hans-Jurgen von (1953–) German composer. He studied in Frankfurt and is best known for his stage compositions: operas *Blutbund* (1974), *Das Diplom* (1974), *Die Leiden des jungen Werthers*, after Goethe (1986), *Chimare* (1986), *63: Dream Palace* (1990, introducing some popular music elements) and *Slaughterhouse Five* (1995); ballets *Die Nacht aus Blei* (1981) and *Werther Szenen* (1989); other pieces include Symphony (1976), Variations for strings (1990), *Sappho-Gesänge* for mezzo and ensemble (1983), oboe concerto (1987), and three string quartets (1973, 1977, 1987).

Bösendorfer, Ignaz (1796–1859) Austrian piano manufacturer. He founded his firm in Vienna in 1828 and was succeeded in 1859 by his son Ludwig (1835–1919). In the 1980s the company developed an electronic pianola that sends details of the music played on it to a computer.

Boskovsky, Willi (1909–1991) Austrian violinist and conductor. He was with the Vienna Philharmonic Orchestra 1933–71, as coleader from 1939. He formed the Vienna Octet in 1948.

He conducted the New Year's Day concerts in Vienna, 1954–79.

Bossi, Renzo (1883–1965) Italian composer, son of composer and organist Enrico Bossi. He studied under his father at the Liceo Benedetto Marcello in Venice and took a composition prize in 1902, when he went to Leipzig to continue studying piano, organ, and conducting, the last under Nikisch. He was conductor at several German opera houses before he went to Milan as assistant conductor at La Scala. Professor of composition at Parma from 1913 and Milan from 1916.

Works include: the operas *Rosa rossa* (after Oscar Wilde) (Parma, 1940), *Passa la ronda!* (Milan, 1919), *La notte del mille*, *Volpino il calderaio* (after Shakespeare's *Taming of the Shrew*) (Milan, 1925), and *Proserpina*; symphonies, *Sinfoniale*, *Fantasia sinfonica*, and *Bianco e nero* for orchestra; violin concerto; chamber music.

Bottesini, Giovanni (1821–1889) Italian double bass player, conductor, and composer. His works include 12 operas and an oratorio. He wrote *Méthode complète de Contre-basse* and many pieces for double bass. As a virtuoso of his instrument he was compared with the violinist Niccolò Paganini.

Bottesini was born at Crema, Lombardy. In 1840 he went on an international concert tour which included engagements at Havana, Paris, Palermo, Barcelona, and Cairo, and established his fame as the greatest master of the double bass. He became director of the Conservatory at Parma.

Works include: the operas *Marion Delorme* (after Victor Hugo, Palermo, 1862), *Ali Baba* (London, 1871), and *Ero e Leandro* (Turin, 1879); double bass concertos with orchestra; much music for double bass and piano.

Bottrigari (Bottrigaro), Ercole (1531–1612) Italian theorist. His *Il Desiderio* (1594) deals with the problems of combining instruments of different families. From 1600 to 1604 he was involved in a controversy with Artusi.

Boucourechliev, André (1925–) French composer and musicologist of Bulgarian origin. He studied in Sofia, Paris, and Darmstadt. He has worked as a music critic and written books on R Schumann, F Chopin, and L van Beethoven. His works are influenced by P Boulez and include the series *Archipel* (from 1967) which allows the performer a wide range of interpretative choices. Other works include: *Texte I* and *II* for tape

(1959–60), *Grodek* for soprano and ensemble (text by Trakl, 1963), *Musiques Nocturnes* for clarinet, harp, and piano (1966), *Ombres* for 11 strings (based on themes from Beethoven's late quartets; first performance Brussels 1970, conductor Boulez), *Amers* for orchestra (1973), piano concerto (1976).

Boughton, Rutland (1878–1960) English composer. He idolized Wagner, and determined to found an English centre of opera on the same lines as Bayreuth. He began in a very modest way at Glastonbury with a series of music dramas on the Arthurian legends, producing *The Immortal Hour* (1914). A special theatre was to be built at Glastonbury, but the project had to be abandoned.

Boughton was born at Aylesbury, England. He studied at the Royal College of Music in London under Charles Villiers Stanford and Walford Davies, but left after a short time, and produced some early orchestral works, conducting for a time at the Haymarket Theatre, London. In 1914, in collaboration with Reginald Buckley, he founded the Glastonbury Festival School of Music Drama, where *The Immortal Hour* was produced; the festival was revived after World War I. In 1922 *The Immortal Hour* had a long run in London, and *Alkestis* was produced there by the British National Opera Company in 1924. From 1926 Boughton was an active member of the Communist Party.

Works include: music dramas *The Birth of Arthur* (1908–09), *The Immortal Hour* (1914), *Bethlehem* (1913), *The Round Table*, *Alkestis* (1922), *The Queen of Cornwall* (1924), *The Lily Maid* (1934); ballets *Choral Dances*, *Snow White*, *The Moon Maiden*; dramatic scene *Agincourt* from Shakespeare's *Henry V*; works for chorus and orchestra *The Skeleton in Armour* (Longfellow), *The Invincible Armada* (Schiller), *Midnight* (E Carpenter), *Song of Liberty*; unaccompanied choral music, two string quartets.

Bouilly, Jean-Nicolas (1763–1842) French writer. He was administrator of a department near Tours during the French Revolution. He wrote libretti for a number of operas (◊rescue opera) for various composers, including Cherubini and Gaveaux. The libretto of Beethoven's *Fidelio* is based on his book for Gaveaux's *Léonore*.

Boulanger, Lili (Juliette Marie Olga) (1893–1918) French composer. She was the younger sister of Nadia Boulanger. At the age of 19, she won the Prix de Rome with the cantata *Faust et Hélène* for voices and orchestra.

She studied first as a pupil of her sister Nadia, then at the Paris Conservatory.

Works include: incidental music for Maeterlinck's *La Princesse Maleine* (1918); two poems for orchestra; cantata *Faust et Hélène* (after Goethe, 1913); psalms with orchestra.

Boulanger, Nadia Juliette (1887–1979) French music teacher and conductor. She studied under Gabriel Fauré at the Paris Conservatory, where she later taught, as well as at the Ecole Normale de Musique and the American Conservatory at Fontainebleau. Many distinguished composers were her pupils, including her sister, Lili Boulanger, Lennox Berkeley, Aaron Copland, Jean Françaix, Roy Harris, Walter Piston, and Philip Glass.

She was the first woman to conduct the Royal Philharmonic, London, in 1937, and the Boston Symphony, the New York Philharmonic, and the Philadelphia Orchestra in 1938. After the outbreak of World War II in Europe in 1939, she went to the USA, returning in 1946.

Works include: incidental music to d'Annunzio's *La città morta* (with Pugno) (1911); cantata *La Sirène* (1908); orchestral works; instrumental pieces, songs.

Boulevard Solitude opera by Henze (libretto by the composer and G Weil), produced Hanover, 17 February 1952. A modern version of the Manon story; lovers Manon and Armand are forced apart by poverty when she must take a rich admirer to support herself and her brother.

Boulez, Pierre (1925–) French composer and conductor. He is the founder and director of ◊IRCAM, a music research studio in Paris opened in 1977. His music, strictly serial and expressionistic in style, includes the cantatas *Le Visage nuptial* (1946–52) and *Le Marteau sans maître* (1955), both to texts by René Char; *Pli selon pli* (1962) for soprano and orchestra; and *Répons* (1981) for soloists, orchestra, tapes, and computer-generated sounds.

Boulez was born at Montbrison on the River Loire. After abandoning studies in mathematics, he studied with Messiaen at the Paris Conservatory, and in 1946 took a course in serial technique with Leibowitz. Also in 1946, he worked for the Renaud-Barrault theatre company and in 1953–54 founded the 'Domaine Musical' with Barrault, which specialized in new music. As a composer he belongs to the avant garde, writing in a style which has its roots in Debussy and Webern and also in the ideas of James Joyce and Mallarmé. He is one of the pioneers of integral serialism, but later introduced freer elements into his music. Boulez is also a leading conductor of advanced new music. He was principal conductor of the BBC Symphony Orchestra 1971–75, and of the New York Philharmonic Orchestra 1971–77, giving notable performances of works by Berg, Bartók, Stravinsky, and members of the Second Viennese School, including Schoenberg's *Moses und Aron* in London in 1974. He conducted Wagner's operas *Parsifal* at Bayreuth 1966, and *The Ring* 1976, and gave the first complete performance of Berg's opera *Lulu* in Paris in 1979.

His early works (including *Flute Sonatina* 1946, *Le Visage Nuptial*, and the first two piano sonatas) are preoccupied with developments and extensions of Webern's serial technique. *Structures* (1952) for two pianos is a turning point in his development, taking account of the concepts of a series of durations, intensities, and timbres first promulgated by Messiaen. Later works, such as *Le Marteau sans maître*, the third piano sonata, and *Pli selon pli* develop these ideas with greater flexibility, eventually leading to the use of open forms (as in the third piano sonata) in which the order of musical material may be decided by the performer. Since the 1960s he has become prominent as a conductor of international standing. He wrote *Boulez on Music Today* (1971).

Works include: ORCHESTRAL ... *explosante fixe* ... (1971–73); *Rituel in memoriam Bruno Maderna* (1974–75); *Répons* for 24 players, six instrumental soloists, and computerized electronics (1981).

VOCAL *Le Soleil des eaux* for solo voices, chorus, and orchestra (after Char); *Le Marteau sans maître* for alto and six instruments (after Char) (1952–57); *Pli selon pli* for soprano and orchestra (after Mallarmé, 1958–62); *e e cummings ist der dichter* for 16 solo voices and 24 instruments (1970, revised 1986).

INSTRUMENTAL three piano sonatas (1946, 1948, 1957); *Livre* for string quartet (1948, revised for string orchestra 1968); *Eclat* for 15 instruments (1965, expanded as *Eclat/Multiples* for 27 instruments, 1966); *Dérive* for small ensemble (1984); *Dérive II* for 11 instruments (1988); *Message esquisse* for cello.

Boult, Adrian Cedric (1889–1983) English conductor. He conducted the BBC Symphony Orchestra 1930–50 and the London Philharmonic 1950–57. He promoted the work of Holst and Vaughan Williams, and was a celebrated interpreter of Elgar.

bourdon French musical term for the drone of an instrument such as the hurdy-gurdy or bagpipes, or for a piece of music imitating a drone accompaniment. See also ◊musette.

Bourgault-Ducoudray, Louis (Albert) (1840–1910) French composer. A lawyer at first, he entered the Paris Conservatory late and took a composition prize in 1862. In 1869 he founded a choral society in Paris with which he gave performances of unfamiliar works. He collected and published Greek and Breton folksongs, and lectured on history of music at the Conservatory from 1878.

Works include: the operas *L'Atelier de Prague* (1858), *Michel Colomb* (1887), *Bretagne*, *Thamara* (1891), *Myrdhin* (1905); satiric play *La Conjuration des fleurs*; *Stabat Mater*, *Symphonie religieuse* for unaccompanied chorus; *Fantaisie en Ut mineur*, *Carnaval d'Athènes*, *Rapsodie cambodgienne*, *L'Enterrement d'Ophélie* (after Shakespeare) for orchestra.

Bourgeois, Derek (David) (1941–) English composer. He studied at Cambridge, and with Howells at the Royal College of Music; appointed lecturer at Bristol University in 1971.

Works include: two symphonies (1960, 1968), variations on a theme of Mozart, for double bass and orchestra (1967), symphonic fantasy *The Astronauts* (1969); *Jabberwocky-Extravaganza* for baritone, chorus, and orchestra (1963); string quartet (1962), two brass quintets (1965, 1972).

Bourgeois gentilhomme, Le/The Bourgeois as Gentleman comedy-ballet by Molière with music by J B Lully, produced Chambord, 14 October 1670.

Incidental music by Richard Strauss to a shortened version of Molière's comedy translated by H von Hofmannsthal, preceding the one-act opera *Ariadne auf Naxos*, produced Stuttgart, 25 October 1912. Strauss afterwards dropped it for a new operatic first act and made a concert suite for orchestra of the incidental music, adding a minuet by Lully (first performed Vienna, 31 January 1920, conductor Strauss).

bourrée French dance form in fast double two time, accented on the second beat, and starting on the upbeat, the music for which is found in the classical ◊suite.

boutade (French 'whim, frolic') 18th-century dance, or sometimes a whole ballet, in a whimsical style; also sometimes an instrumental piece of the same character.

Boutique fantasque, La/The Fantastic Toyshop ballet by Respighi, arranged from

The opening of Bach's famous Bourrée from his Cello Suite no. 3.

music by Rossini (choreographed by Leonid Fedorovich Massin), produced London, Alhambra Theatre, 5 June 1919. The music consists mainly of small pieces written by Rossini in his retirement for the amusement of his friends.

bow a stick holding lengths of stretched horsehair which is drawn across the strings of a member of the violin or viol family in order to produce sound vibrations in the string. Before the 17th century bows were convex, but changes in violin technique prompted the development of concave bows, perfected by François Tourte (1747–1835) at the end of the 18th century.

Unusual instruments that have been played with a bow include the ◊glass harmonica and ◊musical saw.

bowing the art of using a bow, or the marking of scores and parts with indications about how to bow.

Bowles, Paul Frederick (1910–) US writer and composer. Born in New York City, he studied music composition with Aaron Copland and Virgil Thomson, writing scores for ballets, films, and an opera, *The Wind Remains* (1943), as well as incidental music for plays. He settled in Morocco, the setting of his novels *The Sheltering Sky* (1949) (filmed 1990) and *Let It Come Down* (1952), which chillingly depict the existential breakdown of Westerners unable to survive self-exposure in an alien culture. Other works include *A Thousand Days for Mokhtar* (1989) and *Too Far from Home* (1994). His autobiography, *Without Stopping*, was published 1972.

Bowles settled permanently in Tangier with his wife, the writer Jane Bowles (1917–1973), after World War II and became greatly influenced by Moroccan storytelling – he later turned to transcribing and translating tales by Mohammed Mrabet and others.

Boyarina Vera Sheloga (Rimsky-Korsakov) see ◊*Pskovitianka*.

Boyce, William (1710–1779) English composer and organist. He wrote church music,

symphonies, and chamber music, but is best known for his song 'Heart of Oak' 1759. He was one of the most respected English composers of his time. Much of his music exhibits a fresh liveliness, particularly his many dance movements.

Boyce was a chorister at St Paul's Cathedral and a pupil of Maurice Greene, whom he succeeded as Master of the King's Musick in 1755. Meanwhile he held various organ posts in London, was appointed composer to the Chapel Royal in 1736, and conductor of the Three Choirs Festival the following year. From 1758 he was organist of the Chapel Royal. Deafness forced him to give up much of his work during his later years. Although his dance movements and fugues show much individuality, based on an idiom bequeathed by Handel, his numerous court odes are more easily forgotten. In recent years his music has been revived.

Works include: stage entertainments *The Chaplet* (1749) and *The Shepherd's Lottery* (1751); masques *Peleus and Thetis* (1740) and Dryden's *Secular Masque* (about 1746); incidental music for Shakespeare's *Tempest*, *Cymbeline* (1746), and *Romeo and Juliet* (1750); pantomime *Harlequin's Invasion* (with M Arne and Aylward, and containing the song 'Heart of Oak'); service settings and anthems; cantatas and odes; 20 symphonies and overtures; 12 trio sonatas; keyboard music; songs, and other pieces. He also completed a notable collection of earlier church music begun by Greene (published under the title *Cathedral Music* in three volumes 1760–73).

Boyd, Anne (1946–) Australian composer. She studied with Peter Sculthorpe at Sydney and with Bernard Rands in York, and was appointed head of the music department at Hong Kong University in 1980. Her music reflects oriental influences and includes some small-scale theatre pieces: *As Far as Crawls the Toad* (1970), *The Rose Garden* (1971), *The Death of Captain Cook* (oratorio, 1978); *The Little Mermaid* (1978), and *The Beginning of the Day* (1980), children's operas; *Black Sun* for orchestra (1989); flute concerto (1992); *Grathawai* for orchestra (1993); three string quartets (1968, 1973, 1991); *Wind across Bamboo* wind quintet (1984); choral and solo vocal music.

Boyhood's End cantata for tenor and piano by Tippett (text by W H Hudson), composed 1943 and performed London, 5 June 1943.

Bozay, Attila (1939–) Hungarian composer. He studied in Budapest at the Bartók Conservatory and with Ferenc Farkas. His music is influenced by serial technique and by Hungarian folksongs.

Works include: the operas *Queen Kungisz* (1969) and *Hamlet* (1984); *Pezzo concertato* for viola and orchestra, *Pezzo sinfonico* for orchestra (1967); *Trapeze and Bars*, cantata (1966); two string quartets (1964, 1971), *Formations* for solo cello (1969).

braccio, da (Italian 'on the arm') in music, suffix originally used to distinguish violins, which are played resting on the arm, from viols, which are played da ◊gamba (on the leg). The term 'viola da braccio' in 17th-century music signifies a violin or viola; today only the viola (German *bratsche*) is so called.

brace a bracket connecting a number of simultaneously played staves, such as the two staves in piano and harp music, or a greater number of staves in a score.

Brack, Georg (Jörg) (lived 16th century) German composer. His part songs were published in collections printed by Schöffer in 1513, Arnt von Aich in 1519, and others.

Bradley, Scott (1914–) US composer of animation film music. Working for the US film-production company Metro-Goldwyn-Mayer (MGM), with Carl Stalling he developed the ◊click-track which enables a composer to write a music track to any desired tempo for a given length of film. He also introduced classical music to *Tom and Jerry* cartoons, arranging Liszt's *Hungarian Rhapsody No. 2* for *Cat Concerto* (1947), and in *The Cat that Hated People* using a twelve-tone row on piccolo to represent Jerry and the same row in reverse played by oboe to represent Tom.

Brahms, Johannes (1833–1897) German composer, pianist, and conductor. He is considered one of the greatest composers of symphonic music and of songs. His works include four symphonies, lieder (songs), concertos for piano and for violin, chamber music, sonatas, and the choral *Ein Deutsches Requiem/A German Requiem* (1868). He performed and conducted his own works.

In 1853 the violinist Joachim introduced him to the composers Liszt and Schumann, who encouraged his work. From 1868 Brahms made his home in Vienna. Although his music belongs to a reflective strain of Romanticism, similar to Wordsworth in poetry, Brahms saw himself as continuing the classical tradition from the point to which Beethoven had brought it. To his contemporaries, he was a strict formalist, in opposition to the romantic sensuality of Wagner. His influence on Mahler and Schoenberg was profound.

Brahms was born at Hamburg, the son of a double bass player, from whom he learnt the rudiments of music as a child. Although intended for an orchestral player, he made such progress on the piano that his parents decided to make a prodigy performer of him when about 11, but his teachers wisely opposed this. He soon afterwards began to compose, but had to play in sailors' taverns and dancing-saloons at night to supplement his parents' earnings. He gave two concerts 1848–49, but did not free himself from the drudgery of playing and teaching until he went on a concert tour with Reményi in 1853, when he met Joachim, Liszt, and other musicians of importance, particularly Robert and Clara Schumann, who took much interest in him. He was intermittently engaged at the court of Lippe-Detmold 1857–60, travelled as a pianist, and worked at Hamburg, where he conducted a ladies' choir. At Hanover in 1859 he premiered his first piano concerto, which, although one of the great masterpieces of the genre, was poorly received by both audience and critics, probably as a result of inadequate rehearsal time.

He first visited Vienna in 1862 and settled there the following year. From 1864 he devoted his time entirely to composition, except for some concert tours on which he played mainly his own works. At Bremen in 1868 he conducted the premiere of his most profound vocal work, *Ein Deutsches Requiem/A German Requiem*; one month later he added the movement *Ihr habt nun Traurigkeit/Though ye now be sorrowful* in memory of his mother. His success as a composer was firmly established during the 1860s, and he became known abroad; but did not complete his first symphony until 1876. It had taken him 15 years and was written in Beethoven's shadow, but after its premiere Brahms was established as the foremost composer of instrumental music of his time. The symphony was soon followed by a more relaxed work in D major. He wrote much during summer holidays in Austria, Germany, and Switzerland, but hardly visited other countries except Italy. In 1877 he refused an honorary doctorate from Cambridge University because he did not wish to go to receive it in person, but accepted a doctorate from Breslau in 1879. In 1881 he was the soloist in the premiere of his second piano concerto. In 1896 he began to suffer seriously from cancer of the liver, the disease from which he died. Brahms was the great compositional conservative of the 19th century. Musicians tended to be classified either as supporters of Brahms or of Wagner, the great innovator of the same period. However, what Brahms lacked in formal invention he more than compensated for in profundity and the perfection of contemporary models.

Works include: CHORUS AND ORCHESTRAL *Ein Deutsches Requiem/A German Requiem* (texts from Luther's translation of the Bible), with baritone and soprano soloists (1857–68), *Rhapsody* for contralto, male chorus, and orchestra (1869), *Gesang der Parzen* (1882).

SYMPHONIES no. 1 in C minor, op. 68 (1855–76), no. 2 in D, op. 73 (1877), no. 3 in F, op. 90 (1883), no. 4 in E minor, op. 98 (1884–85).

CONCERTOS two for piano, no. 1 in D minor, op. 15 (1854–58), no. 2 in B♭, op. 83 (1878–81); violin in D, op. 77 (1878); violin and cello in A minor, op. 102 (1887).

CHAMBER two string sextets, op. 18 in B♭ (1860), op. 36 in G (1865); three string quartets; two string quintets, op. 88 in F (1882), op. 111 in G (1890); three piano quartets, op. 25 in G minor (1861), op. 26 in A (1861), op. 60 (1855–75); piano quintet op. 34 in F minor (1864); clarinet quintet op. 115 in B minor (1891); three piano trios, op. 8 in B (1854, revised 1890), op. 87 in C (1880–82), op. 101 in C minor (1886); horn trio op. 40 in E♭ (1865); two cello sonatas, op. 38 in E minor (1862–65), op. 99 in F (1886); three violin sonatas (1879–88); trio for clarinet, cello, piano (1891); two sonatas for clarinet or viola op. 120 in F minor and E♭ (1894).

SOLO PIANO includes three sonatas (1852–53); Variations on themes by Schumann, Handel (op. 24, 1861), Paganini (op. 35, 1863), and Haydn (version for two pianos of work for orchestra, 1873); rhapsodies, intermezzos, and other pieces.

ORGAN includes 11 chorale preludes op. 122 (1896).

VOCAL: numerous part songs; the song cycles *Die Schöne Magelone* op. 33 and *Vier ernste Gesänge* for low voice and piano op. 121; more than 200 Lieder (1852–86).

Brand, Max (1896–1980) Polish-born Austrian composer. His opera *Maschinist Hopkins*

(1929) is one of the outstanding works of the 'machinist' period of the 1920s; it was banned by the Nazis and not heard again complete until produced by the BBC (British Broadcasting Corporation) in 1986. He also experimented with electronic music and wrote *The Astronauts, an Epic in Electronics* in 1962.

He studied in Vienna under Schreker and Hába. He settled in the USA in 1940 but returned to Austria in 1975.

Works include: opera; scenic oratorio *The Gate* (1944); symphonic poems, chamber music.

Brandenburg Concertos a series of six orchestral concertos by J S Bach, dedicated 1721 to the Margrave Christian Ludwig of Brandenburg: I, F, for three oboes, two horns, bassoon, *violino piccolo*, strings, and continuo; II, F, for recorder, oboe, trumpet, violin, strings, and continuo; III, G, for three violins, three violas, three cellos, bass, and continuo; IV, G, for two recorders, violin, strings, and continuo; V, D, for flute, violin, harpsichord, strings, and continuo; VI, B♭, for two violas, two bass viols, cello, bass, and continuo.

Brandenburgers in Bohemia, The/Braniboři v Čechách opera by Smetana (libretto by K Sabina), produced Prague, Czech Theatre, 5 January 1866. Brandenburgers invade Bohemia, and are thrown out.

Brandts-Buys, Jan (1868–1933) Dutch composer. He won a state prize as a youth and studied at Frankfurt. Most of his operatic successes were produced in Germany and Austria.

Works include: the operas *Das Veilchenfest* (Berlin, 1909), *Le Carillon, Die Schneider von Schoenau* (Dresden, 1916), *Der Eroberer* (Dresden, 1918), *Mi-carême, Der Mann im Mond* (1922), *Traumland, Ulysses; Oberon Romancero* for orchestra; three piano concertos; suite for strings, harp, and horn; string quartets; quintet for flute and strings; piano trios; piano works; songs.

branle a French dance in 2–2 or 3–2 time dating from the 15th century and cultivated until the 18th, called brawl in England.

brass band instrumental ensemble consisting of ◊brass and sometimes ◊percussion instruments. The brass usually comprises (in descending order of pitch) the cornet, flugelhorn, tenor horn, B♭ baritone, euphonium, trombone, and bombardon (bass tuba). The brass band developed during the 19th century from the military band, and was particularly associated with the manufacturing towns of Lancashire and Yorkshire. Classical composers have written for the medium, including Elgar in his *Severn Suite* (1930).

brass instrument any of a class of musical instruments made of brass or other metal, including trumpets, bugles, trombones, and horns. The function of a reed is served by the lips, shaped and tensed by the mouthpiece, acting as a valve releasing periodic pulses of pressurized air into the tube. Orchestral brass instruments are derived from signalling instruments that in their natural or valveless form produce a directionally focused range of tones from the harmonic series by overblowing to as high as the 16th harmonic. They are powerful and efficient generators, and produce tones of great depth and resonance.

In the symphony orchestra the brass instruments are the French horn, trumpet, trombone, and tuba. In the brass band they comprise the cornet, flugelhorn, tenor horn, B♭ baritone, euphonium, trombone, and bombardon (bass tuba).

Brautwahl, Die/The Choice of a Bride opera by Busoni (libretto by composer based on a story by E T A Hoffmann), produced Hamburg, 13 April 1912. Orchestral suite in five movements performed Berlin, 2 January 1913. Albertine has two men over 300 years old among her suitors; she marries her favourite, the young painter Edmund, after he passes a test.

bravura (Italian 'bravery') musical term indicating that a passage demands brilliant virtuoso standards. It is associated especially with Romantic 19th-century music, such as many of Liszt's piano works.

break the change in tone-quality between different registers of voices and of wind instruments, a natural defect which may be more or less successfully corrected by technical means.

breaking the 17th-century practice of varying a theme by dividing it into figurations of smaller note-values, as in divisions (variations). Breaking the ground was the same process if the theme was on a ground-bass.

Brecht, Bertolt (1898–1956) German poet and playwright. He was associated with Kurt ◊Weill from 1928 and has been credited with the text of the ◊*Dreigroschenoper*; most of it is now known to be by Elisabeth Hauptmann, one of his several female collaborators. Brecht had more say in Weill's *Happy End* (1929), ◊*Aufstieg und Fall der Stadt Mahagonny* (1930), and *Der Jasager*. From 1948 Brecht's Berliner Ensemble encouraged social realism and theatrical innovation, spawning a whole

generation of original stage producers. See also ◊*Lehrstück*.

Brehm, Alvin (1925–) US composer, conductor, and double bass player. He studied at Juilliard with Wallingford Riegger. As a soloist he performed with such groups as the Contemporary Chamber Ensemble (1969–73), the Group for Contemporary Music (1971–73), and the Chamber Music Society of Lincoln Center (1984–89); he has also led modern music as a conductor, from 1947.

Works include: concertina for violin and strings (1975), piano concerto (1977), sextet for piano and wind quintet (1984), tuba concerto (1982).

Brenet, Michel (1858–1918), pseudonym of Marie Bobillier French musicologist. He wrote studies of J Okeghem, G P da Palestrina, G F Handel, J Haydn, P Grétry, and H Berlioz.

Bretón, Tomás (1850–1923) Spanish composer. He was director of Madrid Conservatory from 1901.

Works include: the operas *Guzman el Bueno* (1875), *Garin, Raquel* (1900), *Farinelli, El certamen de Cremona, Tabaré*, and *Don Gil* (1914); zarzuelas *Los amantes de Teruel, La Dolores, La verbena de la paloma* (1894) and about 30 others; oratorio *Apocalipsia* (1882); *Las escenas andalazas, Salamanca, En la Alhambra* for orchestra; violin concerto; three string quartets, piano quintet, sextet for wind, piano trio.

breve (Latin 'short') the shortest note of 13th-century music. Since the subsequent addition of many other shorter notes, it is now the longest, equal in duration to eight ◊crotchets. It is rarely used and is notated by an unfilled white note-head (often in the shape of a square) with two vertical lines attached to its left and right side.

Brian, (William) Havergal (1876–1972) English composer. His works (many unperformed, and most unpublished) include five operas (among them a Faust after Goethe), songs, and choral music (including settings of Blake and of Shelley's 'Prometheus Unbound'). He wrote 32 symphonies in visionary Romantic style, including the *Gothic* (1919–27) for large choral and orchestral forces; he wrote the last 21 between the ages of 81 and 92.

Brian was born at Dresden, Staffordshire. The son of a potter, he was self-taught in composition but before World War I was regarded as a leading 'modern'. He became an organist and music teacher in Staffordshire and wrote criticism at Manchester from 1905.

Later he moved to London, where he made a precarious living under great difficulties. Some of his early music was conducted by Wood and Beecham, although he did not hear any of his 32 symphonies performed until 1954 at the age of 78, when his eighth symphony was produced by the BBC (British Broadcasting Corporation). The largest symphony, no. 1 *The Gothic*, was not performed until 1961. Despite the meagre prospects of hearing his own works performed during the early years – most of his 32 symphonies are still unpublished – Brian continued to compose.

Works include: the operas *The Tigers* (1916–29; first performance BBC, 1983), *Turandot* (1950), *The Cenci* (1952), *Faust* (1956), *Agamemnon* (1957); 32 symphonies (1919–68); three *English Suites*, *Hero and Leander*, overtures *For Valour* (Whitman) and *Dr Merryheart*, *Festal Dance*, *Fantastic Variations on Old Rhymes*, symphonic poem *In Memoriam* for orchestra; *By the Waters of Babylon*, *The Vision of Cleopatra*, and a setting from Shelley's 'Prometheus' for chorus and orchestra (1937–44); Heine's 'Pilgrimage to Kevlaar' for chorus and orchestra; songs; part songs.

Bride of Messina, The/Nevěsta Messinská opera by Fibich (libretto by O Hostinský, based on Schiller's drama *Die Braut von Messina*), produced Prague, Czech Theatre, 28 March 1884.

bridge a support for the strings of an instrument that determines its length and transmits vibration to the body. In violins, lutes, guitars, and other instruments the bridge is fixed, but in the Indian tambura (long lute) and Japanese koto (zither), bridges are movable to change the tuning. The ◊monochord of music theory also has a movable bridge.

Bridge, Frank (1879–1941) English composer. His works include the orchestral suite *The Sea* (1912), and *Oration* (1930) for cello and orchestra. He taught English composer Benjamin Britten.

Bridge was born at Brighton and studied at the Royal College of Music, London, where Charles Stanford was his composition master. He also learned the violin, viola, and conducting. He went on to play viola in various quartets and gained varied experience as operatic and concert conductor, but later devoted his time to composition, under the patronage of Elizabeth Sprague Coolidge, though he also taught Britten privately. He won Cobbett Prizes for chamber music 1905–15 and honourable mention for his E minor

string quartet at Bologna in 1906. He won acclaim for such accessible works as *The Sea*, *Lament* (1915) for strings, and *There is a Willow* (1928). However, starting with the Piano Sonata (1924), his music explores dissonance to a greater degree, including bitonality. His third and fourth string quartets (1927, 1937) show an advanced harmonic idiom, not far removed from the music of Berg. He was well known as a teacher; his pupil Britten's *Variations on a theme of Frank Bridge* (1937) are based on a theme from his master's Idyll no. 2 for string quartet 1906.

As a composer he possessed a formidably polished technique, and in his inter-war compositions developed a radical cosmopolitan idiom, influenced by the atonality of Schoenberg. He is now recognized as one of the finest composers of his generation, particularly in the field of chamber music.

Works include: the opera *The Christmas Rose* (1918–29; produced London, 1932); symphonic poem *Isabella* (1907), suite *The Sea* (1911), rhapsody *Enter Spring* (1927), tonepoem *Summer* for orchestra; Lament for strings; *There is a willow grows aslant a brook* (on a passage in *Hamlet*); *Phantasm* for piano and orchestra (1931), *Oration* for cello and orchestra (1930), *Rebus* overture (1940) and *Allegro moderato* for strings (1941). Four string quartets (1901–37), two piano trios, Fantasy quartet and several smaller pieces for string quartet, piano quintet, Fantasy Trio and quartet for piano and strings, string sextet, Rhapsody for two violins and viola, *Divertimenti* for wind instruments, violin and piano sonata, cello and piano sonata; numerous piano works including sonata, four *Characteristic Pieces*, suite *A Fairy Tale*, three Improvisations for the left hand; violin, viola, cello, and organ pieces; choruses; songs.

bridge passage a transitional passage in a composition, the transition between first and second subjects in a sonata-form movement.

Briegel, Wolfgang Carl (1626–1712) German composer. He was organist at Schweinfurt and Gotha; from 1671 to his death music director at Darmstadt. He wrote operas and ballets, sacred works for several voices including seven cantatas, *Evangelische Gespräch* and *Evangelischer Blumengarten* (1660–81), pieces for three and four instruments, convivial and funeral songs for several voices, and hymns.

Briganti, I/The Brigands opera by Mercadante (libretto by J Crescini, based on Schiller's drama *Die Räuber*), produced Paris, Théâtre Italien, 22 March 1836.

Brigg Fair, the fair at Brigg, Lincs rhapsody for orchestra by Delius on a Lincolnshire folksong, actually a set of variations, or a kind of passacaglia, composed 1907, performed Basel, 1907; first English performance Liverpool, 18 January 1908.

brillant (French, *brillante*) word used either as an adjective in titles or as a direction showing how a particular passage is to be performed.

brindisi (Italian 'a toast') drinking of someone's health, a drinking song, especially in opera, for example in Donizetti's *Lucrezia Borgia*, Verdi's *Macbeth*, *Traviata*, and *Otello*, or Mascagni's *Cavalleria rusticana*.

brio (Italian 'spirit, fire, brilliance') in music, a word often used in the direction *con* ('with') *brio*, spiritedly.

brisé (French 'broken') an arpeggio in keyboard or harp music; détaché bowing in string music.

Britain, Radie (1903–1994) US composer. She studied in Chicago and with Marcel Dupré in Paris; piano with Leopold Godowsky, and taught privately in Hollywood. Much of her music is evocative of her native southwest scenery, including the orchestral pieces *Heroic Poem* (1929), *Light* (1935), *Ononaga Sketches* (1939), *Serenata sorrentina* (1946), *Cactus Rhapsody* (1953), *Cosmic Mist*, symphony (1962), *Brothers of the Clouds*, for male voices and orchestra (1962); chamber and vocal music.

Britten, (Edward) Benjamin, Baron Britten (1913–1976) English composer. He often wrote for the individual voice; for example, the role in the opera *Peter Grimes* (1945), based on verses by George Crabbe, was written for his life companion, the tenor Peter Pears. Among his many works are the *Young Person's Guide to the Orchestra* (1946); the chamber opera *The Rape of Lucretia* (1946); *Billy Budd* (1951); *A Midsummer Night's Dream* (Shakespeare) 1960; and *Death in Venice* (after Thomas Mann) (1973).

Born in Lowestoft, Suffolk, Britten was educated at Gresham's School, Holt, Norfolk. He studied piano with Harold Samuel and composition with Frank Bridge. Later, with a scholarship, he studied under Benjamin and Ireland at the Royal College of Music. He worked in the USA 1939–42, then returned to England and devoted himself to composing at his home in Aldeburgh, Suffolk, where he and Pears established an annual music festival in 1948. His oratorio *War Requiem*

(1961) combines the liturgical text with poems by Wilfred Owen, and was written for the rededication of Coventry Cathedral in 1962.

Britten's earliest published work was a Sinfonietta for chamber orchestra, 1932. He was represented at the International Society for Contemporary Music festivals of 1934, 1936, and 1938. He worked for the GPO film unit 1935–37. His first international success was the *Variations on a theme of Frank Bridge*, played at the Salzburg Festival in 1937. This was followed by a number of works which established him as the leading English composer of the day, especially the stark *Sinfonia da Requiem* (1940) and the *Serenade* (1943). He was also an excellent pianist and conductor. In 1945 his second opera, *Peter Grimes*, established him as a dramatist; it was succeeded by further operas, including the chamber opera *The Turn of the Screw* (1954). Other large-scale operas are *The Rape of Lucretia*, *Albert Herring* (after Maupassant 1947), *Billy Budd*, *Gloriana* (1953), *Noyes Fludde* (1958) and *The Little Sweep* for children (1949), *A Midsummer Night's Dream*, *Owen Wingrave* (after Henry James, 1971, commissioned for television), and *Death in Venice*. Much of Britten's music is inspired by words, as shown by the many song cycles, the *Spring Symphony* (1949), and the *Nocturne* (1958); most of his tenor songs and roles were written for Pears. He had a close artistic association with Shostakovich and Rostropovich from 1960.

By intellectual conviction and personal disposition Britten was an outsider; the themes of lost innocence, persecution, and isolation are constantly repeated in his music, especially the operas. Once treated with caution by both conservatives and the avant garde, he has now reached a wider acceptance.

Works include: STAGE operas *Peter Grimes* (M Slater, after Crabbe, 1945), *The Rape of Lucretia* (R Duncan, 1946), *Billy Budd* (E M Forster and Crozier, after Melville, 1951, revised 1960), *Gloriana* (W Plomer, 1953), *The Turn of the Screw* (M Piper, after James, 1954), *A Midsummer Night's Dream* (Shakespeare, 1960), and *Death in Venice* (Piper, after Mann, 1973); ballet *The Prince of the Pagodas* (1957).

CHORAL including *A Ceremony of Carols* (1942), cantatas *Rejoice in the Lamb* (C Smart, 1943) and *Saint Nicolas* (Crozier, 1948), *Spring Symphony* (1949), *War Requiem* (1961).

ORCHESTRAL including *Variations on a theme of Frank Bridge* for strings (1937), *Sinfonia da Requiem* (1940), concertos for piano and for violin (1938–39), cello symphony (1963).

VOICE AND ORCHESTRA *Les Illuminations* (A Rimbaud, 1939) for high voice and strings, *Serenade* (various poets) for tenor, horn, and strings, *Nocturne* (various poets, 1958), *Phaedra* for mezzo and orchestra (1975).

CHAMBER AND INSTRUMENTAL including four string quartets (1931 revised 1974; nos. 1–3, 1941, 1945, 1975); cello sonata, three suites for solo cello; *Lachrymae* on song by Dowland for viola and piano (also with strings); *Six Metamorphoses after Ovid* for solo oboe.

SONG CYCLES *Seven Sonnets of Michelangelo* (1940), *The Holy Sonnets of John Donne* (1945), *Winter Words* (Hardy, 1953), *Five Canticles* (1947–74).

Brixi, Franz Xaver (1732–1771) Bohemian organist and composer. After various church posts he became Kapellmeister of Prague Cathedral in 1756.

Works include: largely church music; 105 Masses, including *Missa Pastoralis* (Christmas Mass); 263 offertories, hymns, and motets; 11 Requiems; 24 Vespers; Litanies, and other pieces; also music for organ, including three concertos, a sinfonia, and other pieces.

Broadwood, John (1732–1812) English piano manufacturer and music editor. He married Barbara, daughter of the Swiss-born harpsichord maker Burkat Shudi, in 1769, and was sole proprietor of Shudi & Broadwood from 1782. By 1781 he had built the first Broadwood grand piano, developed from Johannes Zumpe's (fl. 1735–83) square pianos.

His son, James Shudi Broadwood (1772–1851), was taken into partnership in 1795, when the firm became John Broadwood & Son. James's brother, Thomas Broadwood, was taken into partnership in 1807, when the name became John Broadwood & Sons. By the middle of the 18th century, 2,500 pianos were manufactured per year, but the firm declined towards the 1880s.

Brockes, (Barthold) Heinrich (1680–1747) German poet. His religious works inspired ◊Handel (Passion), ◊Telemann (ditto). Part of his Passion oratorio libretto was used by Bach in the *St John Passion*.

broken consort term for a mixed chamber ensemble of Renaissance and early Baroque instruments.

Brook, Barry S(helley) (1918–) US musicologist. He took his PhD in Paris (1959) and has taught there and in the USA (Juilliard from 1977). He has coordinated international bibliographical projects and is the joint editor of the complete works of Pergolesi (1986–).

He has also issued *The Symphony, 1720–1840* and *French Opera in the 17th and 18th Centuries*.

Bros, Juan (1776–1852) Spanish composer of church music. He was director by turns at the cathedrals of Málaga, León, and Oviedo.

Brossard, Sébastien de (1655–1730) French composer. He studied philosophy and theology at Caen and was self-taught in music. He lived at Caen until 1683, when he went to Paris and worked at Notre-Dame, later at Strasbourg. In 1687 he became *maître de chapelle* at the cathedral there and in 1698 music director at Meaux Cathedral. Although he was a prolific composer he is more famous for his dictionary of music (1703, the first in France).

Brown, Christopher (1943–) English composer. He studied with Lennox Berkeley and Boris Blacher. Much of his music has a spiritual content: cantata *David* (1970), organ concerto (1979), Magnificat (1980), *The Vision of Saul* (1983), *Landscapes* for soprano, chorus, and orchestra (1987).

Brown, Earle (1926–) US composer. He pioneered ◊graph notation (a method of notating controlled improvisation by graphical means) and mobile form during the 1950s, as in *Available Forms II* (1962) for ensemble and two conductors. He was an associate of John ◊Cage and was influenced by the visual arts, especially the work of Alexander Calder and Jackson Pollock.

Works include: *Available Forms I*, *Available Forms II* for 98 players and two conductors (1961–62); two octets for eight magnetic tapes; *Light Music* for electric lights, electronic equipment, and instruments; *Sign Sounds* for chamber ensemble (1972), *Windsor Jambs* for soprano and orchestra (1979); *Folio II* for instruments (1981); *Sounder Rounds* for orchestra (1982); *Tracer* for ensemble and tape (1984).

Brown, Howard Mayer (1930–1993) US musicologist. He studied at Harvard and was professor at University of Chicago from 1967. His writings include *Music in the French Secular Theater, 1400–1550* (1963), *Music in the Renaissance* (1976), and *Major Unpublished Works in a Central Baroque and Early Classical Tradition* (1977– ; planned in 60 volumes). He founded Collegium Musicum at Chicago, for the performance of medieval and Renaissance music.

Browne, John (fl. c. 1490) English composer who contributed more pieces than anyone else to the Eton Choirbook and now seems the major English composer of his generation.

browning an English form of *fancy* for viols, similar to the 'In Nomine', but based on a folk tune instead of a plainsong theme.

Bruce, (Frank) Neely (1944–) US composer and pianist. He studied at the University of Illinois and taught at the Wesleyan University from 1974. He founded the American Music/Theater Group 1977 and has also given premieres as a solo pianist. His music has progressed from serialism to Native American influences: chamber operas *Pyramus and Thisbe* (1965), *The Trials of Psyche* (1971), and *Americana* (1978–83); concerto for percussion and orchestra (1967), violin concerto (1974), *Orion Rising* for orchestra (1988); *Eight Ghosts* for four singers and electronics; keyboard music and songs; chamber pieces with voice.

Bruch, Max (1838–1920) German composer. He was professor at the Berlin Academy 1891. He wrote three operas, including *Hermione* (1872). Among the most celebrated of his works are the *Kol Nidrei* (1881) for cello and orchestra, violin concertos, and many choral pieces.

Bruch learnt music as a child from his mother, who was a singer. Later, with a scholarship, he studied with Ferdinand Hiller (1811–85), Carl Reinecke, and Ferdinand Breunung. He visited Leipzig, Munich, and other musical centres to gain further experience and in 1863 produced his opera *Die Loreley* at Mannheim, having obtained permission from the poet Emmanuel von Geibel to use the libretto originally written for Mendelssohn. After two appointments at Koblenz and Sondershausen, he lived first in Berlin and then at Bonn, wholly devoted to composition. From 1880 to 1883 he was conductor of the Liverpool Philharmonic Society, and in 1881 he married the singer Clara Tuczek. From 1883 to 1890 he conducted at Breslau and in 1891 became professor of composition at the Hochschule in Berlin, retiring to Friedenau in 1910. Until recently only the popular G minor violin concerto has allowed Bruch to emerge from the shadow of Brahms; revivals of such works as the oratorio *Odysseus* (1872), the opera *Die Loreley*, and chamber music such as the Septet have allowed a more balanced view of the composer.

Works include: the opera *Die Loreley* (Mannheim, 1863); works for solo voices, chorus, and orchestra: *Odysseus* (after Homer, 1872), *Das Lied von der Glocke* (Schiller, 1879), *Achilleus* (after Homer), *Das Feuerkreuz* (after Scott's 'Lay of the Last Minstrel'); three violin concertos (1868, 1878, 1891), *Scottish Fantasia* for violin, harp, and orchestra (1880); *Kol Nidrei* (1881) for cello and orchestra; Concerto in E minor for clarinet, violin, and orchestra, op. 88; string quintet in A minor (1919), many choruses; instrumental pieces; piano music; songs.

Bruckner, (Josef) Anton (1824–1896) Austrian Romantic composer. He was cathedral organist at Linz 1856–68, and professor at the Vienna Conservatory from 1868. His works include many choral pieces and 11 symphonies, the last unfinished. His compositions were influenced by Wagner and Beethoven.

Bruckner was the son of a country schoolmaster, and was intended to follow the same profession. On the early death of his father in 1837 he was taken in as a choirboy by the monastery of St Florian. There he learnt the organ and was appointed organist in 1845. By this time he had begun to compose, notably the Requiem in D minor, but was dissatisfied with his poor technique and went to study counterpoint with Simon Sechter in Vienna in 1855. He was cathedral organist at Linz 1855–68, and wrote much in his spare time, including the first recognized symphony, *Linz*. On visiting Munich for the production of *Tristan* 1865, he became an ardent Wagnerian. The early progress of his work was hindered by his identification, in the minds of influential critics, with the music of Wagner; a more apposite comparison, perhaps, is with Beethoven, particularly the Ninth Symphony. Bruckner's music typically is imbued with a similar kind of spirituality; this is illustrated by the abundance of early religious works, and the late Te Deum. In addition, Bruckner's orchestra tended not to be as massive as Wagner's.

He was appointed professor at the Vienna Conservatory in 1868, when his first symphony received its first performance at Linz, and remained in the capital for the rest of his life, but visited Nancy, Paris, and London as organ virtuoso in 1869 and 1871. His third symphony, strongly influenced by Wagner, had its first performance at Vienna in 1873 but was a failure. Wide success came after the first performance of the seventh symphony in 1884. He was pensioned in 1891 and received an honorary doctorate from the University of Vienna.

Bruckner's symphonies went through several editions and revisions, first through well-meaning cuts and alterations made by Franz Schalk and the composer himself. The later editions by Robert Haas, succeeded by

Leopold Novak, attempt to return to Bruckner's original thoughts.

Works include: SYMPHONIES F minor (1863), D minor ('no. 0', about 1863–64, revised 1869), no. 1 in C minor (1865, revised 1868–84), no. 2 in C minor (1871, revised 1873–77), no. 3 in D minor (1873, revised 1874–77), no. 4 in E♭ ('Romantic'; 1874, new scherzo 1878, new finale 1880), no. 5 in B♭ (1875–76), no. 6 in A (1879–81), no. 7 in E (1881–83), no. 8 in C minor (1884–87 and 1889–90), no. 9 in D minor (1891–94).

CHORAL Mass no. 1 in D minor (1864, revised 1876–82), no. 2 in E minor with wind accompaniment (1866, revised 1869–82), no. 3 in F minor (1867, revised 1876–93); also Te Deum in C for soloists, chorus, and orchestra (1881–84), five Psalm settings (1852–92), many motets.

INSTRUMENTAL string quintet in F (1879).

Bruhns, Nicolaus (1665–1697) German organist, string player, and composer. His elaborate preludes and fugues and sacred concertos form an important link between Buxtehude and Bach.

He was first employed in Copenhagen, and was then town organist at Husum, Slesvig-Holstein. He wrote cantatas, motets with orchestra, and organ music.

Brumel, Antoine (c. 1460–c. 1515) French composer. He is regarded as one of Josquin Desprez's most important contemporaries and wrote 15 surviving masses, including *Et ecce terrae motus* for 12 voices, and *L'homme armé*, and *Missa pro defunctis*, both for four voices.

He also wrote sequences, antiphons, motets, chansons, and instrumental music based on popular melodies of the day. He was a singer at Chartres Cathedral in 1483, a canon at Laon in 1497, and from 1498 to 1501 choirmaster at Notre-Dame in Paris. In 1506 he went to the court of the Duke of Ferrara, Italy, where he may have died.

Bruneau, (Louis Charles Bonaventure) Alfred (1857–1934) French composer and critic. The son of a painter, he learnt music including cello from his parents, who played violin and piano, and took a cello prize at the Paris Conservatory as a pupil of Franchomme. Afterwards he studied composition with Massenet and played in Pasdeloup's orchestra. In 1887 he produced his first opera; the next two were based on works by Zola, who himself wrote the libretti for the next three stage works. The first of these, however, failed in 1897 because Bruneau and Zola were ardent supporters of Dreyfus. After Zola's death Bruneau wrote his own libretti, some still based on Zola's work. He wrote in a style indebted to Wagner, yet softened by the gentler lyricism of the French tradition, somewhat reminiscent of Gounod and Massenet.

Works include: the operas *Kérim* (1887), *Le Rêve* and *L'Attaque du moulin* (after Zola, 1893), *Messidor*, *L'Ouragan* (1901) and *L'Enfantroi* (libretti by Zola), *Lazare*, *Naïs Micoulin* and *Les Quatre Journées* (after Zola), *Le Tambour*, *Le Roi Candaule*, *Angélo, tyran de Padoue* (1928), *Virginie*; ballets *Les Bacchantes* (after Euripides, 1931) and *Le Jardin de Paradis*; incidental music to his adaptation of Zola's *La Faute de l'Abbé Mouret*; Requiem (1895), choral symphony *Léda*, *La Belle au bois dormant* and *Penthésilée*; cantata *Geneviève de Paris*; *Ouverture héroïque* for orchestra; vocal duets; songs *Chansons à danser* and two books of *Lieds de France* (all words by Catulle Mendès).

brunette (French 'a dark-haired girl') light love song of a type current in 17th–18th-century France, originally so called because of the association of the words with dark girls.

Brussilovsky, Evgeny (1905–1981) Russian composer. In 1933 he was commissioned to do research in Kazakh folk music and went to live at Alma-Ata, the capital of Kazakhstan. There he wrote operas in the national idiom.

Having lost both his parents, he joined the army at 16, but was released in 1922 in order to develop his talent at the Moscow Conservatory. He was expelled in 1924 for non-attendance, due to serious illness, but although very poor, managed to go to Leningrad and induced Maximilian Steinberg to teach him at the conservatory there.

Works include: the operas *Kiz-Ji-Bek* (1934), *Er-Targhin* (1937), and *Jalbir*; eight symphonies (1931–72); instrumental pieces; piano pieces; songs.

Bruzdowicz, Joanna (1943–) Polish composer. She studied with Kazimierz Sikorski and with Messiaen and Pierre Schaeffer in Paris, and has founded electronic music studios in Paris and Brussels.

Works include: musical dramas *The Penal Colony* (Tours, 1972), *The Trojan Women* (Paris, 1973), *The Gates of Paradise* (Warsaw, 1989), *Tides and Waves* (Barcelona, 1992), *Maison neuve* (Montreal, 1992); symphony (1974); concerto for piano (1974), violin (1975), double bass (1982); cantatas, chamber and instrumental music.

Bryars, (Richard) Gavin (1943–) English composer. He studied music privately and has been professor of music at De Montford University from 1985. His earlier compos-

itions were influenced by the ideas of Erik
Satie and John Cage; he later turned to Greek
myth for inspiration.

Works include: *The Sinking of the Titanic*
(1969), *My First Homage* (1978), *The English
Mail-Coach* (1980), and *Homage to Vivier* (1985)
for small ensemble; opera *Medea*, (1984, after
Euripides); *Pico's Flight* for orchestra (1986);
two string quartets (1985, 1990); *Cadman
Requiem* (1989); *The Black River* for soprano
and organ (1991); *The Green Ray* for saxophone and orchestra (1991).

Bucci, Mark (1924–) US composer. He
studied at Juilliard and with Aaron Copland.
He composes in an energetic, diatonic style
and has written the operas *The Boor* (1949,
after Chekhov), *The Dress* (1953), *Sweet Betsy
from Pike* (1953), *Tale for a Deaf Ear* (1957), *The
Hero* (1965), and *Midas* (1981); musicals,
including *The Caucasian Chalk Circle* (1948),
The Adamses (1956), and *The Second Coming*
(1976).

buccina musical instrument, the Roman
bugle horn, used in the Roman army for
signalling.

Bucenus, Paulus (fl. 1567–84) German
composer. He worked as a church musician
at Riga, where he may have died.

Works include: a *St Matthew Passion* (1578),
Masses, motets, *Sacrae Cantiones*.

Buchardo, Carlos López (1881–1948) Argentine composer. He studied in Buenos
Aires and with Roussel in Paris. On returning
to Argentina he became director of the
National Conservatory at Buenos Aires.

Works include: the operas *El sueño de Alma*
(1914), *Escenas argentinas* for orchestra (1920);
piano pieces; songs.

*Buch der hängenden Gärten, Das/The
Book of the Hanging Gardens* 15 songs for
soprano and piano by Schoenberg, op. 15
(texts by Stefan George), composed 1908–09,
performed Vienna, 14 January 1910.

*Buch mit sieben Siegeln, Das/The Book
with Seven Seals* oratorio by Franz Schmidt
(text from the Apocalypse); composed 1935–
37, performed Vienna, 15 June 1938.

Büchner, Georg (1813–1837) German poet
and playwright whose works inspired ◊*Blind
Man's Buff* (P M Davies), ◊*Dantons Tod*
(Einem), Robert Müller-Hartmann (*Leonce
und Lena*), Franz Syberg (ditto), Rudolf
Wagner-Régeny (*Günstling*), Julius Weismann
(*Leonce und Lena*), and ◊*Wozzeck* (A Berg and
M Gurlitt).

**Buchner, Johann (Hans von Constantz)
(1483–1538)** German composer. He wrote

sacred and secular songs, and organ pieces.
His *Fundamentum* is a didactic (self-taught)
work incorporating organ music for the
liturgical year.

He was probably a pupil of Paul Hofhaimer. He worked at Konstanz Cathedral, but
left in 1526, because of its growing Protestantism, and went to Überlingen.

Budavari Te Deum work by Kodály for
soloists, chorus, and orchestra, performed
Budapest Cathedral, 11 September 1936.

buffa (Italian 'comic') see ◊opera buffa.

buffo (Italian 'comic', also 'comedian') in
music, a singer of comic parts, used especially
as adjective; *tenore buffo, basso buffo*.

bugle compact valveless treble brass instrument with a shorter tube and less flared bell
than the trumpet. Constructed of copper
plated with brass, it has long been used as a
military instrument for giving a range of
signals based on the tones of a harmonic
series. The bugle has a conical bore whereas
the trumpet is cylindrical.

**Bühnenweihfestspiel (*Bühne* 'stage';
Weihe 'consecration'; *Fest* 'festival'; *Spiel*
'play')** description given by Wagner to
Parsifal, which he did not wish to call an
'opera' or a 'music drama'.

Bukofzer, Manfred (1910–1955) German-
born US musicologist. He studied at Heidelberg, Berlin, and Basel, and went to the USA
in 1939, where after various appointments he
became professor at University of California,
Berkeley. He specialized in medieval, particularly English, music and edited the complete works of Dunstable. His most important
book is *Studies in Medieval and Renaissance
Music* (1950).

Bull, John (c. 1562–1628) English composer
and keyboard virtuoso. He was a choirboy in
the Chapel Royal in London under Blitheman
and became organist of Hereford Cathedral in
1582. On Blitheman's death in 1591 he became
organist of the Chapel Royal. He gained his
music doctorate at both Oxford (1592) and
Cambridge (1589). In 1596 he was appointed
first professor of music at Gresham College.
In 1601 he travelled abroad when Thomas
Byrd, son of William Byrd, acted as his
deputy at Gresham College. He married
Elizabeth Walter in 1607 and gave up his
professorship, which could be held only by
single men. In 1613 he left England, apparently to escape punishment for adultery, and
became organist at the archducal chapel in
Brussels. In 1617 he was appointed organist at
Antwerp Cathedral, where he remained to his

death. Much of his technically brilliant music for the virginals is in the collection *Parenthia* (1613).

Works include: anthems, including the 'Star' anthem *Almighty Lord*; secular vocal works for several voices; canons; a laud for the Blessed Virgin in Flemish; numerous organ and virginal pieces; some works for viols.

Bull, Ole (Borneman) (1810–1880) Norwegian violinist and composer. He wrote two concertos and many other works for the violin. He was largely self-taught, since his father insisted on his studying theology. In 1829 he visited Louis Spohr at Kassel and in 1832 first made his mark as a public player in Paris. He founded the Norse Theatre at Bergen in 1850.

While in Paris, he married a Frenchwoman, appeared with Chopin and Ernst, and went on to visit Italy with great success. He went to England first in 1836 and to the USA in 1843. In 1870 he was married a second time, to an American.

Buller, John (1927–) English composer. From 1959 he studied with Anthony Milner and in the 1970s produced a series of works based on James Joyce's *Finnegan's Wake*. The opera *Bakxai* (after Euripides) was premiered by English National Opera 1992.

Works include: *The Cave* for flute, clarinet, trombone, cello, and tape (1970), two *Night Pieces* from *Finnegan's Wake* for soprano, clarinet, flute, piano, and cello (1971), *Finnegan's Floras* for chorus, percussion, and piano (1972), *Le Terrazze* for 14 instruments and tape (1974), *Familiar*, string quartet (1974), *The Theatre of Memory* for orchestra (1981), *Towards Aquarius* for ensemble (1983), *Kommos* for chorus, soloists, and electronics (1981), *Of Three Shakespeare Sonnets* for mezzo and ensemble (1983), *Bakxai* opera (1992), *Bacchae Metres* for orchestra (1993), *Mr Purcell's Maggot* (1994).

bullroarer, or whizzer, whizzing stick, lightning stick musical instrument used by Australian Aborigines for communication and during religious rites. It consists of a weighted aerofoil (a rectangular slat of wood about 15 cm/6 in to 60 cm/24 in long and about 1.25 cm/0.5 in to 5 cm/2 in wide) whirled rapidly about the head on a long cord to make a deep whirring noise. It is also used in many other parts of the world, including Britain.

Native American peoples used it as an instrument of sympathetic magic, its noise representing the wind that accompanies rain,

in order to induce, by mimicry, the rain itself. Some Australian Aborigines use it to frighten women away from tribal councils and rituals in which only men are allowed to participate. The women are told that the noise is the voice of the presiding god.

Bülow, Hans Guido Freiherr von (1830–1894) German conductor and pianist. He studied with Wagner and Liszt and in 1857 married Liszt's daughter Cosima. From 1864 he served Ludwig II of Bavaria, conducting first performances of Wagner's *Tristan und Isolde* and *Die Meistersinger*. His wife left him and married Wagner in 1870.

He studied law at Leipzig University and piano with Friedrich Wieck there. At first he was exclusively a Wagnerian as a conductor and gave the first performances of *Tristan und Isolde* 1865 and *Die Meistersinger* 1868, but after his wife went to live with Wagner became more enthusiastic about Brahms without abandoning Wagner. He conducted the first performance of Brahms's fourth symphony in 1885. He made many tours both as a conductor and as a pianist; as a soloist he gave the first performance of Tchaikovsky's first piano concerto in Boston in 1875.

Buona figliuola, La/The Good Girl also *La Cecchina*, opera by Piccinni (libretto by Goldoni, based on Richardson's *Pamela*), produced Rome, Teatro delle Dame, 6 February 1760. Marchese della Conchiglia loves Cecchina, but his sister opposes their marriage because Cecchina is of a lower social class. Problems are resolved when the humble maid is revealed to be the daughter of a baron.

Buonamente, Giovanni Battista (died 1642) Italian violinist and composer. He was an imperial court musician from 1622, and maestro di cappella at the Franciscan monastery of Assisi from 1633. He wrote sonatas for two violins and bass, and music for mixed teams of instruments.

Buovo d'Antona/Bevis of Hampton opera by Traetta (libretto by Goldoni, based on the Anglo-Norman 13th-century romance), produced Venice, Teatro San Moisè, 27 December 1758. Revived Venice 1993, in edition by Alan Curtis. Knight Buovo returns from exile to unite with Druisina and drive out evil Duke Maccabuono.

Burbero di buon cuore, Il/The Good-hearted Grumbler opera by Vicente Martín y Soler (libretto by Lorenzo da Ponte, based on Goldoni's French comedy *Le Bourru bienfaisant*), produced Vienna, Burgtheater, 4

January 1786. Mozart wrote two extra arias for it when it was revived, Vienna, 9 November 1789, and Haydn an additional duet for its production in London, 1794. Bachelor Ferramondo in complication with bankrupt nephew and comely niece.

burden in old vocal music, the refrain sung at the end of each verse; in English medieval carols, the refrain or chorus.

Burgon, Geoffrey (1941–   ) English composer. He studied with Peter Wishart and Lennox Berkeley at the Guildhall School of Music. His music shows a range of influences, including jazz and medieval French music. He is best known for his themes for successful TV series, including *Brideshead Revisited*.

Works include: the opera *Hard Times* (1991, after Dickens); ballets *The Golden Fish* (1964), *Ophelia* (1964), *Persephone* (1979), and *The Trial of Prometheus* (1988); *Brideshead Variations* and *The World Again*, for orchestra (1981 and 1983); *Think on Dredful Domesday* (1969), *Magnificat* (1970), *Veni Spiritus*, *Orpheus* and *Revelations*, all for soloists, chorus, and orchestra (1979–84); *Songs of the Creation* for chorus and organ (1989), *A Vision* for tenor and strings (1991); other works for chorus, and for voice and piano or chamber ensemble.

Burian, Emil František (1904–1959) Czech singer, actor, author, stage manager and composer. He studied at the Prague Conservatory, joined the Dada Theatre in Prague and was director of the dramatic studio of the Brno National Theatre in 1929–30; he also founded a voice band, which sang to given rhythms without definite pitch, accompanied by percussion.

Works include: the operas *Alladine and Palomides* (after Maeterlinck, 1923), *Before Sunrise* (1924), *Bubu de Montparnasse, Mr Ipokras, Fear*; ballets *The Bassoon and the Flute* (1925), *Manège, Autobus*; choruses; chamber music, songs.

Burkhard, Willy (1900–1955) Swiss composer. He studied at the Bern School of Music, at Leipzig with Sigfrid Karg-Elert (1877–1933) and Robert Teichmüller (1863–1939), at Munich with Walter Courvoisier (1875–1931), and later in Paris with Max d'Olone (1875–1959). He became piano professor at Bern Conservatory and conducted choirs and an amateur orchestra. In 1937 he settled at Davos to devote himself entirely to composition.

Works include: the opera *Die schwarze Spinne* (after Gotthelf, 1948); oratorios *Musikalische Übung* (Luther, 1934) and *Das Gesicht*

Jesajas (1933–35), Te Deum, choral suite *Neue Kraft*, festival cantata *Le Cantique de notre terre*, cantata *Das Jahr* and others, Psalm xciii for chorus and organ; *Christi Leidensverkündung* for tenor, chorus, and organ; two symphonies, *Ulenspiegel* variations for orchestra; Fantasy, Little Serenade, and concerto for string orchestra; two violin concertos, organ concerto (1945); two string quartets, piano trio, two trio sonatas; Variations and Fantasy for organ; numerous song cycles, including *Frage*, two on poems by Rilke, one on poems by Morgenstern.

burla (Italian 'jest, trick, practical joke') in music, a humorous piece, rather more boisterous than a scherzo.

burlesca see ◊burla.

burlesque another name sometimes used for the ◊burletta in England.

burletta (Italian 'a little joke') a form of light comic opera or operetta in 18th- and 19th-century England.

Burmeister, Joachim (1564–1629) German music theorist. In treatises published 1599, 1601, and 1606 he codified as *figurae* the various technical and expressive devices used by 16th-century composers.

'Burning Fiery Furnace, The' church parable by Britten (libretto by W Plomer), produced Orford Church, Suffolk, 9 June 1966. In honour of visiting Israelites, Babylonian King Nebuchadnezzar organizes a feast, but throws the guests into a furnace when they do not worship his idols. Saved by an angel, they do not burn.

Burrell, Diana (1948–   ) English composer. She studied at Cambridge and has played the viola in various orchestras. Her music is skilfully crafted.

Works include: *Albatross* (1987); *Landscape* (1988), *Scene with Birds* (1989), and *Resurrection* (1993) for orchestra; choral works *Missa Sancta Endeliente* (1980), *Creator of the Stars of Night* (1989), *You Spotted Snakes* (1991), and *Night Songs* (1991); *Concertante* (1985) and *Archangel* (1987) for ensemble; wind quintet (1990); *Arched Form with Bella* for organ (1990); *Sequence* for cello and tape (1993); *Anima* for strings (1993); viola concerto (1994); *Gulls and Angels* for string quartet (1994).

Burt, Francis (1926–   ) English composer. He studied at the Royal Academy of Music and with Boris Blacher in Berlin. He was resident in Vienna from 1957; professor of composition at Hochschule für Musik from 1973.

Works include: the operas *Volpone* (1960) and *Barnstaple, or Someone in the Attic* (1969); ballet *The Golem* (1962); *Iambics* (1953), *Espressione orchestrale* (1959), *Fantasmagoria* (1963), and *Morgana* (1986) for orchestra; *Und Gott der Herr sprach*, for soloists, chorus, and orchestra (1983); string quartet (1953); *Echoes* for flute and ensemble (1989).

Burton, Avery (c. 1470–c. 1543) English composer. He is known as the composer of a Mass, *Ut re mi fa sol la*, in the Forrest-Heyther part-books (this is probably not the Mass of 1494) and of a Te Deum for organ.

In November 1494 he was paid 20 shillings by Henry VII for composing a Mass; in 1509 he became a gentleman of the Chapel Royal. In 1513 he went to France with the Chapel Royal, a Te Deum of his being sung after Mass at Tournai in September; in June 1520 he was present at the historic meeting between Henry VIII of England and Francis I of France, known as the Field of the Cloth of Gold. His name disappears from the records of the Chapel Royal after 1542.

Burton, Stephen (Douglas) (1943–) US composer. He studied in Vienna and Salzburg and with Henze, and taught at George Mason University, Virginia, from 1974. His music is eclectic in character.

Works include: the operas *An American Triptych* (three one-act operas after Craine, Hawthorne, and Melville, 1974), *The Duchess of Malfi* (after Webster, 1978) and *Aimée* (1983); *Stravinskiana* for flute and orchestra (1972), Variations on a Theme of Mahler, for chamber orchestra (1982); violin concerto (1983); chamber and vocal music.

Busby, Thomas (1755–1838) English organist and composer. He sang at Vauxhall as a boy with great success, and later became a pupil of Battishill. He worked at a music dictionary with Samuel Arnold, and was appointed church organist at St Mary's, Newington, Surrey, around 1780. He gained a doctorate of music at Cambridge in 1801. He wrote several books on music, including a history (1825).

Works include: incidental music for Cumberland's *Joanna of Montfaucon* (an English version of Kotzebue's *Johanna von Montfaucon*), Holcroft's *Tale of Mystery*, Anna Maria Porter's *Fair Fugitives* and Lewis's *Rugantino*; oratorios *The Prophecy* (from Pope's *Messiah*; c. 1784, performed Haymarket, 1799) and *Britannia*; settings of odes by Pope and Gay.

Busch, Fritz (1890–1951) German conductor. Like his brother Adolf Busch, he renounced German citizenship, and left Germany for Buenos Aires in 1933. He conducted the Glyndebourne Opera from 1934 to his death, giving the first performances there of *Figaro*, *Così fan tutte*, *Don Giovanni*, and *Macbeth*, and the British premiere of *Idomeneo*.

He studied at the Cologne Conservatory and after working with various German theatres and orchestras, became conductor of the Stuttgart Opera in 1918 and music director of the Dresden Staatsoper in 1922. He conducted there the first performances of Strauss's *Intermezzo* 1924 and *Die Ägyptische Helena* 1928, Busoni's *Doktor Faust* 1925, and Hindemith's *Cardillac* 1926.

Busenello, Gian Francesco (1598–1659) Italian librettist and poet who is best known for his libretto for Monteverdi's *L'Incoronazione di Poppea* (1642); also libretti for Cavalli's *Gli amori d'Apollo e di Dafne* (1640), *Didone* (1641), and *Statira* (1655).

Bush, Alan Dudley (1900–1995) English composer. He adopted a didactic simplicity in his compositions in line with his Marxist beliefs. He wrote a large number of works for orchestra, voice, and chamber groups. His operas include *Wat Tyler* (1948–51) and *Men of Blackmoor* (1955), both of which had their first performances in East Germany.

Bush studied composition with John Ireland and piano with Artur Schnabel. He became professor at the Royal Academy of Music, conductor of the London Labour Choral Union, and in 1936 chairman of the Workers' Music Association.

Works include: the operas *The Press-Gang* (1946), *Wat Tyler* (1948–51), *The Spell Unbound* (1953), *Men of Blackmoor* (1955), *The Sugar Reapers* (1966), and *Joe Hill: the Man who Never Died* (1970); incidental music for Shakespeare's *Macbeth*, Sean O'Casey's *The Star Turns Red*, and Patrick Hamilton's *The Duke in Darkness*; choral work *The Winter Journey* (Randall Swingler) and others; symphony no. 2 'Nottingham' (1949), no. 3 *Byron* (1960), no. 4 *Lascaux* (1983) and other orchestral music; piano concerto with chorus (Swingler), violin concerto, *Concert Suite* for cello and orchestra (1952); string quartet, piano quartet, *Dialectic* for string quartet (1929); instrumental pieces with piano; piano and organ music, including 24 preludes for piano (1977).

Bush, Geoffrey (1920–) English composer. He is mainly self-taught in composition, but had much valuable advice from the composer John Ireland.

Busnois, Antoine

Bush became a choirboy at Salisbury Cathedral in 1928, went to Lancing College in 1933, and graduated from Balliol College, Oxford, in 1940. He received a doctorate from Oxford in 1946. His studies were interrupted by war service at a hostel for evacuee children.

Works include: five operas including *Spanish Rivals* (1948); *Twelfth Night*, entertainment for chorus and orchestra; overtures *In Praise of Salisbury* and *The Rehearsal* for orchestra, Divertimento for string orchestra, two symphonies (1954, 1957); concerto for piano and strings, *Sinfonietta concertante* for cello and chamber orchestra, oboe concerto, rhapsody for clarinet and string quartet; sonatas for violin and piano, and trumpet, and piano; two piano sonatinas; *Portraits* and *La Belle Dame sans merci* (Keats) for unaccompanied chorus; songs.

Busnois, Antoine (c. 1430–1492) French composer. He was a pupil of Okeghem and was in the service of the Burgundian court until 1482, when he became music director at the church of Saint-Sauveur at Bruges.

Works include: two Masses, Magnificat, hymns, 61 songs for three or four voices; motets, including *Fortunata desperata*, used later by Josquin des Prés.

Busoni, Ferruccio Dante Benvenuto (1866–1924) Italian pianist, composer, and music critic. Much of his music was for the piano, but he also composed several operas including *Doktor Faust*, completed by Philipp Jarnach after Busoni's death. His work shows the influence of Liszt and his ballet score for *Doktor Faust* shows his debt to Bizet. Specimens of his style at its best are to be found in his later sonatinas, *Sarabande und Cortège* from *Faust*, and the monumental *Fantasia contrappuntistica* for piano. An apostle of Futurism, he encouraged the French composer Edgard Varèse.

Busoni was born at Empoli, near Florence. He appeared as a pianist in public at the age of seven, and later studied at Graz and Leipzig. He taught at the Helsinki Conservatory in 1889, at Moscow in 1890 (where he married the Swede Gerda Sjöstrand), and in Boston, USA, 1891–94. He settled in Berlin for good in 1894, but travelled widely as a pianist and during World War I lived first at Bologna as director of the Conservatory and then at Zurich. At Bologna he hoped to influence Italian music, and to prove that he was himself an Italian composer, but was disappointed.

He rejected Wagnerian music-drama, and sought to re-establish links with great composers of the past, notably J S Bach and Mozart, and the commedia dell'arte. His opera *Doktor Faust* was first performed in 1925; missing sketches were located in 1974 and were used for a new edition by Antony Beaumont, which was performed in Bologna in 1985 and at the London Coliseum in 1986. His ideas on aesthetics, especially his *Sketch of a New Aesthetic of Music* 1907, were attacked by conservatives such as Hans Pfitzner.

As a pianist Busoni was considered to have the most powerful individuality and greatest technical mastery since Liszt and Rubinstein. As a composer he is sometimes regarded as a formidable intellect whose works rarely live up to his ambition; he was admired alike by Mahler and Schoenberg (one premiered his *Berceuse élégiaque* 1909, and the other arranged it) but it may be his Italianate pieces which are the most readily accessible.

Works include: STAGE *Die Brautwahl* (1908–11), *Arlecchino* and *Turandot* (1916–17), *Doktor Faust* (1916–24).

ORCHESTRAL violin concerto (1897), piano concerto, with male chorus in finale (1903–04), *Berceuse élégiaque* (1909), *Indianisches Tagebuch*, book two, 'Gesang vom Reigen der Geister' (1915), *Concertino* for clarinet and orchestra (1918), *Sarabande und Cortège*, studies for *Doktor Faust* (1919).

CHAMBER two string quartets (1881, 1887), two violin sonatas (1890, 1898).

PIANO *Elegien*, seven pieces (1907), *Indianisches Tagebuch*, book one (1915), *Fantasia contrappuntistica* (1910, as *Grosse Fuge*; revised 1910 and 1912; version for two pianos 1921), six sonatinas (1910–20). Also editions and arrangements of Bach for piano, including D minor Chaconne.

Büsser, (Paul-) Henri (1872–1973) French conductor and composer. He conducted Debussy's *Pelléas et Mélisande* at its first production in 1902 and made an orchestral version of *Printemps*.

He was a pupil of Widor and Guilmant at the Paris Conservatory, and won the Prix de Rome in 1893. He was successively organist at Saint-Cloud, conductor of the choral class at the Conservatory, and director of Niedermeyer's school. In 1921 he was appointed professor of composition at the conservatory.

Works include: the operas *Daphnis et Chloé* (1897), *Colomba* (after Mérimée), *Les Noces corinthiennes* (1922), *La Pie borgne*, *Le Carrosse du Saint-Sacrement* (Mérimée) (1948); Masses and motets; *Hercule au jardin des Hespérides*,

Suite funambulesque, and other orchestral works; choruses, songs.

Bussotti, Sylvano (1931–) Italian composer. After producing some early works in a relatively traditional style, he turned to a graphical manner of composing, which is influenced by John Cage and attempts to suggest the type of improvisation required. His music can be very poetic and evocative; his chief work is the opera *Lorenzaccio*.

Bussotti was born at Florence. He studied at the Florence Conservatory and with Max Deutsch in Paris. His interests lie equally in painting, music, and the theatre, and his scores often contain either considerable elements of graphic design (as in *Five pieces for David Tudor* 1959) or are 'action scripts' (such as *Le Passion selon Sade* 1969) which outline theatrical action and music.

Works include: the operas *Lorenzaccio* (1972), *Nottetempo* (1976), *La Racine* (1980), *L'Ispirazione* (1988), and *Fedra* (1988); *Torso* for voice and orchestra; *Fragmentations* for harp; *Five piano pieces for David Tudor* (1959); *Pour clavier* for piano; *Pearson Piece* for baritone and piano; cantata *Memoria* (1962); Requiem (1969); *Opus Cygne* for flute and orchestra (1979).

Bustini, Alessandro (1876–1970) Italian composer. He studied at the Accademia di Santa Cecilia in Rome, where he later became professor.

Works include: the operas *Maria Dulcis* (based on a story in Berlioz's *Soirées de l'orchestre*) (Rome, 1902), *La città quadrata*, and *L'incantesimo di Calandrino*; funeral Mass for Victor Emmanuel II; two symphonies (1899, 1909), symphonic poem *Le tentazioni*; two string quartets; sonatas for violin and piano and viola and piano, piano pieces.

Buths, Julius (1851–1920) German pianist and conductor. He worked at Düsseldorf from 1890, and was director of the conservatory there and conductor of the Lower Rhine Festival, where he introduced Edward Elgar's *Dream of Gerontius* in 1901.

Butler, Martin (1960–) English composer. He studied at the Royal College of Music, London and at Princeton, USA, and has attended Luciano Berio's electronic music studio in Florence. His music admits a variety of influences, including jazz.

Works include: *From an Antique Land* for ensemble (1982); *The Flight of Coll* for orchestra (1983); string quartet (1984); *Dance Fragments* for ensemble (1984); *Cavalcade* for orchestra (1985); *The Sirens' Song*, opera (1986); *Tin Pan Ballet* (1986); *Night Machines*

for tape (1987); *To See the Beauties of the Earth* for chorus (1987); *Songs and Dances from a Haunted Place* for string quartet (1988); *Fixed Doubles* (1989) and *O Rio!* (1990) for orchestra; *Jazz Machines* for ensemble (1990); wind quintet (1991); opera *Craig's Progress* (1994).

Butterfly (Puccini). See ◊*Madama Butterfly*.

'Butterfly', or 'Butterfly's Wing' Study nickname sometimes given to Chopin's piano Study in Gb major op. 25 no. 9.

Butterley, Nigel (Henry) (1935–) Australian composer. He studied at New South Wales Conservatory and with Priaulx Rainier in London. His music has progressed from a style influenced by Bartók, Hindemith, and Shostakovich to the avant garde.

Works include: the opera *Lawrence Hargrave Flying Alone* (1988); *Meditations of Thomas Traherne* for orchestra (1968), violin concerto (1970), symphony (1980), *From Sorrowing Earth* for orchestra (1990); three string quartets (1965, 1974, 1979) and clarinet trio (1979).

Butterworth, Arthur (1923–) English composer and conductor. In his compositions he has drawn primarily on local pastoral traditions, although he has also considered 12-note composition.

He was appointed conductor of the Huddersfield Philharmonic Orchestra in 1964.

Works include: three symphonies (1957, 1965, 1975) and an arrangement of Elgar's Introduction and Allegro for brass band (1976).

Butterworth, George (Sainton Kaye) (1885–1916) English composer. He collected folk songs, and cultivated folk dancing and composition, but enlisted on the outbreak of World War I and was killed in action. He suggested the idea for Vaughan Williams's *London Symphony* (1911–13), and the work is dedicated to his memory.

Butterworth was born in London. He was educated at Eton and Oxford, and studied music briefly at the Royal College of Music in London. His songs, *A Shropshire Lad* and *Bredon Hill*, are regarded as among the finest in English music. He was killed at Pozières in the Battle of the Somme, shortly after being awarded the Military Cross.

Works include: Rhapsody *A Shropshire Lad* (1912) and Idyll *The Banks of Green Willow* (1913) for orchestra; *Bredon Hill* (1912); two song cycles on Housman's 'Shropshire Lad'; Sussex folk songs arranged; carols set for chorus; a few other choral pieces and songs.

Buus, Jacques (c. 1500–1565) Flemish composer and organist. He first published some work in France, but went to Italy and in 1541 became organist at St Mark's in Venice, succeeding Baldassare da Imola. He went to Vienna on leave in 1550, but never returned and became organist at the court of Ferdinand I.

Works include: motets, madrigals; French chansons; ricercari for organ.

Buxheimer Orgelbuch large German manuscript of keyboard music (not all of it necessarily for organ) datable c. 1470. It contains mostly ornamented arrangements of sacred and secular vocal works; also several versions of the *Fundamentum organisandi* by Paumann and some liturgical organ music. The upper part is written on a staff of (usually) seven lines, the lower part(s) in letters. In some pieces the use of pedals is indicated.

Buxtehude, Dietrich (1637–1707) Danish composer. In 1668 he was appointed organist at the Marienkirche, Lübeck, Germany, where his fame attracted J S Bach and Handel. He is remembered for his organ works and cantatas, written for his evening concerts (*Abendmusiken*); he also wrote numerous trio sonatas for two violins, viola da gamba, and harpsichord.

From 1668 he was organist of St Mary's Church, Lübeck. From 1673 he gave pre-Christmas *Abendmusiken* at which his vivid and vocally elaborate cantatas were performed, for example *Das neugeborne Kindelein*. His vocal sacred concertos to Latin texts are in a style recalling Venetian models. He was the greatest organ composer of the period preceding J S Bach, who is alleged to have walked 200 miles to hear him play.

Works include: concerted works for chorus and orchestra (*Abendmusiken*); church cantatas, all with German texts, except a sequence of seven, *Membra Jesu nostri* (1680); sonatas for strings; organ music, including chorale preludes; suites for harpsichord.

buysine, or buzine medieval musical instrument, a large horn dating from the 13th century. It originates from a long Saracen trumpet, which survived until the 16th century as a ceremonial instrument.

By an Overgrown Path/Po zarostlém chodníčka work for piano in ten movements by Janáček (1901–11). The movements are titled: 1. Our evenings; 2. A blown-away leaf; 3. Come along with us; 4. The Virgin of Frýdek; 5. They chattered like swallows; 6. One cannot tell; 7. Good night; 8. In anguish; 9. In tears; 10. The little owl continues screeching.

Byrd, William (1543–1623) English composer. His sacred and secular choral music, including over 200 motets and Masses for three, four, and five voices, exemplifies the English polyphonic style.

Probably born in Lincoln, Byrd studied under Thomas ◊Tallis as one of the children of the Chapel Royal in London. He became organist at Lincoln Cathedral in 1563. He married Juliana Birley there in 1568, and was elected a Gentleman of the Chapel Royal in 1569, but continued his duties at Lincoln until 1572, when he became organist of Queen Elizabeth's Chapel Royal jointly with Tallis. In 1575 Queen Elizabeth granted Byrd and Tallis an exclusive licence for printing and selling music and they dedicated to her their *Cantiones sacrae* published that year.

Byrd married for the second time in about 1587. In 1593 he bought Stondon Place near Stapleford-Abbott, Essex, where he remained for the rest of his life, as far as his duties in London would let him. He was frequently involved in litigation and was several times prosecuted for recusancy as a Roman Catholic, but remained in favour with the Queen.

Byrd's popular reputation rests with his three great Masses, in three, four, and five parts, in which his contrapuntal mastery is most fully displayed. Other aspects of his genius are found in the ornate *Cantiones sacrae* and the large body of consort songs and instrumental music.

Works include: three Masses; 17 Latin motets in the *Cantiones sacrae* by Tallis and Byrd; 61 Latin motets in two books of *Cantiones sacrae*; 99 Latin motets in two books of *Gradualia*; about 50 motets in manuscript form; four Anglican services; about 61 anthems; some miscellaneous English church music; *Psalmes, Sonets and Songs* (18 nos.); *Songs of Sundrie Natures* (47 nos.); *Psalmes, Songs and Sonnets* (32 nos.); four separate madrigals (others are in those three books); consort songs, canons; rounds; fantasies for strings, seven *In Nomines* for strings, ten pieces for strings on plainsong tunes, some miscellaneous music for strings; about 100 virginal pieces, among them fantasias, preludes, grounds, variations, pavans, and galliards, and other dances.

Byron, George Gordon (1788–1824) English poet. Hector Berlioz was inspired by *Childe Harold's Pilgrimage* (1812) and *The Corsair* (1814) to write *Harold en Italie* (1834) and the *Corsaire* overture (1831). Giuseppe Verdi wrote his opera *Il Corsaro* in 1848. Schumann wrote incidental music to Byron's play in 1852 and he, Wolf, Mendelssohn, and Busoni set individual poems. Arguably one of the most compelling of all Byron settings is Schoenberg's *Ode to Napoleon* for reciter, string quartet, and piano (1942), which plays on the comparison between Bonaparte and Hitler.

Byzantine chant the name given to the Christian chant of the Greek-speaking Orthodox Church. In 330 Constantine the Great made Byzantium (henceforth Constantinople) capital of the Roman Empire; but only in 527, with the coronation of Justinian I as Emperor, did Byzantine liturgy, art, and music gain supremacy throughout the Empire. Other important dates are 726–843 (the iconoclastic age), 1054 (the final break from Roman Catholicism), and 1453 (the sack of Constantinople by the Turks). During the course of the 11th century the introduction of new hymns was forbidden, and the power of the Byzantine Empire was broken with the establishment of the Latin Empire (1204–61). However, the restoration of the Eastern Empire in 1261 led to a renaissance which lasted for a century, followed by a gradual deterioration until the end of the Empire.

Byzantine music and liturgy were dominated by its hymns, which adorned the Offices rather than the Mass. The *troparion* (later *sticheron*) was an intercalation between the verses of a psalm. The *kontakion* was a sermon in verse, sung after the reading of the Gospel at the Morning Office. At the end of the 7th century it was replaced by the *kanon*, consisting of nine odes of nine stanzas each: each ode had its own melody. Finally acclamations to the Emperor were sung throughout the period; unlike music actually sung in church, these were accompanied by instruments, especially the organ.

Byzantine music, notated in neumes, is based on a system of eight modes (*echoi*), defined by characteristic melodic formulas as well as by tonality. The verse itself is Semitic in origin. The comparative simplicity of earlier and middle Byzantine music gave way, at the end of the period, to a highly embellished style in which the balance between verse and music tended to be destroyed.

C

C the keynote, or tonic, of the scale of C major.

C.A. abbreviation for **col arco**, meaning 'with the bow'.

cabaletta a short aria with repeats which the singer could freely embellish as a display of virtuosity. In the 19th century the term came to be used for the final section of an elaborate aria.

Cabanilles, Juan (Bautista José) (1644–1712) Spanish organist and composer. In 1665 he was appointed organist of Valencia Cathedral, a post he held until his death. He was regarded as one of the great organ composers of his time, writing mostly *tientos*, pieces similar to the ◊ricercare.

Cabezón, Antonio de (1510–1566) Spanish organist and composer. Although blind from early childhood, he studied with Tomás Gómez at Palencia and became chamber organist and harpsichordist to Charles V, remaining at court under Philip II, and accompanying him to England on his marriage to Mary I. He composed music for organ, vihuela, and other instruments.

cabrette (French dialect for *chevrette*, 'she-kid') musical instrument, a variety of ◊musette from the Auvergnat region in France.

caccia, da (Italian 'hunting') suffix used to describe music or instruments associated with the hunt, for example the oboe da caccia, precursor of the ◊cor anglais, and corno da caccia, or hunting horn.

Caccini, Francesca (1587–c. 1640) Italian singer and composer. She was taught by her father, Giulio ◊Caccini.

Works include: the opera *La liberazione di Ruggiero* (1625); ballets *Il ballo delle zigane* (1615) and *Rinaldo innamorato* (after Tasso); sacred and secular cantatas for one and two voices, and other pieces.

Caccini, Giulio (c. 1545–1618) Italian singer, lutenist, and composer. He wrote short vocal pieces in recitative style and sang them to the theorbo, which led to larger essays of the kind, set to scenes by Count Giovanni Bardi, and eventually to Rinuccini's libretto for the opera *Euridice*, first set by Jacopo Peri and immediately afterwards by Caccini in 1602. In 1604–05 he visited Paris with his daughter, Francesca ◊Caccini.

Caccini was born in Tivoli or Rome, and was taken to Florence by Cosimo I de' Medici around 1565. He was successful as a singer there, and became known throughout Italy. He used to attend Count Bardi's salon in Florence, and was credited with the invention of a new style of song, the *stile recitativo*, which developed there. The first mention of Caccini as a composer dates from 1589, when he composed music for the marriage of Grand Duke Ferdinando I. In 1600 he was appointed musical director at the court of the Medici family, and remained in their service until his death.

His two songbooks, *Le nuove musiche*, published in 1602 and 1614, contain pieces for solo voice and figured bass. The first has a preface on the new style of singing and composition adopted by Caccini, and embellishments in the music that were usually improvised are written out in full.

Works include: the operas *Euridice* and *Il rapimento di Cefalo* (both 1602); *Nuove musiche* containing madrigals and arias for voice and continuo.

cachucha (Spanish) an Andalusian dance in quick, energetic 3–4 time.

Cadéac, Pierre (lived 16th century) French composer. He was master of the choirboys at Auch (near Toulouse) in 1556. He composed Masses, motets, and chansons, including

perhaps the 'Je suis désheritée' ascribed to him by the music publisher Pierre Attaingnant in 1539 (but to 'Lupus' by the same publisher in 1533). This famous piece was used as the basis of numerous Masses in the 16th century, including one by Palestrina.

cadence the closing progression of a chord sequence, usually of two chords linked by a note in common. A cadence defines the

Cadence, from Latin cado + 'I fall' Traditional forms are, in the key of C major

(a) perfect (US authentic): dominant to tonic

(b) plagal: subdominant to tonic

(c) imperfect: tonic to dominant:

(d) deceptive (or interrupted): dominant to a chord other than the tonic (usually the submediant or subdominant):

(e) the so-called Phyrigan cadence, where the fall is in the lowest part (this derives it's name from the Phrygian mode):

Apart from these traditional forms any harmonic progression which suggests finality, if only temporarily, is technically a cadence.

completion of a musical sentence in relation to a starting tonality.

A **perfect cadence** (V–I) corresponds to a full close, a **plagal cadence** (IV–I) corresponds to a weak close, and an **imperfect cadence** (I–V) corresponds to a half close. Transitional cadences, including the **interrupted cadence** (V–VI), resolving on a minor chord, and the **Phrygian cadence** are harmonically rhetorical flourishes.

cadence-phrase the final group in the exposition of a sonata movement, leading to the close in a key other than the tonic.

cadenza an unaccompanied exhibition passage in the style of an improvisation, inserted by the soloist at the climax of a concerto movement.

The practice of improvising a cadenza largely ceased around 1780, composers thereafter supplying their own in written form. Recently, however, the practice of the interpreter composing a cadenza has re-emerged, with Stockhausen writing new cadenzas for Haydn and Mozart and Nigel Kennedy recording Beethoven's 1805 *Violin Concerto* with a cadenza of his own devising.

Cadi dupé, Le/The Cadi Duped opera by Gluck (libretto by P R Lemonnier), produced Vienna, Burgtheater, December 1761. The judge wants to divorce his wife Fatima, taking young Zelmira instead. She refuses him, so he takes revenge by engaging her to an apparently destitute man, who turns out to be her lover, Nouradin.

Cadman, Charles Wakefield (1881–1946) US composer. He studied at Pittsburgh and became organist, chorus conductor, and critic there. He explored Native American music and used it in some of his works. After a visit to Europe in 1910 he became organist in Denver, and later settled in Los Angeles.

Works include: the operas *The Garden of Mystery* (1925), *The Land of Misty Water* (1909–12), *The Garden of Death, Shanewis/The Robin Woman* (1918), *A Witch of Salem* (1926), *The Willow Tree*; cantatas for mixed and male voices; *Thunder-bird* suite (1914), *Oriental Rhapsody, Dark Dancers of the Mardi Gras* for orchestra; *American Suite* and *To a Vanishing Race* for string orchestra; string quartet (1917), piano trio; violin and piano sonata, sonata and suite *Omar Khayyám* for piano; songs.

Cadmus et Hermione opera by Lully (libretto by Quinault), produced Paris, Opéra, 27 April 1673. Cadmus loves Hermione, but Mars has promised her to the giant Draco. Cadmus proves his bravery by killing a dragon. After complications introduced by the gods, all ends happily.

Caduta de' giganti, La/The Fall of the Giants opera by Gluck (libretto by F Vanneschi), produced London, King's Theatre, Haymarket, 7 January 1746.

Caffarelli (1710–1783), real name Gaetano Majorano Italian castrato alto. A pupil of N Porpora, he made his operatic debut in Rome, 1726, in Sarro's *Valdemaro*. He sang for Handel in London in 1738, creating the title roles in *Faramondo* and *Serse*.

Cage, John (1912–1992) US composer. His interest in Indian classical music led him to the view that the purpose of music was to change the way people listen. From 1948 he experimented with instruments, graphics, and methods of random selection in an effort to generate a music of pure incident. For example, he used 24 radios, tuned to random stations, in *Imaginary Landscape No 4* (1951). His ideas profoundly influenced late 20th-century aesthetics.

Cage studied briefly with Arnold Schoenberg, also with Henry Cowell, and joined others in reacting against the European music tradition in favour of a freer idiom open to non-Western attitudes. Working in films during the 1930s, Cage assembled and toured a percussion orchestra incorporating ethnic instruments and noisemakers, for which *Double Music* (1941) was composed (with Lou Harrison). He invented the ◊prepared piano, in which different objects are inserted between the strings, altering the tone and the sound produced, to tour as accompanist with the dancer Merce Cunningham, a lifelong collaborator.

Cage was the most prominent pioneer and exponent of such 'experimental' concepts as indeterminacy, chance (◊aleatory music), and silence, his ideas having had a very considerable influence in both the USA and Europe. He worked to reduce the control of the composer over the music, introducing randomness and inexactitude and allowing sounds to 'be themselves'. Influenced by oriental ideas, he attempted to relegate the supremacy of the composer. In a later work, *4 Minutes and 33 Seconds* (1952), the pianist sits at the piano reading a score for that length of time but does not play. He also explored electronic music.

Cage's essays and writings were collected in, for example, *Silence* (1961) and *For the Birds* (1981).

Works include: STAGE *Europeras I–IV* (1987–91), ballet *The Seasons* (1947).

ORCHESTRAL concerto for prepared piano and chamber orchestra (1951); *Etcetera* (1973).

PERCUSSION AND ELECTRONICS *Construction I in Metal* for percussion sextet (1939); *Imaginary Landscape I* for turntables, frequency recordings, muted piano, and cymbal (1939); *Living Room Music* for percussion quartet (1940); *Construction II* and *III* and *Imaginary Landscape II* and *III*, all for percussion ensemble (1940–42); *Imaginary Landscape IV* (March no. 2) for 12 radios, 24 players, and conductor (1951); *Imaginary Landscape V* for tape (1952); *Fontana Mix* for tape or other instruments (1958).

CHAMBER string quartet (1950); *4′ 33″* (no sound intentionally produced, 1952); *HPSCHD* for seven harpsichords, or tape machines; *Cheap Imitation* for violin (1977); 30 pieces for string quartet (1984).

PIANO AND PREPARED PIANO *Sonatas and Interludes* (1946–48); *Music of Changes* (1951); *Water Music* (1952); *One* (1988); *Swinging* (1989).

VOCAL many works, including *Song Books*, *Solos for Voice 3–92* (1970); *Hymns and Variations for 12 amplified voices* (1978); *Litany for the Whale* for two voices (1980).

Ça Ira (French 'It will go on') song of the French Revolution, written by a street singer, Ladré, and set to an existing tune by Bécourt, a drummer of the Paris Opéra.

calando (Italian 'lowering') in musical notation, indicating a progressive softening, as in ◊diminuendo, but also to an extent a progressive slowing down, as in ◊ritardando.

calata an Italian lute dance of the early 16th century, similar to the French *basse danse*. It was written in duple time, but had a triple rhythm of three-bar groups.

Caldara, Antonio (1670–1736) Italian composer. He was a pupil of Giovanni Legrenzi at Venice, and after travelling much and working in Rome and Madrid, he settled in Vienna as vice-conductor under Johann Fux in 1716, writing music for court celebrations there and in Salzburg. He was the first to set many of the libretti of Metastasio.

Works include: about 100 operas and other stage works, including *Ifigenia in Aulide* (1718), *Lucio Papirio, Gianguir* (1724), *Don Chisciotte* (1727), *La pazienza di Socrate con due moglie* (with Reutter, 1731), *Il Demetrio, Sancio Panza, Achille in Sciro* (1736); church music, oratorios, cantatas, madrigals, canons; trio sonatas, quartets, septet.

Caldwell, Sarah (1924–) US conductor and producer. In 1976 she became the first woman conductor at the New York Metropolitan Opera House, conducting *La Traviata*.

She staged her first opera while a student at Tanglewood; founded the Boston Opera Company 1957 and gave the first US performances of *War and Peace, Moses und Aron* (as producer), *Benvenuto Cellini*, and the original versions of *Boris Godunov* and *Don Carlos*. She gave the first US performance of *The Ice Break* in 1979.

caledonica musical instrument, an alto ◊bassoon invented by the Scottish bandmaster Meik around 1820. It was played with a clarinet reed mouthpiece.

Calife de Bagdad, Le opera by Boieldieu (libretto by C G de Saint-Just), produced Paris, Opéra-Comique, 16 September 1800. Isaoun loves Zétulbe, but wants her to love him for himself, not his riches. He courts her in disguise and wins her heart.

calinda, or calenda an African-American dance introduced into the West Indies and later cultivated in the southern USA, originally an African ritual dance accompanied by drums, which remained a feature of its music. Delius makes use of it in *Koanga*.

Calino casturame see ◊Callino casturame.

Calisto, La opera by Cavalli (libretto by G Faustini, after Ovid's *Metamorphoses*), produced Venice, Teatro Sant' Apollinare, 1651; known today in a free realization by Raymond Leppard (Glyndebourne, 26 May 1970), and in editions by Paul Daniel and René Jacobs. Jupiter assumes the identity of Diana in order to seduce soprano Callisto.

Callcott, John Wall (1766–1821) English organist and composer. Having obtained a deputy organist's post, he found time to compose and in 1785 gained three of the four prizes offered by the Catch Club. Two years later he took part in founding the Glee Club. In 1809 he went insane, and died having reached letter P of a music dictionary, feeling unable to proceed further.

The son of a bricklayer, he had no regular music teaching, but picked up much knowledge from Samuel Arnold and Benjamin Cooke. When Haydn came to England, Callcott studied instrumental writing under him, but continued to write glees and catches with great success, and obtained a doctorate from Oxford University in 1800.

Works include: the setting of Joseph Warton's *Ode to Fancy* (1785); anthem for Arnold's funeral; scena on the death of Nelson; a book of psalms edited with Arnold, with some new tunes; numerous glees, catches, and canons.

Callino casturame (probably corruption from Irish 'Cailín ó chois Siúire mé') 'I am a girl from beside the [river] Suir'; a tune mentioned in Shakespeare's *Henry V* (IV. iv) and set by 16th-century composers, including Byrd.

Calm Sea and Prosperous Voyage (Beethoven and Mendelssohn) see ◊*Meeresstille und Glücklicke Fahrt*.

Calvisius, Seth (1556–1615) German scholar and musician. He was cantor of St Thomas's School, Leipzig, and music director of its church from 1594. In addition to writing several learned books on music, he compiled collections of vocal music and composed motets, hymns, and other pieces.

Calzabigi, Raniero da (1714–1795) Italian literary critic and author. From 1762 he collaborated with Gluck in the more dramatically convincing 'reform' operas: *Orfeo ed Euridice* (1762), *Alceste* (1767), and *Paride ed Elena* (1770).

His first libretti were in the dry, formal style of Metastasio. After living in Paris and Vienna for a time, he returned to Italy in the 1770s. His last work, set by Paisiello, returns to his earlier manner.

Cambert, Robert (c. 1628–1677) French composer. His *Pomone* (1671) was the first French opera to be staged in public. Most of his music is lost. He was ousted by Lully and went to live in London in 1673.

He studied harpsichord with Jacques Chambonnières, was organist at the church of Saint-Honoré in Paris, and was appointed musical director at the court of Anne of Austria, mother of Louis XIV. He was associated with the poet Pierre Perrin, who in 1669 had obtained a grant of monopoly for the performance of musical stage works in the French language; their opera *Pomone* was performed in 1671. He also composed the music for Perrin's *Pastorale*, performed at the Château d'Issy in 1659; it was claimed, though erroneously, to be the earliest French comedy in music, or opera. Lully's intrigues transferred Perrin's monopoly into his own hands, and Cambert left Paris to settle in London.

Works include: a comedy with music *La Muette ingrate* (1658); a pastoral performed at Issy and another, *Les Peines et les plaisirs de l'amour* (1671); operas *Ariane, ou Le Mariage de Bacchus, Pomone* (1674); a trio for Brécourt's *Jaloux invisible; airs à boire*.

Cambiale di matrimonio, La/The Marriage Contract, opera by Rossini (libretto by G

Rossi, based on a comedy by C Federici), produced Venice, Teatro San Moisè, 3 November 1810. Rossini's first opera to be performed. Tobias Mill is keen to sell off his daughter Fanny, but young Milfort intervenes.

camera, concerto da, or camera, sonata de (Italian 'chamber concerto or sonata') secular work written for performance at home or at concerts, as distinct from a concerto or sonata; *da chiesa*, 'for the church'.

camerata (Italian 'society') a group of intellectuals meeting for cultural exchanges, in particular one at Florence under Count Giovanni de' Bardi in c. 1573–87 and strongly influenced by Girolamo Mei's research into ancient Greek music. The earliest operas seem to have emerged from their deliberations.

cameriera (Italian 'chambermaid') term used in Italian opera, especially of the 17th and 18th centuries, in the same way as *servetta/servant-girl* is used for soubrette parts.

Cameron, Basil (1884–1975) English conductor. He studied in Berlin 1902–06, and as a conductor in Torquay adopted, but only up to the war, the name Basil Hindenburg in an attempt to negate the usual prejudice against conductors with English names. He was engaged with seaside orchestras 1912–30, then conducted orchestras in San Francisco and Seattle before returning to the UK in 1938. He assisted Wood, then Boult, with the Prom Concerts from 1940; in September 1945 he conducted the first European performance of Arnold Schoenberg's piano concerto.

Camilla, Trionfo di Camilla, opera by Giovanni ◊Bononcini.

Cammarano, Salvatore (1801–1852) Italian librettist. He wrote various stage pieces before the libretto for Donizetti's *Lucia di Lammermoor* in 1835; his other libretti included *Roberto Devereux, Belisario*, and *Poliuto*. His first libretto for Giuseppe Verdi was *Alzira*, in 1841; later *La battaglia di Legnano, Luisa Miller*, and most of *Il Trovatore*. Also wrote the libretti for Pacini's *Saffo* and Mercadante's *La Vestale* and *Medea*.

Campagnoli, Bartolomeo (1751–1827) Italian violinist and composer. After studying with Pietro Nardini, he worked in Italy, Germany, and Paris. He wrote concertos, sonatas, duets, and other pieces for violin; flute music; caprices for viola; also an important work on violin playing, *Metodo per violino*.

Campana Sommersa, La/The Sunken Bell opera by Respighi (libretto by C Guastalla, after G Hauptmann's *Die versunkene Glocke*); 1923–27, first performed Hamburg, 24 November 1928. Bell-maker Enrico falls for the elf Rautendelein, and deserts his wife. At the news of his wife's suicide he rejects Rautendelein, but dies because he cannot live without her.

Campanella, La the third of Liszt's *Études d'exécution transcendante d'après Paganini* for piano, composed 1838, already used by him 1831–32 for the *Grande Fantaisie de bravoure sur la Clochette*. The theme is that of the finale of Paganini's violin concerto in B minor, op. 7, a rondo in which harmonics are combined with a bell.

Campenhout, François van (1779–1848) Belgian tenor and composer. He sang in Belgium, Holland, and France until 1827. During the 1830 revolution he wrote the Belgian national anthem, 'La Brabançonne'.

Works include: the operas *Grotius, Le Passepartout,* and *L'Heureux Mensonge;* church music; choruses; songs.

Campian, Thomas see Thomas ◊Campion.

Campiello, Il/The Square opera by Wolf-Ferrari (libretto by M Ghisalberti, after Goldoni), produced Milan, La Scala, 12 February 1936. A slice of working-class Venetian life.

Campioli (lived 18th century), real name Antonio Gualandi Italian castrato alto. He made his operatic debut in Berlin in 1708, and sang in Handel's operas in London, 1731–32; he sang Argone in the first performance of *Sosarme* (1732).

Campion, Thomas (1567–1620) English poet and musician. He was the author of the critical *Art of English Poesie* 1602 and four books of *Ayres* 1601–17, for which he composed both words and music.

The *Art of English Poesie* is an attack on the use of rhyme and a plea for the adoption of unrhymed metres formed on classical models, such as are used in Campion's own 'Rose-cheeked Laura, Come'. He also wrote *Poemata* 1595, in Latin, containing poems, elegies, and epigrams.

Campion was born in Witham, Essex. Educated at Cambridge and other European universities, he then studied law, but left this profession and practised medicine in London.

He published a first collection of airs to the lute with Philip Rosseter in 1601 and four more followed between about 1613 and 1617, all the words of the songs being his own. He composed masques that are among the best of their kind, and produced many fine lyrics notable for their metrical finish. His songs are verbally delicate, and he composed most of his own settings for them; the balance between the lyrics and the music is sensitive and satisfying. The best known are 'There is a Garden in her Face' and 'My Sweetest Lesbia, Let Us Live and Love', a translation from Catullus.

In 1613 he published a book on counterpoint, and wrote the poetry for *Songs of Mourning* on the death of Prince Henry, set by Coprario. His poem 'Neptune's Empire' was set for chorus and orchestra by Ernest Walker.

Works include: five books of airs to the lute (over 100) and three separate earlier songs; songs for the production of four masques, 1607–13, including *The Mask of Flowers.*

Campioni, Carlo Antonio (1720–1788) Italian composer. He was in the service of the Grand Duke of Tuscany at Florence and the King of Sardinia.

Works include: Requiem and other church music, trio sonatas, duets for two violins and for violin and cello; keyboard music.

Campra, André (1660–1744) French composer. He held various provincial organist's posts and settled in Paris in 1694, when he was appointed music director at Notre-Dame, where his motets soon attracted large congregations. He became equally famous as a stage composer, bringing out about 40 dramatic works which earned him great fame and made a link between the work of Lully and Rameau. After many years of neglect, his works are now being revived and recorded.

He was born at Aix-en-Provence, where he learnt music at the church of Saint-Sauveur. His first stage work was the opera-ballet *L'Europe galante* (1697); his last was the opera, *Achille et Déidamie* (1735).

Works include: the operas and opera-ballets *L'Europe galante* (1697), *Le Carnaval de Venise* (1699), *Hésione, Tancrède, Iphigénie en Tauride* (with Desmarets, 1704), *Alcine, Hippodamie* (1708), *Les Festes vénitiennes, Idoménée* (1712), *Le Jaloux trompé, Achille et Déidamie* (1735), and others; pasticcios *Fragments de Lully* and *Télémaque* (the latter with pieces by Charpentier, Colasse, Desmarets, Marais, and Rebel senior); entertainments *Amaryllis, Les Festes de Corinthe, Le Génie de la Bourgogne, Les Noces de Vénus* (1740), and others; a Mass, cantatas, motets, and psalms.

canary, also canarie or canaries a dance in quick triple time with a dotted rhythm, possibly originating from the Canary Islands.

cancan high-kicking stage dance in fast duple time (2/4) for women (solo or line of dancers), originating in Paris about 1830. The music usually associated with the cancan is the *galop* from Offenbach's *Orphée aux enfers/ Orpheus in the Underworld* (1858).

cancel US term for natural, sharp.

canción Spanish, meaning 'song'.

cancionero Spanish, meaning 'a song-book'.

cancrizans (from Latin *cancer*, 'crab', 'crab-wise') term used for the device of repeating a musical phrase or theme backwards, note for note. 'Canon cancrizans' is a canon in which one part or more proceed normally while another one or more go backwards. In serial music the reversed form of the series is sometimes called cancrizans instead of the more usual *retrograde*.

Candide comic operetta by Bernstein (libretto by L Hellman, after Voltaire), produced Boston, 29 October 1956; revised 1973 and produced New York, City Opera, 13 October 1982. In spite of all the evidence to the contrary, Candide (tenor) believes everything in life is for the best. He eventually decides, after many adventures, that his philosophy was mistaken, and resolves to build a new life.

Canis, Corneille (Cornelis de Hond) (c. 1510/1520–1561) Flemish composer. He was choirmaster of Charles V's imperial chapel in the Netherlands from 1548, and later became chaplain to the Emperor Ferdinand in Prague. He wrote church music, chansons, and other pieces.

Cannabich, (Johann) Christian (1731–1798) German violinist, conductor, and composer. After studying with Johann Stamitz in Mannheim and Niccolò Jommelli in Rome, he became Konzertmeister of the Mannheim orchestra in 1758 and director of instrumental music in 1774. From 1778 he worked in Munich. His conducting was admired by Mozart, who taught Cannabich's daughter Rosa in 1777 and wrote a piano sonata for her.

Works include: operas, ballets, including *Renaud et Armide* (1768), symphonies, chamber music.

Cannon, Philip (1929–   ) English composer. He studied with Imogen Holst and later at the Royal College of Music with Gordon Jacob (composition) and Pierre Tas (violin). This was followed by some study with Hindemith. After a period of lecturing at Sydney University, he returned to the Royal College of Music in 1952.

Works include: three operas; string quartet (1964) and other chamber music, vocal and choral music including *Lord of Light*, oratorio

for soloists, chorus, and orchestra (1980), piano compositions; two symphonies, including *Son of Man*, for the UK's entry to the European Community.

canon an echo form for two or more parts employed in classical music, for example by two solo violins in an orchestral movement by Vivaldi or J S Bach, as a means of generating pace and advertising professional skill.

Canonic variations may also introduce a difference in starting pitch between the voices, creating ambiguities of tonality; the highest expression is the ◊fugue. A cryptic form of canon cultivated as a form of calling card by composers since 1600 requires the same fragment of music to be performed by different players in different clefs and from different viewpoints, for example Schoenberg's 'Legitimation als Canon/Canonic Licence' from the *Three Satires* 1925–26, dedicated to George Bernard Shaw.

cantabile (Italian 'singable') in musical notation, indicating a singing and lyrical style (of playing). It implies a full, rich tone and legato touch.

cantata an extended work for voices, from the Italian, meaning 'sung', as opposed to ◊sonata ('sounded') for instruments. A cantata can be sacred or secular, sometimes uses solo voices, and usually has orchestral accompaniment. The first printed collection of sacred cantata texts dates from 1670.

Cantata Academica work by Britten for soloists, chorus, and orchestra, composed 1959 on Latin texts, for the 500th anniversary of Basel University; first performed Basel, 1 July 1960.

Cantata Misericordium work by Britten for tenor, baritone, small chorus, and chamber orchestra (text by P Wilkinson), composed for the centenary of the International Red Cross, first performed Geneva, 15 September 1963, conductor Ansermet.

Cantata on the Death of the Emperor Joseph II work by Beethoven for soloists, chorus, and orchestra (text by S A Averdonk). The cantata was commissioned from Beethoven in Bonn after the death of the Emperor on 20 February 1790, but was not performed. The manuscript was probably seen by Haydn, on his return from his first visit to England, and led to his offering Beethoven lessons in Vienna. Not performed until 1884, the cantata contains an anticipation of a theme from the last scene of *Fidelio*.

(a) 'standard'

(b) by inversion

(c) by diminution

(a) 'standard'; (b) by inversion; and (c) by diminution. If the imitation is exact the canon is termed 'strict'; if it is modified by the addition or omission of accidentals it is 'free as to intervals'. A canon may proceed (1) by inversion, with one part going up where the other goes down and vice versa (illustration (b)); (2) by augmentation, with one part in notes twice or more the length of the other (illustration (c)); (3) by diminution, with one part in notes half or less the length of the other; (4) by retrograde motion (canon cancrizans), with one part going backwards while the other goes forwards. Various combinations of these forms are also possible. A canon may be accompanied by one or more independent parts. Two or more canons can occur simultaneously.

Cantata Profana, A kilenc csodaszarvas/ The Nine Enchanted Stags work by Bartók for tenor, baritone, chorus, and orchestra, composed 1930, first performed in BBC (British Broadcasting Corporation) concert, 25 May 1934.

Cantelli, Guido (1920–1956) Italian conductor. He quickly made his way in Italy and abroad as a conductor whose gifts were second only to Toscanini's. He conducted the National Broadcasting Company Symphony Orchestra from 1949 and the Philharmonia, London, from 1951.

He studied at the Milan Conservatory and, after escaping from a German prison camp and a Fascist prison hospital in World War II, began to conduct concerts with the Scala orchestra in Milan. He was killed in an air accident.

Canteloube (de Malaret), (Marie) Joseph (1879–1957) French composer. In 1900 he began to collect and study French folk song, particularly of the Auvergne region, of which he published several collections. He is best known for his four volumes of folk-song arrangements *Chants d'Auvergne* 1923–30.

He studied with d'Indy at the Schola Cantorum in Paris, and lectured on French music and folk song from 1923.

Works include: the operas *Le Mas* (1910–13) and *Vercingetorix* (produced 1933); symphonic poems *Vers la princesse lointaine* and *Lauriers*; *Pièces françaises* for piano and orchestra; *Poème* for violin and orchestra; *Dans la* *montagne* for violin and piano; songs with orchestra and with piano; many folk-song arrangements.

Canterbury Pilgrims, The opera by Stanford (libretto by G A à Beckett, after Chaucer), produced London, Drury Lane Theatre, 28 April 1884.

canticle in the Roman Catholic or Anglican liturgies, a hymn or song of praise based on scripture and similar to a psalm, but whose text does not originate in the Book of Psalms. An example of a canticle is the ◊Magnificat of Anglican evensong.

Canticles series of five works by Britten: no. 1 *My beloved is mine* (text by F Quarles), for high voice and piano, first performed Aldeburgh, 1 November 1947; no. 2 *Abraham and Isaac* (text from Chester miracle play), for alto, tenor, and piano, first performed Nottingham, 21 January 1952; no. 3 *Still falls the rain* (text by E Sitwell), for tenor, horn, and piano, first performed London, 28 January 1955; no. 4 *The Journey of the Magi* (text by T S Eliot), for countertenor, tenor, baritone, and piano, first performed Aldeburgh, 26 June 1971; no. 5 *The Death of Narcissus* (text by Eliot), for tenor and harpsichord, first performed Schloss Elmau, 15 January 1975.

Canticum Sacrum (ad honorem Sancti Marci nominis) work by Stravinsky, in honour of St Mark's, Venice, for tenor, baritone, chorus, and orchestra; composed 1955, first performed Venice, 13 September 1956.

Canti di Prigionia/Songs of Captivity work by Dallapiccola for chorus, two pianos, two harps, and percussion (texts by Mary Stuart, Boethius, and Savanarola); composed 1938–41 in protest against Italian fascism, first performed Rome, 11 December 1941.

cantigas (Spanish 'canticles') Spanish sacred songs for single voice of the 13th century, mostly in honour of the Virgin Mary, allied in form to the French *virelai* and the Italian *lauda*.

cantilena a sustained, flowing melodic line, especially when sung *legato* or played in the manner of such singing.

cantillation chanting in unison in the Jewish synagogue service.

cantino the E string of the violin.

cantiones sacrae (Latin 'sacred songs') title often given to collections of Latin motets in the 16th and 17th centuries.

canto (Italian 'song') in instrumental as much as in vocal music, usually the part of a composition which has the chief melody. The direction *marcato il canto* indicates that such a melody is to be emphasized.

canto carnascialesco (Italian 'carnival song') a Florentine part-song of the 15th–16th centuries with secular, often ribald, words, sung in carnival processions.

canto fermo see ◊cantus firmus.

cantometrics influential but controversial analytical system, developed by Alan Lomax and Victor Grauer in the late 1960s for a world-wide study of folk song. Musical factors relating to song style are submitted to statistical analysis and correlated with appropriate social and cultural data, with a view to delineating the role of song in its cultural context.

cantor (Latin *cantare*, 'to sing') in Roman Catholicism and Judaism, the prayer leader and choirmaster, responsible for singing solo parts of the chant. The position can be held by any lay person. In Protestant churches, the music director is known as the cantor.

cantus firmus (Latin 'fixed song') in music, any familiar melody employed in counterpoint as a reference for the invention of an accompanying melody.

In early music, multiple parts were composed one at a time, each referring to the cantus firmus, but not to any other, with sometimes strange harmonic results, for example the final cadence E minor–G major–F major.

Canyons aux étoiles, Des/From the Canyons to the Stars work by Messiaen for piano, horn, and orchestra, composed 1970–74, first performed New York, 20 November 1974.

canzona (Italian 'ballad') 16th-century instrumental form modelled on vocal polyphony, adopted by Frescobaldi, J S Bach, Andrea Gabrieli, and Giovanni Gabrieli.

canzonet (from Italian *canzonetta*, 'little song') light songs written in England round about 1600, either for several voices with or without instruments or for a single voice with lute accompaniment. Later simply a song in England, such as Haydn's English Canzonets.

canzonetta (Italian 'little song') often synonymous with ◊canzona in 16th–17th-century Italy; later a light song or short and simple air in an opera, for example.

canzoniere Italian, meaning 'song-book'.

Cape, Safford (1906–1973) US conductor and musicologist. At Brussels in 1933 he founded the Pro Musica Antiqua, for the performance of medieval and Renaissance music. He made many recordings for the Anthologie Sonore and History of European Music in Sound, and established the European Seminar on Early Music at Bruges and Lisbon in 1961.

Capella, Martianus Minneus Felix (lived 4th–5th centuries) Latin philosopher and writer on the liberal arts, active in Carthage. His De musica, widely read from the 9th century onwards, is the ninth and last book of his De nuptiis Philologiae et Mercurii. His treatise, deriving in part from Varro, had considerable influence on later medieval theorists. It was also largely based on Peri mousikēs by Aristedes Quintillianus, especially as concerns musical terminology, classification, and aesthetics of music.

Capirola, Vincenzo (1474–after 1548) Italian lutenist and composer. His collection of lute music, which dates from about 1517, is among the most important early manuscripts of the repertory.

Caplet, André (1878–1925) French conductor and composer. He was much influenced by Debussy, who allowed him to orchestrate a part of Le Martyre de Saint Sebastien, which Caplet premiered in 1911.
Works include: the symphonic study Le Masque de la Mort rouge (after Poe, 1909); Epiphanie for cello and orchestra (1923); Mass for unaccompanied voices; Le Miroir de Jésus for voices, string quintet, and harp (1924); Le Pie Jésus for voice and organ; Suite persane for ten wind instruments; Conte fantastique (after Poe) for harp and string quartet (an arrangement of Le Masque de la Mort rouge); Sonata de chiesa for violin and organ; children's suite for piano duet; song cycles Prières, La Croix douloureuse, Trois Fables de La Fontaine, Cinq Ballades françaises. He orchestrated Debussy's Children's Corner and conducted the first performance of Le Martyre de Saint Sébastien (1911).

Capriccio opera by Richard Strauss (libretto by C Krauss and the composer), produced Munich, Staatsoper, 28 October 1942. An elegant 'conversation piece' in which composer Flamand and poet Olivier compete for the affections of Countess Madeleine; a deconstructionist opera about opera.
Work by Janáček in four movements for piano left hand and orchestra; composed 1926, first performed Prague, 2 March 1928.
Work by Stravinsky for piano and orchestra; composed 1929, first performed Paris, 6 December 1929, conductor Ansermet.

capriccio (Italian 'caprice') in music, an all-purpose name for a lightweight piece, often in the style of a ◊fugue, combining technical virtuosity with entertainment.

Capriccio espagnol/Spanish Caprice orchestral work by Rimsky-Korsakov, written as a display piece for the St Petersburg Orchestra, finished 4 August and performed St Petersburg, 17 December 1887. It contains brilliant solo parts for most of the principal instruments and for the brass in groups. It was originally intended to be for violin and orchestra, a companion-piece to Rimsky-Korsakov's Russian Fantasy.

Capriccio italien/Italian Caprice orchestral work by Tchaikovsky, composed during a visit to Rome in 1880 and first performed Moscow, 18 December 1880.

Caprichos, Los fantasia for orchestra by Henze; composed 1963, first performed Duisburg, 6 April 1967.

Capuleti e i Montecchi, I/The Capulets and Montagues opera by Bellini (libretto by F Romani, based on Shakespeare's sources for Romeo and Juliet), produced Venice, Teatro La Fenice, 11 March 1830. Juliet romanced by a mezzo Romeo. Bellini's example persuaded Berlioz to set the play as an extended symphony with voices.

Caractacus cantata for solo voices, chorus, and orchestra by Elgar, op. 35 (libretto by H A Acworth), composed in 1898 and produced Leeds Festival, 5 October 1898. Ancient Briton battles the Romans.
Music by Arne for a dramatic poem by W Mason (published 1759), performed London Covent Garden, 6 December 1776.

Carafa (di Colobrano), Michele Enrico (1787–1872) Italian composer. On the failure of his first opera he enlisted in the bodyguard of Murat, then king of Naples, took part in the Russian campaign in 1812 and was decorated by Napoleon, after whose fall he returned to music. He produced operas not only in Italy but in Vienna and Paris, where he settled in 1827 and became very popular. He was professor of composition at the Paris Conservatory, 1840–58.
Works include: about 35 operas, Il fantasma (1805), Il vascello d'occidente, Gabriella di Vergy (1816), Ifigenia, Berenice, Le Solitaire, La Violette (1828), La Fiancée de Lammermoor, and Elisabetta in Derbyshire (after Scott, 1818), Masaniello (competing with Auber's Muette de Portici, 1827), La Prison d'Edimbourg (after Scott's Heart of Midlothian), Jeanne d'Arc (after Schiller, 1821).

Carattaco opera by J C Bach (libretto by G G Bottarelli), performed London, King's Theatre, 14 February 1767.

Cardew, Cornelius (1936–1981) English composer and pianist. He belonged at one time to the avant-garde school, whose ideas are much influenced by John Cage, but he later espoused Marxist principles and published a book, *Stockhausen Serves Imperialism* 1974. In 1969 he founded the Scratch Orchestra for nonperformers, who are free to produce any sounds or no sounds on conventional or improvised instruments. His works have been widely performed in Europe.

Cardew was born at Winchcombe, Gloucestershire. He studied at the Royal Academy of Music with, among others, Howard Ferguson. In 1958 he went to Cologne to study electronic music, also working with Stockhausen until 1960.

Works include: *Octet 1959*; 193-page graphic score *Treatise* (1967); *The Great Learning* (1970); *Autumn 60* for orchestra; *A Bun* for orchestra; *The East is Red* for violin and piano (1972), *The Old and the New* for soprano, chorus, and orchestra (1973); piano music.

Cardillac opera by Hindemith (libretto by F Lion, based on E T A Hoffmann's story *Das Fräulein von Scudéri*), produced Dresden, 9 November 1926; revised version produced Zurich, 20 June 1952. Goldsmith Cardillac murders his clients to recover his handywork. After stabbing his daughter's fiancé, Cardillac reveals he is a murderer and a mob kills him.

Carestini, Giovanni (c. 1705–c. 1760) Italian castrato alto. He first appeared in Rome in 1721, and sang in Handel's operas in London, 1733–35, creating roles in *Arianna in Creta*, *Ariodante*, and *Alcina*.

Carey, Henry (1687–1743) English poet and musician. He wrote the song 'Sally in Our Alley'. 'God Save the King' (both words and music) has also been attributed to him.

Carey was a pupil of Thomas Roseingrave and Francesco Geminiani. He wrote libretti for Lampe's operas *The Dragon of Wantley*, *Margery*, and *Amelia*.

Works include: cantatas and songs to his own words; ballad operas *The Contrivances* (1729), *A Wonder, or the Honest Yorkshireman* (1735), *Nancy, or the Parting Lovers* (1739), and others; songs for Vanbrugh and Cibber's *The Provok'd Husband*.

carillon bell-ringing mechanism in which a manual keyboard, and often pedals, played like an organ, are connected by wires to the beaters of up to 70 static bells. The bells are usually hung in a tower, often in a church. Carillons are found throughout Europe and the USA; mechanized carillons were the forerunners of musical clocks and boxes.

Carissimi, Giacomo (1605–1674) Italian composer. He was chapel master at the church of Sant' Apollinare in Rome, and is famous for his reform of the recitative, and for being practically the inventor of the cantata. He wrote sacred and secular cantatas and motets. His music is distinguished by its pure style and its exquisite melodies, and his followers included the elder Bononcini and Alessandro Scarlatti.

He was born at Marino, near Rome. He was maestro di cappella at Assisi 1628–29; then went to Rome, where he held a similar post at the church of Sant' Apollinare attached to the German College 1630–74. He pioneered the use of expressive solo aria as a commentary on the Latin biblical text. He wrote five oratorios, including *Jephtha* (1650).

Works include: Masses, motets; *Lauda Sion* and *Nisi Dominus* for eight voices; oratorios *History of Job, Baltazar, Abraham and Isaac, Jephtha* (c. 1650), *The Last Judgement, Jonah*; sacred cantatas; vocal duets.

Carlton, Richard (c. 1558–c. 1638) English composer. He was educated at Cambridge, and later became vicar at St Stephen's Church, Norwich, and a minor canon at the cathedral. He published a book of madrigals in 1601 and contributed to *The Triumphes of Oriana*.

carmagnole (from Carmagnola in northern Italy) wild song and dance that accompanied the peasant costume of the same name, from Piedmont and the Midi, worn by southern French revolutionaries to Paris in 1793. The song and dance were very popular with the revolutionaries during the Terror in Paris.

The refrain of each verse was: 'Vive le son, vive le son / Dansons la Carmagnole / Vive le son du canon!'.

Carmen opera by Bizet (libretto by H Meilhac and L Halévy, based on the story by Mérimée), produced Paris, Opéra-Comique, 3 March 1875. Don José caught between gypsy Carmen and original love Micaela. Obsessed by Carmen, who soon rejects him, José turns to crime, eventually killing her outside a bullring.

Carmina Burana medieval Latin verse miscellany compiled from the work of wandering 13th-century scholars and including secular (love songs and drinking songs) as well as religious verse. Carl Orff composed a cantata based on the material in 1937.

Carnaval/Carnival suite of piano pieces on the notes AS (German Es = E flat; also As = A♭) C H (German = B♮) by Schumann, op. 9, the letters representing the only musical ones in Schumann's surname and the town of Asch in Bohemia, the home of Ernestine von Fricken, with whom he was in love in 1834–35, when he wrote the work. She is alluded to in the piece entitled *Estrella*; other persons referred to are Clara Wieck in *Chiarina*, Chopin and Paganini under their own names, and Schumann himself in his two different imaginary characters of *Florestan* and *Eusebius*.

Ballet on Schumann's music, orchestrated by Glazunov and others (choreographed by Fokin), produced Paris, Opéra, 4 June 1910.

Carnaval des animaux, Le/The Carnival of the Animals suite ('grand zoological fantasy') by Saint-Saëns for chamber orchestra with two pianos, privately performed and not intended by the composer to be published. It contains a number of humorous musical allusions.

Carnaval romain, Le/The Roman Carnival concert overture by Berlioz, op. 9, written in 1843 on material from the opera *Benvenuto Cellini* of 1834–38, first performed Paris, 3 February 1844.

Carnegie Hall largest concert hall of New York (seating 3,000), opened 1891.

It is named after the millionaire philanthropist Andrew Carnegie (1835–1919). It has a distinctive rich ◊acoustic.

Carnival concert overture by Dvořák, op. 92, composed 1891 and forming, with *Amid Nature* and *Othello*, a cycle with thematic connections originally called *Nature, Life and Love*.

Suite by Schumann; see ◊*Carnaval*.

carol song that in medieval times was associated with a round dance; today carols are associated with festivals such as Christmas and Easter.

Christmas carols were common as early as the 15th century. The custom of singing carols from house to house, collecting gifts, was called wassailing. Many carols, such as 'God Rest You Merry Gentlemen' and 'The First Noel', date from the 16th century or earlier.

Caron, Philippe Firmin(ius) (fl. 1450–80) Flemish or French composer, much praised by writers of the time. Four of his Masses and nearly 20 chansons survive. He may have had some connection with the Burgundian court,

although it has proved impossible to identify him firmly with any surviving documentation. Called 'Firminius Caron' in Tinctoris's *Liber de Arte Contrapuncti* (1477).

Carpani, Giuseppe (Antonio) (1752–1825) Italian poet and writer on music. He settled in Vienna, and was friend and biographer of Franz Joseph Haydn. His book on the composer was plagiarized by Stendhal.

Carpenter, John Alden (1876–1951) US composer. He learnt music privately and studied with Paine while a student at Harvard University, and (briefly) with Elgar in Rome in 1906, later at Chicago with Bernhard Ziehn. Although a businessman, he composed much in a varied style. *Skyscrapers* features red traffic lights operated by a keyboard.

Works include: the ballets *Krazy-Kat* (produced 1921), *Skyscrapers*, and *The Birthday of the Infanta* (after Wilde, 1919); *Song of Faith* for chorus and orchestra; symphonies, *Adventures in a Perambulator* (1915) and *Sea Drift* (after Whitman) for orchestra; concertino for piano and orchestra, violin concerto; string quartet (1927), piano quintet; many songs including *Gitanjali* cycle (Tagore).

Carr, Benjamin (1768–1831) US composer and publisher. He was the first to publish the song 'Yankee Doodle' in the USA and his ballad opera *The Archers, or Mountaineers of Switzerland* first performed in New York in 1796, is the first US opera of which music parts survive.

Arriving in Philadelphia in 1793, he founded a music publishing business there, becoming known as the Father of Philadelphia Music. He was cofounder of the Musical Fund Society in 1820 and was also active in New York and Baltimore as a publisher, concert promoter, and organist.

Carré work by Stockhausen for four orchestras, four choruses, with four conductors, first performed Hamburg, 28 October 1960.

Carré, Michel (1819–1872) French librettist. He collaborated with Jules Barbier (1822–1901) on texts for most French opera composers of their time. They used works by Shakespeare, Goethe, Molière, and Corneille to provide material to suit the bourgeois tastes of contemporary audiences.

Carrillo, Julián (1875–1965) Mexican composer. He studied at the National Conservatory at Mexico City, won a violin prize, and made further studies at Leipzig and Ghent Conservatories. Returning to Mexico in 1905, he was active as a violinist and conductor as well as a composer. He experimented in his later works with music using small fractional divisions of the scale.

Works include: the operas *Ossian* (1902), *Mexico in 1810* (1909), and *Xulitl* (1920, revised 1947); two Masses, Requiem; six symphonies, (1901–48), three suites, overture *8 de Septiembre*, symphonic poem *Xochimilco* for orchestra; fantasy for piano and orchestra, concerto for flute, violin, and cello; four string quartets, piano quintet, string sextet, four violin and piano sonatas; 40 works in fractional scales, including *Ave Maria* for chorus, *Fantasía Sonido 13* for chamber orchestra, *Preludio a Cristóbal Colón* for soprano and ensemble.

Carrosse du Saint-Sacrement, Le/The Coach of the Holy Sacrament opera by Lord Berners (libretto from Mérimée's play), produced Paris, Théâtre des Champs-Elysées, 24 April 1924. Viceroy of Peru lends his mistress his new carriage.

Carse, Adam (1878–1958) English music scholar and composer. He studied in Germany and at the Royal Academy of Music, London. He was assistant music master at Winchester College 1909–22 and professor at the Royal Academy of Music from 1923. He made a special study of instruments and the orchestra, and left a collection of early wind instruments to the Horniman Museum, London.

Carter, Elliott Cook (1908–   ) US composer. He created intricately structured works in Schoenbergian serial idiom, incorporating 'metrical modulation', an adaptation of standard notation allowing different instruments or groups to remain synchronized while playing at changing speeds. This practice was first employed in his *String Quartet No 1* (1950–51), and to dense effect in *Double Concerto* (1961) for harpsichord and piano. In his eighth decade, his music has shown a new tautness and vitality, as in *Three Occasions for Orchestra* (1986–89).

He was educated at Harvard University, where he studied music with Walter Piston; later he was a pupil of Nadia Boulanger in Paris. From 1960 to 1962 he was professor of composition at Yale University and in 1960 was awarded the Pulitzer Prize. From 1972 he taught at the Juilliard School, New York. Carter's music is many-layered and of extreme rhythmic complexity, sometimes recalling Charles Ives, with cross-rhythms and different rhythms played simultaneously.

Works include: STAGE opera *Tom and Lily* (1934), ballet *Pocahontas* (1939).

ORCHESTRAL symphony no. 1 (1942, first performance 1944), *Holiday Overture* (1944, first performance 1948), *Variations* (1953–55, first performance 1956), piano concerto (1965, first performance 1967), *Concerto for Orchestra* (1969, first performance 1970), *A Symphony of Three Orchestras* (1976, first performance 1977), *Penthode* for chamber orchestra (1985), *Partita* (1993), *Adagio Tenebroso* (1995).

INSTRUMENTAL piano sonata (1946), cello sonata (1948), five string quartets (1951, 1959, 1971, 1986, 1995), *Night Fantasies* for piano (1980), *Triple Duo* for paired instruments: flute/clarinet, violin/cello, piano/percussion (1982), quintet for piano and wind (1992).

SOLO VOCAL *A Mirror on Which to Dwell* for soprano and nine players (six settings of Elizabeth Bishop, 1975), *In Sleep, in Thunder*, song cycle for tenor and 14 players (texts by Robert Lowell, 1981).

Carvalho, João de Sousa (1745–1798) Portuguese composer. He studied at Naples and taught at Lisbon on his return to Portugal.

Works include: 15 Italian operas, including *Perseo* (1779), *Testoride Argonauta* (1780), *Penelope* (1782), *L'Endimione* (1783); Masses and other church music with orchestra; harpsichord sonatas.

Carver, Robert (c. 1490–after 1546) Scottish monk and composer. He was a canon of Scone Abbey. His work was influenced by such major Flemish contemporaries as Josquin des Prés and Henricus Isaac.

Works include: Masses (one in 10 parts), motets (one in 19 parts), and other church music.

Cary, Tristram (Ogilvie) (1925–   ) English composer. He has been a pioneer in the performance of electronic music in Britain and has experimented with the concept of environmental sound; he founded his own electronic studio and was an influential teacher at the Royal College of Music. Appointed dean at Adelaide University in 1982. Works include the cantata *Peccata mundi* (Cheltenham, 1972) and stage and film music.

Casals, Pablo (Pau) (1876–1973) Catalan cellist, composer, and conductor. He was largely self-taught. As a cellist, he was celebrated for his interpretations of J S Bach's unaccompanied suites. He wrote instrumental and choral works, including the Christmas oratorio *The Manger*.

He was an outspoken critic of fascism who openly defied Franco, and a tireless crusader for peace.

Casals was born in Tarragona. His pioneer recordings of Schubert and Beethoven trios 1905, with French violinist Jacques Thibaud and French pianist Alfred Cortot, launched his international career and established the popularity of the cello as a solo instrument, notably the solo suites of J S Bach recorded 1916. In 1919 he founded the Casals Orchestra in Barcelona, which he conducted until leaving Spain 1939 to live in Prades in the French Pyrenees, where he founded an annual music festival. In 1956 he moved to Puerto Rico, where he launched the Casals Festival 1957. He toured extensively in the USA.

Casanova, André (1919–) French composer. He studied the 12-note technique with Leibowitz. His works include trio for flute, viola, and horn, piano pieces, and songs.

Casella, Alfredo (1883–1947) Italian composer. He reacted strongly against the too exclusive and melodramatic operatic tendencies in the Italy of his time and aimed at reviving the classical Italian, predominantly instrumental music. His own work moved from the influence of Debussy and Mahler through atonality and towards neoclassicism. In 1924 he founded, with d'Annunzio and Malipiero, an association for the propagation of modern Italian music.

He was born at Turin, where his father was a teacher at the Liceo. In 1896 he went to the Paris Conservatory to study piano under Diémer and composition under Fauré. From 1912 he directed popular concerts at the Trocadero, Paris. At the start of World War I he went to Rome and taught piano at the Liceo di Santa Cecilia.

Works include: the operas *La donna serpente* (after Gozzi, 1928–31), *La favola d'Orfeo* (1932), *Il deserto tentato*; ballets *Il convento veneziano* and *La giara* (after Pirandello); three symphonies, suite *Italia*, *Elegia eroica*, *Pagine di guerra*, *Introduzione, aria e toccata* (1933), concerto for orchestra; *A notte alta*, *Partita*, and *Scarlattiana* for piano and orchestra; concerto for violin, cello, organ, and orchestra; *Notte di maggio* for voice and orchestra (1914); concerto and five pieces for string quartet and other chamber music; cello and piano sonata; many piano works including sonatina and *Sinfonia, arioso e toccata*; two suites for piano duet; numerous songs.

Caserta, Anthonello (Marotus) da (c. 1365–after 1410) Italian composer. His works include eight French songs, several in the most complex three-voice style of the ars

subtilior, and eight simpler Italian songs, mostly in two voices.

Caserta, Philipottus da (c. 1350–after 1390) Italian composer and theorist. He composed works for the Papal Court of Clement VII (1378–94) and for the Milanese court of Bernabò Visconti (1354–85), and probably taught Johannes Ciconia. His works include one Credo, six French ballades (several in the most complex ars subtilior style), and three treatises on music.

Casken, John (1949–) English composer. His work has been influenced by Polish music and serialism.

He studied at Birmingham University with John Joubert and Peter Dickinson. He was a featured composer at Bath Festival 1980. In 1981 he was appointed lecturer at Durham University.

Works include: the opera *Golem* (1990); piano concerto (1980), *Masque* for oboe, two horns, and strings (1982); *Erin* for double bass and small orchestra (1983), *Orion over Farne* (1984), *Maharal Dreaming* (1989), cello concerto (1991), *Darting the Skiff* for strings (1993); *Kagura* for 13 wind instruments (1973), *Amarantos* for nine players (1978), *Fonteyn Fanfares* for 12 brass instruments; string quartet (1982); *Ligatura* for organ; *Clarion Sea* for brass quintet (1985), piano quintet (1990).

Cassandra opera by Gnecchi (libretto by L Illica), produced Bologna, Teatro Comunale, 5 December 1905. In 1909 the Italian critic Giovanni Tebaldini created a sensation by pointing out that Strauss's *Elektra*, which did not appear until that year, contained passages strikingly resembling Gnecchi's music.

cassation an 18th-century musical term, similar to divertimento and serenade, for a work in several movements suitable for open-air performance. The origin of the word is uncertain.

Casse-Noisette (Tchaikovsky) see ◊*Nutcracker*.

Cassiodorus, Flavius Magnus Aurelius (c. 487–c. 580) Roman senator, ecclesiastical historian, and theologian. He wrote no specifically musical work, but the music theory contained in his *Institutiones* (about 560), deriving largely from Aristoxenus, caused him to be regarded, with Boethius and Isidore of Seville, as one of the three founders of medieval music theory.

castanets Spanish percussion instrument made of two hollowed wooden shells, originally chestnut wood (Spanish *castaña*). They are held in the palm and drummed together by the fingers to produce a rhythmic accompaniment to dance.

Orchestral castanets or 'clappers', mounted on a handle, were employed by silent-film effects musicians to imitate the sound of a galloping horse, hence the phrase 'to run like the clappers'.

Castelnuovo-Tedesco, Mario (1895–1969) Italian composer. He studied at the Instituto Musicale Cherubini at Florence and later with Pizzetti. At the age of 15 he wrote *Cielo di settembre* for piano (later orchestra) and in the 1925 he gained a prize for his opera *La Mandragola* (after Machiavelli). He settled in USA in 1939, at first at Larchmont, New York, and then at Los Angeles.

He was born at Florence. In 1939, being a Jew, he was forced by Mussolini's racial laws to leave Italy and settled in the USA, later becoming a US citizen and establishing himself as a film composer.

Works include: six operas, including *La Mandragola* (1926) and *Bacco in Toscana* (1931); Shakespearean concert overtures, twelve concertos for various instruments, including second guitar concerto (1953); three string quartets (1929, 1948, 1964); sonatas for many instruments; numerous piano pieces, including *Questo fu il carro della morte* (1913); settings of all the songs in Shakespeare's plays (in English) for voice and piano, and other songs.

Castiglioni, Niccolo (1932–   ) Italian composer and pianist. His music is eclectic in style, influenced by Debussy, Messiaen, Webern, and Cage, and remarkable for its frequently delicate textures. He has also pursued a career as a concert pianist.

He studied with Ghedini at the Milan Conservatory.

Works include: *Impromptus I–IV* for orchestra; *Rondels* for orchestra; *Movimento continuato* for piano and small ensemble (1959), *Gymel* for flute and piano; *Inizio di movimento* for piano; *A Solemn Music I* for soprano and chamber orchestra (after Milton, 1963); *Sinfonia* (1969).

Castore e Polluce/Castor and Pollux opera by Vogler (libretto based on one by C I Frugoni), produced Munich, 12 January 1787. Weber wrote variations for piano on an air from it, op. 5.

Castor et Pollux opera by Rameau (libretto by P J J Bernard), produced Paris, Opéra, 24 October 1737; revised version produced June 1754. Based on the Greek myth; Pollux to the rescue of twin brother Castor, with help from Jupiter.

castrato a high male voice of unusual brilliance and power achieved by castration before puberty, regarded as the ideal timbre for heroic roles in opera by composers from Monteverdi to Wagner. Castrati were mainly, but not exclusively, active in 17th- and 18th-century Italy, where they sang soprano and alto parts in theatres and churches. Recordings preserve the voice of Alessandro Moreschi (1858–1922), the last male soprano of the Sistine Chapel.

Castration interrupts the normal growth of the vocal folds in the larynx at puberty, preventing the mature male voice from descending in pitch, while allowing vocal prowess to benefit from adult growth in all other respects.

Catalani, Alfredo (1854–1893) Italian composer. He studied first with his father, an organist, and produced a Mass at the age of 14. He went on to study at the Paris Conservatory from 1871 and later taught at the Milan Conservatory.

Works include: the operas *La Falce* (1875), *Elda* (1880), *Dejanice* (1883), *Edmea*, *Loreley* (1890), and *La Wally* (1892); Mass; symphonic poem *Ero e Leandro*, and other pieces.

Catalogue d'oiseaux piano work by Messiaen in seven books based on his notations of birdsong, composed 1956–58, first performed Paris, 15 April 1959.

catch a part-song, in vogue in England from the early 17th to the 19th centuries, in which the voices follow each other in the manner of a canon or round, with the difference in the most characteristic examples that the words, thus mixed up, acquire new and ludicrous meanings, often of an indecent nature in the 17th century.

Caterina Cornaro opera by Donizetti (libretto by G Sacchero), produced Naples, Teatro San Carlo, 12 January 1844; revived in 1972 with a concert performance in London and a production in Naples. Venetian Caterina loves Gerardo but has been sworn to Lusignano, King of Cyprus. The competing wooers are reconciled when Lusignano saves Gerardo's life.

catgut strings term used to distinguish the strings of musical instruments from those made of metal or artificial material. Although still often so called, they are not made of the bowels of cats but of sheep. In general, they have a mellower sound and generate less volume than metal strings.

catline, also catling, catlin, catleen in 16th-century music, a kind of roped and polished gut string, particularly for low pitches on viols and lutes; by the late 18th century it could refer to any high gut string.

Catone in Utica opera by Vinci (libretto by Metastasio), produced Rome, Teatro delle Dame, 19 January 1728. Marcia, daughter of Cato (ruler of Utica) secretly loves Caesar, but Cato wants her to marry Arbace. When Caesar's armies overrun the Uticans and Cato commits suicide, Marcia is sworn to hatred against Caesar.

Also versions by Hasse (Turin, 1731), Vivaldi (Verona, 1737), J C Bach (Naples, 1761), and Paisiello (Naples, 1789).

'Cat's Fugue, The' popular name for Domenico Scarlatti's G minor harpsichord sonata (no. 30 in Kirkpatrick's list). Its bizarre subject has been taken to represent a cat picking its way along a keyboard. (Experiments suggest that no cat would hit upon this particular succession of intervals.)

Catulli Carmina scenic cantata by Orff (text from poems by Catullus), the second of three works together called *Trionfi* (other two are *Carmina Burana* and *Trionfo di Afrodite*), produced Leipzig, 6 November 1943.

Causton, Thomas (c. 1520–1569) English composer. Gentleman of the Chapel Royal in London. He wrote services, anthems, psalms, and contributed to Day's *Certaine Notes* and *Whole Psalmes*, 1563.

Cavalieri, Emilio de' (c. 1550–1602) Italian composer. He was long in the service of Ferdinando de' Medici at Florence. He was in close touch with the group of professional and amateur musicians known as the camerata, and with them worked towards the evolution of opera; in 1600 he produced *Euridice*, with text by Ottavio Rinuccini and music by Giulio Caccini and Jacopo Peri, the first opera of which the music is extant.

Cavalieri was born in Rome, where he was organist at the Oratorio del Crocifisso 1578–84. In 1589 he oversaw the production of a lavish series of *intermedi* ('interludes'), to celebrate the marriage of Ferdinando to Christine of Lorraine. His own works were still dramatic pieces to be performed in concert form. They include the following, all set to words by Lelio Guidiccioni: *Il satiro, La disperazione di Fileno*, and *Il giuoco della cieca* (all lost), and *La rappresentatione di Anima, et di Corpo*, an allegory produced in 1600 and the first play set throughout to music.

Cavalleria rusticana/Rustic Chivalry opera by Mascagni (libretto by G Menasci and G Targioni-Tozzetti, based on G Verga's play), produced Rome, Teatro Costanzi, 17 May 1890. Turiddu loves Lola, now married to Alfio. Former love Santuzza tells Alfio of the infidelity; Alfio challenges Turiddu to a duel and kills him.

Cavalli, (Pietro) Francesco (1602–1676) Italian composer. He was organist at St Mark's, Venice, and the first to make opera a popular entertainment with such works as *Equisto* (1643) and *Xerxes* (1654), later performed in honour of Louis XIV's wedding in Paris. Twenty-seven of his operas survive.

cavata (Italian 'a thing carved or engraved') in music, a short arioso following a recitative, especially in the early 18th century.

cavatina short operatic aria, consisting of one section without repetition of text, unlike the aria's usually three-part division; for example 'Porgi amor' from Mozart's *Le Nozze di Figaro/The Marriage of Figaro* (1786). Also, an instrumental piece of songlike quality, for example a movement of Beethoven's String Quartet No. 13 (1826).

Cavazzoni, Marco Antonio (c. 1490–c. 1560) Italian composer, father of Girolamo Cavazzoni. The two *ricercari* from his *Recerchari, Motetti, Canzoni* for organ, published in Venice in 1523, are toccatalike pieces designed as preludes to the two motet arrangements; the *Canzoni* are arrangements of French chansons and the forerunners of the Italian instrumental ◊canzone.

Cavendish, Michael (c. 1565–1628) English composer. Born into a noble family, he seems to have held no appointments. He contributed to East's *Whole Booke of Psalmes* in 1592 and published a volume of his own compositions in 1598, dedicated to Lady Arabella Stuart, his second cousin; the volume contained 20 airs to the lute, or with three other voices, and eight madrigals. He also contributed a madrigal to *The Triumphes of Oriana*.

Caverne, La/The Cave opera by Lesueur (libretto by P Dercy, from an episode in Lesage's *Gil Blas*), produced Paris, Théâtre Feydeau, 16 February 1793.

Cazden, Norman (1914–1980) US composer. He studied at Juilliard and with Walter Piston at Harvard. He worked as a pianist with dance groups, and collected folk music.

Works include: *The Lonely Ones*, ballet (1944), symphony (1948), *Songs from the Catskills*, for band (1950), viola concerto (1972); wind quintet (1966) and other chamber music; songs.

C clef the clef, derived from an ornamental letter C, which indicates that the line on

Soprano   Mezzo-soprano   Alto   Tenor

All five C clefs were formerly used; the baritone F clef is often substituted for the last.

which it is placed represents middle C. Only two C clefs are in use today: the alto, for the viola, and the tenor, for the tenor trombone and the upper register of the bassoon, cello, and double bass.

cebell a dance occurring in English 17th-century music, similar to the ◊gavotte.

Cecilia, St (lived 2nd or 3rd century AD) Christian patron saint of music. She was martyred in Rome, and is said to have sung hymns while undergoing torture. Feast day 22 November.

There are many compositions in her honour; for example, Henry Purcell's *Ode on St Cecilia's Day* (1692) and Benjamin Britten's *Hymn to St Cecilia* (1942).

cédez (French imperative 'cede, give, surrender'; 'hold back') in music, a direction used by Debussy and some other French composers to indicate a *ritenuto*.

celesta musical instrument, a keyboard ◊glockenspiel producing high-pitched sounds of glistening purity. It was invented by Auguste Mustel of Paris in 1886 and first used to effect by Tchaikovsky in *The Nutcracker* ballet 1890.

Celestina, La opera by Pedrell (libretto based on an anonymous 15th–16th-century Spanish dialogue novel, *La comedia de Calisto y Melibia*, sometimes attributed to Fernando de Rojas), not produced.

cello common abbreviation for **violoncello**, bass member of the ◊violin family and lowest-pitched member of the string quartet. Its four strings are tuned C2, G2, D3, and A4. In the 17th and 18th centuries a version was made with a fifth string tuned E4. Its solo potential was recognized by J S Bach, and a concerto repertoire extends from Haydn (who also gave the cello a leading role in his string quartets), and Boccherini to Dvořák, Elgar, Britten, Ligeti, and Lukas Foss. The *Bachianas Brasilieras 1* by Villa-Lobos is scored for eight cellos, and Boulez's *Messagesquisse* (1977) for seven cellos.

cellone (Italian 'big cello') modern ◊cello of large size made by Stelzner of Dresden,

capable of being played seated and intended to supply a double bass instrument for chamber music. It has four strings tuned in perfect fifths two octaves below the violin.

Cello Symphony work by Britten for cello and orchestra, op. 68, composed 1963 and performed Moscow, 12 March 1964 by Rostropovich.

Celos aun del ayre matan/Jealousy, even of the air, is deadly opera on the subject of Cephalus and Procris by Juan Hidalgo (libretto by Calderón), produced Madrid, Buen Retiro, 5 December 1660. The first Spanish opera.

cembalo short form of clavicembalo, an accompanying ◊harpsichord, a musical instrument.

Cendrillon/Cinderella opera by Isouard (libretto by C G Etienne, after Perrault), produced Paris, Opéra-Comique, 22 February 1810.

Opera by Massenet (libretto by H Cain, after Perrault), produced Paris, Opéra-Comique, 24 May 1899. Prominence given to Cinderella's father, the hen-pecked Pandolphe.

Cenerentola/Cinderella opera by Wolf-Ferrari (libretto by M Pezzè-Pescolato, after Perrault), produced Venice, Teatro La Fenice, 22 February 1900.

Cenerentola, La, ossia La bontà in trionfo/ Cinderella, or The Triumph of Goodness opera by Rossini (libretto by J Ferretti, based on Etienne's text for Steibelt's opera), produced Rome, Teatro Valle, 25 January 1817. Fairy tale with a Freudian subtext substitutes bracelet for slipper.

cent in acoustics, unit by which musical intervals are measured, a cent being a hundredth part of a semitone in an equal-tempered scale.

Céphale et Procris opera by Grétry (libretto by Marmontel), produced Versailles, at court, 30 December 1773; first Paris performance, Opéra, 2 May 1775. Cephalus tests his wife's fidelity by courting her in disguise.

Cephalus and Procris opera by Araia (libretto, in Russian, by A P Sumarokov), produced St Petersburg, at court, 10 March 1755.

Ce qu'on entend sur la montagne/What is heard on the Mountain symphonic poem by Liszt, based on a poem by Victor Hugo; composed 1848–49, first performed Weimar, February 1850.

Ceremony of Carols, A eleven settings by Britten for treble voices and harp; composed 1942, first performed Norwich, 5 December 1942.

Cererols, Joan (1618–1676) Spanish composer and musician. He joined the monastery at Montserrat as a choirboy, became a novice in 1636, and remained there until his death as director of music. His works are often for double chorus and include a *Missa de batalla*, for 12 voices, two Requiems, a Magnificat, and the antiphon *Alma redemptoris mater*.

Cerha, Friedrich (1926–   ) Austrian composer and violinist. In 1958, with Kurt Schwertsik, he founded Die Reihe, an organization devoted to the performance of new music. His completion of Act 3 of *Lulu* from Berg's short score was performed in Paris in 1979.

He studied musicology at Vienna University and also composition with Alfred Uhl. He became director of the electronic studios of the Vienna Music Academy in 1960.

Works include: *Espressioni Fondamentali* for orchestra; *Relazioni Fragile* for harpsichord and chamber orchestra; *Intersecazioni* for violin and orchestra; *Spiegel I–VII* (1960–68); concerto for violin, cello, and orchestra (1975); *Baal*, opera (1974–79; first performance Salzburg, 1981); *Baal-Gesänge* for baritone and orchestra (1982); concerto for flute, bassoon, and orchestra (1982); *Requiem für Hollensteiner* (1983); *Keintat* for voice and 11 instruments (1983); *Der Rattenfänger*, opera (1987).

Cernohorský, Bohuslav Matěj (1684–1742) Bohemian composer, theorist, and friar. He travelled to Italy, where he was cathedral organist at Padua 1710–15 and at Assisi 1715–20 and 1731–41, and is believed to have taught Tartini and Gluck. He was a highly valued composer of church and organ music, but most of his works were destroyed by fire in 1754.

Certon, Pierre (died 1572) French composer. He was in the Sainte-Chapelle in Paris in 1532, and became choirmaster there before 1542 and chaplain in 1548. As a canon of

Notre-Dame at Melun he founded an annual service there.

Works include: Masses, about 50 motets, psalms, canticles, about 200 chansons.

Cesaris, Johannes (fl. c. 1385–c. 1420) French organist and composer. He is mentioned (with Johannes Carmen and Johannes Tapissier) by Martin le Franc in his poem 'Le Champion des dames' 1441–42, as having 'astonished all Paris' in the recent past. One motet and several chansons survive.

Cesti, (Pietro) Antonio (1623–1669) Italian composer. His work includes church music and sacred cantatas, but it was as an opera composer that he became most famous, his 15 operas being produced at Venice, Lucca, Innsbruck, Florence, and Vienna. *Il pomo d'oro*, first performed at Vienna in 1667, is the most elaborately spectacular baroque opera known to musical history.

After serving as a choirboy at Arezzo he became a Minorite friar in 1637. He was a pupil of Giacomo Carissimi in Rome, and in 1645 was appointed maestro di cappella at Volterra Cathedral. In 1653, having previously become a priest, he entered the service of the court at Innsbruck and remained there, with a brief interval as a tenor in the papal chapel, for 13 years. From 1666 to 1669 he was vice-Kapellmeister in Vienna.

Works include: the operas *L'Orontea* (1649), *Il Cesare amante* (1651), *Alessandro il vincitor di se stesso, L'Argia, La Dori* (1657), *Tito, Nettuno e Fiora festeggianti* (1666), *Il pomo d'oro, Semiramide, Le disgrazie d'Amore* (1667); motets; cantatas.

Chabrier, (Alexis) Emmanuel (1841–1894) French composer. He wrote *España* (1883), an orchestral rhapsody, and the light opera *Le Roi malgré lui/The Reluctant King* (1887). His colourful orchestration inspired Debussy and Ravel.

Born at Ambert, Puy-de-Dome, he studied law and was employed at the Ministry of the Interior, but cultivated music as a gifted amateur. Having produced two operettas in 1877 and 1879, he devoted himself entirely to composition. From 1884 to 1885 he was chorus master at the Château d'Eau theatre, where he assisted Lamoureux to produce two acts of Wagner's *Tristan und Isolde*. He also brought out selections from his opera *Gwendoline* (1885), which was performed as a whole in Brussels in 1886. After the production of *Le Roi malgré lui*, the run of which was interrupted by the fire of 25 May 1887 at the Opéra-Comique, he came under the influence of Wagner.

A colourful and ebullient figure (characteristics which were reflected in his music), Chabrier was one of the most entertaining letter-writers among French composers.

Works include: the operas *Le Roi malgré lui*, *Gwendoline* (1885), and *Briséis* (unfinished, one act performed Paris, 1897); operettas *L'Etoile* and *Une Education manquée* (1879); rhapsody *España* (1883) and *Joyeuse Marche* for orchestra; *La Sulamite* for mezzo, chorus, and orchestra; ten *Pièces pittoresques*, *Habanera* and *Bourrée fantasque*, and other pieces for piano; three *Valses romantiques* for two pianos; songs.

chace (Old French *chasse*; 'chase, hunt') 14th-century term for ◊canon, because the parts 'chase' each other.

chaconne piece of music derived from a dance form, possibly of Spanish origin, in three time, constructed over a ◊ground bass. An example is the aria 'Dido's Lament' from Purcell's opera *Dido and Aeneas* (1689), in which the inevitability of the bass line conveys a sense of Dido's inescapable fate.

chacony see ◊chaconne.

Chadwick, George (Whitefield) (1854–1931) US composer. He studied at Boston, Leipzig, and under Rheinberger in Munich. He returned to the USA in 1880 and became organist at Boston, then professor at the New England Conservatory and its director in 1897.

Works include: the operas *Tabasco* (1894), *Judith*, *The Padrone* (1912), and others; works for chorus and orchestra *The Viking's Last Voyage*, *The Song of the Viking*, *Lovely Rosabelle*, *The Lily Nymph*, *Phoenix expirans*, and others; three symphonies (1882–94), symphonic poems *Cleopatra*, *Aphrodite*, *Angel of Death*, *Tam o'Shanter* (after Burns), overtures *Rip van Winkle*, *Thalia*, *Melpomene*, *Adonis* (after Shelley), *Euterpe*, and others, *Symphonic Sketches*, *Sinfonietta*, *Suite symphonique*; five string quartets (1878–98) piano quintet; songs with orchestra and with piano; piano and organ works; church music, part-songs.

Chagrin, Francis (1905–1972) Anglo-Romanian composer. He studied at Zurich, Bucharest and, with Dukas and Nadia Boulanger, in Paris; later with Seiber in London, where he joined the French section of the BBC (British Broadcasting Corporation) Overseas Service in 1941. In 1943 he founded the Committee for the Promotion of New Music.

Works include: incidental music for Shaw's *Heartbreak House* and Gozzi's *Re cervo*; music for films and broadcasts; Prelude and Fugue and suites for orchestra; two symphonies; piano concerto; chamber music; piano pieces; over 100 songs.

Chailly, Luciano (1920–) Italian composer. He studied in Bologna and Milan, and with Hindemith at Salzburg. He was artistic director at La Scala, Milan, 1968–71, and at the Milan Conservatory from 1969. His style is neoclassical, with some serial and electronic effects.

Works include: the operas *Il canto del cigno* (Bologna, 1957), *Una demanda di matrimonio* (after Chekhov; Milan, 1957), *Procedura penale* (Como, 1959; English translation by A Jacobs as 'Trial by Tea-Party'), *Il Mantello*, 'surrealist opera' (Florence, 1960), and *L'Idiota* (after Dostoevsky, Rome, 1970).

Chalet, Le opera by Adam (libretto by E Scribe and A H J Mélesville), produced Paris, Opéra-Comique, 25 September 1834.

chalumeau short, thickset double-reed wind instrument, ancestor of the ◊clarinet. It is also the term used to describe the dark lowest register of clarinet tone.

chamber music music intended for performance in a small room or chamber, rather than in the concert hall, and usually written for instrumental combinations, played with one instrument to a part, as in the ◊string quartet.

Chamber music developed as an instrumental alternative to earlier music for voices such as the madrigal, which allowed accompanying instruments little freedom for technical display. At first a purely instrumental style, it developed through Haydn and Beethoven into a private and often experimental medium, making unusual demands on players and audiences alike. During the 20th century, the limitations of recording and radio encouraged many composers to scale down their orchestras to chamber proportions, as in Alban Berg's *Chamber Concerto* (1923–25) and Stravinsky's *Agon* (1953–57).

early developments The string quartet of Allegri is believed to be the first example of its kind, while among English composers who wrote 'fantasy trios', or 'fancies', were Byrd and Gibbons. In the 17th and early 18th centuries the harpsichord generally provided a bass line. The chamber sonata with a figured bass accompaniment was established by the great Italian school of violinists – such as Vivaldi and Corelli. From the 18th century, a new type of chamber music was tried out by Haydn, in which members of a string quartet play on equal terms, with no additional keyboard instrument. Haydn also developed the classical ◊sonata form in his chamber music. His quartets influenced those of Mozart, who in turn influenced Haydn's later works. The last quartets of Beethoven show many striking departures from the original classical framework.

later developments In the 19th century chamber music found its way into the concert hall, sometimes taking on a quasi-orchestral quality, even in the work of Brahms. The early 20th-century French school of Impressionists, such as Debussy and Ravel, experimented with chamber music forms, and, during the period which followed, developments such as ◊atonality and ◊polytonality have found expression in chamber music. Twentieth-century composers of chamber music include Berg, Webern, Hindemith, Stravinsky, Prokofiev, Shostakovich, Kodály, Bartók, Ireland, Bliss, Tippett, Rubbra, Copland, and Roy Harris.

chamber opera a type of opera written for few singers without chorus and a small orchestra often consisting entirely of solo instruments. Well-known examples are Strauss's *Ariadne auf Naxos* (1916) and Britten's *The Turn of the Screw* (1954).

chamber orchestra small orchestra, consisting of about 25 players. This was the standard orchestral size until the 19th century, when expanding wind sections, followed by a compensatory increase in the number of string players, increased the proportions to the size of the modern symphony orchestra. During the 20th century the chamber orchestra has once again become fashionable, partly as a reaction against the Romantic legacy of Wagner (which included the use of large-scale instrumental forces), partly as a result of economic conditions, and partly as a result of the ◊authenticity movement and the interest in ◊early music. Famous chamber orchestras include the Academy of St Martin-in-the-Fields and the Orpheus Chamber Orchestra.

chamber organ small ◊organ with one or two manuals (keyboards), suitable for playing figured-bass accompaniments or 18th-century solo concertos.

chamber pitch see ◊Kammerton.

Chamber Symphony title given by Schoenberg to his op. 9 (1906) for 15 solo instruments and arranged by him for orchestra in 1922 and 1935. A second work with the same title was begun 1906 and completed 1939.

Chambonnières, Jacques Champion, Sieur de (c. 1602–1672) French harpsichordist and composer. He was in the service of Louis XIII and XIV, and also worked for a time in

Sweden. He taught several of the later harpsichordists, including Couperin and d'Anglebert, and published two books of harpsichord pieces, illustrating an important stage in the evolution of explicitly noted ornamentation.

Chaminade, Cécile (Louise Stéphanie) (1857–1944) French pianist and composer. She studied with various masters, including Benjamin Godard for composition. She began to compose at the age of eight, and at eighteen gave her first concert. She toured widely in France and England.

Works include: comic opera *La Sévillane;* ballet *Callirhoë* (1888); *Symphonie lyrique* for chorus and orchestra; suites for orchestra; *Concertstück* for piano and orchestra (1896); two piano trios; numerous light piano pieces; songs.

Chandos Anthems twelve anthems by Handel, composed c. 1717–20 for the Earl of Carnarvon, later Duke of Chandos, for performance in his private chapel at Canons near Edgware.

chanson song type common in France and Italy, often based on a folk tune that originated with the ◊troubadours. Josquin ◊des Prés was a chanson composer.

chanson de toile (French 'cloth song') French medieval song which tells its story or performs its actions with reference to a female, not a male, character. Hence the name, which refers to spinning or weaving.

Chansons de Bilitis, Trois songs for voice and piano by Debussy (texts by P Louÿs) composed 1892, first performed Paris, 17 March 1897 (version with orchestra performed Paris, 20 February 1926). Incidental music for two flutes, two harps, and celesta, composed 1900, first performed Paris, 7 February 1901; arranged by Boulez with the addition of a reciter, performed London, 23 March 1965.

Chansons madécasses three songs by Ravel for voice, flute, cello, and piano (texts by E Parny), composed 1925–26, first performed Paris, 13 June 1926.

chant ritual incantation by an individual or group, for confidence or mutual support. Chants can be secular (e.g. football supporters' chants) or religious. Ambrosian and ◊Gregorian chants are forms of ◊plainsong.

Chant du Rossignol, Le symphonic poem in three movements by Stravinsky, based on music from his opera *The Nightingale*, arranged 1917, first performed Geneva, 6 December 1919, conductor Ansermet; ballet version performed Paris, Opéra, 2 February 1920.

chanter the pipe of the ◊bagpipes on which the melody is played.

chanterelle (French 'the singing one') in music, the E string of the violin or (less often) the highest string of any stringed instrument.

chant-fable (French 'song-fable') a 13th-century narrative interspersed with songs.

Chapel Royal in the UK, a group of musicians and clergy serving the English monarch. Dating back at least to 1135, the Chapel Royal fostered many of England's greatest composers, especially prior to the 18th century, when many great musical works were religious in nature. Members of the Chapel Royal have included Tallis, Byrd, and Purcell.

There are chapels royal, in the sense of chapel buildings, at the former royal palaces of St James's, Hampton Court, the Tower of London (St John the Evangelist, and St Peter ad Vincula), and Windsor Castle (with a royal chapel also in Windsor Great Park), and a royal church at Sandringham, Norfolk.

Chaplet, The musical stage entertainment by Boyce (libretto by M Mendez), produced London, Drury Lane Theatre, 2 December 1749.

Char, René (1907–1988) French poet. His works inspired Pierre ◊Boulez (*Le Visage Nuptial*, *Le Soleil des eaux*, *Le Marteau sans maître*).

Charakterstück (German 'character or characteristic piece') a short instrumental piece of music outlining some definite mood, human character, or literary conception.

Charpentier, Gustave (1860–1956) French composer. He went into business at Tourcoing at the age of 15, but a scholarship enabled him to study music at the Lille and Paris Conservatories. At the latter he was a pupil of Massenet, and won the Prix de Rome for his cantata *Didon* in 1887. In 1902 he founded the Conservatoire Populaire Mimi Pinson, providing free instruction in music for working-class girls. His fame rests mainly on his opera about Paris working-class life, *Louise* (1900).

Works include: the operas *Louise* (produced 1900) and *Julien* (1913); cantata *Didon* (1887); symphonic drama for solo voices, chorus, and orchestra, *La Vie du poète* (afterwards used in *Julien*); orchestral suite *Impressions d'Italie* (1889); *Fête du couronnement de la Muse* (later used in *Louise*); *Impressions fausses* (Verlaine) and *Sérénade à Watteau* for voice and orchestra (1896); *Poèmes chantés* and five

poems from Baudelaire's 'Fleurs du mal' for voice and piano.

Charpentier, Marc-Antoine (c. 1645–1704) French composer. He wrote incidental music in Italian style to plays by Molière, including *Le Malade imaginaire/The Hypochondriac* (1673). Later in life, as official composer to the Sainte Chapelle, Paris, he composed sacred music in French style and the opera *Médée* (1693).

Chartreuse de Parme, La/The Carthusian Monastery of Parma opera by Sauguet (libretto by A Lunel, based on Stendhal's novel), produced Paris, Opéra, 16 March 1939.

Chasse, La/The Hunt nickname of Haydn's symphony no. 73, in D major, composed in 1781; also of his string quartet in Bb major, op. 1 no. 1, written c. 1755.

Chasseur maudit, Le/The Accursed Huntsman symphonic poem by Franck, based on a ballad by Bürger, composed 1882. First performed Paris, Société Nationale, 31 March 1883.

Chausson, Ernest (1855–1899) French composer. His early music was influenced by Massenet and Wagner, and includes the symphonic poem *Viviane* (1882); he later turned to 18th-century French musical models. He was a pioneer of cyclic form. A fastidious, perhaps too self-critical artist, Chausson was one of the most important successors in the line of Franck.

Chausson was born in Paris, where he attended the Conservatory for less than a year in 1880 and then became a pupil of Franck until 1883. Of independent means, he never held an official appointment, but helped to found the Société Nationale de Musique and was its secretary 1889–99. He died in a cycling accident, the first person to do so.

Works include: the operas *Le Roi Arthus* (1886–95), *La Légende de Sainte Cécile* (1891), and others; incidental music to Shakespeare's *Tempest*; symphony in Bb major (1890), symphonic poem *Viviane* (1882); *Poème de l'amour et de la mer* for voice and orchestra (1882–90); string quartet (unfinished), concerto for violin and piano with string quartet (1891), piano trio, piano quartet, *Chanson perpétuelle* for voice, string quartet and piano; piano and organ pieces; 10 op. nos. of songs.

Chávez, Carlos Antonio de Padua (1899–1978) Mexican composer and pianist. His music incorporates national and pre-Columbian folk elements, for example *Chapultepec: Republican Overture* (1935). He composed a number of ballets, seven symphonies, and concertos for both violin and piano.

He was taught music as a child by his brother and two casual teachers, but later went to Europe and New York to gain experience. He was founder-director of the Mexico Symphony Orchestra 1928–48 (he later became its conductor), and director of the National Conservatory 1928–34. He held a post in the Department of Fine Arts, and was a leading figure in the cultural life of his country, doing much to explore Mexican folk music.

Works include: the opera *Panfilo and Lauretta* (1953, produced in New York , 1957), ballets *El fuego nuevo*, *Los cuatro soles*, and *Caballos de Vapor/Horse Power*; *Sinfonía de Antígona*, *Sinfonía proletaria*, and *Sinfonía India* for orchestra; concertos for harp and for piano and orchestra; *Energía* for instrumental ensemble *El sol* for chorus and orchestra; three string quartets (1921, 1932, 1944); sonata for four horns; piano pieces.

Checkmate ballet by Bliss (choreographed by N de Valois), produced by Sadler's Wells Ballet, Paris, Théâtre des Champs-Élysées, 15 June 1937; first London performance Sadler's Wells, 5 October 1937.

chef d'attaque the leader of an orchestra, so called because great importance was always attached in France to unanimity of bowing and attack in orchestral string playing.

chekker 14th–16th-century keyboard instrument used in England, France, and Spain. In the latter countries it was called *échiquier*, *exaquir*, and similar names. The instrument is clearly a forerunner of the ◊harpsichord and ◊clavichord.

Chérubin opera (comédie chantée) in three acts by Massenet (libretto by F de Croisset and H Cain, after the play by Croisset), produced Monte Carlo, 14 February 1904; not produced in the USA until 1989 (Santa Fe) and England 1993 (Covent Garden). Seventeen-year-old Chérubin is spoiled for choice but settles for Nina.

Cherubini, Luigi (Carlo Zanobi Salvadore Maria) (1760–1842) Italian composer. His first opera *Quinto Fabio* (1779) was produced at Alessandria. Following his appointment as court composer to King George III of England in 1784, he settled in Paris, where he produced a number of dramatic works including *Médée* (1797), *Les Deux Journées* (1800), and the ballet *Anacréon* (1803). After 1809 he devoted himself largely to church music.

He was born in Florence, where his father was a musician at the Teatro della Pergola. He studied first with his father, then under various masters, notably Alessandro and Bartolomeo Felici. At the age of 16 he had written an oratorio, Masses, and other pieces. About 1778, with a grant from the Grand Duke, he went to study with Giuseppe Sarti at Venice and in 1780 produced his first opera, *Quinto Fabio*. His second opera *Lodoïska* (1791), set in Poland, was a huge success. In London he produced *La finta principessa* (1785) and *Giulio Sabino* (1786), and was appointed composer to George III, but left for Paris in 1786.

After a brief return to Italy he settled permanently in Paris in 1788. There he produced his first French opera, *Démophon* (1788), to a libretto by Marmontel. He soon became very busy conducting and writing operas, though without much success. In 1795 he married Cécile Tourette. In 1806 he produced *Faniska* in Vienna, where it had been specially commissioned, and met Beethoven, who admired his work and whose only opera *Fidelio* was influenced by it. On his return to France he lived, retired and embittered, at the Prince de Chimay's country residence and there wrote church music as well as more operas. In 1815 he composed an overture and a symphony for the Philharmonic Society, London. In 1816 he and Lesueur became attached to the royal chapel with large salaries and in 1822 he became director of the Conservatory, where he often confronted the precocious Berlioz. In 1833 he produced his last work for the theatre, *Ali Baba, ou les Quarante Voleurs*. Henceforward he devoted himself to church music, and his Requiem in D minor (1836) is one of his finest works. In his last years he was affected by depression and unsettled by an uneasy relationship with the authorities.

As a composer, he is, with Gluck, an austere representative of a nobler classical style in French opera; as a teacher his influence was harmful in restricting his pupils by the narrow rules of an earlier age. Beethoven greatly admired him, but Cherubini neither understood nor appreciated Beethoven. Mendelssohn was the only young contemporary whom he openly praised.

Works include: the operas *Armida abbandonata* (1782), *Alessandro nell' Indie*, *Demetrio*, *Ifigenia in Aulide*, *Lodoïska* (French), *Médée* (1797), *Les Deux Journées/The Water Carrier* (1800), *Anacréon, ou L'Amour fugitif* (1803), *Faniska*, *Pimmalione*, *Les Abencérages* (1813), *Bayard à Mézières*, *Ali Baba, ou Les Quarante*

Voleurs (1833); ballet-pantomime *Achille à Scyros*; ten Masses and two coronation Masses, two Requiems (one for male voices) and other choral works; symphony in D major and overture for orchestra; six string quartets (1834–37), string quintet; songs.

chest of viols set of ◊viols (usually six) of various sizes in a cupboard or chest, an article of furniture which was often found in well-to-do English households of the 16th and 17th centuries.

chest voice the lower register of the human voice, the chest being the source of sound production. It contrasts with the higher range available from the ◊head voice. In the 19th century and earlier there was disagreement concerning the precise use of the term, some claiming that only head (high) and chest voices exist, others claiming that a third, middle register is also available. Today there is less concern about these distinctions.

Cheval de bronze, Le/, The Bronze Horse opera by Auber (libretto by E Scribe), produced Paris, Opéra-Comique, 23 March 1835.

Chevreuille, Raymond (1901–1976) Belgian composer. He was mainly self-taught, although he took some courses at the Brussels Conservatory. His works are in a harmonically advanced idiom.

Works include: a chamber opera *Atta Troll* (1952), three ballets; symphony with vocal quartet, *Evasions* for soprano and chamber orchestra, *Saisons* for baritone and chamber orchestra; concerto for three woodwind instruments, cello concerto; six string quartets (1930–45).

Chezy, Wilhelmine (or Helmina) von (1783–1856), born von Klencke German dramatist and novelist. He wrote the libretto of Carl Maria von Weber's *Euryanthe* and Franz Schubert's *Rosamunde.*

chiavette (Italian 'little keys') clefs other than those normal in 16th- and early 17th-century vocal music, used either to avoid leger-lines or to indicate transposition, for example the tenor clef might be used for a bass part, the treble clef for a soprano part, and so on.

Chihara, Paul (1938–) US composer. He studied with Boulanger in Paris and Pepping in Berlin. He taught at University of California, Los Angeles 1966–74, and was composer-in-residence with the San Francisco Ballet from 1980. His music has employed serial and aleatory techniques.

Works include: a viola concerto (1963); string quartet (1965); *Magnificat* (1966); *Red-*

wood for viola and percussion (1967); *Rain Music*, tape collage (1968); *Forest Music* for orchestra, *Ceremony* series for various instrumental groups (I–V, 1971–75); *Missa Carminum* (1976); symphony (1982); *Sequoia* for string quartet and tape (1984); ballets *Mistletoe Bride* (1978) and *The Tempest* (1980).

Child, William (c. 1606–1697) English composer and organist. He was educated at Bristol Cathedral and was appointed one of the organists at St George's Chapel, Windsor in 1632. At the Restoration he received a court appointment and in 1663 received a doctorate from Oxford University.

Works include: about 25 services, about 50 anthems, motet *O bone Jesu*, 20 psalms for three voices with continuo, chants, Magnificat, 'in Gamut', Te Deum and Jubilate and other church music; secular vocal pieces, catches and ayres; two suites of dances for viols.

Childhood of Christ (Berlioz). See ◊*Enfance du Christ.*

Child of our Time, A oratorio by Tippett for soloists, chorus, and orchestra composed 1939–41, inspired by persecution of Jews following assassination of a Nazi envoy in Paris. Tippett's own text includes African-American spirituals; first performed London, 19 March 1944.

Children's Corner a set of piano pieces, with English titles, by Debussy, composed 1906–08, dedicated to his daughter Claude-Emma Debussy (Chouchou): 1. *Doctor Gradus ad Parnassum*; 2. *Jimbo's Lullaby*; 3. *Serenade for the Doll*; 4. *The Snow is Dancing*; 5. *The Little Shepherd*; 6. *Golliwogg's Cake-Walk.* First performed Paris, 18 December 1908; orchestral version by André Caplet performed New York, 1910.

Childs, Barney (1926–) US composer. He studied at Oxford and Stanford Universities, and with Carter and Copland. He was professor of composition at the University of Redlands, California, 1976–92. His music belongs to the avant garde, and allows the performer a large degree of freedom through improvisation and 'self-generating structures'.

Works include: two symphonies (1954, 1956); eight string quartets (1951–74); two violin sonatas (1950, 1956); *Interbalances*, six pieces for various groups (1941–64); *When Lilacs Last in the Dooryard Bloom'd* (after Whitman, for soloists, chorus, and band, 1971); *Couriers of the Crimson Dawn*, for any instruments (1977); *13 Classic Studies for the*

Contrabass (1981); *Sunshine Lunch and Like Matters* for bass clarinet and ensemble (1984); horn octet (1984); concerto for timpani and orchestra (1989).

Chinese block, or temple block percussion instrument in the shape of a hollow wooden box. It produces a dry, rapping sound when struck.

Chinese pavilion musical instrument shaped like a tree or pagoda and hung with brass plates and small bells, shaken to make a jingling noise and used in military bands, especially in the 18th century. It was popularly called 'Jingling Johnny' or 'Turkish Crescent'.

chitarrone (Italian 'big guitar') musical instrument, a long-necked bass lute (archlute) incorporating freely vibrating bass strings which are twice the length (sounding an octave lower) of up to seven double courses of manually stopped strings, used in Renaissance and early Baroque ensembles to provide a firm and resonant bass line.

Chlubna, Osvald (1893–1971) Czech composer. He was a pupil of Janáček and later professor at the Brno Conservatory. He scored the last act of Janáček's *Sarka* (staged 1925) and gave an upbeat ending to *From the House of the Dead* (1930).

Works include: the operas *Catullus's Vengeance* (1917), *Alladine and Palomides* (after Maeterlinck) (1922), *Nura* and *The Day of Beginning*; cantatas *Lord's Prayer*, *Minstrel's Child* and others; *Symphony of Life and Love*, symphonic poems *Dreams*, *Before I Go Dumb*, *Two Fairy Tales*, *Song of my Longing*; overture *Fairy Land*, two suites for orchestra; *Sinfonietta* for chamber orchestra; five string quartets, piano music, songs.

choir body of singers, usually of sacred music, of more than one voice to a part, whose members are able to sight read music and hold a melody. A traditional cathedral choir of male voices is required to sing responses, hymns, and psalms appropriate to the church calendar.

The choir was the principal medium for the development of Renaissance polyphony, with instruments initially reading from vocal parts and only subsequently evolving distinct instrumental styles. The Venetian antiphonal style of Monteverdi and Gabrieli treats voices and instruments as opposing choirs. During the 19th century choir festivals became a popular feature of musical life, promoting mixed-voice choral singing by amateur groups.

choir organ third manual (keyboard) of an ◊organ, characterized by quiet stops and pipes appropriate for accompanying a church choir. Often the pipes of the choir organ are housed separately from the rest, located behind the organist's back instead of being grouped together with the other pipes, usually in front of and above the player.

It was formerly often a small instrument set apart from the principal organ in a church, and used separately to accompany the choir.

Chopin, Frédéric François (1810–1849) Polish composer and pianist. He made his debut as a pianist at the age of eight. As a performer, Chopin revolutionized the technique of pianoforte-playing, turning the hands outward and favouring a light, responsive touch. His compositions for piano, which include two concertos and other works with orchestra, are characterized by great volatility of mood, and rhythmic fluidity.

From 1831 he lived in Paris, where he became known in the fashionable salons, although he rarely performed in public. In 1836 the composer Liszt introduced him to George Sand (Madame Dudevant), with whom he had a close relationship 1838–46. During this time she nursed him in Mallorca for tuberculosis, while he composed intensively and for a time regained his health. His music was used as the basis of the ballet *Les Sylphides* by Fokine 1909 and orchestrated by Alexander Gretchaninov (1864–1956), a pupil of Rimsky-Korsakov.

Chopin's father was professor of French at Warsaw. Chopin began piano lessons at the age of six, played at a musical evening aged seven (when he first published a work, a Polonaise in G minor), and in public at eight. From 1822 he took composition lessons with Józef Elsner, and made great progress in composition and improvisation. He left the Warsaw Conservatory in 1827 and played in Vienna in 1829. On his return he fell in love with the singer Konstancja Gładkowska, who appeared at the third of his public concerts in 1830; but he left Poland that year, playing in Vienna and Munich and visiting Stuttgart, where he heard of the taking of Warsaw by the Russians during the November Uprising. He went to Paris in October 1831 and decided to remain there. He appeared frequently in public and gave private lessons, especially in French and Polish aristocratic circles.

He met Maria Wodzińska at Dresden in 1835 and at Marienbad in 1836; they fell in love and became secretly engaged, but the engagement was broken off by her family. In

1838 he visited George Sand at Nohant, where she held house parties in the summer. Most summers were spent at Nohant until 1847, when a family quarrel between Sand and her children led to one with Chopin and they parted. The last ten years of his life were a continual struggle against illness, and he gave his last public concert in February 1848, but continued to teach and play at private houses. His pupil Jane Stirling took him to Scotland in August 1848 for a rest at the country house of her brother-in-law, Lord Torphichen. Chopin afterwards played at Manchester, Glasgow, and Edinburgh, and went to London in November. In January 1849 he was back in Paris in a critical state of health and finance, but was supported by wealthy friends until his death.

Chopin's music, written almost exclusively for solo piano, was (along with Liszt's) the most important of the 19th century in the development and perfection of a Romantic style. It is entirely original, with an apparent melodic simplicity that usually masks a variety of more complex undercurrents of harmony and rhythm. He was among the first to use the thumb freely on black keys. Many of his pieces, with eerie or echo effects or fairylike accompaniments, depend for their adequate rendering on the use of a particularly subtle kind of finger technique and pedalling, and are a good test of the varied resources of the skilled pianist.

Works include: two concertos in E minor and F minor (1829–30); four other works with orchestra including *Andante Spianato* (1834); 50 Mazurkas in 13 sets (1830–49), 27 Studies, 26 Preludes (24 in all keys), op. 28 (1836–39), 19 Nocturnes, 14 Waltzes (1827–41), 16 Polonaises, 4 Ballades in G minor, F, A♭, F minor (1831–42), 4 Impromptus, 4 Scherzos in B minor, B♭ minor, C♯ minor, E (1831–39), three Rondos, three sonatas in C minor (1828), B♭ minor (1839), B minor (1844), *Barcarolle* in F♯, *Berceuse*, *Bolero*, Fantasy in F minor, *Tarantella* and other miscellaneous piano pieces; piano trio (1829); cello and piano sonata (1832).

Chopsticks a childish little waltz played on the piano by children with the forefingers of each hand, to which the name refers by analogy with the two sticks with which the Chinese eat their food.

'Chopsticks' Variations a set of variations for piano (three hands, the second player playing a variant in 2–4 time of the above with one hand) by Borodin, Cui, Liadov, and Rimsky-Korsakov, written before 1880, when a second edition appeared and Liszt contributed a new variation of his own.

Choral (English 'chorale') Lutheran hymn. The German word was originally used to mean the choral parts of Latin chant, and by extension plainsong in general, a meaning which it still bears today. At the Reformation it took on the secondary meaning of the monophonic congregational singing of the Lutheran liturgy, many of the melodies being adaptations from the plainsong itself; hence the term *Choralbearbeitung/chorale arrangement* to denote any kind of setting of such melodies. The English word is simply an adaptation of the German in its Lutheran sense, the final 'e' being added to make the pronunciation clear and to avoid confusion with the adjective 'choral'.

chorale traditional hymn tune of the German Protestant Church; see ◊Choral.

chorale cantata term used for a form of church cantata, especially by Bach, which draws on the text and, usually, music of a Lutheran hymn. The chorale words and melody may (rarely) be present in each movement of the cantata (in *Christ lag in Todesbanden*), or some verses may be replaced by free paraphrases of the text or completely new material set as recitatives or arias. Treatment varies from the simple harmonizations found as the last movement of many cantatas to the complexity of the massive fantasia-like chorus which opens *Ein' feste Burg*.

chorale fantasy a type of organ composition in which a hymn tune is freely treated.

choral prelude a type of organ piece for church use by Bach; introducing the tune of the hymn about to be sung by the congregation and artistically elaborating it by contrapuntal treatment or by the provision of an original accompaniment.

'Choral Symphony' popular name for Beethoven's ninth symphony in D minor, op. 125, on account of its last movement, a setting of Schiller's ode *An die Freude/To Joy* for solo quartet, chorus, and orchestra. Composed c. 1817–24, first performed Vienna, 7 May 1824.

chord a group of three or more notes sounded together. The resulting combination of tones may be either harmonious or dissonant.

chording a term used to designate either the spacing of the notes in a chord in composition or the performance of them strictly in tune in relation to each other.

chordophone one of the four main classes of musical instrument used in the original ◊Sachs-Hornbostel system, the others being ◊idiophone, ◊aerophone, and ◊membranophone. In this class of instruments, the sound emanates from the vibration of a string stretched between fixed points. Thus violins and lutes are chordophones.

Chorley, Henry F(othergill) (1808–1872) English music critic, librettist, and author. He contributed to the *Athenaeum* from 1830.

Choron, Alexandre (Etienne) (1771–1834) French music scholar and composer. Among his books are a music encyclopedia and treatises on music study, part-writing, and plainsong.

Works include: a Mass, a *Stabat Mater*, psalms, hymns.

Chorton (German 'choir-pitch') the pitch to which church organs in Germany were tuned in the 17th–18th centuries. It was higher, usually by a whole tone, than *Kammerton* ('chamber pitch'), and it is for this reason that Bach transposed the woodwind parts in his cantatas up, or alternatively transposed the organ parts down. The strings could, as necessary, play at either pitch.

chorus body of usually untrained male and female singers of secular unison songs, or providing the refrain element of solo verse song. A stage chorus in opera or musicals is normally a trained body of singers providing a dispersed accompaniment in four or more parts to principal soloists.

Chout/The Buffoon ballet in six scenes, op. 21, by Prokofiev (scenario by the composer, from a story by A Afansyev), composed 1915, revised 1920; produced Paris, Ballets Russes, 17 May 1921. Symphonic Suite from the ballet arranged 1920, first performed Brussels, 15 January 1924.

Chou Wen-chung (1923–) Chinese-born US composer. His music reflects oriental and avant-garde influences and includes *Nocturnal*, editions of *Ameriques* (1972), and *Octandre* (1980). He was appointed professor at Columbia University in 1972.

He studied in the USA from 1946, at first with Slonimsky and Luening, and with Varèse 1949–54.

Works include: *Landscapes* for orchestra (1949); *Metaphors* for wind orchestra (1961); *Pien* for piano, percussion, and wind (1966); *Beijing in the Mist* for chamber ensemble (1986); *Echoes from the Gorge* for percussion quartet (1989); *Windswept Peaks* for violin,

cello, clarinet, and piano (1990) choral and piano works, film music.

Christelflein, Das opera by Pfitzner (libretto by I von Stach and the composer), produced Munich, 11 December 1906, conductor Mottl. A dying girl gets her Christmas tree before an elf takes her to heaven.

Christmas Concerto Corelli's Concerto grosso, op. 6. no. 8.

Christmas Eve/Notch Pered Rozhdestvom opera by Rimsky-Korsakov (libretto by the composer, based on Gogol's story), produced St Petersburg, 10 December 1895.
See also ◊*Vakula the Smith*.

Christmas Oratorio a series of six cantatas by Bach (1734) designed for separate performance between Christmas and Epiphany. Not originally intended for performance as one composite work.

Christmas Symphony (Haydn) see ◊*Lamentatione*.

Christophe Colomb opera by Milhaud (libretto by P Claudel), produced in Germany, Berlin, Staatsoper, 5 May 1930, conductor Kleiber. The work makes use of film. In the final scene, Queen Isabella rides to heaven on a mule provided by Columbus.

Christophorus, oder Die Vision einer Oper opera by Schreker (libretto by the composer), composed 1925–29 but the original production was banned by the Nazis; first performed Freiburg, 1 October 1978. A student attempts to write an opera based on the life of St Christopher, but the characters of the legend become confused with his own friends.

Christus oratorio by Liszt (words from the Bible and the Roman Catholic liturgy), composed 1855–66, first performed Weimar, 29 May 1873.

Oratorio by Mendelssohn (words by Chevalier Bunsen), began 1844, resumed 1847, but left unfinished.

Christus am Oelberg/Christ at the Mount of Olives oratorio by Beethoven, op. 85 (libretto by F X Huber), produced Vienna, 5 April 1803.

chromatic (from Greek chrōmatikos, 'coloured') scale proceeding entirely by semitones, that is, taking in all the notes available in traditional Western music. Chromatic harmony consists of chords using notes not included in the scale of the prevailing key and thus, in notation, involving the use of many accidentals.

Chromatic Fantasy and Fugue a keyboard work in D minor by Bach, written c. 1720,

An ascending and descending chromatic scale beginning on C.

revised c. 1730. The adjective refers to the harmonies of the fantasy and the subject of the fugue.

chromatic harp French ◊harp which has strings for all the notes of the chromatic scale. They are not all strung parallel, but are slightly crossed, so that except where they actually intersect they stand away from each other in two ranges, one representing the diatonic scale of C major, the other the sharps or flats, like the white and black notes on the piano.

The normal harp has strings tuned to the scale of C♭ major, but each string can be raised in pitch by a semitone or a whole tone with the aid of pedals.

chromaticism the use of enriched harmonies for added expression, practised by 19th-century composers mainly of French and Russian schools, for example Rimsky-Korsakov, Skriabin, Debussy, Ravel, Messiaen, Honegger, and Dutilleux.

Chromatic harmonies are ambiguous consonances rather than expressionist dissonances, influenced by the sounds of music imported from Indonesia and Japan and heard, for example, at the Paris Exposition 1889, which influenced Debussy. Chromaticism is associated with the introduction of new timbres to the symphony orchestra including the celesta, glockenspiel, and xylophone.

chromatic madrigal 1. madrigal making free use of chromatic harmony; 2. in 16th-century Italy, *a madrigale cromatico* was one using black notes as the basis of measurement and hence moving at a brisk speed.

chromatic scale musical scale proceeding by semitones. In theory the inclusion of all 12 notes makes it a neutral scale without the focus provided by the seven-tone diatonic major or minor scale; in practice however, owing to small deviations from equal temperament, it is possible for a trained ear to identify the starting point of a randomly chosen chromatic scale.

Chronochromie/Time-colour work for orchestra in seven sections by Messiaen; composed 1960, first performed Donaueschingen, 16 October 1960, conductor Rosbaud.

Chrysander, (Karl Franz) Friedrich (1826–1901) German music scholar and editor. He lived in England for some time, researching material for his great biography of Handel, which was published 1858–67, though never completed. He also edited Handel's complete works. Other works of his on old music are valuable, but he was violently opposed to all of what he called 'modern' music (that is, music written after the time of Handel).

church mode, or authentic mode in music, one of eight modes or scales developed by the medieval church, centring on the notes D, E, F, or G, and using the notes of the C major scale. See ◊mode.

Chute de la Maison Usher, La/The Fall of the House of Usher opera by Debussy (libretto by himself, based on E A Poe's story), worked at between 1908 and 1918, but never completed. Realizations of Debussy's fragments were performed at Yale University and Frankfurt, 1977.

ciaccona Italian spelling of ◊chaconne, a piece of music.

Ciconia, Johannes (c. 1335 or c. 1373–1411 or 1412) Liègeois composer and music theorist. His only clearly documented activity is as choirmaster at Padua Cathedral from about 1401, though another man of the same name was born about 1335 and was active earlier in Avignon. He was perhaps the most important and influential composer of his generation. His works include Mass movements, motets, and secular works in both French and Italian. There is also a treatise, *Nova musica*.

He began to study music around 1385, as a choirboy at Saint-Jean l'Evangeliste, Liège. Before 1400 he went to Padua where he became choirmaster and a canon at the cathedral, posts which he retained until his death. His motets show an advanced approach to imitation; some of them are ceremonial works, and date largely from the time he spent in Padua. They include two isorhythmic pieces in honour of the city's bishop.

Cid, Der opera by Cornelius (libretto by composer, based on Corneille's drama), produced Weimar, 21 May 1865.

Cid, Le opera by Massenet (libretto by A P d'Ennery, L Gallet, and E Blau, based on Corneille's drama), produced Paris, Opéra, 30 November 1885. Chimène loves Rodrigue; when Rodrigue's father is appointed guardian to the king's son, Chimène's father insults Rodrigue, who then kills him in a duel. Chimène seeks revenge against Rodrigue, but forgives him after he has saved Spain in battle.

Cilea, Francesco (1866–1950) Italian composer. He produced his first opera in 1889, while still a student at Naples Conservatory. The publisher Sonzogno then commissioned a second, which was produced at Florence in 1892. Cilea was professor at the Reale Instituto Musicale, Florence, 1896–1904.

Works include: the operas *Gina* (1889), *La Tilda*, *L'Arlesiana* (after Daudet), *Adriana Lecouvreur* (after Scribe, 1902), *Gloria*; cello and piano sonata; numerous piano works.

Cimadoro, Giovanni Battista (1761–1805) Italian composer. He successfully produced the dramatic works *Ati e Cibeli* (1789), *Il ratto di Proserpina* (Venice, 1791), and 'scena lyrica' *Pimmalione* in Italy, but settled in London 1791. Other works include concerto for double bass and vocal pieces.

Cimarosa, Domenico (1749–1801) Italian composer. He wrote more than 60 operas, including the witty *Il matrimonio segreto/The Secret Marriage* (1792). He also wrote orchestral and keyboard music.

He studied at Naples, where his masters included Sacchini and Piccinni, and produced his first opera there in 1772. Later he lived by turns in Rome and Naples, became famous with several operas, travelled much, and in 1787 went to the court of Catherine II at St Petersburg, Russia. In 1791 the Emperor Leopold II invited him to Vienna to succeed Antonio Salieri as court Kapellmeister. There he produced his most successful opera, *Il matrimonio segreto* (1792), based on *The Clandestine Marriage* by Colman and Garrick; it was encored in its entirety at its premiere. His engagement in Vienna ended the same year, when, on the death of Leopold, Salieri was reappointed. Cimarosa returned to Naples, where he became maestro di cappella to the

king. He was imprisoned because of his involvement in the Neapolitan rising of 1799. On his release he set out for St Petersburg, but died at Venice on the way, allegedly by poison.

Works include: over 60 operas, including *Le stravaganze del conte*, *L'Italiana in Londra* (1779), *Il pittore parigino*, *La ballerina amante* (1782), *L'Olimpiade*, *Artaserse* (1784), *L'impresario in augustie*, *Cleopatra* (1789), *Idalide*, *Il matrimonio segreto*, *Le astuzie femminili* (1794), *Il marito disperato*, *L'impegno superato*, *Gli Orazi ed i Curiazi*, *Penelope* (1795), *Achille all' assedio di Troia*; Masses, oratorios, cantatas.

Cimarrón, El work by Henze for baritone, flute, guitar, and percussion (text from *The Autobiography of a Runaway Slave*, by E Montejo), first performed Aldeburgh, 22 June 1970.

cimbalom musical instrument, a Hungarian pedestal ◊dulcimer modernized during the 19th century from a gypsy instrument. It consists of a box-shaped resonator over which strings are stretched laterally, the performer playing front to back rather than across, using light beaters. The sound is brittle, not unlike a ◊fortepiano. Composers include Stravinsky in *Renard* (1922) and Kodály in the orchestral suite *Háry János* (1927).

Cinderella see ◊Cendrillon and ◊Cenerentola.

Cinesi, Le/The Chinese Ladies opera by Caldara (libretto by Metastasio), produced Vienna, at court, Carnival 1735. Four friends while away the time acting out legends.

Opera by Gluck (libretto ditto), produced Schlosshof, near Vienna, at court, 24 September 1754.

cinquepace (from French cinq pas, 'five steps'; also colloqial 'sink-a-pace') a dance of the 16th century in quick 3–4 time and requiring movements in groups of five paces. The name was used both for the galliard following the pavane and for the tordion concluding the basse danse. Shakespeare makes a pun on it in *Much Ado about Nothing*.

ciphering the escape of sound from organ pipes by a fault in or damage to the mechanism.

Circassian Bride, The opera by Bishop (libretto by C Ward), produced London, Drury Lane Theatre, 23 February 1809.

Circe and Penelope two parts of a cyclic opera, *Ulysses*, by Keiser (libretto by F C Bressand), produced Brunswick, February 1696.

circular canon a canon whose tune, instead of coming to an end, returns to the beginning and may be repeated *ad infinitum*. The round, *Three blind mice*, is a familiar example.

Circus Polka work for piano by Stravinsky, to accompany the elephants in the Ringling Bros' circus; scored for wind band by D Raksin, 1942; arranged by the composer for orchestra, first performed Cambridge, Massachusetts, 13 January 1944.

Ciro in Babilonia, o sia La caduta di Baldassarre/Cyrus in Babylon or The Fall of Belshazzar opera by Rossini (libretto by F Aventi), produced Ferrara, 14 March 1812. Belshazzar is 'found wanting' Amira, wife of King Cyrus, who has been defeated by the Babylonians. Cyrus faces execution, but his fate improves when his forces counterattack.

cithara ancient musical instrument resembling a lyre but with a flat back. It was strung with wire and plucked with a plectrum or (after the 16th century) with the fingers. The bandurria and laud, still popular in Spain, are instruments of the same type.

citole medieval plucked musical instrument, related to the ◊cittern and once confused with the gittern by music historians. It became obsolete in the late 14th century.

cittern plucked stringed instrument, usually almond shaped, with a flat back and a fretted fingerboard. It originated about 1500, is easy to play, and was a popular alternative to the lute. Larger forms include the bandurria and the orpharion. It was superseded in the 19th century by the guitar.

The cittern usually had four pairs of wire strings tuned in either of two ways.

Clapp, Philip Greeley (1888–1954) US composer. After graduating from Harvard University he studied with Max von Schillings at Stuttgart, and in London. Following several academic appointments he became professor of music at the University of Iowa.

Works include: cantata *A Chant of Darkness* (H Keller); 12 symphonies (1908–44), piano concerto in B minor, *Fantasy on an Old*

Plainchant for cello and orchestra, *Dramatic Poem* for trombone and orchestra; songs with orchestra; string quartet and other pieces.

clarinet any of a family of single-reed woodwind instruments of cylindrical bore. The clarinet did not establish itself in the orchestra until after the middle of the 18th century. In their concertos for clarinet, Mozart and Weber exploited the instrument's range of tone from the dark low register rising to brilliance, and its capacity for sustained dynamic control. The ability of the clarinet both to blend and to contrast with other instruments makes it popular for chamber music and as a solo instrument. It is also heard in military and concert bands and as a jazz instrument.

The clarinet was developed from the double-reed chalumeau by German instrument maker J C Denner about 1700 and was occasionally used in the Baroque orchestra as an instrument of trumpetlike tone. In the 19th century Theobald Boehm made the essential modifications producing the modern chromatic instrument, revealed by Berlioz as having a raucous and strident side to its character in the final 'Witches' Sabbath' movement of the *Symphonie fantastique/Fantastic Symphony* (1830). A broad range of clarinets remain in current use, including soprano B♭ and A (standard orchestral clarinets), alto F (military band), B♭ bass, piccolo E♭ and D, and sinuous contrabasses in E♭ and B♭, the latter sounding two octaves lower than the soprano B♭, and virtually inaudible on its own.

The sounding compass of the A clarinet (top); of the B flat (centre); and of the E flat (bottom).

clarinette d'amour (French 'love clarinet')
large ◊clarinet made in continental Europe
between the late 18th century and around
1820, usually a major third or fourth lower
than the clarinet in C.

clarino (Italian 'clarion') name given to the
trumpet in the 17th and 18th centuries, also
the name of the highest register of the
instrument, from C above middle C upwards,
which was regularly used for florid passages
in the works of Bach and his contemporaries.
In the early 18th century the name was
sometimes equivalent to clarinet, for which
the normal Italian term was *clarinetto*.

Clari, or The Maid of Milan opera by Bishop
(libretto by J H Payne, based on Marmontel's
story *Laurette*), produced London, Covent
Garden, May 1823. It contains the song *Home,
sweet home*, not only as a song, but as a kind of
Leitmotiv or theme song occurring in various
forms.

Clarke, Jeremiah (c. 1674–1707) English
composer. Organist at St Paul's, he composed
'The Prince of Denmark's March', a harpsichord piece that was arranged by Henry
Wood as a 'Trumpet Voluntary' and wrongly
attributed to Purcell.

He was a pupil of John Blow at the Chapel
Royal, organist at Winchester College 1692–
95, and in 1699 was appointed organist at St
Paul's Cathedral in London. He was sworn
Gentleman-extraordinary of the Chapel Royal
in 1700 and organist in 1704. He committed
suicide, supposedly after an unhappy love
affair.

Works include: anthems; odes on the
Assumption of the Blessed Virgin, in praise
of Barbadoes and *O Harmony*; setting of
Dryden's 'Alexander's Feast' (1697), operas
The Island Princess (with D Purcell and
Leveridge) (1699), *The World in the Moon*
(Settle, with D Purcell) (1697); incidental
music for Shakespeare's *Titus Andronicus*,
Sedley's *Antony and Cleopatra*, and other
plays; harpsichord music, including *The
Prince of Denmark's March* ('Trumpet Volun-
tary').

Clarke, Rebecca (1886–1979) English viola
player and composer. In a competition in the
USA in 1919 for a work for viola and piano
she won the prize with a sonata, second only
to Ernest Bloch's Suite. She settled in the USA
at the outbreak of war in 1939 and married
the pianist James Friskin (1886–1967) in 1944.

She studied at the Royal Academy of Music
in London.

Works include: Psalm for chorus; piano
trio (1921); viola and piano sonata, Rhapsody

for cello and piano (1923), duets for viola and
cello; songs for voice and violin and for voice
and piano; instrumental pieces.

Classical a term commonly used to denote
the period of Haydn, Mozart, and Beethoven,
as opposed to the later Romantic period and
earlier Baroque period.

classical music term used to distinguish
'serious' music from ◊pop music, rock music,
◊jazz, and ◊folk music. It is generally used to
refer to Western art music – that is, music for
the concert hall or church written in the
tradition which originated with European
music of the Middle Ages and passed
through the Renaissance, Baroque, Classical,
and Romantic styles.

The term is also used (usually with a capital
C) for music of the Classical period of music
history, to distinguish it from ◊Baroque music
and ◊Romantic music. Music of the Classical
era emphasized elegance and simplicity more
than personal expression and emotion. The
Classical period lasted from about 1750 to
about 1830, and included the music of
composers such as Mozart and Haydn.

Classical music term used specifically to
refer to the period between approximately
1750 and 1830, in which composers' concerns
for form and symmetry were analogous to
those of the ideals of Classical Greek and
Roman art and philosophy. As epitomized by
the Viennese Classical School of Haydn,
Mozart, and Beethoven, Classical music is
characterized by the growth of clear formal
and sectional elements, especially ◊sonata
form; clear and often symmetrical harmonic
and melodic relationships from phrase to
phrase and section to section, influenced in
part by the study of rhetoric (for example, the
use of ◊antecedent / ◊consequent phrases);
and the development from Baroque ◊polyph-
ony and ◊counterpoint to the melodic style of
◊homophony with distinct and subordinate
accompaniments.

'Classical Symphony' symphony no. 1 in D,
op. 25, by Prokofiev, written in emulation of
Haydn, performed Petrograd (St Petersburg),
21 April 1918.

Claudel, Paul (1868–1955) French poet and
dramatist. His works and thought inspired
◊Milhaud (◊*Christophe Colomb*, ◊*Homme et son
désir*, *Protée*, *Annonce faite à Marie*, Aeschylus
translations and songs) and ◊Honegger
(*Danse des morts, Soulier de satin*, ◊*Jeanne d'Arc
au bûcher*).

Claudine von Villa Bella play for music by J
W Goethe.

Music by F Schubert (libretto from Goethe's play); all three acts were composed in 1815 but the manuscripts of Acts 2 and 3 were used as firelighters by the servants of Josef Hüttenbrenner. Overture and Act 1 performed Vienna, Gemeindehaus Wieden, 26 April 1913.

clausula an interpolation in regular rhythm into 12th- and 13th-century ◊organum, without words, but either sung to the syllable of the text immediately preceding it or played by instruments or both together. The lowest (tenor) part, which in the main portions of the music is in very long notes, here moves at a quicker speed, the notes being arranged in a rhythmical pattern. Numerous clausulae were also designed apparently as independent pieces. In later usage the term meant 'cadential formula'.

clavecin French term for ◊harpsichord, a musical instrument popular in the 16th–18th centuries.

claves musical percussion instrument of Latin American origin, consisting of small hardwood batons struck together.

clavicembalo, often abbreviated to cembalo alternative name for the ◊harpsichord, a musical instrument.

clavichord small domestic keyboard instrument. Of delicate tone, the clavichord was developed in the 16th century on the principle of the ◊monochord. Notes are sounded by a metal blade striking the string. The sound is clear and precise, and a form of vibrato (◊bebung) is possible by varying finger pressure on the key. It was superseded in the 18th century by the ◊fortepiano.

In the 'fretted' clavichord each string is used for two adjacent notes, the note depending on the position in which the string is struck. The two adjacent notes therefore cannot be sounded simultaneously. 'Fretless' clavichords have a separate string for each note. The first clavichords had few strings, using a keyboard-based array of metal tangents combining the function of plectrum and bridge to define and produce a range of pitches. Later instruments increased the number of strings.

clavicytherium (Latin) musical instrument, a ◊harpsichord whose wing-shaped body stands upright instead of being placed horizontally as in the grand piano.

clavier general term for an early ◊keyboard instrument.

***Clavierübung* (German 'keyboard practice')** a collection of keyboard music by Bach,

published in four parts: I (1731), six partitas; II (1735), Italian concerto and French overture; III (1739), organ prelude and fugue in E♭ major framing 21 chorale preludes on the catechism and four manual *duetti*; IV (1741 or 1742), 'Goldberg' variations.

claviorganum musical instrument that combines harpsichord and organ mechanisms. It dates from the late 16th century and was made in various forms until the 18th century.

Clay, Frederic (1838–1889) English composer. He wrote light operas and the cantata *Lalla Rookh* (1877), based on a poem by Thomas Moore.

He was born in Paris, and studied under Molique and Hauptmann at Leipzig. He began by writing light operas for amateurs 1859–60, but produced *Court and Cottage* at Covent Garden in London in 1862.

Works include: light operas *Princess Toto, Don Quixote* (1876), *The Merry Duchess* (1883), *The Golden King*, and others; incidental music for Shakespeare's *Twelfth Night*; cantatas *The Knights of the Cross* and *Lalla Rookh* (Moore), the latter including 'I'll sing thee songs of Araby'; songs 'She wandered down the mountainside', 'The Sands of Dee'.

clef a symbol prefixed to a five-line stave indicating the pitch range to which the written notes apply. Introduced as a visual aid in plainchant notation, it is based on the letter G (treble clef), establishing middle C (C4) as a prime reference pitch, G4 a fifth higher for higher voices, and F3 a fifth lower for lower voices.

The C clef is now comparatively rare, except for viola, cello, and bassoon; for most other instruments the G and F clefs are standard.

Clemens non Papa (c. 1510–c. 1556), alternative name of Jacques Clément Franco-Flemish composer. Clemens was a prolific composer known chiefly for his sacred works, especially his settings of *souterliedekens*, the Dutch psalms. He produced over 400 works, including Masses, motets, psalms in Flemish, and chansons.

The reason for the *non Papa* ('not the pope') in his name is uncertain, though it was probably coined as a joke, for Pope Clement VII died in 1534, and the name was not used in a publication until 1545.

He was succentor at Bruges cathedral 1544–45, and in late 1550 was at 's-Hertogenbosch. He also spent some time in Ypres, and had links with Leyden and Dort. His three-voice psalms were the first polyphonic settings of the psalms in Dutch, with the use of popular song melodies as *cantus firmi*. All but one of his Mass settings are parody settings on chansons and motets by contemporary composers.

Clementi, Aldo (1925–) Italian composer. He studied with Petrassi and Maderna, who influenced him towards 12-note serialism. His works are densely structured and include *Informels* (1961–63); concerto for wind orchestra and two pianos (1967); stage series *Blitz* (1973); *Collage 4* (1979) and *Es* (1981); concerto for piano and 11 instruments (1986).

Clementi, Muzio (1752–1832) Italian pianist and composer. He settled in London in 1782 as a teacher and then as proprietor of a successful piano and music business. He was the founder of the present-day technique of piano playing, and his series of progressive studies, *Gradus ad Parnassum* (1817), is still in use.

Clementi was born in Rome, where he studied as a child, and at the age of nine was appointed to a post as organist. He afterwards studied under Santarelli and Carpani, and by the age of 14 had composed several contrapuntal works. He attracted the attention of Peter Beckford, MP, a cousin of the author of Vathek, who brought him to England, where Clementi continued to pursue his studies until the year 1773 when he published his first piano sonatas and appeared with spectacular success as a virtuoso pianist and composer. He was conductor of the Italian Opera in London 1777–80, after which he toured extensively on the Continent, in 1781 playing before the Viennese court in competition with Mozart (who thought little of him). Back in London, Johann Baptist Cramer and John Field were his pupils. He was associated with the publishers and piano manufacturers Longman & Broderip, upon whose bankruptcy in 1798 he reestablished the firm in partnership with Longman. His interest in the company (trading under a constantly changing variety of names) continued until his death. He was again on tour in Europe 1802–10, taking Field with him to St Petersburg, where the latter remained. In 1807 he met Beethoven in Vienna. From 1810, apart from occasional further travels, he remained in England.

On his return to England he founded a business as pianoforte-maker and musical publisher in London. John Field was his assistant and pupil there, and in 1802 Clementi took Field on a continental tour. In 1813 he assisted in forming the Philharmonic Society. He left about 70 sonatas, symphonies

and overtures. He died at Evesham and is buried in the cloisters of Westminster Abbey.

Works include: four symphonies; about 60 piano sonatas; 100 progressive piano studies entitled *Gradus ad Parnassum*; capriccios and other piano pieces; sonatas for various instruments and piano; chamber music.

***Clemenza di Scipione, La*/The Clemency of Scipio** opera by J C Bach, produced London, King's Theatre, Haymarket, 4 April 1778. Scipio holds prisoners after victory at Carthage. Luceius attempts to rescue his love, Arsinda, but is captured. Facing execution, he is saved when Arsinda threatens suicide and Scipio shows mercy.

***Clemenza di Tito, La*/The Clemency of Titus** opera by Gluck (libretto by Metastasio), produced Naples, Teatro San Carlo, 4 November 1752.
Opera by Mozart (libretto ditto, altered by Caterino Mazzolà), produced Prague, to celebrate the coronation of the Emperor Leopold II as King of Bohemia, 6 September 1791. Titus forgives Vitellia and Sextus for plotting against him.
See also ◊*Tito Vespasiano*.

Cleofide opera by Hasse (libretto by M A Boccardi, based on Metastasio's *Alessandro nell'Indie*), produced Dresden, at court, 13 September 1731. Alexander the Great falls for Cleophis but she remains faithful to Porus.

Cleopatra, Die betrogene Staats-Liebe, oder Die unglückselige Cleopatra, Königin von Egypten opera by Mattheson (libretto by F C Feustking), produced Hamburg, Theatre beim Gänsemarkt, 20 October 1704. Based on Shakespeare's play and the events described in Plutarch's *Lives*.

Cleopatra e Cesare opera by Graun (libretto by G C Bottarelli, based on Corneille's *La Mort de Pompée*), produced Berlin, Opera, 7 December 1742. Written for the inauguration of that theatre. Revived Berlin 1992 (250th anniversary).

Cléopâtre opera by Massenet (libretto by L Payen), produced Monte Carlo, 23 February 1914.

click-track in film music, a technique to aid the coordination of music and film action invented by composers Carl Stalling and Scott ◊Bradley. Holes punched in the soundtrack of a composer's working print click at a desired tempo measured in frames, allowing a composer to construct a musical phrase to climax at a precise moment in the film action.

A metronome tempo of 144 beats per minute, for example, is equivalent to one hole every ten frames of film. A feature of cartoon films from 1937, the click-track was also employed by the composer Max ◊Steiner for feature romance films, in which context it is called 'Mickey-Mousing'.

Clochette, La/The Little Bell opera by Duni (libretto by L Anseaume), produced Paris, Comédie-Italienne, 24 July 1766.

Clochette, La, ou Le Diable page/The Little Bell, or The Devil as Page opera by Hérold (libretto by E G T de Lambert), produced Paris, Opéra-Comique, 18 October 1817. Schubert wrote two songs for the Vienna production in 1821.

'Clock Symphony' the nickname of Haydn's symphony no. 101, in D major (no. 9 of the 'Salomon' symphonies), written for London in 1794. The name derives from the ticking motion of the accompanying figuration in the slow movement.

Clori, Tirsi, e Fileno large-scale Italian cantata for two sopranos, alto, and chamber ensemble by Handel; composed 1707. First modern revival, London, 1984.

Club Anthem an anthem composed jointly by Blow, Humfrey, and W Turner c. 1664, when they were choirboys at the Chapel Royal. It is a setting of the words 'I will always give thanks'.

cluster the effect of playing simultaneously and without emphasis all the notes within a chosen interval. It was introduced by US composer Henry Cowell in the piano piece *The Banshee* (1925), for which using a ruler on the keys is recommended. Its use in film and radio incidental music symbolizes a hallucinatory or dreaming state, presumably because it resembles an internalized disturbance of normal hearing.

The cluster effect is also heard in *Ecuatorial* (1933–34) by Varèse, Stockhausen's *Piano Piece X* (1961), and Ligeti's *Volumina* (1962) for organ, using the player's forearms. Cluster writing for strings features in Penderecki's *Threnody for the Victims of Hiroshima* (1960), and for voices in Ligeti's *Lux Aeterna*.

Cluytens, André (1905–1967) Belgian conductor. He studied piano at Antwerp Conservatory. He first worked for his father as a chorus trainer at the Théâtre Royal in Antwerp, where he later conducted opera.

He then held numerous posts in France, including director of the Paris Opéra Comique, 1947–49. In 1955 he conducted Richard Wagner's *Tannhäuser* at Bayreuth. US debut 1956, with the Vienna Philharmonic Orchestra; Viennese Staatsoper from 1959.

Coates, Albert (1882–1953) English conductor and composer (mother Russian). He was sent to school in England and entered Liverpool University; he returned to Russia to enter his father's business but was sent to the Leipzig Conservatory. He studied conducting with A Nikisch and conducted opera at several German theatres before he was engaged at St Petersburg, where he conducted R Wagner's dramas at the Mariinsky Theatre. He fled to England during the Revolution in 1919 and settled in London for good, conducting Wagner's *Tristan* and the *Ring* at Covent Garden; he led the first public performance of Holst's *The Planets* (1920).

Works include: the operas *Assurbanipal, Samuel Pepys, Pickwick* (Covent Garden, 1936), and *Gainsborough's Duchess*; symphonic poem *The Eagle*, Russian Suite for orchestra; piano pieces.

Coates, Eric (1886–1957) English composer. He is remembered for the orchestral suites *London* (1933), including the 'Knightsbridge' march; 'By the Sleepy Lagoon' (1939); 'The Dam Busters March' (1942); and the songs 'Bird Songs at Eventide' and 'The Green Hills of Somerset'. He is best known as the composer of the signature tune for BBC Radio's 'Desert Island Discs' (the *By the Sleepy Lagoon*).

Coates was born at Hucknall, Nottinghamshire. He studied at the Royal Academy of Music in London and became a viola player in a quartet and in the Queen's Hall Orchestra, but later devoted himself to the composition of light and popular music. His autobiography, *Suite in Four Movements*, was published in 1953.

Cobbold, William (1560–1639) English organist and composer. He was organist at Norwich Cathedral 1599–1608, and was one of the ten musicians who harmonized the tunes in East's Psalter of 1592. In 1601 he contributed a madrigal to *The Triumphes of Oriana*. Among his other few surviving works are 11 consort songs.

Coccia, Maria Rosa (1759–1833) Italian composer. At the age of 16 she passed a severe examination at the Accademia di Santa Cecilia in Rome and an account of her brilliant success was published. In 1780 another eulogy of her was issued with letters from the teacher Giovanni Battista Martini, the librettist Pietro Metastasio, and the castrato singer Farinelli.

Works include: Magnificat for voices and organ, written at 15, *Dixit Dominus* and a cantata, but most are lost.

Cochlaeus, Johannes (Johann Dobnek) (1479–1552) German cleric and music scholar. He was a Roman Catholic and an opponent of Luther, in office at Cologne, Worms, Mainz, and Frankfurt. He wrote a treatise on music, and composed odes.

Cockaigne (In London Town) concert overture by Elgar, op. 40, composed 1900, first performed London, Philharmonic Society, 20 June 1901.

Coclico (Coclicus), Adrianus Petit (1499 or 1500–1592) Flemish composer. He became a Protestant and went to Wittenberg in 1545. After holding various posts in Germany he went to the Danish court at Copenhagen. He published a treatise entitled *Compendium musices* and a collection of psalm settings entitled *Consolationes piae*.

coda (Italian 'tail') in music, a concluding section of a movement added to emphasize the destination key.

codetta (Italian 'little tail') a small form of ◊coda, not appearing as a rule at the end of a movement, but rather rounding off a section of such a movement, or a theme or group of themes, thus assuming the function of a bridge-passage.

Coelho, Rui (1892–1986) Portuguese composer. He studied at Lisbon and later with Humperdinck, Bruch, and Schoenberg in Berlin. He became music critic of the *Diario de Noticias* at Lisbon and in 1924 won a prize with his second opera.

Works include: the operas *Crisfal* (1919), *Belkiss* (1924), *Inés de Castro* (1925), *Tá-Mar* (1936), and *Entre giestas* (1946); symphonic poems *5 Sinfonias camoneanas*, *Promenade d'été*; chamber music; piano pieces; songs.

Coerne, Louis (Adolphe) (1870–1922) US conductor and composer. He studied in Europe and at Harvard University. After filling an organist's post at Buffalo and conducting there and at Columbus, he became associate professor at Smith College, Northampton, Massachusetts, and also taught at Harvard. Later he held other distinguished teaching posts and visited Germany, where some of his works were performed.

Works include: the operas *A Woman of Marblehead*, *Zenobia* (1902, produced Bremen, 1905), and *Sakuntala* (after Kalidasa); incidental music to Euripides' *Trojan Women*; six-part Mass; symphonic poem *Hiawatha* (after Longfellow) and other works for orchestra; violin concerto, string quartet in C minor, three piano trios in canon; songs.

Coffee Cantata name given to J S Bach's secular cantata BWV 211 (c. 1734–35), *Schweigt stille, plaudert nicht.* The libretto by Picander deals in a humorous way with the then new vogue for drinking coffee.

Cohn, Arthur (1910–) US composer, conductor and writer. He studied at Juilliard and conducted in Philadelphia 1942–65. His books include *Twentieth-Century Music in Western Europe* (1961) and *The Encyclopedia of Chamber Music* (1990). He has written six string quartets (1928–45), a flute concerto (1941), and *Kaddisch* for orchestra (1965).

col (Italian 'with the') musical term, as in *col arco*, 'with the bow'.

Colas Breugnon opera by Kabalevsky (libretto by V Bragin after R Rolland's novel), produced Leningrad, 22 February 1938; revised 1953 and 1969. Carpenter Colas recalls his colourful life, in which he revenges himself on the Duke who has destroyed his creations.

Colasse, Pascal (1649–1709) French composer. In about 1677 he obtained an appointment at the Opéra from Lully, in whose works he wrote some of the subordinate parts.

He studied at the Maîtrise de Saint-Paul and the Collège de Navarre in Paris. In 1683 he became one of the four superintendents of the royal chapel, each of whom had to direct the music for three months per year, and two years later he shared with Lalande the appointment of royal chamber musician. In 1696 he was appointed maître de musique de chambre.

Works include: the operas *Achille et Polyxène* (with Lully, 1687), *Thétis et Pélée* (1689), *Enée et Lavinie* (1690), *Jason, La Naissance de Vénus* (1696), *Polyxène et Pyrrhus*, and others; motets, *Cantiques spirituels*, and other church music.

Coleman, Charles (died c. 1664) English composer. He was chamber musician to Charles I and after the Civil War music teacher in London. He received a doctorate in music from Cambridge in 1651, and was appointed composer to Charles II in 1662. With Cooke, Hudson, H Lawes, and Locke he contributed music to Davenant's *Siege of Rhodes* (entertainment at Rutland House), 1656.

Coleman, Edward (died 1669) English singer, lutenist, and composer, son of Charles Coleman. He composed incidental music to Shirley's play *Contention of Ajax and Achilles* in 1653, contributed songs to *Select Musicall Ayres and Dialogues* the same year, and pieces of his appeared in Playford's *Musical Companion* in 1672.

Both he and his wife sang in *The Siege of Rhodes* in 1656. He became a Gentleman of the Chapel Royal on its re-establishment in 1660 and succeeded Lanier in the royal band in 1662.

Coleridge-Taylor, Samuel (1875–1912) English composer. He wrote the cantata *Hiawatha's Wedding Feast* (1898), a setting in three parts of Longfellow's poem. The son of a West African doctor and an English mother, he was a student and champion of traditional black music.

He sang at a church at Croydon as a boy, and entered the Royal College of Music as a violin student in 1890, but also studied composition under Charles Stanford. He had works performed while still at college and in 1899 he was represented at the North Staffordshire Festival at Hanley. He was appointed conductor of the Handel Society in 1904, and visited the USA that year, as well as in 1906 and 1910; but otherwise devoted all his time to composition and private teaching. In the last years of his life he did some teaching at the Guildhall School of Music, London.

Works include: the opera *Thelma* (1907–09); settings for solo voices, chorus, and orchestra of portions from Longfellow's 'Hiawatha' (three parts, 1898), Coleridge's 'Kubla Khan' (1905), Noyes's 'A Tale of Old Japan'; 'Five Choral Ballads' (Longfellow), 'Sea Drift' (Whitman) for chorus; oratorio *The Atonement*; incidental music for Shakespeare's *Othello* and Stephen Phillips's *Herod*, *Ulysses*, *Nero*, and *Faust* (after Goethe); symphony in A minor; violin concerto in G minor; nonet for strings and wind, piano quintet, clarinet quintet, string quartet in D minor, and other chamber music; piano music, songs.

colla parte (Italian 'with the part') in music, a direction indicating that the accompaniment to a vocal or instrumental solo part is to follow the soloist in a passage performed without strict adherence to the tempo.

collegium musicum (Latin 'musical fraternity') in 18th-century Germany, an association for the performance of chamber and orchestral music. Today the term is used in universities to refer specifically to an ensemble performing early music.

col legno (Italian 'with the wood') musical direction indicating that a passage for a string instrument or a group of such instruments is to be played by striking the strings with the stick of the bow.

Collin, Heinrich Joseph von (1771–1811) Austrian poet. His chief connection with music is the drama *Coriolan* for which Beethoven wrote an overture. Stadler wrote incidental music for his tragedy *Polyxena*.

Collingwood, Lawrance (1887–1982) English conductor and composer. He was chorister at Westminster Abbey and organ scholar at Exeter College, Oxford; he lived in Russia for a time and worked with Albert Coates at the St Petersburg Opera; he married there and returned to England during the Revolution. He was principal conductor at Sadler's Wells 1931–46, and conducted the UK first performances of Rimsky-Korsakov's *Snow Maiden* (1933) and *The Tale of Tsar Saltan* (1937).

Works include: the opera *Macbeth* (1934), symphonic poem for orchestra, two piano sonatas.

Colombe, La/The Dove opera by Gounod (libretto by J Barbier and M Carré, after La Fontaine), produced Baden-Baden, 3 August 1860. Sylvie in rivalry with another Florentine lady.

Colonna, Giovanni Paolo (1637–1695) Italian composer. He studied in Rome with Giacomo Carissimi, Antonio Abbatini, and Orazio Benevoli. He became organist of San Petronio at Bologna in 1659 and maestro di cappella in 1674.

Works include: the opera *Amilcare di Cipro* (1692) and other dramatic works; Masses, motets, psalms, litanies; oratorios.

Colonne, Edouard (actually Judas) (1838–1910) French violinist and conductor. He was the first to popularize Berlioz and was well known for his performances of Wagner, Tchaikovsky, and other composers then unknown in France. He founded the Concerts Colonne.

coloratura a rapid ornamental vocal passage with runs and trills. A **coloratura soprano** is a light, high voice suited to such music.

colour the quality or timbre of an instrument or voice. A 'dark' sound denotes a thick, heavy sonority while a 'light' sound describes a thinner, more transparent sonority. Alexander Skriabin invented a keyboard which would project colours on to a screen in order to reflect the mood and character of the music.

colour music composers referring to or using colour (light):

Bantock, *Atalanta in Calydon*, during the performance of which the concert-room is to be lighted in a different colour for each movement.

Bliss, *Colour Symphony*, each movement of which bears the name of a colour as title.

Schoenberg, *Die glückliche Hand*, in which coloured light plays a part, as noted in the score.

Skriabin, *Prometheus*, which contains an optional part for the *tastiera per luce*, designed to throw differently coloured lights.

Colporteur, Le, ou L'Enfant du bûcheron/ The Pedlar, or The Woodcutter's Child opera by Onslow (libretto by F A E de Planard), produced Paris, Opéra-Comique, 22 November 1827.

Combattimento di Tancredi e Clorinda, II/ The Combat of Tancredi and Clorinda dramatic cantata by Monteverdi (text by Tasso, from Canto XII, *Gerusalemme liberata*), performed Venice, Palazzo Mocenigo, 1624. Published in Monteverdi's *Madrigali guerrieri e amorosi*, 1638.

combination tone an acoustical phenomenon in which a third faint tone is heard when two notes are sounded loudly together. The frequency of the combination tone is the difference between the numerical frequencies of the two notes. For example, given note 1 = 500 Hz, and note 2 = 300 Hz, the combination tone is: 500 Hz − 300 Hz = 200 Hz. Combination tones are often used and manipulated in ◊electronic music.

comédie lyrique an 18th-century French name for comic opera.

Comedy on a Bridge/Veselohra na moste opera for radio in one act by Martinů (libretto by the composer, after V K Klicera), produced Prague Radio, 18 March 1937. Bridge connects two feuding villages.

come prima (Italian 'as at first') musical direction indicating that the opening section of a movement is to be played again exactly as before, or that a passage is to be treated in the same manner as before.

come sopra (Italian 'as above') musical direction asking the player to repeat the manner of performance of a passage heard earlier.

'Come, thou monarch of the vine' song by Schubert, from Shakespeare's *Antony and Cleopatra*, translated by F von Mayerhofer as *Trinklied*, 'Bacchus', and composed in Germany in 1826.

'Come, ye sons of art, away' ode by Purcell for the birthday of Queen Mary II, 1694 (text probably by N Tate).

commedia per musica (Italian 'comedy for music') Neapolitan term of the 18th century for comic opera.

common chord the nontechnical term for a major or minor ◊triad.

common time alternative name for 4/4 time. The symbol C which denotes common time originates in music of the Middle Ages in which triple time (three beats in a bar) was considered perfect (as it reflected the Holy Trinity) and notated by a circle (the perfect geometric shape), and duple time (two beats in a bar) was considered imperfect and notated by a broken circle.

Communion the last item of the Proper of the Roman Mass. Originally a psalm with antiphon before and after each verse, only the antiphon is now retained. In general style the Communion resembles the Introit.

comparative musicology the term used up to the middle of the 20th century to describe the branch of musicology which examines the music of different cultures – especially non-Western cultures (German *vergleichende Musikwissenschaft*). Since about 1950 the word ◊'ethnomusicology' has replaced it in common usage.

compass the range of notes covered by a voice or instrument.

Compenius, Heinrich, the elder (c. 1525–1611) German music theorist and composer, the eldest member of a family of organ builders who also worked in Denmark. His son Esaias Compenius (died 1617) built the organ at Frederiksborg Castle and was co-author with Michael Praetorius of *Orgeln Verdingnis* (*Organographia*). Esaias's brother Heinrich Compenius the younger (died 1631) built the organ at Magdeburg Cathedral. Heinrich's nephew Johann Heinrich Compenius (died 1642) built the organ at St Mauritius, Halle, for Samuel Scheidt.

Compère, Loyset (c. 1445–1518) French composer. He started as a chorister at Saint-Quentin Cathedral, later became a canon, and was eventually appointed its chancellor.

composition

Works include: Masses, magnificats, and other church music; also many secular songs with French and Italian words.

composition the process of combining sounds creatively to yield a work; also, the work itself.

compound intervals any intervals exceeding the compass of an octave, so called, as distinct from simple intervals, because they differ from the latter only in width, not in character; thus, a major tenth is essentially the same as a major third.

compound time a metre in which each beat divides into three units. For example, 6/8 consists of two beats, each of three quavers.

computer-generated music music in which a computer has been used by the composer, generating or synthesizing the properties and timbre of sound; also, music which is generated by a computer's response to a series of commands, which are designed by a composer and fed to the machine on a computer program. A computer is often used in compositions which use elements of chance, as in a ◊stochastic work.

Comte Ory, Le/Count Ory opera by Rossini (libretto by Scribe and C G Delestre-Poirson), produced Paris, Opéra, 20 August 1828. Young Count Ory and his page Isolier pursue Countess Adèle, dressed first as pilgrims, then as nuns. They must escape before Adèle's husband returns.

Comus masque by Milton, with music by Henry ◊Lawes, produced Ludlow Castle, 29 September 1634.
The same with alterations by Dalton and music by Arne, produced London, Drury Lane Theatre, 4 March 1738.

con (Italian 'with') musical term, as in *con espressione*, 'with expression'.

con amore (Italian 'with love, with affection') in music, indicating an enthusiastic manner of performance.

concento (Italian 'union, agreement') in music, the playing of the notes of a chord exactly together.

concert originally, as in the English 'consort', the singing or playing together under any conditions; now a public performance of music, except that of an opera or as a rule that given by a single performer, which is more often called a recital.

concertante term in music descriptive of an orchestral concerto in which a number of instruments perform solo, as in the sinfonia concertante works of Haydn and Mozart.

concertato (Italian 'concerted') a musical work or portion of a composition written for several persons to perform together.

concerted music any music written for several soloists to perform together. Any chamber music or a quartet or other ensemble in an opera or oratorio is concerted music, but the opera or oratorio itself is not, neither is, for example, a symphony or a choral part song.

Concertgebouw (Dutch 'concert building') Amsterdam's principal concert hall, built 1888. The Concertgebouw Orchestra is in residence here.

concertina musical instrument, a portable reed organ related to the ◊accordion but smaller in size and hexagonal in shape, with buttons for keys. Metal reeds are blown by wind from pleated bellows which are opened and closed by the player's hands. It was invented in England in the 19th century.

concertino (Italian 'little concert or little concerto') in the former sense the concertino is a group of solo instruments playing alternately with the orchestra (*ripieno*) in a work of the *Concerto grosso* type; in the latter a concertino is a concerto for a solo instrument formally on a smaller scale.
Examples include that by Janáček for piano, clarinet, horn, bassoon, two violins, viola; composed 1925, first performed Brno, 16 February 1926; also by Stravinsky for string quartet, composed 1920; revised 1952 for 12 instruments, first performed Los Angeles, 11 November 1957.

concert master the leader of an orchestra, usually the principal violinist.

concerto composition, usually in three movements, for solo instrument (or instruments) and orchestra. It developed during the 18th century from the **concerto grosso** form for string orchestra, in which a group of solo instruments (concerto) is contrasted with a full orchestra (ripieno).
Corelli and Torelli were early concerto composers, followed by Vivaldi, Handel, and Bach (*Brandenburg Concertos*). Mozart wrote about 40 concertos, mostly for piano. Recent concertos by Ligeti (*Double Concerto* 1972 for flute and oboe), Berio (*Concerto for Two Pianos* 1972–73), and Carter (*Violin Concerto* 1990) have developed the concerto relationship along new lines.

concerto grosso (Italian 'grand consort') musical term for orchestra transferred to the musical form predating the 18th-century symphony. The concerto grosso was a composition for a relatively small ensemble featuring a solo instrumental group or concertino in opposition to an accompanying group or ripieno.

concert pitch standard pitch to which concert ensembles tune up. In a symphony orchestra it is normally the pitch A4, which is common to instruments of the string orchestra. It is given by the oboe, otherwise by the concert master (principal violin) or deputy, or by the piano or organ if featured, as their tuning is fixed in advance.

In military and brass bands, concert pitch is B♭, for the reason that wind instruments in general are historically tuned to B♭ or a related dimension (the pitch of B♭ expressing a wavelength of specific measure).

The standard frequency associated with concert A4 pitch is 440 Hz (cycles per second) but this is subject to variation, some orchestras preferring 438 Hz, others tending towards 442 Hz, with slight but consequential effects on individual and ensemble tone. Prior to 1700 the pitch standard was local and set by the chapel organ, of which a number of Renaissance and Baroque examples survive with values for A4 between a low extreme of 380 Hz and a high of 610 Hz. In 1862 Hermann ◊Helmholtz gave a value for A4 of 431 Hz, an increase on 18th-century concert pitch. The revival of ◊authentic early music practices after 1970 has led to agreement on standards of 460–465 Hz for High Renaissance music, 415 Hz for Baroque and Classical music, and 430 Hz for Romantic music.

Concertstück (German, also *Konzertstück*, 'concerto piece') in music, title sometimes given to works of the concerto type for solo instrument and orchestra which are not fully developed concertos. *Concertstücke* are often in one movement or in several connected sections. Although German, the title has been used by composers in other countries, e.g. Chaminade and Pierné in France, Cowen in England.

Conchita opera by Zandonai (libretto, in French, by M Vaucaire, translated into Italian by C Zangarini, based on P Louÿs' novel *La Femme et le pantin*), produced Milan, Teatro dal Verme, 14 October 1911. The libretto was originally written for Puccini. Mateo teased by lover Conchita until he gets tough.

concord the sounding together of notes in harmony that satisfies the ear as being final in itself and requiring no following chord to give the impression of resolution.

Concord Sonata work for piano by Ives in four movements: *Emerson, Hawthorne, The Alcotts, Thoreau*, after the Concord, Massachusetts, group of writers admired by Ives; composed 1909–15, first complete performance New York, 20 January 1939, by John Kirkpatrick.

concrete music (French *musique concrète*), music created by reworking natural sounds recorded on disc or tape, developed 1948 by Pierre Schaeffer and Pierre Henry in the drama studios of Paris Radio. **Concrete sound** is prerecorded natural sound used in electronic music, as distinct from purely synthesized tones or noises.

conducting the direction of a performance by visual gestures. Groups of more than about six performers have nearly always needed someone to ensure ensemble and consistency of interpretation, and there is iconographic evidence of conductors in Egypt and Sumeria from the third millennium BC, just as there is for medieval chant choirs. With the rise of written polyphony, however, ensembles tended to be small and musical direction normally lay in the hands of a leading performer – in the Baroque era often controlling the ensemble from an organ, harpsichord or (particularly in Classical music) from the violin. Conducting with a baton as an independent activity arose mainly in the 19th century, particularly with Spontini, Spohr, and Mendelssohn; and the earliest professional career conductor seems to have been Otto Nicolai (1810–49). But until the 20th century the most important conductors were usually primarily composers.

conductor the director of an orchestra who beats time, cues entries, and controls the overall expression and balance of a performance.

Conductors of ballet and opera are normally resident, on a full-time contract, available for the ongoing preparation of new repertoire. Conductors for symphony orchestras are more often freelance, star performers in their own right, under temporary contract for concert or recording purposes and thus more reliant on the expertise of orchestras.

conductus a 12th–13th-century vocal composition originally processional in character and written for one or more voices. The basic melody of a *conductus* was generally a tune specially composed. A *conductus cum cauda* was a polyphonic composition ending with an elaborate tail-piece without words (*cauda*, Latin 'tail'). In the polyphonic *conductus* the parts normally move in the same rhythm.

conga Afro-Cuban barrel drum, long and narrow in shape, played with the fingers and palms; also an Afro-Cuban ballroom dance in duple time (2/4), with a syncopated rhythm.

Congreve, William (1670–1729) English dramatist and poet. His works inspired F Austin (*The Way of the World*), J Eccles (ditto, *Love for Love*, *Semele*, and *Ode for St Cecilia's Day*), ◊Finger (*Love for Love* and *Mourning Bride*), ◊*Judgement of Paris* (J Eccles, Finger, D Purcell, and Weldon), Philidor (*Ode for St Cecilia's Day*), ◊Purcell (*Double Dealer and Old Bachelor*), ◊*Semele* (Handel), and ◊Wellesz (*Incognita*).

Connolly, Justin (Riveagh) (1933–) English composer. He studied at the Royal College of Music with Peter Fricker, and was appointed professor there in 1966. He taught at Yale University in the early 1960s and his music has been influenced by Milton Babbitt and Elliott Carter.

Works include: six sets of *Triads* (trios) for various instrumental ensembles (1964–74), five sets of *Obbligati* for various chamber ensembles (1965–81), *Antiphonies* for 36 instruments (1966), two sets of *Poems of Wallace Stevens* for soprano, clarinet, and piano (1967–70), *Rebus* for orchestra (1970), *Diaphony* for organ and orchestra (1977), *Sentences* for chorus, brass, and organ (to poems by Thomas Traherne 1979), oratorio *The Marriage of Heaven and Hell* (text by Blake); *Chimaera* for dancer, alto, baritone, and ensemble (1979), *Fourfold from the Garden Forking Path* for two pianos (1983); *Spelt from Sibyl's Leaves* for six solo voices and ensemble (1989), *Cantata* for soprano and piano (1991), symphony (1991).

Conradi, Johann Georg (died 1699) German composer. He was one of the earliest composers of German operas, which include *Die schoene und getreue Ariadne* (1691), *Diogenes Cynicus*, *Numa Pompilius*, *Der tapffere Kayser Carolus Magnus* (1692), *Der Verstöhrung Jerusalem*, and *Der wunderbar-vergnügte Pygmalion*. He also wrote sacred music, and was music director at Ansbach 1683–86 and director of the Hamburg opera 1690–93.

Consecration of the House (Beethoven.) See ◊Weihe des Hauses.

consecutive an adjective used to describe the progression of intervals of the same kind in similar motion.

consequent in musical analysis, the second phrase of a symmetrical two-phrase unit. Following the 'questioning' antecedent phrase, the consequent phrase often ends on a more stable harmony. Antecedent/consequent phrases are most typical of compositions from the Classical period.

Conservatoire National Supérieur de Musique the chief school of music in Paris, opened 1795 with Sarrette as director, having grown out of the Ecole Royale du Chant, established in 1784 under the direction of Gossec. Later directors were Cherubini, Auber, A Thomas, Dubois, Fauré, Rabaud, Delvincourt, M Dupré, and Loucheur.

conservatory a school or college of music which specializes in preparing students for a career in performance or composition. The term originated in 16th-and 17th-century Italy with orphanages that taught music to a high standard. Famous conservatories include the ◊Juilliard School in New York, the Conservatoire in Paris, and the ◊Royal College of Music in London.

console the part of an ◊organ which is directly under the control of the player's hands and feet.

consonance a combination of two or more tones that is pleasing to the ear. It is the opposite of a ◊dissonance, and is judged consonant by the absence of a ◊beat frequency.

It differs from ◊harmony in referring to the tuning (intonation) of voices and instruments, and applies equally to unison tuning, for example of double-course string instruments, and tuning by intervals.

consort a chamber ensemble of Renaissance or Baroque instruments of uniform sonority, for example recorders or viols. A nonuniform ensemble, comprising mixed instruments, is called a broken consort.

Constant, Marius (1925–) Romanian-born French composer and conductor. He studied in Paris with Messiaen and Honegger; directed Ballets de Paris 1956–66, and was music director of Ars Nova, an ensemble promoting new music 1963–71. His early compositions were impressionistic; in his later works he turned to serialism. He collaborated with Peter Brook in his reductions of *Carmen* and *Pelléas et Mélisande*.

Works include: the operas *La Serrure* and *Le Souper* (both 1969), *La Tragédie de Carmen* (1981); ballets *Jouer de flute* (1952), *Haut Voltage* (1956), *Cyrano de Bergerac* (1960), *Paradise Lost* (1967), *Candide* (1970), *Le Jeu de Sainte Agnès* ('ecclesiastical action' for singers, dancers, actors, organ, electric guitar, trombone, and percussion; 1974); piano concerto (1954), *Turner*, 3 essays for orchestra (1961), *Winds* for 13 wind instruments and double bass (1968), *14 Stations* for 92 percussion instruments and ensemble (1970), *103 Regards dans l'eau* for violin and orchestra (1981); *Pelléas and Mélisande Symphony* (1986); *Des droits de l'homme*, oratorio (1989).

Consul, The opera by Menotti (libretto by the composer), produced Philadelphia, 1 March 1950. Freedom fighter John Sorel must emigrate to evade the secret police. His wife Magda tries to obtain a visa at the consulate, but fails. John is arrested and Magda commits suicide.

contano (Italian 'they count', accent on first syllable) musical direction in a vocal or instrumental part of a work where the performers have a prolonged rest, warning them to count bars in order to make sure of coming in again at the proper moment.

Conte Caramella, Il opera by Galuppi (libretto by Goldoni, partly based on Addison's comedy *The Drummer, or The Haunted House*), produced Verona, 18 December 1749.

Contesa dei numi, La/The Contest of the Gods, opera by Gluck (libretto by Metastasio), produced Copenhagen, at court, 9 April 1749, to celebrate the birth of Prince Christian, later Christian VII.

Contes d'Hoffmann, Les/The Tales of Hoffmann opera by Offenbach (libretto by J Barbier and M Carré, based on a play of their own and on stories by E T A Hoffmann), produced Paris, Opéra-Comique, 10 February 1881, after Offenbach's death. He did not finish it; the scoring is partly by Guiraud. Hoffmann tells of doomed love for Olympia, Antonia, and Giulietta.

Conti, Francesco Bartolomeo (1681–1732) Italian lutenist and composer. He was theorbo player to the Austrian court in Vienna 1701–05, and again from 1708. He was appointed court composer in 1713.

   Works include: the operas *Alba Cornelia* (1714), *Clotilda, Il trionfo dell' Amore, I satiri in Arcadia, Don Chisciotte in Sierra Morena* (1719), *L'Issipile, Pallade trionfante* (1722), and others; stage serenades; oratorios, cantatas.

Conti, Gioacchino (1714–1761) Italian soprano castrato. A rival of ◊Caffarelli. He sang in Rome from 1730 and at Covent Garden, London, 1736–37, in the first performances of Handel's *Atalanta, Arminio, Giustino*, and *Berenice*. He sang in Italy and Spain until 1755 in operas by Hasse, Jommelli, and Galuppi. He was praised for his expressive singing in a high range.

continental fingering the fingering of piano music now in universal use, with the fingers

marked 1–5 from the thumb. This system has displaced the so-called English fingering, marked + for the thumb and 1–4 for the other fingers, which however, was by no means in use throughout the whole history of English keyboard music.

continuo abbreviation for **basso continuo**; in music, the bass line on which a keyboard player, often accompanied by a bass stringed instrument, built up a harmonic accompaniment in 17th-century Baroque music.

contra- a prefix attached to the name of certain instruments or organ stops denoting a lower pitch (usually an octave below).

contrabass alternative name for the ◊double bass, a musical instrument.

contrabassoon musical instrument, a larger version of the ◊bassoon, sounding an octave lower.

contrafactum (Latin 'counterfeit') in music, a vocal composition in which the original words have been replaced by new ones, either secular words substituted for sacred, or vice versa. In the 16th century, the Reformation was responsible for several changes of this kind, especially from Latin to vernacular words in the conversion of plainsong melodies to hymn tunes.

contralto low-register female voice, a high (falsetto) male voice, or a low boy's voice; also called an ◊alto. ·

contrapunctus see ◊counterpoint.

contrapuntal a work employing ◊counterpoint, multiple parts of imitative melody.

contrary motion the movement of two voices in opposite directions from each other; the opposite of parallel motion. The strictest form of contrary motion is ◊inversion, in which one voice plays the mirror image of the other. For example, two voices which sing simultaneously: C4–G4–F4 and C4–F3–G3.

contratenor (Latin 'against the tenor') in the 14th and 15th centuries, a singing voice in the same range as the tenor. It was used to embellish three-part vocal music; the other parts were the melody and the tenor. Later, when four-part songs became popular, the contratenor part was split into the *altus* 'high' and *bassus* 'low' parts, and these, in turn developed into the modern contralto and bass parts.

contredanse see ◊country dance.

Convenziene ed inconvenienze teatrali, II one-act opera (*farsa*) by Donizetti (libretto by the composer, after A S Sografi), performed Naples, Teatro Nuovo, 21 November 1827.

Sometimes given in modern revivals under the spurious title *Viva la Mama*. A satirical commentary on the 'conveniences' or agreed rules, concerning the rank of contemporary Italian singers.

Converse, Frederick Shepherd (1871–1940) US composer. In 1910 his *Pipe of Desire* became the first US opera to be performed at the New York Metropolitan Opera House. From 1917 to 1919 he served in the army and in 1930 became Dean of the New England Conservatory, a post which he held until 1938.

Although intended for a commercial career, he studied music at Harvard University under John Paine. Later he studied piano with Carl Baermann and composition with George Chadwick at Boston, and took a finishing course at Munich. After his return to the USA he held teaching posts at Boston and Harvard until 1907.

Works include: the operas *The Pipe of Desire* (1905), *The Sacrifice* (1910), *The Immigrants* (1914), and *Sinbad the Sailor*; *Job* for solo voices, chorus, and orchestra, *Laudate Dominum* for male voices, brass, and organ; five symphonies (1920–40), orchestral tone-poems *Endymion's Narrative* (1901), *The Mystic Trumpeter* (after Whitman, 1905), *Ormazd*, *Ave atque vale*, *Song of the Sea*, *Flivver Ten Million*, romance *The Festival of Pan* for orchestra; *Night and Day* for piano and orchestra (after Whitman); *Hagar in the Desert* for contralto and orchestra, *La Belle Dame sans merci* for baritone and orchestra (Keats, 1902); three string quartets; piano trio; sonata and concerto for violin and piano; piano pieces; songs.

Convitato di pietra, Il/The Stone Guest opera by Fabrizi (libretto by G B Lorenzi), produced Rome, 1787.

Convitato di pietra, Il, o sio Il dissoluto opera by Righini (librettist unknown), produced Prague, 1776. A setting of the Don Juan legend, produced 11 years before Mozart's.

Conyngham, Barry (1944–) Australian composer. He studied with Peter Sculthorpe and Takemitsu and taught at University of Melbourne from 1975, and was a visiting scholar at Minnesota and Pennsylvania State Universities. His music reflects oriental and modern French influences.

Works include: music theatre pieces *Ned* opera (1975–78), *The Apology of Bony Anderson* (1978), *Fly* opera (1984), and *Bennelong* puppet opera (1988); *Crisis: Thoughts in a City* (1968), *Five Windows* (1969); concerto for orchestra (1981), *Vast* I–IV for orchestra (1987); con-

certos, vocal and chamber music (string quartet, 1979).

Cooke, Arnold (1906–) English composer. He was educated at Repton School and Caius College, Cambridge, where he was awarded a music degree in 1929. From that year to 1932 he was a pupil of Hindemith in Berlin, and in 1933 was appointed professor of harmony and composition at the Royal Manchester College of Music. In 1938 he settled in London; and was appointed professor of composition at Trinity College of Music, London, in 1947.

Works include: the operas *Mary Barton* (1949–54), *The Invisible Duke* (1976); cantata *Holderneth* for baritone, chorus, and orchestra; six symphonies (1946–84), two clarinet concertos, concert overture for orchestra, Passacaglia, Scherzo, and Finale for string orchestra, piano concerto; four Shakespeare sonnets for voice and orchestra; five string quartets (1933–78), and other chamber music.

Cooke, Benjamin (1734–1793) English organist and composer. He was a pupil of Johann Pepusch, whom he succeeded in 1752 as conductor to the Academy of Ancient Music. In 1757 he was appointed choirmaster at Westminster Abbey in succession to Bernard Gates (c. 1685–1773). He was awarded doctorates in music from Cambridge University in 1775, and from Oxford in 1782, when he became organist of St Martin-in-the-Fields, London.

Works include: services, anthems (some for special occasions), psalms, chants, and hymns; ode for Delap's tragedy *The Captives*; *Ode on the Passions* (Collins), odes for Christmas Day, on Handel, on Chatterton, and for the King's recovery, ode *The Syren's Song to Ulysses*; glees, catches, and canons; orchestral concertos; organ pieces; harpsichord lessons.

Cooke, Deryck (1919–1976) English musicologist. His best-known works include the book *The Language of Music* (1959) and his performing version of Mahler's unfinished tenth symphony, heard in London on 13 August 1964 (revised 1972).

He studied privately and at Cambridge University. From 1947 to 1959 he worked for the British Broadcasting Corporation, devoting much time to writing and broadcasting.

Coperario, John (c. 1570–1626) adopted name of John Cooper, English lutenist, viol player, and composer. He studied in Italy and on his return, about 1604, adopted the Italianized name of Coperario or Coprario. He taught the children of James I and was the master of William and Henry Lawes. In 1625 he was appointed composer-in-ordinary to Charles I.

Works include: *The Masque of the Inner Temple and Gray's Inn* (F Beaumont), *The Masque of Flowers*; *Funeral Teares* on the death of the Earl of Devonshire, *Songs of Mourning* on the death of Prince Henry (words by Campion); anthems; works for viols and for viols and organ; fancies for the organ based on Italian madrigals; lute music; songs and other pieces.

Copland, Aaron (1900–1990) US composer. His early works, such as his piano concerto 1926, were in the jazz idiom but he gradually developed a gentler style with a regional flavour drawn from American folk music. Among his works are the ballets *Billy the Kid* (1939), *Rodeo* (1942), and *Appalachian Spring* (1944) (based on a poem by Hart Crane). Among his orchestral works is *Inscape* (1967).

Born in New York, Copland studied in France with Nadia Boulanger, and taught from 1940 at the Berkshire Music Center, now the Tanglewood Music Center, near Lenox, Massachusetts. He took avant-garde European styles and gave them a distinctive American pitch. His eight film scores, including *The Heiress* (1949), set new standards for Hollywood.

He began to learn the piano at the age of 13 and studied theory with Rubin Goldmark; he later went to France and became a pupil of Boulanger at the American conservatory at Fontainebleau. In 1924 a Guggenheim scholarship enabled him to spend two more years in Europe. He was represented for the first time at an International Society for Contemporary Music festival at Frankfurt in 1927, and won a prize in American music with his *Dance Symphony* in 1930. He was first influenced by Stravinsky and Boulanger but later assimilated local American styles, notably in the ballets *Billy the Kid* and *Appalachian Spring*. His chamber music is more introspective and complex in character. He did much to promote American music, and also wrote and lectured extensively. He toured widely as a conductor of his own and other American music.

Works include: the opera *The Tender Land* (1952–54); ballets *Billy the Kid* (1938), *Rodeo*, *Appalachian Spring* (1943–44); school opera *The Second Hurricane*; music for films includes *Of Mice and Men*; orchestral works: three symphonies, (1925, 1933, 1946), *Music for the Theatre*, *Symphonic Ode*, *A Dance Symphony*, *Statements*, *El Salón México* (1933–36), *Music for the Radio*, *An Outdoor Overture*, *Quiet City*

(1939), *Letter from Home*, *Danzón Cubano*; *Lincoln Portrait* for orator and orchestra (1942), piano concerto (1926), clarinet concerto (1948), *Connotations* for orchestra (1962), *Inscape* (1967), *Three Latin American Sketches* (1972). *The House on the Hill* and *An Immorality* for female chorus; two pieces for string quartet; sextet for clarinet, strings, and piano; piano quartet; nonet; violin and piano sonata; piano sonata, piano pieces.

Coppélia, ou La Fille aux yeux d'émail/ Coppelia, or The Girl with Enamel Eyes ballet by Delibes (scenario by C Nuitter and A Saint-Léon; choreographed by L Mérante), produced Paris, Opéra, 25 May 1870.

Coptic chant the music of the Christian Church in Egypt, which from the middle of the 5th century has been Monophysite. There was a primitive system of notation by the 10th century, but nothing definite is known about the chant in its original form. It still flourishes today, and is characterized by the use of percussion instruments.

Coq d'or (Rimsky-Korsakov). See ◊*Golden Cockerel*.

cor anglais, or English horn musical instrument, an alto ◊oboe, pitched a fifth lower than the oboe in F, with a distinctive tulip-shaped bell and warm nasal tone. It is heard to pastoral effect in Rossini's overture to *William Tell* (1829), and portraying a plaintive Sasha the duck in Prokofiev's *Peter and the Wolf* (1936).

The cor anglais has many famous solos in the orchestral repertoire, including the Franck symphony, Berlioz's *Symphonie fantastique*, Dvořák's *New World* symphony, and Sibelius's tone poem *The Swan of Tuonela*.

corda (Italian 'string') musical term, as in **una corda** or **u.c.** ('one string') directing a pianist to depress the ◊soft pedal, which moves the hammers so that they strike only one or two strings per key instead of the usual three. **Tre corde** ('three strings') or **tutte le corde** ('all the strings') reverses the marking. (See also ◊due corde.)

cordatura (Italian 'crying together') in music, the notes to which a string instrument is tuned, such as G, D, A, E for the violin. Any change in the normal tuning made temporarily is called *scordatura*.

Cordier, Baude (fl. 1400 or shortly before) French composer. Recent research makes it seem likely that he was the harpist Baude Fresnel (d. 1397–98), who was employed at the court of Philip the Bold from 1384. Of his ten surviving chansons two are particularly famous because of their notation: 'Belle, bonne', written out in the form of a heart; and 'Tout par compas', written down in a circle.

Corelli, Arcangelo (1653–1713) Italian composer and violinist. Living at a time when the viol was yielding to the violin, he was one of the first virtuoso exponents of the Baroque violin and his music, marked by graceful melody, includes a set of *concerti grossi* and five sets of chamber sonatas.

Born at Fusignano, near Milan, he studied in Bologna and in about 1685 settled in Rome, under the patronage of Cardinal Pietro Ottoboni, where he lived at the palace of his patron and published his first violin sonatas. He visited Modena and Naples, conducted at the Roman residence of Queen Christina of Sweden, collected pictures, and taught many violin pupils, including Francesco Geminiani and Pietro Locatelli. Corelli's music is richer in contrapuntal and harmonic interest than that of any other Italian Baroque master, and has been admired for the poise, balance, and brilliance of its style.

Works include: a set of 12 *Concerti grossi* op. 6, including no. 8 in G minor, *'fatto per la notte di nattale'* (Christmas); five sets of chamber sonatas.

Corigliano, John (1938–) US composer. His brilliant and romantic extravaganza *The Ghosts of Versailles* was staged at the New York Metropolitan Opera House in 1991.

He studied with Otto Luening at Columbia University and privately with Paul Creston; and in 1973 began teaching at Lehmann College, New York.

Works include: violin sonata (1963), *Elegy* for orchestra (1966), piano concerto (1968), clarinet concerto (1977), *Hallucinations* for orchestra (1981); incidental music for plays by Sophocles, Molière, and Sheridan; *Naked Carmen*, arrangement of Bizet for singers, pop and rock groups, synthesizer, and instruments; *Echoes of Forgotten Rites* for orchestra (1982); Symphony (1990); opera *The Ghosts of Versailles* (1991).

Coriolan Beethoven's overture, op. 62, to the play of that name by Heinrich von Collin, composed 1807 and produced with the play in March of that year. Apart from its subject the play has no connection with Shakespeare's *Coriolanus*.

cornamuse Renaissance capped double-reed woodwind musical instrument of straight bore and with a clear, reedy tone.

Corneille, Pierre (1608–1684) French poet and dramatist. His works inspired M-A ◊Charpentier (*Polyeucte* and *Andromède*), ◊Der Cid and ◊Le Cid (Cornelius and Massenet), ◊Cleopatra e Cesare (Graun), ◊Dukas (*Polyeucte* overture), ◊Flavio (Handel), ◊Lully (dipe), ◊Martyrs (Donizetti), ◊Poliuto (Pacini), ◊Polyeucte (Gounod), ◊Rieti (*Illusion comique*), ◊Roberto Devereux (Mercadante), ◊Sacchini (*Gran Cid*), ◊Tito Vespasiano (Caldara and Hasse), and J ◊Wagenaar (*Cid*).

Corneille, Thomas (1625–1709) French poet and dramatist, brother of Pierre ◊Corneille. His works inspired J B Lully (◊Bellérophon, ◊Psyché) and M-A ◊Charpentier (*Pierre philosophale*, ◊Médée, and two plays with Visé).

Cornelius, Peter (1824–1874) German composer and author. After failing as an actor, he began to study music, first with Siegfried Dehn in Berlin 1845–50, and from 1852 with Liszt at Weimar, where he joined the New German School of musicians and wrote eloquently about them in Schumann's *Neue Zeitschrift*, without however succumbing to Wagnerian influence in his own work. He sought out Wagner in Vienna in 1858 but declined to follow him to Munich in 1865 for the premiere of *Tristan und Isolde*.

Works include: the operas *Der Barbier von Bagdad* (1855–58), *Der Cid* (1860–62) and *Gunlöd* (unfinished); choral works *Trauerchöre* and *Vätergruft*; duets for soprano and baritone; songs including cycles *Liedercyclus*, *Weihnachtslieder* (1859), *Brautlieder* (1856–58).

Corner, Philip (1933–) US composer. He studied in Paris with Messiaen and in New York with Luening and Cowell; teacher at Rutgers University from 1972. His works show the influence of Cage, minimalism, and Asian music.

Works include: theatre music *Carrot Chew Performance* (1963), *Rationalize Outside Sounds* (1966), *Metal Meditations* (1973), *Democracy in Action* (1979); *This Is It .... This Time* for orchestra (1959); ensemble works, including *Composition With or Without Beverly* (1962); *Flares*, mixed media (1963); series *'Gamelan'* from 1975; piano music and works in graphic notation.

cornet three-valved brass-band instrument, soprano member (usually in B♭) of a group of valved horns developed from the coiled posthorn in Austria and Germany about 1820–50 for military band use. Of cylindrical bore, its compact shape and deeper conical bell allow greater speed and agility of intonation than the trumpet, at the expense of less tonal precision and brilliance. A small E♭ cornet is standard in brass bands alongside a B♭ cornet section.

The cornet is typically played with vibrato, and has its own repertoire of virtuoso pieces, heard in brass band concerts and contests, and consisting of voicelike airs, character pieces, Victorian dance forms, and sets of variations in antique ◊divisions style. A famous early exponent was the Frenchman Arban, for whom Berlioz wrote an optional ◊obbligato for the cornet in his *Symphonie fantastique*. The cornet is a featured solo in Stravinsky's ballet *Petrushka* (1911) and *The Soldier's Tale* (1919), though its part is now more usually played by the trumpet. It should not be confused with the ◊cornett.

cornett musical instrument, the woodwind precursor of the orchestral brass cornet, of narrow conical bore and with finger holes and a cup mouthpiece. It was often made of wood, or of ivory covered with leather. Its clear, trumpetlike tone made it a favoured instrument of Renaissance ◊broken consorts and Baroque orchestras, and although superseded by brass instruments in the 18th century, the cornett remained popular with military and church bands until well into the 19th century.

Members of the cornett family include the straight soprano **mute cornett**, a curved alto **cornetto**, S-shaped tenor **lysarden**, and double S-shaped **serpent**.

corno di bassetto Italian name for the ◊basset horn, a musical instrument.

In 1888–89 Bernard Shaw wrote music criticism for *The Star* under the pseudonym of C di B.

Cornyshe, William (died 1523) English composer. He was attached to the courts of Henry VII and Henry VIII, not only as a musician, but also as an actor and producer of interludes and pageants. He was made a Gentleman of the Chapel Royal in about 1496, and succeeded William Newark as Master of the Children in 1509. He wrote music for the court banquets and masques and officiated in France at the Field of the Cloth of Gold in 1520.

Several other musicians of the period also had the surname Cornyshe, including a William Cornyshe senior (died c. 1502), who was the first recorded master of the choristers at Westminster Abbey c. 1480–90.

Works include: motets, Magnificats, *Ave Maria*; secular songs, some with satirical words, for instruments and voices, including a setting of Skelton's *Hoyda, Jolly Rutterkin*.

coronach, Gaelic (Gaelic 'crying together') a funeral cry, or in its more cultivated musical form a dirge.

Coronation Anthems four anthems by Handel, composed for the coronation of George II and performed at the ceremony in Westminster Abbey, 11 October 1727. 1. 'Zadok the Priest', 2. 'The King shall rejoice', 3. 'My heart is inditing', 4. 'Let thy hand be strengthened'. A number of other composers, from H Cooke in the 17th century to Vaughan Williams in the 20th, have written anthems for coronations in England.

'Coronation' Concerto the nickname of Mozart's piano concerto in D, K537 (dated 24 February 1788), performed by him at Frankfurt at the coronation festivities for Leopold II, 15 October 1790.

'Coronation' Mass Mozart's Mass in C K317 (dated 23 March 1779), so called because it is said to have been written to commemorate the crowning in 1751 of a miraculous image of the Virgin Mary.

Coronation Ode work by Elgar in six sections for soloists, chorus, and orchestra, op. 44; composed 1901–02, first performed Sheffield, 2 October 1902. Finale is 'Land of Hope and Glory', based on tune from *Pomp and Circumstance* march no. 1.

Corregidor, Der/The Mayor opera by Wolf (libretto by R Mayreder, based on P A de Alarcón's story *El sombrero de tres picos/The Three-cornered Hat*), produced Mannheim, 7 June 1896. Frasquita tries to avoid Don Eugenio's amorous advances while her husband Tio Lukas is detained by the Don's men. Incorrectly believing that Frasquita has been unfaithful, Lukas sets out to seduce the Don's wife, Donna Mercedes. After mistaken identities are resolved, Frasquita and Lukas are reunited.

corrente see ◊courante.

Corrette, Michel (1709–1795) French organist, teacher, and composer. He held various organist's posts from 1737, and between 1737 and 1784 published 17 methods on performing practice; these included *L'école d'orphée* 1738, for violin, *Les amusements du Parnasse* 1749, for harpsichord, *Le parfait maître à chanter* 1758, *Les dons d'Apollon* 1762, for guitar, *Les délices de la solitude* 1766, for cello, *Nouvelle methode pour apprendre la harpe* 1774, and *Le berger galant* 1784, for flute.

Works include: the ballets *Les âges* (1733) and *Le lys* (1752); sacred music, including motets, Te Deum (1752), Laudate Dominum (1766), *Trois leçons de ténèbres* for low voice and organ (1784); secular vocal pieces including ariettes and cantatas; concertos for musette, vielle, flute, and violin; sonatas, organ and harpsichord music.

Corri, Domenico (1746–1825) Italian conductor, publisher, and composer. He was a pupil of Nicola Porpora. He settled at Edinburgh in 1771 as conductor (of the Music Society), publisher, and singing-master. He failed in business and settled in London around 1790, when he set up in partnership with Jan Dussek, who married his daughter Sophia in 1792. Apart from music, he also wrote theoretical works, including a music dictionary.

Works include: the operas *Alessandro nell' Indie* (1774) and *The Travellers* (1806); instrumental sonatas, rondos and other pieces; songs including *Six Canzones dedicated to Scots Ladies*.

Corsaire, Le overture by Berlioz, op. 21, composed in Italy, 1831, rewritten in Paris, 1844, first performed Paris, 19 January 1845, as *La Tour de Nice*; final version (*Le Corsaire*) first performed Brunswick, 8 April 1854.

Corsaro, Il/The Corsair opera by Verdi (libretto by F M Piave, based on Byron's poem), produced Trieste, 25 October 1848. The Pasha of Coron captures Corsair Corrado, who falls in love with Gulnara, a slave in the harem. She frees him and kills her master, and together they return to Corrado's home, where they find his betrothed, Medora, dying.

Corsi, Jacopo (1561–1602) Italian nobleman and amateur composer. He was involved in the initiation of opera at Florence. Peri's *Dafne* was produced at his house in 1598 and he took some share in its composition.

Corteccia, (Pier) Francesco di Bernardo (1502–1571) Italian organist and composer. He made a substantial contribution to the development of the madrigal; many of those he wrote were for particular occasions, the most famous being those composed for the wedding of Duke Cosimo I de' Medici to Eleonora of Toledo in 1539. He also wrote a considerable amount of liturgical music, though this is more conservative in style than his secular compositions.

From 1515 he served the church of S Giovanni Battista, Florence, in various capacities and was organist there 1535–39. In 1531 he was appointed organist at the church of San Lorenzo, Florence, and from 1539 was maestro di cappella to Duke Cosimo I. For the marriage of Cosimo's son Francesco to Joanna

of Austria in 1565 he collaborated with the elder Alessandro Striggio on music for Giovanni Battista Cini's intermezzo *Psiche ed Amore*. Corteccia also wrote a prologue, five *intermedii*, and an epilogue for Antonio Landi's comedy *Il comodo*, which was performed at the wedding banquet. The *intermedii* were written for solo singers, ensemble, and varying combinations of instruments to depict different times of the day; they were published in Corteccia's madrigal collection of 1547

Works include: hymns in four parts, canticles and responses, madrigals; pieces for four–eight voices and instruments.

Cortot, Alfred (Denis) (1877–1962) French pianist and conductor. After serving as a *répétiteur* at Bayreuth he founded the Société des Festivals Lyriques at Paris and conducted the first performance in France of *Götterdämmerung* in 1902. In addition to his continuous activity as a pianist and conductor he gave many lectures on piano technique and interpretation and collected a valuable library of rare works.

He studied at the Paris Conservatory, where he gained the *premier prix* in 1896. In 1905 he formed a piano trio with Jacques Thibaud and Pablo Casals. From 1907 to 1917 he taught at the Paris Conservatory and in 1918 was joint founder of the Ecole Normale de Musique. He was charged with Nazi collaboration in 1944.

Cosa rara (Martín y Soler). See ◊*Una cosa rara*.

Così fan tutte, o sia La scuola degli amanti/ All women do it, or The School for Lovers opera by Mozart (libretto by L da Ponte), produced Vienna, Burgtheater, 26 January 1790. Ferrando and Guglielmo test the fidelity of Dorabella and Fiordiligi by swapping partners and courting them in disguise.

Costa, Michael (Michele Andrea Agniello) (1808–1884) Italian-born English conductor and composer of Spanish descent. He studied in Naples and produced his first two operas at the Conservatory there 1826–27, and wrote a Mass, three symphonies and other works. In 1829 he was sent to Birmingham by Zingarelli to conduct a work by that composer at the Festival, but by a mistake was made to sing tenor instead. He then settled in London, wrote many ballets and operas and perfected the orchestra at the Opera; in 1846 he was appointed conductor of the Philharmonic Society and Covent Garden opera, and he became the most important festival conductor.

Works include: the operas *Il delitto punito*, *Il sospetto funesto*, *Il carcere d'Ildegonda*, *Malvina*, *Malek Adhel* (1838), *Don Carlos* (1844); ballets *Kenilworth*, *Une Heure à Naples*, *Sir Huon*; oratorios *La passione*, *Eli*, *Naaman*; Mass for four voices, *Dixit Dominus*; symphony; vocal quartet *Ecco il fiero istante*.

Costanza e Fortezza/Constancy and Fortitude opera by Fux (libretto by P Pariati), produced Prague, Hradžin Palace, at the coronation of the Emperor Charles VI as king of Bohemia, and birthday of the Empress Elizabeth Christina, 28 August 1723. Etruscans in siege of Rome; composed in elaborate style and staged in great splendour.

Cotton, John (lived 12th century), also known as John of Afflighem English or Flemish music scholar. He was the author of a Latin treatise on music which seems to have been widely distributed in manuscript form; six copies are preserved in various European libraries.

Couleurs de la cité céleste work by Messiaen for piano, 13 wind, xylophone, marchimba, and 4 percussion; composed 1963, first performed Donaueschingen, 17 October 1964, conductor Boulez.

counterpoint the art of combining different forms of an original melody with apparent freedom while preserving a harmonious effect. Giovanni Palestrina and J S Bach were masters of counterpoint.

It originated in ◊plainsong, with two independent vocal lines sung simultaneously (Latin *punctus contra punctum* 'note against note').

countersubject a melody which follows the opening subject (principal melody) in a ◊fugue. Typically, when the second voice enters with the subject, the first voice (which previously sang or played the subject) begins the countersubject as a contrapuntal complement to the subject.

countertenor the highest natural male voice, as opposed to the ◊falsetto of the male ◊alto. It was favoured by the Elizabethans for its heroic brilliance of tone.

It was revived in the UK by Alfred Deller (1912–1979).

country dance an English dance which became very popular in France in the 18th century and was called *Contredanse* there, having appeared as *Contredanse anglaise* in publication as early as 1699. It spread to other countries, being called *Contratanz* or *Kontretanz* in Germany and Austria. It lost not only its rustic name but also its rustic nature on the continent, where it was used for ballroom dancing and cultivated by composers of distinction, including Mozart and Beethoven.

coup d'archet (French 'stroke of the bow') the bow attack in string playing.

coup de glotte (French 'stroke of the glottis') in singing, a trick whereby vowel sounds are preceded by a kind of click in the throat produced by a momentary cutting off of the breath-stream.

It is effective as an inflection and insisted on as a point of good technique by many singing teachers, while others consider it harmful to the voice.

Inversion

An example by Bach of double counterpoint. The second system reverses the position of each line.

Couperin, François le Grand (1668–1733) French composer. He is the best-known member of a musical family which included his uncle Louis Couperin (c. 1626–1661), composer for organ and harpsichord. A favoured composer of Louis XIV, Couperin composed numerous chamber concertos and harpsichord suites, and published a standard keyboard tutor *L'Art de toucher le clavecin/The Art of Playing the Harpsichord* 1716 in which he laid down guidelines for fingering, phrasing, and ornamentation.

Couperin, Louis (c. 1626–1661) French composer, harpsichordist, and organist. He is regarded as one of the finest keyboard composers of the 17th century; among his 215 surviving pieces are allemandes, courantes, sarabandes, chaconnes, and pascailles for harpsichord, preludes, fugues, and plainsong versets for organ, and fantaisies for chamber ensemble.

His father, Charles Couperin (c. 1595–1654), was a musician. Louis was sponsored by Jacques Chambonnières, a court musician, and was active in Paris from at least 1651; in 1653 he became the first member of his family to hold the organist's post at Saint-Gervais. He was a treble viol player at court and took part in several ballet performances, including *Psyché* 1656.

coupler an appliance whereby two manuals (keyboards) of an organ or a manual and the pedals can be so connected that while only one is being played the stops controlled by the other are brought into action. Special couplers can also be used to double the notes played automatically an octave above or below.

couplet (French 'I believe') a verse or stanza in a poem. In music, a strophic song, generally of a light and often of a humorous type, in which the same music recurs for each verse. Also the forerunner of the ◊episode in the ◊rondo form, occurring in the French rondeau as cultivated by Couperin and others, where a main theme returns again and again after statements of various *couplets* between.

courante (French 'running') 17th-century French court dance. Initially fast in tempo, with an emphasis on mime, it later became codified in a much slower and graver form. It was a favourite dance of Louis XIV. The music for the dance formed one of the standard movements of a Baroque ◊suite. The Italian courante is in quick triple time (3/8 or 3/4), with continuous 'running' figures in the melody. The French courante is in a more moderate triple time (3/2) or compound duple time (6/4), and often exploits the rhythmic disruption of changing from one metre to the other. Bach uses this variety in the courantes of his famous *French Suites* c. 1722.

course on a musical instrument, a group of strings which are tuned to the same pitch and are played as one string. Lutes, some guitars, and mandolins have double courses, harpsichords have triple courses, and pianos range from heavy single courses in the bass to quadruple courses in the extreme treble. The 12-string guitar is a modern example of a double-course instrument, each pair tuned to the octave rather than to the unison.

While the original purpose of doubling of strings may have been to increase loudness, an additional factor is improved liveliness of tone caused by beat interference of near-unison strings, an important factor in the tuning of a modern concert grand piano.

Covent Garden popular name of the Royal Opera House at Covent Garden, London. The present building was completed 1858 after two previous ones burnt down. The Royal Ballet is also in residence here.

Cowell, Henry Dixon (1897–1965) US composer and theorist. His pioneering *New Musical Resources* (1930) sought to establish a rationale for modern music. He worked with Percy Grainger 1941 and alongside John Cage. Although remembered as a discoverer of piano effects such as strumming the strings in *Aeolian Harp* (1923), and for introducing clusters, using a ruler on the keys in *The Banshee* (1925), he was also an astute observer and writer of new music developments.

Cowell also wrote chamber and orchestral music and was active as a critic and publisher of 20th-century music.

Cowen, Frederic (Hymen) (1852–1935) English composer and conductor. He was conductor by turns of the London Philharmonic Society, at Liverpool and Manchester.

He studied in London, Leipzig, and Berlin. **Works include:** the operas *Pauline* (1876), *Thorgrim*, *Signa* (1893), and *Harold* (1895); operettas and incidental music; oratorios *The Deluge* (1878), *St Ursula*, *Ruth* (1887), *The Veil*, and others; cantatas *The Corsair*, *The Sleeping Beauty*, *St John's Eve*, *Ode to the Passions* (Collins), *John Gilpin* (Cowper); jubilee (1897) and coronation (1902) odes; cantatas for female voices, anthems, part songs. Six symphonies (1869–98: no. 3 *Scandinavian*, no. 4 *Welsh*, no. 6 *Idyllic*); four concert overtures, *Sinfonietta*, *Indian Rhapsody* and other works for orchestra; concerto and *Concertstück* for piano and orchestra; string quartet (1866), piano trio; many piano pieces; about 300 songs.

Cowie, Edward (1943–) English composer. Several of his works are based on the story of the Australian criminal Ned Kelly. His interest in painting is reflected in the *Choral Symphony* of 1982, subtitled *Symphonies of Rain, Sea and Speed*.

After studying with Alexander Goehr, Peter Fricker, and Witold Lutoslawski he taught in England, Germany, and Australia.

Works include: the operas *Commedia* (1978) and *Kelly* (1980–82); *Kate Kelly's Roadshow* for mezzo and ensemble (1982); *Concerto for Orchestra* (1980), two symphonies: (*The American* and *The Australian*, 1980–82), two clarinet concertos (1969, 1975), harp concerto (1982); *Endymion Nocturnes* for tenor and string quartet (1973, revised 1981), *Kelly Choruses* for voices and harp (1981), *Missa Brevis* (Mass for Peace, 1983), *Ancient Voices* for four voices (1983); four string quartets (1973–83), *Kelly Passacaglia* for string quartet (1980).

Cowper, Robert (c. 1474–between 1535 and 1540) English composer. He was clerk of King's College, Cambridge 1493–95, and wrote sacred pieces and carols, notably those in *XX songs ix of iii partes and xi of three partes* 1530.

Cradle will Rock, The 'play with music' in ten scenes by Marc Blitzstein. The Federal Theater banned the work because it depicted class warfare in Steeltown, USA. At the first performance on 16 June 1937 the cast sang from stalls seats, with the composer at a piano. Orson Welles directed.

Craft, Robert (1923–) US conductor and writer on music. From 1948 he was closely associated with Stravinsky, and influenced his conversion to serial technique in the early 1950s. He collaborated with Stravinsky in recording his music, and was the first to record the complete works of Anton Webern. He also recorded much of Schoenberg's music.

He studied at the Juilliard School. At Santa Fe in 1963 he conducted the first US performance of Berg's opera *Lulu* (two-act version). With Stravinsky he compiled six volumes of 'conversations' (1959–69). Other books include *Stravinsky in Photographs and Documents* (1976).

Cramer, Johann Baptist (1771–1858) German-born composer, pianist, and teacher. He is most famous for his 84 studies for piano

1804 and 1810, which are still used today. He composed in a conservative style for his day, trying to emulate the music of Mozart. As a pianist he was admired for his technical command and ◊legato touch. He was one of a group of composers known as the ◊London Pianoforte School.

He was taken to London as a young child, and was taught by his father, Wilhelm Cramer (1746–99), a violinist. He later went to Muzio Clementi for piano study, and first appeared in public in 1781. In 1824 he established a music publishing business. He lived abroad from 1835 to 1845.

Works include: 9 piano concertos; 2 piano quartets and quintets; 124 piano sonatas, 2 volumes of 42 studies each, 16 later studies, 100 daily exercises, and other pieces.

Crawford (Seeger), Ruth (Porter) (1901–1953) US composer. She compiled many folksong anthologies, including *American Folk Songs for Children* (1948), and wrote hundreds of her own piano accompaniments. Her own compositions are regarded as anticipating certain later developments in music.

She studied at the Chicago Conservatory and with Charles Seeger, whom she later married.

Works include: suite for piano and woodwind quintet (1927), nine piano preludes (1924–28), string quartet (1931), *Risselty, Rosselty* for small orchestra (1941), *2 Ricercari* for voice and piano (1932).

Creation Mass (Haydn) see ◊*Schöpfungsmesse*.

Creation, The/Die Schöpfung oratorio by Haydn (libretto by Gottfried van Swieten after an English model, now lost, based on Genesis and Milton's *Paradise Lost*), produced Vienna, Schwarzenberg Palace, 29 April 1798.

Credo the third item of the Ordinary of the Mass. Its text dates from the Council of Nicea (325), and its use was ordered in the Mozarabic and Gallican liturgies in 589. It was not introduced into the Roman liturgy until 1071. Later medieval melodies are also known.

crescendo, or cresc. (Italian 'growing') in musical notation, indicating an increase in the loudness of a passage by constant degrees. *Crescendo poco a poco* ('growing little by little') means that the crescendo should progress more gradually. The opposite marking is 'decrescendo' or 'diminuendo'.

Crescentini, Girolamo (1762–1846) Italian male soprano. He made his first appearance in Rome in 1783, and sang in London in 1785–

Choir and congregation

Credimus in unum Deum, Pa - trem o - mni - pot - en - tem

Choir and congregation

Cre - di -mus in u - num De - - um Pa - trem o - - - mni - pot- en - tem

Priest: Choir:

Cre - do in u - num De - um, Pa - trem o - mni - pot - en - tem

The example shows (i) the Mozarabic, (ii) the Gallican, and (iii) the Roman plainsong variants of the Credo.

87. In Italy he sang in the first performances of Rispoli's *Ipermestra* (1785), Cimarosa's *Gli Orazi* (1797), Zingarelli's *Meleagro* (1798), and Federici's *Ifigenia* (1809).

Creston, Paul (1906–1985), adopted name of Joseph Guttovegio US composer and teacher. His music uses jazzy rhythms and a rich orchestral palette.

He studied piano and organ, but was self-taught in harmony, theory, and composition. He also did research in music therapy, aesthetics, acoustics, and the history of music. In 1938 he was awarded a Guggenheim Fellowship.

Works include: 6 symphonies (1941–82), 15 concertos, including one for two violins, much orchestral music; choral works, many based on texts by Whitman; chamber music; songs.

Cristofori, Bartolommeo di Francesco (1665–1731) Italian harpsichord maker, inventor of the piano. In 1709 he constructed a *gravicembalo col piano e forte* ('harpsichord with softness and loudness'), consisting of a harpsichord frame with a new ♭action mechanism: hammers hitting the strings instead of plucking them, allowing for the first time a gradation of soft to loud.

He worked first at Padua and then at Florence. Three of his pianos survive, dated 1720, 1722, and 1726.

Critic, The, or An Opera Rehearsed opera by Stanford (libretto by L C James, adapted from Sheridan's play), produced London, Shaftesbury Theatre, 14 January 1916.

Croce, Giovanni (1557–1609) Italian priest and composer. He was a pupil of Zarlino, at Venice, where he worked at St Mark's and succeeded Donati as maestro di cappella in 1603. He wrote motets, psalms, madrigals, and *capricci* for voices.

Crociato in Egitto, Il/The Crusader in Egypt opera by Meyerbeer (libretto by G Rossi), produced Venice, Teatro La Fenice, 7 March 1824. Crusader Armando, disguised as El-mireno, has secretly married the Sultan's daughter, Palmide. In a struggle between Islam and Christianity, Sultan Aladino eventually allows Palmide to accompany Armando to Europe after the crusader saves Aladino's life.

Croesus, Der hochmütige, gestürzte und wieder erhabne Croesus opera by Keiser (libretto by L von Bostel after the Italian of N Minato), produced Hamburg, Theater beim Gänsemarkt, Carnival, 1710. King Croesus battles against King Cyrus and loses. Croesus' mute son, Atis, now able to speak, returns to court and tests the fidelity of Elmira. About to execute Croesus, Cyrus has a change of heart. The happy ending is complete when Atis and Elmira are to marry.

Croft, William (1678–1727) English organist and composer. His most famous work is his setting of the Burial Service, which is still in use. Much other church music survives, including two volumes of anthems published under the title *Musica Sacra* in 1724. Other works include theatrical pieces and keyboard music.

He was a chorister of the Chapel Royal under John Blow. He later became organist of St Anne's, Soho, from 1700 and, with Jeremiah Clarke, of the Chapel Royal from 1704.

He was Master of the Children there and organist of Westminster Abbey from 1708, succeeding Blow. He received a doctorate in music from Oxford University in 1713.

crook in brass wind instruments, especially horns, a detachable piece of tubing that can be fitted to alter the length of the tube and thus change the tuning.

Crosse, Gordon (1937–) English composer. His works, sometimes showing the influence of Britten, include the operas *The Grace of Todd* (1969) and *The Story of Vasco* (1974). He has also written children's theatre pieces and the oratorio *Changes* (1966).

Born at Bury, Lancashire, he was educated at Oxford University and then undertook two years' research into 15th-century music. He studied under Egon Wellesz and later under Goffredo Petrassi in Rome. He has taught at Birmingham University, the University of Essex, and at King's College, Cambridge.

Works include: the operas *Purgatory* (1969), *The Grace of Todd* (1969); ballet *Young Apollo* (1984); two symphonies (1964 and 1976), two violin concertos (1962, 1969), *Dreamsongs* for orchestra (1979), *Array* for trumpet and strings (1986); *Quiet* for wind band (1987); string quartet (1980); piano trio (1986); pieces for children: *Meet my Folks* (Hughes), *Potter Thompson* and *Holly from the Bongs*.

cross-fingering a method of fingering woodwind instruments which omits some intermediate holes. It is often convenient, and may sometimes be necessary for high notes.

cross relation alternate name for ◊false relation, a musical term.

cross rhythms either the simultaneous presentation of opposing rhythmic patterns within the same metre (for example one part playing two notes per beat while another part plays three notes per beat, '2 against 3'), or the superimposition of at least two different and unrelated metres (for example 3/4 in one part and 4/4 in another).

Crotch, William (1775–1847) English composer. He was a child prodigy who played the organ at the age of four, went to Cambridge at the age of 11 to assist Randall at the organs of Trinity and King's Colleges, and produced an oratorio *The Captivity of Judah* there in 1789. In 1788 he moved to Oxford to study theology. In 1790 he began to study music and was appointed organist at Christ Church, Oxford; he succeeded Philip Hayes

as professor in 1798. On the establishment of the Royal Academy of Music in London in 1822 he became its first principal.

Works include: oratorios *Palestine* (1805–11) and *The Captivity of Judah* (two settings); *Ode to Fancy* (J Warton) and ode for the installation of Lord Grenville as Chancellor of Oxford University, ode for the accession of George IV; funeral anthem for the Duke of York; anthems and chants, motet *Methinks I hear*; glees; concertos and fugues for organ.

crotchet, US quarter note in music, a note value one-quarter the duration of a ◊semibreve. It is written as a filled black note-head with a stem. It is the basic unit of beat for the most frequently used time signatures (2/4, 3/4, 4/4, and so on).

Crozier, Eric (1914–1994) English librettist and stage director. He wrote the libretti for Britten's *Albert Herring* (1946), *Saint Nicolas* (1948), *Let's Make an Opera* (1949), and *Billy Budd* (with E M Forster) (1951).

He studied in London and Paris and produced plays for British Broadcasting Corporation (BBC) television 1936–39. He was associated with Britten from 1945 and cofounded with him the English Opera Group in 1947 and the Aldeburgh Festival in 1948. He produced the premiere of *Peter Grimes* 1945 and its US first performance (at Tanglewood) 1946; *The Rape of Lucretia* (at Glyndebourne) 1946. He also translated operas by Verdi, Mozart, and Richard Strauss.

Crucible, The opera in four acts by Robert Ward (libretto by composer and B Stambler after Arthur Miller's play), produced New York City Opera, 26 October 1961. Seventeenth-century New England witchcraft trial seen as precursor of Cold War anticommunist hysteria.

Crüger, Johann (1598–1662) German theorist and composer. He was cantor at St Nicholas' Church, Berlin, from 1622, and wrote several chorales which were later used by J S Bach. He also wrote manuals on singing and composition.

Works include: *Praxis pietatis melica* containing hymn tunes with bass, *Geistliche Kirchen-Melodien* containing hymn tunes prescribed by Martin Luther, set for four voices with instruments (1649), Magnificats; secular songs.

Crumb, George Henry (1929–) US composer of imagist works. His music employs unusual graphics and imaginative sonorities, such as the ◊musical saw in *Ancient Voices of Children* (1970), settings of poems by the Spanish poet Lorca.

He studied in Berlin with Boris Blacher and at the University of Michigan with Ross Lee Finney. His early work was influenced by Schoenberg, and he has also used aleatory techniques.

Works include: the orchestral pieces *Variazoni* (1959), *Echoes of Time and the River* (1967); *Star-Child* for soprano, children's voices, male speaking choir, bell ringers, and orchestra, performed New York, 1977, conductor Boulez), *A Haunted Landscape* for instrumental ensemble (1984); *Night Music* for soprano and ensemble (1963), four books of madrigals for soprano, with various instrumental ensembles (1965–69), *11 Echoes of Autumn* for violin, flute, clarinet, piano (1965), *Ancient Voices of Children* for soprano and ensemble (1970), *Black Angels* for amplified string quartet, *13 Images from the Dark Land* (1970); *Voice of the Whale*, with electronics (1972), *Federico's Little Songs* for soprano, flute, and percussion (1986); four books of *Makrokosmos* for amplified piano and percussion (1972–79); *Processional* for piano (1983), *An Idyll for the Misbegotten* for amplified flute and three percussionists (1985), *Zeitgeist* for two amplified pianos (1987).

crumhorn ('curved horn') any of a Renaissance woodwind family of musical instruments with a double reed enclosed in a cap, and with soprano, alto, tenor, and bass members. It has a narrow cylindrical bore and is curved upwards like a walking stick held upside down. It dates from the 15th century and emits a buzzing tone.

Crusell, Bernhard Henrik (1775–1838) Finnish composer and clarinettist. He was a member of the military band at Svaeborg Castle, Finland, before moving to Stockholm in 1791, where he studied with the Abbé Vogler. In 1798 he went to Berlin and in 1803 studied with Henri-Montan Berton and François Gossec in Paris. A leading clarinet virtuoso of his day, he also worked at the Stockholm Opera; translating and conducting for the first time in Sweden operas by Beethoven, Rossini, Meyerbeer, and Auber.

Works include: the opera *Den lilla slavinnan/The Little Slave Girl* (1824); three clarinet concertos (1811, 1818, 1828), Concertante for horn, bassoon, clarinet, and orchestra (1816), Concertino for bassoon and orchestra; three quartets for clarinet and strings (1811, 1817, 1823), three clarinet duos (1821), Divertimen-

to for oboe and strings (1823); 37 songs for four-part chorus.

crwth, also called crot, crotta, crotte or rotte (Welsh 'crowd') early bowed string instrument, ancestor of the ◊violin family.

Cry work by Giles Swayne for 28 amplified voices, depicting the creation of the world; composed 1978, first performed London, 23 July 1980.

csárdás a Hungarian dance consisting of a slow movement called *lassú* and a quick one called *friss*.

Cubana, La, oder Ein leben für die Kunst/ La Cubana, or a Life for the Arts vaudeville by Henze (text by M Enzensberger, after M Barnet); composed 1973, first performed New York, NET theatre, 4 March 1974; stage premiere Munich, Theater am Gärtnerplatz, 28 May 1975.

cue a few notes printed in small music type in instrumental or vocal parts of a musical work, serving as a guide to show where the performer is to come in after a lengthy rest.

Cui, César Antonovich (1835–1918) Russian composer and writer, of French parentage. An army engineer by profession, he became a member of 'The ◊Five' group of composers and was an enthusiastic proponent of Russian nationalist music in the press. Despite this, his own musical tastes tended towards the France of Auber and Meyerbeer in the operas *Angelo* (1876), based on Victor Hugo, and *Le Flibustier/The Buccaneer* (1889), based on a play by Jean Richepin.

Cui composed some attractive vocal and piano miniatures, and ten operas, including *A Prisoner in the Caucasus* (1857–58), first performed 1883, and *William Ratcliff* (1861–68), first performed 1869. He also collaborated with Borodin, Mussorgsky, Rimsky-Korsakov, and Minkus on the opera-ballet *Mlada*, and completed Mussorgsky's *Sorochintsy Fair*.

Cui was educated at the High School of Wilno, where his father, a French officer left behind in the retreat from Moscow in 1812, was professor of French. He had some lessons in music from Moniuszko, but was sent to the School of Military Engineering at St Petersburg in 1850, where he became subprofessor in 1857. He became an authority on fortifications and remained an amateur in music, but he joined Balakirev's circle of Russian nationalist composers and became one of the 'Five', though the least exclusively Russian among them. He became a critic in 1864 and did much literary work for the nationalist cause.

Works include: OPERA *The Mandarin's Son* (1859, produced 1878), *A Prisoner in the Caucasus* (after Pushkin), *William Ratcliff* (after Heine, 1869), *Angelo* (after Hugo), *Le Flibustier* (libretto by J Richepin), *The Saracen* (after Dumas senior, 1889), *A Feast in Time of Plague* (Pushkin, 1900), *Mam'zelle Fifi* (after Maupassant), *Matteo Falcone* (after Mérimée) and *The Captain's Daughter* (1911).

OTHER works for chorus with and without orchestra; four suites and other works for orchestra; string quartets in C minor (1890) and D (1907); 15 op. nos. of piano pieces, three pieces for two pianos; various instrumental pieces; about 25 op. nos. of songs including settings of Pushkin, Lermontov, Nekrassov, Richepin, and Mickiewicz.

Cummings, Conrad (1948–) US composer. He studied at Yale, Stanford, and Tanglewood, and has worked at the Columbia-Princeton Electronic Music Center and at Institut de Recherche et de Co-ordination Acoustique-Musique (IRCAM), Paris. Teacher at the Oberlin Conservatory from 1980. His music draws on Baroque models as well as electronic resources.

Works include: OPERA *Eros and Psyche* (1983), *Cassandra* (1985, revised as a dramatic scene), *Positions* (1956) (1988, after 1950s sex manuals), *Insertions* (1988), *Photo-Op* (1989), and *Tonkin* (after an incident in the Vietnam War, 1993).

OTHER *Subway Songs* for four-track tape (1974), *Movement* for orchestra (1975), *Skin Songs* for soprano and ensemble (1978), *Dinosaur Music* for ten-track tape and 14 loudspeakers (1981), *Music for Starlore* for stereo tape (1982).

cummings, e(dward) e(stlin) (1894–1962) US poet whose works inspired Richard R ◊Bennett (*Love Songs*), Luciano ◊Berio (*Circles*), Pierre ◊Boulez (*Cummings ist der Dichter*), Peter ◊Dickinson (songs), D ◊Erb (*Cummings Cycle*), E ◊Harper (*seven poems by e e c*), and Roger ◊Smalley (septet for soprano and ensemble).

Cummings, W(illiam) H(ayman) (1831–1915) English organist, tenor, and scholar. He sang under Felix Mendelssohn's direction as a boy and later made an edition of 'Hark! the Herald Angels Sing' to music from Mendelssohn's *Festgesang*. He sang in the J S Bach's Passions and conducted the Sacred Harmonic Society; cofounded the Purcell Society and edited three volumes for it; wrote a biography of H Purcell, 1881. He also wrote on Blow, Arne, and Handel (biography, 1904). He was principal of the Guildhall School of Music and Drama 1896–1910.

cummings ist der dichter/cummings is the poet work by Boulez for 16 voices and 24 instruments; composed 1970, first performed Stuttgart, 25 September 1970; work in progress. Title allegedly arose as the result of a misheard telephone conversation, concerning the name of the poet who provided the work's text (e e cummings).

Cunning Little Vixen, The/Příhody lišky Bystroušky opera by Janáček (libretto by the composer after R Těsnohlídek's verses for a comic strip published serially in a Brno newspaper during 1920). Composed 1921–23, produced Brno, 6 November 1924. Vixen is captured, but escapes, marries, and raises a litter. She is shot by a poacher, but her spirit survives in her cubs.

Cupid and Death masque by James Shirley with music by Locke and C Gibbons, performed London, before the Portuguese ambassador, Leicester Fields, 26 March 1653.

Curioso indiscreto, Il/Indiscreet Curiosity opera by Anfossi (librettist unknown), produced Rome, Teatro della Dame, February 1777. Mozart wrote two extra soprano arias for this when it was produced in Vienna, 30 June 1783. Marchese Calandrino tests fidelity of Clorinda, who falls in love with the Contino, the Marchese's friend.

Curlew River church parable in one act by Britten (libretto by W Plomer after the Japanese Noh play *Sumidagawa*), produced Orford Church, Suffolk, 12 June 1964. Ferryman conveys madwoman to her son's grave; during prayer, an angel restores her sanity.

Curran, Alvin (1938–) US composer. He studied with Elliott Carter at Yale, and at Rome cofounded the group Musica Electronica Viva in 1966; he has also given solo performances at festivals of new music.

Works include: *Songs and Views from the Magnetic Gardens* (1975); *Light Flowers, Dark Flowers* (1977); *The Works* (1980); *Maritime Rites* for foghorns, ships, and rowing boats full of singers (1984); *Crystal Psalms*, with six choruses (1988); *Electric Rags I* and *II* (1985, 1989).

curtain tune an old term sometimes used in the place of 'act tune' for an ◊intermezzo or entr'acte in the incidental music for a play.

curtal capped double-reed Renaissance woodwind instrument, ancestor of the ◊bassoon, of folded conical bore and mild reedy tone, also known as the **dulcian**.

Curtis, Alan (1934–   ) US conductor, harp-sichordist, and musicologist. He is an author-ity on early keyboard music and has edited for recording and produced several 17th-century operas, including Monteverdi's *L'in-coronazione di Poppea*, Cavalli's *Erismena*, and Cesti's *Il Tito* at Innsbruck, 1983.

He studied at Michigan and Illinois Uni-versities and with Gustav Leonhardt in Amsterdam.

Curtis Institute of Music music school in Philadelphia, USA, founded by Mary Louise Bok 1924 in memory of her father Cyrus Curtis. Since 1928 students have not had to pay tuition fees. Directors have included Josef Hofmann (1926–38), Efrem Zimbalist (1941–68), Rudolf Serkin (1968–76), John de Lancie (1977–85), and Gary Graffman (from 1986).

Curwen English family of music education-ists and publishers:

John (1816–1880), founded the Tonic Sol-fa method of music notation (originated in the 11th century by Guido d'Arezzo), in which the notes of the diatonic major scale are named by syllables (doh, ray, me, soh, lah, te) to simplify singing by sight; he established the Tonic Sol-fa Association in 1853 and the publishing firm in London in 1863.

John Spencer (1847–1916), son of John. He studied at the Royal Academy of Music under Macfarren, Sullivan, and Prout, carried on his father's work and began the competition festival movement in England with the Stratford (East London) Festival in 1882.

Annie (Jessy), born Gregg, later Matlock (1845–1932), wife of John Spencer. She stu-died at the Royal Irish Academy of Music, married in 1877 and wrote a number of books on a music-teaching method of her own.

cut time alternative for ◊alla breve, a musical term.

cyclic form in musical analysis, a multi-movement work in which the same motif, theme, melody, or other notable compos-itional element is used throughout, at times in a different context or manifestation from its original form. Early examples include works by Handel and Vivaldi, but not until the 19th century did this technique reach its fruition, in works including Beethoven's Fifth Sym-phony 1808, Liszt's Piano Sonata in B Minor 1853, and compositions based on the theories of Wagner's ◊leitmotif and Berlioz's 'idée fixe' (a repeated ◊theme).

cyclic mass a misleading term for a setting of the Ordinary of the Mass in which there is

some kind of thematic connection between the movements.

cymbal ancient percussion instrument of indefinite pitch, consisting of a shallow circular brass dish suspended at the centre; either used in pairs clashed together or singly, struck with a beater. Smaller finger cymbals or **crotala**, of ancient origin but used in the 20th century by Debussy and Stock-hausen, are precise in pitch. Turkish or 'buzz' cymbals incorporate loose rivets to extend the sound.

Cymon opera by Michael Arne (libretto by D Garrick, based on Dryden's *Cymon and Iphigenia*), produced London, Drury Lane Theatre, 2 January 1767.

Cyrano opera by W Damrosch (libretto by W J Henderson, based on Rostand's play *Cyrano de Bergerac*), produced New York Metropoli-tan Opera, 27 February 1913.

Cyrano de Bergerac opera by Alfano (li-bretto by H Cain, based on Rostand's play), produced in Italian translation, Rome, Teatro Reale, 22 January 1936. Cyrano has a nose for amorous trouble, writing love letters for the verbally inept Christian, who loves Roxane.

Cythère assiégée, La/Cytherea Besieged opera by Gluck (libretto by C S Favart, based on Longus' *Daphnis and Chloe*), produced Vienna, Burgtheater, spring 1759. Scythian warriors lay siege to Cytherea but fall for her attendant nymphs.

Czaar und Zimmermann (Lortzing). See ◊*Zar und Zimmermann*.

czakan woodwind instrument of the ◊flute type, probably originating from Transylvania but very fashionable in Vienna around 1830, made in the shape of a walking stick and often used as such.

Czernohorsky see Bohuslav ◊Cernohorský.

Czerny, Carl (1791–1857) Austrian pianist, teacher, and composer. He was first taught the piano by his father, played brilliantly at the age of ten, and became a pupil of Beethoven about that time; he also took advice from Hummel and Clementi. Not liking to appear in public, he took to teaching and soon had an enormous following of pupils, among which he chose only the most gifted. This left him enough leisure for composition, which he cultivated so assidu-ously as to produce almost 1,000 works. He is chiefly remembered for his books of graded studies and technical exercises used in piano teaching, including the *Complete Theoretical* *and Practical Pianoforte School* (1839) which is still in widespread use.

Works include: 24 Masses, 4 Requiems, 300 graduals and offertories; many symphonies, overtures; concertos; string quartets and trios; choruses; songs and, most numerous of all, masses of piano music, including studies, exercises, preludes, and fugues in all the keys and endless arrangements of other composers' works.

D

D the second note, or supertonic, of the scale of C major.

D Deutsch, followed by a number, indicates listing of work by Schubert in the thematic catalogue by O E Deutsch.

d the tonic note in any key in tonic sol-fa notation, pronounced 'doh'.

da capo (Italian 'from the top') term in written music instructing a player that the music at that point starts from the beginning. It is abbreviated to 'D.C.'. A companion instruction is dal segno ('from the sign').

da capo al fine (Italian 'from the beginning to the end') musical phrase in which the performer is asked to go back to the beginning; with the simple *da capo*, the composition is not to be repeated as a whole, but only to the point where the word *fine* ('end') appears.

da capo aria a distinctive type of vocal piece for a single voice (though duets and other ensemble pieces may be in the same form) consisting of three sections, the third of which is a repetition of the first, while the middle section is a contrast based sometimes on similar and sometimes on wholly different thematic material. The da capo aria was cultivated in the second half of the 17th and first half of the 18th century (up to the earlier works of Gluck), notably by A Scarlatti, Handel, Bach, Hasse, and Jommelli.

Dafne opera by Schütz (libretto by Martin Opitz, partly translated from Rinuccini), produced Torgau, Hartenfels Castle, at the wedding of Georg, Landgrave of Hesse, and Sophia Eleonora, Princess of Saxony, 23 April 1627. The music has not survived.

Dafne, La opera by Gagliano (libretto by O Rinuccini), produced Mantua, at the ducal court, January 1608.
   Opera by Peri (libretto ditto), produced Florence, Palazzo Corsi, Carnival 1597. The first Italian opera and first opera on record anywhere. After belittling Cupid, Apollo falls victim to the arrows of love, pursuing an unyielding Daphne.

Dafni opera by Astorga (libretto by E Manfredi), produced Genoa, Teatro Sant' Agostino, 21 April 1709.

Dahl, Ingolf (1912–1970) German-born US composer. After study in Cologne and Zurich he moved to the USA in 1935, teaching at the University of Southern California from 1945. His earlier work was dissonant and expressionistic; he later came under Stravinsky's influence.
   Works include: Concerto for saxophone and wind orchestra (1949), Symphony Concertante for two clarinets and orchestra (1953), *The Tower of St Barbara* for orchestra (1955), piano quartet (his first serial work, 1957), *Elegy Concerto* for violin and orchestra (1963), *Aria Sinfonica* (1965), *Intervals* for strings (1970).

Dahlhaus, Carl (1928–1989) German musicologist. A prolific writer on music theory and history, his books and articles cover an enormous range of topics and periods; he is best known for his studies in 19th-century music and history. Extremely influential in German-speaking musicology, and increasingly so in English-speaking circles from the early 1980s when his major works began to be translated. Dahlhaus believed that music cannot be divorced from the society and culture which produces it; therefore, an understanding of musical history can only flow from an understanding of history in a wider sense. He was influenced by the historical theories of Hegel and Marx, and by the philosophical approach to music taken by Adorno. His theoretical writings include *Esthetics of Music* (1967) and *Foundations of Music History* (1977); historical studies include *Nineteenth-Century Music* (1980), *Ludwig van Beethoven* (1987) and the articles collected as *Schoenberg and the New Music* (1987).

Dalayrac, Nicolas-Marie (1753–1809), originally d'Alayrac French composer. In 1777 he published six string quartets, and two small operas were performed privately in 1781. The following year he made his debut with *L'Eclipse totale* at the Théâtre Italien. He changed his name from its aristocratic form during the Revolution, and adapted operatic airs to lyrics with Republican sentiments.

He first intended to study law, then in 1774 went to Versailles to embark on a military career, but his main interest was music and he took lessons in composition from Honoré Langlé (1741–1807).

Works include: about 60 operas, including *Nina ou la Folle par amour* (1786), *Les Deux petits Savoyards, Camille, Adolphe et Clara* (1799), *Maison à vendre*; 36 string quartets.

Dalby, Martin (1942–) Scottish composer. He studied at the Royal College of Music with Herbert Howells (composition) and Frederick Riddle (viola). He has been influenced by jazz and by Spanish music; from 1965 he has held administrative posts in London and Glasgow.

Works include: symphony (1970), *Concerto Martin Pescatore*, for strings (1971), viola concerto (1974), *Nozze di Primavera* for orchestra (1984); *Keeper of the Pass* for soprano and instruments (1971), *Orpheus* for chorus, narrator, and 11 instruments (1972), *Call for the Hazel Tree*, for chorus and electronics (1979); *Yet still she is the Moon*, brass septet (1973), *Aleph* for eight instruments (1975), *Man Walking*, octet for wind and strings (1980); two piano sonatas (1985, 1989).

Dalcroze, Emile Jaques- see ◊Jaques-Dalcroze.

Dale, Benjamin (1885–1943) English composer. He studied at the Royal Academy of Music in London, where he later became professor of composition and warden.

Works include: cantata *Before the Paling of the Stars* (1912), and *Song of Praise* for chorus and orchestra (1923); violin and piano sonata.

Dalibor opera by Smetana (libretto in German, by J Wenzig, translated into Czech by E Špindler), produced Prague, Czech Theatre, 16 May 1868. Milada attempts to rescue imprisoned Dalibor, but her plan is betrayed and both die in a final battle.

Dallam, Thomas (c. 1570–after 1614) English organ builder. He built organs for King's College, Cambridge, and Worcester Cathedral. He travelled to Constantinople in 1599–1600 with a mechanical organ, a present from Queen Elizabeth I to the Sultan.

Robert Dallam (1602–1665), **Ralph Dallam** (d. 1673) and **George Dallam**, also organ builders, were probably members of the same family.

Dallapiccola, Luigi (1904–1975) Italian composer. Initially a Neo-Classicist, he adopted a lyrical twelve-tone style after 1945. His works include the operas *Il prigioniero/The Prisoner* 1949 and *Ulisse/Ulysses* 1968, as well as many vocal and instrumental compositions.

Dallapiccola was born at Pisino, Istria. For political reasons his family were moved to Graz in 1917, where his decisive first contacts with music (especially opera) were made. The family returned to Italy in 1921, where Dallapiccola studied at the Florence Conservatory and in 1931 became professor. In 1956 he was appointed professor at Queen's College, New York. His mature music, while using serial techniques, modified them to allow for a more lyrical style than is usual, not avoiding tonal references, thematic structures, and harmonic progressions.

He first attracted international attention at pre-1939 festivals of the International Society for Contemporary Music (ISCM). His *Songs of Captivity* were prompted by the fascist racial laws of 1938, and represent the expression in music of an imprisonment which was as much mental as physical. This 'protest music', with its theme of mental persecution, was continued in his later opera *Il prigionero* 1944–48 (after *La Torture par l'esperance* by Villiers de l'Isle Adam) and the choral *Songs of Liberty* 1951–55. His early opera *Volo di notte* 1937–39 (after Antoine de Saint-Exupéry) makes tentative use of serial techniques which were brought to fruition in his highly personal and poetic manner in the group of *Greek Lyrics* 1942–45. In the 1950s Dallapiccola was much influenced by Webern, and his own personal style gave way to a less poetic and more cerebral expression. Nevertheless his supremacy as a vocal writer was maintained on the large oratorio *Job* 1950, and *Requiescant* 1957–58, and small works such as

Goethe Lieder 1953, *Cinque canti*, 1956, *Preghiere*, 1962, and *Parole di San Paolo*, 1964. His large opera *Ulysses*, 1968, the fruit of ten years' work, reveals a return to his earlier poetic style. Dallapiccola was not successful with instrumentalism in spite of his excellence as an orchestrator. He had great influence in postwar Italy, and played a dominant part in the cultural renaissance of that country.

Works include: OPERA *Volo di notte* (after Saint-Exupéry, 1937–39), *Il Prigionero* (1944–48), *Ulisse* (1960–68); ballet *Marsia* (1942–43).

VOICES AND ORCHESTRAL *Canti di prigionera* (1941), *Canti di liberazione* (1955), *Concerto per la notte di natale* for soprano and orchestra (1957), *Tre laudi*.

ORCHESTRAL *Piccolo concerto* for piano and orchestra (1941), *Tartiniana*, divertimento for violin and chamber orchestra (1951), *Piccola musica notturna* (1954; for chamber ensemble 1961). Music for three pianos; *Liriche anacreontiche Roncevals*, cycle of Greek and other songs; *Ciaccona, intermezzo e adagio* for solo cello (1945).

dal segno (Italian 'from the sign') term in written music instructing a player that the music at that point recommences from a place other than the beginning, indicated in the score by a crossed 'S', sign. The abbreviated form is 'D.S.'. To start from the beginning, the instruction is da capo ('from the top').

Dame blanche, La/The White Lady opera by Boieldieu (libretto by Scribe, based on Scott's *Guy Mannering* and *The Monastery*), produced Paris, Opéra-Comique, 10 December 1825. It contains some Scottish tunes. At auction George Brown prevents the castle from falling into the wrong hands. With help from orphan Anna, it is revealed that George is actually the missing heir Julien Avenel.

Damett, Thomas (1389 or 1390–c. 1437) English composer. He was at the Chapel Royal 1413–31, and was canon of Windsor from 1431 until his death. Works of his are included in the Old Hall manuscript.

Damnation de Faust, La dramatic cantata by Berlioz (words by composer and A Gandonnière, based on Goethe's drama), composed 1846, incorporating the *Huit Scènes de Faust* of 1828; first performed Paris, Opéra-Comique, 6 December 1846; produced as an opera, Monte Carlo, 18 February 1893.

Damoiselle élue, La/The Blessed Damsel cantata for soprano, mezzo, and female chorus and orchestra by Debussy, set to French translation by Gabriel Sarrazin of

Rossetti's poem in 1887–88. First performed Paris, Salle Erard, 8 April 1893.

Dämon, Der/The Demon dance pantomime by Hindemith, scenario by M Krell; composed 1922 and performed Darmstadt, 1 December 1923. Concert suite for small orchestra arranged 1923.

damper pedal on a piano, an alternative name for the ◊sustaining pedal. The tone is sustained because the pedal lifts the dampers off the strings. Not to be confused with the damping pedal.

damping pedal on a piano, the 'soft' pedal, which on a grand piano shifts the hammers of the instrument so that they touch only two strings or a single string for each note, instead of three or two. For this reason its use is often indicated by the words *una corda* ('one string'). This outdated term should not be confused with the ◊damper pedal.

Damrosch, Walter (Johannes) (1862–1950) US conductor and composer, son of Leopold Damrosch. He studied in Germany and settled in the USA in 1871, and became conductor of the New York Oratorio and Symphonic Societies in 1885. He was director of the Damrosch Opera Company 1894–99, giving the first US performances of several operas by Wagner.

Works include: the operas *The Scarlet Letter* (after Hawthorne, 1896), *Cyrano de Bergerac* (after Rostand, 1913), *The Dove of Peace*, *The Man without a Country* (1937); incidental music to Euripides' *Electra*, *Iphigenia in Aulis*, and *Medea*; *Abraham Lincoln's Song* for baritone solo, chorus, and orchestra; Te Deum; violin and piano sonata; songs.

Danaïdes, Les opera by Salieri (libretto by F L du Roullet and L T de Tschudy, partly based on and translated from Calzabigi's *Ipermestra* intended for Gluck, composed by Millico), produced Paris, Opéra, 26 April 1784. When Danaus orders his fifty daughters to kill their husbands, Hypermestra alone refuses for love of Lyncaeus.

dance of death (German *Totentanz*; French *danse macabre*) popular theme in painting of the late medieval period, depicting an allegorical representation of death (usually a skeleton) leading the famous and the not-so-famous to the grave. One of the best-known representations is a series of woodcuts (1523–26) by Hans Holbein the Younger. It has also been exploited as a theme in music, for example the *Danse macabre* of Saint-Saëns 1874, an orchestral composition in which the xylophone was introduced to represent dancing skeletons.

Dance Rhapsody two works for orchestra by Delius: no. 1 composed 1908, first performed Hereford Festival 8 September 1909, conductor Delius; no. 2 composed 1916, first performed London, 23 October 1923, conductor Wood.

Dances of Galánta orchestral work by Kodály, composed for the 80th anniversary of the Budapest Philharmonic Society, first performed Budapest, 11 December 1936.

Dances of Marchosszék work for piano by Kodály, composed 1927. Version for orchestra first performed Dresden, 28 November 1930, conductor F Busch.

Dance Suite work for orchestra in six movements by Bartók, composed 1923 for the fiftieth anniversary of the merging of Pest, Buda and Obuda into Budapest. First performed Budapest, 19 November 1925, conductor E Dohnányi. Version for piano 1925.

Dandrieu, Jean François (1682–1738), or d'Andrieu French organist and composer. He succeeded his uncle, Pierre Dandrieu, as organist of the church of Saint-Barthélemy in Paris, and in 1704 he became organist at Saint-Merry. He was appointed organist of the royal chapel in 1721. He wrote a book on harpsichord accompaniment.

Works include: a set of symphonies *Les Caractères de la guerre* (1718); trios for two violins and bass; violin sonatas; organ pieces; three volumes of harpsichord pieces.

Daniel-Lesur, Adopted name of Daniel Jean Yves Lesur (1908–   ) French organist and composer. In 1938 he became professor of counterpoint at the Schola Cantorum in Paris. He was also appointed organist at the Benedictine abbey. With Baudrier, Jolivet, and Messiaen, he formed the group known as 'La Jeune France' in 1936.

His teachers included Charles Tournemire and George Caussade (1873–1936).

Works include: the operas *Andrea del Sarto* (1969), *Ondine* (1982), and *La reine morte* (1987); *Suite française* for orchestra (1935); *Passacaille* for piano and orchestra (1937); *Le Voyage d'Automne* for voices and orchestra (1990); *Fantasie Concertante* for cello and orchestra (1993); suite for string trio and piano; three Heine songs for voice and string quartet; *Noëls* and suite *Le Carillon* for piano; *La Vie intérieure* for organ; songs.

Daniel, Play of/Danielis Ludus a medieval liturgical music drama dealing with the story of Daniel in the lions' den. It was written by

students of Beauvais between 1227 and 1234 and intended almost certainly for performance after matins on the feast of the Circumcision (1 January).

Danse, La last of three entrées which make up Rameau's opéra-ballet *Les fêtes d'Hébé* (libretto by A G de Montdorge), produced Paris, Opéra, 21 May 1739. Often heard as a separate item.

Danse Sacrée et Danse Profane work by Debussy for harp and strings; composed 1903, first performed Paris, 6 November 1904.

Danses Concertantes work for chamber orchestra by Stravinsky; composed 1942, in Hollywood, first performed Los Angeles, 8 February 1942.

Dante Alighieri (1265–1321) Italian poet. His works and thought inspired compositions such as the ◊Dante Sonata and ◊Dante Symphony (Liszt); Dante's ◊*Francesca da Rimini* inspired operas by Goetz, Nápravník, Rakhmaninov, and Zandonai; symphonic fantasy by P Tchaikovsky; *Françoise de Rimini* (opera, A Thomas); and *Generali*; see also ◊Wolf-Ferrari (*Vita Nuova*).

Dante and Beatrice symphonic poem by Bantock, first performed London, Music Festival, 1911.

Dante Sonata a one-movement sonata by Liszt, entitled *Aprilès une lecture du Dante*, in the Italian volume of his *Années de pèlerinage*, composed 1837–39, revised 1849. Liszt called it a *sonata quasi fantasia*.

Dante Symphony a symphony by Liszt based on Dante's *Divina commedia*, composed 1855–56, first performed Dresden, 7 November 1857. There are two movements, *Inferno* and *Purgatorio*.

Dantons Tod/Danton's Death opera by Einem (libretto by Boris Blacher and composer, based on Georg Büchner's drama), produced Salzburg, 6 August 1947. During the French Revolution, the evil Robespierre spreads rumours that Danton is an aristocrat. After the trial Danton is guillotined; Lucile, the wife of his friend Desmoulins (also killed) longs for death.

Danza, La opera in one act by Gluck (libretto by Metastasio), performed Vienna, Laxenberg, 5 May 1755.

Danzi, Franz (1763–1826) German cellist and composer. He was a minor member of the Mannheim school of symphonists. A pupil of Georg Vogler, he was a member of the court band at Mannheim and from 1778, at Munich.

He was Kapellmeister to the court of Württemberg at Stuttgart, and later at Karlsruhe.

Works include: the operas *Die Mitternachtsstunde* (1788), *Turandot* (after Gozzi, 1817); church music; symphonies, concertos and concertantes; chamber music.

Daphne opera in one act by Richard Strauss (libretto by Joseph Gregor), produced Dresden, 15 October 1938. Daphne spurns Apollo and sprouts into a laurel tree.

Daphnis et Alcimadure pastoral by Mondonville (libretto, in the Languedoc dialect, by the composer), produced Fontainebleau, at court, 4 November 1754, first Paris performance, Opéra, 29 December 1754.

Daphnis et Chloé ballet by Ravel (scenario after Longus, choreography by Fokin), produced Paris, Théâtre du Chatelet, 8 June 1912.

Da Ponte, Lorenzo (Conegliano Emmanuele) (1749–1838) Italian librettist. He is renowned for his collaboration with Mozart in *The Marriage of Figaro* 1786, *Don Giovanni* 1787, and *Cosí fan tutte* 1790. His adaptations of contemporary plays are deepened by a rich life experience and understanding of human nature.

Born in Ceneda (now Vittorio Veneto), he studied to take holy orders, proving a skilful versifier in both Italian and Latin.

Appointed as a professor in literature at Treviso Seminary 1773, his radical views and immoral behaviour led to his banishment from Venice 1779. Travelling to Vienna, he was appointed as librettist to the New Italian Theatre 1781 on the recommendation of Salieri. His first major success was in adapting Beaumarchais's comedy for Mozart's *The Marriage of Figaro. Don Giovanni* and *Cosí fan tutte* followed, together with libretti for other composers. In 1805 he emigrated to the USA, eventually becoming a teacher of Italian language and literature.

Daquin, Louis Claude (1694–1772), or d'Aquin French organist, harpsichordist, and composer. He studied under Louis Marchand and played before Louis XIV as a child prodigy at the age of six. At 12 he was appointed organist of Petit Saint-Antoine in Paris. In 1727 he was Rameau's successful rival for the post of organist at Saint-Paul, and in 1739 succeeded Dandrieu at the Chapel Royal. He is especially remembered as one of the great French representatives of harpsichord music.

Works include: cantata *La Rose*; harpsichord pieces including *Le Coucou*; *Noëls* for organ or harpsichord.

Dardanus opera by Rameau (libretto by C A L de La Bruère), produced Paris, Opéra, 19 November 1739). Iphise loves her father's enemy Dardanus, but Teucer wants his daughter to marry Antenor. Captured by Antenor, Dardanus later escapes and slays an avenging sea monster, saving Antenor. Dardanus and Iphise are united.

Opera by Sacchini (libretto ditto, altered by N F Guillard), produced Versailles, at court, 18 September 1784; first Paris performance, Opéra, 30 November 1784.

dargason an English country dance and folksong at least as old as the 16th century. Holst used it in his *St Paul's Suite*.

Dargillières (lived 16th century) Parisian family of instrument makers, including **Anthoine** (c. 1518–1572). He was 'faiseur d'orgues de la Chapelle du roi', and built various church organs in Paris. His son **Roch** (born 1559) built numerous organs in the Paris neighbourhood, including those at Rouen (St Michael) and Chartres (cathedral).

Dargomizhsky, Aleksandr Sergeievich (1813–1869) Russian composer. He studied music as an amateur at St Petersburg and led the life of a dilettante. After meeting Mikhail Glinka in 1833 he set to work on his first opera. After the next stage attempt he devoted himself mainly to songs between 1856 and 1860, including many of a satirical nature anticipating those of Mussorgsky. In 1864 he visited western Europe, but was able to gain a hearing only in Belgium, where he performed his orchestral fantasies. On his return he associated himself with Balakirev's nationalist group, without actually joining it. He set Pushkin's poem 'The Stone Guest', based on the story of Don Juan, as an opera word for word. It was left unfinished at his death, but was completed, on his directions, by Cui and orchestrated by Rimsky-Korsakov in 1872.

Dargomizhsky was born in Tula. He showed musical talent at an early age and was taught to play the piano and violin; by the age of 11 he had made some attempt at composition. He entered the civil service in St Petersburg but retired in 1835 after four years and, moving in fashionable circles, became well known as an amateur pianist and a composer of dilettante drawing-room songs. It was his chance meeting with Mikhail Glinka, who lent him his notes taken during his studies with Siegfried Dehn in Berlin, which gave his talents a more serious bias, and the two composers may be said together to have symbolized the pretensions of Russian musical genius at this period; but whereas Glinka's music was idealistic and lyrical, Dargomizhsky's was realistic and dramatic.

Though inferior to Glinka, Dargomizhsky is a figure of some importance in the history of Russian opera: his first opera was *Esmeralda* 1839, based on Victor Hugo's *Notre-Dame de Paris*; however, it was not accepted for the Imperial Opera until 1847. This was followed by a cantata on 'The Triumph of Bacchus', a dramatic poem by Pushkin, which he converted into a ballet-opera in 1867. Then came the opera *Rusalka or The Watersprite* 1855, for the libretto of which Dargomizhsky again turned to Pushkin. This opera, superior to *Esmeralda*, gradually won a permanent place in the Russian repertory. Dargomizhsky's association with Mily ◊Balakirev and his circle gave him a leading part in the formation of a national and progressive school of Russian music. Dargomizhsky's own views on opera resembled those of Gluck and Wagner in the adaptation of the music to the dramatic import of the text.

Works include: the operas *Esmeralda* (after Hugo, 1847), *Rusalka* (after Pushkin, 1856), *Rogdana* (unfinished). *The Stone Guest* (Pushkin, completed by Cui and Rimsky-Korsakov; produced posthumously 1872): ballet *Bacchus' Feast:* a duet for an opera *Mazeppa;* orchestral fantasies *Kazatchok, Baba-Yaga* and *Mummers' Dance; Tarantelle slave* for piano duet; about 90 songs, vocal duets, trios, quartets, choruses.

Dart, (Robert) Thurston (1921–1971) English harpsichordist and musicologist. His pioneer reinterpretations of Baroque classics such as Bach's *Brandenburg Concertos* helped to launch the trend towards authenticity in early music.

dastgah melodic mode, used as a basis for improvisation or composition in Persian music.

Daughter of the Regiment (Donizetti). See ◊*Fille du Régiment, La*

Davenant, William (1606–1668), or D'Avenant English poet and playwright. His works inspired Banister (*Circe*); W ◊Lawes (*Triumph of the Prince d'Amour* and *Unfortunate Lovers*); ◊Locke (*Macbeth*); Pepys ('Beauty retire'); ◊Siege of Rhodes (Locke, H Lawes, H Cooke, Coleman and Hudson).

David opera in five acts and 12 scenes by Milhaud (libretto by A Lunel), written to celebrate the establishment of Jerusalem as the capital of Judea, produced Jerusalem, 1 June 1954. Founder of Jerusalem fathers Solomon out of Bathsheba.

David, Félicien-(César) (1810–1876) French composer. He settled in Paris in 1841 and made a great success with his oriental descriptive symphony *Le Désert* 1844, inspired by his travels in Palestine. He was one of the first Western composers to introduce oriental scales and melodies into his music.

He was born at Cadenet, Vaucluse, and learnt music at the cathedral of Aix-en-Provence and from 1825 at a Jesuit college, and began to compose early. He entered the Paris Conservatoire in 1830, travelled in the East in 1833–35, and after his return began to make a name as a composer of quasi-oriental music. He wrote symphonies, chamber music, and songs. Once highly popular, his music is now almost entirely forgotten.

Works include: the operas *La Perle du Brésil* (1851), *Herculanum* (1859), *Lalla-Roukh* (after Moore, 1862), *Le Saphir*, and *La Captive* (withdrawn); oratorio *Moïse au Sinaï;* mystery *Eden;* motets and hymns; descriptive symphony *Le Désert* and *Christophe Colomb;* four symphonies; four string quartets; 24 string quintets, two nonets for wind; *Mélodies orientales* for piano; songs.

David, Johann Nepomuk (1895–1977) Austrian composer. He was a choirboy at St Florian and studied at the Vienna Academy. He taught composition successively at Leipzig, Salzburg, and Stuttgart, and published analytical studies of classical composers.

Works include: eight symphonies (1936–65), two partitas for orchestra, two concertos for string orchestra; flute concertos, two violin concertos, *Requiem chorale* for soli, chorus, and orchestra; three string quartets, four string trios, and other chamber music; three cello sonatas; chorale preludes and other works for organ.

Davidde Penitente/The Penitent David cantata by Mozart, K469 (libretto probably by L da Ponte), made up in March 1785, mainly from portions of the unfinished C minor Mass, K427, of 1782–83. Only two arias are new.

Davidsbündlertänze/Dances of the League of David a set of 18 piano pieces by Schumann, op. 6, composed in 1837, the title alluding to the *Davidsbund* (league of David) association.

Davie, Cedric Thorpe (1913–1983) Scottish composer and organist. He studied at the Scottish National Academy of Music in

Glasgow, the Royal Academy of Music in London, and later the Royal College of Music there, where he was a pupil of R O Morris, Vaughan Williams, and Gordon Jacob, gaining the Cobbett and Sullivan Prizes in 1935. He also studied piano with Egon Petri in Germany, and composition with Kodály at Budapest and Kilpinen at Helsinki. He was head of music at St Andrews University from 1945.

Works include: the opera *Gammer Gurton's Needle*, ballad opera *The Forrigan Reel* (James Bridie); concerto for piano and strings; string quartet; violin and piano sonata, sonatinas for cello and piano and flute and piano; eight *Little Songs*.

Davies, (Henry) Walford (1869–1941) English composer and broadcaster. His compositions include the cantata *Everyman* 1904, the 'Solemn Melody' 1908 for organ and strings, chamber music, and part songs. He also wrote sacred music and pieces for children. He was a popular radio broadcaster, particularly in his British Broadcasting Corporation (BBC) series, *Music and the ordinary listener* 1926–30.

He was educated at St George's Chapel, Windsor, under Walter Parratt (1841–1924), and at the Royal College of Music in London, where Charles Stanford was his composition master. He held various organist's appointments, and graduated in music from Cambridge University in 1898, when he was appointed organist and choirmaster at the Temple Church. He was professor of music at the University of Wales, Aberystwyth, from 1919. He resigned from the Temple in 1923 and became organist at St George's, Windsor, in 1927. In 1934 he succeeded Elgar as Master of the King's Musick.

Davies, Peter Maxwell (1934–) English composer and conductor. His music combines medieval and serial codes of practice with a heightened Expressionism as in his opera *Taverner* 1972, based on the life and works of the 16th-century composer John Taverner. Other works include the opera *The Lighthouse* 1980. He was appointed conductor of the British Broadcasting Corporation (BBC) Scottish Symphony Orchestra in 1985.

Davies was born in Manchester. After training at the Royal Manchester College of Music alongside the British composers Alexander Goehr and Harrison Birtwistle, he studied with the Italian composer Goffredo Petrassi (1904–). From 1959 to 1962 he taught music at Cirencester Grammar School, and in 1962 went to the USA to study with the US

composer Roger Sessions at Princeton University. Since 1970 he has been based in Orkney.

Works include: STAGE *Nocturnal Dances* (1970), *Taverner*, opera (1972), *The Martyrdom of St Magnus*, chamber opera (1977), *The Two Fiddlers*, opera for children (1978), *The Lighthouse*, chamber opera (1980), opera *Resurrection* (1987), ballet *Caroline Mathilde* (1990), opera *The Doctor of Myddfai* (1996).

ORCHESTRAL *Worldes Blis* (1968), *Vesalii Icones* for dancer, cello, and ensemble (1969), *Ave Maris Stella*, for chamber ensemble (1975), six symphonies (1976, 1981, 1985, 1989, 1994, 1996), violin concerto (1986), ten Strathclyde concertos, for various instruments (1987–95).

VOCAL *O Magnum Mysterium*, four carols a cappella (1960), *Eight Songs for a Mad King* for voice and ensemble (1969), *Hymn to St Magnus* for mezzo and instruments (1972), *Miss Donnithorne's Maggot* for mezzo and ensemble (1974), *Fiddlers at the Wedding* for mezzo and instruments (1974), *Black Pentecost* for mezzo, baritone, and orchestra (1982), *Into the Labyrinth*, cantata (1983).

Davis, Anthony (1951–) US composer and jazz pianist. He studied at Yale University and has been active in jazz ensembles in the USA and abroad; he was director of Episteme, and cofounded Advent in 1973. He has performed in New York with members of the Advancement of Creative Musicians.

Works include: the operas *X: the Life and Times of Malcolm X*, premiered at New York City Opera 1986, and *Under the Double Moon*, St Louis 1989; piano concerto *Wayang V* (1985); *Notes from the Underground* for orchestra (1988); violin concerto (1988).

Davy, Richard (c. 1467–c. 1507) English composer. He was educated at Magdalen College, Oxford, where he was organist and choirmaster 1490–92. He later became chaplain to Anne Boleyn's grandfather and father 1501–15. He wrote motets, Passion music for Palm Sunday, part songs, and other pieces.

D.C. abbreviation for **da capo** (Italian 'from the beginning').

'Death and the Maiden' Quartet Schubert's string quartet in D minor D810, begun March 1824, finished or revised January 1826, and first performed Vienna, 1 February 1826. It is so called because the second movement is a set of variations on the introduction and the second half of his song, *Der Tod und das Mädchen* (D531, 1817, text by M Claudius), which consists of Death's quiet and reassuring answer to the girl's agitated plea to be spared. The work is sometimes heard today in an arrangement for string orchestra by Mahler.

Death and Transfiguration (Strauss). See ◊*Tod und Verklärung*.

Death in Venice opera by Britten (libretto by Myfanwy Piper, after Thomas Mann), produced Snape, Maltings 16 June 1973). Writer Aschenbach, believer in order, is seduced by the passion of Venice; his frustrated love of beauty and of the boy Tadzio destroys his ideals and finally himself.

Death of Klinghoffer, The opera in two acts by John Adams (libretto by Alice Goodman, based on the Palestinian hijacking of the *Achille Lauro*, 1985), produced Brussels, Théâtre de la Monnaie, 19 March 1991.

Debora e Jaele/Deborah and Jael opera by Pizzetti (libretto by composer), produced Milan, Teatro alla Scala, 16 December 1922. Loosely based on the Biblical story, Sisera, here the king of Canaa, faces a conflict between love for Jael and duty. Later Jael splits the sleeping Sisera's skull, rather than leave him to a worse death before the victorious Israelites.

Deborah oratorio by Handel (words by S Humphreys), produced London, King's Theatre, Haymarket, 17 March 1733.

Debussy, (Achille-) Claude (1862–1918) French composer. He broke with German Romanticism and introduced new qualities of melody and harmony based on the wholetone scale, evoking oriental music. His work includes *Prélude à l'après-midi d'un faune/ Prelude to the Afternoon of a Faun* 1894, illustrating a poem by Mallarmé, and the opera *Pelléas et Mélisande* 1902.

Among his other works are numerous piano pieces, songs, orchestral pieces such as *La Mer* 1903–05 and *Trois Nocturnes* 1899, and the ballet *Jeux* 1910–13. Debussy also published witty and humorous critical writing about the music of his day, featuring the fictional character Monsieur Croche 'antidilettante' (professional debunker), a figure based on Erik ◊Satie.

Debussy was the son of a shopkeeper. He took his first piano lessons at the age of seven, and from 1870 was taught for three years by Mauté de Fleurville, a former pupil of Chopin. He entered the Paris Conservatory 1873, studying with Lavignac and Marmontel, and later with Emile Durand. At 17 he failed to win a piano prize, but entered a composition class in 1880. For the next two summers he was domestic musician to Nadezhda von Meck, Tchaikovsky's former patroness, whose children he taught and who took him first to Switzerland and Italy and to Russia the following year. He won the Prix de Rome in 1884 and went to Rome the next year, but left in 1887, before the statutory three years were completed. During these years he began to reject the prevalent Wagnerian currents in music of the day, forging a new path towards impressionism. Debussy's ideal was that music should have the effect of continuous improvisation. He began to compose seriously in the new manner for which he became known with a French translation of Dante Gabriel Rossetti's *Blessed Damozel*, completed in 1888. He was influenced by Satie in 1891 and performed his first important mature work, the prelude to Mallarmé's poem 'L'Après-midi d'un faune', in 1894. In 1899 he married a dressmaker, Rosalie (Lili) Texier, and in the same year completed his *Nocturnes*, a symphonic triptych for orchestra. He became music critic for the *Revue blanche* 1901; and the following year produced his only finished opera, a setting of Maeterlinck's *Pelléas et Mélisande*. The opera was described by its conductor, André Messager, as opening a window on the whole world of modern music; clear themes and strong contrasts are replaced by atmospheric depictions of mood. Debussy left his wife in 1904 for Emma Bardac, whom he married after divorcing his first wife in 1905. A private, depressive man of wide culture, Debussy was a friend of writers and painters, and himself a penetrating critic. During his last decade he was generally acclaimed, but was also suffering from terminal cancer.

Debussy's approach to certain chords as 'sound-events' in themselves, important for their own colour and sensuous qualities even more than as stages in a harmonic progression, indicated a new path for Western music. His style is an inspired amalgam of Massenet and Mussorgsky with a smattering of Liszt and hints from his friend Satie (and later, more clearly, the shade of the Wagner he affected to despise); yet his influence affected composers as diverse as Ravel, Stravinsky, Bartók, Varèse, Messiaen, and Boulez, and continues to the present day.

Works include: STAGE opera *Pelléas et Mélisande* (1902); incidental music to d'Annunzio's *Le Martyre de Saint Sébastien* (1911); ballet *Jeux* (1913).

VOCAL three *Chansons de France* (Charles d'Orléans) for unaccompanied chorus; songs including sets *Ariettes oubliées* (Verlaine), two sets of *Fêtes galantes* (Verlaine), *Chansons de*

Bilitis (Pierre Louÿs) (1898), *Trois Poèmes de Stéphane Mallarmé.*

ORCHESTRAL *Prélude à l'Après-midi d'un faune* (1895) *Trois Nocturnes* (1899), *La Mer* (1905) and *Trois Images* for orchestra (1912).

CHAMBER AND PIANO string quartet (1893); sonatas for cello and piano; flute, viola, and harp; and for violin and piano (1915–17); many piano pieces including *Suite bergamasque*, suite *Pour le Piano* (1901), *Trois Estampes* (1903), *L'île joyeuse* (1904), two sets of three *Images*, suite *Children's Corner*, two sets of 12 *Préludes* (1910, 1913), and 12 *Etudes* (1915); *En blanc et noir* (1915) for two pianos.

Decius, Nikolaus (c. 1485–after 1546) German Lutheran pastor and theologian. He wrote the words and composed or adapted the music of three chorales, anticipating even Martin Luther in this field.

decrescendo, or decresc. (Italian 'decreasing') in musical notation, indicating a decrease in the loudness of a passage by constant degrees. *Decrescendo poco a poco* means that the decrescendo should progress more gradually. An alternative marking is 'diminuendo'. The opposite marking is 'crescendo'.

Dedekind, Constantin Christian (1628–1715) German poet and composer. He studied at Dresden and in 1654 became a member of the Saxon court chapel and Konzertmeister in 1666. He arranged words for sacred music dramas.

Works include: psalms, sacred and secular vocal music, concertos for voices and instruments.

de Falla, Manuel Spanish composer; see ◊Falla, Manuel de.

degree the position of a note in a scale. The first degree of C major is therefore C, the second is D, the third is E, and so on. Alternative terms for the seven degrees of a scale are, starting with the first degree: tonic, supertonic, mediant, subdominant, dominant, submediant, and leading note.

Deidamia opera by Handel (libretto by P A Rolli), produced London, Theatre Royal, Lincoln's Inn Fields, 10 January 1741. Handel's last opera. Achilles dresses up as a girl but Deidamia discovers his secret; when Ulysses makes advances to Deidamia, Achilles reveals himself and joins Ulysses to fight at Troy.

Delage, Maurice (Charles) (1879–1961) French composer. He travelled to the east and incorporated exotic elements into his music, which includes *Quatre poèmes hindous* 1913, for soprano and nonet.

He began to study music comparatively late in life, and was a pupil of Ravel.

Works include: overture to a ballet *Les bâtisseurs de ponts* (after Kipling), symphonic poem *Conté par la mer* and other orchestral works; piano pieces; songs.

Delalande, Michel-Richard (1657–1726) French organist and composer for the court of Louis XIV. His works include grand motets and numerous orchestral suites.

Delannoy, Marcel (François Georges) (1898–1962) French composer. A painter and architect at first, he was mainly self-taught in music.

Works include: the operas *Le Poirier de misère* (1925), *Philippine* (1937), *Fête de la danse*, *Ginevra* (1942); ballet-cantata *Le Fou de la dame*, ballets *La Pantoufle de vair* and *L'Eventail de Jeanne* (with others); incidental music for Aristophanes' *Peace* and other plays; symphonies and *Figures sonores* for orchestra, *Sérénade concertante* for violin and orchestra; string quartets; many songs.

Delibes, (Clément Philibert) Léo (1836–1891) French composer. His lightweight, perfectly judged works include the ballets *Coppélia* 1870 and *Sylvia* 1876, and the opera *Lakmé* 1883.

Delibes studied at the Paris Conservatory, where Adolphe Adam was his composition master. He became accompanist at the Théâtre Lyrique in 1853 and was organist successively at two churches. Later he became accompanist and chorus master at the Opéra and in 1881 professor of composition at the Conservatory.

Works include: the operas *Maître Griffard* (1857), *Le Jardinier et son seigneur* (1863), *Le Roi l'a dit* (1873), *Jean de Nivelle*, *Lakmé* (1883), *Kassya* (unfinished); ballets *La Source* (with Minkus), *Coppélia* (on E T A Hoffmann's story *Olympia*), *Sylvia*, *Le Pas des fleurs*; divertissement for Adam's ballet *Le Corsaire*; incidental music for Hugo's *Le Roi s'amuse*; operettas *Deux Sous de charbon* (1856), *Deux Vielles Gardes*, *L'Omelette à la Follembûche* (1859), *Le Serpent à plumes* (1864), *L'Ecossais de Chatou* and others; Mass; cantata *Alger*; dramatic scene *La Mort d'Orphée*; songs; children's choruses.

Delius, Frederick Theodore Albert (1862–1934) English composer. His haunting, richly harmonious works include the opera *A Village Romeo and Juliet* 1901; the choral pieces *Appalachia* 1903, *Sea Drift* 1904, *A Mass of Life* 1905; orchestral works such as *In a Summer*

Garden 1908 and *A Song of the High Hills* 1911; chamber music; and songs.

Delius was born in Bradford. His father was a well-to-do businessman and wished him to follow a commercial career, but music was cultivated in the home and Delius worked steadily at music by himself, although he had little systematic teaching. In 1884 he went to Florida as an orange planter and came under the influence of Thomas Ward, organist at Jacksonville. In 1886, after some teaching in USA, he went to the Leipzig Conservatory for a short time, but found its conservative teaching uncongenial. While there, he met the Norwegian composer Grieg, who influenced Delius's romantic style of composition and persuaded his father to allow him to devote himself to composition. From 1889 Delius lived in France, mainly in Paris, and in 1897 he settled at Grez-sur-Loing, near Fontainebleau, with the German painter Jelka Rosen, whom he later married.

A concert of his works was given in London in 1899 and he became known here and there in Germany. He had assimilated early influences of Wagner, Grieg, and Debussy, and found his own voice in *Koanga* 1904, *Paris: Song of a Great City* 1899, and *A Village Romeo and Juliet*. From 1907 important first performances were given in England: Thomas Beecham conducted *Paris* in 1908 and *A Mass of Life* in 1909, and Henry Wood conducted *Sea Drift* in 1908. He contracted syphilis and in 1922 was attacked by paralysis, which gradually increased until four years later he was helpless and totally blind. He continued to compose, however, with the assistance of Eric Fenby, who acted as his amanuensis from 1928.

Works include: OPERA *A Village Romeo and Juliet* (1901; produced 1907), *Fennimore and Gerda* (1919).

CHORAL WITH ORCHESTRA *Sea Drift* (1904), *A Mass of Life* (1904–05), *A Song of the High Hills*.

ORCHESTRAL *Paris* (1899), *Brigg Fair* (1907), *In a Summer Garden*, *On hearing the First Cuckoo in Spring* (1911), *Summer Night on the River* (1913), *North Country Sketches*, *Eventyr* (after Asbjørnsen's fairy-tales, 1917); concertos for piano, violin, cello and violin and cello (1897, 1915, 1916, 1921).

OTHER chamber music: three violin and piano sonatas.

Dello Joio, Norman (1913–) US composer. His works combines the influences of jazz, Italian opera, and the Catholic church, and includes three operas based on the story of Joan of Arc.

He studied at the Juilliard Graduate School in New York with Wagenaar, and later with Hindemith at Yale School of Music. He was professor of music at Boston University 1972–79.

Works include: the operas *The Ruby* (1953), *The Triumph of St Joan* (1959), and *Blood Moon* (1961); symphonic ballet *On Stage*; *Western Star* for solo voices, narrator, chorus, and orchestra; sinfonietta, ballet suite *Duke of Sacramento* (1942), symphonic movement *Silvermine* for orchestra, *Colonial Variations* for orchestra (1976), concertos for piano, two pianos, harp, and flute; *Variations on a Bach Chorale* for orchestra (1985); Mass (1976); quartet and trio for woodwind, trio for flute, cello, and piano; violin and piano sonata, *Duo concertante* for cello and piano, sonatina for cello solo; suite and *Duo concertante* for two pianos; two sonatas, suite and two preludes for piano.

Del Mar, Norman Rene (1919–1994) English conductor, composer, and horn player. He founded the Chelsea Symphony Orchestra 1944, and was a guest conductor with leading orchestras. He conducted an enormously wide range of music, but was especially known for his Mahler, Elgar, and other late Romantics, above all Strauss, and was noted for his clear interpretations of complex scores. He also composed two symphonies, a string quartet, and a number of horn pieces.

books He wrote three volumes on Richard Strauss 1960–72, as well as *Orchestral Variations* 1981 and *Companion to the Orchestra* 1987.

career Del Mar was born in London and was educated at Marlborough public school. At the Royal College of Music he studied violin, piano, and horn; conducting with Constant Lambert, and composition with R O Morris and Vaughan Williams. In World War II he played the horn in the RAF Central Band.

With the Chelsea Symphony Orchestra he performed what were then little-known modern works such as Mahler's Second and Ninth Symphonies. He became Thomas Beecham's assistant with the Royal Philharmonic Orchestra 1947, conducting Strauss in the composer's presence. He was principal conductor of the English Opera Group 1949–56, and met Benjamin Britten and conducted his *Let's Make an Opera* and *The Rape of Lucretia* at the Aldeburgh Festival 1949.

He was appointed chief conductor of several orchestras (including the British Broadcasting Corporation (BBC) Scottish Orchestra 1960, the Göteborg Symphony

Orchestra, Sweden, 1968, the Academy of the BBC 1974–77, and the Århus Symphony Orchestra, Denmark, 1985–88) but not of any of the major London orchestras. He was also a professor of conducting at the Guildhall School of Music 1953–60 and the Royal Academy of Music 1974–77.

Delsarte, (François) Alexandre (Nicolas Chéri) (1811–1871) French music teacher and theoretician. Teaching at the Paris Conservatoire, he devised a system of body movements designed to develop coordination, grace, and expressiveness, which greatly inspired the pioneers of modern dance, such as Emile ◊Jaques-Dalcroze and Ted Shawn.

He divided the movements of the human body into three categories: eccentric, concentric, and normal; and the expressions into three zones: head, torso, and limbs.

Del Tredici, David (1937–) US composer. His early music contains several settings of Joyce: *I Hear an Army* 1964 for soprano and string quartet, *Night Conjure-Verse* 1965 for voices and instruments, and *Syzygy* 1968 for soprano, horn, bells, and chamber orchestra. Since 1968 his music been concerned with Lewis Carroll's 'Alice' stories.

He studied at Berkeley and with Roger Sessions at Princeton. His compositions on the 'Alice' theme include: *Pop-Pourri*, for voices, rock group, and orchestra (1968), *The Lobster Quadrille* for soprano, folk music ensemble, and orchestra (1969, revised 1974), *Vintage Alice* (1971; same forces), *An Alice Symphony* (1976), *Final Alice*, for orchestra (1976), *Child Alice*, for soprano and orchestra, in four parts: *In Memory of a Summer Day*, *Happy Voices*, *All in the Golden Afternoon*, and *Quaint Events* (1977–81; performed separately in St Louis, San Francisco, Philadelphia, and Rotterdam, 1980–83; first complete performance Aspen, 1984); *March to Tonality* for orchestra (1985); *Haddock's Eyes* for soprano and ensemble (1986); *Steps* for orchestra (1990).

Demetrio/Demetrius libretto by Metastasio. Opera by Caldara, produced Vienna, at court, 4 November 1731. Further settings by Hasse (1732), Gluck (1742) and Jommelli (1749). Cleomice, new queen of Syria, must choose a husband. She loves Alcestis, a commoner, whom rival Olinto orders to leave the country. When it is revealed that Alcestis is in fact Prince Demetrius, the marriage goes ahead.

Demetrio e Polibio opera by Rossini (libretto by V Vigano-Mombelli). Rossini's first opera, it was written while he was a student at the Bologna Conservatory, from 1806; produced Rome, Teatro Valle, 18 May 1812. Demetrio, king of Syria, finds his long-lost son at the court of King Polibio.

demisemiquaver, US 32nd note in music, a note value 1/32nd the duration of a ◊semibreve. It is written as a filled black note-head with a stem and three flags (tails).

Demofoonte, rè di Tracia/Demophoon, King of Thrace libretto by Metastasio. Opera by Caldara, produced 4 November 1733. Further settings by Gluck (1743), Jommelli, (1743, the first of four), Graun (1746) and Hasse (1748). King Demophoön wants to sacrifice a virgin to appease Apollo, but the intended victim (Dirce) is secretly married to his son, Timanthes. Many twists in the plot, but a happy ending.

Demon, The opera by A Rubinstein (libretto, in Russian, by P A Viskovatov, based on Lermontov's poem), produced St Petersburg, 25 January 1875. Revived Wexford, 1994. Demon kills Tamara's lover but she is rescued by an angel.

Démophoon opera by Cherubini (libretto by Marmontel, based on Metastasio's *Demofoonte*, produced Paris, Opéra, 5 December 1788. Cherubini's first French opera.

Demuth, Norman (1898–1968) English composer and author. He was educated as a choirboy at St George's Chapel, Windsor, and at Repton School. He studied music at the Royal College of Music in London and became professor of composition at the Royal Academy of Music there in 1930. His books include studies of Franck, Ravel, and Roussel.

Works include: five operas, including *Volpone* (after Jonson) and *The Oresteia* (Aeschylus); five ballets; four symphonies, two piano concertos; three sonatas for violin and piano, string trio, string quartet.

De natura sonoris two works by K Penderecki: no. 1 for orchestra; first performed Royan, France, 7 April 1966; no. 2 for wind, percussion and strings; first performed New York, 3 December 1971.

Dench, Chris (1953–) English composer. He is self-taught and a leading member of the avant garde; his music has been performed by the London Sinfonietta, Ensemble InterContemporain, and the Arditti Quartet. He has appeared at Darmstadt, the Venice Biennale, and the International Society for Contemporary Music's World Music Days.

Works include: *Helical* for piano (1975), *Caught Breath of Time* for flute (1981), *Enonce* for 15 players (1984), *Strangeness* for string quartet (1985), *4 Darmstadter Aphorismen* (1986–89); *Sulle Scale della Fenice* for flute (1989), *Dark Neumes* for guitar, six brass, and amplified ensemble (1989).

Denisov, Edison (1929–) Russian composer. An early Soviet exponent of serial and electronic music, he studied at Moscow Conservatory with Vissarion Shebalin and taught there from 1960.

Works include: the opera *L'écume des jours* (1981), and ballet *Confession* (after de Musset, 1984), *The Four Girls* opera after Picasso, (1986); concertos for cello (1972), flute (1975), violin (1978), flute and oboe (1978), bassoon and cello (1982), oboe (1986), and clarinet (1989); symphony (1987); string trio (1969), piano trio (1971), clarinet and piano quintets, with strings (1987), Octet (1992), Requiem (1980).

Density 21.5 work for solo flute by Varèse; first performed New York, 16 February 1936. Title refers to the specific gravity of platinum.

Dent, Edward J(oseph) (1876–1957) English musicologist and composer. His books include works on Alessandro Scarlatti, Mozart's operas, English opera, Handel, and Busoni, and his compositions include polyphonic motets and a version of *The Beggar's Opera*. He was president of the International Society for Contemporary Music from its foundation in 1922 until 1938.

He was educated at Eton and at Cambridge University, where he was professor of music 1926–41. He was a governor of Sadler's Wells Opera, for which he translated many works, and was on the editorial board of the *New Oxford History of Music*.

Dering, Richard (c. 1580–1630), or Deering English organist and composer. He became a Catholic and went to Brussels in 1617 as organist to the convent of English nuns, but returned to England to become organist to Henrietta Maria on her marriage to Charles I in 1625.

Works include: *Cantiones sacrae* for several voices, motets, anthems; canzonets for three and four voices, quodlibets on street cries; fancies and other pieces for viols.

De Sabata, Victor (1892–1967) Italian conductor and composer. He studied under his father, a chorus master at the Teatro alla Scala, Milan, and at the Milan Conservatory with Orefice and others. He later became conductor at La Scala and at the Royal Opera in Rome, and conducted at the Monte Carlo Opera from 1918 (including the first performance of *L'Enfant et les Sortilèges* in 1925).

He visited the USA in 1938, conducted Wagner's *Tristan* at Bayreuth in 1939, and visited London with the Scala company in 1950, conducting Verdi's *Otello* and *Falstaff* at Covent Garden.

Works include: the operas *Lisistrata* (after Aristophanes), *Il macigno*, *Mille e una notte* (1931); incidental music for Shakespeare's *Merchant of Venice*; symphonic poems *Juventus*, *La notte di Platon*, *Gethsemani*, suite for orchestra.

descant a high-pitched line for one or more sopranos, added above the normal soprano line (melody) of a hymn tune; a high-pitched instrument of a family, such as the descant recorder (known in the USA as soprano recorder); or an improvised melody sung against a written voice part, also known as faburden, fauxbourdon, or ◊discant).

Older English writers used the term descant to mean ◊counterpoint.

Descartes, René (1596–1650) French philosopher. He wrote a book on music, *Compendium musicae* (1618), in which he outlined the relationship between the physical aspect of sound and its perception by the listener.

Déserteur, Le opera by Monsigny (libretto by J M Sedaine), produced Paris, Comédie-Italienne, 6 March 1769.

Déserts work by E Varèse for wind instruments, percussion, and magnetic tapes *ad lib*; composed 1953–54; first performed Paris, 20 December 1954, conductor Scherchen. Early use is made here of electronic sound.

Desmarets, Henri (1661–1741) French composer. He was educated at the court of Louis XIV. At the end of the 17th century he secretly married the daughter of a dignitary at Senlis and fled to Spain, becoming music superintendent to Philip V in 1700. In 1708 he became music director to the Duke of Lorraine at Lunéville.

Works include: the operas and ballets *Didon* (1693), *Circé, Théagène et Chariclée* (on Heliodorus's *Aethiopica*, 1695), *Les Amours de Momus, Vénus et Adonis, Les Fêtes galantes* (1698), *Iphigénie en Tauride* (with Campra) and *Renaud ou La Suite d'Armide* (1722), motet and Te Deum for the marriage of Princess Elisabeth Thérèse to the King of Sardinia; church music written early in his career under the name of Goupillier.

Desprez, Josquin Franco-Flemish composer; see ◊Josquin Desprez.

Dessau, Paul (1894–1979) German composer. His work includes incidental music to Bertolt Brecht's theatre pieces; an opera, *Der*

Verurteilung des Lukullus/The Trial of Lucullus 1949, also to a libretto by Brecht; and numerous choral works and songs.

From 1910 he studied at the Klindworth-Scharwenka Conservatory in Berlin and later in Hamburg, where in 1913 he became a coach at the opera. In 1933 he went to Paris, where he studied Schoenberg's serial method with René Leibowitz. He conducted all over Germany, but was forced to leave and in 1939 went to New York. He collaborated with Brecht from 1942, when they met as political exiles in the USA, returning with him to East Berlin 1948.

Works include: the operas *Das Verhör des Lukullus* (1949; produced 1951), *Puntila* (1959; produced 1966), *Lanzelot* (1969), *Einstein* (1973), *Leonce und Lena* (1979); children's operas *Das Eisenbahnspiel, Tadel der Unzuverlässigkeit*; concertino for solo flute, clarinet, horn, and violin; a piano sonata; much vocal and orchestral music, film and incidental music.

dessus (French 'top' of the viols) musical instrument, the treble ◊viol.

Destouches, André Cardinal (1672–1749) French composer. A sailor at first, then a musketeer, he studied with André Campra and produced his first stage work, *Issé*, in 1697. He held various court appointments and was director of the Opéra 1728–31.

Works include: the operas *Amadis de Crèce* (1699), *Marthésie, Omphale, Callirhoé, Télémaque et Calypso* (1714), *Sémiramis* (1718), *Les Stratagèmes de l'Amour*; heroic pastoral *Issé*; comedy-ballet *Le Carnaval et la folie*; ballet *Les Eléments* (with Lalande, 1721), cantatas (*Enone*) and *Sémélé*.

détaché (French 'detached, separated') a bowing style in string playing. In quick passages the bow changes direction so that each note is clearly separated, but without the sound being perceptibly interrupted, as in *staccato*.

Dettingen Te Deum a Te Deum composed by Handel to celebrate the victory of Dettingen won on 26 June 1743. First performed London, Chapel Royal, 27 November 1743.

Deuteromelia the second part of a collection of canons, rounds and catches published by Ravenscroft in London in 1609, the first part being *Pammelia*.

Deutsches Requiem (Brahms). See ◊*German Requiem*.

Deutsche Tänze (German 'German dances') type of country dance in 3–4 (slow waltz) time, cultivated by Mozart, Beethoven,

Schubert and others. The adjective 'Deutsche' was frequently used alone in titles.

Deux Avares, Les/The Two Misers opera by Grétry (libretto by C G F de Falbère), produced Fontainebleau, at court, 27 October 1770; first Paris performance, Comédie-Italienne, 6 December 1770.

Deux Chasseurs et la Laitière, Les/The Two Huntsmen and the Milkmaid opera by Duni (libretto by L Anseaume, after La Fontaine), produced Paris, Comédie-Italienne, 21 July 1763.

Deux Journées, Les/The Two Days: better known as The Water-Carrier opera by Cherubini (libretto by J N Bouilly), produced Paris, Théâtre Feydeau, 16 January 1800. Fugitive Armand and his wife Constance are helped by water-seller Mikéli. After several incidents Armand must reveal his identity to save Constance, but at that moment news arrives that the ban against the couple has been lifted.

Deux Petits Savoyards, Les/The Two Little Savoyards opera by Dalayrac (libretto by G J Marsollier), produced Paris, Comédie-Italienne, 13 January 1789.

developing variation the technique of varying a musical motive so that each of its different occurrences remains identifiably related to the original form of the motive. The term was coined by Schoenberg, particularly in relation to the works of Brahms. See ◊motivic analysis.

development the central process of sonata form, in which thematic material presented in the opening statement is combined and extended.

Devil and Kate, The/Čert a Káča opera by Dvořák (libretto by A Wenig), produced Prague, Czech Theatre, 23 November 1899. Kate is carried off to hell after announcing that she would dance even with the Devil, but her tongue gets her thrown out.

Devils of Loudun, The/Diably z Loudun opera by Penderecki (libretto by composer after John Whiting's play *The Devils*), based on a narrative by Aldous Huxley which describes a case of diabolic possession in a 17th-century convent of Ursuline nuns (Father Grandier is accused of bewitching them); first performed Hamburg, 20 June 1969.

Devil's Opera, The opera by Macfarren (libretto by G Macfarren, the composer's father), a satire on the diabolic elements in works like Weber's *Freischütz*, Meyerbeer's

Robert le Diable, and Marschner's *Vampyr*, produced London, Lyceum Theatre, 10 September 1838.

Devil's Trill (Tartini). See ◊*Trillo del Diavolo.*

Devil's Wall/Certova stena opera by Smetana (libretto by E Krasnohorska), produced Prague, Czech Theatre, 29 January 1882. Smetana's last completed opera. Javek searches for a wife for Vok, but Beneš wants him to stay single and thereby receive Vok's inheritance. The Devil, in league with Beneš, tries to drown Vok in a monastery but the beautiful Hedvika warns Vok. Beneš repents, and Vok marries Hedvika.

Devin du village, Le/The Village Soothsayer opera by Rousseau (libretto by composer), produced Fontainebleau, at court, 18 October 1752, with overture and recitatives by Pierre de Jélyotte (1713–87) and Francœur; Paris, Opéra, 1 March 1753, with music all by Rousseau. Soothsayer unites discordant couple, Colin and Colette.

Devisenarie (German 'device aria') type of aria of the 17th and 18th centuries in which the first word or words occur separately in the voice-part, as though the singer were announcing a title, before the first line of the text or more is sung continuously, often after a further instrumental passage.

de Vitry, Philippe French composer; see ◊Vitry, Philippe de.

dhola musical instrument, a deep-toned Indian drum, barrel-shaped and played at both ends. It is played with the hands and, depending on how and where it is struck, produces a flexible tone that rises from bass to the tenor register.

dhrupad (Hindi 'fixed verse') vocal genre of north Indian (Hindustani) music, characterized by an extensive unmetred introduction (*alap*), a composed text setting of between two and four sections (*sthayi, antara,* and sometimes *sanchari* and *abhog*), and improvised development. Although less common than the ◊khyal, it is considered to be the oldest variety of north Indian classical music still performed, and is highly prestigious.

Diabelli, Anton (1781–1858) Austrian publisher and composer. He was the original publisher of Beethoven, Haydn, and Schubert. He is most famous today for appearing in the title of Beethoven's *Diabelli Variations* 1823, which formed part of a contribution by 50 composers, each of whom was asked to compose a piece based on a waltz theme written by Diabelli himself.

He was educated for the priesthood, but studied music with Michael Haydn. He went to Vienna as piano and guitar teacher and joined Peter Cappi in his publishing firm in 1818; it became Diabelli & Co. in 1824.

Works include: the operetta *Adam in der Klemme* (Vienna, 1809); Masses; many piano pieces, including the little waltz on which Beethoven wrote the 33 variations op. 120, and other pieces.

'Diabelli' Variations (Beethoven). See ◊Diabelli and ◊Vaterländischer Künstlerverein.

Diable à quatre, Le, ou La Double Métamorphose ballad opera with airs arranged by F A Danican Philidor (libretto by J M Sedaine, based on Coffey's *Devil to Pay*), produced Paris, Opéra-Comique, 19 August 1756.

Diable dans le beffroi, Le/The Devil in the Belfry opera by Debussy (libretto by himself, based on Edgar Allan Poe's story), worked on in 1903 but not completed.

diabolus in musica (Latin 'the devil in music') in music, a medieval warning against the use of the tritone – the interval of the augmented fourth (such as C–F♯ or F–B), which was looked at askance as a melodic progression.

Dialogues des Carmélites, Les opera by Poulenc (libretto by G Bernanos), produced Milan (La Scala), 26 January 1957. During the French Revolution the sisters of the Carmelite order are condemned to death. The opera follows the contrasting Blanche and Constance, who meet the same fate.

Diamants de la Couronne, Les/The Crown Diamonds opera by Auber (libretto by Scribe and J H V de Saint-Georges), produced Paris, Opéra-Comique 6 March 1841.

Diamond, David (Leo) (1915–) US composer. His works are written in a neo-classical style and include *Rounds* 1944 for string orchestra.

He studied at the Eastman School of Music at Rochester and later at the American Conservatory at Fontainebleau with Nadia Boulanger. After his return to the USA he was awarded several composition prizes.

Works include: 11 symphonies (1941–89), sinfonietta, serenade, variations, *Psalm, Elegy in Memory of Ravel* and ballet suite *Tom* for orchestra; concerto and *Rounds* for string orchestra (1944); violin concerto (1936–67), *Hommage à Satie* and ballade for chamber orchestra, concertos for piano, cello, and violin (2) with chamber orchestra; *A Night Litany* (Ezra Pound) for chorus and three madrigals for unaccompanied chorus (James

Joyce) *Choral Symphony: To Music* (1967); *A Secular Cantata* (1976); ten string quartets (1943–76), string trio; sonatina for violin and piano, cello and piano sonata, partita for bassoon and piano; sonata and sonatina for piano; 52 preludes and fugues for piano.

diapason the principal stop of an organ, which gives the instrument its characteristic tone quality. Diapasons may be 'open', producing a bright colour, or 'stopped', producing a muffled but sweet tone. The equivalent stop on a German-built instrument is the Prinzipal. In French usage, 'diapason' means tuning fork, hence 'diapason normal' is the equivalent of ◊concert pitch.

diapente the interval of the fifth. In old music canons at the fifth were called epidiapente when answered in the fifth above, and subdiapente when answered below.

diaphony, (Latin *diaphonia*) see ◊dissonance.

Diary of one who disappeared/Zápisník zmizelého cycle of 22 songs by Janáček for tenor, mezzo, three women's voices, and piano; composed 1917–21, performed Brno, 18 April 1921.

diastole (from Greek 'distinction, differentiation') old term, in use to the middle of the 18th century, for the divisions of music into sections or phrases.

diatonic scale a scale consisting of the seven notes of any major or minor key.

Dibdin, Charles (1745–1814) English singer, author, and composer. He began his career as a singing actor at Covent Garden, where his pastoral *The Shepherd's Artifice* was produced in 1764. Over 100 dramatic works followed. In 1789 he began his series of 'Table Entertainments', in which he was author, composer, narrator, singer, and accompanist. One of the

most successful, *The Oddities*, contained the song 'Tom Bowling'. Many other sea-songs achieved great popularity.

He began singing as a chorister at Winchester Cathedral, went to London at the age of 15, and made his stage debut in 1762. In 1778 he was appointed composer to Covent Garden Theatre, and during the 1780s dabbled in theatrical management with variable success. A projected journey to India came to nothing, but the fundraising travels which were to have financed it provided material for his *Musical Tour* 1788. Towards the end of his life a publishing venture made him bankrupt, and he was saved from destitution by a public subscription. He wrote an account of his professional life and other literary works.

Works include: over 100 dramatic pieces, including *Lionel and Clarissa* (1768), *The Padlock, The Ephesian Matron, The Captive, The Ladle* (1773), *The Trip to Portsmouth, The Seraglio* (1776), *Rose and Colin, The Touchstone, The Milkmaid, Tom Thumb, Harvest Home* (1787); over 30 'Table Entertainments' containing innumerable songs.

Dibdin, Thomas John (1771–1841) English dramatist and songwriter. He is said to have written about 200 plays, including the pantomime *Mother Goose* 1807 and the patriotic *The Mouth of the Nile* 1798, and 2,000 songs, many of them sea songs and ballads.

Dichterliebe/Poet's Love song cycle by Schumann, op. 48 (16 poems by Heine), composed 1840.

Dickinson, Peter (1934–) English composer and teacher. He was professor at Keele University 1974–84. He studied at Cambridge University and at the Juilliard School, New York. While in the USA he met John Cage and Edgard Varèse; other influences have been Satie and Stravinsky.

Major

Minor (melodic)

Minor (harmonic)

Three commonly used diatonic scales.

Works include: *Vmusicitas*, ballet (1959), music-theatre piece *The Judas Tree* (1965); *Monologue* for strings (1959), *Transformations*, *Homage to Satie* for orchestra (1970); piano concerto (1978–84), violin concerto (1986); settings of poems by W H Auden, Dylan Thomas, Alan Porter, e.e. cummings, and Emily Dickinson for voice and piano (1956–71); *Mass of the Apocalypse* for female chorus and four percussion (1984); two string quartets; piano and organ music.

didjeridu, or didgeridoo musical lip-reed wind instrument, made from a hollow eucalyptus branch 1.5 m/4 ft long and blown to produce rhythmic, booming notes of relatively constant pitch. It was first developed and played by Australian Aborigines.

Dido and Aeneas opera by Purcell (libretto by N Tate, after Virgil), produced Chelsea, London, Josias Priest's boarding school ('by young gentlewomen'), December 1689. Aeneas sails off while Dido laments.

Dido, Königin von Carthago opera by Graupner (libretto by Heinrich Hinsch), produced Hamburg, Theater beim Gänsemarkt, spring 1707. Dido is pursued by Numidian King Iarbas, as Aeneas receives sailing orders from Mercury and Venus.

Didon/Dido opera by Piccinni (libretto by Marmontel), produced Fontainebleau, at court, 16 October 1783, first Paris performance, Opéra, 1 December 1783.

Didone abbandonata/Dido Forsaken Opera by Hasse (libretto Metastasio), produced Hubertusburg, near Dresden, 7 October 1742. Further settings by Jommelli (1747) and Traetta (1757).

Didone, La/Dido opera by Cavalli (libretto by G Busenello), produced Venice, Teatro San Cassiano, Carnival 1641. Dido accepts love of Iarbas, as Aeneas departs for Italy.

Dienstag aus Licht/Tuesday from Light opera in two acts by Stockhausen, the fourth of a projected seven (libretto by composer), first performed Lisbon, 10 May 1992. The day named after Mars depicts philosophical and martial battles between Michael and Lucifer.

Diepenbrock, Alphons (1862–1921) Dutch composer. At first a philologist, he was self-taught in music.

Works include: incidental music for Aristophanes' *The Birds*, Sophocles' *Electra* (1920), Goethe's *Faust*, Vondel's *Gysbrecht van Amstel*, *Stabat Mater*, Te Deum for solo voices, chorus, and orchestra, Mass; songs with orchestra; chamber music; songs.

Dieren, Bernard van (1887–1936) Dutch-born British composer. A scientist by training, he had little musical experience, apart from violin playing, before the age of 20, when he began to compose. In 1909 he settled in London as correspondent to foreign newspapers, after making serious music studies, which he continued in Germany in 1912, when his real creative career began. He wrote a book on the sculptor Jacob Epstein and a volume of musical essays, *Down among the Dead Men* 1935.

Works include: the opera *The Tailor* (R Nichols, 1917); symphony on Chinese poems for solo voices, chorus, and orchestra; *Les Propous des beuveurs* (Rabelais) for chorus and orchestra; *Beatrice Cenci*, orchestral epilogue to Shelley's drama (1909), overture *Anjou*; serenade for small orchestra, overture for chamber orchestra; *Diafonia* for 17 instruments and baritone (Shakespeare sonnets, 1916), *Fayre eies* (Spenser) for baritone and chamber orchestra; six string quartets (1912–28); three unaccompanied choruses; sonata and three studies for unaccompanied violin, and other pieces.

Dièse, or Dièze (French 'sharp') in music, the sign for sharp (♯).

Dies irae/*Day of wrath* the sequence from the Mass for the Dead originally associated with a distinct plainsong theme which has been frequently used or quoted by various composers, for example:

Bantock, Witches' Dance in incidental music to *Macbeth*.

Berlioz, Witches' Sabbath in *Fantastic Symphony*, and Requiem.

Dallapiccola, *Canti di prigionia*.

Davies (Maxwell), *St Michael*.

Liszt, *Totentanz* for piano and orchestra.

Miaskovsky, symphony No. 6.

Rakhmaninov, Rhapsody on a Theme by Paganini for piano and orchestra and Symphonic Dances, op. 45.

Respighi, *Impressioni brasiliane*.

Saint-Saëns, *Danse macabre* for orchestra.

Stevenson (Ronald), *Passacaglia on DSCH*.

Tchaikovsky, Theme and Variations in Suite No. 3 for orchestra and song *In Dark Hell*.

Vaughan Williams, *Five Tudor Portraits* for chorus and orchestra (lament for Philip Sparrow).

A recent theory claims the Dies Irae as the 'hidden' theme of Elgar's 'Enigma' Variations.

diesis in ancient Greece, either the interval between a fourth and two 'major' tones or a quarter-tone. In modern acoustics, either the great diesis is the difference between four minor thirds and an octave, or the enharmonic diesis is the difference between an octave and three major thirds.

Dietrich, Albert (Hermann) (1829–1908) German composer and conductor. He wrote a violin and piano sonata jointly with Schumann and Brahms in 1853, though his most successful works were his songs. He was court music director at Oldenburg from 1861.

Works include: the opera *Robin Hood* (1879); incidental music to Shakespeare's *Cymbeline* (performed London, 1896); symphony in D minor; choral and orchestral works; horn concertos; chamber music.

digital method of sound recording in which audio signals are converted into a series of electronically-represented pulses, determined by the voltage of the sound. This information can be stored for reproduction or manipulation in the case of composition in the electronic medium.

Dillon, James (1950–　) Scottish composer. His music has had Renaissance and non-Western influences and is densely composed. Works by him have ben featured at Bath, Darmstadt, Warsaw, and Paris festivals.

Works include: *Babble* for 40 voices (1976), *Cumha* for 12 strings (1978), *Once Upon a Time* for 12 instruments (1980), *Spleen* for piano (1980), *Come Live With Me* for mezzo and four instruments (1981), string quartet (1983), *Le Rivage* for wind quintet (1984), *Windows and Canopies* (1985), *Helle Nacht* for orchestra (1987), *Shrouded Mirrors* (1988), *Blitzschlag* (1991), string quartet no.2 (1991), *Viriditas* (1993).

diminished term used to describe intervals normally 'perfect' (fourths, fifth, octaves) or 'minor' (seconds, thirds, sixths, sevenths) which have been made a semitone narrower.

Perfect and diminished intervals.

diminished seventh an interval consisting of a minor ◊seventh which is contracted (diminished) by one semitone, to create an interval of nine semitones (for example A–G♭); alternatively, a **chord** consisting of a minor seventh which is contracted (diminished) by one semitone. If every voice of the chord is filled in, there is also a minor third and a

diminished fifth, for example A–C–E♭–G♭. This chord, which consists only of a series of minor thirds, is ambiguous harmonically and therefore useful in modulation (moving from one key to another).

The example illustrates two of the three possible diminished 7th chords.

diminuendo (Italian 'diminishing') in musical notation, indicating a decrease in the loudness of a passage by constant degrees. *Diminuendo poco a poco* means that the diminuendo should progress more gradually. An alternative marking is 'decrescendo'. The opposite marking is 'crescendo'.

diminution a reduction of interval size, of chord, loudness level, or note values of a theme.

Dimitrij opera by Dvořák (libretto by M Červinková-Riegerová), produced Prague, Czech Theatre, 8 October 1882. The subject is the 'false Dimitri', the pretender who also figures in Mussorgsky's *Boris Godunov*. Having assumed the throne, Tsar Dmitrij marries Marina and then falls in love with Xenie. Jealous, Marina reveals that Dmitrij is in fact the son of a peasant. The opera ends when Prince Šujský shoots him.

d'Indy, Vincent French composer; see ◊Indy, Vincent d'.

Dinorah (Meyerbeer). See ◊*Pardon de Ploërmel, Le*.

Dioclesian (Purcell). See ◊*Prophetess, The*.

direct a sign used in plainsong notation and often in early music in staff notation, indicating at the end of the stave the position of the first note at the beginning of the following one.

dirge (Latin *Dirige Domine*, from the Office for the Dead) song of lamentation for the dead. A poem of mourning is usually called an ◊elegy.

discant, or descant in medieval music, a form of ◊polyphony, originally an improvisation technique in which one voice had the ◊cantus firmus (fixed melody) whilst another or several others extemporized a free accompanying part or parts. It is found in early medieval ◊plainsong such as ◊organum.

discord a combination of notes jarring to the ear. See ◊dissonance.

disjunct motion see ◊motion.

Dissoluto punito, Il (Mozart). See ◊*Don Giovanni*.

dissonance a combination of two or more tones displeasing to the ear. It is the opposite of a ◊consonance, and is judged dissonant by the presence of a ◊beat frequency.

Equal ◊temperament involves a measure of deliberate distuning of intervals to allow free ◊modulation between keys. On the harpsichord and piano, the effect is disguised by making unison strings (courses) internally dissonant, an effect also improving tonal sustain.

Dissonance Quartet string quartet no. 19 in C, K465 by Mozart, composed 1785. The dissonant introduction to the first movement gives the work its name.

dissonant counterpoint technique developed by the US composer Charles ◊Seeger and espoused by, amongst others, Ruth ◊Crawford and Carl ◊Ruggles. In dissonant counterpoint, the traditional definitions of dissonant and consonant intervals are reversed, so that the composer deliberately avoids using traditionally consonant intervals (thirds, fourths, fifths and sixths) except as passing harmonies. The technique seeks to replace the traditional rules of counterpoint, rather than extending them in the manner of Schoenberg's atonal works.

Distratto, Il nickname of Haydn's symphony no. 60 in C major, so called on account of its being an adaptation of the incidental music to *Der Zerstreute* (1775), a German version of Regnard's *Le Distrait*.

dital harp alternative name for the ◊harp lute, a musical instrument.

Dittersdorf, Karl Ditters von (1739–1799), originally simply Karl Ditters Austrian composer and violinist. He spent much of his life in Vienna, where his most popular opera, *Doktor und Apotheker*, was produced in 1786. Michael Kelly's *Reminiscences* contain an account of Dittersdorf playing string quartets with Haydn, Mozart, and Johann Baptist Vanhal.

Dittersdorf was educated in the household of Prince Hildburghausen in Vienna, he studied composition with Giuseppe Bonno. He played in the orchestra of the Imperial Opera in Vienna 1761–63, and then travelled

to Italy with Gluck, achieving great success as a violinist. In 1765 he succeeded Michael Haydn as Kapellmeister to the Bishop of Grosswardein, and from 1769 to 1795 served the Prince Bishop of Breslau in the same capacity. He was ennobled in 1773, and henceforth called himself von Dittersdorf. During his last years he was in the service of Baron Stillfried at Rothlhotta. His autobiography, dictated shortly before his death, was published in 1801.

Works include: over 40 operas, including *Amore in musica, Betrug durch Aberglauben, Doktor und Apotheker* (1786), *Hieronimus Knicker* (1789), *Das rothe Kaeppchen, Die Hochzeit des Figaro* (after Beaumarchais), and others; oratorios *Isacco* (1766), *Davidde Penitente* (1771), *Esther, Giobbe* (1786); Masses and other church music; over 100 symphonies, including 21 on Ovid's *Metamorphoses*; concertos; divertimenti, chamber music.

Diversions work by Britten for piano, left hand, and orchestra; composed 1940, revised 1954, first perfomed Philadelphia, 16 January 1942, Paul Wittgenstein soloist.

divertimento a suite of 18th-century music written for light entertainment, usually in four to nine movements, for a small string, wind, or mixed ensemble. Mozart wrote 25, entitling them, in addition to 'divertimento', 'serenades' and 'cassations'.

divertissement mainly a term connected with ballet, where it means a set of varied dances with no particular plot. In music a suite, particularly of arrangements or pieces based on familiar tunes, an entertaining piece of any kind or a fantasy of a lighter sort, such as Schubert's *Divertissement à la hongroise*. In 18th-century French usage a dance interlude, with or without songs, in a play or opera; also sometimes a short play with dances and songs.

Divine Poem, The title of symphony no. 3 in C minor, op. 43 by Skriabin, first performed Paris, 29 May 1905, conductor Nikisch. The work's three movements, titled 'Struggles', 'Delights', and 'Divine Play', reflect Skriabin's mystic beliefs.

divisi, or div. (Italian 'divided') in orchestral compositions, associated with passages of double notes, directing players reading one part (for example first violins) to divide into groups and play only one note per instrument, rather than trying to play both notes at once. It appears most often in orchestral string parts.

divisions an old method of improvising ◊variations by dividing the basic note values of a theme into smaller fractions representing higher tempi in proportion to the original time values (see ◊diminution).

The medieval extension of harmonic ratios to tempo can be found in the keyboard variations of Mozart, Beethoven, and Brahms; in the late 20th century Stockhausen has reinvented the concept by introducing a tempo scale equivalent to equal temperament, with metronomic values graduated within the 'tempo-octave' 60–120 beats per minute.

division viol musical instrument, a bass ◊viol of moderate size on which ◊divisions were often played in the 17th century.

Djamileh opera by Bizet (libretto by L Gallet, based on Musset's *Namouna*), produced Paris, Opéra-Comique, 22 May 1872. Haroun changes his mistress every month, but Djamileh, who has fallen in love with him, returns in disguise, winning his heart.

djembe single-headed goblet-shaped drum from Senegambia in West Africa, with a high pitched tone. Played with the hands.

Djinns, Les/The Genii symphonic poem by Franck for piano and orchestra, based on verses from Hugo's *Les Orientales*, composed 1884; first performed Paris, 15 March 1885.

DMus abbreviation for **Doctor of Music**.

do the old name for the note C (see ◊solmization), still used in Latin countries. In tonic sol-fa notation the tonic note in any key, represented by the symbol **d**, pronounced doh.

Docteur Ox, Le opéra bouffe by Offenbach (libretto by P Gille and A Mortier, based on a Jules Verne story), produced Paris, Théâtre des Variétés, 26 January 1877.

dodecaphony music composed according to the ◊twelve-tone system of composition.

Dodge, Charles (1942–) US composer. He specializes in electronic music. His work has been performed at the Tanglewood, Warsaw, and Stockholm festivals and by the New York and Los Angeles Philharmonic Orchestras.

He studied with Gunther Schuller and Otto Luening at Columbia University; and studied computer music at Princeton.

Works include: *Changes* (1970), *Earth's Magnetic Field* (1970), *Extensions* (1973), *Palinode* with orchestra (1976), *The Waves* with soprano (1984), *Song Without Words* (1986), *The Voice of Binky* (1989).

Dodgson, Stephen (1924–) English composer and broadcaster. Best known for his guitar concertos, he has also written for the clavichord and harpsichord.

Other works include piano quartet, Symphony for wind (1974), *Epigrams from a Garden* for mezzo and clarinets (1977), concertos for bassoon (1969), clarinet (1983), and trombone (1986); string quartet (1986); songs.

doh the name for the tonic note in any key in tonic sol-fa, so pronounced, but in notation represented by the symbol **d**.

Dohnányi, Ernst (Ernö) von (1877–1960) Hungarian pianist, conductor, composer, and teacher. As a pianist his powers were prodigious, while as a composer he drew upon the classical German tradition, especially Brahms. His compositions include *Variations on a Nursery Song* 1914 and *Second Symphony for Orchestra* 1948.

Born in Bratislava, he studied under Carl Forstner, the cathedral organist at his native town, until 1893, when he went to the Hungarian Academy at Budapest, where he studied piano under Stephan Thomán and composition under Hans Koessler. In 1897 he had some lessons from d'Albert and appeared as a pianist in Berlin and Vienna. He visited England in 1898 and the USA in 1899, and made many more tours, but eventually became better known as a composer. From 1908 to 1915 he was professor of piano at the Hochschule in Berlin and in 1919 became conductor of the Budapest Philharmonic Orchestra and director of the city's conservatory. He premiered Bartók's four orchestral pieces in Budapest 1922.

Rumoured to have been friendly with the Nazis during the 1930s and 1940s, he left Hungary in 1944 and subsequently settled in the USA.

Works include: the operas *Aunt Simona* (Dresden, 1913), *The Tower of Voivod* (Budapest, 1922), and *The Tenor* (1929); ballet *Pierrette's Veil*; symphonies in F minor, D minor, and E major, suite in F♯ minor and *Suite en valse* for orchestra; two piano concertos and *Variations on a Nursery Song* for piano and orchestra (1913); two violin concertos, *Concertstück* for cello and orchestra; three string quartets, piano quintet, sextet for violin, viola, cello, clarinet, horn, and piano; serenade for string trio; sonatas for violin and piano and cello and piano; 12 op. nos. of piano music, including a passacaglia, four rhapsodies, *Humoresques in form of a Suite*, *Ruralia hungarica*; songs.

Doktor Faust opera by Busoni (libretto by composer) based on the Faust legend and Marlowe's *Dr Faustus* (1589); not based on Goethe. Left unfinished at Busoni's death and completed by Jarnach: produced Dresden, 21 May 1925. First produced in Britain, London, Coliseum, 25 April 1986, given in a new edition by Antony Beaumont (first heard at Bologna 1985) in which the dying Faust transfers his soul to the corpse of a child.

Doktor und Apotheker/Doctor and Apothecary opera by Dittersdorf (libretto by G Stephanie, junior), produced Vienna, Burgtheater, 11 July 1786. Gotthold and Leonore are forbidden to marry by their warring fathers, but after complications and disguises, the couple are united.

dolce (Italian 'sweet') in musical notation, indicating sweet, soft expression.

dolce stil nuovo (Italian 'sweet new style') a style of Italian lyric verse written between about 1250 and 1300. It was characterized by musicality, the spiritualization of courtly love, and a mystical and philosophical strain in the analysis of love. It was expressed in sonnets, *canzoni*, and ballads. The style was developed by Guido Guinizelli (c. 1240–76), Cavalcanti, and above all Dante, whose lyrics in his *Vita nuova*, inspired by his love for Beatrice, are the finest examples of the *docle stil nuovo*. It greatly influenced ◊Petrarch and through him many later Italian poets.

The term was coined by Dante in *Purgatorio* XXIV 57.

dolcian musical instrument, an early form of ◊bassoon.

Dolly suite of six children's pieces for piano duet by Fauré, op. 56, composed in 1893, orchestra for a ballet by Rabaud in 1896; first produced Paris, 23 January 1913. It is dedicated to the daughter of Mme Emma Bardac, later Debussy's second wife. As in the case of Debussy's *Children's Corner*, the title and two of the sub-titles seem to suggest some English association: 1. *Berceuse*; 2. *Mi-a-ou*; 3. *Le Jardin de Dolly*; 4. *Kitty-Valse*; 5. *Tendresse*; 6. *Le Pas espagnol*.

Dolmetsch, (Eugène) Arnold (1858–1940) English musician and instrument maker, born into a Swiss family settled in France. Together with his family, including his son Carl (1911–), he revived interest in the practical performance of solo and consort music for lute, recorders, and viols, and established the Baroque soprano (descant) recorder as an inexpensive musical instrument for schools.

He worked in Boston, USA, and Paris, France, as a restorer and maker of early musical instruments before establishing his workshop in Haslemere, England, 1917.

Dolmetsch studied violin under Henry Vieuxtemps at Brussels, but turned his interests to early music and instruments. He worked with the piano firm of Chickering at Boston, 1902–09, and then with that of Gaveau in Paris until 1914, when he moved to England and set up his own workshop for harpsichords, viols, lutes, recorders, and other instruments at Haslemere. He arranged periodical festivals of early music and brought up a family to take part in them with various instruments. He edited early music and wrote a book on interpretation.

Domaines work by Boulez for solo clarinet and 21 instruments; 1968, first performed Brussels, 20 December 1968.

Domestic Symphony (R Strauss). See ◊*Symphonia domestica*.

dominant the fifth note of the diatonic scale, for example, G in the C major scale. The chord of the dominant is related to the tonic chord by the dominant note, which corresponds to its third harmonic. Classical modulation involves a harmonic progression from the tonic to the dominant and back. The return may be a symmetrical journey, as in the binary form of a sonata by Scarlatti, or an abrupt resolution of dominant to tonic chords in a 'perfect' cadence.

Domino noir, Le/The Black Domino comic opera by Auber (libretto by Scribe) produced Paris, Opéra-Comique, 2 December 1837.

Dom Sébastien, Roi de Portugal/Dom Sebastian, King of Portugal opera by Donizetti (libretto by Scribe), produced Paris, Opéra, 13 November 1843. Crusade against the Moors led by King of Portugal Dom Sebastian. Although defeated by the Moors, Sebastian is saved by amorous Zayda. Sebastian returns to Spain to find the throne has been usurped by his uncle, who throws the couple into prison; they are shot when they try to escape.

Donatoni, Franco (1927–) Italian composer. He studied in Rome with Pizzetti; has been influenced by him, and has used serial and, more recently, aleatory techniques.

Donatoni was born at Verona. He studied at the Accademia di Santa Cecilia in Rome with Ildebrando Pizzetti. At first his works were modelled on a Bartokian idiom, but after meeting the serialist composer Bruno Maderna in 1953 he took up integral serialism and produced his highly cerebral *For Grilly*

1960 as well as the *String Quartet II* 1958 and *Doubles* 1961. He· tends to dense, heavily decorated writing, which has intensity but lacks clarity, especially in such concentrated orchestral scores as *Per orchestra* 1962, *Strophes*, and *Sezioni*. He is regarded as a leader of avant-garde music in Italy.

Works include: Concerto for bassoon and strings (1952), Divertimento for violin and chamber orchestra (1954), *Black and White*, for 37 strings (1964), *Doubles II* for orchestra (1970), *Portrait* for harpsichord and orchestra (1976); four string quartets (1950–63), *Etwas ruhiger in Ausdruck*, for chamber ensemble (1968; title from no. 2 of Schoenberg's piano pieces op. 23); *Spiri* for string quartet and ensemble (1977), *Tema* for woodwind and strings (1981), *Refrain* for eight instruments (1986), *Flag* for 13 instruments (1987), *Chantal* for flute, clarinet, harp, and string quartet (1990). Vocal music includes *The Book with Seven Seals*, oratorio for soloists, chorus and orchestra (1951), and *Serenata* for soprano and 16 instruments (1959; text by Dylan Thomas), and *Arias* for soprano and orchestra (1978); *Atem*, opera in two acts (1985); *In canda II* for orchestra (1994); *Luci II* for bassoon and cornet (1996).

Don Carlos opera by Verdi in five acts (libretto by F M Méry and C Du Locle, based on Schiller's drama), produced Paris, Opéra, 11 March 1867. Verdi's second French opera. Revised in four acts, in Italian, and produced Milan, La Scala, 10 January 1884. Don Carlos (heir to the throne) and Elisabeth love each other, but she has been promised to Carlos' father, King Philip. After the marriage, the lovers are discovered; Elisabeth withdraws to a monastery, where Carlos meets her. Philip arrives to hand his son over to the Inquisition, but Carlos is taken into the cloister by his grandfather's ghost.

Don Chisciotte della Mancia opera by Paisiello (libretto by G B Lorenzi), performed Naples, Teatro dei Fiorentini, summer 1769. Version by Henze performed Montepulciano, 1 August 1976.

Don Chisciotte in corte della duchessa/ Don Quixote at the Duchess's Court opera by Caldara (libretto by G C Pasquini, based on Cervantes), produced Vienna, 6 February 1727.

Don Chisciotte in Sierra Morena/Don Quixote in the Sierra Morena opera by Conti (libretto by Zeno and P Pariati, based on Cervantes), produced Vienna, 11 February 1719.

Don Giovanni/Don Juan Opera by Mozart (first title: *Il dissoluto punito, ossia Il Don Giovanni: The Rake Punished, or Don Juan*) (libretto by Lorenzo da Ponte), produced Prague, 29 October 1787. In Vienna, with additions, Burgtheater, 7 May 1788. Dangerous Don has a catalogue of conquests, but he can't convince the Commendatore, murdered father of Donna Anna, who returns to drag him down to Hell.

Don Giovanni di Mañara (Alfano) ◊*Ombra di Don Giovanni*.

Don Giovanni Tenorio, ossia Il convitato di pietra/Don Juan Tenorio, or The Stone Guest opera by Gazzaniga (libretto by G Bertati, based on Tirso de Molina), produced Venice, Teatro San Moisè, 5 February 1787.

Donington, Robert (1907–1990) English instrumentalist and musicologist. He edited music, wrote learned articles, performed with various teams on early instruments, and produced books on instruments and ornaments, including *The Interpretation of Early Music* 1963.

He was educated at St Paul's School, London, and Oxford University, and studied early instruments and interpretation of music with Arnold Dolmetsch at Haslemere. He also published *Wagner's Ring and its Symbols* 1963 and *The Rise of Opera* 1981.

Donizetti, (Domenico) Gaetano (Maria) (1797–1848) Italian composer. He created more than 60 operas, including *Lucrezia Borgia* 1833, *Lucia di Lammermoor* 1835, *La Fille du régiment* 1840, *La Favorite* 1840, and *Don Pasquale* 1843. They show the influence of Rossini and Bellini, and are characterized by a flow of expressive melodies.

Donizetti studied at Bergamo and at the Liceo Filarmonico at Bologna. He entered the army to avoid following his father's trade and while at Venice in 1818 produced his first opera, *Enrico di Borgogna*. The opera which made his name widely known was *Anna Bolena*, produced in 1830 at Milan, although by this time he had already produced over 30 operas. His *Lucia di Lammermoor*, produced at Naples in 1835, was his greatest success. He excelled not only in serious operas, where he showed a gift for melody and mastery of dramatic ensembles, but also in comic operas, such as *La Fille du régiment* 1840, *L'elisir d'amore* 1832, and *Don Pasquale* 1843. In 1839–40 and 1843 he visited Paris and produced operas there. At about this time, his physical and mental health began to fail, and he became paralysed in 1845.

Donizetti's operas demanded capable singers, and first found favour through such great singers as Giuditta Grisi and Luigi Lablache; more recently, singers such as Maria Callas, Joan Sutherland, and Montserrat Caballé have helped find a new audience, in particular for the recently neglected serious works.

Works include: OPERA more than 70: *Zoraida di Granata* (Rome, 1822), *L'ajo nell'imbarazzo* (Rome, 1824), *Emilia di Liverpool* (Naples, 1824), *Gabriella di Vergy* (composed 1826, performed Naples, 1869), *Il borgomastro di Saardam* (Naples, 1827), *Le convenienze ed inconvenienze teatrali* (Naples, 1827), *Il Giovedi Grasso* (Naples, 1828), *Alina, regina di Golconda* (1828), *Elisabetta, o Il castello di Kenilworth* (Naples, 1829), *Anna Bolena* (Milan, 1830), *Gianni di Parigi* (Milan, 1831), *Fausta* (Naples, 1832), *Ugo, conte di Parigi* (Milan, 1832), *L'elisir d'amore* (Milan 1832), *Il furioso all'isola di San Domingo* (Rome, 1833), *Torquato Tasso* (Rome, 1833), *Lucrezia Borgia* (Milan, 1833), *Rosmonda d'Inghilterra* (Florence, 1834), *Maria Stuarda* (Naples, 1834), *Gemma di Vergy* (Milan, 1834), *Marino Faliero* (Paris, 1835), *Lucia di Lammermoor* (Naples, 1835), *Belisario* (Venice, 1836), *Il campanello di notte* (Naples, 1836), *L'assedio di Calais* (1836), *Pia de' Tolomei* (Venice, 1837), *Roberto Devereux* (Naples, 1837), *Maria di Rudenz* (Venice, 1838), *La fille du régiment* (Paris, 1840), *La favorite* (Paris, 1840), *Maria Padilla* (Milan, 1841), *Linda di Chamounix* (Vienna, 1842), *Caterina Cornaro* (Naples, 1842), *Don Pasquale* (Paris, 1843), *Dom Sébastien* (Paris, 1843).

Poliuto (Naples, 1848; composed 1838 for Naples, it was banned and produced in Paris in 1840 as *Les Martyrs*), *Le duc d'Albe* was written for Paris in 1840 but not produced; the score was completed by M Salvi and others and produced at the Teatro Apollo, Rome, on 22 March 1882.

Don Juan symphonic poem by Richard Strauss, op. 20, based on Lenau's poem, composed 1887–88, first performed Weimar, 11 November 1889.

Don Juan de Mañara opera by Goossens (libretto by Arnold Bennett), produced London, Covent Garden, 24 June 1937.

Don Juan legend for musical treatments, see Franco◊ Alfano (*L'ombra di Don Giovanni*), Boris◊ Assafiev (*The Seducer of Seville*), Carnicer (*Don Giovanni Tenorio*), Vincenzo ◊Fabrizi, Righini (*Il convitato di pietra*), Aleksandr ◊Dargomizhsky (*Stone Guest*), ◊*Don Giovanni* (Mozart), ◊*Don Giovanni Tenorio* (Gazzaniga), ◊*Don Juan* (R Strauss), ◊*Don Juan de Mañara* (Goossens), *Don Juan Mañara* Enna, ◊Ferreira,

◊Graener (*Don Juans letztes Abenteuer*), ◊*Ombra di Don Giovanni* (Alfano), ◊Purcell (Shadwell's *Libertine*), ◊Salazar (*Don Juan en los infiernos*), E ◊Schulhoff (opera), ◊Shebalin (*Stone Guest*), ◊Tomasi (*Don Juan de Mañara*).

Donna ancora è fedele, La/The Lady is still Faithful opera by Pasquini (libretto by D F Contini), produced Rome, Palazzo Colonna, 19 April 1676.

Donna del Lago, La/The Lady of the Lake opera by Rossini (libretto by A L Tottola, based on Scott's poem), produced Naples, Teatro San Carlo, 24 September 1819. In Scotland King James V loves Ellen, the daughter of rebel Douglas. She in turn loves Malcolm, but must marry Douglas' ally Roderick. After Roderick is killed, James spares the captive Douglas and sanctions marriage between Ellen and Malcolm.

Donna Diana opera by Reznicek (libretto by composer based on Moreto's comedy, produced Prague, German Theatre, 16 December 1894. Haughty Diana is humbled by persistent suitor.

Donna serpente, La/The Serpent-Woman opera by Casella (libretto by C Lodovici, based on Gozzi's comedy), produced Rome, Teatro Reale, 17 March 1932. Wagner's *Die Feen* was on the same subject. Fairy Miranda marries Altidor against the wishes of her father, Demogorgòn, who forces her to test most cruelly Altidor's devotion. When eventually he fails the test she is turned into a snake, but thanks to the magic of wizard Geònca and Altidor's bravery, Miranda is restored.

Donne curiose, Le/The Inquisitive Ladies opera by Wolf-Ferrari (libretto by L Sugano, based on Goldoni's comedy), produced Munich, in German, 27 November 1903. Gourmet men suspected of infidelities by their inquisitive womenfolk.

Donnerstag aus Licht/Thursday from Light first opera by Stockhausen from projected opera cycle **Licht**. The work is semi-autobiographical: the three acts are titled *Michael's Youth*, *Michael's journey around the earth* (a huge concerto for trumpet and orchestra) and *Michael's homecoming*; composed 1978–81, produced Milan, La Scala, 3 April 1981.

Don Pasquale comic opera by Donizetti (libretto by composer and G Ruffini), based on Angelo Anelli's *Ser Marcantonio*, composed by Pavesi in 1810), produced Paris, Théâtre Italien, 3 January 1843. Pasquale disapproves of match between nephew Ernesto and Norina, but changes his mind after a mock marriage to 'Sofronia', Norina in disguise.

Don Quichotte opera in five acts by Massenet (libretto by H Cain, based on Cervantes and Jacques Le Lorrain's comedy, *Le Chevalier de la longue figure*), produced Monte Carlo, 19 February 1910. Quichotte recovers Dulcinea's necklace from bandits, but she rejects him.

Don Quixote symphonic poem by R Strauss, op. 35, based on Cervantes, composed 1897, first performed Cologne, 8 March 1898. The work is described as 'Fantastic Variations on a theme of knightly character' and contains important solo parts for cello (Don Quixote) and viola (Sancho Panza).

Don Quixote, The Comical History of play by Thomas Durfey, based on Cervantes, with music by Purcell and others, composed parts i and ii, 1694, by Purcell and Eccles; part iii, 1695, by Akeroyde, Courteville, Pack, Morgan and D Purcell. i. produced London, Dorset Gardens, May 1694; ii. ditto June 1694; iii. London, Drury Lane Theatre, November 1695.

Doppio Concerto work by Henze for oboe, harp and strings, written for Heinz and Ursula Holliger and performed by them Zurich, 2 December 1966.

doppio movimento (Italian 'double movement') in music, a direction indicating that a new tempo is to be exactly twice as fast as the one it displaces.

Dorati, Antál (1906–1988) US conductor, born in Hungary. He toured with ballet companies 1933–45 and went on to conduct orchestras in the USA and Europe in a career spanning more than half a century. Dorati gave many first performances of Bartók's music and recorded all Haydn's symphonies with the Philharmonia Hungarica.

He studied at the Budapest Academy of Music with Bartók and Kodály. He first conducted at the age of 18. In 1947 he became a US citizen and in 1948 conductor of the Minneapolis Symphony Orchestra. He was chief conductor of the British Broadcasting Corporation (BBC) Symphony Orchestra 1963–67, of the Royal Philharmonic Orchestra 1975–78, and of the Detroit Symphony Orchestra 1977–81. He also composed, and made a number of successful arrangements of pieces including J Strauss's *Graduation Ball*.

Dorfbarbier, Der/The Village Barber comic opera by Schenk (libretto by J and P Weidmann), produced Vienna, Burgtheater, 30 October 1796.

Dorian mode one of the ◊church modes, a scale D–C, centred around and beginning on D, which uses only the notes of the C major scale.

'Dorian' Toccata and Fugue organ work in D minor by Bach, so called on account of its notation without key-signature, the B♭ being inserted where necessary as an accidental.

Dori, La, ovvero La schiava fedele/Doris, or The Faithful Slave opera by Cesti (libretto by A Apolloni), produced Innsbruck, Hof-Saales, 1657. Dori, disguised as a man, is sold as a slave to Arsinoe, her sister. Complicated plot ends happily with sisters' marriage to Tolomeo and Oronte.

Dorn, Heinrich (Ludwig Egmont) (1804–1892) German composer, teacher, and conductor. He was a pupil of Carl Friedrich Zelter in Berlin, taught of Robert Schumann at Leipzig, and was opera conductor at Hamburg and Riga, where he succeeded Richard Wagner in 1839. He later became conductor at the Royal Opera and professor in Berlin.

Works include: the operas, *Die Rolands-knappen* (1826), *Die Nibelungen* (1854); ballet *Amors Macht*; Requiem; cantatas; orchestral works; piano music; songs.

Dostoevsky, Feodor Mikhailovich (1821–1881) Russian novelist. His works and thought inspired R ◊Chailly (*L'Idiota*); ◊*From the House of the Dead* (Janáček); ◊*Gambler* (Prokofiev); ◊*Grossinquisitor* (Blacher); ◊*Idiot* (Henze); Vladimir ◊Rebikov (*Christmas Tree*); Daniel ◊Ruyneman (*Brothers Karamazov*); Heinrich ◊Sutermeister (*Raskolnikov*).

dot (1) above or under a note normally indicates *staccato*. Uses other than this are: (*a*) in 18th-century violin music, a series of dots with a slur indicates notes to be detached without changing the bow; (*b*) in 18th-century clavichord music, a series of dots with a slur above or under a single note indicates repeated pressure on the key; (*c*) in older French music, dots above or under a succession of quavers or semi-quavers could mean the observance of equal note-values (*notes égales*), as opposed to the current fashion of lengthening or shortening such notes alternately (*notes inégales*). (2) A dot to the right of a note normally lengthens it by half. See ◊dotted notes.

dotted notes notes with a dot placed on their right, with the effect of prolonging them by half their original value. A double dot has the effect of adding another half of the smaller value to the original note, which is thus lengthened by three-quarters of its value. Double dots were introduced by Leopold Mozart, before whose time their effect could not be precisely indicated in notation, though it was often produced at will by the interpreter, especially in slow movements written in singly dotted rhythm, such as the slow introductions in Lully's and Handel's overtures.

dot-way a 17th-century system of musical notation for recorders, with staves where each line represented a fingerhole, while dots placed over the lines showed which fingers were to be kept down for each note.

double the old French name for a type of musical variation that was merely a more highly ornamented version of a theme previously played in plainer notes.

double bar a pair of bar-lines placed very close together and marking off a principal section of a musical composition, such as the end of the exposition and beginning of the development in a sonata or symphony. It may be preceded or followed by repeat signs, or both, in which case the music before and/or after it must be repeated.

double bass large, bowed four-stringed (sometimes five-stringed) musical instrument, the bass of the ◊violin family. It is descended from the bass viol or violone. Until 1950, after which it was increasingly superseded by the electric bass, it also provided bass support (plucked) for jazz and dance

8ve lower

8ve lower

8ve lower

The double bass has four strings, formerly three, tuned (top or centre). The first of these is the one in general use. The range can be artificially extended either by tuning down the bottom string or by the addition of a fifth string. In the latter case the instrument is normally tuned as shown in the bottom illustration. If the C string is tuned down to B, this will continue the tuning in fourths.

bands. Performers include Domenico Dragonetti, composer of eight concertos, the Russian-born US conductor Serge Koussevitsky (1874–1951), and the jazz player and composer Charles Mingus. The double bass features in the well-loved 'Elephants' solo, No 5 of Saint-Saëns' *Carnival of the Animals* 1897.

The double bass is tuned in fourths (E1, A1, D2, G2).

double bassoon, or contrabassoon musical instrument, a ◊bassoon with a range an octave lower than that of the ordinary instrument.

double bass viol alternative name for the ◊violone, a musical instrument.

double chant a chant in two sections used in the Anglican Church and covering two verses of a psalm.

double concerto a concerto for two solo instruments, such as Bach's D minor for two violins, Mozart's E♭ major for two pianos, Brahms's A minor for violin and cello, Elliott Carter's for piano and harpsichord.

double counterpoint see ◊counterpoint.

double dots see ◊dotted notes.

double flat an accidental, ♭♭, lowering the note before which it stands by a whole tone.

double fugue a ◊fugue consisting of two subjects (principal melodies). Of two types, one consists of three sections: a fugue on subject A, a fugue on subject B, and a fugue combining A and B. The other consists of a fugue in which both subjects are introduced at the beginning of the piece and combined throughout.

double sharp an accidental, 𝄪, raising the note before which it stands by a whole tone.

double stopping on a stringed musical instrument, the technique of producing two notes simultaneously by ◊stopping two separate strings.

doucemelle, French keyboard instrument in use around the 15th century; a forerunner of the ◊piano. Also an alternative name for the ◊dulcimer.

Dowland, John (c. 1563–c. 1626) English composer of lute songs. He introduced daring expressive refinements of harmony and ornamentation to English Renaissance style in the service of an elevated aesthetic of melancholy, as in the masterly *Lachrymae* 1605.

Dowland, Robert (c. 1591–1641) English lutenist and composer, son of John ◊Dowland. He was appointed lutenist to Charles I on his father's death in 1626. He composed lessons for the lute, and published a book of airs by continental composers.

downbeat the downward movement of a conductor's hand or baton, signifying the starting point or strong beat of a musical bar.

down bow in the playing of string instruments, the movement of the bow in the direction from the heel to the point.

Down by the Greenwood Side dramatic pastoral in one act by Birtwistle (libretto by M Nyman), for soprano, five actors and chamber ensemble; performed Brighton, Pier Pavilion, 8 May 1969. St George is defeated by the Black Knight but revives under the vernal earth magic of the Green Man.

Draeseke, Felix (August Bernhard) (1835–1913) German composer. He studied at the Leipzig Conservatory and with Liszt at Weimar. He later taught at Dresden, Lausanne, Munich, and Geneva, and finally settled at Dresden in 1876, where he became professor of composition at the Conservatory in 1884.

Works include: the operas *Gudrun* (1884), *Herrat*, and *Merlin* (1903–05); Requiem, trilogy of oratorios *Christus*, Easter scene from Goethe's *Faust* for solo voices, chorus, and orchestra (1907); five symphonies, overtures for orchestra, including *Penthesilea* (after Kleist); concerto for piano, violin, and cello; three string quartets, string quintet; many piano works including a sonata.

drag in playing the ◊snare drum, a stroke preceded by a group of grace-notes, usually three or four.

Draghi, Antonio (c. 1634–1700) Italian composer. He began his career as a singer at Venice. In 1658 he went to Vienna to take up a court appointment, and was appointed Hofkapellmeister in 1682. He was also a librettist for other composers, including Bertali, Ziani, and the Emperor Leopold I.

Works include: 67 operas, including *Timone misantropo*, after Shakespeare (1696), 116 smaller stage pieces, about 40 oratorios, cantatas, hymns, and other pieces.

drame lyrique a modern French term for a serious opera.

dramma (per musica) (Italian 'drama (for music)') 18th-century term for opera; actually plays written especially for the purpose of being set to music.

dramma giocoso (Italian 'jocular drama') name occasionally used for *opera buffa* in the later 18th century; Mozart's original designation of *Don Giovanni*.

Drátenik/The Tinker opera by Škroup (libretto by J K Chmelenský), produced Prague, 2 February 1826. The first Czech opera.

Dream of Gerontius, The oratorio by Elgar, op. 38 (words selected from Cardinal John Henry Newman's poem), first performed Birmingham Festival, 3 October 1900.

Dreigroschenoper, Die/The Threepenny Opera operetta by Weill (libretto based on Elisabeth Hauptmann's German version of Gay's *Beggar's Opera*, with some additions by Brecht), produced Berlin, Theater am Schiffbauerdamm, 31 August 1928. Mack the Knife escapes the gallows.

Drei Pintos, Die/The Three Pintos unfinished opera by Weber (libretto by T Hell, based on Carl Ludwig Seidel's story *Der Brautkampf*), partly composed 1821; produced in an edition completed by Mahler, Leipzig, 20 January 1888. Don Pinto's misadventures on his way to wooing Clarissa. He is impersonated by her true love Don Gomez, who eventually marries her.

drone an accompanying constant tone or harmony, usually octave or fifth. It is a feature of many classical and folk traditions, and is produced by many instruments of folk music, including the Indian vina, bagpipes, and hurdy-gurdy. Drone effects in written music include the organ ◊pedal point and the ◊musette dance form.

Drone is also the name given to the three lower pipes of the bagpipes, which produce a fixed chord above which the melody is played on the ◊chanter; also a bowed instrument with a single string stretched on a stick over a bladder; sometimes called a bumbass.

Among examples of drone in the concert repertoire are Wagner's overture to *Das Rheingold/The Rhinegold* 1853–54 and the mystery chord of Schoenberg's third orchestral piece 'Farben'/'Chord Colours' from the *Five Pieces for Orchestra* 1909.

drone bass an unvaryingly sustained bass on any composition, resembling the drone of a bagpipe.

Druckman, Jacob (1928–1996) US composer. His earlier works were mainly chamber pieces; he later turned to writing orchestral music, including *Windows* 1972, for which he won a Pulitzer Prize.

He studied at the Juilliard School and in Paris. He directed electronic music centres at Princeton and Yale Universities.

Works include: violin concerto (1956), *Dark upon the Harp* for mezzo, brass quintet, and percussion (1962); *The Sound of Time* for soprano and orchestra (1965); *Animus I–IV* for mezzo, instruments, and tape (1966–77), *Windows* for orchestra (1972); *Lamia* for soprano and orchestra (1974); *Chiaroscuro* for orchestra (1976); Viola concerto 1978); *Aureole* for orchestra (1979); *Prism*; three pieces for orchestra after music from operas by M A Charpentier, Cavalli, and Cherubini (1980); three string quartets (1948, 1961, 1981); *Athenor* for orchestra (1985).

drum any of a class of percussion instruments including **slit drums** made of wood, **steel drums** fabricated from oil containers, and a majority group of **skin drums** consisting of a shell or vessel of wood, metal, or earthenware across one or both ends of which is stretched a membrane of hide or plastic. Drums are struck with the hands or with a stick or pair of sticks; they are among the oldest instruments known.

tuned drums Most drums are of indeterminate low or high pitch and function as rhythm instruments. The exceptions are steel drums, orchestral ◊timpani (kettledrums), and Indian ◊tabla which are tuned to precise pitches. Double-ended African kalungu ('talking drums') can be varied in pitch by the player squeezing on the tension cords: higher tension over the playing drumhead results in a higher pitch. Frame drums, including the Irish bodhrán and Basque tambour, are smaller and lighter in tone and may incorporate jingles or rattles.

orchestral and military drums Orchestral drums consist of timpani, tambourine, snare, side, and bass drums, the latter either single-headed (with a single skin) and producing a ringing tone, called a gong drum, or double-headed (with two skins) and producing a dense booming noise of indeterminate pitch. Military bands of footsoldiers employ snare and side drums, and among cavalry regiments a pair of kettledrums mounted on horseback are played on ceremonial occasions.

pop and jazz drums Dance-band drums have evolved from the 'traps' of Dixieland jazz into a battery of percussion employing a range of stick types. In addition to snare and foot-controlled bass drums, many feature a scale of pitched bongos and tom-toms, as well as suspended cymbals, hi-hat (foot-controlled double cymbals), cowbells, and temple blocks. Recent innovations include the rotary tunable rototoms, electronic drums, and the drum machine, a percussion synthesizer.

Drum Mass (Haydn). See ◊*Paukenmesse.*

'Drum-Roll' Symphony/Symphonie mit dem Paukenwirbel nickname of Haydn's symphony no. 103 in E♭ major (composed for London, 1795), so called because it opens with a timpani roll.

Dryden, John (1631–1700) English poet, dramatist and satirist. His works inspired numerous musical settings, such as ◊*Acis and Galatea* (Handel); ◊*Albion and Albanius* (Grabu); ◊*Alexander's Feast* (Handel); ◊*Almahide* (G Bononcini); ◊Boyce (*Secular Masque*); J ◊Clarke (*Alexander's Feast*); Clayton (ditto); ◊*Cymon* (M Arne); G B Draghi (*Ode for St Cecilia's Day*); J Eccles (*Spanish Friar*); Pelham ◊Humfrey (*Conquest of Granada* and *Indian Emperor*); ◊*Indian Queen* and ◊*King Arthur* (Purcell); ◊*Ode for St Cecilia's Day* (Handel); ◊Purcell (*Amphitryon, Aureng-Zebe, Cleomenes, Love Triumphant, Spanish Friar, Tyrannic Love* and *Oedipus*); Nicholas ◊Staggins (*Conquest of Granada* and *Marriage à la Mode*).

D.S. abbreviation for **dal segno** (Italian 'from the sign').

Dubois, (François Clément) Théodore (1837–1924) French composer. He studied at Rheims and then at the Paris Conservatory, where he won the Prix de Rome in 1861. Returning to Paris in 1866, he was active as an organist and teacher, and succeeded Saint-Saëns as organist at the Madeleine in 1877. From 1896 to 1905 he was director of the Conservatory. His treatises on harmony, counterpoint, and fugue are still in use.

Works include: the operas *La Guzla de l'Emir* (1873), *Le Pain bis* (1879), *Aben-Hamet, Xavière* (1895); ballet *La Farandole*; Requiem, *Messe de la Délivrance* and other Masses, motets and other church music; oratorios, *Les Sept Paroles du Christ* and *Paradis perdu*; orchestral works.

due corde (Italian 'two strings') in music, direction to a pianist to depress the ◊soft pedal halfway (as in Beethoven's Piano Sonata in A Flat 1822) so that the hammer hits two of the three strings for each note, or directing a violinist to use two strings, which affects the timbre, even though the passage in question could be played on one string.

Due Foscari, I/The Two Foscari opera by Verdi (libretto by F M Piave, based on Byron's drama), produced Rome, Teatro Argentina, 3 November 1844. The Doge's son Jacopo has been accused of murder. He is first imprisoned, then exiled, against the pleas of his wife, Lucrezia. It is revealed too late that Jacopo is innocent: he dies upon leaving Venice.

Due litiganti (Sarti). See ◊*Fra due litiganti.*

Duenna, The, or The Double Elopement
opera by Thomas Linley, father and son
(libretto by Sheridan), produced London,
Covent Garden 21 November 1775. Sheridan
was son-in-law of Linley senior.

Opera by Roberto Gerhard (libretto by
composer and C Hassall after Sheridan), first
performed by the British Broadcasting Corporation (BBC), broadcast 23 February 1949;
stage premiere Madrid, 21 January 1992.
Luisa is inclined to Antonio but must marry
Isaac Mendoza. After mistaken identities and
twists in the plot, the opera ends with a triple
wedding: Luisa marries Antonio, Luisa's
brother Ferdinand marries Clara, and Isaac
Mendoza marries Margaret, Luisa's duenna.
see also ◊*Betrothal in a Monastery.*

duet, or duo music or ensemble of two voices
or instruments. A piano duet is normally two
players sharing a single instrument (also
called 'piano four-hands'); a piano duo is
two players on two pianos.

Dufay, Guillaume (c. 1400–1474) Flemish
composer. He wrote secular songs and sacred
music, including 84 songs and eight masses.
His work marks a transition from the style of
the Middle Ages to the expressive melodies
and rich harmonies of the Renaissance.

Dukas, Paul Abraham (1865–1935) French
composer and teacher. His scrupulous orchestration and chromatically enriched harmonies were admired by Debussy. His small
output includes the opera *Ariane et Barbe-
Bleue/Ariane and Bluebeard* 1907, the ballet *La
Péri/The Peri* 1912, and the animated orchestral scherzo *L'Apprenti sorcier/The Sorcerer's
Apprentice* 1897.

Dukas studied at the Paris Conservatory,
where his teachers included Théodore Dubois
and Ernest Guiraud. He taught the orchestral
class there 1910–13 and was then appointed
professor of composition; in 1926 he also
began teaching at the Ecole Normale, and
held both posts until his death. Among his
pupils at the Conservatory was Olivier
Messiaen.

He wrote very little, composing slowly and
with extreme care. His opera *Ariane et Barbe-
Bleue* is among the finest French operas of its
day, premiered four years before Bartók
wrote *Duke Bluebeard's Castle* 1918.

Works include: the opera *Ariane et Barbe-
Bleue* (Maeterlinck, 1907); ballet *La Péri* (1912);
symphony in C major, (1896), overture to
Corneille's *Polyeucte*, *L'Apprenti sorcier* (on
Goethe's poem 'Der Zauberlehrling'); sonata
in E♭ minor, *Variations on a theme by Rameau*,

Prélude élégiaque on the name of Haydn and *La
Plainte, au loin, du faune* (in memory of
Debussy) for piano; *Sonnet de Ronsard* and
Vocalise for voice and piano; *Villanelle* for
horn and piano, and other pieces, including
unpublished overtures to Shakespeare's *King
Lear* and Goethe's *Götz von Berlichingen.*

**Duke Bluebeard's Castle/A kékszakállú
hercegvára** opera in one act by Bartók
(libretto by B Balázs); composed 1911, produced Budapest, 24 May 1918, conductor
Tango. Inquisitive bride Judith tours Bluebeard's blood-spattered castle and joins his
former wives in eternal gloom.

Dukelsky, Vladimir (1903–1969) Russian-
born US composer. Under the influence of
Gershwin he wrote light music under the
name of Vernon Duke, but cultivated an
advanced modern style under his own name.
In 1924 Diaghilev heard his piano concerto
and commissioned him to write a work for
the Ballets Russes.

He studied at Moscow and Kiev, where his
teachers included Reinhold Glière. He went
to live in Constantinople in 1920 and settled
in New York in 1922.

Works include: the operetta *Yvonne* (1926);
ballets *Zéphir et Flore* and *Public Gardens*;
oratorio *The End of St Petersburg* (1937); four
symphonies, *Dédicaces* for soprano, piano,
and orchestra, piano concerto; string quartet;
violin sonata; song cycle *Triolets of the North*
(Feodor Sologub); Three Chinese songs and
other songs.

dulce melos (Latin 'sweet melody') keyboard instrument, also known as the ◊chek-
ker.

dulcian an organ stop of reedy quality,
usually of 16-foot pitch (sounding an octave
lower than written); also an alternative name
for the ◊curtal.

dulciana an open ◊diapason organ stop of
delicate tone. It may embrace 4 ft, 8 ft, or 16 ft
pipes.

dulcimer musical instrument, a form of
◊zither, consisting of a shallow open trape-
zoidal soundbox across which strings are
stretched laterally; they are horizontally
struck by lightweight hammers or beaters. It
produces clearly-differentiated pitches of
consistent quality and is more agile and
wide-ranging in pitch than the harp or lyre.
In Hungary the dulcimer is known as a
cimbalom, and is a national instrument.

Of Middle Eastern origin, the dulcimer
spread into Europe about 1100 and was
introduced to China and Korea about 1800.

Examples include the Iraqi *santir*, Chinese *yang shin*, Russian *chang*, Korean *yangum*, and Swiss *hackbrett*.

dulcitone keyboard instrument producing its sound on a set of tuning forks, similar to the ◊celesta.

Dumanoir, Guillaume (1615–c. 1697) French violinist and composer. As the 'Roi des Violons' (the head of the guild of violin players) he came into conflict with the dancing-masters, whom he wished to compel to contribute to the violinists' guild of Saint-Julien. Being unsuccessful in this, he wrote the abusive pamphlet *Le Mariage de la musique avec la danse/The Marriage of Music and Dance* 1664. He composed dance music which was liked by Louis XIV, who appointed him ballet master of the royal pages.

He was the son of Guillaume Dumanoir, whom he succeeded as head of the Confrérie de Saint-Julien (the violinists' guild). He renewed his father's quarrel with the dancing masters, resigning in 1685. Before that he had quarrelled with Lully over the privilege of training orchestra musicians and lost a lawsuit against him in 1673.

Dumbarton Oaks concerto in E♭ for chamber orchestra by Stravinsky; composed 1937–38, performed Washington, DC, at Dumbarton Oaks, the private estate of R W Bliss, 8 May 1938. First public performance Paris, 4 June 1938.

dumka a lament, which in music takes the form of a slow piece alternating with more animated sections, as in Dvořák's *Dumky* Trio.

'Dumky' Trio a piano trio by Dvořák, op. 90, composed 1891.

Dunhill, Thomas (Frederick) (1877–1946) English composer. He was assistant music master at Eton College 1899–1908, and organized concerts for chamber music and for the promotion of British music in London during the early years of the century. He entered the Royal College of Music in 1893, where Charles Stanford was his composition master, and where he later became professor of composition.

Works include: the operas *The Enchanted Garden* (1928), *Tantivy Towers* (A P Herbert, 1931), and *Happy Families*; ballets *Dick Whittington* and *Gallimaufry*; symphony in A minor, *Elegiac Variations* in memory of Parry and overture *Maytime* for orchestra; *Triptych* for viola and orchestra; piano quartet, two piano trios, five quintets.

Duni, Egidio Romoaldo (1708–1775) Italian composer. He wrote about ten serious operas in Italy, beginning with *Nerone* 1735, which was a great success. In 1757 he settled in Paris, where he became a leading composer of opéras comiques, notably *Le peintre amoureux de son modèle* 1757.

He studied under Francesco Durante in Naples.

Works include: the operas *Nerone* (1735), *Le caprice amoureux*, *Le peintre amoureux de son modèle* (1757), *L'isle des fous*, *Le milicien*, *Les deux chasseurs et la laitière* (1763), *La fée Urgèle*, *La clochette*, *Les moissonneurs*, *Les sabots* (1768).

Dunstable, John (c. 1385–1453) English composer of songs and anthems. He is considered one of the founders of Renaissance harmony.

Duparc, (Marie Eugène) Henri Fouques (1848–1933) French composer. His songs are memorable for their lyric sensibility. Only 16 of them survive.

He was educated by Jesuits at the Collège de Vaugirard, where he learned piano from César Franck, and afterwards took private lessons in composition from him. His few works include the symphonic poem *Lenore* 1875, and a nocturne, *Aux étoiles*, but he is chiefly remembered for his songs, among them 'Invitation au voyage' and 'Phydile'. He was a fierce critic of his own work and destroyed a number of compositions. He never took any share in official musical life, but continued to compose at intervals until 1885, when he began to suffer from an incurable nervous complaint and retired to Switzerland.

Works include: the symphonic poem *Lénore* (on Bürger's poem, 1875) and nocturne *Aux Etoiles*; motet *Benedicat vobis Dominus*; 16 songs including *Phydilé*, *Invitation au voyage*, *Soupir*, *La vague et la cloche*, *Extase*, *Le manoir de Rosemonde* and *Lamento*; and several afterwards destroyed.

duplet group of two notes occupying the time of three.

duple time a metre in which the bar may be divided into two beats, as in 2/4 and 6/8.

Dupré, Marcel (1886–1971) French organist and composer. He was appointed professor of organ at the Paris Conservatory in 1926 and organist at Saint-Sulpice in 1936, succeeding Widor. From 1954 to 1956 he was director of the Conservatory.

He played Bach from memory at the age of ten, and in 1898 was appointed organist of the church of Saint-Vivien at Rouen. He produced an oratorio in 1901. After that he studied piano, organ, and composition at the Paris Conservatory and won the Prix de Rome in 1914 as a pupil of Widor. He was organist at Notre-Dame 1916–22 during the illness of Louis Vierne. His pupils at the Conservatory included Jehan Alain and Olivier Messiaen.

Works include: the oratorio *Le Songe de Jacob*, motets and *De Profundis*; two symphonies; concerto for organ and orchestra (1934), violin and piano sonata; cello pieces; songs; many organ works including *Symphonie-Passion*, 79 chorales, *Le Chemin de la Croix*.

dur (German 'hard') in music, the German equivalent of 'major' when referring to a key, as in *'C dur'* (C major). *Dur* is the opposite of *moll*.

Durand, Auguste Frédéric (1770–1834), born Duranowski Polish-born French violinist and composer. A virtuoso violinist, he was renowned for his technique and was a significant influence on Paganini.

Duranowski, August Fryderyk see Auguste Frédéric ◊Durand.

Durante, Francesco (1684–1755) Italian composer. His works consist largely of church music, also sonatas, toccatas, and other pieces for harpsichord. Unusually for a Neapolitan composer, he wrote no operas.

He was educated at Naples, where in 1742 he became maestro di cappella at the Conservatorio di S Maria and in 1745 at that of S Onofrio. His pupils included Tommaso Traetta, Giovanni Paisiello, Antonio Sacchini, Giovanni Pergolesi, and Niccolò Piccinni.

Durchführung (German 'through-leading') in music, term for the ◊development or working-out section of a movement in sonata form.

durchkomponiert (German 'set through-out') in music, a descriptive term for a song in which the words are set to music continuously, not strophically with the same music repeated for each verse.

Durey, Louis (1888–1979) French composer. He did not study music until the age of 22, and in 1914 he enlisted on the outbreak of World War I. In 1916, during leave, he came under the influence of Satie and joined the group known as Les Six, but was the first to secede from it in 1921. In 1923 he went to live in seclusion in southern France, writing very little.

Works include: the opera on Mérimée's *L'Occasion* (1925); incidental music to Hebbel's *Judith* (1918); three string quartets, piano

trio, string trio; song cycles with chamber music or piano.

durezza (Italian 'hardness') term now used in the direction *con durezza* to indicate that a harsh or unyielding manner of performance is required. Up until the 17th century the term was used for discord.

Durfey, Thomas (1653–1723), or D'Urfey English playwright and poet. His works inspired ◊Akeroyde (*Don Quixote*); Ralph Courteville, (ditto); ◊*Don Quixote, The Comical History of*, (Purcell and others); G B Draghi (*Wonders in the Sun*); J Eccles (*Don Quixote*); Mathew ◊Locke (*Fool turned Critic*); D ◊Purcell (*Cynthia and Endymion*); H ◊Purcell (*Fool's Preferment, Marriage-Hater Matched, Richmond Heiress, Sir Barnaby Whigg* and *Virtuous Wife*); William ◊Turner (*Fond Husband* and *Madam Fickle*).

Durkó, Zsolt (1934–) Hungarian composer. His music breaks away from local influences and favours the avant garde.

He studied in Budapest and with Goffredo Petrassi in Rome.

Works include: the opera *Moses* (produced Budapest 1977); *Organismi* for violin and orchestra (1964), *Dartmouth Concerto* for soprano and orchestra (1966), *Fioriture* for orchestra (1966), *Altimara* for chorus and orchestra (1968), *Funeral Oration*, oratorio (1972), *Turner Illustrations* for orchestra (1976); two string quartets (1966, 1969), *Impromptus in F* for flute and ensemble (1984); wind octet (1988); *Ilmarinen* for chorus (1989).

Durón, Sebastián (1660–1716) Spanish composer, an early exponent of Spanish opera. He was organist at Seville Cathedral 1680–85. In 1691 he became organist at the court of Madrid and was appointed maestro de capilla in 1702.

Not having supported the Bourbon succession, he seems to have gone into exile in 1706.

Works include: the operas and zarzuelas *Muerte en amor es la ausencia, Apolo y Dafne, Selva encantada de Amor, Las nuevas armas de Amor, La guerra de los gigantes, Salir el amor del mundo*; incidental music for a comedy, *Jupiter*; two ballets.

Dürr, Alfred (1918–) German musicologist. He studied at the University of Göttingen. From 1953 he edited the *Bach-Jahrbuch* and has been principal contributor to the Bach *Neue Ausgabe* (complete works). Bach's cantatas are at the centre of his research.

Dürr, Walter (1932–) German musicologist. He studied at Tübingen University and taught there from 1962; from 1965 he was joint editor of the *Neue Schubert-Ausgabe* at Tübingen. Other fields of study are Mozart and the Italian madrigal.

Duruflé, Maurice (1902–1986) French organist and composer. He learnt music in the choir school of Rouen Cathedral 1912–18, and then studied at the Paris Conservatory under Louis Vierne, Charles Tournemire, and Paul Dukas. He was appointed organist at the church of Saint-Etienne-du-Mont in 1929.

Works include: Requiem for chorus and orchestra (1947); *Messe-cum jubilo* (1966); chorale on *Veni Creator*, suite and many other works for organ; *Prelude, Recitative and Variations* for flute, viola, and piano; three dances for orchestra.

Dušek, Franz (František Xaver) (1731–1799) Bohemian pianist and composer. He wrote about 40 symphonies and 20 string quartets.

He was a pupil of Georg Wagenseil in Vienna. Dušek himself later taught in Prague, and was the master of many famous pupils. He and his wife Josefa (1754–1824) were friends of Mozart, who worked on his opera *Don Giovanni* at their home in Prague.

Dussek, Jan Ladislav (1760–1812) Bohemian (Czech) composer and pianist. A virtuoso pianist, his compositions, which include over 40 piano sonatas and 15 piano concertos, often display technically challenging passages, by the standard of his day. Composing more fully textured (and often more harmonically adventurous) music than most of his contemporaries, Dussek foreshadowed many of the musical developments of the 19th century. He was one of a group of composers known as the ◊London Pianoforte School.

Dussek was an accomplished pianist at the age of five and an organist at nine. He was educated at a Jesuit College and Prague University, where he read theology. He had shown early promise, and in about 1779 went to the Netherlands, where he held organ posts at Malines and Bergen-op-Zoom. He gave up his organist's career about 1782, and won great success in Amsterdam and The Hague as a pianist and composer. Concert tours took him to Hamburg (where he studied with C P E Bach), Berlin, and St Petersburg, where he entered the service of Prince Radziwill, spending the next two years on the latter's estate in Lithuania. He played before Marie Antoinette in Paris in 1786, and after a visit to Italy returned there in 1788. At the French Revolution he fled to London,

where he first appeared at one of Salomon's concerts in 1790. In 1792 he married the singer and pianist Sophia Corri (1745–1847), and joined his father-in-law's firm of music publishers. The business failed, and in 1800 he went to Hamburg to escape his creditors. More travels followed. He was with Prince Louis Ferdinand of Prussia 1803–06, then in the service of the Prince of Isenburg and, finally, Talleyrand.

His piano music uses the instrument in a novel and congenial way. His sonatas show many striking anticipations of later composers; his influence on Beethoven was particularly important.

Works include: incidental music for *The Captive of Spilburg* (London, 1798) and Sheridan's *Pizarro* (both with Kelly); three overtures and serenade for orchestra; Mass (1811); three string quartets, two piano quartets, piano quintet, about 20 piano trios; about 12 sonatas for piano duet, sonata for two pianos; piano music; about 18 concertos, about 32 sonatas, about 25 rondos, about 20 sets of variations, various miscellaneous pieces; about 65 sonatas with violin or flute.

Dutilleux, Henri (1916–) French composer. He wrote instrumental music in elegant Neo-Romantic style. His works include *Métaboles* 1962–65 for orchestra and *Ainsi la nuit/Thus the Night* 1975–76 for string quartet.

He studied at the Paris Conservatory and won the Prix de Rome in 1938; he was appointed professor at the Conservatory in 1970. His music is regarded as being in the tradition of Ravel, Debussy, and Messiaen.

Works include: two symphonies (performed Paris, 1950 and Boston, 1959); ballets *Le loup* (1953) and *Summer's End* (1981), *La giole* for voice and orchestra (1944), *Cinq métaboles* for orchestra, first performance Cleveland, 1965), *Tout un monde lointain* for cello and orchestra (1970), *Timbres, espaces, mouvement* for orchestra (first performance Washington, 1978), *Ainsi la nuit* for string quartet (1976); *L'arbre des songes* for violin and orchestra (1985), *Mystère de l'instant* for 24 strings, cimbalom, and percussion (1989), *Le jeu des contraires* for piano (1989), *Diptyque, Les citations* for oboe, harpsichord, double bass, and percussion (1991).

Duval, François (c. 1673–1728) French violinist and composer. He was a member of Louis XIV's '24 violons du roi'. His violin sonatas are written in the Italian style and were published as the first of their kind in 1704. He wrote numerous books of sonatas for violin and bass and two violins and bass.

Dvořák, Antonín Leopold (1841–1904)
Czech composer. His Romantic music extends the Classical tradition of Beethoven and Brahms and displays the influence of Czech folk music. He wrote nine symphonies; tone poems; operas, including *Rusalka* (1900); large-scale choral works; the *Carnival* (1891–92) and other overtures; violin and cello concertos; chamber music; piano pieces; and songs. International recognition came with two sets of *Slavonic Dances* 1878 and 1886. Works such as his *New World Symphony* (1893) reflect his interest in American folk themes, including black and Native American music. He was director of the National Conservatory, New York, 1892–95.

Dvořák was the son of a village innkeeper and butcher. He heard only popular and simple church music as a child, but developed remarkable gifts. He was sent to the organ school at Prague in 1857, began to compose two years later, and joined an orchestra as violinist. He later played viola in the orchestra of the Bohemian Provisional Theatre at Prague, conducted by Wagner from 1862, and from 1866 by Smetana. Eleven years later he became organist of the church of St Adalbert, Prague. In 1865 he wrote the song cycle *Cypresses*, inspired by his hopeless love of his pupil, Josefina Čermaková. In 1873 he married Anna, Josefina's sister, and produced his first compositions to receive attention, including the 3rd symphony; earlier works had been strongly influenced by Wagner. During this period he wrote many songs, overtures, and symphonies, and in 1874 produced his opera *King and Charcoal-Burner*, which was not a success. The same year he received for the first time the Austrian state prize for composition. One member of the committee was the composer Brahms, who befriended Dvořák and introduced him to his publisher, Simrock. The *Slavonic Rhapsodies* and *Dances* of 1878 brought an essentially nationalist character to his music, and their publication brought him international fame. They were followed by the first of his great string quartets, the E♭ op. 51, and the powerful 6th Symphony: in the former work folk elements are most obvious, in the latter the presence of Brahms is felt.

Dvořák first visited England in 1884 to conduct the *Stabat Mater* in London. In 1885 he bought the country estate of Vysoká, which remained his home. In 1891 he received an honorary doctorate from Cambridge University, and was appointed professor at Prague Conservatory, where he became director in 1901. In 1892–95 he was

director of the new National Conservatory in New York, and spent some holidays at the Czech colony of Spillville, Iowa. The premiere of the *New World Symphony* at Carnegie Hall was one of the greatest successes of his career.

In 1896 he paid the last of his many visits to England, where he had produced several works at the music festivals. The mighty and classically modelled 7th symphony was premiered in London in 1885, and the cello concerto followed ten years later; Josefina, his first love, died during its composition, and in memory of her the slow section of the finale quotes her favourite song from *Cypresses*.

Works include: OPERA *Dimitrij* (1882), The *Jacobin* (1889), *The Devil and Kate* (*Čert a Káča*, 1899), *Rusalka* (1901), *Armida* (1904).

CHORAL WITH ORCHESTRA (some with solo voices): *Stabat Mater* (1877), *Requiem* (1890); *Te Deum*; four sets of vocal duets; 68 songs.

ORCHESTRAL nine symphonies, including no. 5 in F, op. 76 (1875); no. 6 in D, op. 60 (1880); no. 7 in D minor, op. 70 (1885); no. 8 in G, op. 88 (1889); no. 9 in E minor, 'From the New World', op. 95 (1893). Five symphonic poems *The Water-Sprite* (1896), *The Noon-day Witch* (1896), *The Golden Spinning-Wheel*, *The Wood-Dove*, *Hero's Song* (1897); seven concert overtures; orchestral works including Serenade in D minor for wind, cello, and bass (1878); *Scherzo capriccioso* (1883), *Symphonic Variations* (1877); two sets of Slavonic Dances; *Serenade* for string orchestra; concertos for piano, violin, and cello (1876, 1880, 1895).

CHAMBER MUSIC 14 string quartets, including no. 12 in F, op. 96 (1893, *American*), no. 13 in G, op. 105 (1895), no. 14 in A♭, op. 106 (1895); two string quintets: in G, op. 77, with double bass (1875), in E♭, op. 97, with viola (1893); four piano trios, including F minor, op. 65 (1883), in E minor, '*Dumky*', op. 90 (1891); piano quintet in A, op. 81 (1887); sonatina (1893) for violin and piano.

PIANO 14 op. nos. of piano pieces, including Theme and Variations, six sets of piano duets, including Slavonic Dances, *Legends*.

Dygon, John (c. 1485–1541) English cleric and composer. He took his Bachelor of Music at Oxford in 1512, probably in 1521 went to Louvain to study with the Spanish humanist Juan Luis Vives, and became a prior at St Austin's Abbey, Canterbury. A motet of his is preserved and a treatise on proportions in Trinity College library, Cambridge.

dynamics symbols indicating relative loudness, changes in loudness such as **crescendo** and **diminuendo**, or loudness in accentuation such as **rinforzando**.

Dynamic markings from Monteverdi to J S Bach were primarily objective indicators of tonal change, occasionally spatial and directional in significance. Dynamic expression emerged slowly during the 18th century as instruments of the orchestra evolved away from fixed registers towards individual freedom of expression, coinciding with the coming of age of the fortepiano, named to advertise its expressive advantages over the fixed-register harpsichord. After 1950 many composers attempted to bring dynamics under serial control, but with only limited success.

Dyson, George (1883–1964) English composer. He wrote choral and orchestral music, including a setting of Chaucer's prologue to the *Canterbury Tales* 1931. In 1937 he was appointed director of the Royal College of Music in succession to Hugh Allen, retiring in 1952.

He studied at the Royal College of Music in London and became music director at Winchester College in 1924, having already taught at Osborne, Marlborough, Rugby, and Wellington, serving in World War I between.

Works include: *The Canterbury Pilgrims* (setting of Chaucer's prologue, 1931) and other compositions for solo voices, chorus and orchestra; orchestral, chamber and piano music; songs.

E

E the third note, or mediant, of the scale of C major.

early music music composed in previous periods. The meaning of the term has changed over the years: originally it denoted Western music composed from the early Middle Ages to the Renaissance. As the ◊authenticity movement grew during the mid-20th century it came to include music of the Baroque period as well. Today there is no precise limitation regarding the qualification of early music, but it is generally accepted to include music as late as the early 19th century. The journal *Early Music,* established 1973, focuses on ◊performance practice and other musicological issues concerning music prior to the Romantic period.

Early Reign of Oleg, The Russian 'opera' or play with music (libretto by Catherine II), music by Pashkeievich, Canobbio and Sarti, produced St Petersburg, at court, Hermitage Theatre, 26 October 1790.

Earth Dances work for orchestra by Birtwistle, first performed London, 14 March 1986.

ear training the development of the sense of pitch, involving elements such as ready distinction of intervals and identification of various types of chords.

Easdale, Brian (1909–) English composer. He wrote *Missa coventrensis* 1962 for the consecration of Coventry Cathedral.

He was educated at Westminster Abbey choir school and the Royal College of Music in London.

Works include: the operas *Rapunzel* (1927), *The Corn King* (1935) and *The Sleeping Children* (1951); incidental music for Eugene O'Neill's *Mourning Becomes Electra;* film music *The Red Shoes; Missa coventrensis* (1962), *Dead March, Tone Poem, Six Poems* for orchestra; piano concerto (1938); string trio; pieces for two pianos; song cycles.

East, Michael (c. 1580–1648) English composer. He was apparently in the service of Lady Hatton in London early in the 17th century and from 1618 was organist of Lichfield Cathedral.

Works include: Evening Service, anthems; six books of madrigals (some with anthems) and a madrigal contributed to *The Triumphes of Oriana;* music for viols.

Easter music-drama see ◊liturgical drama.

Easter Oratorio/Kommt, eilet und laufet work by J S Bach performed as a church cantata 1725 and revised 1732–35 as an oratorio.

Eastman School of Music US conservatory, in Rochester, NY, founded 1912 and taken over 1917 by George Eastman (1854–1932). It became part of the University of Rochester 1921, with Howard Hanson as director 1924–64; he was succeeded by Walter Hendl, 1964–72, and Robert S Freeman from 1972. The Cleveland Quartet has been its quartet-in-residence.

Eaton, John (1935–) US composer. He studied with Sessions and Babbitt at Princeton, and taught at Indiana University from 1970. His works use microtones, serial techniques, and synthesizer called syn-ket; his operas *Ma Barker* (1957), *Heracles* (1968), *Myshkin* (1973), *The Tempest* (1985), *The Reverend Jim Jones* (1989).

Eben, Petr (1929–) Czech composer. His works are mostly chamber and vocal pieces, and reflect his interest in religion and myth.

He studied in Prague and has taught at the university there.

Works include: a piano concerto (1961); oratorio *Apologia Sokrates* (1964); *Ubi caritas et amor* for chorus (1965); wind quintet (1965); *Faust* for organ (1980); string quartet (1981); *Curses and Blessings*, ballet (1980); organ concerto (1983); piano trio (1986); *Hommage à Dietrich Buxtehude* for organ (1987); two *Invocations* for trombone and organ (1989).

Eberlin, Johann Ernst (1702–1762) German organist and composer. He was esteemed as a composer of church music.

He settled in Salzburg in 1724, where he became organist to the court and cathedral in 1729, and Kapellmeister in 1749.

Works include: several operas, to texts by Metastasio, over 50 Masses; 12 Requiems; offertories and other pieces; several oratorios; organ music.

Ebony Concerto work by Stravinsky for clarinet and orchestra, composed 1945 for Woody Herman and his band and performed by them, New York, 25 March 1946.

Eccard, Johann (1553–1611) German composer. His works were chiefly choral pieces. As a Lutheran composer, Eccard made much use of the chorale melodies in his works. The collection of sacred pieces which he published in 1597 contains simple harmonizations, but in other volumes he developed the complex chorale motet, of which he was one of the major exponents.

He was a pupil of David Köler in the choir school attached to the Weimar court chapel, 1567–71, and then of Orlande de Lassus in the Hofkapelle at Munich. From the late 1570s he was in the service of Jacob Fugger at Augsburg, and in 1579 joined the chapel of the Margrave of Brandenburg-Ansbach at Königsberg; he was assistant Kapellmeister there until 1604 when he succeeded to the senior post. In 1608 the new Elector Joachim Friedrich of Brandenburg in Berlin appointed Eccard Kapellmeister at his Berlin court, and Eccard continued to serve his successor, Johann Sigismund. His music was still printed 30 years after his death.

Works include: motets, chorales (some harmonized, some newly composed by him); sacred songs; secular German songs for several voices, wedding songs, odes, festival songs.

échappée (French, short for *note échappée*, 'escaped note') in music. the progres-

An échappée between the notes E and D in the top voice of this example.

sion between two adjacent notes which deviates by at first taking a step in the opposite direction and then taking the second note aimed at by an interval of a third.

Echelle de soie, L'/The Silken Ladder opera by Gaveaux (libretto by F A E de Planard), produced Paris, Opéra-Comique, 22 August 1808. The original of Rossini's *Scala di seta*.

echo musical effect. In composition, various echo effects have been used in many ways; Lassus's madrigal *Olà, che buon eco*, the witches' chorus in Purcell's *Dido and Aeneas*, the *Echo* piece in Bach's B minor clavier partita, the *Scène aux champs* in Berlioz's *Fantastic Symphony*, or the second act of Humperdinck's *Hänsel und Gretel*.

Echo et Narcisse opera by Gluck (libretto by L T de Tschudy), produced Paris, Opéra, 24 September 1779. Echo is in despair when Narcissus prefers his own reflection to her. She dies from grief, but when Narcissus recovers his senses she is restored to life.

Eclat work by P Boulez for 15 instruments; first performed Los Angeles, 26 March 1965. Expanded as *Éclat/Multiples* and performed London, 21 October 1970.

ecossaise (French 'Scottish one') dance long supposed to be of Scottish origin but no longer considered so. As a fashionable ballroom dance in the early 19th century, it was in fairly animated 2–4 time, about halfway between the polka and the galop in speed. Among the composers who cultivated it were Beethoven, Schubert, and Chopin. The German *Schottisch* (usually written *Schottische* in English) is the same thing.

Écuatorial work by E Varèse for bass voice, eight brass, piano, organ, two odes Martenots, and six percussion (text is a Spanish translation of a prayer from the sacred book of the Maya Quiché, the *Popul Vuh*), first performed New York, 15 April 1934, conductor Nicolas Slonimsky.

Edelmann, Johann Friedrich (1749–1794) Alsatian pianist and composer. He became famous in Paris through the patronage of his pupil, Baron Dietrich. He was a friend of Gluck, and Mozart thought well of his piano compositions. He apparently played a discreditable part during the French Revolution, and died on the guillotine.

Works include: the operas *Ariane dans l'île de Naxos* (1782), *La Bergère des Alpes* (1781) and *Diane et l'Amour* (1802); symphonies; keyboard concertos and sonatas.

Eder, Helmut (1916–) Austrian composer. He studied in Stuttgart and with Carl Orff in Munich. He co-founded the electronic music school at Linz Conservatory, 1959, and professor at the Salzburg Mozarteum from 1967. His music progressed towards electronics from neo-classicism and serialism.

Works include: OPERA *Oedipus* (1960), *Der Kardinal* (1965), *Der Aufstand* (1975), *Georges Dandin* (1979), *Mozart in New York* (1991).

BALLET *Moderner Traum* (1957), *Anamorphose* (1963), and *Die Irrfahrten des Odysseus* (1965).

OTHER five symphonies (1950–80), three violin concertos (1963, 1964, 1982), cello concerto (1981), concertino for classical orchestra (1984); string quartet (1948), clarinet quintet (1982).

Edgar opera by Puccini (libretto by F Fontana, based on Musset's *La Coupe et les lèvres*), produced Milan, La Scala, 21 April 1889. Edgar loves Fidelia, but runs away with moorish Tigrana when she is threatened by villagers. Regretting the loss of Fidelia, he decides to join soldiers in battle. Later reunited with Fidelia, who stabs Tigrana.

Edipo Re/King Oedipus opera in one act by Leoncavallo (libretto by G Forzano, after Sophocles), produced Chicago, 13 December 1920.

Eduardo e Cristina opera in two acts by Rossini (libretto by G Schmidt, written for Pavesi, altered by A L Tottola and G Bevilacqua-Aldovrandini), produced Venice, Teatro San Benedetto, 24 April 1819. Pastiche, assembled from *Ricciardo e Zoraide*, *Ermione* and *Adelaide di Borgogna*.

Education manquée operetta in one act by Chabrier (libretto by E Leterrier and A Vanloo), produced privately Paris, 1 May 1879. Paris, Théâtre des Arts, 9 January 1913. Count Gontran is educated in the facts of life.

Edwards, Richard (c. 1522–1566) English composer. A pupil of the musician, physician, and Greek scholar George Etheridge of Thame, he entered Corpus Christi College, Oxford, in 1540, and transferred to Christ Church on its foundation in 1546. He was appointed Master of the Children of the Chapel Royal in London in 1561, and wrote two plays for them. He was also a playwright,

producing *Palamon and Arcite* before Queen Elizabeth and also writing *Damon and Pithias*, and a poet, compiling and contributing to a book of verse, *The Paradise of Dainty Devices*.

Works include: music to his own *Damon and Pithias*; part songs *In Going to My Naked Bed* and *O the Silly Man*.

Edwards, Ross (1943–) Australian composer. He studied in Sydney and Adelaide, with Peter Sculthorpe and Maxwell Davies. He was lecturer at the New South Wales conservatory from 1976.

Works include: *Quen Quaeritis*, children's nativity play (1967); *Etude* for orchestra (1969); *Mountain Village in a Clearing Mist* for orchestra (1973); string quartet (1982); piano concerto (1982); *Christina's World*, theatre piece (1983); series *Maninya I–V* for chamber ensemble with voices (1981–86); *Reflections* for piano and three percussion (1985); *Flower Songs* for chorus and percussion (1986); *Maninyas* for violins and orchestra (1988); *Varregh* for solo percussion and orchestra (1989).

Egdon Heath work for orchestra by Holst, after the Dorset landscape described by Hardy in *The Return of the Native* (1878). Commissioned by the New York Symphony Orchestra and performed 12 February 1928 in New York.

Egisto, L'/Aegisthus opera by Cavalli (libretto by G Faustini), produced Venice, Teatro San Cassiano, autumn 1643. First modern revival Santa Fe 1974, in a free realization by Raymond Leppard. Egisto and Clemene resolve to find their original lovers after being separated by pirates. They become involved in love triangles which eventually resolve happily.

Egk, Werner (1901–1983) German composer. He wrote music for the opening of the Berlin Olympics in 1936.

He was mainly self-taught and began to compose to broadcasting commissions. He settled near Munich and succeeded Paul Graener as head of the faculty of composition in the Nazi Reichsmusikkammer. From 1936 to 1940 he conducted at the Berlin Staatsoper and from 1950 to 1953 was director of the Hochschule für Musik in Berlin.

Works include: the operas *Columbus* (1932; produced 1942), *Die Zaubergeige* (1935), *Peer Gynt* (1938), *Circe* (1945), *Irische Legende* (after Yeats, 1953), *Der Revisor* (after Gogol, 1957), *Die Verlobung in San Domingo* (1963); ballets *Joan de Zarissa* and *Abraxas* (1948); dance suite *Georgica* for orchestra; violin concerto

(*Geigenmusik*, 1936), *Französische Suite* (after Rameau, 1949), *Spiegelzeit* for orchestra (1979).

Egmont incidental music by Beethoven for Goethe's tragedy of that name, op. 84, written in 1809–10 for a revival at the Burgtheater in Vienna on 15 June 1810.

Egyptian Helen, The (R Strauss). See ◊*Ägyptische Helena*.

Eichendorff, Joseph von (1788–1857) German poet and novelist. His works were used in Robert ◊Franz (songs); Mark ◊Lothar (*Freier*); Hans ◊Pfitzner (*Von deutscher Seele*); Othmar ◊Schoeck (*Schloss Dürande, Wandersprüche* and songs); Robert ◊Schumann (*Liederkreis*); six songs by Johannes ◊Brahms; 16 by Schumann; 28 (including eight early) by Hugo ◊Wolf.

Eighteen-Twelve Overture (Tchaikovsky). See ◊*Year 1812.*

eilen (German 'to hurry') musical term; as opposed to *nicht eilen,* 'do not hurry'.

Eimert, Herbert (1897–1972) German composer and critic. In 1951 he founded an electronic studio at the Cologne branch of West German Radio. He wrote extensively on modern music.

He studied music and musicology at Cologne Conservatory and University 1927–1933. He worked for German radio and edited the *Kölnische Zeitung* 1936–45 and from 1955 edited *Die Reihe.*

Works include: *Glockenspiel* (1953); *Etüden über Tongemische; Requiem für Aikichi Kuboyama* (1962); choral and chamber music and electronic pieces.

Eine kleine Nachtmusik (Mozart). See ◊*Kleine Nachtmusik.*

Einem, Gottfried von (1918–1996) Austrian composer. His opera *Der Besuch der alten Dame* 1971 was based on a stage vehicle for the actress Ingrid Bergman.

He worked at the Wagner theatre at Bayreuth in 1938, and at the Staatsoper in Berlin; and studied further in London and Vienna. A plan to study with Hindemith was frustrated when the latter was suspended by the Nazis in 1934, and Einem and his mother were themselves arrested by the Gestapo. After his release he studied with Boris Blacher, with whom he wrote the libretto for his first opera and secured a post at the Dresden Staasoper. In 1948, after the success of *Dantons Tod,* he was invited to help to direct the festival at Salzburg, where he later lived.

Works include: the operas *Dantons Tod* (on Büchner's drama, 1947), *Der Prozess/The Trial*

(after Kafka, 1953), *Der Besuch der alten Dame* (after Dürrenmatt, 1971); *Kabale und Liebe* (after Schiller, 1976), *Jesu Hochzeit* (1980), *Prinz Chocolat* (1983), and *Tuliphant* (1990); ballet *Prinzessin Turandot* (after Gozzi); *Capriccio* and concerto for orchestra; 'Philadelphia' symphony (1960); piano concerto; *Bruckner Dialog* for orchestra (1971), *Wiener Symphonie* (1976), *Ludi Leopoldini* (1980); piano pieces; Hafiz songs; three string quartets (1975, 1977, 1980); wind quintet (1976).

Einleitung (German 'introduction') see ◊introduction.

Ein musikalischer Spass (Mozart). See ◊*Musikalischer Spass.*

Einstein, Alfred (1880–1952) German musicologist. He revised Riemann's *Musiklexicon* 1912, 1922, and 1929; and Köchel's Mozart catalogue 1937. He also wrote works on German viola da gamba music, on Gluck and Mozart, a short history of music, and in particular specialized in the study of the Italian madrigal, on which he wrote a monumental book 1949. He also published *Schubert* 1951.

A pupil of Adolf Sandberger, he took his doctor's degree in 1903. He became editor of the *Zeitschrift für Musikwissenschaft* in 1918, and was music critic of the *Berliner Tageblatt* from 1929. In 1933 he went into exile from Germany, settling first in London, then at Florence, and lastly in Northampton, Massechusetts, USA, where he was professor at Smith College.

Einstein on the Beach opera by Philip Glass (text by Robert Wilson), produced Avignon, 25 July 1976; New York Metropolitan Opera 21 November 1976 (at Lincoln Center but not with Metropolitan Opera Company). Text includes poems by a mentally-impaired man; references are made to Patty Hearst and pop idols David Cassidy and the Beatles. The audience is invited to come and go at will during the 4½ hours of performance.

Eisler, Hanns (1898–1962) German composer. He collaborated with the playwright Bertolt Brecht, but their work displeased the Nazis, and both men fled Nazi Germany for the USA. Eisler returned to East Berlin in 1950. The music he wrote for the new communist state consisted chiefly of songs and music for stage and films.

He studied with Schoenberg in Vienna and won a composition prize in 1924. He taught in Berlin 1925–33, but emigrated to the USA when a price was put on his head for his interest in music for the proletariat and in anti-Nazi activities. He was appointed professor at the New School of Social Research there, but left the USA in 1948, living first in Vienna and then returning to East Berlin.

Works include: the operas *Galileo* (1947) and *Johannes Faustus* (1953), didactic plays *Mother* (after Gorky's novel, 1931), *Hangmen Also Die, For Whom the Bell Tolls; The Roundheads and the Pointedheads* and others; *Die Massnahme* (1930), *Lenin-Requiem* (1937), *Solidaritätslied* (1930), *Kinderlieder* (1951) and *Schweyk in Zweiten Weltkrieg* (1957), all to texts by Brecht; music for numerous films; *German Symphony* for solo voices, chorus, and orchestra (1935–39), cantatas, choral ballads, proletarian songs, and other pieces; orchestral suites on Russian and Jewish folk songs; string quartet (1937), nonet (1939), two septets (1941, 1947), piano quintet (1944); chamber cantata *Palmström* for speech-song, flute, clarinet, violin, and cello; *Zeitungsausschnitte* for voice and piano; *Ernste Gesänge* for baritone and orchestra (1962).

Eitner, Robert (1832–1905) German musicologist and bibliographer. He was founder of the Gesellschaft für Musikforschung in 1868, editor of the *Monatshefte für Musikgeschichte*, compiler of the *Quellen-Lexicon* (a catalogue of the contents of music libraries) and other bibliographical works.

Elder, Mark Philip (1947–) English conductor. He was music director of the English National Opera (ENO) 1979–92 and of the Rochester Philharmonic Orchestra, USA, 1989.

Elder worked at Glyndebourne from 1970, conducted with the Australian Opera from 1972, and joined the ENO 1974. As principal conductor of the ENO, he specializes in 19th- and 20th-century repertoire.

electroacoustic music see ◊acousmatic music.

electrochord electrophonic piano invented by Vierling of Berlin 1929–33. It produces its notes by the conversion of electrical waves into audible sounds.

electronde electrophonic musical instrument that produces notes from the air. The notes it produces are graded according to the chromatic scale by means of a switch, and are not indeterminate in pitch like those of the aetherophone or ◊theremin. It was invented by Martin Taubman of Berlin in 1929.

electronic music music composed mainly of electronically generated and modified sounds. The term was first used in 1954 to describe music made up of synthesized sounds recorded on tape, to distinguish it from *musique concrète* (◊concrète music), but later included music for electronic sounds with traditional instruments or voices.

Karlheinz Stockhausen was a pioneer of electronic music, and his *Gesang der Jünglinge/ Song of the Youths* 1955–56, for boy's voice and electronic sounds, was one of the first important pieces in this style. Luciano Berio also composed music using a mixture of electronic and traditional instruments, such as *Differences* 1957 for chamber ensemble and tape. Other composers working in the early years of electronic music were Milton Babbitt, Bruno Maderna, and Edgard Varèse.

The development of portable electronic instruments in the late 1950s meant that electronic music could be played live and no longer had to be created in a studio and recorded on tape. Computer technology has also greatly improved the range and versatility of electronic instruments. Composers such as Pierre Boulez and Iannis Xenakis have written electronic pieces using the latest computer technology, and many other composers now incorporate electronic instruments in their work.

early electronic music The synthesis of musical sounds was first made possible early in the 20th century by the invention of the thermionic valve. The first experiments in this field gave rise to various musical instruments such as the ◊theremin, ◊ondes Martenot, and electronic organ, in which the sound is produced by means of oscillators, transformed by filters, and fed out of loudspeakers. The development of 'pure' electronic music only came about after the perfection of the tape recorder in 1950; before then electronic instruments tended to be used to augment traditional ensembles or as solo instruments mimicking or replacing acoustic ones, and no idiomatic style for these new instruments had been developed.

the Cologne studio In 1951 a studio was set up at Cologne Radio under the direction of Herbert Eimert. Its aim was to use only sounds synthesized by electronic oscillators as the raw material for electronic manipulation, as distinct from the *musique concrète* practised in Paris, which used only external sounds, both musical and unmusical, for its material. The methods of using these two sorts of material, however, were similar, making use of electronic filters, intensity control, reverberation, and tape manipulation. One of the most important composer pioneers in the field was Stockhausen, who was director of the Cologne studio from 1963.

His later compositions, such as *Mikrophoponie I* 1964 and *Mikrophoponie II* 1965, and work by other composers in the Cologne studio went further in the direction of using external sounds as well as electronic sound, thus merging *musique concrète* and pure electronic music. In the late 1950s composers began to use prerecorded electronic music in conjunction wih 'live' instruments in pieces such as Stockhausen's *Kontakte* for piano, percussion, and tape 1959–60.

equipment A typical electronic music studio of that time would contain a number of oscillators or sound sources, producing basic wave forms and noise, and a number of devices for treating these sound sources: filters, to alter the tone quality of a sound by eliminating or emphasizing certain harmonics in its harmonic series; envelope shapers, to control the attack, duration, and intensity curve of a sound; reverberation units, to provide resonance; and ring modulators, by which one sound modulates another to produce dramatic changes in quality. In addition, very slow wave forms were used to control the ◊pitch, intensity, duration, ◊timbre, and other parameters of the sounds generated by the oscillators, allowing a certain amount of preprogramming of the studio without the aid of computer techniques.

computers and electronic music After 1960, with the arrival of the purpose-built synthesizer developed by Robert Moog, Peter Zinovieff, and others, interest switched to computer-aided synthesis, culminating in the 4X system installed at the Institut de Recherche et de Co-ordination Acoustique/ Musique (◊IRCAM) in Paris. The application of computers to electronic music has introduced greater flexibility, allowing whole compositions to be programmed and stored in memory banks. This, along with the advent of digital recording techniques, has eliminated the need for laborious tape editing. The computer can be used to control and sequence the sounds and their characteristics, and also to synthesize any desired wave form. This has made it possible to produce complex electronic music live in the concert hall, without the necessity of recording it on tape first, and even to manipulate the sounds of the various instruments during the performance, as in Boulez's . . . *explosante fixe* . . . 1973– (work in progress).

electronics and popular music The electronic music of the 1960s, particularly the work of Stockhausen, had a profound influence on many jazz and rock musicians. Miles Davis in particular found inspiration for his jazz/rock fusion, and paved the way for future developments in the field. Groups such as Weather Report incorporated electronic instruments into their ensembles, and the expressive capabilities of the synthesizer were particularly suited to the style which had evolved from free jazz. In the world of rock and pop, electronic instruments were also becoming more prevalent from the early 1960s. At the more popular end of the spectrum, the Beach Boys used an ondes Martenot in their hit 'Good Vibrations', while more progressive bands such as Emerson, Lake and Palmer, and Pink Floyd explored the possibilities of the newly invented ◊Moog synthesizer. The use of electronically generated music continued throughout the 1970s and 1980s, especially in dance music, where in some cases it totally replaced conventional guitars and drums. For some rock musicians, notably Frank Zappa, the use of electronic instruments helped to bridge the gap between rock and 'serious' music; a trend that has continued through to the present in the work of composers such as Brian Eno.

electrophone any of a class of musical instruments that generate their tone by electronic means.

elegy (from Greek *elegeia*) in poetry, a piece of sorrowful and usually commemorative character; in music either a vocal setting of such a poem or an instrumental piece suggesting the mood awakened by it.

Elegy for Young Lovers opera by Henze (libretto by W H Auden and Chester Kallman), produced Schwetzingen, Schlosstheater, 20 May 1961; first British production Glyndebourne, 13 July 1961. Poet gains inspiration from mountainside death of lovers.

Elektra opera by R Strauss (libretto by H von Hofmannsthal, a much modernized reinterpretation of Sophocles), produced Dresden, Royal Opera, 25 January 1909. After Clytemnestra kills their father, Elektra and Orestes decide to take revenge.

Elgar, Edward (William) (1857–1934) English composer. Although his celebrated oratorio *The Dream of Gerontius* 1900 (based on the written work by theologian John Henry Newman) was initially unpopular in Britain, its good reception in Düsseldorf 1902 led to a surge of interest in his earlier works, including the *Pomp and Circumstance Marches* 1901. His *Enigma Variations* 1899 brought him lasting fame.

Among his later works, which tend to be more introspective than the earlier ones, are oratorios, two symphonies, a violin concerto, chamber music, songs, and the symphonic poem *Falstaff* 1913, culminating in the poignant cello concerto of 1919. After this piece, Elgar published no further music of significance. He concentrated on transcriptions and made some early gramophone recordings of his own work.

Elgar was the son of a music dealer who was also organist at St George's Roman Catholic Church, Worcester. He was self-taught as a composer, and at the age of 12 wrote music for a little domestic play, *The Wand of Youth*. He was sent to work in a solicitor's office at 15, though he preferred to help at his father's shop. From the age of 16 he was employed locally as a teacher, played bassoon in a wind quintet, and joined the Worcester Glee Club. In 1879 he became a leader of the Worcester Philharmonic and was conductor of the Glee Club and of the band at the county psychiatric hospital at Powick, for which he arranged much music. He also played organ at his father's church and became a member of W C Stockley's orchestra at Birmingham, which gave the first public performance of his *Sérénade mauresque*. In 1889 he married Caroline Alice Roberts and they lived in London until 1891.

In 1890 the Three Choirs Festival (held at Worcester that year) included for the first time a work of his, the *Froissart* overture. This is the first work in which Elgar reveals his characteristic confidence of manner and mastery of orchestration. Choral works, including *Scenes from the Saga of King Olaf* 1896 and *Caractacus* 1898, were heard at festivals, and the *Enigma Variations* for orchestra were conducted by Hans Richter 1899. *The Dream of Gerontius* was produced at Birmingham Festival in 1900 and at the Lower Rhine Festival, Düsseldorf, Germany, in 1901 and 1902. An Elgar Festival at Covent Garden Theatre, London, in 1904 brought him greater recognition, and he was knighted that year. He was professor of Music at Birmingham University 1905–06.

His first symphony was performed by Richter in Manchester and London in 1908, and its immense success led to 100 further performances throughout Europe. Fritz Kreisler premiered the Violin Concerto in 1910. During World War I he wrote much topical music and afterwards the valedictory cello concerto and three chamber works. After the death of his wife in 1920 he wrote only some small pieces and incidental music. He was

Master of the King's Music from 1924. At his death he left unfinished a third symphony and an opera, *The Spanish Lady*, based on Ben Jonson's play *The Devil is an Ass*.

Elgar's songs, chamber music, and smaller works are often poetic, but add nothing to a reputation founded on *Gerontius*, the symphonies, and the symphonic study *Falstaff* 1913, which reveal a highly individual mastery of orchestration.

Works include: ORCHESTRAL two symphonies (1908, 1911); concert overtures *Cockaigne* (1901), *In the South* (1904); many miscellaneous orchestral works, including *Enigma* variations (1899), *Introduction and Allegro* for strings (1905), symphonic study *Falstaff* (1902–13); violin concerto (1910), cello concerto (1919).

VOCAL cantatas *Caractacus* (1898), *The Music Makers* (1902–12); oratorios *The Dream of Gerontius* (1900), *The Apostles*, *The Kingdom*.

CHAMBER string quartet, E minor, piano quintet, A minor (1919), violin and piano sonata, E minor (1918); songs for solo voice, including cycle *Sea Pictures* with piano or orchestra (1897–99); *Severn Suite* for brass band.

Elijah/Elias oratorio by Mendelssohn (words from the Old Testament), produced first in the English version at the Birmingham Festival, 26 August 1846; first German performance Hamburg, 7 October 1847.

Elisa opera by Fux (libretto, in Italian, by P Pariati), produced at court at Laxenburg Palace near Vienna, 25 August 1719.

Elisabetta regina d'Inghilterra/Elizabeth, Queen of England opera by Rossini (libretto by G Schmidt), produced Naples, Teatro San Carlo, 4 October 1815. The overture was taken from *Aureliano in Palmira* and afterwards used for *Il barbiere di Siviglia*. Elizabeth I imprisons Leicester when he marries Mathilde, daughter of Mary, Queen of Scots. She later releases him and survives an assassination attempt by the treacherous Norfolk.

Elisir d'amore, L'/The Love Potion opera by Donizetti (libretto by F Romani, based on Scribe's *Le Philtre*, composed by Auber), produced Milan, Teatro della Canobbiana, 12 May 1832. Simple Nemorino hopes to win landowner Adina with a love potion from the fraud Dulcamara. At first she spurns him, ready to marry Belcore, but then falls genuinely in love with him, without the help of the bogus potion.

Eliza, ou Le voyage aux glaciers du Mont St Bernard opera by Cherubini (libretto by J A de R Saint-Cyr), produced Paris, Théâtre Feydeau, 13 December 1794.

Ellis, David (1933–) English composer. He studied at the Royal Manchester College of Music and worked as an administrator with the British Broadcasting Corporation (BBC) from 1964. He was Head of Music for BBC North 1978–86, and artistic director of the Northern Chamber Orchestra from 1986.

Works include: the opera *Crito* (1963); *Sinfonietta* (1953), violin concerto, piano concerto (1962), *Fanfares and Cadenzas* for orchestra (1968), *February Music* for cello and chamber orchestra (1977), *Circles* (1979); *Suite franglaise* for strings (1987); choral music includes *Sequentia I–V* for soloists, chorus, and orchestra (1962–75); string trio (1954), wind quintet (1956); piano sonata (1956); string quartet (1980).

Eloy, Jean-Claude (1938–) French composer. He studied with Milhaud and Boulez; other influences include Varèse, Webern, and oriental music. He worked at electronic music studio, Cologne, with Stockhausen.

Works include: *Etude III* for orchestra (1962); *Equivalences* for wind and percussion (1963); *Polychronies* for chamber ensemble (1964); *Kamakala* for chorus and three orchestral groups (1971); *Kshara-Akshara* for soprano, chorus and three orchestral groups (1974); *Shanti* for six solo voices and electronics (1972–74); *Fluctuante-Immuable* for orchestra (1977); *Yo-In* (Reverberations) for four tapes and percussion (1980).

El Salón México symphonic sketch by Copland, named after a Mexico City nightclub and including local colour and tunes. First performed Mexico City, 27 August 1937, conducted by Carlos Chávez.

Elsner, Ksawery Józef (1769–1854) Polish composer of Swedish descent. Being intended for medicine, he had little music teaching in his youth, but learnt the violin and some harmony at Breslau and studied more assiduously on going to Vienna. In 1791 he became violinist at the Brno Theatre and the next year conductor at Lwów. He went to Warsaw as theatre conductor in 1799, establishing a music society there in 1815 and became the first director of the Conservatory opened in 1821. He was the formative teacher of F Chopin.

Works include: 27 operas (22 in Polish, *Król Łokietek* (1818), ballets and melodramas; *Stabat Mater*, church music; 11 symphonies; 6 string quartets; instrumental pieces.

Elwell, Herbert (1898–1974) US composer. He studied with Bloch in New York and with Nadia Boulanger in Paris. He was head of composition at the Cleveland Institute 1928–45, and teacher at Oberlin Conservatory from 1946.

Works include: ballet *The Happy Hypocrite* (1925); *I Was With Him*, cantata (1937); *Introduction and Allegro* for orchestra (1942); *Blue Symphony* for voice and string quartet (1944); *Lincoln: Requiem Aeternam* (1946); two string quartets; piano sonata.

embellishment an alternative name for ◊ornamentation.

embouchure the position of the lips and tension of the facial muscles required to produce a good tone on a brass or woodwind instrument.

Emerald Isle, The unfinished operetta by Sullivan, completed by German (libretto by B Hood), produced London, Savoy Theatre, 27 April 1901.

Emma di Resburgo/Emma of Roxburgh opera by Meyerbeer (libretto by G Rossi), produced Venice, Teatro San Benedetto, 26 June 1819. It was Meyerbeer's first major success, but Weber opined that he had imitated Rossini.

Emmanuel, (Marie François) Maurice (1862–1938) French musicologist and composer. He wrote several learned books on the musical idiom, Greek music, modal accompaniment, Burgundian folk song, and other subjects.

He studied at the Paris Conservatory and was a pupil of François Gevaert at Brussels. After various appointments as a historian and musician he became professor of music history at the Conservatory in succession to Louis Bourgault-Ducoudray in 1907 and retained the post until 1936.

Works include: the operas *Prométhée enchaîné* (1916–18) and *Salamino* (1921–28, both after Aeschylus); operetta *Pierrot peintre* (1886); incidental music for Plautus' *Amphitryon*; two symphonies, *Suite française*, *Ouverture pour un conte gai*, *Zingaresca* for orchestra; three *Odelettes anacréontiques* for voice, flute, and piano (1911); violin and piano and cello and piano sonatas; *Sonate bourguignonne* and six sonatinas for piano; *In memoriam matris* and *Musiques* for voice and piano.

'Emperor' Concerto nickname for Beethoven's E♭ major piano concerto, op. 73.

Emperor Jones opera by Gruenberg (libretto by K de Jaffa, based on Eugene O'Neill's play), produced New York, Met, 7 January

1933. Escaped convict Brutus Jones rules Caribbean island, exploiting the locals until they rebel against him and he commits suicide.

'Emperor' Quartet see ◊*Emperor's Hymn.*

Emperor's Hymn, The *Gott erhalte Franz den Kaiser* (words by L L Haschka), composed by Haydn and first sung to celebrate the Emperor's birthday, 12 February 1797. Also used by Haydn as a theme for variations in the string quartet op. 76 no. 3 (known as the 'Emperor' Quartet). Later adopted as the Austrian national anthem. It is well-known in England as a hymn-tune.

Empfindsamer Stil (German 'sensitive style') term applied to music by some German 18th-century composers, especially C P E Bach and Quantz, who sought to make their music directly expressive of feeling. See ◊*Affektenlehre.*

Encina, Juan del (1468–1529) Spanish poet, playwright, and composer. He cultivated especially the ◊villancico, a form resembling the French ◊virelai. Over 60 of his songs are contained in a manuscript at Madrid, the *Cancionero Musical de Palacio.*

Encina studied at Salamanca University and entered the service of the Duke of Alba at Toledo. His poems were published at Salamanca in 1496. In 1498 he went to Rome, where he held a post at the court of the Spanish pope. While there he produced the *Farsa de Placida e Vittoriano* and composed many songs for his own plays. He was archdeacon of Málaga Cathedral 1508–19, and of León Cathedral from 1519 until his death.

encore (French 'again') in music, an unprogrammed extra item, usually short and well known, played at the end of a concert to please an enthusiastic audience.

Ende einer Welt, Das/The End of a World radio opera in two acts by Henze (libretto by W Hildesheimer), performed Hamburg, 4 December 1953; revised for the stage 1964 and produced Frankfurt, 30 November 1965.

end pin alternative term for the ◊tail pin of a cello or double bass.

Enée et Lavinie/Aeneas and Lavinia opera by Colasse (libretto by B de Fontenelle, after Virgil), produced Paris, Opéra, 16 December 1690.

Opera by Dauvergne (libretto ditto), produced Paris, Opéra, 14 February 1758.

Enescu, George (1881–1955) Romanian violinist and composer. In 1899 he began his career as a virtuoso violinist and teacher of the instrument; Yehudi Menuhin and Arthur Grumiaux were among his pupils.

He studied at the Vienna Conservatory 1888–93, and then went to Paris to finish his violin studies with Marsick and to study composition with Jules Massenet, André Gedalge, and Gabriel Fauré.

Works include: the opera *Oe(lig)dipe* (after Sophocles, 1921–31; produced 1936); five symphonies (1905, 1912–14, 1916–21, with chorus and piano solo, and tenor and chorus); *Poème roumain/Romanian Rhapsodies,* suites and intermezzi, and other pieces for orchestra; string octet (1900), wind dectet (1906), two piano quintets (1894, 1940), two piano quartets (1909, 1943), two string quartets (1920, 1953), two piano trios (1897, 1916); three violin and piano sonatas (1897, 1899, 1926), two cello sonatas (1898, 1935); suites and other works for piano; songs.

Enfance du Christ, L'/The Childhood of Christ oratorio by Berlioz, op. 25, for solo voices, chorus, and orchestra, composed 1850–54, first performed Paris, 10 December 1854.

Enfant et les sortilèges, L'/The Child and the Spells opera in one act by Ravel (libretto by Colette), produced Monte Carlo, 21 March 1925. Spoiled child faces all the animals he has tortured; he redeems himself by tending a wounded squirrel.

Enfant prodigue, L'/The Prodigal Son lyric scene by Debussy (libretto by E Guinand), written for the Prix de Rome and published 1884; produced as an opera, London, Covent Garden, 28 February 1910 with Perceval Allen, conducted by Pitt. see ◊Prodigal Son.

Engel, Carl (1883–1944) US musicologist. He studied at Strasbourg and Munich and settled in the USA 1905. He was appointed chief of the music division of the Library of Congress, Washington, DC, 1922, and succeeded Sonneck as editor of the *Musical Quarterly* 1929. One of the organizers and 1937–38 president of the American Musicological Society. He published many articles and books on music, including essay collections *Alle Breve: from Bach to Debussy* (1921) and *Discords Mingled* (1931).

English Cat, The opera ('a story for singers and instrumentalists') in two acts by Henze (libretto by Edward Bond after Balzac's *Peines de coeur d'une chatte anglaise*), produced Schwetzingen, 2 June 1983. All cats: Minette must marry Lord Puff. She is seen with Tom, and is taken to divorce court for adultery.

Minette is drowned, Tom is stabbed and 'the lawyers will make a huge profit'.

English horn alternative name for the ◊cor anglais, a musical instrument of the oboe family.

English Suites six keyboard suites by Bach, composed by 1724–25.

Englund, (Sven) Einar (1916–) Finnish composer. His music is influenced by Sibelius and Shostakovich. He has taught at the Sibelius Academy.

He studied with Selim Palmgren in Helsinki and with Copland at Tanglewood.

Works include: seven symphonies (1946–88), cello concerto (1954), two piano concertos (1955, 1974), concerto for 12 cellos (1981), violin concerto (1981), serenade for strings (1983), piano trio (1982), flute concerto (1985), string quartet (1985), suite for cello, *The Last Island* (1986).

enharmonic (of a musical harmony) capable of alternative interpretations, used as a link between passages of normally unrelated key. For example, an enharmonic modulation from C♯ to F major plays on the equivalence, in keyboard terms, of the notes E♯ and F.

enigma canon a canon written down in a single part with no indication where the subsequent entries of the other parts are to occur, the performers being left to guess how the music fits by solving a riddle.

enigmatic scale Italian 'scala enigmatica'. Verdi's term for the curious scale on which he constructed his *Ave Maria* for four voices, composed c. 1889.

'Enigma' Variations a set of orchestral variations by Elgar, op. 36, entitled *Variations on an Original Theme*, composed 1898, first performed London, 19 June 1899, conductor Richter. Each variation is a musical portrait of some person indicated only by initials or by a nickname, all of whom have, however, been identified. The word 'Enigma' appears over the theme. See Cipriani ◊Potter.

Enoch Arden melodrama for reciter and piano by Strauss, op. 38 (a setting of Tennyson's poem in German translation by A Strodtmann), first performed Munich, 24 March 1897 (performed in Vienna, 13 January 1899, with Zemlinsky at the piano).

En Saga (Sibelius). See ◊*Saga, En*.

ensalada (Spanish 'salad') a kind of burlesque madrigal cultivated in Spain in the 16th century, in dramatic form, like Vecchi's *Amfiparnaso*, not intended for stage performance. Also a ◊quodlibet.

ensemble (French 'together') any group of musicians, usually a group of instrumentalists playing chamber music, and especially a group larger than a quartet. Normally, each member of an ensemble plays a different part; but in an orchestra there may be several players playing the same music. In opera, the word often refers to a section where several solo singers perform together.

Entflieht auf leichten Kähnen double canon for chorus *a cappella* by Webern, op. 2; composed 1908, first performed Fürstenfeld, 10 April 1927.

Entführung aus dem Serail, Die/The Elopement from the Harem opera by Mozart (libretto by C F Bretzner [*Belmont und Constanze*] altered by G Stephanie, junior), produced Vienna, Burgtheater, 16 July 1782. Constanze resists the amorous Pasha Selim, who keeps her locked up. Belmonte (her true lover) and Pedrillo attempt to rescue her but are caught. The Europeans expect execution but are shown mercy by the Pasha.

entr'acte (French 'between acts') orchestral music played between the acts of an opera or play.

entrée (French 'entrance, entry') in the 17th and 18th centuries, a piece of music in a stately rhythm accompanying the entry of processions in ballets and other stage pieces; also, more generally, an introduction or prelude to any work, but more especially a ballet or opera where it accompanies the rise of the curtain; an entrée could also be the beginning of each new scene in a ballet.

entries the appearances of the subject in the different parts of a fugue.

entry a 17th- and 18th-century English term for ◊prelude.

Éolides, Les symphonic poem for orchestra by Franck, on a poem of the same name by Leconte de Lisle; composed 1876, first performed Paris, 13 May 1877.

Eötvös, Péter (1944–) Hungarian conductor and composer. He was music director of the Ensemble Intercontemporain, Paris,

The enigmatic scale on C.

1979–91. As principal guest conductor for the British Broadcasting Corporation (BBC) Symphony Orchestra from 1985, he conducted the first performance of Birtwistle's *Earth Dances* in 1986.

He studied at Budapest and Cologne. In 1981 he gave the first performance of Stockhausen's *Donnerstag aus Licht*, at La Scala, Milan, and premiered Reich's *Desert Music* 1984.

Works include: *Hochzeitmadrigal* for six soloists (1963/1976), and *Chinese Opera* for chamber orchestra (1984).

Ephesian Matron, The comic serenata by Dibdin (libretto by I Bickerstaffe), produced London, Ranelagh House, 12 May 1769.

Epic of Gilgamesh, The oratorio by Martinů for soloists, speaker, chorus, and orchestra; composed 1954–55, first performed Basel, 24 January 1958, conductor Sacher. The work's three sections are titled *Gilgamesh*, *The death of Enkidu* and *Invocation*.

episode a passage or section of a ◊fugue linking appearances of the subject (principal melody), usually non-thematic in nature and often forming sequences in order to modulate (move from one key to another) before the subject establishes a new key; or in a ◊rondo, one of a variety of sections appearing between and contrasting with the recurring principal theme.

equale (Italian, plural equali, 'equals') term used for instrumental pieces, especially trombones (Beethoven's equale), written for a group of similar instruments.

equal temperament a type of ◊temperament (tuning of a scale) in which every semitone within an octave is exactly equal.

Equivoci, Gli/The Doubles opera by Storace (libretto by L da Ponte, based on Shakespeare's *Comedy of Errors*, produced Vienna, Burgtheater, 27 December 1786). Identical couples cause comic confusion.

Equivoci nel sembiante, Gli/Dissimilarity in Similarity opera by Alessandro Scarlatti (libretto by D F Contini), produced Rome, Teatro Capranica, 5 February 1679. Scarlatti's first opera. Nymph Lisetta and sister Clori in love with shepherd Eurillo, and with Armindo, disguised as Eurillo.

Erard, Pierre (1796–1855) French piano and harp maker. He joined his uncle Sébastien ◊Erard in business.

Erard, Sébastien (1752–1831) French piano and harp maker. He introduced mechanical

improvements that enhanced key and pedal action.

His firm was established about 1777 and produced its first grand piano in 1796. He opened a shop in London in 1792. He was the uncle of Pierre Erard.

Erb, Donald (1929–) US composer. His works are influenced by jazz and neoclassical techniques, and also employ electronics. His early career was as a trumpeter in dance bands.

He studied at the Cleveland Institute and with Boulanger in Paris. He has taught in Cleveland, Bloomington, and at the Southern Methodist University in Dallas.

Works include: *Symphony of Overtures* (1964), *The Seventh Trumpet*, for orchestra (1969), cello concerto (1975), trumpet concerto (1980); *The Last Quintet* for woodwind (1982), *Fantasy for Cellist and Friends* (1983); clarinet concerto (1984); concerto for orchestra (1985); concerto for brass and orchestra (1986); *Cummings Cycle* for mixed chorus and orchestra (1963), *New England's Prospect* for choruses and orchestra (1974); electronic music included *The Purple-roofed Ethical Suicide Parlor* (1972) and *Autumnmusic* (1973).

Ercole amante/Hercules as Lover opera by Cavalli (libretto by F Buti), produced Paris, Tuileries, 7 February 1662. The only opera specially written for Paris by Cavalli. The ballet music was by Lully. The title alludes to the marriage of Louis XIV. Hercules wants Iole, but she hates him for having killed her father, who consented to her marriage with Hercules' son, Hyllus. Hercules imprisons his son and is about to marry Iole when she saves herself by giving him a deadly shirt to wear.

Erickson, Robert (1917–) US composer. He studied at the Chicago Conservatory and with Krenek at Hamline. He was professor at the University of California, San Diego, from 1967. His music has progressed from serialism, through electronic means, to *musique concrète*.

Works include: chamber concerto (1960), concerto for piano and seven instruments (1963), concerto for siren and other flyers, for orchestra (1965), cardenitas, for singer, seven musicians and tape (1968), *Pacific Sirens* for instruments and tape (1969), *East of the Beach* for small orchestra (1980), *Auroras* for orchestra (1982), *Sierra* for voice and chamber orchestra (1984), *Solstice* for string quartet (1985).

Erismena opera by Cavalli (libretto by A Aureli), performed Venice, Teatro San Apollinare, 1656. Modern editions by L Salter

(BBC, 1967) and A Curtis (1974). Erismena dresses as an Armenian soldier to pursue seducer Idraspe.

Eritrea opera by Cavalli (libretto by G Faustini), performed Venice, Teatro San Apollinare, 1652. An edition by Jane Glover was conducted by her at the Wexford Festival in 1975. Disguised as her dead brother, captured Eritrea falls for Egyptian prince.

Erkel, Ferenc (1810–1892) Hungarian composer. In creating the Hungarian opera, he was responsible for its distinctive national style. His own most important operas are *Hunyadi László* 1844 and *Bánk Bán* 1861, both based on Hungarian historical events. Erkel was important in all fields of Hungarian music and composed Hungary's national anthem in 1844.

Erkel was born at Bekesgyula and studied at Pozsony (now Bratislava). As a pianist and conductor, he organized musical life at Kolozsvar in his early days. In 1825 he became music director of the Hungarian theatre in Buda, in 1836 assistant conductor of the German theatre in Pest, and in 1838 conductor of the National Theatre. He founded the Budapest Philharmonic Society in 1853 and was director of the Academy of Music 1875–89.

Works include: the operas *Bátori Mária* (1840), *Hunyadi László* (1844), *Bánk Bán* (1861), *Dózsa György*, *Brankovics György* (1874), *Névtelen Hősök*, *István Király/King Stephen*); piano music; songs, and other pieces.

***Erlkönig, Erl* (real name Alder) King,** a ballad by Goethe, set by Schubert in 1815 at the age of 18, first sung in public by Johann Michael Vogl, Vienna, 7 March 1821, published as op. 1 that year.

Ernani opera by Verdi (libretto by F M Piave, based on Victor Hugo's drama *Hernani*), produced Venice, Teatro La Fenice, 9 March 1844. The first of Verdi's operas produced outside Milan. Outlawed Ernani and Don Carlos, King of Spain, both in love with Elvira. Don Carlos becomes Holy Roman Emperor, Ernani marries Elvira, Silva (guardian and former fiancé of Elvira) gets revenge.

Ernelinde, Princesse de Norvège opera by Philidor (libretto by A H H Poinsinet), produced Paris, Opéra, 24 November 1767.

Ernste Gesänge (Brahms). See ◊*Vier ernste Gesänge*.

Eroe cinese, L'/The Chinese Hero opera by Bonno (libretto by Metastasio), produced Vienna, Schönbrunn Palace, at court, 13 May 1752.

Ero e Leandro/Hero and Leander opera by Bottesini (libretto by Boito, at first intended for himself), produced Turin, Teatro Regio, 11 January 1879.

Opera by Mancinelli (libretto ditto), first produced as a cantata, in England, Norwich Festival, 8 October 1896; first stage production Madrid, Teatro Real, 30 November 1897.

'Eroica' Symphony Beethoven's symphony No. 3 in E♭ major, op. 55, composed 1803–04. It was to have been entitled *Bonaparte*, but on hearing that Napoleon had declared himself Emperor, Beethoven renamed it *Sinfonia Eroica, composta per festeggiare il souvenire di un grand'uomo/Heroic symphony, composed to celebrate the memory of a great man.*

'Eroica' Variations Beethoven's piano variations and fugue, op. 35 (composed 1802), so called because they used the same theme as the finale of the 'Eroica' symphony. The theme, however, was taken from one' of Beethoven's dances, and the variations were written before the symphony.

Erreur d'un moment, L', ou La Suite de Julie/The Error of a Moment, or The Sequel to Julie opera by Dezède (libretto by J M B de Monvel), produced Paris, Comédie-Italienne, 14 June 1773.

Erwartung monodrama for soprano and orchestra by Schoenberg (libretto by Marie Pappenheim), composed 1909 but first produced Prague, 6 June 1924, conductor Zemlinsky, with Marie Gutheil-Schoder. Solitary woman searches through a wood for her lover; she finds his murdered body, which prompts an array of stark emotions.

Esclarmonde opera by Massenet (libretto by E Blau and L de Gramont), produced Paris, Opéra-Comique, 15 May 1889. Esclarmonde, daughter of the King of Byzantium, uses magic powers to seduce the knight Roland. She is later exorcised and forced to renounce him, but Roland wins her back at a tournament, becoming king.

Escobar, Pedro (c. 1465–after 1535) Portuguese composer. He spent much of his life in Spain, where he was maestro de capilla at Seville early in the 16th century. He composed church music and secular pieces for three and four voices.

Esmeralda opera by Fabio Campana (1815–82) (libretto by G T Cimino, based on Victor Hugo's novel, *Notre-Dame de Paris*), produced St Petersburg, 30 December 1869.

Opera by Dargomizhsky (libretto by composer translated from Victor Hugo's libretto based on his *Notre-Dame de Paris*, and written for Louise Angélique Bertin [1805–77] for her opera produced Paris, 1836), produced Moscow, 17 December 1847.

España rhapsody for orchestra by Chabrier of Spanish tunes collected by the composer during a visit to Spain in 1882–83; composed 1883, first performed Paris, 4 November 1883. Waldteufel later made a ballroom waltz of it.

espressione (Italian 'expression') term used in musical notation.

espressivo, or espr., (Italian 'expressive') term used in musical notation.

Esquivel Barahona, Juan de (c. 1565–after 1613) Spanish composer. He was maestro de capilla at Salamanca Cathedral in 1608 and at Ciudad-Rodrigo 1611–13. His Masses and motets were published in two volumes in 1608, and a volume of miscellaneous sacred works in 1613. An *Officium pro defunctis/Mass for the dead* survives in manuscript form.

essential discord a chord which is dissonant according to acoustic theory, but whose notes belong to the key in which a composition or passage is written and has become sufficiently current to be introduced without preparation.

Estampes/Engravings a set of three piano pieces by Debussy, composed 1903; 1. *Pagodes*, 2. *Soirée dans Grenade*, 3. *Jardins sous la pluie*.

estampida (Provençal; French *estampie*) an instrumental dance form of the 13th and 14th centuries, related to the troubadour/trouvère repertory. Its form consisted of several *puncta* (sections), each played twice, with first- and second-time endings, called *ouvert* and *clos*. Frequently the *ouvert* and *clos* endings, which often comprised the greater part of each *punctum*, were the same throughout the piece, resulting in a great deal of repetition.

Esther oratorio by Handel. First performed as a masque entitled *Haman and Mordecai* (libretto probably by Pope and Arbuthnot, after Racine), Canons, near Edgware, c. 1720. Subsequently recast, with additional words by Samuel Humphreys, and performed as an oratorio in London, at first privately to celebrate Handel's birthday and then at King's Theatre, Haymarket, 2 May 1732.

Oratorio by Dittersdorf (libretto by S I Pintus), performed Vienna, 21 December 1773. During the interval of a revival of the work, 16 December 1785, Mozart's piano

concerto no. 22, K482 received its first performance.

estinto (Italian 'extinct, dead') musical direction indicating that a passage is to be performed in a toneless manner.

estompé (French 'stumped, shaded off') in musical direction, damped, muffled; frequently used by Debussy where he asks for a veiled or dull tone.

Es war einmal/Once upon a time opera by Zemlinsky (libretto by Drachmann), produced Vienna, Hofoper, 22 January 1900. The opera was conducted by Mahler, who assisted Zemlinsky in revising the work. Princess married to a gypsy fits the wedding dress offered by a mystery prince, her husband in disguise.

Eternal Gospel, The/Věčné evangelium legend by Janáček for soprano, tenor, chorus, and orchestra (text by J Vrchlický), composed 1914, revised 1924. First performed Prague, 5 February 1917.

Et expecto resurrectionem mortuorum work in five sections by O Messiaen for 18 woodwind, 16 brass, and three percussion, composed 1964 to commemorate the dead of two World Wars. First performed Paris, Sainte-Chapelle, 7 May 1965, conductor Baudo.

ethnomusicology expanding earlier definitions of the field as the study of non-Western musics, 'ethnic music' or 'world music', ethnomusicology is the anthropological study of music as a culture-specific phenomenon and a universal aspect of human social behaviour. It developed out of late 19th-century studies of 'exotic' Asian scales in Europe and studies of Native American music in the USA. Since the 1950s there has been a gradual process of incorporation of the insights offered by **comparative musicology**, with its emphasis on collection, documentation, systematization, classification, transcription, and analysis with the **anthropology of music**, with its emphasis on extended periods of field work, participant observation, the learning of vocal and instrumental performance skills by researchers, and the search for the social functions of music.

Ethnomusicologists attempt to describe music cultures as whole systems or 'music cultures' but the general trend has been towards studies focused on specific theoretical problems, such as the role of music in healing, the cultural role and symbolism of musical instruments, and the relationship of musical aesthetics, values, and social power.

Ethnomusicologists find themselves increasingly concerned with the ethics of fieldwork and the politics of representation, the music of migrant populations, the relationship between music, ethnicity, and identity in the construction of place, and a study of popular musics worldwide.

See: ◊comparative musicology, ◊organology, ◊cantometrics.

Etler, Alvin (1913–1973) US composer. His music is influenced by serialism and shows concern for textural elements.

He studied at the Cleveland Institute and with Hindemith at Yale University, and he taught at Smith College 1949–73.

Works include: two sinfoniettas (1940, 1941), concerto for orchestra (1957), concerto for wind quintet and orchestra (1962), concerto for string quartet and orchestra (1968), concerto for cello and chamber group (1971); concerto for violin and wind quintet (1958); two string quartets (1963, 1965).

Etoile du Nord, L'/The North Star opera by Meyerbeer (libretto by Scribe), produced Paris, Opéra-Comique, 16 February 1854. Disguised Katherine joins Russian army and warns Tsar Peter of conspiracy.

Etoile, L' opéra bouffe by Chabrier (libretto by E Leterrier and A Vanloo), produced Paris, Théâtre Bouffes-Parisiens, 28 November 1877. On the advice of an astrologer, a superstitious king cancels the execution of Lazuli, a pedlar who has insulted him.

etouffé (French 'stifled, smothered') musical direction to deaden the tone on instruments where it is liable to vibrate after being sounded, as on the harp or the kettledrums.

Etranger, L'/The Stranger opera by d'Indy (libretto by composer), produced Brussels, Théâtre de la Monnaie, 7 January 1903.

Ettinger, Max (1874–1951) German composer. He studied in Berlin and Munich and lived at both places until 1933, when he went into exile in Italian Switzerland.

Works include: the operas Clavigo (after Goethe, 1926), *Judith* (after Hebbel), *Frühlingserwachen* (after Frank Wedekind, 1928), *Juana* (after Georg Kaiser), *Dorlores* (1931); oratorios *Königin Esther; Moses, Weisheit des Orients* (from Omar Khayyám) for solo voices, chorus and orchestra; string quartet (1945).

étude (French 'study') musical exercise designed to develop technique.

Etudes symphoniques a set of 12 concert studies for piano by Schumann, op. 13, at first entitled *Etudes en forme de variations*, composed 1834. They are variations on a theme by the father of Ernestine von Fricken, with whom Schumann was in love at that time, but they are dedicated to Sterndale Bennett, in whose honour Schumann introduced into the finale a theme from Marchschner's *Ivanhoe* opera *Der Templer und die Jüdin*: a song in praise of England. Five further variations are sometimes now given.

etwas (German 'somewhat, rather') in music, term used in conjunction with an adjective denoting speed or character, such as *etwas langsam*.

Eugene Onegin opera by Tchaikovsky (libretto by composer and K S Shilovsky, based on Pushkin's poem-novel), produced by students of the Conservatory, Moscow, 29 March 1879. First professional performance Moscow, Bolshoi, 23 January 1881. Onegin rejects Tatiana's proposal by letter, but realizes too late by Act III that he loves her after all; she is now married to Prince Gremin.

eunuch flute early woodwind instrument with a mouthpiece containing a membrane that vibrates when the player sings into it. It dates back to the 16th century at least, but was never much more than a toy.

eunuch singers see ◊castrato.

euphonium musical instrument, a tenor four-valved brass band instrument of the bugle type, often mistaken for a tuba, and called a **baryton** in Germany. It is used chiefly in brass and military bands.

euphony suavity and harmoniousness of sound, the opposite of cacophony.

The compass of the euphonium.

eurhythmics practice of coordinated bodily movement as an aid to musical development. It was founded about 1900 by the Swiss musician Emile ◊Jaques-Dalcroze, professor of harmony at the Geneva conservatoire. He devised a series of 'gesture' songs, to be sung simultaneously with certain bodily actions.

Euridice, L' opera by Caccini (libretto by Ottavio Rinuccini), produced Florence, Palazzo Pitti, 5 December 1602. Orfeo's bride, Euridice, dies from a snake bite, but is allowed to return from Hades after divine intervention.

Opera by Peri (libretto ditto), produced Florence, Palazzo Pitti, 6 October 1600.

Euripides (fl. c. 484–406 BC) Greek dramatist. His tragedies, based on mythology and early history, inspired the following musical settings: ◊*Alkestis* (Boughton and Wellesz); ◊*Bakchantinnen, Die* (Wellesz); ◊*Bassarids, The* (Henze); Daniel ◊Börtz (*Backanterna*); Buller (*Bakxai*); Louise ◊Coerne (*Trojan Women*); W ◊Damrosch (*Electra, Iphigenia in Aulis, Medea*); John ◊Foulds (*Trojan Women*); Giorgio ◊Ghedini (*Baccanti, Ifigenia in Tauride*); C ◊Gray (*Trojan Women*); ◊*Ifigenia in Aulide* (Caldara, Cherubini, Graun, Zingarelli); ◊*Ifigenia in Tauride* (Galuppi, Maio and Traetta); ◊*Iphigénie en Aulide* (Gluck); ◊*Iphigénie en Tauride* (Campra, Gluck and Piccinni); ◊Schürmann (*Getreue Alceste*); Vladimir ◊Senilov (*Hippolytus*); Nicolas ◊Slonimsky (*Orestes*); V ◊Thomson (*Medea*); Ernst ◊Toch (*Bacchantes*); ◊*Troades* (Reimann); Charles ◊Wood (*Ion and Iphigenia in Tauris*).

Europe Galante, L' opera-ballet by Campra (libretto by A H de la Motte), produced Paris, Opéra, 24 October 1697. The work's four entrées are entitled *La France, L'Espagne, L'Italie, La Turquie,* and depict the amorous inclinations of each country.

Euryanthe opera by Weber (libretto by H von Chézy), produced Vienna, Kärntnertortheater, 25 October 1823. Lysiart in league with evil Eglantine to prove Euryanthe, Adolar's bride, unfaithful. They trick her and Lysiart succeeds in winning a bet, thereby ruining Adolar. Later the innocent Euryanthe is vindicated.

evensong an evening service of the Anglican Communicon in which most of the liturgy is sung in ◊Anglican chant. It also contains hymns, psalms, and the canticles ◊Magnificat and ◊Nunc Dimittis.

Éventail de Jeanne, L'/Joan's Fan ballet by Auric, Delannoy, Ferroud, Ibert, Milhaud, Poulenc, Ravel, Roland-Manuel, Roussel, and Schmitt (choreography by Alice Bourgat), produced Paris, in private, 16 June 1927; Opéra, 4 March 1929.

Eventyr/Once upon a time ballad for orchestra by Delius after fairy tales by P C Asbjørnsen (1812–85), composed 1917 and dedicated to Henry Wood, who gave the first performance in London, 28 June 1919.

Everyman incidental music for Hugo von Hofmannsthal's German version of the 15th-century English morality play, *Jedermann*, by Sibelius, op. 83, composed 1916, first performed Helsinki, National Theatre, 5 November 1916. Six monologues from Everyman

were set by Frank Martin for baritone and piano in 1943; orchestral version 1949.

Evocations three symphonic poems by Roussel, composed 1910–12: 1. *Les Dieux dans l'ombre des cavernes*; 2. *La Ville rose*; 3. *Aux bords du fleuve sacré*; first performed Paris, Société Nationale, 18 May 1912.

Symphonic suite by Bloch, composed 1937; first performed San Francisco, 11 February 1938. Three movements: *Contemplation, Houang/God of War, Renouveau.*

Ewen, David (1907–1985) US writer on music. He moved to the USA in 1912 and studied in New York; University of Miami from 1965. In 50 years he published more than 80 music reference books, *Dictators of the Baton* (1943), *Encyclopedia of the Opera* (1955, revised 1971), *The World of 20th-Century Music* (1968), *Composers Since 1900* (1969), *Musicians Since 1900* (1978), and *US Composers* (1982).

Excursions of Mr Brouček/The, Výlety pana Brouček, opera by Janáček (libretto by the composer with F Gellner, V Dyke, F S Procházka and others, after two novels by S Čech), produced Prague, 23 April 1920. Not produced in Britain until Edinburgh, 5 September 1970, by the Prague National Theatre Company. Part I depicts sausage-eating Brouček amidst aesthetic, vegetarian moon-dwellers; part II concerns the 1420 Czech defence in battle of their Hussite faith. Brouček is almost punished for cowardice but returns to the present.

Expert, Henri (1863–1952) French musicologist. He studied, and later taught, at Niedermeyer's school in Paris, and was also a pupil of Franck and Gigout. He was professor of music at the Ecole des Hautes Etudes Sociales and librarian of the Conservatory library. He edited a series of early French music, *Les Maîtres musiciens de la renaissance française* and *Monuments de la musique française,* of settings of Ronsard's poetry, early songs, church and harpsichord music.

'. . . explosante-fixe . . .' work by P Boulez for unspecified forces. Given with flute, clarinet, and trumpet in London on 17 June 1971; with same forces, plus strings and computer-controlled electronics, New York Philharmonic Orchestra, conductor P Boulez, on 5 January 1973. Further revised under P Boulez, with the British Broadcasting Corporation (BBC) Symphony Orchestra in Rome, on 13 May 1973.

exposition the opening statement of a classical sonata, concerto, or symphony first movement, in which the principal themes are clearly outlined.

expression signs or words providing a dramatic context for the interpretation of neutral performance indicators for tempo, dynamics, phrasing, and so on.

expressionism use of melodic or harmonic distortion for expressive effect, associated with Schoenberg, Hindemith, Krenek, and others.

expression marks in musical composition, all the indications by which composers indicate their wishes as to the manner of performance of a work, especially from the dynamic point of view (*forte, piano, crescendo, diminuendo*); they may extend also to matters of speed and rhythm (*rallentando, rubato,* or *accelerando*). Expression marks were little used before the 18th century and hardly at all before the 17th century.

extemporization see ◊improvisation.

extended technique in general, nontraditional methods of obtaining sounds from musical instruments. Many 20th-century composers have experimented with extended techniques of various sorts, particularly for wind instruments. An early example is the use of percussive keystrokes in Varèse's *Density 21.5* for solo flute (1930), in which the performer makes an audible sound by hitting the keys of the flute hard when changing note. Other examples of extended technique for woodwind include multiphonics (splitting the note so that two separate

harmonics are heard; a technique often achieved accidentally by beginners, but extremely difficult to control deliberately), humming into the mouthpiece, and so forth.

extravaganza (from Italian 'stravaganza') word sometimes used for a composition of an unusual nature, especially for a light and fantastic stage piece with music, such as Gilbert and Sullivan's *Trial by Jury*.

Eybler, Joseph Leopold von (1765–1846)
Austrian composer. He attempted to complete Mozart's Requiem (1791) and suffered a stroke while conducting it in 1833. After holding various appointments in Vienna, he was chief Kapellmeister to the Austrian court 1824–33.

He was a pupil of Johann Albrechtsberger.

Works include: the opera *Das Zauberschwert* and others; oratorio *Die vier letzten Dinge* (1810), Requiem in C minor (1803, for Empress Maria Theresa), cantata *Die Hirten bei der Krippe*, seven Te Deums, 32 Masses, offertories, graduals, and other church music; symphonies; chamber music, piano pieces, and other pieces.

Ezio/Aetius libretto by Metastasio, first set by Porpora (Venice, 1728); other settings by Handel (1732); Jommelli (1741); Gluck (1750) and Hasse (1755). General Aetius and Emperor Valentinian both love Fulvia. Maximus, her father, plays them off against each other to try and gain the throne. After much complication, Aetius and Fulvia are united and Maximus is pardoned.

F

f abbreviation for ◊forte (loud).

fa the old name for the note **F** (see ◊solmization), still used in Latin countries, and in tonic sol-fa notation the sub-dominant note in any key represented by the symbol **f**, pronounced fa.

Faber, Heinrich (before 1500–1552) German theorist and composer. He was the author of a music textbook for beginners, *Compendiolum musicae pro incipientibus*, which was first published at Brunswick in 1548 and ran into numerous editions. There is some church music to Latin and German texts.

fabliau (old French 'fable') troubadour ballad with narrative words, distinct from the love songs sung by the troubadours.

Fabricius, Werner (1633–1679) German organist and composer. After pursuing other studies at Leipzig University, including law, he became music director at St Paul's Church there in 1656 and, in addition, at St Nicolas' Church in 1658. He was also a public notary.

He studied under his father, Albert Fabricius, who was organist at Flensburg; his other teachers were Thomas Selle and Heinrich Schiedemann at the Hamburg Gymnasium.

Works include: motets, hymn tunes; sacred and secular songs for several voices; suites for viols and other instruments.

Fabrizi, Vincenzo (1764–after 1812) Italian composer. He had written 14 operas by the time he was 24; many of them were short comic pieces, performed all over Italy. His *Il convitato di pietra (Don Giovanni Tenorio)* was premiered at Rome in 1787, the same year as Mozart's *Don Giovanni* was given in Prague,

and rivalled the success of Mozart's work for several years.

faburden see ◊fauxbourdon.

Façade diversion by Walton (poems by Edith Sitwell), privately produced London, Chenil Gallery, Chelsea; first public performance London, Aeolian Hall, 12 June 1923. Two concert suites arranged later for enlarged orchestra and for piano duet. Produced as a ballet (choreography by Frederick Ashton), London, Cambridge Theatre, 26 April 1931.

Fackeltanz (German 'torch dance') dance in which each performer carries a torch.

fadinho (Portuguese *fado*) type of popular song performed in Portuguese towns, in the streets and cafés, accompanied by the guitar and enlivened by dancing.

Fago, Nicola (1677–1745) Italian composer, nicknamed Il Tarantino after his birthplace. He was educated at the Conservatorio della Pietà dei Turchini in Naples. He was maestro di cappella at the Conservatorio di S Onofrio, 1704–08, and at the Conservatorio della Pietà, 1705–40. His works consist mainly of church music but he also wrote four or more operas including *Radamisto* (1707) and *Cassandra* (1711), oratorios, and other works.

Fagott German name for the ◊bassoon, a musical instrument.

fagotto (Italian 'fagot or bundle') alternative name for the ◊bassoon, a musical instrument.

Faidit, Gaucelme (c. 1160–c. 1215) Provençal ◊troubadour. He was at first a jongleur, and travelled with his wife, Guilhelma Monja, to various European courts. In 1202 he accompanied Boniface III of Montserrat to the Fourth Crusade and several of his songs exhort the young and strong to take part in the holy war. Among his patrons were Richard the Lion-Heart (whose death he lamented in a beautiful *planh*), Raymond d'Agoult, and Geoffrey of Brittany.

Fairies, The opera by John Christopher Smith (libretto by composer, based on Shakespeare's *A Midsummer Night's Dream*), produced London, Drury Lane, 3 February 1755.

Fair Maid of Perth (Bizet). See ◊*Jolie Fille de Perth*.

Fair Maid of the Mill (Schubert). See ◊*Schöne Müllerin*.

Fair Melusina (Mendelssohn). See ◊*Schöne Melusine*.

Fair of Sorotchintsy (Mussorgsky). See ◊ *Sorotchintsy Fair*.

Fairy Queen, The semi-opera by Purcell (libretto adapted from Shakespeare's *A Midsummer Night's Dream* by Elkanah Settle), produced London, Dorset Gardens Theatre, April 1692. The plot broadly follows that of Shakespeare's play, without setting any of the words. Revived by the English National Opera for the Purcell tercentenary, 1995.

Fairy's Kiss *The/Le Baiser de la fée* ballet in four scenes by Stravinsky, based on songs and piano pieces by Tchaikovsky, produced Paris, Opéra, 27 November 1927, choreographed by Nijinska. Suite for orchestra, Divertimento, 1934.

Fairy Tale, Pohádka, work by Janáček for cello and piano, after the tale *Czar Berendei* by V A Zhukovsky, first performed Brno, 13 March 1910, revised c. 1923.

fa-la a light 16th–17th-century English composition for several voices of the ◊ballett type. Its name derives from the syllables to which the refrain was sung.

Falconieri, Andrea (1586–1656) Italian composer. He lived successively at Parma, Florence, Rome, and Modena, and also visited Spain. He was maestro di cappella at Naples from 1650.

Works include: motets, madrigals, instrumental pieces.

fall a ◊cadence (such as 'dying fall' in Shakespeare).

Fall, Leo (1873–1925) Austrian composer. He studied at the Vienna Conservatory and became conductor at Berlin, Hamburg, and Cologne. He wrote c. 25 works for the stage, chiefly operettas, including *Die Dollarprinzessin* (1907), *Eternal Waltz*, *Die geschiedene Frau* (*The Girl in the Train*), *Der liebe Augustin* (*Princess Caprice*), and *Madame Pompadour*.

Falla, Manuel de (1876–1946), full name Manuel Maria de Falla y Matheu Spanish composer. The folk idiom of southern Spain is an integral part of his compositions. His opera *La vida breve/Brief Life* 1905 (performed 1913) was followed by the ballets *El amor brujo/Love the Magician* 1915 and *El sombrero de tres picos/The Three-Cornered Hat* 1919, and his most ambitious concert work, *Noches en los jardines de España/Nights in the Gardens of Spain* 1916. He also wrote songs and pieces for piano and guitar.

He was born in Cádiz, and began to study the piano in Madrid at the age of eight. In 1902 he produced a zarzuela, *Los amores de Inés*, written with very little tuition in composition. This had no success, and he studied composition 1902–04 at the Madrid Conservatory with Felipe Pedrell, the founder of the modern national Spanish school of composition. In 1905 he won two prizes for piano playing and for his opera *La vida breve*. He lived in Paris 1907–14, where he was influenced by the Impressionist composers Debussy, Ravel, and Dukas, but returned to Spain and settled in Madrid on the outbreak of World War I. The production of *La vida breve* at Nice and Paris in 1913 and of the ballet *The Three-Cornered Hat* in London in 1919 spread his reputation. In 1921 he moved to Granada and became more exclusively a nationalist composer again; but had later works performed in England, Paris, and New York. In 1939 he moved to Argentina, where he died at Alta Gracia, leaving unfinished his most ambitious work, the cantata *L'Atlántida*, on which he had worked since 1928.

Works include: OPERA *La vida breve* (1904–05), *El retablo de maese Pedro* (for puppets after Cervantes's *Don Quixote*, 1923); ballets *El amor brujo* (1915), *El sombrero de tres picos/The Three-Cornered Hat*.

INSTRUMENTAL AND SOLO VOCAL *Noches en los jardines de España* for piano and orchestra (1911–15); *Psyché* for mezzo-soprano, flute, violin, viola, cello, and harp (1924); concerto for harpsichord, flute, oboe, clarinet, violin, and cello (1923–26); *Fantasia baetica* for piano; *Homenaje: pour le tombeau de Debussy* for guitar; seven popular Spanish songs.

false relation, or cross relation in harmony, the appearance of different voices (independent parts) of two notes which bear the same note name but not the same pitch, either simultaneously or in close succession; that is, where one is modified by a flat or sharp, and the other is a natural. For example, false relations occur if an E♭ in the soprano voice is followed in the next chord by an E♮ in the tenor voice. In traditional harmony and counterpoint, false relations are not encouraged because harmonic alterations in one voice, as represented by a modifying sharp or flat, are resolved most smoothly within the same voice.

falsetto the tone-production of male singers resulting in notes above their normal pitch in the female (soprano or alto) register, and sounding like an unbroken voice. Falsetto is the voice normally cultivated by male countertenors.

falsobordone see ◊fauxbourdon.

Falstaff opera by Verdi (libretto by Boito, based on Shakespeare's *Merry Wives of Windsor* and *King Henry IV*), produced Milan, La Scala, 9 February 1893. Falstaff hopes to solve his money problems by seducing Alice Ford and Meg Page; he realizes his folly when he is tipped into the Thames.

Symphonic study by Elgar, op. 68 (based on Shakespeare's *King Henry IV* and references to Falstaff in *King Henry V*), composed 1913, performed Leeds Festival, 2 October 1913. ◊*At the Boar's Head*; ◊*Lustigen Weiber von Windsor*; ◊*Sir John in Love*.

Falstaff, ossia Le tre burle/Falstaff, or The Three Jests opera by Salieri (libretto by C P Defranceschi, after Shakespeare), produced Vienna, Kärntnertortheater, 3 January 1799. Beethoven wrote an early set of piano variations on the opera.

Fanciulla del West, La/The Girl of the [Golden] West opera by Puccini (libretto by G Civinini and C Zangarini, based on David Belasco's play), produced New York Metropolitan Opera, 10 December 1910. Jack Rance the sheriff and Dick Johnson the bandit compete for Minnie's affections. Realizing that Dick is an outlaw, Jack hunts him down and prepares to lynch him, but Minnie arrives in time to save the day.

fancy old English term equivalent to the Italian *fantasia*, that is, a polyphonic composition for a consort of viols, ◊broken consort, or keyboard instrument. Fancies had no definitely determined form, but always made considerable use of counterpoint and were generally divided into a number of sections, played without a break but not thematically connected.

fandango an 18th-century Spanish dance in moderate to fast triple time (3/8 or 3/4), danced by a couple with the accompaniment of a guitar and castanets. Fandangos are

found in Mozart's *Le Nozze di Figaro/The Marriage of Figaro* 1786, Gluck's *Don Juan* 1761, and Rimsky-Korsakov's *Capriccio espagnol/Spanish Capriccio* 1887.

fanfare a ceremonial short and brilliant tune for trumpets, or a piece for other instruments imitating the effect of trumpets. Written traditionally for valveless (natural) instruments, fanfares typically include notes of the major ◊triad and ◊diatonic scale. An example of a fanfare is the introduction to Act II of Wagner's *Tristan und Isolde* 1865.

Faniska play with music by Cherubini (libretto, in German, by Josef Sonnleithner), produced Vienna, Kärntnertortheater, 25 February 1806.

Fantaisie (Italian 'fantasia'; German 'Fantasie') see ◊fantasia.

Fantaisies symphoniques title for Martinů's sixth and last symphony; composed 1953 to celebrate the 75th anniversary of the founding of the Boston Symphony Orchestra. First performed Boston, 12 January 1955, conductor Munch.

fantasia, or fantasy, phantasy, fancy in music, a free-form instrumental composition for keyboard or chamber ensemble, originating in the late Renaissance, and much favoured by English composers Dowland, Gibbons, and Byrd.

It implies the free manipulation of musical figures without regard to models of form. Later composers include Telemann, J S Bach, and Mozart.

Fantasia Concertante on a Theme of Corelli work for strings by Tippett, based on Corelli's Concerto Grosso op. 6 no. 2, composed 1953 for the tercentenary of his birth. First performed Edinburgh, 29 August 1953.

Fantasia Contrappuntistica work for piano composed 1910, with sub-title 'Grosse Fuge', by Busoni. Based on Contrapunctus XVIII of Bach's *The Art of Fugue* and completes the last unfinished fugue, with extra subject of Busoni's own. Two more versions for solo piano by 1912 and version for two pianos 1921, first performed Berlin, 16 November 1921.

Fantasia on a Theme by Thomas Tallis work for double string orchestra and string quartet by Vaughan Williams, based on no. 3 of nine psalm tunes (1567) by Tallis, first performed Gloucester, 6 September 1910.

Fantasia on a theme of Handel work by Tippett for piano and orchestra, composed 1939–41. First performed London, 7 March

1942. Written while Tippett was in conflict with wartime government as a conscientious objector: just over a year after the first performance he spent three months in Wormwood Scrubs prison.

Fantasiestück (German 'fantastic piece') short instrumental piece of a free or fantastic character, rather less extended as a rule than a fantasy and keeping to a single movement and mood, whereas the latter is usually in several connected sections.

'Fantastic Symphony' (Berlioz). See ◊*'Symphonie fantastique'.*

Faramondo opera by Handel (libretto by A Zeno, altered), produced London, King's Theatre, Haymarket, 3 January 1738. In medieval France, King Gustaavo plots revenge against Faramondo, the alleged murderer of one of his sons. An unusually convoluted plot also deals with deceptions and love rivalries.

farandole, French, a dance of Provence, probably of Greek origin. It is danced by large groups of people in procession through the streets and accompanied by pipe and tabor. The music is in 6–8 time, so that the example in Bizet's *Arlésienne* music is not traditionally correct, though very evocative.

farce (from Latin *farcire*, 'to stuff, to lard') in 18th-century opera, a comic scene introduced into a serious work. Hence a complete comic opera so interpolated, or simply a comic opera in one act (Italian *farsa*). The modern sense of the term in English (an absurdly comic play) is derived from this. In earlier English the verb had the meaning it still has in French of stuffing food with seasoning, and in music it was used for the practice of interpolating words in the *Kyrie eleison.*

Farewell, Absence and Return (Beethoven). See ◊*Adieux, l'absence et le retour.*

'Farewell' Symphony nickname of Haydn's symphony no. 45 in F♭ minor, composed 1772 as a hint to Prince Esterházy that the orchestra would welcome leave of absence. In the finale the players leave one by one until only two violins remain.

Farinelli (real name Carlo Broschi) (1705–1782) Italian castrato soprano. He was a pupil of Porpora, in whose *Eumene* he made his debut in Rome in 1721. He sang with great success in many European cities, including Vienna and London. He remained in the service of the European court 1737–59, singing every night in private for Philip V, then Ferdinand VI. He retired to Bologna.

Farkas, Ferenc (1905–   ) Hungarian composer. After travelling to enlarge his experience and holding two posts at provincial schools of music, he was professor of composition at the Academy of Dramatic Art in Budapest 1949–75.

He studied at the Budapest Conservatory and with Respighi in Rome.

Works include: the opera *The Magic Cupboard* (1942); musical plays and operettas; opera *A Gentleman from Venice*, produced at Budapest, 1991; ballet *Three Vagabonds*; incidental music (including Shakespeare's *Timon of Athens, As You Like It,* and *Romeo and Juliet*); cantata *Fountain of St John*; symphonies and other orchestral works, chamber music, piano music, songs.

Farmer, John (c. 1570–   ) English composer. He wrote a treatise on the polyphonic setting of plainsong tunes.

He was organist of Christ Church Cathedral at Dublin 1595–99, and then went to London.

Works include: psalm tunes set for four voices contributed to East's Psalter; madrigals; instrumental pieces.

Farnaby, Giles (c. 1563–1640) English composer. He wrote madrigals, psalms for the *Whole Booke of Psalms* 1621, edited by Thomas Ravenscroft (1582–1633), and music for virginals (an early keyboard instrument), over 50 pieces being represented in the 17th-century manuscript collection the ◊*Fitzwilliam Virginal Book.*

He lived in London, where he married in 1587, and took a degree in music at Oxford University in 1592.

Works include: 20 canzonets for four and one for eight voices, madrigals, psalm tunes set for four voices in East's Psalter; over 50 virginal pieces.

Farnaby, Richard (c. 1594–   ) English composer, son of Giles ◊Farnaby. In 1608 he became apprentice to Sir Nicholas Saunderson of Fillingham, Lincolnshire; in 1614 he married. He wrote 52 keyboard pieces which were included in the *Fitzwilliam Virginal Book,* compiled by Francis Tregian who died in 1619.

Farquhar, George (1678–1707) Irish dramatist. His works inspired J E Eccles (*Stage Coach*); Gottfried ◊Finger (*Sir Harry Wildair*); Richard ◊Leveridge (*Constant Couple, Recruiting Officer, Love and a Bottle*); Daniel ◊Purcell (*Beaux's Stratagem, Constant Couple, Inconstant*).

Farrant, Richard (c. 1530–1580) English organist and composer. He was a Gentleman of the Chapel Royal in London until 1564, when he became organist and choirmaster at St George's Chapel, Windsor. He also wrote music for the Blackfriar's Theatre, London.

Works include: service in A minor (usually sung in G minor), anthems 'Call to Remembrance' and 'Hide not Thou Thy Face', and other church music, songs for plays produced by him with the choirboys before Queen Elizabeth; keyboard pieces in the Mulliner Book.

farsa, or farsa per musica (Italian 'farce', or 'farce for music') Italian term of the early 19th century for a type of comic opera in one act, such as Rossini's *La cambiale di matrimonio*.

Farthyng, Thomas (died 1520) English composer. He worked at King's College, Cambridge, as chorister, 1477–83, and as clerk, 1493–99. He was appointed at the Chapel Royal, 1511–20. He wrote church music and secular songs.

Fasch, Carl Friedrich (Christian) (1736–1800) German harpsichordist and composer. He was appointed second harpsichordist (with C P E Bach) to the court of Frederick the Great in 1756, but the outbreak of the Seven Years War (1756–63) cost him his position and forced him to live by teaching. In 1791 he founded the Berlin Singakademie, the choral society which he conducted until his death.

He was a pupil of his father, Johann Friedrich ◊Fasch, and later of Johann Hertel at Strelitz. He was conductor of the court opera in Berlin 1774–76.

Works include: oratorio *Giuseppe riconosciuto* (1774), Mass for 16 voices, cantatas, psalms, and other church music; also some instrumental music.

Fasch, Johann Friedrich (1688–1758) German organist and composer; father of Carl Friedrich ◊Fasch. He founded the collegium musicum at Leipzig, travelled after 1714, held various posts at Gera, Greitz, and in the service of Count Morzin at Lukaveč, Bohemia, and in 1722 was appointed Kapellmeister at Zerbst. He was famous as a composer in his day, though his works were not published until after his death.

He was a pupil of Kuhnau at St Thomas's School, Leipzig.

Works include: four operas including *Die getreue Dido* (1712); Masses, a Requiem, church cantatas, motets, a Passion; about 90 orchestral suites, 60 concertos, trios, sonatas,

and other pieces; many of his vocal pieces are now lost.

Faun and Shepherdess song-suite for mezzo and orchestra by Stravinsky (text by Pushkin); composed 1906, first performed St Petersburg, 4 February 1908; in the same concert the E♭ symphony, dedicated to Rimsky-Korsakov, was given its first performance.

Fauré, Gabriel (Urbain) (1845–1924) French composer. He wrote songs, chamber music, and a choral *Requiem* 1888. He was a pupil of Saint-Saëns, became professor of composition at the Paris Conservatoire 1896, and was its director 1905–20.

Fauré studied at Niedermeyer's school of music in Paris 1854–66, and became church organist at Rennes in the latter year. He returned to Paris in 1870, became organist first at Saint-Sulpice and then at Saint-Honoré, and choirmaster at the Madeleine in 1877, being appointed organist there in 1896, a post he held until 1905. He had many distinguished composition pupils, including Ravel, Enescu, and Koechlin.

His early music, notably the song cycle *La bonne chanson*, 1st violin sonata and 1st piano quartet, was lyrical and contemplative in nature. His best known work, the *Requiem*, also dates from this period. He adopted a terser, more rigorous style at the turn of the century, with the opera *Prométhée*, and continued in this style with the piano quintets and cello sonatas.

Works include: STAGE opera *Pénélope* (1913); incidental music *Pelléas et Mélisande* (Maeterlinck, 1898).

ORCHESTRAL *Pavane* (1887), suite *Masques et bergamasques* (1919).

CHAMBER two piano quintets (D minor, C minor, 1906, 1921), two piano quartets (C minor, G minor, 1879, 1886); string quartet (1924), piano trio (1923); two sonatas for violin and piano (A major, E minor, 1876, 1926), two sonatas for cello and piano; pieces for violin and piano, cello and piano, and flute and piano.

VOCAL Requiem for solo voices, chorus, and orchestra (1887–90); *Messe basse* for female voices and organ; 11 miscellaneous religious vocal pieces.

SOLO PIANO 34 op. nos. of piano music, including five Impromptus, 13 Barcarolles, four Valses-caprices, eight Nocturnes, Theme and Variations, nine Preludes; *Dolly*, six pieces for piano duet.

SOLO VOCAL 96 songs including cycles *Poème d'un jour*, *La bonne chanson* (1893, Verlaine), *La*

Chanson d've (Charles van Lerberghe, 1906–10), *L'Horizon chimérique*.

Faust episodes from Lenau's *Faust*: two orchestral pieces by Liszt, *Night Procession* and *Dance in the Village Inn* (first *Mephisto Waltz*), composed c. 1860, first performed Weimar, 8 March 1861.

Opera by Gounod (libretto by J Barbier and M Carré, based on Goethe's drama), produced Paris, Théâtre Lyrique, 19 March 1859.

Opera by Spohr (libretto by J K Bernard, founded on the Faust legend without reference to Goethe's work, not completed at that time), produced Prague, 1 September 1816. Revised without spoken dialogue 1852 and produced London, Covent Garden, 4 April 1852.

Overture by Wagner, not for Goethe's drama, but a kind of symphonic poem on it, composed Paris, 1839–40 ·after hearing Beethoven's symphony at the Conservatory; first performed Dresden, 22 July 1844; rewritten 1854–55 and performed at Zurich, 23 January 1855.

Adolphe ◊Adam (ballet); Samuel ◊Arnold (*Dr Faustus*); Nils ◊Bentzon (*Faust III*); ◊Damnation de Faust (Berlioz); ◊Doktor Faust (Busoni); ◊Mefistofele (Boito); Henri ◊Pousseur (*Votre Faust*); Hermann ◊Reutter (*Doktor Johannes Faust*); ◊Schnittke (*Historia von D Johann Fausten*); ◊Szenen aus Goethes 'Faust' (Schumann).

Fausta, Empress Fausta, wife of Constantine I opera by Donizetti (libretto by D Gilardoni), produced Naples, Teatro San Carlo, 12 January 1832. Not related to the Faust legend. Fausta, wife of the Emperor Constantine, loves her stepson, Crispo, who loves Beroe. Crispo rejects Fausta, but charges are nonetheless brought against him for supposedly loving the queen. He is condemned to death and Fausta poisons herself.

Fausto/Faust opera by Louise Angélique Bertin (1805–1877) (libretto, in Italian, by composer, based on Goethe's drama), produced Paris, Théâtre Italien, 8 March 1831. The first *Faust* opera and the only one by a woman. Bertin was the sister of Berlioz's editor of the *Journal des Débats*; Berlioz may have had a hand in the work; at any rate he probably suggested the subject.

'Faust-Symphonie, Eine' symphony by Liszt, based on Goethe's drama, 'in three character pictures': 1. *Faust*; 2. *Gretchen*; 3. *Mephistopheles*, with final chorus 'Alles Vergängliche ist nur ein Gleichnis'; finished without the chorus, 19 October 1854, chorus added 1857 and revised 1880; first performed

Weimar, Court Theatre, 5 September 1857, on the occasion of the unveiling of the Goethe-Schiller monument. The work is dedicated to Berlioz. It was performed at Bayreuth (conductor Barenboim) on the centenary of Liszt's death, 31 July 1986.

fauxbourdon ('false bass') name given to a wide variety of technical procedures in the 15th–16th centuries, usually involving improvisation. As originally used by Dufay and others, the term implied the use of chains of 6–3 chords, the middle part being 'improvised' by doubling the top part a fourth lower throughout; later, different techniques were employed to achieve the same effect. The English used their version of the word for a similar process, the three parts being improvised straight from plainsong (at first in the middle, later in the top part). The fauxbourdon itself (that is, the lowest part) was also used as the basis of entirely new compositions.

In the later 15th and early 16th centuries, the use of the term in both France and England was enormously extended to include techniques in which the idea of 6–3 chords was entirely lost. It is to this final stage in its history that the Italian use of the term belongs, meaning initially a kind of fauxbourdon in four parts with the 'true' bass supplied beneath the false one, and ultimately nothing more than simple declamatory composition in note-against-note style.

Faux Lord, Le/The False Lord opera by Piccinni (libretto by G M Piccinni, the composer's son), produced Paris, Comédie-Italienne, 6 December 1783.

Favart, Charles Simon (1710–1792) French playwright and librettist. He wrote ◊Bastien und Bastienne (Mozart); ◊Cythère assiégée (Gluck); ◊Löttchen am Hofe (J A Hiller); ◊Rosina (Shield); and for Franz ◊Süssmayr (*Soliman II*).

Favola d'Orfeo, La/The Story of Orpheus opera by Monteverdi (libretto by A Striggio), produced Mantua, at the court of the Hereditary Prince Francesco Gonzaga, Carnival 1607. Revived in a version by d'Indy and given in concert performance, Paris, 1904; staged Oxford 1925, under Westrup. Also versions by Malipiero, Orff, Hindemith, Leppard, and Harnoncourt.

Opera by Casella (libretto by C Pavolini, after A Ambrogini [Poliziano (1454–1494)]), produced Venice, Teatro Goldoni, 6 September 1932.

favola per musica (Italian 'story for music') early Italian term for opera of a legendary or mythological character; actually a story of that kind in dramatic form written for the purpose of being set to music.

Favorite, La opera by Donizetti (libretto, in French, by A Royer and G Vaëz, with Scribe's assistance), produced Paris, Opéra, 2 December 1840. Fernand falls in love with King Alphonse's mistress, Léonor, without knowing her true identity. After their marriage he finds out and feels dishonoured, retreating to a monastery. Later Léonor contracts a fatal illness, and as she dies is reconciled with Fernand.

Fayrfax, Robert (1464–1521) English composer. He was a Gentleman of the Chapel Royal on the accession of Henry VIII, with whom he attended the Field of the Cloth of Gold in 1520.

He became organist and choirmaster at St Albans Cathedral before 1502. He gained a degree in music at Cambridge University in 1501 (for his Mass *O quam glorifica*), and a doctorate in 1504; he received a doctorate from Oxford in 1511.

Works include: six cyclic Masses, motets, two Magnificats, *Stabat Mater*; songs for several voices, and other pieces.

Feast at Solhaug, The incidental music for Ibsen's play by H Wolf for a production of a German translation by Emma Klingenfeld, Vienna, 21 November 1891.

Fedé, Jehen (c. 1415–c. 1477) French composer. He was well known in his day as a writer of sacred and secular music, but only six pieces believed to be by him have survived.

He was vicar of Douai 1439–40, a papal singer 1443–45; at the Sainte Chapelle in 1449; at the court of Charles VII 1452–53; at St Peter's, Rome in 1466; and a member of Louis XI's chapel 1473–74.

Fedeltà premiata, La dramma pastorale giocoso by Haydn (libretto by G Lorenzi), performed Eszterháza, 25 February 1781; successfully revived in recent years at the Camden and Glyndebourne Festivals. The goddess Diana demands a sacrifice of two faithful lovers unless one hero offers to take their place. Fileno and Celia face this danger, but when Fileno offers his life to save Celia's, Diana shows mercy.

Fedora opera by Giordano (libretto by A Colautti, based on Sardou's play), produced Milan, Teatro Lirico, 17 November 1898. Fedora's husband, Vladimir, is murdered.

After tracking down the killer, Count Loris, Fedora learns that the motive was revenge for an affair Vladimir had had with Loris' wife. The two fall in love, but come to a bad end when Vladimir's father takes revenge.

Fedra/Phaedra opera by Pizzetti (libretto G d'Annunzio's tragedy), produced Milan, La Scala, 20 March 1915. Phaedra, wife of Theseus, loves her stepson, Hippolytus, who rejects her. She makes Theseus believe Hippolytus has raped her, and Hippolytus is then killed. Phaedra takes poison, but unlike the version in Greek myth, she remains defiant to the end.

Feen, Die/The Fairies opera by Wagner (libretto by composer, based on Gozzi's comedy, *La Donna serpente*), composed 1833, when Wagner was aged 20, and not staged in his lifetime; produced Munich, 29 June 1888; rehearsed by Richard Strauss, who was not allowed to conduct the performance. Dramatic ideas from *Die Feen* are developed in Strauss's opera *Die Frau ohne Schatten* (1919). Ada, half fairy, marries King Arindal on the condition that he does not ask about her true identity. He fails, and she is turned to stone, but Arindal restores her and the two leave for fairyland.

Fée Urgèle, La, ou Ce qui plaît aux dames/ The Fairy Urgéle, or What Pleases the Ladies opera by Duni (libretto by C S Favart, based on a story by Voltaire, founded on Chaucer's *Tale of the Wife of Bath*), produced Fontainebleau, at court, 26 October 1765; first performed Paris, Comédie-Italienne, 4 December 1765. In 7th-century France, knight Robert is imprisoned and can be released only when he successfully answers a riddle. To find the answer he agrees to marry the crone La Vieille, who turns out to be his lover, Marton.

Felciano, Richard (1930–) US composer. He studied with Milhaud and Dallapiccola, and worked at the University of California at Berkeley.

Works include: the opera *Sir Gawain and the Green Knight* (1964); *Contractions* for woodwind quintet (1965); *Mutations* for orchestra (1966); *Soundspace for Mozart* for flute and tape (1970); *Galactic Rounds* for orchestra (1972); *In Celebration of Golden Rains* for organ and gamelan (1977); *Salvatore Allende* for ensemble (1983); *Palladio* for violin, piano and percussion (1989).

Feldman, Morton (1926–1987) US composer. An associate of John Cage and Earle Brown in the 1950s, he devised an indeterminate notation based on high, middle, and low instrumental registers and time cells of fixed duration for his *Projection* series for various ensembles 1950–51, later exploiting the freedoms of classical notation in a succession of reflective studies in vertical tone mixtures including *Madame Press Died Last Week at 90* 1970.

He studied with Stefan Wolpe and Wallingford Riegger. Influenced by abstract expressionist painting, he introduced the element of chance into his music, indicating often only an approximation of what is to be played.

Works include: *Durations I–V* (1960–61); *Extensions I–V* (1951–60); *Vertical Thoughts I–V* (1963); *Two Instruments* for cello and horn; *For Franz Kline* for soprano, violin, cello, horn, chimes, and piano; *De Kooning* for piano, cello, violin, horn, and percussion (1963); ballet *Ixion*; *The Swallows of Salangan* for chorus and 76 instruments; *The Viola in my Life I–IV* (1970–71); *The Rothko Chapel* for viola, chorus, and percussion (1972); *Neither*, monodrama to text by Beckett for soprano and orchestra (1977); series of works with orchestra, featuring cello, string quartet, piano, oboe, flute, and violin (1972–79); two string quartets (1979, 1983); *Trio* (1980); *The Turfan Fragments* for orchestra (1980); *Triadic Memories* for piano (1981); *For John Cage* (1982); *Three Voices* for three sopranos, or voice and tape (1982); violin concerto (1984).

Feldpartie, or Feldpartita (German 'field suite') old German term for suites written for wind instruments and played in the open on military occasions.

Félix, ou L'Enfant trouvé/Felix, or The Foundling opera by Monsigny (libretto by J M Sedaine), produced Fontainebleau, at court, 10 November 1777; first Paris performance, Comédie-Italienne, 24 November 1777. Monsigny's last opera.

Fellowes, Edmund H(orace) (1870–1951) English clergyman and musicologist. He was educated at Winchester College and Oxford, and attached to St George's Chapel, Windsor, as minor canon from 1900. He was awarded an honorary doctorate of music at Dublin, 1917 and Oxford, 1938. He wrote books on the English madrigal, Byrd and O Gibbons, and edited *The English Madrigal School*, English lutenist songs, Byrd's works and co-edited *Tudor Church Music*.

Felsztyński, Sebastian (c. 1490–c. 1544) Polish composer. He studied at Kraków University. He wrote church music, and compiled a hymn-book for Sigismund I in 1522.

Felton, William (1715–1769) English organist and composer. He became famous as a performer on the organ and harpsichord, for which he wrote concertos and lessons. The celebrated *Felton's Gavotte* was a set of variations in one of the concertos.

Felton was educated at Manchester and Cambridge, he became a clergyman, a vicar-choral, and later a minor canon at Hereford Cathedral.

feminine adjective used to describe a cadence or phrase which ends on an unstressed beat of the bar, most typically the second beat.

Fenby, Eric William (1906–) English composer and writer on music. From 1928–34 he acted as amanuensis to Delius, who was living blind and paralysed at Grez-sur-Loing, and helped him to commit *Songs of Farewell*, *A Song of Summer*, *Fantastic Dance-Idyll*, and other late works to paper. He published a memoir, *Delius as I knew him* 1936 (revised 1981).

He became an organist at the age of 12 and studied music with A E Keeton. He was professor of harmony at the Royal Academy of Music 1964–77.

Works include: symphonic, overture *Rossini on Ilkla Moor*, and other pieces.

Fennell, Frederick (1914–) US conductor. He founded the Eastman Wind Ensemble in 1952 and made many successful recordings with it. He was conductor-in-residence at the University of Miami School of Music, Florida 1965–80.

He studied at the Eastman School and conducted the Little Symphony and Symphonic Band 1939–65.

Fennelly, Brian (1937–) US composer. He studied at Yale University and has been professor at New York University. His music draws on a wide range of sources.

Works include: *Evanescences* for ensemble (1969); string quartet (1971); *In Wildness is the Preservation of the World*, fantasy for orchestra after Thoreau (1975); series *Tesserae*, for various instrumental groups (1971–81); *Quintuplo* for brass quintet and orchestra (1978); *Scintilla* for cello and orchestra (1981); *Winterkill* for chorus and piano (1981); saxophone concerto (1984); brass quintet (1987); *On Civil Disobedience* (1992–93).

Fennimore und Gerda opera in 11 pictures by Delius (libretto, in German, by composer, based on P Jacobsen's novel *Niels Lyhne*), produced Frankfurt, 21 October 1919. Erik and Niels love Fennimore. She marries Erik and thier relationship sours. Later Erik is accidentally killed; the last two pictures concentrate on Niels' romance with Gerda.

Feo, Francesco (1691–1761) Italian composer. He was a pupil of Gizzi and Fago at the Conservatorio della Pietà della Turchini in Naples, and later of Pitoni in Rome. He produced his first opera, *L'amor tirannico*, in Naples, 1713. He was maestro di cappella of the Conservatorio St Onofrio, 1723–28, and of the Conservatorio dei Poveri, 1739–43. Jommelli and Pergolesi were among his pupils.

Works include: the operas *Siface* (1723), *Ipermestra*, *Arianna* (1728), *Andromaca* (1730), *Arsace* (1740) and others; Masses and other church music.

Feragut, Beltrame (or Bertrand) (c. 1385–c. 1450) French composer who travelled in France and Italy. His motet *Excelsa civitas Vincencia* was written in honour of a new bishop of Vicenza, Francesco Malipiero, in 1433. A few other sacred works survive.

Feramors opera by Anton Rubinstein (libretto, in German, by J Rodenberg, based on Moore's 'Lalla Rookh'), produced Dresden, 24 February 1863. Kashmiri Princess Tulipchuk loves Feramors but must marry the Khan of Bbukhara. The two men turn out to be the same person.

Ferguson, Howard (1908–   ) Irish composer and pianist. He was a professor at the Royal Academy of Music 1948–63; made many editions of early keyboard works, and was active as an accompanist.

He was educated at Westminster School and the Royal College of Music in London as a pupil of R O Morris.

Works include: the ballet *Chaunteclear* (1948); partita and four *Diversions on Ulster Airs* for orchestra; concerto for piano and strings (1951); Octet (1933); two violin and piano sonatas, four pieces for clarinet and piano; sonata and five bagatelles for piano; two ballads for baritone and orchestra; three *Medieval Carols* for voice and piano; *The Dream of the Rood* for soprano or tenor, chorus, and orchestra.

fermata (Italian 'pause') prolonging a note or rest beyond its normal length. For very short pauses a square sign was invented by Vincent d'Indy, but this device never found general acceptance. In *da capo* arias the fermata sign over the final chord of the first section indicates where the aria is to end after the repeat. In a chorale, or a chorale prelude, it indicates the end of a line.

Fernand Cortez, ou La Conquête de Mexique/Hernäen Cortés, or The Conquest of Mexico opera by Spontini (libretto by J A Esménard and V J E de Jouy, based on a tragedy by Piron), produced Paris, Opéra, 28 November 1809. Cortez' brother Alvar is a prisoner of the Aztecs; Cortez' Aztec lover Amazily, seen as a traitor by her own people, offers her life to save Alvar, but Cortez rescues her in the nick of time.

Fernando operetta by Schubert (libretto by A Stadler), composed 1815; never performed in Schubert's lifetime; produced Magdeburg, 18 August 1918 (concert performance Vienna, 1905). Fernando rescued from life as a hermit after killing his brother-in-law.

Ferne Klang, Die/The Distant Sound opera by Schreker (libretto by composer) produced Frankfurt, 18 August 1912. Young couple Fritz and Greta separate to seek their fortunes: the 'Distant Sound'. Fritz becomes a composer and Greta a courtesan. They meet years later and he dies in her arms.

Ferneyhough, Brian John Peter (1943–   ) English composer. His uncompromising, detailed compositions include *Carceri d'invenzione*, a cycle of seven works inspired by the engravings of Piranesi 1981–86, *Time and Motion Studies* 1974–77, and string quartets.

He studied in Birmingham and with Lennox Berkeley at the Royal Academy of Music, and undertook further study in Amsterdam and with Klaus Huber in Basel. He has taught at the Freiburg Musikhochschule and at Darmstadt, Germany. His music is of the advanced avant garde, and includes electronic devices.

Works include: *Prometheus* for wind sextet (1967), *Sonatas* for string quartet, *Epicycle* for 20 strings (1969), *Missa Brevis* for 12 voices (1971), *Firecycle Beta* for orchestra with five conductors (1971), *Sieben Sterne* for organ, *Transit* for six voices and chamber orchestra (1975), *La Terre est un Homme* for orchestra (1978), *Funerailles* for strings and harp (two versions), String quartet no. 2 (1980), *Carceri d'Invenzione*, for chamber ensemble (1982), for flute and chamber orchestra (1984), *Etudes Transcendantals* for voices and ensemble (1984); *Intermedio alla Ciaccona* for violin (1980); *Mnemosyne* for bass flute and tape (1986); third and fourth string quartets (1987, 1990); *Kurze Schatten* for guitar (1983–89); *Trittico per G S* for double bass (1989).

Ferrabosco, Alfonso (1543–1588) Italian composer. He was the most important of the Italian musicians who lived in England in the 16th century. He wrote madrigals, lute pieces, and motets. Many of his works appear in *Musica Transalpina*.

He was born at Bologna, son of the singer and composer Domenico Ferrabosco (1513–1574). He settled in London before 1562; left the service of Queen Elizabeth I in 1569, after becoming involved in a murder case, and returned to Italy on leave, which he extended until 1572. In 1578 he left England for good and entered the service of the Duke of Savoy at Turin, leaving his children in England.

Works include: motets, madrigals, and other pieces.

Ferrabosco, Alfonso (c. 1575–1628) English composer of Italian descent. He was left behind, being probably illegitimate, when his father Alfonso Ferrabosco left England in 1578. He was trained in music at Queen Elizabeth's expense, he became one of James I's court musicians, and succeeded John Coprario as Composer of Music to the King in 1626.

Works include: songs for masques (Ben Jonson) *The Masque of Blackness, Hymenaei, The Masque of Beauty, The Hue and Cry after Cupid, The Masque of Queens, Love freed from Ignorance and Folly*; fancies for viols; lessons for lyra viol; ayres with lute and bass viol; contributions to Leighton's *Teares or Lamentacions*.

Ferrari, Benedetto (c. 1597–1681) Italian music theorist, playwright, and composer. The final duet of his opera *Il pastor regio* (Bologna, 1641) may have been used as the duet at the end of Monteverdi's *L'incoronazione di Poppea*.

He lived at Venice, where he began to produce music dramas with words and music of his own in 1637. In 1645 he went to the court of Modena, where he remained until 1662, except for a visit to Vienna 1651–53. He was then dismissed, but re-appointed in 1674.

Works include: the operas *Armida* (1639), *La ninfa avara* (1641), *Il pastor regio* (1640), *Proserpina rapita*, and others; oratorio *Sansone*; three books of *Musiche varie a voce sola*.

Ferreira, Manuel (died 1797) Spanish composer and conductor. He was attached to a Madrid theatre for which he wrote incidental music for plays and light operas which are early examples of tonadillas (short stage pieces, often of a satirical nature).

Works include: the opera *El mayor triunfo de la mayor guerra*, numerous light operas, incidental music to plays by Calderón, Moreto, and others, including Antonio de Zamora's *Don Juan*.

Ferretti, Giovanni (c. 1540–1609) Italian composer and priest. He was maestro di cappella at Ancona Cathedral from 1575; then worked at the Santa Casa in Loreto. Apart from a few sacred works, he specialized in the lighter types of madrigal, publishing five books of *Canzoni alla Napolitana* (1573–1585).

Fervaal opera by d'Indy (libretto by composer, based on and altered from Tegnér's *Axel*), produced Brussels, Théâtre de la Monnaie, 12 March 1897. Fervaal can save his people only if he renounces love, but he falls for Guilhen. Defeated by the Saracens, he carries Guilhen's body away, pledging a new age of Christianity.

festa teatrale (Italian 'theatrical feast or festival') 18th-century type of opera of a festive kind, especially one expressly written for an occasion, such as a royal or princely patron's wedding. The subject of the libretto was usually mythological and allegorical. Mozart's *Ascanio in Alba* (1771) is an example.

Festes vénitiennes, Les/The Venetian Feasts opera by Campra (libretto by A Danchet), produced Paris, Opéra, 17 June 1710. Revived Aix-en-Provence, 1975. Prologue followed by five (originally three) acts: independent love stories.

Festin de l'araignée, Le/The Spider's Banquet ballet by Roussel (choreography by G de Voisins, based on Henri Fabre's *Souvenirs entomologiques*), produced Paris, Théâtre des Arts, 3 April 1913.

Festing, Michael (Christian) (c. 1680–1752) English violinist and composer. He was music director of the King's Theatre from 1737 and of Ranelagh Gardens from 1742.

He was a pupil of Geminiani in London. He made his first appearance there in 1724 and became Master of the King's Musick in 1735.

Works include: paraphrase of the third chapter of Habakkuk, Milton's *Song on May Morning* (1748), Addison's *Ode for St Cecilia's Day* and other odes, cantatas; symphonies; concertos and sonatas for various instruments; songs.

Fêtes de l'Amour et de Bacchus, Les/The Feasts of Cupid and Bacchus pastorale by Lully (libretto by Quinault, with Molière and I de Benserade), produced Paris, Opéra, 15 November 1672. A pastiche from his and Molière's *comédies-ballets*.

Fêtes de Thalie, Les/Thalia's Feasts opera-ballet by Mouret (libretto by J de Lafont), produced Paris, Opéra, 19 August 1714. Prologue followed by three independent 'entrées' (acts) about love: 'La fille', 'La veuve', 'La femme'.

**Fêtes d'Hébé, Les, ou Les Talens lyriques/
Hebe's Feasts, or The Lyrical Gifts** opera-
ballet by Rameau (libretto by A M de
Montdorge), produced Paris, Opéra, 21 May
1739. Divinities gather on the banks of the
Seine to celebrate gifts to the lyric stage: *La
poésie, La musique, La danse*.

Fétis, François Joseph (1784–1871) Belgian
musicologist. He wrote a *a Biographie universelle des musiciens* 1835–44, an unfinished
Histoire générale de la musique 1869–76, and
many theoretical works. He also wrote
several operas. He is seen as the founder of
modern musical lexicography and probably
the most prolific musicologist ever, though
his work is often highly unreliable.

He was born at Mons, and was trained by
his father and at Paris. He was appointed
organist and professor of music at Douai in
1813; professor at the Paris Conservatory in
1821; and director of the Brussels Conservatory and chapel master to Leopold I in 1833.
In 1827 he founded the Revue Musicale.

Feuersnot/Fire Famine opera by Richard
Strauss (libretto by Ernst von Wolzogen),
produced Dresden, 21 November 1901. As
revenge against the mocking and chaste
Diemut, Konrad casts a spell by which all
the town's lights are extinguished until
Diemut yields to Konrad's desires.

Février, Henri (1875–1957) French composer. He studied under Massenet and Fauré
at the Paris Conservatory.

Works include: the operas *Monna Vanna*
(after Maeterlinck, 1909), *Ghismonda* (1918), *La
Damnation de Blanchefleur, La Femme nue*
(1932), *L'Île désenchantée*, operetta *Sylvette*
(with Delmas); comic operas *Le Roi aveugle,
Agnès dame galante, Carmosine* (after Musset);
songs .

ff abbreviation for ◊fortissimo, very loud.

f holes, or ff holes the sound-holes of
instruments of the ◊violin family, so called
because of their shape.

Fiamma, La/The Flame opera by Respighi
(libretto by C Guastalla after H W Jenssen),
produced Rome, Teatro Reale, 23 January
1934. Silvana, wife of Basilio, falls in love with
her stepson, Donello, using magic to seduce
him. The two are found together; Basilio
drops dead, and Silvana is tried for witchcraft. She realizes the futility of her passion
and is condemned to death.

Fibich, Zdeněk (1850–1900) Czech composer. His music is personal rather than national, and was considerably advanced and
daring for its time. After studying in France

and Germany, and having taught in Poland
for a time, he returned to Czechoslovakia in
1874 and conducted at the National Theatre
in Prague. He retired in 1881 to devote
himself entirely to composition, and wrote
over 600 works of various kinds.

Fibich was born at Šerbořic near Čáslav.
Very precociously gifted, he studied at the
Leipzig Conservatory under Carl Richter and
Salomon Jadassohn (1831–1902), also piano
under Ignaz Moscheles. He also studied in
Paris 1868–69 and Mannheim 1869–70.

He wrote seven operas and a trilogy of
melodramas (spoken text accompanied by
music) entitled *Hippodamia* 1891, the most
ambitious work of the kind ever produced;
also choral works, three symphonies and
other orchestral music, melodramas with
orchestra and with piano, chamber and piano
music, and songs.

Works include: the operas *Bukovin* (1874),
Blaník (1881), *The Bride of Messina* (after
Schiller, 1884), *The Tempest* (after Shakespeare), *Hedy* (after Byron's 'Don Juan'), *Šárka*
(1897), *Pad Arkuna*; melodramas *Christmas
Eve, Eternity, The Water-Sprite, Queen Emma,
Haakon*, and the trilogy *Hippodamia* (1891);
incidental music to Vrchlický's comedy *A
Night at Karlstein*; three symphonies, overtures, symphonic poems *Othello* and *The
Tempest* (both after Shakespeare), and four
others; two string quartets (1874, 1879), piano
quartet, piano trio, quintet for piano, violin,
cello, clarinet, and horn; piano sonata, 350
pieces *Moods, Impressions and Memories* for
piano; songs, vocal duets.

Fida ninfa, La/The Faithful Nymph opera by
Vivaldi (libretto by S Maffei), produced
Verona, Teatro Filarmonico, 6 January 1732.
It was published in Cremona in 1964, in an
edition by R Monterosso. Licori is pursued by
pirate Oralto but remains true to Osmino.

fiddle any instrument from a widespread
family of bowed lutes consisting of one or
more strings stretched the full length of a
fingerboard terminating in a soundbox. The
timbre of a fiddle depends on the resonance
of the soundbox, which depends on the
frequency of the sound vibration. The lower
the frequency (the lower the pitch of the note)
the larger the soundbox needed to produce a
full tone. 'Fiddle' is also the colloquial name
given to instruments of the violin family.

Most fiddles are flat-backed; the 13th-
century **rebec**, however, is tear-shaped and
has a convex back like a lute. Many fiddles
incorporate ◊sympathetic strings which vi-

brate when the string next to them is sounded, enriching the overall effect.

The **American Apache fiddle** has a hollow tubular body, often made of cactus; the **Middle East spike fiddle** rests on the leg and has a dish-shaped soundbox; **African fiddles** take many forms, including the shoe-like rebab; **Asian fiddles** include the Japanese *ko-kiu*, the Mongolian *morinchur*, and the Chinese *erh-hu*. **Medieval and Renaissance fiddles** held at the shoulder are the immediate predecessors of the violin.

In folk fiddle traditions, from the gypsy music of Eastern Europe to US country music, the violin was widely adopted as the successor to the fiddle. In Norway, four sympathetic strings were added to create the Hardanger fiddle.

Fiddler's Child, The, *Šumařovo dítě*, ballad for orchestra by Janáček, after a poem by S Čech, composed 1912. First performed Prague, 14 November 1917.

Fidelio, oder Die eheliche Liebe/Fidelio, or Wedded Love opera by Beethoven (libretto by J Sonnleithner, based on Bouilly's libretto of *Léonore, ou L'Amour conjugal* written for Gaveaux), produced Vienna, Theater an der Wien, 20 November 1805, conductor Beethoven, with the overture *Leonora No.2*; revised version, with overture *Leonora No. 3*, same theatre, 29 March 1806, conductor Seyfried; overture *Leonora No. 1* written for the first performance but abandoned as unsuitable; second revision produced Vienna Kärntnertortheater, 23 May 1814, with *Fidelio* overture in E major. Political prisoner Florestan is rescued by his disguised wife (Leonore/Fidelio) when the evil Pizarro arrives to kill him.

Field, John (1782–1837) Irish-born composer and pianist. He is often regarded as one of a group of composers known as the London Pianoforte School, and all of his works include the piano, reaching their peak artistically with his ◊nocturnes, a genre he named and devised. These anticipate Chopin's nocturnes by 20 years, especially regarding their forward-looking textures and ◊passage work.

As an apprentice to Muzio Clementi, he travelled throughout Europe demonstrating instruments for the firm of piano makers established by his master. In 1803 he settled in St Petersburg, where he composed most of his mature music.

Field was the son of a violinist at the Dublin theatre. He was taught music and the piano by his grandfather, an organist. On

moving to London he was apprenticed to Muzio Clementi, who taught him and at whose piano warehouse he was employed to show off the instruments by improvisation. He made his first public appearance at Giordani's concerts at Dublin in 1792 and in London in 1794. In 1802 Clementi took him to Paris, Germany, and Russia. He left him behind at St Petersburg in 1803, where he became a piano teacher and in 1808 married a Mlle Percheron. In 1822 he settled at Moscow, where he had as great a success as he had had in the new capital. He travelled much as a pianist, visiting London in 1832, and afterwards Paris, Switzerland, and Italy. At Naples he was taken ill and lay in hospital for months until a Russian family took him back to Moscow, where he died soon after his return.

Works include: seven piano concertos (1799–1822); 17 nocturnes, four sonatas and many rondos, fantasies, variations, and other pieces for piano; piano quintet and other chamber music; works for piano duet.

Fielding, Henry (1707–1754)) English novelist and dramatist, author of ballad operas *The Intriguing Chambermaid*, *The Lottery*, *Miss Lucy in Town*, *Don Quixote in England*, and others. His works inspired T A Arne; Monro (*Temple Beau*); *Tom Jones* (Philidor).

Field Mass work by Martinů for baritone, male chorus, and orchestra, composed 1939 in Paris. First performed Prague, 28 February 1946, conductor Kubelik.

Fierrabras/The Braggart opera by Schubert (libretto by Kupelwieser, after Calderón, taken from A W von Schlegel's *Spanisches Theater*), composed 1823, but not performed during Schubert's lifetime; produced Karlsruhe, 9 February 1897. French Roland loves Moorish Princess Florinda; her brother Fierrabras loves Charlemagne's daughter Emma, who in turn loves Eginhard. Moorish leader Boland imprisons Roland and other knights, but Charlemagne arrives victorious to save the day.

Fiery Angel, The/Ogenny Angel opera in five acts by Prokofiev (libretto by composer after novel by V Bryusov), composed 1919–27. First performed (concert) Paris, 25 November 1954; produced Venice, 29 September 1955. Themes from the opera are used in Prokofiev's third symphony, in C minor, op. 33; composed 1928, first performed Paris, 17 May 1929, conductor Monteux. Renata, possessed by the spirit of her former lover, Heinrich, fails to find release in the passion of admirer Ruprecht. She is ordered to be burned when she enters a convent and involves the nuns in diabolic possession.

fifara 17th-century name for the transverse ◊flute, a musical instrument.

fife (German *pfeife*) small transverse ◊flute, originally with finger holes, without keys, and of similar range to the ◊piccolo. Of Swiss origin, the fife is a popular military-band instrument, played with the side drums and associated with historic parades. The name is now used for a military flute in B♭, with six finger holes and several keys.

Fifine at the Fair orchestral fantasy by Bantock on Robert Browning's poem, composed 1901, first performed Birmingham Music Festival 1912.

fifth an interval of five diatonic notes, consisting of three whole tones and a semitone, for example C–G. A fifth is an example of a 'perfect interval' because it remains the same in both major and minor keys. A fifth may be augmented (by one semitone), for example C–G♯, or diminished (by one semitone), for example C–G♭.

Figaro character of dramatic fiction. He made his first appearance in ◊Beaumarchais's plays *The Barber of Seville* 1775, *The Marriage of Figaro* 1784, and *The Other Tartuffe* 1792. Since Beaumarchais's time Figaro has become the type of ingenious roguery, intrigue, and cunning, who displays the utmost sang-froid in all his daring deceptions. He appears conspicuously in Mozart's opera *The Marriage de Figaro* 1786 and Rossini's *The Barber of Seville* 1816, both operas being based on the plays of the same names.

Figaro (Mozart). See ◊*Nozze di Figaro*.

Figlia del reggimento see ◊*Fille du Régiment*.

figuration the persistent use of decorative or accompanying figures of similar type throughout a piece of music.

figure a short musical phrase, especially one that assumes a distinctive character in the course of a composition.

figured bass in 18th-century music, notation of a leading harpsichord or organ part indicating the bass line in standard notation, and the remaining music by numeric chord indications, allowing the player to fill in as necessary.

It arose because the keyboard player often doubled as conductor, and is still practised by session musicians.

figured chorale a hymn-tune setting, especially for organ, in which the plain notes of the melody are surrounded by more rapid patterns of notes, usually all of the same kind of formation.

Figures-Doubles-Prismes work for orchestra by Boulez, first performed Strasbourg, 10 January 1964; an expansion of *Doubles* for orchestra, first performed Paris, 16 March 1958.

filar la voce, or filar il tuono, (Italian; French *filer la voix*, 'spin the voice'; or *filer le son*, 'spin the tone') in singing, to sustain the voice on a long-drawn soft note, without crescendo or diminuendo.

fileuse ('spinner', from *filer*, 'to spin') name of a type of instrumental piece with rapid figurations of various kinds suggesting the motion of a spinning-wheel and often, in its melody, a spinning-song. There are familiar examples by Raff and Fauré (in the latter's incidental music for *Pelléas et Mélisande*), and Mendelssohn's Song without Words, op. 67 No. 4, although not so entitled, conforms to the type, being in fact nicknamed *Spinnerlied* in German, though called *The Bee's Wedding* in English. The prototype of the fileuse was vocal, e.g. the spinning-choruses in Haydn's *Seasons* (Winter) and Wagner's *Flying Dutchman*, Schubert's song *Gretchen am Spinnrade*.

Fille du Régiment, La/The Daughter of the Regiment opera by Donizetti (libretto by J H V de Saint-Georges and J F A Bayard), produced Paris, Opéra-Comique, 11 February 1840. Donizetti's first French opera. Marie, found as an infant, has been brought up by the regiment. Tonio becomes a soldier in order to marry her. After complications by Marie's newly-discovered relatives, all ends happily.

film score in contemporary usage, music specially written to accompany a film on the soundtrack. In the early days of cinema a symphonic poem was composed as a loosely-aligned accompaniment to a major silent film, or background music was improvised or assembled by pit musicians with the aid of a Kinothek theme catalogue. With the arrival of optical sound on film came the fully synchronized Hollywood film score. Composers in the European Romantic tradition, including Erich Korngold, Max Steiner, and Franz Waxman, initially tried to adapt the symphonic style to the faster-moving screen action; a more successful transition was made by animated film music specialists, such as Scott ◊Bradley. After 1950 a younger generation including Alec North and Elmer Bernstein adopted simpler, jazz-oriented idioms.

Composers for silent films include Saint-Saëns, Arthur Honegger, and Edmund Meisel, whose music for Eisenstein's *Battleship Potemkin* 1925 was banned by the authorities. Composers for sound film include Georges Auric, Aaron Copland, Prokofiev, William Walton, Bernard Herrmann, and Ennio Morricone.

Filosofo di campagna, II/The Country Philosopher opera by Galuppi (libretto by Goldoni), produced Venice, Teatro San Samuele, 26 October 1754. Eugenia loves Rinaldo but has been promised to Nardo, whom she has not yet met. Eugenia's sister Lesbina impersonates Eugenia and falls in love with Nardo. Complications are followed by marriage.

final the tonic note of the modes on which the scales of the authentic modes begin and end. In the plagal modes the final is on the fourth above the starting-note. See ◊modes.

final (French 'finale') see ◊finale.

finale a normally fast final movement of a classical four-movement work, or an elaborate conclusion of an opera incorporating a variety of ensembles.

Finck, Hermann (1527–1558) German composer and theorist. He wrote a theoretical book, *Practica musica* in five volumes. Works include motets, sacred songs and wedding songs for several voices.

He studied at the University of Wittenberg, where he taught music from 1554. In 1557 he was appointed organist in Wittenberg, but died the following year at the age of 31.

Fine, Irving (1914–1962) US composer. His music has reflected two of the major trends of the 20th century – Neo-Classicism and atonality.

He studied at Harvard with Walter Piston and in Paris with Boulanger; and taught at Harvard 1939–50 and Brandeis University 1950–62.

Works include: *Toccata concertante* (1948), *Partita* for wind quintet, *Alice in Wonderland*, suite for chorus and orchestra (1949), *Mutability*, six songs for mezzo and piano (1952), string quartet (1952), *Serious Song* (1955), *Blue Towers* for orchestra (1959), *Diversions* for orchestra (1958), *Symphony* (1962).

Fine, Vivian (1913–) US composer and pianist. She studied in Chicago 1919–31 and with Roger Sessions 1934–42. She began performing contemporary piano works in 1931 and taught at Bennington College, Vermont 1964–87.

Works include: the ballet *Alcestis* (1960) and chamber opera *The Woman in the Garden* (1978); *A Guide to the Life Expectancy of a Rose*, for soprano, tenor, and chamber ensemble (1956); *Paen* for narrator, women's voices, and brass ensemble (1969); *Drama for Orchestra* (1982); *Poetic Fires* for piano and orchestra (1984); *After the Tradition* for chamber orchestra (1988).

Fingal's Cave, also called Hebrides concert overture by Mendelssohn, op. 26, composed in recollection of a visit to the Hebrides in 1829, Rome, December 1830; revised version, London, summer 1832. (The first score was entitled *Die einsame Insel/The Lonely Island*).

Finger, Gottfried (or Godfrey) (c. 1660–1730) Moravian composer. Nothing is known of his career until he went to London about 1685, working under the patronage of James II. He left in 1702, piqued at having gained only the fourth prize after John Weldon, John Eccles, and Daniel Purcell for the composition of Congreve's masque *The Judgement of Paris*.

On leaving London he went to Berlin, where he entered the service of Sophia Charlotte, Queen of Prussia. Later he lived in the Palatinate and wrote some operas for Neuburg and Heidelberg.

Works include: the operas *The Virgin Prophetess* (Settle), *Sieg der Schönheit über die Helden* (1706), *L'amicizia in terzo* (in part); masques *The Loves of Mars and Venus* (Motteux, with Eccles) and *The Judgement of Paris* (Congreve, 1701); incidental music (some with D Purcell) for Lee's *Rival Queens*, *The Wive's Excuse*, *Love for Love* and *The Mourning Bride* (both Congreve), *Love at a Loss*, *Love makes a Man* (Cibber), *The Humours of the Age* (Southerne), *Sir Harry Wildair* (Farquhar) and *The Pilgrim* (Vanbrugh); concertos and sonatas for various instruments; pieces for violin and flute (with Banister), and other pieces.

fingerboard in string instruments, the upper surface and continuation of the neck, against which the fingers press the strings to alter their length and therefore their pitch.
Violins have smooth fingerboards, allowing the player scope to alter the pitch continuously; other instruments, such as the guitar and lute, have ◊frets attached or inlaid to regulate intonation.

fingered tremolo see ◊tremolo.

fingering notation directing the player to use specific fingers on specific notes. In piano music '1' represents the thumb, '2' the index finger, and so on. In orchestral string music

'1' represents the index finger, '2' the middle finger, and so on.

finite canon a canon sung through once, without repetition of its phrases.

Finke, Fidelio Friedrich (1891–1968) German composer. He became inspector of the German music schools in Czechoslovakia in 1920 and director of the German Academy of Music in Prague in 1927.

He studied at the Prague Conservatory with his uncle Romeo Fidelio and with Vitězslav Novák for composition. He taught there from 1915.

Works include: the opera *Die Jacobsfahrt* (1936); *Pan* symphony, overture, and other works for orchestra; two string quartets.

Finlandia symphonic poem for orchestra by Sibelius, op. 26, composed in 1899 (revised 1900; first performed Helsinki, 2 July 1900). It has become a work for national celebrations in Finland, being based on material sounding like Finnish patriotic songs, the whole of which, however, is the composer's own invention, not folk music.

Finney, Ross Lee (1906–   ) US composer. His compositions have attempted a reconciliation between tonal and serial music.

He was educated at Carleton College, Minnesota, and studied music at Minnesota University and later in Paris and Vienna with Nadia Boulanger and Alban Berg; he also studied with Roger Sessions at Harvard University.

Works include: Overture to a Social Drama for orchestra; four symphonies (1942–72); piano concerto, violin concerto; *John Brown* for tenor, male chorus, and chamber orchestra; eight string quartets (1935–60), piano trio; violin and piano sonata; four piano sonatas; eight Poems for soprano, tenor, and piano.

Finnissy, Michael (1946–   ) English composer. He studied at the Royal College of Music with Bernard Stevens and Humphrey Searle. He taught in the music department at the London School of Contemporary Dance 1969–74.

Works include: the operas *The Undivine Comedy* (Paris 1988) and *Thérèse Raquin* (London 1993); *Mysteries*, eight separately performable music theatre pieces with Latin texts from the Bible: 1. *The Parting of Darkness*, 2. *The Earthly Paradise*, 3. *Noah and the Great Flood*, 4. *The Prophecy of Daniel*, 5. *The Parliament of Heaven*, 6. *The Annunciation*, 7. *The Betrayal and Crucifixion*, 8. *The Deliverance of Souls*; *Orfeo* for soloists and instruments (1975), *Mr Punch* for voice and instruments

(1977), *Vaudeville* for mezzo, baritone, instruments, and percussion (1983); seven piano concertos (two for piano alone), *Offshore* for orchestra, *Pathways of Sun and Stars* for orchestra (1976); *Jeanne d'Arc* for soprano, tenor, cello, and small orchestra (1971), *Babylon* for mezzo and ensemble, *Sir Tristan* for soprano and ensemble (1979), *Ngano* for mezzo, tenor, chorus, flute, and percussion (1984); string trio (1986); *Red Earth* (1988) and *Eph-phatha* (1989) for orchestra; *Obrecht Motetten* I–IV for various instrumental groups (1989–92); *In stiller Nacht* for violin, cello, and piano (1990); *Cambridge Codex* for flute, violin, cello, and two bells (1991); *Two Motets* for countertenor and guitar (1992); *Nine Romantics* for piano (1992); string quartet (1986).

Finta giardiniera, La/The Pretended Garden-Girl opera by Anfossi (libretto by R de Calzabigi), produced Rome, Teatro delle Dame, Carnival 1774.

Opera by Mozart (libretto ditto), produced Munich, 13 January 1775. Count Belfiore has fled, believing he has killed Countess Violante in a quarrel. However, she seeks him amorously, disguised as Sandrina, a gardener.

Finta semplice, La/The Pretended Simpleton opera by Mozart (libretto by M Coltellini), composed for Vienna, 1768, but not performed there; produced Salzburg, 1 May 1769). Fracasso and Simone marry Giacinta and Ninetta, as Giacinta's brothers fall for the Baroness Rosina, sister of Fracasso.

Finte gemelle, Les/The Pretended Twins opera by Piccinni (libretto by G Petrosellini), produced Rome, Teatro Valle, 2 January 1771.

Finto Stanislao, Il/The False Stanislas opera by Gyrowetz (libretto by F Romani), produced Milan, La Scala, 5 August 1818. The libretto was used by Verdi in 1840 for *Un giorno di Regno*.

Finzi, Gerald (1901–1956) English composer. His music owes something to English pastoral traditions, but more to his literary heritage: settings of Milton, Crashaw, Shakespeare, and Traherne show a vivid response to verbal imagery.

Finzi was born in London. He studied privately with Edward Bairstow and R O Morris. He was professor of composition at the Royal Academy of Music, London 1930–33, and afterwards went to live in the country to give his whole time to composition.

Works include: incidental music for Shakespeare's *Love's Labour's Lost*; festival anthem (Crashaw), *Intimations of Immortality* (Wordsworth, about 1938, revised 1950) and *For St Cecilia* (Edmund Blunden) for chorus and orchestra; three Elegies (Drummond) and seven part songs (Robert Bridges) for unaccompanied chorus, *New Year Music* for orchestra, *Romance* for strings; *Introit* for violin and small orchestra, concerto for clarinet and strings (1949), cantata *Dies Natalis* (Traherne) for high voice and orchestra (1926–39), *Farewell to Arms* (Ralph Knevet and George Peele) for tenor and small orchestra, two Sonnets by Milton for ditto; *Interlude* for oboe and string quartet, Prelude and Fugue for string trio; five Bagatelles for clarinet and piano; Thomas Hardy song cycles *By Footpath and Stile* for baritone and string quartet (1922), *A Young Man's Exhortation* (1926–29), *Earth and Air and Rain* and *Before and After Summer*; five Shakespeare songs, *Let us Garlands Bring*.

Fioravanti, Valentino (1764–1837) Italian composer. He was a pupil of Sala at one of the Naples Conservatories. He produced his first opera in Rome in 1784, worked as conductor at Lisbon from 1803 and visited Paris in 1807, returning to Italy to become maestro di cappella at St Peter's in Rome.

Works include: the operas *Le avventure di Bertoldino* (1784), *Le cantatrici villane* (1799), *I virtuosi ambulanti* (1807), *Ogni eccesso è vizioso* and 66 others; church music .

fioritura (Italian 'flowerings, flourishes, decorations') in music, ornamental figures elaborating a plainer melodic passage, either according to the composer's notation or improvised according to the performer's invention.

fipple flute a term describing a whistle, such as the Baroque ◊recorder, that has a plug or 'fipple' inserted in the mouthpiece to direct the flow of air precisely at the aerofoil.

Firebird, The/Zhar Ptitsa ballet by Stravinsky (choreography by Fokin), produced Paris, Opéra, 25 June 1910, conductor Gabriel Pierné.

'Fire Symphony' nickname of a symphony by Haydn, No. 59, in A major, composed c. 1766–68.

Fireworks fantasy for large orchestra by Stravinsky, composed 1908 to celebrate the marriage of Nadezhda Rimsky-Korsakov, his teacher's daughter, to Maximilian Steinberg, St Petersburg 17 June 1908. The score was revised for smaller forces and performed 22 January 1910.

'Fireworks Music' Handel's *Music for the Royal Fireworks*, a suite of pieces originally for wind band, was composed for the celebrations of the Peace of Aix-la-Chapelle, first performed London, Green Park, 27 April 1749.

Firsova, Elena (1950–) Russian composer. Her music is in a variety of instrumental forms, many of them small scale, and was first heard outside the USSR in Paris and Venice in 1979. She made her British debut in 1980 with *Petraca's Sonnets* 1976.

She studied at the Moscow Conservatory, and has learned from Edison Denisov. One of several composers who chose to live in the West after the collapse of Communism, she was professor and composer-in-residence at Keele University, Lancashire, in 1993.

Works include: the operas *Feast in Time of Plague* (1972) and *The Nightingale and the Rose* (1991); cello concerto (1973), two violin concertos (1976, 1983), four chamber concertos (1978, 1982, 1985, 1988), concerto for violin and 13 strings (1993); *Chamber Music* (1973), *Stanzas* (1975), *Autumn Music* (1988) and *Cassandra* (1993) for orchestra; four string quartets (1970, 1974, 1980 – in memoriam Igor Stravinsky – and 1989); *Spring Sonata* for flute and piano (1982); *The Night Demons* for cello and piano (1993); *Petraca's Sonnets* for voice and ensemble (1976) and settings of Pasternak, Mayakovsky, Mandelstam, and Shakespeare for voice and instruments; *Silentium* for mezzo and string quartet (1991), *Distance* for voice, clarinet, and string quartet (1992); *Music for 12* (1986) and *Odyssey* for ensemble (1990); *Before the Thunderstorm* for soprano and ten instruments (1995); piano sonata (1986).

first-movement form term sometimes used for 'sonata form'; however, there are some first sonata movements in other forms (variations) while there are any number of slow movements and still more of finales in regular sonata form.

'First of May, The' symphony no. 3 in E♭, op. 20, by Shostakovich. The finale is a choral tribute to International Workers' Day (text by S Kirsanov) but the first performance in Leningrad on 21 January 1930 did not gain official approval. Shostakovich met with further trouble in his next work, *Lady Macbeth of the Mtsensk District*, denounced in *Pravda* and by Stalin.

Fischer, Edwin (1886–1960) Swiss pianist and conductor. In addition to his activities as a soloist he also conducted orchestras in Lübeck, Munich, and Berlin. He edited a number of early keyboard works and wrote books on Bach and on Beethoven's piano sonatas.

He studied at the Basel Conservatory, where he later taught for several years. He returned to Switzerland in 1942 and was a successful teacher in Lucerne and elsewhere.

Fischer, Johann Caspar Ferdinand (c. 1665–1746) German composer. From 1692 he was Kapellmeister to the Margrave of Baden in Schlackenwerth (Bohemia) and Rastatt. His keyboard music includes *Ariadne Musica* 1715, a series of 20 preludes and fugues, each in a different key, and thus a precursor of Bach's *Das Wohltemperierte Clavier*.

Other works include *Musicalisches Blumen-Büschlein* (a collection of keyboard suites in the French style), *Musicalischer Parnassus* (nine suites named after the Muses), *Blumenstrauss* (organ preludes and fugues on the eight modes), *Le Journal de Printemps* (suite for orchestra with trumpets *ad lib*), and church music.

Fischietti, Domenico (c. 1720–c. 1810) Italian composer. He was a pupil of Durante and Leo in Naples, where he produced his first opera 1742. He worked as conductor in Prague, then became Kapellmeister in Dresden 1766–72, and at Salzburg Cathedral 1772–79.

Works include: the operas *Lo Speziale* (with V Pallavicini, 1754), *Il Signor Dottore*, *Il Mercato di Malmantile*, *La Ritornata di Londra* (all on libretti by Goldoni) and c. 20 others; church music.

Fišer, Luboš (1935–) Czech composer. He studied in Prague, where his two operas, *Lancelot* and *The Good Soldier Schweik*, were produced 1961 and 1962. He emigrated to the USA 1971 and became composer-in-residence with the US Wind Symphony Orchestra at Pittsburgh. His music often returns to myth and religion for inspiration.

Works include: the ballet *Changing Game* (1972); two symphonies (1956, 1960); 15 Prints after Dürer's *Apocalypse*, for orchestra (1965); *Requiem* (1968); *Lament over the Destruction of the City of Ur*, for soloists, narrators, chorus and bells (1969); *Kretzer Etude* for chamber orchestra (1974); *Serenade for Salzburg* (1977); *Albert Einstein* for organ and orchestra (1979); piano concerto (1980); *Centaurs* for orchestra (1983); string quartet (1955), cello sonata (1975), piano trio (1978), and five piano sonatas (1955–78).

Fitelberg, Jerzy (1903–1951) Polish-born US composer. He played percussion in his father's orchestra as a boy and studied composition at the Warsaw Conservatory and under Schreker in Berlin. He settled in Paris in 1933 and in New York in 1940. His fourth string quartet (1937) received an Elizabeth Sprague Coolidge award.

Works include: Concert Pieces, *Sinfonietta* (1946), *Polish Pictures*, *Nocturne* and two suites for orchestra, symphony for strings, piano, harp and percussion, concerto for strings; two piano concertos (1929, 1934), two violin concertos, cello concerto; five string quartets (1926–45), string trio, woodwind quintet; Suite for violin and piano, sonatina for two violins, duo for violin and cello, sonata for cello solo; piano sonata and pieces.

Fitzwilliam Virginal Book manuscript collection of 297 mainly English 17th-century compositions for keyboard instruments copied by Francis Tregian and acquired by Richard Fitzwilliam (1745–1816) who bequeathed it to Cambridge University. Among composers represented are William Byrd, John Bull, and Giles Farnaby.

Five Movements for String Quartet work by Webern; composed 1909, first performed Vienna, 8 February 1910. Version for string orchestra 1929, first performed Philadelphia, 26 March 1930.

Five Orchestral Pieces/Fünf Orchesterstücke work for large orchestra by Schoenberg, op. 16, composed 1909 revised 1922; first performed London, 3 September 1912, conductor Wood. Schoenberg gave the five pieces the titles *Premonitions*, *The Past*, *Chord-Colours*, *Peripetie*, *Endless Recitative*.

Schoenberg's pupil, Webern, wrote Five Pieces for orchestra 1911–13, first performed Zurich, Innternational Society for Contemporary Music (ISCM) concert, 22 June 1926 (four of the five pieces last for less than one minute). Webern's five posthumous pieces for orchestra (1913) were performed Cologne, 13 January 1969.

Five, The, also known as The Mighty Five or The Mighty Handful (Russian *Moguchaya kuchka*) term applied by art critic Vladimir Stasov (1824–1906) to the St Petersburg group of five composers – Mily Balakirev, Alexander Borodin, César Cui, Modest Mussorgsky, and Nicolai Rimsky-Korsakov – whose establishment of a distinctively Russian nationalist idiom he promoted.

Five Tudor Portraits choral suite by Vaughan Williams on poems by Skelton. 1. Ballad, *The Tunning of Elinor Rumming*; 2. Intermezzo, *My Pretty Bess*; 3. Burlesca, *Epitaph on John Jayberd of Diss*; 4. Romanza, *Jane Scroop: Her*

Lament for Philip Sparrow; 5. Scherzo, *Jolly Rutterkin*. For mezzo-soprano, baritone, chorus, and orchestra, first performed Norwich Festival, 25 September 1936.

Flackton, William (1709–1798) English organist and composer. He was a bookseller, but played the organ and violin, and also taught and composed harpsichord and string music, including works for viola.

flageolet musical instrument, a whistle flute of tapered bore popular in France and England as a town-band instrument during the 17th–19th centuries.

flam on the ◊side drum, a double stroke, as distinct from a roll.

flamenco generic term applied to a particular body of *cante* (song), *baile*, (dance) and *toque* (solo guitar music) from Andalusia in southern Spain. It has attracted worldwide interest and flamenco clubs can be found in places as far apart as the USA, Japan, and Germany, as well as all the major cities throughout Spain. It is also known as *cante gitano* (gypsy song) and *cante hondo* (deep song). Despite the varied conjectures concerning its origin, consensus points to the early history and development of *cante flamenco* to Andalusia.

flat a note or a key that is played lower in pitch than the written value, indicated by the ♭ sign or key signature. It can also refer to inaccurate intonation by a player.

flautando (Italian 'fluting') in music, a flute-like tone produced by drawing the bow lightly over the strings of a violin, near the end of the fingerboard.

flautino (Italian 'little flute') small ◊recorder, either the descant recorder or the flageolet, also called *flauto piccolo* in the early 18th century (for example in Handel's *Rinaldo*).

flauto traverso the transverse ◊flute, that is the modern flute held horizontally. as distinct from the recorders and similar flutes played vertically.

Flavio, rè de' Longobardi/Flavius, King of the Lombards opera by Handel (libretto by N F Haym, partly based on P Corneille's *Cid*), produced London, King's Theatre, Haymarket, 14 May 1723. Set in a mythical Britain; Guido kills the father of his lover Emilia in a duel; King Flavio restores Guido to her after his execution is threatened.

Flavius Bertaridus, König der Longobarden/Flavius Bertaridus, King of the Lombards opera by Telemann (libretto by C G Wendt), produced Hamburg, Theater beim Gänsemarkt, 23 November 1729.

flebile Italian 'plaintive, mournful'.

Flecha, Mateo (1481–c. 1553) Spanish monk and composer. He was a pupil of Juan Castelló at Barcelona, and became maestro de capilla to the Infantas of Castile, the daughters of Charles V. He later became a Carmelite and settled in the monastery of Poblet.

Flecha, Mateo (1530–1604) Spanish monk and composer. He was taught by his uncle Mateo ◊Flecha (1).Works by the two Flechas (not always distinguishable) include church music, madrigals, *ensaladas* (burlesque madrigals), and other pieces. A stage work of his, *El Parnaso*, is believed to have been performed at Madrid in 1561.

He was in the service of the Emperor Charles V until 1558 and of Philip II. He then went to Prague in the service of the Emperor Maximilian, and after the Emperor's death in 1576 he remained there until 1599. After this he joined the abbey of Solsona as a Franciscan monk.

Fledermaus, Die/The Flittermouse, The Bat operetta by J Strauss, junior (libretto by C Haffner and R Genée, based on a French vaudeville, *Le Réveillon*, by H Meilhac and L Halévy, taken from a German comedy, *Das Gefängnis*, by R Benedix), produced Vienna, Theater an der Wien, 5 April 1874. Rosalinde, husband Eisenstein, and lover Alfred mixed up in a practical joke at Prince Orlofsky's ball.

Flem, Paul Le see ◊Le Flem.

flicorno Italian brass instrument used in military bands, corresponding to the ◊saxhorn and ◊flugelhorn.

Fliegende Holländer, Der/The Flying Dutchman opera by Wagner (libretto by composer, based on Heine's *Memoiren des Herrn von Schnabelewopski*, Marryat's novel *The Phantom Ship* and other sources), produced Dresden, 2 January 1843. Dutchman condemned by blasphemy to sail his ship forever until redeemed by the love of a faithful woman; Senta is ready to die for him.

Flood, The musical play by Stravinsky (text by Robert Craft from Genesis and the York and Chester miracle plays); composed 1961–62, first performed Colombia Broadcasting System (CBS) TV, 14 June 1962. First stage performance Hamburg, 30 April 1963, conductor Craft.

Florentinische Tragödie, Eine opera in one act by Zemlinsky (text from the blank-verse drama *A Florentine Tragedy* by Wilde, in German translation by M Meyerfeld); composed 1915–16, produced Stuttgart, 30 January 1917, conductor Max von Schillings. Performed in a Hamburg Opera production 1983 at Edinburgh and in 1985 at Covent Garden. Jealous husband Simone kills Guido in a duel and is reunited with wife Bianca over the corpse.

Florida suite for orchestra by Delius, composed 1886–87 and dedicated to the people of Florida (it had been Delius's ambition to become an orange planter). Performed privately in Leipzig 1888; first public performance London, 1 April 1937, conductor Beecham. Not published until 1963. The four movements are titled *Daybreak*, *By the River*, *Sunset*, and *At Night*.

Floridante, Il opera by Handel (libretto by R A Rolli), produced London, King's Theatre, Haymarket, 9 December 1721. Floridante loves Elmira, adopted daughter of usurper King Oronte. Oronte also loves Elmira, and threatens Floridante with death. At the last moment Oronte is overpowered; Floridante and Elmira become king and queen.

Flos Campi/Flower of the Field work by Vaughan Williams in six movements for viola, wordless chorus, and small orchestra, first performed London 10 October 1925, with Lionel Tertis, conductor Wood.

Floss der Medusa, Das/The Raft of the Medusa 'popular and military oratorio' by Henze (text by E Schnabel), for soloists, chorus, and orchestra, dedicated to the memory of Ché Guevara. The projected first performance in Hamburg on 9 December 1968 had to be cancelled when members of the chorus, revolting students, and the police came into conflict. First performed (concert) Vienna 29 January 1971; stage production Nuremberg, 15 April 1972. The *Medusa* of the title was a French frigate abandoned at sea in 1816. The officers escaped in lifeboats and cut adrift the entire crew on a single raft.

Flothuis, Marius (1914–   ) Dutch composer. He was artistic director of the Concertgebouw Orchestra 1955–74; and was appointed professor of musicology at the University of Utrecht in 1974.

He studied with Hans Brandts-Buys.

Works include: concertos for flute, horn, violin, chamber orchestra; *Sinfonietta Concertante* for clarinet, saxophone, and chamber orchestra; cello sonata; *Partita* for two violins (1966), *Romeo's Lament* for horn (1975), *Hommage à Mallarmé* for voice, flute, cello, and piano (1980), sonata for oboe, horn, and harpsichord (1986), *Preludio e Fughetta* for three trumpets (1986).

Flotow, Friedrich Adolf Ferdinand, Freiherr von (1812–1883) German composer. He wrote 18 operas, including *Martha* 1847.

Flotow was born at Teutendorf, the son of a nobleman. He went to Paris in 1827 and studied music under Antonín Reicha and others. He began to produce operas at aristocratic houses and wrote incidental music for the play *Alessandro Stradella* at the Palais-Royal in 1837 (it was enlarged into an opera in 1844). Over the next two years he contributed musical numbers to Albert Grisar's operas *Lady Melvill* 1838 and *L'Eau Merveilleuse* 1839, and in 1839 he made his first public stage success with *Le Naufrage de la Méduse*, based on an incident in 1816 involving a French ship whose crew were left adrift on a raft while the officers escaped in lifeboats.

His greatest success came with *Martha*, produced at Vienna in 1887; its blend of German sentiment and Italian ardour made it popular for many years in Europe and at the New York Metropolitan Opera House. He was intendant of the court theatre at Schwerin 1856–63. He then returned to Paris, but went to live near Vienna in 1868.

Works include: French, German, and Italian operas, including *Le Naufrage de la Méduse*; 1839), *L'Esclave de Camoëns* (1843), *Stradella* (1844), *L'Âme en Peine*, *Martha* (1847), *Rübezahl*, *L'Ombre*, *Il Fior d'Harlem*, *Rob Roy* (after Scott); ballets *Lady Henriette* (with Burgmüller and Deldevez, on which *Martha* was based later), *Die Libelle*, and *Tannkönig*; incidental music to Shakespeare's *A Winter's Tale* (1859); *Fackeltanz*, overtures, and other pieces for orchestra; chamber music, songs.

flourish in old English, a fanfare, but in modern music terminology a short figure used as an embellishment rather than as a theme.

Floyd, Carlisle (1926–   ) US composer. His first opera, *Susannah*, was produced at the University of Houston in 1955 and at New York City Opera in 1956; it has since become one of the most widely produced of all US operas.

He studied at Syracuse University and privately with Rudolf Firkušny.

Other stage works include *Wuthering Heights* (Santa Fe, 1958), *The Passion of Jonathan Wade* (New York , 1962), *The Sojourner and Mollie Sinclair* (Raleigh, S Carolina, 1963), *Markheim* (New Orleans, 1966), *Of Mice and Men*, after Steinbeck (Seattle, 1970), *Bilby's Doll* (Houston, 1976), *Willie Stark* (Houston, 1981), *All the King's Men* (1981).

flue pipes the majority of pipes in an ◊organ, which generate sound by directing air over a narrow rigid edge (as when a person blows across the top of a bottle). The other pipes are known as reeds.

Flügel (German 'wing') German name for the grand ◊piano, which is wing-shaped.

flugelhorn valved brass instrument of the ◊bugle type. It is made in three sizes: soprano, alto, and tenor, and is used in military and brass bands. In Britain only the alto instrument, in B♭, is used, normally only in brass bands. The alto flugelhorn has a similar range to the cornet but is of mellower tone.

flute, or transverse flute side-blown woodwind instrument of considerable antiquity. The flute is difficult to master but capable of intricate melodies and expressive tonal shading. The player blows across an end hole, the air current being split by the opposite edge, which causes pressure waves to form within the tube. The fingers are placed over holes in the tube to create different notes. The standard soprano flute has a range of three octaves or more.

The instrument originated in Asia about 900 BC. European flutes can be traced back to about 1100, and include the military fife, subsequently developed by the Hotteterre family of instrument-makers into the single-key Baroque flute. Today's orchestral chromatic flutes with extensive keywork derive from further modifications in the 19th century by Theobald Boehm. Now more usually made of metal (even silver, gold, or platinum) than wood, they include the soprano flute in C4, the higher piccolo in C5, the alto in G3, and the bass flute in C3, a rarity in the orchestra but much in vogue during the avant-garde 1950s as a concert instrument and an evocative accompaniment to films of the **nouvelle vague** era.

The flute has an extensive concert repertoire, including familiar pieces by J S Bach, Mozart, and the pastoral refrain of Debussy's *L'Après-midi d'un faun/Afternoon of a Faun* 1894. Vivaldi wrote a number of concertos for piccolo, and Maderna has composed for alto and bass flutes. Performers include James Galway and the Italian Severino Gazzelloni (1919–).

The compass of the flute.

flûte à bec (French 'beak flute') French name for the fipple flute, flageolet, or ◊recorder, a musical instrument.

flûte douce (French 'sweet flute') alternative name for the ◊recorder, a musical instrument.

flutter-tonguing a technique used mainly in playing the flute and clarinet, in which the player rolls an R while playing, creating a fluttering tone.

Flying Dutchman see ◊*Fliegende Holländer*, and ◊*Vaisseau-fantôme*.

Foerster, Josef Bohuslav (1859–1951) Czech composer. He held various appointments as organist, teacher, and critic. He wrote six operas, incidental music for plays, church and secular choral music, five symphonies and other orchestral works, two violin concertos and a cello concerto, chamber music, numerous piano pieces and songs, and about 30 recitations with piano accompaniment.

Foerster was born at Dětenice, Bohemia, and studied at Prague Organ School. From 1893 he lived for ten years at Hamburg, where he worked as a music teacher and critic and his wife, Berta Foerster-Lauterer (1869–1936), sang at the opera. After 1903 they lived in Vienna, where he taught at the Conservatory, but from 1918 until his retirement in 1931 he was professor of composition in Prague.

Works include: the operas *Deborah* (1893), *Eva*, *Jessica* (on Shakespeare's *Merchant of Venice*, 1905), *The Invincibles*, *The Heart*, *The Fool*; incidental music for Vrchlický's *Samson*, Strindberg's *Lucky Peter's Journey*, Schiller's *Maria Stuart*, and other plays; *Stabat Mater* and other works for chorus and orchestra, five symphonies (1887–1929), six suites, four symphonic poems, and two overtures for orchestra; two violin concertos; five string quartets, three piano trios, quintet for wind instruments; two violin and piano sonatas, cello and piano sonata; works for piano, organ, and harmonium; ten recitations with piano accompaniment; songs, part songs.

Fogliano, Ludovico (died after 1538) Italian music theorist and composer, brother of Giacomo Fogliano. He sang in the papal chapel and was choirmaster at Modena Cathedral. His *Musica Theorica* was published in 1529, and a single *frottola* was included in Ottaviano Petrucci's ninth book, published in 1508.

Folia, La/The Folly in music, term used for melody found in popular dances and songs of the Baroque period. First mentioned by Francisco de Salinas in 1577, the melody was first used as the basis for variations in 1604 and later variations have been by Corelli, Albicastro and Marais (c. 1700), A Scarlatti and C P E Bach (1778). Liszt uses the theme in his *Rhapsodie Espagnole*, Rakhmaninov in his *Variations on a theme of Corelli*, (dedicated to Fritz Kreisler, first performed Montreal, 12 October 1931), and Henze in *Aria de la folia española* (1977).

folk music traditional music, especially from rural areas, which is passed on by listening and repeating, and is usually performed by amateurs. The term is used to distinguish it from the ◊classical music of a country, and from urban popular or commercial music. Most folk music exists in the form of songs, or instrumental music to accompany folk dancing, and is usually melodic and rhythmic rather than harmonic in style.

Each country has its own styles of folk music, based on distinctive ◊scales and ◊modes, and often played on instruments associated with that culture alone, such as the Scottish ◊bagpipes, the Russian ◊balalaika, or the Australian ◊didjeridu. A number of composers of classical music have used folk music in their own pieces to give them a particular national character, and in the late 19th century the use of folk tunes was a prominent feature of ◊nationalism in music.

In the 20th century a number of people, such as the composers Zoltán ◊Kodály and Béla ◊Bartók, and the musicologists Cecil ◊Sharp and Alan Lomax, have transcribed and recorded folk music to preserve it for the future. Since World War II, a renewed interest – especially among young people – led to a 'folk revival'. Traditional folk music was performed to a much wider audience, and songwriters such as Pete Seeger, Joan Baez, and Bob Dylan composed popular songs in a folk style.

Elements of folk music have also been combined with rock and pop music, and form an important part of world music.

folk *vs* classical The term 'folk music' is generally used to describe music of an aural/oral tradition performed by amateurs, particularly in rural areas, to distinguish it from the classical, urban, or commercial music of a particular country or culture. This definition, however, makes it only relevant to cultures that have a classical, art music tradition (such as China, India, Europe, and North America); other countries tend not to recognize the distinction. The influence of western music

around the world, and in particular western popular music, has thrown the traditional music of many countries into sharp contrast; this nonwestern music has recently been categorized with genuine folk music as world music or roots music.

origins All music is thought to have its beginnings in storytelling, worksongs, and ritual, and these are the basic forms still prevalent in folk music around the world. The ballad, often unaccompanied, is the most common genre of folk song, and probably evolved as a means of memorizing traditional stories to be passed on from generation to generation. The worksong was used to establish a regular rhythmic accompaniment to repetitive physical work, often in a call and response pattern. Instrumental folk music is usually restricted to accompaniment for folk dance, and has its roots in rituals – especially those associated with specific events in the rural calendar such as harvest, midwinter, and the beginning of spring.

the study of folk music In Europe at the end of the 19th century there was a resurgence of interest in folk music, partly because of a fear that it might be lost to posterity in face of increasing urbanization, and partly to establish 'schools' of composition with some form of national identity to distinguish them from the mainstream (that is, Germanic) classical music of the time. There was also a wider interest in music of other cultures, which led to the establishment of the new discipline of ethnomusicology. As the 20th century progressed, organizations began to form for the preservation and study of folk music, and musicologists transcribed and later recorded performances of traditional folk music from all over the world. In 1931, the first international folk festival was held in Copenhagen, Denmark. Many such festivals are now held in almost every country in the world. Internationally, folk songs and music are studied and published by the International Folk Music Council, founded in 1947, and the Society for Ethnomusicology, founded in 1956.

folk music in the British Isles Interest in ballad poetry in the late 18th century led to the discovery of a rich body of folk song in Europe, but it was not until the late 19th century that there was any systematic collection of folk music. In England, this was seen in the transcription and preservation of folk tunes by such people as the Rev Sabine Baring-Gould and Cecil ◊Sharp. The Folk Song Society was founded in 1898 and became the English Folk Dance and Song

Society in 1911. In true Victorian fashion, they bowdlerized much of the material they collected, and edited out much of the sophisticated ornamentation and rhythmic complexity, which they felt to be 'primitive', or simply poor performance. The collection of folk music continued through the first half of the 20th century, with important contributions made by Ralph ◊Vaughan Williams (whose collections not only influenced his own music but have been a significant source to the present day), A L Lloyd, and Ewan MacColl; and a unique and invaluable collection gathered by several generations of the Copper family of Sussex. Although recognizably different styles of folk music can be seen within the countries of the British Isles, a rough classification can be made by national boundaries: English, Scottish, Irish, and Welsh folk music all have distinctive characteristics.

In England, folk song is generally in the ballad tradition, either unaccompanied or with a simple concertina or melodeon accompaniment, and, typically for a maritime nation, there is also a large number of shanties. The two folk-dance traditions, Morris dancing and country dance and their many regional variations, each have their own associated tunes, usually played on a pipe and drum, fiddle, or concertina.

Scottish folk music can be divided roughly into two styles: Highland (associated with the Gaelic language), and Lowland (associated with the Scots language). Unusually for a true oral folk tradition, most Scottish folk songs are by known composers and poets whose names have been passed down with their songs, which are mainly in the form of unaccompanied ballads. Instrumental music includes dance music for fiddle and concertina, and a uniquely Scottish genre, the pibroch, a form of theme and variations specifically for the bagpipes.

Irish folk song can similarly be divided according to language, with distinct musical traditions for both Irish and English lyrics. Dances such as the jig and the reel are typical in Irish instrumental music, and are played on the fiddle and pipe, and Irish versions of the harp and bagpipes, almost invariably with the rhythmic accompaniment of the bodhrán, a kind of drum. Much of the traditional repertoire has been preserved and played by groups such as the Chieftains.

Although there is a long tradition of musical culture in Wales, very little true folk music has survived. Welsh traditional music, like Scottish folk music, is mostly by known poets and composers, but because of its association with the Bardic culture, this is perhaps more accurately regarded as a classical rather than a folk culture.

folk revival in the UK The post-World War II folk revival in the USA had a counterpart in the UK, with both a renewed interest in traditional folk music and a new generation of songwriters and performers in a folk style. The 1960s saw the appearance of performers in many different folk styles: the Watersons, who popularized traditional unaccompanied folk singing; groups such as Pentangle and the Incredible String Band, and the singer Donovan produced new music in a folk style; and folk-rock bands such as Fairport Convention and Steeleye Span brought some of the folk repertoire to a new audience by performing using the instruments of the rock band, as well as introducing new songs in a folk idiom. This folk revival continued through the 1980s, and was furthered by rock guitarist Richard Thompson and such groups as the Pogues (formed 1983), while the singer/songwriter Billy Bragg continued in the tradition of the political protest song. In recent years, there has been a growing interest in roots, or world, music, encompassing traditional as well as modern music from many cultures.

Bibliography: Grove Dictionary of Music and Musicians Oxford Dictionary of Music, Larousse Encyclopedia of Music, Oxford Companion to Popular Music, Penguin Encyclopedia of Popular Music.

folksong (◊Volkslied), a traditional song of often great but indeterminate antiquity, whose origins and composer are unknown, but which has been preserved by being handed down orally from generation to generation, often in several different versions or corruptions.

Folquet de Marseille (died 1231) Provençal ◊troubadour. His output consists mainly of love songs, sober in tone and moralizing in content. The son of a wealthy merchant, he became a Cistercian monk and, in 1205, bishop of Toulouse, in which capacity he was a notorious persecutor of the Albigensian heretics.

Fomin, Evstigney Ipatovich (1761–1800) Russian composer. He studied under Martini at Bologna and later became conductor in St Petersburg. His opera *The Americans* is about the Spanish conquest of the Americas.

Works include: the melodrama *Orfey i Evridika* (1792) and operas *Boyeslav* (1786),

Orpheus (1792), *Clorinda and Milo, The Americans* (1800), *The Golden Apple*.

Foote, Arthur (William) (1853–1937) US organist and composer. He held organ appointments at Boston for many years. His compositions are chiefly chamber and choral pieces, and include *A Night Piece* for flute and strings 1922.

He studied at the New England Conservatory at Boston and later with John Paine at Harvard.

Works include: cantatas on Longfellow's 'The Farewell of Hiawatha' (1885), 'The Wreck of the Hesperus' (1887), and 'The Skeleton in Armour' (1891); overture *In the Mountains*, prologue to *Francesca da Rimini*, and three suites for orchestra; cello concerto; three string quartets (1883–1901), piano quartet, piano quintet, two piano trios; choral works; organ and piano pieces; songs.

Ford, Thomas (c. 1580–1648) English lutenist and composer. He was in the service of Henry, Prince of Wales in 1611, and was appointed one of the musicians to Charles I in 1626.

Works include: *Musick of Sundrie Kindes* (1607) with airs to the lute (also to be performed in four vocal parts), catches and rounds; two anthems contributed to Leighton's *Teares and Lamentacions* and others including *Miserere my Maker*, dances for lute.

forefall see ◊appoggiatura ('from below').

foreground see ◊structural level.

Forest (died c. 1446) English composer, possibly the John Forest who was canon and later dean of Wells, dying there in 1446. His motet *Qualis est dilectus tuus* was included (together with the beginning of *Ascendit Christus*, ascribed to Dunstable in a continental manuscript) among the latest additions to the Old Hall manuscript. Other sacred music survives in continental sources.

forlana, or furlana an old Italian dance in 6–8 time. A classical example of its use is in Bach's Overture (Suite) in C for orchestra and a modern one in Ravel's *Tombeau de Couperin*.

form the large-scale structure and overall design of a composition, providing a coherent framework for the effective presentation of musical ideas. Short pieces do not require complicated forms because the thematic material is usually sufficiently coherent in itself. The simplest forms are **binary form**, which consists of two sections often separated by a double bar (marking off a section), and simple **ternary form**, which consists of one section followed by a contrasting section,

followed by the return of the first section. Most larger-scale forms are expansions and developments of these two basic types, carefully using a balance of thematic development and transformation, repetition, variation, and contrast. Examples include **sonata form** and **rondo form**. During the 19th century, when Romantic composers such as Wagner fought against standard Classical forms, the alternative structure of a literary text or idea often came to replace the traditional, more technical, compositional forms.

Formé, Nicolas (1567–1638) French composer. He was a clerk and singer in the Sainte-Chapelle in Paris 1587–92, then became a countertenor in the royal chapel and succeeded Eustache du Caurroy as choirmaster and composer there in 1609. Although almost dismissed from the Sainte-Chapelle for not conforming to the ecclesiastical rules, he returned there in 1626 and, as a favourite musician of Louis XIII, enjoyed special privileges. Only his church music survives.

Works include: Masses, motets, Magnificat, and other church music.

Förster, (Emanuel) Aloys (1748–1823) German oboist and composer. He wrote a treatise on thorough-bass. He was a prolific composer of piano and chamber pieces. Beethoven acknowledged his debt to Förster in the composition of string quartets.

After two years as a military bandsman, 1766–68, he lived as a freelance teacher and composer, first in Prague, then from 1779 in Vienna.

Works include: 48 string quartets; four string quintets; six piano quartets, and other chamber music; piano concertos, sonatas, variations and other pieces.

Forster, Georg (c. 1510–1568) German music publisher and composer. He published five sets of German songs, the *Frische Teutsche Liedlein* 1539–56, some of which he wrote himself; he also composed sacred and Latin works.

forte, or f (Italian 'strong') in musical notation, a direction to play loudly.

Forte, Allen (1926–) US music theorist. He is known for his formulation of set-series, particularly to explain atonal music. His major works are *The Structure of Atonal Music* (1973) and *The Harmonic Organization of The Rite of Spring* (1978).

fortepiano early 18th-century piano invented by Italian instrument maker Bartolommeo Cristofori in 1709. It has small, leather-bound hammers and harpsichord strings. Unlike the harpsichord, it can produce a varying intensity of tone, depending on the pressure of the player's touch, hence the name, which means 'loud-soft' in Italian.

It was rendered obsolete by technical developments, but has been revived by performers working with period instruments. Present-day performers include Trevor Pinnock, Gustav Leonhardt, and Jörg Demus.

forte piano, or fp (Italian 'loud, soft') in music, of dynamics, loud then immediately soft.

fortissimo, or ff (Italian 'very strong') in musical notation, a direction to play very loudly.

Fortner, Wolfgang (1907–1987) German composer. He studied with Hermann Grabner. From 1931 to 1954 he taught theory and composition at the Evangelical Church Music Institute in Heidelberg, where he founded and conducted a chamber orchestra. In 1954 he became professor of composition at the German Music Academy in Detmold, and in 1957 succeeded Genzmer at the Musikhochschule in Freiburg im Breisgau. His music shows the influence of Reger and Hindemith. He also used serial techniques in later years, approaching integral serialism.

Works include: *Bluthochzeit* (after Lorca, 1956; revised 1963), *Corinna* (1958), *In seinem Garten liebt Don Pimperlin Belison* (after Lorca, 1962), *Elisabeth Tudor* (1972); ballet *Die Weisse Rose* (after Wilde); *Deutsche Liedmesse, Marianische Antiphonen* for unaccompanied chorus; symphonies; *Sinfonia concertante* for chamber orchestra; concertos for various instruments and small orchestra; four string quartets (1929–75), *Suite* for solo cello (1932), *5 Bagatelles* for wind quintet (1960).

Forty-Eight (Preludes and Fugues) (Bach). See ◊*Wohltemperierte Clavier, Das.*

Forza d'amor paterno, La/The Force of Paternal Love opera by Stradella (librettist unknown), produced Genoa, Teatro del Falcone, Carnival 1678.

Forza del destino, La/The Force of Destiny opera by Verdi (libretto by F M Piave, based on the drama by A P de Saavedra, Duke of Rivas, *Don Alvaro, o La fuerza de sino*), produced St Petersburg, 10 November 1862; first performed in Italy, Rome, Teatro Apollo, 7 February 1863. Leonora and Alvaro elope together, but he accidentally kills her father and the two are separated in their flight. Leonora's brother Carlo searches to find her 'seducer', to avenge the dishonour fallen

upon the family. After a series of coincidences, Leonora and Alvaro die together.

Foss, (born Fuchs) Lukas (1922–) US composer and conductor. His stylistically varied works, including the cantata *The Prairie* 1942 and *Time Cycle* for soprano and orchestra 1960, express an ironic view of tradition.

Born in Germany, Foss studied in Berlin with Julius Goldstein; from 1933 he studied piano in Paris with Lazare Lévy and composition with Noel Gallon. In 1937 he went with his parents to the USA, and studied at the Curtis Institute in Philadelphia. Later he studied with Hindemith at Yale University; in 1944 he gave the Boston first performance of Hindemith's *Four Temperaments* for piano and strings. In 1945 he won a Guggenheim Fellowship and in 1950 a Fulbright Fellowship. He became professor of composition at California University in 1953.

He has composed much: in the 1940s he wrote vocal music in neoclassical style; in the mid-1950s he began increasingly to employ improvisation. He has also written chamber and orchestral music in which the players reproduce tape-recorded effects.

Works include: the operas *The Jumping Frog of Calaveras County* (after Mark Twain, 1950), *Griffelkin* (television opera, 1955), *Introductions and Goodbyes* (libretto by Foss and Menotti); ballet *Gift of the Magi*; cantata *The Prairie* (after Carl Sandberg), oratorio *A Parable of Death* (Rilke, 1952); *Time Cycle* for soprano and ensemble (1960), *American Cantata* for tenor, chorus, and orchestra (1976), *Thirteen Ways of Looking at a Blackbird* for soprano, flute, piano, and percussion (1978), *Round a Common Centre* for voice and ensemble (1979), *De Profundis* (1983), *With Music Strong* for mixed chorus and ensemble (1988); two piano concertos (1944, 1951); three symphonies (no. 3 *Symphony of Sorrows*, 1988); *Orpheus* for cello, oboe, and clarinet; *Solomon Rossi Suite* (1975), *Renaissance Concerto* for flute and orchestra (1986), *American Landscapes*, guitar concerto (1989); three string quartets (1947, 1973, 1975), brass quintet (1978), percussion quartet (1983), horn trio (1984), *Taski* for six instruments (1986), *Central Park Reel* for violin and piano (1989); incidental music to *The Tempest*.

Fossa, Johannes de (c. 1540–1603) German or Flemish composer. He wrote six Masses and other sacred works. He succeeded Roland de Lassus as Kapellmeister at the Munich court in 1594.

Foster, Stephen Collins (1826–1864) US songwriter. He wrote about 175 sentimental popular songs including 'My Old Kentucky Home' 1853 and 'Beautiful Dreamer' 1864, and rhythmic minstrel songs such as 'Oh! Susanna' 1848 and 'Camptown Races' 1850. Almost wholly self-taught in music, he published his first song as early as 1842.

Foulds, John (Herbert) (1880–1939) English composer and conductor. He joined a theatre orchestra in Manchester at the age of 14 and the Hallé Orchestra in 1900. He worked at various opera houses abroad, gave concerts for the forces during World War I ,and wrote *A World Requiem* 1919–21 for the war dead. He later conducted various music societies in London.

Works include: incidental music for Kalidasa's *Sakuntala*, Euripides' *Trojan Women*, and several others; *A Vision of Dante* (concert opera 1905–08), *A World Requiem* for solo voices, chorus, and orchestra (1919–21); *Epithalamium*, *Keltic Suite* (1911), and *Suite Fantastique* for orchestra; *Holiday Sketches*, *Suite française*, and *Gaelic Dream Song* for small orchestra; *Idyll* for string orchestra; *Mood Pictures* for violin and piano; *Variations* and *Essays in the Modes* for piano.

Fourier transform the mathematical technique by which a complex sound wave can be broken down into its constituent simple waves or partials. Essential to techniques of sound synthesis which produce or manipulate sounds identical to those produced by live instruments.

Four Last Songs/Vier letzte Lieder sequence of songs for soprano and orchestra by Strauss, composed 1948; his last work. First performed London, 22 May 1950, with Flagstad and Furtwängler. First three texts are by Hermann Hesse; *Frühling, September, Beim Schlafengehen*. No. 4 by Eichendorff: *Im Abendrot*.

Four Saints in Three Acts opera in four acts by Virgil Thomson (libretto by Gertrude Stein), produced in concert form at Ann Arbor, Michigan, 20 May 1933 and on the stage at Hartford, Connecticut, 8 February 1934. It deals with the deeds of 16th-century Spanish saints.

Four Sea Interludes concert work by Britten, derived from his opera *Peter Grimes* (first performed London, 1945). The four sections are titled *Dawn, Sunday Morning, Moonlight* and *Storm*; first performed Cheltenham, 13 June 1945.

Four Seasons, The/Le quattro Stagioni four violin concertos by Vivaldi in E, G minor, F, and F minor, depicting the seasons. The first four of 12 violin concertos op. 8 pub. 1725 in Amsterdam as 'The contest between harmony and invention'.

Four Serious Songs (Brahms). See ◊*Vier ernste Gesänge*.

Four Temperaments, The title for symphony no. 2, op. 16, by Nielsen; composed 1901–02, first performed Copenhagen, 1 December 1902.

Four Temperaments, Theme and Variations, The work for piano and string orchestra by Hindemith. Commissioned by Balanchine and composed 1940; first performed (concert) Boston, 3 September 1944, Lukas Foss as soloist. Stage production New York, City Ballet, 20 November 1946. The four main sections are titled *Melancholy, Sanguine, Phlegmatic* and *Choleric*.

fourth an interval of four diatonic notes consisting of two whole tones and a semitone, for example C–F. A fourth is an example of a 'perfect interval' because it remains the same in both major and minor keys. A fourth may be augmented (increased by a semitone), for example C–F♯.

A fourth may be perfect; it can also be augmented or diminished.

Fowler, Jennifer (1939–) Autralian composer, resident in London from 1969. She studied in Perth and at the electronic music studio in Utrecht.

Works include: *Look on this Oedipus* (1973), *Chant with Garlands* (1974), and *Ring out the Changes* for orchestra; *Revelation* for string quintet (1971); *Chimes, Fractured* for ensemble (1970), *The Arrows of St Sebastian I and II* for ensemble (1981); *Line Spun with Stars* for piano trio (1983); *Echoes from an Antique Land* for ensemble (1983); *Threaded Stars* harp solo (1983); *Between Science and the World* for wind quintet (1987); *We Call it to You, Brother* for ensemble (1988); *And Ever Shall Be* for mezzo and ensemble (1989); *Reeds, Reflections* for oboe and string trio (1990).

Fox Strangways, A(rthur) H(enry) (1859–1948) English musicologist, critic, and editor. He was educated at Wellington College and Balliol College, Oxford, he also studied in Berlin. After teaching at Dulwich and Wellington Colleges until 1910, and visiting India, on the music of which he wrote a book (*The Music of Hindostan*), he became assistant critic of *The Times* in London in 1911 and chief critic of the *Observer* 1925. He founded *Music and Letters* 1920 and edited it until 1936. He also wrote a biography of Cecil Sharp and translated many songs (some with Steuart Wilson), by Schubert, Brahms, and Wolf.

fp abbreviation for **forte piano**, loud then immediately soft.

Fra Diavolo, ou L'Hôtellerie de Terracine/ Brother Devil, or the Inn at Terraccina opera by Auber (libretto by Scribe), produced Paris, Opéra-Comique, 28 January 1830. Lorenzo on the hunt for the bandit Fra Diavolo, who plans to kill Zerlina, Lorenzo's love. He catches the criminal and gets the girl.

Fra due litiganti il terzo gode/Between Two Litigants the Third Makes Profit opera by Sarti (libretto altered from Goldoni's *Le Nozze*), produced Milan, La Scala, 14 September 1782. Mozart quotes a tune from it in the second-act finale of *Don Giovanni*: it was first produced in Vienna, 28 May 1783. Set against a background of feuding Count and Countess, steward Masotto wins the heart of serving maid Dorina after outmanoeuvring rivals Titta and Mingone.

Françaix, Jean (1912–   ) French composer. His music is noted for its wit and brilliance, and shows the influence of Satie and Les Six.

Françaix was born at Le Mans. He studied under his father, who was director of the Conservatory there, and with Nadia Boulanger in Paris. He showed great talent at an early age and a great facility in his writing.

Works include: the operas *Le Diable boiteux* (1938), *La Main de gloire* (1950), *Paris à nous deux* (1954), *La princesse de Clèves* (1965); ballets *Beach* and *Le Roi nu* (after Hans Andersen); two symphonies (1932, 1953), *Suite concertante*; *L'horloge de flore* for oboe and orchestra (1959); *Divertissement* for string trio and orchestra; piano concerto (1936) and concertino, flute concerto (1966), Fantasy for cello and orchestra. Concertos for violin (1970, 1979), double bass (1974), bassoon and strings (1979), guitar and strings (1983), trombone and wind (1984), flute and clarinet (1991); Cassazione for three orchestras (1975), *Mozart new-look* for double bass and ten wind instruments (1981), Concerto for 15 soloists

and orchestra (1988); *Petit Quatuor* for strings, quintet for flute, harp and strings, two wind quintets (1948, 1987), octet (1972), *Danses Exotiques* for 12 players (1986), *Dixtuor* for wind and string quintet (1986), *Elegie* for wind instruments (1990), Suite for four saxophones (1990); songs and piano music.

Francesca da Rimini opera by Generali (libretto by P Pola, based on Dante), produced Venice, Teatro La Fenice, 26 December 1829.

Opera by Nápravník (libretto by O O Paleček and E P Ponomarev, based on a play by Stephen Phillips, *Paolo and Francesca*, and farther back on Dante), produced St Petersburg, 9 December 1902. After a part of Dante's 'Inferno'. Francesca must marry the crippled Gianciotto, but she falls in love with his brother, Paolo. After learning of her infidelity, Gianciotto sets a trap and kills the pair.

Opera by Rachmaninov (libretto taken from scenes of Pushkin's play, with additions by Modest Tchaikovsky, based on Dante), produced Moscow, 24 January 1906.

Opera by Zandonai (libretto by T Ricordi, based on d'Annunzio's tragedy, and farther back on Dante), produced Turin, Teatro Regio, 19 February 1914.

Symphonic fantasy by Tchaikovsky, op. 32 (based on Dante), composed 1876, first performed Moscow, 9 March 1877.

Unfinished opera by Goetz, completed by Ernst Frank (libretto by composer), produced Mannheim, 30 September 1877.

See also ◊*Françoise de Rimini*; ◊*Paolo e Francesca*.

Francesco Canova da Milano (1497–1543) Italian lutenist and composer. Known as *Il divino* ('the divine'), he was the finest composer of lute music before John Dowland. He was in the service first of the Duke of Mantua, about 1510, and then of Pope Paul III from 1535. He was a prolific composer, publishing and contributing to several books of lute pieces.

Franchetti, Alberto (1860–1942) Italian composer. He studied first in Italy, then with Draeseke at Dresden and at the Munich Conservatory under Rheinberger. He was director of the Cherubini Conservatory, Florence, 1926–28.

Works include: the operas *Asrael* (1888), *Cristoforo Colombo* (1892), *Fior d'Alpe, Signor di Pourceaugnac* (after Molière, 1897), *Germania, La figlia di Jorio* (after d'Annunzio), *Notte di leggenda, Glauco* and (with Giordano) *Giove a Pompeii* (1921); symphony in E minor.

Franck, César Auguste (1822–1890) Belgian composer. He was a pioneer of cyclic form, and his harmonic style was influenced by his experience as a church organist. His music, mainly religious and Romantic in style, includes the *Symphony in D Minor* 1866–68, *Symphonic Variations* 1885 for piano and orchestra, the *Violin Sonata* 1886, the oratorio *Les Béatitudes*/*The Beatitudes* 1879, and many organ pieces.

Franck was born at Liège. A precociously gifted child, especially as a pianist, he made a concert tour in Belgium at the age of 11. Sent to Paris in 1835 to study, he entered the Conservatory in 1837; there he won prizes each year until he left in 1842. He returned to Belgium, but settled permanently in Paris in 1844. In 1848 he married a young actress and was appointed organist at the church of Saint-Jean-Saint-François in 1851. In 1853 he became choirmaster and in 1858 organist at Sainte-Clotilde. He was particularly noted for his skill in improvisation. He was appointed professor of the organ at the Conservatory in 1872.

Franck gathered together a circle of young, eager students, including d'Indy, Chausson, Lekeu, and Duparc, and with them pursued the study of polyphonic and symphonic music; he was the founder of a special branch of modern French music, one which absorbed the innovations of Wagner without loss of individuality.

He became a chevalier of the Legion of Honour in 1885 and two years later, in January 1887, a festival of his music was held.

Works include: ORCHESTRAL symphony in D minor (1888); symphonic poems, *Les Eolides* (1876), *Le Chasseur maudit* (after Burger), *Psyché* (with chorus); *Les Djinns* and *Variations symphoniques* for piano and orchestra.

CHORAL WITH ORCHESTRA (some with solo voices): *Les Béatitudes* (1870), *Rédemption* (1874), *Rébecca*, Psalm 101; *Paris: chant patriotique* for tenor and orchestra; *Messe solennelle* for bass and organ; Mass for three voices, organ, harp, cello, and double bass; three motets, three offertories, and other small sacred vocal works.

CHAMBER piano quintet (1879), string quartet; sonata for violin and piano (1886).

KEYBOARD AND SONGS about 16 works for piano, including *Prélude, Choral et Fugue* and *Prélude, Aria et Final*; nine works for organ, including six *Pièces pour Grand Orgue*.

Franckenstein, Clemens von (1875–1942) German composer. He studied in Vienna and later at Munich with Thuille and at Frankfurt with Knorr. After a visit to the USA he conducted the Moody-Manners Opera Company in England, 1902–07, then worked at the court theatres of Wiesbaden and Berlin, and in 1912 became general intendant of the Munich court theatres.

Works include: the operas *Griseldis* (1898), *Rahab* (1911) and *Des Kaisers Dichter* (1920); ballet *Die Biene*; orchestral works: variations on a theme by Meyerbeer, Dance Suite, Serenade, Rhapsody, Praeludium, Symphonic Suite, *Das alte Lied*, four Dances, *Festival Prelude*, chamber music; piano works; songs.

Francœur, François (1698–1787) French violinist and composer. He joined the Paris Opéra orchestra at the age of 15 and there met François Rebel, with whom he worked for the rest of his life. They collaborated on several operas, of which *Pyrame et Thisbé* 1726 was the first.

He was a pupil of his father, Joseph Francœur, who was a double bass player at the Opéra. In 1720 he published his first violin sonatas, and in 1723 went with Rebel to Prague for the coronation of Charles VI. After his return to Paris in 1726 he gradually rose to the highest positions in French music, being appointed composer to the court in 1727; member of the king's band in 1730; inspector of the Opéra in 1743 and director in 1757; superintendent of the king's music in 1760 (he held the last three jointly with Rebel).

His nephew, Louis Joseph Francœur (1738–1804), was also a violinist and composer and was for a time director of the Opéra.

Works include: the operas, composed jointly with Rebel, beginning with *Pyrame et Thisbé* (1726), ballets, violin sonatas, and other pieces.

Françoise de Rimini, Francesca da Rimini, opera by A Thomas (libretto by J Barbier and M Carré, based on Dante), produced Paris, Opéra, 14 April 1882.

Franco of Cologne (lived mid-13th century) French music theorist. He wrote an *Ars cantus mensurabilis* which survives in seven manuscripts. It expounds the system of notation in his day, now called 'Franconian'.

An anonymous monk of Bury St Edmunds, writing of Parisian music in the 13th century, refers to a 'Franco primus', apparently a Parisian, who also wrote on the same subject.

Francs-Juges, Les/The Judges of the Secret Court unfinished opera by Berlioz (libretto by H Ferrand), composed 1827–28; first performance of the overture Paris, 26 May 1828. The rest was discarded or used elsewhere, as in the *Symphonie fantastique*.

Frankel, Benjamin (1906–1973) English composer and teacher. He studied the piano in Germany and continued his studies in London while playing jazz violin in nightclubs. His output includes chamber music and numerous film scores, notably *The Man in the White Suit* 1951 and *A Kid for Two Farthings* 1955.

He picked up a precarious living as a music teacher, café pianist, and jazz-band violinist while attending the Guildhall School of Music in the daytime. He gradually improved his living by working as an orchestrator and theatre conductor, finally succeeding as a conductor and composer of film music. In his published work he became an early English exponent of serial technique.

His reputation in the film world grew with music for *The Seventh Veil* 1945, *The Years Between* 1946, and *Dear Murderer* 1947. In his mature works, which include eight symphonies, an important violin concerto 1951, *The Aftermath* (Robert Nichols) for tenor and orchestra, four string quartets, and other chamber works, he successfully espoused serial methods in conjunction with a strong feeling for tonality.

Works include: music for many films, *Pezzo sinfonico* for orchestra, *Solemn Speech and Discussion* and *Music for Young Comrades* for string orchestra, *The Aftermath* (Robert Nichols) for tenor, strings, trumpet, and drums; eight symphonies (1952–72); violin concerto; five string quartets, *Three Sketches* for string quartet, string trio, trio for clarinet, cello, and piano, *Early Morning Pieces* for oboe, clarinet, and bassoon; violin and piano sonata, sonatas for unaccompanied violin and viola, *Sonata ebraica* for cello and harp, *Elégie juive* for cello and piano; Passacaglia for two pianos; piano pieces.

Franz, Robert (1815–1892), born Knauth, German composer. He was one of the best exponents of German songs, the first of which he published in 1843 and which attracted the attention of Schumann, Mendelssohn, Liszt, and others. His output of Lieder (songs), though influenced by Schubert and Schumann, was characterized by its striving toward simplicity and the style of folk song.

After much parental opposition he became a pupil of Friedrich Schneider at Dessau in 1835, and after two years returned home, devoting himself to study and composition without being able to secure a musical post. He then became a church organist and choral conductor, also lecturer at Halle University. Much troubled by increasing deafness and a nervous complaint, he had to retire in 1868, but did much work in editing the older choral classics.

Works include: more than 350 songs to texts by Burns, Eichendorff, Lenau, Geibel, Heine, Müller, and Goethe; church music; part songs.

Frauenliebe und-Leben/Woman's Love and Life song cycle by Schumann, op. 42 (eight poems by Adelbert von Chamisso), composed 1840.

Frau ohne Schatten, Die/The Woman without a Shadow opera by R Strauss (libretto by H von Hofmannsthal), produced Vienna, Opera, 10 October 1919. The Empress searches for her shadow, the symbol of fertility, in order to save her husband from being turned to stone. In contrast, Barak's wife is willing to sell her shadow, but is eventually united with her husband, while the Empress gains her own shadow.

Fredegunda opera by Keiser (libretto by J U König, from the Italian by Francesco Silvani), produced Hamburg, Theater beim Gänsemarkt, March 1715.

Frederick II (the Great) (1712–1786) king of Prussia, flautist, and composer. He learnt music from Gottlob Hayne, the Berlin Cathedral organist, and in 1728 had flute lessons from Johann Quantz. In 1734 he established a private band at his castle at Rheinsberg and on his accession to the throne in 1740 established a court band at Berlin and Potsdam. Johann Graun, Quantz, and C P E Bach were in his service.

Works include: part of the opera *Il rè pastore* (Metastasio) and the libretti for several operas by Graun; over 120 instrumental works, many with prominent flute parts.

Fredigundis opera by Franz Schmidt (libretto by B Warden and I M Welleminsky, after F Dahn); composed 1916–21, produced Berlin, 19 December 1922. Fredegundis murders the wife of King Chilpenich and becomes queen, but a poison she prepares for a rival is drunk by her husband and daughter.

free-reed instrument musical wind instrument such as the ◊mouth organ, ◊accordion, or ◊harmonium, that employs tuned metal tongues vibrating at a predetermined frequency as valves controlling the escape of air under pressure. Free reeds do not ◊overblow, but the mouth organ can be made to 'bend' the pitch by varying the air pressure.

Freischütz, Der/The Freeshooter opera by Weber (libretto by F Kind, based on a story in Apel and Laun's *Gespensterbuch*), produced

Berlin, Schauspielhaus, 18 June 1821. Max invokes the 'Black Huntsman' to help win a shooting competition and Agathe. He is banished for his use of the supernatural, but is allowed to return in a year to marry.

French horn musical brass instrument, a descendant of the natural hunting horn, valved and curved into a circular loop, with a funnel-shaped mouthpiece and wide bell.

French overture see ◊overture.

French sixth see ◊augmented 6th chords.

French Suites six keyboard suites by Bach, composed mainly at Cöthen c. 1722 and completed by c. 1724. They differ from the *English Suites* in having no preludes.

Frescobaldi, Girolamo (1583–1643) Italian composer and virtuoso keyboard player. He was organist at St Peter's, Rome 1608–28. His compositions included various forms of both instrumental and vocal music, and his fame rests on numerous keyboard toccatas, fugues, ricercari, and capriccios in which he advanced keyboard technique and exploited ingenious and daring modulations of key.

He studied at Ferrara under the cathedral organist Luzzasco Luzzaschi, and first gained a reputation as a singer. It was reported that 20,000 people came to hear his first recital at St Peter's in Rome. He was given leave of absence 1628–33, during which time he served as organist to Ferdinand II, Duke of Tuscany. He also worked in Brussels, Mantua, and Florence. Johann Froberger was among his pupils. Bach owned a copy of his *Fiori musicali* (1635); it contains various pieces for use in the Mass.

Works include: two Masses, a Magnificat, motets and madrigals; ricercari, canzoni, toccatas, and other pieces for organ and for harpsichord; fantasies for instruments in four parts; madrigals.

Frescoes of Piero della Francesca, The work for orchestra in three movements by Martinů, depicting three of the frescoes by Piero at Arezzo; composed 1955, first performed Salzburg, 28 August 1956, conductor Kubelik.

fret on the fingerboard of a plucked or bowed string instrument, an inlaid ridge of a material such as gut, wood, ivory, or metal, or a circlet of nylon, against which a string is pressed to shorten its vibrating length and therefore change pitch. Frets enable the player to play in tune with certainty, since the vibrating length of the string is fixed by the fret.

Freunde von Salamanka, Die/The Friends of Salamanca operetta by Schubert (libretto by J Mayrhofer), composed 1815, but never performed in Schubert's lifetime; produced with a new libretto by G Ziegler, Halle, 6 May 1928. Don Alonso wins Countess Olivia with the help of his friends.

Fricker, Peter Racine (1920–1990) English composer. His music avoided local pastoral influences and learned instead from continental neo-classical and serial models.

He studied at the Royal College of Music in London and later with Mátyás Seiber. His wind quintet won the Clements Prize in 1947 and his first symphony won the Koussevitsky Award.

Works include: the radio operas *The Death of Vivien* and *My Brother Died* (1954); ballet *Canterbury Prologue* (after Chaucer); oratorio *A Vision of Judgment* (1957–58); *Whispers at the Curtains* for baritone, chorus, and orchestra (1984); five symphonies (1948–76); *Prelude, Elegy and Finale* for strings; violin and viola concertos, *Concertante* for three pianos and strings; wind quintet, four string quartets (1947–76); violin and piano sonata; organ sonata.

Friede auf Erden/Peace on Earth work for chorus *a cappella* by Schoenberg (text by C F Mayer); composed 1907, first performed Vienna, 9 December 1911, conductor Schreker.

Friedenstag/Peace Day opera by R Strauss (libretto by J Gregor, who first suggested it to Stefan Zweig, based on Calderón's play *La redención de Breda* and Velázquez's picture illustrating that), produced Munich, 24 July 1938. Besieged town faces self-destruction rather than defeat. At the last moment a peace is declared and enemies meet as brothers.

Froberger, Johann Jacob (1616–1667) German organist and composer. He was court organist at Vienna and travelled to England, France, Germany, and the Low Countries performing keyboard music.

He studied under his father, who was a singer, and later Kapellmeister, at Stuttgart. He was appointed court organist in Vienna on the accession of the Emperor Ferdinand III in 1637, and remained there until 1657, but spent 1637–41 in Italy as a pupil of Frescobaldi. In 1662 he went to London, where he is said to have arrived destitute, having been twice robbed on the way. In later years he lived in the house of Sibylla, Dowager Duchess of Württemberg, at her retreat at Héricourt.

Works include: harpsichord suites, many pieces for organ and harpsichord including toccatas, ricercari, and 30 suites.

'Frog' Quartet the nickname of Haydn's string quartet in D major, op. 50 No. 6, the finale of which is supposed to have a 'croaking' theme.

Froissart concert overture by Elgar, op. 19, composed 1890 and performed at the Worcester Festival of that year on 9 September, conductor Elgar. The title refers to the French historian Jean Froissart (1338–1404). Elgar prefaced the score with a quotation from Keats: 'When chivalry lifted up her lance on high'.

Fromm, Andreas (1621–1683) German composer. He was cantor at the Marienkirche and professor at the Pädagogium of Stettin in the middle of the 17th century.

Works include: the oratorios *Actus Musicus* (one of the earliest known in German), and *Vom reichen Mann und Lazarus* (1649); *Dialogus Pentecostalis*.

'From My Life' (Smetana). See ◊*Aus meinem Leben*.

From the House of the Dead (Janácek). See ◊*House of the Dead, From the*.

'From the New World' (Dvořák). See ◊*'New World' Symphony*.

Frosch (German 'frog') in music, the heel of the violin bow. The direction 'am Frosch' found in German scores means that a passage is to be bowed near the heel of the bow.

frottola an early 16th-century Italian song, originating in Milan, for several voices or for solo voice and instruments, forerunner of the madrigal but less polyphonically elaborate. The term is used in a general sense to cover numerous different forms: *strambotto*, *oda*, or *capitolo*, and also in a particular sense, to mean a song in several stanzas with a refrain or burden (*ripresa*) sung complete at the beginning and (usually) curtailed, but often with a musical extension, after each stanza; the same music serves for both refrain and stanza.

Frye, Walter (fl. c. 1450–75) English composer. His *Ave Regina Caelorum Mater Regis* was copied into 13 continental manuscripts and is found in three arrangements for keyboard in the *Buxheimer Orgelbuch*.

He is believed to have been a choral conductor at Ely Cathedral in the 1440s and later joined the London Guild of Parish Clerks. He wrote three Masses (*Flos Regalis*, *Nobilis et Pulchra*, and *Summa Trinitati*), chansons, and antiphons.

Fuchs, Robert (1847–1927) Austrian composer. He was professor at the Vienna Conservatory 1875–1912, where Mahler, Wolf, Zemlinsky, and Schreker were among his pupils. His serenades are still sometimes performed in Germany.

Works include: two operas, *Die Königsbraut* (1889) and *Die Teufelsglocke* (1893); Mass; symphony in C major, five Serenades (four for strings); piano concertó; chamber music.

fuga (Italian 'flight') in earlier times one of the Italian terms for canon, another being caccia.

fuga ricercata see ◊ricercare.

fugato (Italian 'fugued') a passage written in the manner of a fugue, occurring merely incidentally in a composition; or a piece in fugal style that cannot be considered to be in the form of a fugue.

fughetta (Italian 'little fugue') in music, unlike a *fugato*, a fughetta is formally a proper fugue, but much more condensed.

fugue (Latin 'flight') in music, a contrapuntal form with two or more subjects (principal melodies) for a number of parts, which enter in succession in direct imitation of each other or transposed to a higher or lower key, and may be combined in augmented form (larger note values). It represents the highest form of contrapuntal ingenuity in works such as J S Bach's *Das musikalische Opfer*/The *Musical Offering* 1747, on a theme of Frederick II of Prussia, and *Die Kunst der Fuge*/The *Art of the Fugue* published 1751, and Beethoven's *Grosse Fuge*/*Great Fugue* for string quartet 1825–26.

Fulda, Adam of (c. 1445–1505) German monk, music theorist, and composer. He wrote a tract on music and composed motets and other pieces.

full close alternative name for a perfect ◊cadence, in which the ◊dominant chord resolves to the ◊tonic.

full organ direction to an organist to couple the manuals (keyboards) together and use all the louder stops.

full score a complete transcript of a composition showing all parts individually, as opposed to a **short score** or **piano score** that is condensed into fewer lines of music.

functional harmony see ◊harmonic analysis.

fundamental in musical acoustics, the lowest ◊harmonic of a musical tone, corresponding to the audible pitch.

The exposition of Bach's fugue in A flat major, Well-tempered Clavier, *Book II, no. 17.*

fundamental bass an imaginary harmonic phenomenon expounded by Rameau. The fundamental bass is the root bass of any chord occurring in a composition, and according to Rameau no composition was aesthetically satisfying unless that bass, either actually present or implied, was in each chord used, proceeding from the one before it to the one after it in accordance with definite rules of musical logic.

fundamental line (German *Urlinie*) in voice-leading analysis, the fundamental line is the deepest level of melodic organization in a tonal work. It consists of a linear descent from a specific note of the tonic chord to the tonic note, written as 3–2–1 or 5–4–3–2–1, or (unusually) 6–5–4–3–2–1. According to Schenker's theory of tonal structure, each note of the fundamental line must be supported by a structural harmony. The first note of the fundamental line is called the *Kopfton* or head-note, and this is often prolonged for the bulk of the piece. A section of the piece before the *Kopfton* appears is called the 'ascent', the section prolonging it is called the 'structure', the section prolonging the other notes of the fundamental line is called the 'descent', and a section prolonging the last note is the 'peroration'.

fundamental structure (German *Ursatz*) in voice-leading analysis, the fundamental structure is the deepest level of harmonic organization in a tonal work. It consists of a two-part contrapuntal figure, the bass line consisting of the progression I–V–I, and the upper line consisting of the fundamental line of the piece, where the first note and the last two notes coincide with the bass. According to ◊Schenker's theory of tonal harmony, it is the presence of the fundamental structure in all well-formed tonal pieces which gives their tonal structure coherence and organic unity. See ◊structural level.

funeral march see ◊march.

Funeral Ode (Bach). See ◊*Trauer-Ode.*

furiant lively Czech dance in 3–4 time with a characteristic effect of cross-rhythm, often used in place of a scherzo by Dvořák and other Czech composers of the national school.

furlong in music, old English name for the ◊forlana.

Furrer, Beat (1954–   ) Swiss-born composer who studied with Roman Haubenstock-Ramati and formed the Société de l'art acoustique ensemble.

Works include: the music drama *Die Blinden* to texts by Rimbaud, Hölderlin, and Maeterlinck (Vienna, 1989); *Risonanze* for orchestra in three groups (1988); *Face de la Chaleur* for five instrumental groups (1991); two string quartets.

Furtwängler, (Gustav Heinrich Ernst Martin) Wilhelm (1886–1954) German conductor. He was leader of the Berlin Philharmonic Orchestra 1924–54. His interpretations of Wagner, Bruckner, and Beethoven were valued expressions of monumental national grandeur, but he also gave first performances of Bartök, Schoenberg's *Variations for Orchestra* 1928, and Hindemith's opera *Mathis der Maler/Mathis the Painter* 1934, a work implicitly critical of the Nazi regime. He ascended rapidly from theatre to opera orchestras in Mannheim 1915–20 and Vienna 1919–24, then to major appointments in Leipzig and Vienna.

Furtwängler studied at Munich with Joseph Rheinberger and Max von Schillings, and early began gaining experience as conductor of concerts and opera at Zurich, Munich, Strasbourg (where he was a deputy to Hans Pfitzner), and Lübeck. After an engagement at Mannheim he followed Arthur Nikisch at the Leipzig Gewandhaus. He made his London debut in 1924, and his New York debut in 1925. He conducted the Vienna Philharmonic Orchestra from 1924 (and was principal conductor 1927–28 and 1933–54). In 1928 he became conductor-in-chief of the Berlin Philharmonic. In 1934 he was obliged to resign his post, when he supported Hindemith against the attacks of Goebbels and other Nazis. He toured infre-

quently but with great success, visiting Bayreuth 1931–44 and Covent Garden, London 1935–38, performing Wagner's *Tristan* and *The Ring*. Furtwängler was also active as a composer, producing three symphonies, a piano concerto, a Te Deum, and some chamber music.

Fussell, Charles C(lement) (1938–   ) US composer and conductor. His music is largely traditional in scope and content. He founded the Group for New Music at the University of Massachusetts in 1974.

He studied at the Eastman School and with Boris Blacher in Berlin.

Works include: the opera *Caligula* (1962); three symphonies (1963, 1964–67, 1978–81); *Northern Lights* for chamber orchestra (portraits of Janáček and Munch, 1979); *Virgil Thomson Sleeping* for chamber orchestra (1981); *Cymbeline*, romance for soprano, tenor, and ensemble (1983); *A Song of Return* for chorus and orchestra (1989); *Wilde* two monologues for baritone and orchestra (1990); *Last Trombones* for five percussionists, two pianos, and six trombones (1990).

Fux, Johann Joseph (1660–1741) Austrian composer and theorist. His rules of ◊counterpoint, compiled in his *Gradus ad Parnassum* 1725, were studied by Haydn and Beethoven, and are still used as a teaching formula by many music schools. He wrote a considerable quantity of sacred music, including 50 masses and 10 oratorios.

Fux was organist to the Schottenkirche in Vienna 1696–1702, became court composer in 1698, second Kapellmeister at St Stephen's Cathedral in 1705 and first in 1712, vice-Kapellmeister to the court in 1713, and Kapellmeister in 1715.

Works include: 18 operas, including *Costanza e fortezza* (1723); 11 oratorios including *Gesù Cristo negato da Pietro* (1719); around 80 Masses and quantities of other church music; 38 trio sonatas; partitas and other pieces for orchestra; keyboard music.

fz, abbreviation for Italian *forzando* musical direction which, placed against a note or chord, indicates that it should be strongly accentuated. The more usual word is *sforzando*, marked *sf.*

G

G the fifth note, or dominant, of the scale of C major.

Gabrieli, Andrea (c. 1533–1585) Italian composer. He was organist at St Mark's, Venice, from 1566, and his music, for example *Concerti* (1587), makes much use of the spatial effects possible within St Mark's, with vocal and instrumental groups separated in contrasting ensembles.

He was a member of a Venetian school which cultivated an antiphonal style suited to the two choir galleries and two organs of St Mark's Church. He became second organist at St Mark's, Venice in 1566 and first organist in 1584. He was a famous teacher and had many distinguished pupils, Italian and foreign, including his nephew Giovanni ◊Gabrieli and the Germans Hans Hassler and Gregor Aichinger.

Works include: Masses, motets, and other church music with instruments; spiritual songs; madrigals, and other pieces for several voices; choruses for Sophocles' *Oedipus Tyrannus*; ricercari for organ.

Gabrieli, Giovanni (c. 1555–1612) Italian composer. He succeeded his uncle Andrea Gabrieli (c. 1533–1585) as organist of St Mark's, Venice. His sacred and secular works include numerous madrigals, motets, and the antiphonal *Sacrae Symphoniae* (1597), sacred canzonas and sonatas for brass choirs, strings, and organ, in spatial counterpoint.

Gaburo, Kenneth (1926–1993) US composer. He studied at the Eastman School and with Petrassi in Rome. He was a professor at the University of Illinois 1955–68, and at San Diego 1968–75. He founded and directed the Studio for Cognitive Studies at San Diego

1975–83; his music was concerned with extending verbal limits within composition, and frequently employed electronics, as in series of *Antiphonies* I–X (1958–89).

Works include: the operas *The Snow Queen* (1952), *Blur* (1956), and *The Widow* (1961); string quartet (1956); *Shapes and Sounds* for orchestra (1960); *A Dot is no Small Thing*, for orchestra (1984).

Gade, Niels Vilhelm (1817–1890) Danish composer. The most important Danish composer of the 19th century. He was a violinist in the royal orchestra at Copenhagen before going to Leipzig, where he was engaged as assistant conductor of the Gewandhaus Orchestra. After returning to Denmark he established a permanent orchestra and became co-director of Copenhagen's Academy of Music.

His teachers included Andreas Berggreen and Christoph Weyse. Having won a composition prize for his *Ossian* overture in 1841, he was enabled to go to Leipzig for further study with a royal grant. There he came into contact with Mendelssohn, who produced his first symphony in 1843 and engaged him to conduct the Gewandhaus concerts in his absence. He returned to Copenhagen in 1848 and worked as organist, conductor, and teacher, becoming court music director in 1861.

Works include: the opera *Mariotta* (1849); cantatas *Baldurs Drom* (1858), *Comala, Erl King's Daughter, Zion, The Crusaders, Den Bjaergtagne* (1873), *Psyche*, and others; eight symphonies (1842–71), overtures *Echoes from Ossian, In the Highland, Hamlet* (after Shakespeare), *Michelangelo*, and others, suite

Holbergiana for orchestra. String quartet, quintet, string octet, piano trios, and other chamber music; four violin and piano sonatas; instrumental pieces; piano sonata in E minor and pieces for piano solo and duet; songs, part songs.

Gafori, Franchino (1451–1522) Italian priest, theorist, and composer. He wrote several theoretical books, including *Theoriça musicae* 1492 and *Practica musicae* 1496, and also composed Masses and other church music. Leonardo da Vinci was among his friends.

He was maestro di cappella at Monticello and Bergamo, and from 1484 was attached to Milan Cathedral.

gagaku traditional court music of Japan with origins in ancient China and 8th-century Japan. The tonal systems, scales, and modes of gagaku are also derived from ancient Chinese theory and practice and each category of gagaku has a separate instrumentation (for example, the use of the 'wagon' zither in Shinto ritual music) and tonal system.

Gagliano, Giovanni Battista da (1584–1651), real name Zenobi Italian composer. He was instructor at the church of San Lorenzo at Florence in 1613, in succession to his brother Marco da ◊Gagliano, and later musician to the Grand Duke of Tuscany.

Works include: motets, psalms, and other church music.

Gagliano, Marco da (1582–1643), real name Zenobi Italian composer, brother of Giovanni Battista da Gagliano. In 1607 he founded the Accademia degl' Elevati for the cultivation of music. His opera *Dafne* (1608), a setting of Rinuccini's libretto, followed Monteverdi's epoch-making *Orfeo* by one year; it also developed early operatic form, to include airs and choruses as well as recitative.

He studied organ and theorbo under Luca Bati at the church of San Lorenzo, Florence, where he was a priest. He became instructor there in 1602 and maestro di cappella in 1608. About 1610 he was appointed maestro di cappella to the Grand Duke of Tuscany. He was in touch with the ducal family of Gonzaga at Mantua, where *Dafne* was produced in 1608. He also wrote music for the wedding of the Duke's son.

Works include: the operas *Dafne*, *La Flora*, *Il Medoro* (music lost); oratorio *La regina Santa Orsola* (1624, music lost); Masses, Offices for the Dead, *Sacrae cantiones*; madrigals.

gagliarda see ◊galliard.

gaillarde see ◊galliard.

Gál, Hans (1890–1987) Austrian composer and musicologist. After the Anschluss (the annexation of Austria by Germany) he took refuge at Edinburgh, where he was lecturer at the University 1945–57.

He was a pupil of Eusebius Mandyczewski in Vienna and lectured at the university there from 1918; he later became director of the Music Academy at Mainz.

Works include: the operas *Der Fischer, Der Arzt der Sobeide* (1919), *Ruth, Die heilige Ente* (1923), *Das Lied der Nacht* (1926), *Die beiden Klaus, Der Zauberspiegel*; *Requiem für Mignon* (from Goethe's *Wilhelm Meister*, 1923) for chorus and orchestra, and other choral works; *Sinfonietta, Ballet Suite, Pickwickian Overture* (after Dickens), and other pieces for orchestra; serenade for strings; piano concerto, violin concerto; four string quartets (1916–71), five Intermezzi for string quartet, serenade for string trio; piano works.

galant (French and German 'courtly') in music, an adjective used to designate a special musical style of the 18th century, especially that of C P E Bach and the Mannheim school. Its main characteristics are elegance, a certain restraint of feeling, formality (often using sonata form), and the abandonment of Baroque counterpoint in favour of a distinct division between melody and accompaniment.

galanteries (French 'courtesies'; German *Galanterien*) extra dances or other pieces added to those which were normal in the Baroque suite or partita (◊allemande, ◊courante, ◊sarabande, and ◊gigue). The most frequently used galanteries were ◊bourrées, ◊minuets, ◊passepieds, ◊chaconnes and, among pieces other than dances, airs.

Galatea, La opera by Schürer (libretto by Metastasio), produced Dresden, at court, 8 November 1746.

Galilei, Vincenzo (c. 1520–1591) Italian composer, theorist, and lutenist. He took part in the discussions which, after his death, helped transform the Florentine camerata into opera; he also wrote theoretical books. Galilei upheld Greek drama against the contemporary madrigal, becoming involved in controversy with his teacher, Gioseffo Zarlino. He was the father of the astronomer Galileo Galilei.

Works include: cantata *Il Conte Ugolino* from Dante, a setting of the Lamentations of Jeremiah (both lost, and both among the earliest music for a single voice with accompaniment); two books of madrigals; pieces for two viols; a lute book in tablature; *Dialogo della musica antica et della moderna* (1581).

galimatias, or galimathias (French 'galli-maufry, farrago, gibberish') musical term, found in Mozart's *Galimathias musicum* (K32) written by him at The Hague in 1766, at age of ten, for the coming of age of William of Orange. It contains the Dutch national air 'Wilhelmus van Nassouwe'.

galliard spirited 16th-century court dance in triple time, originating from Lombardy, Italy. It was a very athletic dance, full of complicated steps, mainly performed by couples and popular in the court of Elizabeth I of England. It became increasingly lascivious in the 17th century. The music for the galliard consists of compound duple time (6/8) with bars of simple triple time (3/4) intermingled to upset the pulse. The galliard is often coupled to a ◊pavane, of contrasting common time (4/4).

Gallican chant Provençal plainsong in use in France until the introduction of the Roman ritual in the 8th century.

Galliculus, Johannes (fl. first half of the 16th century), or Alectorius, or Hähnel German theorist and composer. He taught at Leipzig 1520–50; wrote a theoretical work *Isagoge [later Libellus] de compositione cantus* and composed a Passion according to St Mark, two Magnificats, a psalm, and liturgical works for Easter and Christmas.

galop (French 'gallop') quick ballroom dance in 2–4 time, a variant of the ◊polka, first appearing under that name in Paris in 1829, but of older German origin, its German name (now *Galopp*) having been *Hopser* 'hopper' or *Rutscher* 'glider'.

galoubet small wind instrument, the pipe used with the accompanying tabor (French *tambourin*).

Galuppi, Baldassare (1706–1785) Italian composer. His serious operas met with indifferent success, but his comic operas are notable, especially those on libretti by Goldoni, the most famous being *Il filosofo di campagna* (1754).

Galuppi was born at Burano, near Venice. He studied with his father and later, after the failure of his first opera in 1722, with Antonio Lotti in Venice. His operatic career proper began in 1728, after which he composed a vast quantity of works. He visited London 1741–43, and produced several operas there. He was appointed second maestro di cappella at St Mark's, Venice in 1748, and first maestro and director of the Ospitale degl' Incurabili in 1762. He was director of Catherine the Great's chapel at St Petersburg 1765–68, writing new operas and Russian sacred music. Thereafter he composed few operas and devoted himself chiefly to oratorios for the Incurabili.

Works include: the operas *Alessandro nell' Indie* (1738), *L'Olympiade, L'Arcadia in Brenta* (1749), *Il Conte Caramella, Il mondo della luna* (1750), *Il mondo alla roversa, La calamità de cuori, Il filosofo di campagna, Le nozze* (1755), *L'amante di tutte, Le tre amanti ridicoli, Il Marchese Villano* (1762), *Ifigenia in Tauride* (1768), and others (over 90 in all); 27 oratorios; church music; instrumental music.

Galway, James (1939–) Irish flautist. He played with the London Symphony Orchestra

This galliard by Byrd opens with a melody related to the pavane also shown here.

1966, the Royal Philharmonic Orchestra 1967–69, and was principal flautist with the Berlin Philharmonic Orchestra 1969–75 before taking up a solo career.

gamba, da (Italian 'on the leg') in music, suffix used to distinguish viols, which are played resting on the leg, from members of the violin family, which are played under the chin, or 'on the arm' (viola da braccio).

Gambler, The/Igrok opera in four acts by Prokofiev (libretto by composer, after the story by Dostoevsky); composed 1915–17, revised 1928, produced Brussels, 29 April 1929; planned for performance in St Petersburg, 1917, but cancelled at the outbreak of the Revolution. Orchestral Suite *Portraits*, op. 49, in four movements; first performed Paris, 12 March 1932. Alexey, in love with Pauline, ruins himself for her sake. He takes to gambling and makes a fortune, but she rejects him.

gamelan percussion ensemble consisting largely of tuned knobbed gongs and keyed metallophones found in Indonesia (especially Java and Bali) and Malaysia. Most modern gamelan are tuned to a 5-note or 7-note system. Gamelan music is performed as an accompaniment for dance and theatre.

gamma (Greek letter Γ) the name of the lowest note of the musical scale known to medieval theory, G on the bottom line of the bass stave. Where the hexachord was based on it, it received the name of 'gamma-ut' (hence ◊'gamut'), and in France the name of the scale is still *gamme*.

gamut in medieval musical theory, the lowest note (G2); also a generic term for scale, or for the entire spectrum of pitches, from the lowest to the highest.

The lowest note of the gamut.

gamut-way a 17th-century term for music written in ordinary notation, as distinct from tablature.

Ganne, (Gustave) Louis (1862–1923) French composer. He conducted the Opéra balls in Paris and orchestras at Royan and Monte Carlo, and became very popular as a composer of ballets and operettas.

He was a pupil of Théodore Dubois and César Franck.

Works include: the operettas *Rabelais, Les Colles des femmes, Les Saltimbanques* (1899) and *Hans le joueur de flûte* (1906); ballet *La Source*

du Nil and several others; popular songs including 'La Marche Lorraine' and 'Le Père la Victoire'; dances *La Tsarine*.

gapped scales any scales containing less than seven notes, such as the pentatonic scale, which has five.

García, José Mauricio Nunes (1767–1830) Brazilian composer. He directed music at Rio de Janeiro Cathedral from 1798 and composed about 20 Masses, the later ones being influenced by Italian opera. His brilliant Requiem of 1816 established his reputation throughout South America.

Garden of Fand, The symphonic poem by Bax, composed 1913, first performed Chicago, 29 October 1920. Fand is a heroine of Irish legend, but in this work the garden of Fand is simply the sea, charged with Irish legendry.

Gardiner, H(enry) Balfour (1877–1950) English composer. He was educated at Charterhouse School and Oxford, and studied music under Knorr at Frankfurt. He became music master at Winchester College for a short time, then devoted himself to composition. He financed and conducted series of concerts at Queen's Hall, 1912–13, including early performances of works by British contemporaries, including the first performance of *The Planets*.

Works include: *News from Wydah* (Masefield) for chorus and orchestra (1912); symphony in D, *English Dance,* Fantasy and *Shepherd Fennel's Dance* (after Hardy) for orchestra; string quartet, string quintet (1905) and other chamber music; *Noel,* five pieces. for piano; part songs.

Gardiner, John Eliot (1943–) English conductor. He first made his mark establishing the Monteverdi Choir 1966, which he continues to conduct. He is an authority on 17th- and 18th-century music, and an exponent of the ◊authenticity movement. He has also recorded modern music.

Gardner, John (Linton) (1917–) English composer. Chamber music of his was heard in London and Paris in the 1930s, but his first great success was the performance of the first symphony at the Cheltenham Festival of 1951.

Gardner was educated at Wellington and Oxford, became music master at Repton School in 1939, and after doing war service was appointed coach at Covent Garden, London. He taught at Morley College, London 1952–76.

Works include: the operas *The Moon and Sixpence* (after Somerset Maugham, 1957) and

Tobermory (1977); symphony and Variations on a Waltz by Nielsen for orchestra (1952); piano concerto (1957), *An English Ballad* for orchestra (1969); Mass in C (1965), *Cantata for Easter* (1970); string quartet (1939), oboe quintet; two piano sonatas; *Intermezzo* for organ; songs.

Garland for the Queen a set of songs for mixed voices dedicated to Queen Elizabeth II on her coronation in 1953, with contributions by Bax, Berkeley, Bliss, Finzi, Howells, Ireland, Rawsthorne, Rubbra, Tippett, and Vaughan Williams.

Garlandia, Johannes de (lived 13th century) scholar and writer on music. He taught at the University of Paris. His two treatises on plainsong (*De plana musica*) and mensural music (*De mensurabili musica*, about 1240), were among the most influential writings of their time.

Gaspard de la Nuit three poems for piano by Ravel after Aloysius Bertrand; 1908, first perfomed Paris, 9 January 1909. The movements are *Ondine*, *Le Gibet*, and *Scarbo*.

Gasparini, Francesco (1668–1727) Italian composer. He wrote over 60 operas, as well as choral and church music. He was also highly regarded as a teacher. His treatise 'L'armonico pratico al cimbalo', was published in 1708.

He was a pupil of Corelli and Pasquini. He later became choirmaster at the Ospedale della Pietà, Venice, and in 1725 was appointed maestro di cappella of the church of St John Lateran, Rome.

Works include: 61 operas, including *Il più fedel fra i vassalli*, *La fede tradita e vendicata* (1704), *Ambleto* (on Shakespeare's *Hamlet*, 1705); oratorios *Mosè liberato dal Nilo*, *La nascita di Cristo*, and *Le nozze di Tobia* (1724); church music; cantatas.

Gassenhauer (German 'street-beater') 16th-century term for a popular dance, which was very soon used to mean a popular song. It survived till the 20th century. The modern term is *Schlager*.

Gassmann, Florian Leopold (1729–1774) Bohemian composer. He settled in Vienna as a ballet composer in 1763. In 1771 he was instrumental in founding Vienna's first music society, the Tonkünstler-Sozietät. He wrote 15 operas, most of them comic, including *L'opera seria* (1769), a satire on contemporary operatic practices, which was revived in Berlin in 1994.

Gassmann studied with Padre Martini in Bologna. He was appointed court Kapellmeister in succession to the younger Georg Reutter in 1772.

Works include: 25 operas, including *Gli uccellatori* (1759), *L'amore artigiano*, *La notte critica* (1768), *La contessina*; oratorio, *La Betulia liberata* (1772); over 50 symphonies; much church music; chamber music.

Gast, Peter (1854–1918), real name Johann Heinrich Köselitz German composer. He studied at the Leipzig Conservatory and later went to Basel as a friend and disciple of Nietzsche, some of whose compositions he revised. Afterwards he lived at Venice and Weimar.

Works include: the operas *Wilbram* (1879), *Orpheus und Dionysos*, *König Wenzel*, *Die heimliche Ehe* (based on the libretto of Cimarosa's *Matrimonio segreto* and farther back on Colman and Garrick's *Clandestine Marriage*, 1891); festival play *Walpurgis* (1903), *Hosanna* for chorus and orchestra; symphonies, symphonic poem *Helle Nächte* and other orchestral works; string quartet, septet, songs.

'Gastein' Symphony a symphony in C major, supposed to have been written by Schubert during a visit to Gastein in Autumn 1825, of which no trace is left. It has been suggested that it is identical with the Grand Duo for piano duet, op. 140, but recent views identify it as the 'Great' C major symphony. It must therefore have been composed in 1825, not, as previously thought, in 1828.

Gastoldi, Giovanni Giacomo (c. 1550–1622) Italian composer. He was maestro di cappella at the church of Santa Barbara, Mantua, 1592–1608; he was then appointed choirmaster at Milan Cathedral.

Works include: a Magnificat and other church music; madrigals; canzoni and balletti for voices and instruments (those of 1591 influenced Morley and Weelkes).

gat (Hindi 'movement', 'action') Hindustani composition type, usually played on plucked stringed instruments such as the ◊sitar and ◊sarod. Most are based on one of a limited number of stereotypical stroke patterns, and comprise two or three sections (*sthayi, antara*, and sometimes *manjha*). The most common type is the Masitkhani gat, named after the 19th-century sitarist Masit Khan, set in the 16-beat metric cycle *teental* at a slow tempo.

Gaudentios (lived 2nd century AD) Greek music theorist. He was the first to formulate a system of eight *tonoi* (modes in the scalic sense) based on the idea of joining the interval of a fourth to that of a fifth with one note common to both.

Gaveau, Etienne (1872–1943) French piano manufacturer. He followed his father **Joseph Gaveau** (1824–1903) and built a factory at Fontenay-sous-Bois in 1896, and a concert hall (Salle Gaveau) in Paris in 1907.

Gaviniès, Pierre (1728–1800) French violinist and composer. His compositions for the violin, including *Les vingt-quatre matinées* 1800, were the most demanding pieces in the violin repertory before Paganini.

He made his first appearance in Paris in 1741, at the Concert Spirituel, of which he was conductor 1773–77. He was professor of violin at the Paris Conservatory from its foundation in 1795.

Works include: the opera *Le Prétendu* (1760); violin concertos; sonatas for violin and bass, violin and piano, two violins, and unaccompanied violin, violin studies *Les vingt-quatre matinées* (1800), violin pieces including the *Romance de G*.

gavotte light-hearted dance in common time (4/4), originating from the Pays de Gap, France, whose inhabitants were called Gavots. Originally a folk dance, it was adopted by the court and continued to develop ever more complicated steps until it could only be performed by professional dancers. The music begins with an ◊upbeat of two crotchets, and the phrases usually begin and end in the middle of each bar. It became popular at the court of Louis XIV (Lully composed several gavottes), later becoming an optional movement of the Baroque ◊suite. The gavotte has been revived by some 20th-century composers, including Prokofiev and Schoenberg, who uses one in his *Suite* 1934.

Gawain opera in two acts by Harrison Birtwistle (libretto by D Harsent after the anonymous medieval poem *Sir Gawain and the Green Knight*), produced London, Covent Garden, 30 May 1991.

Gay, John (1685–1732) English poet and playwright. He wrote ◊*Acis and Galatea*

(Handel); ◊*Beggar's Opera*; (odes) ◊Busby; ◊*Dreigroschenoper* (Weill); ◊Polly.

Gaztambide y Garbayo, Joaquín (Romualdo) (1822–1870) Spanish conductor and composer. He studied at Pamplona and the Madrid Conservatory. After a stay in Paris he became a theatre manager and conducted in Madrid.

Works include: 44 zarzuelas, including *La mensajera*, *El estreno de una artista*, *El valle de Andorra*, *Catalina*, *Los Magyares*, *El juramento*, and *La conquista de Madrid*.

Gazza ladra, La/The Thieving Magpie opera by Rossini (libretto by G Gherardini, based on the French melodrama, *La Pie voleuse*, by J-M T B d'Aubigny and L C Caigniez), produced Milan, La Scala, 31 May 1817. Ninetta condemned to death for stealing silverware but released when a magpie is identified as the culprit.

Gazzaniga, Giuseppe (1743–1818) Italian composer. Of his 44 operas, *Don Giovanni o sia Il convitato di pietra* 1787 was an immediate forerunner of Mozart's opera of the same title, (which was produced later the same year in Prague); it has been revived at Wexford and elsewhere in recent years.

He was a pupil of Nicola Porpora and Niccolò Piccinni in Naples, where his first opera was produced in 1768. Later, he lived chiefly in Venice, until his appointment as maestro di cappella at Crema Cathedral in 1791. His works also include oratorios, a symphony, and three piano concertos.

Gebrauchsmusik (German 'utility music') term for a species of work written for practical use and best translated as 'workaday music'. It was common among German composers in the 1920s and 1930s. Hindemith's published works of the kind (several are unpublished) are: *Spielmusik* for strings, flutes, and oboes (1927); four three-part *Songs for Singing Groups*; an educational work for concerted violins in first position (1927); *Music to Sing or Play* (five nos. for various

The opening of Bach's gavotte from his French Suite no. 5.

vocal or instrumental combinations); *Lesson* for two male voices, narrator, chorus, orchestra, a dancer, clowns, and community singing (1929); *Let's Build a Town*, a musical game for children (1930); *Plöner Musiktag* (1932; four nos. for various vocal and instrumental combinations). Some other composers, such as Milhaud in France, Copland in the USA, and Weill and Orff in Germany, have done similar work.

Geburtstag der Infantin, Der/The Birthday of the Infanta pantomime by Schreker after the story by Wilde; composed 1908, first performed Vienna, 27 June 1908. Orchestrated in 1923 as a suite for large orchestra and performed Amsterdam, 18 October 1923, conductor Mengelberg; new ballet scenario by Schreker, 1926, under title *Spanisches Fest*, performed Berlin 22 January 1927, conductor Leo Blech. Wilde's story was set as an opera by Zemlinsky in 1920–21; Der ◊*Zwerg*.

gedackt, sometimes gedact, properly *gedeckt* (German 'covered') musical term meaning 'stopped'. It refers to ◊diapason organ stops producing a muted 8-ft tone.

gedämpft (German 'damped') musical term meaning 'muted, muffled', used to refer to drums.

Geduldige Socrates, Der/The Patient Socrates opera by Telemann (libretto by J U von König, after Minato), produced Hamburg, 28 January 1721. Socrates has his patience tried by the squabbling of his two wives.

Geharnischte Suite second suite for orchestra by Busoni; composed 1895, revised 1903, first performed Berlin, 1 December 1904. (*Geharnischte*, 'armoured man'.)

Geheime Königreich, Das/The Secret Kingdom fairy-tale opera in one act by Krenek (libretto by composer; 1926–27, produced in a triple bill with *Der Diktator* and *Schwergewicht*, Wiesbaden, 6 May 1928. King and queen find the answer in the forest to the riddle 'What contains the whole world in itself?'.

Geheimnis des entwendeten Briefes, Das chamber opera by Blacher (libretto by H Brauer after E A Poe's story *The Mystery of the Purloined Letter*). The first performance was planned for 2 February 1975 but postponed after Blacher's death on 30 January; produced Berlin, 14 February 1975.

Geibel, Emanuel von (1815–1884) German poet. His works inspired ◊Jensen (*Spanisches Liederbuch*); (Bruch and Mendelssohn) ◊Loreley; ◊Schumann (*Vom Pagen und der Königstochter*); (H Wolf) ◊*Spanisches Liederbuch*; Volbach (*Vom Pagen und der Königstochter*).

Geige (German 'fiddle') the familiar German name of the ◊violin.

Geiringer, Karl (Johannes) (1899–1989) Austrian-born US musicologist. He studied in Berlin and Vienna and was librarian at the Vienna Gesellschaft der Musikfreunde, 1930–38. He was resident in the USA from 1940 and professor of music history and theory at Boston University, 1941–62. He became professor of music at the University of California, Santa Barbara, 1962–72. He edited Haydn's music and published a monograph *Haydn: A Creative Life in Music* in 1946. He also wrote on Brahms (1935), musical instruments (1943), and the Bach family (1954).

Geisslerlieder (German 'flagellants' songs') sacred German monophonic songs of the Middle Ages in the Italian *laude* tradition and particularly cultivated at the time of the Black Death in 1349. The chief manuscript source is the *Chronikon* of Hugo von Reutlingen, which also describes how the singing was accompanied by penitential rites performed by the *Geissler* ('flagellants').

Gellert Lieder six songs by Beethoven for voice and piano to texts by C F Gellert, op. 48; composed c. 1802. The titles are, 1. *Bitten*; 2. *Die Liebe des Nächsten*; 3. *Vom Tode*; 4. *Die Ehre Gottes aus der Natur*; 5. *Gottes Macht und Vorsehung*; 6. *Busslied*.

Gelosie fortunate, Le/The Fortunate Jealousies opera by Anfossi (libretto by F Livigni), produced Venice, Teatro San Samuele, autumn 1786. Mozart added an aria to it on its production in Vienna, 2 June 1788.

Gelosie villane, Le/The Rustic Jealousies opera by Sarti (libretto by T Grandi, based on a comedy by Goldoni), produced Venice, Teatro San Samuele, November 1776.

gemel see ◊gymel.

Geminiani, Francesco (1687–1762) Italian violinist and composer. His treatise *The Art of Playing the Violin* 1751 was the first violin tutor ever published. His music was influenced by Corelli and is typically brilliant in fast movements and expressive in slow movements. He lived in London, Paris, and Dublin.

Geminiani was born at Lucca. He studied music under Alessandro Scarlatti and Corelli. In 1714 he visited England, where he very quickly became famous and decided to settle. A few years later he went to Dublin, and afterwards divided his time between England and Ireland. His teaching introduced modern violin technique to England, and he wrote several theoretical works.

Works include: concerti grossi, violin sonatas, cello sonatas, trio sonatas, keyboard pieces.

Gemma di Vergy opera by Donizetti (libretto by E Bidera, based on the elder Dumas's play, *Charles VII chez ses grands vassaux*), produced Milan, La Scala, 26 December 1834. Count of Vergy wants to annul marriage with infertile wife Gemma. Her slave Tamas stabs new wife Ida then kills himself; Gemma grieves.

gemshorn an obsolete type of recorder made from an animal's horn (especially that of a cow or goat). It disappeared from use during the 16th century. The name is also used for an organ stop of light, sweet tone, with conical pipes and usually 4-foot pitch (one octave above that written).

Generalbass (German 'general bass') see ◊thorough-bass.

Generali, Pietro (1773–1832) Italian composer. He studied under Giovanni Masi in Rome and in 1802 produced his first opera there. In 1817–21 he conducted opera at Barcelona, and later became maestro di cappella at Novara Cathedral.

Works include: about 60 operas, including *Gli amanti ridicoli*, *Il Duca Nottolone*, *La villana in cimento*, *Le gelosie di Giorgio*, *Pamela nubile* (after Richardson, *via* Goldoni's comedy, 1804), *La calzolaia*, *Misantropia e pentimento* (after Kotzebue), *Gli effetti della somiglianza*, *Don Chisciotte* (after Cervantes), *Orgoglio ed umiliazione*, *L'idolo cinese*, *Lo sposo in bersaglio*, *Le lagrime di una vedova* (1808), *Adelina* (1810), *La moglie giudice del marito*, *I baccanali di Roma* (1816), *Francesca da Rimini* (after Dante); Masses and other church music; cantata *Roma liberata*.

general MIDI, musical instrument digital interface or GM standard set of 96 instrument and percussion 'voices' that can be used to encode musical tracks which can be reproduced on any GM-compatible synthesizer, or ◊MIDI.

general pause, or G.P. in music, a rest in an orchestral work of at least one full bar for the entire orchestra, often appearing suddenly after a climax.

It originated in 18th-century Germany.

Genet, Elzéar (Carpentras) (c. 1470–1548) French composer. He wrote secular works to both Italian and French texts, and numerous Masses, motets, hymns, and Magnificats. He was a papal singer to Julius II in 1508 and maestro di cappella under Pope Leo X 1513–21, as well as being at the court of King Louis XII some time between those dates.

Genoveva opera by Schumann (libretto by composer, altered from one by R Reinick based on the dramas of Tieck and Hebbel), produced Leipzig, 25 June 1850. Genoveva's husband Siegfried departs for battle and entrusts his castle to Golo, who loves Genoveva. After being rejected, he frames her for adultery and is about to execute her, when Siegfried returns and the couple are reconciled.

Gentle Shepherd, The ballad opera (libretto by Allan Ramsay), produced Edinburgh, Taylor's Hall, 29 January 1729. It was first published (1725) as a pastoral comedy, and is therefore not, as is sometimes said, the first ballad opera, since *The Beggar's Opera* (1728) was staged earlier. Patie, of noble birth but brought up as a shepherd, wants to marry humble Peggy, but he believes it would be socially impossible. Later it turns out that she too is of noble blood.

Genzmer, Harald (1909–) German composer. His compositions include choral, orchestral, and chamber pieces. He taught composition at the Hochschule für Musik at Freiburg im Breisgau 1946–57, and was appointed professor at the Munich Hochschule in 1957.

He studied first in Marburg and later with Hindemith in Berlin.

Works include: the cantata *Racine* (1949); Mass in E; symphony no. 1, *Bremen symphony*; concertos for piano, cello, oboe, flute (2), trautonium (2); two string quartets; sonatas for violin, flute, and other chamber music.

George, Stefan (1868–1933) German poet. His works were used in A ◊Berg's compositions (*Wein*; *Lyric Suite*); A ◊Schoenberg's *Buch der hängenden Gärten*; and A ◊Webern's songs op. 3 and op. 4.

Gerber, Heinrich Nicolaus (1702–1775) German organist and composer. He was court organist at Sonderhausen from 1731. He improved and invented instruments, including the ◊Strohfiedel. He was the father of Ernst Ludwig Gerber.

He studied at Leipzig University under J S Bach.

Works include: a hymn-book with figured basses; variations on chorales for organ; music for harpsichord, organ, harp.

Gerbert, Martin (1720–1793) German music historian. He entered the Benedictine monastery of St Blasien in 1737 and was ordained priest in 1744, and abbot in 1764. He published a history of church music in 1774 under the title *De cantu et musica sacra*, and a collection of medieval music treatises in 1784.

Gerhard, Roberto (1896–1970) Spanish-born British composer. He studied with Enrique Granados and Arnold Schoenberg and settled in England in 1939, where he composed twelve-tone works in Spanish style. He composed the *Symphony No. 1* 1952–55, followed by three more symphonies and chamber music incorporating advanced techniques.

His achievement was to unite atonal methods with the colours and rhythms of his native Spain; some of his later music, notably the Third Symphony (*Collages*, 1960) allows some avant-garde techniques. His opera *The Duenna* 1947 received its British premiere 1992 (it was premiered in Wiesbaden, Germany, 1957).

Gerhard was born at Valls, near Barcelona. Although a choirboy and a tentative pianist and composer from an early age, he began serious music studies late, owing to parental opposition. He studied piano with Granados and composition with Carlos Pedrell at Barcelona 1915–22 and then composition with Schoenberg in Vienna 1923–28. He taught at Barcelona 1929–38, was in charge of the music department of the Catalan Library, for which he edited music by 18th-century Catalan composers, translated various music treatises into Spanish, and contributed to the literary weekly *Mirador*. Pedrell introduced him as a composer and he began to make his way in Spain and Latin America.

He settled in England after the Spanish Civil War in 1938, and lived in Cambridge, first on a research studentship at King's College, then for the rest of his life off his compositions, which included occasional, radio, and film music as well as more substantial works.

Works include: the opera *The Duenna* (after Sheridan, 1945–47); ballets *Ariel* (1934), *Soirées de Barcelone* (1938), *Don Quixote* (after Cervantes), *Alegrias* (1942), and *Pandora* (1944); oratorio *The Plague* (after Camus, 1964); music for radio plays *Cristobal Colón* and *Adventures of Don Quixote* (Eric Linklater after Cervantes); four symphonies (1952–67, no. 3 *Collages* for orchestra and magnetic tape); concerto for orchestra (1965); *Epithalamion* for orchestra (1966), violin concerto (1943); *Cancionero de Pedrell*, *Serranillas*, and *Cançons i Arietes* for voice and orchestra, *Hymnody* for 11 players (1963); *Concert for eight*; nonet (1956), two string quartets (1955, 1962); piano trio (1918), wind quintet; *Gemini* for violin

and piano; cantata for solo voices, chorus, and orchestra; song cycle *L'infantament meravellós de Shaharazada* (1917) and other songs; various arrangements of old Spanish music.

Gerle, Hans (c. 1500–1570) German lutenist, violist, and lute-maker. He was the son of Conrad Gerle (d. 1521), also a lute-maker. He published a book on viol and lute playing and two collections of lute pieces in tablature.

German, Edward (1862–1936), born Edward German Jones English composer. He is remembered for his operettas *Merrie England* 1902 and *Tom Jones* 1907, and he wrote many other instrumental, orchestral, and vocal works.

He studied at Shrewsbury and the Royal Academy of Music in London 1880–87. He became an orchestral violinist and in 1888 music director of the Globe Theatre, writing incidental music for various productions, including well-received music for Henry Irving's version of *Henry VIII* 1892. In 1901 he completed *The Emerald Isle*, left unfinished by Sullivan. He had his enduring success the following year, with *Merrie England*, often performed by amateur opera companies.

Works include: the light operas *The Rival Poets* (1886, revised 1901), *Merrie England* (1902), *The Princess of Kensington*, *Tom Jones* (after Fielding), *Fallen Fairies* (W S Gilbert); incidental music for Shakespeare's *Richard III*, *Henry VIII*, *Romeo and Juliet*, *As You Like It*, *Much Ado about Nothing*, Anthony Hope's *Nell Gwyn*, and others; two symphonies, symphonic suite in D minor, symphonic poem *Hamlet*, symphonic suite *The Seasons*, *Welsh Rhapsody*, *Theme and Six Diversions* and other orchestral works; Coronation March and Hymn for George V; chamber music and many songs.

German flute name for the transverse ◊flute in England in the 18th century.

German Requiem, A work for chorus, soprano and baritone solo, and orchestra by Brahms, op. 45, composed 1866–69, first performed Leipzig, 18 February 1869, conductor Reinecke. The original name, *Ein deutsches Requiem*, means that Brahms did not set the liturgical Latin text, but a choice of his own from Luther's translation of the Bible.

German sixth see ◊augmented 6th chords.

Gero, Jhan (fl. 1540–55) Franco-Flemish composer. He lived in Venice and was connected with the music printers Antonio Gardane (Gardano; 1509–69) and Girolamo

Scotto (1505–72). He composed motets, madrigals, and a highly successful book of duos, published 1541.

Gershwin, George (1898–1937), born Jacob US composer.

His musical comedies, mostly to lyrics by his brother **Ira Gershwin** (1896–1983), were among Broadway's most successful in the 1920s and 1930s, including *Strike up the Band* 1927, *Funny Face* 1927, and *Girl Crazy* 1930. He also wrote concert works including the tone poems *Rhapsody in Blue* 1924 and *An American in Paris* 1928. His opera *Porgy and Bess* 1935 incorporated jazz rhythms and popular song styles in an operatic format.

Successful songs from the Gershwin brothers' musicals include 'I Got Rhythm', ''S Wonderful', and 'Embraceable You'.

Gershwin was born in Brooklyn, New York. He worked as a pianist in a music publisher's office 1914–17, and wrote songs (his first was published in 1916) and a musical comedy, *La, La, Lucille* 1919. Although his scores to musicals made him famous, his 'serious' work, including *Rhapsody in Blue* and *Piano Concerto in F* 1925, earned him much critical acclaim. *Of Thee I Sing* 1931, a collaboration between the Gershwin brothers, was the first musical to win a Pulitzer prize.

Although his melodic gift was long recognized, it took many years for his masterpiece, *Porgy and Bess*, to reach a wide audience; it was not staged at the New York Metropolitan Opera House until 1985, and had to wait until 1986 for its premiere by a British company, at Glyndebourne.

Works include: the opera *Porgy and Bess* (1935); many musical comedies including *Lady Be Good* and *Of Thee I Sing* (1931); music for several films; *An American in Paris* (1928) and *Cuban Overture* (1932) for orchestra; *Rhapsody in Blue* (1924) and concerto for piano and orchestra (1925); a large number of popular songs, including 'Lady Be Good', 'I Got Rhythm', 'The Man I Love', 'Embraceable You', and 'Love Walked In'.

Gervaise, Claude (lived 16th century)

French arranger and composer. He composed a considerable amount of dance music for various instruments, and several books of chansons, 1541–57.

Gesang der Jünglinge/The Song of the Youths

work by Stockhausen for sung and spoken boys' voices, electrically processed and relayed through five loudspeakers; text from the *Book of Daniel*, on three Hebrew youths undergoing ordeal by fire in Babylon. First performed Cologne, 30 May 1956.

Geschöpfe des Prometheus, Die/The Creatures of Prometheus

ballet by Beethoven (choreographed by Salvatore Vigano), produced Vienna, Burgtheater, 28 March 1801.

Gese, Bartholomäus (1555 or 1562–1613), or Barthel Göss,

German theologian and composer whose works were important in the development of the Protestant Passion. He was cantor at the Marienkirche, Frankfurt, from 1593 until his death.

Works include: Masses (one on themes by Lassus), motets, psalms, hymns, sacred songs, and other pieces, all for the Lutheran Church; Passion according to St John; wedding and funeral music.

Gesius, Bartholomäus see ◊Gese, Bartholomäus.

Gestalt (German 'shape, formation')

word that has gained currency as a musical term in German-speaking countries, used in music analysis and in philosophical or aesthetic discussions on music to designate a musical idea as it comes from the composer's mind in what is supposed to be a kind of primeval or pre-existing form.

gestopft (German 'stopped, obstructed')

in music, notes played on the horn with the hand inserted into the bell to produce an altered sound. Formerly this technique enabled the player to obtain extra notes not in the series of natural harmonics, a device made unnecessary by the valve horn.

Gesualdo

opera by Alfred Schnittke (libretto by Richard Bletschacher), produced Vienna, Staatsoper, 26 May 1995.

Gesualdo, Carlo (c. 1561–1613), prince of Venosa

Italian composer and lutenist. His compositions, which comprise sacred and secular vocal music, and some instrumental pieces, are noted for their complex (modern-sounding) harmonic structure, most unlike the work of his contemporaries. His highly chromatic madrigals (in six books 1594–1611), set to emotional, passionate texts, have been admired in the 20th century by Stravinsky, among others.

In 1590 he had his wife and her lover murdered; he married Leonora d'Este of Ferrara in 1593, and lived at the court in Ferrara until 1596.

Gesualdo took his music studies seriously in his youth and became a very accomplished lutenist. He married his first cousin Maria d'Avalos, a Neapolitan noblewoman, in 1586. Though only 21, she had already been married twice and had children. She bore him a son, but became the lover of Fabrizio Caraffa, 3rd Duke of Andria; Gesualdo had them both murdered on the night of 16 October 1590. In 1594 he went to the court of Ferrara and married Leonora d'Este there, but returned to his estate at Naples in 1596, where he spent the rest of his life in a state of profound depression.

His work is notable for its expressive power and chromatic harmony. In 1960 Stravinsky orchestrated three of Gesualdo's madrigals, to mark the 400th anniversary of his birth. He is the subject of Alfred Schnittke's second opera, *Gesualdo*.

Works include: seven books of madrigals (the last posthumously published of pieces composed in 1594); two books of *Sacrae cantiones*, responds for six voices.

Getreue Alceste, Die/The Faithful Alcestis opera by Schürmann (libretto by J U König), produced Brunswick, February 1719.

Gevaert, François Auguste (1828–1908) Belgian music historian, theorist, and composer. He studied at Ghent and worked as organist there; later travelled in Spain, Italy, and Germany. He was director of music at the Paris Opéra, 1867–70, and of the Brussels Conservatory from 1871. He wrote several treatises on history, plainsong, and theory.

Works include: the operas *Hugues de Zomerghem* (1848), *La Comédie à la ville*, *Georgette* (1848), *Le Billet de Marguerite*, *Les Lavandières de Santarem* (1855), *Quentin Durward* (after Scott, 1858), *Le Diable au moulin*, *Château Trompette*, *La Poularde de Caux* (1861), *Les Deux Amours*, *Le Capitaine Henriot*; Requiem for male voices and orchestra (1853), Christmas cantata, psalm *Super flumina*, cantatas *De nationale verjaerdag* and *Le Retour de l'armée*; orchestral *Fantasia sobre motivos españoles*.

Gezeichneten, Die/The Stigmatized opera by Schreker (libretto by composer; composed 1913–15, produced Frankfurt, 25 April 1918. Crippled Alviano loves Carlotta, but loses her to the handsome Tamare. Carlotta dies as Alviano kills his rival.

Ghedini, Giorgio Federico (1892–1965) Italian composer. He made editions of music by Monteverdi, the Gabrielis, and Frescobaldi. He studied at Turin and Bologna, at first intending to be a conductor. He later taught at the conservatories of Turin, Parma, and Milan, but eventually devoted himself to composition.

Ghedini was born at Cuneo, Piedmont. He studied at Milan Conservatory, where he eventually became director. A follower of Alfredo Casella, his best orchestral pieces are among the neoclassical works which come closest to the spirit of the Italian instrumentalism of Vivaldi's lifetime. He wrote one opera, *Billy Budd* (after Melville), in 1949, but is most renowned for his orchestral pieces such as *Partita* 1926, *Architetture* 1940, and *Concerto dell' Albatro* 1945.

Works include: eight operas, including *Le baccanti* (after Euripides, produced Milan, 1948), and *Billy Budd* (after Meville, produced Venice, 1949); incidental music for Euripides' *Iphigenia in Tauris*; two Masses and various choral works; *Partita*, symphonies, *Concerto dell' Albatro* (after Melville's *Moby Dick*) for orchestra; concertos for piano, two pianos, two cellos and violin; concerto for violin and flute with chamber orchestra; wind quintet, piano quartet; two string quartets and other chamber music; violin and piano sonata; piano works; songs.

Gherardello da Firenze (c. 1320/25–1362/63) Italian composer. He wrote sacred works, madrigals, and other pieces, but is famous especially for his caccia (canonic hunting-song) 'Tosto che l'alba del bel giorno appare'.

Gherardeschi, Filippo Maria (1738–1808) Italian composer. He was a pupil of Padre Martini at Bologna, 1756–61, and became maestro di cappella at the cathedrals of Volterra and Pistoia, and finally, from c. 1766 to his death, at S Stefano in Pisa. He was also music director to the court of the Grand Duke of Tuscany.

Works include: seven operas, church music, keyboard music.

Ghiselin, Jean (c. 1455–c. 1511), or Verbonnet Flemish composer. He was active especially in Ferrara. The music printer Ottaviano Petrucci of Venice published several of his works between 1501 and 1507. He composed Masses (a volume was published in 1503), motets, songs, and other pieces.

Ghislanzoni, Antonio (1824–1893) Italian baritone, novelist, music editor, and librettist. He edited the *Gazzetta musicale* of Milan and collaborated on the libretto for Verdi's *Aida*, as well as writing c. 85 libretti of his own.

Ghosts of Versailles, The opera in two acts by John Corigliano (libretto by W H Hoffmann, after Beaumarchais), produced New York Metropolitan Opera, 19 December 1991. Beaumarchais himself makes a ghostly appearance, and attempts to rescue Marie Antoinette from the guillotine.

'Ghost' Trio the nickname given to Beethoven's piano trio in D major, op. 70 no. 1, on account of its slow movement in D minor, which has a mysterious, gloomy and haunting theme, accompanied frequently by string tremolos. Sketches for the work appear on the same sheet as sketches for a projected opera on Macbeth.

Ghro, Johann (c. 1575–1627), or Groh German organist and composer. He was organist at Meissen 1604–12 and later became music director at Wesenstein.

Works include: intradas, pavanes, galliards, and other pieces for several instruments; sacred music.

Giacobbi, Girolamo (1567–c. 1629) Italian composer. He was maestro di cappella at the church of San Petronio at Bologna 1604–08.

Works include: operas and intermedi: *Andromeda* (produced Salzburg, 1618; perhaps first opera outside Italy), *L'Aurora ingannata, Amor prigioniero, La selva dei mirti, Il Reno sacrificante*; motets, psalms, and other church music.

Giacomelli, Geminiano (c. 1692–1740) Italian composer. He was a pupil of Capelli at Parma, and possibly later of A Scarlatti. He was maestro di cappella at Parma, 1719–27 and 1732–37; at Piacenza, 1727–32; at Loreto from 1738.

Works include: the operas *Ipermestra* (1724), *Cesare in Egitto* (1735) and c. 16 others; two oratorios, other sacred works; concert arias.

Giannettini, Antonio (1648–1721) Italian composer. He sang at St Mark's, Venice, c. 1674–86, and was maestro di cappella at the ducal court of Modena from 1686. He produced his first opera, *Medea in Atene*, at Venice, 1675.

Works include: the operas, *Temistocle* (1683), *Artaserse* (1705), oratorios, cantatas, motets, psalms.

Giannini, Vittorio (1903–1966) US composer, brother of Dusolina Giannini. He studied at Juilliard with Rubin Goldmark and taught there from 1939, and taught at Curtis Institute from 1956. His music reflects his Italian ancestry.

Works include: the operas *Lucedia* (1934), *The Scarlet Letter* (1938), *Beauty and the Beast* (1938), *The Taming of the Shrew* (1953), *The Harvest* (1961) and *The Servant of Two Masters* (1967); symphony *In Memoriam Theodore Roosevelt* (1935) and four numbered symphonies; three divertimenti; piano concerto

(1937), *Stabat Mater* and Requiem (1937); chamber music and songs.

Gianni Schicchi (Puccini). See ◊*Trittico*.

'Giant's Fugue' the nickname of Bach's fugal chorale prelude on 'Wir glauben all', in Part III of the *Clavierübung*, so named because of a striding figure in the pedals.

Giardini, Felice de (1716–1796) Italian violinist and composer. He played in the opera orchestras at Rome and Naples, visited Germany in 1748, and then settled in London, where he succeeded Michael Festing as leader of the Italian opera orchestra at the King's Theatre in 1752. He played and taught there until 1784, when he retired to Italy, but he reappeared in London in 1790 and died during a tour of Russia.

Giardini was born at Turin. He was a chorister at Milan Cathedral and later a pupil of Giovanni Battista Somis at Turin.

Works include: the operas *Enea e Lavinia* (1764), *Il rè pastore* (1765), and others; incidental music for William Mason's *Elfrida*; oratorio *Ruth* (with Avison); 12 violin concertos; 21 string quartets, six string quintets, seven sets of string trios; sonatas for violin and piano; violin duets.

Giasone/Jason opera by Cavalli (libretto by G A Cicognini), after the Greek myth *Jason and the Argonauts*; produced Venice, Teatro San Cassiano, probably 5 January 1649. Jason gets the fleece and falls in love with Medea, but in the end returns to his first love, Hypsipyle.

Gibbons, Orlando (1583–1625) English composer. He wrote sacred anthems, instrumental fantasias, and madrigals including *The Silver Swan* for five voices 1612. From a family of musicians, he became organist at Westminster Abbey, London, in 1623.

Gibbons was brought up at Cambridge, where he took a degree in music in 1606. He was a singer at the Chapel Royal from 1603 and organist there from about 1615 until his death. Oxford awarded him an honorary doctorate in 1622, and the following year he was appointed organist at Westminster Abbey. He died suddenly at Canterbury while waiting to officiate at Charles I's marriage service, for which he had written music.

Works include: Anglican church music (5 services, about 13 full anthems, and about 25 verse anthems); 20 madrigals; *Cries of London* for voices and strings, 30 fantasies for strings, 4 *In Nomine* for strings, 2 pavanes and 2 galliards for strings; 16 keyboard fantasies, 6

sets of variations for keyboard and other keyboard pieces.

Gibbs, C(ecil) Armstrong (1889–1960) English composer. He was educated at Winchester College and Trinity College, Cambridge, where he studied music with Dent, and later at the Royal College of Music in London, where he became a professor of composition.

Works include: incidental music to Maeterlinck's *The Betrothal* (1921); comic opera *The Blue Peter* (A P Herbert, 1923); play with music *Midsummer Madness* (Clifford Bax); Nativity play *The Three Kings*; cantata *The Birth of Christ* (1929), Passion according to St Luke, choral symphony *Odysseus; La Belle Dame sans merci* (Keats, 1928), *The Highwayman* (Alfred Noyes) and *Deborah and Barak* for chorus and orchestra; symphony in E major; string quartet in A major; songs.

Gibbs, Joseph (1699–1788) English organist and composer. He was an organist at various Essex churches, finally at St Mary-le-Tower, Ipswich from 1748 until his death. His most important publication is a set of eight violin sonatas (dating from about 1746); six string quartets (from about 1777) and organ music also survive.

Gibson, Alexander (1926–1995) Scottish conductor. He cofounded Scottish Opera in 1962: *Les Troyens* 1969 and *Der Ring des Nibelungen* 1971 were notable achievements.

He studied in Scotland and London, and spent the 1950s with Sadlers Wells Opera and the British Broadcasting Corporation (BBC) Scottish Symphony Orchestra. He was principal conductor with the Scottish National Orchestra 1959–84. His US debut was with the Detroit Symphony Orchestra in 1970, and he was principal guest conductor with the Houston Symphony Orchestra from 1981. In 1990 he conducted *Tosca* with Scottish Opera, *Otello* for Kentucky Opera, and *Tristan* at the Bruckner Festival, Linz.

giga (Italian 'jig') see ◊jig.

gigue lively dance form which developed in two directions, one French, one Italian (*giga*), probably from the 16th-century English jig. The French variety, popular in France during the early 1700s, is in a moderate or fast tempo (6/4 or 6/8) while the Italian variety is quicker (12/8).

In musical notation, the writing of the French form is characterized by wide leaps and dotted rhythms. It is more contrapuntal than most other dance forms of the period, similar in style to a ◊fugue with an inverted subject (principal melody) for the second theme. The Italian variety is characterized by 'running' figures and few leaps. It is non-fugal with a more obvious harmonic framework. The gigue came to be used, more often than not, as the last movement of a Baroque ◊suite. Composers of the more common French form include Bach, Handel, and Froberger.

Gilbert, Anthony (1934–) English composer. He studied at Morley College under Anthony Milner and Walter Goehr. Has taught in Manchester and London and has worked as a music editor.

Works include: *Sinfonia* for chamber orchestra (1965); *Regions* for two chamber orchestras (1969); *The Scene Machine*, one-act opera produced Kassel (1971); *Cantata* (1972); Symphony (1973); *The Chakravaka Bird*, song drama for radio (1977); *Towards Asavari* for piano and small orchestra (1978); *Vasanta with Dancing* for chamber ensemble (1981); *Beastly Jingles* for soprano and ensemble (1984); *Dream Carousels* for wind orchestra (1988); *Certain Lights Reflecting* for soprano and orchestra (1989); two string quartets (1986–87); *Tree of Singing Names* for chamber orchestra (1989, revised 1993); *Upstream River* for narrator and ensemble (1991).

Gilbert, Henry (Franklin Belknap) (1868–1928) US composer. He studied at Boston and became a businessman, but later devoted himself to composition. He often used ragtime and African-American tunes for his thematic material.

Works include: ballet *The Dance in Place Congo* (after G W Cable); symphonic prologue to Synge's *Riders to the Sea* (1913); *Salammbô's Invocation to Tanith* (after Flaubert) for soprano and orchestra; *Indian Sketches* and *Hymn to America* for chorus and orchestra; *Americanesque, Comedy Overture on Negro Themes* (1906), three *American Dances, Negro Rhapsody, Legend*, and *Negro Episode* for orchestra; *The Island of Fay* (after Poe, 1923); *Indian Scenes* and *Negro Dances* for piano; *Pirate Song* (Stevenson) for voice and piano; edition of 100 folk songs.

Gilbert, W(illiam) S(chwenck) (1836–1911) English playwright and librettist. He wrote libretti for operettas with music by Sullivan, ◊Gondoliers, ◊Grand Duke, ◊HMS Pinafore, ◊Iolanthe, ◊Mikado, ◊Patience, ◊Pirates of Penzance, ◊Princess Ida, ◊Ruddigore, ◊Sorcerer, The, ◊Thespis, ◊Trial by Jury, Utopia Limited, ◊Yeoman of the Guard.

Giles, Nathaniel (c. 1558–1634) English organist and composer. He was organist of Worcester Cathedral 1581–85, and then became organist and choirmaster of St George's

Chapel, Windsor. In 1596 he became organist and choirmaster of the Chapel Royal in London, and took the official titles of Gentleman and Master of the Children on the death of William Hunnis in 1597. He collaborated with the playwright Ben Jonson at Blackfriars Theatre, London, from 1600.

He received a doctorate in music from Oxford University in 1622.

Works include: services, anthems, motets; madrigal 'Cease now, vain thoughts'.

Gilson, Paul (1865–1942) Belgian composer. He was appointed professor of harmony at the Brussels Conservatory in 1899 and of Antwerp Conservatory in 1904. He was also music critic of the newspapers *Le Soir*, 1906–14, and then of *Le Midi*.

His teachers included François Gevaert. He won the Belgian Prix de Rome in 1889.

Works include: the operas *Prinses Zonneschijn* and *Zeevolk* (1895); ballets *La Captive* and *Daphne*; oratorio *Le Démon* (after Lermontov); *Francesca da Rimini* (after Dante) for solo voices, chorus, and orchestra (1892); *La mer* for reciter and orchestra (1892).

Ginastera, Alberto Evaristo (1916–1983) Argentinian composer. His early works, including his *Pampeana No. 3* 1954, are mostly in a nationalistic style, but after 1958 he turned to modern techniques of ◊serialism, aleatory rhythms (see ◊aleatory music), and the use of microtones. He is best known for his operas, which renounce his earlier nationalist style for more advanced atonal techniques: *Don Rodrigo* 1964, *Bomarzo* 1967, and *Beatrix Cenci* 1971.

He studied with Athos Palma at the National Conservatory of Buenos Aires and graduated in 1938. He visited the USA 1945–47, and from 1948 taught in Buenos Aires, where he was director of the Centre for Advanced Musical Studies from 1963. After *Bomarzo* was banned in Argentina for alleged obscenities in the ballet, he left Buenos Aires and lived in the USA from 1968 and Europe from 1970.

Works include: the operas *Don Rodrigo* (1964), *Bomarzo* (1967), *Beatrix Cenci* (1971); ballets *Panambi* (1940) and *Estancia*; psalms for chorus and orchestra; *Variacones concertantes* for orchestra (1953), *Concerto per corde* (1965), *Estudos sinfónicos* (1967), two piano concertos (1961, 1972), violin concerto (1963), two cello concertos (1968, 1980), three string quartets (1948, 1953, 1973), three piano sonatas (1952, 1981, 1982), piano quintet (1963), cello sonata (1979); cantata *Bomarzo* for narrator, baritone, and orchestra (1964).

Gines Pérez, Juan (1548–1612) Spanish composer. He held a church appointment in his native town at the age of 14. He was maestro di cappella and director of the choir school at Valencia 1581–95. In 1595 he returned home as canon at Orihuela Cathedral.

Works include: motets, psalms; secular Spanish songs; contributions to the Mystery play performed annually at Elche, near Alicante.

Gintzler, Simon (c. 1500–after 1550) German composer. His collection of lute music was published in Venice in 1547, and he also contributed to Hans Gerle's *Eyn Newes ... Lautenbuch*, published in Nuremberg in 1552.

Gioconda, La opera by Ponchielli (libretto by Boito, based on Victor Hugo's *Angelo*), produced Milan, La Scala, 8 April 1876. Gioconda loves Enzo, but so does Laura. The evil Barnaba does his best to thwart everyone's happiness, eventually causing Gioconda's suicide.

giocoso (Italian 'jocose') in musical notation, merry, humorous.

Gioielli della Madonna, I/The Jewels of the Madonna opera by Wolf-Ferrari (libretto by E Golisciani and C Zangarini), produced, in German, Berlin, Kurfürsten-Oper, 23 December 1911. Gennaro wins Mariella by stealing the jewels of the Madonna, but rival Raffaele intervenes and the lovers kill themselves.

Giordani, Tommaso (c. 1730–1806) Italian composer. The son of a travelling opera impresario, he produced his first opera with his father's company in London in 1756. He subsequently lived chiefly in London (he was director at the King's Theatre, Haymarket 1768–83) and Dublin, and composed a large number of theatrical works for both cities. He was unrelated to either Carmine or Giuseppe Giordani.

Works include: the operas *La comediante fatta cantatrice* (1756), *L'eroe cinese* (1766), *Love in Disguise* (1766), *Il padre e il figlio rivali*, *Artaserse*, *Il re pastore* (1778), *Phillis at Court*, and others, about 50 in all; songs for Sheridan's *The Critic*; oratorio, *Isaac*; church music; concertos and sonatas for piano and other instruments; string quartets, trios; songs.

Giordano, Umberto (1867–1948) Italian composer. He was a popular composer in the tradition of romantic realism that was the vogue at the end of the 19th century, and most of his themes were melodramatic. He is best known for the operas *Andrea Chénier*

1896, set in the French Revolution, *Fedora* 1898, and the comic *Il rè/The King* 1929.

Giordano was born at Foggia, the son of an artisan. He was allowed to learn music as best he could, but in the end studied at the Naples Conservatory under Paolo Serrao. He attracted the attention of the publisher Edoardo Sonzogno (1836–1920) with the opera *Marina* 1889, written while he was still a student, and soon became very successful with a series of stage works.

Works include: the operas *Marina* (1889), *Mala vita* (1892), *Regina Diaz* (1894), *Andrea Chénier* (1896), *Fedora* (after Sardou, 1898), *Siberia* (1903), *Marcella, Mese Mariano, Madame Sans-Gêne* (after Sardou and Moreau, 1915), *Giove a Pompei* (with Franchetti), *La cena delle beffe* (1924), *Il rè*.

Giorno di regno, Un, ossia Il finto Stanislao/A Day's Reign, or The False Stanislas opera by Verdi (libretto by F Romani, used earlier by Gyrowetz, ◊*Finto Stanislao*), produced Milan, La Scala, 5 September 1840. It is Verdi's only comic opera except *Falstaff*. Belfiore is disguised as King Stanislaus to protect the sovereign. A comedy in which he prevents his love, the widow Marchesa, from marrying another.

Giovanna d'Arco/Joan of Arc opera by Verdi (libretto by T Solera, based on Schiller's drama *Die Jungfrau von Orleans*), produced Milan, La Scala, 15 February 1845. Joan rallies the troops of defeated Charles VII of France. Although denounced as a follower of Satan by her father, Giacomo, she goes on to save the day, but falls in battle.

Giovanna di Guzman (Verdi). See ◊*Vêpres siciliennes*.

Giovannelli, Ruggiero (c. 1560–1625) Italian composer. After holding various church apointments in Rome, he succeeded Palestrina as maestro di cappella at St Peter's in 1594, and was maestro di cappella of the Sistine Chapel 1614–24. At the request of Pope Paul V he contributed to a new edition of the Gradual.

Works include: Masses, Miserere, and other church music; six books of madrigals, one of canzonette and villanelle.

Giovannini (died 1782) Italian composer. The customary identification of Giovannini with the Comte de St Germain remains without proof. The only works extant under the name Giovannini are a handful of songs (including 'Willst du dein Herz mir schenken' in Bach's *Anna Magdalena Notebook*) and eight violin sonatas.

Giove in Argo/Jupiter in Argos opera by Lotti (libretto by A M Lucchini), produced Dresden, Redoutensaal, 25 October 1717, the new opera house not being ready. The latter was opened with the same work 3 September 1719. (An English adaptation of the same libretto, under the title *Jupiter in Argos*, was set by Handel, produced London, King's Theatre, 1 May 1739.)

Gioventù di Enrico V, La/The Youth of Henry V opera by Pacini (libretto by J Ferretti, partly based on Shakespeare's *Henry IV*), produced Rome, Teatro Valle, 26 December 1820.

Gipps, Ruth (1921–) English composer, pianist, and oboist. In 1944–45 she played second oboe and English horn in the City of Birmingham Symphony Orchestra. She conducted the London Repertoire Orchestra 1955–86, and was a professor at the Royal College of Music from 1967.

She studied under her mother at the Bexhill School of Music and later under Vaughan Williams at the Royal College of Music in London.

Works include: the ballet *Sea Nymph*; five symphonies (1942–80), other orchestral music, including six concertos, and chamber works.

Giraud de Borneil (1156–1200), or Guiraut de Bornelh, Provençal ◊troubadour. He was a professional poet who wrote in most of the lyric genres. His love songs, often complex in thought and expression despite his defence of a simple style, were praised by Dante for their moral seriousness.

Girdlestone, C(uthbert) M(orton) (1895–1975) English scholar. He was educated at the Sorbonne in Paris and at Cambridge, where he became lecturer in French. He was professor of French at King's College, Newcastle-upon-Tyne, 1926–61, and wrote the books *Mozart et ses concertos pour piano* and *Jean-Philippe Rameau*.

Girl of the Golden West (Puccini). See ◊*Fanciulla del West, La*.

Giselle, ou Les Wilis ballet by Adam (choreography by Jean Coralli, on a story by Heine, adapted by Théophile Gautier), produced Paris, Opéra, 28 June 1841.

gittern medieval guitar with four strings, played with a plectrum. It survived in England until around 1400; the term was then applied to other members of the guitar family in the 16th–17th centuries.

Giuliano opera by Zandonai (libretto by A Rossato, based on Flaubert's *Saint Julien* *l'Hospitalier*), produced Naples, Teatro San Carlo, 4 February 1928.

Giulietta e Romeo/Juliet and Romeo opera by Vaccai (libretto by F Romani, after Shakespeare's sources for Romeo and Juliet), produced Milan, Teatro della Canobbiana, 31 October 1825.
Opera by Zandonai (libretto by A Rossato, after Shakespeare), produced Rome, Teatro Costanzi, 14 February 1922.
Opera by Zingarelli (libretto by G M Foppa), produced Milan, La Scala, 30 January 1796.

Giulio Cesare opera by Malipiero (libretto by composer, based on Shakespeare's *Julius Caesar*), produced Genoa, Teatro Carlo Felice, 8 February 1936.

Giulio Cesare in Egitto/Julius Caesar in Egypt opera by Handel (libretto by N F Haym), produced London, King's Theatre, Haymarket, 20 February 1724. Caesar beats off rivals in love and war to marry Cleopatra.

Giulio Sabino opera by Sarti (libretto by P Giovannini), produced Venice, Teatro San Benedetto, January 1781.

Giuramento, Il/The Vow opera by Mercadante (libretto by G Rossi, based on victor Hugo's *Angelo*), produced Milan, La Scala, 10 March 1837. Manfredo commands Bianca to take poison after her adultery with Viscardo, but envious Elaisa substitutes a sleeping potion.

Giustini, Lodovico (1685–1743) Italian composer and organist. In 1732 he published a book of sonatas, probably the first published music written specifically for the piano, as distinct from music for keyboard instruments in general.

Giustinian, Leonardo (1383–1446) Italian poet. He wrote love poems for musical settings, some of which he provided himself, which were called after him as late as the 16th century.

Giustino opera by Handel (altered libretto from Nicolo Beregani), produced London, Covent Garden, 16 February 1737. Giustino joins Anastasius in battle against Vitalian. Later Giustino and Vitalian join forces to defeat the usurping Amantius, who has imprisoned Anastasius. The opera concludes with Giustino united with Leocasta, whom he has rescued earlier.

giusto (Italian 'just', 'strictly') term used in musical notation, as in *tempo giusto*.

Glagolitic Mass work by Janáček for soloists, chorus, organ, and orchestra (text by M Weingart from Ordinary of the Mass in 9th-century Slavonic). Five main sections are *Gospodi pomiluj*, *Slava*, *Veřuju*, *Svet*, *Agneče Božij*; composed 1926, first performed Brno, 5 December 1927.

Glanville-Hicks, Peggy (1912–1990) Australian composer. In 1938 her choral suite was performed at the International Society for Contemporary Music festival in London.
She studied at the Melbourne Conservatory and from the age of 19 under Vaughan Williams, Gordon Jacob, and R O Morris at the Royal College of Music in London. She won a scholarship in 1932 and another in 1935, which enabled her to travel and to study further with Wellesz in Vienna and Nadia Boulanger in Paris. In 1939 she married the composer Stanley Bate, with whom she went to the USA, living in New York until 1958 and Greece from 1959.

Works include: the operas *Cædmon* (1934), *The Transposed Heads* (1953), *The Glittering Gate* (1959), *Nausicaa* (1961), *Sappho* (1963); Sinfonietta, *Prelude* and *Scherzo*, *Span*, *Suite*, and *Music for Robots* for orchestra; choral suite (Fletcher) for women's voices, oboe, and strings; piano concerto, flute concerto; *Concertino da camera* for flute, clarinet, bassoon, and piano; six Housman songs.

Glareanus, Henricus (1488–1563), real name Heinrich Loris Swiss theorist. He studied the relationship between the Greek and the church modes and wrote treatises, notably *Isagoge in musicen* 1516 and *Dodecachordon* 1547, containing his new theory of 12 church modes.
He studied music at Berne and Cologne, and taught at Basel from 1515 and again from 1522, after holding a professorship in Paris from 1517 on the recommendation of Erasmus of Rotterdam. In 1529 he settled at Freiburg im Breislau, Germany.

Glass, Louis (Christian August) (1864–1936) Danish composer. He is best known for his symphonies, which include no. 3 *Skovsymfoni/Wood Symphony* 1901 and no. 5 *Svastica* 1911.
Glass studied at the Brussels Conservatory and came under the influence of César Franck. He was a contemporary of Nielsen but his music more often recalls Austrian models of the same period. Some of his symphonies have been revived in recent years by Edward Downes.

Works include: the symphonies: no. 1 (1893), no. 2 (1899), no. 3 *Skovsymfoni/Wood Symphony* (1901), no. 4 (1911), no. 5 *Svastica* (1911), no. 6 *Skjoldungeaet/Birth of the Scyldings* (1926); concertos for oboe, violin, and cello;

four string quartets (1890–1906); string sextet (1892); piano quintet (1896); cello sonata and two violin sonatas; piano music and songs.

Glass, Philip (1937–) US composer. As a student of Nadia Boulanger, he was strongly influenced by Indian music; his work is characterized by repeated rhythmic figures that are continually expanded and modified. His compositions include the operas *Einstein on the Beach* 1976, *Akhnaten* 1984, *The Making of the Representative for Planet 8* 1988, and the *'Low' Symphony* 1992 on themes from David Bowie's *Low* album.

He studied at the Juilliard School and with Boulanger in Paris. Under the influence of Indian and North African music he has evolved a technique (minimalism) whereby melodic ideas are not developed but juxtaposed in 'timeless' repetitions. He won early fame in New York with the four-hour *Einstein on the Beach*, and this success was consolidated with the Gandhi opera *Satyagraha* 1980 and the pharaonic *Akhnaten* 1984. Later works seemed to have lacked fresh musical ideas, but creative renewal came with an opera for Columbus Day, given at the New York Metropolitan Opera House in 1992.

Works include: *Einstein on the Beach* (Avignon and New York Metropolitan, 1976); *Satyagraha* (Rotterdam, 1980); *The Photographer* (Amsterdam, 1982); *Civil Wars* (1982–84); *Akhnaten* (Stuttgart, 1984); *The Juniper Tree* (Cambridge, Massachusetts, 1985, with Robert Moran), *The Fall of the House of Usher* (Cambridge, 1988), *The Making of the Representative for Planet 8* (Houston, 1988), *1,000 Airplanes on the Roof* (Vienna Airport, 1988), *Hydrogen Jukebox* (Charleston, South Carolina, 1990), *The Voyage* (New York Metropolitan, 1992); also instrumental ensemble works, including *Music with Changing Parts* (1970), *Music in 12 Parts* (1971–74); violin concerto (1987) and string quartet (1993).

glass harmonica, or armonica musical instrument based on the principle of playing a wine glass with a wet finger. It consists of a graded series of glass bowls nested on a spindle and resting in a trough part-filled with water. Rotated by a foot pedal, it emits pure tones of unchanging intensity when touched either by the fingers or mechanically. It was devised by Benjamin Franklin; Mozart, Beethoven, and Schubert all wrote pieces for it.

Glazunov, Aleksandr Konstantinovich (1865–1936) Russian composer. He achieved fame with his first symphony, which was written when he was only 17. He absorbed a range of influences, from his teacher Rimsky-Korsakov's orchestrational skill to Tchaikovsky's lyricism. His own style fits between that of the Russian national school of The ◊Five and that of the western European 'cosmopolitan' composers. He made a significant impact as a teacher on the following generation of composers, including Prokofiev and Shostakovich.

Glazunov was born at St Petersburg. After being taught music at home as a child, he studied with Rimsky-Korsakov from 1880 and finished his course in 18 months, having a first symphony ready for performance early in 1882. Belaiev arranged a concert of his works in 1884 and began to publish them. He visited western Europe in 1884, and his music thereafter reconciled current European musical trends with Russian influences from Tchaikovsky and Borodin. In 1897 he conducted the premiere of Rachmaninov's 1st symphony, allegedly while drunk. He was appointed director of the St Petersburg Conservatory in 1905, and wrote little after that to augment his enormous earlier output. He completed several of Borodin's unfinished works, notably the overture to *Prince Igor*. He left Russia in 1928 and settled in Paris.

Works include: STAGE ballets *Raymonda* (1897) and *The Seasons* (1899); eight symphonies (1881–1906); symphonic poem *Stenka Razin* (1885); violin concerto (1904), two piano concertos, concerto for saxophone.

INSTRUMENTAL AND VOCAL seven string quartets (1881–1930), string quintet; many works for piano including two sonatas and Theme and Variations.

glee a part song, usually for male voices, in not less than three parts, much cultivated by English composers in the 18th and early 19th centuries. The word is derived from the Anglo-Saxon *gliw* ('entertainment'), particularly musical entertainment. Webbe, Stevens, Callcott, Horsley, Attwood, Battishill, Cooke, and others cultivated the glee.

Gleichnisarie see ◊parable aria.

gliding tone musical tone, continuously rising or falling in pitch between preset notes, produced by a synthesizer.

Glière, Reinhold Moritzovich (1875–1956) Russian composer. He made research into Azerbaijani, Uzbek, and Ukrainian folk song and based some of his later works on it. In 1939 he became chairman of the Organizing Committee of USSR composers.

He learnt the violin as a child, but soon began to compose and was sent to the Kiev School of Music and later to the Moscow

Conservatory, where he was taught by Arensky, Taneiev, and Ippolitov-Ivanov. He taught at the Gnessin School of Music in Moscow and at the Kiev Conservatory, of which he became director in 1914, but settled in Moscow in 1920 (professor of composition at the Conservatory until 1941). Among his pupils was Prokofiev, who said of him 'Glière is fat and middle-aged, rather like a well-fed cat'.

Works include: the operas *Shakh-Senem* (1926), *Leyli and Mejnun* (1937), *Rachel* (after Maupassant's *Mlle Fifi*), *Ghulsara* (1949); ballet *The Red Poppy*, 1927; incidental music for Sophocles' *Oedipus Rex*, Aristophanes' *Lysistrata*, Beaumarchais's *Marriage of Figaro*, and others; three symphonies (No. 3, *Ilia Muromets*, 1909–11), three symphonic poems, concert overtures; harp concerto, concerto for soprano and orchestra; fantasy for wind instruments; four string quartets (1900–48); three string sextets, string octet; many instrumental pieces; 18 op. nos. of piano music, 22 op. nos. of songs.

Glinka, Mikhail Ivanovich (1804–1857) Russian composer. He broke away from the prevailing Italian influence and turned to Russian folk music as the inspiration for his opera *A Life for the Tsar* (originally *Ivan Susanin*) 1836. His later works include the opera *Ruslan and Lyudmila* 1842 and the instrumental fantasia *Kamarinskaya* 1848. He is often regarded as the founder of Russian music, exerting a strong influence on two generations of composers, most notably Mussorgsky, Tchaikovsky, and Stravinsky.

The son of a wealthy landowner, Glinka was born on his father's estate at Novospasskoye. He was sent to school at St Petersburg 1817–22. He picked up lessons casually, including some piano lessons from John Field, and also studied violin and theory. At his father's wish he worked in the Ministry of Communications 1824–28, but he gave it up, not being obliged to earn a living and wishing to devote himself to music. He visited Italy

1830–33, where he had lessons from Francesco Basili at Milan, then Vienna, and lastly Berlin, where he studied under Siegfried Dehn. On his father's death he returned to Russia, settled in St Petersburg, and married in 1835. There he worked at *A Life for the Tsar* and succeeded in having it produced in 1836; it was an immediate success, combining nationalist musical elements with a patriotic tale composed at a time of unrest. *Ruslan and Ludmilla* was delayed by domestic troubles and the separation from his wife in 1841, and was produced in 1842. In 1844 he visited Paris and Spain, in 1848 Warsaw, and France again in 1852–54. It was during a visit to Berlin, 1856–57, that he died.

He freed Russian opera from German and Italian influences and at the same time introduced harmonic innovations that were to bear fruit in the work of nearly all the later nationalist Russian composers. He wrote a vast amount of music for one who was trained so late, including over 80 songs, and died comparatively early.

Works include: the operas *A Life for the Tsar* (formerly *Ivan Sussanin*, 1836) and *Ruslan and Ludmilla* (1842); incidental music to Count Kukolnik's *Prince Kholmsky*; orchestral works: *Jota aragonesa* (*Capriccio brillante*), *A Night in Madrid* (1851), *Kamarinskaya* (1848), *Valse-Fantaisie*; string quartet in F major; trio for clarinet, bassoon, and piano; sextet for piano and strings; about 40 piano pieces; Polish hymn and *Memorial Cantata* for chorus; about 85 songs; some vocal duets and quartets.

glissando a rapid uninterrupted scale produced by sliding the finger across a keyboard or harp strings, or along the fingerboard of a violin or guitar. In wind instruments, it corresponds to a gliding tone, a famous example being the clarinet glissando at the start of Gershwin's *Rhapsody in Blue* 1924.

Globokar, Vinko (1934–) Yugoslav composer and trombonist. His avant-garde virtuosity encouraged Stockhausen, Kagel, and Berio to write works for him.

The plainsong melody of the Gloria found in Mass XV of the Vatican edition.

He studied in Ljubljana and at the Paris Conservatory; and later with Leibowitz and Berio. In 1968 he was appointed professor of trombone at the Cologne Musikhochschule. With Heinz Holliger he gave the UK first performance of Takemitsu's *Gemeaux* at Edinburgh in 1989. He was the featured composer at Dartington in 1992.

His own music includes *Voie* for narrator, chorus, and orchestra (1965); *Fluide* for 12 instruments (1967); *Traumdeutung* for 4 choruses and instruments (1967); *Concerto grosso* for 5 solo players, orchestra, and chorus (1970); *Ausstrahlungen* for soloists and 20 players (1971); *Carrousel* for 4 voices and 16 instruments (1977); *Discours I–IX* for various instruments (1967–93); *Les Emigrés* (1982–86); *L'Armonia Drammatica* (1986–889); *Labour* (1992); *Blinde Zeit* (1993).

glockenspiel tuned percussion instrument of light metal bars mounted on a carrying frame for use in military bands or on a standing frame for use in an orchestra (in which form it resembles a small xylophone or celesta). It is played with hammers or via a piano keyboard attachment.

Gloria (Latin *Gloria in excelsis Deo*, 'Glory to God in the highest') second item of the Ordinary of the Mass, following immediately after the Kyrie. Although the Ambrosian Gloria is sung to an even simpler tone, the melody printed with Mass XV of the Vatican edition is probably the oldest.

Gloriana opera by Britten (libretto by William Plomer), produced London, Covent Garden, 8 June 1953. Robert Devereux, Earl of Essex, and Lord Mountjoy compete for Queen Elizabeth I's attention. Essex is appointed to suppress an Irish rebellion but fails, himself becoming rebellious to the Crown. Reluctantly the Queen has him beheaded.

Glover, Jane (1949–) English conductor and musicologist. She studied at Oxford University, where she wrote a doctoral thesis on Francesco Cavalli, which was later published as a book. She made her professional debut as a conductor at the Wexford Festival in 1975, with her own edition of Cavalli's *Eritrea*.

She started her Glyndebourne career as chorus mistress, then as conductor on tour 1982–85, conducting *Don Giovanni* at the Festival in 1982. She was artistic director of the London Mozart Players 1984–92, and made her Covent Garden debut in 1988 with Mozart's *Die Entführung*. In 1989 she conducted English National Opera's production

of *Don Giovanni*, and in 1992 Gilbert and Sullivan's *Princess Ida*.

Gluck, Christoph Willibald von (1714–1787) Bohemian-German composer. His series of 'reform' operas moved music away from the formal conventions of the day, in which the interests of singers predominated; in particular, endless recitative was replaced by orchestral accompaniments, which improved dramatic flow. In 1762 his *Orfeo ed Euridice/Orpheus and Eurydice* revolutionized the 18th-century conception of opera by giving free scope to dramatic effect. It was followed by *Alceste/Alcestis* 1767 and *Paride ed Elena/Paris and Helen* 1770.

In 1774 his *Iphigénie en Aulide/Iphigenia in Aulis*, produced in Paris, brought to a head the fierce debate over the future of opera in which Gluck's French style had the support of Marie Antoinette, while his Italian rival Niccol Piccinni had the support of Madame du Barry. With *Armide* 1777 and *Iphigénie en Tauride/Iphigenia in Tauris* 1779, Gluck won a complete victory over Piccinni.

Born in Erasbach, Bavaria, the son of a forester, he left home in face of his parent's opposition to music and matriculated at Prague University in 1731. About 1735 in Vienna he entered the service of Prince Melzi, with whom he went to Italy. He may have studied under Sammartini in Milan, where he made his debut as an opera composer in 1741 with *Artaserse* (libretto by Metastasio). A number of operas followed, all in the conventional Italian form. He went to England, perhaps with Prince Lobkowitz, in 1745, possibly visiting Paris on the way. In London, where he met Handel, he produced two operas and appeared as a performer on the glass harmonica. In about 1747 he joined the Mingotti touring opera company, of which he subsequently became Kapellmeister, and travelled widely.

Gluck married in 1750 and settled in Vienna two years later, being connected with the court as Kapellmeister to Maria Theresa from 1754, though without official title (only in 1774 was he appointed court composer). Under the management of Count Durazzo the Viennese theatre moved away from conventional *opera seria*, and Gluck wrote a number of French *opéras-comiques*. The dramatic ballet *Don Juan*, embodying the choreographer Jean-Georges Noverre's ideas on modern dance, was produced in 1761.

In *Orfeo ed Euridice*, Gluck and his librettist Calzabigi realized in opera the current demands for greater dramatic truth in the theatre. The aims of this 'reform' were set out in the prefaces to *Alceste* and *Paride ed Elena*. In many ways, such as prominent use of the chorus and ballet, these works adopted features of French opera, and Gluck now turned to Paris, where *Iphigénie en Aulide* was produced in 1774, followed by French versions of *Orfeo* and *Alceste* in 1774 and 1776, and *Armide* in 1777. Gluck was reluctantly involved in a squabble between his supporters and the partisans of Piccinni, but this was decisively closed by the triumph of his *Iphigénie en Tauride* 1779. His last opera for Paris, *Echo et Narcisse* 1779, was unsuccessful, and he returned to Vienna, where he remained until his death.

Gluck's idea of a drama in which music and stage action are fully integrated had a profound influence on later composers. Wagner's concept of the *Gesamtkunstwerk* ('total art-work') is an obvious successor. Although *Orfeo ed Euridice* has remained popular, the rest of Gluck's output is still relatively neglected.

Works include: the *Opere serie Artaserse* (1741), *Demetrio, Demofoonte* (1743), *Il Tigrane, La Sofonisba* (1744), *Ipermestra, La caduta de' giganti* (1746), *Artamene, Le nozze d'Ercole e d'Ebe, Semiramide riconosciuta* (1748), *La Contesa dei numi, Ezio* (1750), *La clemenza di Tito* (1752), *Le Cinesi, Antigono, Il re pastore, Il Telemaco*; French *opéras-comiques*, including *L'Isle de Merlin* (1758), *La Cythère assiégée, L'Arbre enchanté, L'Ivrogne corrigé, Le Cadi dupé* (1761), *La Rencontre imprévue* (1764); 'reform' operas *Orfeo, Alceste, Paride ed Elena* (1770); French operas for Paris *Iphigénie en Aulide* (1774), *Orphée et Euridice*, and *Alceste* (both French versions of the earlier Italian operas), *Armide* (1777), *Iphigénie en Tauride, Echo et Narcisse* (1779); ballets *Don Juan* (1761), *Semiramide* (1765), and others; a number of symphonies, eight trio sonatas, a setting of *De profundis* for chorus and orchestra (1787), and seven settings of Klopstock's *Odes*.

Glückliche Hand, Die/The Lucky Hand opera by Schoenberg (libretto by composer); composed 1913, produced Vienna, Volksoper, 14 October 1924. Symbolic drama in which artist/Man is made to face choice between worldly success and spiritual truth.

Glyndebourne site of an opera house in East Sussex, England, established 1934 by John Christie (1882–1962). Operas are staged at an annual summer festival and a touring company is also based there. It underwent extensive rebuilding work in the early 1990s.

Gnecchi, Vittorio (1876–1954) Italian composer. He studied music at Milan. His first opera, given at Bologna in 1905, was at the centre of great controversy in 1909, when Strauss's *Elektra* appeared and showed striking similarities to Gnecchi's music.

Works include: the operas *Cassandra* (after Homer's *Iliad*, 1905), and *La Rosiera* (1927); heroic poem for orchestra *Notte nel campo di Holoferne*.

Gnessin, Mikhail Fabianovich (1883–1957) Russian composer and teacher. He studied with Rimsky-Korsakov and Liadov at the St Petersburg Conservatory and in Germany from 1911 to 1914. He settled at Rostov in 1914, at Moscow in 1923 and became professor at the Leningrad Conservatory 1936; his pupils included Khachaturian and Khrennikov. His work is influenced by Jewish music.

Works include: the operas *Youth of Abraham* (1921–23) and *The Maccabees*; incidental music for plays, including Sophocles' *Antigone* and *Oedipus Rex* (1915), Gogol's *The Revisor*, Blok's *The Rose and the Cross*; *The Conqueror Worm* (after Poe), 1905–17 for solo voices, chorus, and orchestra (1926); *Symphonic Fragment* (after Shelley), *Song of Adonis* and *Fantasia in the Jewish Style* for orchestra; *Requiem* for piano quintet, *Variations on Jewish Themes* and *Azerbaijan Folksongs* for string quartet, sextet *Adygeya*; violin and piano sonata in G minor, *Sonata-Ballade* for cello and piano; songs with orchestra; song cycles to words by Alexander Blok, Sologub; Jewish folk-song arrangements.

Godard, Benjamin (Louis Paul) (1849–1895) French composer. In 1878 he tied with Théodore Dubois in gaining the prize in a competition organized by the municipality of Paris with the dramatic symphony *Le Tasse* for solo voices, chorus, and orchestra. In 1885 he established a series of 'modern concerts' without success.

He studied violin and composition at the Paris Conservatory, and became a viola player in chamber music.

Works include: the operas *Pedro de Zalamea* (1884), *Jocelyn* (1888), *Le Dante* (1890), *La Vivandière, Les Guelfes*; incidental music to Shakespeare's *Much Ado about Nothing* and Fabre's *Jeanne d'Arc*; *Scènes poétiques* (1879), dramatic poem *Diane, Symphonie-Ballet, Symphonie gothique, Symphonie orientale*, and *Symphonie légendaire* for orchestra; two violin concertos, two piano concertos; three string quartets (1883–93), two piano trios; five violin and piano sonatas; piano pieces; over 100 songs.

God Save the King/Queen British national anthem. The melody resembles a composition by John ◊Bull and similar words are found from the 16th century. It has also been attributed to Henry ◊Carey. In its present form it dates from the Jacobite Rebellion of 1745, when it was used as an anti-Jacobite Party song.

In the USA the song 'America', with the first line 'My country, 'tis of thee', is sung to the same tune. Variations on the 'America' theme were composed by Charles Ives 1891.

Goebel, Reinhard (1952–) German conductor and violinist. He studied in Cologne and with Gustav Leonhardt in Amsterdam. He founded the Musica Antiqua Cologne in 1973 and has given many concerts of early music throughout Europe, the Americas, and the Far East.

He performed at York Festival, England, in 1989 with music by Legrenzi, Schmelzer, and Biber. Recordings include Telemann's *Tafelmusik*.

Goehr, (Peter) Alexander (1932–) German-born English composer. He was professor of music at Cambridge from 1976. A lyrical but often hard-edged serialist, he nevertheless usually remained within the forms of the symphony and traditional chamber works, and more recently turned to tonal and even NeoBaroque models. Works include the opera *Arden muss sterben/Arden Must Die* 1966, the music theatre piece *Naboth's Vineyard* 1968, and *Metamorphosis/Dance* 1974.

Goehr, Walter (1903–1960) German-born British conductor and composer. He gave the first performances of Britten's *Serenade* and Tippett's *A Child of our Time*. He also made editions of Monteverdi's *Vespers* of 1610 and *Poppea*.

He studied with Schoenberg in Berlin, conducting the Radio Orchestra there 1925–31. In 1933 he moved to London and was music director of the Columbia Graphophone Company until 1939. He conducted Morley College concerts from 1943.

He is the father of Alexander ◊Goehr

Works include: symphony, radio opera, incidental, and chamber music.

Goethe, Johann Wolfgang von (1749–1832) German poet, novelist, dramatist, and philosopher. His most significant influence in the world of music has been through his drama ◊*Faust*. Successful settings of other dramas have been made by Beethoven (*Egmont*), Mendelssohn (*Die erste Walpurgisnacht*), Brahms (*Rinaldo*), Thomas (*Mignon*), and

Massenet (*Werther*). Much of Goethe's poetry was created with musical setting in mind. Many of Schubert's greatest Lieder are based on Goethe, although the poet failed to recognize his genius, preferring simple strophic settings.

Works include: some of Schubert's Goethe Lieder are *An den Mond, Erlkönig, Der Fischer, Ganymed, Gretchen am Spinnrade, Heidenröslein, Kennst du das Land?, Der Musensohn, Nähe des Geliebten, Prometheus*, and *Wanderers Nachtlied*.

J André (*Erwin und Elmire*); ◊*Apprenti sorcier* (Dukas); Nils ◊Bentzon (*Faust III*); Blangini (*Die Letzten Augenblicke Werthers*); Johannes ◊Brahms (*Gesang der Parzen, Rinaldo*); ◊*Claudine von Villa Bella* (Schubert and Reichardt); Paul ◊Dukas (*Apprenti sorcier* and *Götz von Berlichingen*); ◊*Egmont* (Beethoven); ◊*Erlkönig* (Schubert); Hans ◊Gál (*Requiem für Mignon*); C ◊Goldmark (*Götz von Berlichingen* and *Meeresstille und glückliche Fahrt*); E T A ◊Hoffmann (*Scherz, List und Rache*); A Hüttenbrenner (*Erlkönig*); Charles ◊Koechlin (*Nuit de Walpurgis classique*); Ernst ◊Křenek (*Triumph der Empfindsamkeit*); C ◊Loewe (*Erlkönig*); ◊*Meeresstille und Glückliche Fahrt* (Beethoven and Mendelssohn); ◊Mendelssohn (*Erste Walpurgisnacht*); ◊*Mignon* (A Thomas); ◊*Rhapsodie*, ◊*Rinaldo* (Brahms); Anton ◊Rubinstein (*Wilhelm Meister*); ◊*Scherz, List und Rache* (Bruch); Othmar ◊Schoeck (*Erwin und Elmire, Dithyrambe* and songs); ◊Schubert (*Claudine von Villa Bella* and 20 Lieder); Robert ◊Schumann (*Requiem für Mignon*); Stiehl (*Jery und Bätely*); ◊*Tasso, lamento e trionfo* (Liszt); V ◊Tomášek (songs); ◊*Veilchen, Das* (Mozart); Georg ◊Vogler (*Erwin und Elmire*); Anton ◊Webern (two choral songs); Egon ◊Wellesz (*Scherz, List und Rache*); ◊*Werther* (Massenet); P ◊Winter (*Scherz, List und Rache* and *Jery und Bätely*); C F ◊Zelter (songs); Johann ◊Zumsteeg (*Clavigo*).

Settings include 5 songs by Brahms, 1 by Mozart (*Veilchen*), 71 by Schubert, 19 by Schumann, 60 (including nine early) by Wolf.

See also ◊Faust and ◊'Faust-Symphonie'.

Gogol, Nikolai Vassilevich (1809–1852) Russian novelist. His works inspired Boris ◊Assafiev (*Christmas Eve*); Arturo ◊Berutti (*Taras Bulba*); ◊*Christmas Eve* (Rimsky-Korsakov); Mikhail ◊Gnessin (*Revisor*); ◊*Marriage, The* (Mussorgsky and Martinů); ◊*May Night* (Rimsky-Korsakov); ◊*Nose, The*, (Shostakovich); ◊*Revisor, Der* (Egk); H ◊Searle (*Diary of a Madman*); A ◊Serov (*Christmas Eve Revels*); ◊*Sorochintsy Fair* (Mussorgsky); ◊*Taras Bulba* (Janáček); ◊*Vakula the Smith* (Tchaikovsky); K Weis (*Revisor*).

'Goldberg Variations' monumental set of 30 variations by Bach for two-manual harpsichord, BWV 998. A wide variety of keyboard technique is explored, in particular the canon, which is developed in each third variation.

Golden Age (Shostakovich). See ◊*Age of Gold*.

Golden Cockerel, The/Zolotoy Petushok opera by Rimsky-Korsakov (libretto V I Bielsky, based on Pushkin's satirical fairy tale), produced Moscow, 7 October 1909, after Rimsky-Korsakov's death. It is his last opera. King Dodon's astrologer presents a golden cockerel, which can warn of trouble. The King falls in love with Queen Shemakha, whom the astrologer names as his price for the cockerel. The King refuses and the cockerel kills him.

Goldene Bock, Der chamber opera by Krenek (libretto by composer), produced Hamburg, 16 June 1964. Jason time-travels to Route 66 in the USA, and divorces Medea when he serves him soup made from the flesh of a Greek shipping magnate.

Golden Legend, The oratorio by Sullivan (on Longfellow's poem), produced Leeds Festival, 1886; revived at Leeds, 15 March 1986, conductor Mackerras.

'Golden Sonata' the nickname given to the ninth (F major) of Purcell's ten *Sonatas of IV Parts* for two violins, cello, and continuo, published posthumously in 1697.

Goldmark, Karoly (Carl) (1830–1915) Austro-Hungarian composer. His best-known work today is the *Rustic Wedding Symphony*, although he established his reputation with the Wagner-influenced opera *Die Königin von Saba/The Queen of Sheba* 1875.

Goldmark was the son of a poor Jewish cantor, who managed to enter him at the Sopron school of music in 1842. He studied violin and made such rapid progress that he was sent to Vienna the next year and entered the conservatory in 1847. During the 1848 Revolution he played at the theatre at Györ in Hungary and was nearly shot as a rebel. In 1850 he returned to Vienna, where he eventually settled as a teacher.

Works include: the operas *Die Königin von Saba* (1875), *Merlin* (1886), *Das Heimchen am Herd* (after Dickens's *Cricket on the Hearth*, 1896), *Die Kriegsgefangene, Götz von Berlichingen* (after Goethe, 1902), and *Ein Wintermärchen* (after Shakespeare's *Winter's Tale*, 1908); symphonic poem *Rustic Wedding* and two symphonies; two Scherzos for orchestra and overtures *Sakuntala* (after Kalidasa), *Penthesilea* (after Kleist), *Im Frühling, Der gefesselte Prometheus, Sappho, In Italien*, and *Aus Jugen-*

dtagen, symphonic poem *Zrinyi; Meeresstille und glückliche Fahrt* (Goethe) for male chorus and horns, other choral works; two violin concertos; string quartet (1860), piano quintet, three piano trios, and other chamber music; two suites and sonata for violin and piano, cello and piano sonata; piano pieces; songs.

Goldmark, Rubin (1872–1936) US composer of Austro-Hungarian descent, nephew of Carl ◊Goldmark. He studied at the Vienna Conservatory and the National Conservatory in New York, where Dvořák was his composition master. He was director of the Colorado College Conservatory 1895–1901, but returned to New York in 1902 and settled as private piano and composition teacher, until, in 1924, he was appointed to the Juilliard Graduate School there.

Works include: *Hiawatha* (after Longfellow, 1900), *Samson* (1914), *Requiem* (on Lincoln's address at Gettysburg), *Negro Rhapsody*, and *The Call of the Plains* for orchestra; string quartet in A major; piano trio in D minor; violin and piano sonata; violin pieces; piano music, songs; choruses.

Goldoni, Carlo (1707–1793) Italian playwright and librettist. His works were used in ◊*Arcadia in Brenta* (Galuppi); ◊*Buovo d'Antona* (Traetta); ◊*Burbero di buon cuore, Il* (Martín y Soler); ◊*Donne curiose, Le* (Wolf-Ferrari); ◊*Filosofo di campagna, Il* (Galuppi); D ◊*Fischietti* (four operas); ◊*Fra due litiganti il terzo gode* (Sarti); P ◊*Generali* (*Pamela nubile*, after Richardson); ◊*Isola disabitata* (G Scarlatti); ◊*Lottchen am Hofe* (J A Hiller); G F ◊*Malipiero* (three operas); ◊*Mondo alla roversa, Il* (Galuppi); ◊*Mondo della luna, Il* (Galuppi and Haydn); G ◊*Paisiello* (*Ciarlone*); ◊*Pescatrici, Le* (Bertoni and Haydn); N ◊*Piccinni* (*Vittorina*); ◊*Quattro rusteghi* (Wolf-Ferrari); Guiseppe Scarlatti (*Portentosi effetti della Madre Natura, I*); ◊*Speziale, Lo* (Haydn); ◊*Tigrane, Il* (Gluck); Usiglio (*Donne curiose*); *Vendemmia* (Gazzaniga); J ◊*Wagenaar* (*Philosophical Princess*); E W Wolf (*Dorfdeputierten*).

Goldschmidt, Adalbert von (1848–1906) Austrian composer. He devoted himself as an amateur to the composition of large-scale works, the first of which, produced in Berlin in 1876, showed remarkable affinities with Wagner's *Ring*, which was not heard until later the same year, at Bayreuth.

Works include: the music-dramas *Die sieben Todsünden* (1876), *Helianthus, Gaea* (trilogy), opera *Die fromme Helene* (after Wilhelm Busch); symphonic poem; about 100 songs, and other pieces.

Goldschmidt, Berthold (1903–) German-born English conductor and composer. He left Germany in 1935 and settled in England. His music then went through a long period of neglect, but the opera *Beatrice Cenci* was given a London concert premiere in 1988 and *Der gewaltige Hahnrei* was revived in Berlin in 1992.

He studied in Berlin, became assistant conductor of the Staatsoper there in 1926, and conducted at the Darmstadt Opera in 1927. In 1931–33 he conducted on Berlin Radio and was artistic adviser to the municipal opera there, but the Nazi régime drove him to England. In 1964 he conducted the first performance of Deryck Cooke's performing version of Mahler's tenth symphony. His clarinet quintet 1983 was premiered in Pasadena in 1985.

Works include: the operas *Der gewaltige Hahnrei* (after Crommelynck, produced Mannheim, 1932) and *Beatrice Cenci* (after Shelley, 1949–50); ballet *Chronica*; overture to Shakespeare's *Comedy of Errors*, symphonies and other orchestral works, including *Ciaconna Sinfonica* (1936, premiered in Vienna 1960, performed under Simon Rattle in Berlin 1987, and heard at the 1993 London Proms); violin, cello, and harp concertos, chamber music, including four string quartets (1925, 1936, 1989, 1992), clarinet quintet, piano trio (1985), string trio (*Retrospectum*, 1991), *Capriccio* for violin (1992).

Goldschmidt, Otto (1829–1907) German pianist and composer. He studied at the Leipzig Conservatory under Mendelssohn and in 1848 went to Paris intending to study with Chopin. In 1849 he went to London, and settled there in 1858. He was accompanist to the singer Jenny Lind, whom he married in 1852. He was the founder of the Bach Choir in 1875.

Works include: the oratorio *Ruth* (1867), cantata *Music* for soprano and female voices (1898); piano concerto; piano trio; two duets for two pianos; studies and pieces for piano; songs.

Golgotha oratorio by Frank Martin for five soloists, chorus, and orchestra (text from the Bible and St Augustine); composed 1945–48, first performed Geneva, 29 April 1949.

Gombert, Nicolas (c. 1495–c. 1556) Flemish composer. His music was admired for its sombre colours and close-knit textures.

Gombert was a pupil of Josquin des Prés. He was in service at the Emperor Charles V's chapel in Flanders from 1562 and became maître des enfants (master of the choirboys)

in 1529; later he became a canon at Tournai and in 1537 went to Spain with 20 singers and held a post in the imperial chapel in Madrid. He was exiled in 1540 for gross indecency with his choirboys.

Works include: 10 Masses, 160 motets, psalms; about 80 chansons.

Gomes, (Antônio) Carlos (1836–1896) Brazilian composer. He studied with Lauro Rossi in Milan, and in 1895 was appointed director of the Conservatory at Pará, but he was delayed at Lisbon by illness and died soon after his arrival. The once-popular opera *Il Guarany* 1870, based on a local Indian legend, has been revived in recent years with Placido Domingo.

Works include: the operas *A noite do castello* (1861), *Joana di Flandres*, *Il Guarany* (1870), *Fosca, Salvator Rosa* (1874), *Maria Tudor* (on Victor Hugo's play, 1879), *Lo schiavo*, *Condor* (1891); revues *Se sa minga* and *Nella luna*; ode *Il saluto del Brasil* (Philadelphia Exhibition, 1876) and cantata *Colombo* (Columbus Festival, 1892).

Gomis, José Melchor (1791–1836) Spanish composer. He was bandmaster at Barcelona, moved to Madrid c. 1817 and in 1823 went to Paris for political reasons. In 1826–29 he taught singing in London, where he published many Spanish songs, and then returned to Paris, where he produced comic operas.

Works include: Spanish monodrama *Sensibilidad y prudencia, ó La aldeana*, French comic operas *Le Diable à Séville* (1831), *Le Revenant* (after Scott, 1835), *Le Portefaix* and *Rock le barbu* (1836); *L'inverno* for four voices and orchestra; songs.

Gondoliers, The, or The King of Barataria operetta by Sullivan (libretto by W S Gilbert), produced London, Savoy Theatre, 7 December 1889. The baby Prince of Baratavia is brought up by gondoliers. Not knowing the heir's true identity, the Inquisitor later appoints Marco and Giuseppe as rulers, but it is eventually revealed that servant Luiz is the true king.

gong percussion instrument originating in ancient China, consisting of a round sheet of metal with a turned-up rim. It is struck with a hammer, which may be covered with any of a range of materials, according to the quality of sound required. A large gong is also called a ◊tam-tam.

Gonzaga, Guglielmo (1538–1587) Duke of Mantua, he succeeded to the duchy in 1556, became a great patron of music, and was himself a composer. He published anonymously a book of madrigals and one of *Sacrae cantiones*.

Goodall, Reginald (1901–1990) English conductor, known for his slow, expansive interpretations of Wagner. He conducted without a baton, and never took curtain calls.

Goodall studied at the Royal College of Music and in Germany. His broad tempi and intensity of expression were regarded as belonging to the best traditions of German conductors. He conducted the first performance of *Peter Grimes* at Sadlers Wells, London, in 1945. In 1946 he joined the staff at Covent Garden, but his gifts were not properly recognized until major success came with Wagner's *Die Meistersinger* at Sadlers Wells in 1968. He conducted *Parsifal* at Covent Garden in 1971; at the London Coliseum he conducted Wagner's *Ring* in 1973 and *Parsifal* in 1986; for Welsh National Opera he conducted *Tristan* in 1979 and *The Valkyrie* in 1984. He also conducted Bruckner's symphonies.

Good-Humoured Ladies, The ballet by Tommasini on music by D Scarlatti (choreography by Massin), produced Rome, Teatro Costanzi, 12 April 1917.

Goodman, Benny (1909–1986) US clarinettist, composer, and band-leader. He played in various jazz and dance bands from 1921. In 1938 he recorded the Mozart quintet with the Budapest Quartet and commissioned Bartók's *Contrasts* (first performance 1939). Copland and Hindemith wrote concertos for him (both first performances 1950).

Goossens, (Aynsley) Eugene (1893–1962) English conductor and composer. As a composer he was prolific in most departments of music and progressive in technique. His works include two operas to libretti by Arnold Bennett: *Judith* 1929, and *Don Juan de Manara* 1937, and much orchestral and chamber music. He was the grandson of Eugène Goossens (1845–1906) and son of Eugène Goossens (1867–1958), both conductors of the Carl Rosa Opera Company. His brother Leon was a leading oboist, and his sisters Marie and Sidonie both renowned as harpists.

After study at Bruges and Liverpool, and under Stanford at the Royal College of Music, he played the violin in the Queen's Hall Orchestra 1911–15. His first appearance as a conductor was in 1916, deputizing for Beecham (with whom he was closely associated for the next few years) in Stanford's *The Critic* 1916. After that he formed an orchestra of his own, giving early English performances of

works by Stravinsky, and conducting the Russian Ballet. As a conductor he was afterwards associated with many famous orchestras in England and the USA, most notably the Cincinnati Symphony Orchestra, which he conducted 1931–46. In 1947 he was appointed director of the New South Wales Conservatory at Sydney and conductor of the symphony orchestra; he returned to England in 1956.

Works include: the operas *Judith* (1929) and *Don Juan de Mañara* (1937); ballet *L'Ecole en crinoline*; two symphonies (1940, 1944), sinfonietta; *Silence* for chorus and orchestra; Fantasy Concerto for piano and orchestra, oboe concerto (1927), violin concerto; two string quartets (1915, 1940).

Goovaerts, Alphonse (Jean Marie André) (1847–1922) Belgian composer and writer on music. He studied at the Jesuit College of Antwerp, and at the age of 15 was obliged by financial losses to take a commercial career; but he studied music thoroughly by himself and in 1866 obtained a post at the Antwerp town library. In 1869 his *Messe solennelle* was performed. In 1874 he was appointed music secretary to Antwerp Cathedral where he established a special choir, for which he copied a vast quantity of old motets of various schools. He began to write on the reform of church music, and in 1898 was appointed keeper of the royal archives in Brussels.

Works include: motets, *Petite Messe*, *Messe solennelle* and other church music; songs, part songs.

gopak, or hopak a Russian folk dance with music of a lively character in quick 2–4 time.

Gorczycki, Grzegorz (c. 1664–1734) Polish composer. He was *Magister cappellae* at Kraków Cathedral from 1698. He wrote motets and other church music.

Gordigiani, Luigi (1806–1860) Italian composer. He was a pupil of his father, Antonio Gordigiani, who died when he was 14, and he had to make a living by writing piano pieces under German names. The Russian Prince Nikolai Demidov and the Polish Prince Józef Poniatowski discovered his great gifts and gave him their patronage, the latter providing him with the libretto for his opera *Filippo*, produced at Florence 1840.

Works include: ten operas; *Canzonette*, *Canti popolari* and other songs (c. 300 in all); duets for female voices; Tuscan airs with piano accompaniment.

Górecki, Henryk Mikolaj (1933–) Polish composer. His study with Messiaen and exposure to avant-garde influences after 1956 led him to abandon a politically correct neoclassical style and seek out new sonorities. He later adopted a slow-moving tonal idiom appealing to revived religious tradition, often on tragic themes from Polish history, as in *Old Polish Music* for orchestra 1969, and his third symphony, *Sorrowful Songs* 1976, which propelled him to fame in the West in 1992.

He studied with Boleslaw Szabelski at Katowice Conservatory 1955–60.

Works include: cantata *Epitafium*; *Symphony no. 1* (1959), *No. 2* for soprano, baritone, chorus, and orchestra (1972), *No. 3* for soprano and orchestra (1973); *Scontri* for orchestra (1960); *Canticum Graduum* for orchestra (1969); *Old Polish Music* for brass and strings (1969); harpsichord concerto (1980); *Concerto-Cantata* for flute and orchestra (1992); *Epitaph* for mixed chorus and instruments (1956); *Genesis III: Monodrama* (1963); *Two Sacred Songs* for baritone and orchestra (1971); *Beatus Vir* for baritone, chorus, and orchestra (1979); chamber: *Quartettino* for wind (1956); sonata for two violins (1957); series *Genesis I–IV* for various instrumental groups (1962–70); *Aria* for tuba and ensemble (1987); *Already it is Dusk* (string quartet no. 1, 1988); *Quasi una fantasia* for string quartet (1991); *Kleines Requiem für eine Polka* for piano and 13 instruments (1993).

Gorzanis, Giacomo (c. 1525–after 1575) Italian composer. He published four books of lute music, including numerous dance-suites in two or three movements. One of these, consisting of a *passo e mezzo* and *padovana* 1561, provides an early example of 'sonata' used as a title. He was blind.

Göss, Barthel see Bartholomäus ◊Gesius. ╮

Gossec, François Joseph (1734–1829) Belgian-born French composer. On the foundation of the Paris Conservatory in 1795 he became one of its directors and professor of composition. As one of the leading composers of the French Revolution, he wrote many works for public ceremonies, often using vast forces. His works include over 30 symphonies, church and chamber music, ballets and theatre music, and 19 operas. After 1800 he wrote little.

Gossec was a chorister at Antwerp Cathedral. In 1751 he went to Paris, where with Rameau's help he obtained a post writing symphonies for La Pouplinière's private orchestra in 1754. He later became music director to the Prince of Condé. He founded the Concert des Amateurs in 1770, and in 1773 took over the direction of the Concert Spirituel. He also produced much chamber music and in 1760 performed a Requiem in which, as in other works, he anticipated the experimental manner of Berlioz. From 1795 to 1816 he was professor of composition at the Conservatory.

Works include: OPERA *Les Pêcheurs, Toinon et Toinette* (1767), *Thésée* (1782), *Rosine* (1786), and others; ballets *Les Scythes enchaînés*, added to Gluck's *Iphigénie en Tauride* (1779), *Mirsa*, and *Callisto*.

ORATORIO *La Nativité* (1774); Requiem (1760), *Dernière Messe des vivants*, motets and other pieces; funeral music for Mirabeau, *Le Chant du 14 juillet, L'Offrande à la liberté*, and other music for the Revolution.

OTHER About 50 symphonies (1756–1809), overtures, and other orchestral works; 12 string quartets, trios, and other chamber music.

Gossett, Philip (1941–) US musicologist. He studied at Princeton (PhD 1970) and taught at the University of Chicago from 1968 (professor and chairman of the music department 1978–84). He was general editor of the critical edition of Verdi's works; joint editor of the Rossini edition from 1979; co-editor with Charles Rosen of *Early Romantic Operas* (New York, 1978–83, in 44 volumes); facsimile edition of *Il Barbiere di Siviglia* (Rome, 1993).

Gothic Symphony the first by Havergal Brian, for soloists, children's choruses, brass band, and orchestra of 180; last of four movements is a setting of the Te Deum. Composed 1919–27, first performed by amateur forces, London, 24 June 1961; first professional performance London, 30 October 1966, to mark Brian's 90th birthday. Broadcast live to the USA by satellite, 25 May 1980.

Götterdämmerung/Twilight of the Gods opera by Wagner (libretto by composer), produced Bayreuth, 17 August 1876. Ring des Nibelungen, Der. Following the conclusion of *Siegfried*, this fourth and final opera of the ◊Ring des Nibelungen cycle opens with the awakening of Brünnhilde. Siegfried, having inadvertently drunk a magic potion, betrays her to Gunther; Gutrune hopes to acquire Siegfried. Meanwhile Hagen, Alberich's son, has conspired to try to gain power and the Ring. Hagen murders Siegfried, but Brünnhilde takes the Ring, returning it to the Rhinemaidens as Valhalla burns.

Gottschalk, Louis Moreau (1829–1869) US composer and pianist. His adoption of Creole and American folk music, Latin American rhythms and dance forms, and striking colouristic effects won the admiration of Berlioz, Liszt, Offenbach, and others. His compositions include *Souvenir d'Andalousie/ Souvenir of Andalusia* 1851 for piano and orchestra and numerous piano pieces, among which are *La Gallina: danse cubaine/La Gallina: Cuban Dance* c. 1868 and *Le Banjo – esquisse américaine/Banjo – American Sketch* 1854–55.

Gottschalk studied in Paris and had much success there as a pianist from his debut in 1844. He toured throughout Europe and, from 1853, North and South America. He died of yellow fever while on tour in Brazil.

Works include: *Escenas campestres* for soprano, tenor, baritone, and orchestra (1860); two symphonic poems, *La nuit des tropiques* and *Montevideo*; numerous piano pieces including *The Dying Poet* and *Grand Fantasy on the Brazilian National Anthem*.

Götz, Hermann (1840–1876) German composer. At first he studied music only incidentally when a student at Königsberg University, but later went to the Stern Conservatory in Berlin. In 1863 he went to Switzerland as organist at Winterthur and in 1867 he settled at Zurich. From 1870 he devoted himself wholly to composition.

Works include: the operas *Der Widerspänstigen Zähmung* (on Shakespeare's *Taming of the Shrew*, 1874) and *Francesca da Rimini* (unfinished, produced Mannheim, 1877); *Nänie* (Schiller) and Psalm cxxxvii for solo voices, chorus, and orchestra; cantata for male voices and orchestra; symphony in F major, *Spring* overture for orchestra; violin concerto in G major (1868), piano concerto in Bb major; piano quintet, piano quartet, piano trio; sonata for piano duet; sonatina, *Genrebilder* and other works for piano; songs.

Goudimel, Claude (c. 1514–1572) French composer. He contributed chansons for several voices to many collections, also four-part settings to a book of odes by the Roman poet Horace and to another of sacred songs (*chansons spirituelles*) by Marc-Antoine de Muret (1526–85) in 1555, and settings of French translations of the psalms, including a complete Protestant psalter.

After studying at Paris University, Goudimel then worked with the publisher Nicolas du Chemin as a proofreader and later as a business partner. He first appeared as a composer in Paris in 1549, when he contributed chansons to a book published by du Chemin. About 1557, having become a Huguenot, he went to live at Metz with the Protestant colony there, and composed his first complete Psalter in 1564. About ten years later he left for Besançon, and afterwards for Lyon, where he died in the massacre of the Huguenots in August 1572.

Goudimel wrote Masses, motets, and chansons, but it is for his psalm settings that he is remembered. They range in style from motet-like works to simple harmonizations.

Works include: five Masses, three Magnificats, psalms in motet form and other works for the Catholic Church; psalms, including a complete psalter, for the Protestant Church; sacred songs and numerous secular chansons for several voices.

Gould, Morton (1913–1996) US composer and conductor. He studied at New York University, and later worked as a pianist at Radio City Music Hall and presented music programmes on radio. His works are much indebted to popular idioms.

Works include: BALLETS *Interplay* (1945), *Fall River Legend*, on Lizzie Borden – America's most famous orphan (1947) and *Fiesta* (1957); ORCHESTRAL *Little Symphony* (1939), four symphonies (1942, 1944, 1947, 1952), three *American Symphonettes* (1922, 1935, 1937), piano concerto (1937), violin concerto (1938), *A Lincoln Legend* (1941), *Spirituals* (1941), viola concerto (1943), *Concerto for Orchestra* (1945), *Dance Variations* for two pianos and orchestra (1953), *Concerto for Tap Dancer* (1953), *Jekyll and Hyde Variations* (1957), *Festive Music* (1965), *Venice* for double orchestra and brass bands (1966), *Vivaldi Gallery* (1967), *Symphony of Spirituals* (1976), *American Ballads* (1976), *Housewarming* (1982), flute concerto (1984), *Chorales and Rags* (1988), *Concerto Grosso* (1988). Also music for Broadway shows, films, and state occasions (including the Los Angeles Olympics, 1984).

Gounod, Charles François (1818–1893) French composer and organist. His operas, notably *Faust* 1859 and *Roméo et Juliette* 1867, and church music, including *Messe solennelle/ Solemn Mass* 1849, combine graceful melody and elegant harmonization. His *Méditation sur le prélude de Bach/Meditation on Bach's 'Prelude'* 1889 for soprano and instruments, based on Prelude No. 1 of Bach's *Well-Tempered Clavier*, achieved popularity as 'Gounod's *Ave Maria*'.

Gounod was born in Paris, the son of a painter. His mother, a good pianist, taught him music from an early age and he was educated at the Lycée Saint-Louis and at the Paris Conservatory, where his masters included Halévy, Paer, and Lesueur. In 1839 he won the Prix de Rome and spent the statutory three years in Rome, studying early Italian church music; his interest in this music culminated in the elaborate *Messe solennelle de Ste Cécile* 1855. After a tour in Austria and Germany he returned to Paris and was appointed organist at the church of the Missions Etrangères. Intending to become a priest, he did not produce any important music until his opera *Sapho* appeared in 1851. In 1852–60 he conducted the united choral societies named Orphéon. His five-act setting of *Faust* for the Paris Opéra in 1859 brought his melodic gift before a huge public and Gounod became the most popular opera composer of his time; his success was consolidated by a saccharine but effective version of *Romeo and Juliet*. While living in London in 1870–75, he founded what later became the Royal Choral Society.

Works include: the operas *Sapho* (1851), *La nonne sanglante* (1854), *Le médecin malgré lui* (on Molière, 1858), *Faust* (after Goethe, 1859), *Philémon et Baucis, La Reine de Saba, Mireille* (after Mistral), *La Colombe, Roméo et Juliette* (after Shakespeare, 1867), *Cinq-Mars* (after Alfred de Vigny), *Polyeucte* (after Corneille, 1878), *Le Tribut de Zamora*; incidental music for Ponsard's *Ulysse*, Legouvé's *Les Deux Reines*, and Barbier's *Jeanne d'Arc*; oratorios *La Rédemption, Mors et Vita, Tobie*; eight cantatas; 16 Masses, Requiem (1895), *Stabat Mater*, Te Deum, *De profundis, Ave verum corpus, Pater noster*, Magnificat and other sacred vocal pieces; two symphonies (1855–56); some piano compositions including the *Funeral March for a Marionette; Méditation sur le premier Prélude de Bach* for soprano, violin, piano, and organ; some smaller choral works; many songs.

Goyescas opera by Granados (libretto, in Spanish, by F Periquet y Zuaznabar), produced New York, Metropolitan, 28 January 1916. Much of the material is taken from the piano work below. Pacquito and Fernando duel over Rosario; Fernando dies in her arms. Two sets of piano pieces by Granados, inspired by paintings of Spanish scenes by Goya, first performed Paris, 4 April 1914: I. *Los requiebros/The Compliments, Coloquio en la reja/Colloquy at the Grilled Window, El fandango del candil/The Fandango of the Lantern, Quejas, ó La maja y el ruiseñor/Plaints, or The Maja and the Nightingale;* II. *El Amor y la Muerte/Love and Death, Epílogo: la serenata del espectro/Epilogue: the Spectre's Serenade.* (A *maja* is the feminine counterpart of *majo*, 'a fop, a dandy'). Granados also wrote a separate *escena goyesca*

for piano: *El pelele* (a puppet or straw-man tossed in a blanket).

Gozzi, Carlo (1722–1806) Italian dramatist. His works inspired F ◊Chagrin (*Re cervo*); F ◊Danzi (*Turandot*); ◊Donna serpente (Casella); ◊Einem (*Turandot*); ◊Feen (Wagner); J P E Hartmann (*Ravnen*); F H ◊Himmel (*Sylphen*); A ◊Jensen (*Turandot*); ◊König Hirsch (Henze); ◊Love for Three Oranges (Prokofiev); R ◊Sessions (*Turandot*); ◊Stenhammar (*Turandot*); ◊*Turandot* (incidental music Weber; operas, Busoni and Puccini).

G.P. abbreviation for ◊general pause, a moment where all players are silent.

Grabmusik/*Funeral music* cantata by Mozart for soloists, chorus, and small orchestra; composed 1767 (when Mozart was ill), performed Salzburg Cathedral, 7 April 1767.

Grabu, Louis (fl. 1665–94), or Grabut, Grebus French violinist and composer. He was appointed composer to Charles II in 1665, and was Master of the King's Musick 1666–74.

Works include: the operas *Ariane, ou le mariage de Bacchus* (1674) and *Albion and Albanius* (libretto by Dryden), 1685.

grace alternative name for embellishment or ◊ornamentation.

grace note an ornamental note written in small type to show that its duration is not counted as a part of the metre of the bar, but must be subtracted from either the following or the preceding full note. When appearing singly, written as a quaver or sometimes a crotchet, it can indicate an appoggiatura ('leaning' note), requiring up to half the value of the next note. If it appears as a semiquaver or as a quaver with a stroke through the stem, it generally appears just on or before the beat, in the manner of an appoggiatura or acciaccatura ('crushed' note). When appearing in a large group, as in a cadenza by Beethoven or a melody by Chopin, the grace notes usually fill in the duration of a single note in the melody, and may (if time permits) be played with greater rhythmic flexibility than in standard notation.

'Gradus ad Parnassum' (Latin 'Steps to Parnassus') a treatise on counterpoint by Fux, published 1725.

A series of 100 instructive and progressive piano pieces by Clementi, published in 1817. The first piece in Debussy's *Children's Corner* for piano alludes satirically to Clementi's collection.

Graener, Paul (1872–1944) German composer. His lieder (songs) and operas were popular in the 1920s, and he was one of a large number of composers who were successful during the Third Reich.

He was a choirboy in Berlin Cathedral and at the age of 16 entered the Veit Conservatory, but soon began to teach himself, and led a wandering life, conducting at various theatres and composing a number of immature works. He was in London 1896–1908 as a teacher at the Royal Academy of Music and conductor at the Haymarket Theatre. He was then appointed director of the New Conservatory in Vienna, and in 1910 became director of the Mozarteum at Salzburg. After some years in Munich he succeeded Reger as professor of composition at the Leipzig Conservatory, but resigned in 1924. In 1930 he became director of the Stern Conservatory in Berlin, and under the Nazi régime was vice-president of the Reichsmusikkammer, being succeeded by Egk in 1941.

Works include: the operas *Der vierjährige Posten* (Körner, 1918), *Das Narrengericht* (1931), *Don Juans letztes Abenteuer* (1914), *Theophano* (Byzanz, 1918), *Schirin und Gertraude*, *Hanneles Himmelfahrt* (after G Hauptmann, 1927), *Friedemann Bach* (1931), *Der Prinz von Homburg* (after Kleist, 1935); choral works; symphonies (*Schmied Schmerz*), *Romantic Fantasy*, *Variations on a Russian folk song*, and other orchestral works; six string quartets, three piano trios, and other chamber music; sonata and suite for violin and piano, suite for cello and piano; piano pieces; over 100 songs.

Grainger, Percy Aldridge (1882–1961) Australian-born US experimental composer and pianist. He is remembered for piano transcriptions, songs, and short instrumental pieces drawing on folk idioms, including *Country Gardens* 1925, and for his settings of folk songs, such as *Molly on the Shore* 1921.

Grainger shared his friend Ferruccio Busoni's vision of a free music, devising a synthesizer and composing machine far ahead of its time.

Grainger was a pupil of his mother and of Louis Pabst at Melbourne. He later studied in Frankfurt, Germany, with James Kwast (1852–1949), Iwan Knorr, and Busoni. He lived in London in 1900–14 and became interested in folk music. He toured Scandinavia in 1909, and settled in the USA in 1914, later becoming naturalized. He made a successful New York debut in 1915, and in 1928 married Ella Viola Ström at the Hollywood Bowl, conducting his *To a Nordic Princess* in honour of the occasion. In 1938

he founded a museum at Melbourne, to house his manuscripts and souvenirs; his request for the museum to display his skeleton after his death was declined.

Works include: compositions for chorus and orchestra with and without solo voices: *Marching Song of Democracy* (1901–17), *The Bride's Tragedy* (Swinburne, 1908), *Father and Daughter* (Faroe folk song), *Sir Eglamore*, *We have fed our seas* (Kipling, 1900–04), *Tribute to Foster*, *Bridal Song*, and others; part songs including *Brigg Fair*, *Morning Song of the Jungle* (Kipling); pieces for small orchestra: *Molly on the Shore* (1907), *Colonial Song*, *Shepherd's Hey* (1913), *Mock Morris, Irish Tune from County Derry* ('Londonderry Air'), clog dance *Handel in the Strand*; suite *In a Nutshell* for two pianos; four Irish dances on themes by Stanford, *Walking Tune*, and other pieces for piano; songs. He edited and arranged hundreds of British and Scandinavian folk songs.

gramophone an instrument (invented by Edison in 1877) that reproduces recorded sound. The early version, known as a phonogram, recorded and reproduced sound by means of cylinders; music is now recorded on magnetic tape, afterwards transferred to a disc of vinylite. The sound waves of the music are reproduced thereon in a continuous groove. In performance the disc revolves, a static needle is brought into contact with the groove, and the 'frozen' sound waves are released and electronically amplified. From 1958 sounds were directed to the listener with greater realism by means of stereophonic recordings, followed in the 1970s by quadraphonic recordings.

A more recent development is the **compact disc**, on which the musical signal is digitally encoded so that it can be decoded by laser with absolutely no wear to the disc, with complete fidelity and with virtually no danger of destroying the disc through careless handling.

Granados, Enrique (1867–1916) Spanish composer and pianist. His piano work *Goyescas* 1911, inspired by the work of the artist Goya, was converted to an opera in 1916.

Granados studied composition with Carlos Pedrell at Barcelona and piano in Paris. Returning to Spain in 1889, he became a well-known pianist and in 1900 he founded the Sociedad de Conciertos Clásicos in Madrid, which he conducted. After a visit to New York for the production the operatic version of *Goyescas* in January 1916, he went down in the *Sussex* when it was torpedoed by a German submarine in the English Channel. He had swum to rescue his wife, but was weighed down with the gold that the New York Metropolitan Opera had paid him for *Goyescas*.

Works include: the operas and zarzuelas *Maria del Carmen* (1898), *Gaziel* (1906), *Goyescas* (based on the piano work), *Petrarca*, *Picarol*, *Follet*, *Liliana*; symphonic poem *La nit del mort*, four suites and other pieces for orchestra; *Cant de las Estrelles* for chorus, organ, and piano; piano trio, *Oriental* for oboe and strings; *Goyescas* (two volumes), ten Spanish Dances, six pieces on Spanish folk songs, *Escenas románticas*, *Escenas poéticas* (1926), *Libro de horas*, Impromptus, children's pieces for piano; songs *Escritas en estilo antiguo*, and a collection of tonadillas.

gran cássa (Italian 'great case, great box') Italian name for the Qbass drum.

grand chœur (French 'great choir', 'full organ') a musical direction that the organ is to be used with all the registers.

Grand Duke, The, or The Statutory Duel operetta by Sullivan (libretto by W S Gilbert), produced London, Savoy Theatre, 7 March 1896. It was Gilbert's last libretto for Sullivan.

Grande-Duchesse de Gérolstein, La operetta by Offenbach (libretto by H Meilhac and L Halévy), produced Paris, Théâtre des Variétés, 12 April 1867. Grand-Duchess has an eye for recruit Fritz, promoting him eventually to the rank of general. When he still prefers to marry peasant Wanda, she turns against him. After complications, a happy ending.

Grande Messe des Morts, Requiem work by Berlioz for tenor, chorus, and orchestra, (composed 1837; revised 1852 and 1867). First performed Paris, 5 December 1837.

Grandi, Alessandro (c. 1575–c. 1630) Italian composer. His church music was in part inspired by the spacious architecture of St Mark's, Venice, and many of his motets are in the concertato style, with singers positioned in different parts of the church to give a 'stereophonic' effect. His later motets employ instrumental accompaniments and anticipate the sacred concertos of Schütz and other North European masters.

Grandi may have studied under Giovanni Gabrieli at Venice. He was maestro di cappella at Santo Spirito, Ferrara, 1610–17, and then at St Mark's, where he sang under Monteverdi's direction and became his deputy in 1620. In 1627 he became choirmaster at the church of Santa Maria Maggiore at Bergamo. He died of the plague.

Works include: five Masses, about 200 motets, psalms; madrigals; cantatas, arias for solo voice.

grand jeu (French 'great play') in music, an alternative term for *grand chœur*, 'full organ'; also the name of a harmonium stop that brings the whole instrument into play.

Grand Macabre, Le opera by Ligeti (libretto by composer and M Meschke, after M de Ghelderode), produced Stockholm, 12 April 1978. London, Coliseum, 2 December 1982, with the original roles of Spermando and Clitoria 'translated' by G Skelton as Amando and Miranda. Nekrotzar returns from the grave in an attempt to destroy the world, but is disappointed when a threatening comet passes by harmlessly.

grand opera type of opera without any spoken dialogue (unlike the *opéra-comique*), as performed at the Paris Opéra in the 1820s to 1880s. Grand operas were extremely long (five acts), and included incidental music and a ballet.

Composers of grand opera include D F E Auber, Giacomo Meyerbeer, and Ludovic Halévy; examples include Verdi's *Don Carlos* 1867 and Meyerbeer's *Les Huguenots* 1836.

grand piano large, wing-shaped form of the pianoforte, with horizontal stringing and soundboard.

Grange, Phillip (1956–) English composer. He studied at York University and with Peter Maxwell Davies. He was a lecturer in composition at Exeter University from 1989.

Works include: piano sonata (1978); *Cimmerian Nocturne* for ensemble (1979); sextet for wind quintet and piano (1980); *The Kingdom of Bones* music theatre (1983); *Variations* (1986); *Concerto for Orchestra* (1988); *Changing Landscapes* (1990). Performances at most major UK festivals, also in Europe and the USA; London Proms, 1983.

Gran Mass/Graner Messe a mass by Liszt for solo voices, chorus, orchestra, and organ, composed in 1855 for the inauguration of a church at Gran (Esztergom) in Hungary and performed there 31 August 1856.

graphic scores scores by 20th-century composers which seek to convey musical ideas by means of nontraditional notation. Some scores are intended to symbolize particular sounds or textures, others allow the interpreter more latitude. Examples are by Feldman, Stockhausen, Cage, Ligeti, Bussotti, and Cornelius Cardew. Graphic scores have been admired as much for their visual as their musical qualities.

graph notation an invented sign language representing unorthodox sounds objectively in pitch and time, or alternatively representing sounds of orthodox music in a visually unorthodox manner. A form of graph notation for speech patterns used in phonetics was adopted by Stockhausen in *Carré/Squared* 1959–60.

Graphic representation of sounds begins with medieval plainchant, which originally aimed at recording the real inflection of a singing voice. Its reappearance in modern times dates from 1856, with the invention by León Scott of the **phonautograph** for recording visual traces of speech sounds. The possibility of drawing sound for direct reproduction was raised by composer Ernest Toch 1928; with the arrival of optical sound on film during the 1930s A M Avraamov and B A Yankovsky in Russia and Rudolf Pfenninger in Germany successfully devised methods of optical waveform synthesis for music production.'

Artists László Moholy-Nagy in Berlin and Jack Ellit in London were experimenting at this time with freely-drawn soundtracks incorporating found images, thumbprints, and so on, of predictable rhythm but noisy character, a technique later adopted by Canadian filmmaker Norman McLaren. In 1940 Villa-Lobos composed *New York Skyline* based on the outline of a photograph projected onto graph paper and thence to music manuscript. Percy Grainger's proposed Free Music Machine 1948, designed by Burnett Cross, applies optical sound principles on a larger scale, a technique continued in digital synthesizers such as the Fairlight. Development of the sound spectograph 1944 by engineers at Bell Telephone Laboratories introduced a much improved projection of audio events in pitch and time, providing a model for Stockhausen's iconic score *Elektronische Studie II/Electronic Study II* 1953–54. John Cage's graphic scores of the 1950s revive memories of film experiments in the 1930s, as may be said of many European composers of graph scores from the period 1959–70.

Graupner, Christoph (1683–1760) German composer. He wrote more than 1,400 cantatas and over a hundred symphonies, as well as operas, chamber music, and keyboard pieces. He was Kapellmeister at Hesse-Darmstadt from 1712, and was elected cantor of St Thomas's, Leipzig, in 1723, but was unable to obtain his release from Darmstadt, so that the post fell to J S Bach.

He was a pupil of Johann Schelle and Johann Kuhnau at St Thomas's, Leipzig, and was harpsichordist at the Hamburg opera under Reinhard Keiser 1707–09, and there produced his first operas. In 1709 he entered the service of the Landgrave Ernst Ludwig of Hesse-Darmstadt as vice-Kapellmeister, becoming Kapellmeister in 1712 on the death of Briegel.

Works include: the operas *Dido* (1707), *Antiochus und Stratonica* (1708), *La costanza vince l'inganno* (1715), and others; over 1,400 church cantatas; 113 symphonies; 87 overtures; about 50 concertos; quantities of chamber music, keyboard music.

grave (Italian 'heavy, serious') musical direction indicating a slow tempo.

gravicembalo 17th-century name for the clavicembalo or ◊harpsichord.

Gray, Cecil (1895–1951) Scottish writer on music and composer. In 1920 he became joint editor of the *Sackbut* with Philip Heseltine, with whom he also wrote a book on the composer Gesualdo (1926), and whose biography as a composer (Peter Warlock) he published. Other books are a *History of Music* 1928, essays 'Predicaments' 1936 and 'Contingencies' 1947, and two works on Sibelius (1931, 1935).

Works include: the operas *Deirdre*, *The Temptation of St Anthony* (after Flaubert), and *The Trojan Women* (after Euripides).

grazia, con (Italian 'with grace') musical direction; 'with grace', Italian *grazioso*.

grazioso Italian 'graceful'; term used in musical notation.

Great Fugue (Beethoven). See ◊*Grosse Fuge*.

great organ the principal manual (keyboard) of an ◊organ, characterized by the most powerful pipes and stops of the instrument. It often has the greatest number of stops, ranging from a wide variety of ◊flue pipes to a selection of reeds.

great staff a theoretical clarification of the relationship of the traditional clefs. On an 11-line stave with, for example, the treble clef four lines from the top and the bass clef, four lines from the bottom, the middle line will represent middle C.

Greaves, Thomas (fl. 1604) English lutenist and composer. He was in the service of Sir Henry Pierpoint, whose wife was a cousin of Michael Cavendish. In 1604 he published the book *Songs of Sundrie Kindes*, containing seven songs to the lute, four songs for voice and viols, and four madrigals.

Grechaninov, Aleksandr Tikhonovich (1864–1956) Russian composer. He studied under Rimsky-Korsakov. He earned a living composing music for the Russian Orthodox Church; left Russia after the Revolution and settled in Paris in 1925. In 1929 he moved to the USA.

Although the son of semiliterate small shopkeepers, Grechaninov managed to study piano at the Moscow Conservatory under Vassily Safonov, but in 1890 he went to St Petersburg as a composition pupil of Rimsky-Korsakov.

Works include: the operas *Dobrinya Nikitich* and *Sister Beatrice* (after Maeterlinck's play, 1910), incidental music for plays; much music for the Russian Church, including 44 complete liturgies; Catholic church music, including Masses and motets; choral works; five symphonies (1894–1936), Elegy for orchestra; concertos for cello, violin, and flute; four string quartets; *Music Pictures* for bass solo, chorus, and orchestra.

Greek opera in two acts by Mark-Anthony Turnage (libretto by composer and J Moore, after S Berkoff's play), produced Munich, Carl-Orff Saal, 17 June 1988. It is an updated version of the Oedipus legend, in troubled urban setting: Eddy kills a café manager and marries his wife, who later turns out to be his mum.

Greek Passion, The opera by Martinů (libretto by composer from the novel by N Kazantzakis); composed 1955–58 in Nice, New York, Pratteln and Rome, produced Zurich, 9 June 1961, conductor Sacher. The villagers of Lyeovrissi prepare for their annual Passion play. Manolios, who is to play Christ, fights for some local refugees, but is killed by Panais, who was to play Judas.

Greene, Maurice (1696–1755) English organist and composer. By the time of his death, he had held all the major musical appointments in England, including organist at St Paul's Cathedral 1718, organist and composer of the Chapel Royal 1727, and Master of the King's Musick 1735. An inheritance in 1750 enabled him to devote time to a collection of English church music, which after his death was completed by Boyce and published under the title *Cathedral Music*.

The son of a clergyman, Greene was a chorister at St Paul's Cathedral, studied the organ there under Richard Brind, and after holding church posts was appointed organist

of St Paul's in 1718. On William Croft's death in 1727 he became organist and composer of the Chapel Royal, and in 1730 succeeded Thomas Tudway as professor at Cambridge University. He was cofounder (with Michael Festing) of the Royal Society of Musicians in 1738.

Works include: over 100 anthems, the most notable published in *Forty Select Anthems* (1743), and other church music; oratorios *The Song of Deborah and Barak* (1732) and *Jephtha* (1737); pastorals *Florimel, or Love's Revenge* (1734), *The Judgement of Hercules* and *Phoebe* (1747); Odes for St Cecilia's Day and other occasions; miscellaneous songs and catches; overtures; organ voluntaries; harpsichord music.

Gregorian chant any of a body of plainsong choral chants associated with Pope Gregory the Great (540–604), which became standard in the Roman Catholic Church.

Gregorian tones the chants of the Gregorian psalmody sung in groups corresponding to the eight church modes (four authentic and four plagal).

Grenon, Nicolas (c. 1380–1456) French composer. He wrote sacred Latin music and chansons.

The earliest mention of Grenon is at Paris in 1399. He later worked at Laon and Cambrai cathedrals and at the Burgundian court chapel under Duke John the Fearless. He was master of the choirboys at the papal chapel 1425–27, and finally returned to Cambrai where he was for many years Guillaume Dufay's neighbour and was probably an influence on the younger composer.

Gresham, Thomas (1519–1579) founder of Gresham College in London. He was knighted 1559. The College was provided for by his will, and among the professorships was one for music, which has continued to the present day. The first professor, appointed 1596, was John Bull.

Gretchen am Spinnrade/Margaret at the Spinning-Wheel Schubert's setting of Gretchen's song in Goethe's *Faust*, Part I, composed 1814 at the age of 17, published as op. 2 in 1821.

Grétry, André Ernest Modeste (1741–1813) Belgian-born French composer. He wrote about 40 operas, and was a leading figure in the development of opéras-comiques. He is best known through the arrangement of his *Zémire et Azor* 1771 made by the conductor Thomas Beecham.

Grétry was a chorister at the church of St Denis, Liège, and received his initial musical training from his father (a violinist) and local church musicians. By 1759 he had already composed some symphonies and church music, which won him a scholarship to study in Rome, where he remained until 1765, when he produced the intermezzo *La vendemmiatrice*. After a time in Geneva he went to Paris in 1767 to make his way as an opera composer. From 1768 he produced a continuous stream of opéras-comiques, the most popular being *Richard Cœur-de-Lion* 1784, an early example of a rescue opera. He was made an inspector of the Paris Conservatory on its foundation in 1795, and the same year became one of the original members of the Institut de France. He published his memoirs in three volumes 1789–97, and wrote other literary works.

Works include: OPERA-COMIQUE *La vendemmiatrice* (1765), *Isabelle et Gertrude, Le Huron* (1768), *Lucile, Le tableau parlant* (1769), *Silvain, Les deux avares, L'amitié à l'épreuve, Zémire et Azor* (1771), *L'ami de la maison, Le Magnifique, La Rosière de Salency, La fausse magie* (1775), *Les mariages samnites* (several versions), *Matroco* (1777), *Le jugement de Midas, Les fausses apparences, ou L'amant jaloux* (1778), *Les evénements imprévus, Aucassin et Nicolette* (1779), *Thalie au Nouveau Théâtre, Théodore et Paulin* (later *L'épreuve villageoise*), *Richard Cœur-de-lion* (1784), *Les méprises par ressemblance, Le comte d'Albert* (1786), *Le prisonnier anglais* (later *Clarice et Belton*), *Le rival confident, Raoul Barbebleue* (1789), *Pierre le Grand, Guillaume Tell* (1791), *Basile, Les deux couvents, Joseph Barra, Callias* (1794), *Lisbeth, Le barbier du village, Elisca*.

Produced at the Paris Opéra: *Céphale et Procris* (1773), *Les trois âges de l'opéra* (1778), *Andromaque, La double epreuve, ou Colinette à la cour, L'embarras des richesses* (1782), *La caravane du Caire, Panurge dans l'île des lanternes* (after Rabelais, 1785), *Amphitryon, Aspasie, Denys le Tyran, La fête de la Raison, Anacréon chez Polycrate* (1797), *Le casque et les colombes* (1801), *Delphis et Mopsa*, and others.

Grétry, Lucile (1772–1790) French composer, daughter of André ◊Grétry. At the age of 13 she composed the opera *Le mariage d'Antonio* which, scored by her father, was successfully produced in 1786 at the Comédie Italienne, followed by *Toinette et Louis* a year later.

Grieg, Edvard (Hagerup) (1843–1907) Norwegian nationalist composer. Much of his music is small-scale, particularly his songs, dances, sonatas, and piano works, strongly identifying with Norwegian folk music. Among his orchestral works are the *Piano Concerto in A Minor* 1869 and the incidental music for Henrik Ibsen's drama *Peer Gynt* 1876, commissioned by Ibsen and the Norwegian government.

Grieg was born in Bergen, the son of a merchant; he was taught piano by his mother from 1849. In 1858 Ole Bull persuaded his parents to send him to study at Leipzig, Germany, and he entered the Conservatory there. In 1863 he went to live in Copenhagen and studied with Niels Gade. In 1864 he met Rikard Nordaak, who fired his enthusiasm for Norwegian national music, and became engaged to his cousin Nina Hagerup, whom he married in 1867, settling as a teacher and conductor at Christiania. He was a director of the Christiania (Oslo) Philharmonic Society in 1866 and played a part in the formation of the Norwegian Academy of Music. In 1869, at Copenhagen, he premiered his most enduring work, the Piano Concerto in A minor. The premiere of Ibsen's *Peer Gynt*, in February 1876 secured Grieg's reputation as the leading Scandinavian composer of the day; the work's colourful and evocative vignettes represent his talent at its best. In 1888–89 he and his wife appeared in London, Paris, and Vienna. He was awarded honorary doctorates by Cambridge University in 1894 and by Oxford in 1906.

Once dismissed by Debussy as 'a pink bonbon stuffed with snow', Grieg is now returning to critical favour. In his music he rapidly developed a style which was characterized partly by its echoes of Norwegian folk song and even more by his own harmonic experiments, whose combination produced music of great strength and individuality. He was primarily a lyrical composer.

Works include: SOLO VOICES, CHORUS, AND ORCHESTRA *Land-sighting, Olaf Trygvason; Bergliot* (Bjørnson) for declamation and orchestra.

CHAMBER AND SOLO VOCAL string quartet in G minor (1878); three sonatas for violin and piano; sonata for cello and piano; 24 op. nos. of piano pieces, including ten volumes of *Lyric Pieces*, sonata in E minor, *Slåtter* (1903); 143 songs, including *Haugtussa* cycle (Garborg, 1895), settings of Ibsen, Bjørnson.

OTHER incidental music for Ibsen's *Peer Gynt* (1874–75) and Bjørnson's *Sigurd Jorsalfar* (1872); *Holberg Suite* for string orchestra (1884); piano concerto in A minor (1868).

Griffes, Charles T(omlinson) (1884–1920) US composer. He studied in Berlin with Humperdinck and taught there for a time. He returned to the USA in 1907, and became a music teacher at a boys' school at Tarrytown, New York. His early death was brought about by ill health and overwork.

Works include: the Japanese mime play *Schojo* (1917); dance drama *The Kairn of Koridwen* (1916); *The Pleasure Dome of Kubla Khan* (after Coleridge) for orchestra (1917); Poem for flute and orchestra; *These things shall be* (J A Symonds) for unison chorus; Sketches on Indian themes for string quartet; piano sonata and pieces; songs.

Grigny, Nicolas de (1672–1703) French organist and composer. He studied under his father – Louis de Grigny (c. 1646–1709), organist at Notre-Dame of Rheims – and in Paris. He was organist of the abbey of Saint-Denis, Paris, 1693–95 and then of Rheims Cathedral. Organ music written by him and published in 1699 was known and copied by J S Bach in his early years.

Grillparzer, Franz (1791–1872) Austrian poet and dramatist. Friend of Ludwig van Beethoven and Franz Schubert. He wrote a funeral oration for the former and a sketched inscription for the latter's gravestone. For works used by composers, see J N ◊Hummel (*Ahnfrau*); C ◊Kreutzer (*Libussa* and *Melusine*); ◊Sappho (Kaun); ◊Schöne Melusine (Mendelssohn and C Kreutzer); ◊Schubert (*Ständchen* and *Mirjams Siegesgesang*); I X ◊Seyfried (*Ahnfrau* and *König Ottokar*); O O ◊Straus (*Traum ein Leben*).

Grisar, Albert (1808–1869) Belgian composer. He was intended for a business career and was sent to Liverpool, but ran away to Paris to study music in 1830. He became a pupil of Reicha, but was driven to Antwerp by the Revolution. He produced *Le Mariage impossible* at Brussels in 1833, and returned to Paris, where he had further operatic successes. He studied with Mercadante at Naples in 1840 and returned to Paris in 1844.

Works include: the operas *Sarah* (after Scott, 1836), *L'an 1000*, *Lady Melvill* (1838), and *L'eau merveilleuse* (both with Flotow), *Le naufrage de la Méduse* (with Flotow and Pilati), *Les travestissements* (1839), *L'Opéra à la cour* (with Boïeldieu, junior), *Gille Ravisseur* (1848), *Les Porcherons* (1850), *Bonsoir M Pantalon*, *Le carillonneur de Bruges* (1852), *Les amours du diable*, *Le chien du jardinier* (1855), *Voyage autour de ma chambre* (after Xavier de Maistre, 1859), *La chatte merveilleuse* (1862), *Bégaiements d'amour*, *Douze innocentes* (1865).

Griselda, La opera by A Scarlatti (libretto after A Zeno), produced Rome, Teatro Capranica, January 1721. The last of Scarlatti's 69 operas, beginning with *Gli equivoci* (1679). Modern edition by L Salter. King Gualtiero tests his wife, Griselda. She must live as a peasant, is threatened with the loss of her son, and is pursued by Ottone. She remains true and is restored as queen.

Grisélidis opera by Massenet (libretto by A Silvestre and E Morand), produced Paris, Opéra-Comique, 20 November 1901. It was revived at the Wexford Festival, 1983. Grisélidis the shepherdess marries the Marquis de Saluces, who has the Devil test her fidelity.

Grocheio, Johannes de (fl. 1300) music theorist of uncertain nationality who worked in Paris around 1300. His *De musica* survives in two manuscripts and is important for the light it throws on the secular music of his day and how it was performed.

Grofé, Ferde (1892–1972) US composer and arranger. He worked as an arranger for the Paul Whiteman band, and in 1924 arranged Gershwin's *Rhapsody in Blue*. His own music includes *Mississippi Suite*, *Hollywood Suite*, and the well-known *Grand Canyon Suite*, which was premiered under Whiteman in 1931.

grosse caisse (French 'great case or chest') French name for the ◊bass drum.

Grosse Fuge/Great Fugue a work for string quartet by Beethoven, op. 133, in a fugal form 'tantôt libre, tantôt recherchée', written 1825 as the finale of the B♭ major string quartet, op. 130, and first performed with it, Vienna, 21 March 1826. Beethoven was persuaded by his publisher that it was too long, difficult, and abstruse for that purpose and subsequently wrote the new finale, now part of op. 130. Also version for two pianos, op. 134.

Also title for first version of Busoni's *Fantasia contrappuntistica* (1910).

Grossin, Estienne (fl. c. 1420), or Grossim French composer. He was chaplain at St Merry, Paris in 1418, and *clerc de matines* at Notre Dame in 1421. He wrote church music and chansons, including a Mass (without *Agnus*) with a part labelled 'trombetta'.

Grossinquisitor, Der/The Grand Inquisitor oratorio by Blacher (text by L Borchard, from Dostoevsky's *The Brothers Karamazov*); composed 1942, first performed Berlin, 14 October 1947.

Grossvater-Tanz (German 'grandfather's dance') believed at one time to be a 17th-century German dance (with words referring to a grandfather's wooing), sung and danced at weddings, and later used as the final dance at balls and therefore called *Kehraus*, 'sweep-out'. Schumann used it both in *Papillons*, op. 2, and *Carnaval*, op. 9, in the latter to stand for the 'Philistines' in the finale. The dance was actually written by Karl Gottlieb Hering (1765–1853).

Grosz, Wilhelm (1894–1939) Austrian com-poser. His music has become associated with Kurt Weill, and a concert of their music was given at the London Proms in 1993.

Grosz studied theory under Guido Adler and composition under Franz Schreker. In 1921 he was appointed conductor at Mann-heim Opera, but returned to Vienna in 1922 to make a living as pianist and composer. From 1928 he worked with a gramophone company in Berlin, and conducted the Kam-merspiele in Vienna 1933–34. He then left Germany and became a refugee in London and New York .

Works include: the operas *Sganarell* (1925) and *Achtung, Aufnahme* (1930); play with music *St Peters Regenschirm*; ballets *Der arme Reinhold* (1928) and *Baby in der Bar*; incidental music to Werfel's *Spiegelmensch* and Haupt-mann's *Die versunkene Glocke*; music for films and radio; Symphonic Variations, serenade, suite, overture to an opera buffa and other pieces for orchestra; Symphonic Dance for piano and orchestra; string quartet; two violin and piano sonatas; three piano sonatas.

ground composition built on a ground bass, or the bass itself.

ground bass a bass line that repeats cyclic-ally, over which an evolving harmonic-melo-dic structure is laid. Examples are the ◊chaconne and ◊passacaglia.

Grout, Donald J(ay) (1902–1987) US musi-cologist. He studied at Syracuse and Harvard Universities and in Strasbourg and Vienna. He taught at Harvard 1936–42, and was professor of music at Cornell University 1945–70. Early opera and works of A Scarlatti were at the centre of his research. His books include *A Short History of Opera* (1948, revised 1965), *A History of Western Music* (1960, revised 1973, 1980 and, with C V Palisca, 1988), and *Mozart in the History of Opera* (1972).

Grove, George (1820–1900) English scholar. He edited the original *Dictionary of Music and Musicians* 1889, which in its expanded and revised form is still one of the standard music reference sources. He was also the first

director of the ◊Royal College of Music. He was knighted in 1882.

Groves, Charles Barnard (1915–) English conductor. Known both as a choral and symphonic conductor, he is an outstanding interpreter of British music, especially the works of Delius. He was knighted in 1973.

Gruber, H(einz) K(arl) (1943–) Austrian composer. He has played the double bass in various Viennese orchestras, and cofounded the avant-garde group **MOB Art and Tone ART**.

He studied at the Vienna Hochschule and with von Einem.

Works include: the melodrama *Die Vertrei-bung aus dem Paradies* for speakers and six instruments (1966), the spectacle *Gomorrah* (1972), 'pandemonium' *Frankenstein!!* for bar-itone and orchestra (1977); stage work *Gloria von Jaxtberg* (1993); Concerto for orchestra (1964), *Manhattan Broadcasts* for chamber orchestra, *Arien* for violin and orchestra, *Demilitarized Zones* for brass band (1979), *Rough Music*, concerto for percussion and orchestra (1983); two violin concertos (1978, revised 1992, and 1988); cello concerto (1989); Mass for chorus, two trumpets, horn, double bass, and percussion (1960), *Reportage aus Gomorrah* for five singers and eight players (1976), *Bring Me the Head of Amadeus*, TV film for the Mozart bicentenary (1991).

Gruenberg, Louis (1884–1964) US pianist and composer. His most successful work was the opera *The Emperor Jones*, premiered at the New York Metropolitan opera house 1933 with Lawrence Tibbett in the title role.

Gruenberg was born in Russia and was taken to the USA at the age of two. He studied in Berlin and Vienna, where he was a piano pupil of Ferruccio Busoni. He first appeared as pianist in Berlin in 1912 and then began to travel, but from 1919 remained in the USA to devote himself wholly to compo-sition.

Works include: the operas *The Bride of the Gods* (1913; libretto by Busoni), *The Dumb Wife*, *Jack and the Beanstalk*, *Emperor Jones* (after Eugene O'Neill, 1931), *Helena of Troy* (1936); children's opera *The Witch of Brocken*; radio opera *Green Mansions* (after W H Hudson); five symphonies, *Hill of Dreams*, *Enchanted Isle*, Serenade for orchestra; violin concerto; *The Daniel Jazz* (V Lindsey), *Animals and Insects*, and *The Creation* for voice and chamber orchestra; *Four Indiscretions* for string quartet, two string quartets, two sonatas for violin and piano; piano pieces.

Gruppen work by Stockhausen for three orchestras, placed in different parts of a hall and playing different music; composed 1955–57, first performed Cologne, 24 March 1959.

gruppetto, or gruppo or groppo in music, one of several similar Italian terms used in the 16th century for trills (rapid oscillation between adjacent notes), and later for the turn (a form of melodic pirouette around a note). As a turn, the gruppetto designates a four-note figure consisting of the note above the principal note, the note itself, the note below, and the note itself. It was often used as an extemporized embellishment, especially by singers.

gruppo, also gruppetto, in music, to 'trill, turn'.

GSM see ◊Guildhall School of Music and Drama.

Guadagni, Gaetano (c. 1725–1792) Italian castrato alto, later soprano. He made his first appearance at Parma in 1747, and went to London in 1748, where he sang in *Messiah*, *Samson*, and *Theodora* (first performance 1750). He later sang in Dublin, Paris, Lisbon, Italy, and Vienna, where he was the first Orpheus in Gluck's *Orfeo* in 1762.

Guadagnini, Giovanni Battista (J B) (1711–1786) Italian violin maker. He worked at Piacenza, Milan, Cremona, Parma, and Turin. His father, **Lorenzo Guadagnini** (before 1695–c. 1748), worked at Piacenza, and may have been a pupil of Stradivari. Giovanni Battista's son, **Giuseppe Guadagnini** (c. 1736–1805), nicknamed *Il soldato* ('the soldier') worked at Como, Pavia, and Turin.

Guarini, Giovanni Battista (1537–1612) Italian poet. See ◊*Pastor fido* (Handel); S ◊Rossi (*Idropica*); E ◊Settle (*Pastor fido*).

Guarnieri, (Mozart) Camargo (1907–1993) Brazilian composer. He was conductor of the Orquestra Sinfônica Municipal, São Paulo, and director of the Conservatory from 1960. He often visited the USA, where many of his works were performed.

He was a pupil of Charles Koechlin in Paris.

Works include: four symphonies; five piano concertos (1936–70), two violin concertos (1940, 1953); chamber music; cello and piano sonata; piano pieces; songs.

Gubaidulina, Sofia (1931–) Russian composer. In 1975 she cofounded the group **Astreya**, for improvisations on folk instruments from Russia and Caucasia. A leading member of the New Music generation of Russian composers, she has often turned to literature and religion for inspiration. She has been resident in Germany since 1991, the year in which her opera-oratorio-ballet, *Prayer for the Age of Aquarius* was premiered.

She studied at the Moscow Conservatory 1954–59 and later with Vissarion Shebalin.

Works include: ORCHESTRAL *Offertorium* violin concerto (1980–86), *Seven Words* for cello, bayan, and strings (1982), *Stimmen ... verstummen* symphony in 12 movements (1986), *Pro et Contra* for large orchestra (1989).

VOCAL *Night in Memphis* cantata (1968–92), *Rubayat* cantata for baritone and orchestra (1969), *Perception* for soprano, baritone, and seven strings (1985), *Hommage à T S Eliot* for soprano and octet (1987), *Aus dem Stundenbuch/From the Book of Hours* for cello, orchestra, male chorus, and female speaker (1991).

CHAMBER piano sonata (1965), four string quartets (1971, 1987, 1987, 1990), *De Profundis* for bayan (1978), *Garten von freuden und Traurigkeiten* for flute, harp, and viola (1988), string trio (1988), *Silenzio* five pieces for bayan, violin, and cello (1991), *Even and Uneven* for seven percussionists (1991).

Guerrero, Francisco (1528–1599) Spanish composer. He published a large number of works, both religious and secular, and earned himself a reputation in Spain second only to that of Tomás de Victoria as a composer of church music in the 16th century. His works include Masses, requiems, motets, psalms, and Passions in a flowing polyphonic style; they were much admired for their complex canonic devices and remained in use long after his death, especially in South America.

He studied under his brother Pedro Guerrero and Fernández de Castilleja at Seville Cathedral, where he was a chorister 1542–46; he also had some lessons from Cristóbal de Morales as a child. In 1546 he was appointed maestro di cappella at the cathedral of Jaén, and after the death of Morales to that of Málaga, though he never lived there, but filled posts at Seville Cathedral from 1549 until he succeeded Castilleja as maestro di cappella in March 1574. He visited Lisbon, Rome (twice), Venice, and in 1588 went to the Holy Land. Many of his works were published in France and Italy.

Works include: 18 Masses, about 150 liturgical pieces, including motets, psalms, vespers, Magnificats, Te Deum; sacred and secular songs.

Guglielmi, Pietro Alessandro (1728–1804) Italian composer. He produced his first opera in Naples in 1757, and thereafter had great success throughout Italy and abroad. He was in England intermittently 1767–72, and also visited Brunswick and Dresden. In 1793 he was appointed maestro di cappella at St Peter's, Rome.

He studied under Durante in Naples.

Works include: about 100 operas, including *Il ratto della sposa* (1765), *La sposa fedele* (1767), *La villanella ingentilita* (1779), *I finti amori*, *La virtuosa di Mergellina* (1785), *L'inganno amoroso*, *La pastorella nobile*, *La bella pescatrice* (1789); oratorios, including *La morte d'Abele*, *La Betulia liberata*, and others; church music, symphonies; chamber music, keyboard music.

Guglielmi, Pietro Carlo (c. 1763–1817) Italian composer, son of Pietro Alessandro ◊Guglielmi. He studied at the Conservatorio di Santa Maria di Loreto in Naples, producing the first of many successful operas in 1794 in Madrid. He also visited London, Lisbon and Paris.

Works include: almost 50 operas, *Amor tutto vince* (1805), *Guerra aperta* (1807); oratorio *La distruzione di Gerusalemme* (1803).

Guglielmo Ratcliff/William Ratcliff opera by Mascagni (libretto by composer, based on Heine's tragedy), produced Milan, La Scala, 16 February 1895. An earlier work than *Cavalleria rusticana*, although produced later. Mary and Count Douglas are to marry, but Ratcliff wants to kill Douglas to avenge his father, killed by Mary's father. In the end he kills Mary and himself as well.

Guido d'Arezzo (c. 990–c. 1050) Italian Benedictine monk and music theorist. He greatly advanced solmization and mutation by adapting the syllables Ut, Re, Mi, Fa, Sol, and La to the hexachord and by demonstrating the hexachordal positions on the fingers by the use of the 'Guidonian hand'.

He lived in Pomposa and Arezzo, and visited Rome. He was once, rather doubtfully, credited with the invention of the music stave, the use of which he certainly encouraged. His chief theoretical work, written about 1026, is entitled *Micrologus de musica*.

Guildhall School of Music and Drama (GSM) music school established 1880 to serve the City of London; it was housed in a new building in 1887 and in another in 1977. Its principal 1978–88 was John Hosier, Ian Horsbrugh from 1988.

Guilelmus Monachus (lived 15th century) music theorist of uncertain nationality who lived in Italy but may possibly have been English. His treatise *De praeceptis artis musicae* contains references to the English use of 'fauxbourdon' and 'gymel'.

Guillaume Tell/William Tell opera by Grétry (libretto by J M Sedaine), produced Paris, Comédie-Italienne, 9 April 1791.

Opera by Rossini (libretto by V J E de Jouy and H L F Bis, based on Schiller's drama), produced Paris, Opéra, 3 August 1829. Rossini's last opera. Swiss patriot William Tell would lead the uprising against the Austrians, but he has been imprisoned. Arnold, once in love with Austrian Mathilde, joins the fight after his father is executed. After the storm, sunny skies for Switzerland.

Guilmant, (Félix) Alexandre (1837–1911) French organist and composer. He toured widely with great success and was professor of organ at the Schola Cantorum in Paris, which he had helped Charles Bordes and Vincent d'Indy to found, and at the Paris Conservatory.

He was a pupil of his father, an organist at Boulogne, where he afterwards held several church appointments, studying briefly in Brussels with Jaak Lemmens in 1860 and moving to Paris in 1871, where he was organist at the Trinité Church until 1901.

Works include: two symphonies for organ and orchestra; eight sonatas and 25 sets of pieces for organ, organ music for church use.

guimbarde French name for the ◊Jew's harp.

Guiraud, Ernest (1837–1892) French composer. He wrote operas, several cantatas, and overtures, and recitatives for Bizet's *Carmen* and Offenbach's *Contes d'Hoffman*; he also finished the orchestration of the latter.

Guiraud was born at New Orleans, the son of a French musician. He studied at the Paris Conservatory and won the Prix de Rome in 1859. He served in the Franco-Prussian war and in 1876 became professor of harmony and accompaniment at the Conservatory, following Massé as the head of the advanced composition class in 1880. Debussy was one of his pupils.

Works include: OPERA *Sylvie* (1864), *En Prison* (1869), *Le Kobold* (1870), *Madame Turlupin*, *Piccolino* (1876), *Galante Aventure*, *Le Feu*, *Frédégonde* (unfinished, completed by Saint-Saëns).

OTHER ballet *Gretna Green* (1873); overture *Arteveld*, *Chasse fantastique* (after Hugo's *Beau Pécopin*), and suite for orchestra; Caprice for violin and orchestra. Recitatives for Bizet's *Carmen* and orchestration of Offenbach's *Contes d'Hoffmann*.

Guiraut de Bornelh alternative spelling of ◊Giraud de Borneil, Provençal troubadour.

Guirlande, La, ou Les fleurs enchantées acte de ballet by Rameau (libretto by J-F Marmontel), produced Paris, Opéra, 21 September 1751. The garlands exchanged by Myrtil and Zélide will only stay fresh as long as they remain faithful.

guitar flat-bodied musical instrument with six or twelve strings which are plucked or strummed with the fingers. The fingerboard is usually fretted (see ◊fret), although some modern electric guitars are fretless. The Hawaiian guitar is laid across the player's lap, and uses a metal bar to produce a distinctive gliding tone. The solid-bodied electric ◊guitar, developed in the 1950s by Les Paul and Leo Fender, mixes and amplifies vibrations from electromagnetic pickups at different points to produce a range of tone qualities.

Derived from a Moorish original, the guitar spread throughout Europe in medieval times, becoming firmly established in Italy, Spain, and the Spanish American colonies. The 20th-century revival owes much to Andrés Segovia, Julian Bream, and John Williams. The guitar's prominence in popular music can be traced from the traditions of the US Midwest; it played a supporting harmony role in jazz and dance bands during the 1920s and adapted quickly to electric amplification.

guitar, electric amplified acoustic guitar employing optional electromagnetic pickups set under the strings to detect vibration, bypassing the soundbox. The solid-bodied instrument developed in the 1950s by Leo Fender and Les Paul has a cutaway body to extend fingering positions, and multiple pickups for harder and softer timbres that can be varied in balance while playing.

The technique of 'humbucking' uses feedback circuits to recycle guitar body reverberation to create indefinite sustain. This allowed the development in the 1970s of a distinctive singing tone by hard-rock lead guitarists.

Other forms include the **double-neck guitar** and the **electric bass**, a guitar version of the string bass.

Composers for electric guitar include Frank Martin, Pierre Boulez, and Luciano Berio.

guitar violoncello alternative name for the ◊arpeggione, a stringed musical instrument.

The open strings of the modern classical guitar.

Gundry, Inglis (1905–   ) English composer. Educated at Oxford, he read law, but turned to literature, writing poems and a novel, *The Countess's Penny*. He studied at Royal College of Music under Vaughan Williams, Gordon Jacob, and R O Morris. After war service in the navy, he became instructor Lieutenant and music adviser to the Admiralty education department, for which he edited a *Naval Song Book*.

Works include: the operas *Naaman: the Leprosy of War* (1937), *The Return of Odysseus* (after Homer, 1938), *The Sleeping Beauty* and *Partisans* (1946); ballet *Sleep*; Variations on an Indian theme and overture *Per mare, per terram* for orchestra; Comedy Overture for small orchestra; *Sostenuto and Vivace* for strings; Fantasy string quartet; songs.

Günther von Schwarzburg opera by Holzbauer (libretto by A Klein), produced Mannheim, at court, 5 January 1777. Günther battles Karl for control of the Holy Roman Empire, finally being poisoned by Karl's mother; admired by Mozart.

Guntram opera by Richard Strauss (libretto by composer) produced Weimar, 10 May 1894. Strauss's first opera; revised version produced Weimar, 22 October 1940. Guntram kills Duke Robert after being attacked by him, but the idealistic minstrel realizes that his deed was caused by love for the Duke's wife, Freihild. Guntram seeks solitude for introspection.

Guridi, Jesús (1886–1961) Spanish composer of Basque descent. He studied at the Schola Cantorum in Paris, also at Liège and Cologne. His music is based on Basque themes.

Works include: the operas *Mirentxu* (1915) and *Amaya* (1920), zarzuela *El caserío* (1926); orchestra and organ music; church music; four string quartets; settings of Basque folksongs.

Gurney, Ivor (Bertie) (1890–1937) English composer and poet. He was a choirboy at Gloucester Cathedral and later studied at the Royal College of Music in London with a scholarship. He suffered much from ill-health and during World War I was badly wounded and shell-shocked. He struggled for a time against poverty, but in 1922 lost his reason. He died of tuberculosis.

Works include: *The Apple Orchard* and *Scherzo* for violin and piano; two sets of piano pieces; song cycles *Ludlow and Teme* (A E Housman) and *The Western Playland*, over 200 songs, some to his own poems. Two volumes of poetry, *Savern and Somme* and *War's Embers*.

Gurrelieder/Songs of Gurra work by Schoenberg for five soloists, speaker, four choruses, and large orchestra, including iron chains (text a German translation of the Danish poems by J P Jacobsen); composed 1900–11, first performed Vienna 23 February 1913, conductor Franz Schreker. First US performance Philadelphia, 8 April 1932, conductor Stokowski.

Gustave III, ou Le Bal masqué/Gustavus III, or The Masked Ball opera by Auber (libretto by Scribe), produced Paris, Opéra, 27 February 1833. See ◊*Ballo in maschera* for plot synopsis.

Gutiérrez, Antonio Garcia (1812–1884) Spanish dramatist. See ◊*Simon Boccanegra* and ◊*Trovatore* (Verdi).

Guy, Barry (1947–) English composer and double bass player. His early interest was in jazz; he later studied at the Guildhall School of Music with Buxton Orr and Patric Standford. Since he formed the Jazz Composers' Orchestra in 1971 his works have combined improvisatory with more controlled avant-garde techniques.

Works include: *D* for 15 solo strings (1972); *Anna* for amplified double bass and orchestra (1974); *Statements III* and *IV* for jazz orchestra (1972–75); string quartet *III* (1973); *Songs from Tomorrow* for 13 instruments (1975); *Voyages of the Moon* for double bass and orchestra (1983); *Blitz*, septet (1984); *rondOH!* for piano, violin, and double bass (1985); *Video Life* for double bass and electronics (1986); ballet for London Contemporary Dance Theatre; *After the Rain* (1992); *Bird Gong Game* (1992); *Witch Gong Game* (1993); *Portraits* (1993).

Guy-Ropartz, Joseph Guy Marie Ropartz (1864–1955) French composer. After studying law, he went to the Paris Conservatory as a pupil of Dubois, Massenet, and Franck. In 1894 he became director of the Nancy Conservatory and in 1919 of that of Strasbourg. Later he retired to Brittany, where he was born.

Works include: four operas, including *Le Pays* (1913); ballet *L'Indiscret*; three Masses, motets, and other church music; five symphonies (1895–1945), *La cloche des morts*, *La chasse du Prince Arthur*; six string quartets (1893–1951); three violin and piano sonatas, two cello and piano sonatas; songs; organ music.

Gwendoline opera by Chabrier (libretto by C Mendès), produced Brussels, Théâtre de la Monnaie, 10 April 1886. Gwendoline, daughter of Saxon leader Armel, is to marry Danish Harald. Armel plans to massacre the Danes during the festivities. Gwendoline tries to warn Harald, but it is too late, then she kills herself.

gymel (from Latin gemellum, 'a twinsong') vocal music in two parts, both of the same range. A characteristic feature is the use of parallel thirds. The term first occurs in the 15th century, when it usually refers to a divided voice-part in a polyphonic composition, but examples are found as early as the 14th century.

Gymnopédies three pieces for piano by Satie, composed 1888. Nos. 1 and 3 (*Lent et triste*, *Lent et grave*) were orchestrated by Debussy and performed Paris, 20 February 1897.

Gymnopédies refers to Greek dances in honour of Apollo, performed by naked men and boys; Debussy's music has become a popular ballet.

Gyrowetz, Adalbert (Vojcěch) (1763–1850), or Jírovec Bohemian composer. He wrote about 40 operas and 100 chamber and piano pieces, mostly in a style resembling Haydn's. He knew Beethoven, and was a pall-bearer at his funeral in 1827.

He learnt music from his father, a choirmaster. He later went to Prague to study law, but continued to work at music. As private secretary to Count Franz von Fünfkirchen, he was expected to take part in the domestic music. He then went to Italy for study under Nicola Sala at Naples and later visited Paris, where symphonies of his had been performed under the name of Haydn. In 1789 the French Revolution drove him to London, where the score of his opera *Semiramis* was burnt in the fire of the Pantheon in 1792. He returned to Vienna soon after, and in 1804 was appointed conductor at the court theatres, where he wrote many works until 1831.

Works include: the Italian operas *Federica ed Adolfo* (1812) and *Il finto Stanislao* (1818), German operas *Agnes Sorel* (1806), *Ida die Büssende* (1807), *Der Augenarzt, Robert, oder Die Prüfung* (1815), *Helene, Felix und Adele, Hans Sachs, Die Junggesellen-Wirtschaft, Der Sammtrock, Aladin* (after Oehlenschläger), *Das Ständchen* (1823), and others; ballet *Die Hochzeit der Thetis* (1816) and others; melodramas *Mirina* and others; comic cantata *Die Dorfschule*; over 60 symphonies, serenades, overtures, and other orchestral works; about 60 string quartets, quintets, numerous trios; about 40 violin and piano sonatas; instrumental pieces, dances; songs.

H

H the German equivalent of B♮.

Haas, Robert (Maria) (1886–1960) Austrian musicologist. He edited the original versions of Bruckner's works 1932–42, and was succeeded in this task by Leopold Nowak. He wrote books on Baroque music, musical performance, Mozart, and Bruckner.

Haas received a doctorate from Prague University and became assistant to the musicologist Guido Adler. He later became a lecturer at Vienna University and director of the music department of the State Library there.

Hába, Alois (1893–1973) Czech composer. Much of his work (after the suite for strings 1917) is based on the division of the scale into quarter-tones. He later employed sixth-tones (as in the fifth quartet 1923), and fifth-tones (as in the 16th quartet 1967). He also wrote some 12-tone music, for example *Fantasia* for nonet 1932.

He gained a knowledge of folk music before he began studying at the Prague Conservatory under Novák. He later became a pupil of Schreker in Vienna and Berlin. While working for Universal Edition in Vienna he gained a good knowledge of Schoenberg's music. He was appointed professor at the Prague Conservatory in 1924.

Works include: opera *Matka/Mother*, produced Munich 1931, Overture and Symphonic Music for orchestra; Fantasy for piano and orchestra; violin concerto; 16 string quartets (1919–67) and other chamber music; piano sonata and other works (some for quarter-tone piano); works for string instruments.

habanera, or havanaise Cuban dance named after the city of Havana. The most popular dance in Latin America during the 19th century, it was the ancestor of other dance forms, including the Argentinian tango. The habanera is usually in slow duple time (2/4) and uses a variety of standard rhythms. There is a celebrated example in Bizet's opera *Carmen* 1875.

Habeneck, François Antoine (1781–1849) French violinist and conductor. He was the founder of the Société des Concerts du Conservatoire in Paris, conductor at the Opéra 1824–47, and gave the first performances of *Guillaume Tell*, *Les Huguenots*, *La Juive*, and *Benvenuto Cellini*. He was the first conductor to cultivate Beethoven's music in France.

He was a pupil of Baillot.

Hacomblene (Hacomplaynt), Robert (c. 1456–1528) English composer. He was scholar of Eton, 1469–72, and of King's College, Cambridge from 1472. He was a Fellow at Cambridge 1475–93, and Provost from 1509 until his death. A *Salve Regina* by him is in the Eton Choirbook.

Haddon Hall operetta by Sullivan (libretto by Sydney Grundy), produced London, Savoy Theatre, 24 September 1892.

Hadley, Henry (Kimball) (1871–1937) US conductor and composer. He studied with his father, with Chadwick at Boston and Mandyczewski in Vienna. He conducted opera in USA and Germany, and in 1909 became conductor of the symphony orchestra at Seattle; San Francisco 1911–15. From 1920 he lived in New York.

Works include: the operas *Safié* (1909), *Azora, Daughter of Montezuma* (1917), *Bianca, Cleopatra's Night* (1920), and *Mirtil in Arcadia*;

Music, The New Earth, and *Resurgam* for solo voices, chorus and orchestra; five symphonies, overtures *In Bohemia, Herod* and to Shakespeare's *Othello,* Symphonic Fantasy, tone poems *Salome, Lucifer,* and *The Ocean.*

Hadley, Patrick (Arthur Sheldon) (1899–1973) English composer. His musical output is small but distinguished, and includes incidental music for Greek plays, choral works *The Trees so High* 1931 and *The Hills* 1944, a rhapsody *One Morning in Spring* for small orchestra, vocal works, church music, and a string quartet.

He was educated at Winchester College and Cambridge University, and studied music at the Royal College of Music in London, where in 1925 he joined the teaching staff. He received a doctorate from Cambridge in 1938, and was appointed lecturer at the university and Professor of Music in succession to Dent 1946–62.

Works include: incidental music to Sophocles' *Antigone;* symphony for baritone and chorus *The Trees so High* (1931), *La Belle Dame sans merci* (Keats) for tenor, chorus, and orchestra, *My Beloved Spake* (Song of Solomon) for chorus and orchestra; cantatas *The Hills* for soprano, tenor, bass, chorus, and orchestra (1944), and *Travellers; Ephemera* (Yeats), and *Mariana* (Tennyson, 1937) for voice and chamber orchestra; string quartet in C major, fantasy for two violins and piano; songs; part songs.

Hadow, W(illiam) H(enry) (1859–1937) English educationist and music scholar. He was educated at Malvern College and Oxford, where later he lectured on music, having studied at Darmstadt and under C H Lloyd. He was principal of Armstrong College, Newcastle-upon-Tyne, 1909–19, and Vice-Chancellor of Sheffield University, 1919–30. He edited the *Oxford History of Music* and wrote volume v thereof, *The Viennese Period;* other books include *Studies in Modern Music* and *English Music.* He also composed chamber music and songs.

'Haffner' Serenade Mozart's Serenade in D major, K250, written at Salzburg in July 1776 for the marriage of Elisabeth Haffner, daughter of the late Bürgermeister Sigmund Haffner, celebrated on 22 July.

'Haffner' Symphony Mozart's Symphony in D major K385, composed in Vienna in summer 1782 for the Haffner family, probably on the occasion of the ennoblement of Sigmund Haffner, junior, on 29 July 1782.

Hagith opera in one act by Szymanowski (libretto by composer after F Dormann); composed 1912–13, while Szymanowski was living in Vienna; produced Warsaw, 13 May 1922. Hagith is stoned to death after she refuses to become a sacrifice for King David.

Hahn, Reynaldo (1874–1947) French composer and conductor. He was popular in Parisian salons as a performer of his own songs, and was admired by Proust. In 1934 he was appointed music critic of *Le Figaro,* and in 1945 became music director of the Paris Opéra. As a conductor he specialized in Mozart and as a composer he wrote much incidental music for plays, two ballets, operas, and operettas.

He was sent to the Paris Conservatory at the age of 11, where his teachers included Massenet. He had his first work published at the age of 14 and his first opera produced at 23.

Works include: OPERA *L'Ile du rêve* (1898), *La Carmélite* (1902), *La Colombe de Bouddha* (1921), *Nausicaa, Le Pauvre d'Assise, La Reine de Saba, Le Temps d'aimer, Brummel* (1931), *Le Marchand de Venise* (after Shakespeare, 1935), and many operettas including *Ciboulette.*

OTHER ballets *La Fête chez Thérèse* (1907) and *Le Dieu bleu* (1912); incidental music for Shakespeare's *Much Ado about Nothing,* Rostand's *Le Bois sacré,* Sacha Guitry's *Mozart* (1925), and others; ode *Prométhée* for solo voices, chorus, and orchestra; symphonic poem *Nuit d'amour bergamasque;* string quartet and other chamber music; piano pieces; songs including cycles *Chansons grises, Chansons latines, Chansons espagnoles.*

hairpins in musical notation, colloquial term for *crescendo* and *diminuendo* marks.

Halévy, Jacques François Fromental (Elias) (1799–1862), born Lévy French composer. His music, which consists almost entirely of operas, is brilliant and charming, rather than profound. Halévy's daughter married Bizet, who finished Halévy's last opera, *Noe,* as *Le Deluge.*

From 1809 he studied at the Paris Conservatory under Cherubini, who was both a friend and a strong musical influence. After twice taking a second prize, he won the Prix de Rome in 1819. He continued to study in Italy, and on his return to Paris tried to gain a foothold on the operatic stage, for which he had already written more than one work. He succeeded with *L'Artisan* in 1827, after which he wrote an enormous number of operas. In the same year he became professor of harmony and accompaniment at the Conservatory, of counterpoint and fugue in 1833, and of composition in 1840.

Works include: OPERA about 40, including *La dilettante d'Avignon*, *Ludovic* (begun by Hérold), *La juive* (1835), *L'éclair*, *Guido et Ginevra*, *Le shérif*, *Le guitarréro*, *La reine de Chypre*, *Charles VI* (1843), *Les mousquetaires de la reine* (1846), *Le val d'Andorre*, *La fée aux roses*, *La tempestà* (in Italian, after Shakespeare, 1850), *La dame de Pique* (after Mérimée), *Le juif errant* (after Sue), *Jaguarita l'indienne* (1855), *La magicienne*, and others; ballets *Yella*, *Manon Lescaut* (after Prévost).

OTHER incidental music to *Prométhée enchaîné* (translated from Aeschylus); cantatas *Les derniers moments du Tasse*, *La mort d'Adonis* and *Herminie*; funeral march and *De profundis* on the death of the Duc de Berry.

Halévy, Ludovic (1834–1908) French novelist and librettist. He collaborated with Hector Crémieux in the libretto for Offenbach's *Orpheus in the Underworld*; and with Henri Meilhac on librettos for Offenbach's *La Belle Hélène* and *La Vie parisienne*, as well as for Bizet's *Carmen*.

half-close an imperfect cadence, such as one in which the dominant chord is preceded by the tonic.

A half-close from C to G major.

Halffter, Cristóbal (1930–) Spanish composer. His music tends towards total serialism. In 1962 he became professor of composition at Madrid Conservatory. He was a lecturer at the University of Navarra 1970–78, and was appointed director of the electronic music studio at Freiburg im Breislau in 1978.

He is the nephew of the brothers Ernesto and Rodolfo Halffter. He studied with Conrado del Campo and Alexandre Tansman.

Works include: the operas *Don Quichotte* (produced Düsseldorf, 1970), *Cantata in expectatione resurrectionis domini* (1962); concertino for string orchestra; *Sinfonia* for three instrumental groups (1963); *Cinco microformas* for orchestra; *Dos movimientos* for timpani and string orchestra; cello concerto (1974); violin concerto (1979), two cello concertos (1979, 1985), Sinfonia ricercata for organ and

orchestra (1982), flute concerto (1982), concerto for violin, viola, and orchestra (1984), piano concerto (1988), *Espejos* for four percussionists and tape (1963); ballet *Saeta*; *Misa ducal*; *Tres piezas* for string quartet; *Formantes* for two pianos; *Tres piezas* for solo flute; sonata for solo violin; *Antifona pascual* for soloists, chorus, and orchestra, *Dona nobis pacem* for mixed chorus and ensemble (1984).

half tone, or half step in music, alternative terms for ◊semitone.

Halka opera by Moniuszko (libretto, in Polish, by W Wolski, based on a story by K W Wójcicki), concert performance Wilno, 11 January 1848; produced Wilno, 28 February 1854; revised version Warsaw, 1 January 1858. The Polish national opera, Wallek-Walewski's opera *Jontek's Revenge* is a sequel to it. Halka commits suicide after she is seduced and abandoned by the nobleman Janusz.

Hall, Henry (c. 1655–1707) English organist and composer. He was a choirboy in the Chapel Royal in London under Cooke. He was appointed organist at Exeter Cathedral in 1674 and at Hereford Cathedral in 1688.

Works include: Te Deum in E♭ major, Benedicite in C minor, *Cantate Domino* and *Deus misereatur* in B♭ major, anthems and other church music; songs, duets, catches.

Halle, Adam de la, or Hale see ◊La Halle.

Hallé, Charles (Carl) (1819–1895) German conductor and pianist. Settling in England 1848, he established and led Manchester's Hallé Orchestra 1858, until his death. As a pianist, he was the first to play all 32 Beethoven piano sonatas in London (also in Manchester and Paris).

Halling a Norwegian dance originating from the Hallingdal between Oslo and Bergen. It is usually in 2–4 time and goes at a moderately quick pace. In its early form, as distinct from that cultivated by Grieg and other composers, its music is played on the Hardanger fiddle.

Haman and Mordecai (Handel). See ◊*Esther*.

Hambraeus, Bengt (1928–) Swedish composer and musicologist. He studied musicology at the University of Uppsala 1947–56, and from 1957 worked for Swedish Radio, at the same time teaching at Uppsala University. He participated in courses at Darmstadt, being chiefly influenced by the work of Webern, Stockhausen, and Boulez.

Works include: *Rota* for three orchestras, percussion, and electronic tape (1964); *Constellation I* for organ; *Constellation II* for recorded tape; *Constellation III* derived from nos. I and II; *Doppelrohr II*, an electronic piece; *Introduzione-Sequenze-Coda*; chamber opera *Experiment X* (1971), church opera *Se nännis kan* (1972).

Hamilton, Iain Ellis (1922–) Scottish composer. His intensely emotional and harmonically rich works include striking viola and cello sonatas; the ballet *Clerk Saunders* 1951; the operas *Pharsalia* 1968 and *The Royal Hunt of the Sun* 1967–69, which renounced melody for inventive chordal formations; and symphonies.

Born in Glasgow, he worked as an aircraft engineer 1939–46, and studied at the Royal Academy of Music 1947–51, where various works of his were introduced. He won the Royal Philharmonic Society prize for his clarinet concerto and the Koussevitsky Award for his second symphony. He was professor at Duke University, North Carolina, USA 1961–81.

Works include: operas *Agamemnon* (1969), *The Royal Hunt of the Sun* (1967–69; produced 1977), *The Catiline Conspiracy* (after Jonson, 1974), *Tamburlaine* (1977), *Anna Karenina* (1981), *Lancelot* (1984); *The Tragedy of Macbeth* (1990); *London's Fair* (1992); ballet *Clerk Saunders*; four symphonies (1950–81); two violin concertos (1952, 1971); two piano concertos (1949, 1967); Variations for strings; *Aurora* for orchestra (1975); *Requiem* (1979), Mass in A (1980), *St Mark Passion* (1982); clarinet quintet, string quartet, flute quartet; Variations for solo violin; viola and piano sonata; pieces for wind instruments and piano; piano sonata; violin concerto; octet for strings (1984).

Hamlet incidental music for Shakespeare's tragedy by Tchaikovsky, op. 67a, including 16 numbers and an abridged version of the *Hamlet* fantasy-overture, op. 67, first performed St Petersburg, 17 November 1888; the play first performed with Tchaikovsky's music, St Petersburg, 21 February 1891.
See also ◊*Ambleto*; ◊*Amleto*; ◊Shakespeare.

Hammerklavier (German 'hammer keyboard instrument') alternative name for the ◊piano, used to distinguish it from the ◊harpsichord, in which the strings are plucked. Beethoven designated his sonatas op. 101 and 106 as 'für das Hammerclavier', and the word is now used as a nickname for the latter sonata.

Hammerschmidt, Andreas (1612–1675) Bohemian composer. He was taken to Freiberg, Saxony in 1626; he became organist there in 1635, and at Zittau in 1639. He wrote much Lutheran church music, which was published in 14 collections 1639–71.

Works include: sacred concertos and madrigals for several voices, sacred dialogues for two voices, odes, motets, and hymns, 17 short Lutheran Masses; thanksgiving for eight voices for the Saxon victory at Liegnitz; dances for viols.

Hammerstein, Oscar, II (1895–1960) US lyricist and librettist. He collaborated with Richard ◊Rodgers over a period of 16 years on some of the best-known US musicals, including *Oklahoma!* 1943 (Pulitzer prize), *Carousel* 1945, *South Pacific* 1949 (Pulitzer prize), *The King and I* 1951, and *The Sound of Music* 1959.

He was a grandson of opera impresario Oscar Hammerstein (I) (1846–1919). He earned his first successes with *Rose Marie* 1924, music by Rudolf Friml (1879–1972); *Desert Song* 1926, music by Sigmund Romberg (1887–1951); and *Show Boat* 1927, music by Jerome Kern. *Show Boat* represented a major step forward in integration of plot and character. After a period of moderate success in film music, he joined Rodgers and began their 16-year collaboration. His adaptation of *Carmen* as a musical (*Carmen Jones*) was premiered in 1943.

His grandfather established the Manhattan Opera House in 1906, in rivalry with the New York Metropolitan. US premieres of *Elektra* and *Pelléas et Mélisande* were given but in 1920 he was bought out by the New York Metropolitan and prevented from mounting opera in New York and other major US cities. A London Opera House, opened at Kingsway in 1911, lasted only two seasons.

Hammond organ electric ◊organ invented in the USA by Laurens Hammond in 1934. It is widely used in gospel music. Hammond applied valve technology to miniaturize Thaddeus Cahill's original 'tone-wheel' concept, introduced draw-slide registration to vary timbre, and incorporated a distinctive tremulant using rotating speakers. The Hammond organ was a precursor of the ◊synthesizer.

Hampton, John (c. 1455–after 1522) English composer. He was master of the choristers at Worcester Priory 1484–1522. He is represented in the Eton Choirbook.

Hanboys, John (lived 15th century) English Franciscan friar and music theorist. His treatise *Summa ... super musicam* is a commentary on ◊Franco of Cologne.

Handbassl (Austrian and South German dialect 'little hand bass') Leopold Mozart's name for the violoncello piccolo, a musical instrument.

hand bells small hand-held bells of various pitches that are rung by a group of performers. They provide a form of practice for 'change ringing' (a team method of ringing full-size church bells using hand ropes). Many pieces of music, including Christmas carols, are easily transcribed for hand bells.

Handel, George Frideric (1685–1759), originally Georg Friedrich Händel German composer, a British subject from 1726. His first opera, *Almira*, was performed in Hamburg in 1705. In 1710 he was appointed Kapellmeister to the elector of Hanover (the future George I of England). In 1712 he settled in England, where he established his popularity with such works as the *Water Music* 1717 (written for George I). His great choral works include the *Messiah* 1742 and the later oratorios *Samson* 1743, *Belshazzar* 1745, *Judas Maccabaeus* 1747, and *Jephtha* 1752.

Visits to Italy 1706–10 inspired a number of operas and oratorios, and in 1711 his opera *Rinaldo* was performed in London. *Saul* and *Israel in Egypt* (both 1739) were unsuccessful, but his masterpiece, the oratorio *Messiah*, was acclaimed on its first performance in Dublin in 1742. Other works include the pastoral *Acis and Galatea* 1718 and a set of variations for harpsichord that were later nicknamed 'The Harmonious Blacksmith'.

Handel was born in Halle. After initial opposition from his father, a barber-surgeon, he studied music with Zachow in Halle, and in 1702 enrolled at the university there to read law, at the same time holding the probationary post of organist at the Domkirche. The next year he abandoned law to become a violinist, and later a harpsichordist, at Keiser's Opera House in Hamburg, and had the operas *Almira* and *Nero* staged in 1705. He travelled in Italy 1706–09, visiting the principal cities and meeting the leading composers. *Agrippina* was successfully produced at Venice in 1709, and he also made a great reputation as a harpsichordist. Other works composed in Italy include the oratorios *La resurrezione* and *Il trionfo del tempo*, solo cantatas, chamber duets, and other pieces. With the support of Steffani he was appointed to succeed the latter as Kapellmeister to the Elector of Hanover in 1710, but left almost immediately on leave of absence for London, where *Rinaldo* was given with great success the next year. Again in London on

leave in 1712, he settled there, never returning to his post in Hanover.

Between 1712 and 1715 Handel staged four operas, and in 1713 wrote a *Te Deum* and *Jubilate* to celebrate the Peace of Utrecht, receiving a life pension of £200 from Queen Anne. On her death in 1714 the Elector of Hanover succeeded to the throne as George I, but apparently took a lenient view of his former Kapellmeister's truancy, for Handel's pension was soon doubled. In 1716 he composed the *Water Music*, to accompany George I on his journey down the River Thames. As music director to the Earl of Carnarvon (later Duke of Chandos) 1717–20, he wrote the *Chandos Anthems, Acis and Galatea*, and the masque *Haman and Mordecai*. From 1720 he directed the opera at the King's Theatre, Haymarket.

With the founding of the Royal Academy of Music in 1720 began Handel's most prolific period as an opera composer, and over the next 20 years he wrote more than 30 works. Opera in Italian met with limited success (Dr Johnson called it 'an exotic and irrational entertainment'), and it was only in recent years that the beauties of *Giulio Cesare, Orlando, Ariodante*, and *Alcina* have been appreciated. The rivalry of the fashionable Italian composer Giovanni Bononcini, and John Gay's ridicule in *The Beggar's Opera* 1728, led him to abandon Italianate opera for English oratorio.

Handel experienced difficulties with the formation of partisan factions round himself and Bononcini, and things were aggravated by internal strife between his two leading ladies, Faustina Bordoni and Francesca Cuzzoni. The popular success of Gay's *The Beggar's Opera* made matters worse, and in that year the Royal Academy of Music went bankrupt. Handel continued to produce operas, acting as his own impresario in partnership with Johann Jakob Heidegger (1666–1749), a Swiss impresario active in London, but rival factions, now of a political nature, again undermined his success, and in the 1730s he increasingly turned to oratorio. *Esther* (a revision of the masque *Haman and Mordecai*), 1732, was followed by *Deborah*, *Saul*, and *Israel in Egypt*.

Handel's last opera was produced in 1741, after which he devoted his time chiefly to oratorio. *Messiah* was the summation of his life's work, composed in a single burst of inspiration but including some elements from earlier music. Its success encouraged him to write 12 more oratorios, some on Old Testament texts (*Samson, Solomon*) others on

Classical mythology (*Semele*). He continued to appear in public as a conductor and organist, playing concertos between the parts of his oratorios, but his health declined and in 1751, despite receiving treatment for cataracts, he became totally blind. His last major public success came in 1749 with the suite for wind instruments, to accompany the Royal Fireworks in Green Park.

Works include: OPERA *Agrippina* (1710), *Rinaldo* (1711), *Radamisto* (1720), *Giulio Cesare* (1724), *Tamerlano* (1724), *Rodelinda* (1725), *Scipione*, *Alessandro* (1726), *Orlando* (1733), *Ariodante* (1735), *Alcina* (1735), *Giustino, Berenice* (1737), *Serse* (1735), *Imeneo* (1740), *Deidamia* (1741); incidental music to Ben Jonson's *The Alchemist* and Smollett's *Alceste*.

ORATORIO *Athalia* (1733), *Saul* (1739), *Israel in Egypt* (1739), *Messiah* (1742), *Samson* (1743), *Belshazzar* (1745), *Judas Maccabaeus* (1747), *Joshua*, *Susanna* (1749), *Solomon* (1749), *Theodora* (1750), *Jephtha* (1752).

OTHER CHORAL WORKS *Acis and Galatea* (1718); *Alexander's Feast* (1736), *Ode for St Cecilia's Day* (1739), *L'Allegro, il Penseroso ed il Moderato* (after Milton), *Semele* (1744); 11 'Chandos' Anthems: (1717–18); anthems for the coronation of George II: *Let thy hand be strengthened*, *My heart is inditing*, *The king shall rejoice*, and *Zadok the priest*; dramatic cantatas: *Apollo e Dafne* (1708) and *Aci, Galatea e Polifemo* (1708); numerous other solo and duo cantatas, including *Armida abandonata* (1707), *Silete venti* (1729); Utrecht *Te Deum* and *Jubilate*.

INSTRUMENTAL trio sonatas and other pieces; 12 *concerti grossi* for strings, 'oboe concertos', organ concertos, *Water Music* (1717), *Music for the Royal Fireworks* (1749), and other pieces; keyboard music, including organ fugues and harpsichord suites.

Handford, Maurice (1929–1986) English conductor and horn player. He studied at the Royal Academy of Music. He was principal horn, Hallé Orchestra, 1949–61; conducted the orchestra from 1966, notably in complex scores by Olivier Messiaen and Witold Lutosławski, but resigned in 1971. He was often heard with regional BBC (British Broadcasting Corporation) orchestras and was principal conductor of the Calgary Philharmonic Orchestra 1971–75.

Handl, Jacob (1550–1591), also known by his Latinized name, Jacobus Gallus Slovenian composer. He was a prolific composer of church music, and wrote 16 Masses, motets, a Te Deum, and a cycle of music for the liturgical year. He also wrote German songs and other secular works, many of which show the influence of Franco-Flemish composers. Contemporary critics complained about the complexity of his music – his four-volume *Opus musicum* 1586–91 included two pieces scored for twenty-four voices.

Handl was born in Ribniča near Ljubljana, and went to Austria in the mid-1560s. He was a singer in the chapel of Emperor Maximilian II in Vienna 1574–75. He then travelled through Austria, Bohemia, Silesia, and Moravia, and was choirmaster to the Bishop of Olomouc 1579–85. By mid-1586 he was cantor at the church of St Jan na Brzehu in Prague, where he remained until his death.

Hansell, Kathleen (Amy Kuzmick) (1941–) US musicologist and organist. She studied at University of Illinois and took her PhD at Berkeley, 1980. She was teacher and organist in Illinois and Iowa, from 1967, and archivist at the Swedish Music History Archive, Stockholm, from 1982. Publications include *Lucio Silla*, for the *Mozart Ausgabe*, editions of Berwald and Hindemith, and *Zelmira* for *Tutte le opere di G Rossini*. She made contributions to *Grove's Dictionary of Music and Musicians* and other lexicographical sources.

Hänsel und Gretel opera by Humperdinck (libretto by A Wette, Humperdinck's sister, from a tale by the Brothers Grimm), produced Weimar, 23 December 1893. Based on the fairy tale; using her gingerbread house as bait, the wicked witch preys on hungry children, but Hänsel and Gretel outwit her, saving themselves and all her previous victims.

Hans Heiling opera by Marschner (libretto by E Devrient, originally written for Mendelssohn), produced Berlin, Opera, 24 May 1833. The gnome Heiling gives up his supernatural powers to live above ground with peasant girl Anna, but he returns to the caves after losing her affections.

Hanson, Howard (1896–1981) US composer. He studied music in New York and at Evanston University, Illinois. After various appointments, he gained the American Prix de Rome, and after his stay in Italy was director of the Eastman School of Music at Rochester, New York 1924–64.

Works include: the opera *Merry Mount* (after Hawthorne, 1934); choral work *The Lament for Beowulf*; seven symphonies (1923–77), symphonic poems *North and West*, *Lux aeterna*, and *Pan and the Priest* for orchestra; string quartet (1923), piano quintet, concerto for piano quintet; piano pieces; songs.

Hans Sachs opera by Lortzing (libretto by composer and F Reger, based on a play by J L F Deinhardstein), produced Leipzig, 23 June 1840. An earlier opera on the subject of Wagner's *Meistersinger*, which was also used before that by Gyrowetz. Sachs loses bride Kunigunde to Eoban in a rigged singing competition, but the Emperor Maximilian intervenes.

Harawi, chant d'Amour et de Mort song cycle by Messiaen for soprano and piano (text by composer), performed Brussels 1946. The first of a trilogy of works inspired by the Tristan legend: others are the *Turangalîla* symphony (1946–48) and *Cinq Rechants* for chorus *a cappella* (1949).

Harbison, John (1938–) US composer. He studied at Harvard and with Sessions at Princeton, and taught at MIT 1969–82; he was composer-in-residence for the Pittsburgh Symphony Orchestra 1982–84.

Works include: the operas *The Winter's Tale* (1979) and *Full Moon in March* (after Yeats, 1979); ballets after Homer *Ulysses' Raft* and *Ulysses' Bow* (1983–84); violin concerto (1980), two symphonies (1981, 1987), concerto for oboe, clarinet, and strings (1985), viola concerto (1990); two string quartets (1985, 1987).

Hardanger fiddle (Norwegian *Hardengerfe-len*) Norwegian ◊violin with four strings and four ◊sympathetic strings, used for playing folk dances.

Many of Edvard Grieg's piano pieces were inspired by the music of the Hardanger fiddle.

Hardy, Thomas (1840–1928) English novelist and poet. His works inspired ◊*Egdon Heath* (Holst); Edward ◊Harper (*Fanny Robin* and *The Mellstock Quire*); Alun ◊Hoddinott (*Trumpet Major*); Dominic ◊Muldowney (*Love music for Bathsheba and Gabriel Oak*); Stephen ◊Paulus (*The Woodlanders*); *Tess* (Camille Erlanger); poems set as songs by, among others, Bax, Britten, Finzi, Holst, and Ireland.

'ark, hark, the lark' song by Schubert from Shakespeare's *Cymbeline*, translated by A W Schlegel as *Ständchen aus 'Cymbeline'* and composed in Germany in 1826.

harmonic a prefix denoting organ pipes, producing harmonic notes from pipes of double, triple, or quadruple speaking length. See ◊harmonics.

harmonica musical instrument, a pocket-sized reed organ blown directly from the mouth, invented by Charles Wheatstone in 1829; see ◊mouth organ.

The ◊glass harmonica (or **armonica**) is based on an entirely different principle.

harmonic analysis a method of describing the chords and progressions used mainly in music of the 18th and 19th centuries. The principles rest on the identification of a chord by its root and by the position of the root within the scale. Thus, a root-position chord on the tonic is designated as I, its first inversion as Ib (or, using the parlance of ◊thorough bass, I⁶) and its second inversion as Ic (or I6/4); further elaborations of the system are all based on figured bass notation. Within diatonic music with straightforward harmonies, the main chords are I, IV and V; II and VI are also common, but III and VII are used more rarely. First inversions are important and used frequently except in structural cadences. Second inversions of triads are normally considered discords and can be used only in particular circumstances.

A further refinement of this system is 'functional harmony', first devised by Heinrich Riemann in his *Vereinfachte Harmonielehre* (1893). Here every chord was described as part of a tonic (I), dominant (V) or subdominant (IV) function. This system, still little practised outside Germany, makes the entire chordal vocabulary of the classical and romantic eras more comprehensible as a logical system; but at the same time many details need to be glossed over and this leads to the use of 'reduction' graphs which describe certain chords as passing chords within a broader progression. Hierarchical reductions of this kind led to the analytical techniques of Heinrich Schenker and his followers.

harmonic bass another name for the acoustic bass organ ◊stop.

harmonic minor scale a kind of minor scale in which the seventh degree is raised by a semitone from its original 'natural' position.

harmonic rhythm the rhythm of harmonic change. For most tonal music, the variety of harmonic rhythm is of considerable importance to the musical effect. Thus it may be noted, for instance, that in many simple melodies of the classical era the harmonic

The harmonic minor scale on C.

rhythm speeds up towards the cadence: the faster chord changes at that point help to clarify the end of the phrase. Another example might be the moment before the recapitulation in sonata-form movements (sometimes called the 'retransition'): here the harmonic rhythm often slows down to a standstill, normally on the dominant, thus not only increasing the tension but allowing for a sudden change in harmonic rhythm at the moment of recapitulation.

harmonics a series of partial vibrations that combine to form a musical tone. The number and relative prominence of harmonics produced determines an instrument's tone colour (timbre). An oboe is rich in harmonics, the flute has few. Harmonics conform to successive divisions of the sounding air column or string: their pitches are harmonious.

harmonic series the composite series of notes that can be produced by a vibrating substance or air column.

Harmonie der Welt, Die/The Harmony of the World opera by Paul Hindemith (libretto by the composer) in five acts, produced Munich, 11 August 1957. Symphony from the opera 1951; first performed Basel 24 January 1952. Based on the life of the astronomer Johannes Kepler (1571–1630), who maintained in *Harmonices mundi* that the planets emit musical sounds in their orbits round the Sun.

Harmoniemesse Mass in B♭ by Haydn, composed 1802 and performed Eisenstadt, 8 September 1802. Title derives from prominent use of wind instruments (German *Harmonie*, 'wind band'). Haydn's last Mass.

Harmoniemusik music for a combination of woodwind and brass instruments with or without percussion, such as a military band.

Harmonious Blacksmith, The name given to the Air and Variations in Handel's E major harpsichord suite (Book I, no. 5, published 1720). Despite the traditional story that Handel composed the piece after hearing a blacksmith singing at his work, the nickname is of 19th-century origin.

harmonium keyboard reed organ of the 19th century, powered by foot-operated bellows and incorporating lever-action knee swells to influence dynamics. It was invented by Alexandre Debain in Paris about 1842.

Widely adopted in Europe and the USA as a home and church instrument, in France and Germany the harmonium flourished as a concert solo and orchestral instrument, being written for by Sigfrid Karg-Elert, Arnold Schoenberg (*Herzgewächse/Heart's Bloom* 1907), and Karlheinz Stockhausen (*Der Jahreslauf/The Course of the Years* 1977).

harmony any simultaneous combination of sounds, as opposed to melody, which is a succession of sounds. Although the term suggests a pleasant or agreeable sound, it is applied to any combination of notes, whether consonant or dissonant. The theory of harmony deals with the formation of chords and their interrelation and logical progression.

The founder of harmonic theory was Jean-Philippe ◊Rameau. In his *Traité de l'harmonie/Treatise on Harmony* 1722, he established a system of chord classification on which subsequent methods of harmony have been based.

Harnasie ballet pantomime by Szymanowski (scenario by J Iwaszkiewicz and J M Rytard); composed 1923–31, produced Prague, 11 May 1935.

Harold en Italie a descriptive symphony by Berlioz, op. 16, for solo viola and orchestra, based on Byron's *Childe Harold*, composed 1834, first performed Paris, 23 November. It was suggested by Paganini, but not played by him.

harp plucked musical string instrument, with the strings stretched vertically and parallel to one member of a triangular framework. A second member of the triangle is a wood and brass soundbox of triangular shape; the third member locates pegs by means of which the strings are tensioned. The orchestral harp is

1   2   3   4   5   6   7   8   9   10   11   12   13   14   15   16

The harmonic series. Those marked x are not in tune with the normal scale. The members of the series have a proportional relation to each other. Thus if the lowest note vibrates at 64 cycles per second (cps), the octave above it will be at 128 cps, the G (no. 3) at 172 cps, middle C at 256 cps, and so on.

the largest instrument of its type. It has up to 47 diatonically tuned strings, in the range B0–C7 (seven octaves), and seven double-action pedals to alter pitch. Before the pedals are depressed, the strings sound the diatonic scale of Cb major, but each note can be raised a semitone or a whole tone by one of the pedals. Thus all the notes of the chromatic scale can be sounded.

Recorded from biblical times, the harp existed in the West as early as the 9th century, and was common among medieval minstrels. At that time it was quite small, and was normally placed on the knees. It evolved in size because of a need for increased volume, following its introduction into the orchestra in the 19th century. Composers for the harp include Mozart, Maurice Ravel, Carlos Salzedo, and Heinz Holliger. The harp has also been used in folk music, as both a solo and accompanying instrument, and is associated with Wales and Ireland.

Harper, Edward (1941–) English composer. He studied at Oxford and with Gordon Jacob, and also at the Royal College of Music; lecturer at Edinburgh University from 1964.

Works include: piano concerto (1969); *Bartók Games* for orchestra (1972); *Ricercari in memoriam Luigi Dallapiccola* for 11 instruments (1975), *Fanny Robin*, opera in one act from an episode in Hardy's *Far from the Madding Crowd* (1975); *seven poems by e e cummings* for soprano and orchestra (1977); *Chester Mass* for chorus and orchestra (1979); clarinet concerto (1982); *Intrada after Monteverdi* for chamber orchestra (1982); *Hedda Gabler*, opera after Ibsen's play (1985); *The Mellstock Quire* opera after Hardy (1987); *Double Variations* for oboe, bassoon, and wind (1989); *In Memoriam* for cello and piano (1990), *The Lamb* for soprano, chorus, and orchestra (1990), *Homage to Thomas Hardy* for baritone and chamber orchestra (1990); string quartet (1986).

harp lute, or dital harp stringed musical instrument invented early in the 19th century. It was derived from instruments of the lute type, but had a larger number of strings held by pegs in the harp-shaped head, about half of them changeable in pitch by a fingerboard, the others remaining open and thus capable of playing only a single fixed note.

'Harp' Quartet the nickname given to Beethoven's string quartet in Eb major, op. 74, composed 1809, because it contains, in the first movement, several arpeggios divided between the instruments.

harpsicall, or harpsicon old English terms, variations of ◊harpsichord.

harpsichord the largest and grandest of 18th-century keyboard string instruments, used in orchestras and as a solo instrument. The strings are plucked by 'jacks' made of leather or quill, and multiple keyboards offering variation in tone are common. However, unlike the piano, the tone cannot be varied by the player's touch. The revival of the harpsichord repertoire in the 20th century owes much to Wanda Landowska and Ralph Kirkpatrick (1911–1984).

In classical orchestral music, such as that of Handel or Haydn, the harpsichord part is a continuo part improvised over a ◊figured bass.

Harpsichords have to be tuned regularly, and may therefore be adjusted in temperament according to repertoire. Famous makers of harpsichords include the English Kirckman and the Flemish Ruckers families. A modern repertoire has developed for the concert harpsichord, with concertos by Elliott Carter 1961, Manuel de Falla 1926, Frank Martin 1952, Bohuslav Martinů 1935, and *Continuum* for solo harpsichord by György Ligeti 1968.

Harris, Roy (Leroy Ellsworth) (1898–1979) US composer. His works, which make use of American folk tunes, include the *Symphony No. 10* 1965 (known as 'Abraham Lincoln') and the orchestral *When Johnny Comes Marching Home* 1935.

His father was a farmer who migrated to California during Harris's boyhood, and at 18 Harris had a farm of his own. In 1916 he enlisted to fight in World War I. In 1918 he returned to the USA and became a music student at the University of California, driving a dairy cart to earn a living. Next he studied under Arthur Farwell for two years and in 1926 produced an Andante for strings for the New York Philharmonic Orchestra. The next two years were spent in Paris studying with Nadia Boulanger. He returned to USA in 1929 and later held posts at the Westminster Choir school at Princeton, New Jersey, Cornell University, Colorado, Logan (Utah), Nashville, and Pittsburgh. His most successful work was his third symphony, declaring American ruggedness at the onset of war. It was premiered under Koussevitsky at Boston 1939.

Works include: CHAMBER AND INSTRUMENTAL three string quartets (1930–39), sextet and quintet for wind and piano, piano quintet; pieces for violin and viola and piano; piano works, including sonatas and *Children's Suite*.

OTHER 13 symphonies (1934–76), *Farewell to Pioneers* (1936); works for orchestra; concerto for violin and orchestra, and *Symphony for Voices* for eight-part unaccompanied chorus.

Harrison, Frank Llewelyn (1905–1987) Irish musicologist and educationist. He studied in Ireland and later under Schrade and Hindemith at Yale University. He was music director at Queen's University, Kingston (Canada), 1935–46, and Professor of Music at Colgate University, Hamilton (New York), 1946–47 and at WA University, St Louis, 1947–52. From 1952 to 1970 he was a lecturer in music, subsequently reader, at Oxford University, and professor of Ethnomusicology at Amsterdam University, 1970–80. He specialized in the study of English medieval music, edited *The Eton Choirbook* (three volumes), and published *Music in Medieval Britain* (1958). He was general editor of the series *Early English Church Music*.

Harrison, Lou (1917–   ) US composer. He has experimented with new sonorities, including novel scales and methods of tuning. He helped promote the music of Varèse, Carl Ruggles, and Henry Cowell, and conducted the first performance of Ives' third symphony in 1946. A visit to the Far East in 1961 inspired much music for the gamelan.

Harrison studied with Cowell and Schoenberg 1937–40. He then taught at Mills College and at the University of California in 1942. From 1945 to 1948 he was a music critic for the *New York Herald-Tribune*. He taught at San José State University 1967–82, and at Mills College 1980–85.

Works include: the opera *Rapunzel* (1959); ballets *Solstice, The Perilous Chapel* (1949), *Almanac of the Seasons, Johnny Appleseed, Changing World*, and others; Prelude and Saraband for orchestra, three symphonies, piano concerto (1985); string quartet set (1979), *Ariadne* for flute and percussion (1987); three suites; *Four Strict Songs* for eight baritones and orchestra in pure intonation (1955); *Recording Piece* for percussion; *Simfony I*; violin concerto with percussion orchestra; string trio; suite for cello and harp; piano music.

Hartmann, Karl Amadeus (1905–1963) German composer. He began composing late in life, but destroyed his early works and turned to serialism under the influence of Webern. After World War II he organized the important 'Musica Viva' concerts in Munich to propagate new music. In 1952 he was elected to the German Academy of Fine Arts and in 1953 became president of the German section of the International Society for Contemporary Music.

He studied with Josef Haas at the Munich Academy and later with Scherchen.

Works include: the chamber opera *Des Simplicius Simplicissimus Jugend* (1934–35; produced 1949), eight symphonies (1936–62); concerto for piano, wind, and percussion, *Musik der Trauer* for violin and strings (1939); two string quartets.

Harty, (Herbert) Hamilton (1879–1941) Irish conductor and composer. After much conducting experience in London he was appointed conductor to the Hallé Orchestra at Manchester in 1920. He gave the first British performance of Mahler's ninth symphony in 1930.

He studied piano, viola, and composition under his father and became an organist at the age of 12. He later became organist at Belfast and at Dublin, where he studied further under Michele Esposito. In 1900 he settled in London as an accompanist and composer and married the soprano Agnes Nicholls. He retired from the Hallé in 1933.

Works include: arrangement of Handel's *Water Music* and *Fireworks Music*, Irish Symphony (1924), *Comedy Overture*, symphonic poem *With the Wild Geese* for orchestra (1910); violin concerto; cantata *The Mystic Trumpeter* (Whitman); *Ode to a Nightingale* (Keats) for soprano and orchestra (1907); many songs.

Harvey, Jonathan Dean (1939–   ) English composer. His use of avant-garde and computer synthesis techniques is allied to a tradition of visionary Romanticism in works such as *Inner Light II* 1977 for voices, instruments, and ◊tape music and *Mortuos plango, vivos voco/I Mourn the Dead, I Call the Living* 1980 for computer-manipulated concrete sounds, realized at ◊IRCAM.

He studied at Cambridge and Glasgow Universities, and was appointed professor at Sussex University in 1980. He has worked with Stockhausen and Babbitt.

Works include: symphony (1966); *Persephone Dream* for orchestra (1973), *Smiling Immortal* for chamber orchestra and tape (1977), *Easter Orisons* for strings (1983); *Madonna of Winter and Spring* (1986), *Lightness and Weight* for tuba and orchestra (1986); cello concerto (1990); ten Cantatas for soloists and various instrumental combinations (1965–76); *Hymn* for chorus and orchestra (composed 1979 for the 900th anniversary of Winchester Cathedral), *Passion and Resurrection*, church opera, performed Winchester 1981; opera *Inquest of Love* (1993); chamber and instrumental music including *Mortuos plango, vivos* *voco* for computer-processed concrete sounds, performed Lille 1980: *Modernsky Music* of 1981, for two oboes, bassoon, and harpsichord, derives its title from one of Schoenberg's 3 Satires op. 28, in which Stravinsky is mocked as 'Modernsky', for apparently following musical fashion. *Curve with Plateaux* for cello (1982), *Valley of Aosta* for 13 players (1988); *Scena* for violin and ensemble (1992); *Chant* for viola (1992).

Háry János ballad opera by Kodály (libretto by B Paulini and Z Harsányi, based on a poem by János Garay), produced Budapest, 16 October 1926. It contains popular Hungarian tunes and begins with an orchestral imitation of a sneeze. Orchestral Suite performed New York, 15 December 1927. János tells tall tales about his youth, spent defeating Napoleon, winning the heart of the Emperor's wife. But all along he remained true to his bride back in his native village.

Hassan, or The Golden Journey to Samarkand incidental music by Delius for the play by James Elroy Flecker; 1920, produced London, His Majesty's, 20 September 1923, with ballets arranged by Fokine. Orchestral suite by Eric Fenby, with instruments including camel bells, performed on BBC (British Broadcasting Corporation) television, 1 August 1933.

Hasse, Johann Adolf (1699–1783) German composer. He began his career as a singer in Hamburg, and produced his first opera, *Antioco*, in 1721. He wrote about 70 operas, and became the most successful opera seria composer of his generation.

Hasse was a tenor at the Hamburg Opera under Reinhard Keiser 1718–19, then at Brunswick, 1719–22, where *Antioco* was produced in 1721. In 1922 he went to Italy and studied with Porpora and Alessandro Scarlatti. After many successful operas for Naples, he became maestro di cappella at the Conservatorio degli Incurabili in Venice in 1727. He married the singer Faustina Bordoni in 1730, and in 1734 went to Dresden as Kapellmeister to the Saxon Court, a post he held for 30 years. He was allowed generous leave of absence, however, and travelled widely, including a visit to London in 1734. In 1764, after the death of the Saxon Elector, he moved to Vienna, then in 1773 to Venice, where he lived for the rest of his life.

Works include: OPERA *Antioco* (1721), *Il Sesostrate* (1726), *Tigrane* (1729), *Artaserse*, *Cleofide* (1731), *Cajo Fabricio* (1732), *Il Demetrio*, *Siroe, rè di Persia* (1733), *Tito Vespasiano* (1735), *Lucio Papirio* (1742), *Didone abbandonata*,

Antigono (1743), *Semiramide riconosciuta* (1744), *Arminio, Leucippo, Demofoonte* (1748), *Attilio Regolo* (1750), *Il Ciro riconosciuto* (1751), *Solimano, Ezio, Olimpiade, Alcide al Bivio* (1760), *Il trionfo di Clelia* (1762), *Partenope, Piramo e Tisbe* (1768), *Ruggiero* (1771), and many others.

OTHER oratorios *I Pellegrini al sepolcro, Sant' Elena al calvario* (1746), *La Conversione di Sant' Agostino* (1750); Masses and other church music; concertos for flute and for violin; solo sonatas, trio sonatas, harpsichord pieces.

Hassell, Jon (1937–) US composer and trumpeter. As a composer and performer he has been involved with minimalism, Balinese music, and electronics. He studied with Stockhausen and Henri Pousseur in Cologne and at the Eastman School.

Works include: *Music for Vibraphones* (1965); *Blackboard Piece with Girls and Loops* (1969); *Goodbye Music* (1969); *Solid State* for two synthesizers (1969); *Superball* (1969); *Landscape Series* (1969–72); *Sulla Strada*, theatre piece after Kerouac's *On the Road* (performed Venice, 1982). Recordings include music from the Far East (*Earthquake Island, Aka-Dhari-Java*).

Hassler, Hans Leo (1564–1612) German organist and composer. He wrote considerable quantities of church music in Latin and German, in addition to many secular songs in German and Italian, and other pieces. He was one of the first Germans to study in Italy, and the polychoral techniques and rich sonorities of his Masses and motets show the influence of the Venetians.

Hassler was born in Nuremberg and was taught by his father, Isaac Hassler (c. 1530–1591), who was himself an organist. After an appointment at Nuremberg he was sent to Venice for further study under Andrea Gabrieli. He was organist to Octavian Fugger at Augsburg 1585–1600; he published many works there and established a wide reputation. Having returned to Nuremberg as organist of the Church of Our Lady, he married and went to live at Ulm in 1604, but soon went into the service of the Emperor Rudolph in Prague. In 1608 he became organist to Christian II, the Elector of Saxony at Dresden, but suffered from tuberculosis and died during a visit with the Elector to Frankfurt.

Although Hassler was a Protestant, his early works are all for the Catholic Church. His German church music is somewhat conservative, and though it often uses Lutheran melodies, it shows the influence of Roland de Lassus. He was famous for his Italian madrigals and canzonettes, and German songs were widely known: the tune of his love song, 'Mein G'müt ist mir verwirret' 1601, was used for the Lutheran hymn, 'O Haupt voll Blut und Wunden' which features in Bach's St Matthew Passion.

Works include: Masses, Magnificats, hymn tunes, motets (including two collections *Sacrae cantiones* and *Sacri concentus*), fugal psalms, and Christian songs; Italian canzonets for four voices, Italian and German madrigals, *Lustgarten neuer teutscher Gesäng* (32 German songs for four–eight voices, 1601); ricercari, toccatas, and other pieces for organ.

Hatton, John (Liptrott) (1808–1886) English composer. He was almost wholly self-taught in music. In 1832 he settled in London, in 1842 became attached to Drury Lane Theatre as composer and in 1844 visited Vienna to produce his opera *Pascal Bruno*. In 1848 he went to the USA and later became music director of the Prince's Theatre, London, where he wrote much incidental music for Kean's productions.

Works include: the operas *Pascal Bruno* (1844) and *Rose, or Love's Ransom* (1864), operetta *The Queen of the Thames*; incidental music for Shakespeare's *Macbeth, Henry VIII, Richard II, King Lear, The Merchant of Venice* and *Much Ado About Nothing*, Sheridan's *Pizarro*, an adaptation of Goethe's *Faust* and other plays; Mass, two services, eight anthems; oratorio *Hezekiah*; cantata *Robin Hood*; over 150 songs, including *To Anthea* (Herrick); many part songs.

Haubenstock-Ramati, Roman (1919–1993) Polish-born Israeli composer. His first works are conservative in idiom, he later moved on to serial and aleatory techniques.

He studied composition in Kraków and Lwów from 1937 to 1940. From 1947 to 1950 he was music director of Radio Kraków and then emigrated to Israel, where he became director of the music library in Tel-Aviv. In 1957 he moved to Paris, living also in Vienna, where he worked for Universal Edition.

Works include: the opera *Amerika* (after Kafka, 1964); *Ulysses*, ballet (1977), *La Symphonie des timbres* for orchestra; *Vermutungen über ein dunkles Haus* for three orchestras; *Papageno's Pocket-size Concerto* for glockenspiel and orchestra (1955); *Recitativo and Aria* for cembalo and orchestra; *Sequences* for violin and orchestra; *Petite Musique de nuit*, mobile for orchestra (1958); *Blessings* for voice and nine players; *Mobile for Shakespeare* for

voice and six players (1960); *Jeux* for six percussion groups; concerto for strings (1977); *Interpolation*, mobile for solo flute; *Ricercari* for string trio.

Hauer, Josef (Matthias) (1883–1959) Austrian composer. He published a series of pamphlets on composition according to his own 12-note system, which was different from Schoenberg's. All his works use this system, which is based on groups of notes he called *Tropen*, derived from the combinations of the 12 notes of the chromatic scale allowed by the agreement of their overtones.

Works include: the opera *Salammbô* (after Flaubert, 1929; performed Vienna, 1983); play with music, *Die schwarze Spinne* (after Jeremias Gotthelf, 1932; performed Vienna, 1966); Mass for chorus, organ, and orchestra; cantata *Wandlungen*; music for Aeschylus' *Prometheus Bound* and tragedies by Sophocles; *Vom Leben* recitation with singing voices and chamber orchestra for broadcasting; sinfonietta, eight suites, seven Dance Fantasies (1928), Concert Piece, *Apocalyptic Fantasy* (1913), *Kyrie* and other pieces for orchestra; symphony for strings, harmonium, and piano; violin concerto, piano concerto; six string quartets (1924–26), quintet for clarinet, violin, viola, cello, and piano; many piano pieces including two sets of Studies and pieces on Hölderlin titles; about 87 *Zwölftonspiele* for different instruments and instrumental combinations; six song cycles to poems by Hölderlin and other songs.

Haunted Tower, The opera by Storace (libretto by James Cobb), produced London, Drury Lane Theatre, 24 November 1789.

Hauptmann, Moritz (1792–1868) German theorist, writer on music, and composer. He studied at Dresden and began to work there, lived in Russia 1815–20, played violin in L Spohr's orchestra at Kassel from 1822 and was cantor at St Thomas's Church in Leipzig from 1842 to his death. He wrote on acoustics, harmony, and fugue.

Works include: the opera *Mathilde* (1826); two Masses, motets and psalms; choruses and part-songs; three sonatas for violin and piano, violin duets; songs.

Hauptwerk the German equivalent of the ◊great organ, the manual (keyboard) of the most powerful pipes and stops.

hautbois (French 'high-wood' or 'loud-wood') in music, term used for smaller members of the ◊shawm family, used in England and France after 1500. 'Hautboy' was the English term for ♢oboe (the shawm's descendant) in the 17th and 18th centuries.

haute-contre alto or high tenor, whether voice or instrument. Hence an old name for the alto or tenor ♢viol and the ♢viola.

Hawkins, John (1719–1789) English music historian and antiquary. Devoted at first to architecture and then to law, he gradually became interested in literature and music. Having married a wealthy woman in 1753, he was able to retire and to undertake, in addition to minor works, his *General History of the Science and Practice of Music*, published in five volumes in 1776, the same year as the first volume of Charles Burney's similar work.

Hawte, William (c. 1430–1497) English composer. He wrote four settings of the *Benedicamus Domino* (Cambridge, Magdalene College, Pepys MS 1236) and a processional antiphon, *Stella caeli*.

Haydn, (Franz) Joseph (1732–1809) Austrian composer. He was a major exponent of the classical sonata form in his numerous chamber and orchestral works (he wrote more than 100 symphonies). He also composed choral music, including the oratorios *The Creation* 1798 and *The Seasons* 1801. He was the first great master of the string quartet, and was a teacher of Mozart and Beethoven.

Haydn was employed by the Hungarian Esterházy family from 1761, being responsible for all the musical entertainment at their palace. His work also includes operas, church music, and songs, and the 'Emperor's Hymn', adopted as the Austrian, and later the German, national anthem.

Born in Lower Austria, the son of a wheelwright, Haydn went at the age of eight as a chorister to St Stephen's Cathedral in Vienna under Georg Reutter (junior). On leaving the choir school about 1749 he lived at first as a freelance, playing violin and organ, and teaching. He was for a time pupil-manservant to the Italian composer Nicola Porpora in Vienna, but in composition he was largely self-taught, studying the works of C P E Bach, Fux's *Gradus ad Parnassum*, and others. From these years date his earliest compositions, especially church music, including two Masses. His first string quartets were written about 1755 for Baron Fürnberg, through whom he obtained the post of music director to Count Morzin in 1759. The next year he entered into what was to prove an unfortunate marriage, and in 1761 took employment with the Esterházy family, in 1766 succeeding

Franz Gregor Werner as Kapellmeister, a post he held for the rest of his life.

At Eszterháza, the magnificent palace in the Hungarian marshes, completed in 1766, where the household now spent the greater part of the year, Haydn wrote the majority of his instrumental music and operas. At first he wrote symphonies and instrumental pieces for the Prince, notably more than 100 trios for the ♢baryton over ten years. Beginning with with symphony no. 22 (the 'Philosopher') 1764 and continuing through the 1760s to no. 49 ('La Passione'), Haydn gained his maturity as a composer, showing inventiveness in each work. The first truly mature string quartets, the set of six op. 20, 1772, continue this developing mastery and were followed by the quartets op. 33, 1781, which include *The Joke* and *The Bird*; they were claimed to be written 'in a quite new and special manner'. In the set of op. 50, 1787, Haydn repays the debt which Mozart had acknowledged when dedicating his own quartets to the older composer.

Though he was isolated in Eszterháza, his fame spread; his works were published abroad, and he received invitations to travel, which, however, his duties obliged him to refuse. In 1786 he was commissioned to compose six symphonies for the Concert de la Loge Olympique in Paris; these works are full of splendid invention and brilliant orchestral effects, declaring for the first time Haydn's genius to the world at large.

On the death of Prince Nikolaus in 1790 the Esterházy musicians were disbanded and Haydn, though retaining his title and salary, was free to accept an invitation from the violinist and impresario J P Salomon to go to England. His first visit to London, 1791–92, for which he composed an opera (not produced) and six symphonies, was a great success, and was followed by another 1794–95, for which a further six symphonies were written. The twelve London symphonies confirmed his reputation as the most original composer of the genre during his time. The wit, melodic inventiveness, and densely woven developments of these works were matched in the great sets of string quartets written 1791–97 (op. 64, op. 71, op. 74, and op. 76).

In 1792 he received an honorary doctorate from Oxford University. On the accession of Prince Nikolaus II in 1795 the Esterházy music establishment was in part revived; but Haydn's duties were light, chiefly involving the composition of a Mass each year for the princess's name day, and giving rise to the six great Masses of 1796–1802. Inspired by the works of Handel he had heard in London, he composed *The Creation* and *The Seasons*. From 1803 he composed little, living in retirement in Vienna.

In spite of huge advances made in the knowledge and performance of Haydn's music in recent years, the sheer range and quantity of his output may be intimidating, so that he still awaits wide recognition, and some of his works are still unpublished.

Works include: OPERA 20 works for the stage, of which seven are lost (all first performances at Eszterháza, unless otherwise stated) *Acide*, festa teatrale (Eisenstadt, 1763), *La cantarina*, intermezzo (Eisenstadt, 1766), *Lo speziale*, dramma giocosa (1768), *Le pescatrici*, dramma giocosa (1770), *L'infedeltà delusa*, burletta (1773), *L'incontro improvviso*, dramma giocosa (1775), *Il mondo della luna*, dramma giocosa (1777), *La vera costanza*, dramma giocosa (1779), *L'isola disabitata*, azione teatrale (1779), *La fedeltà premiata*, dramma pastorale giocosa (1781), *Orlando Paladino*, dramma eroicomico (1782), *Armida*, dramma eroico (1784), *L'anima del filosofo* (now known by its alternative title of *Orfeo ed Euridice*, written for London 1791 but not performed; first known production Florence, 10 June 1951, with Callas and Christoff). Marionette operas *Philemon und Baucis* (1773), *Hexen-Schabbas* (1773, lost), *Dido* (1776, lost), *Die Feuerbrunst* (1776), *Die Bestrafte Rachbegierde* (1779).

MASSES 14 *Missa 'Rorate coeli desuper'* (1748), *Missa brevis* in F (1749), *Missa Cellensis, Cäcelienmesse* in C (1766), *Missa in honorem BVM, Grosse Orgelmesse*, in Eb (1771), *Missa Sancti Nicolai*, in G (1772), *Missa brevis* in B flat, *Kleine Orgelmesse* (1778), *Missa Cellensis, Mariazeller Messe* (1782), *Missa Sancti Bernardi* (*Heiligmesse*) Bb (1796), *Missa in tempore belli, Paukenmesse*, in C, (Vienna, 26 December 1796); Mass in D minor, *Nelson Mass* (Eisenstadt, 23 September 1798); Mass in Bb, *Theresienmesse* (1799); Mass in Bb, *Schöpfungsmesse* (Eisenstadt, 13 September 1801); Mass in Bb, *Harmoniemesse* (Eisenstadt, 8 September 1802). A fragment of the lost Mass *Sunt bona mixta malis*, (about 1769) was discovered in Ireland 1983.

CANTATAS AND ORATORIOS *Stabat Mater* (1767), *Applausus* (Zwettl, 17 April 1768), *Il ritorno di Tobia* (Vienna, 2 April 1775), *Die Sieben letzten Worte unseres Erlösers am Kreuze/Seven Last Words* (Vienna, 26 March 1796), *Die Schöpfung/The Creation*, (Vienna, 29 April 1798), *Die Jahreszeiten/The Seasons* (Vienna, 24 April 1801). Also Te Deum in C (1800).

SYMPHONIES 104 nos. 1–5 (1758–60); nos. 6–8, *Le Matin, Le Midi, Le Soir* (1761); nos. 9–21 (about 1762); no. 22 in Eb, *The Philosopher*

(1764); nos. 23–25 (1764); no. 26 in D minor, *Lamentatione* (1770); nos. 27–29 (1765); no. 30 in C, *Alleluja* (1765); no. 31 in D, *Hornsignal* (1765); nos. 32–42 (about 1768) no. 43 in Eb, *Mercury* (1772); no. 44 in E minor, *Trauersinfonie* (1772); no. 45 in F♯ minor, *Farewell* (1772); no. 46 in B and no. 47 in G (1772); no. 48 in C, *Maria Theresa*, and no. 49 in F minor, *La Passione* (about 1768); nos. 50–52 (1773); no. 53 in D, *The Imperial* (1778); nos. 54–59 (1774); no. 60 in C, *Il Distratto* (1774); nos. 61–72 (about 1779); no. 73 in D, *La Chasse* (1782); nos. 74–81 (1781–84); nos. 82–87 *Paris Symphonies*; no. 82 in C, *The Bear*, no. 83 in G minor, *The Hen*, no. 84 in Eb, no. 85 in Bb, *La Reine*, no. 86 in D, no. 87 in A (1785–86); no. 88 in G, no. 89 in F, no. 90 in C, no. 91 in Eb (1787–8); no. 92 in G, *The Oxford* (1789); nos. 93–104 *London Symphonies* no. 93 in D, no. 94 in G, *The Surprise*, no. 95 in C minor, no. 96 in D, *The Miracle*, no. 97 in C, no. 98 in Bb, no. 99 in Eb, no. 100 in G, *The Military*, no. 101 in D, *The Clock*, no. 102 in Bb, no. 103 in Eb, *The Drumroll*, no. 104 in D, *The London* (1791–95).

CONCERTOS four for violin, in C, D, A, and G (1769–71); two for cello in C and D (1761 and 1783); organ concerto in C (1756); concerto for violin and harpsichord (1766); harpsichord concertos in F, G, and D (1771–84); for trumpet in Eb (1796); Sinfonia concertante in Bb for oboe, violin, cello, and bassoon (1792); five concertos for lire organizzate (about 1786); five concertos for oboe, flute, horn, and bassoon are either lost or spurious.

STRING QUARTETS The usually given number of 83 is incorrect; from this must be subtracted the set of six op. 3, now known to be by Romanus Hoffstetter, and the arrangement of *The Seven Last Words*, hitherto counted as seven separate quartets. Op. 1 nos. 1–6 (about 1757); op. 2 nos. 1, 2, 4, and 6 (about 1762); op. 9 nos. 1–6 (about 1771); op. 17 nos. 1–6 (about 1772), op. 20, nos. 1–6, *Sun Quartets* in Eb, C, G minor, D, F minor, A (1772); op. 33 nos. 1–6, *Russian Quartets* in B minor, Eb (*The Joke*), C (*The Bird*), Bb, G, D (1781); op. 42 in D minor (1785); op. 50 nos. 1–6 in Bb, C, Eb, F♯ minor, F, and D (*The Frog*) (1787); op. 54 nos. 1–3 in G, C, and E (1788); op. 55 nos. 1–3 in A, F minor, and Bb (1790); op. 64 nos. 1–6 in C, B minor, Bb, G, D (*The Lark*), and Eb (1791); op. 71 nos. 1–3 in Bb, D, and Eb (1795); op. 74 nos. 1–3 in C, F, and G minor (*The Rider*) (1796); op. 76 nos. 1–6 in G, D minor (*The Fifths*), C (*The Emperor*), Bb (*The Sunrise*), D, Eb (1797); op. 77 nos. 1 and 2 in G and F (1802); op. 103 in D minor (1803).

OTHER INSTRUMENTAL 32 piano trios, 126 baryton trios and other chamber music; 60

piano sonatas (1760–94), five sets of variations for piano including F minor (1793); solo songs, part songs, arrangements of Scottish and Welsh folk songs. 12 Canzonettas to English words for solo voice and piano including 'My mother bids me bind my hair', 'Sailor's Song', and 'She never told her love' (1794–95); Solo cantatas *Arianna a Naxos* (1789) and *Berenice che fai* (1795).

Haydn, (Johann) Michael (1737–1806) Austrian composer, brother of Franz Joseph ◊Haydn. As well as a great deal of church music, including over 30 Masses, he also wrote about 40 symphonies, some chamber music, and an opera.

He was a chorister at St Stephen's Cathedral in Vienna under Reutter from about 1745. In 1757 he was appointed Kapellmeister to the Archbishop of Grosswardein, Hungary, became Konzertmeister to the Archbishop of Salzburg in 1762, and was cathedral organist there from 1781. Apart from occasional visits to Vienna, he remained in Salzburg till his death, in 1801 refusing the post of vice-Kapellmeister (under his brother Joseph) to Prince Esterházy.

Works include: 32 Masses including *Missa Hispanica* (1786), two Requiem Masses, including C minor Requiem, for Archbishop Sigismund, 1771, which influenced Mozart's Requiem, eight German Masses, six *Te Deum* settings, 117 Graduals, 45 Offertories, 27 Holy Week Responsories, and other pieces; opera *Andromeda e Perseo* (1787), German *Singspiele* and other music for the stage, oratorios; cantatas; 46 symphonies including one with a slow introduction by Mozart (K444: Mozart's '37th' symphony); five concertos; six string quintets; 11 string quartets; keyboard music.

'Haydn' Quartets the familiar name of Mozart's six string quartets dedicated to Haydn: G major, K387 (1782), D minor, K421 (1783), E♭ major, K428 (1783), B♭ major, K458 (1784), A major, K464 (1785), C major, K465 (1785).

'Haydn' Variations a set of variations by Brahms for orchestra, op. 56a, or for two pianos, op. 56b on a theme called the 'St Anthony Chorale' from a Divertimento for wind instruments, attributed formerly to Haydn, where it is also treated in variation form. First performed of the orchestral version, Vienna, 2 November 1873.

Hayes, William (1708–1777) English organist and composer. He was organist at Worcester Cathedral from 1731 and organist and master of the choristers at Magdalen College, Oxford from 1734; he was appointed professor in 1742. He introduced many of Handel's works to Oxford, Bath, and Winchester; his own works were indebted to Handel.

He was the father of Phillip Hayes.

Works include: the oratorios *The Fall of Jericho* and *David* (about 1776), 16 psalms, Te Deum in D, 20 anthems, masques *Circe* (1742) and *Peleus and Thetis*; Odes *When the fair consort* (1735), *Where shall the Muse* (1751), *O that some pensive Muse* (Ode to the memory of Handel, about 1760), *Ode on the Passions* (about 1760) and *Daughters of Beauty* (1773); six cantatas, concertos, and trios.

Haym, Nicola Francesco (1678–1729) Italian cellist, librettist, and composer of German descent. He went to London in 1702, and with Dieupart and Clayton was active in establishing Italian opera there. From 1713 he wrote several libretti for Handel, including *Teseo*, *Radamisto*, *Giulio Cesare*, and *Rodelinda*; he also wrote for Bononcini and Ariosti. His own works include a Latin oratorio and a serenata, anthem *The Lord is King*, and two sets of trio sonatas.

Hayman, Richard (1951–) US composer. He studied at Columbia University, and later learned from Cage and Boulez. Early employment included renovating church organ pipes. In 1975 wrote *Dali*, commissioned by the artist and inscribed on a toothpick. *It is not here* was realized in Morse Code at the Museum of Modern Art, New York, 1974. His later works include *sleep whistle* (1975), which the composer performs while asleep in a store window, and *roll*, executed while lying down in the street and covered by Hindu bells. *Dreamsound* was performed at Berkeley, California, in 1976.

Hayne van Ghizeghem (c. 1445–between 1472 and 1497) Franco-Flemish composer. His life is documented only for the years 1457–72, which he spent at the court of Burgundy. His entire surviving output is of French chansons, several of which were among the most successful of their age, including 'De tous biens plaine', 'Allez regretz', and 'Amours, amours'.

head voice the upper register of the human voice, referring to the head as the area of sound production. The head voice of a male singer is called ◊falsetto. However, there has been disagreement (in the 19th century and earlier) concerning the precise use of the term, some claiming that only head voice and ◊chest voice (the lower register) exist, others claiming that a third middle register is also important. Today, there is less concern about these distinctions.

Heart's Assurance, The song cycle by Tippett for high voice and piano (poems by Sidney Keyes and Alun Lewis); commissioned by Peter Pears and performed by him and Britten in London on 7 May 1951.

Heath, John (lived 16th century) English composer. His morning and communion services were printed by John Day in 1560, but had already been in use about 1548. There is also an anthem and a part song, and a keyboard piece in the Mulliner Book is almost certainly his.

He is not to be confused with the John Heath of Rochester, who wrote English church music and died in 1668; this may have been his grandson.

'Hebrides' Overture (Mendelssohn). See ◊*Fingal's Cave.*

Heckel, Johann Adam (1812–1877) German instrument maker. He founded the family firm at Biebrich in 1831 and became the foremost German bassoon maker, making many improvements to the instrument.

Heckelclarina musical instrument specially created by the firm of Heckel at Biberich, Germany, for the playing of the shepherd's pipe part in Act III of Wagner's *Tristan und Isolde.*

heckelphone musical instrument, a wide-bore baritone ◊oboe in B♭. It was introduced by the German maker Wilhelm Heckel (1856–1909) and adopted by Richard Strauss in the opera *Salome* 1905.

Hedley, Arthur (1905–1969) English writer on music. He studied at Durham University. In 1946 he became correspondent of the Chopin Institute at Warsaw. He authored a book on Chopin and many articles. His collection of Chopin manuscripts and related material is in the Museo de Chopin, Majorca.

heel in stringed musical instruments, the end of the bow held by the player.

Heiligmesse *Holy Mass, Missa Sancti Bernardi von Offida,* in B♭, composed 1796 by Haydn as a companion to the *Missa in tempore belli/Mass in time of war.*

Heimchen am Herd, Das/The Cricket on the Hearth opera by Goldmark (libretto by A M Willner, based on Dickens's story), produced Vienna, Opera, 21 March 1896. May is to marry Tackleton, owner of a doll factory, after her love Edward, a sailor, goes to sea. Edward returns and the two marry.

Heimkehr aus der Fremde, Die/The Return from Abroad; better known as Son and Stranger operetta by Mendelssohn (libretto by K Klingemann), produced Leipzig, 10 April 1851. Kauz has to leave town in a hurry after he tries to impersonate the son of a magistrate.

Heine, Heinrich (1797–1856) German poet. His works and thought inspired Havergal ◊Brian (*Pilgrimage to Kevlaar*); ◊*Dichterliebe* (Schumann); ◊*Der Fliegende Holländer* (Wagner); ◊*Giselle* (Adam); *Guglielmo Ratcliff* (Mascagni); *Wallfahrt nach Kevlaar* (◊Humperdinck); ◊*Liederkreis* (Schumann); ◊*Schwanengesang* (Schubert); ◊*William Ratcliff* (Cui). Six songs by Brahms, six by Schubert, and 39 by Schumann.

Heinichen, Johann David (1683–1729) German composer and theorist. After training as a lawyer, he became a composer of operas and other pieces. He also wrote two important treatises on figured bass.

He studied under Schelle and Kuhnau in Leipzig, then practised law in Weissenfels, but in 1709 returned to Leipzig as an opera composer. The following year he went to Italy to study, and remained there until 1716. In 1717 he was appointed Kapellmeister to the Elector of Saxony in Dresden, where he lived until his death.

Works include: operas, numerous Masses, motets, and other church works, cantatas, symphonies, orchestral suites, solo and trio sonatas.

Heinö, Mikko (1958–) Finnish composer. He studied in Berlin, and at the Helsinki University, where he taught from 1977 until 1985, when he became professor of musicology at University of Turku. His works include five piano concertos, horn concerto, concerto for orchestra, *Brass Mass, Wind Pictures* for choir and orchestra. Books include *The Twelve Tone Age in Finnish Music* (1986) and *Postmodern Features in New Finnish Music* (1988).

Heinrich, Anthony Philip (1781–1861) Bohemian-born US composer. Popular throughout the main US music centres of the time, New York, Boston, and Philadelphia, he became known as the 'Beethoven of America'. Heinrich's experiences of the frontier included a deep awareness of Native American music, and in *The Jubilee* 1841, a work for soloists, chorus, and orchestra, he depicts the story of the British colonists in America.

He emigrated to the USA in 1810, settling first in Philadelphia then moving to Kentucky in 1817; at Lexington he conducted the first known performance of a Beethoven symphony in America. His first compositions date from 1818; they include the collection of songs and violin and piano pieces entitled *The Dawning of Music in Kentucky, or the Pleasures of Harmony in the Solitudes of Nature*. His orchestral music, often for huge forces and developing from models by Haydn and Beethoven, dates from 1831 with *Pushmataha, a venerable Chief of Western Tribe of Indians*; later such works include *The Treaty of William Penn with the Indians* 1834, *The Ornithological Combat of Kings* 1847, and *The Wildwood Troubadour* 1834–53. He visited Europe from 1827 and his *Ornithological symphony* was performed at Graz, Austria, in 1836. Other works include *The War of the Elements and the Thundering of Niagara* c. 1845, for orchestra and *A Chromatic Ramble of the Peregrine Harmonist*, for piano. His status in the history of American music is suggested by his nickname, 'Father Heinrich'.

Heidenleben, Ein/A Hero's Life symphonic poem by Richard Strauss, composed autumn 1898. First performed Frankfurt, 3 March 1899. The work is autobiographical.

Heliogabalus Imperator 'allegory for music' by Henze, after M Enzensberger; composed 1971–77, first performed Chicago, 16 November 1972, conductor Solti.

Heller, Stephen (1813 or 1814–1888) Hungarian pianist and composer. At the age of nine he caused some sensation as a boy pianist. He studied in Paris, and worked there as a pianist and teacher until his death, becoming one of the group which included Berlioz, Chopin, Liszt, and Halle. He wrote entirely for the piano, except two works with violin entitled *Pensées fugitives*, in collaboration with Heinrich Ernst, and achieved an individual style of great lyrical charm.

Heller was born at Pest. He studied with Anton Halm in Vienna, made his first public appearance at Pest in his teens, and later went on tour in Germany. He lived at Augsburg 1830–38 after a long illness, working quietly at composition, and settled in Paris in 1838. In 1850 and 1862 he visited England.

Works include: four sonatas, a very large number of studies, variations, and fantasies on operatic tunes, five Tarantellas, Caprice on Schubert's *Trout*, several sets entitled *Im Walde, Promenades d'un solitaire* (after Rousseau's letters on botany), *Blumen-, Frucht- und Dornenstücke* (after Jean Paul, 1853), *Dans le bois, Nuits blanches*, and other pieces.

Helm, Everett (1913–   ) US composer and writer. He studied at Harvard with Walter Piston, and later with Malipiero and Vaughan Williams. He has appeared widely as teacher and lecturer and has written books on Bartók (1965) and Liszt (1972).

Works include: two piano concertos (1951, 1956); *Adam and Eve*, medieval adaptation (1951); *Le Roy fait battre tambour*, ballet (1956); *Sinfonia da camera* (1961); string quartets, woodwind quintet (1967).

Helmholtz, Hermann (Ludwig Ferdinand) von (1821–1894) German scientist. After holding three professorships in physiology he turned to physics, of which he became professor at Berlin University in 1871. He specialized in the musical aspects of acoustics and in 1863 published his *Lehre von den Tonempfindungen als physiologische Grundlage für die Theorie der Musik* (translated by A J Ellis as *On the Sensations of Tone*).

Helmholtz resonator spherical vessel of metal or glass with an opening and an earpiece on opposite sides, from a harmonic series of 19 such vessels constructed for German physicist Hermann Helmholtz (1821–1894) as an instrument of acoustic analysis. Placed in the ear, it acts as an acoustic filter, allowing only sounds of a particular pitch to be heard. Helmholtz also used resonators in series with tuning forks as sound sources in pioneering experiments in synthesizing instrumental timbres.

The ear canal acts in a similar way, enhancing frequencies in the range 1,000–4,000 Hz.

hemidemisemiquaver, or US 64th note in music, a note value 1/64th the duration of a ◊semibreve. It is written as a filled black notehead with a stem and four flags (tails).

hemiola rhythmic device based on the ratio 3:2, in which two bars of triple time are articulated in the manner of three bars in duple time. It was much favoured by Brahms, and also by Baroque composers for use in passages approaching a ◊cadence.

Hemmel, Sigmund (died 1564) German composer. He composed the first complete polyphonic metrical psalter in Germany (published at Tübingen in 1569). He also wrote German and Latin sacred songs, and a Mass.

Henrici, Christian Friedrich (known as Picander) (1700–1764) German poet and cantata librettist. From 1726 he was involved in a collaboration with J S Bach, which resulted in the texts for the *St Matthew Passion, St Mark Passion*, and part of the *Christmas Oratorio*. He also furnished libretti for many of Bach's occasional vocal works and some of the church cantatas.

After study in Wittenberg he moved to Leipzig in 1720. He was well known as a playwright and published five volumes of poems, under the title *Ernst schertzhafte und satyrische Gedichte*.

Henry, Pierre (1927–) French composer. He worked with Pierre ◊Schaeffer at the Groupe de Recherche de Musique Concrète 1950–58; their collaborations include *Symphonie pour un homme seul* 1950 and the opera *Orphée* 1953. After leaving Schaeffer's studio he founded a private electroacoustical studio at Apsome in 1958.

He studied with Messiaen and Nadia Boulanger.

Works include: ballets *Haut Voltage* (1956), *Le Voyage* (1962), *Messe pour le temps présent* (1967), and *Nijinsky, clown de Dieu* (1971); *Messe de Liverpool* (1967), *Gymkhana* (1970), *Ceremony* (1970), *Futuriste I* (1975).

Henry VIII (1491–1547) King of England, 1509–47. He composed or arranged several songs found in a manuscript (British Museum, Add 31,922) dating from his reign, and a three-part motet *Quam pulchra es*.

Henry VIII opera by Saint-Saëns (libretto by L Détroyat and P A Silvestre, produced Paris, Opéra, 5 March 1883. Henry defies the Pope to marry Anne Boleyn.

Henze, Hans Werner (1926–) German composer. His immense and stylistically restless output is marked by a keen literary sensibility and seductive use of orchestral coloration, as in the opera *Elegy for Young Lovers* 1959–61 and the cantata *Being Beauteous* 1963. Among recent works are the opera *Das Verratene Meer/The Sea Betrayed* 1992.

He studied with Fortner at Heidelberg and Leibowitz in Paris. He is influenced by Schoenberg, though not strictly a 12-note composer, and has also done much to further the ballet in Germany; in 1950–52 he was ballet adviser to the Wiesbaden Opera. In 1953 he moved to Italy, where his music became more expansive, as in the opera *The Bassarids* 1966. Following the student unrest of 1968 he suddenly renounced the wealthy musical establishment in favour of a militantly socialist stance in works such as the abrasive *El Cimarrón* 1969–70 and *Voices* 1973, austere settings of 22 revolutionary texts in often magical sonorities. The opera *We Come to the River* 1976 and the ballet *Orpheus* 1980 were written in collaboration with Edward

Bond. In recent years Henze has returned to the musical past, and has become increasingly lyrical and elaborate: his reconstruction of Monteverdi's *Il Ritorno di Ulisse* was staged at Salzburg in 1985.

Works include: STAGE *Elegy for Young Lovers*, chamber opera (Schwetzingen and Glyndebourne, 1961), *Der junge Lord*, comic opera (Berlin, 1965), *The Bassarids*, opera seria (Salzburg, 1966), *Orpheus*, ballet by Edward Bond (Stuttgart, 1979), *The English Cat*, chamber opera (Schwetzingen, 1983).

ORCHESTRAL eight symphonies (1947–1993); two violin concertos (1948, 1978), two piano concertos (1950, 1967), *Doppio Concerto* for oboe, harp, and strings (1966), *Requiem* (nine spiritual concertos) for piano, trumpet, and chamber orchestra (1992).

VOCAL MUSIC five *Neapolitan Songs* for baritone and orchestra (1956), *Nocturnes and Arias* for soprano and orchestra (1957), *Kammermusik* for tenor, guitar, and chamber orchestra (1958), *Ariosi* for soprano, violin, and orchestra after Tasso (1963), *Versuch über Schweine/Essay on Pigs*, 1969), *Das Floss der Medusa*, oratorio to the memory of Ché Guevara (1968), *El Cimarrón*, for baritone and ensemble (1970), *Voices*, for mezzo, tenor, and instruments (22 revolutionary texts; 1973).

CHAMBER MUSIC five string quartets (1947–77), *Royal Winter Music*, two sonatas for guitar on Shakespearean characters (1975–79).

heptachord a scale of seven notes.

Herbert, Victor (1859–1924) Irish-born US conductor and composer. In 1893 he became conductor of the 22nd Regiment Band, also composing light operettas for the New York stage. He was conductor of the Pittsburgh Philharmonic 1898–1904, returning to New York to help found the American Society of Composers, Authors, and Publishers (AS-CAP) in 1914.

The second of his two cello concertos, written in 1894, inspired Dvořák to write his own cello concerto.

Born in Dublin, Republic of Ireland, Herbert trained as a cellist at the Stuttgart Conservatory, and began his professional musical career in Vienna, Austria. He emigrated to the USA in 1886 and played with the New York Metropolitan Opera and Philharmonic Orchestra.

Works include: the operas *Natoma* (1911) and *Madeleine* (1914), operettas *The Wizard of the Nile* (1895), *Babes in Toyland* (1903), and over 30 others; cantata *The Captive*; symphonic poem *Hero and Leander* and three suites for orchestra; Serenade for strings; songs.

Hercules secular oratorio by Handel (libretto by T Broughton), produced London, King's Theatre, Haymarket, 5 January 1745.

Herder, Johann Gottfried von (1744–1803) German philosopher, philologist and author, influential in the forming of the early-Romantic idea of music as an independent art. His poetic works inspired J C F ◊Bach (*Brutus*, oratorios and cantatas); Adolph ◊Jensen (*Stimmen der Völker*); ◊Prometheus (Liszt); Johann ◊Reichardt (*Morning Hymn*).

Hermannus Contractus (1013–1054), Hermann the Cripple German music scholar and composer. He studied at the monastery of Reichenau in Switzerland and became a Benedictine monk. He wrote musical treatises and composed hymns, sequences, and other pieces.

Hermann von Salzburg (lived 14th century) Austrian monk and composer. He belonged to the tradition of the Minnesinger but also wrote a few polyphonic pieces and a love song addressed to a lady acquaintance of the Archbishop of Salzburg.

Hermione opera by Bruch (libretto by E Hopffer, based on Shakespeare's *Winter's Tale*), produced Berlin, Opera, 21 March 1872.

Hernried, Robert (1883–1951) Austrian-born US scholar and composer. He studied in Vienna, and after a career as opera conductor 1908–14 he held various teaching posts and professorships in Germany and the USA, where he emigrated 1934. In 1946 he was appointed professor at Detroit University. He wrote several books and over 300 articles.

Works include: the operas *Francesca da Rimini* (after Dante) and *The Peasant Woman*; Mass; over 60 choral works; concert overture for orchestra; chamber music and songs.

Hero and Leander see ◊Ero e Leandro.

Hérodiade/Herodias opera by Massenet (libretto by P Milliet and 'Henri Grémont' (Georges Hartmann), based on a story by Flaubert), produced Brussels, Théâtre de la Monnaie, 19 December 1881. Salome, the abandoned daughter of Hérodiade, loves John the Baptist and kills herself rather than yield to Herod.

Hérodiade orchestral recitation by Hindemith, after Mallarmé; composed 1944, first performed Washington, DC, 30 October 1944, with the Martha Graham dance group.

Hérold, (Louis Joseph) Ferdinand (1791–1833) French composer. He had considerable success with the operas *Zampa* 1831 and *Le Pré aux Clercs* 1832, but is best known today for the ballet *La fille mal gardée* 1828.

Hérold was born in Paris and studied under his father, the pianist François Joseph Hérold (1755–1802). Later he was taught by Fétis, Louis Adam, Catel, and Méhul, and won the Prix de Rome in 1812. In Rome and Naples, where he became pianist to Queen Caroline, he wrote several instrumental works, and the comic opera *La jeunesse de Henri V*. Returning to Paris in 1816, he collaborated with Boieldieu in the opera *Charles de France*, and in 1817 began to produce operas of his own. He was accompanist at the Théâtre Italien from 1820 until 1827, when he married Adèle Elise Rollet and became choirmaster at the Opéra. About this time he began to suffer seriously from tuberculosis, from which he died.

Works include: OPERA *Les Rosières* (1817), *La Clochette* (1817), *Le premier venu*, *Les troqueurs* (1819), *L'amour platonique*, *L'auteur mort et vivant* (1820), *Le muletier* (1823), *Lasthénie*, *Le lapin blanc*, *Vendôme en Espagne* (with Auber), *Le Roi René* (1824), *Marie*, *L'illusion*, *Emmeline* (1829), *L'auberge d'Auray* (with Carafa), *Zampa* (1831), *Le pré aux clercs* (1832), *Ludovic* (unfinished, completed by Halévy).

BALLET *Astolphe et Joconde* (1827), *La sonnambule* (1827), *Lydie*, *La fille mal gardée*, *La Belle au bois dormant* (after Perrault).

OTHER incidental music for Ozaneaux's *Dernier jour de Missolonghi*; two symphonies; four piano concertos; cantata *Mlle de la Vallière*, *Hymne sur la Transfiguration*; three string quartets; two sonatas, variations, rondos, and other pieces for piano.

Heroldt, Johannes (c. 1550–1603) German composer. His works include a setting of the *St Matthew Passion* for six voices, published at Graz in 1594.

Hero's Life (Richard Strauss). See ◊Heldenleben, Ein.

Herrmann, Bernard (1911–1975) US film composer. His long career began with *Citizen Kane* 1941; besides Orson Welles, he collaborated with Alfred Hitchcock (*North by Northwest* 1959 and *Psycho* 1960), François Truffaut (*Fahrenheit 451* 1966), and Martin Scorsese (*Taxi Driver* 1976). He wrote his best scores for thrillers and mystery movies, and was a major influence in the establishment of a distinctively American musical imagery.

Born in New York, he won a composition prize at the age of 13 and began studying with Phillip James at New York University and later at the Juilliard Graduate School of Music. He joined CBS (Columbia Broadcasting System) in 1933 as a composer and conductor of music for drama and documentary programmes, and worked with Orson Welles on a number of radio projects before making his film debut. An eclectic stylist, he made his own orchestrations and sought out many new and exotic instruments for special effects and authentic colour.

Works include: the opera *Wuthering Heights* (1948–50; produced Portland, Oregon, 1982), cantatas *Moby Dick, Johnny Appleseed;* symphonic poem *City of Brass; Fiddle Concerto;* symphony; string quartet; film scores including *Citizen Kane, Psycho,* and *The Birds.* His last film music was for *Taxi Driver* (1976).

hertz (Hz) term for frequency in musical pitch, corresponding to cycles per second, and named after the German physicist Heinrich Hertz (1857–1894). For example, the phrase A 440 Hz means the note A (A4) of the frequency 440 cycles per second.

Hervé (1825–1892), real name Florimond Ronger French composer. He studied music as a choirboy, then with Elwart and Auber. He was organist at various Paris churches, including Saint-Eustache, and later theatre manager, operetta singer, librettist, and conductor.

Works include: more than 80 operettas, *Don Quixote et Sancho Pança* (after Cervantes, 1848), *Le Hussard persécuté, La Fanfare de Saint-Cloud, Les Chevaliers de la Table Ronde* (1866), *L'il crevé, Chilpéric, Le Petit Faust, Les Turcs* (parody of Racine's *Bajazet,* 1869), *La Belle Poule, Le Nouvel Aladin, Frivoli* (1886); ballets *Dilara, Sport, La Rose d'Amour, Cléopâtre, Les Bagatelles;* symphony *The Ashanti War* for solo voices and orchestra (1874); many light songs.

Herz, Das/The Heart opera by Pfitzner (libretto by H Mahner-Mons); composed 1930–31, produced Berlin and Munich, 12 November 1931. Pfitzner's last opera. Dr Athanasius attempts the diabolic resuscitation of the Duke's dead son, but the price is his wife's heart. He is condemned for sorcery, but atones.

Herzgewächse work by Schoenberg for high soprano, celesta, harmonium, and harp, op. 20; composed 1911. First British performance BBC (British Broadcasting Corporation) concert, 1 December 1960.

Herzogenberg, Heinrich von (1843–1900), Baron H Peccaduc Austrian composer and conductor. He studied at the Vienna Conservatory and settled at Leipzig in 1872. He conducted the Bach society there 1875–85, before becoming professor of composition at the Berlin Hochschule für Musik. His wife, Elisabeth von Herzogenberg (1842–1892) was a fine amateur pianist and pupil of Brahms.

Works include: Mass (1895), Requiem (1891), psalms; oratorios *Die Geburt Christi* and *Die Passion,* cantata *Columbus;* three symphonies, no. 1 entitled *Odysseus;* five string quartets (1876–90), two piano trios, two string trios; two violin and piano sonatas, cello and piano sonata; two sets of variations for two pianos, many piano pieces and duets; fantasies for organ; songs, vocal duets, part songs.

Heseltine, Philip (Arnold) real name of the English composer Peter ◊Warlock.

heterophony form of group music making found in folk music worldwide, in which the same melody line is presented simultaneously in plain and individually embellished forms.

Heuberger, Richard (Franz Josef) (1850–1914) Austrian music critic and composer. He studied engineering at first, but at the age of 26 devoted himself to music, becoming a choral conductor in 1878 and a critic in 1881. His best-known work is *Der Opernball/Ball at the Opera House*

Works include: the operas *Abenteuer einer Neujahrsnacht* (1896), *Manuel Venegas* (1889), *Miriam* (later *Das Maifest* 1894), *Barfüssele;* operettas *Der Opernball* (1898), *Ihre Excellenz, Der Sechsuhrzug, Das Baby, Der Fürst von Düsterstein, Don Quixotte* (after Cervantes); ballets *Die Lautenschlägerin* and *Struwwelpeter.*

Heure espagnole, L'/The Spanish Hour opera in one act by Ravel (libretto by Franc-Nohain, based on his own comedy), produced Paris, Opéra-Comique, 19 May 1911. Mule-driver Ramiro and poet Gonzalve keep good time with clockmaker's wife Concepción.

hexachord not a chord in the true sense, but a group of six individual notes. Introduced in the 11th century as a method of sight-singing, a series of overlapping scalar hexachords embraced the entire compass of notes. In the 20th century the term was redefined by composers using the ◊twelve-tone system, particularly Schoenberg and Webern, as being half of a twelve-tone (twelve-note) row, allowing further compositional manipulation.

hexachord fantasy a type of composition cultivated particularly by 16th–17th-centuries. English composers, a piece based on the first six notes of the scale, ascending or

Hexachordum durum:

Hexachordum naturale:

Hexachordum molle:

The three hexachords on G, C, and F respectively.

descending. The pieces were often entitled 'Ut, re, mi, fa, sol, la'.

Hexameron a collective piano work, published in 1837, consisting of bravura variations on the March in Bellini's *Puritani* by Liszt, Thalberg, Pixis, Herz, Czerny, and Chopin, with an introduction, finale and connecting passages by Liszt.

hey old country dance similar to the ◊reel, and probably to the ◊canary.

Heyden, Sebald (1499–1561) German theologian and music theorist. His explanations of the musical notation of his time are particularly valuable.

Heyns, Cornelius (lived 15th century) Flemish composer. He was succentor at St Donatian in Bruges 1452–53 and 1462–65. His Mass *Pour quelque paine* has also been attributed to Okeghem.

Heyse, Paul (Johann Ludwig) (1830–1914) German poet and novelist. See ◊*Italienisches Liederbuch* (H Wolf); Adolph ◊Jensen (*Spanisches Liederbuch*); ◊*Spanisches Liederbuch* (H Wolf).

Hiawatha three cantatas for solo voices, chorus and orchestra by Coleridge-Taylor, a setting of parts of Longfellow's poem: 1. *Hiawatha's Wedding Feast*, 2. *The Death of Minnehaha*, 3. *Hiawatha's Departure*, first performed as a whole, London, 22 March 1900.

Hidalgo, Juan (c. 1614–1685) Spanish composer. He was influential in the introduction of Italian-style operas to Spain, and collaborated with the playwright Calderón in the composition of several operas, including *Celos aun del aire matan* 1660, the first known Spanish opera.

He was a harpist and harpsichordist in the royal chapel at Madrid, and is said to have invented an instrument called the *claviharpa*.

Works include: the operas *Celos aun del aire matan* (libretto by Calderón, 1660) and *Los celos hacen estrellas* (libretto by Guevara); incidental music to various plays by Calderón including *Ni Amor se libra de Amor*.

hidden fifths, hidden octaves the movement of two parts in the same direction to a fifth or an octave. In many contrapuntal styles this is to be avoided, especially when involving the top or bottom line. Textbooks in formal counterpoint gave them this title as having an effect similar to that of consecutives.

Highland fling Scottish dance step, rather than a dance itself, although that is often so called. The music is that of the Strathspey and the step is a kick of the leg backwards and forwards.

Hignard, (Jean Louis) Aristide (1822–1898) French composer. He was a pupil of Halévy at the Paris Conservatory, where he gained the second Prix de Rome in 1850.

Works include: the operas *Hamlet* (after Shakespeare; composed 1868 but not produced until 1888, owing to success of Thomas' *Hamlet*), *Le Colin-Maillard*, *Les Compagnons de la Marjolaine* and *L'Auberge des Ardennes* (all on libretti by Jules Verne and Michael Carrol) and eight others; choruses; *Valses concertantes* and *Valses romantiques* for piano duet; songs.

Hildegard, Saint (1098–1179), also known as 'Hildegard of Bingen' German abbess and musician. She was educated at the Benedictine nunnery of Disisbodenberg, where she became abbess in 1136. She wrote monophonic music for the church which shows some departures from traditional plainsong style. She wrote music to her own poetry from 1140, collected in the 1150s as *Symphonia armonie celestium revelationum* (77 poems based on the liturgical calendar). The morality play *Ordo virtutum* concerns the struggle of virtue against the devil and contains 82 melodies.

Hill, Alfred (1870–1960) Australian composer, conductor and teacher. His early career was in Leipzig; he moved to New Zealand in 1902 and became influenced by Maori music. He was professor at New South Wales Conservatory 1915–35.

Works include: eight operas, *Tapu* (1903), *A Moorish Maid* (1905), *Giovanni, the Sculptor* (1914); ten symphonies (1896–1958); 17 string quartets, six sonatas for violin and piano.

Hillemacher, Paul (Joseph Wilhelm) (1852–1933) and Lucien (Joseph Edouard) (1860–1909) French composers, brothers who wrote all their works in collaboration. They studied at the Paris Conservatory, where Paul won the Prix de Rome in 1876 and Lucien in 1880.

Works include: the operas *Saint-Mégrin* (1886), *La Légende de Sainte Geneviève*, *Une aventure d'Arlequin* (1888), *Le régiment qui passe* (1894), *Le Drac*, *Orsola*, *Circé* (1907); mimed dramas *One for Two* and *Fra Angelico*; incidental music for Haraucourt's *Héro et Léandre* and for George Sand's *Claudie*; symphonic legend *Loreley* and other orchestral works; chamber music, songs, part songs.

Hiller, Ferdinand (1811–1885) German pianist, conductor, and composer. He succeeded Mendelssohn as conductor of the Leipzig Gewandhaus 1843–44. From 1850 he lived at Cologne, where he founded the Conservatory.

He was taught music privately as a child and appeared as a pianist at the age of ten. In 1825 he went to Weimar to study under Hummel. After a brief return to Frankfurt he lived in Paris 1828–35, where he taught and gave concerts. He produced his first opera at Milan in 1839 and his first oratorio at Leipzig in 1840, then studied with Giuseppe Baini in Rome, lived at Frankfurt, Leipzig and Dresden, became conductor at Düsseldorf 1847 and at Cologne 1850, where he remained.

Works include: the operas *Romilda* (1839), *Die Katakomben* (1862), *Der Deserteur* (1865); oratorios *Die Zerstörung Jerusalems* (1840) and *Saul*; cantatas *Nala und Damajanti*, *Prometheus*, *Rebecca*, and others, including one from Byron's 'Hebrew Melodies'; four symphonies, four overtures (including one to Schiller's *Demetrius*), and other orchestral works; two piano concertos (1835, 1861), violin concerto (1875); three string quartets, three piano quartets, five piano trios; violin and cello sonata; sonata, 24 studies, *Modern Suite*, and many other works for piano; songs, part songs.

Hiller, Johann Adam (1728–1804) German composer. He spent the greater part of his life at Leipzig, where he was the central figure in the musical activity of the city. He founded subscription concerts and a musical weekly, and was one of the originators of the German *Singspiel*, of which he wrote many successful examples 1766–82.

He was a chorister under Homilius in Dresden, and studied law at Leipzig University. After a short period in the service of Count Brühl he returned to Leipzig, working

as a flautist, singer, and conductor. In 1763 he founded subscription concerts on the model of the Paris Concert Spirituel, these becoming the Gewandhaus concerts in 1781. He also produced a musical weekly, *Wöchentliche Nachrichten*, 1766–70. He left Leipzig in 1785, but after some short-term posts returned to succeed Doles as municipal music director and Cantor of St Thomas's.

Works include: *Singspiele*: *Der Teufel ist los* (after Coffey's *The Devil to Pay*, 1766), *Lisuart und Dariolette*, *Lottchen am Hofe* (1767), *Die Muse*, *Die Liebe auf dem Lande* (1768), *Die Jagd*, *Der Dorfbalbier* (1771), *Der Aerndtekranz*, *Der Krieg* (1772), *Die Jubelhochzeit*, *Das Grab des Mufti*, *Das gerettete Troja*; settings of Gellert's odes and other choral works; cantatas; 100th Psalm; instrumental music; also many theoretical and critical writings on music.

Hiller, Lejaren (1924–) US composer. He learned from Sessions and Babbitt and co-created the first computer composition (*Illiac Suite* 1957). He directed the experimental music studio at the University of Illinois 1958–68, and was appointed professor of music at the State University of New York, Buffalo, in 1968.

Works include: two symphonies (1953, 1960), piano concerto (1949), seven string quartets (1949–79), six piano sonatas (1946–72); *Computer Cantata* (1963), seven *Electronic Studies* (1963), *Rage over the Lost Beethoven* (1972); *The Fox Trots Again* for chamber orchestra (1985). He collaborated with Cage on *HPSCHD* for 1–7 harpsichords and 1–51 tapes (1968).

Hilton, John (2) (1599–1657) English organist and composer, possibly the son of John Hilton. He took a degree in music at Cambridge University in 1626 and two years later became organist at St Margaret's Church, Westminster.

Works include: services and anthems; madrigals, *Ayres, or Fa La's* for three voices (published 1627; the last English madrigal publication); *Elegy on the death of Wm Lawes* for three voices and bass; collection of catches, rounds, and canons *Catch that catch can* (1652); songs, fantasies for viols, hymn 'Wilt Thou forgive that sin where I begun' from Donne's 'Divine Poems'.

Himmel, Friedrich Heinrich (1765–1814) German harpsichordist, pianist, and composer. He read theology at Halle University, but later under the patronage of Frederick William II of Prussia studied music at Dresden under Johann Naumann and in Italy, where he produced two operas. Appointed court Kapellmeister in Berlin in 1795, he was still able to travel and visited Russia, Scandinavia, Paris, London, and Vienna.

Works include: the operas *Il primo navigatore* (1794), *La morte di Semiramide* (1795), *Alessandro* (1799), *Vasco da Gama* (1801), *Frohsinn und Schwärmerei, Fauchon das Leyermädchen* (1804), *Die Sylphen, Der Kobold* (1813), oratorio *Isacco*; funeral cantata for the King of Prussia; Masses, Te Deum, motets, psalms and other church music; instrumental music, songs.

Hindemith, Paul (1895–1963) German composer and teacher. His operas *Cardillac* 1926, revised 1952, and *Mathis der Maler/Mathis the Painter* 1933–35, are theatrically astute and politically aware; as a teacher in Berlin 1927–33 he encouraged the development of a functional modern repertoire ('Gebrauchsmusik'/'utility music') for home and school.

In 1939 he emigrated to the USA, where he taught at Yale University and was influential in promoting a measured neoclassical idiom of self-evident contrapuntal mastery but matter-of-fact tone, exemplified in *Ludus Tonalis* for piano 1942 and the *Symphonic Metamorphoses on Themes of Carl Maria von Weber* 1944. In later life he revised many of his earlier compositions to conform with a personal theory of tonality.

He was taught the violin as a child and entered the Hoch Conservatory at Frankfurt, where he studied under Arnold Mendelssohn and Sekles. Later he played in the Frankfurt Opera orchestra and was leader there 1915–23; in 1921 he founded a string quartet (the Amar-Hindemith quartet) with the Turkish violinist Licco Amar, in which he played viola. The quartet was disbanded in 1929, the year in which he premiered Walton's viola concerto in London.

Works of his were heard at the Donaueschingen festival in 1921 and at the International Society for Contemporary Music festival at Salzburg in 1922. His one-act operas of 1921–22 scandalized audiences and some musicians, and he had an early reputation as an iconoclast. His Kammermusik series, begun in 1922, sought to re-establish the musical values of the Baroque concerto; *Cardillac* uses neoclassical forms, although its story of a goldsmith who murders his clients to regain his work recalls the savagery of Hindemith's early pieces for the stage.

From 1927 he taught composition at the Berlin Hochschule für Musik, and his music was conducted by Furtwängler and Klemperer, but the Nazis proscribed his works as degenerate art. His opera *Mathis der Maler* was therefore produced at Zurich, Switzerland, in 1938; a three-movement symphony from the opera was premiered at Berlin in 1934 by Fürtwangler, prompting a temporary break with the Nazi authorities. For some years after 1933 he was at Ankara in an official capacity to reorganize Turkish music education. In 1939 he emigrated to the USA, where he taught at Yale University, but in 1946 he returned to Europe and was active for several years as a conductor.

In his late, largely orchestral works, Hindemith sought further to establish the values of tonality and Classical restraint. The vision of astronomer Johannes Kepler in his last opera, *Die Harmonie der Welt*, suggests the composer himself striving to hear the sounds emitted by the planets as they circle the sun, oblivious to the harsher musical realities around him.

Works include: OPERA *Cardillac* (after E T A Hoffmann, 1926), *Mathis der Maler* (1938), *Harmonie der Welt* (1957); ballet *Nobilissima Visione* (1938).

ORCHESTRAL *Kammermusik* nos. 1–7 (1922–27; see separate entry), *Mathis der Maler*, symphony from the opera (1934), *Der Schwanendreher*, concerto after folk songs, for viola and small orchestra (1935), *Trauermusik* for viola and strings (1936), *Nobilissima Visione*, suite from the ballet (1938), cello concerto (1940), Symphony in Eb (1940), *Theme and Variations 'The Four Temperaments'* for piano and strings (1940), *Symphonic Metamorphosis on Themes of Carl Maria von Weber* (1943), *Symphonia Serena* (1946), clarinet concerto (1947), horn concerto (1949).

CHAMBER AND KEYBOARD six string quartets (1918–45); 16 sonatas for various instruments, including four for solo viola; *Ludus tonalis*: 12 fugues with prelude and postlude, and other works for piano; three organ sonatas.

CHORAL AND SOLO VOCAL *Das Marienleben*, 15 songs for soprano and piano (texts by Rilke, 1922–23); Requiem, after Walt Whitman's 'When Lilacs Last in the Dooryard Bloom'd' (1946).

Hin und Zurück/There and Back opera in one act by Hindemith (libretto by M Schiffer after an English revue), produced Baden-Baden, 17 July 1927. The plot, concerning a jealous husband, goes into reverse at half way. At the first performance the part of the errant, palindromic wife was sung by Otto Klemperer's wife, Johanna.

Hippolyte et Aricie/Hippolytus and Aricia opera in five acts by Rameau (libretto by S J de Pellegrin), produced Paris, Opéra, 1 October 1733. Hippolytus and Aricia are in love. Believing her husband Theseus to be dead, Phaedra confesses love for her stepson Hippolytus, who rejects her. Theseus returns and condemns his son for what appears to be an attack on Phaedra. Hippolytus is carried off by a sea monster, but survives and is reunited with Aricia.

See also ◊Ippolito ed Aricia.

Hirt auf dem Felsen, Der/The Shepherd on the Rock song by Schubert D965, for piano and soprano with clarinet obbligato (text by W Muller and H von Chezy); commissioned by Anna Milder-Hauptmann (1785–1838), the first Leonore in *Fidelio* (1805). With *Die Taubenpost*, Schubert's last work; composed October 1828.

Histoire du soldat/The Soldier's Tale action for a narrator, actors, and dancers by Stravinsky (libretto by C F Ramuz), produced Lausanne, 28 September 1918, conductor Ansermet.

Histoires Naturelles song cycle by Ravel for voice and piano; composed 1906, first performed Paris, 19 March 1907. The five animals depicted are *The Peacock*, *The Cricket*, *The Swan*, *The Kingfisher*, and *The Guineafowl*.

Hitchcock, (Hugh) Wiley (1932–) US musicologist. He studied in Michigan and Paris (with Nadia Boulanger), and was appointed professor of music at Brooklyn College in 1971. His research interests involve US music history and the music of the French Baroque. He was editor for the Americas in the *New Grove Dictionary of Music and Musicians* and co-editor of the *Grove Dictionary of US Music*. Other publications include *Music in the United States* (1969, 1975, 1988), *Les oeuvres de Marc-Antoine Charpentier* (1982), and editions of Caccini, Leo, and Lully.

HMS Pinafore operetta by Sullivan (libretto by W S Gilbert), produced London, Opéra Comique, 25 May 1878. The first work by Gilbert and Sullivan to be a worldwide success.

Hoboken, Anthony van (1887–1983) Dutch musicologist. He studied in Frankfurt and Vienna and in 1927 founded a manuscript archive in the National Library in Vienna; an almost complete thematic catalogue of Haydn's works was published in 1957 and 1971. Haydn's works are commonly designated 'Hob.'. with a roman numeral denoting group classification (for example opera, symphony), followed by an Arabic numeral for a work within a group.

Hobrecht, Jacob see ◊Obrecht.

Hochzeit des Camacho, Die/Camacho's Wedding opera by Mendelssohn (libretto by C A L von Lichtenstein, based on Cervantes' *Don Quixote*), produced Berlin, Schauspielhaus, 29 April 1827. Quiteria loves Basilio but must marry the rich Camacho. At the wedding Basilio feigns attempted suicide; Camacho allows him to marry Quiteria so that he may die a happy man. The subterfuge is revealed, but Camacho accepts the lovers' union.

hocket word similar to 'hiccup' and derived from the French equivalent *hoquet*. It is used for a device in medieval vocal and instrumental music, consisting of phrases when broken up by rests, in such a way that when one part is silent another fills the gap. Also a piece written in this style.

Hoddinott, Alun (1929–) Welsh composer. His works, conservatively inclined and mostly orchestral, include five symphonies, a clarinet concerto, four Welsh Dances, much chamber music, and an oratorio.

He studied at the University College of South Wales, Cardiff, where he was appointed professor of music in 1967. He was artistic director of Cardiff Festival of 20th-Century Music 1966–89.

Works include: the operas *The Beach of Falseá* (1974), *Murder, The Magician* (1976), *The Rajah's Diamond* (1979), *The Trumpet Major*, after Hardy (1981); eight symphonies (1954–92), four Sinfoniettas (1968–71), *Variants*, *Night Music* for orchestra, two clarinet concertos (1954, 1986), oboe concerto, three piano concertos, organ concerto (1967), *Doubles* for oboe, harpsichord, and strings (1982), Triple concerto for violin, cello, and piano (1986), *Noctis Equi* for cello and orchestra (1989); choral music; clarinet quartet, three string quartets (1966, 1984, 1988), string trio; ten piano sonatas.

Hoffmann, Amadeus (Ernst Theodor Wilhelm) (1776–1822) German composer and writer. He composed the opera *Undine* 1816, but is chiefly remembered as an author and librettist of fairy stories, including 'Nussknacker/Nutcracker' 1816. His stories inspired ◊Offenbach's *Tales of Hoffmann*.

Hoffmeister, Franz Anton (1754–1812) Austrian music publisher and composer. Beethoven and Mozart were among his clients. The best known of his nine operas was *Der Königssohn aus Ithaka* 1803. Whether by accident or design, many of his works were ascribed to Haydn.

He started in Vienna as a law student but in 1783 established his publishing firm. With Kühnel in Leipzig he established a bureau which later became the publishing house C F Peters. He wrote 66 symphonies, about 60 concertos, including 25 for flute, 42 string quartets, and 18 string trios.

Hoffmeister Quartet string quartet no. 20, in D major, by Mozart (K499); composed 1786 and published by F A ◊Hoffmeister.

Hofmann, Leopold (1738–1793) Austrian composer. He was Kapellmeister at St Stephen's Cathedral in Vienna from 1772. He belongs to the Viennese school of symphonists.

Works include: church music, symphonies, concertos.

Hofmannsthal, Hugo von (1874–1929) Austrian poet and dramatist. See ◊*Ägyptische Helena* (R Strauss); ◊*Alkestis* (Wellesz); ◊*Arabella* (R Strauss); ◊*Ariadne auf Naxos* (ditto); ◊*Bourgeois gentilhomme* (ditto); ◊*Elektra* (ditto); ◊*Everyman* (Sibelius); ◊*Frau ohne Schatten, Die* (R Strauss); ◊*Josephslegende* (ditto); F ◊Martin (*Jedermann*); ◊*Oedipus und die Sphinx* (Varèse); Reuss (*Tor und der Tod*); ◊*Rosenkavalier, Der* (R Strauss); A ◊Tcherepnin (*Hochzeit der Sobeide*); H ◊Unger (*Tor und der Tod*); Wagner-Régeny (*Bergwerk zu Falun*); ◊Wellesz (*Alkestis, Lied der Welt* and *Leben, Traum und Tod*); ◊Zemlinsky (*Das gläserne Herz*).

Holby, Lee (1926–) US composer. He studied at the Curtis Institute and in Rome and Salzburg, and is best known for his operas, influenced by Menotti: *The Scarf* (after Chekhov, produced Spoleto 1958), *Beatrice* (after Maeterlinck, 1959), *Natalia Petrovna* (after Turgenev, 1964), *Summer and Smoke* (after T N Williams, 1971); also incidental music to Webster's *The Duchess of Malfi* (1957).

Holborne, Anthony (1584–1602) English composer. He was in the service of Queen Elizabeth I. His collection *The Cittharn Schoole* 1597 contains pieces for cittern and bass viol, as well as three-part songs by his brother William. A further collection, *Pavans, Galliards, Almains and Other Short Aeirs*, was published in 1599.

Holbrooke, Joseph (or Josef) (1878–1958) English composer. After a hard struggle as a pianist and conductor he came under the patronage of Lord Howard de Walden, who wrote the libretti for his dramatic trilogy *The Cauldron of Annwen* 1912–16. Other works (many on subjects from Edgar Allan Poe) include ballets, symphonic poems, and a great deal of chamber music.

He studied at the Royal Academy of Music.

Works include: the operas *Pierrot and Pierrette* (1909; revised 1924 as *The Stranger*), *The Snob, The Wizard,* and the trilogy *The Cauldron of Annwen* (*The Children of Don* (1912), *Dylan* (1914), and *Bronwen* (1916)); ballets *The Red Mask* (after Poe), *The Moth and the Flame, Coromanthe,* and others; *Dramatic Choral Symphony* and *The Bells* for chorus and orchestra (both after Poe, 1903); symphonic poems *The Raven* (1900), *Ulalume* and *The Masque of the Red Death* (all after Poe); violin concerto (1917); six string quartets (including *Pickwick Club* after Dickens), piano music and songs.

Hölderlin, Johann Christian Friedrich (1770–1843) German poet. See Hans Erich ◊Apostel (songs); Benjamin ◊Britten (*Hölderlin Fragmente*); Brahms ◊*Schicksalslied*; Richard ◊Strauss (three hymns).

Höller, York (1944–) German composer. He studied at the Cologne Musikhochschule under Zimmermann and Alfons Kontarsky, and came under the influence of Boulez at Darmstadt. He has worked at the electronic studio at Cologne.

Works include: the operas *Der Meister und Margarita* (1989) and *Caligula* (1992); *Topic* for orchestra (1967), cello sonata (1969), piano concerto (1970), *Horizont,* electronic (1972), *Chroma* for orchestra (1974), *Tangens,* electronic (1973), *Antiphon* for string quartet (1977), *Arcus* for orchestra (1978), *Moments musicaux* for flute and piano (1979), *Mythos* for orchestra (1980), *Traumspiel* for soprano, orchestra, and tape (1983), *Improvisation sur le nom de Pierre Boulez* for 17 instruments (1985), *Fanal* for trumpet and orchestra (1990), *Pensées* for piano, orchestra, and tape (1991), *Aura* for orchestra (1992), *Pas de deux* for cello and piano (1993).

Holliger, Heinz (1939–) Swiss oboist and composer. He has created avant-garde works in a lyric expressionist style, including *Siebengesang/Sevensong* 1967 for amplified oboe, voices, and orchestra. He has given first performances of works written for him by Berio, Krenek, Henze, and Stockhausen.

He studied oboe and piano in Bern and Paris, and composition with Veress in Bern and Boulez in Paris. He has won several prizes for his oboe playing.

Works include: cantata *Himmel und Erde* for tenor and chamber group (1961); *Studie* for soprano, oboe, and cello with harpsichord; *Improvisation* for oboe, harp, and 12 string instruments (1963); *Pneuma* for 34 wind instruments and percussion (1970), *Come and*

Go, chamber opera (1977), *Engführung* for chamber orchestra (1984), *Der ferne Klang* for ensemble (1984), *Tonscherben* for orchestra (1985), *What Where*, chamber opera (1988), *Scardanelli-Zglus* 1–4 (1975–91); sonata for oboe and piano; sonata for oboe solo; string quartet (1975).

Holloway, Robin (Greville) (1943–) English composer. His music, which shows a textural and harmonic eclecticism, has been influenced by German Romanticism.

He studied at Cambridge, and was later appointed lecturer there.

Works include: the opera *Clarissa* (1968–76; first performance 1990); *Scenes from Schumann*, seven paraphrases for orchestra (1970) and *Fantasy-Pieces*, on the Heine *Liederkreis* of Schumann, for 13 players (1971). Other works include two Concertos for Orchestra (1969, 1979); *Serenata Notturna* for four horns and orchestra (1982); *Clarissa Symphony*, for soprano, tenor, and orchestra (1981); *Serenade in G* (1986); *Inquietus* for chamber orchestra, in memory of Peter Pears (1986); Concerto for clarinet and saxophone (1988), violin concerto (1989), *The Spacious Firmament* for chorus and orchestra (1989), *Wagner Nights* for orchestra (1989), *Serenade for Strings* (1990), *Summer Music* and *Winter Music* for ensemble (1991, 1992).

Holman, Peter (1946–) English harpsichordist, director, and writer. He studied at King's College, London, with Thurston Dart. He founded the early music group Ars Nova while still a student; cofounded with Roy Goodman the Parley of Instruments (1979); and gave many performances in the UK and Europe with Renaissance and early Baroque string consort music. He was music director of Opera Restor'd from 1985, performing 18th-century English masques and operas in authentic style. He was professor at the Royal Academy of Music, London, and joint artistic director of the Boston Early Music Festival. Publications include *The Violin at the English Court, 1540–1690* (1993) and a book on Purcell for the tercentenary (1995). His edition of Arne's *Artaxerxes* was performed in London under Roy Goodman, 1995.

Holmboe, Vagn (1909–) Danish composer. Denmark's most distinguished composer after Nielsen, Holmboe has published 10 symphonies, 12 string quartets, 13 chamber concertos, and many other pieces, including the *Requiem for Nietzsche* 1963–64. With his wife, the Romanian pianist Meta Graf, he explored Romanian folk music.

He studied with Knud Jeppesen (1892–1974) and Finn Høffding in Copenhagen and Ernst Toch in Berlin. From 1940 to 1949 he taught at the Institute for the Blind in Copenhagen, and thereafter at the Copenhagen Conservatory.

Works include: the opera *Fanden og Borgmesteren* (1940); ballet *Den galsindede Tyrk*; 12 symphonies (1935–88); 13 chamber concertos (1939–56), 20 string quartets (1948–75), three violin sonatas.

Holmès, Augusta (Mary Anne) (1847–1903), born Holmes Irish naturalized French pianist and composer. Although her parents were against her taking up music, she played the piano and sang as a child prodigy and began to compose under the name of Hermann Zenta. Later she studied with César Franck.

Works include: the operas *Héro et Léandre*, *La montagne noire* (1895), *Astarté, Lancelot du Lac*; choral works *Les Argonautes* (on Homer's 'Iliad', 1881), psalm 'In exitu', ode *Ludus pro patria* and *Ode triomphale*; symphony on Ariosto's 'Orlando furioso', *Lutèce* and *Pologne*, symphonic poem *Irlande* (1882); song-cycle *Les Sept Ivresses*.

Holoman, D(allas) Kern (1947–) US musicologist and conductor. He studied in North Carolina and played the bassoon in an orchestra there before becoming the founding director of the Early Music Ensemble, 1973–79. He was chair of the music department at Davis, California, 1980–88. The music of Berlioz formed the centre of his research, and he has published on the composer's creative process (1980), a Catalogue (1987), and a biography (1989).

Holst, Gustav(us Theodore von) (1874–1934) English composer of distant Swedish descent. He wrote operas, including *Sávitri* 1908 and *At the Boar's Head* 1924; ballets; choral works, including *Hymns from the Rig Veda* 1908–12 and *The Hymn of Jesus* 1917; orchestral suites, including *The Planets* 1914–16; and songs. He was a lifelong friend of Ralph ◊Vaughan Williams, with whom he shared an enthusiasm for English folk music. His musical style, although tonal and drawing on folk song, tends to be severe. He was the father of Imogen Holst (1907–), musicologist and his biographer.

Holst's father was a music teacher and his mother a pianist, and he had early experience as organist and choral and orchestral conductor in a small way. In 1892 he went to the Royal College of Music in London, but disliked the keyboard instruments and studied composition under Charles Stanford.

Suffering from neuritis, he took up the trombone instead of the piano, and on leaving played in the orchestra of the Carl Rosa Opera Company, and later in the Scottish Orchestra. In 1903 he became music master at a school in south London, and in 1905 at St Paul's Girls' School, where he remained to his death. In 1907 he was appointed music director at Morley College for Working Men and Women; in 1912 he conducted there the first modern performance of Purcell's *Fairy Queen*. From 1919 he taught composition at the Royal College of Music and 1919–23 at Reading College. He had to wait a long time for recognition; Balfour Gardiner had arranged a private performance of *The Planets* 1918, and with its public premiere the following year, Holst achieved the first real success of his career. In 1923 he conducted at the University of Michigan and his opera *The Perfect Fool* (a satire on Wagnerism) was given at Covent Garden. The choral symphony after Keats was given at the 1925 Leeds Festival and in 1928 his bleak tone poem after Hardy, *Egdon Heath*, was premiered by the New York Symphony Orchestra. The *Choral Fantasia* was first heard 1931 and the *Brook Green Suite* 1933.

Side by side with the influence of English folk music was that of Indian literature (*Sávitri* is the story from the *Mahābhārata*), and a number of choral hymns and songs are set to texts from the Rig-Veda, translated by Holst from the Sanskrit. He was also influenced by the early music of Weelkes and Byrd.

Works include: OPERA *The Wandering Scholar, Sávitri* (1908; produced 1916), *At the Boar's Head* (on Shakespeare's *Henry IV*, 1925).

CHORAL Choral hymns from the *Rig Veda* with orchestra (1908–12), *The Hymn of Jesus* for chorus and orchestra (1917), choral symphony (Keats) for soprano, chorus, and orchestra (1925).

ORCHESTRAL *A Somerset Rhapsody* (1907), *Beni Mora* suite (1910), *The Planets* (1914–16), *Egdon Heath* for orchestra (after Thomas Hardy, 1927); *St Paul's* suite for strings; *Fugal Concerto* for flute, oboe, and strings, concerto for two violins and orchestra (1929); *A Moorside Suite* for brass band. Nine hymns from the *Rig-Veda* for voice and piano (1908).

Holt, Simon (1958–) English composer. He studied at the Royal Northern College of Music with Anthony Gilbert and was featured composer at the 1985 Bath Festival. He has written pieces to commissions from the Nash Ensemble and London Sinfonietta.

Works include: *Syrensong* (1987), and *Walking with the river's roar* (1991) for orchestra; ensemble pieces *Mirrormaze* (1981), *Shadow Realm* (1983), *Burlesca obscura*, clarinet quintet (1985), *Danger of the Disappearance of Things* for string quartet (1989), *Sparrow Flight* (1989) and *Icarus Lamentations* (1992); vocal works with ensemble *Wyrdchanging* (1980), *Canciones* (1986), *Ballad of the Black Sorrow* (1988), *A Song of Crocuses and Lightning* (1989), *Tangara* (1991), *A Knot of Time* (1992); *Lunas Zauberschein* for mezzo and bass flute (1979); piano music.

Holzbauer, Ignaz (1711–1783) Austrian composer. Originally intended for a career in law, he was largely self-taught in music, and visited Italy to complete his studies. Director of the court opera in Vienna intermittently 1742–50, he was appointed Kapellmeister in Stuttgart in 1751, and two years later to the court of the Elector Palatine in Mannheim, where the orchestra under Johann Stamitz was the most famous of the time. During visits to Italy on leave of absence he produced several operas, and in Mannheim produced the German opera *Günther von Schwarzburg*. As a composer of symphonies he belongs to the Mannheim School.

Works include: the operas *Il figlio delle selve* (1753), *L'isola disabitata* (1754), *Nitetti* (1758), *Alessandro nell' Indie*, *Tancredi*, *Günther von Schwarzburg* (1777); oratorios *La Passione* (1754), *Isacco* (1757), *La Betulia liberata* (1760); Masses, motets and other church music; 65 symphonies; concertos, chamber music.

Holzbläser (German 'woodblowers') German name for woodwind instruments.

Holzblasinstrumente German name for ◊woodwind instruments.

Holztrompete (German 'wooden trumpet') musical instrument designed for use in the third act of Wagner's *Tristan und Isolde*, actually a revival of the ◊cornett, but provided with a valve.

Homer Greek poet. His *Iliad* and *Odyssey* inspired Max ◊Bruch (*Achilles* and *Odysseus*); Gnecchi (*Cassandra*); Heger (*Bettler Namenlos*); Herzogenberg (*Odysseus* symphony); ◊Holmès (*Argonautes*); ◊*Homerische Welt* (Bungert); ◊*Ritorno d'Ulisse in patria, Il* (Monteverdi, Henze); ◊*Ulisse* (Dallapiccola).

Homerische Welt/Homeric World operatic tetralogy by Bungert (libretto by composer, based on Homer's 'Odyssey'):

I. *Kirke/Circe*, produced Dresden, 29 January 1898.

II. *Nausikaa/Nausicaa*, produced Dresden, 20 March 1901.

III. *Odysseus Heimkehr/The Return of Ulysses*, produced Dresden, 12 December 1896.

IV. *Odysseus Tod/The death of Ulysses*, produced Dresden, 30 October 1903.

Bungert's attempt to create a Wagnerian cycle, but based, like Berlioz's *Troyens* and Taneiev's *Oresteia*, on classical Greek subjects.

'Homme armé, L'' (French 'the armed man') name of an old French secular song, the tune of which was often used by composers of the 15th and 16th centuries as *cantus firmus* for their Masses, which were then designated by that name.

Homme et son désir, L'/Man and his Desire ballet by Milhaud (words, 'plastic poem', by Paul Claudel, choreographed by Jean Borlin), produced Paris, Théâtre des Champs-Élysées, 6 June 1921.

homophonic (from Greek 'alike-sounding') term applied to music in which the individual lines making up the harmony have no independent significance, that is to say, for most purposes chordal.

homophony music comprising a melody lead and accompanying harmony, in contrast to **heterophony** and **polyphony** in which different melody lines of equal importance are combined.

Honegger, Arthur (1892–1955) Swiss composer. He was one of the group of composers known as ◊Les Six. His work was varied in form, for example, the opera *Antigone* 1927, the ballet *Skating Rink* 1922, the oratorio *Le roi David/King David* 1921, programme music (*Pacific 231* 1923), and the *Symphonie liturgique/Liturgical Symphony* 1946. He also composed incidental music for Abel Gance's silent movie classics *La roue/The Wheel* 1923 and *Napoléon* 1927.

Honneger was born at Le Havre, and was given his first music lessons there by the organist R C Martin. He then studied at the Zurich Conservatory 1909–11, and at the Paris Conservatory 1911–13. After that he became a private pupil of Widor and d'Indy and in 1914 began to compose. Though always in touch with Switzerland, he belonged mainly to the French school. He married the composer Andrée Vaurabourg, who was also attached to 'Les Six', though less closely.

Works include: OPERA stage oratorios *Le roi David* (1921), *Judith*, *Jeanne d'Arc au bûcher* (Paul Claudel, 1938).

INCIDENTAL MUSIC for *Phædre* (d'Annunzio, 1926), *Oedipe-Roi* (Sophocles, 1948).

ORCHESTRAL AND VOCAL WITH ORCHESTRA *La danse des morts* (Claudel) for solo voices, chorus, and orchestra (on Holbein), *Chant de joie*, prelude to Shakespeare's *Tempest*, *Mouvements symphonique*: *Pacific 231*, *Rugby* and No. 3 (1923–33), five symphonies (1930–51), *Prélude, Arioso et Fugue* (on B.A.C.H., *Pastorale d'été* (1920); cello concerto; Five Poems by Guillaume Apollinaire for voice and orchestra (1910–17).

CHAMBER AND SOLO VOCAL two violin and piano sonatas, sonatas for viola and piano, cello and piano, clarinet and piano.

hopak see ◊gopak.

Horenstein, Jascha (1898–1973) Russian-born conductor. He went with his family to Germany as a child, and studied with Max Bode in Königsberg, Adolph Busch in Vienna, and composition with Schreker in Berlin. He was appointed conductor of the Düsseldorf Opera in 1926 and settled in the USA in 1941; he gave the first US performance of Busoni's *Doktor Faust* there in 1964. Well known in Schubert, Bruckner, and Mahler, he conducted the first performances of Berg's Three Movements for strings (Berlin, 1929) and *Altenberg Lieder* (Rome, 1953). He conducted *Parsifal* at Covent Garden a few weeks before his death.

Horizon Chimérique, L' song cycle by Fauré, op. 118 (texts by Jean de la Ville de Mirmont); composed 1921, first performed Paris, 13 May 1922, with Charles Pinzéra.

horn member of a family of lip-reed wind instruments used for signalling and ritual, and sharing features of a generally conical bore (although the orchestral horn is of part conical and part straight bore) and curved shape, producing a pitch of rising or variable inflection.

Many horns are based on animal horns, for example the shofar of Hebrew ritual and the medieval oliphant and gemshorn, and shells, for example the conch shell of Pacific island peoples. Horns in metal originated in South America and also Central Asia (Tibet, India, Nepal), and reached Europe along with the

The normal compass of the horn. One or two higher and lower notes are possible. The modern keyed horn is built in F and high B flat, with four valves, one of which transposes the instrument from the lower to the higher pitch.

technology of metalwork in the Bronze Age. The familiar hunting horn, unchanged for many centuries, was adapted and enlarged in the 18th century to become an orchestral instrument, its limited range of natural harmonics extended by a combination of lip technique and hand stopping within the bell and the use of extension crooks for changes of key.

The modern valve horn is a 19th-century hybrid Bb/F instrument; the name **French horn** strictly applies to the earlier *cor à pistons* which uses lever-action rotary valves and produces a lighter tone. The **Wagner tuba** is a horn variant in tenor and bass versions devised by Wagner to provide a fuller horn tone in the lower range. Composers for horn include Mozart, Haydn, Richard Strauss, Weber, Schumann (*Konzertstück* for four horns 1848), Ravel, and Benjamin Britten (*Serenade for Tenor, Horn, and Strings* 1943).

Hornbostel, Erich (Moritz) von (1877–1935) Austrian musicologist. He is most famous (with Curt Sachs) for his part in the Sachs-Hornbostel classification of musical instruments, still employed by most scholars and museums.

He studied physics and philosophy at Vienna and Heidelberg, and in 1906 became head of the gramophone archives in Berlin for the recording of ethnic music, on which he wrote several learned works. In 1933 he left Germany and went to New York; in the following year he went to London and Cambridge.

Horne, David (1970–) Scottish pianist and composer. He studied in Edinburgh and at the Curtis Institute (1989), and at Harvard. He has won prizes at Huddersfield Festival, as composer, and BBC Young Musician of the Year (piano section). He has performed solo concerts with the CBSO, London Sinfonietta and Scottish National Orchestra; Prokofiev's Third Concerto at the 1990 Proms. His compositions include string quartet (1988), *Splintered Unisons* and *Towards Dharma* for ensemble (1988–89), *Light Emerging* for orchestra (1989), *Northscape* for chamber orchestra (1992), and a piano concerto (1992).

hornpipe English dance popular between the 16th and 19th centuries, associated especially with sailors. During the 18th century it changed from triple time (3/4) to common time (4/4). Examples include those by Purcell and Handel.

hornpipe obsolete wind instrument, once common to Celtic cultures, consisting of a wooden pipe with a single-reed mouthpiece on one end, and a horn for the bell.

Horn Signal, Symphony with the nickname of Haydn's symphony no. 31 in D major, composed 1765, so called because of the horn fanfares at the beginning and end.

Horst-Wessel-Lied song introduced by the Nazis as a second German national anthem. The text was written to a traditional tune by Horst Wessel (1907–1930), a Nazi 'martyr'.

Horvat, Milan (1919–) Croatian conductor. He studied at Zagreb and was conductor of the Zagreb Philharmonic Orchestra 1946–53 and 1958–69; chief conductor of the Radio Telefis Eireann (RTE) Symphony Orchestra at Dublin, 1953–58. He was principal of Zagreb Opera 1958–65, giving many Yugoslav first performances; Austrian Radio Symphony Orchestra 1969–75, with many concerts as guest elsewhere in Europe (Salzburg Festival 1970, Krzysztof Penderecki's *St Luke Passion*). He was conductor of the Zagreb Symphony Orchestra from 1975. Recordings include music by Shostakovich and Hindemith.

Horwood, William (died 1484) English composer. He became master of the choristers at Lincoln Cathedral in 1477. His music, consisting of Latin antiphons and a Magnificat, is included in the Eton Choirbook; a fragmentary *Kyrie* has also survived.

Hothby, John (c. 1410–1487) English Carmelite, music scholar, composer, and doctor of theology. He graduated at Oxford and lectured there in 1435. He probably travelled in Spain, France, and Germany, and settled in Florence around 1440; he possibly also lived in Ferrara. He was called Giovanni Ottobi in Italy, and was at Lucca from c. 1468 to 1486. He taught there, but was recalled to England by Henry VII. He wrote a number of theoretical treatises. Some of his sacred and secular compositions were entered in the Faenza Codex .

Hotteterre, Jacques-Martin (1674–1763) French flautist, bassoonist, and instrument maker. He came from a family of woodwind instrument makers and composers responsible for developing the orchestral Baroque flute and bassoon from folk antecedents. A respected performer and teacher, he wrote a tutor for the transverse flute and composed trio sonatas and suites for flute and bassoon.

Developments of the oboe from the shawm, the bassoon from the curtal, and the transverse flute from the cylindrical flute are often credited to members of the Hotteterre family.

Jacques Hotteterre called himself *Le Romain* after an early visit to Italy. From 1708 at the latest he was a bassoonist in the Grands Hautbois and was a flautist in the service of the king. His book *Principes de la flûte traversière* 1707 was the first such treatise to be published; it was followed by *L'art de préluder sur la flûte traversière* and *Méthode pour la musette* 1737.

House of the Dead/From the, Z Mrtvého Domu opera in three acts by Janáček (libretto by the composer, after Dostoevsky), produced Brno, 12 April 1930. Various prisoners in a Siberian gulag recall their earlier lives. The opera is framed by the incarceration and eventual release of the political prisoner, Alexandr.

Housman, A(lfred) E(dward) (1859–1936) English poet and Latin scholar. His poems from *A Shropshire Lad* and *Last Poems* were set to music by many composers, including Barber, Butterworth, Gurney, Ireland, Moeran, C W Orr, Somervell, and Vaughan Williams.

Hovhaness, Alan (1911–) US composer. Much of his work is influenced by Indian and other oriental music. A prolific composer, he destroyed a great deal of his work in 1940.

He studied piano with Heinrich Gebhard and composition with Converse and Martinů.

Works include: ten operas; 63 symphonies (1939–88), *And God Created Whales* (1970) including taped part for humpbacked whale, two *Armenian Rhapsodies* for strings, 23 concertos (1936–80) including *Elibris* for flute and strings; *Lousadzak* for piano and strings; concerto for trumpet and strings; *Sosi* for violin piano, percussion, and strings; *Arekeval* for orchestra; concerto for orchestra; *Ad Lyram* for orchestra; chamber music including five string quartets (1936–76).

Howard, Samuel (1710–1782) English organist and composer. He was a pupil of Croft at the Chapel Royal and later of Pepusch. He was organist at the churches of St Clement Danes and St Bride. He received a doctorate in music from Cambridge in 1769. He assisted Boyce in compiling his *Cathedral Music*.

Works include: anthems and other church music; pantomimes, *The Amorous Goddess*, or *Harlequin Married* and *Robin Goodfellow*; cantatas and songs.

Howells, Herbert Norman (1892–1983) English composer, organist, and teacher. His works are filled with an 'English' quality, as with those of Elgar and Vaughan Williams.

Often elegiac in expression, as in some of the *Six Pieces for Organ* 1940, much of his music after the mid-1930s reflects his mourning over the death of his son. He wrote choral and chamber music, as well as solo works, both sacred and secular.

Howells studied under Herbert Brewer at Gloucester Cathedral and later under Charles Stanford at the Royal College of Music in London, where he became professor of composition. Later, having been first sub-organist at Salisbury Cathedral, he lived a retired life 1917–20 owing to poor health. He succeeded Holst as music director at St Paul's Girls' School 1936–62, and was professor of music at London University 1952–62. His best-known work is the *Hymnus Paradisi* 1938, written in memory of his son, in which he escapes the influence of Vaughan Williams and other pastoralists.

Works include: CHAMBER clarinet quintet; two organ sonatas; oboe sonata, clarinet sonata; *Lambert's Clavichord* and *Howells' Clavichord* for clavichord; piano pieces; much church music, including *Collegium Regale*, for unaccompanied choir (1944); songs, especially to words by Walter de la Mare.

OTHER *Hymnus Paradisi* for soli, chorus, and orchestra (1938); *Procession, Paradise Rondel*; concerto for strings (1939), two piano concertos (1913, 1924); *Stabat Mater* (1963).

Hoyland, Vic(tor) (1945–) English composer. Works of his have been featured at the Bath, Aldeburgh, and California Contemporary Music Festivals, and he has directed performances of electronic music, including Stockhausen's *Momente* in London, 1994.

He studied at York University with Bernard Rands and Robert Sherlaw-Johnson. In 1993 he was appointed senior lecturer at the Barber Institute, Birmingham.

Works include: *Em* for 24 voices (1970); *Ariel* for voice and ensemble (1975); *Serenade* for 14 players (1979); *Xingu*, music theatre (1979); *Michelangiolo* for baritone and ensemble (1981); *Quartet Movement* (1982); quintet for brass (1985); string quartet (1985); *In Transit* for orchestra (1987) *Of Fantasy, Of Dreams and Ceremonies* for 13 strings (1989); Trio (1990); piano quartet (1990); Chamber Concerto, with piano (1993).

Hubay, Jenö (originally Eugen Huber) (1858–1937) Hungarian violinist and composer. He travelled much, edited and completed some of Vieuxtemps' works, and became violin professor at the Brussels Conservatory in 1882 and at the Budapest

Conservatory in 1886, of which he was director 1919–34.

A pupil of his father Karl Huber, he appeared as a prodigy at the age of 11, but later went to study with Joachim in Berlin.

Works include: the operas *Alienor* (1891), *A Cremonai Hegedüs* (after Coppée's *Luther de Crémone*, 1894), *A Falu Rossza, Karenina Anna* (after Tolstoy, 1915), *Az álarc*, and others; four symphonies; four violin concertos; *Sonate romantique* for violin and piano; many violin pieces, studies.

Huber, Hans (1852–1921) Swiss composer. After attending seminary at Solothurn, he studied music under Carl Munzinger there and later at the Leipzig Conservatory. After teaching in Alsace, he settled at Basel 1877. In 1889 he became professor at the Conservatory there and succeeded Selmar Bagge as its director 1896, retiring 1918.

Works include: the operas *Weltfrühling* (1894), *Kudrun* (1896), *Simplicius* (1912), *Die schöne Bellinde, Frutta di mare* (1918); Masses, cantatas.; nine symphonies (No. 2 on pictures by Böcklin) and other orchestral works *Sommernächte, Serenade, Carneval* and *Römischer Carneval*; four piano concertos, violin concerto; much chamber music; piano music; songs, including Hafiz cycle.

Huber, Klaus (1924–) Swiss composer. His music combines avant-garde techniques with a strong religious awareness.

He studied with Willy Burkhard at the Zurich Conservatory and with Blacher in Berlin. From 1950 he taught violin in Zurich and from 1960 music history at the Lucerne Conservatory.

Works include: cantata for voices and four instruments *Des Engels Anredung an die Seele* (1957); oratorio *Mechthildis* for alto voice and chamber orchestra (1957). *Auf die ruhige Nacht-Zeit* for soprano and chamber group (1958); *Soliloquia* for soloists, chorus, and orchestra; *Sonata da chiesa* for violin and organ, *Concerto per la Camerata* (1955), *Tempora*, violin concerto (1970); *Jot, oder Wann kommt der Herr Züruck* opera (1973); *Turnus* for orchestra and tape (1974); *Litania instrumentalis* for orchestra (1975); *Von Zeit zu Zeit*, string quartet (1985); *Protuberanzen* for orchestra (1986); *Spes contra spem* for voice, narrator, and orchestra (1988).

Hughes, Anselm (actually Humphrey Vaughan) (1889–1974) English music scholar and Anglican Benedictine, Prior of Nashdom Abbey. He was a member of the Editorial Board of the *New Oxford History of Music*, editor of volume ii and joint editor of volume iii.

Hughes, Gervase (1905–) English composer. He studied at Oxford, and in 1926 joined the music staff of the British National Opera Company; he later conducted at various theatres. In 1933 he left the music profession, but after World War II took to composing again. He wrote books on Sullivan (1960) and Dvořák (1967).

Works include: the opera *Imogen's Choice*, operettas *Castle Creevy* and *Venetian Fantasy*; symphony in F minor, *Overture for a Musical Comedy* for orchestra; piano music, songs.

Hugh the Drover, or Love in the Stocks opera by Vaughan Williams (libretto by Harold Child), produced London, RCM, 4 July 1924. Itinerant Hugh wins Mary in a boxing contest and both are released from the stocks to lead a wandering life.

Hugo, Victor (1802–1885) French poet, novelist and dramatist. See Balfe (◊*Armourer of Nantes, The*), Franz ◊Liszt (*Ce qu'on entend ...*); César ◊Cui (*Angelo*); Aleksandr ◊Dargomizhsky (*Esmeralda* and *Notre-Dame de Paris*); Léo ◊Delibes (*Le Roi s'amuse*); César Franck (◊*Djinns*); Verdi (◊*Ernani*); Campana, Dargomizhsky (◊*Esmeralda*); Gabriel ◊Fauré (songs); Amilcare Ponchielli (◊*Gioconda, La*; Mercadante (◊*Giuramento, Il*; Donizetti (◊*Lucrezia Borgia*); Carlos Gomes (◊*Maria Tudor*; Franz Liszt (◊*Mazeppa*); F Schmidt (◊*Notre Dame*); Carlo Pedrotti (*Marion Delorme*); Amilcare ◊Ponchielli (ditto); Verdi (◊*Rigoletto*); Glover, Marchetti, and Mendelssohn (◊*Ruy Blas*); Wagner-Régeny (*Der Günstling*).

Huguenots, Les opera by Meyerbeer (libretto by Scribe and Emile Deschamps), produced Paris, Opéra, 29 February 1836. Amorous conflict set against 16th-century religious massacres.

Hulda opera by César Franck (libretto by C Grandmougin, based on a play by Bjørnson), not performed in Franck's lifetime; produced Monte Carlo, 8 March 1894. In 11th-century Norway, Hulda seeks revenge on Aslak and his clan, who killed her family. All end up dead.

Humfrey, Pelham (1647–1674) English composer. At the Restoration in 1660 he entered the re-established Chapel Royal in London under Henry Cooke, joined John Blow and William Turner in the composition of the so-called 'club anthem', and was sent abroad for study by Charles II in 1664. On his return from France and Italy in 1667 he became a Gentleman of the Chapel Royal, where in

1672 he succeeded Cooke as Master of the Children.

Works include: music to Shakespeare's *Tempest* (1674), Dryden's *Conquest of Granada* and *The Indian Emperor*, Crowne's *History of Charles VIII*, and Wycherley's *Love in a Wood*; anthems; odes, sacred songs, airs for one and two voices.

Hummel, Ferdinand (1855–1928) German pianist, harpist, and composer. After playing piano and harp in public as a child, he studied at Kullak's Conservatory in Berlin and later had a success with realistic operas.

Works include: the operas *Mara* (1893), *Angla* (1894), *Ein treuer Schelm* (1894), *Assarpai*, *Sophie von Brabant* (1899), *Die Beichte* (1899), *Die Gefilde der Seligen*; incidental music for 14 plays by Wildenbruch and others; symphony, overture; piano concerto, fantasy for harp and orchestra; choral works; chamber music; piano pieces.

Hummel, Johann Nepomuk (1778–1837) Austrian pianist and composer. Following in the steps of Mozart (his teacher), his melodies are graceful if somewhat overly symmetrical and 'square'. He was known as a conservative in his lifetime, clinging to a decaying tradition in the face of growing Romanticism. In ꞌaddition to his keyboard works, which include seven concertos, he wrote choral and chamber works and operas.

He learnt music at first from his father, the conductor Joseph Hummel, who had gone to Vienna in 1785 as conductor of the Theater auf der Wieden. By that time Johann was already a brilliant pianist and Mozart took him as a pupil for two years. In 1787 he went on tour in Germany, Holland, Scotland, and England and had further lessons from Clementi in London, where he stayed until 1792. In 1793 he was back in Vienna, studying composition with Albrechtsberger, Haydn, and Salieri. In 1803 he visited Russia and was music director to Prince Esterházy 1804–11. In 1816–19 he held a similar post at the court of Württemberg at Stuttgart and was at the court of Weimar 1819–22 and from 1833 to his death, undertaking extensive concert tours in between and spending much time in London. He was a friend of Beethoven and was the original dedicatee of Schubert's last three piano sonatas. He married the singer Elisabeth Röckl (1793–1883).

Works include: the operas *Die Rückfahrt des Kaisers* (1814) and *Mathilde von Guise* (1810); ballets *Hélène et Paris* (1807), *Das belebte Gemälde*, *Sappho*; pantomime *Der Zauberring* (1811), incidental music to Grillparzer's *Die Ahnfrau*; Masses and other church music; seven piano concertos; trumpet concerto (1803), chamber music; sonatas for piano with another instrument; piano sonatas, rondos, variations.

humoresque 19th-century French and English title (German *Humoreske*) for a short instrumental piece characterized by a lively and capricious nature. Famous examples include humoresques for piano by Schumann 1839 and Dvořák 1894.

Humperdinck, Engelbert (1854–1921) German composer. He studied in Cologne and Munich and assisted Richard Wagner in the preparation of *Parsifal* at Bayreuth in 1882. He wrote the musical fairy operas *Hänsel und Gretel* 1893, and *Königskinder/King's Children* 1910.

He was born at Siegburg. He studied under F Hiller at the Cologne Conservatory and later with F Lachner and Rheinberger at Munich. In 1879 he met Wagner in Italy and acted as his assistant at Bayreuth 1881–82. Later he travelled in France, Italy, and Spain and taught at the Barcelona Conservatory 1885–87. In 1890–96 he taught at the Hoch Conservatory at Frankfurt and was for a time music critic of the newspaper *Frankfurter Zeitung*. His enduring success, *Hänsel und Gretel*, was premiered at Weimar in 1893 under Richard Strauss. In 1900 he became director of the Meisterschule for composition in Berlin.

Works include: the operas *Hänsel und Gretel* (1893), *Dornröschen* (1902), *Die Heirat wider Willen* (1905), *Königskinder* (1910), *Die Marketenderin*, *Gaudeamus*; play with music *Königskinder* (an earlier version of the opera); spectacular pantomime *The Miracle*; incidental music to Shakespeare's *Merchant of Venice* (1905), *Winter's Tale* (1906), *The Tempest* (1906), and *Twelfth Night*, Maeterlinck's *The Blue Bird* (1912), Aristophanes' *Lysistrata*; choral works *Das Glück von Edenhall* (Uhland), *Die Wallfahrt nach Kevlaar* (Heine); *Humoreske* and *Maurische Rhapsodie* for orchestra; part songs, songs.

Humphries, John (c. 1707–c. 1740) English composer. He published six solos for violin and bass and two sets of concertos. He may be the J S Humphries who published a set of sonatas for two violins in about 1733.

Hungarian Sketches work for orchestra by Bartók, arranged from piano pieces including *Four Dirges* and *Three Burlesques*, 1931; first performed Budapest, 26 November 1934. Movements are titled *An evening in the village,*

Bear dance, Melody, Slightly tipsy, and *Swineherd's Dance.*

Hunnenschlacht/Battle of the Huns symphonic poem by Liszt inspired by Kaulbach's fresco, composed 1857; first performed Weimar, 29 December 1857.

'Hunt' Quartet the familiar nickname of Mozart's B♭ major string quartet, K458, because the opening suggests hunting horns.

Hunyady László opera by Erkel (libretto by B Egressy), produced Budapest, 27 January 1844. The chief Hungarian national opera. After surviving one plot against him, politician László is imprisoned by the palatine Gara, the father of László's fiancée Mária, who promises his daughter to the king in exchange for László's death. László survives three blows of the executioner's sword, but the fourth kills him.

Huon de Bordeaux medieval French romance. See ◊*Oberon, König der Elfen* (Wranitzky) and ◊*Oberon, or The Elf King's Oath* (Weber).

hurdy-gurdy musical instrument, usually with six strings, resembling a violin in tone but using a form of keyboard to play a melody on the top string, while drone strings provide a continuous harmony. An inbuilt wheel, turned by a handle, sets the strings vibrating.

Hurlstone, William (Yeates) (1876–1906) English pianist and composer. He studied at the Royal College of Music in London, having already published waltzes for piano at the age of nine. He was professor of counterpoint at the Royal College of Music from 1905 to his early death.

Works include: Fantasy-Variations on a Swedish Air and suite *The Magic Mirror* for orchestra (1896); piano concerto (1896); string quartet in E minor, piano and wind quintet, piano quartet, Fantasy string quartet (1906); sonatas for violin and piano, cello and piano, bassoon and piano, suite for clarinet and piano.

Husa, Karel (1921–) Czech-born US composer and conductor. He studied at Prague Conservatory and with Boulanger and Honegger in Paris. He emigrated to the USA in 1954, and was professor Cornell University from 1961. He has been influenced by Czech folk music, neoclassicism, and serialism.

Works include: Sinfonietta (1947), *Trois Fresques* (1949), Divertimento for strings (1949), Symphony (1954), *Fantasies* (1957), Mosaïques (1961), Concerto for brass quintet and orchestra (1970), trumpet concerto (1974), Monodrama (1976), *The Trojan Women*, ballet for orchestra (1981); *Symphonic Suite* (1984), Concerto for Orchestra (1980), concertos for organ, trumpet, and cello (1987–88); three string quartets (1948–68); 12 *Moravian Songs*; Variations for piano quintet (1984).

Husitská concert overture by Dvořák, op. 67, composed 1883, first performed Prague, reopening of the National Theatre, 13 November 1883. Based on the 10th-century St Vaclav chorale and the 15th-century Hussite hymn.

Huston, Scott (1916–) US composer. He studied with Howard Hanson at the Eastman School and taught at the Cincinnati Conservatory 1952–88. His works include opera *Blind Girl* (New York 1984), six symphonies (No. 6, *The Human Condition*, 1982), *Sounds of the Courtesans* for voice and ensemble (1985), and *The Unpredictable Pendulum of Temperaments*, for dancers and ensemble (1988).

hymn song in praise of a deity. Examples include Akhenaton's hymn to the Aton in ancient Egypt, the ancient Greek Orphic hymns, Old Testament psalms, extracts from the New Testament (such as the 'Ave Maria'), and hymns by the British writers John Bunyan ('Who would true valour see') and Charles Wesley ('Hark! the herald angels sing'). The earliest sources of modern hymn melodies can be traced to the 11th and 12th centuries, and the earliest polyphonic settings date from the late 14th century. Gospel music and carols are forms of Christian hymn singing.

During the period between the Reformation and 1822, no singing was allowed in services of the Established Church apart from the reciting of the psalms. The Free Churches, however, included hyms singing; the most important collection was *Collected Hymns for the Use of People Called Methodists* 1780, and these hymns were sung in Established Churches from 1822. Perhaps the most famous collection of hymns in the English language is *Hymns Ancient and Modern* 1860, which included both Methodist hymns and many new hymns by members of the Oxford Movement, including J M Neale and John Henry Newman.

Notable Christian hymn writers include Reginald Heber (1783–1826) ('From Greenland's icy mountains'), Henry Francis Lyte (1793–1847) ('Abide with me'), John S B Monsell (1811–1875) ('Fight the good fight'), and Sabine Baring-Gould (1834–1924) ('Onward Christian soldiers'). William Blake's poem 'Jerusalem' was set to music by Hubert

Parry. Vaughan Williams edited the *English Hymnal* 1906, writing new hymns as well as giving new arrangements to many existing ones. Less conventional is Benjamin Britten's 'Hymn to St Cecilia' 1942.

Hymne au Saint Sacrément work for orchestra by Messiaen; composed 1932, first performed Paris, 23 March 1933. First US performance New York, 13 March 1947, conductor Stokowski.

Hymnen/Anthems work for electronic instruments by Stockhausen, which reprocesses a selection of the world's national anthems; composed 1966, first performed Cologne, 30 November 1967. Also in versions with added soloists and, shorter, with orchestra.

Hymn of Jesus, The work by Holst for three choruses and orchestra, op. 37 (text Holst's translated from the Apocryphal Acts of St John); composed 1917 and dedicated to Vaughan Williams, first performed London, 25 March 1920.

Hymn of Praise/Lobgesang Mendelssohn's symphonic cantata, op. 52, in which three movements of a symphony precede the choral portion; produced Leipzig, St Thomas's Church, 25 June 1840; in English, Birmingham Festival, 23 September 1840.

Hymn of the Nations (Verdi). See ◊*Inno delle nazioni.*

Hymnus Amoris/Hymn of Love work by Nielsen for soloists, adult and children's choruses, and orchestra (text in Danish by A Olrik, in Latin by J L Heiberg); composed 1896, first performed Copenhagen, 27 April 1897, conductor Nielsen.

Hyperprism work by Edgard Varèse for wind and percussion; first performed New York, 4 March 1923.

I

Iberia four sets of piano pieces by I Albéniz, representing different parts of Spain, composed at various times before 1909; I. *Evocación, El Puerto, Fête-Dieu à Séville*; II. *Triana, Almeria, Rondeña* III. *El Albaicin, El Polo, Lavapiés*; IV. *Málaga, Jérez, Eritaña*.

Ibéria (Debussy). See ◊*Images pour Orchestre*.

Ibert, Jacques François Antoine (1890–1962) French composer. Although writing in a variety of genres and styles, his music is generally considered light, due in large part to his seven often witty operas. However, his music reflects its subject matter: in his ◊symphonic poem *La Ballade de la geôle de Reading* (1922) he captures the horror of Oscar Wilde's poem, while in his Flute Concerto 1934 he involves the full technical range of the solo instrument.

He studied at the Paris Conservatory and won the Prix de Rome in 1919. He became director of the French Academy in Rome in 1937 and returned there after World War II. From 1955 to 1957 he was director of the Opéra-Comique in Paris.

Works include: STAGE seven operas, two ballets, and contribution to *L'Eventail de Jeanne*; incidental music to Labiche's *Le Chapeau de paille d'Italie* and other plays; film music including *Don Quichotte*.

ORCHESTRAL suites *Escales* (1992) and *Paris, Symphonie Concertante* for oboe and strings (1949), *Divertissement* for chamber orchestra (1930); concertos for piano, for saxophone, and for cello and wind.

Ice Break, The opera by Tippett (libretto by composer), produced London, Covent Garden, 7 July 1977, conductor C Davis. Soviet dissident Juri joins his wife Nadia and son Juri in the USA, Nadia dies, father and son fall out, and son is injured in a race riot. Father and son are reconciled in the end.

Ideale, Die/The Ideals symphonic poem by Liszt, based on a poem by Schiller, composed 1857; first performed Weimar, 5 September 1857 at the unveiling of the Goethe-Schiller monument.

idée fixe Berlioz's term for a theme (in the *Fantastic Symphony*) which recurs in varying forms in the course of a composition as an allusion to some definite idea.

idiophone one of the four main classes of musical instruments used in the original ◊Sachs-Hornbostel system, the others being ◊aerophone, ◊membranophone, and ◊chordophone. In instruments which are idiophones, the sound emanates from the vibration of 'the substance of the instrument itself'. Thus, bells and gongs are included, as are castanets and glass harmonicas.

Idiot, Der ballet-pantomime by Henze (scenario by I Bachmann after Dostoevsky), produced Berlin, 1 September 1952.

Idoménée/Idomeneus opera by Campra (libretto by A Danchet), produced Paris, Opéra, 12 January 1712.

Idomeneo, rè di Creta, ossia Ilia ed Idamante/Idomeneus, King of Crete, or Ilia and Idamantes opera by Mozart (libretto by G B Varesco, based on the French libretto by A Danchet), produced Munich, 29 January 1781. Not given at Covent Garden, London, until 1978; New York Metropolitan Opera 1982. Returning Cretan king must sacrifice his son to fulfil his promise to the gods.

Idyll work for string orchestra in seven movements by Janáček; 1878, first performed Brno, 15 December 1878.

Idyll: Once I passed through a populous city work by Delius for soprano, baritone, and orchestra (text from Walt Whitman); composed 1930–32, with reworkings from the then unperformed opera *Margot-la-Rouge*, 1901–02; first performed London, 3 October 1933, conductor Wood. Delius's last work.

Ifigenia in Aulide/Iphigenia in Aulis opera by Caldara (libretto by A Zeno), produced Vienna, 4 November 1718.
Opera by Cherubini (libretto by F Moretti), Turin, Teatro Regio, 12 January 1788.
Opera by Graun (libretto by L de Villati, after Racine's *Iphigénie en Aulide*), produced Berlin, Royal Opera, 13 December 1748. Frederick II of Prussia probably collaborated.
Opera by Zingarelli (libretto by F Moretti), produced Milan, La Scala, 27 January 1787. (All libretti based ultimately on Euripides.)

Ifigenia in Tauride/Iphigenia in Tauris opera by Galuppi (libretto by M Coltellini, based on Euripides), produced St Petersburg, at court, 2 May 1768.
Opera by Traetta (libretto ditto), produced Vienna, Schönbrunn Palace, at court, 4 October 1763.
See ◊*Iphigénie en Tauride* for plot synopsis.

Ifigenia, L' opera by Jommelli (libretto by M Verazi), produced Rome, Teatro Argentina, 9 February 1751.

Île de Merlin, L', ou Le Monde renversé/Merlin's Island or the World Upside-down opera by Gluck (libretto by L Anseaume), produced Vienna, Schönbrunn Palace, at court, 3 October 1758. Pierrot and Scapin are rewarded with love and happiness on miraculous island, courting Merlin's nieces Argentine and Diamantine.

Illica, Luigi (1857–1919) Italian playwright and librettist. He is best known for his libretti for Puccini's *Manon Lescaut*, *La Bohème* (with G Giacosa), *Tosca*, and *Madama Butterfly*.
The first of his 88 libretti was for Smareglia's *Il vassallo di Szigeth* (produced Vienna, 1889); he also collaborated with Catalani, Giordano, Mascagni, and D'Erlanger.

Illuminations, Les song cycle by Britten for high voice and strings (text nine prose poems by A Rimbaud, 1872–73); composed 1938–39, first performed London, 30 January 1940.

Images two sets of piano pieces by Debussy: first series composed 1905, *Reflets dans l'eau*, *Hommage à Rameau*, *Mouvement*, first perfomed Paris, 3 March 1906; second series,

composed 1907, *Cloches à travers les feuilles*, *Et la lune descend sur le temple qui fut*, *Poissons d'or*, first performed Paris, 21 February 1908.

Images pour Orchestre three symphonic pieces by Debussy: *Gigues* (originally *Gigues tristes*), composed 1906–11; *Rondes de printemps*, composed 1909; *Ibéria (Par les rues et par les chemins*, *Les Parfums de la nuit*, and *Le Matin d'un jour de fête*), finished 1908. *Ibéria* first performed Paris, 20 February 1910, conductor Pierné; first performed three pieces Paris, 26 January 1913, conductor Pierné.

Imbrie, Andrew (Welsh) (1921–) US composer and pianist. He studied with Sessions and at the University of California, at Berkeley; he was professor there from 1960. He writes in standard forms, with 12-note technique.
  Works include: three symphonies (1966–70), concertos for violin (1954), cello (1972), piano (1973, 1974) and flute (1977); five string quartets (1942–87), cello sonata (1969); operas *Christmas in Peebles Town* (1964) and *Angle of Repose* (1976); Requiem for soprano, chorus and orchestra (1984).

Imeneo/Hymeneus opera by Handel (libretto adapted from S Stampiglia), composed 1738, produced Lincoln's Inn Fields, London, 22 November 1740. Handel's penultimate opera. Athenian Rosmene has promised her hand to Tirinto, but marries Imeneo, who has rescued her from pirates. The moral: gratitude and reason should triumph over the passions.

imitation a ◊contrapuntal device in which a theme or motif is repeated in different vocal or instrumental parts. The strictest form of imitation is the ◊canon, in which every voice has, in turn, exactly the same notes and rhythms as the one before it. In a ◊fugue the subject (principal melody) is treated imitatively, before a greater degree of contrapuntal freedom occurs in a non-thematic episode (a passage linking appearances of the subject). The use of imitation in composition can be traced back to early forms of ◊polyphony from about 1200.

Immortal Hour, The opera by Boughton (libretto by composer, adapted from plays and poems by Fiona Macleod), produced Glastonbury, 26 August 1914. King Eochaidh falls in love with fairy princess Etain, who cannot remember her true identity. She is later reclaimed by Midir; the Lord of Shadows mercifully kills Eochaidh so that he will not suffer.

imperfect cadence see ◊half-close.

Impériale, L' nickname of Haydn's symphony no. 53 in D major, composed c. 1775.

Impresario in angustie, L'/The Impressario in Distress opera by Cimarosa (libretto by G M Diodati, similar to that of Mozart's *Schauspieldirektor*), produced Naples, Teatro Nuovo, October 1786.

Impresario, The (Mozart). See ◊*Schauspieldirektor.*

impressionism a style of composition emphasizing instrumental colour and texture. The term was first applied to the music of Claude Debussy.

impromptu a 19th-century character piece in the style of an improvisation. Composers of piano impromptus include Schubert and Chopin.

improvisation a principal means of artistic expression among oral cultures, including popular music and jazz in the West. It is based on standard models, including modes, ◊raga, or scales of specific significance, and on standard rhythms, or familiar melodies combining modal and rhythmic components.

A composer/performer creates a fresh and personal interpretation of a model at each performance, one showing understanding of the emotional history of the original, and bringing an ingenious artistry to bear on expression and decoration. Successful improvisation relies on the awareness of an audience, knowing the prototype, and freely responding to refinements of artistic variation. Organists are taught improvisation as a technique, and improvisation was also a principal technique of silent film accompaniment.

Improvisation sur Mallarmé two works by P Boulez after Stéphane Mallarmé: no. 1 for soprano, harp, tubular bells, vibraphone and four percussion; composed 1957, first performed Hamburg, 13 January 1958, conductor Rosbaud. Also for soprano and orchestra, first performed Donaueschingen, 20 October 1962, conductor Boulez. No. 2, same forces as 1. i, with piano; composed 1957, first performed 13 January 1958.

incalzando (Italian 'persuading, urging forward') in musical direction, accelerating the pace.

incidental music accompanying music to stage or film drama that, in addition to setting a mood (see ◊background music), is also part of the action, as in Thomas ◊Arne's music (including songs) for the stage, music for ◊masques, and so on.

Incognita opera by Wellesz (libretto by E Mackenzie, on Congreve's story), produced Oxford, 5 December 1951. Amorous intrigues and mistaken identities.

Incontro Improvviso, L'/The Unforeseen Meeting opera by Haydn (libretto by K Friberth, translated into Italian from Dancourt's *La Rencontre imprévue*, composed by Gluck), produced Eszterháza, 29 August 1775. Prince Ali and Princess Rezia were once lovers, but were captured by pirates and separated. Rezia, now the favourite of the Egyptian sultan, escapes with newly found Ali, thanks to the help of slave Osmin.

Incoronazione di Poppea, L'/The Coronation of Poppaea opera by Monteverdi (libretto by Busenello, based on Tacitus), produced Venice, Teatro Saints Giovanni e Paolo, autumn 1643. Modern editions by Westrup (first British production, Oxford 1927), Krenek, d'Indy, Malipiero, Ghedini, Leppard, Norrington, Harnoncourt and Curtis. It was the first opera not to be based on a mythical or religious theme. Poppea defeats her rivals and weds Nero.

Indes galantes, Les/Love in the Indies opera-ballet by Rameau (libretto by L Fuzelier), produced Paris, Opéra, 23 August 1735. The four entrées are *Le turc généreux, Les Incas du Pérou, Les fleurs, Les sauvages.* Revived New York, 1961; London, 1972.

indeterminacy the absence of specific instruction concerning a significant element of a composition. A mobile piece is unspecific in terms of the order of sections; a graphic score is indeterminate in notation or timing. All music is indeterminate to some degree, since no two live performances can be totally alike.

Indeterminacy as an aesthetic goal of the avant garde around 1950–70 aims, by stripping away the means of achieving an exact performance, to re-establish extemporization as an element of virtuosity, and to provoke new discoveries. With the aid of multichannel tape recording, pop musicians in the 1970s developed an art of composing by experiment from taped initial ideas. Composers of indeterminate music include ◊Berio, ◊Stockhausen, and the Polish composer Roman Haubenstock-Ramati (1919–). After 1970, indeterminacy became a music education cause, aimed at releasing repressed creativity.

India, Sigismondo d' (c. 1582–1629) Italian composer. His highly chromatic madrigals have been valued as second only to those of ◊Monteverdi.

He left his native Sicily to work as director of music at the Turin court of the Duke of Savoy 1611–23. His madrigal collections were published in eight books 1606–24 at Milan and Venice. In 1625 his sacred drama *Sant' Eustachio* was produced in Cardinal Maurizio's palace at Rome. The following year he moved to Modena. Other important influences on his style came from Luca Marenzio and the chromaticism of Gesualdo.

Indianische Fantasie work by Busoni for piano and orchestra op. 44, based on Native American themes (Busoni was professor at New England Conservatory 1891–94); composed 1913, first performed Berlin, 12 March 1914.

Indian music classical musical culture represented in north India, Pakistan, Nepal, and Bangladesh by the Hindustani tradition, and in south India and Sri Lanka by the Karnatic tradition. An oral culture of great antiquity, allied to Muslim traditions of the Middle East and Central Asia, it resembles the medieval European troubadour tradition of composer-performer, being an art of skilful extemporization in a given mood (rasa), selecting from a range of melody prototypes (ragas) and rhythmic formulae (talas), understood in the same way as in the West 'blues' defines a mood, a scale, and a form, and 'boogie-woogie' an associated rhythm.

Indian music is geared to the time of day, and a composition/performance is not fixed in duration. An ensemble consists of a melody section, featuring voice, sitar, sarod, surbahar, violins, shrill reed woodwinds, or harmonium, solo or in combination; a drone section featuring the vina or tambura, providing a resonant harmonic ground; and a rhythm section of high and low tuned hand drums. The music has a natural buoyancy, the melody effortlessly rising, in contrast to the tonal gravitational pull exerted in European tonal music. The sounds of Indian music are rich in high frequencies, giving an impression of luminous radiance. Popular awareness of Indian music in the West increased after world tours since the 1950s by virtuosos Ravi Shankar (sitar) and Ali Akhbar Khan (sarod). In Britain, a tradition of popular music thrives among expatriate communities and in schools.

Indian Queen, The play by Dryden and Robert Howard, produced 1664; adapted as a semiopera with music by Henry and Daniel Purcell, produced London, Drury Lane Theatre, 1695. Mexican Queen Zempoalla fights invading Peruvian forces led by Montezuma.

He discovers she has overthrown the legitimate queen, who is revealed to be Montezuma's long-lost mother.

Indigo und die vierzig Räuber/Indigo and the Forty Robbers operetta by J Strauss, junior (libretto by M Steiner), produced Vienna, Theater an der Wien, 10 February 1871. Strauss's first operetta.

Indy, (Paul Marie Théodore) Vincent d' **(1851–1931)** French composer. He studied under César Franck, and was one of the founders of the *Schola Cantorum*. His works include operas (*Fervaal* 1897), symphonies, tone poems (*Istar* 1896), and chamber music.

Although born in Paris, he belonged to a noble family of the Ardèche district in the Vivarais. His mother died at his birth and he was brought up by his paternal grandmother, a good musician. At the age of 11 he was sent to Louis Diémer for the piano and Albert Lavignac for theory, and later studied piano under Jean Marmontel. In 1870 he published his first works and served in the defence of Paris against the Prussian army. To please his family he studied law, but was determined to be a musician and went for advice to Franck, who offered to teach him. He also joined Edouard Colonne's orchestra as a timpanist to gain experience. Jules Pasdeloup gave the first performance of one of his works, the overture to Schiller's *Piccolomini*, afterwards part of his *Wallenstein* trilogy.

Next to Franck he admired Liszt, with whom he spent two months at Weimar in 1873, and Wagner, whose first *Ring* cycle he attended at Bayreuth in 1876. He helped the conductor Lamoureux introduce Wagner's music to Paris (*Lohengrin*, 1887) and revived works by Rameau, Gluck, and Monteverdi (*Poppea* in his own edition). In 1894 he joined Charles Bordes, together with Guilmant, in founding the *Schola Cantorum*; he taught there until his death and had many pupils of the highest distinction, including Edgard Varese. From 1912 he also directed the orchestral class at the Conservatory.

Works include: STAGE operas *Fervaal* (1897), *L'Etranger*.

ORCHESTRAL symphonic variations *Istar* (1896), *Jour d'été à la montagne* (1905); *Symphonie sur un chant montagnard français* (*Symphonie cévenole*) for piano and orchestra (1886).

CHAMBER three string quartets (1890, 1897, 1929), string sextet and piano quintet (1924), trios for piano, violin, and cello, suite for trumpet, two flutes and string quartet; sonata for cello and piano.

PIANO AND SONGS 18 op. nos. of piano works, including sonata in E major, *Thème varié*; 90 *Chansons populaires du Vivarais* arrangements of 12 French folk songs for unaccompanied chorus.

Inextinguishable, The/Det Undslukkelige title of Nielsen's fourth symphony; composed 1915–16, first performed Copenhagen, 1 February 1916, conductor Nielsen.

Inez de Castro opera by Persiani (libretto by S Cammarano), produced Naples, Teatro San Carlo, 28 January 1835. It was written for Malibran.

Infantas, Fernando de las (1534–after 1609) Spanish composer, descendant of the Fernández family of Córdoba. He is known by the name Infantas because one of his ancestors conveyed the infantas Constanza and Isabella to Bayonne, occupied by the English in the 14th century, before their respective marriages to John of Gaunt and Edmund Langley. His compositions attracted the attention of the Bishop of Córdoba, the Archduke Charles of Austria. He settled in Rome around 1559, but took holy orders in 1584 and to Paris; he had returned to Spain by 1608.

Works include: motets, some for special occasions, such as the death of the Emperor Charles V (1558) and the battle of Lepanto (1571), a setting of Psalm xcix.

infinite canon canon contrived to make the end overlap with the beginning, so that it can be repeated to infinity.

Inganno felice, L'/The Happy Deceit opera by Rossini (libretto by G M Foppa), produced Venice, Teatro San Moise, 8 January 1812. Falsely accused of adultery, the abandoned Isabella is reunited with her husband.

Ingegneri, Marc Antonio (c. 1545–1592) Italian composer. He learnt music from V Ruffo at Verona Cathedral and, around 1570 became maestro di cappella at Cremona Cathedral. Monteverdi was his pupil there.

Works include: two books of Masses, three books of motets, one of hymns and eight of madrigals; also 27 responsories for Holy Week (long attributed to Palestrina).

Inghelbrecht, D(ésiré-) E(mile) (1880–1965) French conductor and composer. He conducted many concerts of modern music in Paris, also the Swedish Ballet in Paris and London. He conducted at the Paris Opéra 1945–50 and founded the French National Radio Orchestra in 1934, conducting it until 1944 and again 1951–58.

Works include: the operas *La nuit vénitienne* (after Musset, 1908) and *La chêne et le* *tilleul* (1960); two operettas; ballets *El Greco* (1920) and *Le Diable dans le beffroi* (1921); Requiem; *Cantique des créatures de Saint François* for chorus and orchestra; *Sinfonia breve* (1930); string quartet; sonata for flute and harp; quintet for strings and harp; *Suite Petite-Russienne* and other piano works; *La Nursery* for piano duet (three books); songs.

In Nature's Realm (Dvořák). See ◊*Amid Nature*.

inner part in polyphonic music (see ◊polyphony), the voices (independent parts) whose registers (instrumental or vocal ranges) are neither the highest nor lowest. In a four-voice choir, for example, the alto and tenor sing inner parts, their registers falling between the soprano and bass. In a string quartet usually the second violin and viola are inner parts between the first violin and cello.

innig (German 'inward, intimate, heartfelt') term frequently used by German romantic composers, especially Schumann, where profound feeling is required in performance.

Innocenza giustificata, L'/Innocence Vindicated opera by Gluck (libretto by G Durazzo, with words for the airs by Metastasio), produced Vienna, Burgtheater, 8 December 1755. Julia's innocence proved by divine intervention.

Inno delle nazioni/Hymn of the Nations cantata by Verdi written for the International Exhibition in London, but produced at Her Majesty's Theatre, 24 May 1862. It introduced national airs in contrapuntal combination.

in nomine an instrumental piece of the later 16th century for viols or keyboard, similar to the fancy or fantasia, but based on a plainsong melody used as a *cantus firmus*. The melody is that of 'Gloria tibi Trinitas', an antiphon for Trinity Sunday, which was used by Taverner as the *cantus firmus* of a Mass with the title *Gloria tibi Trinitas*. Part of the *Benedictus* of this Mass, beginning at the words 'In nomine Domini', was arranged as an instrumental piece, and this seems to have suggested to other composers the idea of writing original instrumental pieces on the same *cantus firmus*. The last composer to write *in nomines* was Purcell.

Inori/Adorations work for soloist(s) and orchestra by Stockhausen, first performed Donaueschingen, 20 October 1974.

In questa tomba oscura a collective work, of which only Beethoven's song remains known today. In 1808 composers were invited to set this poem by Giuseppe Carpani, probably at the invitation of Countess Rzewuska in

Vienna. Among the 63 composers who responded were, apart from Beethoven, Asioli, Cherubini, Czerny, Paer, Reichardt, Righini, Salieri, Tomášek, Weigl, and Zingarelli.

Insanguine, Giacomo (1728–1795) Italian composer. He studied at the Conservatorio di Sant' Onofrio at Naples, where he taught from 1767, eventually becoming maestro di cappella. Between 1756 and 1782 he produced 21 operas; other works include Masses and other church music, cantatas, and arias.

instrumentation the art of composing for particular musical instruments in a manner appropriate to their range and sound. ◊Orchestration is similar in meaning, usually referring specifically to instruments in an orchestral setting.

intavolatura ('tablature') a 16th- and 17th-century musical term used for publications issued for keyboard instruments and written on two staves, as distinct from instrumental music printed in score or in separate parts.

Intégrales work for small orchestra and percussion by Varèse; composed 1923, first performed New York, 1 March 1925, conductor Stokowski.

integral serialism a type of ◊serialism pioneered by Boulez and Stockhausen in the early 1950s that brings as many musical elements as possible under serial control. This technique applies not only to pitch, but also to dynamics, duration, and timbre.

intendant manager or director of an opera house or other theatre in Germany, especially one attached to a court in former times.

interdominant musical term used to describe temporary dominants in the keys in which episodes may appear in the course of a composition, other than the dominant of the prescribed key. The same as the German *Zwischendominante*.

interlude piece or passage of music played between two other works or sections. This may occur between scenes of an opera, for example, as in Britten's *Sea Interludes* from *Peter Grimes* 1945. In the 18th century, interludes were played between the verses of a hymn or psalm. In the latter case, the organist often improvised passages and so there are few remaining printed examples. Exceptions include certain organ chorales, such as Bach's *In dulci jubilo*.

intermède musical term; 'interlude, intermezzo'.

intermedii, or *intermezzi* in 15th- and 16th-century Italy, musical or dramatic interludes

played between the acts of a play or during the intervals of a banquet. The musical *intermedii* consisted of instrumental pieces played out of sight of the audience. The dramatic *intermedii* were stage spectacles performed by singers, dancers, and actors in costume. These were broadly similar to the English ◊interlude.

In its combination of music and drama, *intermedii* can be regarded as an important forerunner of opera.

Intermedii were first performed during the intervals of Renaissance plays – the court of 15th-century Ferrara was particularly important in their development. Sometimes the subject matter of the *intermedii* was connected with that of the play, though more often unrelated pastoral scenes with allegorical figures were presented. The Medici court in Florence was also the scene of many of the most lavish entertainments. The most spectacular was that performed in 1589 at the wedding of Christine of Lorraine and Ferdinando de' Medici, for which the music was provided by leading composers, including Marenzio and ◊Caccini.

intermedio see ◊intermezzo.

intermezzo a one-act comic opera, such as Pergolesi's *La Serva Padrona/The Maid as Mistress* 1732; also a short orchestral interlude played between the acts of an opera to denote the passage of time. By extension, an intermezzo can also be a short piece to be played between other more substantial works, such as Brahms's *Three Intermezzos for Piano* 1892.

Intermezzo opera by Richard Strauss (libretto by composer) produced Dresden, 4 November 1924. The material of the libretto is autobiographical. Composer Robert Storch is in trouble when his wife Christine reads a misdirected love letter.

Internationale international revolutionary socialist anthem; composed 1870 and first sung 1888. The words by Eugène Pottier (1816–1887) were written shortly after Napoleon III's surrender to Prussia; the music is by Pierre Degeyter. It was the Soviet national anthem 1917–44.

interpretation the manner in which a performer plays a work. Except in the case of prerecorded electronic music, which excludes the performer altogether, the limitations of notation mean that a composer cannot indicate the most subtle levels of dynamics, expression, articulation, and other details of ◊performance practice. Inevitably the performer is responsible for these, although during some periods it has been the convention for the musician to take greater liberties than during others. For instance, the 18th-century performer had much greater freedom than the 20th-century performer, not only to alter a composer's dynamics and articulation without criticism, but also, to a degree, to change the notes themselves.

interval the pitch difference between two notes, expressed in terms of the diatonic scale, for example a fifth, or as a harmonic ratio, 3:2.

In the Mists, V mlhách, work by Janáček in four movements for piano; composed 1912.

In the South, Alassio concert overture by Elgar, op. 50, composed during a visit to Italy 1903 and published in 1904. First performed London, 16 March 1904, conductor Elgar.

Intimate Letters/Listy důverné subtitle of Janáček's second string quartet, composed 1928 and inspired by his unrequited love for Kamilla Stoesslová, 38 years his junior, and to whom he wrote almost daily letters during the last ten years of his life. First performed Brno, 11 September 1928; one month after Janáček's death.

intonation the means by which a performer maintains correct tuning. Pitch accuracy requires continuous slight adjustments of pitch in those instruments for which it is feasible. For orchestral violins, violas, cellos, and double basses, pitch is adjustable by finger positioning (instruments losing pitch as a result of atmospheric conditions are retuned between movements). Woodwind instruments are of relatively fixed pitch, but a note may 'bend' using a combination of finger and breath technique, or be shifted microtonally by adopting a different fingering. Trumpets are equipped with a tuning slide, controlled by the little finger; horns can be modified in pitch by inserting the left hand into the bell.

intonazione (Italian 'intonation') 16th-century musical term for a prelude, especially one for organ used in church to precede a service.

Into the Labyrinth cantata for tenor and orchestra by Maxwell Davies (text by G Mackay Brown), first performed Kirkwall, Orkney, 22 June 1983.

intrada (Italian, now entrada, 'entrance, entry') musical term; ◊introduction, prelude.

introduction a section preceding the main body of a work. Many symphonies of the 18th century featured a slow introduction (includ-

ing works by Haydn, Mozart, and Beethoven), and this practice is sometimes transferred to quartets and keyboard works, as in Beethoven's *Sonata Pathétique* 1799. The introduction may be related motivically or thematically to the rest of the work, as in the *Pathétique*, or it may be more independent, as in Elgar's *Introduction and Allegro* 1905 for strings.

Introduction and Allegro work for string quartet and string orchestra by Elgar; composed 1904–05, first performed London, 8 March 1905, conductor Elgar.
Title of Ravel's Septet for harp, string quartet, flute and clarinet; composed 1906, first performed Paris, 22 February 1907.

Introit (Latin *introitus*, 'entrance') the first item of the Proper of the Mass, accompanying the entry of the ministers. Originally a complete psalm with antiphon before and after each verse, it was reduced in the Middle Ages to its present form of antiphon, psalm-verse, *Gloria Patri* and repeat of antiphon or ary The antiphon is a freely-composed melody, the psalm being sung to a slightly ornate psalmtone.

invention a term not commonly used by composers, but made famous by Bach in his *15 Inventions* for keyboard 1720. In two parts, each composition is contrapuntal and highly imitative, based upon a short melodic motif or phrase. Bach's so-called 'three-part inventions' were not named as such by the composer, but rather the term 'sinfonia' was used instead (*15 Sinfonias* 1723).

Inventions the title given to Bach's two sets of short keyboard pieces written strictly in two and three parts respectively, and probably designed as technical studies. He called the three-part set 'symphonies', but there is no essential difference in character between them and the two-part inventions.

inversion the mirror image of a melody used in counterpoint; alternatively a chord in which the natural order of notes is rearranged.

A root position triad on C with first and second inversions.

invertible counterpoint see ◊counterpoint.

Invisible City of Kitezh, The Legend of the See ◊*Legend of the Invisible City of Kitezh and Maiden Fevronia*.

Invitation to the Dance (Weber). See ◊*Auf-forderung zum Tanz*.

Iolanta opera in one act by Tchaikovsky (libretto by Modest Tchaikovsky, Tchaikovsky's brother, based on Hertz's play *King René's Daughter*), produced St Petersburg, 18 December 1892. Blind Iolanta's sight is restored in response to amorous interest from Vaudemont.

Iolanthe, or The Peer and the Peri operetta by Sullivan (libretto by W S Gilbert), produced London, Savoy Theatre, 25 November 1882, and New York, Standard Theatre, same date. Phyllis loves Strephon, but his half-fairy parentage and the Lord Chancellor cause problems. Fairy mother Iolanthe intervenes and the couple are united.

Ione, old Italian spelling **Jone** opera by Petrella (libretto by G Peruzzini, based on Bulwer-Lytton's novel *The Last Days of Pompeii*), produced Milan, La Scala, 26 January 1858.

Ionian mode a ◊mode that is equivalent to the major scale. On a piano, it is the scale from C to B using only the white notes.

Ionisation work by Edgard Varèse for 13 percussion, piano, and two sirens; 1931, first performed New York 6 March 1933, conductor Nicolas Slonimsky.

Ipermestra/Hypermnestra opera by Gluck (libretto by Metastasio), produced Venice, Teatro San Giovanni Cristostomo, 21 November 1744. Warned by an oracle, King Danaus orders his daughter to kill her betrothed, Lynceus, on their wedding night. She cannot do it, and instead separates from him. A happy ending after complications.

Iphigénie en Aulide/Iphigenia in Aulis opera by Gluck (libretto by F L L du Roullet, based on Racine and further back on Euripides), produced Paris, Opéra, 19 April 1774. Gluck's first opera for the Paris stage, though not his first French work. Agamemnon must sacrifice his daughter, Iphigénie, in order to gain favourable winds to sail for Troy. At the last moment she is saved by the goddess Diana, who leaves a deer in her place.

Iphigénie en Tauride/Iphigenia in Tauris opera by Desmarets and Campra (libretto by J F Duché and A Danchet), produced Paris. Opéra, 6 May 1704.

Opera by Gluck (libretto by N F Guillard), produced Paris, Opéra, 18 May 1779.

Opera by Piccinni (libretto by A C Dubreuil), produced Paris, Opéra, 23 January 1781.

A sequel to *Iphigénie en Aulide*; Iphigénie has been transported to Tauris from the sacrificial altar by Diana. Orestes, Iphigénie's brother, arrives in the barbaric kingdom to return a statue of Diana to Greece. After being captured, a happy ending.

(All libretti based on Euripides.)

See also ◊*Ifigenia, L'*.

Ippolito ed Aricia/Hippolytus and Aricia opera by Traetta (libretto by C I Frugoni, translated from S J de Pellegrin's libretto for Rameau's *Hippolyte et Aricie*, 1733), produced Parma, 9 May 1759.

Ippolitov-Ivanov, Mikhail Mikhailovich (1859–1935) Russian composer. His compositions show a strong influence from the Caucasus; he wrote a book on Georgian folk music, and his symphonic suite *Caucasian Sketches* 1894 is probably his most popular work. He orchestrated the rediscovered St Basil scene from Mussorgsky's *Boris Godunov* 1925 and added three acts to Mussorgsky's unfinished opera *The Marriage* 1931.

He studied under Rimsky-Korsakov at the St Petersburg Conservatory. In 1884 he was appointed conductor of the Imperial Opera at Tiflis, and in 1893 professor at the Moscow Conservatory, of which he was director 1906–22. He composed seven operas, as well as cantatas, choral works, and orchestral, chamber, and instrumental music. His memoirs were published as *Fifty Years of Russian Music* 1934.

Works include: OPERA *Ruth* (1887), *Azra, Assia* (after Turgenev's story, 1900), *Treachery* (1910), *Ole from Norland* (1916), *The Last Barricade*, also completion of Mussorgsky's *Marriage* (1931)

OTHER *Hymn to Labour* for chorus and orchestra (1934), two symphonies, *Caucasian Sketches* (1894), *Iberia, Armenian Rhapsody* (1895), *Mtsyri* (after Lermontov), *From Ossian, Episode from Schubert's Life, Turkish Fragments* (1930), *Musical Scenes from Uzbekistan, The Year 1917, Catalonian Suite*, and other pieces for orchestra; two string quartets; *An Evening in Georgia* for harp and wind instruments; violin and piano sonata; piano and other instrumental pieces; cantatas for chorus and piano; 116 songs.

IRCAM, L'Institut pour la Recherche et Co-ordination Acoustique-Musique research institute founded by the French government as part of the Georges Pompidou Centre in Paris and opened in 1977 under the directorship of Pierre ◊Boulez. IRCAM aims to combine scientific research into acoustics, psychology, and the development of computer applications in music with compositional activity and performance of contemporary works by its body of musicians, the Ensemble InterContemporain. Composers commissioned to work at IRCAM collaborate with computer programmers to produce their works. Notable examples of works produced at IRCAM include *Répons* by Boulez (1981–82), *Mortuos Plango, Vivos Voco* by Jonathan ◊Harvey (1980) and the mime interludes from *The Mask of Orpheus* by Harrison ◊Birtwistle (1986).

Ireland, John Nicholson (1879–1962) English composer. His works include the mystic orchestral prelude *The Forgotten Rite* 1917 and the piano solo *Sarnia* 1941. Benjamin Britten was his pupil.

He was born at Bowdon, Cheshire, and was educated at Leeds Grammar School and at the Royal College of Music, studying under Stanford 1893–1901. Apart from organist's appointments, and his later composition professorship at the Royal College of Music, he devoted himself entirely to creative work. His pupils included Britten, Moeran, and Searle. In 1932 he received an honorary doctorate from Durham University. His music is small scale, and influenced by Debussy and early Stravinsky.

Ireland's first compositions were concerted chamber music and songs. Two violin sonatas followed, and these established his reputation at once. His best-known subsequent works are a pianoforte sonata, a symphonic rhapsody *Mai-Dun* 1921, and a piano concerto 1930. He also wrote a large number of songs, one of the best known being the setting of Masefield's 'Sea Fever'. Several song cycles are important, and all his songs are distinguished by his sensitive choice of words from the finest English poetry, and by the lyrical beauty and sincerity of their music, which is also found in the piano music.

Works include: FILM MUSIC *The Overlanders* (1946–47); *These Things shall be* (John Addington Symonds) for chorus and orchestra (1936–37).

ORCHESTRAL prelude *The Forgotten Rite* (1913), *A London Overture* (1936); *Concertino pastorale* for string orchestra (1939); concerto in E flat for piano and orchestra; *A Downland Suite* for brass band.

CHAMBER two violin and piano sonatas, cello and piano sonata, fantasy-sonata for clarinet and piano; piano sonatina and many shorter pieces such as *Sarnia* (1941); song settings including *Five poems by Thomas Hardy* (1926).

Iris opera by Mascagni (libretto by L Illica), produced Rome, Teatro Costanzi, 22 November 1898. Abducted by Osaka and Kyoto, Iris

is thrown into Kyoto's brothel. She kills herself when her father finds out.

Irische Legende opera by Egk (libretto by composer) after Yeats's drama *The Countess Cathleen*, 1898), produced Salzburg, 17 August 1955, conductor Szell; revised 1970. Benevolent Countess sells her soul to rescue famine-stricken people.

Irish Symphony Stanford's third symphony, in F minor, op. 28, composed 1887, first performed London, 27 June.

Irmelin opera in 3 acts by Delius (libretto by composer), produced Oxford, 4 May 1953, conductor Beecham. Composed 1890–92. Much courted Irmelin is rescued from her suitors by Nils, a prince brought up as a swineherd.

Irrelohe opera by Schreker (libretto by composer), composed 1919–23, produced Cologne, 27 March 1924, conductor Klemperer. Count Henry of Irrelohe rises above the reputation of his rapist father, marrying Eva and defending her against Peter.

Isaac, Henricus (Heinrich) (c. 1450–1517) Flemish composer. He was a prolific composer of songs and instrumental music, and wrote a *Choralis Constantinus* consisting of 58 offices for the whole year; but he is popularly remembered for the song 'Innsbruck ich muss dich lassen', later harmonized by J S Bach. His wide travel is reflected in the various national influences in his music. He was a major contemporary of Josquin Desprez, Jacob Obrecht, and Pierre de La Rue.

Isaac was born at Brabant. In about 1484, when he seems to have been at Innsbruck and in touch with Paul Hofhaimer there, he went via Ferrara to Florence as musician to the Medici family. He sang in the choir at the chapel of San Giovanni at Florence, and was regularly employed at the cathedral from 1485. He visited Rome in 1489, and married Bartolomea Bello, the daughter of a wealthy butcher.

Lorenzo de' Medici died in 1492 and since his successor, Pietro, kept a less lavish household, Isaac accepted an invitation from the Emperor Maximilian, who visited Pisa in 1496, to join the Imperial court, just then about to be transferred from Augsburg to Vienna. He seems to have visited Innsbruck again to be formally appointed and was possibly appointed in Augsburg too. His duties were not arduous, so that he was able to live by turns in Vienna, Innsbruck, Constance (all connected with the court), and Italy. He also spent much time at the court of

Ercole d'Este, Duke of Ferrara, and during his last years he remained at Florence.

Works include: many Masses, about 50 motets, sequences, Lamentation *Oratio Jeremiae*, 58 four-part settings of the offices under the title *Choralis Constantinus*, the first polyphonic cycle of liturgical works for the ecclesiastical year: Webern wrote a dissertation on the *Choralis Constantinus* in 1906; four-part Monodia on the death of Lorenzo de' Medici (words by Poliziano); many German, Italian, French, and Latin songs (including 'Innsbruck, ich muss dich lassen', which may not be his own tune), 58 instrumental pieces in three–five parts, 29 domestic pieces in two–five parts.

Isabeau *leggenda drammatica* by Mascagni (libretto by L Illica), produced Buenos Aires, 2 June 1911, conductor Mascagni. Disobedient Isabeau is condemned by her father, King Raimondo, to ride naked before the populace. The townspeople pity her and do not watch. The only exception, Folco (with whom Isabeau falls in love) is killed.

Isidor of Seville (c. 560–636) philosopher and theologian. He was Archbishop of Seville from 599. His contribution to music theory is contained in book III of his *Etymologiae* (largely a summary of Cassiodorus), and he deals with practical matters of church music in *De Ecclesiasticis Officiis*.

Isis opera by Lully (libretto by Quinault), produced Saint-Germain, 5 January 1677 and first performed Paris, April 1677.

Isle of the Dead, The symphonic poem by Rachmaninov, after a painting by A Böcklin; composed 1907, first performed Moscow, 1 May 1909.

Isola disabitata, L'/The Desert Island opera by Haydn (libretto by Metastasio), produced Eszterháza, 6 December 1779. Shipwrecked sisters Constanza anad Silvia are rescued by husband Germando and lover Enricompany Also settings by Giuseppe Scarlatti (Venice, 1751) and Traetta (Bologna, 1768).

isometric (from Greek 'equally metrical') a manner of writing vocal music in several parts mainly in block chords, that is, in the same rhythm.

isorhythm a form in which a given rhythm cyclically repeats, although the corresponding melody notes may change. It was used in European medieval music, and is still practised in classical Indian music. The composers Berg, Cage, and Messiaen used isorhythmic procedures.

isorhythmic (from Greek 'equally rhythmic') modern term for a method of construction used by composers for polyphonic music in the 14th and 15th centuries. One or more of the parts were arranged in a rhythmic pattern several bars long, which was repeated throughout the piece, sometimes with changes of tempo (indicated by the use of smaller note values, or different mensuration signs).

Isouard, Nicolò (1775–1818) Maltese composer of French descent. Educated at a military academy in Paris, he had to leave France at the Revolution, and after a time in Malta studied music in Palermo and in Naples under Sala and Guglielmi. He made his debut as an opera composer in Florence with *L'avviso ai maritati* in 1794. The following year he was appointed organist to the Order of St John of Malta in Valetta, and later became maestro di cappella there. Leaving Malta in 1799 he settled in Paris, where he produced many operas and also appeared as a pianist.

Works include: over 40 operas, *L'avviso ai maritati*, *Artaserse* (1794), *Le Tonnelier* (1801), *Michel-Ange* (1802), *Cendrillon* (1810), *Le Billet de loterie* (1811), *Joconde, Jeannot et Colin, Aladin ou La Lampe merveilleuse* (1822).; Masses, motets, cantatas, and other vocal works.

Israel in Egypt oratorio by Handel (words from the Bible and the Prayer Book version of the psalms), composed 1738, performed London, King's Theatre, Haymarket, 4 April 1739.

'Israel' Symphony symphony by Bloch, composed 1912–16, first performed New York, 3 May 1916.

Issé opera by Destouches (libretto by A H de la Motte), produced Fontainebleau, at court, 7 October 1679; first Paris performance, Opéra, 30 December 1697. Apollo woos Issé, disguised as shepherd Philemon.

issimo Italian superlative ending denoting an extreme quality, as in *pianissimo* (softest) or *fortissimo* (loudest).

Istar symphonic variations by d'Indy, op. 42, first performed Brussels, 10 January 1897. The work is based on the Babylonian legend of Ishtar's descent into limbo, and illustrates her disrobing at the seven stations of her progress by the devices of presenting the variations first, in diminishing complexity, and stating the theme only at the end, in bare octave unison.

Istel, Edgar (1880–1948) German musicologist. He studied at Munich; composition with Volbach and Thuille, and musicology with

Sandberger. He lived and taught there until 1913, when he went to Berlin as lecturer on music. In 1920 he was in Madrid and later moved to the USA. His books include works on Wagner, Cornelius, Paganini, and especially on various aspects of opera.

istesso tempo, l' (Italian from lo stesso tempo, 'the same pace') a musical direction given where a change is indicated in the time-signature, but the composer wishes the music to continue at the same pace or beat in the new rhythm. The change is thus merely one of metre, not of movement.

Italiana in Algeri, L'/The Italian Girl in Algiers opera by Rossini (libretto by A Anelli), produced Venice, Teatro San Benedetto, 22 May 1813. Captured Isabella outwits amorous Mustafà and is reunited with Lindoro.

Italian Concerto a harpsichord work in three movements by Bach, published (together with the 'French Overture') in the second part of the *Clavierübung* in 1735. The two manuals of the harpsichord are used to reproduce the contrast between *concertino* and *ripieno* characteristic of the *concerto grosso*.

Italian in Londra, L'/The Italian Girl in London opera by Cimarosa (libretto by G Petrosellini), produced Rome, Teatro Valle, 28 December 1778. Livia arrives in London to search for her lover Arespingh, who has abandoned her. Arespingh is torn between his arranged marriage and Livia, whom he still loves. In the end he chooses Livia.

Italian overture see ◊overture.

Italian sixth see ◊augmented sixth chords.

'Italian' Symphony Mendelssohn's fourth symphony, op. 90, in A major and minor, begun in Italy, 1831 and finished in Berlin, 31 March 1833; first performed London, 13 May 1833, conducted by the composer.

Italienisches Liederbuch/Italian Song Book Hugo Wolf's settings of Italian poems in German translated by Paul Heyse, composed (22 nos.) 1890–91 and (24 nos.) 1896.

Ivanhoe opera by Sullivan (libretto by J R Sturgis, based on Scott's novel), produced London, Royal English Opera House (now Palace Theatre), 31 January 1891. Rowena and Rebecca compete for errant knight Ivanhoe.

Ivan le Terrible opera by Bizet (libretto by A Leroy and H Trianon, first offered to Gounod and abandoned by him), composed in 1865 and accepted for production by the Théâtre Lyrique in Paris, but withdrawn by the composer. The first performance (concert)

took place at Mühringen (Württemberg) in 1946. First stage performance Bordeaux, 12 October 1951. Tsar Ivan defeats assassination attempt and marries Princess Marie.

Ivan Susanin opera by Cavos (libretto by Prince A A Shakhovskoy), produced St Petersburg, 31 October 1815. The subject is that on which Glinka's *Life for the Tsar* was based in 1836.
The title given to Glinka's *Life for the Tsar* in Soviet Russia.

Ivan the Terrible (Rimsky-Korsakov) see ◊*Pskovitianka*.

Ives, Charles Edward (1874–1954) US composer. He experimented with ◊atonality, quarter tones, clashing time signatures, and quotations from popular music of the time. He wrote five symphonies, including *Dvorakian Symphony No. 1* 1895–98 and *Holidays Symphony* 1904–13; chamber music, including the *Concord* sonata; and the orchestral works *Three Places in New England* 1903–14 and *The Unanswered Question* 1908.

Much of Ives' music is in a polytonal idiom, and occasionally employs ◊microtones. In addition, he experimented with conflicting rhythms, dissonant harmony and counterpoint, chord clusters, and the spatial presentation of music. He also made frequent use of hymn and folk tunes. He composed in isolation, without much thought for the ease of performer or publisher, earning his living very successfully from his own insurance company. Ives stopped composing around 1920, but it was only after his death that his music was widely played and appreciated.

Born in Danbury, Connecticut, he studied at Yale University under H Parker and D Buck, and wrote his first symphony there 1895–98. He was already impatient with tradition and from an early age he was interested by disparate sounds occurring simultaneously; the occasion when he heard two bands playing different tunes made a lasting impression. He moved to New York in 1898, working as an insurance agent and setting up his own agency in 1907. A second symphony (1900–02) was written in his spare time, and the Third (1904–11) impressed Mahler, then conductor at the New York Metropolitan Opera.

Much of his music was written from 1910, but by 1918 his health was suffering. He gradually retired from business and took to revising earlier works rather than writing new ones. The huge *Concord* sonata was published in 1919, but not performed until 1939. Its first performance (by John Kirkpatrick) was greeted with acclaim, in spite of its complexities. His orchestral music was taken up first by Eugene Goossens at New York in 1927, then by Nicolas Slonimsky. The Third Symphony was premiered at New York under Lou Harrison in 1946 but the Fourth was not performed until 11 years after Ives' death, under Stokowski. Leonard Bernstein was also a successful champion of the symphonies.

Works include: ORCHESTRAL four symphonies: no. 1 in D minor (1896–98), no. 2 (1897–1901), no. 3 (1901–04, for chamber orchestra, *The Camp Meeting*, no. 4 (1910–16); *New England Holidays* (*Washington's Birthday, Decoration Day, Fourth of July, Thanksgiving*; 1904–13); *Three Places in New England* (Orchestral Set no. 1: *The St Gaudens in Boston Common, Putnam's Camp, Redding, Connecticut*, and *The Housatonic* at Stockridge; 1903–14); Orchestral Set no. 2: *An Elegy to our Forefathers, The Rockstrewn Hills Join in the People's Outdoor Meeting*, and *From Hanover Square North at the end of a Tragic Day*; 1909–15); *Central Park in the Dark* (1898–1907); *The Unanswered Question* (1908).

CHORAL *General William Booth Enters into Heaven* for bass, chorus, and orchestra (1914); ten Psalm settings, including *Psalm 90* (1924); *Three Harvest Home Chorales* for chorus, brass, double bass, and organ (1898–1912).

CHAMBER string quartet no. 2 (1907–13); four sonatas for violin and piano (1902–15); *From the Steeples and the Mountains* for brass quintet (1901).

PIANO AND SONGS Piano sonata no. 2 (*Concord, Massachusetts, 1840–1860: Emerson, Hawthorne, The Alcots, Thoreau*; 1909–15); organ music; 114 songs (1884–1921).

Ivrogne corrigé, L'/The Reformed Drunkard opera by Gluck (libretto by L Anseaume on a fable by La Fontaine), produced Vienna, Burgtheater, April 1760. Drunkard Mathurin is reformed by a chorus of demons in disguise. In the process he allows his niece to marry the man of her choice.

J

Jachet (or Jaquet) da Mantova (died 1559)
Flemish singer and composer. He was attached to San Pietro Cathedral at Mantua 1527–58, and wrote Masses, Magnificats, motets, psalms, hymns, and other pieces.

jack the mechanism in the virginal, harpsichord, and similar instruments by which the strings are plucked. In a piano the jack accommodates the fall of the hammer from the string.

Jackson, Francis (1917–) English organist and composer. He studied at Durham University and with Edward Bairstow; he succeeded him as organist at York Minster in 1946. He is well known as a recitalist, most often heard in Vierne and Franck. His own works include a *Te Deum* and *Jubilate* (1964), Symphony in D minor for orchestra, and *Sonata giocosa* for organ (1972).

Jackson, William (1730–1803) English organist and composer. He learnt music as a choirboy in Exeter Cathedral, then studied in London. He became music teacher at Exeter and from 1777 held various appointments at the cathedral there.

Works include: the operas *The Lord of the Manor* (1780) and *The Metamorphosis* (1783); a stage piece *Lycidas* (based on Milton, 1767), Te Deum, services, anthems and other church music; setting of Pope's ode *The Dying Christian*; various vocal pieces and songs; harpsichord sonatas.

Jacob, Gordon (Percival Septimus) (1895–1984) English composer and conductor. An eminent specialist in orchestration, as a composer he was prolific in music always ideally suited to the chosen medium. His works include ballet and film music, two symphonies, three suites, variations and other works for orchestra, concertos for various instruments, and chamber music.

Jacob was born in London. He studied under Charles Stanford and Charles Wood at the Royal College of Music, London, and became professor of orchestration there in 1926.

Works include: the ballets *The Jew in the Bush* and *Uncle Remus* (after J C Harris); music for films; sinfonietta (1942), variations on an air by Purcell and on an original theme for orchestra, *Passacaglia on a Well-known Theme* ('Oranges and Lemons') for orchestra (1931); two symphonies (1929, 1944) and *Denbigh* suite for strings, Divertimento for small orchestra; concertos for piano, violin, viola, oboe, bassoon, and horn; clarinet concerto (1980); suite for military band; quartets for oboe and strings, and clarinet and strings and other chamber music; instrumental pieces.

Jacobin, The opera by Dvořák (libretto by M Cervinková-Riegrová); composed 1887–88, produced Prague, 12 February 1889; revised 1897. Bohuš returns to father's favour after false accusations by cousin Adolf.

Jacobsen, Jens Peter (1847–1885) Danish poet and novelist. For settings, see ◊*Fennimore und Gerda* (Delius); ◊*Gurrelieder* (Schoenberg); Ebbe Hamerik (*Marie Grubbe*).

Jacques, Reginald (1894–1969) English organist and conductor. He studied at Oxford and held various posts there before founding the Bach Choir, London, in 1931; conductor until 1960. He founded the Jacques Orchestra 1936 and gave many wartime concerts. He is well known for performances of the Bach passions with traditional forces and style.

Jacquet, Elizabeth see ◊La Guerre.

Jagd, Die/The Hunt opera by J A Hiller (libretto by C F Weisse, based on J M Sedaine's libretto for Monsigny's *Le Roi et le fermier*), produced Weimar, 29 January 1770. Röschen loves Töffel, but can only marry after her brother, Christal, has married his fiancée, who has been kidnapped by the evil Count. She escapes, and the King arrives to bless the two marriages.

Jakobsleiter, Die/Jacob's Ladder oratorio by Schoenberg; composed 1917–22, unfinished. Scoring completed by Winfried Zillig, first performed Vienna 16 June 1961, conductor Kubelik.

Jaleo Spanish dance in moderate 3–8 time, accompanied by castanets.

Janáček, Leoš (1854–1928) Czech composer. He became director of the Conservatory at Brno 1919 and professor at the Prague Conservatory 1920. His music, highly original and influenced by Moravian folk music, includes arrangements of folk songs, operas (*Jenůfa* 1904, *The Cunning Little Vixen* 1924), and the choral *Glagolitic Mass* 1926.

Janáček was the son of a poor schoolmaster; he became a choirboy at the monastery of the Austin Friars at Brno. He later earned his living as a music teacher and went to the Organ School in Prague for study. He conducted various choral societies, made some desultory studies at Leipzig and Vienna, and in 1881 returned to Brno to found an organ school there. He had meanwhile become involved with Moravian folk music, collecting, harmonizing, and performing folk songs; their influence is heard in his first mature work, the opera *Jenůfa*, begun in 1894 and staged at Brno in 1904. Although it was a success, wider recognition did not come until the its production in Prague in 1916, which was followed by a production in Germany.

The last ten years of Janáček's life saw a great burst of creative activity, with the composition of many new works that are full of exuberance, expressive power, and characteristic jagged rhythms. The opera *The Excursions of Mr Brouček* was premiered at Prague in 1920, and the following year the rhapsody after Gogol, *Taras Bulba*, was given in Brno. Much of his astonishing later music, in particular the opera *Káta Kabanová* and the second string quartet 'Intimate Letters', was inspired by his unrequited love for Kamila Stösslová, to whom he wrote constant letters in the last decade of his life. Many scenes in his operas, as well as the song cycle *Diary of a Young Man Who Disappeared*, seem to have an

epistolatory basis; they are often brief vignettes in which the characters communicate with one another in a confiding, confessional manner.

He made close studies of folk song and speech, which he applied to his vocal music; speech rhythms were particularly important to Janáček in the portrayal of a character's mood. His vocal music often reflects this, and moves fluently between neutral speech-dominated patterns and moments of intense emotion and expressive power. Although he was not an orthodox religious believer, Janáček's music suggests an articulate pantheism, with a profound sympathy for the human condition and an ecstatic celebration of the natural world and the part of a creator in it.

Works include: OPERA nine, including *Jenůfa* 1904), *The Excursions of Mr Brouček* (1920), *Káta Kabanová* (1921), *The Cunning Little Vixen* (1924), *The Makropoulos Case* (1926), *From the House of the Dead* (1930).

VOCAL *Glagolitic Mass* for solo voices, chorus and orchestra (1926), numerous choral works, including *Rikadla* (1927).

ORCHESTRAL rhapsody *Taras Bulba* (on Gogol, 1918), Sinfonietta for orchestra (1926); concertino for piano and chamber orchestra (1925), *Capriccio* for piano left hand and ensemble (1926).

CHAMBER two string quartets (one on Tolstoy's *Kreutzer Sonata*, 1923, no. 2 *Intimate Letters*, 1928), wind sextet *Mládí/Youth*, *By an Overgrown Path* (for piano, 1901–08); *The Diary of a Young Man who Disappeared* (1921) for voices and piano.

Janequin, Clément (c. 1472–c. 1560) French composer of chansons and psalms. He was choirmaster at Angers Cathedral 1534–37 and then based in Paris from 1549.

His songs of the 1520s–30s are witty and richly textured in imitative effects, for example 'Le Chant des oiseaux'/'Birdsong', 'La Chasse'/'The Hunt', and 'Les Cris de Paris'/ 'Street Cries of Paris'.

'La Bataille de Marignan'/'The Battle of Marignan' 1515 incorporates the sounds of warriors fighting.

Japanische Festmusik work for orchestra by Strauss, op. 84; composed for the 2,600th anniversary of the Japanese Empire; first performed Tokyo, 11 December 1940; less than a year before Pearl Harbor. See also ◊*Sinfonia da Requiem.*

Jaques-Dalcroze, Emile (1865–1950) Swiss composer and teacher. He is remembered for his system of physical training by rhythmical movement to music (◊eurhythmics), and founded the Institut Jaques-Dalcroze in Geneva 1915.

He studied with Delibes in Paris, with Bruckner and Fuchs in Vienna, and at the Geneva Conservatory, where in 1892 he became professor of harmony. There he invented his system of teaching music by co-ordination with bodily movement.

Works include: the operas *Le violon maudit* (1893), *Janie* (1894), *Sancho Panza* (after Cervantes, 1897), *Le bonhomme jadis* (1906), *Les jumeaux de Bergame*, *La fille au vautour* (after W von Hillern's *Die Geier-Wally*); festival play *La fête de la jeunesse et de la joie* (1932); choral works *La veillée*, *Festival vaudois*; suite for orchestra; two violin concertos (1902, 1911); three string quartets; piano music and songs.

Jarnach, Philipp (1892–1982) German composer of Catalan/French descent. He studied with the composer Busoni and completed his unfinished opera *Doktor Faust* 1925 from the material then available after Busoni's death. Further sketches were completed by Antony Beaumont for performance in 1985. Jarnach's own works, in Italianate neoclassical style, include orchestral and chamber music.

He studied piano with Edouard Risler (1873–1929) and composition with Albert Lavignac in Paris. In 1914 he went to Switzerland and taught counterpoint at the Zurich Conservatory 1918–1921, he then settled in Berlin and continued his studies with Busoni.

Works include: prelude to *Prometheus*, suite *Winterbilder* (1915), *Prologue to a Tournament*, *Sinfonia brevis*, *Morgenklangspiel* (1925), Prelude No. 1, *Musik mit Mozart* for orchestra (1935), string quartet and quintet (1916, 1920); violin and piano sonata, two sonatas for unaccompanied violin; *Konzertstück* for organ; sonatina and other works for piano; songs with orchestra and with piano.

Järnefelt, (Edvard) Armas (1869–1958) Finnish composer. He is chiefly known for his 'Praeludium' 1907 and the lyrical 'Berceuse' 1909 for small orchestra, from music for the drama *The Promised Land*.

After studying under Wegelius, Busoni, and Massenet at Helsinki, Berlin, and Paris respectively, he conducted at various German theatres and 1898–1903 at Helsinki. He was appointed conductor of the Opera there in 1903 and was conductor at Stockholm 1907–32. He often conducted works by Sibelius and gave the first Swedish performances of works by Mahler and Schoenberg.

Works include: incidental music to *The Promised Land*; choral works; orchestral music

including *Praeludium* (1907) and *Berceuse* (1909) for small orchestra; songs.

jazz polyphonic syncopated music, characterized by solo virtuosic ◊improvisation, which developed in the USA at the turn of the 20th century. Initially music for dancing, often with a vocalist, it had its roots in black American and other popular music. Developing from ◊blues and spirituals (religious folk songs) in the southern states, it first came to prominence in the early 20th century in New Orleans, St Louis, and Chicago, with a distinctive flavour in each city.

Traits common to all types of jazz are the modified rhythms of West Africa; the emphasis on improvisation; western European harmony emphasizing the dominant seventh and the clash of major and minor thirds; characteristic textures and ◊timbres, first exemplified by a singer and rhythm section (consisting of a piano, bass, drums, and guitar or a combination of these instruments), and later by the addition of other instruments such as the saxophone and various brass instruments, and later still by the adoption of electrically amplified instruments.

Jean de Paris opera by Boieldieu (libretto by C G de Saint-Just), produced Paris, Opéra-Comique, 4 April 1812. The King has chosen the Princess of Navarre as a bride for the Dauphin. Disguised as simple Jean, the Dauphin meets her and falls in love.

Jeanne d'Arc au bûcher/Joan of Arc at the Stake dramatic oratorio by Honegger (libretto by Paul Claudel), produced Basel, 12 May 1938.

Jeffreys, George (c. 1610–1685) English composer. He was steward to Lord Hatton of Kirby, Northamptonshire, and was also a member of the Chapel Royal, and organist to Charles I at Oxford in 1643 during the Civil War.

Works include: services, anthems, over 120 motets, sacred solos and duets, carols; music for masques and plays; secular songs, duets, and other pieces; fancies for strings and virginals.

Jemnitz, Alexander (1890–1963) Hungarian composer and critic. He studied at the Budapest Conservatory, then with Reger at Leipzig and lastly with Schoenberg in Berlin, where he also taught. Later he returned to Budapest.

Works include: the ballet *Divertimento* (1947); Prelude and Fugue, seven *Miniatures* for orchestra (1947); choral music; string quartet, two string trios (1924, 1927), trios for various other instruments, Partita for two violins, three violin and piano sonatas, sonata for viola and cello.

'Jena' Symphony a symphony in C major discovered at Jena in 1909 and attributed to Beethoven because it bears the inscription 'par L van Beethoven' in an unidentifiable hand; it is now known to be by Friedrich Witt (1771–1837). Edited by Fritz Stein and first performed by him, Jena, 17 January 1910.

Jenkins, John (1592–1678) English composer, lutenist, and string player. He composed both in the traditional English style and in the new Italian fashion, and wrote a large quantity of music for consorts of viols, which was popular with amateur players.

He lived under the patronage of the gentry and nobility, especially Sir Hamon L'Estrange in Norfolk and Lord North, whose sons, including Roger, he taught music. His last patron was Sir Philip Wodehouse at Kimberley.

Works include: fancies and consorts for viols and violins with organ anthems and psalms; Elegy on the death of W Lawes, *Theophila, or Love's Sacrifice* (Benlowes), *A Divine Poem* for voices; rounds; songs.

Jenkins, Newell (1915–) US conductor and scholar. He studied in Dresden and with Carl Orff in Munich. He made his debut with *Dido and Aeneas* at Freiburg im Breisgau in 1935. He founded the Yale Opera Group in 1940 and conducted the Bologna Chamber Orchestra 1948–53. As music director of the Clarion Music Society, New York from 1957, he gave performances of J M Kraus, Steffani, Monteverdi, and Cavalli. He worked as a lecturer at University of California at Irvine, 1971–79, and made recordings of operas by Mayr and Rossini, Kraus's Funeral Ode, and Cherubini's Mass in D Minor.

Jensen, Adolph (1837–1879) German pianist and composer. He studied under various teachers and visited Russia and Copenhagen, where he got to know Niels Gade. He was back at Königsberg 1860–66, taught the piano in Berlin for the next two years, and then lived at Dresden, Graz, and elsewhere for his health.

He was the grandson of the organist and composer Wilhelm Jensen (died 1842).

Works include: the opera *Die Erbin von Montfort* (1858–65; adapted to a new libretto based on Gozzi's *Turandot* by Kienzl after his death); cantatas *Jephthas Tochter* (1864), *Der Gang der Jünger nach Emmaus* (1865), *Donald Caird* (Scott, 1875), and *Adonisfeier*; concert overture and *Geistliches Tonstück* for orchestra; about 25 op. nos. of piano music and settings of Heyse and Geibel (*Spanisches Liederbuch*) and Herder.

Jenůfa opera by Janáček (libretto by composer after G Preissova; known in Czech as *Její Pastorkyňa/Her Foster-daughter*); composed 1894–1903, produced Brno, 21 January 1904. Revised 1906–16 and performed Prague 26 May 1916 with some reorchestration by the conductor, Karel Kovařovic (1862–1920). Jenůfa is to marry Steva, but she is disfigured by Steva's half-brother Laca, who later wins her love. Her step-mother the Kostelnička hides her while she bears Steva's child. After Steva rejects Jenůfa the Kostelnička drowns the baby, but later must pay the price.

Jephtas Gelübde/Jephtha's Vow opera by Meyerbeer (libretto by A Schreiber), produced Munich, 23 December 1812. Meyerbeer's first opera.

Jephte oratorio by Carissimi; composed by 1650 and published in several modern editions; realized by Henze and performed London, 14 July 1976.

Jephté/Jephtha opera by Montéclair (libretto by S J de Pellegrin), produced Paris, Opéra, 28 February 1732. After making a vow to the gods, Israelite general Jephtha must sacrifice his daughter Iphthé for success on the battlefield.

Jephtha oratorio by Handel (libretto by T Morell), produced London, Covent Garden, 26 February 1752.

Jérusalem title of the French version of Verdi's opera *I Lombardi alla prima crociata*.

Jessonda opera by Spohr (libretto by E H Gehe, based on Lemierre's tragedy *La Veuve de Malabar*), produced Kassel, 28 July 1823. Portuguese general Tristan discovers his long-lost love Jessonda is to be immolated, but has sworn not to interfere in local ceremonies. He is free to rescue her, and does so, after the Indians break a cease fire.

Jesus and the Traders/Jezus es a kufarok motet by Kodály for mixed voices a cappella, composed 1934.

jeté (French 'thrown') in music, a style of bowing on string instruments. The upper part of the bow is made to fall lightly on the string so that it rebounds several times during the downward motion and repeats notes in a rapid staccato.

Jeu de Cartes/Card Game ballet in three deals by Stravinsky; composed 1936 in Paris, produced New York Metropolitan Opera 27 April 1937, with choreography by Balanchine.

Jeune Henri, Le/The Young Henry opera by Méhul (libretto by J N Bouilly, originally intended for Grétry and called *La Jeunesse de Henri IV*), produced Paris, Opéra-Comique, 1 May 1797. The overture called *La Chasse du jeune Henri* was known as a concert piece long after the opera was forgotten. The worthy deeds of Henry, who kills a wolf and wins a race, magnanimously giving up his prize.

Jeune Sage et le vieux fou, Le/The Wise Youth and the Old Fool opera by Méhul (libretto by F B Hoffman), produced Paris, Opéra-Comique, 28 March 1793.

Jeux ballet by Debussy (choreography by Nizhinsky), composed 1912 and produced Paris, Théâtre du Châtelet, 13 May 1913.

Jeux d'enfants suite for piano duet by Bizet, op. 22, composed 1871; *Petite Suite* for orchestra arranged from five pieces of it, 1872, first performed Paris, 2 March 1873.

Jewels of the Madonna (Wolf-Ferrari). See ◊*Gioielli della Madonna, I* .

Jew's harp musical instrument consisting of a two-pronged metal frame inserted between the teeth, and a springlike tongue plucked with the finger. The resulting drone excites resonances in the mouth. Changes in the shape of the mouth cavity will vary the pitch of these resonances to produce a melody.

jig a dance popular in the British Isles during the 16th century, which is thought to have developed into the ◊gigue, later commonly used as the last movement of a Baroque ◊suite.

Joachim, Joseph (1831–1907) Hungarian-born German violinist, composer, and conductor. He visited England every year from 1862, and in 1877 conducted the first British performance of Brahms's first symphony; he took part in the first performance of the Double Concerto, 1887. He was the dedicatee of Dvořák's concerto, but refused to play it.

He made his first appearance at the age of seven. He studied at the Vienna Conservatory and in Leipzig, where he came under the influence of Mendelssohn and played under him at the Gewandhaus concerts in 1843. In the following year he played Beethoven's violin concerto in London. He was leader of the orchestra at Weimar 1849–53, and at Hanover 1853–68. In 1868 he was appointed director of the Berlin Hochschule für Musik. He founded the Joachim quartet in 1869.

Works include: overtures for orchestra to Shakespeare's *Hamlet* and *Henry IV*, in commemoration of Kleist and on two comedies by Gozzi; three violin concertos (including 'Hungarian'), variations for violin and orchestra.

Joan of Arc see ◊*Giovanna d'Arco*; ◊*Jeanne d'Arc au bûcher*; and ◊*Maid of Orleans, The*.

Job masque for dancing by Vaughan Williams (choreography by Ninette de Valois, settings by Gwendolen Raverat, based on Blake's illustrations to the Book of Job), produced London, Cambridge Theatre, 5 July 1931.

Oratorio by Parry (words from the Book of Job), produced Gloucester Festival, 1892.

Jochum, Eugen (1902–1987) German conductor. He studied piano and organ at Augsburg Conservatory (1914–22) and composition at the Munich Academy of Music (1922–24). After some time as a *répétiteur* in Munich and Kiel, he conducted at Mannheim and Duisburg, becoming music director of the Hamburg Staatsoper 1934–45. From 1949 he was conductor of the Munich Radio Orchestra. His US debut, with the Concertgebouw Orchestra, was in 1961. He conducted Bartók and Stravinsky during World War II in Hamburg and was well known in Bach and Bruckner.

Johannes de Garlandia see ◊Garlandia, Johannes de.

Johnny Strikes Up (Krenek). See ◊*Jonny spielt auf*.

Johnson, John (c. 1540–1595) English lutenist and composer. He was attached to Queen Elizabeth's court and possibly also to the household of Sir Thomas Kitson at Hengrave Hall, Suffolk, and in London 1572–74. He took part in Leicester's entertainments at Kenilworth Castle in 1575. He wrote lute solos and duets.

Johnson, Robert (c. 1583–1633) English lutenist and composer, presumed to be a son of John Johnson (c. 1540–95). He was taught music at the expense of Sir George Carey, husband of Sir Thomas Kitson's granddaughter, in whose household he was brought up, and was appointed lutenist to James I in 1604. He taught Prince Henry and remained in his post under Charles I.

Works include: songs for several voices; songs to the lute; catches; pieces for viols; also songs in Shakespeare's *Tempest*, in Fletcher's *Valentinian*, and *The Mad Lover*.

Johnson, Robert (c. 1500–1554) Scottish priest and composer. He fled to England as a heretic and settled at Windsor, where he may have been chaplain to Anne Boleyn. He wrote Latin motets, English services and prayers, in nomines for instruments, and songs.

Johnson, Robert Sherlaw (1932–) English composer and pianist. He studied at Durham University, the Royal Academy of Music, and in Paris (authority on Messiaen). Has taught at Leeds and York Universities and, from 1970, Oxford.

Works include: the opera *The Lambton Worm* (produced Oxford, 1978); *Carmen Vernalia* for soprano and chamber orchestra (1972); *Where the Wild Things Are* for soprano and tape (1974); *Festival Mass of the Resurrection* for chorus and orchestra (1974); *Anglorum Feriae* for soprano, tenor, chorus, and orchestra (1977); *Veritas veritatis* for six voices (1980); piano concerto (1983); three piano sonatas; two string quartets (1966, 1969).

Joio, Norman dello see ◊Dello Joio.

Jolas, Betsy (1926–) French composer. Most of her compositions are for small groups of instruments or voices, and she has experimented with substituting voices for instruments, as in *Quatuor II* 1964.

She studied at Bennington College, New York 1940–46, and at the Paris Conservatory with Milhaud and Messiaen. She also taught at the Conservatory from 1974 and has taught widely in the USA.

Works include: the operas *Le pavillon au bord de la rivière* (1975), *Le cyclope* (1986) and *Schliemann* (1989); *Musique d'hiver* for organ and small orchestra (1971), *Trois Recontres* for string trio and orchestra (1973) and *Stances* for piano and orchestra (1978); *D'un opéra de voyage* (1967), *Etats* (1969), *How Now* (1973), and *Préludes-Fanfares-Interludes-Sonneries* (1983) for ensemble; two string quartets (1973, 1989), string trio (1990), keyboard music and songs.

Jolie Fille de Perth, La/The Fair Maid of Perth opera by Bizet (libretto by J H V de Saint-Georges and J Adenis, based on Scott's novel), produced Paris, Théâtre Lyrique, 26 December 1867. Catherine and Smith are united, despite competition from the Duke of Rothsay and a case of mistaken identity.

Jolivet, André (1905–1974) French composer. He was interested in primitive forms of religion, magic, and mysticism, and believed that music is a cosmic force endowed with magical properties. His music is intended to convey such magical qualities; it employs a wide range of rhythmic and dynamic effects to produce an appropriately receptive mood in the listener. His work includes symphonic works, ballets, and chamber pieces, as well as music for films and plays.

He was a pupil of Le Flem and Varèse, and formed the group 'La Jeune France' with Yves Baudrier, Jean Yves Daniel-Lesur, and Messiaen in 1936. He became director of music at the Comedie Française in 1945.

Works include: the opera *Dolorès* (1947); two ballets; oratorio *La Vérité de Jeanne* (1956); three symphonies (1953, 1959, 1964); concertos for trumpet (2), flute, piano, harp, bassoon, and ondes Martenot; string quartet; sonata and suite *Mana* for piano, songs.

Jommelli, Niccolò (1714–1774) Italian composer. During his lifetime he was famous as an opera composer throughout Italy and in Vienna, writing over 50 opera serie and more than 20 comic operas. He also wrote sacred cantatas, oratorios, and Masses.

He studied with Francesco Durante, Francesco Feo, and Leonardo Leo in Naples, made his debut as an opera composer there in 1737, and soon achieved widespread fame. He was Kapellmeister to the Duke of Württemberg at Stuttgart 1753–69. He then returned to Naples, but was unable to recapture his old success in Italy; he had developed the dry conventions of the Metastasian opera seria, but the Neapolitans were turning their attentions to comic opera.

Works include: the operas *Ricimero* (1740), *Ezio* (three settings: 1741, 1748, 1758), *Semiramide* (1741), *Sofonisba* (1746), *Artaserse* (1749), *Ifigenia in Aulide* (1751), *Talestri, Attilio Regolo* (1753), *Fetonte, La clemenza di Tito* (two settings: 1753, 1765), *Pelope, Il matrimonio per concorso, La schiava liberata, Armida* (1770), *Ifigenia in Tauride* (1771); oratorios *Isacco, Betulia liberata* (1743), *Santa Elena al Calvario,* and others; Passion oratorio, *Miserere,* Masses and other church music; cantatas; symphonies and other instrumental music.

Jones, Daniel (Jenkyn) (1912–1993) Welsh composer. He began composing at a very early age and later produced a large quantity of music, including 12 symphonies.

He studied at University College, Swansea, where he read English, and later at the Royal Academy of Music in London. He studied conducting with Sir Henry Wood and composition with Harry Farjeon.

Works include: the operas *The Knife* (1963) and *Orestes* (1967); incidental music for *Under Milk Wood* (Dylan Thomas); twelve symphonies (1944–90); symphonic poems *Cystuddiau Branwen, Cloud Messenger*; concertino for piano and orchestra; eight string quartets, string quintet, five string trios, violin sonata, cello sonata, piano sonata, sonata for kettledrums, wind septet, wind nonet.

Jones, John (1728–1796) English organist and composer. He was appointed organist of the Middle Temple in 1749; in 1753 became organist of Charterhouse, succeeding Pepusch; and was appointed organist of St Paul's Cathedral in 1755. He wrote chants, harpsichord lessons, and other pieces.

Jones, Robert (c. 1485–c. 1536) English composer. He was a Gentleman of the Chapel Royal from 1513. He composed a song, 'Who shall have my fair lady', a Mass, *Spes nostra*, and a Magnificat.

Jones, Robert (c. 1570–c. 1617) English lutenist and composer. He worked for several patrons and took a degree in music at Oxford University in 1597. In 1610, with Philip Rosseter and others, he obtained a patent to train children for the Queen's revels, and in 1615 they were allowed to erect a theatre in Blackfriars, but its opening was subsequently prohibited.

Works include: madrigals, five books of *Songs and Ayres* to the lute, anthems.

Jongen, Joseph (1873–1953) Belgian composer. He taught at the conservatories of Liège and Brussels. Most of his compositions are orchestral or chamber pieces.

He studied at the Liège Conservatory. He was awarded a prize from the Académie Royale in 1893 and the Belgian Prix de Rome in 1897. After teaching for a short time at the Liège Conservatory, he went to Rome and later travelled in Germany and France, taking up a professorship at Liège in 1903. In 1914–18 he was in England as a war refugee, but returned to Liège until 1920, when he became professor at the Brussels Conservatory, of which he was later appointed director.

Works include: the ballet *S'Arka*; symphony (1910), *Fantaisie sur deux Noëls wallons* (1902), symphonic poem *Lalla Rookh* (after Thomas Moore, 1904), *Impressions d'Ardennes* (1913), *Tableaux pittoresques* (1917), *Passecaille et Gigue* for orchestra (1930); *Pièce symphonique* for piano and wind orchestra, violin concerto, harp concerto (1944), suite for viola and orchestra, *Symphonie concertante* for organ and orchestra (1926), concerto for wind quintet (1923); three string quartets (1894, 1916, 1921), two serenades for string quartet, piano trio; two violin and piano sonatas, cello sonata; *Sonata eroica* for organ; songs.

Jongleur de Notre Dame, Le/Our Lady's Juggler opera by Massenet (libretto by M Léna on a story by Anatole France in *L'Etui de nacre*, based on a medieval miracle play), produced Monte Carlo, 18 February 1902. Juggler Jean, having given up street performances, enters a monastery. As a tribute, he performs before a statue of the Virgin, and expires amidst a sacred halo.

Jonny spielt auf/Johnny Strikes Up opera by Krenek (libretto by composer), produced Leipzig, Munich, Opera, 10 February 1927. Composer Max woos prima donna Anita, but she is more interested in the violinist, Daniello. Max finds new inspiration from life, and is reunited with Anita.

Jonson, Ben(jamin) (1573–1637) English poet and dramatist. For settings, see Handel (◊*Alchemist, The*); Salieri (◊*Angiolina, ossia Il matrimonio per susurro*); George ◊Auric (*Volpone*); ◊Ferrabosco (masques); Henry Haringston ('Drink to me only'); ◊Lanier (*Lovers made Men* and *Vision of Delight*); ◊Lothar (*Lord Spleen*); Bliss (◊*Pastoral*); R Strauss (◊*Schweigsame Frau, Die*), Elgar (◊*Spanish Lady*); ◊Vaughan Williams (*Pan's Anniversary*).

Joplin, Scott (1868–1917) US composer and pianist. He first came to attention as a pianist at brothels in St Louis and Chicago. He achieved fame with *Maple Leaf Rag* in 1899, and was considered the leading exponent of 'classic rag', in which the standard syncopated rhythm was treated with some sophistication. He published *The Entertainer* 1902 and formed the Scott Joplin Opera Company 1903, for the performance of his opera *A Guest of Honour* (music lost). *Treemonisha*, an opera about a black baby girl found under a tree by a woman called Monisha, was completed 1911 and performed in concert 1915. Joplin's last years were ruined by syphilis. His posthumous fame was initiated with a revival of *Treemonisha* at Atlanta in 1972 and continued in 1974, when *The Entertainer* was one of the best-selling discs. Joplin was awarded a posthumous Pulitzer Prize in 1976.

Joseph opera by Méhul (libretto by A Duval), produced Paris, Opéra-Comique, 17 February 1807. Weber wrote piano variations, op. 28, on a romance from it. Joseph, sold into slavery by his brothers, is successful in Egypt. He later meets them and tests their remorse.

Joseph and his Brethren oratorio by Handel (libretto by J Miller), performed London, Covent Garden, 2 March 1744. Blind Jacob is reunited with his long-lost son.

Josephs, Wilfred (1927–) English composer. As well as film and television music, he has written nine symphonies, concertos, and chamber music. His works include the *Jewish Requiem* 1969 and the opera *Rebecca* 1983.

He studied at the Guildhall School of Music and in Paris. His *Requiem* of 1963 won first prize in a La Scala competition.

Works include: the opera *Rebecca* (after Hollywood rather than du Maurier; produced Leeds 1983); dramatic works for children and for TV; ballets *The Magic Being* (1961), *La Répétition de Phèdre* (1965), *Equus* (1978) and *Cyrano de Bergerac* (1985); ten symphonies (1955–85); two piano concertos, violin concerto, clarinet concerto (1975), concerto for viola and chamber orchestra (1983); *Mortales* for soloists, chorus, and orchestra (texts by Blake, Shelley, Nashe, and Luther; first performance Cincinnati, 1970); four string quartets (1954–81), octet (1964), two violin sonatas, piano trio (1974).

Josephslegende ballet in one act by Strauss (scenario by H Kessler and Hugo von Hofmannsthal); composed 1912–14, produced Paris, Opéra, 14 February 1914, Ballet Russe.

Joshua oratorio by Handel (libretto by T Morell), performed London, Covent Garden, 23 March 1748.

Josquin Desprez (1440–1521), or des Prés Franco-Flemish composer. His synthesis of Flemish structural counterpoint and Italian harmonic expression, acquired in the service of the Rome papal chapel 1484–1503, marks a peak in Renaissance vocal music. In addition to masses on secular as well as sacred themes, including the *Missa 'L'Homme armé'/Mass on 'The Armed Man'* 1504, he also wrote secular chansons such as 'El Grillo'/'The Cricket' employing imitative vocal effects.

Josten, Werner (1885–1963) German-born US composer and conductor. He studied in Munich, Geneva (with Jaques-Dalcroze), and Paris. In 1918 he became assistant conductor at the Munich Opera, but in 1920 emigrated to the USA. He was appointed professor at Smith College, Northampton, Massachusetts, in 1923; conducted the first US performance of *L'Incoronazione di Poppea* (1926); he also led *Orfeo* (1929) and the US premieres of Handel's *Giulio Cesare* (1927), *Rodelinda* (1931), and *Serse* (1928). In 1938 he gave the first modern revival of Fux's *Costanza e fortezza* (1723).

Works include: ballets *Batouala* (1931), *Joseph and his Brethren* (1936), *Endymion* (1933); *Crucifixion* for bass solo and chorus, *Hymnus to the Quene of Paradys* for contralto solo, women's chorus, strings, and organ, *Ode for St Cecilia's Day* for solo voices, chorus, and orchestra (1925); symphony in F major, serenade, symphonic movement *Jungle* (on Henri Rousseau's picture 'Forêt exotique',

1929) for orchestra; symphony and two *Concerti sacri* for strings and piano.

jota Spanish dance, especially of Aragon and Navarre. It dates from the 12th century and is said to derive its name from the Moor Aben Jot. It is in quick 3–4 time. The music is played on instruments of the guitar type and often accompanied by castanets and other percussion.

Joubert, John (1927–) South African composer. He studied at Cape Town University and the Royal Academy of Music in London. He was a lecturer at Hull University 1950–62, and at Birmingham University 1962–86.

Works include: the operas *Antigone* (1954), *In the drought* (1956), *Silas Marner* (1961), *Under Western Eyes* (1968); cantatas *The Leaves of Life* and *Urbs beata*; three motets; symphonic prelude, two symphonies (1956, 1971), *In Memoriam, 1820* for orchestra; violin concerto (1954), piano concerto; two string quartets (1950, 1977) and other chamber music; choral works; songs.

Jour de Fête a collective work for string quartet: 1. *Les Chanteurs de Noël* (Glazunov); 2. *Glorification* (Liadov); 3. *Chœur dansé russe* (Rimsky-Korsakov).

Jubel-Ouvertüre/Jubilee Overture concert overture by Weber, op. 59, composed 1818 as a companion piece to the *Jubel-Cantate* for the 50th anniversary of the accession of the King of Saxony, Frederick Augustus, and performed Dresden, 20 September. It concludes with the tune of 'God save the King'.

Judas Maccabaeus oratorio by Handel (libretto by T Morell), composed 9 July–11 August 1746, produced London, Covent Garden, 1 April 1747.

Judgement of Paris, The masque by Congreve, for the composition of which a prize was advertised in the *London Gazette* in 1700, the first four prizes being won by Weldon, Eccles, D Purcell, and Finger in 1701. Eccles's setting produced London, Dorset Gardens Theatre, 21 March; Finger's 27 March 1701. The libretto was later set by G Sammartini, produced Cliveden, Buckinghamshire, 1 August 1740, and by Arne, produced Drury Lane, London, 12 March 1742.

Judith opera by Natanael Berg (1879–1957), (libretto in Swedish, by composer, based on Hebbel's drama), produced Stockholm, 22 February 1936. Biblical blood-letting, as Holofernes is decapitated.

Oratorio by Arne (libretto by I Bickerstaffe), performed London, Drury Lane Theatre, 27 February 1761.

Oratorio by Parry (libretto from the Bible), performed Birmingham Festival, 1888.

Play with music by Honegger (libretto by R Morax), produced Mézières, open-air Théâtre du Jorat, 13 June 1925; operatic version, Monte Carlo, 13 February 1926.

Juditha triumphans devicta Holofernes barbarie oratorio by Vivaldi (text by J Cassetti), performed Venice 1716. Sometimes given in modern revivals as a stage work, as at Camden Festival, London, 1984.

Juha opera in three acts by Merikanto (libretto by Aino Ackté), composed 1920–22; produced Lahti, Music College, 28 October 1963. Juha drowns himself when the truth of his wife's infidelity is revealed.

Juif polonais, Le/The Polish Jew opera by Camille Erlanger (libretto by H Cain and P B Gheusi, based on Erckmann-Chatrian's novel), produced Paris, Opéra-Comique, 11 April 1900. The subject is that of the play *The Bells*, in which Irving made his greatest popular success.

Juilliard School music school and college founded in New York 1924, financed by the will of Augustus D Juilliard, a cotton merchant. One of the world's leading conservatories, it moved in 1969 to its current location, the newly built Lincoln Center. The Juilliard Quartet was founded in 1946 by the school's president William Schumann, and became famous initially for its interpretation of Bartók's works.

Juive, La/The Jewess opera by Halévy (libretto by Scribe), produced Paris, Opéra, 23 February 1835. Prince Leopold, posing as a Jew, woos Rachel, the apparent daughter of Jewish goldsmith Eléazar. When Rachel discovers the deception, and that Leopold is married, she denounces him. All three face trial for inter-racial love, and Rachel and Eléazar are executed.

Julie opera by Dezède (libretto by J M B de Monvel), produced Paris, Comédie-Italienne, 28 September 1772. Mozart wrote piano variations (K264) on the air 'Lison dormait' in 1778.

Julien, ou La Vie du poète/Julian, or The Poet's Life opera by G Charpentier, sequel to *Louise* (libretto by composer), produced Paris, Opéra-Comique, 4 June 1913. Julien's artistic fantasies and peregrinations.

Julietta, or The Key to Dreams lyric opera by Martinů (libretto by composer, after the play by G Neveux); composed 1936–37, produced Prague, National Theatre, 16 March 1938. Michel and Julietta meet and part in a disturbing dream world where reality and fantasy mingle.

Julius Caesar (Handel and Malipiero). See ◊*Giulio Cesare.*

Junge Lord, Der/The Young Lord opera by Henze (libretto by Ingeborg Bachmann, after Wilhelm Hauff), produced Berlin, Deutsche Oper, 7 April 1965. Milord Edgar, a simian in disguise, makes a monkey of German townspeople.

Junge Magd, Die/The Young Girl six songs for alto, flute, clarinet, and string quartet by Hindemith (texts by George Trakl); first performed Donaueschingen, 31 July 1922.

Jungfernquartette (German 'maiden quartets') another nickname for Haydn's six string quartets, op. 33, also known as 'Russian quartets' and more generally as 'Gli Scherzi'.

Jungfrun i Tornet/The Maiden in the Tower opera in one act by Sibelius (libretto by Hertzberg); composed 1896 for Robert Kajanus's Helsinki Orchestra and orchestra school, first performed 7 November 1896. Imprisoned maiden is released to lover.

Juon, Paul (1872–1940) Russian composer. He studied with Taneiev and Arensky in Moscow and with Bargiel in Berlin, where he settled and was later appointed professor at the Hochschule für Musik by Joachim.

Works include: ballet *Psyche*; symphony in A, serenade and other works for orchestra; three violin concertos (1909, 1913, 1931), *Episodes concertantes* for violin, cello, piano, and orchestra; chamber symphony, five pieces for string orchestra; three string quartets (1898, 1904, 1920), sextet for piano and strings, two piano quintets (1906, 1909), two piano quartets (1908, 1912), piano trios (1901, 1915), Divertimento for wind and piano, ditto for clarinet and two violas; instrumental pieces; *Satyrs and Nymphs*, *Preludes*, and *Capriccios* for piano.

'Jupiter' Symphony nickname (not the composer's own) given to Mozart's last symphony, K551 in C major, finished 10 August 1788.

justiniana a type of 16th-century *villanella* for three voices, the words of which satirized the Venetian patricians. There is no connection between this and the *villanella* set to poetry of the type originated by Leonardo Giustinian.

just intonation singing or instrumental playing in what is said to be the pure natural scale, not that artificially fixed on keyboard instruments by equal temperament.

K

Kabale und Liebe opera by Einem (libretto by composer after Schiller's tragedy, 1784), first performed Vienna, Staatsoper, 17 December 1976.

Kabalevsky, Dmitri Borisovich (1904–1987) Russian composer and pianist. While he was known in the West for his keyboard and instrumental works, his reputation in the USSR was based upon vocal works, including the opera *The Taras Family* 1947. Kabalevsky's work mirrored the Soviet authorities' policy of 'Socialist Realism' in his transparent Neo-Classical style.

As a result, his work is more immediately accessible than that of his contemporaries Prokofiev and Shostakovich, who were frequently criticized by the government. He helped guide the official course of music in the USSR after World War II.

He was born at St Petersburg, and entered the Skriabin School of Music at Moscow when his family settled there in 1918. He studied piano and became a composition pupil first of Sergey Vasilenko and Georgy Catoire, afterwards of Nikolai Myaskovsky. He later became professor of composition there.

Works include: the operas *The Golden Spikes, Colas Breugnon* (after Romain Rolland's 1938 novel), *Before Moscow* (1943), and *Nikita Vershinin* (1955); incidental music for Shakespeare's *Measure for Measure*, Sheridan's *School for Scandal* and an adaptation of Flaubert's *Madame Bovary*; film music *Poem of Struggle, Our Great Fatherland* and *People's Avengers* for chorus and orchestra; four symphonies (no. 3 *Requiem for Lenin*); three piano concertos (1931–53), violin concerto, two cello concertos; two string quartets (1928,

1945); three sonatas, two sonatinas, and other piano music; Requiem; songs.

Kabeláč, Miloslav (1908–1979) Czech composer. He studied composition at the Prague Conservatory 1928–31 with K B Jirák and later also the piano at the Master School. In 1932 he joined the staff of Czech Radio.

Works include: eight symphonies (1941–70); cantatas *Mystery of Time, Do not retreat*; two overtures; wind sextet; suite for saxophone and piano; violin and piano pieces; choral music.

Kabuki Japanese theatrical form popular since the Edo period (1603–1868) and the source of many musical genres. There are two main kinds of Kabuki play: *jidaimono* or pseudo-historical pieces and *sewamono* or stories dealing with the cultural life of the Edo period. There are also modern plays. Musical instruments are played onstage (accompanying dance or providing narrative comment) or offstage (programmatic music) and Kabuki music uses percussion, flutes, shamisen (long-necked lutes), and vocals.

Kadosa, Pál (1903–1983) Hungarian composer and pianist. He studied with Kodály at the Budapest Academy and taught piano at Fodor Conservatory 1927–43. He was professor at the Budapest Academy from 1945. His compositions are influenced by Bartók.

Works include: the opera *The Adventure of Huszt* (1951); five cantatas (1939–50); eight symphonies (1941–68); four piano concertos (1931–66); two violin concertos (1931, 1941); concerto for string quartet and chamber orchestra (1936); three string quartets (1934–57); two string trios (1930, 1955); two piano sonatas (1926–60).

Kagel, Mauricio (1931–) Argentine composer of advanced tendencies. He studied in Buenos Aires, and settled in Cologne, Germany, in 1957. He has evolved a very complex style, employing serial and aleatory techniques, permutations of different languages, light effects, and aural distortions.

Works include: *Anagrama* for four soloists, speaking chorus, and chamber ensemble (1958); *Sur scène*, theatrical piece in one act for speaker, mime, singer, and three instruments (1962); *The Women*, dramatic scene for three female voices, three actresses, a dancer, chorus of women, and electronic tapes; *Match* for three players; *Diaphony* for chorus, orchestra, and two projectors (1964); *Transición I* for electronic sounds; *Transición II* for piano, percussion, and two tapes; *Hetrophonie* for an orchestra of solo instruments; string sextet; *Ludwig Van*, film score (1970); *Staatstheater*, 'ballet for nondancers', with instruments including chamber pot (1971); opera, *Die Erschöpfung der Welt* (produced Stuttgart, 8 February 1980), *Sankt–Bach–Passion* (1985); piano trio (1985); *A Letter* for mezzo and orchestra (1986); *Dance School* ballet (1988); *Quodlibet* for women's voices and orchestra (1988); third string quartet (1988); *Fragende Ode* (1989).

Kaiser Quartett (Haydn). See *ϕ'Emperor' Quartet*.

Kajanus, Robert (1856–1933) Finnish conductor and composer. He studied at the Helsinki and Leipzig Conservatories, and also studied composition with Johan Svendsen in Paris. He founded the orchestra of the Helsinki Philharmonic Society in 1882, with which later he paid several important visits to foreign countries, giving many early performances of works by Sibelius. He was director of music at Helsinki University 1897–1926.

Works include: symphony *Aino* (on an incident from the *Kalevala*), and other pieces.

Kalabis, Viktor (1923–) Czech composer. He studied at the Prague Academy and Charles University. He was manager of the music department at Prague Radio, 1953–72.

Works include: five symphonies (1956, 1961, 1971, 1972, 1976); Concerto for Orchestra (1966), and nine instrumental concertos; two nonets, two wind quintets, seven string quartets; sonatas for violin, cello, clarinet, and trombone (1967–82); ballet on *Alice in Wonderland, Two Worlds* (1980); Incantations for 13 wind instruments (1988).

Kalcher, Johann Nepomuk (1764–1827) German organist and composer. He studied at Munich, where he became court organist in

1798. Weber was one of his pupils. He wrote Masses, symphonies, organ music, and songs.

Kalinnikov, Vassily Sergeyevich (1866–1901) Russian composer. He was educated at a seminary, where he conducted the choir. In 1884 he went to Moscow and, in spite of great poverty, obtained a musical education at the Philharmonic Society Music School. After conducting Italian opera for the 1893–94 season, he was found to suffer from tuberculosis and from that time lived mainly in the Crimea, devoted to composition.

Works include: incidental music to Alexey Tolstoy's *Tsar Boris* (1899); cantatas *St John Chrysostom* and *Russalka*; two symphonies, suite, two Intermezzi and two sketches for orchestra; string quartets; piano pieces; songs.

Kalkbrenner, Friedrich (Wilhelm Michael) (1785–1849) German pianist, teacher, and composer. He studied under his father, Christian Kalkbrenner (1755–1806) and at the Paris Conservatory. He made his first public appearance in Vienna in 1803, returning to Paris in 1806. He lived in London as teacher and performer 1814–23 and then settled in Paris as a member of the piano firm of Pleyel, but continued to teach and perform.

Works include: four piano concertos (1823–35), concerto for two pianos; piano septet, sextet and quintet; piano school with studies appended, sonatas, variations and numerous other works for piano.

Kalliwoda, Johan Vaclav (1801–1866) Bohemian violinist and composer. He studied at the Prague Conservatory 1811–17 and played in the orchestra 1817–22. He then became music director to Prince Fürstenberg at Donaueschingen until his retirement in 1866.

Works include: the opera *Blanka*; seven symphonies (1826–43); concertinos for violin, for clarinet, and other instruments; three string quartets; violin duets, violin pieces.

Kálmán, Imre (1882–1953) Hungarian composer. He had great success with the operetta *Tatárjárás* 1908 (produced in New York and elsewhere as *The Gay Hussars*).

He studied in Budapest, then lived in Vienna until 1938. He moved to Paris in 1939, and in 1940 emigrated to the USA, where he lived in New York and Hollywood.

Works include: *Der gute Kamerad* (1911), *Der Zigeunerprimas* (1912), *Die Csárdásfürstin* (1915), *Die Faschingsfee* (1917), *Gräfin Mariza* (1924), *Die Zirkusprinzessin* (1924), and *Der Teufelsreiter*.

Kalomiris, Manolis (1883–1962) Greek composer. He studied in Athens, Constantinople, and Vienna. He taught at Kharkov 1906–10 and then settled in Athens as professor at the Conservatory. From 1919 he was director of the Hellenic Conservatory there until 1926, when he founded the National Conservatory and became its director.

Works include: the operas *The Master Builder* (after N Kazantzakis, 1915), *The Mother's Ring* (after J Kambyssis, 1917), *Anatoli* and *The Haunted Waters* (after Yeats, 1950–52); incidental music; two symphonies; symphonic poems for orchestra; chamber music; piano works; songs.

Kamarinskaya fantasy for orchestra on two Russian themes by Glinka, composed 1848 and known only in an edition revised by Rimsky-Korsakov and Glazunov.

Kamieński, Maciej (1734–1821) Hungarian-Polish composer. He studied in Vienna and settled at Warsaw in about 1760. He produced the first Polish opera there on 11 May 1778.

Works include: the opera *Happiness in Unhappiness* and five others in Polish and two in German; church music, cantata for the unveiling of the Jan III Sobieski monument.

Kammermusik German term for ◊chamber music.

Kammermusik/Chamber Music seven works by Hindemith composed 1921–27; no. 1 for small orchestra, first performed Donaueschingen, 31 July 1922, conductor Scherchen; no. 2 for piano and 12 instruments, first performed Frankfurt 31 October 1924, conductor Clemens Krauss; no. 3 for cello and ten instruments, first performed Bochum, 30 April 1925, conductor Hindemith; no. 4 for violin and chamber orchestra, first performed Dessau, 25 September 1925; no. 5 for viola and chamber orchestra, first performed Berlin, 3 November 1927, conductor Klemperer; no. 6 for viola d'amore and chamber orchestra, first performed Cologne, 29 March 1928; no. 7 for organ and chamber orchestra, first performed Frankfurt, 8 January 1928.

Kammerton (German 'chamber-pitch') pitch to which orchestral instruments in Germany were tuned in the 17th–18th centuries. It was lower, by a whole tone or more, than the *Chorton* (choir-pitch) used for church organs, and it was for this reason that Bach, in his Leipzig cantatas, transposed the organ parts down a tone in order to make them agree with the orchestra. The transposition applied only to the organ parts; the orchestral parts could be used as they stood.

kapellmeister (German 'chapel master') chief conductor and chorus master, also resident composer for a private chapel, responsible for musical administration.

Kapellmeistermusik (German 'conductor's music') contemptuous term for a musical work which betrays creative weakness and has no merit but that of a knowledge of rules and glib craftsmanship.

Karajan, Herbert von (1908–1989) Austrian conductor. He dominated European classical music performance after 1947. He was principal conductor of the Berlin Philharmonic Orchestra 1955–89, artistic director of the Vienna State Opera 1957–64, and of the Salzburg Festival 1956–60. A perfectionist, he cultivated an orchestral sound of notable smoothness and transparency; he also staged operas and directed his own video recordings. He recorded the complete Beethoven symphonies three times, and had a special affinity with Mozart and Bruckner, although his repertoire extended from Bach to Schoenberg.

Karel, Rudolf (1880–1945) Czech composer. He studied composition under Dvořák at the Prague Conservatory. In 1914, on holiday in Russia, he was interned as an Austrian subject, then taught at Taganrog and Rostov-on-Don, fled to Siberia and eventually escaped to Czechoslovakia, where he became professor at the Prague Conservatory. He died tragically in a concentration camp.

Works include: the operas *Ilsa's Heart* (1909) and *Godmother's Death* (1932); incidental music to Knud Hamsun's *The Game of Life*; *Awakening*, symphony for solo voices, chorus, and orchestra; two symphonies, *Renaissance* and *Spring*, symphonic poems *The Ideals* and *Demon*, suite, fantasy, Slavonic dances. for orchestra; violin concerto, three string quartets (1902–36).

Karelia incidental music in nine movements by Sibelius; composed 1893, first performed Viipuri, 13 November 1893. Suite for orchestra in three movements op. 11, 1893.

Karetnikov, Nikolai (1930–1994) Russian composer. From the time of his Fourth Symphony 1963, he was obliged to compose and publish in secrecy, owing to his political dissent. His opera *Til'Ulenshpigel* was written and recorded over five years with the cooperation of friends; dubbed the first *samizdat* opera and premiered at Bielefeld, Germany, in 1993.

He studied with Shebalin at the Moscow Conservatory.

Works include: *The Mystery of Apostle Paul,* opera oratorio (1972–87), Chamber suite *From Shalom-Aleham* (1986), quintet for piano and strings (1990), and *Six Spiritual Songs* (1992).

Karg-Elert, Sigfrid (1877–1933) German composer. After studying at Leipzig he devoted himself to the European harmonium. His numerous concert pieces and graded studies, including *66 Choral Improvisations* 1908–10, exploit a range of impressionistic effects such as the 'endless chord'.

He became professor at the conservatories of Magdeburg and Leipzig. He was a brilliant pianist, but was persuaded by Grieg to devote himself to composition.

Works include: a symphony, two piano concertos (1901, 1913); string quartet; violin and piano sonatas; sonata and other works for piano; over 100 songs; pieces for harmonium and many organ works, including 66 chorale improvisations (1908–10), 24 preludes and postludes, Sonatina, passacaglia, fantasy and fugue in D major, *Chaconne, Fugue-Trilogy and Chorale,* ten characteristic pieces, three symphonic chorales, seven *Pastels from Lake Constance* (1919), six *Cathedral Windows* (1923), 54 variation-studies *Homage to Handel.*

Karłowicz, Mieczysław (1876–1909) Polish composer. The son of a noble family, he travelled much as a child and learnt the violin in Prague, Dresden, and Heidelberg, and soon played chamber music with his parents, a cellist and a pianist. He later studied at Warsaw, where his composition teacher was Zygmunt Noskowski, and afterwards with Heinrich Urban in Berlin. He also studied conducting with Arthur Nikisch at Leipzig. He settled at Zakopane in the Tatra mountains in 1908 and was killed in a climbing accident.

Works include: incidental music to *Biała Gołąbka;* symphony in E minor, symphonic poems *Returning Waves* (1907), *The Sad Story (Preludes to Eternity), Stanisław i Anna Oświęcimowie* (1912), *An Episode of the Masquerade,* serenade (1897), *Lithuanian Rhapsody* for orchestra; violin concerto (1902); songs.

Karl V opera by Krenek (libretto by composer), produced Prague, German Opera, 15 June 1938; revised version, Vienna, 1984. Reminiscences of Emperor Charles V, presented as an anti-Nazi parable, but not appreciated by Viennese authorities, and cancelled in rehearsal, 1934.

Kashchei the Immortal/Kashchei Bessmertny opera by Rimsky-Korsakov (libretto

by composer), produced Moscow, 25 December 1902. Kashchei is the wizard of Russian fairy lore who appears also in Stravinsky's *Firebird* ballet.

Kastner, Jean Georges (Johann Georg) (1810–1867) Alsatian composer and theorist. He studied theology at home, but produced an opera *Die Königin der Sarmaten* and was sent by the Strasbourg town council to study with Berton and Reicha at the Paris Conservatory. He wrote a treatise on orchestration, a manual on military music, and methods for various instruments.

Works include: operas, cantatas and songs.

Káta Kabanová opera by Janáček (libretto by V Červinka, based on Ostrovsky's play *Groza*), produced Brno, 23 November 1921. Adulterous Káta is driven to suicide in the Volga.

Katerina Izmailova (Shostakovich). See ◊*Lady Macbeth of the Mtsensk District.*

Kauer, Ferdinand (1751–1831) Austrian composer. He studied at Znaim and Vienna, where he was appointed leader and second conductor at the Leopoldstadt Theatre, for which he wrote music for about 100 pantomimes and farces, as well as operettas and operas.

Works include: the operas *Das Donauweibchen* (1798), *Das Waldweibchen;* oratorio *Die Sündflut;* trio *Nelsons grosse See-Schlacht.*

Kaun, Hugo (1863–1932) German composer. He had written over 150 works before he was 16 and studied with Kiel at the Berlin Academy of Arts. In 1884 he went to USA as a pianist, but had to give up that career owing to an injury; in 1887 he settled in Milwaukee, but returned to Berlin in 1901, teaching composition first at the Academy and from 1922 at the Klindworth-Scharwenka Conservatory.

Works include: the operas *Der Pietist, Sappho* (1917), *Der Fremde* (1920) and *Menandra* (1925); several choral works; three symphonies, *Minnehaha und Hiawatha* (after Longfellow), symphonic prologue *Marie Magdalene,* humoresque *Falstaff* (after Shakespeare) and other orchestral works; four string quartets, piano quintet, two piano trios, octet; violin and piano sonata.

Kay, Ulysses Simpson (1917–1995) US composer. He studied with Howard Hanson at the Eastman School and with Hindemith at Tanglewood. Professor, Lehman College, New York, 1968–88.

Works include: the operas *The Boor* (after Chekhov; composed 1955, produced 1968),

The Juggler of our Lady (composed 1956, produced 1962), *The Capitoline Venus* (1971), *Jubilee* (1976); Suite for Strings (1949), *Song of Jeremiah*, cantata (1954), Serenade for Orchestra (1954), Fantasy Variations for orchestra (1963), *Scherzi musicali* for chamber orchestra (1971); two string quartets (1953, 1956), piano quintet (1949); choral pieces and songs.

kazoo simple wind instrument adding a buzzing quality to the singing voice on the principle of 'comb and paper' music.

Keats, Donald (Howard) (1929–) US composer. He studied at Yale and Columbia Universities until 1953, and was professor of music at the University of Denver from 1975. His music is basically tonal, and includes setting of Eliot (*The Hollow Men*), Cummings (*Anyone Loved in a Pretty How Town*) and Yeats (*A Love Triptych*). Other works include two symphonies (no. 2 Elegiac, 19960), two string quartets (1951, 1965), piano sonata (1966) and *Música Instrumentalis* for nine instruments (1980).

Keiser, Reinhard (1674–1739) German composer. As chief composer to the Hamburg Opera, he composed over 100 operas, making Hamburg the most distinguished operatic centre in Germany.

A pupil of Schelle at St Thomas's School, Leipzig, he worked at Brunswick from 1692 under Johann Kusser, whom he succeeded as chief composer to the Hamburg Opera in 1695. He was appointed Kapellmeister to the Danish Court in Copenhagen in 1723, and returned to Hamburg as Cantor of the cathedral in 1728.

Works include: the operas *Basilius, Circe* (1702), *Penelope* (1702), *Der geliebte Adonis, Augustus, Orpheus* (1702), *La forza della virtù, Stoertebecker und Joedge Michaels, Die verdammt Statt-Sucht* (1703), *Nebucadnezar* (1704), *Octavia, Masagniello furioso* (1706), *Desiderius* (1709), *Croesus* (1710), *Fredegunda* (1715), *Die grossmüthige Tomyris* (1717), *Ulysses, Der lächerliche Printz Jodelet* (1726), and others; Passion oratorios *Der für die Sünde der Welt gemartete und sterbende Heiland Jesus* (text by Brockes, 1712), *Der blutige und sterbende Jesus* (Hunold, 1704); cantatas; motets; instrumental music.

Kelemen, Milko (1924–) Croatian composer. His mature style employs serial and aleatory techniques.

He studied at the Zagreb Conservatory with Štjepan Sulek (1914–1986).

Works include: the operas *König Ubu* (1965), *State of Siege* (after Camus' *The Plague*, 1970) and *Apocalyptica* ballet-opera (1979);

Koncertantne Improvizacije for string (1955); *Concerto giocoso* for chamber orchestra; concertos for violin and bassoon; concertino for double bass and strings; *Symphonic Music 57*; *Abecedarium* for strings (1973); *Mageia* for orchestra (1979); *Dramatico* for cello and orchestra (1985); *Fantasmas* for viola and orchestra (1986); *Memoirs* for string trio (1987); *Sonnets* for string quartet (1988); nonet (1988); *Games* song cycle; piano sonata.

Keller, Gottfried (1819–1890) Swiss poet and novelist. Six of his poems were set by Hugo Wolf. See also ◊*Kleider Machen Leute* (Zemlinsky); ◊*Romeo und Julia auf dem Dorfe* (Delius); Othmar ◊Schoeck (*Gesangfest im Frübling, Lebending begraben, Gaselen, Unter Sternen, Sommernacht* and songs); Otto ◊Vrieslander (songs).

Keller, Hans (1919–1985) Austrian-born British journalist and critic. In 1959 he joined the British Broadcasting Corporation (BBC) in London. He had much influence on broadcasting policy, and in his programmes of functional analysis he sought to elucidate structure and ideas by musical example, rather than verbal explanation.

After studying in Vienna he fled to England in 1938; he played the violin and viola in various ensembles before joining the BBC. An apparent mastery of his adopted language led to a prolific career as a journalist; natives were sometimes bemused by a certain subjectivity and love of paradox. He wrote the libretto for Benjamin Frankel's opera *Marching Song* BBC 1983 and *The Great Haydn Quartets* 1986.

Kelley, Edgar Stillman (1857–1944) US composer and writer on music. He studied at Chicago and Stuttgart, and on his return to the USA became organist and critic in California, where he also made a study of Chinese music. He then taught at Yale University, in Berlin, and from 1910, at the Cincinnati Conservatory.

Works include: the operetta *Puritania* (1892); incidental music for Shakespeare's *Macbeth*; orchestral suite on Chinese themes, *Aladdin, Gulliver* symphony (after Swift), *New England Symphony*, suite *Alice in Wonderland* (after Lewis Carroll, 1913); cantata *Pilgrim's Progress* (after Bunyan, 1918), *Wedding Ode* for tenor, male chorus and orchestra; *My Captain* (Whitman) and *The Sleeper* (Poe) for chorus; variations for string quartet, string quartet, piano quintet; piano pieces; songs.

Kelly, Bryan (1934–) English composer who studied with Gordon Jacob and Herbert Howells; he has written extensively for brass band and for educational use. He was professor of composition at Royal College of Music 1962–84; he then moved to Italy.

Works include: *The Tempest* Suite, for strings (1967); *Edinburgh Dances* and Concertante Music, for brass band (1973); *Stabat Mater*, for soloists and orchestra (1970); *Latin Magnificat*, for chorus and wind instruments (1979); two symphonies (1982, 1986); *The Spider Monkey Uncle King*, opera pantomime (1971); *Herod, do your worst*, nativity opera (1968).

Kelly, Michael (1762–1826) Irish tenor, actor, and composer. He made his operatic debut at Naples in 1781. He began composing dramatic works in 1789, and produced over 60. His entertaining *Reminiscences* 1826, though not fully reliable, contain valuable information on his contemporaries, especially Mozart.

He studied with Michael Arne and others, and went to Naples in 1779 to study with Fedele Fenaroli (1730–1818) and Giuseppe Aprile (1732–1813). At the Court Opera in Vienna, 1784–87, he was the first Basilio and Curzio in Mozart's *The Marriage of Figaro* 1786. He returned to London in 1787.

Works include: dramatic works *A Friend in Need* (1797), *The Castle Spectre, Blue Beard* (1798), *Pizarro* (Sheridan, 1799), *The Gipsy Prince* (1801), *Love laughs at Locksmiths* (1803), *Cinderella, Polly* (1813).

Kelterborn, Rudolf (1931–) Swiss composer. He studied with J Handschin and Willy Burkhard, Blacher, and Fortner. In 1960 he became an instructor at the Detmold Music Academy, and was director of the Basel Academy from 1983. In his music he tends towards integral serialism.

Works include: the operas *Die Errettung Thebens* (1963), *Kaiser Jovian* (1967), *Ein Engel kommt nach Babylon* (1977); *Der Kirschgarten* (after Chekhov, 1984); *Julia* (1991); *Metamorphosen* for orchestra (1960); concertino for violin and chamber orchestra; concertino for piano and chamber orchestra; suite for woodwind, percussion and strings; sonata for 16 solo strings (1955); *Cantata Profana* for baritone, chorus and 13 instruments (1960); cantata *Ewige Wiederkehr* for mezzo, flute and string trio (1960); cello concerto (1962); chamber music for various instrumental groups including five string quartets (1954–70), *5 Fantasien* for flute, cello and harpsichord; *7 Bagatellen* for wind quintet; *Metamorphosen* for piano; *Meditation* for six wind instruments.

kemence heavy, short-necked fiddle of Rajasthan, NW India, played by the Manghaniyar caste of musicians and poets.

Kempe, Rudolf (1910–1976) German conductor. Renowned for the clarity and fidelity of his interpretations of the works of Richard Strauss and Wagner's *Ring* cycle, he conducted Britain's Royal Philharmonic Orchestra 1961–75 and was musical director of the Munich Philharmonic from 1967.

Kempff, Wilhelm Walter Friedrich (1895–1991) German pianist and composer. He excelled at the 19th-century classical repertory of Beethoven, Brahms, Chopin, and Liszt. He resigned as director of the Stuttgart Conservatory when only 35 to concentrate on performing; later he played with Pablo Casals, Yehudi Menuhin, and Pierre Fournier.

Kendale, Richard (died 1431) English grammarian and music theorist. A short musical treatise by him is included in the manuscript written down by John Wylde, precentor of Waltham Holy Cross Abbey, c. 1460 (British Museum, Lans. 763).

Kepler, Johannes (1571–1630) German philosopher, astronomer, and writer on music. He was an early supporter of the Copernican view of the solar system, which placed the Sun at its centre, and was the first to propose that the orbits of the planets are eliptical. His *Harmonices Mundi* (1619) elaborates various music theories; book five elaborates on the ancient Greek doctrine of Pythagoras that the planets emit musical sounds in their orbits round the Sun. Kepler's theories form the basis of Paul ◊Hindemith's opera *Die ◊Harmonie der Welt* (1957).

Kerle, Jacob van (c. 1531–1591) Flemish composer. He spent some time in Italy, partly in Rome in the service of Otto von Truchsess, Cardinal-Archbishop of Augsburg, in whose service he was 1562–75. He was with the Cardinal at Augsburg at times, and may have attended the Council of Trent with him 1562–63. Later he became canon of Cambrai, but was often in Vienna and Prague attending on the Emperor Rudolf.

Works include: *Preces*, commissioned by the Cardinal of Augsburg in 1562, Masses, motets, Te Deums, Magnificats, hymns, *Sacrae cantiones*.

Kerll, Johann Caspar (1627–1693), also Kerl, Keril, Gherl (or, in Italian, Cherll, Giovanni Gasparo) German organist and composer. He wrote 11 operas, all of which are now lost. Of his other compositions, 18 Masses and other church music survive, as well as secular pieces. He excelled in writing for the organ.

He settled early in Vienna as a pupil of Giovanni Valentini; then studied in Rome with Carissimi and probably studied the organ with Frescobaldi. He was in the service of the Elector of Bavaria in Munich 1656–74. He returned to Vienna as a private teacher, and was appointed court organist there in 1677, but went back to Munich in 1684.

Works include: the operas *Oronte, Erinto, Le pretensioni del sole* (1667), *I colori geniali;* Masses, motets, and other church music; sonatas for two violins and bass; toccatas, ricercari, and other works for organ.

Kerman, Joseph (Wilfred) (1924–) US music scholar and critic. He studied in London, New York, and Princeton, and was professor at the University of California from 1960; Oxford 1971–74. He is an authority on William Byrd. His books include *Opera as Drama* (1956), *The Beethoven Quartets* (1967), and *Musicology* (1985).

Kern, Jerome David (1885–1945) US composer. Many of Kern's songs have become classics, notably 'Smoke Gets in Your Eyes' from his musical *Roberta* 1933. He wrote the operetta *Show Boat* 1927, which includes the song 'Ol' Man River'.

Based on Edna Ferber's novel, *Show Boat* was the first example of serious musical theatre in the USA.

Kern studied with Paolo Gallico and Alexander Lambert in New York. He turned to the composition of musical comedy and other light music, writing dozens of hit songs and musicals from 1904 and Hollywood movies from the beginning of the sound era 1927. He worked mainly with lyricist Otto Harbach but also with Ira Gershwin, Oscar Hammerstein II, Dorothy Fields, and Johnny Mercer.

Works include: musical comedies *Sunny* (1925), *Show Boat* (1927), *Music in the Air* (1932), *Roberta* (1933), and others; film music.

Kertész, István (1929–1973) Hungarian conductor. Zoltan Kodály was among his teachers. After gaining experience at the Budapest Opera, he left Hungary during the 1956 uprising. He was musical director of the Cologne Opera from 1964 until his death and brought the company to London in 1969.

His UK debut was with the Royal Liverpool Philharmonic Orchestra in 1960; he was principal conductor of the London Symphony Orchestra 1965–68. He led G Verdi's *Un Ballo in maschera* at Covent Garden, 1966. He is noted for his interpretations of Mozart and

Dvořák, and also heard in Britten, Prokofiev, Bartók, Stravinsky, and Henze. He drowned while swimming near Tel-Aviv.

kettledrum see ◊timpani.

Keuris, Tristan (1946–) Dutch composer. He studied at Utrecht with Ton de Leeuw 1963–69. He was head of composition at the Sweelinck Conservatory, and lectured in the USA, Norway, and Berlin.

Works include: quintet for orchestra (1967); *Choral Music* (1969); *Soundings* for orchestra (1970); alto saxophone concerto (1971); *Sinfonia* (1975); *Serenade* (1976); piano concerto (1980); *Movements* for orchestra (1982); two string quartets (1982, 1985); violin concerto (1984); *Symphonic Transformations* (Houston Symphony Orchestra commission, 1987); *To Brooklyn Bridge* for 24 voices and ensemble (1988); *Five Pieces* for brass quintet (1988); *Catena: Refrains and Variations* for 31 wind instruments, percussion, and celesta (1989); organ concerto (1993).

key the ◊diatonic scale around which a piece of music is written. For example, a passage in the key of C major uses mainly the notes of the C major scale, and harmonies made up of the notes of that scale. The first note of the scale is known as the ◊tonic; it gives the name of the key and is the note on which the music usually starts and finishes.

Most music does not remain in one key, but moves to related keys by using ◊chromatic notes in a process known as ◊modulation. This adds contrast and creates tension, which is relieved when the music returns to the 'home' key. The use of keys forms the basis of ◊tonality.

The term is also used for the lever on ◊keyboard instruments, such as the piano or organ, which the player presses in order to produce a note; and for the levers on ◊woodwind instruments which players press to cover the note holes out of the reach of their fingers.

Key, Francis Scott (1779–1843) US lawyer and poet. He wrote the song 'The Star-Spangled Banner' while Fort McHenry, Baltimore, was besieged by British troops 1814; since 1931 it has been the national anthem of the USA.

Key was born in Maryland. He served as US attorney for the District of Columbia 1833–41.

keyboard a set of 'keys' (levers worked by the fingers or feet) arranged in order of the pitches of notes they control, forming part of various keyboard instruments and enabling the performer to play a much larger number of strings or reeds than could otherwise be controlled. The keyboard is a major innovation of Western music, introduced to medieval instruments of the organ type (including the portative organ and the reed organ), and subsequently transferred to Renaissance stringed instruments such as the ◊clavichord and ◊hurdy-gurdy. Keyboard instruments were designed to enable precise and objective reproduction of musical intervals.

The clavichord was first developed as a demonstration ◊monochord, to which the addition of a keyboard brought flexibility and reliability in demonstrating the relationship of string length (position of the tangent, equivalent to a key-operated bridge) to pitch. Keyboards introduced consistent scaling to pitch space at the time that the Mercator projection was revolutionizing geographical mapmaking. Instrument makers seized on the user-friendly keyboard mechanism to create new markets for amateur and domestic use, creating in the clavichord a mechanized plectrum guitar, in the harpsichord a mechanized lute, in the hurdy-gurdy a keyboard viol, and in the fortepiano a mechanized dulcimer.

key bugle, also Kent bugle musical instrument, a type of ◊bugle with side holes covered with keys similar to those used on woodwind instruments. It was invented in the early 19th century.

keynote the ◊tonic: the note on which the scale begins and ends, which determines the key of a piece of music in major or minor and after which that key is named.

key relationships these may be close or remote, based largely on the similarity of key signatures; for instance, in the key of C major the relation of the tonic chord (C) with the dominant (G) is close.

The relation of C minor with E♭ major (its relative major) is also close, whereas the relation of C major with E♭ major is less close. Transference from one key to another may be abrupt or may be effected by modulation.

key signature sharps or flats indicating a prevailing key; the symbols for these are inserted on the score at the beginning of a musical stave, after the ◊clef. A key signature without sharps or flats signifies C major or A minor, or that the music is ◊atonal.

A change of key signature during a piece is indicated by a double bar at which any cancellation of elements of the previous key signature is shown by natural signs (♮) prior to or incorporated in the new key signature.

Khachaturian, Aram Il'yich (1903–1978) Armenian composer. His use of folk themes is shown in the ballets *Gayaneh* 1942, which includes the 'Sabre Dance', and *Spartacus* 1956.

His father, a bookbinder, was able to send him to study in Moscow only after the Revolution. He entered the Gnesin School of Music there and studied under Mikhail Gnesin in 1923; from 1929 until 1937 he studied at the Moscow Conservatory under Sergey Vasilenko and Myaskovsky. He studied the folk songs of Russian Armenia and other southern regions, which influenced his compositions. He was successful with a pre-war symphony and piano concerto, but was denounced in the composers' purge of 1948 and as a result turned to patriotic film and ballet music.

Works include: ballets *Happiness* (1939), *Gayaneh* (1942), and *Spartacus* (1954), incidental music for Shakespeare's *Macbeth*, Lope de Vega's *Widow of Valencia*, Pogodin's *Kremlin Chimes*, Kron's *Deep Drilling*, Lermontov's *Masquerade*, and others; film music *Song of Stalin* for chorus and orchestra; three symphonies (1932–47), *Dance Suite* and *Solemn Overture*, 'To the End of the War' for orchestra; marches and pieces on Uzbek and Armenian

Tonic/dominant and relative major/minor relationships are close; C major and E flat major are not closely related.

themes for wind band; concertos for piano, violin, cello, and violin and cello; string quartet (1932), trio for clarinet, violin, and piano; sonata and pieces for violin and piano; piano music, part songs; songs for the Russian army.

Maj.	Min.
C	A
G	E
D	B
A	F♯
E	C♯
B	G♯
F♯	D♯
C♯	A♯
C♭	A♭
G♭	E♭
D♭	B♭
A♭	F
E♭	C
B♭	G
F	D

The complete series of key signatures in order of increasing complexity by sharps, returning towards C major through the flat keys.

Khamma ballet-pantomime in two scenes by Debussy (scenario W L Courtney and M Allan), composed in short score 1911–12, orchestrated by Koechlin 1912–13; first performed (concert) Paris, 15 November 1924, conductor Pierné. First stage performance Paris, Opéra-Comique, 26 March 1947.

khorovod a type of ancient Russian folksong sung in chorus of two or more parts in a primitive kind of counterpoint. It was sung mainly at religious and family festivals and on seasonal occasions.

Khovanshchina unfinished opera by Mussorgsky (libretto by composer and V V Stassov), produced as completed and scored by Rimsky-Korsakov after Mussorgsky's death, St Petersburg, 21 February 1886. Shostakovich also added to Rimsky-Korsakov's work. The plot is based on historical events surrounding the opponents of Tsar Peter the Great: Prince Khovansky, head of the militia, the Regent Sofia as represented by the actions of Prince Golitsin, the 'Old Believers' as personified by Marfa. All come to an unhappy end.

Khrennikov, Tikhon Nikolaievich (1913–) Russian composer. He was secretary of the Union of Soviet Composers from 1948; and was made a Hero of Socialist Labour in 1973. He played a prominent part in the Stalinist-inspired denunciations of Prokofiev and Shostakovich; and renewed his attacks with the emergence of the New Music generation of composers, Schnittke and Sofia Gubaidulina.

He was taught music at home, but entered the Gnesin School of Music at Moscow in 1929 and the Conservatory in 1932 as a pupil of Shebalin.

Works include: the operas *The Brothers* (*In the Storm*, 1939); *Mother* (after Gogol, 1957); incidental music for Shakespeare's *Much Ado about Nothing*, an adaptation of Cervantes' *Don Quixote*, and others, film music for *The Pigs and the Shepherd*; three symphonies (1955–73); three piano concertos (1933–82); piano pieces; songs to words by Pushkin and Burns; war songs.

khyal (Hindi 'thought', 'idea') vocal genre of north Indian (Hindustani) music. Characterized by a text setting (usually in two sections, *sthayi* and *antara*) and a wide variety of improvisation techniques, most distinctively 'tan', melismatic flourishes which can be highly elaborate. The most commonly heard vocal genre in the tradition.

Kielflügel (German 'quill-wing') German name for the ḍharpsichord, so named from the quills that pluck the strings and the wing shape of the instrument's body.

Kilpinen, Yrjö (1892–1959) Finnish composer. He had a few lessons in theory at the Helsinki Conservatory and in Berlin and Vienna, but was otherwise self-taught. Like Sibelius, he was enabled by a government grant to devote himself to composition. He was one of the finest song composers of the 20th century, and wrote over 500 songs to Finnish, Swedish, and German texts.

Works include: cello sonata, viola da gamba sonata; piano sonatas; over 500 songs on Finnish, Swedish, and German poems.

Kim, Earl (1920–) US composer. In its precision and rhythmic subtlety, his music reflects his Korean origins. He was professor of music at Harvard 1967–90.

He studied at University College of Los Angeles with Schoenberg in 1939, and with Bloch and Sessions at Berkeley.

Works include: the opera *Footfalls*, 1981; *Dialogues* for piano and orchestra (1959); violin concerto (1979); 12 caprices for violin (1980); *Now and Then* for soprano, flute, viola, and harp (1981); *Where Grief Slumbers* for soprano, harp, and strings (1982); *The 11th Dream* for soprano, baritone, piano, violin, and cello (1989); *Three Poems in French* for soprano and string quartet (1989); *Some thoughts on Keats and Coleridge* for chorus (1990).

Kindermann, Johann Erasmus (1616–1655) German composer and organist. He studied with J Staden and in common with other German composers of his time probably visited Venice, where he would have met Frescobaldi and Cavalli. From 1640 he was organist at the Egidienkirche, Nuremberg.

Works include: vocal pieces *Cantiones Jesu Christi* (1639), *Friedens Clag* (1640), *Concentus Salomonis* (1642), *Opitianischer Orpheus* (1642), *Musica catechetica* (1643), *Gottliche Liebesflamme* (1651); nine cantatas, and other pieces; instrumental works *Harmonia organica* (1645), 27 Canzoni, nine sonatas; 30 suite movements; and other pieces.

Kinderszenen/Scenes from childhood thirteen piano pieces by Schumann, op. 15; composed 1838.

Kindertotenlieder/Songs of Dead Children cycle of five songs by Mahler, with orchestra or piano, to poems by Rückert; composed 1902, first performed Vienna, 29 January 1905, conductor Mahler.

King, Robert (lived 17th–18th centuries) English composer. He joined the royal band in 1680 on the death of John Banister, received a licence to give concerts in 1689, and took a degree in music at Cambridge University in 1696.

Works include: incidental music for Crowne's *Sir Courtly Nice* and many other plays; Shadwell's Ode on St Cecilia's Day, Motteux's Ode for John Cecil, Earl of Exeter; many songs for one and more voices.

King and Charcoal-Burner/Kral a Uhli opera by Dvořák (libretto by B Guldener), produced Prague, Czech Theatre, 24 November 1874. Dvořák's first opera to be produced. King Matyáš, lost in the forest, talks to Liduška, daughter of charcoal burner Matěj. Young Jeník becomes jealous and embarks on a glorious military career before he is united with her.

King Arthur, or The British Worthy semi-opera by Purcell (libretto by Dryden), produced London, Dorset Gardens Theatre, 1691. Arthur and Merlin fight Saxon leader Oswald to establish a united Britain and rescue the beloved Emmeline.

King Charles II opera by Macfarren (libretto by M D Ryan, based on a play by J H Payne), produced London, Princess's Theatre, 27 October 1849.

King Christian II incidental music by Sibelius for a play by A Paul; composed 1898, first performed Helsinki, 28 February 1898, conductor Sibelius. Suite for orchestra in six movements, 1898. First British performance London, 26 October 1901, conductor Wood.

Kingdom, The oratorio by Elgar, op. 51 (libretto compiled from the Bible by the composer), Part II of a trilogy of which I is *The Apostles* and III was never completed. First performed Birmingham Festival, 3 October 1906.

King Goes Forth to France, The/Kuningas lahtee Ranskaan opera in three acts by Aulis Sallinen (libretto by P Haavikko), produced Savonlinna Festival, 7 July 1984. Also staged at Santa Fe (1986) and Covent Garden (1987). A future prince seizes power from the prime minister, and facing a new ice age leads an army south into France.

King Lear incidental music for Shakespeare's tragedy by J André, produced Berlin, 30 November 1778.

Incidental music by Balakirev, produced St Petersburg, 1861.

Overture by Berlioz, op. 4, composed in Italy, 1831, first performed Paris, 9 November 1834.

Opera by Frazzi (1922–28, produced Florence, 1939).

Verdi worked at the Shakespearean subject for many years, but never brought the opera anywhere near completion, and his skhes were destroyed after his death, at his own wish. See ◊*Re Lear*.

For opera by Reimann, see ◊*Lear*.

'King of Prussia' Quartets (Mozart). See ◊*'Prussian' Quartets.*

King Olaf cantata for solo voices, chorus, and orchestra by Elgar, op. 30, set to words by Longfellow altered by H A Acworth, produced at the N Staffordshire Festival, Hanley, 30 October 1896.

King Priam opera in three acts by Tippett (libretto by composer), produced by the company of the Royal Opera, Covent Garden, at Coventry, 29 May 1962. Judgement of Paris followed by the destruction of Troy.

King Roger opera by Szymanowski (libretto by composer and J Iwaszkiewicz), produced Warsaw, 19 June 1926. Queen Roxane and her husband Roger are converted by a wandering shepherd-prophet, Dionysus in disguise.

King Stephen (Beethoven). See ◊*König Stephan.*

Kinkeldey, Otto (1878–1966) US musicologist. After a general academic education in New York and Berlin, he studied music with MacDowell 1900–02 while he was a schoolmaster and chapel organist. After further studies at the university and academy for church music in Berlin, he became organ teacher at a similar institution at Breslau (Wrocław in modern-day Poland), and later lecturer and professor of musicology. Returning to the USA in 1914 he was alternately chief of the music division of the New York Public Library and professor at Cornell University. He wrote a dissertation on 16th-century keyboard music and many valuable contributions to periodicals.

Kinsky, Georg (1882–1951) German music scholar and editor. Self-taught in music, he worked at first at the Prussian State Library in Berlin and then became curator until 1927 of the Heyer Museum of musical instruments, of which he compiled a valuable catalogue. From 1921 he was also active at the Cologne Conservatory, from which he retired 1932. His books include a *History of Music in Pictures*, works on instruments, and a catalogue of Beethoven's works.

Kirbye, George (c. 1565–1634) English composer. He first appeared as the most copious contributor, except John Farmer, to Thomas East's psalter *The Whole Book of Psalmes* 1592. In 1598 he married Anne Saxye, and he seems to have lived at that time at Rushbrooke near Bury St Edmunds, Suffolk, as domestic musician at the residence of Sir Robert Jermyn. In 1597 he dedicated his book of 24 madrigals to Jermyn's daughters. In 1601 he contributed a madrigal to *The Triumphes of Oriana.*

Works include: motets, a hymn; madrigals; pavane for viols.

Kircher, Athanasius (1601–1680) German mathematician, philosopher, and music scholar. He was professor at the Jesuit College of Würzburg, but was driven from Germany in 1633 by the Thirty Years' War. He travelled to Avignon, Vienna, and in 1637 to Rome, where he settled for the rest of his life. His chief musical literary work is *Musurgia universalis* 1650.

Kirckman, Jacob (1710–1792) German-born organist and composer. He settled in London about 1730 and founded a family firm of harpsichord makers which dominated the British market during the late 18th century and moved into piano manufacture in 1809.

Kirkpatrick, John (1905–1991) US pianist and scholar. He studied at Princeton and with Nadia Boulanger in Paris, and performed works by many modern US composers, in particular Charles Ives. In 1939 he gave the first performance in New York of the *Concord Sonata*, vital in the wider recognition of the music of Ives; he also made a significant academic contribution in this respect.

Kirkpatrick, Ralph (1911–1984) US harpsichordist and musicologist. He published a number of scholarly editions, including Bach's *Goldberg Variations* and an important book on Domenico Scarlatti (published in 1953) which gives definitive listings for all the sonatas given 'Kk' nos.

He studied piano at home and theory at Harvard, and went on to study with Nadia Boulanger in Paris. In Paris he took harpsichord lessons with Landowska, as well as working with Arnold Dolmetsch in Haslemere, Surrey. He received a Guggenheim Fellowship in 1937 and toured Europe studying early manuscripts. In 1940 he was appointed to Yale University.

Kirnberger, Johann Philipp (1721–1783) German theorist and composer. He was a pupil of J S Bach in Leipzig 1739–41. After various posts, he entered the service of Frederick the Great as a violinist in 1751. Appointed Kapellmeister and teacher of composition to Princess Amalia of Prussia in 1758, he increasingly abandoned performance and composition to devote his time to theoretical writings. Among many treatises the most important is *Die Kunst des reinen Satzes*, in which he promoted the conservative musical values of J S Bach. His compositions include cantatas, motets and instrumental music.

Kiss, The/Hubička, opera by Smetana (libretto by E Krásnohorská, based on a story by K Svetlá, produced Prague, 7 November 1876. Vendulka declines a kiss from widower Lukaš, for fear of offending the spirit of his dead wife. The pair are later united.

kit diminutive ◊violin, formerly used by dancing masters, who on account of its small size and narrow shape were able to carry it in the long pockets of their tail coats. It is therefore known in French as *pochette* and in German as *Taschengeige*.

Kitezh (Rimsky-Korsakov). See ◊*Legend of the Invisible City of Kitezh and Maiden Fevronia*.

kithara plucked string instrument of ancient Greece. See ◊lyre.

Kjerulf, Halfdan (1815–1868) Norwegian composer. He studied in Germany, and wrote a large number of songs that combine Norwegian folk tunes with German Romanticism.

At his father's desire he studied law at Christiania University, but on the death of his father in 1840 he decided to devote himself to music. He taught, and published some songs, even before he had done much in the way of theoretical study. In about 1850 he received a government grant to study at Leipzig for a year, and on his return he tried to establish classical subscription concerts, with little success. He became a friend of Bjørnsterne Bjørnson (1832–1910), who wrote many poems especially for him to set.

Works include: choruses and quartets for male voices; piano pieces; over 100 songs.

Klagende Lied, Das/The Song of Lamentation cantata by Mahler (text by composer) for soloists, chorus, and orchestra; first version 1880 in three parts: *Waldmärchen, Der Spielmann, Hochzeitstück*. Revised 1888 with part one omitted, first performed Vienna, 17 February 1901, conductor Mahler; first performed original version Vienna, 8 April 1935, conductor Arnold Rosé.

Klaviatur German name for a musical ◊keyboard.

Klavier German name for the ◊piano, but see also ◊clavier.

Klavierübung (J S Bach) see ◊*Clavierübung*.

Klebe, Giselher (1925–) German composer. He studied at the Berlin Conservatory with Kurt von Wohlfurt and later with Josef Rufer and Blacher. From 1946 to 1949 he worked for Berlin Radio. His music follows the traditions of Schoenberg and Webern.

Works include: OPERA *Die Räuben* (after Schiller, 1957), *Die tödlichen Wünsche* (1959), *Alkmene* (1961), *Figaro lässt sich scheiden* (1963), *Jacobowsky und der Oberst* (1965), *Ein wahrer Held* (after Synge, 1975), *Das Mädchen aus Domrémy* (1976), *Des Rendez-vous* (1977), *Der jüngste Tag* (1980), and *Die Fastnachtsbeichte* (1983).

OTHER *Con moto* for orchestra, five symphonies (1951–77), *Divertissement joyeux* for chamber orchestra, *Zwitschermaschine* for orchestra (after Paul Klee); concerto for violin, cello and orchestra(1954); concertos for cello, organ, clarinet and harpsichord (1957, 1980, 1985, 1988); ballet *Pas de trois*; *Geschichte der lustigen Musikanten* for tenor, chorus and five instruments; wind quintet, two sonatas for solo violin, viola sonata, three string quartets (1949, 1963, 1981); double bass sonata (1971).

Kleiber, Erich (1890–1956) Austrian conductor. He was appointed music director of the Berlin Staatsoper in 1923, and gave several important premieres, in particular that of *Wozzeck* 1925, of which he also conducted the first British stage performance in 1952. Differences with the Nazis obliged him to resign his Berlin post, and in 1937 he left Germany for Argentina, but returned to Europe in 1948. His son Carlos Kleiber is also a conductor.

After apprentice years in Darmstadt and Düsseldorf, he became music director of the Staatsoper, Berlin in 1923, making his debut with *Fidelio*. He made his London concert debut in 1935, with the London Symphony Orchestra, and in 1938 conducted *Der Rosenkavalier* at Covent Garden. He made his New York debut in 1930. Differences with the Nazis over artistic policy obliged him to resign his Berlin post, and from 1937 to 1949 he was active in Buenos Aires, becoming an Argentine citizen in 1938. He returned to Europe in 1948, conducting the London Philharmonic Orchestra, and in Florence in 1951 gave the first known performance of Haydn's last opera, *Orfeo ed Euridice*, with Maria Callas.

Kleider Machen Leute opera by Zemlinsky (libretto by L Feld after G Keller), produced Vienna, Volksoper, 2 December 1910). Nettchen and other villagers assume that travelling tailor Strapinski is a count. Nettchen falls in love with him, but her feelings remain unchanged after his lowly origins are revealed.

Kleine Nachtmusik, Eine (German 'Little Serenade') Mozart's own title for his serenade in G major for strings, K525, finished 10 August 1787.

Kleist, (Bernd) Heinrich (Wilhelm) von (1777–1811) German poet, novelist, and dramatist. See Felix ◊Draeseke (*Penthesilea* overture); Karoly ◊Goldmark (ditto); Paul ◊Graener (*Prinz von Homburg*); Joseph ◊Joachim (commemoration overture); Heinrich ◊Marschner (*Prinz von Homburg*); ◊*Penthesilea* (Schoeck); Hans ◊Pfitzner (*Käthchen von Heilbronn*); ◊*Prinz von Homburg, Der* (Henze); Wagner-Régeny (*Zerbrochene Krug*); Hugo ◊Wolf (*Penthesilea*).

Klemperer, Otto (1885–1973) German conductor. He was celebrated for his interpretation of contemporary and Classical music (especially Beethoven and Brahms). He conducted the Los Angeles Orchestra 1933–39 and the Philharmonia Orchestra, London, from 1959.

Klengel, Julius (1859–1933) German cellist and composer. He joined the Leipzig Gewandhaus orchestra at the age of 15, began to travel as a virtuoso in 1875, and in 1881 became leading cellist in the orchestra and professor of cello at the Leipzig Conservatory.

He studied cello with Emil Hegar and composition with Salomon Jadassohn (1831–1902).

Works include: four cello concertos, double concertos for violin and cello and two cellos, *Hymnus* for 12 cellos; *Caprice in form of a Chaconne* for cello solo, many cello pieces and studies.

Klindworth, Karl (1830–1916) German pianist and conductor. He was a pupil of Franz Liszt, and arranger of music for his instrument, including vocal scores of Richard Wagner's works. He lived in London as pianist, conductor and teacher 1854–68, then became piano professor at the Moscow Conservatory, but returned to Germany in 1884 and opened a school of music in Berlin in 1893. His adopted daughter Winifred Williams (1897–1980) married Siegfried Wagner.

Klingsor, Tristan (Léon Leclère) (1874–1966) French poet. See ◊*Shéhérazade* (Ravel).

Klopstock, Friedrich (1724–1803) German poet. His works inspired C P E ◊Bach (*Morgengesang am Schöpfungstage*); Christoph Willibald von ◊Gluck (odes); Jean François

◊Lesueur (*Mort d'Adam*); Giacomo ◊Meyerbeer (sacred cantatas); ◊*Resurrection Symphony* (Gustav Mahler); Corona Schröter (songs); Christian Friedrich Schwenke (odes); Ludwig ◊Spohr (*Vater unser*); Maximilian ◊Stadler (*Frühlingsfeier*); Philipp Wolfrum (*Grosse Hallelujah*). Thirteen songs were set by Schubert.

Klotz (lived 17th–18th centuries) German family of violin makers in Mittenwald, including **Matthias** (1653–1743), who worked for a time at Florence and Cremona, but returned to Mittenwald in about 1683; three sons, **Georg** (1687–1737), **Sebastian** (1696–1775), and **Johann Carl** (1709–1769).

At least 18 members of succeeding generations are known.

Kluge, Die/The Clever Girl opera by Orff (libretto by composer, after Grimm), produced Frankfurt, 20 February 1943.

Knaben Wunderhorn, Des/The Youth's Magic Horn German anthology of old folk poetry. The 13 *Des Knaben Wunderhorn* songs which Gustav Mahler scored for voice and orchestra in 1900, are: 1) *Der Schildwache Nachtlied*; 2) *Verlor'ne Muh*; 3) *Trost im Ungluck*; 4) *Wer hat dies Liedlein erdacht?*; 5) *Das irdische Leben*; 6) *Des Antonius von Padua Fischpredigt*; 7) *Rheinlegendchen*; 8) *Lied des Verfolgten in Turm*; 9) *Wo die schönen Trompeten blasen*; 10) *Lob des hohen Verstandes*; 11) *Es sungen drei Engel*; 12) *Urlicht*; 13) *Das himmlische Leben*. See ◊Mahler (songs, nine with piano, 13 with orchestra) and Otto ◊Vrieslander (songs).

Knappertsbusch, Hans (1888–1965) German conductor. He studied at the Cologne Conservatory with Steinbach and Lohse (1909–12) and then took various positions as an opera conductor. In 1922 he became conductor at the Munich Staatsoper, where he remained until 1938, when he became director of the Vienna Staatsoper. In 1937 he made his Salzburg opera debut (Richard Strauss's *Der Rosenkavalier*) and conducted his only opera in London (R Strauss's *Salome*, Covent Garden). He was guest conductor at the Wiener Philharmoniker 1947–64. He was best known for his performances of Wagner, especially *Parsifal*, which he conducted at Bayreuth from 1951.

Knecht, Justin Heinrich (1752–1817) German organist and composer. He worked as an organist and conductor in Biberach from 1771, and was vice-Kapellmeister in Stuttgart 1806–08.

Works include: a symphony entitled *Le Portrait musical de la nature* (about 1784) which has a programme similar to that of Beethoven's 'Pastoral' Symphony.

Kniegeige (German 'knee fiddle') German name for the Ọviola da gamba, a musical instrument.

Knipper, Lev Konstantinovich (1898–1974) Russian composer. His early work shows the influence of Stravinsky, but after 1932 he wrote in a more popular idiom, as in the symphony *Poem of Komsomol Fighters* 1933–34 with its mass battle songs. He is known in the West for his song 'Cavalry of the Steppes'.

knot alternative name for the ornamental fretwork sound hole of many flat-bellied string instruments and keyboard instruments, more generally called a rose.

Knot Garden, The opera by Tippett (libretto by composer), produced London, Covent Garden, 2 December 1970, conductor C Davis. Under the auspices of psychoanalyst Mangus, Faber and Thea overcome marital difficulties; gay couple Mel and Dov separate when Mel's lust is directed towards Thea's sister, Denise.

Knussen, (Stuart) Oliver (1952–) English composer and conductor. An eclectic and prolific composer, his works include the opera *Where the Wild Things Are* 1983, based on the children's story by Maurice Sendak.

He studied in the USA with Gunter Schuller.

Works include: the operas *Where the Wild Things Are* (1983) and *Higglety Pigglety Pop* (1985; produced at Glyndebourne); three symphonies (1966–79); Concerto for Orchestra (1970); *Coursing* for chamber orchestra (1979); *Chiara* for orchestra (1986); *Hums and Songs of Winnie-the-Pooh* for soprano and ensemble (1970–83), *Trumpets*, for soprano and three clarinets (1975); *Late Poems and an Epigram of Rainer Maria Rilke* for soprano (1988); *Whitman Settings* for soprano and orchestra (1991); *Sonya's Lullaby* for piano (1978); *Variations* for piano (1989); *Songs Without Voices* for eight instruments (1992).

Koanga opera by Delius (libretto by C F Keary, based on G W Cable's novel *The Grandissimes*), produced Elberfeld, in Germany, 30 March 1904. Uncle Joe tells the story of Koanga, a slave-prince who falls in love with slave-girl Palmyra. Plantation owner Perez prevents the wedding. Koanga kills him and is himself captured and killed. Palmyra commits suicide.

Koch, (Sigurd Christian) Erland ̦ von (1910–) Swedish composer. His compositions are chiefly instrumental and based on folk music.

He studied at the Stockholm Conservatory and later in London, Paris, and Dresden.

Works include: four symphonies (1938–53); symphonic poem *A Tale from the Wilderness, Symphonic Episode, Symphonic Dance*; three piano concertos (1936–72); violin concerto; suite for chamber orchestra; six string quartets (1934–63); string trio; violin and piano sonata; piano works; songs.

Köchel, Ludwig (Alois Ferdinand) Ritter von (1800–1877) Austrian naturalist and music bibliographer. He lived at Salzburg 1850–63 for the purpose of compiling his thematic catalogue of Mozart's works, published in 1862 (sixth edition 1964).

Kodály, Zoltán (1882–1967) Hungarian composer and educationalist. With Béla Bartók, he recorded and transcribed Magyar folk music, the scales and rhythm of which he incorporated in a deliberately nationalist style. His works include the cantata *Psalmus Hungaricus* 1923, a comic opera *Háry János* 1925–27, and orchestral dances and variations. His 'Kodály method' of school music education is widely practised.

Kodály learnt the violin as a child, sang in a cathedral choir, and tried to compose without systematic instruction. In 1900, after living in small provincial towns, he entered the University of Budapest to study science, but also became a pupil at the Conservatory. He studied Hungarian folk song and in 1906 wrote his university thesis on it; in the same year his *Summer Evening* was premiered in Budapest. He collected folk songs in collaboration with Bartók 1907–14. He was appointed professor at the Conservatory and deputy director in 1919.

His music was performed at the International Society for Contemporary Music festivals from their inception in 1923. Beatrice Harrison gave London performances in 1924 of his finest chamber work, the sonata for solo cello, and further recognition on the international stage came with the premieres of the *Háry János* suite 1927 and the *Dances from Marosszek* 1930. The popular *Psalmus Hungaricus* was performed in London and New York from 1927; Henry Wood programmed *Summer Evening* and *Dances from Galanta* at the London Promenade concerts in 1930 and 1931.

Variations on a Hungarian Folksong (Peacock) was composed for the Concertgebouw Orchestra in 1939 and the *Concert for Orchestra* for the Chicago Symphony Orchestra in 1941. His final work for orchestra was the symphony in C 'In memoriam Arturo Toscanini', which was premiered at Lucerne under Ferenc Fricsay in 1961. In 1945 Kodály became president of the newly founded Hungarian Arts Council, and in 1967 was awarded the Gold Medal of the Royal Philharmonic Society. In 1960 he received an honorary doctorate in music from Oxford University.

Works include: ORCHESTRAL *Summer Evening* (1906), *Ballet Music* and *Suite*, for *Háry János* (1925–27), *Dances of Galánta* (1933), *Marosszék Dances* (1930), *Variations on a Hungarian Folksong, The Peacock* (1939).

CHAMBER AND VOCAL two string quartets (1909, 1918); duo for violin and cello (1914); sonatas for cello solo (1915) and for cello and piano (1909); 21 works for chorus with and without orchestra, including *Psalmus Hungaricus, Budavari Te Deum* (1936), *Missa brevis.*

OTHER play with music *Háry János* (1926).

Koechlin, Charles (1867–1950) French composer. He never appeared as an executive musician or held any official appointment, but devoted himself largely to composition and the writing of some theoretical books as well as studies of Debussy and Fauré. Other influences on his music were Ravel, Poulenc, and Stravinsky.

He studied at the Paris Conservatory, where his teachers included Massenet and Fauré. He exercised a considerable influence on younger French composers, not least through his theoretical writings. His output is vast and leaves hardly any category of music unprovided, and although he sought no success and obtained little, his work is of high quality and lasting interest.

Works include: seven pieces inspired by Kipling's *Jungle Book* (Three Poems for soli, choir, and orchestra, op. 18; symphonic poems *La course de printemps, La méditation de Parun Baghat, La loi de la Jungle, Les Bandar-Log); Seven Stars Symphony* (on film stars including Greta Garbo, Marlene Dietrich, and Charlie Chaplin); *Symphonie d'hymnes* (1910–33); *Le Docteur fabricius,* symphonic poem (1944); chamber music: three string quartets; sonatas for violin, viola, cello, flute, oboe, clarinet, bassoon, and horn, all with piano; 13 sonatinas for piano; choruses, songs.

Koffler, Józef (1896–1943) Polish composer. After studying with Schoenberg, he began to cultivate the 12-note system, the first Polish composer to do so. Later he became professor at the Lwów State Conservatory, but was killed during a Nazi roundup of Jews near Kraków.

He studied composition with Hermann Theodor Otto Grädener (1844–1929) and musicology with Guido Adler (1855–1941) in Vienna.

Works include: ballet *Alles durch M.O.W.;* three symphonies (no. 3 performed at London, 1938) and *Polish Suite* for orchestra, 15 variations for string orchestra; string trio (performed Oxford, 1931), cantata *Die Liebe* for voices, viola, cello, and clarinet; piano music, 40 *Polish Folksongs, Musique de ballet, Musique quasi una sonata,* sonatina, and other pieces; four poems for voice and piano.

Kokkonen, Joonas (1921–) Finnish composer. His early work was neoclassical in spirit; later influences were Bach, Sibelius, and Bartók. He was professor of composition at the Sibelius Academy, Helsinki.

He studied with Palmgren and Hannikainen at the Sibelius Academy, Helsinki.

Works include: the opera *Viimeiset Kiusaukset/The Last Temptations,* produced Helsinki 1975, London 1979); five symphonies (1960–82), *Music for Strings* (1957), cello concerto (1969); *Missa a cappella* (1963), Requiem (1983); piano trio (1948), three string quartets (1959, 1966, 1976), *Sinfonia da camera* for 12 strings (1962), *... durch einen spiegel* for 12 strings and harpsichord (1977), *Improvvisazione* for violin and piano (1982), *Il Paesaggio* for chamber orchestra (1987).

Kokoschka, Oskar (1886–1980) German poet, playwright, and painter. His works inspired Hindemith (◊*Mörder, Hoffnung der Frauen*) and Křenek (◊*Orpheus und Eurydike*).

Kolb, Barbara (1939–) US composer. She has taught theory and composition in New York and has directed the Third Street Music School Settlement from 1979. She was resident at the electronic studio ◊IRCAM, Paris 1983–84.

She studied composition and clarinet at Hartt College and with Lukas Foss and Gunther Schuller at the Berkshire Music Center.

Works include: *Trobar clus* for 13 instruments (1970); *Soundings* for 11 instruments and tape (1972); *Frailties* for tenor, tape, and orchestra (1971); *Musique pour un vernissage* for ensemble (1977); *The Point that Divides the Wind* for organ and 4 percussionists (1981); *Millefoglie* for chamber orchestra (1988); *The Enchanted Loom* for orchestra (1989); *Voyants* for piano and chamber orchestra (1991); *Clouds* for organ, piano, and tape (1992); *All in Good Time* for orchestra (1993).

kolenda, modern-day kolęda a type of Polish folk song (carol) sung at Christmas, some specimens dating back to the 13th century.

Kollmann, August Friedrich Christoph (1756–1829) German organist; theorist, and composer. He held a post at Lüne, near Lüneburg, but in 1782 went to London, where he was appointed sacristan and cantor of the German Chapel, St James's. He wrote many theoretical works, and also composed a piano concerto and chamber music.

Kol Nidre/All Vows work for cello and orchestra by Bruch, composed 1881. Also version for cello and piano.

Work by Schoenberg for speaker (rabbi), chorus, and orchestra, op. 39; composed autumn 1938, first performed Los Angeles, 4 October 1938, conductor Schoenberg.

kolo Siberian dance in quick 2–4 time. The 15th of Dvořák's *Slavonic Dances* for piano duet is a kolo.

Kondracki, Michał (1902–) Polish composer. He studied with Karol Szymanowski at Warsaw and with Paul Dukas and Nadia Boulanger in Paris, returning to Poland in 1931.

    Works include: the opera *Popieliny* (1934); ballet *Legend of Kraków* (1937); *Cantata ecclesiastica* and humorous cantata *Krasula*; orchestral works *Little Mountain Symphony*, symphonic action *Metropolis* (1929), toccata and fugue, symphonic picture *Soldiers march past, Match*, partita for small orchestra, nocturne for chamber orchestra; piano concerto.

Kondrashin, Kiril (1914–1981) Russian conductor. He conducted opera in Leningrad and Moscow 1936–56. He was principal conductor of the Moscow Philharmonic Orchestra 1960–75 and assistant conductor of the Concertgebouw Orchestra from 1975. He recorded the Shostakovich symphony and gave the first performances of no 13 (1962) and the second violin concerto (1967). He conducted at the Hollywood Bowl one month before his death.

König Hirsch/The Stag King opera by Henze (libretto by H von Cramer after Gozzi's *Re Cervo*, 1762), produced Berlin, 23 September 1956. Revised as *Il Re Cervo* 1962 and produced Kassel, 10 March 1963. First staging of complete score in original version at Stuttgart, 5 May 1985. King Leandro assumes the shape of a stag and his treacherous chancellor, Tartaglia, magically transforms himself to the King's appearance, and orders a stag hunt. Tartaglia is killed by the assassin Coltellino who, under contract from Tartaglia himself, believes him to be the King. All rejoice.

Königin von Saba, Die/The Queen of Sheba opera by C Goldmark (libretto by S H Mosenthal), produced Vienna, Opera, 10 March 1875. King Solomon's diplomat Assad forsakes his fiancée Sulamith for a secret affair with the Queen of Sheba. Assad blasphemes publicly, placing the Queen above the gods; he is banished to the desert, where he is reconciled with Sulamith and dies.

Königskinder/King's Children opera by Humperdinck (libretto by E Rosmer), produced as a play with accompanying music, Munich, 23 January 1897; the operatic version produced New York Metropolitan Opera 28 December 1910. Goose-girl escapes from the witch and is united with the King's son, but both are rejected by the townspeople, and die after eating the witch's poisoned bread.

König Stephan incidental music by Beethoven, op. 117, for Kotzebue's play written for the opening of the new theatre at Pest and performed there 9 February 1812.

Kontakte work by Stockhausen for piano, percussion and four-track tape (1959–60, first perfomed Cologne, 11 June 1960).

Kontrapunkte work by Karlheinz Stockhausen for six wind instruments, piano, harp, violin, and cello, 1952–53; first performed Cologne, 26 May 1953.

Konzertmeister (German 'concert master') the leader of an orchestra.

Konzertstück see ◊Concertstück.

Kopfton see ◊fundamental line.

kora plucked harp-lute with twenty-one strings from West Africa. Used by professional male musicians known as *jalolu* (singular *jali*) of the Mandinka people of Gambia and Senegal. The kora primarily accompanies narrations, recitations, and songs in honour of a patron.

Korn, Peter (Jona) (1920–) German-born US composer and conductor. After studies with Rubbra in London, he moved to the USA in 1941, continuing his studies with Ernst Toch and Schoenberg. He founded the Los Angeles New Orchestra in 1948 and was its conductor until 1956. In 1967 he was appointed director of the Strauss Conservatory at Munich.

    Works include: the opera *Heidi* in Frankfurt (1963, first performance 1978); three symphonies (1946, 1952, 1956), violin concerto (1965), *Beckmesser* variations for orchestra (1977), trumpet concerto (1979); two string quartets (1950, 1963), wind quintet (1964), piano trio (1975), octet (1976), duo for viola and piano (1978).

Korngold, Erich Wolfgang (1897–1957) Austrian-born US composer. He began composing while still in his teens and achieved early recognition when his opera *Die tote Stadt/Dead City* was premiered simultaneously in Hamburg and Cologne 1920. In 1934 he moved to Hollywood to become a composer for Warner Brothers. His film scores, in richly orchestrated and romantic style, include *The Adventures of Robin Hood* 1938 and *Of Human Bondage* 1945.

Kossuth symphonic poem in ten tableaux by Bartók; composed 1903, first performed Budapest, 13 January 1904.

koto Japanese musical instrument; a long ◊zither of ancient Chinese origin, having 13 silk strings supported by movable bridges. It rests on the floor and the strings are plucked with ivory plectra, producing a brittle sound.

Kotzebue, August (Friedrich Ferdinand) von (1761–1819) German playwright. See Pietro ◊Generali (*Misantropia e pentimento*); Beethoven (◊*König Stephan*); Albert ◊Lortzing (*Wildschütz*); Johann ◊Reichardt (*Kreuzfahrer*); Peter Ritter (*Eremit auf Formentara*); Beethoven (◊*Ruins of Athens*); Antonio ◊Salieri (*Hussiten vor Naumburg*); Franz ◊Süssmayr (*Wildfang*); Schubert (◊*Teufels Lustschloss, Des*); Paul ◊Wranitzky (music for plays).

Koukourgi (Cherubini). See ◊*Ali Baba, ou Les Quarante Voleurs*.

Koussevitsky, Sergei (1874–1951) Russian musician and conductor. He is well known for his work in the USA. He established his own orchestra in Moscow in 1909, introducing works by Prokofiev, Rachmaninov, and Stravinsky. Although named director of the State Symphony after the Bolshevik Revolution 1917, Koussevitsky left the USSR for the USA, becoming director of the Boston Symphony Orchestra in 1924.

Koussevitsky was trained at a conservatory in Moscow, becoming a recognized virtuoso on the double bass; he later specialized as a soloist on the instrument and toured Europe. He first appeared as a conductor in Berlin 1908. In 1924 he was appointed conductor of the Boston Symphony Orchestra, and in 1934 founded the annual Tanglewood summer music festival in W Massachusetts. He commissioned Stravinsky's *Symphony of Psalms* in 1931 and in 1943 Bartók's Concerto for orchestra. Other works he premiered include the Mussorgsky/Ravel *Pictures* 1922, Prokofiev's first violin concerto 1923 and second

symphony 1925, and Bernstein's second symphony 1949. The Koussevitsky Music Foundation, set up as a memorial to his wife, commissioned Britten's *Peter Grimes* 1945, among other works.

Kozeluch (Kotzeluch, Koželuh), Leopold (1747–1818) Bohemian composer. He was a pupil of his cousin Johann Anton Kozeluch (1738–1814), and studied law at Prague University, but devoted himself entirely to composition from 1771. In 1778 he went to Vienna and succeeded Mozart as Imperial composer in 1792.

Works include: the operas *Didone abbandonata*, *Judith*, *Deborah*, and others; oratorio *Moisé in Egitto* (1787); 24 ballets and 3 pantomimes; 11 symphonies; 22 piano concertos and several for other instruments; 6 string quartets, 63 trios; piano sonatas, folksong arrangements.

Kraft, Anton (1749–1820) Bohemian cellist and composer. Beethoven's Triple Concerto was composed for him, and he played in the first performance of Beethoven's seventh symphony 1813. Haydn's D major cello concerto was once ascribed to Kraft.

Originally intended for a career in law, he was engaged by Prince Esterházy as principal cellist in 1778, remaining until 1790 and receiving tuition in composition from Haydn. He was subsequently in the service of Prince Grassalkovich and (from 1795) Prince Lobkowitz.

Works include: concertos, sonatas, and other pieces for cello, duets for two cellos.

Kraft, William (1923–) US composer and timpanist. He founded and directed the Los Angeles Percussion Ensemble, giving the US first performances of Stockhausen's *Zyklus* and Boulez's *Le marteau sans maître*. He was principal with the Los Angeles Philharmonic Orchestra 1955–81 and composer-in-residence 1981–85.

He studied at University College of Los Angeles, then at Columbia University 1949–52, with Henry Brant and Otto Luening.

Works include: *Concerto Grosso* (1961); Concerto for four percussion and orchestra (1966); *Triangles* for percussion and ten instruments (1969); piano concerto (1973); timpani concerto (1983); *Weavings* for string quartet and percussion (1984); *Contextures II* for soprano, tenor, and chamber orchestra (1984); *A Kennedy Portrait* for narrator and orchestra (1988); horn concerto (1988).

krakowiak a Polish dance from the region of Kraków, sometimes introduced into ballets and ballrooms in the 19th century under the name of *Cracovienne*. In its original form it was danced by all the assembled couples and sometimes words were sung to it. It is in quick 2–4 time. The best-known example is Chopin's concert rondo op. 14 (1828).

Krämerspiegel/The Shopkeeper's Mirror cycle of 12 songs for voice and piano by Richard Strauss (texts by A Kerr); composed 1918 and includes ironic references to German publishers: no. 2 *Einst kam der Bock als Bote*, refers to Berlin publishing firm, Bote und Bock. First performed Berlin, 1 November 1926.

Kraus, Joseph Martin (1756–1792) German composer. He settled in Sweden and became director of music to the King. His opera *Proserpina* 1781 was revived at the Drottningholm Theare, near Stockholm, in 1981 .

He studied law and philosophy at Mainz, Erfurt, and Göttingen, and studied composition with Georg Vogler. He went to Stockholm and remained there as a theatre conductor, becoming music director in 1781. In 1782–87 he travelled widely with a grant from the King of Sweden. In 1788 he succeeded Francesco Uttini as Kapellmeister at Stockholm.

Works include: the operas *Soliman II, Aeneas at Carthage* (produced 1799), *Proserpina* (1781), church music; *Funeral Cantata for Gustavas III* (1792); symphonies and overtures; string quartets.

Krauss, Clemens (1893–1954) Austrian conductor. From 1912 he conducted at several opera houses in Germany and Austria, including Vienna and Berlin. He was closely associated with Richard Strauss, both as a conductor, and in the case of *Capriccio*, as joint librettist; he conducted the first performances of *Arabella, Friedenstag,* and *Die Liebe der Danae.*

He studied with Hermann Theodor Otto Grädener (1844–1929) and Richard Heuberger at the Vienna Conservatory. In 1922 he became conductor at the Vienna Staatsoper and in 1924 opera intendant and conductor of the Museum concerts at Frankfurt. In 1929–34 he was director of the Vienna and in 1934–36 of the Berlin Staatsoper, after which he directed the Opera at Munich. He married the singer Viorica Ursuleac (1894–1985).

Krebs, Johann Ludwig (1713–1780) German organist, harpsichordist, and composer. He was a pupil of J S Bach at Leipzig from 1726, and became organist at Zwickau, Zeitz, and Altenburg.

Works include: Magnificat, settings of the Sanctus; trios; sonatas, suites, fugues, choruses, with variations, and other pieces for clavier; flute sonatas, organ music.

Krehbiel, Henry (Edward) (1854–1923) US music critic and author. After studying law at Cincinnati, he became music critic to the *Cincinnati Gazette,* 1874, and to the *New York Tribune,* 1880. He edited Thayer's life of Beethoven, collected and wrote on African-US folksongs and wrote many books including studies of opera, of Richard Wagner's works, and of US musical life.

Kreidekreis, Der/The Chalk Circle opera by Zemlinsky (libretto by composer after Klabund); 1932, produced Zurich, 14 October 1933. Zemlinsky's last completed opera. Prostitute Haitang becomes Empress of China after Prince Pao reveals he is the father of her child.

Kreisler, Fritz (1875–1962) Austrian violinist and composer. He was a US citizen from 1943. His prolific output of recordings in the early 20th century introduced a wider public to classical music from old masters such as J S Bach and Couperin to moderns such as de Falla and Rachmaninov. He also composed and recorded romantic pieces in the style of the classics, often under a pseudonym.

He gave the first performance of Elgar's *Violin Concerto* 1910, dedicated to him by the composer.

He appeared as an infant prodigy at the age of seven. He studied at the Vienna Conservatory under Joseph Hellmesberger and Jacques Auber, and at the Paris Conservatory under Joseph Massart and Delibes, winning the gold medal at the age of 12. After touring in the USA in 1889 he returned to Austria to study medicine. After his military service and a period of intense study, he reappeared as a soloist in Berlin in 1899 and again toured in the USA. After three months' service in the Austrian army in 1914 he was discharged on account of wounds and returned to the USA, where he eventually made his home. He made frequent tours in Europe and gave the first performance of Elgar's violin concerto (10 November 1910). He was best known for his broad-toned and emotionally committed performances of the Brahms and Beethoven violin concertos. His compositions include a string quartet, the operetta *Apple Blossoms* 1919, and a number of violin solos, some of which he at first tried to present as the work of 18th-century composers.

Kreisleriana a cycle of piano pieces by Schumann, op. 16, composed in 1838 and dedicated to Chopin. The title is borrowed from the musician Kreisler in E T A Hoffmann's stories *Fantasiestücke in Callots Manier*.

Krejčí, Iša (1904–1968) Czech composer. He was a pupil of Novák and Jirák. After working for some time at Bratislava, he returned to Prague and joined the radio service.

Works include: the opera *Confusion at Ephesus* (on Shakespeare's *Comedy of Errors*, 1946), operatic scene *Antigone* (after Sophocles, 1934), sinfonietta for orchestra; *Little Ballet* for chamber orchestra; string quartet in D major, nonet, trios for oboe, clarinet, and bassoon and clarinet, double bass and piano; sonatina for clarinet and piano; songs.

Krenek, Ernst (1900–1991) Austrian-born US composer and theorist. Following early popular success with the jazz-influenced operas *Jonny spielt auf/Johnny Strikes Up* 1926 and *Leben des Orest/Life of Orestes* 1930, he supported himself as a critic while working on the ambitious twelve-tone opera *Karl V/Charles V* 1938. He moved to teaching posts in the USA in 1939 but remained in contact with postwar developments in extended serialism and aleatoric music with *Quaestio Temporis/In Search of Time* 1957, and with electronic music in *Spiritus intelligentiae sanctus* 1956.

His writings include the study *Johannes Ockeghem* 1953 and *Horizon Circled* 1974.

Krenek studied with Franz Schreker in Vienna and Berlin. In the 1920s he appeared at several of the smaller festivals in Germany and 1925–27 was conductor at the operas of Kassel, Wiesbaden, and other smaller towns in order to gain experience in operatic stagecraft. His first wife was Gustav Mahler's daughter Anna. After the success of *Jonny spielt auf*, he worked in 12-note music as a disciple of Schoenberg. In 1933, when the Nazi régime gained the upper hand, he settled in Vienna and worked on behalf of progressive Austrian composers, but he was opposed by the Fascists and his *Karl V* was banned at the Vienna Staatsoper. He left Austria for the USA in 1937, where he later became Dean of the School of Fine Arts and director of the music department at Hamline University, St Paul 1942–47; he lived in California from 1948. His book *Über neue Musik*, first published in Vienna in 1937 and then translated and revised as *Music Here and Now* (New York, 1939) is a defence of the 12-note system.

Amends for the hostile treatment he received in Vienna were made with the 1990 first performance of his 1930 musical satire *Kehraus um St Stephan* – a revision of *Karl V*

had been given at Vienna in 1984. Belated recognition in his homeland was also shown with the 1988 Salzburg Festival premiere of his 1935 oratorio *Symeon der Stylit*.

Works include: OPERA *Jonny spielt auf* (1927), *Leben des Orest* (1930), *Karl V* (1938), *Der goldene Bock* (1964).

CHORAL MUSIC *Lamentatio Jeremiae Prophetae* (1941).

ORCHESTRAL five symphonies (1921–50), two *Concerti grossi*; four piano concertos (1923–50), two violin concertos (1924, 1954), cello concerto; theme and 13 variations for orchestra (1931).

CHAMBER AND SOLO VOCAL 8 string quartets (1921–52); 25 songs, song cycles *Reisebuch aus den österreichischen Alpen*, *Gesänge des späten Jahres*.

Kreutzer, Conradin (1780–1849) German conductor and composer. He held the post of Kapellmeister in Stuttgart, Donaueschingen, Vienna, and Cologne. His most successful composition was the opera *Der Verschwender* 1834.

He first learnt music as a choirboy, then went to Freiburg im Breislau to study law, but gave it up for music. He travelled in Switzerland as a pianist and singer and in 1804 went to Vienna to study composition with Johann Albrechtsberger. After conducting at the court of Stuttgart and Donaueschingen, he returned to Vienna and became conductor at the Kärntnertortheater for three periods between 1822 and 1840 and of the Josefstadttheater 1833–40. Later he worked at Cologne and Paris, and again in Vienna.

Works include: the operas *Conradin von Schwaben* (1812), *Die Alpenhütte* (1815), *Libussa* (libretto by Grillparzer, 1822), *Melusine* (libretto ditto, 1833), *Das Nachtlager von Granada* (1834), *Cordelia* and about 25 others; incidental music to plays including Raimund's *Der Verschwender* (1834); oratorio *Sending Moses* (1814); church music; chamber music; piano works; male-voice part songs and songs.

Kreutzer, Rodolphe (1766–1831) French violinist and composer of German descent. Beethoven dedicated his violin sonata op. 47 to him, known as the *Kreutzer Sonata*.

Kreutzer was born at Versailles, and was taught mainly by his father. When he was 16 the French queen Marie Antoinette appointed him first violin in the royal chapel, where he learnt much from hearing Nicola Mestrino (1748–89) and Giovanni Battista Viotti. Later he became leader at the Théâtre Italien, where he began to write operas of his own. He toured much and became violin professor at the Paris Conservatory in 1795. In 1798 he went to Vienna in the suite of Count Bernadotte and got to know Beethoven. He often played violin duets with Pierre Rode, and on the latter's departure to Russia in 1801, Kreutzer became leader at the Paris Opéra. He later held court appointments under both Napoleon I and Louis XVIII. He compiled a *Méthode de violon* with the violinist Pierre Baillot.

Works include: the operas *Jeanne d'Arc à Orléans* (1790), *Paul et Virginie* (after Saint-Pierre), *Lodoïska* (1791), *Imogène, ou la gageure indiscrète* (after Boccaccio, 1796), *Astyanax, Aristippe* (1808), *La mort d'Abel* (1810), *Mathilde* and many others; ballets *Paul et Virginie, Le carnaval de Venise, Clari*, and others; 19 violin concertos (1783–1810), 4 *Symphonies concertantes*; 15 string quartets; 15 trios; sonatas, caprices, studies, airs with variations for violin.

'Kreutzer' Sonata nickname of Beethoven's A-major violin and piano sonata, op. 47, composed in 1803 and dedicated to R Kreutzer. The work is the subject of Tolstoy's novel *The Kreutzer Sonata*, in which it has a disastrous effect on the morals of the characters. Beethoven and George Bridgetower gave the first performed on 17 May 1803.
Subtitle of Janáček's first string quartet, composed 1923–24, based on lost piano trio of 1908–09. First performed Prague, 17 September 1924.

Křička, Jaroslav (1882–1969) Czech composer. He taught in Russia, and on his return to Prague in 1909 became conductor of the Glagol choral society. He was director of the Prague Conservatory 1942–45.
He studied at the Prague Conservatory 1902–05, and came under the influence of Vitězslav Novák, enlarged his experience in Berlin, and then went to Russia, teaching at the music school of Ekaterinoslav.
Works include: the operas *Hypolita* (after one of Maurice Hewlett's *Little Novels of Italy*, 1916) and *The Gentleman in White* (after Wilde's *Canterville Ghost*, 1929); several operas for children; choral works *The Temptation in the Wilderness* (1922) and many others with and without orchestra; symphony in D minor, symphonic poems *Faith*, overture to Maeterlinck's *Blue Bird* (1911), *Polonaise* and *Elegy on the Death of Rimsky-Korsakov, Children's Suite* for small orchestra (1907), *Nostalgia* for string orchestra; three string quartets (1907–39), violin and piano sonata; piano music and songs.

Krieger, Johann (1651–1735) German organist and composer. He was court organist at Bayreuth 1671–77, and later became organist and town music director at Zittau.
He was taught by his brother, Philipp ◊Krieger.
Works include: plays with music; sacred and secular songs for several voices with instruments; organ works; six partitas, preludes and fugues for clavier.

Krieger, Johann Philipp (1649–1725) German organist and composer, brother of Johann ◊Krieger. He travelled in Italy and studied under Johann Rosenmüller at Venice. He then entered the service of the Duke of Saxe-Weissenfels, and was chamber musician and organist at Halle from 1677 and music director at Weissenfels from 1712.
Works include: the opera *Der grossmütige Scipio* (1690) and others; plays with music; church music; arias for one–four voices with instruments; sonatas for violin and viola da gamba; *Partien* for wind instruments.

Krips, Josef (1902–1974) Austrian conductor. He studied in Vienna with Mandyczewski and Weingartner, and became a violinist in the Volksoper there. In 1924 he began his career as a conductor and from 1926 to 1933 was general music director at Karlsruhe. In 1933 he became a conductor at the Vienna Staatsoper and in 1935 professor at the Vienna Academy of Music.
He made his Salzburg Festival debut in 1935 with *Der Rosenkavalier*; he returned in 1946, with *Don Giovanni*. During World War II he lost these positions, but rejoined the Vienna Staatsoper in 1945; he took the company to Covent Garden in 1947, conducting Mozart's three Da Ponte operas; he returned with the Covent Garden company in 1963, with *Don Giovanni*. From 1950 to 1954 he was conductor at the London Symphony Orchestra; San Francisco Symphony Orchestra 1963–70, New York Metropolitan Opera from 1967 (*Zauberflöte*).

kriti (Telugu 'work', 'composition') an important genre of south Indian (Carnatic) music. Essentially a song in three sections (*pallavi, anupallavi, charanam*), it is often performed with the addition of improvised sections. Kritis also form an important part of the solo instrumental repertoire. Important composers include Tyagaraja (1767–1847) and Muttuswami Dikshitar (1775–1835).

Krommer, Franz (originally Kramář, František Vincenc) (1759–1831) Moravian violinist, organist, and composer. His symphonies and chamber pieces are similar in style to those of Mozart and Haydn. Having been an organist 1776–84, he went to Hungary and later became music director to Prince Grassalkovich in Vienna. In 1818 he succeeded Leopold Kozeluch as court music director.

Works include: two Masses; music for wind band; symphonies; 69 string quartets and quintets.

Krumhorn German spelling of ◊crumhorn, a Renaissance double-reed woodwind instrument.

Krumpholz, Johann Baptist (1742–1790) Bohemian harpist and composer. He grew up in Paris, travelled as a virtuoso, and was in the service of Prince Esterházy 1773–76, receiving tuition in composition from Haydn. After further travels he settled in Paris, and was responsible for some notable improvements to his instrument. When his wife deserted him for the composer J L Dussek, he drowned himself in the river Seine.

Works include: 8 concertos, 32 sonatas for harp; 2 symphonies for harp and small orchestra; harp duets.

Kubelik, (Jeronym) Rafael (1914–1996) Czech conductor and composer. He is the son of violinist Jan Kubelik. His works include symphonies and operas, such as *Veronika* 1947. He was musical director of the Royal Opera House, Covent Garden, London, 1955–58.

Kubelik, Jan (1880–1940) Czech violinist and composer. He performed in Prague at the age of eight, and became one of the world's greatest virtuosos; he also wrote six violin concertos.

Kubik, Gail (1914–1984) US violinist and composer. She studied at the Eastman School of Music, Rochester, New York , and won several composition prizes.

Works include: ballet *Frankie and Johnnie* for dance band and folk singer (1946); *In Praise of Johnny Appleseed* (Vachel Lindsay) for baritone, chorus, and orchestra; three symphonies (1949–57); suite for orchestra; two violin concertos, *American Caprice* for piano and 32 instruments; two *Sketches* for string quartet, piano trio, wind quintet, *Trivialities* for flute, horn, and string quartet.

Kuhlau, (Daniel) Frederik (Rudolph) (1786–1832) German-born Danish composer. His music spans the end of the Classical period and the beginning of the Romantic style. During the French occupation he went to Denmark to escape conscription and became a flautist in the court orchestra at Copenhagen. In 1825 he visited Vienna and met

Beethoven, who composed a punning canon on his name.

A child of poor parents, he picked up musical knowledge at Brunswick and Hamburg.

Works include: the operas *Røverborgen* (1814), *Trylleharpen* (1817), *Lulu* (1824), and several others; incidental music for Heiberg's *Elverhøj* (1828); piano works; flute pieces.

Kuhnau, Johann (1660–1722) German organist, harpsichordist, composer, and writer on music. He was J S Bach's predecessor in the post of cantor at St Thomas's, Leipzig. His biblical sonatas for harpsichord are early examples of ◊programme music.

He was cantor at Zittau and went to Leipzig in 1682. In 1684 he became organist at St Thomas's Church, in 1700 was appointed music director of the university and the churches of St Nicholas and St Thomas, and in 1701 became cantor of St Thomas's.

Other works include motets on hymn-tunes and other church music; partitas and other pieces for harpsichord, including seven sonatas entitled *Frische Clavier-Früchte*, and the six sonatas *Biblische Historien* (1700).

Kullak, Theodor (1818–1882) German pianist and composer. He was intended for a career in law and at some time studied medicine, but in 1842 decided definitely in favour of music and went to Vienna to finish his piano studies with Carl Czerny. In 1846 he became court pianist to the King of Prussia and settled in Berlin, founding a conservatory with Julius Stern and Adolph Marx there in 1850, and one of his own in 1855.

Works include: a piano concerto in C minor; piano trio; duets for piano and violin; a vast number of piano pieces, studies.

Kullervo symphonic poem by Sibelius for soloists, chorus, and orchestra, based on legends from the *Kalevala*. Withdrawn after its first performance in Helsinki on 28 April 1892 and not heard again until after Sibelius's death in 1957.

Opera in two acts by Sallinen (libretto by composer, after A Kivi), produced Los Angeles, Music Center, 25 February 1992. Raised in violence and alienation, Kullervo commits violence on all around him, before his own suicide.

Kunst der Fuge, Die/The Art of Fugue Bach's last work, left unfinished at his death in 1750. A series of examples of the art of fugal and canonic writing, all based on the same theme. See also ◊per arsin et thesin.

Kupferman, Meyer (1926–) US composer and clarinettist. He made his debut as soloist in New York in 1946. He taught at Sarah Lawrence College from 1951. His music derives from jazz, electronics, and serialism.

Works include: the operas *In a Garden* (1949) and *Doctor Faustus Lights the Lights* (1953), both after Gertrude Stein; two piano concertos (1948, 1978); 11 symphonies (1950–83); concerto for cello and jazz band (1962); violin and clarinet concertos (1976, 1984); *Savage Landscape* for orchestra (1989); five string quartets; *Sound Phantoms*, ten pieces for chamber ensemble, no. 10 (1981); *Top Brass Five* for five trumpets (1989); *Wicked Combinations*, song cycle for mezzo and piano (1989); *A Crucible for the Moon* for soprano, alto saxophone, and percussion orchestra (1986).

Kurtág, György (1926–) Hungarian composer. Early influences were Bartók and Kodály; later he employed a post-Webern serial technique, in which mosaics of sound are used to build a larger compositional picture.

He studied in Budapest and Paris.

Works include: string quartet (1959); eight Duets for violin and cimbalom (1961); *In Memory of a Winter Sunset*, for soprano, violin, and cimbalom (1969), string quintet (1971); *Splinters*, for solo cimbalom (1975); *Homage to Luigi Nono*, for chamber ensemble (1980); *Messages of the Late Miss R V Troussova* for soprano and chamber ensemble (1980); *Scenes from a Novel* for soprano and ensemble (1981); *Attila-József Fragments* for soprano (1981); *Kafka Fragmente* for soprano and violin (1986); *Requiem for the Beloved* for soprano and piano (1987); *Officium Breve* for string quartet (1989); double concerto for piano, cello, and two chamber ensembles (1990); *Samuel Beckett: What is the Word* for alto voices and ensemble.

Kurzwellen/Shortwaves work by K Stockhausen for electronics and four short-wave radios; first performed Bremen, 5 May 1968. Developed as *Beethausen, opus 1970, von Stockhoven*.

Kvapil, Jaroslav (1892–1958) Czech composer. He studied with Janáček at Brno and was later appointed professor of organ and counterpoint at the Organ School there. In 1911–13 he continued studying at the Leipzig Conservatory, and on his return to Brno became professor of piano and composition at the Conservatory and conductor of the Philharmonic Society.

Works include: four symphonies, variations and fugue for orchestra; cantata for baritone solo, chorus and orchestra; six string quartets, piano quintet, piano trio; two violin and piano sonatas, cello and piano sonata; piano sonata and pieces; songs.

Kyrie eleison/Greek 'Lord have mercy' the words spoken or sung at the beginning of the Mass in the Catholic, Orthodox, and Anglican Churches. Following the Introit, it has three parts of text: Kyrie Eleison, Christe Eleison, Kyrie Eleison, each of which is repeated three times, reflecting the Holy Trinity.

In musical setting, the first item of the Ordinary of the Mass. Originally it was not part of the Mass but of various Litanies, at the head of which it still stands. In the Mass it has a nine-fold structure, and the simplest melodic form consisted of eight repetitions of a simple melody followed by a quite different melody for the ninth clause.

This melody closely resembles that still used for the Litany Kyries for Rogationtide and Holy Saturday. Other musical forms in common use were: *aaa bbb aaa'*; *aaa bbb ccc'*; and *aba cdc efe'* (a stroke represents an extended form of the phrase concerned).

1.2.3.	Ky - ri - e - le - i -son
4.5.6.	Chri-ste e - le - i -son
7.8.	Ky - ri - e - le - i -son

9. Ky-ri - e - - - - le - i - son

A kyrie in which the plainsong melody is varied only on the ninth and final time.

L

l the submediant note in any key in tonic sol-fa notation, pronounced Lah.

La the old name for the note A (see ◊solmization), still used in Latin countries, and in tonic sol-fa notation the submediant note in any key, represented by the symbol l, pronounced Lah.

La Barbara, Joan (1947–) US composer and vocal performer. She was a vocalist with Steve Reich and Musicians 1971–74, and worked with Philip Glass 1973–76. Her performances involve novel techniques of sound production, rather than singing as such. She gave the first performances of works by Cage, Morton Feldman, and her husband, Morton Subotnick.

She undertook vocal studies with Phyllis Curtin at Tanglewood and in New York, and studied composition at New York University.

Works include: *Hear What I Feel* for amplified voice (1974), *Space Testing* for acoustic voice (1976), *Chandra* for amplified solo voice, men's voices, and chamber orchestra (1978), *Winds of the Canyon* for voice and tape (1982), *The Solar Wind I-III* for voice(s) and ensembles (1983–84), *Loose Tongues* for eight amplified solo voices and tape (1985), *Urban Tropics*, sound portrait (1988), *Conversations* for low voice (1988), *In the Dreamtime*, self-portrait sound collage (1990), *Awakenings*, for chamber ensemble (1991), *Klangbild Köln/ Sound Portrait of Cologne* (1991).

Lac des cygnes (Tchaikovsky). See ◊*Swan Lake*.

Lächerliche Prinz Jodelet, Der/The Ridiculous Prince Jodelet opera by Keiser (libretto by J P Praetorius, based on P Scarron's comedy, *Jodelet, ou Le Maître valet*), produced Hamburg, Theater beim Gänsemarkt, 1726.

Lachrimae John Dowland's collection of 21 dances for 5 bowed instruments with lute (London, 1604). Its opening pavane, *Lachrimae antiquae*, is a version of his song *Flow my teares* (first published 1600), though in its original form it was probably a pavan for solo lute. In the early 17th century the piece appeared in many other arrangements for different ensembles and by different hands, usually with the title *Lachrimae*.

Lachrymae work for viola and piano by Britten, '*Reflections on a song of John Dowland*'; composed 1950, first performed Aldeburgh, 20 June 1950. Arranged for viola and string orchestra 1976, first performed Recklinghausen, 3 May 1977.

lacrimoso (Italian 'tearful') term used in musical notation.

Lady Macbeth of the Mtsensk District/Lady Macbeth Mtsenskago Uyezda opera by Shostakovich (libretto by A Preis and composer, based on a novel by N S Leskov), produced Moscow, 22 January 1934. Very successful at first, but afterwards discountenanced as decadent by the Soviet government. Revised as *Katerina Izmailova* and produced 1963. Tormented by her father-in-law Boris, Katerina Izmaylova has an affair with Sergei while her ineffectual husband, Zinovy, is away. Boris discovers Sergei and brutally whips him, but Katerina has her revenge by poisoning Boris. Suspicious, Zinovy returns and beats her, but Sergei intervenes and kills him. The police are informed and the couple are led away. In a group of convicts, Sergei flirts with a young prisoner to provoke Katerina. She throws her rival off a bridge, and jumps into the rapids herself.

Lady of the Lake, The songs by Schubert set to German translations from Scott's poem by P A Storck 1825 and published 1826 as op. 52.1. Ellen's first song, 'Soldier, rest!'; 2. Ellen's second song, 'Huntsman, rest!'; 3. Ellen's third song, 'Ave Maria'; 4. Norman's song, 'The heath this night'; 5. Lay of the Imprisoned Huntsman, 'My hawk is tired'. Op. 52 contains two more poems from Scott's work, 'Boating Song' for male chorus and 'Coronach' for female chorus.

La Grotte, Nicolas de (c. 1530–c. 1600) French composer and keyboard player. He published settings of poems by Ronsard in 1569 and examples of *musique mesurée à l'antique*. In 1583 he published with Claude Le Jeune pieces for the *Balet comique de la Royne*.

La Guerre, Elisabeth-Claude de (1666 or 1667–1729), born Jacquet French harpsichordist and composer from Jacquet family of musicians and instrument-makers. A pupil of her father, Claude Jacquet (died 1702), she showed early promise and attracted the patronage of Louis XIV and later Mme de Montespan, being particularly gifted at improvisation. She married the organist and composer Marin La Guerre (1658–1704) before 1684.

Works include: the opera *Céphale et Procris* (1694); cantatas; *Te Deum* and other church music; violin sonatas, trio sonatas, harpsichord music.

Lah the name for the submediant note in any key in Tonic Sol-fa, so pronounced, but in notation represented by the symbol l

La Halle, Adam de (c. 1230–c. 1288), or La Hale French poet and composer. He was educated for the priesthood, but fell in love and married a young girl, whom he left to rejoin the Church at Douai around 1263. In 1282 he went to Naples with the Comte d'Artois.

Works include: the stage pieces *Le jeu d'Adam, ou de la feuillée* and *Le jeu de Robin et de Marion* (1285); motets; chansons.

La Hèle, Georges de (1547–1586), or Helle Flemish composer. He wrote Masses, motets, and chansons; some of his works were destroyed in a fire at Madrid in 1734.

He was a chorister at the royal chapel in Madrid in his youth. In 1578 he was choirmaster at Tournai Cathedral, but was probably back in Spain by 1580. He won two

prizes at the Puy de Musique at Evreux in 1576.

lai (French; later English lay) a medieval lyrical poem in pairs of stanzas in different metrical forms; also the music set to such poems.

Lajtha, László (1892–1963) Hungarian folksong expert and composer. He studied at the Music High School at Budapest, specializing in folk music, and joined the folklore department of the National Museum in 1913. He was professor at the Budapest Conservatory 1919–49.

Works include: three ballets including *Lysistrata* (1933) and *Capriccio* (1944); two Masses and other choral works; ten symphonies (1936–61); violin concerto; ten string quartets and other chamber music; sonatas for violin, cello, and piano.

Lakmé opera by Delibes (libretto by E Gondinet and P Gille), produced Paris, Opéra-Comique, 14 April 1883. Brahmin priest Nilakantha opposes an affair between his daughter Lakmé and English officer Gerald. After being stabbed, Gerald is nursed by Lakmé, who poisons herself when she realizes that Gerald must return to his duties.

Lalande, Michel-Richard de (1657–1726) French organist and composer. He taught himself to play the violin, bass viol, and harpsichord. On being refused admission to Lully's orchestra, he took up the organ and secured organist's appointments at three churches. He failed to obtain the post of court organist, but was given charge of the princesses' musical education and became maître de chapelle in 1704.

He learnt music as a chorister at the church of Saint-Germain-l'Auxerrois in Paris. In 1683 he was appointed one of the superintendents of the royal chapel, and was appointed master of the royal chapel in 1704. In 1684 he married the court singer Anne Rebel, who died in 1722; his second wife, whom he married in 1723, was Mlle de Cury, daughter of one of the court surgeons.

Works include: BALLETS AND OPERA-BALLETS *Ballet de la jeunesse* (1686), *Le Palais de Flore* (1689), *Adonis* (1696), *Myrtil et Mélicerte* (1698), *Les Fées* (1699), *L'Amour fléchi par la Constance*, *L'Hymen champêtre* (1700), *Ballet de la Paix*, *Les Folies de Cardenio* (from Cervantes' *Don Quixote*, 1720), *Ballet de l'inconnu*, *Les Eléments* (with Destouches, 1725), *L'Amour berger*, *Eglogue, ou Pastorale en musique*, *Les Fontaines de Versailles*.

OTHER 70 motets with orchestral accompaniment; cantata *Le Concert d'Esculape*; *Trois*

Leçons des Ténèbres, Miserere for solo voice; music for the royal table, including *Sinfonias pour les soupers du Roi.*

Lalla-Roukh opera by F David (libretto by H Lucas and M Carré, based on Moore's *Lalla Rookh*), produced Paris, Opéra-Comique, 12 May 1862.

Lallouette, Jean François (1651–1728) French violinist and composer. From 1668 to 1677 he was violinist and conductor at the Paris Opéra, but Lully dismissed him for claiming collaboration in his *Isis,* which may have been true, for he was said to have often assisted Lully.

He studied violin with Guy Leclerc and composition with Lully. In 1693 he became maître de chapelle at Rouen Cathedral, in 1695 at Notre-Dame at Versailles, and in 1700 at Notre-Dame in Paris.

Works include: dramatic interludes and ballets; Masses, motets, Misereres.

Lalo, (Victor Antoine) Edouard (1823–1892) French composer. His Spanish ancestry and violin training are evident in the *Symphonie espagnole* 1873 for violin and orchestra, and *Concerto for Cello and Orchestra* 1877. He also wrote an opera, *Le roi d'Ys/The King of Ys* 1887.

He first studied violin and cello at the Lille Conservatory and then violin at Paris, taking composition lessons privately at the same time. In 1855 he became viola player in the Armingaud-Jacquard quartet. He wrote little until 1865, the year of his marriage to Mlle Bernier de Maligny, who sang his songs in public. Gradually his success grew both in the opera house and the concert room.

His most popular works during his lifetime were the opera *Le roi d'Ys* and the ballet *Namouna.* He is best known today for the five-movement *Symphonie espagnole* for violin and orchestra, and the cello concerto.

Works include: the operas *Fiesque* (after Schiller, composed 1866–67), *Le roi d'Ys* (1888), *La Jacquerie* (unfinished, completed by Coquard, performed 1895); pantomime with choruses *Néron;* ballet *Namouna* (1882); symphony in G minor (1886), *Divertissement, Rhapsodie norvégienne* and scherzo for orchestra, two aubades for small orchestra, concerto, *Symphonie espagnole* (1874), *Fantaisie norvégienne* (1878), *Romance-Sérénade* (1879) and *Concerto russe* (1879) for violin and orchestra, concertos for piano and for cello; string quartet (later revised as No. 2), three piano trios; violin and piano sonata and a number of pieces, cello and piano sonata and pieces; *La Mère et l'enfant* for piano duet; over 30 songs and two vocal duets; church music.

Lambe, Walter (c. 1452–c. 1500) English composer. His known music was all included in the Eton Choirbook: it consists of a Magnificat and five votive antiphons (a sixth can be completed from another manuscript; another is partially lost, and four more completely so).

He was King's Scholar at Eton in 1467 (aged 15), and clerk at St George's, Windsor, from 1479 to 1499 or later, acting as master of the choristers 1480–84 (at first jointly with William Edmunds).

Lambert, Constant (1905–1951) English composer, conductor, and critic. His works include *Horoscope* and *The Rio Grande,* which react against contemporary English pastoralism and look to jazz and early Stravinsky for inspiration.

Lambert was born in London, the son of the painter George Washington Lambert. He studied at the Royal College of Music in London, where he studied under Vaughan Williams. While he was still a student, Diaghilev commissioned the ballet *Romeo and Juliet* from him and produced it at Monte Carlo in 1926. It was followed by Pomona at Buenos Aires in 1927. He began to make his mark as a conductor of ballet with the Camargo Society and was later engaged to conduct ballet at the Sadlers Wells Theatre, with which he appeared in Paris in 1937, having already conducted at the International Society for Contemporary Music Festival at Amsterdam in 1933. He also became a concert conductor, was for a time music critic to the journal *Referee,* and published a book of criticism, *Music Ho! A Study of Music in Decline* 1934.

Works include: ballets *Romeo and Juliet* (Monte Carlo, 1926), *Pomona* (Buenos Aires, 1927), *Horoscope* (London, 1938); incidental music for Shakespeare's *Hamlet;* music for films *Merchant Seamen* and *Anna Karenina* (after Tolstoy); *Summer's Last Will and Testament* (Nash), masque for baritone solo, chorus, and orchestra (1932–35); *The Rio Grande* for piano, orchestra, and chorus (1927); dirge in Shakespeare's *Cymbeline* for voices and orchestra; *Music for Orchestra, Aubade héroïque* for small orchestra; concerto for piano and chamber orchestra; piano sonata; four poems by Li-Po for voice and piano.

Lamentatione name (apparently authentic) given to Haydn's symphony no. 26 in D minor, composed c. 1768, on account of the use it makes of a chant associated with the Lamentations of Jeremiah.

Lamentations the Lamentations of Jeremiah used in the Roman Catholic service at matins in Holy Week; originally sung in plainsong and still surviving in that form, but from the early 16th century also used in polyphonic settings.

lamento (Italian 'lament') plaintive aria in early 17th-century Italian opera conventionally placed before the tragic culmination of the plot. The best known example is the *Lamento d'Arianna*, the only surviving fragment from Monteverdi's *Arianna*.

Lamoureux, Charles (1834–1899) French violinist and conductor. In 1881 he founded the Concerts Lamoureux, at which he made a great deal of orchestral music, including Wagner's, known to a wide public.

He studied violin and theory at the Paris Conservatory, joined a theatre orchestra, then played at the Paris Opéra. In 1860 he helped to found a chamber music society for the introduction of new works, and conducted choral works by Bach, Handel, and others in the 1870s. He then became conductor at the Opéra. He toured Russia in 1893 and gave regular concerts in London from 1896.

Lampe, John Frederick (Johann Friedrich) (1703–1751) German bassoonist and composer. He left Brunswick about 1725 and settled in London, but went to Dublin in 1748 and to Edinburgh in 1750. He married Isabella Young, sister of Thomas Arne's wife.

Works include: burlesque operas *The Dragon of Wantley* (1757) and *Margery, or A Worse Plague than the Dragon* (1738; libretti by Carey), mock opera *Pyramus and Thisbe* (from Shakespeare's *Midsummer Night's Dream*, 1745), masque *The Sham Conjurer* (1741); music for Carey's *Amelia*; about ten other stage works; cantata to celebrate the suppression of the Stuart rebellion; songs.

Lampugnani, Giovanni Battista (1706–1786) Italian composer. Successful throughout Italy as an opera composer, he went to London in 1743 to take over the opera at the King's Theatre from Baldassare Galuppi, but later returned to Milan, where he wrote his five comic operas 1758–69.

He studied in Naples, and made his debut as an opera composer there in 1732. From 1779 he was maestro al cembalo at the Teatro alla Scala.

Works include: about 30 operas, including *Semiramide* (1741), *Rossane, Tigrane* (1747), *Artaserse, Siroe* (1755), *L'amor contadino* (1760); also trio sonatas, church music.

Lancelot and Elaine symphonic poem no. 2 by MacDowell, op. 25, based on the Arthurian legend, composed 1888.

Landarzt, Ein/A Country Doctor radio opera by Henze after the story by Kafka; broadcast Hamburg, 29 November 1951; revised for Dietrich Fischer-Dieskau as a monodrama, 1964; first performed Berlin, 12 October 1965. Radio opera revised for stage 1964, first performed Frankfurt, 30 November 1965. Doctor's macabre night-call to village boy.

Landi, Stefano (c. 1586–1639) Italian singer and composer. He was maestro di cappella at Padua about 1620 and in Rome from 1624, and sang alto in the Papal Chapel from 1630. His sacred opera *Il Sant' Alessio* has been successfully revived at Rome and Innsbruck in 1981 and at Los Angeles in 1988.

Works include: the operas *La morte d'Orfeo* (1619) and *Il Sant' Alessio* (1631); Masses and psalms; madrigals and cantatas; arias for one voice.

Landini, Francesco (c. 1325–1397) Italian organist, lutenist, composer, and poet. He was one of the chief exponents of the Italian ♭ars nova. Although blind from early childhood, he became a skilled player of various instruments, in particular the portative organ, and was organist at the church of San Lorenzo, Florence 1369–96.

He was born in Florence and spent most of his life there, but also visited Venice, where he was highly acclaimed. As a composer he is remarkable for his madrigals and *caccie*, both forms that later underwent considerable development.

Works include: madrigals, *ballate*, and other pieces.

Landini sixth a cadence in music of the 14th and 15th centuries named after Francesco Landini, of whose vocal works it is a feature. The idiom is not confined to Italian music nor is there any evidence to suggest that Landini invented it.

The Landini sixth in C major.

ländler Austrian country dance in 3/4 or 3/8 time, in which couples spin and clap. It was very popular in the late 18th century and composers, such as Mozart, Beethoven, and Schubert, wrote music in the rhythm of the dance.

Landon, H(oward) C(handler) Robbins (1926–) US musicologist. He has devoted himself particularly to the study of late 18th-century music and has published a number of articles and books, including *The Symphonies of Joseph Haydn* (1955), *The Collected Correspondence and London Notebooks of Joseph Haydn*, and *Haydn: Chronicle and Works*, five volumes (1976–80).

He studied at Swarthmore College and Boston University. Since 1947 he has lived in Europe. He has also published *Haydn: His Life and Music* 1988, and editions of numerous works by Haydn, including several operas and the complete symphonies. He has published books on Beethoven (1970) and Mozart as a Mason (1983), and also in 1983 edited recently discovered material for Handel's Roman Vespers. Other works include *Mozart's Last Year* 1988, *Mozart: The Golden Years* 1989, *Mozart and Vienna* 1991, and *Vivaldi, Voice of the Baroque* 1993.

Landowska, Wanda Luiza (1877–1959) Polish harpsichordist and scholar. She founded a school near Paris for the study of early music, and was for many years one of the few artists regularly performing on the harpsichord. In 1941 she moved to the USA.

She toured widely and settled in France, where in 1927 she opened a school for the study of early music at Saint-Leu-la-Forêt, near Paris. She wrote books and articles on aspects of early music. Falla's harpsichord concerto 1923–26, and Poulenc's *Concert Champêtre* 1927–28 were composed for her. In 1933 she gave the first public performance of the Goldberg Variations, and recorded the Well-Tempered Clavier 1949–56.

Lang, Paul Henry (1901–1991) Hungarian-born US musicologist. In 1924 he went to the University of Paris and four years later to the USA. He became professor of musicology at Columbia University in New York in 1939. In 1945 he was appointed editor of the *Musical Quarterly*. Among his writings are *Music in Western Civilization* (1941) and *George Frideric Handel* (1966).

Langlais, Jean (1907–1991) French organist and composer. He held several organist's appointments at Paris churches, lastly at Sainte-Clotilde. Blind himself, he taught organ and composition to blind pupils at the Institut des Jeunes Aveugles. His best-known works are for organ, but he also wrote many others.

He was educated at an institute for the blind and studied organ under André Marchal, also blind, later with Dupré at the Paris

Conservatory, where he also studied composition with Dukas.

langsam (German 'slow'; langsamer 'slower') term used in musical notation.

Lanier, Nicholas (1588–1666), or Laniere English painter, flautist, singer, and composer of French descent. In 1613, with John Coperario and others, he composed a masque for the marriage of the Earl of Somerset and in 1617 he not only set Ben Jonson's *Lovers made Men*, but sang in it and painted the scenery.

He was probably taught by his father, John Lanier, a sackbut player. In 1625 he was sent to Italy to collect pictures for the royal collection, and in 1626 was appointed Master of the King's Musick. He lived in the Netherlands during the Commonwealth, but resumed his post at the Restoration. Several other members of his family were musicians in the royal service.

Works include: masques *Lovers made Men* and. *The Vision of Delight* (Jonson, 1617); cantata *Hero and Leander*, New Year's songs; vocal dialogues, songs.

Lanner, Joseph (Franz Karl) (1801–1843) Austrian violinist and composer. He composed country dances and waltzes, in which he was Johann Strauss's greatest rival.

He was born in Vienna, the son of a glove-maker, and taught himself to play the violin. Anxious to conduct an orchestra, he began by forming a string quartet, in which Strauss, senior, played viola. They performed at various taverns, playing his arrangements of selections from favourite operas. He was engaged to conduct the orchestra at dances, visited provincial cities with his own band, and finally conducted the court balls in turn with Strauss.

Works include: over two hundred waltzes, country dances, quadrilles, polkas, galops, marches.

Lantins, Arnold de (died 1432) Flemish composer from the diocese of Liège. He was in Venice in 1428 and was included (with Dufay) in a list of papal singers in 1431. He composed chansons, motets and a Mass, *Verbum incarnatum*.

Lantins, Hugo de (fl. early 15th century) Flemish composer, possibly brother of Arnold de ◊Lantins. Like Arnold he visited Italy, and in 1420 wrote an epithalamium for Cleofe Malatesta di Pesaro. Two of his five motets connect him with Venice (1423) and Bari respectively. He also wrote numerous chansons.

Laparra, Raoul (1876–1943) French composer. He studied at the Paris Conservatory. His *Habanera* was given at Covent Garden 1910, New York Metropolitan 1924. He was killed in an Allied air raid near Paris.

Works include: the operas *Peau d'âne* (1899), *La Habanera* (1908), *La Jota* (1899), *Le Joueur de viole*, *Las Toreras* (1929), *L'Illustre Fregona*; *Un Dimanche basque* for piano and orchestra; string quartet; songs.

La Pouplinière, Alexandre Jean Joseph le Riche de (1693–1762), or Poupelinière French music patron. He was farmer-general of taxes and amassed a huge fortune. He kept a private orchestra, had Rameau living in his house for several years and studied under him, and patronized a number of other composers and performers, including Mondonville.

Lara, Isidore de (1858–1935), actually Cohen English composer. He studied composition with Mazzucato and singing with Lamperti at the Milan Conservatory, and later went to Lalo in Paris. He returned to London and became well known in wealthy drawing rooms as a song composer and performer. Later he came under the patronage of the Princess of Monaco, which enabled him to have his operas staged in the grand manner.

Works include: OPERA *The Light of Asia* (1892), *Amy Robsart* (after Scott's *Kenilworth*, 1893), *Moïna* (1897), *Messaline* (1899), *Soléa*, *Sanga*, *Nail*, *Les Trois Masques* (1912), *The Three Musketeers* (after Dumas, 1921), and others.

OTHER cantata *The Light of Asia* (first version of the opera); many songs.

largamente (Italian 'broadly, spaciously') in music, an indication that a movement or phrase is to be played in a broad manner.

large the largest note value in the medieval system of measured musical notation. It was known in Latin as *duplex longa* or *maxima*, and was divisible into two longs.

larghetto musical tempo indication for a slow movement, less slow than a *largo*.

largo (Italian 'large, broad, wide, spacious') musical tempo indication for a slow movement denoting a broad style as much as a slow pace. See also ◊larghetto.

'Largo' the popular name for the aria 'Ombra mai fù/Shade never was' from Handel's opera *Serse* (*Xerxes*), more generally known as an instrumental piece published in all kinds of arrangements. The familiar title is not even the original tempo indication, which is larghetto.

Lark Ascending, The romance for violin and orchestra by Vaughan Williams, composed 1914, first performed London, Queen's Hall, 14 June 1921, conductor Boult.

'Lark' Quartet a nickname sometimes given to Haydn's string quartet in D, op. 64 No. 5, on account of the exposed high first-violin passage at the opening.

Larsen, Jens Peter (1902–1988) Danish musicologist. He studied at Copenhagen University and taught there from 1928, becoming professor in 1945. He was organist at Vangede Church, 1930–45. He edited several works by Haydn and other composers, and authored *Die Haydn-Überlieferung*, *Die Haydn Kataloge*, and *Handel's 'Messiah'*. He wrote an entry for Haydn in the *New Grove's Dictionary of Music and Musicians* (1980).

Larsen, Libby (1950–) US composer. She studied at the University of Minnesota with Dominick Argento. In 1993 she became artistic director of the Hot Notes Series, giving performances with synthesized sound.

Works include: the operas *Tumbledown Dick* (1980), *Frankenstein, the Modern Prometheus* (1990), and *Mrs Dalloway* (1993); *Symphony: Water Music* (1985); *Coming Forth into Day* oratorio (1985); *Sonnets from the Portuguese*, song cycle for soprano and chamber ensemble (1989); Piano concerto: 'Since Armstrong' (1990); *Ghosts of an Old Ceremony*, dance (1991); Third Symphony 'Lyric' (1991); Marimba concerto (1992); *Quartet: Schoenberg, Schenker and Schillinger*, for string quartet (1991); *Mary Cassat*, for mezzo, trombone, and orchestra (1994).

Larsson, Lars-Erik (1908–1986) Swedish composer, conductor, and critic. His works vary between traditional and more modern styles. For instance, the ten *Two-Part Piano Pieces* 1932 introduced the ◊twelve-tone system to Swedish music, while his *Sinfonietta*, composed in the same year, is contrapuntal and neo-Baroque in style. However, despite the dichotomy in his work, the characteristic that threads Larsson's music together is his gift of lyricism.

He studied at the Royal Academy of Music at Stockholm, and later in Leipzig and Vienna, where he was a pupil of Berg. He was a conductor for Swedish radio 1937–54; professor of composition at Stockholm Conservatory 1947–59; and director of music at Uppsala University 196'.–66.

Works include: the opera *The Princess of Cyprus* (1937); incidental music to Shakespeare's *Winter's Tale*; three symphonies (1927–45), two concert overtures, lyric suite for orchestra; sinfonietta for strings (1932), divertimento for chamber orchestra; saxophone concerto.

La Rue, Jan (1918–   ) Indonesian-born US musicologist. He studied at Harvard and Princeton, and was at New York University from 1957. He has written particularly about style analysis and 18th-century music, striving for objectively verifiable conclusions.

La Rue, Pierre de (c. 1460–1518) Flemish composer. He is regarded as the equal of his contemporaries, Josquin Desprez, Henricus Isaac, Jacob Obrecht, and Antoine Brumel.

He was a pupil of Ockeghem, and was in the service by turns of the court of Burgundy, Charles V, and Margaret of Austria. He was appointed prebendary of Courtrai and later of Namur.

Works include: 31 Masses, seven Magnificats, Requiem, 38 motets; chansons.

Laserna, Blas (1751–1816) Spanish composer. He became official composer to several Madrid theatres in 1779.

Works include: numerous tonadillas, comic opera *La gitanilla por amor* (1791); incidental music for plays by Calderón, Lope de Vega, Moreto, Ramón de la Cruz's *El café de Barcelona* (1788), and others, lyric scene *Idomeneo* (1792), and other pieces.

Lassen, Eduard (1830–1904) Danish-born conductor and composer. He was taken to Brussels at the age of two, later studied at the Conservatory there, and took the Belgian Prix de Rome in 1851. Unable to get his first opera staged at Brussels, he took it to Liszt at Weimar, who produced it in 1857. He was music director there from 1858 and conductor of the opera from 1860. He conducted the first performance of Saint-Saëns's *Samson et Dalila* (1877).

Works include: the operas *Landgraf Ludwigs Brautfahrt* (1857), *Frauenlob* (1860), *Le Captif;* including music to Sophocles' *Oedipus,* Goethe's *Faust* and *Pandora,* Calderón's *Circe,* and Hebbel's *Nibelungen* (1876; the year of the first production of *The Ring,* at Bayreuth); festival cantata, Te Deum; *Biblische Bilder* for voices and orchestra; two symphonies, *Beethoven* and *Festival* overtures.

Lassus, Orlande de (Orlando di Lasso) (1532–1594) Flemish composer. The abundance, variety and polyphonic ingenuity of his music places him as one of the greatest composers of the Renaissance.

He seems to have gone to Italy as a boy, and he travelled there and served in various noble households, in Sicily, Naples, and

Milan. In 1553–54 he was choirmaster at St John Lateran in Rome, after which he returned home and settled for two years at Antwerp, where in 1555–56 he began to publish his first works. In 1556 he went to Munich and entered the service of the Duke of Bavaria. There he married Regina Weckinger in 1558, and in 1563 became chief Kapellmeister in succession to Daser. He made a visit to Venice in 1567 to find musicians for Munich, and to Ferrara. In 1570 he was ennobled by the Emperor Maximilian.

After a visit to Paris in 1571 Charles IX offered him a post as chamber musician, but he returned to Munich after the king's death in 1574. That year he went to Rome to present Pope Gregory XIII with a volume of Masses and received the order of the Golden Spur. In spite of an offer from Dresden, he remained attached to the Bavarian court to the end. His Latin motets were collected and published in 1604 by his sons Ferdinand and Rudolph under the title *Magnum opus musicum*.

Works include: more than 2,000 compositions: about 60 Masses, four Passions, 101 Magnificats, Requiem, about 500 motets, *Sacrae cantiones,* psalms (including seven penitential psalms); madrigals, Italian *canzoni,* French chansons, German songs for several voices.

Last Judgement, The the English title of Spohr's oratorio *Die letzten Dinge,* produced Kassel, 25 March 1826.

Latrobe, Christian Ignatius (1757–1836) English clergyman and composer. He studied at the college of the Moravian Brethren at Niesky in Upper Lusatia and in 1795 became secretary of the English branch. He dedicated three sonatas to Haydn, with whom he made friends during the latter's visits to England. He edited Moravian hymn-tunes and six volumes of German and Italian church music.

Works include: *Dies irae* (1823), Te Deum, Miserere (1814), anthems and other church music; instrumental sonatas; airs to poems by Cowper and Hannah More.

Lauda Sion a sequence sung at Mass on the Feast of Corpus Christi in the Roman Church, words by St Thomas Aquinas, c. 1264. Cantata by Mendelssohn written for a festival at Liège and performed there on 11 June 1846.

laudi spirituali Italian sacred songs of the 13th century and later, with words in the vernacular, at first for single voice and later in parts. Their centre of origin was Florence.

Laudon Symphony nickname of Haydn's symphony no. 69 in C, composed c. 1778 and dedicated to Field Marshal Baron Gideon Ernst von Loudon.

Lavignac, (Alexandre Jean) Albert (1846–1916) French musicologist. He studied at the Paris Conservatory, where he became professor in 1882. He was founder and first editor of the *Encyclopédie de la musique* (1913–16); also wrote many technical treatises and a study on Richard Wagner.

lavolta, or Italian *volta* or French *volte* an old dance in 3–2 time, probably of Italian origin, since the jump that was a feature of it retained the Italian word *volta*.

Lavotta, János (1764–1820) Hungarian violinist and composer. He was one of the outstanding exponents of *verbunkos* music.

He was of noble birth, but left home on his father's remarriage and became a professional musician, at the same time following a legal career. He became very fashionable in Vienna and Budapest, conducted at various theatres, but took to drink and ended in decay.

Lawes, Henry (1596–1662) English composer. His works include music for Milton's masque *Comus* 1634. His brother **William Lawes** (1602–1645) was also a composer, notably for viol consort.

Lawes, William (1602–1645) English composer. Like his brother Henry ◊Lawes, he studied with John Coperario and became a musician at Charles I's court. He joined the Royalist army during the Civil War and was killed by a shot during the siege of Chester.

Works include: music for Shirley's masque *The Triumph of Peace* (with Ive, 1634) and Davenant's *The Triumph of the Prince d'Amour* and *The Unfortunate Lovers* (1638); anthems and psalms; music for consorts of viols; airs for violin and bass; catches and canons; airs and dialogues for one and more voices.

Layolle, François de (Francesco dell' Aiolle) (1492–c. 1540) French organist and composer. He was Benvenuto Cellini's music teacher; worked at church of SS Annunziate, Florence, until 1518. His son Aleman Layolle afterwards taught Cellini's daughter and became organist at Lyon by 1521.

Works include: Masses, motets; canzoni, madrigals.

leader the usual English name for the principal first violin in an orchestra or of a string quartet or other chamber music team. In the USA, especially in journalism, the conductor is often called 'leader'; the usual US term for the leading first orchestral violin is Concertmaster, from German *Konzertmeister*.

leading motif (German *Leitmotiv*) a short theme associated with a personage, object, or idea in an opera or other work, quoted at appropriate moments or worked up symphonically. Its chief exponent is Wagner, but it was not his invention, for it occurs in earlier compositions.

leading note the seventh note of an ascending ◊diatonic scale, so called because it 'leads' inevitably to the upper tonic or key note. It is tuned ◊sharp in minor keys to maintain its leading character.

The leading note is very dissonant in relation to the tonic, but consonant in relation to the chord of the fifth, or dominant. Typically the transition from leading note to tonic is expressed in the V–I 'perfect' ◊cadence.

Lear opera by Reimann (libretto by C Henneberg after Shakespeare), produced Munich, 9 July 1978. King Lear disowns faithful daughter Cordelia after she is unable to express her love for him, dividing his kingdom between treacherous daughters Goneril and Regan instead. Lear becomes insane and all end up dead.

Leben des Orest/The Life of Orestes opera by Křenek (libretto by composer), produced Leipzig, 19 January 1930. Orestes travels from early matricide to eventual forgiveness.

Le Brun, Jean (lived 15th century) French priest and composer. He wrote motets and chansons.

Lechner, Leonhard (c. 1553–1606) Austrian composer. He was music director 1584–85 to Count Eitel Friedrich of Hohenzollern at Hechingen and in 1595 was appointed to a similar post at the court of Württemberg at Stuttgart.

After studying with Lassus in the court chapel at Munich, he became a schoolmaster at Nuremberg in 1570. In 1579 he began to publish a revised edition of Lassus's works.

Works include: Masses, motets, Magnificat, psalms, introits, wedding motet for the Elector Johann Georg I of Saxony; sacred and 160 secular German songs for two–five voices in seven published books; St John Passion (1594).

Leclair, Jean-Marie (1697–1764) French composer and violinist. Originally a dancer and ballet-master, he composed ballet music, an opera, *Scylla et Glaucus* 1746, and violin concertos.

Leclair was born at Lyon. He began his career as a dancer, and in 1722 was a ballet master in Turin, but while there turned to the violin, studying with Giovanni Battista Somis. In 1728 he settled in Paris, where he had great success as a player and composer. He was a member of the royal orchestra 1734–36, then went to Holland, returning to Paris after various travels in 1743. For a time he was in the service of Don Philip of Spain at Chambéry, and joined the orchestra of the Duke of Gramont in 1748. He met his death at the hand of an unknown murderer.

Works include: the opera *Scylla et Glaucus* (1746; concert performance London, 1979); ballets and 'divertissements'; 12 violin concertos; 48 violin sonatas; violin duets; trio sonatas.

Lecocq, (Alexandre) Charles (1832–1918) French composer. His first operetta, *Le Docteur Miracle* 1857, won joint first prize with a work by Bizet in a competition organized by Offenbach. However, he had no great success until he produced *Fleur de Thé* in 1868, and until then supplemented his income by teaching and organ playing. After that he made a fortune with his many operettas.

Lecocq was born in Paris, where he studied at the Conservatory 1849–54.

Works include: the opera *Plutus* (1886); operettas *Les cent vierges*, *La fille de Madame Angot* (1872), *Giroflé-Girofla* (1874), *La petite mariée* (1875), *Le petit duc* (1878), *Camargo* (1878), *Ninette*, *Barbe-bleue*, and about 40 others; orchestral works; violin and piano sonata; sacred songs for women's voices *La chapelle au couvent*; instrumental pieces; piano works; songs.

Leçons des Ténèbres settings of the Lamentations of Jeremiah for performance at matins on the last three days of Holy Week. See also ◊Lamentations.

ledger line, or leger line in music, notation used to indicate exceptionally high or low notes, consisting of short lines added above or below the ◊stave. In music prior to the Classical period it was common to change clefs in order to avoid using ledger lines. For example, if a part reading bass clef became too high, the composer would notate tenor clef. This practice is continued for cello and bassoon writing but not for other instruments such as the keyboard. The first known example of a ledger line occurs in an organ book of 1523.

Lee, Nathaniel (c. 1653–1692) English playwright. See Gottfried ◊Finger (*Rival Queens*, with D Purcell); Henry ◊Purcell (*Oedipus*,

Massacre of Paris, *Sophonisba* and *Theodosius*); Nicholas ◊Staggins (*Gloriana*).

Lees, Benjamin (1924–) Russian-born US composer. He was taken to the USA as a child, and studied piano in San Francisco and Los Angeles. After serving in the US Army 1942–45, he studied at University of California at Los Angeles, theory, harmony and composition with Halsey Stevens, Ingolf Dahl, and Ernst Kanitz, also taking private lessons from George Antheil. In 1955 he won a Guggenheim Fellowship and in 1956 a Fulbright Fellowship.

Works include: the operas *The Oracle* (1955) and *The Gilded Cage* (1971); five symphonies (1953–86; no. 3 for string quartet and orchestra); concertos for violin, oboe and piano (2); *Profile* for orchestra, concerto for orchestra, *Declamations* for string orchestra and piano; *Visions of Poets*, a dramatic cantata (1961); concerto for brass and orchestra (1983); *Portrait of Rodin* for orchestra (1984), horn concerto (1992); four string quartets (1951, 1955, 1982, 1989), three violin sonatas (1953, 1972, 1991), cello sonata (1981), piano trio (1983); four piano sonatas (1949, 1950, 1956, 1963), violin sonata; piano music.

Leeuw, Ton de (1926–) Dutch composer. His chief interest is in experimental music, and he has been influenced by *musique concrète* as well as serialism.

He studied composition in Paris with Messiaen and Thomas de Hartmann. He became interested in musical folklore and in 1961 toured India to collect material.

Works include: the TV opera *Alceste* (1963), opera *De Droom/The Dream*, 1965): oratorio *Job* (1956); two symphonies, *Ombres* for orchestra and percussion, concertos for piano and string orchestra; *Spatial Music I–IV*, *Litany of Our Time* (1965–68), *Resonances* for orchestra (1985), concerto for guitar and strings (1989); two string quartets (1958, 1964); *Apparences I* for cello (1987); choral and piano music; electronic pieces.

LeFanu, Nicola (1947–) English composer, daughter of Elizabeth Maconchy. She studied at Oxford and with Wellesz and Petrassi. She lectured at Morley College, London 1970–75, and in 1977 was appointed lecturer at King's College, London.

Works include: the operas *Dawnpath* (1977), *Blood Wedding* (1992), and *Wild Man* (1995), ballet *The Last Laugh* for soprano, tape, and chamber orchestra (1972); *Preludio* for strings (1967; revised 1976), *The Hidden Landscape* for orchestra (1973), *Columbia Fall* for percussion, harp, and strings (1975), *Farne* for orchestra (1979); *Variations* for piano and orchestra (1982); concerto for alto saxophone and orchestra (1989); *The Valleys shall Sing* for chorus and wind (1973), *For we are the Stars* for 16 voices (1978), *Like a Wave of the Sea* for chorus and ensemble of early instruments (1981), *Stranded on my Heart* for tenor, chorus, and strings (1984); *The Silver Strand* for chorus (1989); Clarinet quintet (1971), *Collana* for six instruments (1976), *Deva* for cello and seven instruments (1979); *Invisible Places* clarinet quintet (1986); *Nocturne* for cello and piano (1988).

Le Flem, Paul (1881–1984) French composer and critic. He was professor at the Schola Cantorum, Paris, chorus master at the Opéra-Comique, conductor of the Chanteurs de Saint-Gervais, and critic for *Comoedia*.

His teachers included d'Indy and Roussel at the Schola Cantorum.

Works include: the operas *Le Rossignol de Saint-Malo* (1942) and *Dahut*; choreographic drama on Shakespeare's *Macbeth*; cantata *Aucassin et Nicolette*; four symphonies (1908–78), *Triptyque symphonique* for orchestra; fantasy for piano and orchestra; chamber music; violin and piano sonata; piano works; choral music.

Le Franc, Guillaume (died 1570) French composer. A Protestant, he fled to Switzerland, and settled at Geneva in 1541. He established a school of music there, becoming master of the children and singer at the cathedral the following year, and edited Calvin's Genevan Psalter, in which Bourgeois and Marot also had a hand. In 1545 he left for the cathedral of Lausanne, and in 1565 issued a new Psalter there with some tunes of his own.

legato (Italian 'tied') term used to describe music that is phrased smoothly and continuously.

Légende de Saint Christophe, La opera by d'Indy (libretto by composer), produced Paris, Opéra, 6 June 1920.

Legende von der heiligen Elizabeth, Die/ The Legend of St Elizabeth of Hungary oratorio by Liszt (words by Otto Roquette), first performed in Hungary, Budapest, 15 August 1865; first produced as an opera, Weimar, 23 October 1881.

Legend of Joseph, The (Strauss) see ◊*Josephslegende*.

Legend of the Invisible City of Kitezh and Maiden Fevronia/Skazhanie o nevidimom gradie Kitezh i dieve Fevronie opera by Rimsky-Korsakov (libretto by V I Bielsky),

produced St Petersburg, 20 February 1907. Revived St Petersburg and London, 1994. A golden mist magically hides the city of Kitezh from the invading Tatars. Fevronia, captured by the barbarians, escapes to her slain groom, Prince Vsevolod, in eternal life in the Invisible City.

Legend of Tsar Saltan, The/Skazka o Tsarie Saltanie opera by Rimsky-Korsakov (libretto by V I Bielsky, after Pushkin), produced Moscow, 3 November 1900. Prince Guidon transforms himself into a tree to rescue his mother and return her to the Tsar.

Leggenda di Sakuntala, La opera by Alfano (libretto by composer, based on Kalldasa's play), produced Bologna, Teatro Comunale, 10 December 1921. The manuscript was destroyed during World War II. Alfano reconstructed the opera for production in 1952, as *Sakuntala*. Sakuntala expires after meeting lover king, but their child becomes a world hero.

leggiero (Italian 'light'; leggieramente 'lightly') in musical notation, term that often implies a detached articulation.

legno (Italian 'wood') in musical notation, from the term *col legno* ('with the wood'), instruction to a string player to tap the string with the wooden part of the bow rather than to draw the bow across the string in the usual manner.

Legrant, Guillaume (fl. 1418–56) Franco-Flemish composer. Between 1419 and 1421 he was a member of the papal chapel. He wrote three chansons, a florid organ piece without title, and a very chromatic *Gloria-Credo* pair.

Legrenzi, Giovanni (1626–1690) Italian composer. He was organist at Bergamo from 1645, then maestro di cappella at Ferrara 1656–65. In 1672 he became director of the Conservatorio dei Mendicanti at Venice and in 1685 maestro di cappella of St Mark's there.

Works include: the operas *Achille in Sciro* (1663), *Eteocle e Polinice* (1675), *La divisione del mondo, Germanico sul Reno* (1676), *Totila, I due Cesari* (1683), *Il Giustino, Pertinace* (1684), and about ten others; Masses, motets, psalms, and other church music; orchestral works; church sonatas.

Lehár, Franz (1870–1948) Hungarian composer. He wrote many operettas, among them *The Merry Widow* 1905, *The Count of Luxembourg* 1909, *Gypsy Love* 1910, and *The Land of Smiles* 1929. He also composed songs, marches, and a violin concerto.

Born at Komárom, the son of a military bandmaster, he studied at the Prague Conservatory, intending to become a violinist, but then became a military bandmaster. His music shows the influence of the southern Slavonic folk tunes and he first tried to win fame as a composer of serious opera as, for example, in *Kukuška* (later renamed *Tatjana*) 1896; but it was in the field of operetta that he achieved real distinction. During his last years he lived in retirement at Ischl.

Works include: the opera *Kukuška* (later called *Tajana*, 1896), operettas *The Merry Widow* (1905), *The Count of Luxembourg* (1909), *Gypsy Love* (1910), *The Three Graces*, *Pompadour*, *Springtime*, *Frasquita* (1922), *Clo Clo*, *The Blue Mazurka*, *Frederica* (1928), *The Land of Smiles* (1929), and many others; symphonic poem *Fieber*, three comedy scenes for orchestra.

Lehmann, Liza (Elizabetta Nina Mary Frederika) (1862–1918) English singer and composer. In 1885 she made her first appearance as a singer at St James's Hall, where she sang for the last time in 1894, when she married Herbert Bedford.

She was taught at first by her mother, Amelia Chambers, herself an accomplished amateur composer. She later studied at Rome, Wiesbaden, and at home with Hamish MacCunn, also singing with Alberto Randegger. The composer David Bedford is her grandson.

Works include: light opera *The Vicar of Wakefield* (after Goldsmith, 1906), musical comedy *Sergeant Brue* (L Housman); incidental music for *Everyman* and other plays; ballads for voice and orchestra; song cycles *In a Persian Garden* (Omar Khayyám), *In Memoriam* (Tennyson).

Lehrstück (German 'didactic piece, educational play') small form of music drama cultivated in Germany in the 1920s–1930s by Eisler, Hindemith, Weill, and other composers, the chief literary exponent being Bertolt Brecht. It was cultivated mainly by the working classes in Germany at first, though later the influence spread to other European countries and to the USA. The Lehrstück makes use of historical material and dialectical discussion for the purpose of enlightening the masses, and it was for a time a counteragent to the Nazi movement until its exponents were forced to emigrate.

The first performance of Hindemith's *Lehrstück*, for soloists, chorus and orchestra (texts by Brecht) was at Baden-Baden, 28 July 1929.

Leibowitz, René (1913–1972) French-Polish composer. After studying with Schoenberg and Webern, he destroyed all his works written before 1937, including six string quartets, and devoted himself entirely to 12-note music. He was known as a leading teacher of 12-note composition and published *Schoenberg et son école* and *Introduction à la musique de douze sons*.

Leibowitz settled in Paris in 1926 and studied in Germany and Austria 1930–33 with Schoenberg and Webern. He conducted works of the 12-note school in the USA 1947–48.

Works include: music drama *La Nuit close* (1949); four unaccompanied choruses; symphonies and variations for orchestra; chamber symphony for 12 instruments, chamber concerto for violin, piano, and 17 instruments, *Tourist Death* for soprano and chamber orchestra (1943), *L'Explication des métaphores* for speaker, two pianos, harp, and percussion; string quartet, ten canons for oboe, clarinet, and bassoon, wind quintet; violin and piano sonata; sontata and pieces for piano; songs.

Leicester, ou Le Château de Kenilworth opera by Auber (libretto by Scribe and A H Mélesville, based on Scott's *Kenilworth*), produced Paris, Opéra-Comique, 25 January 1823. Leicester's friendship with Elizabeth I makes his wife superfluous.

Leich (German 'lay') medieval type of German song similar to the French *lai*.

Leichtentritt, Hugo (1874–1951) German musicologist. He studied with Paine at Harvard University and later at the Hochschule für Musik in Berlin, where he became professor at the Klindworth-Scharwenka Conservatory. In 1933 he left Germany as a refugee from the Nazi régime and returned to the USA to join the staff of Harvard University. His books include studies of Keiser, Handel, Chopin, Busoni and the motet.

Leigh, Walter (1905–1942) English composer. He studied at Cambridge and with Hindemith in Berlin. In 1932 a work of his was performed at the International Society for Contemporary Music festival in Vienna. He enlisted during World War II and was killed in action.

Works include: the comic operas *The Pride of the Regiment, Jolly Roger* (1933); pantomime *Aladdin* (1931); revues *Nine Sharp* and *Little Revue*, 1939; incidental music to Aristophanes' *Frogs*, Shakespeare's *Midsummer Night's Dream*; overture *Agincourt*, *Music for*

String Orchestra, Three Pieces for Amateur Orchestra; concertino for harpsichord and strings; three movements for string quartet (1929), trio for flute, oboe, and piano and sonatina for viola and piano; songs.

Leighton, Kenneth (1929–1988) English composer. He was lecturer at Edinburgh University 1956–68, and at Oxford University 1968–70. From 1970 he was professor at Edinburgh University.

He studied at Queen's College, Oxford and with Petrassi in Rome. He won several prizes for composition.

Works include: the opera *Columba* (1980); concerto for strings; two symphonies (1964, 1974); three piano concertos (1951–69), violin concerto, cello concerto; string quartet, two violin sonatas; three piano sonatas; Fantasy-Octet, 'Homage to Percy Grainger' (1982); choral works.

Leinsdorf, Erich (1912–1993) Austrian-born US conductor. He was music director with the Boston Symphony Orchestra 1962–69, and principal conductor with the West Berlin Radio Symphony Orchestra 1977–80.

Leinsdorf studied with Paul Emerich and Hedwig Kammer-Rosenthal at the Vienna Gymnasium. In 1934 he became assistant to Bruno Walter and Toscanini at the Salzburg Festival and later appeared as a conductor in Italy, France, and Belgium. In 1938 he was engaged as an assistant conductor at the New York Metropolitan Opera, making his debut with *Die Walküre*, and becoming chief conductor 1939–43. He served in the US Army from 1944 and returned to the New York Metropolitan 1958–62.

leitmotif, German Leitmotiv (German 'leading motive') in music, a recurring theme or motive used to illustrate a character or idea. Wagner frequently used this technique in his operas, and it was later adopted in music for film.

Leitner, Ferdinand (1912–   ) German conductor. He studied in Berlin with Schreker, Schnabel and Muck, and conducted in Berlin, Hamburg and Munich before moving to Stuttgart. He was music director until 1969 and led many productions of Wieland Wagner; also gave first performances of Orff's *Oedipus der Tyrann* (1959) and *Prometheus* (1968). He made his US debut at Chicago 1969 (*Don Giovanni*). He was at the Zurich Opera 1969–84 and was principal conductor of the Hague Philharmonic Orchestra 1976–80. He was a well-known conductor of Bruckner and Mozart, and gave operas by Berg and Busoni (the only recording of *Doktor*

Faust). He conducted Mozart's C-minor Mass at Salzburg, 1985, *Tannhäuser* at Chicago (1988) and *Ariadne auf Naxos* for Radio Audizioni Italiane (RAI) at Turin, 1989.

Le Jeune, Claude (or Claudin) (c. 1530–1600) Franco-Flemish composer. He worked for most of his life in Paris. Having become a Huguenot, he tried to escape from Paris during the siege of 1588, and his manuscripts were saved from seizure by the Catholic soldiers by his colleague Jacques Mauduit, himself a Catholic. Later Le Jeune became chamber musician to the king. Like Jean-Antoine de Baïf (1532–1589) and Mauduit, he was an exponent of *musique mesurée*.

Works include: motets, psalms set to rhymed versions in measured music and also to tunes in the Genevan Psalter set for three voices; chansons; madrigals; instrumental fantasies, and other pieces.

Lekeu, Guillaume (1870–1894) Belgian composer. In 1891 he won second prize in the Belgian Prix de Rome with the lyric scene *Andromède*, and was thought likely to become the leading representative of the Belgian school had he not died at a very early age.

Lekeu was born at Heusy, Verviers. He studied with Franck and d'Indy in Paris. His most memorable works are an Adagio for strings, a string quartet, a piano trio, a piano quartet (finished by d'Indy), a violin sonata, and a piano sonata.

Works include: a symphonic study on Shakespeare's *Hamlet* (1887), *Fantaisie sur deux airs populaires angevins* for orchestra; Adagio for string quartet and orchestra; Introduction and Adagio for brass; *Chant lyrique* for chorus and orchestra; piano quartet (completed by d'Indy), piano trio; violin and piano sonata (1891), cello and piano sonata (completed by d'Indy); three piano pieces; *Trois Poèmes* for voice and piano.

Lélio, ou Le Retour à la Vie/Lélio, or The Return to Life 'lyric monodrama' by Berlioz for an actor, solo voices, chorus, piano, and orchestra, op. 14, composed in 1831 as a sequel to the *Symphonie fantastique* and first performed with the latter, Paris Conservatory, 9 December 1832.

Lemminkäinen's Return symphonic legend by Sibelius, op. 22, one of four on subjects from the *Kalevala*, composed 1893–95, first performed Helsinki, 13 April 1896. The other three are *The Swan of Tuonela*, *Lemminkainen and the Maidens of Saari*, *Lemminkainen in Tuonela*.

'Leningrad' Symphony Shostakovich's seventh symphony, op. 60, awarded the Stalin prize 1942 and first performed in Kuibishev, by the evacuated Bolshoi Theatre Orchestra of Moscow, 5 March 1942. The Nazi march in the first movement is parodied by Bartók in his Concerto for Orchestra (1944).

lento (Italian 'slow') in musical notation, slightly slower than, or approximately the same tempo as ♩adagio, depending on the historical period in which the music was written.

Leo, Leonardo (Lionardo Oronzo Salvatore de) (1694–1744) Italian composer. His comic operas (often in Neapolitan dialect) were ranked with those of Pergolesi and had a great influence on later Italian masters of the genre. He also wrote much church music. Piccinni and Jommelli were among his pupils.

He was a pupil of Provenzale and Fago at the Conservatorio della Pietà dei Turchini, Naples 1709–13, where his first oratorio was performed in 1712. Appointed supernumerary organist to the court at Naples in 1713, he rose to become maestro di cappella just before his death. He taught at the Conservatorio della Pietà from 1715 (appointed primo maestro in 1741) and the Conservatorio S Onofrio from 1725 (appointed primo maestro in 1739).

Works include: OPERA *Sofonisba* (1718), *Lucio Papirio*, *Caio Gracco* (1720), *La 'mpeca scoperta* (in Neapolitan dialect, 1723), *Timocrate*, *Il trionfo di Camilla*, *La semmeglianza di chi l'ha fatta*, *Il Cid*, *Catone in Utica* (1729), *La clemenza di Tito* (1735), *Demofoonte*, *Farnace* (1736), *Siface*, *Ciro riconosciuto*, *L'amico traditore*, *La simpatia del sangue*, *L'Olimpiade* (1737), *Vologeso*, *Amor vuol sofferenza* (*La finta Frascatana*, 1739), *Achille in Sciro* (1740), *Scipione nelle Spagne* (1740), *Il fantastico* (*Il nuovo Don Chisciotte*), after Cervantes, 1743), and about 40 others.

OTHER oratorios *Il trionfo della castità di S Alessio* (1713), *Dalla morte alla vita* (1722), *La morte di Abele*, *S Elena al Calvario* (1734), *S Francesco di Paolo nel deserto* and others; Masses, motets, psalms, and other church music; concerto for four violins, six cello concertos; harpsichord pieces.

Leoncavallo, Ruggero (1858–1919) Italian operatic composer. He played in restaurants, composing in his spare time, until the success of *I Pagliacci*/*The Strolling Players* 1892. His other operas include *La Bohème*/*Bohemian Life* 1897 (contemporary with Puccini's version) and *Zaza* 1900.

He studied piano privately at first and then entered the Naples Conservatory, which he left in 1876 with a master diploma. He went to Bologna to attend Carducci's lectures in literature, and was on the point of producing his first opera, *Chatterton* there, but was swindled and found himself penniless. He made a precarious living by giving lessons and playing the piano at cafés, but later managed to travel widely as café pianist. He then began a trilogy on the Italian Renaissance, *Crepusculum*, with *I Medici*, but never produced the planned two following works, *Savonarola* and *Cesare Borgia*. In the meantime he made an enormous success with *I Pagliacci* at Milan in 1892 and soon all over Italy.

La Bohème at Venice in 1897 suffered from the appearance of Puccini's work on the same subject, and in spite of a commission for a German opera for Berlin, *Der Roland von Berlin*, in 1904, he never repeated the success of *Pagliacci*. He wrote all his own libretti and some for other composers.

Works include: OPERA *Chatterton* (after Alfred de Vigny, composed 1876, produced 1896), *I Medici*, *I Pagliacci* (1892), *La Bohème* (after Murger, 1897), *Zaza*, *Der Roland von Berlin* (after Willibald Alexis, 1904), *Maia* (1910), *Gli zingari*, *Goffredo Mameli*, *Edipo rè* (after Sophocles, 1920), *Tormenta* (unfinished); operettas *A chi la giarettiera* (1919), *Il primo bacio*, *Malbruk* (1910), *La reginetta delle rose* (1912), *Are you there?* (1913), *La candidata*, and *Prestami tua moglie*.

OTHER ballet *La vita d'una marionetta*; symphonic poem *Serafita* (after Balzac's novel).

Leoni, Leone (c. 1560–1627) Italian composer. He was maestro di cappella of Vicenza Cathedral from 1588.

Works include: Masses, motets (some in many parts with instruments), *Sacrae cantiones*, psalms, Magnificats and other church music, sacred and secular madrigals.

Leoninus, Leonius (fl. c. 1163–1201), now sometimes called Léonin French poet, theologian, and composer. First documented in 1179, he was active mainly at Notre-Dame, Paris, for which he is said to have composed the *Magnus liber organi* containing at least 42 settings of music for the Mass and Office in two voices. This formed the basis of the great Notre-Dame repertory later elaborated by Perotinus Magnus and others.

Leonora, ossia L'amore conjugale/***Leonora, or Wedded Love*** opera by Paer (libretto by G Cinti, based on Bouilly's libretto for Gaveaux), produced Dresden, 3 October

1804. See Beethoven's ◊*Fidelio, oder Die eheliche Liebe* for plot synopsis.

Leonora Overtures (Beethoven). See ◊*Fidelio, oder Die eheliche Liebe.*

Léonore, ou L'Amour conjugal/Leonora, or Wedded Love opera by Gaveaux (libretto by J N Bouilly, based on a real event), produced Paris, Théâtre Feydeau, 19 February 1798. A forerunner and model of Beethoven's ◊*Fidelio, oder Die eheliche Liebe.*

Leopold I (1640–1705) Holy Roman Emperor. He composed an opera, *Apollo deluso*, to a libretto by his court musician Antonio Draghi in 1669, and contributed to numerous other operas by the same composer. His oratorios include *Il sagrifizio d'Abramo* (1660), *Il figliuol prodigo* (1663), and *Il lutto dell'universo* (1668).

Leopolita, Martinus (Marcin Lwowczyk) (c. 1540–1589) Polish composer who might have studied under Sebastian Felsztyna and Jan Jeleń of Tuchola. He was a member of the College of Roratists (*Cappella Rorantistarum*), established at the Royal Chapel at the Wawel royal residence in Kraków in 1543, and court composer there from 1560.

Works include: Masses, including *Missa Paschalis*, motets; secular songs for several voices, and other pieces.

Leppard, Raymond John (1927–) English conductor and musicologist. His imaginative reconstructions of Monteverdi and Cavalli operas did much to generate popular interest in early opera and to stimulate academic investigation of the performance implications of early music manuscript scores.

He studied at Cambridge and made his debut as a conductor in London in 1952. From 1960 he was a regular conductor of English Chamber Orchestra, and of the BBC Northern Symphony Orchestra 1973–80. He conducted *Solomon* at Covent Garden in 1959 and Monteverdi's *L'incoronazione di Poppea* at Glyndebourne in 1964. This was the first of several realizations of Venetian opera, all of which attracted negative scholarly comment for making too many transpositions, having too much music from other sources, and instrumental parts realized in too lavish a manner. However, Leppard's versions of Monteverdi, and of Cavalli's *L'Ormindo, La Calisto, L'Egisto*, and *Orione*, have been popular with the public. Leppard also produced Monteverdi's *Ballo delle ingrate* in 1958, and Cavalli's Messa Concertata. He made his US concert debut at New York in 1969, his opera debut at Santa Fe in 1974, with *Egisto*, and his New York Metropolitan debut in 1978, with

Billy Budd. He has been based in the USA since 1976, being principal guest conductor of the St Louis Symphony Orchestra from 1984 and of the Indianapolis Symphony Orchestra from 1986.

Leroux, Xavier (Henri Napoléon) (1863– 1919) Italian-born French composer. He studied at the Paris Conservatory, one of his masters being Massenet, and gained the Prix de Rome in 1885. He became harmony professor there in 1896 and edited the periodical *Musica*.

Works include: OPERA *Evangeline* (1885), *Astarté, La Reine Fiammette* (after Catulle Mendès, 1903), *William Ratcliff* (after Heine, 1906), *Théodora, Le Chemineau* (1907), *Le Carillonneur* (1913), *La Fille de Figaro* (1914), *Les Cadeaux de Noël*, 1814, *Nausithoé, La Plus Forte, L'Ingénu*.

OTHER incidental music to Sardou and Moreau's *Cléopâtre* (1890), Aeschylus's *The Persians* and Richepin's *Xantho chez les courtisanes*; cantatas *Endymion* (1885) and *Vénus et Adonis* (1897); overture *Harald*; Mass with orchestra; motets; numerous songs.

L'Escurel, Jehannot de (died c. 1303) French composer. His 34 secular works, all but one of which are monophonic, are included in the same manuscript as the *Roman de Fauvel*.

Lessel, Franz (Franciszek) (1780–1838) Polish-Austrian composer. He studied medicine in Vienna, but became a pupil of Haydn, whom he looked after until his death. He then returned to Poland and lived with Prince Czartoryski's family until they were driven away by the Revolution. The rest of his life was unsettled.

Works include: three Masses, Requiem and other church music; five symphonies; piano concerto; chamber music; piano sonatas and fantasies.

Les Six (French 'The Six') a group of French composers: Georges Auric, Louis Durey (1888–1979), Arthur Honegger, Darius Milhaud, Francis Poulenc, and Germaine Tailleferre (1892–1983). Formed 1917, the group had Jean Cocteau as its spokesman and adopted Erik ◊Satie as its guru; it was dedicated to producing works free from foreign influences and reflecting contemporary attitudes. The group split up in the early 1920s.

lesson a 17th–18th-century term for a keyboard piece, generally of an instructive character.

Lesueur, Jean François (1760–1837) French composer. He wrote operas and much church music and introduced some orchestral innovations anticipating Berlioz, who was his pupil.

He was born at Drucat, near Abbeville, and first learnt music as a choirboy at Abbeville. He then held church appointments at Amiens and Paris. After 1781 he became musical director successively at Dijon Cathedral, Le Mans, Tours, Saints Innocents, Paris, 1784, and Notre-Dame, Paris, 1786. He was allowed to use a full orchestra at Mass and to open the proceedings with an overture. This aroused a controversy which led to his resignation, and he spent 1788–92 in the country, devoted to the composition of operas. In 1793 he was appointed professor at the school of the National Guard and in 1795 one of the inspectors at the newly opened Conservatory. In 1804 he succeeded Paisiello as maître de chapelle to Napoleon, after whose fall he was appointed superintendent and composer to the chapel of Louis XVIII. In 1818 he became professor of composition at the Conservatory, where his pupils included Berlioz and Gounod.

Works include: the operas *Télémaque* (1796), *La caverne* (1793), *Paulin et Virginie* (after Saint-Pierre, 1794), *Ossian, ou Les bardes* (1804), *Le triomphe de Trajan* (with Persuis, 1807), *La mort d'Adam* (after Klopstock, 1809), and some others; Mass and Te Deum for Napoleon's coronation, three Solemn Masses, *Stabat Mater*, motets, psalms and other church music; oratorios *Messe de Noël*, *Debora*, *Rachel*, *Ruth et Noémi*, *Ruth et Boaz*; cantatas.

letters, music based on composers have sometimes amused themselves by turning names or other words into notes representing in musical nomenclature the letters of which they are formed, or as many as can be thus used. In English the letters A to G can be thus represented; in German H (B♮) and S (Es is equivalent to E♭) can be added, and in French and Italian the syllables Do, Re, Mi, Fa, Sol, La, Si may be used. In France a system was devised for the works on the names of Fauré and Haydn listed below, whereby the notes A to G were followed by further octaves named from H onwards. Examples include:

Abegg (supposed friends of Schumann's): Schumann, *Variations on the Name of Abegg* for piano, op. 1.

Asch (the birthplace of Ernestine von Fricken): Schumann, *Carnaval* for piano op. 9.

Bach ♭B.A.C.H.. See also Faber, below.

Bamberg (the maiden name of Cui's wife): Cui, scherzo for piano duet (on BABEG and CC = César Cui).

Belaiev: Borodin, Glazunov, Liadov and Rimsky-Korsakov, string quartet on 'B-la-F'.

Faber: canon in seven parts by Bach, dated 1 March 1749, sung over a ground or *Pes* on the notes F. A. B♭. E. and marked 'F A B E Repetatur', thus forming the name Faber, which may be a Latin form of some German surname derived from some kind of manual labour. The canon also bears an inscription in Latin containing the following acrostics on the names of Faber and Bach: 'Fidelis Amici Beatum Esse Recordari' and 'Bonae Artis Cultorem Habeas'.

Fauré: pieces by Aubert, Enescu, Koechlin, Ladmirault, Ravel, Roger-Ducasse, and Schmitt contributed to a Fauré number of the *Revue musicale* in 1924.

Gade: Schumann's piano piece so entitled in *Album für die Jugend*. Rheinberger, fughetta for organ.

Gedge: Elgar, allegretto for violin and piano on GEDGE, dedicated to the Misses Gedge.

Haydn: Ravel, *Menuet sur le nom d'Haydn* for piano.

Sacha: Glazunov, *Suite sur le thème du nom diminutif russe* for piano, op. 2.

Schumann (letters SCHA only): *Carnaval* (inversion of the letters ASCH).

Leveridge, Richard (c. 1670–1758) English bass and composer. He appeared as a singer mainly in pantomimes, but also in Italian opera, his career extending from 1695 to 1751. As a composer he is remembered for his songs.

Works include: incidental music for Shakespeare's *Macbeth* (1702), Farquhar's *The Recruiting Officer*, *Love and a Bottle*, and (with D Purcell) *The Constant Couple*, Vanbrugh's *Aesop* and other plays; masque *Pyramus and Thisbe* (after Shakespeare, 1716); songs, including 'The Roast Beef of Old England'.

Levi, Hermann (1839–1900) German conductor. He conducted the first performance of Wagner's *Parsifal* at Bayreuth; at first, Wagner objected that a Jew should conduct what was essentially a Christian opera, but nevertheless accepted him as 'the ideal Parsifal conductor'. He continued at Bayreuth until 1894, and conducted at Wagner's funeral.

He studied with V Lachner at Munich and at the Leipzig Conservatory. After various appointments he became director of the Munich court theatre 1872–96, where he conducted his own editions of Mozart's operas.

Levin, Robert D (1947–) US pianist and musicologist. Mozart has been at the centre of his research and he has published completions of various works.

He studied with Nadia Boulanger 1960–64 and graduated from Harvard University in 1968. He has given solo and chamber concerts throughout the USA, Europe, and Japan from 1970; and was pianist with the New York Philomusica from 1971. His completions of works by Mozart include the D minor Requiem and a four wind concertante that has conjectural orchestration but retains the wind parts of the concerto known as K297b (with clarinet replaced by original flute). He has made recordings with Malcolm Bilson and Melvyn Tan.

Lewis, Anthony (Carey) (1915–1983) English musicologist, conductor, and composer. He edited and conducted operas by Purcell, Rameau, and Handel. He was professor of music at Birmingham University 1947–68 and principal of the Royal Academy of Music, London 1968–82.

He was educated at Wellington College and Cambridge University, studying music at the latter, and went on to study at the Royal College of Music in London and with Nadia Boulanger in Paris. He was on the music staff of the BBC 1935–47 (except during his war service 1939–45), where he organized various music series including the music for the Third Programme (later Radio Three).

Works include: Choral Overture for unaccompanied voices; Elegy and Capriccio for trumpet and orchestra; horn concerto.

L.H. in musical notation, abbreviation for **left hand**, directing a pianist to use the left hand. This is usually in order to facilitate a technically difficult passage, dividing the notes between both hands rather than playing the passage solely with the right hand. It can also be notated in French as M.G. (*main gauche*) or in Italian as M.S. (*mano sinistra*). The opposite is R.H. ('right hand').

L'Héritier, Jean (c. 1480–after 1552) French composer. He wrote Masses, motets, and other pieces.

He was a pupil of Josquin Desprez. In the 1520s he was in Rome, and was music director to the Cardinal de Vermont at Avignon 1540–41.

L'Homme armé see ◊Homme armé.

Liadov, Anatol Konstantinovich (1855–1914) Russian composer. He wrote especially well for the piano, but also composed orchestral works which made him a distinguished member of the national Russian school.

Liadov was born at St Petersburg, where he studied under his father and later with Rimsky-Korsakov at the St Petersburg Conservatory. He became a teacher there in 1878, and his pupils included Prokofiev and Myaskovsky. The Imperial Geographical Society commissioned him, with Balakirev and Liapunov, to collect folk songs in various parts of Russia. His gift was essentially reclusive and small-scale; Stravinsky described his relief at not getting the commission for The Rite of Spring from Diaghilev.

Works include: symphonic poems Baba Yaga (1904), The Enchanted Lake (1909), Kikimora (1909), two orchestral scherzos, The Inn-Muzurka, Polonaise in Memory of Pushkin for orchestra; choral settings from Schiller's Bride of Messina and Maeterlinck's Sœur Béatrice, three choral works for female voices; about 40 op. nos. of piano pieces, including Birulki/Spillikins), ballads 'From Days of Old', 'Marionettes', 'Musical Snuff-Box', variations on a theme by Glinka and on a Polish song, 'From the Book of Revelation', studies, preludes, mazurkas, and other pieces; songs, folk-song settings (1903).

Liapunov, Sergey Mikhailovich (1859–1924) Russian pianist and composer. From 1891 to 1902 he was assistant director of the Imperial Chapel, and from 1910 professor at the St Petersburg Conservatory. He fled to Paris to escape the Russian Revolution.

He studied at Nizhny-Novgorod and at the Moscow Conservatory. In 1893 the Imperial Geographical Society commissioned him, with Balakirev and Liadov, to collect Russian folk songs.

Works include: two symphonies (1887, 1910–17), Ballad, Solemn Overture, Polonaise and symphonic poem Hashish for orchestra; two piano concertos (1890, 1909), rhapsody on Ukrainian themes for piano and orchestra (1908); numerous piano pieces, including suite Christmas Songs, and other pieces; folk-song settings.

Liberté '14 tableaux inspirés par l'histoire du peuple de France', music by Delannoy, Honegger, Ibert, Lazarus, Milhaud, Roland-Manuel, Rosenthal, Tailleferre, and others, produced Paris, Théâtre des Champs-Élysées, May 1937.

libretto (Italian 'little book') the text of an opera or other dramatic vocal work, or the scenario of a ballet.

Libuše opera by Smetana (libretto in German, by J Wenzig, Czech translation by E Spindler), produced Prague, Czech Theatre, 11 June 1881. Libuše, new queen of Bohemia, must choose a husband to help her rule after her quarreling brothers Chrudos and Šťáhlov refuse to obey her authority. Peasant Přemsyl is the lucky man.

licenza (Italian 'licence', 'freedom') in musical notation, from the term *con licenza* ('with freedom'), direction to the performer to take liberties with the tempo, using ◊rubato and other forms of expression.

Lichnovsky, (Prince) Karl (1761–1814) Polish aristocrat, resident in Vienna. After early patronage of Mozart, he was introduced to Beethoven by Haydn. Beethoven's early chamber works were played at his house before publication, notably the string quartets op. 18, with the Schuppanzigh quartet.

Licht/Light cycle of seven projected operas by Stockhausen, one for each day of the week. See ◊*Dienstag aus Licht*, ◊*Donnerstag aus Licht*, ◊*Montag aus Licht*, ◊*Samstag aus Licht*.

Lidarti, Christian Joseph (1730–after 1793) Austro-Italian composer. He was in the service of the Cavalieri di S Stefano in Pisa 1757–84.

He was taught by his uncle, Giuseppe Bonno, in Vienna and later by Jommelli in Italy.

Works include: trio sonatas, catches, and glees.

Lidholm, Ingvar (1921–) Swedish composer. From 1947 to 1956 he was conductor of the Örebro Symphony Orchestra.

He studied at the Stockholm Conservatory with, among others, Hilding Rosenberg and Tor Mann. Later he studied in Italy and France, and also with Mátyás Seiber.

Works include: the opera *The Dutchman* (after Strindberg, 1967), concerto for string orchestra, *Toccata e canto* for chamber orchestra (1944), *Ritornell* for orchestra (1956); concertino for flute, cor anglais, oboe, and bassoon; *Greetings from an Old World* for orchestra (1976); *Kontakion* for orchestra (1978); *De Profundis* for chorus; *Cantata* for baritone and orchestra; string quartet, four pieces for cello and piano, sonata for solo flute.

Liebe der Danae, Die/Danae's Love opera by Richard Strauss (libretto by Josef Gregor), intended for production at the Salzburg Festival and given public dress rehearsal on 16 August 1944. Production postponed owing to war; produced there 14 August 1952. (The title was originally *Der Kuss der Danae/Danae's Kiss*.) Danae, who spurns all men, is pursued by King Midas and Jupiter, favouring the 'golden touch' of Midas. She then falls genuinely in love with him, and continues to love him after vengeful Jupiter makes him destitute.

Liebe im Narrenhaus, Die/Love in the Madhouse opera by Dittersdorf (libretto by G Stephanie, junior), produced Vienna, Kärntnertor-theater, 12 April 1787. Constanze has been promised to lunatic asylum director Bast, so her lover Albert feigns insanity. When Albert inherits a fortune the lovers are allowed to marry.

Lieberson, Peter (1946–) US composer. He studied in New York with Milton Babbitt, Charles Wuorinen, and Donald Martino. He studied Buddhism 1976–81 and was inspired to write his piano concerto of 1983.

Works include: in a serial idiom *Tashi Quartet* 1979; *Lalita (Chamber Variations)* for ten instruments 1984; *Drala* for orchestra 1986; *Gesar Legend* for orchestra 1988; *Raising the Gaze* for seven instruments 1988; and *Wind Messengers* for 13 instruments 1990.

Liebert, Reginaldus (lived early 15th century) French composer. His main work is a complete Mass (Ordinary and Proper) of the Blessed Virgin Mary for three voices.

He probably succeeded Nicolas Grenon at Cambrai in 1424. A Gautier Liebert, composer of three *rondeaux*, was a singer in the papal chapel in 1428.

Liebeslieder/Love Songs a set of waltzes by Brahms for piano duet with solo vocal quartet *ad lib*, op. 52, composed 1869. There is a second set of *Neue Liebeslieder*, op. 65, written in 1874.

Liebesverbot, Das, oder Die Novize von Palermo/The Love-Ban, or The Novice of Palermo opera by Wagner (libretto by composer, based on Shakespeare's *Measure for Measure*), produced Magdeburg, 29 March 1836. Viceroy Friedrich outlaws pleasure but desires Isabella. Friedrich having imprisoned her brother Claudio, Isabella is willing to sacrifice herself for Claudio's agreed release, but she sends Friedrich's wife to the rendezvous. Friedrich's hypocrisy is exposed; a happy ending.

lied (German 'song', plural lieder) musical dramatization of a poem, usually for solo voice and piano; referring to Romantic songs of Schubert, Schumann, Brahms, and Hugo Wolf.

Lieder eines fahrenden Gesellen/Songs of a Wayfarer song cycle by Mahler for low voice and piano (texts by Mahler); composed 1884, orchestrated c. 1895 and performed in this version Berlin, 16 March 1896, conductor Mahler. Titles of songs are 1. *Wenn mein Schatz Hochzeit macht/When my sweetheart gets married*, 2. *Ging heut' Morgen übers Feld/I walked this morning through the fields*: thematically related to the first movement of the contemporary first symphony; 3. *Ich hab ein glühend Messer in der Brust/I have a burning knife in my breast*; 4. *Die zwei blauen Augen/The two blue eyes*. Also heard in version with chamber ensemble by Schoenberg.

Liederkreis title used for two sets of songs by Schumann: nine Heine settings op. 24 and 12 Eichendorff settings op. 39 (both 1840). See also ◊song cycle.

Lieder ohne Worte thirty-six piano pieces by Mendelssohn in the form and character of songs exploiting the principle of accompanying melody rather than polyphonic textures. Vol. I, op. 19, nos. 1–6 (1830–32); II, op. 30, 7–12 (1833–7); III, op. 38, 13–18 (1836–37); IV, op. 53, 19–24 (1841); V. op. 62, 25–30 (1842–43); VI, op. 67, 31–6 (1843–45). The only titles which are Mendelssohn's own are those of the three *Venezianische Gondellieder* (*Venetian Barcarolles*), nos. 6, 12, and 29, the *Duetto*, no. 18, and the *Volkslied*, no. 23.

Liederspiel (German 'song-play') play with songs similar to the *Singspiel*. The term was first used by Reichardt in 1800. It may also mean 'song cycle', as in Schumann's *Spanisches Liederspiel*.

Lied von der Erde, Das/The Song of the Earth symphony for mezzo, tenor, and orchestra by Mahler (so called by the composer, but not numbered among his other symphonies). The words are from Hans Bethge's anthology of German translations of Chinese poetry, *Die chinesische Flöte*: 1. (Li-Tai-Po) *Das Trinklied vom Jammer der Erde/The Drinking-Song of Earth's Misery*; 2. (Tchang-Tsi) *Der Einsame im Herbst/The Lonely One in Autumn*; 3. (Li-Tai-Po) *Von der Jugend/Of Youth*: 4. (ditto) *Von der Schönheit/Of Beauty*; 5. (ditto) *Der Trunkene im Frühling/The Drunkard in Spring*; 6. (Mong-Kao-Yen and Wang-We) *Der Abschied/The Farewell*). Composed 1908; first performed Munich, 20 November 1911, after Mahler's death.

Lieutenant Kijé symphonic suite by Prokofiev, arranged in 1934 from film music composed 1933. The five movements are *Birth of Kijé, Romance, Wedding, Troika, Burial*; first performed Paris, 20 February 1937, conductor Prokofiev.

Life in the Times of the Tsar, A/Zhizn za Tsaria; now Ivan Susanin opera by Glinka (libretto by C F Rosen), produced St Petersburg, 9 December 1836. Ivan Susanin delays the wedding of his daughter Antonida to Bogden Sobinin because of invading Poles who are hunting down the Tsar. Knowing where the Tsar is hiding, Susanin deliberately leads the Poles astray, knowing that he will be killed when the deception is discovered. Susanin willingly sacrifices his life for the Tsar; his bravery is praised by all.

ligature the adjustable metal brace used to attach the reed to the mouthpiece of an instrument of the clarinet family.

ligature notation used in the 13th–16th centuries in which two or more notes are combined to form a single symbol. Depending on the shape of the ligature, the same group of notes could indicate different rhythms. In addition to its rhythmic implications, a ligature indicates that only one syllable is to be sung for the duration of its notes, similar in function to a modern slur marking in vocal works (also known as a ligature, or ◊tie).

Ligeti, Andras (1953–) Hungarian conductor. He studied violin at the Budapest Academy and was leader of the Hungarian State Opera House Orchestra, 1976–80. He conducted concerts in Europe and Canada, and was associate conductor with the Budapest Symphony Orchestra from 1985 (tours of the UK and the USA). He made his UK debut with the BBC Symphony Orchestra in 1989, and with the BBC Philharmonic Orchestra in 1991 (Bartók's *Bluebeard's Castle* and Mahler's 5th symphony).

Ligeti, György Sándor (1923–) Hungarian-born Austrian composer. He developed a dense, highly chromatic, polyphonic style in which melody and rhythm are sometimes lost in shifting blocks of sound. He achieved international prominence with *Atmosphères* 1961 and *Requiem* 1965, which achieved widespread fame as background music for Stanley Kubrick's film epic *2001: A Space Odyssey* 1968. Other works include an opera *Le grand macabre* 1978, and *Poème symphonique* 1962, for 100 metronomes.

Ligeti studied composition with Sándor Veress and Ferenc Farkas at the Budapest Music Academy 1945–49, becoming an instructor there 1950–56. In 1956 he went to the Studio for Electronic Music at Cologne, and in

Modern equivalent

Various ligatures (left), with literal and modern representations (right).

1959 was appointed instructor at the International Courses for New Music at Darmstadt. In 1961 he was visiting professor of composition at the Stockholm Music Academy, and eventually settled in Vienna. His mature music is experimental in nature, featuring complex textures which he called 'micropolyphony', in which the individuality of a large number of separate parts is subsumed, giving the impression of a slowly changing single mass.

Works include: the opera *Le grand macabre* (produced Stockholm 1978); *Artikulation* for electronic sounds (1958); *Apparitions* for orchestra (1959); *Atmosphères* for large orchestra (1961); *Poème symphonique* for 100 metronomes; *Aventures* for soprano, alto, and baritone with seven instruments (1962); *Nouvelles aventures* for soprano and seven instruments; Requiem for soloists, chorus, and orchestra (1965; Kyrie used in film *2001*); *Lux aeterna* for 16 solo voices; cello concerto (1967); *Ramifications* for string orchestra (1969); Chamber Concerto for 13 instruments (1970); *San Francisco Polyphony* for orchestra (1974); Trio for violin, horn, and piano (1982), *3 Phantasien* and *Hungarian Studies*, both for 16 voices (1983); *Etudes* for piano (1985); Piano concerto (1985–88); *Nonsense Madrigals*

for six voices (1988); violin concerto (1990); *L'escalier du diable* for piano (1993).

Lighthouse, The chamber opera in one act by Peter Maxwell Davies (text by composer, based on 1900 disappearance of three Outer Hebridean lighthouse keepers); composed 1979, first performed Edinburgh, 2 September 1980.

Light of Life, The/Lux Christi oratorio by Elgar for soloists, chorus, and orchestra, op. 29 (text by E Capel-Dure from the Scriptures; composed 1896, first performed Worcester, 10 September 1896, conductor Elgar.

'Lilliburlero' a satirical song sung in Ireland after the appointment of General Talbot to the lord-lieutenancy in 1687. It is not likely that the earlier attribution of the tune to Purcell is justified: it was probably a popular melody merely arranged by him, much as 'The Prince of Denmark's March' was arranged by J Clarke.

Lima, Jeronymo Francisco de (1743–1822) Portuguese composer and organist. He was elected to the Brotherhood of St Cecilia, visited Italy, and in 1798 became conductor of the Royal Opera at Lisbon.

Works include: the opera *Le nozze d'Ercole e d'Ebe* (1785) and five others (all Italian); church music; cantatas.

Limburgia, Johannes de (lived late 14th and early 15th century) French composer. He worked at churches in Liège 1408–19, and in Italy from about 1430. His 50 or so compositions (all church music) include a complete Mass (three and four voices) and 16 motets.

Lincoln Portrait, A work by Copland for orchestra, and a speaker, who declaims portions of Lincoln's speeches, first performed by Cincinnati Symphony Orchestra, 14 May 1942.

Linda di Chamounix opera by Donizetti (libretto by G Rossi, after a vaudeville, *La Grâce de Dieu*), produced Vienna, Kärntnertortheater, 19 May 1842. Poor Linda loves the viscount Carlo, who has disguised himself as a destitute painter. She follows him to Paris and learns his true identity, but goes mad upon learning of his supposed marriage to another woman. Carlo reassures her and Linda recovers.

Lindblad, Adolf Fredrik (1801–1878) Swedish composer and singing teacher. He studied with Carl Zelter in Berlin and in 1827 settled at Stockholm as a teacher of singing. Jenny Lind was among his pupils.

Works include: the opera *Frondörerna* (1835); two symphonies; seven string quartets; duo for violin and piano; vocal duets, trios and quartets; numerous songs.

linear counterpoint a term for a kind of counterpoint in 20th-century music which regards the individuality of melodic lines as more important than the harmony they produce in combination.

Linley, Elizabeth Ann (1754–1792) English soprano, daughter and pupil of Thomas ◊Linley. She first sang in her father's concerts in Bath. She made her London debut in 1770, but after her marriage to Sheridan in 1773 retired from singing. Her portrait was painted by Gainsborough and Reynolds.

Linley, Thomas (1733–1795) English singing master and composer. He studied with Thomas Chilcot, the organist of Bath Abbey, and with Paradisi in London; he settled at Bath as singing teacher and concert promoter. From 1774 he managed the oratorios at Drury Lane Theatre in London jointly with Stanley and from 1786 with Arnold. Sheridan became his son-in-law in 1773, and he and his son, also Thomas, wrote music for Sheridan's play *The Duenna* in 1775. In 1776 he moved to

London and bought Garrick's share in Drury Lane Theatre, where he managed the music and wrote music for various pieces.

Works include: the opera *The Royal Merchant* (1767); music for Sheridan's *Duenna* (1781) and *School for Scandal* (the song 'Here's to the maiden'), *The Carnival of Venice* (1781), *The Gentle Shepherd, Robinson Crusoe* (pantomime by Sheridan, after Defoe), *The Triumph of Mirth, The Spanish Rivals* (1784), *The Strangers at Home* (1785), *Love in the East* (1788), and other plays; adaptations from Grétry: *Zelmire and Azor* and *Richard Cœur de Lion*; accompaniments for *The Beggar's Opera*; music for Sheridan's monody on the death of Garrick; six elegies for three voices; 12 ballads; cantatas, madrigals.

Linley, Thomas (1756–1778) English violinist and composer, son and pupil of Thomas ◊Linley. He was also a pupil of Boyce, later of Nardini in Florence, where he struck up a friendship with the young Mozart in 1770. On his return to England he played in his father's concerts, and collaborated with him in the composition of *The Duenna* in 1775. He was drowned in a boating accident.

Works include: the opera *The Cadi of Bagdad* (1778); music for Shakespeare's *The Tempest* (1777) and Sheridan's *The Duenna* (with his father); oratorio *The Song of Moses* (1777); *Ode on the Witches and Fairies of Shakespeare*; anthem 'Let God arise'; violin concerto, several elegies.

Linley, Mary (1758–1787) English singer, daughter and pupil of Thomas ◊Linley. She sang at festivals and gave oratorio performances, but retired on her marriage to Richard Rickell, commissioner of stamps and dramatist, who wrote *The Carnival of Venice* for his father-in-law and altered Ramsay's *Gentle Shepherd* for him.

Linley, William (1771–1835) English composer and government official, son and pupil of Thomas ◊Linley; also a pupil of Abel. He held official posts in India, but in between was Sheridan's partner in the management of the Drury Lane Theatre, for which he composed some unsuccessful works. He settled in London in 1806 as writer and composer.

Works include: pantomimes *Harlequin Captive, The Honey Moon, The Pavilion*; songs to Shakespeare's plays; glees.

'Linz' Symphony Mozart's symphony in C major, K425, composed at the house of Count Thun at Linz, where Mozart and his wife stayed on their return from Salzburg to Vienna, and performed there 4 November 1783.

Lioncourt, Guy de (1885–1961) French musicologist and composer. He studied under d'Indy at the Schola Cantorum in Paris and later taught there. In 1918 he gained a prize with a musical fairy tale, *La Belle au bois dormant* (after Perrault).

Works include: the opera *Jean de la lune,* liturgical drama *Le Mystère d'Emmanuel* (1924); church music; cantata *Hyalis le petit faune* (Samain, 1909–11) and sacred cantatas; chamber music.

Lionel and Clarissa opera by Dibdin (libretto by I Bickerstaffe), produced London, Covent Garden 25 February 1768.

lira (Italian) in music, a generic name given to various early bowed string instruments, such as the rebab, or rebec, and the crwth in earlier times.

lira da braccio (Italian 'arm lyre') bowed string instrument current in the 16th and early 17th centuries. It had seven strings, two or more of which served as drones. As the name implies, it was played on the arm.

lira da gamba (Italian 'leg lyre') musical instrument, a larger version of the lira da braccio, played between the legs. The number of strings, including drones, varied from 11 to 15.

lira organizzata Italian name for the vielle organisée, a musical instrument.

Lissenko, Nikolai Vitalievich (1842–1912) Russian composer. He studied natural science, but while making researches in ethnography he became interested in Ukrainian folk song, specimens of which he began to collect. He then studied at the Leipzig Conservatory and later with Rimsky-Korsakov at St Petersburg. He settled at Kiev.

Works include: the operas *Taras Bulba* (after Gogol, produced 1903), *Sappho, The Aeneid* (after Virgil), and others; operettas; cantatas and other choral works; *Ukrainian Rhapsody* for violin and piano; piano pieces; songs, settings of Ukrainian folk songs.

l'istesso tempo (Italian 'the same tempo') in musical notation, direction given when a change is indicated in the time signature, the composer intending the music remain at the same pace despite the new rhythm.

Liszt, Franz (1811–1886) Hungarian pianist and composer. An outstanding virtuoso of the piano, he was an established concert artist by the age of 12. His expressive, romantic,

and frequently chromatic works include piano music (*Transcendental Studies* 1851), Masses and oratorios, songs, organ music, and a symphony. Much of his music is programmatic; he also originated the symphonic poem. Liszt was taught by his father, then by Carl Czerny. He travelled widely in Europe, producing an operetta *Don Sanche* in Paris at the age of 14. As musical director and conductor at Weimar 1848–59, he championed the music of Berlioz and Wagner.

Retiring to Rome, he turned again to his early love of religion, and in 1865 became a secular priest (adopting the title Abbé), while continuing to teach and give concert tours for which he also made virtuoso piano arrangements of orchestral works by Beethoven, Schubert, and Wagner. He died at Bayreuth in Germany.

Liszt's father, a steward of the Esterházy family's property, was Hungarian, his mother Austrian. At the age of nine he gave a concert at Sopron and in 1823 he had advanced so amazingly that his father took him to Vienna and Paris, where he had immense success. In 1824–25 he paid two visits to England and another in 1827. His father died that year, and he was taken to Paris by his paternal grandmother, who looked after his education there. He remained there, and after a period of religious mysticism under the influence of Lamennais, achieved great success and fame as a pianist, his flamboyant stage manner having almost as much to do with his success as his dazzling technique. In Paris he came into contact with the Romantics, including Berlioz, Chopin, Paganini, and George Sand, and in 1833 he began his liaison with the Countess d'Agoult. They went to live at Geneva in 1835, where a daughter, Blandine, was born, followed by another, Cosima , who became first Hans von Bülow's and then Wagner's wife, at Como in 1837. A son, Daniel, was born in Rome 1839. During this time Liszt wrote the *Album d'un voyageur* first published complete in 1842 (several of the pieces reappeared in the first book of *Années de Pèlerinage* 1855).

He travelled widely as a pianist and made much money. In 1840 he collected funds for the Beethoven memorial at Bonn, and often played for charitable purposes organized on a large scale. He paid further visits to England 1840–41, playing before Queen Victoria, and he toured Russia, Turkey, and Denmark 1842–44. He and the Countess separated in 1844, and the following year he visited Spain and Portugal; two years later, at Kiev, he met Princess Caroline Sayn-Wittgenstein, the wife of a wealthy Russian landowner, who fell in love with him and in 1848 left with him for Weimar, where he was engaged as conductor and music director to the grand-ducal court for certain periods of the year. He produced many new operas there, including Wagner's *Lohengrin* 1850 and Berlioz's *Béatrice et Bénédict* 1862, and settled down to write various works, some on a very large scale, having previously confined himself almost exclusively to piano music. His piano sonata of 1853, followed by the *Faust* and *Dante* symphonies, were revolutionary for their extension of sonata form in a cyclic process extending for several movements, and for their use of limited motifs that become transformed as a means of development. His chief orchestral writings are connected with his Weimar career, and the music of this period had a profound influence on his contemporaries: echoes of the opening theme of Liszt's *Faust* symphony appear in Sieglinde's solo scene at the end of *Die Walküre* act II by Wagner, while traces of *Dante* symphony survive in *Parsifal* by the same composer.

He retired to Rome in 1861, and took minor orders in 1865, becoming an abbé, and henceforward many of his works were of a sacred character: *Missa solemnis* 1855, and other Masses, *Christus* 1862–66, Psalms and the Requiem for male voices and organ. Becoming president of the Budapest Academy of Music in 1875, he lived in Budapest, Weimar, and Rome from this date. In his last years he often visited his daughter Cosima at Bayreuth, and irritated Wagner with his new-found religious fervour. In his last piano works he adopted a totally new, modern style which his contemporaries found incomprehensible. Liszt was the most important figure of musical Romanticism, influencing not only his own age but also the following century.

Until recently, Liszt's posthumous reputation has not been high; his lifestyle has distracted attention from his music. Frequent modern performances of the symphonies and symphonic poems, as well as the work of such pianists as Leslie Howard, Alfred Brendel, and Mikhail Rudy, have revealed a more thoughtful and serious composer.

Works include: ORCHESTRAL *Faust* and *Dante* symphonies (1854–57 and 1856); 13 symphonic poems for orchestra, including *Les Préludes* (1848); two piano concertos in E♭ (1849, revised 1853, 1856) and A (1839, revised 1849–61), *Totentanz*.

VOCAL AND ORGAN oratorio *Christus* (1862–67); a number of other choral works; 55 songs; fugue on B.A.C.H., fantasy (1885) and fugue on *Ad nos, ad salutarem undam* and a few other organ works.

PIANO a vast number of piano compositions, including three volumes of *Années de pèlerinage* (1866–77), 12 *Etudes d'exécution transcendante* (1851), two *Légendes, Liebsträume* (three nocturnes, originally songs), sonata in B minor (1853), 20 Hungarian Rhapsodies; innumerable transcriptions for piano including operatic pieces, symphonies, waltzes, and songs.

Litaniae Lauretanae (Latin 'Litanies of Loreto') litany sung in honour of the Virgin Mary in the Roman Church, dating probably from the 13th century. It has its own plainsong melody, but has also been set by composers, including Palestrina, Lassus, and Mozart.

litany a supplicatory chant consisting of a series of petitions with an infrequently changing response to each. The best-known litanies in the Roman Church are the Litany of the Saints, sung on Holy Saturday and during Rogationtide, and the 13th-century ◊*Litaniae Lauretanae*. The reformed churches have also adopted the litany, excluding references to the saints, as in Cranmer's litany, still used in the Anglican Church.

Literes, Antonio (1673–1747) Spanish bass viol player and composer. He was a member of the royal band in Madrid from 1693. He is often confused with his son, a well-known organist, who was also called Antonio.

Works include: the operas *Júpiter y Danae, Los Elementos, Dido y Eneas*; zarzuela *Coronis*; 14 psalm settings; eight Magnificat settings.

Litolff, Henry (Charles) (1818–1891) Anglo-Alsatian composer, pianist, and publisher. He travelled widely as a concert pianist until 1851, and produced his best opera, *Les Templiers*, at Brussels in 1886.

His father was Alsatian, his mother English. As a boy of 13 he became a pupil of Moscheles for piano, made his first appearance in 1832, and at 17 left for France, having married against his parents' wishes. He was a concert pianist until 1851, when he acquired a music publishing business at Brunswick, marrying as his second wife the widow of the former owner. But he soon left his adopted son Theodor Litolff in charge and settled in Paris, where later he married again, a Comtesse de la Rochefoucauld.

Works include: the operas *Les Templiers* (1886) and *Héloïse et Abelard* (1872); oratorios *Ruth and Boaz*; five piano concertos including no. 4 (1852) with the popular Scherzo, violin concerto; overture *Robespierre* and others; chamber music; piano works.

'Little Russian' Symphony Tchaikovsky's second symphony in C minor, op. 17, also called *Ukrainian* symphony, composed 1872, performed Moscow, 18 February 1873.

Little Slave Girl, The/Den lilla slavinnan opera by Crusell (libretto by composer), produced Stockholm, 18 February 1824.

liturgical drama a medieval church representation of Bible and other stories. It originated, probably in France, in a 10th-century trope to the Introit for Easter Day, which takes the form of a dialogue for the Angel and the Marys at the sepulchre. In the second half of the century it was transferred to Matins. The music was originally an extension of plainsong but in course of time came to consist of original compositions. Later subjects treated include the Walk to Emmaus, the Nativity, Epiphany, the Massacre of the Innocents, Old Testament stories and the lives of the saints. The texts were generally in Latin but sometimes also in the vernacular.

liturgy in the Christian church, any written, authorized version of a service for public worship, especially the Roman Catholic ◊Mass.

Its development over the centuries has had a direct impact on music and composition, because until the Renaissance the church had a near monopoly in the West on skilled musicians and composers, whose work therefore catered to the service.

lituus (Latin) the Roman cavalry trumpet. In the 18th century it occasionally meant 'horn'.

Liuzzi, Fernando (1884–1940) Italian musicologist and composer. He studied with Fano and later with Reger and Mottl and Munich. He became professor of harmony at the Conservatories of Parma and of Florence successively, and professor of music history at Rome University 1927–28. He edited Italian *laudi*, arranged performances of Vecchi's *Amfiparnaso* (Florence, 1938) and of Sophocles' *Oedipus Rex* with A Gabrieli's music (Rome, 1937). He wrote books on the *laudi*, on Italian musicians in France, a volume of critical studies *Estetica della musica*, and also numerous learned articles.

Livietta e Tracollo intermezzo by Pergolesi (libretto by T Mariani), produced Naples, Teatro San Bartolommeo, between the acts of Pergolesi's serious opera *Adriano in Siria*, 25 October 1734. Livietta encourages petty thief and trickster Tracallo to reform.

Livre pour quatuor work in six movements for string quartet by Boulez; composed 1948–49, performed Donaueschingen and Darmstadt 1955–62. Revised as *Livre pour cordes*, for string orchestra and performed Brighton, 8 December 1969, conductor Boulez.

Lloyd, George (1913–) English composer. His father wrote the libretti for his three operas, the first of which was produced at Penzance in 1934 and the second at Covent Garden in 1938.

He studied violin with Albert Sammons and composition with Harry Farjeon. He was severely wounded in World War II.

Works include: the operas *Iernin* (1934), *The Serf* (1938) and *John Socman* (1951); 12 symphonies (1932–88); four piano concertos; two violin concertos; *Symphonic Mass* for chorus and orchestra (1992).

Lloyd, John (c. 1475–1523), also Floyd English composer. He sang at the funeral of Prince Henry in 1511 and was present at the Field of the Cloth of Gold in 1520.

Lloyd, Jonathan (1948–) English composer. He studied with Roxburgh 1965–69 at the Royal College of Music and worked with Tristram Cary at the electronic studio there. Later he studied with Pousseur and Ligeti. He has worked as street musician and was composer-in-residence at Dartington College 1978–79.

Works include: *Cantique* for small orchestra (1968), *Everthing Returns* for soprano and orchestra (1978), *Toward the Whitening Dawn* for chorus and chamber orchestra (1980), *Fantasy* for violin and orchestra (1980), *If I Could Turn You On* for soprano and chamber orchestra (1981), *Rhapsody* for cello and orchestra (1982), viola concerto (1980); *Wa Wa Mozart* for piano and orchestra (1991); *There* for guitar and strings (1991); *Tolerance* for orchestra (1993); five symphonies (1983–89); *Three Dances, Waiting for Gozo* and *Won't it Ever be Morning*, for ensemble (1980–82); *John's Journal* for saxophone and piano (1980), two string quintets (1982), *Almeida Dances* for clarinet, piano and string quartet (1986); *Mass for six voices* (1983); *Revelation* for eight voices (1990).

Lloyd Webber, Andrew (1948–) English composer. His early musicals, with lyrics by Tim Rice, include *Joseph and the Amazing Technicolor Dreamcoat* 1968, *Jesus Christ Superstar* 1971, and *Evita* 1978, based on the life of the Argentine leader Eva Perón. He also wrote *Cats* 1981, based on T S Eliot's *Old Possum's Book of Practical Cats, Starlight*

Express 1984, *The Phantom of the Opera* 1986, and *Aspects of Love* 1989.

Other works include *Variations for Cello* 1978, written for his brother **Julian Lloyd Webber** (1951–) who is a solo cellist, and a *Requiem Mass* 1985, which was not regarded as making a significant contribution to the liturgical music of the 20th century.

Along with Tim Rice, he won the Golden Globe in January 1997 for best original song for 'You Must Love Me' from *Evita*.

Lobe, Johann Christian (1797–1881) German flautist, composer, and writer on music. He wrote five operas, which were produced at Weimar, where he was a member of the court orchestra.

He studied at the expense of the Grand Duchess of Weimar, Maria Pavlovna, appeared as a solo flautist at Leipzig in 1811, and then joined the court orchestra at Weimar, where his operas were produced. He left in 1842 and four years later became editor of the *Allgemeine Musikalische Zeitung* at Leipzig; he also published several books on music.

Works include: the operas *Wittekind* (1819), *Die Flibustier* (1829), *Die Fürstin von Granada* (1833), *Der rote Domino* (1835), and *König und Pächter* (1844); two symphonies, overtures; piano quartets.

Lobgesang see ◊*Hymn of Praise.*

Lobkowitz, (Prince) Joseph Franz Maximilian (1772–1816) Bohemian aristocrat and patron of music, resident in Vienna; he had sole direction of the Viennese theatres from 1807. He commissioned Haydn's string quartets op. 77 and was a cosponsor of *The Creation* and *The Seasons*. The Eroica Symphony was first performed in his house, and Beethoven dedicated the quartets op. 18 and fifth and sixth symphony, the Triple Concerto, the string quartet op. 74, and *An die ferne Geliebte* to him.

Lobo, Alonso (c. 1555–1617) Spanish composer. He was a choirboy at Seville Cathedral and assistant to the maestro di cappella from 1591; in 1604 he became maestro di cappella there himself. He was influenced by Palestrina, Victoria, and Guerrero.

Works include: *Liber primus missarum* (1602), containing six Masses and seven motets; Credo romano, three passions, Lamentations, psalms, hymns.

Lobo, Duarte (1565–1646), also called Lopez or Lupus Portuguese composer. He was widely known as a composer of poly-phonic church music, which he published in six books.

He studied under Manuel Mendes (1547–1605) at Evora and later became choirmaster there. Afterwards he went to Lisbon with an appointment to the Royal Hospital and became maestro di cappella at the cathedral about 1590.

Works include: Masses, offices for the dead, canticles, motets, and much other church music.

Locatelli, Pietro (1695–1764) Italian violinist and composer. After travelling widely and establishing a reputation as a virtuoso, he settled at Amsterdam in 1729, where he established public concerts.

He was a pupil of Corelli in Rome.

Works include: a set of 12 concerti grossi, op. 1, and solo concertos; sonatas; studies, caprices and other pieces for violin.

Locke, Matthew (c. 1622–1677), or Lock English composer. He is remembered for the music he wrote for masques such as Shirley's *Cupid and Death* 1653, and his incidental and vocal music for plays, notably *Psyche* 1675. He was a vigorous and acrimonious defender of 'modern music', writing in 1666 a pamphlet defending his church music and in 1672 opening a controversy with Thomas ◊Salmon. Purcell wrote an elegy on his death.

He was a choirboy at Exeter Cathedral under Edward Gibbons. In 1648 he visited the Netherlands, and having returned to London collaborated in Shirley's masque *Cupid and Death* performed before the Portuguese ambassador in 1653. In 1656 he wrote the *Little Consort* for viols in three parts for William Wake's pupils and the same year he was one of the composers who took part in the setting of Davenant's *Siege of Rhodes*. He was Composer in Ordinary to the King and for Charles II's coronation in 1661 he wrote instrumental music for the procession. In 1663, having turned Roman Catholic, he became organist to Queen Catherine.

Works include: OPERA Davenant's *The Siege of Rhodes* (with Coleman, Cooke, Hudson, and H Lawes, 1656), *Psyche* (with G B Draghi).

OTHER masque, Shirley's *Cupid and Death* (with C Gibbons, 1653); incidental music to Stapylton's *The Stepmother*, Shakespeare's *Macbeth* altered by Davenant and containing material from Middleton's *The Witch*, and for Shadwell's version of Shakespeare's *Tempest* (1674), song in Durfey's *The Fool turned Critic*; Kyrie, Credo, anthems, Latin hymns; consorts for viols in three and four parts; songs in three parts, duets; songs for one voice with accompaniment.

loco (Italian 'place') in music, a term used to counteract previous notation ('8ve') calling for the performance of music at an octave higher or lower than normal; it indicates that the music is to return to its normal 'place' on the stave.

Loder, Edward (James) (1813–1865) English composer. He first learnt music from his father, John David Loder (1788–1846), a violinist and music publisher, and in 1826–28 studied with F Ries at Frankfurt. After a second period of study there he settled in London and was induced by Arnold to set an opera, *Nourjahad*, for the New England Opera House, under which name the Lyceum Theatre opened with it in 1834. He was theatre conductor in London and later in Manchester. About 1856 he began to suffer from a disease of the brain.

Works include: OPERAS AND PLAYS WITH MUSIC *Nourjahad* (1834), *The Dice of Death* (1835), *Francis I* (a concoction from his songs), *The Foresters* (1838), *The Deerstalkers* (1841), *The Night Dancers* (1846), *Robin Goodfellow* (1848), *The Sultana*, *The Young Guard*, *Raymond and Agnes*.

OTHER masque *The Island of Calypso* (1852); string quartets; numerous songs, including *12 Sacred Songs*, and *The Brooklet* (a translation of Wilhelm Müller's *Wohin* set by Schubert in *Die schöne Müllerin*).

Loder, Kate (Fanny) (1825–1904) English pianist and composer. She wrote chamber music and an opera, *L'elisir d'amore*. She was a cousin of Edward Loder.

She studied at the Royal Academy of Music in London, where she later became professor of harmony. She made her first appearance in 1844, when she played Medelssohn's G minor concerto. The first performance in England of Brahms's Requiem took place at her house on 7 July 1871, the accompaniment being played on the piano by herself and Cipriani Potter.

Works include: the opera *L'elisir d'amore*, and other pieces.

Lodoïska opera by Cherubini (libretto by C F Fillette-Loraux), produced Paris, Théâtre Fey-dau, 18 July 1791. Evil Count Dourlinski imprisons Lodoïska in order to force her to agree to marry him. Count Floreski rescues her with the help of some Tatar warriors.

Opera by Rodolphe Kreutzer (libretto by J C B Dejaure), produced Paris, Comédie-Italienne, 1 August 1791.

Lodoïska opera by Mayr (libretto by F Gonella), produced Venice, Teatro Le Fenice, 26 January 1796. Plot similar to ◊*Lodoïska*, but Lodoiska is imprisoned by a Count Boleslao and rescued by a Lovinski.

Lodoletta opera by Mascagni (libretto by G Forzano, after Ouida), produced Rome, Teatro Costanzi, 30 April 1917. Dutch flower-seller follows poet to Paris but dies of cold when she gets there.

Loeffler, Charles Martin (Tornow) (1861–1935) Alsatian-born US composer. He went to the USA in 1881, and played in Damrosch's orchestra, in quartets, and with touring companies. In 1882 he joined the Boston Symphony Orchestra, where he remained, sharing the first desk with the leader, until 1903. In 1887 he became a US citizen.

Before Alsace was lost to France in the 1870–71 war, Loeffler, whose father was an agricultural chemist and an author who wrote under the name of 'Tornow', was taken to Smela, near Kiev, and it was there that he was first given violin lessons. The family later moved to Debreczin in Hungary and about 1873 to Switzerland. There he decided to become a violinist and went to Berlin to study with Rappoldi, Kiel, Bargiel, and lastly Joachim. Later he had a period of study with Massart and Guiraud in Paris, joined the Pasdeloup Orchestra and that of a wealthy amateur, where he remained until his emigration to the USA in 1881.

Works include: the psalm 'By the waters of Babylon' for women's voices and instruments, *Beat! Beat! Beat! Drums!* (from Whitman's 'Drum Taps', 1917) for male voices and orchestra, *Evocation* for women's voices and orchestra; chamber music.

Loewe, (Johann) Carl (Gottfried) (1796–1869) German composer. He is remembered chiefly for his songs and settings of narrative poems such as 'Archibald Douglas' and 'Tom the Rhymer'.

He was a choirboy at Cöthen, and in 1809 went to the grammar school at Halle. Encouraged by Jérôme Bonaparte, then king of Westphalia, he devoted himself to composition and later, at Halle University, the study of theology. Jérôme's flight in 1813 deprived him of his income, but he managed to make a living and in 1820 became professor and cantor at Stettin, and was appointed music director and organist in 1821. He visited Vienna in 1844, London in 1847, Sweden and Norway in 1851, and France in 1857. In 1864 he suffered from a six weeks' coma and was asked to resign in 1866, when he went to live at Kiel. He died there after a similar attack.

Works include: the operas *Die Alpenhütte* (1816), *Rudolf der Deutsche* (1825), *Malekadhel* (after Scott's *The Talisman*, 1832), *Neckerein* (1833), *Die drei Wünsche* (1834), *Emmy* (after Scott's *Kenilworth*, 1842); oratorios *Die Zerstörung Jerusalems* (1829), *Palestrina* (1841), *Hiob, Die Auferweckung des Lazarus* (1863), and 12 others; symphonies; concertos; piano solos and duets; numerous songs and ballads, including Goethe's 'Erlkönig', Fontane's German versions of 'Archibald Douglas', 'Tom the Rhymer'.

Loewe, Frederick (1904–1988) German-born US composer. He worked on Broadway from the 1930s and began a collaboration with the lyricist Alan Jay Lerner in 1942. Their joint successes include *Brigadoon* 1947, *Paint Your Wagon* 1951, *My Fair Lady* 1956, *Gigi* 1958, and *Camelot* 1960.

Born in Berlin, the son of an operatic tenor, he studied under Ferruccio Busoni, and in 1924 went with his father to the USA.

Loewenstern, Matthaeus (Apelles) von (1594–1648) German poet and composer. He probably studied at the University of Frankfurt-and-the-Oder. Having been schoolmaster and cantor at Leobschütz, he entered the service of the Duke of Oels-Bernstadt.

Works include: choruses for Opitz's tragedy *Judith*; Latin and German motets; sacred concertos; book of 30 sacred songs to words of his own entitled *Frühlings-Mayen*.

Logroscino, Nicola (1698–after 1765) Italian composer. He was chiefly a composer of *opera buffa*, though his first known opera was not written until 1738.

He was a pupil at the Conservatorio di Santa Maria de Loreto 1714–27, and held an organ post in Conza 1728–31. From 1747 he taught counterpoint at the Conservatory in Palermo.

Works include: the operas *Inganno per inganno* (1738), *L'Inganno felice* (1739), *Ciommetella correvata* (1744), *Il Governadore* (1747), *Giunio Bruto* (1748), *Leandro, Li zíte, Don Paduano, La Griselda* (1752), *Le finte magie* (1756), and many others; oratorio *La spedizione di Giosué* (1763); two settings of the *Stabat Mater*; church music.

Lohengrin opera by Wagner (libretto by composer), produced Weimar, Court Theatre, by Liszt, 28 August 1850. Elsa marries knight Lohengrin but loses him after asking his name and dies of grief when he leaves her.

Lohet, Simon (c. 1550–1611) German organist and composer. He was appointed organist to the court of Württemberg at Stuttgart in 1571.

Works include: pieces in fugal style, canzoni, and hymn-tune fantasies for organ.

Lombardi alla prima crociata, I/The Lombards at the First Crusade opera by Verdi (libretto by T Solera, founded on a romance by T Grossi, produced Milan, La Scala, 11 February 1843. Taken prisoner by the Muslims, Griselda falls in love with her captor Oronte. They resolve to run away together, but he dies in battle, and she returns to the victorious Christians.

London College of Music school founded in 1887, mainly for part-time students. It now caters for around 300 full-time students. Michael Berkeley was composer-in-residence 1987–88. Director was John McCabe.

London Pianoforte School name given to a group of composer-pianists working in London at the turn of the 19th century. They pioneered the Romantic style of keyboard playing, based on a ◊legato touch, and began to develop a more complex harmonic language that ultimately replaced the Classical style. Composers of the London Pianoforte School include Muzio Clementi, Jan Dussek, John Field, and John Cramer.

London Symphony ◊Haydn's symphony no. 104, in D major (no. 12 of the 'Salomon' symphony), written for performance in London in 1795.

London Symphony, A the second symphony by Vaughan Williams, composed 1912, first performed London, 27 March 1914; revised version London, Queen's Hall, 4 May 1920.

long the name of a note value in old mensural notation, half the value of the large and equal to either two or three breves.

Long Christmas Dinner, The/Der Lange Weihnachtsmal opera in one act by Hindemith (libretto by Thornton Wilder), produced Mannheim, 17 December 1961; first produced in English, Juilliard School, New York, 1963. Ninety Christmas dinners over the four generations of a family.

Longueval, Antoine de (fl. 1507–22) French composer. He was a singer in the royal chapel, and wrote three motets, a chanson, and a Passion, formerly attributed to Obrecht, based on all four gospels. Very little is known about his life.

Loqueville, Richard de (died 1418) French composer. He was in the service of Duke

Robert of Bavaria in 1410 and *maître de chant* at Cambrai Cathedral from 1413 until his death. He wrote church music and chansons in the Burgundian style of his day. He probably taught Dufay.

Loreley opera by Bruch (libretto by E Geibel, originally written for Mendelssohn), produced Mannheim, 14 June 1863. Leonore falls in love with Count Otto, unaware of his imminent marriage to Countess Bertha. When she discovers the deception she sells her soul in exchange for beauty. Otto then rejects Bertha in favour of Leonore, but Bertha dies of grief, Otto then commits suicide, and evil spirits claim Leonore.

Unfinished opera by Mendelssohn (libretto by E Geibel). Only the first-act finale, an *Ave Maria* and a chorus of vintners exist.

See also ◊*Lurline*.

Lorenz, Alfred (Ottokar) (1868–1939) Austrian conductor and writer on music. After various other appointments he became conductor at Coburg-Gotha in 1898; but he retired, took a degree in 1922, became lecturer at Munich University in 1923, and professor in 1926. He edited Richard Wagner's literary works and Carl Maria von Weber's early operas, and wrote several books on the form of Wagner's music dramas, on the history of western music and on Alessandro Scarlatti's early operas.

Lorenzani, Paolo (1640–1713) Italian composer. He spent much of his life in France, where, as director of music to Queen Marie-Thérèse, he was influential in popularizing Italian music. After her death in 1683, his influence declined, and he returned to Italy in 1694.

He was a pupil of Benevoli in Rome. In 1675 he went to Sicily and became maestro di cappella at the cathedral of Messina. In 1678 the French viceroy, Marshal de Vivonne, induced him to go to Paris, where he was one of the superintendents of the queen's music 1679–83. After her death he became maître de chapelle at the Theatine monastery, where he wrote motets. His opera *Orontée* was produced at Chantilly in 1688 by order of the Prince de Condé. In 1694 he returned to Rome as maestro di cappella of the Papal chapel.

Works include: the operas *Nicandro e Fileno* (1681) and *Orontée* (1688); motets and Magnificats; cantatas; Italian and French airs.

Lortzing, (Gustav) Albert (1801–1851) German composer, singer, conductor, and librettist. Although not well known outside Germany, such operas as *Undine* and *Der*

Wildschütz occupy in his homeland a similar position enjoyed by the works of Gilbert and Sullivan in Britain.

He had some lessons with Rungenhagen in Berlin as a child, but since his parents were travelling actors, he had to obtain his general and musical education as best he could. He learnt the piano, violin, and cello and studied such theoretical works as he could find. He married in 1823 and found it difficult to make a living in a travelling opera company. His first stage work, *Ali Pascha von Janina*, was produced at Münster in 1828 and repeated at Cologne, Detmold, and Osnabrück. In 1833–34 he was able to lead a more settled life, being engaged as a tenor and actor at the Leipzig municipal theatre. The first two comic operas he wrote there were very successful, and so was his adaptation from Kotzebue, *Der Wildschütz*, in 1842, when he gave up acting. Two short terms as a conductor at Leipzig and Vienna were unsuccessful. He had a large family by this time and fell upon more and more difficult times. The conductorship at a suburban theatre in Berlin in 1850 merely humiliated him without doing much to relieve the situation.

Works include: OPERA *Die beiden Schützen* (1837), *Zar und Zimmermann* (1837), *Hans Sachs* (1840), *Casanova*, *Der Wildschütz* (after Kotzebue, 1842), *Undine* (after de La Motte Fouqué, 1845, *Der Waffenschmied* (1846), *Zum Grossadmiral*, *Rolandsknappen* (1849), *Regina*, and others; operettas *Ali Pascha von Janina* (1824), *Die Opernprobe oder Die vornehmen Dilettanten* (1851).

OTHER oratorio *Die Himmelfahrt Christi* (1828); incidental music for plays including Goethe's *Faust*, Grabbe's *Don Juan und Faust* (1829), Scribe's *Yelva*; plays with music *Der Pole und sein Kind* (1832), *Der Weihnachtsabend* (1832), *Szenen aus Mozarts Leben* (with music adapted from Mozart, 1832); part songs, songs.

Lotario opera by Handel (librettist unknown, based on Antonio Salvi's *Adelaide*, not, as Burney says, on Matteo Noris's *Berengario*), produced London, King's Theatre, Haymarket, 2 December 1729. Strife in 10th-century Italy as Queen Adelaide's husband is killed by Berengario, who wants her to marry his son Idelberto. Held prisoner, she appeals to King Lotario of Germany, who defeats Berengario and rescues Adelaide.

Lothar, Mark (1902–1985) German composer. He studied at the Berlin Musikhochschule with Schreker (composition), Juon (harmony), and Krasselt (conducting).

Later he had lessons with Wolf-Ferrari and others. After appointments as director of music at two Berlin theatres, he was in charge of the music at the Bavarian Staatstheater in Munich 1945–55.

Works include: the operas *Tyll* (1928), *Lord Spleen* (after Ben Jonson's *Epicoene*, 1930), *Münchhausen* (1933) and *Schneider Wibbol* (Berlin, 1938), *Rappelkopf* (Munich, 1958), *Der Widerspenstige Heilige* (Munich, 1968); incidental music for Eichendorff's *Die Freier* and other plays; *Narrenmesse* for male chorus; *Orchesterstücke* and suite for orchestra; serenade for chamber orchestra; music for film and radio; piano trio; piano pieces; songs.

Lottchen am Hofe/Lottie at Court opera by J A Hiller (libretto by C F Weisse after Goldoni and C S Favart), produced Leipzig, 24 April 1767.

Lotti, Antonio (c. 1667–1740) Italian composer. His operas and church music spanned the late Baroque and early Classical styles.

He was a pupil of his father and of Legrenzi in Venice. Appointed singer at St Mark's 1687, he rose to become second organist in 1692, first organist in 1704, and finally maestro di cappella in 1736. He produced his first opera, *Il trionfo dell' innocenza* in Venice in 1692 (*Giustino* 1683, commonly ascribed to him, is by Legrenzi). He visited Dresden 1717–19 as an opera composer, but after his return to Italy devoted himself entirely to church music.

Works include: OPERA *Porsenna* (1713), *Irene Augusta* (1713), *Polidoro* (1714), *Alessandro Severo*, *Constantino* (for Vienna, 1716, with Fux and Caldara), *Giove in Argo* (1717), *Ascanio*, *Teofane* (1719), and others.

OTHER oratorios *Il voto crudele* (1712), *L'umilità coronata in Esther* (1714), *Gioa*, *Giuditta*; Masses, Requiems, Misereres, motets, and other church music.

Louise opera by G Charpentier (libretto by composer, produced Paris, Opéra-Comique, 2 February 1900. Louise joins lover Julien against her parents' wishes.

loure (French) originally a special type of ◊bagpipe, found especially in Normandy, France; later the name of a dance in fairly slow 6–4 time.

Lourié, Arthur (Vincent) (1892–1966) Russian-born US composer of French descent. He studied for a short time at the St Petersburg Conservatory, but was self-taught later. He was appointed director of the music section of the Ministry of Public Instruction in 1918,

but left in 1921. He settled first in France, then from 1941 in the USA.

Works include: the operas *A Feast in Time of Plague* (after Pushkin, 1935), and *The Blackamoor of Peter the Great* (1961); ballet *Le Masque de neige* and others; two symphonies; *Sonate liturgique* for orchestra, piano and chorus; *Ave Maria*, *Salve Regina* and other church music; *Regina coeli* for contralto, oboe, and trumpet (1915), *Improperium* for baritone, four violins and double bass (1923); *Canzona di Dante* for chorus and strings; Japanese Suite for voice and orchestra; three string quartets; sonata for violin and double bass; three piano sonatinas; song cycles *Elysium* (Pushkin, 1918) and *Alphabet* (A Tolstoy).

Love for Three Oranges, The/Liubov k trem Apelsinam opera by Prokofiev (libretto by composer, based on Gozzi's comedy *Fiaba dell' amore delle tre melarancie*), produced in French translation, Chicago, Auditorium, 30 December 1921. The March from it has become popular. In an imaginary realm the Prince's melancholy is cured by the jester Truffaldino. Enraged, Fata Morgana (who was plotting against the prince) casts a spell by which the Prince becomes obsessed by three oranges. But the oranges contain princesses, one of whom the Prince marries.

Love in a Village opera by Arne (libretto by I Bickerstaffe), produced London, Covent Garden, 8 December 1762. Partly a ballad opera and pasticcio, Arne having introduced popular songs and airs by Handel, Galuppi, Geminiani and others.

Love of the Three Kings (Montemezzi). See ◊*Amore dei tre re, L'*.

Löwe, Ferdinand (1865–1925) Austrian conductor. He studied at the Vienna Conservatory and taught there, 1884–97. From 1896 to 1898 he conducted the Wiener Singakademie, and from 1900 to 1904 the Musik-Gesellschaft concerts. He held further posts in Munich, Budapest, and Berlin, and was director of the Vienna Academy of Music from 1919 to 1922. He championed the symphonies of Bruckner, in spurious editions.

Lowinsky, Edward (E)lias (1908–1985) German-born US musicologist. He studied in Stuttgart and Heidelberg. He became a US citizen in 1947. He taught at Queens College, New York (1947–56), Berkeley (1956–61), and at the University of Chicago. He was editor of the series *Monuments of Renaissance Music* (1964–77). Josquin, Lassus, Willaert, and Gombert featured prominently in his research.

Lualdi, Adriano (1885–1971) Italian composer and music critic. He was critic to the *Secolo* at Milan and in 1936 to the *Giornale d'Italia* in Rome. He later became director of the Naples Conservatory. He was a political conservative and supporter of Mussolini. He studied with Wolf-Ferrari at Venice.

Works include: the operas *Le Nozze di Haura* (1908; staged 1943), *La figlia del rè* (1922), *Le furie del Arlecchino* (1915), *Il diavolo nel campanile* (after Poe, 1925), *La Granceola* (1932); ballet *Lumawig e la Saetia*; choral pieces; *La leggenda del vecchio marinaio*, *Suite adriatica*, colonial rhapsody *Africa*, three folk tunes *Samnium* for orchestra; *Sire Halewyn* for soprano and orchestra; *La rosa di Saron* for tenor and orchestra; string quartet in E major; violin and piano sonata; passacaglia for organ; songs and other pieces.

Lucia di Lammermoor opera by Donizetti (libretto by S Cammarano, based on Scott's *Bride of Lammermoor*), produced Naples, Teatro San Carlo, 26 September 1835. Lucia loves the family enemy Edgardo, but her brother Enrico forces her to marry Arturo. When Edgardo finds out, Lucia goes mad and kills Arturo. Edgardo commits suicide from grief.

Lucier, Alvin (1931–) US composer. His *Music for Solo Performer* (1965) uses amplified brain signals in harmony with percussion instruments. In 1966 he founded the Sonic Arts Union (with Gordon Mumma and Robert Ashley), for the performance of electronic music.

He studied at Yale University 1950–54, and at Brandeis 1958–60, becoming choral director there 1962–70. He was professor at Wesleyan University 1970–84.

Works include: *Vespers* (1969); *The Queen of the South* with closed circuit TV system (1972); *Bird and Person Dying* (1975); *Shape of Sounds from the Board* for piano (1979); sound installation (1983); *Serenade* for 13 winds and pure wave oscillator (1985); *Music for Men, Women and Reflecting Walls* (1986); *Salmon River Valley Songs* (1986); *Fidelio-trio* (1988); *Navigations* for string quartet (1991).

Lucio Papiro opera by Caldara (libretto by A Zeno), produced Vienna, 4 November 1719. Opera by Hasse (libretto ditto), produced Dresden, at court, 18 January 1742.

Lucio Silla opera by J C Bach (libretto by G de Gamerra, with alterations by Metastasio), produced Mannheim, at court, 4 November 1774. Opera by Mozart (libretto ditto), produced Milan, Teatro Regio Ducal, 26 December 1772. Banished Cecilio returns to Rome to try to rescue fiancée Giunia from the dictator Sulla. Cecilio, after failing in an assassination attempt, is condemned to die by Sulla, but the dictator shows compassion when Giunia declares her love.

Lucio Vero opera by Pollarolo (libretto by A Zeno), produced Venice, Teatro San Giovanni Crisostomo, 1700. Opera by Sacchini (libretto ditto), produced Naples, Teatro San Carlo, 4 November 1764.

Lucrezia Borgia opera by Donizetti (libretto by F Romani, based on Victor Hugo's tragedy), produced Milan, La Scala, 26 December 1833. Gennaro, unknowingly the son of Lucrezia Borgia, defaces her family crest with his friends. To avenge her honour, Lucrezia intends to poison his friends, but not Gennaro himself, who she knows is her son. The plot misfires and he dies as well.

Ludford, Nicholas (c. 1485–c. 1557) English composer. He wrote seven festal Masses, motets, a Magnificat, and a unique set of seven Masses for the daily Mass of Our Lady. He was long active at the Royal Chapel of St Stephen, Westminster.

Ludovic opera by Hérold, left unfinished and completed by Halévy (libretto by J H V de Saint-Georges), produced Paris, Opéra-Comique, 16 May 1833. Chopin wrote piano variations on an air from it, op. 12.

Ludwig, Friedrich (1872–1930) German musicologist. His comprehensive studies of 13th- and 14th-century music remain indispensable.

He studied at Marburg and Strasbourg Universities. He became a lecturer at Strasbourg in 1905 and professor at Göttingen in 1911, where he was later appointed rector.

Ludwig II (1845–1886) King of Bavaria from 1864, when he succeeded his father Maximilian II. He supported Austria during the Austro-Prussian War 1866, but brought Bavaria into the Franco-Prussian War as Prussia's ally and in 1871 offered the German crown to the king of Prussia. He was the composer Richard Wagner's patron and built the Bayreuth theatre for him. Declared insane 1886, he drowned himself soon after.

Luening, Otto (1900–1996) US composer. He studied at Munich and in Zurich with Philipp Jarnach, and privately with Ferruccio Busoni. He was appointed to Columbia University in 1949, and in 1951 began a series of pioneering compositions for instruments and tape, some in partnership with Vladimir Ussachevsky (1911–) (*Incantation* 1952, *A Poem in Cycles and Bells* 1954). In 1959 he became codirector, with Milton Babbitt and Ussachevsky, of the Columbia-Princeton Electronic Music Center. He taught at the Juilliard School 1971–73.

Works include: the opera *Evangeline* (1928–33, produced New York 1948); flute concertino (1923), *Kentucky Concerto* (1951), *Wisconsin Symphony* (1975); *Potawatomi Legends* for chamber orchestra (1980), *Symphonic Fantasias* I–IX (1924–88); three string quartets (1919–28); many chamber suites and sonatas for violin, flute, and cello; *Green Mountain Evening* for six instruments (1988); electronic music, including *Rhapsodic Variations*, with Ussachevsky (1954).

Luigini, Alexandre (Clément Léon Joseph) (1850–1906) French violinist, conductor, and composer. He studied at the Paris Conservatory, became leader at the Grand Théâtre of Lyon in 1869, and its conductor in 1877. In 1897 he became conductor of the Opéra-Comique in Paris.

Works include: the operas *Faublas* (after Louvet de Couvray, produced 1881) and *Les Caprices de Margot* (produced 1877); ballets; cantata *Gloria victis*; *Ballet égyptien* (1875), *Ballet russe*, *Carnaval turc*, and other light works for orchestra.

Luisa Miller opera by Verdi (libretto by S Cammarano, based on Schiller's drama *Kabale und Liebe*), produced Naples, Teatro San Carlo, 8 December 1849. Luisa loves Rodolfo, but is forced to declare love for Wurm in exchange for the release of her father, Miller, who has been imprisoned by Count Walther. Feeling betrayed, Rodolfo poisons Luisa and himself before learning the truth.

Lully, Jean-Baptiste (1632–1687), adopted name of Giovanni Battista Lulli French composer of Italian origin. He was court composer to Louis XIV. He composed music for the ballet, for Molière's plays, and established French opera with such works as *Alceste* 1674 and *Armide et Rénaud* 1686. He was also a ballet dancer.

The son of a miller, he had little education and learnt to play the guitar and violin without much guidance. At first he joined a group of strolling players, but in 1646 was discovered by the Chevalier de Guise and taken to France, where he entered the household of Mlle de Montpensier, the king's cousin, as a scullion; but when she found that he was musical she made him a personal servant and leader of her string band. In 1652 he passed into the service of Louis XIV, who was then 14. Lully became a ballet dancer, a violinist in the king's '24 violins', and a composer. In 1658 he began to compose

ballets of his own, having contributed to some since 1653 in which the king himself danced. In 1661 he became a French citizen and Composer to the King's Chamber Music and in 1662 Music Master to the Royal Family; he continued to enjoy royal protection, in spite of his open homosexual activity, which at that time was punishable by death.

His first opera, *Cadmus et Hermione*, appeared in 1673, when he obtained a royal patent granting him the monopoly of operatic production and annulling a previous patent given to Pierre Perrin and Robert Cambert. The Académie Royale de Musique, as the Opéra was first called, was opened in 1672 with a pasticcio from earlier works of his, *Les festes de l'Amour et de Bacchus*. Most of his operas were written in collaboration with Philippe Quinault, and most of the ballets with Molière. His last complete opera was *Acis et Galatée* 1686; by this time he had transformed French operatic style, developing the formal French overture and introducing a declaimed accompanied recitative, which replaced the former recitative with harpsichord accompaniment. In 1687 he injured his foot with the staff with which he conducted a Te Deum to celebrate the king's recovery, and died of blood poisoning. His opera *Achille et Polyxène*, left unfinished, was completed by Colasse.

Works include: OPERA *Alceste* (1674), *Thésée* (1675), *Atys*, *Isis* (1677), *Psyché* (1678), *Persée*, *Amadis de Gaule* (1684), *Armide et Renaud* (1686).

COMEDY-BALLETS all with Molière, including *Le Sicilien*, *Les Amants magnifiques* (1670), *Le Bourgeois Gentilhomme* (1670).

BALLETS (some possibly by Boësset and others) *Ballet de Xerxès* (for Cavalli's opera, 1660), *Ballet des saisons*, *Ballet des Muses* (1666), *Ballet de Flore* (1669), *Le Triomphe de l'Amour* (1681), *Le Temple de la paix* (1685). Church music, Miserere, *Plaude laetare*, Te Deum, *De profundis*, motets for double chorus.

Lulu unfinished opera by Berg (libretto by composer), based on Frank Wedekind's plays *Erdgeist* and *Die Büchse der Pandora*), Acts 1 and 2 and a fragment of 3 produced Zurich, 2 June 1937. Third act realized by Friedrich Cerha; first complete performance Paris, 24 February 1979, conductor Boulez. Femme fatale leaves a trail of corpses but is killed by Jack the Ripper.

Lumsdaine, David (1931–) Australian-born British composer. Educated in Sydney, he moved to London in 1952 and studied with Seiber at the Royal Academy of Music.

In 1970 he was appointed lecturer at Durham University, and founded an electronic studio there.

Works include: *Episodes* (1969) and *Shoalhaven* (1982) for orchestra, *Mandala II* and *III* for chamber orchestra; *Mandala V* (1988) for orchestra; *Easter Fresco* for soprano and ensemble (1966); *Round Dance* for sitar, tabla, flute, cello, and piano (1989); *Mandala IV* for string quartet (1983).

lunga pausa (Italian 'long pause') in musical notation, indicating a long ◊rest.

Lupo, Thomas English composer and player of stringed instruments. His father Joseph (died 1616), his uncle Ambrose (died 1591), and his son Theophilus (fl. 1628–42) are also known as composers, but Thomas is distinguished by his pavanes and fantasies for viol consort, particularly in five and six voices.

Lurline opera by V Wallace (libretto by E Fitzball), produced London, Covent Garden, 23 February 1860. The subject is that of the German legend of the Loreley.

lusingando, or lusinghiero (Italian 'wheedling, coaxing') a musical direction to perform a piece or passage in a charming, alluring manner.

Lusitano, Vicente Portuguese music theorist and composer. He was known as Vicente de Olivença in Portugal, but was called Lusitano ('the Portuguese') in Rome, where he settled about 1550. In 1551 he had a dispute with Nicola Vicentino, which was settled in his favour, with Ghiselin Danckerts and Bartolomeo Escobedo as judges. He published a treatise on *cantus firmus* in 1553.

Works include: motets *Epigrammata*, and other pieces.

Lustigen Weiber von Windsor, Die/The Merry Wives of Windsor comic opera by Nicolai (libretto by S H Mosenthal, after Shakespeare), produced Berlin, Opera, 9 March 1849. German version of Falstaff's amorous adventures.

Lustige Witwe, Die/The Merry Widow operetta by Lehár (libretto by V Léon and L Stein), produced Vienna, Theater an der Wien, 30 December 1905. Baron Zeta wants Count Danilo to marry the widow Hanna Glawari for her money, but the two fall geuinely in love, although they hide their feelings at first. All ends well.

lute member of a family of plucked stringed musical instruments of the 14th–18th centuries, including the mandore, theorbo, and chitarrone. Lutes are pear-shaped with up to seven courses of strings (single or double), plucked with the fingers. Music for lutes is written in special notation called ◊tablature and chords are played simultaneously, not arpeggiated as for guitar. Modern lutenists include Julian Bream and Anthony Rooley (1944–   ).

Lutes are descendants of earlier Eastern instruments. In Western use, members of the lute family were used both as solo instruments and for vocal accompaniment, and were often played in addition to, or instead of, keyboard instruments in larger ensembles and in opera.

The notation of lute music, tablature, uses a stave made up of 6 lines rather than the normal 5 and letters rather than notes. Of the 13 or 14 strings on a lute, 6 can be held down against the keyboard like a guitar, whilst the remainder are bass notes which are played by the thumb. The 6 lines on the stave represent the 6 strings. The letters of the alphabet indicate which fret the string must be held down against. The bass notes are shown by letters and numbers, and curved lines across the top of the stave are used to represent the rhythm.

The open strings typical of the lute during the 16th century.

lute-harpsichord musical instrument made for Bach in 1740, called *Lautenclavicymbel*, with gut strings and a keyboard.

luthier originally a lute-maker, later, by transference, a maker of string instruments in general.

Lutosławski, Witold (1913–1994) Polish composer and conductor. His output includes three symphonies, *Paroles tissées/Teased Words* 1965 for tenor and chamber orchestra, dedicated to the singer Peter Pears, and *Chain I* for orchestra 1981. For 30 years he conducted most of the world's leading orchestras in his own compositions, and was greatly influential both within and beyond his native land.

His early major compositions, such as *Variations on a Theme of Paganini* 1941 for two pianos and *First Symphony* 1947, drew some criticism from the communist government. After 1956, under a more liberal regime, he adopted avant-garde techniques, including improvisatory and ◊aleatoric (chance) forms, in *Venetian Games* 1961.

Lutosławski was born in Warsaw while it was still part of the Russian Empire. He spent part of his early childhood in Moscow – the family moved there in 1915 to escape from the German Army – where his father was arrested by the Bolsheviks and summarily executed in 1918. He returned to Warsaw and began piano and violin lessons. From the age of 15 he also studied composition with Witold Maliszewski, who was teaching at the Warsaw Conservatory. At the same time he studied mathematics at Warsaw University. Military service in 1937 and World War II interrupted his career.

His *First Symphony* occupied him on and off 1941–47, but it was condemned at its first performance 1949. He had made no concessions either to the Nazis or to the Stalinist regime. Only his 'functional' music – film and theatre music or pieces based on folk melodies – received a hearing.

In his 'serious' music he worked to produce a new musical language based on 12-note harmony, first revealed in his *Musique funèbre* 1958. He was taken with the idea of aleatoric operations 1960 after hearing music by the US composer John Cage. *Venetian Games* was the first piece in which he used this technique, after which came the *String Quartet 1964, Livre pour orchèstre* 1968, the *Cello Concerto* 1970, and many other compositions.

Lutosławski was sensitive to poetry, and also composed vocal works, including *Les Espaces du sommeil/Spaces of Sleep* 1975 and *Chantefables et chantefleurs* 1990, the latter to verses by the French surrealist poet Robert Denos.

Works include: ORCHESTRAL four symphonies (1941–92), *Concerto for Orchestra* (1954), *Venetian Games* for small orchestra (1961); cello concerto (1970), *Mi Parti* for orchestra (1976), Concerto for oboe, harp, and chamber orchestra (1982), *Chain I* for chamber orchestra (1983), *Chain II* for violin and orchestra (1984), *Chain III* (1986), piano concerto (1988).

VOCAL *Paroles tissées* for voice and orchestra (1965), *Les espaces du sommeil* for baritone and orchestra (1975), *Chantefleurs et Chantefables* for soprano and orchestra (1990).

CHAMBER string quartet (1964); *Grave* for cello and piano (1981), *Variations* on a theme of Paganini for two pianos.

Lutyens, (Agnes) Elizabeth (1906–1983) English composer. Her works, using the twelve-tone system, are expressive and tightly organized, and include chamber music, stage, and orchestral works. Her choral and vocal works include a setting of the Austrian philosopher Ludwig Wittgenstein's *Tractatus* and a cantata *The Tears of Night*. She

also composed much film and incidental music.

The youngest daughter of architect Sir Edwin Lutyens, she married BBC director of music Edward Clark. Her autobiography *A Goldfish Bowl* was published in 1973.

She studied viola and composition at the Royal College of Music in London, the latter with Harold Darke, and later with Caussade at the Ecole normale de musique in Paris. In a lecture at Dartington in the 1950s she coined the term 'Cowpat Music' to describe the work of such composers as Vaughan Williams, Delius, and Holst, who turned to pictorial pastoralism in their music.

Works include: OPERA *Infidelio* (1956, produced 1973) and *Time Off? Not a Ghost of a Chance* (produced 1972); ballet *The Birthday of the Infanta* (after Oscar Wilde, 1932); chamber cantata *Winter the Huntsman* (Osbert Sitwell), *Bienfaits de la lune* (Baudelaire) and other choral works; three symphonic preludes, *Petite Suite, Divertissement*, and other orchestral works

OTHER viola concerto, *Lyric Piece* for violin and orchestra; six chamber concertos (1939–48); 12 string quartets (1938–82), string trio, *Suite gauloise* for wind octet; *Aptote* for solo violin, sonata for solo viola; piano music, suite for organ; *O saisons, o châteaux* (Rimbaud, 1946), and other works for voice and chamber ensemble, including *And Suddenly it's Evening* for tenor and 11 instruments (1967), *Essence of our Happiness* for tenor and ensemble (1968), *Vision of Youth* (1970), *Dirge for the Proud World* (1971), *The Tears of Night* (1971), *Elegy for the Flowers* (1978), two *Cantatas* (1979), *Echoes* (1979), *Fleur du Silence* for tenor and ensemble (1980), *Mine Eyes, My Bread, My Spede* for tenor and string quartet (1980); songs.

Luyton, Karel (c. 1556–1620) Flemish organist and composer. He was in the service of the Emperor Maximilian II at Prague in 1576, and when Maximilian died, was appointed to the Emperor Rudolf II in the same capacity. He succeeded Philippe de Monte as court composer from 1603.

Works include: Masses, motets, Lamentations, *Sacrae cantiones*; Italian madrigals; *Fuga suavissima* and *Ricercare* for organ.

Luzzaschi, Luzzasco (c. 1545–1607) Italian organist and composer. He wrote some sacred works, but his madrigals are his best-known compositions. His skilfully composed five-part madrigals were his most popular works; the later ones show an increased use of homophony.

Luzzaschi was a pupil of Cipriano de Rore at Ferrara and in 1561 became a singer at the Este court there. In 1564 he became court organist, and was also active as a composer and teacher; Frescobaldi was one of his organ pupils. By 1570 he was directing the duke's chamber music, and by 1576 was his organist and maestro di cappella. He was also organist at Ferrara Cathedral and the Accademia della Morte. Here he composed madrigals for the celebrated 'singing ladies' of Ferrara, a group of virtuoso singers who performed for private audiences. His *Madrigali per cantare, et sonare a 1–3 soprani* 1601 contains some of these pieces with their fully notated keyboard accompaniments, which were long kept secret. From 1597 Luzzaschi served Cardinal Pietro Aldobrandini, who controlled Ferrara when the city passed to the papacy.

Works include: motets, *Sacrae cantiones*; madrigals; organ music, and other pieces. His *Madrigali per cantare et sonare* (1601) are for three voices and have keyboard accompaniments.

Lvov, Aleksey Feodorovich (1798–1870) Russian composer. He studied with his father, Feodor Lvov, an authority on church music and folk song, who succeeded Bortniansky as director of the Imperial Chapel in 1825. His son, who rose to high rank in the army and became adjutant to Nicholas I, succeeded him there 1837–61. He was a good violinist and founded a string quartet at St Petersburg. He became deaf and retired in 1867.

Works include: the operas *Bianca e Gualtiero* (1844), *Undine* (after Fouqué, 1847) and *The Bailiff* (1854); much church music; violin concerto; fantasy *The Duel* for violin and cello; Russian Imperial hymn 'God save the Tsar' (1833), quoted by Tchaikovsky in his *1812* overture.

Lyadov, Anatol see Anatol ◊Liadov.

Lydian mode one of the church ◊modes, a scale F–E centred around and beginning on F, which uses only notes of the C major scale. It is also a scale of ancient Greece, the equivalent of the modern major scale.

lyra one of two different musical instruments: either an alternative spelling of ◊lira, or a percussion instrument with tuned steel bars or plates which are played with hammers, similar to the Stahlspiel, used in English military bands and made for them in the shape of a lyre.

lyra viol, also 'lero viol', 'leero viol', or 'viol lyra way' musical instrument, a small bass ◊viol, tuned in various ways and played from a tablature (the form of notation used for lute music). It was in use in England around 1650–1700.

lyre stringed musical instrument of great antiquity. It consists of a hollow soundbox with two curved arms extended upwards to a crosspiece to which four to ten strings are attached. It is played with a plectrum or the fingers. It originated in Asia, and was widespread in ancient Greece and Egypt.

Tuned to a given ◊mode, it provided a pitch guide for vocal melody and embellishment.

lyre-guitar, or Apollo lyre six-stringed musical instrument produced in France near the end of the 18th century, built to suggest the shape of the ancient Greek lyre, but with a fretted fingerboard.

lyrical of melodic, songful quality.

Lyric Suite work for string quartet in six movements by Berg; composed 1925–26, first performed Vienna 8 January 1927. Movements 2, 3, and 4 were arranged for string orchestra and performed Berlin, 31 January 1929, conductor Horenstein. Berg quotes from *Tristan* and Zemlinksy's *Lyric Symphony* and bases the work's note-row on the name of Hanna Robettin-Fuchs, with whom he had an affair. An alternative vocal finale, with text a translation by Stefan George of Baudelaire, was performed New York, 1 November 1979.

Lyrische Symphonie/Lyric Symphony work by Zemlinsky in seven movements for soprano, baritone, and orchestra (text by Tagore in a German translation by the composer); composed 1922–23, first performed Prague, 4 June 1924, conductor Zemlinsky (two days later Zemlinsky conducted the first performance of Schoenberg's *Erwartung*). The format of the Lyric Symphony is modelled on *Das Lied von der Erde*, although the content is Zemlinsky's own.

lyzarden, or lyzardyne; also lizard or lysard in music, an old English name for the bass cornett or corno torto, the predecessor of the ◊serpent, which came into use in the 17th century.

M

Macbeth incidental music by Locke for Davenant's version of Shakespeare's play, produced London, Dorset Gardens Theatre, summer 1674. There were later productions with music by D Purcell, Eccles, Leveridge.

Opera by Bloch (libretto by E Fleg, after Shakespeare), produced Paris, Opéra-Comique, 30 November 1910.

Opera by Collingwood (libretto by composer, chosen from Shakespeare), produced London, Sadler's Wells, 12 April 1934.

Opera by Verdi (libretto by F M Piave and A Maffei, after Shakespeare), produced Florence, Teatro della Pergola, 14 March 1847; revised version (French libretto by C Nuitter and A Beaumont) produced Paris, Théâtre Lyrique, 21 April 1865. Lady Macbeth takes centre stage in Italian version.

Overture by Spohr, op. 75.

Symphonic poem by Richard Strauss, op. 23, composed 1886–87, revised 1890, first performed Weimar, 13 September 1890.

McBride, Robert (1911–) US composer. He studied and took the Bachelor of Music at Arizona University; he obtained the Guggenheim Fellowship in 1937. Later he joined the faculty of Bennington College.

Works include: ballet *Show Piece; Mexican Rhapsody* (1934) and *Prelude to a Tragedy* for orchestra; fugato for 25 instruments, *Workout* for 15 instruments (1936); prelude and fugue for string quartet; sonata *Depression* for violin and piano, *Workout* for oboe and piano, *Swing Music* for clarinet and piano (1938); dance suite for piano, *Lament for the Parking Problem* for trumpet, horn and trombone (1968).

McCabe, John (1939–) English composer and pianist. As a pianist he often performed the sonatas of Haydn. His own compositions include much orchestral and chamber music. He was director of the London College of Music 1983–90.

He studied at the Royal Manchester College of Music and in Munich.

Works include: the operas *The Play of Mother Courage* (1974) and *The Lion, the Witch and the Wardrobe* (1969); ballets *Mary, Queen of Scots* (1976) and *Don Juan* (1973); three symphonies (1965, 1971, 1978), *Variations on a theme of Hartmann* (1964), *The Chagall Windows* (1974), *The Shadow of Light* (1979); concerto for orchestra (1982), three piano concertos (1966, 1970, 1976), two violin concertos (1959, 1980); *Notturni ed Alba* for soprano and orchestra (1970), *Stabat Mater* for soprano, chorus, and orchestra (1976); three string quartets (1960, 1972, 1979); piano and organ music, songs.

MacCunn, Hamish (1868–1916) Scottish composer and conductor. He had an overture *Cior Mhor* performed at the Crystal Palace at the age of 17. After 1890 he conducted the Carl Rosa Opera Company for some time, and also conducted Edward German's light operas at the Savoy Theatre.

He studied with Parry and Stanford at the Royal College of Music in London. In 1889 he married a daughter of the painter John Pettie.

Works include: the operas *Jeanie Deans* (after Scott, 1894), *Diarmid* (1897), and *Breast of Light* (unfinished); light operas *The Golden Girl* (1905) and *Prue*; music for *The Masque of War and Peace* and *Pageant of Darkness and Light*; cantatas *The Moss Rose* (1885), *Lord Ullin's Daughter* (Thomas Campbell, 1888), *The Lay of the Last Minstrel* (after Scott), *Bonny*

Kilmeny (James Hogg), *The Cameronian's Dream* (James Hyslop, 1890), *Queen Hynde of Caledon* (Hogg), *The Death of Parcy Reed*, *The Wreck of the Hesperus* (Longfellow, 1905), and others; Psalm 8 for chorus and organ; overture *The Land of the Mountain and the Flood*; ballads 'The Ship o' the Fiend' and 'The Dowie Dens o' Yarrow', three descriptive pieces *Highland Memories* for orchestra; three Romantic pieces for cello and piano (1914).

MacDermot, Galt (1928–) US composer. He wrote the rock musical *Hair* 1967, with lyrics by Gerome Ragni and James Rado. It challenged conventional attitudes about sex, drugs, and the war in Vietnam.

In the UK, the musical opened in London 1968, on the same day stage censorship ended.

MacDowell, Edward Alexander (1860–1908) US Romantic composer. He was influenced by Liszt. His works include the *Indian Suite* 1896 and piano concertos and sonatas. He was at his best with short, lyrical piano pieces, such as 'To a Wild Rose' from *Woodland Sketches* 1896.

Returning to the USA after several years in Germany, he played his *Second Piano Concerto in D Minor* 1889, his most successful longer work, in New York City. He was one of the first US composers to receive international acclaim.

After learning the piano at home, he went to the Paris Conservatory in 1876, where he studied piano under Marmontel and theory under Savard. Afterwards he worked with Louis Ehlert at Wiesbaden in 1878, and the following year entered the Frankfurt Conservatory, where Raff taught him composition. In 1881 he became piano professor at the Darmstadt Conservatory, and in 1882 was invited by Liszt to play his first piano concerto at Zurich. He returned to the USA in 1884 and married Marian Nevins, who had been his pupil at Frankfurt. After another period at Frankfurt and Wiesbaden he went home for good and settled at Boston in 1888, making his first public appearance in the USA there in November. In 1896 he was appointed head of the new music department at Columbia University, New York and was awarded an honorary doctorate in music by Princeton University. He resigned in 1904, but continued to teach and compose. In 1904 he began to suffer from mental illness which afflicted him until his death.

Works include: symphonic poems *Hamlet and Ophelia* (after Shakespeare, 1885), *Lancelot and Elaine*, *Lamia* (after Keats, 1889); two suites (no. 2 *Indian*) for orchestra; two piano concertos (1882, 1889); six orchestral works; 26 op. nos. of piano solos, including four sonatas, two *Modern Suites*, 24 studies, *Woodland Sketches*, *Sea Pieces*, *Fireside Tales*, *New England Idylls*, also two books of technical exercises; two sets of pieces for piano duet; 42 songs; 26 part songs.

Macfarren, George (Alexander) (1813–1887) English composer and educationist. He edited works by Purcell and Handel and was principal of the Royal College of Music, London from 1876.

A pupil of C Lucas from 1827, he entered the Royal Academy of Music in 1829 and became a professor there in 1834 and principal in 1876. In 1845 he married the German contralto and translator Natalia Andrae (1828–1916). In the 1870s his eyesight began to fail and he eventually became blind, but he continued to work at composition and to teach.

Works include: OPERA *The Devil's Opera* (1838), *The Adventures of Don Quixote* (after Cervantes, 1846), *King Charles II* (1849), *Robin Hood* (1860), *Jessy Lea* (1863), *She Stoops to Conquer* (after Goldsmith, 1864), *The Soldier's Legacy*, *Helvellyn*; masque *Freya's Gift*; oratorios *St John the Baptist* (1873), *The Resurrection* (1876), *Joseph* (1877), *King David*.

OTHER cantatas *Emblematical Tribute on the Queen's Marriage* (1840), *The Sleeper Awakened*, *Lenora*, *May Day*, *Christmas*, *The Lady of the Lake* (after Scott, 1876); much church music; symphony in F minor and seven others (1831–74), overtures to Shakespeare's *Hamlet*, *Romeo and Juliet*, and *The Merchant of Venice*, Schiller's *Don Carlos* (1842), overture *Chevy Chase* and other orchestral works; violin concerto; five string quartets and other chamber music; sonatas for various instruments.

MacGregor, Joanna (1959–) English pianist and composer. She has written music for theatre, radio, and television. In 1993 she gave the premiere of Birtwistle's *Antiphonies*, under Boulez, and has performed other modern repertory by Berio, Xenakis, Ligeti, and Takemitsu.

She studied at Cambridge with Hugh Wood, at the Royal Academy of Music in London, and with Van Cliburn in Texas. She made her London debut in 1985 and has since appeared with all the leading British orchestras. She gave the first performance of Wood's Concerto at the 1991 London Proms and returned in 1993 for Messiaen's *Turangalîla-*

Symphonie. She founded the Contemporary Music platform in London 1991–93.

McGuire, Edward (1948–) Scottish composer. He studied at the Royal Academy of Music 1966–70 and in Stockholm. He played flute with the folk group The Whistlebinkies from 1973. His works have been performed at the Edinburgh Festival and London Promenade concerts.

Works include: the operas *The Loving of Etain* (1990) and *Cullercoats* (1993); ballets *Peter Pan* (1989) and *The Spirit of Flight* (1991); orchestral music *Calgacus* (1977), guitar concerto (1989), *A Glasgow Symphony* (1990), *Scottish Dances* (1990), trombone concerto (1991), and *Symphonies of Scots Songs* (1992); *Symphonies of Trains* (1992), *Sidesteps* (1992), and *Zephyr* (1993) for ensemble; *Loonscapes* (1983) and *The Web* (1989) for soprano and ensemble; *Elegy* for piano trio (1990), *Eastern Echoes* (1991) and *Fountain of Tears* (1992) for flute and guitar, *Remembrance* for oboe trio (1993); piano music.

Machaut, Guillaume de (1300–1377) French poet and composer. Born in Champagne, he was in the service of John of Bohemia for 30 years and, later, of King John the Good of France. He gave the ballade and rondo forms a new individuality and ensured their lasting popularity. His *Messe de Nostre Dame* about 1360, written for Reims Cathedral, is an early masterpiece of *ars nova*, 'new (musical) art', exploiting unusual rhythmic complexities.

Machover, Tod (1953–) US composer and cellist. He studied with Dallapiccola in Florence and with Elliott Carter at the Juilliard School, New York. He was director of musical research at ◊IRCAM, Paris 1980–85. In 1985 he was appointed director of Experimental Media Facility, Media Laboratory at the Massachusetts Institute of Technology.

Works include: concerto for amplified guitar and ensemble (1978), *Nature's Breach* (1985), and *Descres* (1985–89), computer-generated opera *Valis* (first performance Paris, 2 December 1987) and *Epithalamion* (1990) for vocal soloists, 25 players and live and recorded electronics.

Mackenzie, Alexander (Campbell) (1847–1935) Scottish composer. He composed prolifically in all genres, perhaps his most notable works being the operas *Colomba* (1883), *The Cricket on the Hearth* (1914) and *The Eve of St John* (1924), and the oratorio *The Rose of Sharon* (1884). He published his autobiography, *A Musician's Narrative*, in 1927.

Born in Edinburgh, Mackenzie studied in Germany and later at the Royal Academy of Music, London, of which, after 14 years as a violinist and teacher at Edinburgh and some years at Florence, he was principal 1888–1924. He was also conductor of the Philharmonic Society 1892–99, and president of the International Musical Society 1908–12. In 1923 he received the Royal Philharmonic Society's gold medal.

Works include: the operas *Colomba* (1883), *The Troubadour* (1886), *The Cricket on the Hearth* (after Dickens, 1914), and *The Eve of St John* (1924); incidental music for *Marmion* and *Ravenswood* (plays based on Scott), Shakespeare's *Coriolanus*, Byron's 'Manfred', and Barrie's *The Little Minister*; oratorios *The Rose of Sharon* (1884), *Bethlehem* (1894), *The Temptation* (after Milton, 1914); cantatas *The Bride*, *Jason*, *The Story of Sayid*, *The Witch's Daughter*, *The Sun-God's Return*; *The Cottar's Saturday Night* (Burns) for chorus and orchestra (1888), suite, Scottish Rhapsody, Canadian Rhapsody, ballad 'La Belle Dame sans merci' (after Keats, 1883), 'Tam o' Shanter' (after Burns), overtures *Cervantes* (1877), *Twelfth Night* (Shakespeare), *Britannia*, and *Youth, Sport and Loyalty* for orchestra; concerto, Scottish Concerto (1897), suite and *Pibroch* suite for violin and orchestra; string quartet (1875); piano quartet, piano trio; violin and piano pieces; organ and piano music; songs; part songs.

MacMillan, James (1959–) Scottish composer. In works such as *The Confessions of Isobel Gowdie*, premiered at the London Promenade concerts in 1990, he has forsaken modern orthodoxies for a more popular approach.

He studied at Edinburgh University and at Durham with John Casken. He was composer-in-residence at Maxwell Davies's Magnus Festival in 1989. He has taught at the Royal Scottish Academy from 1990.

Works include: the chamber opera *Tourist Variations* (1991) and opera *Inès de Castro* (1993); music theatre *Busqueda* (1988) and *Visitatio Sepulchri* (1993); *Into the Ferment* for ensemble and orchestra (1988), *Tryst* for orchestra (1989), *The Berserking*, piano concerto (1990), *Sinfonietta* (1991), *Veni, Veni Emmanuel*, percussion concerto for Evelyn Glennie (1992), *Epiclesis*, trumpet concerto (1993), *VS* for orchestra (1993); *Tuireadh (Requiem)* for clarinet and string quartet (1991), *Scots Song* for soprano and chamber quintet (1991); music for band, choral pieces and piano music.

Maconchy, Elizabeth (1907–1994) English composer of Irish descent. She composed a great deal of chamber music, including a remarkable series of ten string quartets, one-act operas, a symphony, and a piano concerto. *And Death Shall Have No Dominion*, for chorus and brass, was performed at the Three Choirs Festival in 1969.

She was born at Broxbourne, Hertfordshire. She studied composition under Vaughan Williams and piano under Arthur Alexander at the Royal College of Music in London; and later studied under Karel Jirák in Prague. Several of her works were performed at the International Society for Contemporary Music festivals abroad and were successful in Belgium and eastern Europe. She married William LeFanu, who translated poems by the Greek poet Anacreon for her. Their daughter is the composer Nicola ◊LeFanu.

Works include: the operas *The Sofa* (1957), *The Departure* (1961), and *The Three Strangers* (1967): performed as a trilogy at Middlesbrough 1977; ballets *Great Agrippa* (from Hofmann's 'Shock-headed Peter') and *The Little Red Shoes* (after Andersen); two motets for double chorus (Donne); *The Leaden Echo and the Golden Echo* (Gerard Manley Hopkins) for chorus and chamber orchestra (1978); symphony and suites for orchestra *The Land* (on a poem by Vita Sackville-West) and *Puck*; piano concerto (1930), violin concerto (1963), concertino for clarinet; *Samson at the Gates of Gaza* for voice and orchestra; Sinfonietta (1976), *Little Symphony* (1981), *Music for Strings* (1983); 13 string quartets (1933–85), string trio, *Prelude Interlude* and *Fugue* for two violins; song-cycle *The Garland* (Anacreon).

Maçon, Le/The Mason opera by Auber (libretto by Scribe and G Delavigne), produced Paris, Opéra-Comique, 3 May 1825.

McPhee, Colin (1901–1964) Canadian-born US composer. His studies with Edgard Varèse much influenced his own music, as did his research into Balinese music 1934–36. His best-known work, *Tabuh-tabuhan* for two pianos and orchestra 1936, uses a combination of Balinese and Western orchestral instruments.

He studied with Gustav Strube (1867–1953) at the Peabody Conservatory, Baltimore, and graduated in 1921. He then studied piano with Arthur Friedheim (1859–1932) at the Canadian Academy of Music, where he played a piano concerto of his own in 1924. Next he studied composition in Paris with Paul le Flem and piano with Isidore Philipp (1863–1958). From 1934 to 1939 he spent much time in Bali and Mexico. He also wrote a number of books on Bali and its music, including *Music in Bali* 1966.

Works include: three symphonies (1955, 1957, 1962); concerto for piano and eight wind instruments (1928), *Tabuh-tabuhan* for two pianos and orchestra (1936); *Balinese Ceremonial Music* for two pianos (1942), and other piano music; four *Iroquois Dances* for orchestra.

Macque, Giovanni de (c. 1551–1614) Flemish composer. He was a pupil of Philippe de Monte. He went to Italy, living in Rome 1576–82, and at Naples from 1586, where he was choirmaster of the royal chapel from 1594. He wrote 14 volumes of madrigals and *madrigaletti*. His other works include motets and keyboard music.

Madama Butterfly opera by Puccini (libretto by Giacosa and L Illica, based on David Belasco's dramatic version of a story by John Luther Long), produced Milan, La Scala, 17 February 1904. US naval officer Pinkerton marries Madam Butterfly while visiting Japan. After fathering a son, he abandons her for an American wife. Honour requires Butterfly's suicide.

Madame Sans-Gêne opera by Giordano (libretto by R Simoni after the play by Sardou and Moreau), produced New York Metropolitan Opera 25 January 1915, conductor Toscanini. Laundress Caterina marries Sergeant Lefèbre and becomes Duchess of Danzig after promotion following the French Revolution. Chastised for her common behaviour, Caterina is summoned before Napoleon, a former washing customer, who forgives her.

Maddalena opera in one act by Prokofiev (libretto by composer after M Lieven); 1911–13, first performed BBC, 25 March 1979: orchestrated by E Downes and conducted by him. Maddalena's husband Genaro and lover Stenio kill each other in a struggle.

Mademoiselle Fifi opera by Cui (libretto in Russian, based on Maupassant's story), produced Moscow, 15 December 1903.

Maderna, Bruno (1920–1973) Italian composer and conductor. He collaborated with Luciano Berio in setting up an electronic studio in Milan in 1954. His compositions combine aleatoric and graphic techniques (see ◊aleatory music, ◊graph notation) with an elegance of sound. They include a pioneering work for live and prerecorded flute, *Musica su due dimensioni* 1952, numerous concertos, and *Hyperion* 1964, a 'mobile opera', consisting of a number of composed scenes that may be combined in several ways.

Maderna was born at Venice. He studied violin and piano, and composition with Alessandro Bustini at the Academy of St Cecilia in Rome, and then took composition and conducting lessons with Malipiero and Scherchen. He conducted throughout Europe, specializing in modern music. In 1954 he founded the Milan Radio Studio di Fonologia Musicale with Berio, pioneering Italian electronic music with *Divertimento, Notturno, Continuo,* and *Le Rire.* He visited the USA in 1965, conducting Nono's *Intolleranza* at Boston and concerts in New York and Chicago.

Works include: *Hyperion,* composite theatre work (performed Venice 1964); concertos for piano, two pianos, flute, oboe; *Introduzione e Passacaglia* for orchestra (1947); *Musica su due Dimensioni* for flute, percussion and electronic tape (1952–58); instrumental works include *Composizione in tre tempi, Improvisizione I, II, Serenata I, II* for 11 and 13 instruments (1946–57); *Studi per il Processo di Franz Kafka* for speaker, soprano and chamber orchestra (1949); electronic music including *Notturno, Syntaxis, Continuo, Dimensioni.*

Madetoja, Leevi (Antti) (1887–1947) Finnish conductor, critic, and composer. He conducted the Helsinki orchestra 1912–14, and afterwards that of Viborg. In 1916 he became a music critic at Helsinki and teacher at the Conservatory there, and began teaching at Helsinki University in 1926.

Maetoja was born at Uleaaborg. He studied at the Conservatory in his native town, then with Järnefelt and Sibelius at Helsinki, and afterwards with d'Indy in Paris and Fuchs in Vienna.

Works include: the operas *Pohjalaisia* (1924) and *Juha* (1935); ballets; three symphonies (1916, 1918, 1926), symphonic poems and overtures; *Stabat Mater;* eight cantatas; piano trio; violin and piano sonata; *Lyric Suite* for cello and piano; piano pieces; songs.

Madonna of Winter and Spring work for orchestra and electronics by Jonathan Harvey; first performed London, 27 August 1986, conductor Peter Eötvös.

madrigal form of secular song in four or five parts, usually sung without instrumental accompaniment. It originated in 14th-century Italy. Madrigal composers include Andrea Gabrieli, Monteverdi, Thomas Morley, and Orlando Gibbons.

madrigal comedy a sequence of madrigals in a quasi-dramatic form. The most famous but not the earliest example is Orazio Vecchi's

L'Amfiparnaso, and similar works of his are *La selva di varie ricreazioni/The Forest of Multifarious Delights, Il convito musicale/The Musical Banquet* and *Le veglie di Siena/The Vigils of Siena.* A similar work, Simone Balsamino's *Novellette,* based on Tasso's *Aminta,* appeared the same year as ◊*L'Amfiparnaso* (1594), but there were earlier ones, notably Striggio's *Il cicalamento delle donne al bucato/The Cackling of Women at the Wash,* and later Vecchi was imitated by Banchieri and others.

Maelzel, Johann Nepomuk (1772–1838) German inventor. His name is invariably linked to the ◊metronome. He did not invent the machine, but appropriated the idea, developing it in 1814.

He settled in Vienna in 1792 and invented various mechanical instruments. In 1808 he was appointed court mechanician there. Later he lived in Paris and from 1826 in the USA. Beethoven's *Battle of Victoria* was originally written for Maelzel's 'Panharmonicon' and the second movement of the eighth symphony imitates the ticking of the metronome. The 'Panharmonicon', first exhibited in Vienna in 1804, was an automatic instrument operated by weights acting on cylinders. Maelzel finished a new version of the 'Panharmonicon' in 1812.

maestoso (Italian 'majestic', 'dignified') term used in musical notation. When used as part of a tempo marking, for example *allegro maestoso,* it modifies it, directing the performer to maintain a dignified character.

maestro (Italian 'master') title given to a distinguished musician, whether composer, performer, or teacher.

maestro al cembalo (Italian 'master at the harpsichord') in the late 17th and 18th centuries, the harpsichord player who not only played continuo in the orchestra but also acted as assistant to the conductor and helped to coach singers.

maestro di cappella (Italian 'chapel master') Italian equivalent of ◊kapellmeister.

Magalhães, Filippe de (c. 1571–1652) Portuguese composer. He studied with Manuel Mendes (1547–1605) at Evora. He was maestro di cappella of the Misericordia at Lisbon and from 1614 of the royal chapel there under the Spanish King Philip III.

Works include: Masses, canticles to the Blessed Virgin, chants.

Magelone Romances a cycle of 15 songs by Brahms, settings of poems from Ludwig Tieck's *Die schöne Magelone/Story of the Fair Magelone,* op. 33, composed 1861–66.

maggiore (Italian 'major key') term used in musical notation, sometimes explicitly stated at a point in a composition where the major key returns after a prolonged section in minor, especially in variations, to prevent the performer from overlooking the change of key.

Magic Flute (Mozart). See ◊*Zauberflöte, Die*.

Magic Fountain, The opera by Delius (libretto by composer and J Bell); composed 1894–95, first performed British Broadcasting Corporation (BBC) broadcast, 20 November 1977, conductor Del March. Explorer Solano seeks a magic fountain with native Indian lover Watawa as a guide. Although she has sworn revenge on white men, she falls in love with him, but both die when they drink the fountain's poisonous water.

Magic Opal, The opera by Albéniz (libretto by A Law), produced London, Lyric Theatre, 19 January 1893.

magic opera a species of opera not unlike the English pantomime, popular particularly on the Viennese stage at the end of the 18th and opening of the 19th centuries, where it was called *Zauberoper*. It consisted of dialogue and musical numbers, had a fairy-tale subject with incidents of low comedy, and contained numerous scenic effects. The outstanding example is Mozart's *Zauberflöte*; others are Müller's *Zauberzither*, Wranitzky's *Oberon*, Süssmayr's *Spiegel von Arkadien*, and Schubert's *Zauberharfe*.

Magnard, (Lucien Denis Gabriel) Albéric (1865–1914) French composer. His masterpieces, the operas *Guercoeur* and *Berenice*, owe something in their structure to the example of Wagner, but also reveal an individual visionary lyricism.

Magnard studied at the Paris Conservatory and in 1888 became a private pupil of d'Indy. As the son of Francis Magnard, editor of *Le Figaro*, he was comfortably off and never held any official posts. He retired to Baron, in Picardy, to devote himself to composition, published his works himself, and never took any trouble to have them performed, though some were brought out by enthusiastic friends. During the very first days of World War I he shot two German soldiers from his window and was killed as a sniper. His house, including several of his manuscripts, was burnt down.

Works include: the operas *Yolande*, (1891), (destroyed), *Guercœur* (partly destroyed 1900; performed 1931) and *Bérénice*; four symphonies, (1890, 1893, 1896, 1913), *Suite dans le style*

ancien, *Chant funèbre*, overture *Hymne à la Justice* and *Hymne à Vénus* for orchestra (1904); string quartet (1903), piano trio, piano and wind quintet; violin and piano sonata, cello and piano sonata; piano pieces; songs.

Magnetton (German 'magnet tone') electrophonic instrument invented by Stelzhammer of Vienna in 1933. It produces its notes by means of electromagnets and is capable of imitating various instruments.

Magnificat in the New Testament, the song of praise sung by Mary, the mother of Jesus, on her visit to her cousin Elizabeth shortly after the Annunciation. It is used in the liturgy of some Christian churches in the form of a ◊canticle based on text from Luke's gospel 1:46–55 ('My soul doth magnify the Lord ...'). It is sung at Roman Catholic vespers and Anglican evensong, either in ◊plainsong or to a composer's setting, as in works by Monteverdi, J S Bach, Palestrina, and Vaughan Williams.

Mahillon, Victor (1841–1924) Belgian music scholar, son of the instrument maker Charles Mahillon (1813–87). He studied at the Brussels Conservatory, where he became curator of the museum of musical instruments. He wrote on acoustics and instruments.

Mahler, Alma (1879–1964), born Schindler Austrian pianist and composer of lieder (songs). She was the daughter of the artist Anton Schindler and abandoned composing when she married the composer Gustav Mahler 1902. After Mahler's death she lived with the architect Walter Gropius; their daughter Manon's death inspired Berg's *Violin Concerto*. She later married the writer Franz Werfel.

Mahler, Gustav (1860–1911) Austrian composer and conductor. His epic symphonies express a world-weary Romanticism in visionary tableaux incorporating folk music and pastoral imagery. He composed nine large-scale symphonies, many with voices, including *Symphony No. 2 'Resurrection'* 1884–86, revised 1893–96, and left a tenth unfinished. He also composed orchestral lieder (songs) including *Das Lied von der Erde/The Song of the Earth* 1909 and *Kindertotenlieder/Dead Children's Songs* 1901–04.

The *Symphony No. 2* second movement, based on a *Ländler* (folk dance in three time), is reinterpreted in stream-of-consciousness mode by Luciano Berio in *Sinfonia* 1968, into which Berio inserts a history of musical references from J S Bach to Stockhausen. The *Adagietto* slow movement from *Symphony*

No. 5 provided a perfect foil for Luchino Visconti's film *Death in Venice* 1971.

Mahler was born in Bohemia (now the Czech Republic), the son of a distillery manager. He showed great talent as a pianist in his childhood, and in 1875 his family, who had moved to Jihlava (Iglau) soon after his birth, succeeded in entering him at the Vienna Conservatory. His piano professor, Julius Epstein, advised him to study composition and conducting. After leaving the Conservatory in 1878 he wrote the first version of his cantata *Das klagende Lied*. His conducting career began in the summer of 1880 in Hall, Upper Austria. Posts followed at theatres in Ljubljana in 1881 and Olmütz in 1882. While in Kassel, 1883–85, he wrote the *Lieder eines fahrenden Gesellen* and began the thematically related first symphony. In 1885 he was conductor at the Prague Opera, where he gave performances of the operas by Mozart and Wagner which were to form the basis of his repertory; his conducting was already noted for its precision of ensemble and individuality and flexibility of tempi. At Leipzig, 1886–88, he was second conductor to Nikisch; his completion of Weber's sketches for *Die drei Pintos* was premiered in 1888. While at Budapest, 1888–89, he led the unsuccessful first performance of his first symphony.

Mahler was chief conductor of the Hamburg Opera 1891–97; while there he furthered his reputation for inspiring high standards of theatrical, as well as musical, performance, and in 1892 he took the company to London, for the first Covent Garden performances of Wagner's *Ring*. In December 1895 he led the Berlin first performance of his *Resurrection* symphony, achieving his first success as a composer; in the same year his brother committed suicide, one of several family tragedies. In 1897 Mahler's timely baptism into the Catholic Church led to his appointment as director of the Vienna Court Opera. In the next ten years he established a magnificent company of singing actors and, most notably with the help of the stage designer Alfred Roller, mounted influential productions which sought to harmonize all aspects of stage and musical experience. He succeeded Hans Richter as conductor of the Vienna Philharmonic Orchestra 1898 but, largely as a result of his autocratic methods, he departed in 1901. Various intrigues at the Opera led to his resignation in 1907. During his years in Vienna Mahler wrote his symphonies nos. 4–8 near a villa on the Wörthersee in Carinthia. In the trilogy of purely

instrumental symphonies (nos. 5, 6, and 7), nos. 5 and 7 suggest a progression from doubt and darkness to an optimistic conclusion; no. 6 is classically proportioned and ends with three enormous hammer blows, the last of which fells the creator. The massive choral 8th symphony ends with a Goethe setting in which human suffering is transformed in a universal acclamation.

In 1902 he had married Alma Schindler; through her teacher, Alexander Zemlinsky, he met the composer Arnold Schoenberg. Their friendship is reflected in the complex polyphony and extreme chromaticism of Mahler's later music. The *Kindertotenlieder* 1904 is the first of several works which integrate vocal music of emotional intensity with sympathetic woodwind accompaniments. This style finds its culmination in *Das Lied von der Erde*, which was begun in the year which saw the death of his daughter Maria, aged four. On 1 January 1908 he made his debut as principal conductor of the New York Metropolitan Opera; due to artistic and personal differences his tenure there and with the New York Philharmonic Society was brief. In 1910 he led the triumphant Munich first performance of his eighth symphony, and the following year returned to Europe for the last time, mortally ill with a bacterial infection of the blood. Mahler's music took many years to gain acceptance – four of the symphonies were not heard in Britain until after 1945 – but he is now established as a founder of 20th-century music.

Works include: ten symphonies; all except the last two were premiered by Mahler: no. 1 in D (1883–88, first performance Budapest, 20 November 1889); no. 2 in C minor with soprano, mezzo, and chorus in finale, *Resurrection* (text by composer and Klopstock); 1887–94, first performance Berlin, 13 December 1895); no. 3 in D minor with alto, womens' and boys' voices (texts from Nietzsche and *Des Knaben Wunderhorn*; 1893–96, first performance Krefeld, 9 June 1902); no. 4 in G with soprano in the finale (1899–1901, first performance Munich, 25 November 1901); no. 5 in C♭ minor (1901–02, first performance Cologne, 18 October 1904); no. 6 in A minor (1903–06, first performance Essen, 27 April 1906); no. 7 in E minor (1904–06, first performance Prague, 19 September 1908); no. 8 in E♭ 'Symphony of a Thousand', with soloists, adults' and boys' choruses (text 9th-century hymn *Veni creator spiritus* in first movement and from Goethe's *Faust* part II in second; 1906, first performance Munich, 12 September 1910); no. 9 in D (1908–09, first performance Vienna, 26 June 1912, conductor Walter); no. 10 in F♭ minor was incomplete at Mahler's death: performing version by Deryck Cooke given in London, 13 August 1964. Cantata *Das klagende Lied* (1878–80); song-cycles *Lieder eines fahrenden Gesellen* (1884), *Kindertotenlieder* (1901–04), three books of early songs, five songs to words by Rückert, many other songs, including settings from *Des Knaben Wunderhorn*, *Das Lied von der Erde*, symphony for mezzo and tenor solo and orchestra (1907–09).

Maid of Orleans, The/Orleanskaya Dieva opera by Tchaikovsky (libretto by composer, based on V A Zhukovsky's translation of Schiller's drama), produced St Petersburg, 25 February 1881. Joan of Arc leads the French to miraculous victories over the English, but her father Thibault denounces her as a sorceress. She runs away and is captured by the English, who burn her at the stake.

main droite, or M.D. (French 'right hand') see ◊R.H.

main gauche, or M.G. (French 'left hand') see ◊L.H.

Mainzer Umzug work by Hindemith for soloists, chorus, and orchestra; composed 1962, first performed Mainz, 23 June 1962, conductor Hindemith.

maître de chapelle see ◊maestro di cappella.

maîtrise (French 'mastership') former French name for the whole establishment of the choir at cathedrals and collegiate churches, including not only all that appertained to their performance in church, but also extending to their accommodation and maintenance. The maîtrises were actually schools of music.

Majo, Gian Grancesco di (1732–1770) Italian composer. He was a pupil of his father, Giuseppe di Majo (1697–1771), maestro di cappella at the court at Naples, and later of Padre Martini in Bologna. He was appointed second organist at court in 1750, but lived chiefly as an opera composer.

Works include: 20 operas, *Ricimero, rè dei Goti* (1758), *Astrea Placata* (1760), *Cajo Fabricio*, *Ifigenia in Tauride* (1764), *Eumene* (unfinished at his death, completed by Errichelli and Insanguine); eight oratorios including *La passione di Gesù Cristo* (1780); five Masses and other church music; cantatas.

major one of the two predominant ◊scales (the other being minor) of the tonal system, characterized by the presence of a major third between the 1st and 3rd degrees. A major key is one based on the major scale. See ◊major interval.

major interval interval between the key note of a major scale and a higher note from the same; seconds, thirds, sixths, and sevenths can be major intervals. If the upper note of the major interval is flattened (or the lower note is sharpened) it becomes a minor interval. If the upper note of a major interval is sharpened (or the lower note is flattened) it becomes an augmented interval. If the upper note of a minor seventh is flattened (or the lower note is sharpened) it becomes a diminished seventh.

Makropoulos Case, The/Več Makropulos opera by Janáček (libretto based on Karel Čapek's play), produced Brno, 18 December 1926. Elena searches with the help and hindrance of lawyers Kolenatý and Prus for the magic document that has prolonged her life for 300 years. She longs for death and young Kristina burns the paper after it is found.

malagueña a Spanish dance, named after the town of Málaga, in moderate to fast ◊triple time (3/8 or 3/4). It can refer to several varieties: an 18th-century dance related to the ◊fandango, an older kind of dance based on a ◊chaconne, with a repeating accompaniment of four harmonies and an improvised melody, or a kind of freely formed emotional song. An example of a stylized malagueña can be found in Albéniz's *Iberia* 1909.

Maldere, Pierre van (1729–1768) Belgian violinist and composer. He travelled as a

Major, minor, and augmented thirds and sixths.

virtuoso 1752–58, visiting Dublin, Paris, and Vienna. On his return to Brussels he entered the service of the Duke of Lorraine. He was director of the Brussels Opera 1763–66.

Works include: the operas *Le Déguisement pastoral* (1756), *Les Précautions inutiles* (1760), *La Bagarre* (1763), and others; symphonies; concertos; sonatas.

male alto in singing, an artificial extension of the highest male-voice register, produced by ◊falsetto, used in Anglican church choirs and in male-voice quartets and choral societies, particularly in glees and part songs.

Malheurs d'Orphée, Les/The Miseries of Orpheus opera by Milhaud (libretto by A Lunel), produced Brussels, Théâtre de La Monnaie, 7 May 1926. Peasant Orphée cannot cure the illness of gypsy Euridice and is killed by her sisters.

Malipiero, Gian Francesco (1882–1973) Italian composer and editor of Monteverdi and Vivaldi. His own works, influenced by Stravinsky and Debussy, include operas in a Neo-Classical style, based on Shakespeare's *Julius Caesar* 1934–35 and *Antony and Cleopatra* 1936–37.

Malipiero was born Venice. In 1898 he began studying violin at the Vienna Conservatory, but on failing an examination turned to composition, returning to Venice in 1899. He graduated from the Bologna Liceo Musicale in 1904. In 1913 he went to Paris, where he attended the first performance of Stravinsky's *The Rite of Spring*. He was professor of composition at Parma University 1921–23 and director of the Liceo Musicale Benedetto Marcello, Venice 1939–53. He edited the complete edition of Monteverdi's works, as well as many of Vivaldi's.

Works include: STAGE operas *Sette canzoni* (1919), *Torneo notturno* (1931), *La favola del figlio cambiato* (libretto by Pirandello, 1934), *Ecuba, I capricci di Callot* (after E T A Hoffmann, 1941), *Venere Prigionera* (1955), *Uno dei dieci* (1971); ballet *Pantea* (1919).

ORATORIOS *San Francesco d'Assisi, La cena, La passione* (1935); eight string quartets (1920–64); including *Rispetti e strambotti, Stornelli e ballate*, and *Canzoni alla madrigalesca*.

ORCHESTRAL *Impressioni dal vero* (three sets, 1913), *Sinfonia in quattro tempi come le quattro stagioni* (1933), *Sinfonia elegiaca, Sinfonie delle campane*, and eight others (1946–69); six piano concertos (1934–58), two violin concertos, cello concerto.

Malipiero, Riccardo (1914–) Italian composer, nephew of Francesco ◊Malipiero. He studied at Milan and Turin and with his uncle in Venice. His early compositions are neo-classical in spirit; he turned to serialism in 1945.

Works include: the operas *Minnie la Candida* (1942), *La Donna è mobile* (1957) and *Battano alla Porta* (1962); three piano concertos (1937–61), two cello concertos (1938, 1957); three symphonies (1949–59), *Cadencias* for orchestra (1964), *Mirages* for orchestra (1966); *Ombre* for orchestra (1986); Requiem (1975); three string quartets (1941, 1954, 1960), piano quintet (1957), *Cassazione* for string sextet (1967); piano music.

Malko, Nikolai (Andreievich) (1883–1961) Russian conductor. He studied at St Petersburg with N Rimsky-Korsakov, A Glazunov, and N Tcherepnin, and at Karlsruhe with F Mottl. After teaching in Moscow and Leningrad, he became conductor of the Leningrad Philharmonic Orchestra in 1926 and gave the first performances of Shostakovich's first and second symphonies, but left Russia in 1928 for Denmark and the USA. He was conductor of the Yorkshire Symphony Orchestra 1954–56 and was appointed conductor of the Sydney Symphony Orchestra in 1957.

Mallarmé, Stéphane (1842–1898) French poet. His works inspired ◊Boulez (*Pli selon pli*); ◊Debussy (three poems); ◊Herodiade (Hindemith); ◊*Improvisation sur Mallarmé* (Boulez); ◊*Prélude à l'Après-midi d'un faune* (Debussy); ◊Ravel (three poems).

Mamelles de Tirésias, Les/The Breasts of Tiresias opéra bouffe in two acts by Poulenc (libretto by G Apollinaire), produced Paris, Opéra-Comique, 3 June 1947. Thérèse, tired of her monotonous life as a wife, becomes a man, Tirésias. Meanwhile her husband takes on the duty of producing children – over 40,000 in one day.

Ma Mère l'Oye/Mother Goose suite by Ravel, written for piano duet in 1908 and published 1910, scored for orchestra and produced as a ballet, Paris, Opéra, 11 March 1915, scenario by Louis Laloy, choreography by L Staats. The movements are based on tales by Perrault: 1. *Pavan of the Sleeping Beauty*; 2. *Hop-o'-my-Thumb*; 3. *Little Ugly, Empress of the Pagodas*; 4. *Colloquy between the Beauty and the Beast*; 5. *The Fairy Garden*.

Manchester group group of musicians who studied together at the Royal Northern College of Music in the early 1950s (then the Royal Manchester College of Music). These were composers Peter Maxwell ◊Davies, Harrison ◊Birtwistle and Alexander ◊Goehr, and pianist John ◊Ogdon. As the New Music

Manchester they undertook many performances of contemporary music.

Manchicourt, Pierre de (c. 1510–1564)
Flemish composer. He worked at Tournai
1539–45, Arras around 1555, and Antwerp
from 1557. In 1561 he took charge of the
Flemish choir of Philip II in Madrid.
Works include: Masses, motets; chansons.

Mancini, Henry (1924–1994) US composer. A
four-time Oscar winner for film music, he
wrote and conducted the music for more than
80 films. His tunes include the song 'Moon
River' from *Breakfast at Tiffany's* 1961 and the
theme to *The Pink Panther* 1963 and its
numerous sequels.

Mancini was born in Cleveland, Ohio,
learned flute and piano, and began arranging
music while in his teens. World War II
interrupted his studies at the Juilliard School
of Music in New York.

He became an arranger for the postwar
Glenn Miller Orchestra and worked on the
film *The Glenn Miller Story* 1954. One of his
most striking early scores was the jazz-tinged
music for Orson Welles's film *Touch of Evil*
1958, and he achieved wider attention with
the music for the TV series *Peter Gunn* 1958–
60. He later scored all the films of Blake
Edwards, maker of the *Pink Panther* series,
and accepted TV assignments as well as
features.

Mancini was also a prolific recording artist,
collecting 20 Grammy awards and six gold
albums. On television, he appeared on a half-
hour musical series, *Mancini Generation*, as
well as in numerous specials, and his concerts
were popular around the world. At the time
of his death he was collaborating with Leslie
Bricusse (1931–) on a stage version of the
film *Victor-Victoria* 1982, for which they
provided music and lyrics.

**Mancinus, Thomas (1550–c. 1612), real
name Mencken** German composer. He was
cantor at the cathedral school of Schwerin,
1572–76, tenor at court in Berlin, 1579–81, and
then in the service of the Duke of Brunswick
at Wolfenbüttel.

Works include: Passions according to St
Matthew and St John, Latin and German
motets and madrigals, secular German songs
for several voices.

mandolin plucked string instrument with
four to six pairs of strings (courses), tuned
like a violin, which flourished 1600–1800. The
fingerboard is fretted to regulate intonation. It
takes its name from its almond-shaped body
(Italian *mandorla* 'almond'). Vivaldi com-

posed two concertos for the mandolin about
1736.

The **Neapolitan mandolin**, a different
instrument which appeared about 1750, is
played with a plectrum and has metal strings.
Composers include Beethoven, Hummel,
Schoenberg, and Stravinsky in *Agon* 1955–57.

mandore small, plucked string instrument of
the ◊lute family.

Mandragola, La/The Mandrake opera by
Castelnuovo-Tedesco (libretto based on Machiavelli's comedy), produced Venice, Teatro
La Fenice, 4 May 1926. Callimaco sleeps with
the beautiful Lucrezia after Ligurio arranges a
supposed magic potion to cure her infertility.

Mandyczewski, Eusebius (1857–1929) Romanian-born Austrian musicologist. He studied at the Vienna Conservatory. In 1887 he
became keeper of the archives of the Vienna
Philharmonic Society and in 1897 professor at
the Conservatory. He co-edited the complete
Schubert and Brahms editions, and Haydn's
works (later abandoned).

Manfred incidental music for Byron's drama
by Schumann, op. 115, composed 1849; first
concert performance of the overture, Leipzig,
Gewandhaus, March 1852. The whole produced with Byron's play, Weimar, 13 June
1852.

Symphony by Tchaikovsky, op. 58, based
on the same play 1885, first performed
Moscow 6 April 1886.

Manfredini, Francesco Onofrio (1684–1762)
Italian composer. His 43 published instrumental works including a set of 12 'Con-
certini', chamber sonatas 1704, 12 *Sinfonie da
chiesa* 1709, and six sonatas published in
London in 1764.

He studied with Torelli and Perti in
Bologna and held appointments in Ferrara
and Monaco before returning to Pistoia by
1727, as maestro di cappella at St Philip's
Cathedral. Four oratorios date from his return
to Pistoia.

Manfredini, Vincenzo (1737–1799) Italian
theorist and composer, son of Francesco
◊Manfredini. After study with his father he
went to Moscow in 1758. He became maestro
di cappella at the court of St Petersburg's
Italian opera company in 1762; until he was
superseded by Galuppi he wrote operas for
Catherine II. After his return to Italy in 1769
he became a teacher and writer on music,
notably *Regole armoniche, o sieno Precetti
ragionati* (1775). His compositions include
settings of Metastasio's *Semiramide* (1760),

Olimpiade (1762), and *Artaserse* (1772), as well as six symphonies and six string quartets.

Männergesangverein (German 'men's singing-association') male-voice choral society.

Mannheim School a group of composers associated with the Electoral court at Mannheim in the mid-18th century. Under the leadership of Johann Stamitz (1717–57) the court orchestra became the most famous of the time, establishing a completely new style of playing, and placing particular emphasis on dynamic contrasts, *crescendo* and *diminuendo*. The Mannheim composers, (in addition to Stamitz) F X Richter, Holzbauer, Beck and Cannabich, made notable contributions to the early development of the symphony, and also influenced later composers such as Mozart and Beethoven.

Manns, August (Friedrich) (1825–1907) German-born British conductor. He began popular Saturday concerts in London in 1856, giving early performances of music by Schubert, Schumann, Wagner, and Berlioz, and conducting the Handel Festival 1883–1900.

At first a cellist and violinist in various bands and orchestras in Germany, he later became a bandmaster. He went to London as sub-conductor at Crystal Palace in 1854, becoming full conductor in 1855, when he enlarged the orchestra.

mano destra, or M.D. (Italian 'right hand') see ◊R.H.

Manon opera by Massenet (libretto by H Meilhac and P Gille, based on Prévost's novel *Manon Lescaut*), produced Paris, Opéra-Comique, 19 January 1884. Manon and Des Grieux fall in love and elope, but De Brétigny persuades Manon to go with him instead. The distraught Des Grieux plans to become a priest, but Manon returns and they are reunited. She is arrested, accused of prostitution, and sentenced to transportation. She dies in Des Grieux' arms.

Manon Lescaut ballet by Halévy (scenario by Scribe, based on Prévost's novel, choreography by Jean-Pierre Aumer), produced Paris, Opéra, 3 May 1830.

Opera by Auber (libretto by Scribe, based on Prévost's novel), produced Paris, Opéra-Comique, 23 February 1856.

Opera by Puccini (libretto, in Italian, by M Praga, D Oliva and L Illica, based on Prévost's novel), produced Turin, Teatro Regio, 1 February 1893. Manon and Des Grieux elope, thwarting the schemes of Geronte, who wants her for himself. Later

Manon lives with Geronte, but on seeing Des Grieux returns to him. In revenge, Geronte has her arrested. She is deported to America, where she dies in Des Grieux' arms.

mano sinistra, or M.S. (Italian 'left hand') see ◊L.H.

Manru opera by Paderewski (libretto by A Nossig after J I Kraszewski's novel *The Cabin behind the Wood*, 1843; composed 1892–1901, produced Dresden, 29 May 1901. Ulana marries young gypsy Manru, but loses him to Asa when he returns to his people.

Mantra work by Stockhausen for two amplified pianos; composed 1969–70, first performed Donaueschingen, 18 October 1970. Pianists also play woodblock and bells, while they contemplate the Indian word *mantra*, or mystical repetition.

manual any of the keyboards of a multikeyboard instrument played by the hands. A harpsichord often has two manuals and an organ has up to four (◊great organ, ◊swell organ, ◊choir organ, and ◊solo organ). The pedal keyboard (pedalboard) of the organ is not a manual.

Manuel Venegas unfinished opera by H Wolf (libretto by M Hoernes, based on Alarcón's *El niño de la bola*), begun 1897. Fragments performed Munich, 1 March 1903.

Manzoni, Giacomo (1932–) Italian composer. His music has featured in festivals at Berlin, Osaka, Prague, and Warsaw. He published a book on Schoenberg in 1975.

He studied at the Milan Conservatory and taught there 1962–69; he also taught at the Bologna Conservatory 1964–74, before returning to Milan.

Works include: the operas *La Sentenza* (1960), *Atemtod* (1965; given by Abbado in the 1965 Salzburg Festival), *Per Massimiliano Robespierre* (1975), and *Doktor Faustus* (after Thomas Mann, 1985); *Masse: Omaggio a Edgard Varèse* for piano and orchestra (1977), *Il deserto cresce*, after Nietzsche, for chorus and orchestra (1992); *Ten Poems of Emily Dickinson* for soprano, string quartet, strings, and harp (1988); string quartet (1971).

Manzoni Requiem name sometimes given to Verdi's Requiem, composed 1873 for the anniversary of the death of Alessandro Manzoni, on which it was first performed at Milan, church of San Marco, 22 May 1874; repeated at La Scala on 25 May. The 'Libera me' is adapted from that contributed by Verdi to the collective Requiem he suggested should be written by various Italian composers on the death of Rossini in 1868, a plan which did not materialize. That the 'Libera me' was not merely taken over as it stood is proved by the fact that it contains allusions to material occurring earlier in the Manzoni Requiem. The 'Lachrymosa' is derived from the prison scene in the first version of *Don Carlos* (1867).

Manzuoli, Giovanni (c. 1720–c. 1780) Italian castrato soprano. He made his Italian debut in Florence (1731). Later he visited Madrid, London, and Vienna. In 1763 he sang in the first performance of Gluck's *Trionfo di Clelia* (Bologna) and in 1765 was in London to create the title role in J C Bach's *Adriano in Siria*. He retired in 1771, after creating Ascanio in Mozart's serenata *Ascanio in Alba*.

Maometto Secondo/Mahomet II opera by Rossini (libretto by C della Valle, Duke of Ventignano), produced Naples, Teatro San Carlo, 3 December 1820. A French version entitled *Le Siège de Corinthe*, was produced Paris, 9 October 1826. Muslim warrior Maometto falls for Anna, but she prefers Calbo, and dies in his defence.

maqam (Turkish *makam*) melodic mode, used as a basis for improvisation or composition in Arab and Turkish musics. See ◊taqsim and ◊dastgah.

maraca one of usually a pair of Latin American percussion instruments, consisting of a gourd partly filled with dry seeds or beans (although there are modern-material versions). Maracas are shaken to produce noise and traditionally form part of the rhythm section of Latin American bands. Classical composers who have written for maracas include Prokofiev in *Romeo and Juliet* 1935.

Marais, Marin (1656–1728) French bass viol player, known as a virtuoso player, and composer. He was a pupil of Sainte-Colombe (died c. 1691–1701) at the Sainte-Chapelle, and later became a member of the royal band and the orchestra at the Paris Opéra, where he studied composition under Lully and co-operated with him in the performance of operas. In 1725 he retired to devote himself to gardening, but continued to teach. He added a seventh string to the bass viol, and wrote five collections of bass viol pieces (1686–1725).

Works include: the operas *Idylle dramatique*, *Alcide* (1693), and *Pantomime des pages* (both with Lully's son Louis), *Ariane et Bacchus* (1696), *Alcyone* (1706), *Séméle* (1709); Te Deum; concertos for violin and bass; trios for flute, violin, and bass; pieces for one and two viols; *La Gamme* pieces for violin, viol, and harpsichord.

Maratona ballet by Henze (scenario by Luchino Visconti); composed 1956, produced Berlin, 24 September 1957.

Marbeck, John see John ◊Merbecke.

Marcabru (lived c. 1130–50), or Marcabrun Provençal ◊troubadour. He was one of the earliest of the troubadours, a Gascon of humble origins (tradition has it that he was a foundling). Many of his poems are in a satirical, moralizing, and realist vein that contrasts sharply with the conventional treatment of courtly love characteristic of many later troubadours. The most famous of his four surviving songs with tunes is the semi-religious 'Pax in nomine Domini'. One of his best-known poems deals with the crusade against the Moors in Spain.

marcato (Italian 'marked, accentuated') a musical direction indicating that a piece or movement is to be played in a decided, energetic manner, to that a part is to be brought out strongly above the accompaniment or surrounding parts in a passage.

Marcello, Benedetto (1686–1739) Italian violinist, composer, and author. His masterpiece is the *Estro poetico-armonico* 1724–26, a musical setting of the first 50 psalms as paraphrased into Italian by Girolamo Giustiniani. As well as composing, he wrote the libretto for Giovanni Maria Ruggieri's (fl. 1690–1720) opera *Arato in Sparta*, and in 1720 published the important satire on contemporary opera *Il teatro alla moda*.

He was born at Venice. A pupil of Gasparini and Lotti, he combined his musical interests with a career in law and the civil service. He also wrote canzoni in the madrigal style, instrumental concertos, an oratorio, and an opera. His brother Alessandro (1669–1747) wrote cantatas and concertos.

Works include: the operas and serenatas *La fede riconosciuta, Arianna*, and others; oratorios *Il pianto e il riso delle quattro stagioni* (1731), *Giuditta, Gioaz* (1726), *Il trionfo della poesia e della musica* (1733); Masses, Misereres, and other church music; *Estro poetico-armonico*, settings of 50 psalm-paraphrases by G A Giustiniani; concertos, sonatas for various instruments.

march, or (Italian) marcia in music, a piece originally intended to accompany marching soldiers or other people in procession, facilitating a regular and repeated drum rhythm. One of the earliest known forms of music, marches are usually in duple time (2/4) or common time (4/4), with a strongly marked beat and regular phrasing. There are various types, distinguished by tempo: the funeral march, slow march, quick march, and, occasionally, double-quick march. The earliest examples of the march in art music are found in the work of Lully and Couperin in the 17th century. The march has been used ever since, from Mozart operas as in *Die Zauberflöte/The Magic Flute* 1791, to Beethoven's *Eroica* symphony 1804, to Elgar's *Pomp and Circumstance Marches* 1901.

Marchand de Venise, Le/The Merchant of Venice opera by Hahn (libretto by M Zamaçoïs, after Shakespeare), produced Paris, Opéra, 25 March 1935.

Marchettus (lived 13th–14th centuries) Italian music theorist. He lived at Cesena and Verona at some time and was in the service of Rainier, Prince of Monaco. He wrote a treatise on the division of the scale and two more on notation, which aroused much opposition.

Marching Song opera by Benjamin Frankel (libretto by H Keller, after John Whiting's play); composed 1972–73 and left in short score at Frankel's death. First performed, in edition by Buxton Orr, BBC 3 October 1983.

marcia musical term; 'march'.

Marenzio, Luca (c. 1553–1599) Italian singer and composer. He is the most important of the Italian madrigalists, having written over 400. His madrigals were introduced into England through music editor Nicholas Yonge's (died 1619) *Musica transalpina* in 1588 and he was in correspondence with Dowland in 1595.

Born at Coccaglio, near Brescia, Marenzio studied with Giovanni Contino (1513–1574), organist at Brescia Cathedral, and published his first work in 1581. Soon afterwards he went to Rome, where he served Cardinal Cristoforo Madruzzo from around 1574 until 1578, when he became maestro di cappella to Cardinal d'Este until 1586. During this time he published many madrigals, and began to gain an international reputation as a composer. In 1588 he entered the service of Ferdinando de' Medici and in 1589 contributed two *intermedi* for wedding festivities in Florence. Later that year he returned to Rome, where he was employed by Virginio Orsini, Duke of Bracciano, until 1593. His next patron, Cardinal Cinzio Aldobrandini, recommended Marenzio as music director to the king of Poland. He was in Warsaw 1596–98, at the court of Sigismondo III of Poland. About the year 1599, however, he returned to

Rome and became organist at the papal chapel.

Marenzio published 18 books of madrigals for four–ten voices 1580–99, as well as five books of villanelles and two books of motets. Many of the madrigals he wrote before 1587 are settings of pastoral texts whose authors include the poet Petrarch; these were widely imitated in Europe, and in England by Thomas Morley. As he grew older, Marenzio's madrigals became increasingly serious in tone, with melancholy texts and more dissonance and chromaticism in the music.

Works include: Mass, motets, *Sacri concenti*; over 400 madrigals, *Villanelle ed arie alla napolitana* (five volumes).

Mareuil, Arnaut de (lived 1170–1200) Provençal ◊troubadour. About 25 of his lyric poems remain, mostly love poems, and some others including the earliest known Provençal verse epistles.

He was born in Mareuil-sur-Belle, in the Dordogne.

Margherita d'Anjou opera by Meyerbeer (libretto in Italian, by F Romani, based on a play by R C G de Pixérécourt), produced Milan, La Scala, 14 November 1820.

Margot-la-Rouge opera in one act by Delius (libretto by B Gaston-Danville); composed 1901–02, vocal score by Ravel 1902. Unperformed in Delius' lifetime but part of score was used in the *Idyll* of 1930. Given in orchestration by Eric Fenby, BBC 21 February 1982; the Delius orchestration was then discovered and given at stage first performed, St Louis 17 June 1983. Old flame Thibault is accidentally killed by Margot's new lover when he lunges at her during an argument. Margot then kills her lover and is arrested.

Maria di Rohan opera by Donizetti (libretto by S Cammarano), produced Vienna, Kärntnertor-theater, 5 June 1843. The Count of Chalais fights a duel to avenge an insult to Maria, wife of the Duc de Chevreuse. Chalais, Maria's former lover, writes her a passionate letter, which is intercepted and delivered to Chevreuse. Chalais kills himself.

Maria di Rudenz opera by Donizetti (libretto by S Cammarano), produced Venice, Teatro La Fenice, 30 January 1838. Maria elopes with Corrado, but he prefers her heiress sister, Matilde. Maria stabs Matilde and, unable to move Corrado, dies of wounds previously inflicted by him.

Maria Stuarda opera in two acts by Donizetti (libretto by G Bardari, after A Maffei's translation of Schiller's *Maria Stuart*), produced Milan, La Scala, 30 December 1835. While in rehearsal at Naples the opera was banned by the King; Donizetti used much of the music in a different work, *Buondelmonte*, which was premiered in Naples on 18 October 1834. *Maria Stuarda* was not staged in London until 1966 and in New York, 1972. Leicester intercedes on,behalf of the imprisoned Mary, but Elizabeth is jealous of the two and signs Mary's death warrant.

Maria Theresa Symphony name given to Haydn's symphony no. 48 in C major, supposedly composed for a visit of the Empress Maria Theresa to Eszterháza in 1773.

Maria Tudor opera by Gomes (libretto by M Praga, based on Victor Hugo's tragedy), produced Milan, La Scala, 27 March 1879. Giovanna, fiancée of Gilberto, is seduced by the disguised Count Fabiano, who is Queen Mary's lover. In a jealous rage Mary arrests both Gilberto and Fabiano. Calling for Fabiano's execution, she intends secretly to substitute Gilberto in his place, but Don Gilberto allows his rival to die instead.

Mariazell Mass the familiar name of Haydn's C-major Mass originally entitled *Missa Cellensis*. Composed 1782 for Anton Liebe von Kreutzner, who on his ennoblement wished to make a votive offering at the Marian shrine at Mariazell.

Marienleben, Das/The Life of Mary cycle of 15 songs for soprano and piano by Hindemith (texts by R M Rilke); composed 1922–23, first performed Frankfurt, 15 October 1923. Revised 1936–48 and performed Hanover, 3 November 1948. Six of the songs were arranged for soprano and orchestra, 1938–48.

Mariés de la Tour Eiffel, Les/The Wedded Pair of the Eiffel Tower ballet by five of 'Les Six': Auric, Honegger, Milhaud, Poulenc, and Tailleferre (scenario by Jean Cocteau), produced Paris, Théâtre des Champs-Élysées, 18 June 1921.

Mariette, Auguste Edouard (Mariette Bey) (1821–1881) French Egyptologist, founder of the museum at Cairo. He outlined the libretto for Verdi's *Aida*, drafted in French by C du Locle and written in Italian by Ghislanzoni.

marimba musical instrument, a bass ◊xylophone, a Mexican variant of an instrument originating in Africa, with wooden rather than metal tubular resonators.

marimba gongs percussion instrument similar to the ◊marimba, but with metal plates instead of wooden strips to produce the notes.

Marin, José (1619–1699) Spanish tenor and composer. He sang in the Encarnación convent at Madrid in his younger years, then became a highwayman and a priest. He fled to Rome after committing murder, and was imprisoned, but at the end of his life had a great reputation as a musician.

Works include: songs with continuo, songs with guitar accompaniment.

Marini, Biagio (c. 1587–1663) Italian composer and violinist. He was employed successively as a violinist at Venice, as music director at the church of Sant' Eufemia at Brescia, at the courts of Parma and Munich, and at Düsseldorf, Ferrara, and Milan.

Works include: psalms, vespers, and other church music; symphonies; sonatas, dances, and other pieces for string instruments, vocal and instrumental chamber music, madrigals, canzonets, sacred songs, and other pieces for several voices.

Marino Faliero opera by Donizetti (libretto by E Bidera, based on Byron's drama), produced Paris, Théâtre Italien, 12 March 1835. Doge of Venice, Faliero, is first betrayed by his unfaithful wife Elena, then executed after engaging in a political conspiracy.

Maritana opera by V Wallace (libretto by E Fitzball, based on the play *Don César de Bazan* by A P d'Ennery and P F Dumanoir), produced London, Drury Lane Theatre, 15 November 1845.

Markevich, Igor (1912–1983) Russian-born Italian conductor and composer. He was conductor of the Lamoureux Orchestra, Paris 1958–61, and of the Monte Carlo Orchestra from 1967.

His parents emigrated and lived in Switzerland, but he went to Paris at the age of 15 and studied composition under Nadia Boulanger. His austere ballet *L'Envol d'Icare/The Flight of Icarus* 1932 influenced Bartók. Early in his career he was a protégé of Diaghilev, and was one of his lovers. He became an Italian citizen during war years. After World War II he concentrated on conducting, specializing in Russian and French composers 1880–1950.

Works include: ballets *Rébus* (1931) and *L'Envoi d'Icare* (1932); cantata *Le Paradis Perdu/Paradise Lost* 1933–35 to words by Milton (performed London, 1935) and others, *Cantique d'Amour, Nouvel Age*, cantata for soprano and male-voice chorus (Jean Cocteau); *Hymnes*, concerto grosso and sinfonietta for orchestra; concerto and partita for piano and orchestra; *Galop* for small orchestra; psalm for soprano and orchestra; serenade for violin, clarinet, and bassoon.

Marmontel, Jean François (1723–1799) French author. He was librettist for Rameau, Grétry, Piccinni, Cherubini and others; defender of Piccinni against Gluck and author of an 'Essai sur les révolutions de la musique en France' (1777).

See ◊*Acante et Céphise* (Rameau); ◊*Antigone* (Zingarelli); ◊*Atys* (Piccinni); ◊*Céphale et Procris* (Grétry); ◊*Clari, or The Maid of Milan* (Bishop, from *Laurette*); ◊*Démophoon* (Cherubini); ◊*Didon* (Piccinni); ◊*Guirlande, La, ou Les fleurs enchantées* (Rameau); ◊*Rameau* (*Lysis et Délie; Les Sybarites*); ◊*Zémire et Azore* (Grétry); ◊*Zemire und Azor* (Spohr).

Mârouf, savetier du Caire/Mârouf, the Cobbler of Cairo opera by Rabaud (libretto by L Népoty, based on a story in the *Arabian Nights*), produced Paris, Opéra-Comique, 15 May 1914. Mârouf escapes wife, marries Sultan's daughter, and steals his treasure.

Marpurg, Friedrich Wilhelm (1718–1795) German theorist and writer on music. From 1749 he lived mainly in Berlin, where he began a music weekly, *Der critische Musicus an der Spree*. This was followed by other critical and theoretical writings, including a notable preface to the second edition of Bach's *Kunst der Fuge*, treatises on subjects including fugue, thorough-bass, and keyboard playing.

In Paris as secretary to General Bodenburg about 1746 he met, among others, Voltaire and Rameau, and was influenced by the latter's theories. He also composed some songs and keyboard music.

Marriage of Figaro (Mozart). See ◊*Nozze di Figaro, Le*.

Marriage, The/Zhenitba unfinished opera by Mussorgsky (libretto taken from Gogol's comedy), composed 1864; never performed in Mussorgsky's lifetime; produced with piano accompaniment, St Petersburg, 1 April 1909; with orchestra, Petrograd, 26 October 1917, with Mussorgsky's *Sorotchintsy Fair*. Podkolesin hires a marriage broker in pursuit of Agafya.

Comic opera by Martinů (libretto by composer, after Gogol); composed 1952, first performed NBC TV, New York, 7 February 1953.

Marschner, Heinrich (August) (1795–1861) German composer. He wrote 13 operas, including *Hans Heiling* 1833, and is regarded as the most important German opera composer between Weber and Wagner.

As a boy he played the piano, sang soprano, and composed tentatively without much instruction. In 1813 he was sent to Leipzig to study law, but met Johann Rochlitz, who induced him to take up music. In 1816 he went to Vienna and Pressburg with a Hungarian, Count de Varkony, and settled in Pressburg, where he composed several operas. In 1823 he became assistant conductor to Weber and Francesco Morlacchi at Dresden. In 1827 he became conductor of the Leipzig theatre and from 1831 to 1859 court conductor at Hanover. He married four times.

Works include: OPERA *Saidar, Heinrich IV und Aubigné* (1820), *Der Kyffhäuserberg* (1822), *Der Holzdieb* (1825), *Lucretia, Der Vampyr* (1828), *Der Templer und die Jüdin* (after Scott's *Ivanhoe*, 1829), *Des Falkners Braut* (1832), *Hans Heiling* (1833), *Der Bâbu* (1838), *Das Schloss am Aetna, Kaiser Adolf von Nassau* (1845), *Austin, Sangeskönig Hiarne* (1863).

OTHER incidental music to Kleist's *Prinz Friedrich von Homburg* and other plays; overture on 'God Save the King' and other orchestral works; male-voice choruses; sonatas; songs.

Marseillaise, La French national anthem; the words and music were composed 1792 as a revolutionary song by the army officer Claude Joseph Rouget de Lisle (1760–1836).

Marsh, John (1752–1828) English amateur composer. He practised as a lawyer until 1783, when a legacy enabled him to retire and devote his time to music, in which he was largely self-taught. He conducted concerts in Chichester and elsewhere, and composed some notable symphonies, also concertos, chamber music, and keyboard music.

Marsh, Roger (1949–) English composer. He studied at York University with Bernard Rands and has been lecturer there from 1988.

Works include: music theatre pieces *Cass* (1970) and *Calypso* (1974); *Not a Soul but Ourselves*, for four, amplified voices (1977), *Point to Point* for ensemble (1981); *Samson*, music theatre (1984); *The Song of Abigail* for soprano and orchestra (1985); *Dying for it*, for ensemble (1987); *The Big Bang* (1989); and *Love on the Rocks*, music theatre (1989); *Stepping Out* for orchestra (1990).

Marteau sans maître, Le/The hammer without a master work by Pierre Boulez for mezzo, flute, guitar, vibraphone, xylorimba, viola, and percussion; composed 1952–54, revised 1957; first performed Baden-Baden, 18 June 1955, conductor Rosbaud.

martellato (Italian 'hammered') in musical notation, percussive, with sharp attacks and detached articulation. The term usually appears in compositions for strings or for piano.

Martelli, Henri (1895–1980) French composer. He studied at the Paris Conservatory under Widor and others.

Works include: the opera *La Chanson de Roland* (1921–23; performed 1967) incidental music; three symphonies (1953–57), symphonic poem *Sur la vie de Jeanne d'Arc*, *Bas-reliefs assyriens* and concerto for orchestra; piano concerto; two string quartets; string quintet; piano pieces; songs.

Martha, oder Der Markt von Richmond/ Martha, or The Market at Richmond comic opera by Flotow (libretto by F W Riese, pseudonym 'W Friedrich', based on a ballet-pantomime, *Lady Henriette, ou La Servante de Greenwich*, by J H V de Saint-Georges, produced Paris, 21 February 1844, with music by F Burgmüller and Deldevez), produced Vienna, Kärntnertortheater, 25 November 1847. Lady Harriet and maid Nancy disguise themselves and meet two young farmers, Plumkett and Lyonel, at a country fair. They fall in love, and complications of differing social class are resolved when Lyonel turns out to be of noble blood.

martin in singing, a baritone voice of exceptional range. It is named after the French singer Jean Blaise Martin (1768–1837), who specialized in comic roles in operas by Dalaryac, Boieldieu, and Méhul.

Martin, Frank (1890–1974) Swiss composer, pianist, and harpsichordist. His works are characterized by delicate colouring in instrumentation and an expressive quality combined in later works with a loosely interpreted ◊twelve-tone system. Composing for both large- and small-scale forces, from orchestra to chamber music, his best known works are the operas *Der Sturm/The Tempest* 1956 and *Monsieur de Pourceaugnac* 1962.

He was born at Geneva, studied there with Joseph Lauber, and in 1928 became professor at the Institut Jaques-Dalcroze. In 1946 he settled at Amsterdam, where he remained even after his appointment as professor of composition at the Cologne Conservatoire. Martin was among the most distinguished composers of his generation.

Works include: the operas *The Tempest* (Shakespeare, 1956), *Monsieur Pourceaugnac* (1963); *Six Monologues from 'Jedermann'* (after Hofmannsthal, 1943), ballet *Die blaue Blume*; incidental music for Sophocles' *Oedipus Coloneus* and *Oedipus Rex* and Shakespeare's

Romeo and Juliet. Mass for double chorus, oratorios *In terra pax* (1945), *Golgotha* (1948); *Le Mystère de la Nativité* (1957–59); symphonic suite *Rhythmes*, *Esquisse*, symphony for orchestra; *Petite Symphonie concertante* for harp, harpsichord, piano, and strings (1945); piano concerto, violin concerto (1951), cello concerto (1966); *Cornet* (Rilke) for contralto and orchestra. Piano quintet, rhapsody for string quintet, string quartet, string trio, piano trio on Irish tunes; *Le vin herbé* for 12 voices, strings, and piano (on the subject of Tristram and Yseult, from Joseph Bédier, 1938–41); two violin and piano sonatas.

Martinez, Marianne (1744–1812) Austrian composer and keyboard player of Spanish descent. She was the daughter of the master of ceremonies to the pope's nuncio in Vienna. Her teachers were Metastasio, Porpora, and Haydn.

Works include: the oratorios *Isacco* (1782) and *Santa Elena al Calvario*, psalms translated by Metastasio, Mass, motets, cantatas; symphonies; overtures; concertos; sonatas.

Martini, Giovanni Battista (or Giambattista, known as Padre Martini) (1706–1784) Italian priest, theorist, teacher, and composer. As the most famous teacher and theorist of his time he attracted many distinguished pupils, including Mozart, and corresponded with musicians throughout Europe. His most important works are *Storia della musica*, the unfinished history of music in three volumes 1757–81, and *Saggio di contrappunto*, a treatise on counterpoint 1773–75.

He was born at Bologna, and received a thorough education from his father and others in violin, harpsichord, singing, and composition. He entered the Franciscan Order in 1721, was ordained priest in 1729, and was appointed maestro di cappella of San Francesco, Bologna in 1725, after which he rarely left his home town. He collected a vast musical and scientific library, and was a prolific composer of sacred vocal music.

Works include: about 1,500 works, with about 1,000 canons; oratorios *L'assunzione di Salomone* (1734), *San Pietro*, *Il sacrificio d'Abramo*; about 32 Masses, motets, psalm settings and other church music; stage works; keyboard works.

Martini, Jean Paul Egide (1741–1816), adopted name of Johann Paul Aegidius Schwartzendorf German organist and composer. He settled in France in 1760 and wrote the first of his 13 operas in 1771. He also wrote the song 'Plaisir d'amour'.

He adopted the name of Martini on settling in Nancy as a music teacher in 1760. Hé was in the service of the Duke of Lorraine (the former King Stanislaus of Poland) at Lunéville 1761–64, he then went to Paris, where he wrote military music and produced his first opera in 1771. After three years' absence during the Revolution, he returned to Paris in 1794 to become one of the inspectors of the Conservatory in 1795 and professor of composition in 1800. At the Restoration in 1814 he was appointed superintendent of the court music.

Works include: the operas *L'Amoureux de quinze ans* (1771), *Le Fermier cru sourd* (1772), *Le Rendezvous nocturne* (1773), *Henry IV* (1774), *Le Droit du Seigneur*, *L'Amant sylphe* (1783), *Sapho*, *Annette et Lubin* (1789), *Ziméo*, and others; two Masses, two Requiems, Te Deum, psalm settings and other church music, cantata for the marriage of Napoleon and Marie-Louise; chamber music; marches and other pieces for military band; songs including 'Plaisir d'amour'.

Martino, Donald (1931–) US composer. He studied with Bacon, Babbitt, and Sessions in the USA, and with Dallapiccola in Florence. He was professor of composition at the New England Conservatory of Music 1970–80, and Harvard from 1983. His works often feature his own instrument, the clarinet: quartet for clarinet and strings (1957); concerto for wind quintet (1964); B,A,B,B,I,T,T for clarinet (1966); cello concerto (1972); *Paradiso Choruses*, oratorio after Dante (1974); Triple Concerto for three clarinets and orchestra (1977); string quartet (1983).

Martinů, Bohuslav Jan (1890–1959) Czech composer. He settled in New York after the Nazi occupation of Czechoslovakia in 1939. His music is voluble, richly expressive, and has great vitality. His works include the operas *Julietta* 1937 and *The Greek Passion* 1959, symphonies, and chamber music.

He studied violin at the Prague Conservatory 1906–13 while playing in the Prague Philharmonic Orchestra. In 1922 he took composition lessons with Joseph Suk at the Prague Conservatory and studied with Albert Roussel in Paris 1923–24, and wrote works influenced by jazz and neoclassicism. Operas with Czech subjects followed during the 1930s, and after arriving in the USA as a refugee in 1941 he confined himself largely to instrumental music. He remained in the USA until 1946, when he became professor of composition at Prague Conservatory, returning to the USA in 1948, where he taught at

Princeton and the Berkshire Music Center. He chose not to return to Czechoslovakia after the Communist takeover in 1948, and lived in Switzerland from 1957. His music is often neoclassical in style, enriched with Czech folk song melody, and with an emphasis on rhythm and counterpoint.

Works include: OPERA *Julietta* (1938); *The Greek Passion* (1961); ballets *La revue de cuisine*, *Špalíček*.

CHORAL *Bouquet of Flowers*, *Field Mass* for solo voices, chorus, and orchestra; *The Epic of Gilgamesh*, oratorio (1955).

ORCHESTRAL six symphonies (1942–53); concerto for double string orchestra, piano, and timpani (1938), tone-poem *The Frescoes of Piero della Francesca* (1955), *Sinfonietta giocosa*, *Memorial to Lidice* (1943), *Tre Ricercari*; five piano concertos (1934–57), two violin concertos, two cello concertos, oboe concerto and various other works for instruments and orchestra.

CHAMBER two piano quintets (1933, 1944), nonet for wind and strings, and much other chamber music, three cello and piano sonatas; *Ritournelles*, and other pieces for piano.

Martín y Soler, Vicente (1754–1806) Spanish composer. He travelled widely, producing operas in Italy, Russia, and Vienna, notably *Una cosa rara* 1786, written in collaboration with the librettist Lorenzo da Ponte.

He was born at Valencia, and was a chorister there. He made his debut as an opera composer in Madrid in 1776, then went to Italy, where he probably studied with Padre Martini, and produced operas successfully in Naples, Turin, and Venice. In Vienna, 1785–88, he composed three operas on libretti by da Ponte, the most successful of which, *Una cosa rara* 1786, for a time eclipsed Mozart's *Marriage of Figaro*; Mozart quotes from it in the supper scene in *Don Giovanni*. Apart from a visit to London 1794–95, he lived from 1788 in St Petersburg, in the service of the Russian court.

Works include: OPERA *Ifigenia in Aulide* (1779), *Ipermestra*, *Andromaca* (1780), *Astartea*, *Partenope*, *L'amor geloso* (1782), *In amor si vuol destrezza* (*L'accorta cameriera*, 1782), *Vologeso*, *Le burle per amore* (1784), *La vedova spiritosa*, *Il burbero di buon cuore* (1786), *Una cosa rara*, *o Bellezza ed onestà* (1786), *L'arbore di Diana* (1787), *Gore Bogatyr Kosometovich* (1789), *Melomania* (Russian), *Fedul and his Children* (Russian; libretti of these three by Catherine II), *Il castello d'Atlante* (1791), *La scuola de' maritati* (1795), *L'isola del piacere* (1795), *Le nozze de contadini spagnuoli*, *La festa del villaggio* (1798).

OTHER prologue *La Dora festeggiante* for *Vologeso*; several ballets; church music; cantatas *La deità benefica* and *Il sogno*; *canzonets*; canons.

Martland, Steve (1958–) English composer. His music eschews classical principles and aspires to 'street cred'. *Babi Yar* for orchestra 1983, had a joint first performance with the Royal Liverpool Philharmonic Orchestra and the St Louis Symphony Orchestra.

He studied with Louis Andriessen at the Hague and with Gunther Schuller at Tanglewood in 1984.

Works include: *Lotta continua* for orchestra and jazz band (1981); *Orc* for horn and chamber orchestra (1984); *Crossing the Border* for strings (1991); *Remembering Lennon* for 7 players (1981); *American Invention* for 13 players (1985); *Patrol* for string quartet (1991); *Terra Firma* for 5 voices and video (1989); *The Perfect Act* for amplified ensemble and voice (1991); piano pieces and tape items.

Martucci, Giuseppe (1856–1909) Italian pianist, conductor, and composer. He travelled widely as a pianist, founded the Quartetto Napoletano for the cultivation of chamber music, and became an orchestral conductor. in 1888 he produced the first Italian performance of Wagner's *Tristan* at Bologna.

He was first taught by his father, a bandmaster, and appeared as a pianist in his childhood. He then studied at the Naples Conservatory 1867–72, and became professor there in 1874. In 1886 he was appointed director of the Liceo Musicale at Bologna and there produced *Tristan* in 1888. In 1902 he returned to Naples as director of the Conservatory.

Works include: the oratorio *Samuele*; two symphonies, *4 piccoli pezzi* for orchestra; piano concertos in D minor, B♭ minor (1878, 1885); piano quintet, two piano trios; cello and piano sonata; various instrumental pieces; variations and fantasy for two pianos; songs, 'Pagine sparse', 'Due sogni', and others.

Martyrdom of St Magnus, The chamber opera in nine scenes by Peter Maxwell Davies (libretto by composer, from 'Magnus' by George Mackay Brown), produced Kirkwall, Orkney, 18 June 1977. Orkney's patron saint murdered by Hakon, Earl of Orkney.

Martyre de Saint Sébastien, Le/The Martyrdom of St Sebastian incidental music by Debussy for the mystery play, written in French, by G d'Annunzio, composed for solo voices, chorus, and orchestra in 1911, first performed Paris, Théâtre du Châtelet, 22 May 1911, in five acts.

Martyrs, Les opera by Donizetti (libretto by Scribe, based on Corneille's *Polyeucte*), produced Paris, Opéra, 10 April 1840. See also ◊*Poliuto*.

Marx, Adolph Bernard (1795–1866) German musicologist and composer. He studied law, but gave it up for music, to which he devoted himself in 1824 he founded the *Berliner Allgemeine Musikalische Zeitung*. In 1830 he became professor of music and in 1850 founded a music school with Kullak and Stern (later Stern Conservatory). He wrote books on the history of music, teaching, on Gluck, Handel, Beethoven, composition, and tone-painting.

Works include: the opera *Jery und Bätely* (Goethe, 1824); melodrama *Die Rache wartet*; oratorios *Johannes der Täufer*, *Moses* (1841), *Nahid und Omar*; instrumental works.

Marx, Joseph (1882–1964) Austrian composer. He studied in Vienna and in 1922 became director of the Academy of Music there in succession to Ferdinand Löwe. From 1947 he was professor at Graz University

Works include: *Autumn Symphony* (1921); *Symphonic Night Music*, *Spring Music* for orchestra; romantic concerto for piano and orchestra; several choral pieces; three string quartets, piano quartet, fantasy for piano trio; violin and piano sonata, cello and piano sonata; c. 120 songs.

Marx, Karl (1897–1985) German composer. He studied natural science at first, but met Carl Orff during World War I and later studied music with him. He was appointed professor of the Munich Academy in 1924 and was conductor of the Bach Society there in 1928. From 1939 to 1945 he taught at Graz Conservatory, becoming professor in 1944, and in 1946 he became professor at the Hochschule für Musik in Stuttgart. He was much occupied with school music.

Works include: a passacaglia for orchestra (1932); concertos for piano, violin, two violins, viola and flute; various choral works, some to words by Rilke; divertimento for wind instruments (1934), string quartet and other chamber music; songs, some to words by Rilke.

marziale musical term; 'martial, warlike'.

Masagniello furioso oder Die neapolitanische Fischer-Empörung/Masagniello enraged, or The Neapolitan Fisherman's Revolt opera by Keiser (libretto by Barthold Feind), produced Hamburg, Theater beim

Gänsemarkt, June 1706. Masagniello leads his people against unfair taxes, but goes mad and is killed.

Masaniello (Auber). See ◊*Muette de Portici, La.*

Mascagni, Pietro (1863–1945) Italian composer. His one-act opera *Cavalleria rusticana/ Rustic Chivalry* was first produced in Rome 1890 in the new verismo or realistic style.

He was born at Livorno; his father, a baker, wished him to study law, but he managed to take lessons in secret at the Instituto Cherubini. On being discovered, he was adopted by an uncle, and soon reconciled with his father by having two works performed at the Instituto. Later, Count Florestano de Larderel paid for his further musical education at the Milan Conservatory, where Ponchielli was among his masters. Not wishing to apply himself to solid study, he ran away with a travelling opera company. After many wanderings and a marriage that forced him to settle at Cerignola near Foggia to make a precarious living by teaching the piano and conducting the local band, he won the first prize in an operatic competition with *Cavalleria rusticana* in 1889, and after its production in Rome the following year, he began to accumulate a great fortune, though his many later operas never repeated its success. Besides operas, he wrote some occasional works, cantatas, and the incidental music for Hall Caine's *The Eternal City*, produced in London in 1902. He became a member of the Italian Academy in 1929.

Works include: OPERA *Cavalleria rusticana* (1890), *L'amico Fritz* (1891), *I Rantzau* (both based on Erckmann-Chatrian), *Guglielmo Ratcliff* (after Heine, 1895), *Silvano*, *Zanetto* (1896), *Iris*, *Le maschere*, *Amica* (1905), *Isabeau* (1911), *Parisina* (d'Annunzio), *Lodoletta* (1917), *Il piccolo Marat* (1921), *Pinotta*, *Nerone* (1935); operetta *Si*.

OTHER incidental music for Hall Caine's *The Eternal City*; *Kyrie*, Requiem in memory of King Humbert; cantata for Leopardi centenary (1898), setting of Italian translation of Schiller's 'Ode to Joy' for chorus and orchestra, cantata *In Filanda*; symphony in C minor, symphonic poem for a film *Rapsodia satanica* (1917).

mascherata (Italian 'masquerade') type of 16th-century *villanella*, sung at masked balls or during fancy-dress processions.

Maschere, Le opera by Mascagni (libretto by L Illica), produced Genoa, Milan, Rome, Turin, Venice and Verona, 17 January 1901. Rosaura wishes to marry Florindo but her

father Pantalone lines up Captain Spaventa for her.

Maschinist Hopkins opera by Max Brand (libretto by composer), produced Duisburg, 13 April 1929. The opera pre-figures several dramatic themes in Berg's *Lulu* and was widely performed in Europe before the rise of the Nazis. First complete post-war performance BBC, London, 9 February 1986. Hopkins saves his factory from closure by Bill, who has murdered his wife's first husband. Hopkins blackmails Bill, who seeks to destroy his enemy's shop, but he falls into the machinery and is killed.

masculine cadence a cadence, or full close; the final note or chord of which falls on a strong accented beat of a bar.

mask see ◊masque.

Maskarade opera by Nielsen (libretto by V Andersen after a play by Holberg); composed 1904–06, first performed Copenhagen, 11 November 1906. Leander meets future wife at masked ball.

Mask of Orpheus, The opera by Birtwistle (libretto by P Zinovieff), composed 1973–84, produced London, Coliseum, 21 May 1986. Main characters in legend seen from three different viewpoints: person, hero, myth.

Mask of Time, The oratorio by Tippett in two parts for soloists, chorus and orchestra; composed 1981–83, first performed Boston, 5 April 1984, conductor C Davis.

Masnadieri, I/The Brigands opera by Verdi (libretto by A Maffei, based on Schiller's drama *Die Räuber*), produced London, Her Majesty's Theatre, 22 July 1847. The only opera commissioned by London from Verdi. Jenny Lind and Lablache appeared in it. Carlo joins band of robbers after betrayal by his brother, Francesco, and disinheritance by his father, Massimiliano. Carlo seeks revenge against Francesco and in the process kills the orphan Amalia.

Mason, Benedict (1954–) English composer. His highly eclectic and allusive music includes *Playing Away*, premiered in Munich in 1994, which was alleged to be the first opera to be based on football.

He studied with Peter Maxwell Davies, and with Pousseur in Liège. He has won several international prizes, including the Siemens Stiftungpreis in 1992.

Works include: *Lighthouses of England and Wales* for orchestra (1987) and *Concerto for the Viola Section* (1990); *The Hinterstoisser Traverse* for 12 players (1986), *Nodding Trilliums and Curved Line Angles* for four solo percussion and 15 players (1990); *Chaplin Operas* for mezzo, baritone, and 22 players (1988), *Seven Self-Referential Songs and Realistic Virelais* for soprano and 16 players (1990); electronic pieces *Six Rilke Songs* (1991), *Animals and the Origins of the Dance* (1992) and *Colour and Information* (1993); *Oil and Petrol Marks on a Wet Road are sometimes held to be spots where a rainbow stood*, for 16 voices (1987); two string quartets (1987, 1993); six Etudes for piano (1988).

masque spectacular and essentially aristocratic entertainment with a fantastic or mythological theme in which music, dance, and extravagant costumes and scenic design figured larger than plot. Originating in Italy, where members of the court actively participated in the performances, the masque reached its height of popularity at the English court between 1600 and 1640, with the collaboration of Ben ◊Jonson as writer and Inigo Jones as stage designer. John Milton also wrote masque verses. Composers included Thomas Campion, John Coperario, Henry Lawes, William Byrd, and Henry Purcell.

The masque had great influence on the development of ballet and opera, and the elaborate frame in which it was performed developed into the proscenium arch.

Masques et bergamasques music by Fauré, op. 112, for an entertainment by René Fauchois produced Monte Carlo, 10 April 1919; Paris, Opéra-Comique, 4 March 1920, with a Watteau setting. It included an overture and three dances, newly composed, as well as the Pavane, op. 50, of 1887 and an orchestral version of the Verlaine song 'Clair de Lune', op. 46 no. 2, of the same year, in which the words 'masques et bergamasques' occur.

Mass the setting of the invariable parts of the Christian Mass, that is the *Kyrie, Gloria, Credo, Sanctus* with *Benedictus*, and *Agnus Dei*. A notable example is J S Bach's *Mass in B Minor*.

The Proper of the Mass consists of additional matter (Introit, Gradual, Alleluia or Tract, Offertory, and Communion), and these are less commonly found as parts of a Mass composition.

The medieval practice of writing the movements of a Mass on plainsong melodies, sung by the tenor, was soon extended to the employment of secular tunes. *L'Homme armé* on the continent and *The Western Wind* in England, for example, were especially favoured for this purpose. In the course of the 16th century, however, more and more

composers wrote wholly original Masses, though the practice of borrowing material from motets or *chansons* was also common. Even in later times the treatment of the Mass remained essentially polyphonic, though not necessarily throughout. Certain portions, 'Et vitam venturi saeculi' at the end of the Credo, were almost invariably set as fugues.

Massé, Victor (actually Félix Marie) (1822–1884) French composer. He studied at the Paris Conservatory, where Halévy was his composition master, and gained the Prix de Rome in 1844. He travelled in Italy and Germany after his stay in Rome; in 1860 became chorus-master at the Paris Opéra and in 1866 professor of composition at the Conservatory.

Works include: OPERAS AND OPERETTAS *La Chambre gothique* (1849), *La Chanteuse violée* (1850), *Galathée* (1852), *Les Noces de Jeannette* (1853), *La Reine Topaze* (1856), *Le Cousin de Marivaux* (1857), *La Fiancée du Diable, Miss Fauvette, Les Saisons, La Fée Carabosse, Mariette la promise* (1862), *La Mule de Pedro* (1863), *Fior d'Aliza* (after Lamartine, 1866), *Le Fils du brigadier* (1867), *Paul et Virginie* (after Saint-Pierre), *La favorita e la schiava, Les Chaises à porteurs, Le Prix de famille, Une Loi somptuaire, Les Enfants de Perrette, La Petite Sœur d'Achille, La Trouvaille* (composed 1873), *Une Nuit de Cléopâtre* (1885).

OTHER *Messe solennelle*; cantata *Le Rénégat*; songs.

Massenet, Jules Emile Frédéric (1842–1912) French composer of operas. His work is characterized by prominent roles for females, sincerity, and sentimentality. Notable works are *Manon* 1884, *Le Cid* 1885, and *Thaïs* 1894; among other works is the orchestral suite *Scènes pittoresques* 1874. He was professor of composition at the Paris Conservatory 1878–96.

His long and successful career included no fewer than 27 operas, mainly for the Paris Opéra and Opéra-Comique, and the Monte Carlo Opera. There have been revivals of some of his lesser-known works since the 1980s.

Massenet was born at Montaud, St Etienne, and entered the Paris Conservatory at the age of 11, studying composition with A Thomas and winning the Prix de Rome in 1863. On his return from Rome in 1866 he married a piano pupil and had his first opera, *La Grand'tante*, produced at the Opéra-Comique the next year. He achieved his first major success with the opera *Le Roi de Lahore* 1877, indulging a current taste for the exotic and oriental.

Similar success came with *Hérodiade* (Brussels, 1881) but lasting fame came with *Manon*, premiered in Paris in 1884, in which Massenet indulged to the full the lifelong sympathy he felt for his central female characters. In *Werther* 1892, the lyrical impulse is balanced with a strong dramatic flair. Later operas such as *Cendrillon*, *Grisélidis*, *Chérubin*, and *Don Quichotte* have found recognition as a result of recent revivals.

Works include: OPERA *Don César de Bazan* (1872), *Le Roi de Lahore* (1877), *Hérodiade* (1881), *Manon* (after Prévost, 1884), *Le Cid* (after Corneille, 1885), *Esclarmonde* (1889), *Le Mage*, *Werther* (after Goethe, 1892), *Le Portrait de Manon*, *La Navarraise* (1894), *Sapho* (after Daudet), *Cendrillon* (1899), *Grisélidis* (1901), *Le jongleur de Notre-Dame* (1902), *Thaïs* (1894), (both after A France), *Chérubin* (1905), *Ariane* (1906), *Thérèse* (1907), *Bacchus*, *Don Quichotte* (after Cervantes, 1910), *Roma*, *Panurge* (after Rabelais), *Cléopâtre* (1914), *Amadis* (composed 1895; produced 1922).

OTHER ballets *Le Carillon*, *La Cigale*, *Espada*; incidental music to Leconte de Lisle's *Les Erynnies*, Racine's *Phèdre*, and other plays. Oratorios *Marie-Magdeleine* (1873), *ve* (1875), *La Vierge*, *La Terre promise* (1900); cantatas *David Rizzio*, *Narcisse*, *Biblis*. 13 orchestral works including *Scènes pittoresques* (1874), *Scènes napolitaines* (1876), and three other similar suites, symphonic poem *Visions*; piano concerto, fantasy for cello and orchestra; about 200 songs; duets; choruses.

mässig musical term; 'moderate'.

Massimilla Doni opera by Schoeck (libretto by A Rüeger, based on Balzac's novel), produced Dresden, 2 March 1937. Massimilla falls for Emilio in Venetian fable, set at La Fenice opera house. Subplot balances the artistic virtues of technique versus passion.

Mass in B minor (Bach). See ◊*B minor Mass*.

Mass of Life, A setting of words from Nietzsche's *Also sprach Zarathustra* for solo voices, chorus, and orchestra by Delius, composed 1904–05, produced (second part only in German) Munich Music Festival, 1908; first complete performance (in English), London, 7 June 1909, conductor Beecham.

Master of the King's/Queen's Music(k) honorary appointment to the British royal household, the holder composing appropriate music for state occasions. The first was Nicholas Lanier, appointed by Charles I 1626; later appointments have included Edward Elgar and Arthur Bliss. The present

holder, Malcolm ◊Williamson, was appointed in 1975.

Master Peter's Puppet Show (Falla). See ◊*Retablo de Maese Pedro*.

mastersinger English for ◊Meistersinger.

Mastersingers of Nuremberg, The (Wagner). See ◊*Meistersinger von Nürnberg, Die*.

Mathias, William (1934–1992) Welsh composer and pianist. He studied at the Royal Academy of Music with Lennox Berkeley and Peter Katin. He was lecturer at University College of North Wales 1959–68, and professor from 1970.

Works include: the opera *The Servants* (1980); *Divertimento* for strings (1958), Concerto for Orchestra (1966), three symphonies (1966, 1983, 1991), *Dance Variations* for orchestra (1977); concertos for piano (1955, 1961, 1968), harp (1970), clarinet (1975), horn (1982); *In Arcadia* for orchestra (1992); *This Worldes Joie* for soloists, chorus, and orchestra (1974); *Lux Eterna* for soloists, chorus, organ, and orchestra (1982), *Let us now praise famous men* for chorus and orchestra (1984); two violin sonatas, wind quintet, two piano sonatas (1964, 1979), two string quartets (1968, 1982).

Mathis der Maler/Matthew the Painter opera by Hindemith (libretto by composer), produced Zurich, 28 May 1938. The painter is Matthias Grünewald (15th–16th centuries). Symphony in three movements performed Berlin, 12 March 1934, conductor Furtwängler: *Engelkonzert* (*Concert of Angels*), *Grablegung* (*Entombment*), *Versuchung des heiligen Antonius* (*The Temptation of St Anthony*). Grunewald at first sides with the peasants against the Church authorities, but retreats into his art after witnessing the cruel reality of life.

Matilde di Shabran, ossia Bellezza e cuor di ferro/Matilde of Shabran or Beauty and Heart of Iron opera by Rossini (libretto by J Ferretti), produced Rome, Teatro Apollo, 24 February 1821. Corradino orders poet Isidoro to murder Matilde for supposedly allowing his enemy Edoardo to escape from the dungeon. When Matilde's innocence is proved, Corradino resolves to commit suicide, but is prevented by Edoardo and his father Raimondo.

Matin, Le, Le Midi, Le Soir et la Tempête/ Morning, Noon, Evening and Storm the original titles of Haydn's symphonies Nos. 6 in D major, 7 in C major and 8 in G major, composed 1761.

matins the first Roman Catholic office (or non-Eucharistic service) of the day. It is also used by the Anglican Church to refer to Morning Prayer.

Matrimonio segreto, II/The Clandestine Marriage opera by Cimarosa (libretto by G Bertati, based on G Colman and D Garrick's play of that name), produced Vienna, Burgtheater, 7 February 1792. Geronimo wants to marry his daughter Elisetta to Count Robinson, but the Count prefers her sister, Caroline, who is already secretly married to Paolino. The marriage is revealed and the Count settles for Elisetta.

Mattei, Stanislao (1750–1825) Italian priest, theorist, and composer. He was a pupil of Padre Martini, whom he succeeded as maestro di cappella at the church of San Francesco in Bologna, and later at San Petronio. From 1804 he was professor at the newly founded Liceo Filarmonico; his pupils included Rossini and Donizetti. He wrote a treatise on playing from figured bass.

Works include: eight Masses and other church music; a Passion; intermezzo *La bottega del libraio*.

Mattheson, Johann (1681–1764) German writer on music, organist, and composer. Among his many writings on music the most important are *Der vollkommene Capellmeister* 1739, *Grundlage einer Ehrenpforte* 1740, and a treatise on thorough-bass.

From the age of nine he sang at the Hamburg Opera, and there produced his first opera in 1699. He became friendly with Handel in 1703 and went with him to Lübeck as a candidate to succeed Buxtehude; but both declined on learning that marriage to Buxtehude's daughter was a condition of the post. After some years as a tutor, then as secretary to the English Legation, he was appointed minor canon and music director at Hamburg Cathedral in 1715, but had to resign in 1728 because of his deafness.

Works include: the operas *Die Pleiades* (1699); *Die unglückselige Cleopatra* (1704), *Henrico IV*, *Boris Goudenow* (1710), and *Nero* (1723); 24 oratorios and cantatas; trio sonatas; keyboard music.

Matthews, Colin (1946–) English composer. He studied at Nottingham University and taught at Sussex University 1972–77. He worked with Deryck Cooke on the performing version of Mahler's tenth symphony and was assistant to Britten 1974–76; he edited and issued several early 'bottom drawer' pieces by Britten. He is the brother of David ◊Matthews.

Works include: two *Sonatas* for orchestra (1975, 1980), cello concerto (1984), *Night's*

Mask for soprano and chamber orchestra (1984); *Ceres* for nine players (1972), *Rainbow Studies* for piano and four wind (1978), three string quartets (1979, 1982, 1993), oboe quartet (1981); *Five Sonnets: to Orpheus* (texts by Rilke) for tenor and harp (1976), *Shadows in the Water* for tenor and piano (1978); *A Rose at Christmas* for unaccompanied voices (1992).

Matthews, David (1943–) English composer. He is the brother of Colin ◊Matthews, with whom he collaborated with Deryck Cooke, on performing version of Mahler's tenth symphony. He graduated in Classics from Nottingham University, and worked as an assistant to Benjamin Britten 1966–69. He published a biography of Tippett in 1980.

Works include: four symphonies (1975, 1979, 1985, 1990); three songs for soprano and orchestra (1971); six string quartets (1970–90); *Songs and Dances of Mourning* for cello (1976); *September Music* for small orchestra (1979); *Serenade* for chamber orchestra (1982); violin concerto (1982); clarinet quartet (1984); *In The Dark Time* for orchestra (1985); Variations for Strings (1986); *Chaconne* for orchestra (1987); *Cantiga* for soprano and ensemble (1988); *The Music of Dawn* for orchestra (1990); oboe concerto (1992); *A Vision and a Journey* for orchestra (1993).

Matthisson, Friedrich von (1761–1831) German poet. He is remembered chiefly for Beethoven's setting of his 'Adelaide'; Schubert set 26 of his poems.

Matthus, Siegfried (1934–) German composer. His music is in a conservative idiom and includes the operas *Der letzte Schuss* 1967, *Noch ein Löffel Gift, Liebling?* 1972, *Omphale* 1976, *Judith* 1984, *Die Weise von Liebe des Cornets Christoph Rilke* 1984, *Graf Mirabeau* 1988, and *Desdemona und ihrer Schwestern* 1992.

He studied in East Berlin during the 1950s, with Wagner-Régeny and Hanns Eisler. In 1964 he was appointed composer-in-residence at the Komische Oper Berlin.

Works include: three symphonies (1969, 1976, 1993), concerto for orchestra (1963), concertos for violin (1968), piano (1970), cello (1975), flute (1978), oboe (1985), and triangle (1985); Vocal Symphony for soprano, baritone, two choruses, and orchestra (1967), *Holofernes Portrait* for baritone and orchestra (1981), *Wem ich zu gefallen suche* for tenor, baritone, and piano (1987); two octets (1970, 1989), string quartet (1972).

Mauduit, Jacques (1557–1627) French lutenist and composer. He was, like his father before him, registrar to the courts of justice in

Paris, but became famous as a musician. In 1588 he saved the manuscripts of his Huguenot friend Claude Le Jeune from destruction by Catholic soldiers, though he was himself a Catholic.

In 1581 he won first prize at the annual Puy de Musique at Evreux, and he was associated with Jean-Antoine de Baïf (1532–1589) in his experiments with *musique mesurée*, though after Baïf's death he relaxed the rigid subordination of music to verbal rhythm in his settings of verse.

Works include: Requiem on the death of the poet Ronsard (1585), motets, chansons, chansonnettes mesurées for four voices, and other pieces.

Maunder, John Henry (1858–1920) English composer and organist. His oratorio *The Martyrs* was performed in Oxford in 1894 and his church cantata *From Olivet to Calvary* 1904 was popular for many years.

He studied at the Royal Academy of Music and later played the organ in various London churches. He first wrote operettas, including *The Superior Sex* and *Daisy Dingle* 1885, but then turned to sacred music.

Má Vlast/My Country cycle of six symphonic poems by Smetana, composed 1874–79 and containing programme works on various aspects of Czech history and geography: 1. *Vyšehrad/The Citadel of Prague*; 2. *Vltava/The River*; 3. *Šárka/The Czech Amazon*; 4. *From Bohemia's Woods and Fields*; 5. *Tabor/The City*; 6. *Blaník/The Mountain*.

Mavra opera in one act by Stravinsky (libretto in Russian, by B Koshno, based on Pushkin's *The Little House at Kolomna*), produced in French translation by J Larmanjat, Paris, Opéra, 3 June 1922. 'Mavra' is Parasha's lover Vasily, a hussar disguised as a cook in her mother's house. However, Mavra is discovered shaving, and her true identity is revealed.

Maw, Nicholas (1935–) English composer. His music is largely traditional in character. He studied with Lennox Berkeley at the Royal Academy of Music 1955–58 and with Nadia Boulanger in Paris 1958–59. He taught at Cambridge University 1966–70 and at Yale.

Works include: Requiem for soprano and contralto soloists, women's chorus, string trio, and string orchestra; comic operas *One Man Show* (1964) and *The Rising of the Moon* (1970); *Nocturne* for mezzo-soprano and orchestra (1958); *Scenes and Arias* for solo voices and orchestra (1962); Sonata for strings and two horns (1967); *La Vita Nuova* for soprano and chamber ensemble (1979); *Morning Music* for orchestra (1982); *Spring Music* for orchestra (1983); *Sonata Notturno* for cello and strings (1985); *Odyssey* for orchestra (1972–85); *The World in the Evening* for orchestra (1988), *Little concert* for oboe, two horns, and strings (1988), *Shahnama* for orchestra (1992); *Life Studies* for 15 solo strings (1973–76); Chamber Music for flute, clarinet, horn, bassoon, and piano (1962); two string quartets (1965, 1982); *Music of Memory* for guitar (1989).

Maximilien opera by Milhaud (libretto by A Lunel, translated from a German libretto by R S Hoffmann, based on Franz Werfel's play, *Juarez und Maximilian*), produced Paris, Opéra, 4 January 1932. Misfortunes of Habsburg monarch in Mexican war.

Maxwell Davies, Peter see Peter Maxwell ◊Davies.

Mayer, Robert (1879–1985) German-born British philanthropist. He founded the Robert Mayer Concerts for Children and the Transatlantic Foundation Anglo-American Scholarships. KCVO 1979.

Maynard, John (1577–after 1614) English lutenist and composer. He was connected with the school of St Julian in Hertfordshire, and at some time in the service of Lady Joan Thynne at Cause Castle in Shropshire.

Works include: pavans and galliards for the lute; an organ piece; lessons for lute and bass viol and for lyra-viol; 12 songs *The XII Wonders of the World*, describing various characters, for voice, lute, and viola da gamba.

May Night/Maïskaya Notch opera by Rimsky-Korsakov (libretto by composer, based on a story by Gogol), produced St Petersburg, 21 January 1880. Levko's wedding to Hanna made possible by help from water sprites.

Mayone, Ascanio (c. 1565–1627) Italian composer. He studied with Jean de Macque in Naples, was appointed organist at the Annunziata, Naples in 1593 and maestro di cappella there from 1621.

Works include: madrigals, and solo and chamber instrumental music. His two volumes of keyboard music, *Capricci per sonar* (1603, 1609) contain canzonas and toccatas in an advanced idiom.

Mayrhofer, Johann (1787–1836) Austrian poet; 47 of his poems were set by Schubert. See also ◊Freunde von Salamanka, Die (Schubert).

Mayseder, Joseph (1789–1863) Austrian violinist and composer. He first appeared in Vienna in 1800, and later held several important appointments, including that of chamber musician to the emperor.

Works include: Mass; three violin concertos; eight string quartets; five string quintets; piano trios and other chamber music, violin duets; piano pieces and studies for violin.

Mazas, Jacques (Féréol) (1782–1849) French violinist and composer. He appeared with a violin concerto written for him by Auber, travelled widely, lived in Paris 1829–37, and was director of the music school at Cambrai 1837–41.

He studied under Pierre Baillot at the Paris Conservatory.

Works include: the opera *Le Kiosque* (1842); two violin concertos; string quartets; violin duets; many violin pieces.

Mazeppa opera by Tchaikovsky (libretto by composer and V P Burenin, based on Pushkin's *Poltava*), produced Moscow, Bolshoi Theatre, 15 February 1884. Mazeppa demands Judge Kochubey's daughter Maria as a wife. Kochubey denounces Mazeppa as a separatist but the Tsar does not believe him. Mazeppa has Kochubey executed and Maria goes insane.

Symphonic poem by Liszt, composed in 1854 on Victor Hugo's poem and on the basis of one of the *Grandes Etudes pour le piano* of c. 1838 and their new version, the *Etudes d'exécution transcendante* of 1851, first performed Weimar, 16 April 1854.

mazurka any of a family of traditional Polish dances from the 16th century, characterized by foot-stamping and heel-clicking, together with a turning movement. The music for the mazurka is in triple time (3/4), with dotted rhythms and the accentuation of weak beats, on which phrases also begin and end. It is found at a variety of speeds, but is usually not as fast as the waltz, which is also formally a more rigid dance than the mazurka. During the 18th and 19th centuries, it spread throughout Europe and was made famous by Chopin's approximately 60 works in the genre. Other composers of the mazurka include Karol Szymanowski, Glinka, and Mussorgsky.

Mazzocchi, Domenico (1592–1665) Italian composer. His music has some of the earliest printed ◊dynamics, including 'crescendo' and 'diminuendo'.

He was in the service of the Aldobrandini Borghese family for 20 years.

Works include: the opera *La catena d'Adone* (1626); oratorios *Querimonia di S Maria Maddalena, Il martirio dei Santi Abbundia ed Abbundanzio* (1641); *Musiche sacre*; madrigals, *Dialoghi e sonetti*.

Mazzocchi, Virgilio (1597–1646) Italian composer, brother of Domenico ◊Mazzocchi. He was maestro di cappella at St John Lateran in Rome, 1628–29, and then at St Peter's until his death.

Works include: the operas *Chi soffre speri* (with Marazzoli, 1637) and *L'innocenza difesa* (1641); psalms for double chorus; *Sacri flores* for two–four voices.

mbira term used in the singular to describe several types of large gourd-resonated lamellophones throughout southeast Africa, especially Zimbabwe. Tuned metal strips are attached to a soundboard and amplified by a gourd or box resonator. Also known to non-Africans as a 'finger piano', 'thumb piano', or 'hand piano'.

Meale, Richard (1932–) Australian composer. He studied as a pianist at New South Wales Conservatory. His later music has been influenced by Boulez, Messiaen, and Indonesian music.

Works include: the operas *Voss* (1979–86) and *Mer de Glace* (1986–91); *Images* for orchestra (1966), *Clouds Now and Then* for orchestra (1969); *Viridian* for strings (1979); Symphony (1994); flute sonata (1960), wind quintet (1970), two string quartets (1974, 1980).

meantone in tuning, the meantone system was a common technique used for keyboard instruments before ◊equal temperament came into general use. It provided for the pure intonation of the key of C major and those lying near it at the expense of the more extreme sharp and flat keys, which is the reason why remote keys were rarely used in keyboard works, before the adoption of equal temperament. There was, for example, a pure F♯ and B♭, but these notes were out of tune when used as G♭ or A♯.

Meares, Richard (died c. 1722) English instrument maker. He made lutes, viols, and other string instruments in London in the second half of the 17th century.

Meares, Richard (died 1743) English instrument maker and music publisher, son of Richard ◊Meares. He succeeded to his father's business, but enlarged it by selling not only instruments, but music books and cutlery, and he began to publish music around 1714, including several operas by Handel, such as *Radamisto*, 1720.

measure US term for ◊bar.

Medea play with music (melodrama) by G Benda (text by F W Gotter), produced Leipzig, 1 May 1775. For plot synopsis, ◊*Medea in Corinto.*

Medea in Corinto opera (*melodramma tragico*) by Mayr (libretto by F Romani); produced Naples, Teatro San Carlo, 28 November 1813. Medea takes revenge on treacherous husband Jason by killing their children and his lover, Creusa.

Médecin malgré lui, Le/Doctor against his Will opera by Gounod (libretto, a small alteration of Molière's comedy by composer, J Barbier and M Carré), produced Paris, Théâtre Lyrique, 15 January 1858. Doctor Sganarelle helps Lucinde escape the attentions of a rich suitor and elope with lover Léandre.

Médée opera by Marc-Antoine Charpentier (libretto by T Corneille), produced Paris. Opéra, 4 December 1693.

Opera by Cherubini (libretto by F B Hoffmann), produced Paris, Théâtre Feydeau, 13 March 1797. Abandoned by Jason, Medea poisons his new wife and kills their two sons.

Opera by Milhaud (libretto by Madeleine Milhaud, the composer's wife), produced Flemish translation, Antwerp, 7 October 1939.

medesimo tempo (Italian 'same time') a musical direction indicating that a change of metre does not imply a change of pace. The more usual term is *l'istesso tempo* (formerly *lo stesso tempo*).

mediant the third note (or degree) of the ◊diatonic scale, for example E in the C major scale. A chord of the ·mediant is a ◊triad (chord of three notes) built upon the mediant note.

Medium, The opera in two acts by Menotti (libretto by the composer, produced Columbia University, New York, 8 May 1946. Fraudulent medium Baba accidentally kills her mute assistant Toby, believing him to be a genuine ghost.

Medtner, Nikolai Karlovich (1880–1951), or Metner Russian composer. His music is almost wholly confined to piano works (including three concertos and 12 sonatas) and to songs, but he also wrote three sonatas and three Nocturnes for violin and piano, and at the end of his life he produced a Quintet for strings and piano. Characteristic titles are *Improvisations, Dithyrambs, Fairy Tales,* and *Novels.*

Medtner was born in Moscow. He studied piano under Vassily Safonov at the Moscow Conservatory, won the Rubinstein Prize

there, and toured Europe as a pianist 1901–02, becoming professor at the Conservatory for a year on his return. He then retired to devote himself to composition. After the Revolution he taught at a school in Moscow and in 1921 went on another tour in the West, but found himself unable to return. He settled in Paris for a time and later in London, where he died.

As a keyboard composer he is as important, and in his way as characteristic, as Chopin or Schumann. His numerous songs are deeply felt and tasteful, with piano parts as important as those for the voice. For their words he relied largely upon Russian and German poets, including Pushkin, Tyutchev, Goethe, and Heine. Sponsored by the Maharajah of Mysore, he made gramophone recordings of many of his own works, including all three concertos.

Works include: three piano concertos (1914–43); piano quintet; three sonatas and three nocturnes for violin and piano; 12 piano sonatas and a great number of pieces for piano including *Fairy Tales* op. 8, 9, 14, 20, 26, 34, 35, 42, 48, 51, *Forgotten Melodies* op. 38–40, *Dithyrambs, Novels, Lyric Fragments, Improvisations, Hymns in Praise of Toil,* and others; *Russian Dance* and *Knight-Errant* for two pianos; sonata-vocalise for voice and piano; 17 op. nos. of songs to words by Pushkin, Tiutchev, Goethe, Heine, Nietzsche, and others.

Meeresstille und Glückliche Fahrt/Calm Sea and Prosperous Voyage two poems by Goethe, set by Beethoven as a cantata for chorus and orchestra in 1815, op. 112, and dedicated to the poet; and used by Mendelssohn as the subject for a concert overture, op. 27, in 1828. Elgar quotes from the latter in the romance of the 'Enigma' Variations.

Mefistofele opera by Boito (libretto by composer, based on Goethe's *Faust*), produced Milan, La Scala, 5 March 1868. Faust gains moment of happiness but loses Margherita after accidentally poisoning her mother. Faust repents and eludes Mephistopheles.

Méhul, Etienne Nicolas (1763–1817) French composer. *Euphrosine* 1790 established him as an opera composer, after which he became one of the most notable composers of the Revolution, his greatest success being *Joseph* 1807.

He became an organist in his home town at the age of ten, and went to Paris in 1778, where Gluck encouraged him to write for the stage. He took piano lessons from Edelmann, and supported himself by teaching until the success of the operas *Euphrosine* 1790 and *Stratonice* 1792. On the foundation of the Conservatory in 1795 he became one of its inspectors. His overture *Le jeune Henri* and operas *Uthal* and *Joseph* are notable for their novel instrumental effects.

Works include: OPERA *Euphrosine et Coradin, ou Le tyran corrigé* (1790), *Cora, Stratonice* (1792), *Le jeune sage et le vieux fou* (1793), *Horatius Coclès, Mélidore. et Phrosine* (1794), *La caverne, Doria, Le jeune Henri* (1797), *Le Pont de Lodi* (1797), *Adrien, Ariodant* (1799), *Epicure* (with Cherubini), *Bion, L'irato, ou L'emporté* (1801), *Une Folie, Le trésor supposé* (1802), *Joanna, Héléna* (1803), *Le baiser et la quittance* (with Kreutzer, Boieldieu, and Isouard, 1803), *L'Heureux malgré lui, Les deux aveugles de Tolède* (1806), *Uthal* (without violins), *Gabrielle d'Estrés, Joseph* (1807), *Les Amazones, Le Prince Troubadour* (1813), *L'Oriflamme* (with Paer, Berton, and Kreutzer, 1814), *La journée aux aventures* (1816), *Valentine de Milan* (unfinished, completed by his nephew Louis Joseph Daussoigne-Méhul (1790–1875).

BALLETS *Le jugement de Paris* (with additions from Haydn and Pleyel), *La dansomanie* (1800), *Daphnis et Pandrose* (1803), *Persée et Andromède* (1810)

OTHER incidental music to Joseph Chénier's *Timoléon*; Mass for the coronation of Napoleon I (not performed); cantatas *Chanson de Roland, Chant lyrique* (for the unveiling of Napoleon's statue at the Institut); patriotic songs 'Chant national du 14 juillet', 'Chant du départ', 'Chant de retour'; symphony; two piano sonatas.

Mei, Girolamo (1519–1594) Italian music theorist. His four surviving works include the *Discorso sopra la musica antica e moderna/ Discourse on ancient and modern music*, published at Venice in 1602.

Meistersinger (German 'master singer') one of a group of German lyric poets, singers, and musicians of the 14th–16th centuries, who formed guilds for the revival of minstrelsy. Hans ◊Sachs was a Meistersinger, and Wagner's opera *Die Meistersinger von Nürnberg/The Mastersingers of Nürnberg* 1868 depicts the tradition.

Meistersinger von Nürnberg, Die/The Mastersingers of Nuremberg music drama by Wagner (libretto by composer), produced Munich, Court Theatre, 21 June 1868. Walter wins Eva in a song contest, but only after tempering his passion with the wisdom of Hans Sachs.

Mel, Rinaldo del (c. 1554–c. 1598) Flemish composer. After serving at the Portuguese court, he went to Rome in 1580, where he entered the service of Cardinal Gabriele Paleotti (1522–97) and may have studied under Palestrina. He was at Liège 1587–91, in the household of Ernst, Duke of Bavaria, but he rejoined Paleotti at Bologna, who appointed him maestro di cappella at Magliano Cathedral.

Works include: motets, *Sacrae cantiones*, a Litany; 12 volumes of *madrigaletti* and spiritual madrigals.

Melartin, Erkki (1875–1937) Finnish composer. He studied at the Helsinki Conservatory, Wegelius being his composition master, and later in Germany. He became professor of composition at the Conservatory in 1901, and conductor at Viipuri 1908–10. He was director of the Conservatory 1911–22.

Works include: the opera *Aino* (1907); ballet *Sininen helmi*; eight symphonies (1902–24), five orchestral suites, symphonic poems; violin concerto; four string quartets; violin and piano sonatas; piano sonata and c. 400 pieces; c. 300 songs.

melisma, plural *melismata* (from Greek 'song') an ornament: in plainsong a group of notes sung to a single syllable; in modern music any short passage of a decorative nature.

melodic minor scale a kind of minor scale in which the sixth and seventh degrees are raised by a semitone when ascending and returned to their original 'natural' positions when descending.

mélodie (French 'a melody or tune') now generally current in French as an exact equivalent of the English 'song' or the German 'Lied'.

melodrama play or film with romantic and sensational plot elements, often concerned with crime, vice, or catastrophe. Originally a melodrama was a play with an accompaniment of music contributing to the dramatic effect. It became popular in the late 18th century, due to works like *Pygmalion* 1770, with pieces written by the French philosopher

The melodic minor scale on E.

Jean-Jacques Rousseau. The early melodramas used extravagant theatrical effects to heighten violent emotions and actions artificially. By the end of the 19th century, melodrama had become a popular genre of stage play.

In melodramas of the 18th century there was no direct correlation between the free rhythm of the actor's voice and the music which was played in strict ◊metre. In addition to self-contained melodramas, some operas of the period included scenes of this style, as in the grave-digging scene in Beethoven's *Fidelio* 1805. Schoenberg developed the genre in his *Pierrot lunaire* 1912, by the inclusion of semi-musical speech called ◊Sprechgesang (German 'speech-song').

Beginning with the early work of ◊Goethe and ◊Schiller, melodrama was popularized in France by Pixérécourt (1773–1844), whose *L'Enfant de mystère* was first introduced to England in an unauthorized translation by Thomas Holcroft as *A Tale of Mystery* 1802. Melodramas were frequently played against a Gothic background of mountains or ruined castles.

melodramma (Italian 'music drama') term for 'opera' current in Italy from the end of the 18th century onwards. See ◊melodrama.

melody (Greek *melos* 'song') in music, a recognizable series of notes played or sung one after the other, a tune. Melody is one of the three main elements of music, the others being ◊rhythm and ◊harmony. In Western music a melody is usually formed from the notes of a ◊scale or ◊mode. A melody, with or without ◊accompaniment, may be a complete piece on its own – such as a simple song. In classical music it is more often used as a ◊theme within a longer piece of music.

melodic structure Melody is often seen as a discrete element in music, distinct from ◊harmony and rhythm, but, certainly in Western music, the three are to a large extent interdependent. Phrases within a melody can often be analysed as sequences of notes implying chords, and thus a harmonic structure; rhythmic motifs may help to underline this structure, or impose their own shape on the melody. Other factors, such as the predominance of ascending or descending phrases, or the width of intervals between notes in the melody, also have an expressive quality.

harmonic structure The harmonic implications of a melody, whether explicit in the form of an accompaniment or not, help to give it a distinctive character, establishing its relationship to an underlying scale, mode, or ◊key. This arouses the expectation in the listener that certain conventions will be followed – although it is often the breach of these conventions that makes a melody truly memorable. It is largely the implicit harmonic or key structure that characterizes the mood of a melody – for example, whether it is in a major or minor key, how far from its 'home' key it modulates, and how chromatic the harmony is (see ◊chromaticism).

rhythmic elements It might be thought that the ◊pitch of the notes of a melody would be the primary distinguishing feature, but this is very often not the case. Rhythmic patterns and ◊tempo can also be an integral part of the melody, to the extent that some melodies are recognizable by their rhythm alone. Conversely, if reduced to notes of the same time-value, many well-known melodies are difficult to identify.

aesthetics of melody What constitutes 'a good tune' has been a matter of considerable debate throughout the history of music, each age having its own criteria for making this judgement. As musical tastes have changed, so each generation has criticized its successor for its lack of melodic beauty. Similarly, music from cultures unfamiliar to the listener is often described as 'tuneless'. As with any branch of aesthetics, there can be no hard-and-fast rules for the construction of a memorable or beautiful melody, but attempts continue to be made to analyse those elements that constitute sound melodic structure.

Melusine (Mendelssohn). See ◊*Schöne Melusine*.

membranophone one of the four main classes of musical instrument used in the original ◊Sachs-Hornbostel system, the others being ◊idiophone, ◊aerophone, and ◊chordophone. In instruments which are membranophones, the sound emanates from the vibration of a tight membrane such as the skin on a side drum. Included in this class of instruments are many percussion instruments of the drum type.

Mendelssohn (-Bartholdy), (Jakob Ludwig) Felix (1809–1847) German composer, also a pianist and conductor. His music has the lightness and charm of Classical music, applied to Romantic and descriptive subjects. Among his best-known works are *A Midsummer Night's Dream* 1827; the *Fingal's Cave* overture 1832; and five symphonies, which include the 'Reformation' 1830, the 'Italian' 1833, and the 'Scottish' 1842. He was instrumental in promoting the revival of interest in J S Bach's music.

Mendelssohn was the son of the banker Abraham Mendelssohn and grandson of the Jewish philosopher Moses Mendelssohn. His branch of the family converted to Christianity and moved to Berlin in 1812. At the age of six he had piano lessons from his mother and at seven from Marie Bigot in Paris. In 1817, back in Berlin, he learnt composition from Carl Zelter, whose friend Goethe he visited at Weimar in 1821. Before that, in 1818, aged nine, he appeared at a public chamber concert, and before he was 13 he had written many works, including the piano quartet op. 1.

His father was wealthy enough to enable him to conduct a private orchestra, and he wrote his first symphony at 15, after writing 13 symphonies for strings. By 1825 he had ready the short opera *Camacho's Wedding*, produced at the family's expense in 1827. Also in 1825 he wrote his first masterpiece, the Octet for strings. At 17 he had written the overture to Shakespeare's *A Midsummer Night's Dream* (the rest of the incidental music followed in 1842). In 1829 he conducted Bach's forgotten *St Matthew Passion* at the Vocal Academy and paid the first of his ten visits to England, conducting the Philharmonic Society in London and taking a holiday in Scotland, where he gathered impressions for the *Hebrides* overture and the 'Scottish' symphony, at which he worked in Italy 1830–31. He finished the 'Italian' symphony in 1833, the year he conducted the Lower Rhine Festival at Düsseldorf, where he was engaged to stay as general music director. He left, however, for Leipzig, where he was appointed 'official' conductor of the Gewandhaus concerts in 1835.

During a visit to Frankfurt he met Cécile Jeanrenaud, descendant of a French Huguenot family, whom he married in March 1837. In September of the same year he conducted *St Paul* at the Birmingham Festival. In 1841 he left for Berlin, having been appointed director of the music section of the Academy of Arts, and there furnished incidental music for several classical plays in Greek, English, and French. He returned to Leipzig late in 1842 and founded the Conservatory there in November, opening it in April 1843. He was still living in Berlin, but resumed his conductorship at Leipzig in 1845, conducting the premiere of his most popular work, the violin concerto. But he was in poor health, and his visit to England to conduct *Elijah* at the Birmingham Festival on 26 August 1846 was

his last but one. The death of his sister Fanny in the spring of 1847 greatly depressed him, and he went to Switzerland too ill to do any work, returning to Leipzig in September completely exhausted.

Mendelssohn's music is most highly valued for its fusion of a Romantic, lyrical impulse with a sure sense of form. Much of his best music, including the octet, the first five string quartets, *St Paul*, and the 'Italian' symphony were written while he was in his teens or twenties; exhaustion through frail health and overwork conspired to prevent him from meeting his full potential, although such late works as the violin concerto and *Elijah* find Mendelssohn returning to his finest vein of inspiration.

Works include: OPERA several; incidental music to Shakespeare's *A Midsummer Night's Dream* (1843).

ORATORIOS *St Paul* (1836) and *Elijah* (1846); Goethe's *Erste Walpurgisnacht* for solo voices, chorus, and orchestra.

ORCHESTRAL 13 symphonies for strings (1821–23), five symphonies, including A minor 'Scottish' (1842), A 'Italian' (1833), D minor 'Reformation' (1832); four concert overtures, *A Midsummer Night's Dream* (1826), *Fingal's Cave* (1830), *The Fair Melusine* (1833), *Ruy Blas* (1839); two concertos and three shorter works for piano and orchestra; violin concerto in E minor.

CHAMBER MUSIC including six string quartets, two string quintets, string octet in E♭ op. 20 (1825); two piano trios, in D minor op. 49 (1839) and C minor op. 66 (1845).

KEYBOARD AND SONGS a large amount of piano music including 48 *Lieder ohne Worte/Songs without words*; six sonatas, and other pieces for organ; over 80 songs; 12 sets of vocal duets and part songs.

Mendelssohn (-Bartholdy), Fanny (Cäcilie) (1805–1847) German pianist and composer. She was encouraged in composition by her family but published very few of her 500 works, most of them piano pieces and Lieder (songs), which have enjoyed a revival. She was the sister of Felix ◊Mendelssohn.

She studied with Marie Bigot in Paris and C F Zelter in Berlin. She was the focal point of her Berlin Salon in the 1830s and played her brother's first piano concerto in public in 1838. Her D minor piano trio of 1846 does not suffer from comparison with the early works of her brother.

Mendès, Catulle (1841–1909) French writer, poet, and dramatist. He wrote libretti for several composers, including Chabrier, Messager, Pierné, Pessard, Massenet, and Debussy. Debussy's work, *Rodrigue et Chimène*, was never finished. He married Judith Gautier (1850–1917), with whom he visited Richard Wagner at Triebschen in Switzerland, 1869; she had an affair with Wagner seven years later at Bayreuth, during the first production of the *Ring*.

See also ◊Bruneau (*Chansons à danser* and *Lieds de France*), *Gwendoline* (◊Chabrier), ◊d'Indy (*Médée*), ◊Leroux (*Reine Fiammette*).

Mengelberg, Willem (1871–1951) Dutch conductor. In 1895 he was appointed conductor of the Concertgebouw Orchestra in Amsterdam. He made it one of the finest orchestras in Europe, giving early performances of works by Strauss and Mahler, including the first complete cycle of Mahler's symphonies at Amsterdam in 1920. However, he fell under a cloud when he openly declared his sympathy with Nazi rule during World War II, and went into exile in Switzerland.

He studied at Cologne, became conductor at Lucerne in 1891, and in 1895 was appointed conductor of the Concertgebouw Orchestra. In 1933 he was appointed professor of music at Utrecht University.

Mennin, Peter (1923–1983) US composer. He studied at the Eastman School and taught composition at the Juilliard School, New York, 1947–58. He was president at the latter from 1962.

Works include: nine symphonies (1942–81), *Sinfonia* for chamber orchestra (1947), *Fantasia* for strings (1948), violin concerto (1950), Concertato, *Moby Dick* (1952), cello concerto (first performance New York, 1956, with Leonard Rose), piano concerto (1958), *Cantata de Virtute*, based on *The Pied Piper of Hamelin* (1969), Symphonic Movements (1971) *Reflections of Emily*, to texts by E Dickinson (1979), flute concerto (1982); two string quartets (1941, 1951), piano sonata (1963).

meno (Italian 'less') term used in musical notation, as in *meno mosso* ('less moved'), meaning slower.

Menotti, Gian Carlo (1911–) Italian-born US composer. He created small-scale realist operas in tonal idiom, including *The Medium* 1946, *The Telephone* 1947, *The Consul* 1950, *Amahl and the Night Visitors* 1951 (the first opera to be written for television), and *The Saint of Bleecker Street* 1954. He also wrote orchestral and chamber music.

Menotti was born at Cadegliano. Very precocious, he went to Philadelphia in 1928 and studied with Rosario Scalero at the Curtis

Institute there. He wrote libretti for his own operas and for Barber's *Vanessa* and *A Hand of Bridge*. His first great success came with *The Medium* 1946, a sensational one-act opera, followed by the one-act comedy *The Telephone* 1947; but most striking of all, if musically no more refined, was the full-length *The Consul*, produced in New York in 1950 and in London in 1951. In 1958 he founded the Festival of Two Worlds at Spoleto, Italy. In his operas he has attempted to introduce some popular elements, including values derived from the Broadway musical.

Works include: OPERA *Amelia goes to the Ball* (1937), *The Telephone, The Medium* (1946), *The Consul* (1950), *Amahl and the Night Visitors* (1951), *The Saint of Bleecker Street* (1954), *Maria Golovin* (1958), *Le dernier sauvage* (1963), *Martin's Lie* (1964), *Help, Help, the Globolinks!* (1968), *The Hero* (1976), *The Most Important Man* (1971), *Tamu-Tamu* (1973), *La loca* (1979), *A Bride from Pluto* (1982), *Goya* (1986), *The Wedding* (1988); radio opera *The Old Maid and the Thief* (1939).

OTHER symphonic poem *Apocalypse* (1951); *Pastorale* for piano and string orchestra, two piano concertos, violin concerto (1952); four pieces for string quartet, *Trio for a Housewarming Party* for flute, cello, and piano; *Poemetti*, piano pieces for children; pieces for carillon; symphony *The Halcyon* (1976).

mensurable music measured or measurable music which can be grouped according to regular successions of beats, as distinct from plainsong, which has no measured rhythmic pulse.

mensural notation the musical notation which, as distinct from ◊modal notation, came into use during the 13th century and for the first time began to indicate the exact value of notes and rests by its symbols.

menuet (French 'minuet') diminutive of *menu*; 'small'.

Menuetto term used by German composers of the 18th century to label their minuets under the impression that they were using an Italian term. The correct Italian is *minuetto*, the German *Menuett*.

Merbecke, John (c. 1505–c. 1585), or Marbeck English composer and writer. He compiled *The Booke of Common Praier Noted* 1550, the first musical setting of an Anglican prayer book. He was lay clerk and organist at St George's Chapel, Windsor from 1531. In 1543 he was arrested and in 1544 tried and condemned for heresy as a Calvinist, but he was pardoned and allowed to retain his office.

His concordance of the English Bible, the first complete edition, was published in 1550. After Edward VI's accession, Merbecke compiled *The Booke of Common Praier Noted*. It was the first book of its kind, and used adaptations of plainsong in addition to music written by Merbecke himself. Merbecke's other surviving works are a large-scale Mass, two motets, and an anthem.

Works include: Mass and two motets (probably early); carol 'A Virgine and Mother'; *The Booke of Common Praier Noted* [set to notes] (1550, first version authorized by Edward VI).

Mercadante, (Giuseppe) Saverio (Raffaele) (1795–1870) Italian composer. He wrote about 60 operas, the most successful of which, *Il giuramento* 1837 and *La Vestale* 1840, have a strong dramatic purpose and seriousness of style that influenced Verdi.

He studied under Niccolò Zingarelli at the Collegio di San Sebastiano at Naples and, having learnt the flute and violin, became leader of the orchestra there. On being dismissed he began to earn his living as a stage composer, producing his first opera at the San Carlo theatre in 1819. After several successes in Italy he won favour in Vienna, visited Spain 1827–29, and in 1833 succeeded Pietro Generali as maestro di cappella at Novara Cathedral. In 1840 he became director of the Naples Conservatory. While at Novara he lost an eye and in 1862 became totally blind.

Works include: about 60 operas, including *Violenza e costanza* (1820), *Elisa e Claudio* (1821), *Caritea, regina di Spagna* (1826), *Gabriella di Vergy* (1828), *I Normanni a Parigi*, *I briganti*, *Il giuramento* (1837), *I due illustri rivali* (1838), *Elena da Feltre*, *Il bravo* (1839), *La Vestale* (1840), *Leonora*, *Gli Orazi ed i Curiazi* (1846), *Virginia*; 20 Masses, motets, psalms, and other pieces; cantata *L'apoteosi d'Ercole* and others; instrumental pieces; songs.

Mercury nickname of Haydn's šymphony no. 43, in E♭ major, composed c. 1771.

Merikanto, Aarre (1893–1958) Finnish composer. His opera *Juha* 1922 has been successfully revived, suggesting an individual style that recalls Janáček.

He studied with Max Reger and others at Leipzig and with Sergey Vasilenko at Moscow. He later became professor at the Helsinki Conservatory.

Works include: the opera *Juha* (1922, staged 1963); ballet *The Abduction of Kylliki*

(on a subject from the *Kalevala*); three symphonies (1916, 1918, 1953), variations and fugue and several suites for orchestra; four violin concertos (1916–54), three piano concertos, two cello concertos, concerto for violin, clarinet, horn, and strings; partita for woodwind and harp; choral works; folk-song arrangements.

Mer, La/The Sea three symphonic sketches by Debussy, *De l'aube à midi sur la mer*, *Jeux de vagues*, and *Dialogue du vent et de la mer*, composed 1903–05, first performed Paris, 15 October 1905.

Merlo, Alessandro (1530–after 1594), called Alessandro Romano or Alessandro della Viola Italian tenor-bass, violist, and composer. He was a pupil of Willaert and Rore, and singer in the Papal Chapel in Rome.

Works include: motets; madrigals, *Canzoni alla Napolitana, villanelle*.

Merope opera by Gasparini (libretto by A Zeno), produced Venice, Teatro San Cassiano, 26 December 1711. Polyphontes overthrows King Cresphontes, executing him and two of his three sons. Aepytus escapes and, after growing up, kills Polyphontus and becomes the rightful king.

Also settings by Jommelli (1741) and Graun (1756).

Merry Widow (Lehár). See ◊*Lustige Witwe, Die*.

Merry Wives of Windsor see ◊*Falstaff*, ◊*Lustigen Weiber von Windsor, Die*, and ◊*Sir John in Love*.

Mersenne, Marin (1588–1648) French monk, mathematician, philosopher, and music theorist. His treatises include the two-volume *Harmonie universelle*, published at Paris 1636–37, with a section on instruments, 'Questions harmoniques de la nature des sons'.

Educated at Le Mans and La Flèche, he became a Minorite friar, and was ordained in 1612. He taught philosophy at Nevers and then studied mathematics and music in Paris, where his colleagues included Descartes and the elder Pascal. He corresponded with scholars in England, Holland, and Italy, the last of which he visited three times.

Merulo, Claudio (1533–1604), adopted name of Claudio Merlotti Italian organist, teacher, and composer. Famous in his lifetime for his organ playing, he is best known today for his keyboard music.

He was appointed organist at Brescia in 1556 and second organist at St Mark's, Venice, in 1557, advancing to first organist in 1564. In 1584 he left Venice, visited the court of Mantua, and became organist to the ducal chapel at Parma.

Works include: intermezzi for Dolce's *Le Troiane* (1566) and Cornelio Frangipani's *La tragedia* (1574); Masses, motets, *Sacrae cantiones*, Litanies; madrigals; toccatas and ricercari for organ.

messa di voce (Italian 'setting or placing of the voice') sustained singing of notes or phrase. **Messa** may also mean a crescendo followed by a diminuendo on a single breath.

Messager, André Charles Prosper (1853–1929) French composer and conductor. As well as composing light operas, such as *La Béarnaise* 1885 and *Véronique* 1898, he was noted as a conductor of Mozart and Wagner, and also as a pianist.

He studied at Niedermeyer's school in Paris, under Fauré and Saint-Saëns. In 1876 he won prizes for a symphony and a cantata and in 1883 produced a completion of an operetta *François les Bas-bleus* left unfinished by Firmin Bernicat. He became conductor of the Opéra-Comique and in 1898 its general director. He was artistic director at Covent Garden, London 1901–06 and joint director of the Paris Opéra 1901–13. His wife was the Irish composer Hope Temple (Dotie Davies, 1859–1938), who had been a pupil of his. In 1902 he conducted the first performance of Debussy's *Pelléas et Mélisande.*

Works include: OPERAS AND OPERETTAS *La fauvette du Temple* (1885), *La Béarnaise, Le bourgeois de Calais* (1887), *Isoline* (1888), *Le mari de la reine* (1889), *La Basoche* (1890), *Madame Chrysanthème* (after Pierre Loti's novel, 1893), *Miss Dollar, Mirette, Le chevalier d'Harmental* (1896), *Les p'tites Michu* (1897), *Véronique* (1898), *Les dragons de l'impératrice* (1905), *Fortunio, Béatrice* (1914), *Monsieur Beaucaire,* (in English, 1919), *La petite fonctionnaire* (1921), *L'amour masqué, Passionnement* (1926), *Coup de roulis.*

OTHER ballets *Les deux pigeons* (1886), *Scaramouche* (1891), *Le chevalier aux fleurs* (1897), *Une aventure de la Guimard* (1900) and others; instrumental pieces; piano duets; songs.

Messe solennelle see ◊Missa solemnis.

Messiaen, Olivier Eugène Prosper Charles (1908–1992) French composer, organist, and teacher. His music is mystical in character, vividly coloured, and incorporates transcriptions of birdsong. Among his works are the *Quartet for the End of Time* 1941, the large-scale *Turangalîla Symphony* 1949, and solo organ and piano pieces. As a teacher at the Paris Conservatoire from 1942, he influenced three generations of composers.

His theories of melody, harmony, and rhythm, drawing on medieval and oriental music, have inspired contemporary composers such as Boulez and Stockhausen.

He was born in Avignon, and spent most of his life in Paris, where he was appointed organist at La Trinité church 1931. He was a devout Christian.

***Messiah* (not *The Messiah*)** oratorio by Handel (words selected from the Bible by Charles Jennens), performed Dublin, Music Hall in Fishamble Street, 13 April 1742; first performance in England, Covent Garden, London, 23 March 1743.

Messidor opera by Bruneau (libretto by E Zola), produced Paris, Opéra, 19 February 1897. Bruneau had already written operas on subjects from Zola's works (*L'Attaque du moulin* and *Le Rêve*), but this was the first for which Zola himself wrote the libretto.

mesto (Italian 'mournful', 'sad') term used in musical notation.

Metamorphosen study in C minor for 23 solo strings by Strauss; composed 1945, in response to the wartime devastation of Europe, in particular the destruction of the opera houses, in which his works were performed throughout World War II. Dedicated to Paul Sacher and the Collegium Musicum; first performed Zurich, 25 January 1946.

Metamorphoses after Ovid, Six (*Pan, Phaeton, Niobe, Bacchus, Narcissus, Arethusa.*) Work for solo oboe by Britten; composed 1951, first performed Thorpeness, 14 June 1951.

metamorphosis the transformation of theme or motif, especially rhythmically while the same notes are retained, as for example the *idée fixe* of Berlioz, the themes in Liszt's symphonic poems, or the *Leitmotive* in Wagner's musical dramas.

metaphor aria see ◊parable aria.

Metastasio, Pietro (1698–1782), real name Trapassi Italian poet and librettist. His first original libretto, *Didone*, was produced in 1724 (music by Sarro). The rigid musical and dramatic conventions imposed by his verse dominated opera until Gluck's reforms of 1762. Operas on his libretti include: *Achille in Sciro, Adriano in Siria, Alessandro nell' Indie, Antigono, Artaserse, Catone in Utica, Cinesi, Clemenza di Tito, Cleofide, Contesa dei numi, Demetrio, Demofoonte, Démophoön, Didone abbandonata, Eroe cinese, Ezio, Galatea, Innocenza giustificata, Ipermestra, Isola disabitata, Lucio Silla, Olimpiade, Partenope, Rè pastore, Ruggiero, Semiramide riconosciuta, Siface, Siroe, Sogno di Scipione, Tito Vespasiano, Trionfo di Clelia.*

See ◊Hasse, ◊Jommelli, and ◊Paisiello.

metre the timescale represented by the beat. Metre is regular, whereas rhythm is irregular.

Metre can be **simple** as in 2/4, 4/8, and so on, where each beat divides into two sub-beats; **compound metre** as in 6/8, 9/8, 12/16, and so on, consists of sub-beats of 'compounded' or aggregated in units of three. The numerical sign for metre is a **time signature**, of which the upper number represents the number of beats in the bar, the lower number the type of beat, expressed as a fraction of a unit (**semibreve**). Hence 3/4 is three crotchet (quarter-note) beats to the bar and 6/8 is two beats each of three quavers (eighth notes).

metronome clockwork device, invented by Johann Mälzel in 1814, using a sliding weight to regulate the speed of a pendulum to assist in setting tempo, particularly in music. It is now largely superseded by silent digital display devices.

Metropolitan Opera Company foremost opera company in the USA, founded 1883 in New York City. The Metropolitan Opera House (opened 1883) was demolished in 1966, and the company moved to the new Metropolitan Opera House at the Lincoln Center.

Meyer, Ernst Hermann (1905–1988) German musicologist and composer. He studied in Berlin and Heidelberg. He lived in London from 1933 to 1948, when he was appointed professor of music sociology at the Humbolt University, Berlin. His books include studies of 17th-century instrumental music and English chamber music from the Middle Ages to Purcell.

Works include: the opera *Reiter der Nacht* (1973); film and chamber music.

Meyer, Leonard B(unce) (1918–) US theorist and aesthetician. He studied at Columbia University and the University of Chicago, and taught at the University of Chicago (1961) and the University of Pennsylvania (1975). His books include *Emotion and Meaning in Music* (1956) and (with Grosvenor Cooper) *The Rhythmic Structure of Music* (1960).

Meyerbeer, Giacomo (1791–1864), adopted name of Jakob Liebmann Meyer Beer German composer. His spectacular operas include *Robert le Diable* 1831 and *Les Huguenots* 1836. From 1826 he lived mainly in Paris, returning to Berlin after 1842 as musical director of the Royal Opera.

His father Herz Beer, a banker, gave him every facility to develop his precocious gifts. He was at first trained as a pianist and had some lessons from Clementi during the latter's stay in Berlin. He played in public at the age of seven, but afterwards studied theory and composition under Carl Zelter, Bernhard Weber, and GeorgVogler, and in 1810 moved to the latter's house at Darmstadt, where he was a fellow student with Carl Maria von Weber. His first opera was produced at Munich in 1812 and the second at Stuttgart in 1813. He then went to Vienna and, hearing Hummel play, he retired for further piano studies, after which he appeared again as a virtuoso.

On Salieri's advice he went to Italy in 1815 to study vocal writing, and produced his first Italian opera at Padua in 1817. In 1823 he tried his luck in Berlin, but without much success, and having produced *Il crociato* at Venice in 1824, went to Paris for its first performance there in 1826. He settled and spent much time there for the rest of his life. He wrote no new work between 1824 and 1831, among the reasons being his father's death, his marriage, and the loss of two children. In 1831 *Robert le Diable* made him sensationally fashionable in Paris. This opera, followed by *Les Huguenots* and *Le Prophète* established Meyerbeer as a master of the French grand opera, with ingredients including strong local colour, a sure sense of history, novel instrumental effects, and extended ballets. In 1842 the King of Prussia appointed him general music director in Berlin. He visited Vienna and London in 1847 and the latter again in 1862, when he represented German music at the Great Exhibition. His health began to fail about 1850, and one of his most evocative operas, *L'Africaine*, was left uncompleted at his death.

Works include: OPERA *Jephthas Gelübde* (1812), *Alimelek, oder Die beiden Kalifen, Romilda e Costanza* (1817), *Semiramide riconosciuta* (1819), *Emma di Resburgo* (1819), *Margherita d'Anjou* (1820), *L'esule di Granata, Das Brandenburger Tor, Il crociato in Egitto* (1824), *Robert le Diable* (1831), *Les Huguenots* (1836), *Ein Feldlager in Schlesin* (1844), *Le Prophète* (1849), *L'Etoile du Nord* (1854), *Le Pardon de Ploërmel* (*Dinorah*), *L'Africaine* (1865), *Judith* (unfinished).

OTHER monodrama *Thevelindens Liebe*; incidental music to Michael Beer's (his brother's) drama *Struensee*, Blaze de Bury's *Jeunesse de Goethe*, and Aeschylus' *Eumenides*; masque *Das Hoffest von Ferrara*; ballet *Der Fischer und das Milchmädchen* (1810); oratorio *Gott und die Natur* (1811); *Stabat Mater*, Te Deum, psalms, and other church music; several cantatas, including two for the Schiller centenary, 1859, seven sacred cantatas (Klopstock) for unaccompanied chorus; March for ditto, three Torch Dances, Coronation March, *Overture in the Form of a March* for the London Exhibition; piano works; songs.

Meyerowitz, Jan (1913–) German-born US composer. He studied in Berlin with Zemlinsky and Rome with Respighi. He moved to the USA in 1946, and became a US citizen in 1951.

Works include: the operas *The Barrier* (1950), *Eastward in Eden* (1951), *Esther* (1957), *Godfather Death* (1961), *Winterballade* (1967); *Silesian Symphony* (1957), oboe concerto (1963), six pieces for orchestra (1967); Cantatas on texts by E Dickinson, Cummings and Herrick; chamber music.

mezzo-, or mezza- (Italian 'half') term used in music of medium range or intensity, as in mezzo-soprano, mezzoforte (mf), and so on. The short form 'mezzo' stands for mezzo-soprano.

mezzo-soprano female singing voice with an approximate range A4–F5, between contralto and soprano.

Janet Baker is a well-known British mezzo-soprano.

mf abbreviation of **mezzo forte** (Italian 'half loud'), medium loud.

Mi the old name for the note E (◊solmization), still used in Latin countries, and in tonic solfa the mediant note in any key, represented by the symbol m, pronounced Me.

Miaskovsky, Nikolai Yakovlevich (1881– 1950) Russian composer. Intending to follow a military career, he entered the St Petersburg Conservatory in 1906, where he studied with Rimsky-Korsakov, Liadov, and Wihtol. His compositions include 27 symphonies and 13 string quartets. Although he was denounced in 1948 with Prokofiev and others for 'formalism', his music is in a tonal, conservative idiom.

He was the son of a Russian military engineer stationed in Poland, whence the family moved successively to Orenburg, Kazan, and Nizhny-Novgorod, where Miaskovsky joined the cadet corps. Intended to follow his father's career, he did not finally take to music until 1907, when he resigned his commission, though he had composed many piano preludes, studied with Glière and Krizhanovsky, and entered the St Petersburg Conservatory in 1906. In 1914–17 he fought on the Austrian front and was badly wounded; in 1921 he became composition professor at the Moscow Conservatory.

Works include: the oratorio *Kirov is with us*; 27 symphonies (1908–50), 2 sinfoniettas, symphonic poems *Silence* (after Poe) and *Alastor* (after Shelley), serenade and *Lyric Concertino* for small orchestra; violin concerto (1938); cello concertino (1945); *Salutatory Overture* on Stalin's 60th birthday (1939); 13 string quartets (1913–49); 2 cello and piano sonatas; 9 piano sonatas and other piano pieces; 13 op. nos of songs.

Michael, Tobias (1592–1657) German composer, son of Roger Michael. He studied as a boy chorister under his father in the Dresden court chapel and became music director at Sondershausen in 1619. In 1631 he succeeded Schein as cantor of St Thomas's Church at Leipzig.

Works include: *Musikalische Seelenlust* containing sacred madrigals for voices and sacred concertos for voices and instruments (1634–37); other church music.

Mi contra Fa medieval designation of the tritone (the forbidden interval of the augmented fourth), the Mi being the mediant of the hard hexachord beginning on G.

microphone receiver which turns sound into electrical signals. The signals, transmitted and amplified, can also be used for radio, television, or recording purposes, or in theatres and public halls for the relaying of speech, song, and taped sound to amplifiers placed at various points of the building.

microtone any precisely determined division of the octave smaller than a semitone.

Examples of quarter-tone divisions are heard in the violin solo parts of Bartók's *Violin Concerto No. 2* 1937–38, Berg's *Chamber Concerto* 1923–25, and Boulez's cantata *Le Visage nuptial/The Bridal Countenance* 1946 rev. 1950–51. The Czech composer Alois Hába (1893–1973) and Mexican Julián Carrillo (1875–1965) composed in smaller divisions, and since 1984 Stockhausen has developed notations of up to 16ths of a tone for basset horn and flute, for example in *Xi* 1986 for basset horn.

Normally microtones belong in the domain of expressive pitch variation, being difficult to notate and perform precisely because most instruments other than the voice or violin family are designed to produce tempered pitches, or have fixed frets or keys. When played against a ◊drone, however, they become more clearly quantifiable as audible ◊beat frequencies.

middle C white note, C4, at the centre of the piano keyboard, indicating the division between left- and right-hand regions and between the treble and bass staves of printed music. Middle C is also the pitch indicated by a C clef, for example, for viola.

Middle C in bass, tenor, alto, and treble clefs.

middleground see ◊structural level.

MIDI, acronym for musical instrument digital interface manufacturer's standard allowing different pieces of digital music equipment used in composing and recording to be freely connected.

The information-sending device (any electronic instrument) is called a controller, and the reading device (such as a computer) the sequencer. Pitch, dynamics, decay rate, and stereo position can all be transmitted via the interface. A computer with a MIDI interface can input and store the sounds produced by the connected instruments, and can then manipulate these sounds in many different ways. For example, a single keystroke may change the key of an entire composition. Even a full written score for the composition may be automatically produced.

Midsummer Marriage, The opera by Tippett (libretto by composer), produced London, Covent Garden, 27 January 1955. Spiritually-minded Mark and Jenifer are matched by more down-to-earth Jack and Bella in magical initiation ceremonies.

Midsummer Night's Dream, A incidental music by Mendelssohn to Shakespeare's play.

Overture composed summer 1826 first performed Stettin in February 1827; the rest of the music composed in 1842 and used for a stage production at Potsdam on 14 October 1843.

Opera by Britten (libretto from Shakespeare), produced Aldeburgh, Jubilee Hall, 11 June 1960. Lovers, fairies, and rustics intermingle in enchanted forest.

See ◊*Songe d'une nuit d'été, Le.*

'Mighty Five', or Mighty Handful group of Russian composers; see The ◊Five.

Mignon opera by A Thomas (libretto by J Barbier and M Carré, based on Goethe's *Wilhelm Meister*), produced Paris, Opéra-Comique, 17 November 1866. Gypsy girl Mignon falls for Wilhelm Meister, who seems more interested in the actress Philine. After

later nursing Mignon, who is injured in a fire, Wilhelm affirms his love. Mignon turns out to be the long-lost Spirata, daughter of the Lord in whose house she recuperates.

Mignone, Francisco (1897–1986) Brazilian composer. He studied at São Paulo Conservatory and later in Milan, and in 1929 became professor at the National Conservatory in Rio de Janeiro.

Works include: the operas *O contratador dos diamantes* (1924), *El jayon/L'innocente* (1927); ballet *Maracatú de Chico-Rei* (1933); clarinet and bassoon concertos; orchestral music; songs, and other pieces.

Migot, Georges (Elbert) (1891–1976) French composer. He studied with various masters, including Widor, and made a speciality of medieval music. In 1917 he made himself known in Paris by giving a concert of his own, and, holding no official post, he relied on his own efforts to keep before the public.

Works include: the opera *Le Rossignol en amour* (1926); ballets *La Fête de la bergère* (1924), *Le Paravent de laque, Les Aveux et les promesses*; Psalm 19 for chorus and orchestra, *The Sermon on the Mount* for solo voices, chorus, organ and strings; 13 symphonies (1919–67), *Les Agrestides, Trois Guirlandes sonores* for strings; *La Jungle* for organ and orchestra; *Le Livre des danseries* for violin, flute and piano and other chamber music; songs.

Mihalovici, Marcel (1898–1985) Romanian composer. He studied with d'Indy in Paris and joined a group of advanced French and Russian composers there after World War I. He was married to the pianist Monique ◊Haas.

Works include: *L'Intransigeant Pluton* (1928); ballets *Karagueuz* (1926), *Divertissement*, and others; *Cortège des divinités infernales* (from the opera), *Introduction au mouvement, Notturno* and fantasy for orchestra; three string quartets (1923, 1931, 1946); string trio; violin and piano sonata, sonatina for oboe and piano.

Mikado, The, or The Town of Titipu operetta by Sullivan (libretto by W S Gilbert), produced London, Savoy Theatre, 14 March 1885. Nanki-Poo loves Yum-Yum, against the Mikado's wishes. However, she must marry Ko-Ko, the Lord High Executioner. The lovers marry and escape decapitation.

Mikołaj z Krakowa (lived 16th century) see ◊Nicolaus de Cracovia.

Mikrokosmos/Microcosm a set of 153 small piano pieces by Bartók, arranged in progressive order of technical difficulty and published in six volumes, setting the player various problems of modern technique, each piece being written on a particular principle or system (special rhythms, time-signatures, chords, intervals, atonal or bitonal combinations), composed 1926–37, published 1940.

Milán, Luis (c. 1500–after 1561) Spanish vihuelist and composer. His works were all published in *El Maestro* 1536, the earliest surviving vihuela collection. They include fantasies and pavans for vihuela, Spanish and Portuguese *villancicos*, Spanish ballads, and Italian sonnets for voice and vihuela. He was one of the first composers to write tempo indications.

He was the son of a nobleman, Don Luis de Milán. He visited Italy and Portugal.

Milanese Chant see ◊Ambrosian Chant.

Milford, Robin (Humphrey) (1903–1959) English composer. He was educated at Rugby and studied music at the Royal College of Music, where his masters were Holst, Vaughan Williams, and R O Morris.

Works include: the oratorio *A Prophet in the Land*; cantata *Wind, Rain and Sunshine, Bemerton Cantatas, Five Songs of Escape* for unaccompanied chorus; symphony, concerto grosso, double fugue for orchestra; violin concerto, *The Dark Thrush* (on Hardy's poem) for violin and small orchestra; *Two Easter Meditations* for organ; piano works; songs; part-songs.

Milhaud, Darius (1892–1974) French composer and pianist. A member of the group of composers known as ◊Les Six, he was extremely prolific in a variety of styles and genres, influenced by jazz, the rhythms of Latin America, and electronic composition. He is noted for his use of ◊polytonality (the simultaneous existence of two or more keys), as in the *Saudades do Brasil* 1921 for orchestra and *L'homme et son désir* 1918.

A pastoral element also runs through many of his works, as in his first string quartet 1912 and six chamber symphonies 1917–22. His Jewish ancestry is evident in the cantata *Ani maamiu* written for the Festival of Israel 1973. Other works include the operas *Christophe Colombe/Christopher Columbus* 1928 and *Bolívar* 1943, and the jazz ballet *La création du monde* 1923.

He studied violin and composition at the Paris Conservatory from 1909, under Gédalge, Widor, and d'Indy. His teachers also included Dukas. He was attaché to the French Legation at Rio de Janeiro 1917–19, and there he met Paul Claudel, who collaborated

frequently with him as a librettist. in 1922 he was represented for the first time at the festival of the International Society for Contemporary Music. In 1940 he went to the USA as professor of music at Mills College, California, and in 1947 became professor of composition at the National Conservatory in Paris.

Works include: STAGE operas include *Christophe Colomb* (1930); ballets *L'homme et son désir* (1918), *Le bœuf sur le toit* (1919), *La création du monde* (1923); incidental music for *Oreste* translated from Aeschylus (*Agamemnon, Les Choëphores,* and *Les Euménides,* 1917–22).

ORCHESTRAL works include 12 symphonies for large orchestra (1940–62), *Suite provençale* (1937), *Saudades do Brazil; Ballade, Le carnaval d'Aix* (1926), *Concertino de printemps* for violin and orchestra (1934).

CHAMBER 18 string quartets (1912–62), wind quintet *La cheminée du Roi René* (1939); sonatas and sonatinas for many instruments with piano; six piano works including *Printemps* (two volumes), *Saudades do Brazil* (two volumes, 1920–21); suite *Scaramouche* (1939) for two pianos.

SOLO VOCAL AND CHORAL 14 books of songs including *Poèmes juifs, Catalogue des fleurs* for voice and chamber orchestra (1920); *Liturgie Comtadine* (1933), *Service Sacré* (1947).

military band musical band attached to military regiments and used by them for their ceremonial occasions, but also often engaged to play for the entertainment of the general public, for example in parks, or at the seaside. It generally includes woodwind, brass, and percussion.

'Military' Symphony Haydn's symphony no. 100 in G major (no. 8 of the 'Salomon' symphonies), composed for London in 1794; so called because of the trumpet call and percussion effects found in the second movement.

Millico, Giuseppe (1737–1802) Italian castrato soprano and composer. He was discovered by Gluck, in whose *Le feste d'Apollo* he sang at Parma in 1769. Engaged by the imperial opera in Vienna, he sang the following year in the first performance of Gluck's *Paride ed Elena*. He later visited London, Paris, and Berlin, and from 1780 lived in Naples.

Works include: the operas *La pietà d'amore* (published 1782), *La Zelinda, Ipermestra, Le Cinesi* (1780); cantata *Angelica e Medoro* (with Cimarosa).

Millöcker, Karl (1842–1899) Austrian composer and conductor. After studying at the

Vienna Conservatory, he became a conductor at Graz in 1864 and at the Harmonietheater in Vienna in 1866. In 1869 he was appointed conductor at the Theater an der Wien in Vienna, and produced operettas for it.

Works include: the operettas *Der tote Gast* (1865), *Die beiden Binder, Diana* (1867), *Die Fraueninsel, Ein Abenteuer in Wien* (1873), *Das verwunschene Schloss* (1878), *Gräfin Dubarry* (1879), *Apajune der Wassermann, Der Bettelstudent* (1882), *Der Feldprediger* (1884), *Der Vice-Admiral, Die sieben Schwaben* (1887), *Der arme Jonathan* (1890), *Das Sonntagskind* (1892), *Gasparone*, and many others; numerous piano pieces.

Mills, Charles (1914–1982) US composer. He studied with a six-year scholarship under Copland, Sessions, and Roy Harris, two years with each, and later devoted himself entirely to composition.

Works include: music for solo dance *John Brown*; 5 symphonies (1940–80), slow movement for string orchestra; concertino for flute and orchestra; prelude for flute and strings; Festival Overture for chorus and orchestra; *Ars poetica* for unaccompanied chorus (1940); chamber symphony for 11 instruments (1939), chamber concerto for 10 instruments, chamber concertino for woodwind quintet, 5 string quartets (1939–59), piano trio in D minor, sonatas for cello, violin, and piano.

Milner, Anthony (1925–) English composer. He taught at Morley College, London, 1947–62, and was then appointed to the Royal College of Music. He was appointed lecturer at King's College, London, in 1965.

He studied piano with Herbert Fryer (1877–1957) and composition with R O Morris and later with Mátyás Seiber.

Works include: three symphonies (1972, 1978, 1986), *Sinfonia Pasquale* for string orchestra, *April Prologue* for orchestra; chamber symphony (1968), concerto for symphonic wind band (1979), concerto for strings (1982); *The Song of Akhenaten* for soprano and chamber orchestra (1954); cantatas *Salutatio Angelica* (1948), *The City of Desolation* (1955), *St Francis, The Water and the Fire* (1961), *Emmanuel Cantata* (1975); Mass for *a cappella* chorus (1951); string quartet (1975), oboe quartet, wind quintet; songs; piano sonata (1989).

Milton opera by Spontini (libretto by V J E de Jouy and M Dieulafoy), produced Paris, Opéra-Comique, 27 November 1804. A second Milton was planned by Spontini in 1838, when he visited England in the summer to study the environment. It was to be entitled *Miltons Tod und Busse für den Königsmord/*

Milton's Death and Expiation for the King's Murder) (libretto by E Raupach), but turned into *Das verlorene Paradies/Paradise Lost*); it remained unfinished.

Milton, John (c. 1563–1647) English composer, father of John Milton the poet. He is said to have received a gold medal from a Polish prince for an In Nomine in 40 parts.

He was educated at Christ Church, Oxford. After being cast out by his father as a Protestant, he went to London, and in 1600 became a member of the Scriveners' Company, marrying Sarah Jeffrey about that time. Having made a fair fortune as a scribe, he retired to Horton in Buckinghamshire in 1632, but after his wife's death moved to Reading about 1640. In 1643 he returned to London, where he lived with his son John.

Works include: various sacred pieces for·several voices; madrigal contribution to *The Triumphes of Oriana*, four vocal pieces contributed to Leighton's *Teares or Lamentacions*; two tunes for Ravenscroft's Psalter; five fancies for viols.

Mines of Sulphur, The opera by R R Bennett (libretto by Beverley Cross), produced London, Sadler's Wells, 24 February 1965, conductor C Davis. Plague-carrying actors punish Boconnion, deserter and murderer.

minim, or US half note in music, a note value, half the duration of a ◊semibreve. It is written as an empty white note-head with a stem. It is the basic unit of beat for the following metres: 2/2, 4/2, and cut time (◊alla breve).

Minimalism movement in abstract art (mostly sculpture) and music towards severely simplified composition. Minimal art developed in the USA in the 1950s in reaction to Abstract Expressionism, shunning its emotive approach in favour of impersonality and elemental, usually geometric, shapes. It has found its fullest expression in sculpture, notably in the work of Carl Andre, who employs industrial materials in modular compositions. In music, from the 1960s, it manifested itself in large-scale statements, usually tonal or even diatonic, and highly repetitive, based on a few 'minimal' musical ideas. Major Minimalist composers are Steve ◊Reich and Philip ◊Glass.

Minnesinger (German 'love-singer') any of a group of 12th- to 14th-century German lyric poets and musicians. They represent a continuation of the French ◊troubadour tradition, their songs dealing mainly with the theme of courtly love, but their musical and literary styles diverged. Many were of noble birth, unlike the later ◊Meistersingers (German 'master singers') who were from the middle classes. Dietmar von Aist, Friedrich von Hausen, Heinrich von Morungen, Reinmar, and Walther von der Vogelweide were well-known Minnesingers.

minor one of the two predominant scales (the other being major) of the tonal system. There are three forms of the minor scale: the harmonic, the melodic, and the less commonly used natural minor. See ◊harmonic minor scale and ◊melodic minor scale.

minore (Italian 'minor') in older music, a word often used as a warning in the course of a composition which is predominantly in a major key.

Minor and major seconds and sevenths.

minor intervals seconds, thirds, sixths, and sevenths which are a semitone smaller than the corresponding major intervals.

Minotaur, The ballet in one act by Elliott Carter; composed 1947, produced New York, 26 March 1947.

minstrel professional entertainer of any kind, but particularly a musician, in the 12th–17th centuries. Most common in the Middle Ages, minstrels were usually in the service of a court or of a member of the aristocracy. In the 19th century, a minstrel was one of a group of white entertainers popular in the USA who painted their faces black and impersonated the music and humour of workers from the Southern plantations.

minuet French country dance in three time adapted as a European courtly dance of the 17th century. The music was later used as the third movement of a classical four-movement symphony where its gentle rhythm provides a foil to the slow second movement and fast final movement.

minuetto the correct Italian name for the minuet (not 'menuetto').

'Minute Waltz' the nickname sometimes given to Chopin's Waltz in D♭ major, op. 64 no. 1.

Miracle in the Gorbals ballet by Bliss (scenario by M Benthall, choreography by Robert Helpmann), produced London, Prince's Theatre, 26 October 1944.

Miracles of our Lady cycle of four one-act operas by Martinů: *The Wise and Foolish Virgins* (libretto by V Nezval after 12th-century French text); *Little Mariken of Nijmegen* (libretto by H Gheon after 15th-century Flemish legend); *The Nativity* (libretto by composer after Moravian folk texts); *The Legend of Sister Pasqualina* (libretto by composer after poem by J Zeyer and folk texts). Composed 1933–34, first performed Brno, 23 February 1935.

'Miracle, The' nickname of Haydn's symphony no. 96, in D major (no. 4 of the 'Salomon' symphonies), written for London in 1791. The name is due to the story that a chandelier fell from the ceiling at the first performance, when the audience miraculously escaped injury; but in fact the accident occurred at the first performance of symphony no. 102 in B♭ major (1794–95).

Miraculous Mandarin, The, A csodálatos mandarin pantomime in one act by Bartók (scenario by M Lengyel); 1918–19, produced Cologne, 27 November 1926.
Orchestral Suite performed Budapest, 15 October 1928, conductor Ernö Dohnányi. The Mandarin of the title is mugged by a prostitute and her gang, but he cannot die until he is sexually united with the woman who has attempted to murder him.

Mireille opera by Gounod (libretto by M Carré, based on the poem 'Mirèio' by F Mistral), produced Paris, Théâtre Lyrique, 19 March 1864. Vincent and Mireille love each other, but they are opposed by her father, who favours the advances of bull-tamer Ourrias. Ourrais injures Vincent and is drowned by water spirits. Mireille undertakes a pilgrimage to see Vincent and dies of exhaustion in his arms.

mirliton toy musical instrument similar to the eunuch flute, also known as ◊kazoo in England.

Miroirs set of five piano pieces by Ravel; composed 1905, first performed Paris, 6 January 1906: *Noctuelles, Oiseaux tristes, Une barque sur l'océan* (orchestral version, first performed Paris, 3 February 1907), *Alborada del gracioso* (orchestral version first performed Paris, 17 May 1919), *La Vallée des Cloches*.

mirror canon, or mirror fugue a canon or fugue in which two or more voices are so inverted that the intervals appear simultaneously upside down as well as right side up, looking on paper like a reflection in water.

Miserere title of a work using the text of Psalm 51, *Miserere mei, Deus* ... (Latin 'have mercy upon me, O God ...'). It is sung (often in ◊plainsong) during the Roman Catholic office (or non-Eucharistic service) of Lauds, at sunrise, during the week preceding Easter Sunday. Simple polyphonic settings of the text have been made by early composers such as Josquin Desprez and Gregorio Allegri (the work of the latter is famous for its embellishments and popular with modern audiences). Later composers have set Misereres, including Verdi in the opera *Il trovatore* 1852.

Miserly Knight, The/Skupoy ritsar' opera in three scenes by Rachmaninov (libretto by composer, after Pushkin) 1903–05, produced Moscow, Bolshoi, 24 January 1906. Poor son and penny-pinching father have money problems.

Missa Latin term for 'Mass'.

Missa parodia (Latin 'parody Mass') term arising from a mistaken conjunction of the words *Missa* and *parodia* which occur separately on the title page of a Mass by the 16th-century composer Jacques Paix. His Mass is described as 'Parodia mottetae Domine da nobis auxilium', that is, it is based on material from the motet cited. Neither in this work nor in any other are the words *Missa* and *parodia* joined together. Many 15th- and 16th-century Mass cycles were based on material from a motet or polyphonic song, usually named in the title.

Missa pro defunctis 'Mass for the dead'. See ◊requiem.

Missa solemnis, or solennis (Latin 'solemn Mass') title sometimes used by composers for a Mass of a particularly festive or elaborate kind, such as Beethoven's op. 123. Schubert also used it, and it occurs in French as *Messe solennelle* (Gounod). The title is now used particularly for Beethoven's work, composed 1818–23; first performed St Petersburg, 7 April 1824. Three sections were given in Vienna on 7 May 1824, in the concert with the first performance of the Choral Symphony.

Miss Julie opera by Ned Rorem (libretto by K Elmslie after Strindberg), produced New York, 5 November 1965. Daughter of the house seduces servant.
Opera by William Alwyn (libretto by composer, after Strindberg); composed 1961–76, first performed BBC 16 July 1977.

misura (Italian 'measure, time') musical term; thus *senza misura*, 'without time, not strictly in time'. Also the Italian term for 'bar'.

Mitridate Eupatore, II/Mithridates Eupator opera by Alessandro Scarlatti (libretto by G F Roberti), produced Venice, Teatro San Giovanni Grisostomo, Carnival 1707. Mitridate gains revenge after his mother, Stratonica, murders his father, Pontos.

Mitridate, Rè di Ponto/Mithridates, King of Pontus opera by Mozart (libretto by V A Cigna-Santi, based on a tragedy by Racine), produced Milan, Teatro Regio Ducal, 26 December 1770. Brothers Sifare and Farnace love Aspasia, the fiancée of Mithridates. Mithridates is reported killed in battle, but returns and learns of the infidelity. Mortally wounded, however, he gives his blessing to Sifare's and Aspasia's union.

mixer in sound recording, equipment that allows an engineer to set a different volume level for each individual sound track so that solos can be highlighted and loud instruments can be kept from dominating softer ones. Multimedia systems that allow recording generally include similar, though not as sophisticated, functions through software. This is useful in applications such as adding background music to a scene where two people are talking and it is important to hear the voices clearly over the music.

Mixolydian mode one of the ◊church modes, the mode or scale G to F centred around and beginning on G, that uses only notes of the C major scale. It was originally a scale of ancient Greece equivalent to the white notes of a piano from B to A.

mixture an organ stop, controlling at least two rows of very high-pitched pipes. It is not used alone, but in conjunction with lower-pitched pipes in order to enrich the tone quality of a pre-existing combination of stops.

Mlada opera-ballet commissioned from Borodin, Cui, Mussorgsky, and Rimsky-Korsakov by the Russian Imperial Theatres in 1782, but never completed (libretto by V A Krilov).
Opera by Rimsky-Korsakov (libretto as above), produced St Petersburg, 1 November 1892. Voyslava has poisoned rival Mlada, the bride of Prince Yaromir. Using magic to try to seduce him, Voyslava is foiled by Mlada's ghost. Yaromir dreams of the murder and kills Voyslava, before joining Mlada's heavenly spirit.

Mládí/Youth suite for wind sextet in four movements by Janáček, first performed Brno,

21 October 1924, by professors of the Brno Conservatory.

mobile a piece consisting of sections the order of which may be varied at will or according to rules of association, so named after the example of Alexander Calder's mobile sculpture. Examples include Henri Pousseur's *Mobile* for two pianos 1956–58, and *Mobile for Shakespeare* 1959 by Roman Haubenstock-Ramati. See also ◊aleatory music.

mock trumpet early English name for the ◊clarinet, a musical instrument.

modal notation a form of notation in use for vocal music in the 12th and early 13th centuries, where the rhythm was determined not by the shapes of individual notes but by the various types of ligature in which they were combined according to one or other of the rhythmic modes.

mode an ancient or exotic scale of five or more pitches to the octave, often identified with a particular emotion, ritual function, time, or season, to which music is composed or improvised.

mode of limited transposition system of ◊modes developed by Olivier ◊Messiaen. These modes may be transposed only a limited number of times, after which the original notes reappear. The modes are fundamental to Messiaen's harmonic language.

moderato (Italian 'moderate') in musical notation, term indicating a tempo between ◊andante (walking pace) and ◊allegro (lively).

modes, rhythmic the classification of the rhythms of medieval music; six patterns were used, corresponding to poetic rhythms.

modulation movement from one ◊key to another. In classical dance music, modulation is a guide to phrasing rhythm to the step pattern.

Electronic modulation of live or prerecorded instrumental sound is also used to create unusual timbres, as in ◊Stockhausen's *Mixtur* 1964–67 for instrumental groups and ring modulation.

Moeran, E(rnest) J(ohn) (1894–1950) English composer. His music belongs to the English pastoral tradition, Delius being among his major influences. His works include two sets of choral songs with Old English words, two rhapsodies, a symphony and other orchestral works, a violin concerto, a cello concerto for his wife, Peers Coetmore (whom he married in 1945), chamber and piano music, many songs, and arrangements of folksongs.

He was born at Heston, Middlesex, and lived in Norfolk in his childhood, where his father was a clergyman. He was educated at Uppingham School and later studied music at the Royal College of Music in London. After serving in World War I he continued his studies with John Ireland. In 1923 he came to

Rhythmic modes as represented by poetic stresses (left), medieval notation (middle), and modern notation (right).

public notice with a concert of his works given in London, but after some years spent there he retired to Herefordshire.

Works include: Magnificat and Nunc Dimittis, Te Deum and Jubilate, two anthems; *Nocturne* for baritone, chorus, and orchestra (1934), *Songs of Springtime* and suite *Phyllida and Corydon* for unaccompanied chorus (1934), *Blue-eyed Spring* for baritone and chorus; madrigals, part songs, and folk-song arrangements, Sinfonietta, two rhapsodies, symphonic impression *In the Mountain Country* for orchestra (1921), two pieces for small orchestra *Whythorne's Shadow* (1931) and *Lonely Waters* (1932), symphony in G minor (1934–37); concertos for piano, violin, and cello (1942–45); string quartet in A minor, string trio in G major, piano trio in D major, sonata for two violins, violin and piano sonata in E minor; song cycle *Ludlow Town* (texts by Housman) for baritone and piano (1920); seven *Poems of James Joyce* for baritone and piano (1929), and other pieces.

Moeschinger, Albert (1897–1985) Swiss composer. He studied at Bern, Leipzig, and Munich, in the latter place under Courvoisier. In 1927 he settled at Bern as professor, but in 1943 he retired to Saas Fee, Ct Valais, and later to Ascona.

Works include: the motet *Gottes Pfad*, cantata *Angelus Silesius*, *Das Posthorn* for male chorus and orchestra, cantata *Tag unseres Volks*, Mass for chorus and organ (1943), part-songs and other choral works; five symphonies, including *Symphonie à la gloire de ...* and suite for orchestra, variations on a theme by Purcell for strings and percussion, divertimento for strings, *Fantasia 1944* for chamber orchestra; five piano concertos, violin concerto; six string quartets, piano quintet, six wind trios.

Moffat, Alfred (1866–1950) Scottish composer and editor. He studied in Berlin, where he worked for a time. He settled in London in the 1890s and edited a large collection of early string music, including many English and French works, also several volumes of Scottish, Welsh, and Irish folk songs.

Moïse/Moses opera by Rossini, French version of *Mosè in Egitto* (libretto by G L Balochi and V J E de Jouy), produced Paris, Opéra, 26 March 1827. ◊*Mosè in Egitto* for plot synopsis.

Moldenhauer, Hans (1906–1987) US musicologist. He studied with Rosbaud in Mainz and was active as a *répétiteur* and conductor in different European cities. In 1939 he went to the USA, where after further studies he became director and then president of the

Spokane Conservatory (WA) and lecturer at the University of Washington. Moldenhauer's most important contribution to scholarship was his recovery of a large number of Webern manuscripts and documents, including some previously unknown works, and their publication. Books on Webern include *The Death of Anton Webern, A Drama in Documents* (1961) and *Anton Webern: Chronicle of his Life and Work* (1978). He became blind in 1980.

Molière, Jean-Baptiste Poquelin (1622–1673) French dramatist. See ◊*Ariadne auf Naxos* (Bourgeois Gentilhomme, Richard Strauss); ◊*Bourgeois gentilhomme, Le* (R Strauss); M-A ◊Charpentier (*Comtesse d'Escarbagnas* and *Malade imaginaire*); ◊*Fêtes de l'Amour et de Bacchus, Les* (Lully); ◊Galuppi (*Vertuouse ridicole*); ◊Grétry (*Amphitryon*); Rolf Liebermann (*School for Wives*); ◊Lully (*Mariage forcé; Amour médicin, Princesse d'Elide, Sicilien, George Dandin, M de Pourceaugnac, Amants magnifiques* and *Bourgeois Gentilhomme*); ◊*Médecin malgré lui, Le* (Gounod); Virgilio Mortari (*Scuola delle mogli*); Henry ◊Purcell (*Female Virtuosos*); J B Quinault (*Bourgeois Gentilhomme* and *Princesse d'Elide*); Erwin ◊Schulhoff (*Bourgeois Gentilhomme*); ◊Shaporin (*Tartuffe*); ◊Franchetti (*Signor di Pourceaugnac*); ◊Szymanowski (*Bourgeois Gentilhomme*); Rudolf Wagner-Régeny (*Sganarelle*); Ermanno Wolf-Ferrari (*Amor medico*).

moll (German 'soft') in music, German equivalent to 'minor' when referring to ◊key, as in *'B moll'* (B minor).

It is the opposite of *dur* ('hard', 'major').

Molter, Johann Melchoir (1696–1765) German composer. He is known today for having written 170 symphonies (strictly, sinfonias). He also wrote 66 concertos, including 6 for clarinet, and a Passion.

He was Kapellmeister at the court at Karlsruhe, where he was responsible for opera production 1722–33. After a time as director of church music at Eisenach 1734–41 he returned to Karlsruhe. He made several visits to Italy.

molto (Italian 'much', 'very') term used in musical notation, as in *allegro molto*, 'very quickly'.

Moments musicals the title, which in correct French should be *Moments musicaux*, of Schubert's six piano pieces op. 94, written 1823–28.

Mompou, Federico (1893–1987) Spanish pianist and composer. He studied at the Barcelona Conservatory and later in Paris, where Isidore Philipp (1863–1958) was his piano master and Marcel Samuel-Rousseau

(1882–1955) taught him composition. He lived at Barcelona again 1914–21, then settled in Paris, returning to Barcelona 1941.

Works include: piano pieces *6 Impresiones intimas* (1911–14), *Scènes d'enfants* (1915–18), *Suburqis*, three *Pessebres* (1914–17), *Cançó i dansa*, *Cants magics*, *Fêtes lointaines*, *Six Charmes* (1920–21), *Dialogues*, *Three Variations* (1921), *Dix Préludes* (1927–51); songs 'L'hora grisa', 'Cançoneta incerta', 'Quatre Mélodies', 'Le Nuage', 'Trois Comptines'.

Mond, Der/The Moon opera by Orff (libretto by composer with Grimm), produced Munich, 5 February 1939. Four boys steal the moon and hang it on a lamp. When they grow old and die, its light wakes the dead, before the moon is returned to the sky.

Mondo alla roversa, Il, o sia Le donne che comandano/The World Upside Down, or Women in Command opera by Galuppi (libretto by Goldoni), produced Venice, Teatro San Cassiano, 14 November 1750. Old Bonafede refuses to allow the marriage of his daughters Clarice and Flaminia to Ecclitico and Ernesto, but is duped into consent in his moonscape garden.

Mondo della luna, Il/The World of the Moon opera by Galuppi (libretto by Goldoni), produced Venice, Teatro San Moisè, 29 January 1750.

Opera by Haydn (libretto ditto), produced Eszterháza, 3 August 1777. Old Bonafede refuses to allow the marriage of his daughters Clarice and Flaminia to Ecclitico and Ernesto, but is duped into consent in his moonscape garden.

Mondonville, Jean Joseph (Cassanea) de (1711–1772) French violinist and composer. During the *Guerre des Bouffons* in 1752 he was chosen as the representative of the French National school, opposing the Italians under the patronage of Mme de Pompadour.

His parents were aristocrats in reduced circumstances, but he succeeded in studying the violin. He settled in Paris in 1733, made his name as a violinist and composer, and appeared at the Concert Spirituel in 1737, for which he wrote motets until 1770. In 1744 he became superintendent of the royal chapel and was director of the Concert Spirituel 1755–62.

Works include: OPERAS AND OPERA-BALLETS *Isbé* (1742), *Le Carnaval du Parnasse* (1749), *Titon et l'Aurore* (1753), *Daphnis et Alcimaduro* (in Provençal, 1754), *Les Fêtes de Paphos* (1758), *Thésée*, *Psyché* (1762), *Erigone*, *Vénus et Adonis*, *Les Projets de l'Amour*.

ORATORIO *Les Israélites au Mont Oreb* (1758), *Les Fureurs de Saül* (1758), *Les Titans*.

OTHER the *Privilège du Roi* set as a cantata; trio sonatas for two violins or flutes and bass; sonatas including *Les Sons harmoniques* for violin and bass; sonatas and pieces for harpsichord with violin or voice; harpsichord works including *Pièces de clavecin en sonates*; organ pieces.

Moniuszko, Stanisław (1819–1872) Polish composer. He founded a national Polish school of opera in many respects comparable to that of Glinka in Russia. The opera *Halka* 1848 became his most famous, in fact the classic Polish folk opera.

After studying at home, he went to Berlin 1837–39 as a pupil of Carl Rungenhagen. On his return he became an organist at Wilno, where he taught, conducted, and produced a one-act operetta in 1839. After several more works that remained unperformed he produced *The Lottery* at Warsaw in 1846. He produced *Halka* there in 1848 (a revised version was produced in 1858). In 1858 he became conductor at the Warsaw Opera and later professor at the Conservatory. Moniuszko also wrote six Masses, a requiem, secular choral works, orchestral pieces, two string quartets, and about 400 songs.

Works include: the opera *Halka* (performed 1848, revised 1857), *Flis*, *Hrabina/The Countess*, 1860), *Verbum nobile* (1860), *Straszny Dwór/The Haunted Mansion*, 1865), *Paria*, *Beata* (1872); incidental music for Shakespeare's *Hamlet* and *Merry Wives of Windsor* and other plays; cantatas *Spectres*, *Crimean Sonnets*, and others; seven Masses (1850–74), Litanies and other church music; overture *Bajka* (*Fairy Tale*); 270 songs, including ballads by Adam Mickiewicz.

Monk, Meredith (Jane) (1942–) Peruvian-born US composer and singer. She studied at Sarah Lawrence College in Bronxville, Ney York, and has appeared worldwide from 1978 with her vocal group Appearances. Her compositions are closely related to her work as an avant-garde performance artist. Her opera *Atlas* was given at Houston, Texas, in 1991.

A Raw Recital for voice and electric organ 1970; *Quarry*, opera for 38 voices and ensemble 1976; *Engine Steps* for tape collage 1983; *Book of Days* for 25 voices, synthesizer, and piano 1985; *Cat Song* for voice 1988; *Waltz* for two pianos 1988.

Monn, Matthias Georg (1717–1750) Austrian composer and organist. His symphony in D major of 1740 is the earliest dated symphony to have four movements with a minuet in third place.

After being a chorister at Klosterneuburg, near Vienna, he was from about 1738 organist of the Karlskirche in Vienna.

Works include: 21 symphonies; ten partitas for string orchestra; six string quartets; seven harpsichord concertos, including one arranged by Schoenberg for cello and orchestra (1933); keyboard music; church music.

Monna Vanna opera by Février (libretto Maeterlinck's play with alterations), produced Paris, Opéra, 13 January 1909.

Opera by Rakhmaninov (libretto ditto); composed (one act) 1907, first performed (concert) Saratoga, New York, 11 August 1984. Monna Vanna's husband Guido, commander of besieged Pisa, is suspicious of the help given to relieve the town.

monochord (Greek 'one string') in music, an ancient scientific instrument consisting of a single string stretched over a soundbox which is graduated to allow the adjustment of a movable bridge. The monochord is used to demonstrate the existence of ◊harmonics, and the proportional relations of ◊intervals.

monocorde (Italian *monocordo*, 'single string') musical direction used in violin music where the composer wishes a passage to be played on one string.

monodrama a musical stage work for a single singer, an opera with a cast of one, as for example Meyerbeer's *Tevelindens Liebe*, Gomis's *Sensibilidad y prudencia*, or Schoenberg's *Erwartung*. See also ◊*Lélio* (Berlioz).

monody declamation by an accompanied solo voice, used at the turn of the 16th and 17th centuries.

monophonic music in a single melodic part, without harmony, as distinct from homophonic, which is melodic music accompanied by harmony, or polyphonic, which is music in a number of melodic parts moving simultaneously.

monothematic in musical analysis, describing a composition based on a single theme. In the 18th century Haydn experimented with the technique: several finales of his symphonies are composed monothematically. Composers of the 19th century were also interested in the idea, sometimes involving it as a means of creating coherent ◊cyclic form. Schubert's *Fantasia* ('Wanderer') 1822 may be argued to approach monothematicism, as may Liszt's Sonata in B Minor for Piano 1854, which presents themes derived from possibly a single ◊motif. Some composi-

tions using the ◊twelve-tone system have another type of monothematic construction, in which only one twelve-note row is manipulated in the work.

Monsigny, Pierre-Alexandre (1729–1817) French composer. His first opera was produced 1759, and his association with Sedaine as librettist soon consolidated his success. After *Félix* 1777, at the height of his fame, he wrote no more. He lost his fortune during the Revolution, but was given an annuity by the Opéra-Comique.

He studied the violin in his youth, but after the death of his father took an official position in Paris in order to support his family. A performance of *La serva padrona* in 1754 re-awakened his musical interests, and he took composition lessons from Pietro Gianotti (died 1765), double-bass player and author.

Works include: the operas and *opéras-comiques Les Aveux indiscrets* (1759), *Le Maître en droit* (1760), *Le Cadi dupé* (1761), *On ne s'avise jamais de tout*, *Le Roi et le fermier* (1762), *Rose et Colas* (1764), *Aline, reine de Golconde* (1766), *L'Isle sonnante* (after Rabelais), *Le Déserteur* (1769), *Le Faucon* (1771), *La Belle Arsène* (1775), *Félix, ou L'enfant trouvé* (1777), and others.

Montag aus Licht/Monday from 'Light' opera in three acts by Stockhausen (libretto by composer), produced Milan, La Scala, 7 May 1988. The inaugural opera of Stockhausen's *Licht* cycle, but the third to be composed, it celebrates 'Eve's Day'; the three acts are titled *Eve's First Birth*, *Eve's Second Birth*, and *Eve's Magic*.

Montagnana, Domenico (c. 1690–1750) Italian violin maker. Possibly a pupil of Antonio Stradivari, he worked first at Cremona, and set up a workshop in Venice in 1721.

Montague, Stephen (1943–   ) US composer. He moved to London in 1975 and toured widely with Philip Mead from 1985 in a piano duo. He was co-founder of the Electro-Acoustic Music Association of Great Britain, and his music has been featured at the Warsaw, Paris, and Edinburgh Festivals and at the John Cage Festival, London.

He studied at Florida State and Ohio State Universities, USA.

Works include: ballets *Median* (1984) and *The Montague Stomp* (1984); *At the White Edge of Phrygia* for chamber orchestra (1983), *Prologue* for orchestra (1984), piano concerto (1988); *Varshavjan Spring* for chorus and chamber orchestra (1973–80), *Sotto Voce* for chorus and electronics (1976), *Boom-box*

Virelai for four male voices (1993); two string quartets (1989, 1992); keyboard music and electronic pieces.

Monte, Philippe de (1521–1603) Flemish composer. He was one of the most important and prolific late Renaissance polyphonists; about 40 of his Masses, 300 motets, 45 chansons, and over 1,100 madrigals survive. Among his friends were the composers Roland de Lassus and William Byrd. Monte's secular music enjoyed widespread popularity, as the distribution of his publications and manuscripts testifies.

Monte was born in Malines, and went to Italy while still young. He served the Pinelli family in Naples 1542–51 as singer, teacher, and composer. In 1554 he left Naples and went to the Netherlands. He was in England 1554–55 as a member of the choir of Philip II of Spain, when he met William Byrd and his family; by 1558 he had returned to Italy. In 1568 he went to Vienna as Kapellmeister to the Emperor Maximilian II, after whose death in 1576 he followed the next emperor, Rudolph II, to Prague. He served the emperor for the rest of his life, and was made a canon of Cambrai Cathedral, but did not reside there.

Many of his Masses are based on motets by contemporary composers. His madrigal settings follow the text closely (most of the texts are by contemporary pastoral poets such as Guarini); his later madrigals are simpler in form and increasingly homophonous.

Works include: around 40 Masses, motets; over 30 books of madrigals, including 1,073 secular and 144 spiritual works. His motet *Super flumina Babylonis* was sent to Byrd in 1583, to which the latter responded with *Quomodo cantabimus* in 1584.

Montéclair, Michel (Pinolet) de (1667–1737) French composer, theorist, and teacher. He studied music as a chorister at Langres Cathedral, later he sang in other churches, and went to Italy in the service of the Prince de Vaudémont. After 1702 he settled in Paris and played the double bass in the Opéra orchestra from 1707 until his death.

Works include: the operas and operaballets *Les Festes de l'été* (1716) and *Jephté* (1732), ballet music for C F Pollaroli's opera *Ascanio*; chamber music, cantatas, and sacred music.

Montemezzi, Italo (1875–1952) Italian composer. He learnt the piano as a child, then went to Milan to be trained for engineering, but wished to take up music. He entered the

Conservatory with some difficulty, but obtained a diploma there in 1900. After the production of his first opera in 1905 he was able to give all his time to composition. From 1939 to 1949 he was in the USA, after which he returned to Italy.

Works include: the operas *Giovanni Gallurese* (1905), *Hellera* (1909), *L'amore dei tre re* (1913), *La Nave* (d'Annunzio, 1918), *La notte di Zoraima* (1931), *La principessa lontana* (after Rostand's *Princesse lointaine*, 1931); *The Song of Songs* for chorus or orchestra; symphonic poem *Paolo e Virginia* (after Saint-Pierre); elegy for cello and piano.

Monteux, Pierre (1875–1964) French conductor. Ravel's *Daphnis and Chloe* and Stravinsky's *The Rite of Spring* were first performed under his direction. He conducted Diaghilev's Ballets Russes 1911–14 and 1917, and the San Francisco Symphony Orchestra 1935–52.

Monteverdi, Claudio Giovanni Antonio (1567–1643) Italian composer. He contributed to the development of the opera with *La favola d'Orfeo/The Legend of Orpheus* 1607 and *L'incoronazione di Poppea/The Coronation of Poppea* 1642. He also wrote madrigals, motets, and sacred music, notably the *Vespers* 1610.

Born in Cremona, he was in the service of the Duke of Mantua about 1591–1612, and was director of music at St Mark's, Venice, from 1613. He was first to use an orchestra and to reveal the dramatic possibilities of the operatic form. His first opera *Orfeo* was produced for the carnival at Mantua in 1607.

Monteverdi was the son of a doctor. He was a chorister at Cremona Cathedral and a pupil of Ingegneri, he then became an organist and viol player and in 1583, aged 16, published sacred madrigals. About 1591 he entered the service of the Duke of Mantua, Vincenzo Gonzaga, as a viol player and singer, and there married the harpist Claudia Cataneo. He was in Gonzaga's retinue in the war against the Turks on the Danube and again in Flanders in 1599. He probably heard Peri's *Euridice* at Florence in 1600, and in 1602 was made music master to the court of Mantua. His wife died in 1607 after a long illness, and in the same year Monteverdi finished his first opera, *La favola d'Orfeo*; this remains the earliest opera to be regularly performed today. His next opera, *Arianna*, now lost except for the famous 'Lament', made him widely famous. Meanwhile Monteverdi had written his first five books of madrigals, which are scarcely less important in the development of their species. In 1610 he dedicated his collection of church music, the *Vespers*, to Pope Paul V; from the opening chorus, based on the Toccata of *Orfeo*, and through to the concluding Magnificat, it is evident that the art of music is moving away for the first time from private use and into the public domain.

When Francesco Gonzaga succeeded his brother to the dukedom in 1612, he quarrelled with Monteverdi, who left for Cremona to wait for a new appointment. This came from Venice in 1613, where he was was appointed maestro to St Mark's, the most coveted church appointment in north Italy. He remained there until his death, adding church music of great splendour to his previous output. He had by this time written much church music and numerous madrigals. His church music makes supremely effective use of the particular architecture of St Mark's, deploying separate groups of instruments and singers in order to exploit antiphonal effects. The nine books of madrigals develop from the small-scale pieces of 1587 to the hugely extended forms in Book 8 of 1638. In 1630 he took holy orders after escaping the plague at Venice. In 1639 the second public opera theatre in Venice, the Teatro dei SS Giovanni e Paolo, was opened with Monteverdi's *Adone*, and *Arianna* was revived the same year when the Teatro di San Moisè was inaugurated. Two further operas survive from this period: *Il ritorno d'Ulisse in patria* 1641, and his last opera *L'Incoronazione di Poppea*, widely performed today in an increasing variety of editions. Monteverdi's work in this genre was highly important and influential in establishing opera during this early period. More broadly, Monteverdi was a key figure in providing the impetus for change in which secular music and music for the general public became increasingly important.

Works include: the operas *Orfeo* (1607), *Arianna* (lost except the 'Lament', 1608), *Il combattimento di Tancredi e Clorinda* (after Tasso, 1624), *Il ritorno d'Ulisse in patria* (1640), *L'incoronazione di Poppea* (1642), and about a dozen lost stage works; ballets *Ballo delle ingrate* (1608) and *Tirsi e Clori* (1619); Masses, Magnificats and psalms; *Vespers* (1610), *Sancta Maria* for voice and eight instruments; 40 sacred madrigals; 21 *canzonette* for three voices; nine books of secular madrigals containing 250, including book VIII, *Madrigali guerrieri e amorosi/Madrigals of love and war* ; 26 madrigals published in various collections; 25 *Scherzi musicali* for one to three voices (1607).

Montezuma opera by Roger Sessions (libretto by G A Borgese); composed 1941–63, produced West Berlin, 19 April 1964.

Monticelli, Angelo Maria (c. 1710–1764) Italian castrato soprano. He made his debut in Rome in 1730, sang in London, 1741–46 (in Gluck's two operas for London, *La caduta dei giganti* and *Artamene*), later in Naples, Vienna and, from 1756, in Dresden under Hasse.

Montsalvatge (Bassols), Xavier (1912–) Catalan composer. He studied with Enrique Morera and Jaime Pahissa at the Barcelona Conservatory, winning the Pedrell Prize in 1936.

Works include: the opera *El gato con botas* (1947); four ballets; *Sinfonia mediterranea* (1949); *Concerto breve* for piano and orchestra (1956), *Poema concertante* for violin and orchestra; orchestral suite *Calidoscopo*; string quartet (1952); songs.

Monumentum pro Gesualdo di Venosa ad CD annum three madrigals recomposed in 1960 by Igor Stravinsky for 12 wind instruments and strings to celebrate the 400th anniversary of Gesualdo's birth. First performed Venice, 27 September 1960. The madrigals are *Asciugate i belli occhi, Ma tu, cagion di quella, Belta poi che t'assenti*.

mood (Latin *modus*) in music, the relationship between the long and the breve in mensural notation.

Moog, Robert US electronic instrument designer; see ◊Moog synthesizer.

Moog synthesizer any of a family of inexpensive analogue ◊synthesizers developed in 1963 by Robert Moog (1934–), incorporating transistorized electronics and voltage control, which brought electronic music synthesis within the reach of composers, performers, and academic institutions. A Moog-designed ◊theremin featured in the Beach Boys' hit 'Good Vibrations' 1966.

Moonlight Sonata the nickname of Beethoven's piano sonata in C♯ minor, op. 27 no. 2, probably due to a description of the first movement by Rellstab.

Moore, Douglas (Stuart) (1893–1969) US composer. He studied at Yale University and with Horatio Parker, Bloch, d'Indy, Tournemire, and Nadia Boulanger. He served in the US Navy in World War I, was an organist and lecturer at Cleveland 1921–25, and taught at Columbia University in New York 1926–62.

Works include: the operas *The Devil and Daniel Webster* (1939), *The Ballad of Baby Doe* (1956), and *Carrie Nation* (1966), operetta *The Headless Horseman* (1936), chamber opera

White Wings (1935); motet *Dedication* for six voices, *Simon Legree* for male chorus, *Perhaps to dream* for female chorus; *A Symphony of Autumn, Overture on an American Tune, Pageant of P T Barnum* (1924), *Moby Dick* (after Herman Melville), *In Memoriam,* symphony in A for orchestra (1945); string quartet; sonata and *Down East* suite for violin and piano; wind quintet, clarinet quintet.

Moore, Jerrold Northrop (1934–) US musicologist. He studied at Yale and was curator of sound recordings there, 1961–70. He resided in England from 1970. He became an authority on Elgar, co-editing the *Elgar Complete Edition* and publishing *Elgar: a Life in Photographs* (1974), *Spirit of England: Edward Elgar in his World* (1984), and *Edward Elgar: A Creative Life* (1984). He also edited Elgar's letters.

Moore, Thomas (1779–1852) Irish poet. From about 1802 he began to publish songs with words and occasionally music by himself, and between 1807 and 1834 he produced collections of Irish tunes with new words of his own. He also produced, in 1811, an opera *M P, or The Blue Stocking* with music by himself and C E Horn. He wrote the tune as well as the words of 'The Last Rose of Summer', used by Flotow in *Martha*. For works used by composers, see W S ◊Bennett (*Paradise and the Peri*); Frederic ◊Clay (*Lalla Rookh*); ◊Feramors (A Rubinstein); ◊*Paradise and the Peri* (Schumann); ◊Spontini (*Nurmahal* and *Lalla Rookh*).

Morales, Cristóbal (c. 1500–1553) Spanish composer. He wrote many masses and motets which rank him among the finest contrapuntists of his time. Palestrina based a mass on his motet *O sacrum convivium*.

He studied at Seville under the cathedral maestro de capilla Fernández de Castilleja. He was maestro di cappella at Avila 1526–30, and some time later went to Rome, where he was ordained a priest and became cantor in the Pontifical Chapel in 1535. In 1545 he was given leave to visit Spain, but did not return, remaining as maestro di cappella at Toledo and Málaga, and serving in the household of the Duke of Arcos at Marchena.

Works include: 21 Masses, 16 Magnificats, 91 motets, Lamentations and other church music; cantatas for the peace conference at Nice (1538) and for Ippolito d'Este; madrigals.

Moran, Robert (1937–) US composer. His music has embraced random choice techniques, minimalism, and multiple synthesizers. His *Smell Piece for Mills College* 1967 was

intended to burn down his alma mater and was followed by the chamber opera *Let's Build a Nut House* 1969.

He studied in Vienna, and with Berio and Milhaud at Mills College. He has performed throughout the USA and Europe as a pianist, and has lectured widely. He directed the West Coast Music Ensemble and taught at the San Francisco Conservatory. His environment piece *Hitler: Geschichten aus der Zukunft* 1981 was too much for the Germans who commissioned it, and was promptly banned; the succeeding *Erlöser*, a music drama in two acts, depicts the rantings of a dying Wagner. A collaboration with Philip Glass on the opera *The Juniper Tree* 1985 prompted a conversion to synthesizer-inspired Romanticism: *Desert of Roses* 1992 is based on the *Beauty and the Beast* story, while *From the Towers of the Moon* 1992 is prompted by an ancient Japanese legend. *The Dracula Diary* 1994 suggested a return to anarchism.

Moravia, Hieronymus de (lived 13th century) music theorist, probably a Dominican friar living in Paris. His *Tractatus de Musica* is a comprehensive compilation dealing mainly with plainsong, with an extensive tonary attached.

mordent a specific type of ◊ornamentation which consists of the rapid alternation (usually only once) of the written note with the note a semitone or whole-tone below it. It begins on the beat rather than before it.

The notation for mordents on D and F, and the approximate execution of each.

Mörder, Hoffnung der Frauen/Murder, the Hope of Women opera in one act by Hindemith (libretto by Oskar Kokoschka); composed 1919, first performed Stuttgart, 4 June 1921, conductor Fritz Busch. Sado-erotic meeting of a Man and a Woman.

Moreau, Jean-Baptiste (1656–1733) French composer. He learnt music as a boy chorister at Angers Cathedral and composed motets as a youth. He was appointed choirmaster at the cathedral of Langres (where he married), and later at Dijon. He went to Paris during the

1680s and found his way into the court, for which he began to write stage pieces. In 1688 he was commissioned to write music for Racine's *Esther* for performance at the young ladies' academy of Saint-Cyr. This earned him a pension for life and an appointment at Saint-Cyr jointly with the organist Nivers and later with Clérambault. He remained under the patronage of the king and Mme de Maintenon. He taught both singing and composition, among his pupils for the former were his daughter Claude-Marie Moreau ,and for the latter Clérambault, Dandrieu, and Montéclair.

Works include: Requiem, motet *In exitu Israel* (1691), *Cantiques spirituels* (Racine), Te Deum for the king's recovery (1687) and other church music; stage divertissements including *Les Bergers de Marly*; chorus for Racine's *Athalie* (1691); *Idylle sur la naissance de Notre Seigneur*; drinking songs.

morendo (Italian 'dying') in musical notation, becoming softer.

Moresca Moorish dance of remote antiquity, first introduced by the Moors into Spain and popular all over Europe by the 15th–16th centuries. Allied to the English Morris Dance, 'morys' being an English variant of 'Moorish'; at any rate one of the latter's features – bells or jingles tied to the legs – belonged to the moresca also.

Morhange, Charles Henri Valentin see ◊Alkan.

Mörike, Eduard (Friedrich) (1804–1875) German poet. His works inspired Othmar ◊Schoeck (songs); Heinrich ◊Sutermeister (*Jorinde*; Max ◊Trapp (*Letzte König von Orplid*). 2 songs were set by Brahms, 3 by Schumann, 57 (including four early) by H Wolf.

Morley, Thomas (c. 1557–c. 1602) English composer. He wrote consort music, madrigals, and airs including the lute song 'It was a lover and his lass' for Shakespeare's play *As You Like It* 1599. He edited a collection of Italian madrigals *The Triumphs of Oriana* 1601, and published an influential keyboard tutor *A Plaine and Easie Introduction to Practicall Musicke* 1597. He was also organist at St Paul's Cathedral, London.

'Morning Heroes' symphony for orator, chorus, and orchestra by Bliss (words by Homer, Li-Tai-Po, Whitman, Robert Nichols and Wilfred Owen), first performed Norwich Festival, 6 October 1930.

Moross, Jerome (1913–1983) US composer. He studied at Juilliard and worked in Hollywood from 1940. He is best known for ballets and ballet-operas: *Paul Bunyan* (1934), *Ameri-*

can Patterns (1937), *Susannah and the Elders* (1940), *The Eccentricities of Davy Crockett* (1946), *The Golden Apple* (1952), *Sorry, Wrong Number* (composed 1983).

Morris, R(eginald) O(wen) (1886–1948) English teacher and composer. He was educated at Harrow, New College, Oxford, and the Royal College of Music in London, where later he became professor of counterpoint and composition. In 1926 he was appointed to a similar post at the Curtis Institute at Philadelphia, but soon returned to England. His books include *Contrapuntal Technique in the 16th Century*, *Foundations of Practical Harmony and Counterpoint*, *The Structure of Music*.

Works include: symphony in D major; violin concerto in G minor, *Concerto piccolo* for two violins and strings; fantasy for string quartet, Motets for string quartet; songs with quartet accompaniment.

Morris dance old English folk dance, deriving its name from the Moorish *Moresca* (old English 'morys', 'Moorish'), introduced into England about the 15th century. It partook of a pageant in character and was danced in various kinds of fancy dress, with jingles tied to the dancers' legs. In some districts elements of the Sword Dance were introduced into it. The music, a great variety of tunes, was played by a pipe and tabor, or more rarely by a bagpipe or violin.

Mors et Vita/Death and [New] Life oratorio by Gounod, a sequel to *The Redemption*, produced Birmingham Festival, 26 August 1885.

Morton, Robert (c. 1430–c. 1476) English singer and composer. He composed French chansons, of which two were among the most popular of their day. He was employed at the court of Burgundy 1457–76, under Philip the Good and Charles the Bold.

Moscheles, Ignaz (1794–1870) Bohemian pianist and composer. He composed about 140 opus numbers, including piano concertos, sonatas, chamber music, and studies for the piano. He was a gifted improviser and introduced some innovations in piano playing later developed by the Liszt school. His correspondence with Mendelssohn was published in 1888, and an English translation of a biography by his wife in 1873.

He was born at Prague, and studied under Dionys Weber at the Conservatory there. He played a concerto in public at the age of 14. He was sent to Vienna and there took lessons in counterpoint from Johann Albrechtsberger and composition from Salieri. He made

Beethoven's acquaintance when he arranged the vocal score of *Fidelio* in 1814. He then began to travel widely, and in 1821 appeared in Holland, Paris, and London. In 1824 he taught Mendelssohn in Berlin and became his lifelong friend; in 1826 he married Charlotte Embden at Hamburg and settled permanently in London as a teacher and soloist, and became one of the directors of the Philharmonic Society. In 1832 he conducted the first performance there of Beethoven's *Missa solemnis*. In 1846 he went to Leipzig at Mendelssohn's invitation to become first piano professor at the new conservatory.

Works include: symphony in C (1829); eight piano concertos (1819–38), including G minor and *Concerto pathétique*; a great number of piano works including *Sonate mélancolique, Characteristic Studies, Allegro di bravura* and numerous sonatas, variations, fantasies, studies, and other pieces; *Hommage à Händel* for two pianos.

Mosè in Egitto/Moses in Egypt opera by Rossini (libretto by A L Tottola), produced Naples, Teatro San Carlo, 5 March 1818. Moses frees the Israelites in Egypt and parts the Red Sea on the way home.

See also ◊*Moïse.*

Moser, Hans Joachim (1889–1967) German singer, musicologist, and composer. He studied with his father, Andreas Moser (1859–1925), who was a violinist and writer on music, author of a biography of Joachim. He was later educated at Berlin, Marburg, and Leipzig, and became professor of musicology at Halle, Heidelberg, and later Berlin. His literary works include a history of German music, studies of medieval string music, Luther's songs, German song, and biographies of Hofhaimer, Schütz, and Bach.

Moses und Aron/Moses and Aaron opera in two acts by Schoenberg (projected third act never composed; libretto by composer), first performed (concert), Hamburg, 12 March 1954; produced Zurich, 6 June 1957 (music composed 1930–32). Moses and his brother Aaron bring God's message to the people, but the Israelites cannot understand Moses' abstract ideas. Aaron leads an orgy around the Golden Calf, but Moses interrupts with the Tablets of the Law.

Mosonyi, Mihály (1815–1870), adopted name of Michael Brand Hungarian composer. He studied at Pozsony (now Bratislava) and was music master to a noble family 1835–42, then settled at Budapest. He changed his German name of Brand in 1859, when he

began to aim at writing Hungarian national music.

Works include: the operas *Kaiser Max auf der Martinswand* (composed 1857), *The Fair Ilonka* (1861), and *Almos*, 1862; both in Hungarian; three Masses; symphonies, symphonic poems *Mourning for Széchényi* and *Festival Music* and other orchestral works; 20 piano pieces in the Hungarian manner; 25 Hungarian folk-song arrangements.

mosso (Italian 'moved') term used in musical notation, as in *più mosso* ('more moved'), meaning faster.

Mossolov, Aleksandr Vassilevich (1900–1973) Russian pianist and composer. His family, which cultivated various branches of art, moved to Moscow in 1904 and in 1921 he entered the Conservatory there, studying under Glière until 1925. He travelled much as a pianist and to study folk music in central Asia.

Works include: the operas *The Dam, The Hero* (1928), *The Signal* (1941); cantatas *Sphinx* (Oscar Wilde) and *Kirghiz Rhapsody*; six symphonies (1929–50), ballet *The Factory* (1927) with realistic sound effects, including a shaken metal sheet, also performed as a concert item with the title *The Iron Foundry* (*Music of Machines*); *Turcomanian Suite* and *Uzbek Dance* for orchestra; two piano concertos (1927, 1935), violin concerto, harp concerto, two cello concertos; string quartet, *Dance Suite* for piano trio; viola and piano sonata; songs to words by Pushkin, Lermontov, and Blok; massed choruses, battle songs.

motet sacred, polyphonic music for unaccompanied voices in a form that originated in 13th-century Europe.

Mother Goose (Ravel). See ◊*Ma Mère l'Oye.*

Mother of Us All, The opera by Virgil Thomson (libretto by G Stein), produced New York Brander Matthews Theatre, Columbia University, 7 May 1947.

motif, or motive in music, a group of at least two notes forming an intelligible, characteristic figure, which through repetition and development forms a foundation for larger figures and themes; one of the most basic units of composition. Often, a single motif will serve as the building block for a variety of themes and accompaniment figures.

Beethoven was one of the greatest masters of motivic composition. The first movement of his Fifth Symphony 1808 is a famous example of the constant recurrence of the four-note motif which forms the first four notes of the piece. Throughout the 19th century, composers relied on motifs to provide compositional coherence in an era in which traditional large-scale structures such as ◊sonata form were beginning to lose their relevance. Motifs continued to be an essential compositional tool to early 20th-century artists, including Schoenberg and Stravinsky. Since the evolution of chance procedures and other avant-garde techniques introduced in the 1950s, many composers have abandoned the motif, but it still remains a vital part of composition. See: ◊motivic analysis; ◊developing variation; ◊musical idea.

motion the succession of notes of different pitch. The word is used only with some adjectival qualification or other: **conjunct motion**, a single part moving by steps of adjoining notes; **contrary motion**, two or more parts moving together in different directions; **disjunct motion**, a single part moving by larger than stepwise intervals; **oblique motion**, one part moving when another stands still; and **similar motion**, two or more parts moving together in the same direction.

motivic analysis method of analysing a piece of music according to its important constituent motives. The method identifies ways in which motives are transformed or developed, and links melodies which contain identical or similar motives. A motive which is linked to all the other motivic material of a piece may be called the fundamental motive. The method is equally applicable to tonal and nontonal music, but limited by having little to say concerning harmonic features of a work. See: Arnold ◊Schoenberg; Hans ◊Keller; ◊developing variation; ◊musical idea.

moto (Italian 'motion') term used in musical notation, as in *andante con moto* ('andante with motion'), meaning faster than the usual ◊andante tempo.

moto perpetuo (Italian 'perpetual motion') musical piece exploiting rapid figuration of a uniform and uninterrupted pattern; also called by the Latin name of *perpetuum mobile*.

motoric rhythm a 20th-century term for rhythm based on one specific note value (quavers, for example), usually in order to sustain or generate energy. ◊Ostinatos (repeating melodic or rhythmic figures) often form motoric rhythms, as in Stravinsky's *The Rite of Spring* 1913.

Mottl, Felix (Josef) (1856–1911) Austrian conductor and composer. He studied at a choir school and at the Conservatory in Vienna, became conductor of the Wagner

Society there and in 1876 was engaged by Richard Wagner to conduct the music on the stage in the production of the *Ring*; gave *Tristan* and *Parsifal* at Bayreuth in 1886. In 1881–1903 he was conductor at the ducal court of Karlsruhe, where he directed the symphonic concerts and the opera, producing many unfamiliar works including the first performance of all five acts of *Les Troyens* (1890). From 1903 he was conductor in Munich. He collapsed while conducting *Tristan* and died shortly after.

Works include: the operas *Agnes Bernauer* (after Hebbel), *Rama* and *Fürst und Sänger*; festival play *Eberstein*; music for O J Bierbaum's play *Pan im Busch*; string quartet (1904); songs.

motto short and well-defined theme usually occurring at the opening of a composition and used again during its course, in its first form or altered, in the manner of a quotation or an allusion to some definite idea. The opening themes in Tchaikovsky's fourth and fifth symphonies are familiar examples.

Mount of Olives, The (Beethoven). See ◊*Christus am Oelberg*.

Mouret, Jean Joseph (1682–1738) French composer. He entered the service of the Duchess of Maine in Paris about 1707 and in 1714 began to write for the stage. He was director of the Concert Spirituel 1728–34, also for a time conductor of the Comédie-Italienne. In 1736 he became insane and was taken to the psychiatric hospital of Charenton.

Works include: the operas and opera-ballets *Les Festes de Thalie, Ragonde, Ariane* (1717), *Les Amours des dieux* (1727), *Le Triomphe des sens* (1732), and others; Mass, two books of motets; cantatas *Cantatilles*; two *Suites de Symphonies*, 47 divertissements for orchestra; two books of *Concerts de chambre*; fanfares.

Mourning Symphony (Haydn). See ◊*Trauer-Sinfonie*.

Moussorgsky see Modest ◊Mussorgsky.

mouth organ any of a family of small portable free-reed wind instruments originating in Eastern and South Asia. The compact **harmonica**, or European mouth organ, developed by Charles Wheatstone in 1829, has tuned metal free reeds of variable length contained in a narrow rectangular box and is played by blowing and sucking air while moving the instrument from side to side through the lips.

As the **mouth harp**, the mouth organ is a staple instrument in Country and Western music. As a melody instrument it achieved concert status through the virtuosity of Larry Adler. All mouth organs bend in pitch in response to variation in pressure of the player's breath.

The Chinese sheng, Japanese sho, and Laotian khen are examples of early mouth organs. These older forms consist of a bundle of up to 17 pitch pipes connected at the base to a common wind chamber and mouthpiece, and played by closing finger holes in the pipes that are to sound, forcing air to escape through the free reeds and creating a variable harmony. There are interesting resemblances with the medieval regal, also a portable free-reed instrument, but incorporating Western refinements of a keyboard and bellows.

Mouton, Jean (c. 1459–1522) French composer. He was in the service of Louis XII and François I, and became canon of Thérouanne, which he left probably on its being taken by the English in 1513, and afterwards of the collegiate church of Saint-Quentin.

He was a pupil of Josquin Desprez.

Works include: 14 Masses, 110 motets, psalms, *Alleluia* and *In illo tempore* for Easter, *Noe, noe, psallite* for Christmas, and other pieces.

mouvement (French 'tempo, pace') movement of a sonata, symphony.

Mouvements de cœur seven songs for bass and piano in memory of Chopin (poems by Louise de Vilmorin): 1. *Prélude*: Henri Sauguet; 2. *Mazurka*: Francis Poulenc; 3. *Valse*: Georges Auric; 4. *Scherzo Impromptu*: Jean Françaix; 5. *Étude*: Léo Preger; 6. *Ballade* (*Nocturne*): Darius Milhaud; 7. *Postlude, Polonaise*: Sauguet.

movable doh the ◊tonic or keynote in the tonic sol-fa system which shifts the tonal centre at each modulation into another key instead of prescribing accidentals.

movement a self-contained composition of specific character, usually a constituent piece of a ◊suite, ◊symphony, or similar work, with its own tempo, distinct from that of the other movements.

Movements work for piano and orchestra by Stravinsky; composed 1958–59, first performed New York, 10 January 1960, with Marchgit Weber, who commissioned the score.

Mozarabic chant one of the important branches of early Latin chant, also called Visigothic, and used in central and southern Spain during the Middle Ages. Liturgically it is associated with the Gallican and Ambrosian rites, pre-dating that of Rome and showing similarities with Eastern liturgies. Its music is found in manuscripts of the 8th–11th centuries, but mostly in undecipherable neumes. Only a few melodies survive in readable form. Roman chant and rite were imposed everywhere by 1076 except in Toledo, and in spite of the attempted revival under Cardinal Francisco de Cisneros (c. 1500), little of the musical tradition has been preserved.

Mozart, (Johann Chrysostom) Wolfgang Amadeus (1756–1791) Austrian composer and performer who showed astonishing precocity as a child and was an adult virtuoso. He was trained by his father, **Leopold Mozart** (1719–1787). From an early age he composed prolifically, and his works include 27 piano concertos, 23 string quartets, 35 violin sonatas, and 41 symphonies including the E♭ K543, G minor K550, and C major K551 ('Jupiter') symphonies, all composed in 1788. His operas include *Idomeneo* 1780, *Entführung aus dem Serail/The Abduction from the Seraglio* 1782, *Le Nozze di Figaro/The Marriage of Figaro* 1786, *Don Giovanni* 1787, *Così fan tutte/Thus Do All Women* 1790, and *Die Zauberflöte/The Magic Flute* 1791. Together with the work of Haydn, Mozart's music marks the height of the Classical age in its purity of melody and form.

Mozart's career began when, with his sister, Maria Anna, he was taken on a number of tours 1762–79, visiting Vienna, the Rhineland, Holland, Paris, London, and Italy. He had already begun to compose. In 1772 he was appointed master of the archbishop of Salzburg's court band, but found the post uncongenial and in 1781 was suddenly dismissed. He married Constanze Weber in 1782, settled in Vienna, and embarked on a punishing freelance career as a concert pianist, composer, and teacher that brought lasting fame but only intermittent financial security. His *Requiem*, unfinished at his death, was completed by a pupil.

His works were catalogued chronologically in 1862 by the musicologist Ludwig von Köchel (1800–1877) whose system of numbering – giving each work a 'Köchel number', for example K354 – remains in use in modified form.

Mozart showed early signs of talent, learnt the harpsichord from the age of three or four, and began to compose under his father's supervision when he was five. With his sister (then aged 11) he was taken to Munich in 1762, then to Vienna, where they played at court. Encouraged by their success, Leopold Mozart set out with the children the following year on a longer tour, which took them first through southern Germany, on to Brussels, and to Paris, where they arrived in November 1763. They appeared at court at Versailles, and four sonatas for violin and harpsichord by Mozart were published in Paris. Moving on to London in April 1764, they played before the royal family and made a sensation in public concerts.

In London Mozart was befriended by J C Bach, three of whose sonatas he arranged as piano concertos, and who also influenced the symphonies and other pieces he wrote at the time. They left for Holland in July 1765, and after several stops on the journey through France and Switzerland returned to Salzburg in November 1766. The next months were spent in study and composition, but in September 1767 the whole family went to Vienna. There Mozart composed his first Mass (C minor, K139) and produced the *Singspiel Bastien und Bastienne*, though intrigues thwarted the performance of the opera *La finta simplice*. Returning to Salzburg in January 1769, Mozart had barely a year at home before setting out with his father on an extended tour of Italy; in Rome he wrote down Allegri's *Miserere* from memory, in Bologna he took lessons from Padre Martini and gained election to the Philharmonic Society with a contrapuntal exercise, and in Milan he produced the opera *Mitridate* with great success in December 1770.

Two further visits to Italy followed, both to Milan, for the performance of the serenata *Ascanio in Alba* in October 1771, and the opera *Lucio Silla* in December 1772. At the performance of *Ascanio*, Johann Hasse is alleged to have said 'This boy will cause us all to be forgotten'. Apart from short visits to Vienna, 1773, and Munich, 1775 for the production of *La finta giardiniera* 1775, most of the next five years was spent in Salzburg, his longest period at home since infancy. In September 1777, in company with his mother, he embarked on a lengthy journey which took them via Mannheim to Paris, where his mother died in July 1778. The main object of this trip was to find suitable employment, but being unsuccessful Mozart returned in January 1779 to the uncongenial post of court organist at Salzburg. One of his finest instrumental works, the *Sinfonia concertante* K364, was written later that year.

His opera seria *Idomeneo* was produced in Munich in January 1781, but later the same year, on a visit to Vienna with the household of the Archbishop of Salzburg, he gave up his post to settle in Vienna as a freelance, living by teaching and playing in concerts. His German opera *Die Entführung aus dem Serail* was produced in July 1782, and the next month he married Constanze Weber, whose sister Aloysia, a notable singer, he had courted unsuccessfully in Mannheim four years before. At the height of his fame as a pianist, 1782–86, he composed many concertos for his own use, but thereafter was increasingly plagued by financial worries, which his appointment in 1787 as court composer on the death of Gluck did little to ease. The first of three operas on libretti by the Italian poet Lorenzo da Ponte, *Le Nozze di Figaro*, was produced in 1786, followed by *Don Giovanni* for Prague, 1787 and *Così fan tutte* 1790. In these works Mozart brought opera to new heights of musical ingenuity, dramatic truth, and brilliance of expression. For almost the first time opera characters are recognizable human beings, rather than stock types.

In 1788 he wrote his last three symphonies, the summation of the Classical symphonic style. Assimilating all he had learned from Haydn and others, he took standard forms and gave them new meaning. A visit to Berlin with Prince Lichnowsky in 1789 took him through Leipzig, where he discussed Bach's music with Doles, Bach's successor, and in 1790 he made a fruitless journey to Frankfurt, hoping to earn money as a pianist. After several lean years, 1791 was one of overwork, which must have contributed to his early death; in addition to the last piano concerto (K595), the clarinet concerto (K622), and several smaller works, he composed the operas *La Clemenza di Tito* (produced in Prague for the coronation of Emperor Leopold II), and *Die Zauberflöte* (produced in Vienna). The Requiem remained unfinished at Mozart's death, and was completed later by his pupil Franz Süssmayr.

While Mozart was not a great innovator in the manner of Haydn and Beethoven, he set creative standards in a wide variety of forms to which later composers could only aspire.

Works include: OPERA *Idomeneo, Rè di Creta* (1781), *Die Entführung aus dem Serail* (1782), *Le nozze di Figaro* (1786), *Don Giovanni* (1787), *Così fan tutte* (1790), *Die Zauberflöte* (1791), *La Clemenza di Tito* (1791). Ballet *Les petits riens* (1778).

CHURCH MUSIC including Motet, *Exsultate, jubilate* for soprano, organ, and orchestra, (K165, 1773), *Kyrie* in D minor (K341, 1781), Mass in C, *Coronation* (K317, 1779), *Vesperae solennes de confessore* (K339, 1780), Mass in C minor, unfinished (K427, 1783), Motet, *Ave verum corpus* (K618, 1791), Requiem Mass in D minor, unfinished (K626, 1791).

SYMPHONIES (41; nos. 1–24 composed 1764–73), no. 25 in G minor (K183, 1773), no. 29 in A (K201, 1774), no. 31 in D. *Paris* (K297, 1778), no. 34 in C (K338, 1780), no. 35 in D, *Haffner* (K385, 1782), no. 36 in C, *Linz* (K425, 1783), no. 38 in D, *Prague* (K504, 1786), no. 39 in E♭ (K543, 1788), no. 40 in G minor (K550, 1788), no. 41 in C, *Jupiter* (K551, 1788). Other music for orchestra includes Divertimenti in D (K136, 1772), in B♭ (K137, 1772), in F (K138, 1772), in B♭ (K287, 1777), in D (K334, 1779–80); Serenades in D (K239, 1776, *Serenata Notturna*), in D (K250, 1776, *Haffner*), in D, for four orchestras (K286, 1777), in D (K320, 1779, *Posthorn*), in B♭ for 13 wind instruments (K361, 1781), in E♭ for eight wind instruments (K375, 1781), in C minor for eight wind instruments (K388, 1782 or 3), in G for strings (K525, 1787, *Eine kleine Nachtmusik*); *Mauerische Trauermusik/Masonic Funeral Music* (K477, 1785).

CONCERTOS 27 for piano, including no. 9 in E♭ (K271, 1777), no. 14 in E♭ (K449, 1784), no. 15 in B♭ (K450, 1784), no. 16 in D (K451, 1784), no. 17 in G (K453, 1784), no. 18 in B♭ (K456, 1784), no. 19 in F (K459, 1784), no. 20 in D minor (K466, 1785), no. 21 in C (K467, 1785), no. 22 in E♭ (K482, 1785), no. 23 in A (K488, 1786), no. 24 in C minor (K491, 1786), no. 25 in C (K503, 1786), no. 26 in D, *Coronation* (K537, 1788), no. 27 in B♭ (K595, 1791); five for violin, including no. 3 in G (K216, 1775), no. 4 in D (K218, 1775), no. 5 in A (K219, 1775); Sinfonia Concertante for violin, viola, and orchestra (K364, 1779); for bassoon in B♭ (K191, 1774); for flute, in G (K313, 1778), for oboe in C (K314, 1778), for flute and harp in C (K299, 1778); for clarinet in A (K622, 1791), Sinfonia Concertante in E♭ for oboe, clarinet, horn, and bassoon (K297b, 1778, judged as spurious by some scholars); four for horn (1782–87).

CHAMBER MUSIC 23 string quartets, nos. 1–13 (1770–73), nos. 14–19 dedicated to Haydn (1782–85) in G (K387), in D minor (K421), in E♭ (K428), in B♭ (K458, *The Hunt*), in A (K464), in C (K465, *Dissonance*), no. 20 in D (K499, 1786, *Hoffmeister*), nos. 21–23 dedicated to King of Prussia (1789–90) in D (K575), in B♭ (K589), in F (K590); six string quintets, including no. 3 in C (K515, 1787), no. 4 in G minor (K516, 1787), no. 5 in D (K593, 1790),

no. 6 in B♭ (K614, 1791); string trio in B♭, Divertimento (K563, 1788); five piano trios; two piano quartets in G minor (K478, 1785), in B♭ (K493, 1786); oboe quartet (K370, 1781); horn quintet (K407, 1782); quintet for piano and wind (K452, 1784); clarinet quintet (K581, 1789); clarinet trio in E♭ (K498, 1786); 17 piano sonatas, including no. 8 in A minor (K310, 1778), no. 9 in D (K311, 1777), nos. 10–13 in C, A and F (K330–333, 1781–84), no. 14 in C minor (K457, 1784), no. 15 in C (K545, 1788), no. 16 in B♭ (K570, 1789), no. 17 in D (K576, 1789); sonata in D for two pianos (K448, 1781); 35 sonatas for violin and piano nos. 1–16 composed 1762–66, no. 17 and nos. 18–23 in 1778; nos. 24–35 from 1781–78. Variations for piano, Fantasia in D minor (K397, 1782 or 1786–87), Fantasia in C minor (K475, 1785), Rondo in A minor (K511, 1787).

SOLO SONGS AND LIEDER including 'Die Zufriedenheit' (K349), 'Oiseaux, si tous les ans' (K307), 'Der Zauberer' (K472), 'Das Veilchen' (K476), 'Als Luise' (K520), 'Abendempfindung' (K523), 'Das Traumbild' (K530), 'Sehnsucht nach dem Frühlinge/Longing for Spring' (K596).

Mozart, (Johann Georg) Leopold (1719–1787) Austrian violinist and composer. He was the father of the composer Wolfgang Amadeus ◊Mozart. His important violin tutor, *Versuch einer gründlichen Violinschule*, was published in 1756.

He was educated at the Jesuit college in Augsburg and at Salzburg University, turned entirely to music in 1739, and first held a post with Count Thurn-Valsassina und Taxis. In 1743 he entered the service of the Archbishop of Salzburg, rising to become court composer in 1757 and vice-Kapellmeister in 1763. In 1747 he married Anna Maria Pertl; of their seven children the only two to survive were Maria Anna and Wolfgang Amadeus.

Works include: church music; symphonies; divertimenti and descriptive pieces for orchestra including 'Musical sleigh-ride', 'Toy Symphony', and other pieces; concertos for various instruments; chamber music, sonatas for violin.

Mozart and Salieri opera by Rimsky-Korsakov (libretto Pushkin's dramatic poem, set as it stands), produced Moscow, 7 December 1898. Now discredited story (though still believed by some) that Salieri poisoned Mozart.

Mozartiana Tchaikovsky's fourth suite for orchestra, op. 61, composed in 1887. It consists of four works by Mozart scored for orchestra by Tchaikovsky: jig and minuet for piano, K475 and 355; motet *Ave, verum corpus*, K618, and variations on a theme from *La rencontre imprévue* by Gluck for piano, K455. First performed Moscow, 26 November 1887.

mp in musical notation, abbreviation for **mezzo piano** (Italian 'half soft'), instructing the musician to play less softly.

Mravinsky, Evgeny (1903–1988) Russian conductor. He often conducted the stage works of Tchaikovsky, and orchestral music by Bartók and Stravinsky.

He studied at the Leningrad Conservatory and was conductor of the Leningrad Philharmonic Orchestra from 1938. Active on behalf of Soviet music, he gave the first performances of Shostakovich's symphonies nos. 5, 6, 8, 9, and 10. He conducted the first performance of Prokofiev's sixth symphony at Leningrad in 1947.

mridangam elongated, barrel drum with two tuned heads. Found in various sizes as an accompaniment to art-music throughout India. Known as *mrdang* or *phakvaj* in northern India, where it is also used in devotional temple music, and *mrdanga* or *khol* in eastern India.

Muck, Carl (1859–1940) German conductor. He was noted for his performances of Bruckner's symphonies. He gave the first Russian performances of Wagner's *Ring* in 1889.

He studied at Heidelberg University and at Leipzig University and Conservatory. In 1880 he began a career as a pianist, but became a conductor at Salzburg, Brno, and Graz in succession, at Prague in 1886, and finally at the Royal Opera, Berlin in 1892. He gave the first Russian performance of the *Ring* in 1889, and conducted Wagner in London and from 1901 at Bayreuth (*Parsifal* until 1930), also the Philharmonic concerts in Vienna. From 1906 to 1918, with an interruption, he conducted the Boston Symphony Orchestra. Arrested as an enemy alien in 1918, he returned to Europe after World War I and conducted in Hamburg 1922–33.

Mudd, Thomas (1560–after 1619) English composer. He went to St Paul's School in London and in 1578 to Cambridge as a sizar for the sons of London mercers.

Works include: services, anthems; dances for three viols.

Muette de Portici, La/The Dumb Girl of Portici opera by Auber (libretto by Scribe and Delavigne), produced Paris, Opéra, 29 February 1828. Carafa's *Masaniello*, on the same subject, had been produced at the Opéra-Comique two months earlier. Auber's work is often called *Masaniello*. The seduction of his sister Fenella inspires Masaniello to lead a peasants' revolt against the Spanish viceroy and his son Alphonse. Horrified by the waste of life, however, Masaniello shows mercy to the nobles and as a result is poisoned by his compatriots.

Muffat, Georg (1653–1704) Austrian organist and composer. In 1678 he was appointed organist to the Archbishop of Salzburg, and after visiting Vienna and Rome went to Passau to become organist to the bishop in 1690.

He studied in Paris, with Lully or members of his school.

Works include: the chamber sonatas *Armonico tributo* (1682), *Auserlesene mit Ernst und Lust gemengte Instrumental-Musik, Apparatus musico-organisticus* for organ (12 toccatas, chaconne, and passacaglia, 1690), *Suaviores harmoniae* (1695), two volumes for harpsichord.

Muldowney, Dominic (1952–) English composer. He studied with Jonathan Harvey at Southampton and with Birtwistle in London. In 1976 he was appointed composer in residence at the National Theatre, London.

Works include: *An Heavyweight Dirge* for soloists and chamber ensemble (1971); *Driftwood to the Flow* for 18 strings (1972); *Klavier-Hammer* for one or more pianos (1973); *Music at Chartres* for 16 instruments (1973); two string quartets (1973 and 1980), *Love music for Bathsheba Evergreen and Gabriel Oak* for chamber ensemble (1974); *Double Helix* for eight players (1977), *Macbeth*, ballet music (1979); five *Theatre Poems*, after Brecht (1981); *The Duration of Exile* for mezzo and chamber ensemble (1982); a realization of *The Beggar's Opera* (1982); piano concerto (1983), saxophone concerto (1984); *The Duration of Exile* for mezzo and ensemble (1983), Sinfonietta (1986), *Ars subtilior* for tape and ensemble (1987), violin concerto (1989); *The Ginger Tree* for piano (1989), concertos for percussion (1991), oboe (1991), and trumpet (1993) .

Mulè, Giuseppe (1855–1951) Italian cellist and composer. He studied Sicilian folk song and found that its roots went back to Greek music; he wrote much incidental music for the performance of Greek plays at Syracuse.

He studied at the Palermo Conservatory, of which he was director 1922–25, when he became director of the Santa Cecilia Conservatory in Rome. He also became secretary to the Fascist syndicate of musicians.

Works include: the operas *La Baronessa di Carini* (1912), *Al lupo, La monacella della fontana* (1923), *Dafni* (1928), *Liolà* (on Pirandello's play, 1935), *Taormina*; music for Greek plays: Aeschylus' *Choephori, Seven against Thebes*, Euripides' *Bacchae, Medea, The Cyclops, Hippolytus, Iphigenia in Aulis, Iphigenia in Tauris*, Sophocles' *Antigone*; incidental music for Corradini's *Giulio Cesare*; oratorio *Il cieco di Gerico* (1910); symphonic poems *Sicilia canora* and *Vendemmia*; *Tre canti siciliani* for voice and orchestra; string quartet; violin and cello pieces.

Müller, Wilhelm (1794–1827) German poet. See ◊*Schöne Müllerin, Die* and ◊*Winterreise* (Schubert).

multiphonics a technique of ◊overblowing a woodwind instrument combined with unorthodox fingering to produce a complex dissonance. Composers of multiphonics include Luciano Berio and Heinz Holliger, and the technique is also used by jazz saxophonists.

Mumma, Gordon (1935–) US composer. In 1957 he cofounded Space Theatre, giving performances with computerized electronics. He worked at an electronic studio, Ann Arbour, from 1958, and at the Merce Cunningham Dance Company from 1968. His works involve use of computer techniques, called cybersonics, and include *Sinfonia* for 12 instruments (1960), *Le Corbusier* (1965), *Mesa* (1966), and *Ambivex* (1972).

Münch, Charles (1891–1968), also known as Munch French conductor. He led the Gewandhaus Orchestra 1926–33 and conducted the Boston Symphony Orchestra 1949–62.

He studied at Strasbourg Conservatory, then went to Berlin for further violin studies with Carl Flesch (1873–1944) and then to Paris, where he studied under Lucien Capet (1873–1928). From 1919 to 1925 he taught violin at Strasbourg Conservatory and led the city orchestra, becoming leader of the Leipzig Gewandhaus Orchestra in 1926. He made his debut as a conductor in 1932 in Paris and after various teaching and conducting posts was conductor of the Boston Symphony Orchestra 1949–62 and in 1951 director of the Berkshire Music Center in Tanglewood. He helped found L'Orchestre de Paris, in 1967.

Mundy, John (c. 1555–1630) English organist and composer. He studied under his father, William Mundy, became a Gentleman of the Chapel Royal in London, and suc-

ceeded Marbeck as one of the organists of St George's Chapel, Windsor, about 1585.

Works include: anthems, *Songs and Psalmes* for three–five voices; madrigals (one in *The Triumphes of Oriana*); virginal pieces including the 'Weather' fantasia.

Munrow, David (1942–1976) English early music specialist and wind-instrument player. He founded the Early Music Consort in 1967 and taught at Leicester University and the Royal Academy of Music, London. He gave frequent performances of medieval and Renaissance music and was a frequent broadcaster. He published *Instruments of the Middle Ages and Renaissance* in 1976.

He died by suicide.

Murail, Tristan (1947–) French composer. He cofounded the Groupe de L'Itinéraire, to promote performances of music which combine electronic and traditional instruments. He has taught computer music at the Institut de Recherche et de Co-ordination Acoustique/Musique (◊IRCAM) and the Paris Conservatory.

He studied with Messiaen at the Paris Conservatory.

Works include: *Couleur de mer* for ensemble (1969); *Altitude 8000* for orchestra (1970); *Cosmos privé* for orchestra (1973); *Les nuages de Magellan* for ondes Martenot and ensemble (1973); *Sables* for orchestra (1974); *Mémoire/Erosion* for horn and 9 players (1976); *Désintégrations* for 17 players and tape (1983); *Sillages* for orchestra (1985); *Vues aeriennes* for horn, violin, cello, and piano (1988); *Les sept paroles du Christ en Croix* for orchestra (1986–89); *Le fou à pattes bleues* for flute and piano (1990).

Murino, Aegidius de (lived 14th century) music theorist and composer of uncertain nationality. He may possibly be the 'Egidius Anglicus' of the Manuscript Chantilly 1047. His treatise *Tractatus de diversis figuris* is about note-forms and motet composition. Two motets and one chanson also survive.

Muris, Johannes de (c. 1300–c. 1350) French mathematician, astronomer, and music theorist. He lived for some time in Paris and worked there as a mathematician and astronomer. The most notable of the music treatises attributed to him is the *Ars novae musicae* 1319.

murky bass an 18th-century term of unknown origin for a bass played in broken octaves on keyboard instruments.

Murrill, Herbert (Henry John) (1909–1952) English composer. He studied at the Royal Academy of Music in London and at Worcester College, Oxford. After holding various organist's posts from 1926, he became professor of composition at the Royal Academy of Music in 1933, joined the music staff of the British Broadcasting Corporation (BBC) in 1936 and became Head of Music in 1950.

Works include: the opera *Man in Cage* (1930); three hornpipes for orchestra; two concertos and three pieces for cello and orchestra; string quartet and other chamber music.

Murschhauser, Franz Xaver Anton (1663–1738) Alsatian composer. He was a pupil of Kerl at Munich, where he became Kapellmeister at the church of Our Lady. In 1721, by a remark made in his treatise on composition, 'Academia musico-poetica', he came into conflict with Johann Mattheson.

Works include: *Vespertinus latriae* for four voices and strings (1700); organ books *Octitonium novum organum, Prototypon longobreve organicum, Opus organicum tripartitum* (1696).

Muset, Colin (lived 12th century) French trouvère (see ◊troubadour) and jongleur. The poems of 15 and the music of 8 of his songs have survived.

musette small French ◊bagpipes; also a dance movement and character piece, imitating the music of a bagpipe, with its ◊drone accompaniment. Musette sections are often found in classical suites, as the trio to a gavotte. A modern 'musette' is found in Schoenberg's *Suite for Piano* 1921.

Musgrave, Thea (1928–) Scottish composer. Her works, in a conservative modern idiom, include concertos for horn, clarinet, and viola; string quartets; and operas, including *Mary, Queen of Scots* 1977.

She studied at Edinburgh University and with Nadia Boulanger in Paris 1950–54; her *Cantata for a Summer's Day* dates from this period. After 1953 she felt the influence of Schoenberg's 12-note method, which is seen in a number of works up until the Sinfonia of 1963. After this she gradually, particularly under the influence of Ives, wrote with greater freedom of dramatic gesture, as in the clarinet concerto 1968, in which the soloist moves around the various groups of the orchestra in performance. She lectured at London University 1959–65, and at the University of California from 1970. Her music has employed serial and improvisatory techniques.

Works include: the operas *The Abbot of Drimock* (1955), *The Decision* (1967), *The Voice of Ariadne* (1974), *Mary, Queen of Scots* (1977), *A Christmas Carol* (1979), *An Occurrence at Owl Creek Bridge* (1981), *Harriet, the Woman Called Moses* (1985), and *Simon Bolivar* (1995); *Scottish Dance Suite* for orchestra, *Divertimento* for string orchestra, *Perspectives* for small orchestra; three chamber concertos for various instruments, Concerto for Orchestra (1967), *Peripateia* for orchestra (1981), *The Seasons* (1988) and *Rainbow* (1990) for orchestra; *Triptych* for tenor and orchestra; *The Five Ages of Man* for chorus and orchestra; string quartet (1958); two piano sonatas; songs.

music art of combining sounds into a coherent perceptual experience, typically in accordance with conventional patterns and for an aesthetic purpose. Music is generally categorized as classical, ◊jazz, ◊pop music, country and western, and so on.

The Greek word *mousikē* covered all the arts presided over by the Muses. The various civilizations of the ancient and modern world developed their own musical systems. Eastern music recognizes subtler distinctions of pitch than does Western music and also differs from Western music in that the absence, until recently, of written notation ruled out the composition of major developed works; it fostered melodic and rhythmic patterns, freely interpreted (as in the Indian raga) by virtuosos.

Middle Ages The documented history of Western music since Classical times begins with the liturgical music of the medieval Catholic Church, derived from Greek and Hebrew antecedents. The four scales, or modes, to which the words of the liturgy were chanted were traditionally first set in order by St Ambrose AD 384. St Gregory the Great added four more to the original Ambrosian modes, and this system forms the basis of Gregorian ◊plainsong, still used in the Roman Catholic Church. The organ was introduced in the 8th century, and in the 9th century harmonized music began to be used in churches, with notation developing towards its present form.

In the 11th century counterpoint was introduced, notably at the monastery of St Martial, Limoges, France, and in the late 12th century at Notre-Dame in Paris (by Léonin and Perotin). In the late Middle Ages the Provençal and French ◊troubadours and court composers, such as Machaut, developed a secular music, derived from church and folk music (see also ◊Minnesingers).

15th and 16th centuries Europe saw the growth of contrapuntal or polyphonic music. One of the earliest composers was the English musician John Dunstable, whose works inspired the French composer Guillaume Dufay, founder of the Flemish school; its members included Dufay's pupil Joannes Okeghem and the Renaissance composer Josquin Desprez. Other composers of this era were Palestrina from Italy, Roland de Lassus from Flanders, Victoria from Spain, and Thomas Tallis and William Byrd from England. ◊Madrigals were developed in Italy by members of the Flemish school and later by native composers, including Giovanni Gabrieli; they were written during the Elizabethan age in England by such composers as Thomas Morley, Orlando Gibbons, and Thomas Weelkes (c. 1575–1623). Notable composers of organ music were Antonio de Cabezon (1500–1566) in Spain and Andrea Gabrieli (c. 1533–1586) in Italy.

17th century The Florentine Academy (Camerata), a group of artists and writers, aimed to revive the principles of Greek tragedy. This led to the invention of dramatic recitative and the beginning of opera. Claudio Monteverdi was an early operatic composer; by the end of the century the form had evolved further in the hands of Alessandro Scarlatti in Italy and Jean-Baptiste Lully in France. In England the outstanding composer of the period was Henry Purcell. ◊Oratorio was developed in Italy by Giacomo Carissimi (1605–1674); in Germany, Heinrich Schütz produced a new form of sacred music.

18th century The early part of the century was dominated by J S Bach and Georg Friedrich Handel. Bach was a master of harmony and counterpoint. Handel is renowned for his dramatic oratorios. In France, their most important contemporaries were François Couperin in keyboard music and Jean-Philippe Rameau in grand opera and ballet; the later operas of Christoph Willibald von Gluck, with their emphasis on dramatic expression, saw a return to the principles of Monteverdi. The modern orchestra evolved out of various movements of the mid-1700s, notably that led by Johann Stamitz (1717–1757) at Mannheim. Bach's sons C P E Bach and J C Bach reacted against contrapuntal forms and developed sonata form, the basis of the classical sonata, quartet, and symphony. In these types of composition, mastery of style was achieved by the Viennese composers Franz Haydn and Wolfgang Mozart. With Ludwig van Beethoven, music assumed new dynamic and expressive functions.

19th century Romantic music, represented in its early stages by Carl Weber, Franz Schubert, Robert Schumann, Felix Mendelssohn, and Frédéric Chopin, tended to be subjectively emotional. Orchestral colour was increasingly exploited – most notably by Hector Berlioz – and harmony became more chromatic. Nationalism became prominent at this time, as evidenced by the intense Polish nationalism of Chopin; the exploitation of Hungarian music by Franz Liszt; the works of the Russians Nikolai Rimsky-Korsakov, Alexander Borodin, Modest Mussorgsky, and, less typically, Pyotr Il'yich Tchaikovsky; the works of the Czechs Antonin Dvořák and Bedřich Smetana; the Norwegian Edvard Grieg; and the Spaniards Isaac Albéniz, Enrique Granados, and Manuel de Falla. Revolutionary changes were brought about by Richard Wagner in the field of opera, although traditional Italian lyricism continued in the work of Gioacchino Rossini, Giuseppe Verdi, and Giacomo Puccini. Wagner's contemporary Johannes Brahms stood for Classical discipline of form combined with Romantic feeling. The Belgian César Franck, with a newly chromatic idiom, also renewed the tradition of polyphonic writing.

20th century Around 1900 a reaction against Romanticism became apparent in the impressionism of Claude Debussy and Maurice Ravel, and the exotic chromaticism of Igor Stravinsky and Alexander Skriabin. In Austria and Germany, the tradition of Anton Bruckner, Gustav Mahler, and Richard Strauss faced a disturbing new world of atonal expressionism in Arnold Schoenberg, Alban Berg, and Anton von Webern.

After World War I neoclassicism, represented by Stravinsky, Sergei Prokofiev, and Paul Hindemith, attempted to restore 18th-century principles of objectivity and order while maintaining a distinctively 20th-century tone. In Paris ◊Les Six adopted a more relaxed style, while composers further from the cosmopolitan centres of Europe, such as Sir Edward Elgar, Frederick Delius, and Jean Sibelius, continued loyal to the Romantic symphonic tradition. The rise of radio and recorded media created a new mass market for Classical and Romantic music, but one which was initially resistant to music by contemporary composers. Organizations such as the International Society for Contemporary Music became increasingly responsible for ensuring that new music continued to be publicly performed. Interest in English folk music was revived by the work of Gustav Holst and Ralph Vaughan-Williams.

Among other important contemporary composers are Béla Bartók and Zoltán Kodály in Hungary; Olivier Messiaen in France; Luigi

Dallapiccola and Luciano Berio in Italy; Dmitri Shostakovich in Russia; and Sir Arthur Bliss, Aaron Copland, Edmund Rubbra, Sir William Walton, Samuel Barber, Benjamin Britten, and Michael Tippett in England and the USA.

modern developments The second half of the 20th century has seen dramatic changes in the nature of composition and in the instruments used to create sounds. The recording studio has facilitated the development of concrete music based on natural sounds, and electronic music, in which sounds are generated electrically, developments implying the creation of music as a finished object without the need for interpretation by live performers. Chance music, promoted by John Cage, introduced the notion of a music designed to provoke unforeseen results and thereby make new connections; aleatoric music, developed by Pierre Boulez, introduced performers to freedom of choice from a range of options. In Germany, the avant-garde works of Karlheinz Stockhausen have introduced new musical sounds and compositional techniques. Since the 1960s the computer has become a focus of attention for developments in the synthesis of musical tones, and also in the automation of compositional techniques, most notably at Stanford University and MIT in the USA, and at IRCAM in Paris.

musica ficta (Latin 'feigned music') in music of the Middle Ages, the theory of nondiatonic notes (those notes not normally present in a simple C major scale). B♭ was the first nondiatonic note allowed, in order to avoid the ◊tritone B–F. Other notes later became sharpened or flattened for similar reasons. Musica ficta also introduced nondiatonic notes in order to create a semitone between the ◊leading note (seventh note of a scale) and ◊tonic (first note of a scale). For example, when the tonic is G the leading note F must become F♯ in order to have the desired semitone.

Musica ficta was not always written using ◊accidentals (sharp, flat, or natural signs), rather it required precise knowledge by the performer of correct theory and practice.

musica figurata (Latin and Italian 'figured or decorated music') ornamenting of plainsong by auxiliary notes or the addition of a descant sung against a fundamental melody.

musical twentieth-century form of dramatic musical performance, combining elements of song, dance, and the spoken word, often characterized by lavish staging and large casts. It developed from the operettas and musical comedies of the 19th century.

operetta The operetta is a light-hearted entertainment with extensive musical content: Jacques Offenbach, Johann Strauss, Franz Lehár, and Gilbert and Sullivan all composed operettas.

musical comedy The musical comedy is an anglicization of the French *opéra bouffe*, of which the first was *A Gaiety Girl* 1893, mounted by George Edwardes (1852–1915) at the Gaiety Theatre, London. Typical musical comedies of the 1920s were *Rose Marie* 1924 by Rudolf Friml (1879–1972); *The Student Prince* 1924 and *The Desert Song* 1926, both by Sigmund Romberg (1887–1951); and *No, No, Nanette* 1925 by Vincent Youmans (1898–1946). The 1930s and 1940s were an era of sophisticated musical comedies with many filmed examples and a strong US presence (Irving Berlin, Jerome Kern, Cole Porter, and George Gershwin). In England Noël Coward and Ivor Novello also wrote musicals.

musical In 1943 Rodgers and Hammerstein's *Oklahoma!* introduced an integration of plot and music, which was developed in Lerner and Loewe's *My Fair Lady* 1956 and Leonard Bernstein's *West Side Story* 1957. Sandy Wilson's *The Boy Friend* 1953 revived the British musical and was followed by hits such as Lionel Bart's *Oliver!* 1960. Musicals began to branch into religious and political themes with *Oh, What a Lovely War* 1963, produced by Joan Littlewood and Charles Chiltern, and the Andrew Lloyd Webber musicals *Jesus Christ Superstar* 1971 and *Evita* 1978. Another category of musical, substituting a theme for conventional plotting, includes Stephen Sondheim's *Company* 1970, Hamlisch and Kleban's *A Chorus Line* 1975, and Lloyd Webber's *Cats* 1981, using verses by T S Eliot. In the 1980s, 19th-century melodrama was popular; for example, *Les Misérables* 1985 (first London performance) and *The Phantom of the Opera* 1986.

musical box toy musical instrument made in various shapes of decorative boxes and containing a cylinder with pins which, turning round by clockwork, twangs the teeth of a metal comb producing the notes of a musical scale. The pins are so arranged as to make the pattern of a piece of music. Several sets of pins can be set in the barrel, only one touching the teeth at a time, a choice of more than one piece being thus capable of being produced by the simple device of shifting the barrel slightly sideways. The musical box industry is traditionally centred in Switzerland.

musical idea term associated with Arnold ◊Schoenberg, who used it to describe the initial musical impulse behind a work. Sometimes the term refers to a single musical motive, which he termed the fundamental motive, and sometimes to a more abstract concept of which the fundamental motive is a single instance. In any case, it is the musical idea which gives a work both its unique character and its organic unity. See ◊motivic analysis.

musical instrument digital interface manufacturer's standard for digital music equipment; see ◊MIDI.

Musical Offering (Bach). See ◊*Musikalische Opfer*.

musical saw musical instrument made from a hand saw. The handle is clasped between the knees with the top of the blade held in one hand so that it forms an S curve. A cello bow is played with the other hand across the back edge of the blade to produce an eerie wailing sound. The pitch is altered by varying the curvature of the blade. Composers include George ◊Crumb.

musical science the ancient Greeks distinguished between **musical sound** as an indicator of Pythagorean concepts of number relation and **musical influences** on human (and animal) behaviour, as recounted in the Orpheus legend.

In general, musical science has sought to rationalize ◊pitch, first into ◊modes, then into ◊scales and ◊temperament, and to quantify ◊timbre, to account for differences between sounds of the same pitch. To this end it has evolved a standard division of the ◊octave allowing for the development of Western ◊tonality, a universal notation for pitch, and keyboard instruments for conducting experiments in tonal relations, all of which prefigure recent digital technologies of information storage and retrieval.

The art of music has developed and adapted the discoveries of musical science for the purposes of artistic expression. The emotional power of music lies in its ability to transcend language and appeal directly to subconscious associations of ◊melody, ◊rhythm, ◊dynamics, and ◊tempo.

musical snuffbox kind of musical box made especially in the 18th century, with a double bottom concealing a mechanical music apparatus beneath its normal contents.

musica recta (Latin 'orthodox music') term used in the 14th and 15th centuries to mean the notes of the gamut as projected by the three kinds of hexachord, that is, the white-note scale from G to e″ but including B♭ as well as B♮ (or, with a key signature of one flat, including E♭ as well as E♮, and so on). Since this was the normal scale, the note B could be sung either flat or natural without special indications. This concept is important for editorial accidentals and *musica ficta*: where there is an alternative, *musica recta* should be operated before *musica ficta*.

musica reservata (Latin 'reserved music') 16th-century term applied to music intended for connoisseurs and private occasions, particularly vocal music which faithfully interpreted the words.

music drama alternative term for 'opera' used by composers, notably Wagner, who felt that the older term implies methods and forms for which they had no use.

music hall British light theatrical entertainment, in which singers, dancers, comedians, and acrobats perform in 'turns'. The music hall's heyday was at the beginning of the 20th century, with such artistes as Marie Lloyd, Harry Lauder, and George Formby. The US equivalent is ◊vaudeville.

Many performers had a song with which they were associated, such as Albert Chevalier (1861–1923) ('My Old Dutch'), or a character 'trademark', such as Vesta Tilley's immaculate masculine outfit as Burlington Bertie. Later stars of music hall included Sir George Robey, Gracie Fields, the Crazy Gang, Ted Ray, and the US comedian Danny Kaye.

history Music hall originated in the 17th century, when tavern keepers acquired the organs that the Puritans had banished from churches. On certain nights organ music was played, and this resulted in a weekly entertainment known as the 'free and easy'. Certain theatres in London and the provinces then began to specialize in variety entertainment. With the advent of radio and television, music hall declined, but in the 1960s and 1970s there was a revival in working men's clubs and in pubs.

Music Makers, The ode for contralto solo, chorus, and orchestra by Elgar, op. 69 (poem by Arthur O'Shaughnessy), first performed Birmingham Festival, 1 October 1912. The work contains a number of quotations from earlier works by Elgar.

musicology the academic study of music, including music history, music analysis, music aesthetics, and ◊performance practice. All areas of music fall under the category of musicology except composition, performance studies, and practical music teaching (pedagogy).

music theatre staged performance of vocal music that deliberately challenges, in style and subject matter, traditional operatic pretensions.

Drawing on English music hall and European cabaret and *Singspiel* traditions, it flourished during the Depression of the 1920s and 1930s as working-class opera, for example the Brecht–Weill *Die Dreigroschenoper/The Threepenny Opera* 1928; in the USA as socially conscious musical, for example Gershwin's *Porgy and Bess* 1935; and on film, in René Clair's *Sous les Toits de Paris/Under the Roofs of Paris* 1930 (music composed by Raoul Moretti) and *A Nous la Liberté/Freedom for Us* 1931 (music by Georges Auric). Composers addressing a similar mood of social unrest in the years after 1968 include Henze (*Essay on Pigs* 1968), Berio (*Recital I* 1972), and Ligeti (*Le Grand Macabre/The Great Macabre* 1978). Since 1970 music theatre has emerged as a favoured idiom for short-term community music projects produced by outreach departments of civic arts centres and opera houses.

Musikalische Opfer, Das/The Musical Offering a late work by Bach (BWV 1079) containing two *ricercari*, a fugue in canon, nine canons, and a sonata for flute, violin and continuo, all based on a theme given to Bach by Frederick II of Prussia during the composer's visit to Potsdam in 1747.

Musikalischer Spass, Ein/A Musical Joke a work in four movements for two horns and strings by Mozart, K522 (composed June 1787), sometimes also known by such names as 'The Village Band'. But the joke is not at the expense of rustic performers; the work is a parody of a symphony by an incompetent composer.

musique mesurée (French 'measured music') method of setting words to music cultivated in 16th-century France by Baïf, Le Jeune, Mauduit and others. The metrical rhythm of the words was based on classical scansion and the musical rhythm followed this exactly, long syllables being set to long notes, and short syllables to short notes.

Mussorgsky, Modest Petrovich (1839–1881) Russian composer. He was a member of the group of five composers ('The ◊Five'). His opera masterpiece *Boris Godunov* 1869, revised 1871–72, touched a political nerve and

employed realistic transcriptions of speech patterns. Many of his works, including *Pictures at an Exhibition* 1874 for piano, were 'revised' and orchestrated by others, including Rimsky-Korsakov, Ravel, and Shostakovich, and some have only recently been restored to their original harsh beauty.

Mussorgsky, born in Karevo (Pskov, Russia), resigned his commission in the army in 1858 to concentrate on music while working as a government clerk. He was influenced by both folk music and literature. Among his other works are the incomplete operas *Khovanshchina* and *Sorochintsy Fair*, the orchestral *Night on the Bare Mountain* 1867, and many songs. He died in poverty, from alcoholism.

The son of well-to-do landowners, Mussorgsky was sent to St Petersburg at the age of ten to prepare for a military school, which he entered in 1852. He joined a regiment in 1856 and he did not seriously think of a music career until he met the composers Dargomizhsky and Balakirev in 1857 and began to study under the latter. He resigned his commission in 1858, but never studied systematically. His family's fortune waned after the liberation of the serfs in 1861, but he was in sympathy with that movement and content to live on the small pay he obtained for a position in the civil service. He finished *Boris Godunov* in its first form in 1869, but it was rejected by the Imperial Opera and he recast it 1871–72, this second version being produced in 1874. It gained wide popularity in an orchestration by Rimsky-Korsakov, but Mussorgsky's original is now more often preferred. He sank into ever more acute poverty and ruined his health with drink, but between 1872 and 1880 managed to complete most of his historical opera, *Khovanshchina*.

Works include: the operas *Salammbô* (after Flaubert, unfinished, 1863–66), *The Marriage* (Gogol, unfinished, 1868, produced 1909), *Boris Godunov* (after Pushkin, 1869, revised 1872), *Khovanshchina* (1886), *Sorochintsy Fair* (after Gogol, unfinished, 1874–80); an act for a collective opera, *Mlada* (with Borodin, Cui, and Rimsky-Korsakov, afterwards used for other works); incidental music for Ozerov's *Oedipus Rex*; *The Destruction of Sennacherib* (after Byron, 1867), and *Jesus Navin* for chorus and orchestra. Four Russian folk songs for male chorus; *Night on the Bare Mountain* for orchestra (later used in *Mlada* [with chorus] and further revised) and three small orchestral pieces; suite *Pictures at an Exhibition* (1874) and 12 small pieces for piano; over 60 songs including cycles *The Nursery* (1870), *Sunless*, and *Songs and Dances of Death* (1875–77).

Mustafà, Domenico (1829–1912) Italian castrato and composer. He was the last male
soprano of the Sistine Chapel, which he
entered in 1848. He was later maestro di
cappella there until 1902, when he was
succeeded by Lorenzo Perosi.

Works include: Miserere, *Tu es Petrus*, *Dies
irae* for seven voices, *Laudate*, and other
church music.

Mustel organ keyboard reed instrument
invented by Victor Mustel (1815–90) of Paris.
It is of the harmonium type, but contains
some improvements, including a device by
which the top and bottom halves of the
keyboard can be separately controlled for
dynamic expression.

muta (Italian 'change') musical direction
used in scores where a change is to be made
between instruments (such as A and B♭
clarinet or different horn crooks) or in tunings
(such as kettledrums, strings of instruments
of the violin family temporarily tuned to
abnormal notes). The plural is *mutano*.

mutation an organ ◊stop which produces a
◊pitch other than the normal wavelength
pitch (8 ft) or one related by octave (16 ft, 4
ft, 2 ft, or 1 ft). For example, a Quint stop (22/
3 ft) produces a pitch an octave and a fifth
higher than the depressed key (for example
the C4 key sounds at G5). Other mutation
stops sound higher by two octaves and a
third, by two octaves and a fifth, or by two
octaves and a flat seventh. They are not
played alone, but with other stops which
sound their proper notes.

mute any device used to dampen the vibration of an instrument and so affect the tone.
Orchestral strings apply a form of clamp to
the bridge – the change is used to dramatic
effect by Bartók in the opening bars of *Music
for Strings, Percussion, and Celesta* 1936. Brass
instruments use the hand or a plug of metal
or cardboard inserted in the bell.

Although the word implies a reduction of
volume, a variety of mutes used in big band
jazz are used principally to vary the quality of
tone, as in Stravinsky's *Ebony Concerto* 1945.

Müthel, Johann Gottfried (1728–1788) German organist, harpsichordist, and composer.

He was appointed court organist to the Duke
of Mecklenburg-Schwerin in 1747. On leave
of absence to study in 1750 he visited J S Bach
in Leipzig just before he died. He also visited
Johann Altnikol in Naumburg, C P E Bach in
Berlin, and Telemann in Hamburg.

He was a pupil of Adolph Kunzen (1720–
81) in Lübeck. From 1755 he was an organist
in Riga.

Works include: concertos, sonatas, and
miscellaneous pieces for harpsichord.

Muzak proprietary name for ◊piped music.

Muzen Siciliens, Die/The Muses of Sicily
concerto by Henze for chorus, two pianos,
wind, and percussion (text from Virgil's
Eclogues), first performed Berlin, 20 September 1966.

Muzio Scevola, Il/Mucius Scaevola opera
by Filippo Mattei (or Amadei), Giovanni
Bononcini and Handel (libretto by P A Rolli),
produced London King's Theatre, Haymarket, 15 April 1721.

Myaskovsky, Nikolay see ◊Miaskovsky.

My Country (Smetana). See ◊*Má Vlast*.

Mysliveček, Josef (1737–1781) Bohemian
composer. Between 1767 and 1780 he wrote
about 30 operas, most to texts by Metastasio,
for the principal theatres in Italy. His oratorio
Abrame ed Isacco 1776 was admired by Mozart.

He studied organ and composition in
Prague, and published there in 1760 a set of
symphonies named after the first six months
of the year. In 1763 he went to study with
Giovanni Battista Pescetti in Venice, and a
year later produced his first opera in Parma.
He also visited Munich, where he met Mozart
in 1777 (they had already met in 1772).

Works include: the operas *Medea* (1764), *Il
Bellerofonte* (1767), *Farnace*, *Demofoonte* (1769),
Ezio, *Il Demetrio* (1773), and others; oratorio
Abramo ed Isacco (1776) and three others;
symphonies; concertos; chamber music;
church music.

Mystic Trumpeter, The scena for soprano
and orchestra by Holst (text by Whitman);
1904, first performed London, 29 June 1905.
Revised 1912 and performed London, 25
January 1913.

N

Nabokov, Nikolai (1903–1978) Russian-born US composer. He studied in Berlin and Stuttgart. He became attached to Diaghilev's Russian Ballet in the 1920s, and later settled in the USA.

Works include: the operas *The Holy Devil* (1958) and *Love's Labour Lost* (1973); ballets *Ode on seeing the Aurora Borealis* (1928), *Union Pacific* (1934) and *Don Quixote* (1965); incidental music to a dramatic version of Milton's *Samson Agonistes*; symphonies, *Sinfonia biblica* for orchestra; piano concerto (1932); three symphonies (1930–68); cantata *Collectionneur d'échos* for soprano, bass, chorus and percussion, 6 Poems of Anna Akhmatova for soprano and orchestra (1966).

Nabucco/Nebuchadnezzar opera by Verdi (libretto by T Solera), produced Milan, La Scala, 9 March 1842. Nabucco's supposed daughter, Abigaille (actually an adopted slave) attempts to seize power.

Nachtanz (German 'after-dance') quicker dance following a slower one, often with the same music in different rhythm in the 15th–16th centuries, especially the galliard following the pavane.

Nacht in Venedig, Eine/A Night in Venice operetta by Johann Strauss, junior (libretto by F Zell and R Genée), produced Berlin, Städtisches Theater, 3 October 1883. Written for the opening of that theatre; first Vienna performance, Theater an der Wien, 9 October 1883. Elderly Delaqua wants to marry his ward, but has double competition.

Nachtlager von Granada, Das/The Night-Camp at Granada opera by Conradin Kreutzer (libretto by K J B von Braunthal, based on a play by Friedrich Kind), produced Vienna, Josefstadt Theatre, 13 January 1834. Crown Prince of Spain helps Gabriela unite with Gomez.

Nachtmusik (German 'night piece') see ◊nocturne.

Nachtstücke und Arien/Nocturnes and Arias work by Henze for soprano and orchestra (text by I Bachmann), first performed Donaueschingen, 20 October 1957, conductor Rosbaud.

Nägeli, Hans Georg (1773–1836) Swiss composer, teacher, and publisher. In 1803 he began to publish a series entitled *Répertoire des clavecinistes* and included in it Beethoven's sonatas op. 31 Nos. 1 and 2, adding four bars to the former, much to the composer's annoyance.

He studied at Zurich and Bern and began to publish music at Zurich in 1792. He established the *Schweizerbund* choral society, which soon formed branches, and reformed music teaching in schools on the lines of Pestalozzi's education system. He also wrote on music education and lectured on music in Switzerland and Germany.

Works include: church and school music; toccatas and other piano pieces; 15 books of popular songs, including 'Freut euch des Lebens' and 'Lied vom Rhein'.

Naich, Hubert (c. 1513–after 1546) Flemish composer. He lived at Rome, where he was a member of the Accademia degli Amici. He published a book of madrigals there about 1540.

nail violin, also nail fiddle or nail harmonica eighteenth-century musical instrument, invented by Johann Wilde, a German violinist living at St Petersburg, Russia. It was a semicircular soundboard studded with nails along the rounded edge, which were scraped with a bow.

Naïs pastoral-héroïque by Rameau (libretto by L de Cahusac); composed for the peace of Aix-la-Chapelle, produced Paris, Opéra, 22 April 1749. The suitors of Naïs are overwhelmed by Neptune.

Naissance de la Lyre, La/The Birth of the Lyre lyric opera in one act by Roussel (libretto by T Reinach, after Sophocles), produced Paris, Opéra, 1 July 1925, with choreography by Nijinska. Symphonic fragments in six movements performed Paris, 13 November 1927, conductor Paray.

nakers (from Arabic through old French *nacaires*) Old English name for the ◊timpani or kettledrums, which were then much smaller and therefore higher in pitch, and could not have their tuning altered. In cavalry regiments they were played on horseback, hung on either side of the horse's neck.

Namensfeier, Name[-Day] Celebration, concert overture by Beethoven, op. 115, in C major, composed 1814, Vienna, Redoutensaal, 25 December 1815, conducted by the composer. The name-day was that of the Austrian emperor, which happened to coincide with the completion of the work; it was not composed specially for that occasion.

Namouna ballet by Lalo (scenario by Charles Nuitter; choreographed by Marius Petipa), produced Paris, Opéra, 6 March 1882.

Nancarrow, Conlon (1912–) US composer. Using a player-piano as a form of synthesizer, punching the rolls by hand, he experimented with mathematically derived combinations of rhythm and tempo in *37 Studies for Piano-Player* 1950–68, works of a hypnotic persistence that aroused the admiration of a younger generation of minimalist composers.

He studied at the Cincinnati College-Conservatory 1929–32 and later with Slonimsky and Sessions in Boston. After involvement in the Spanish Civil War he lived in Mexico 1940–81. His music is notated by perforating piano player rolls, although it has been played by other means – the string quartet no. 3 was given its first performance in 1988 by the Arditti Quartet.

Works include: *Blues and Prelude* for piano (1935), *Toccata* for violin and piano (1935), Septet (1940), Sonatina for piano (1940), trio for clarinet, bassoon, and piano (1943), Suite for orchestra (1943), three string quartets.

Nanino, Giovanni Bernardino (c. 1560–1623) Italian composer. He studied under his brother, went to Rome, and from 1591 to 1608 was maestro di cappella at the church of San Luigi de' Francesi there, later at that of San Lorenzo in Damaso. He made early use of the basso continuo.

Works include: motets, psalms and other church music some with organ accompaniment; five-part madrigals.

Napolitana a light song for several voices, allied to the *villanella* and cultivated at Naples especially in the 16th and 17th centuries.

Nápravník, Eduard Franzevich (1839–1916) Czech composer and conductor. As principal conductor of the Mariinsky Theatre, St Petersburg, he gave the first performance of Mussorgsky's opera *Boris Godunov* 1874.

He studied music precariously as a child, being the son of a poor teacher, and was left an orphan and destitute in 1853, but succeeded in entering the Organ School in Prague, where he studied with Kittel and others, and became an assistant teacher. In 1861 he went to St Petersburg as conductor of Prince Yusupov's private orchestra, became organist and assistant conductor at the Imperial theatres in 1863, second conductor in 1867 and chief conductor, succeeding Liadov, in 1869, holding the post until his death; he gave the first performances of *Boris Godunov*, five operas by Tchaikovsky, including *The Maid of Orleans*, *Mazepa*, and *The Queen of Spades*, and five by Rimsky-Korsakov, including *May Night*, *The Snow Maiden*, and *Christmas Eve*. He also conducted concerts of the Russian Music Society.

Works include: the operas *The Nizhni-Novgorodians* (1868), *Harold* (1886), *Dubrovsky* (1895), and *Francesca da Rimini* (on Stephen Phillips's play, 1902); incidental music for Alexei Tolstoy's *Don Juan* (1892); ballads for voices and orchestra *The Voyevode*, *The Cossack*, and *Tamara* (after Lermontov); four symphonies (1860–79), no. 3 *The Demon* (after Lermontov), suite, *Solemn Overture*, marches and national dances for orchestra; concerto and fantasy on Russian themes for piano and orchestra, fantasy and suite for violin and orchestra; three string quartets (1873–78), string quintet (1897), two piano trios, piano quartet; violin and piano sonata, two suites for cello and piano; string instrument and piano pieces.

naqqara kettledrum of the Islamic world, the Caucasus, and Central Asia. It is used in military, religious, and ceremonial music. Made of silver, copper, brass, wood, or pottery the naqqara are usually played in pairs with the skin drum heads tuned at different pitches and beaten with a stick.

Narciso, Narcissus, opera by Domenico Scarlatti (libretto by C S Capece), produced Rome, private theatre of Queen Maria Casimira of Poland, 20 January 1714, under the title of *Amor d'un' ombra*. Performed in London, 31 May 1720, with additional music by T Roseingrave, under the new title.

Nasolini, Sebastiano (c. 1768–c. 1816) Italian composer. He was a pupil of Bertoni in Venice, and in 1787 was appointed *maestro al cembalo* at the opera in Trieste, and 1788–90 maestro di cappella at the cathedral there. From 1790 he devoted himself to opera composition.

Works include: the operas *Nitteti* (1788), *Andromaca* (1790), *La morte di Cleopatra* (1791), *Eugenia* (1792), *Le feste d'Iside* (1794), *Merope*, *La morte di Mitridate* (1796), *Il medico di Lucca* (1797), *Gli umori contrari* (1798), *Il ritorno di Serse* (1816).

national anthem patriotic song for official occasions. The US national anthem, 'The Star-Spangled Banner', was written 1814 by Francis Scott ◊Key and was adopted officially 1931. In Britain 'God Save the King/Queen' has been accepted as such since 1745, although both music and words are of much earlier origin. The German anthem 'Deutschland über Alles/Germany before Everything' is sung to music by Haydn.

The French national anthem, the ◊'Marseillaise', dates from 1792.

Countries within the Commonwealth retain 'God Save the King/Queen' as the 'royal anthem', adopting their own anthem as a mark of independence. These include 'Advance Australia Fair' 1974–76 and from 1984 'O Canada', written 1882 and adopted gradually through popular usage. The anthem of united Europe is Schiller's 'Ode to Joy' set by Beethoven in his Ninth Symphony.

nationalism the adoption by 19th-century composers of folk idioms with which an audience untrained in the classics could identify. Nationalism was encouraged by governments in the early 20th century for propaganda purposes in times of war and political tension. Composers of nationalist music include Smetana, Sibelius, Grieg, Dvořák, Nielsen, Kodály, Copland, Elgar, Shostakovich, and Stephen Foster.

Nattiez, Jean-Jacques (1945–   ) Canadian musicologist. As director of the Groupe de Recherches en Sémiologie Musicale at the University of Montreal from 1974, he is important for developing the use of semiotics in musical analysis, as first expounded in his book *Fondements d'une sémiologie musicale* 1975.

natural, ♮, in music, a sign cancelling a sharp or flat. A **natural trumpet** or **horn** is an instrument without valves, thus restricted to playing natural harmonics.

naturale (Italian 'natural') musical direction indicating that a voice or instrument, after performing a passage in some unusual way (such as *mezza voce* or muted), is to return to its normal manner.

Naumann, Johann Gottlieb (1741–1801) German composer. At the age of 16 he accompanied the Swedish violinist Wesström to Hamburg, then to Italy, where he studied with Tartini, Hasse, and Padre Martini. Produced his first opera in Venice in 1763, and the following year was appointed to the court at Dresden as second composer of church music. Revisited Italy to produce operas 1765–68 and 1772–74, and in 1776 became Kapellmeister in Dresden, where, apart from visits to Stockholm, Copenhagen and Berlin, he remained till his death. His opera *Gustav Vasa* was revived in Stockholm, 1991.

Works include: the operas *Achille in Sciro* (1767), *La clemenza di Tito* (1769), *Solimano*, *Armida* (1773), *Ipermestra*, *Amphion* (1778), *Cora och Alonzo* (1782), *Gustaf Vasa*, 1786; all three in Swedish, *Orpheus og Euridice* (in Danish, 1786), *Protesilao* (with Reichardt), *La dama soldato* (1790), *Aci e Galatea* (1801) and others; 21 Masses and other church music, 13 oratorios.

Navarraise, La/The Girl of Navarre opera by Massenet (libretto by J Claretie and H Cain, based on the former's story *La Cigarette*), produced London, Covent Garden, 20 June 1894. Anita's attempts to win dowry by assassinating military leader.

Navarro, Juan (c. 1530–1580) Spanish composer. He was highly regarded as a polyphonist, and his church music was popular in Spain, Portugal, and Mexico for some time.

After the death of Cristóbal Morales in 1553 he competed unsuccessfully for the post of maestro de capilla at Málaga Cathedral, but he later obtained a similar post in Salamanca. He visited Rome in 1590, where his nephew Fernando Navarro Salazar arranged for the publication of some of his church music.

Works include: psalms, hymns, Magnificats and other church music, madrigals and other pieces.

Naylor, Bernard (1907–1986) English composer, conductor, and organist. He studied at the Royal College of Music in London with Vaughan Williams and Holst; he conducted in Winnipeg and Montreal from 1932, and settled in Canada in 1959.

Works include: 12 motets in two sets (1949, 1952), *The Annunciation according to St Luke* for soloists, chorus and orchestra (1949); *Variations* for orchestra (1960); string trio (1960); *Stabat Mater* (1961); *The Nymph and the Faun* for mezzo and ensemble (text by Marvell, 1965); *Three Sacred Pieces* for chorus and orchestra (1971).

Naylor, Edward (Woodall) (1867–1934) English organist, musicologist, and composer. He studied at Cambridge and the Royal College of Music in London, and after two appointments as organist there he returned to Cambridge in 1897 to become organist at Emmanuel College, taking the doctorate in music degree at the university. He lectured and wrote on music, published a book on *Shakespeare and Music*.

Works include: the opera *The Angelus* (produced Covent Garden 1909); cantata *Arthur the King* (1902); part songs; piano trio in D major.

Neapolitan sixth a chord consisting of a minor third and a minor sixth on the subdominant of the key, which came into vogue in the 17th century. It occurs most often in a cadential progression in a minor key.

The Neapolitan sixth in an A minor cadence.

Neapolitan Songs, Five/Fünf neapolitanische Lieder work by Henze for baritone and orchestra (to an anonymous 17th-century text), first performed Frankfurt, 26 May 1956, with Fischer-Dieskau.

Nebra, José (Melchor de) (1702–1768) Spanish organist and composer. He wrote religious and secular works for the stage. In 1751 he was made vice-maestro de capilla at the royal chapel in Madrid under Francesco Corselli (c. 1702–78), who neglected his duties for the composition of Italian operas, and by 1757 he had completely reorganized the court music.

He became organist at the Convent of the Descalzas Reales in Madrid and principal organist at the royal chapel in 1724. After the destruction of the library there in the fire of 24 December 1734, he and Antonio Literes Carrión (1673–1747) were commissioned to replace the lost church music and to restore what had survived. In 1758 he composed a requiem (*Pro defunctis*) for eight voices, flute, and strings for the funeral of Queen Barbara of Braganza, who had been Domenico Scarlatti's patroness.

Works include: 57 stage works; requiem, Miserere, psalms and other church music; villancico for four voices.

neck on a stringed musical instrument, the narrow piece of wood which projects from the ◊soundbox, supporting the ◊fingerboard. At its end is the peg box, which secures the strings.

Neefe, Christian Gottlob (1748–1798) German conductor and composer. He studied in Leipzig under Hiller, whom he succeeded as conductor of a touring opera company in 1776. He settled in Bonn in 1779, where he was appointed court organist three years later. Beethoven was his pupil from the age of 11. The French occupation of Bonn in 1794 cost him his post, and from 1796 he was music director of the Bossann theatre company in Dessau.

Works include: the operas *Die Apotheke* (1771), *Adelheid von Veltheim, Amors Guckkasten* (1772), *Die Einsprüche* (1772), *Heinrich und Lyda* (1776), *Sophonisbe, Zemire und Azor* (1776) and others; incidental music for Shakespeare's *Macbeth*; church music; chamber music.

Neel, Boyd (1905–1981) English conductor. He founded the Boyd Neel String Orchestra in 1933 and gave the first performance of Britten's *Variations on theme of Frank Bridge* at Salzburg in 1937. The orchestra was renamed

Philomusica of London in 1957. He was dean of Toronto Conservatory 1953–70.

Neidhart von Reuental (c. 1180–c. 1240) German Minnesinger. A younger contemporary of Walther von der Vogelweide, his music survived in print during the Renaissance. Several of his songs are preserved; many others are attributed to him.

He went on a crusade 1217–19 and settled in Austria on his return.

Neidhart von Reuental (c. 1180–c. 1240) German Minnesinger. He went on a crusade in 1217–19 and settled in Austria on his return. Several songs of his are preserved; many others are attributed to him. A younger contemporary of Walther von der Vogelweide, his music survived in print during the Renaissance.

neighbour-note, or neighbouring harmony note in a melodic line which is not harmonized, and which moves by step away from a harmonized note, or by step onto a harmonized note, or away and then back again. In voice-leading analysis, a neighbouring harmony is one in which a neighbour-note is harmonized, this harmony being subordinate to the main harmony. See: ◊passing notes; ◊prolongation.

Nelson Mass the name given to Haydn's Mass in D minor, composed 1798. It is sometimes said that the fanfares in the Benedictus commemorate Nelson's victory in the battle of the Nile; in fact Haydn cannot have heard the news of the battle until after the Mass was finished. His own title was *Missa in angustiis*. Performed Eisenstadt, 23 September 1798.

Nenna, Pomponio (c. 1550–before 1613) Italian composer. He lived mainly at Naples and taught Gesualdo, Prince of Venosa 1594–99. He moved to Rome about 1608.

Works include: two books of responsories and nine books of madrigals.

neo-Bechstein piano electrophonic piano invented by Vierling of Berlin 1928–33 and further developed by Franco and Nernst, producing its notes by the conversion of electrical waves into audible sounds.

neoclassical in 20th-century music, term describing a deliberate combination of Baroque or Classical forms such as sonata form, fugue, and so on, and modern harmony, for example Prokofiev's 'Classical' *Symphony No 1* 1916–17, Stravinsky's ballet *Apollo* 1927–28, and Busoni's opera *Doktor Faust* 1916–24.

neomodal modern music using new derivations from the modes, harmonized, transposed, or otherwise altered.

Nero opera by Rubinstein (libretto, in French [*Néron*], by J Barbier), produced, in German, Hamburg, Municipal Theatre, 1 November 1879.

See also ◊*Nerone*.

Nerone/Nero opera by Boito (libretto by composer), begun 1879, but left unfinished at Boito's death in 1918. Produced, edited by Tommasini and A Toscanini, Milan, La Scala, 1 May 1924. Corrupt Romans and spiritual Christians in conflict as the city burns.

Nessler, Viktor (Ernst) (1841–1890) German composer. He was well known for his opera *Der Trompeter von Säckingen* 1884, which was often conducted by Mahler.

He studied theology at Strasbourg, but took to music and produced a French opera there in 1864. He then went to Leipzig, where he became a choral and afterwards an operatic conductor.

Works include: the operas *Fleurette* (1864), *Die Hochzeitreise*, *Dornröschens Brautfahrt* (1867), *Nachtwächter und Student*, *Am Alexandertag*, *Irmingard* (1876), *Der Rattenfänger von Hameln* (1879), *Der wilde Jäger* (1881), *Der Trompeter von Säckingen* (after Scheffel's poem, 1884), *Otto der Schütz* (1886), *Die Rose von Strassburg* (1890); part songs.

Neues vom Tage/News of the Day opera by Hindemith (libretto by M Schiffer), produced Berlin, Kroll Opera, 8 June 1929, conductor Klemperer. The opera was condemned by Goebbels in 1934: 'in their eagerness to make a sensation atonal musicians exhibit naked women in the bathtub on stage in the most obscene situations'. (Exactly 50 years later Peter Hall's wife, Maria Ewing, took a nude bath in the Glyndebourne production of *Poppea*.)

Neukomm, Sigismund von (1778–1858) Austrian composer. As a chorister at Salzburg Cathedral he was a pupil of M Haydn, who in 1798 sent him to J Haydn in Vienna. In 1806 he went to Sweden and Russia, becoming conductor at the Tsar's German theatre in St Petersburg. He returned to Vienna in 1809 and went to live in Paris soon after, succeeding Dussek in 1812 as pianist to Talleyrand. From 1816 to 1821 he was maestro de capilla to Pedro I of Brazil, with whom he returned to Lisbon, after the revolution, afterwards travelling with Talleyrand. In 1829 he visited London, meeting Mendelssohn, and lived there and alternately in Paris for the rest of his life.

Works include: the opera *Alexander in Indien* (1804), *Niobé* (1809) and others; 48 Masses and Requiem for Louis XVI; oratorios *Mount Sinai, David* and six others; incidental music for Schiller's *Braut von Messina* (1805); songs.

Neumann, František (1874–1929) Czech composer and conductor. He started in a commercial and military career, but went to study music at the Leipzig Conservatory. After filling various chorus-master's and conductor's posts at German and Czech theatres, he went to Brno as chief conductor at the National Theatre. He conducted the first performances of Janáček's *Káta Kabanová, The Cunning Little Vixen, Šárka,* and *The Makropoulos Case.*

Works include: the operas *Idalka, Die Brautwerbung* (1901), *Liebelei* (on Schnitzler's play, 1910), *Herbststurm* (1919), *Beatrice Caracci* (1922); melodrama *Pan;* ballets *In Pleasant Pastures, The Peri, Pierrot;* Masses and motets; symphonic poem *Infernal Dance,* suite *The Sunken Bell, Moravian Rhapsody,* overtures, etc. for orchestra; octet, piano trio; choruses, songs.

Neumark, Georg (1621–1681) German poet and musician. In 1657 he published a collection of sacred and secular songs, *Musikalische-poetischer Lustwald;* some were set to music by himself, including the hymn 'Wer nur den lieben Gott lässt walten'.

neumes signs in Eastern chant and Western plainsong (and in some medieval song-books) indicating the single notes or groups of notes to which each syllable was to be sung. Originally not set on staves, but merely marked above the words and showing neither precise length nor exact pitch, they served as reminders of tunes already known to the singers.

New England Holidays unnumbered symphony by Ives, composed 1904–13: 1. *Washington's birthday* 2. *Decoration Day* 3. *The Fourth of July* 4. *Thanksgiving.* First performed New York, 10 January 1931, conductor Slonimsky.

Newlin, Dika (1923–) US musicologist and composer. Her writings include studies of Bruckner, Mahler, and Schoenberg; also translations, particularly of Schoenberg's writings: *Schoenberg Remembered: Diaries and Recollections, 1938–76* 1980.

She studied privately with Sessions and Schoenberg and then taught at Western Maryland College and Syracuse University.

In 1952 she established a music department at Drew University, New Jersey. She has also composed for various media, especially chamber music.

Newman, John Henry (1801–1890) English cardinal and poet. See ◊*Dream of Gerontius* (Elgar).

New Music (German *Die Neue Musik*) term invented to describe the atonal and serial music of the ◊Second Viennese School (Schoenberg, Berg, and Webern) and their followers. Used by Webern in the title of his autobiographical manifesto, 'The Path to the New Music', and especially by the critics Theodor ◊Adorno and Carl ◊Dahlhaus.

'New World' Symphony Dvořák's Ninth Symphony in E minor, op. 95, with the subtitle *From the New World,* because it was written in the USA. Composed 1893, first performed New York Philharmonic Society, 16 December 1893.

New Year opera in three acts by Tippett (libretto by composer), produced Houston, 5 October 1989. Neurotic psychologist Jo Ann finds time-traveller Pelegrin and true love. He teaches her how to be independent before leaving again for the future.

nexus set see ◊set complex.

ngoni plucked lute of the Manding peoples of West Africa. Commonly found with three strings, the ngoni is played exclusively by men from the professional musicians' caste and is used to accompany praise-singing and historical narrative.

Nibelung Saga/Nibelungenlied ancient Teutonic epic in the Middle High German dialect. See Heinrich ◊Dorn (*Nibelungen*); Felix ◊Draeseke (*Gudrun*); ◊Ring des Nibelungen (Wagner); ◊Sigurd (Reyer).

Nibelung's Ring, The (Wagner). See ◊*Ring des Nibelungen.*

Niccolini, Giuseppe (1762–1842) Italian composer. He was at first very successful in opera, but was eventually driven from the stage by Rossini. He was maestro di cappella at Piacenza Cathedral from 1819.

He studied under Giacomo Insanguine at the Conservatorio di Sant' Onofrio, Naples.

Works include: the operas *I baccanti di Roma* (1801), *Traiano in Dacia* (1807), *Coriolano* (1808), and about 40 others; Masses and other church music.

Nicholson, George (1949–) English composer who studied with Bernard Rands and David Blake. His music is largely for chamber groups.

Works include: Overture, seven winds (1976), *Recycle*, 11 instruments (1976), *The Arrival of the Poet in the City*, melodrama for actor and seven instruments (1983), Chamber concerto (1980), Brass quintet (1977), *Aubade* for soprano and five instruments (1981), *Movements* for seven instruments (1983), *Stilleven* for five instruments (1985), *Blisworth Tunnel Blues* for soprano and ensemble (1986), *Sea-Change* for 14 strings (1988), cello concerto (1990), flute concerto (1993).

Nicholson, Richard (died 1639) English organist and composer. In 1595 he became choirmaster and organist at Magdalen College, Oxford, took a degree in music there in 1596, and became the first professor of music there in 1627.

Works include: anthems, madrigals (one in *The Triumphes of Oriana*), music for viols, 'dialogue' (or song-cycle) for three voices 'Joane, quoth John'.

Nicodé, Jean Louis (1853–1919) German-Polish conductor and composer. In 1856 his family moved to Berlin, where Nicodé studied, first under his father and from 1869 at the Neue Akademie der Tonkunst. Afterwards he taught there and arranged concerts at which he appeared as pianist, toured in the Balkans with Désirée Artot and in 1878 became professor at the Dresden Conservatory. From 1885 he devoted himself to conducting and composition.

Works include: the symphonic ode *Das Meer* for solo voices, male chorus, orchestra and organ (1889); symphonic poems *Maria Stuart* (after Schiller, 1880), *Die Jagd nach dem Glück*, *Gloria*, symphonic variations for orchestra; romance for violin and orchestra; cello and piano sonata; sonata and numerous pieces for piano; songs, including cycle *Dem Andenken an Amarantha* (1886); male-voice choruses.

Nicolai, (Carl) Otto (Ehrenfried) (1810–1849) German composer and conductor. In 1847 he was appointed director of the cathedral choir and the Court Opera in Berlin, where he died of a stroke, two months after the production of his *Merry Wives of Windsor*; after initial rejection, this soon became his most popular opera, and is still often heard in Germany.

He studied the piano as a child, but was so unhappy at home that in 1826 he ran away and was sent to Berlin by a patron the following year for study under Carl Zelter and Bernhard Klein. In 1833 another patron sent him to Rome as organist in the Prussian Embassy chapel, and there he studied under

Giuseppe Baini. He returned there after a year at the Kärntnertortheater in Vienna 1837–38. He became court Kapellmeister in Vienna in 1841 and founded the Philharmonic concerts there in 1842.

Works include: the operas *Enrico II* (later *Rosmonda d'Inghilterra*, 1839), *Il templario* (1840), *Odoardo e Gildippe*, *Il proscritto* (later *Die Heimkehr des Verbannten*, 1841), *Die lustigen Weiber von Windsor* (after Shakespeare, 1849); Mass for Frederick William IV of Prussia, Requiem, Te Deum; Symphonic Festival Overture on 'Ein' feste Burg' for the jubilee of Königsberg University.

Nicolaus de Cracovia (Mikołaj z Krakowa) (lived 16th century) Polish organist and composer. He was in the service of the royal court, and wrote organ music that is included in two manuscripts: that of Jan of Lublin 1537–48 and the Kraków Tablature 1548.

Nielsen, Carl August (1865–1931) Danish composer. His works combine an outward formal strictness with an inner waywardness of tonality and structure. They include the Neo-Classical opera *Maskarade/Masquerade* 1906, a *Wind Quintet* 1922, six programmatic symphonies, numerous songs, and incidental music on Danish texts. He also composed concertos for violin 1911, flute 1926, and clarinet 1928; chamber music; and piano works.

Being poor as a youth, he joined a military band at the age of 14, but at 18 succeeded in entering the Copenhagen Conservatory as a pupil of Niels Gade. In 1891 he entered the royal orchestra and was its conductor 1908–14. He also became conductor of the Music Society and director of the Conservatory. He was one of the most remarkable late Romantic symphonists, combining traditional forms with a new and original approach to tonality; the first symphony is an example of progressive tonality, ending in a different key to the initial one. Later symphonies developed a complex, rhythmically driven polyphony. The third symphony, *Espansiva*, is the first of these great works in which thematic formation is achieved within closely controlled forms. In the fifth symphony, chaos is threatened by a side drummer who is instructed to obliterate the rest of the orchestra; order is restored in a triumphant conclusion.

Works include: the operas *Saul og David* (1902), *Maskarade* (after Holberg, 1906); incidental music for Oehlenschäger's *Aladdin* and many other plays; *Hymnus Amoris* for chorus and orchestra (1897); *Springtime on Fyn*

for soloists, chorus, and orchestra (1922); *Hymn to Art* for vocal soloists and wind instruments (1929); three motets for unaccompanied chorus; six symphonies 1. in G minor (1892), 2. *The Four Temperaments* (1902), 3. *Espansiva* (1911), 4. *The Inextinguishable* (1916), 5. (1922), 6. *Sinfonia semplice* (1925), *Saga-Dream*, symphonic rhapsody for orchestra; violin concerto (1911), flute concerto (1926), *An Imaginary Journey to the Faroes*, rhapsody (1927), clarinet concerto (1928); four string quartets (1887–1919), two string quintets, wind quintet (1922) and other chamber music; two violin and piano sonatas; *Commotio* for organ (1931); suites and other piano works; songs.

Nielsen, Hans (c. 1580–c. 1626) Danish lutenist and composer. After learning music as a choirboy in the royal chapel at Copenhagen, he studied with Giovanni Gabrieli at Venice 1599–1606, and with the English lutenist Richard Howett at Wolfenbüttel 1606–08. After that he was lutenist at the Danish court until 1611, when he was dismissed and went to Heidelberg University. In 1623 he was appointed vice-director of the royal chapel in succession to Mogens Pedersøn.

Nielsen, Riccardo (1908–1982) Italian composer of Scandinavian descent. He studied at the Liceo Musicale of Bologna and at Salzburg, and was influenced by Casella.

Works include: the monodrama *L'Incubo* (1948), radio opera *La via di Colombo* (1953); incidental music for *Maria ed il Nazzareno*; Psalms for male voices and orchestra (1941); concerto for orchestra (1936), two symphonies (1933, 1935); capriccio and *Sinfonia concertante* for piano and orchestra, violin concerto (1932); divertimento for bassoon, trumpet, violin, viola, and cello, trio for oboe, bassoon, and horn (1934), Adagio and Allegro for cello and 11 instruments; sonatas for violin and piano, and cello and piano; *Musica* for two pianos (1939), sonata and *ricercare*, chorale and toccata on BACH for piano; *Laude di Jacopone da Todi* and *Tre satire di Giusti* for voice and piano.

niente (Italian 'nothing') word generally used in connection with *quasi* ('so to speak', 'almost') when extreme softness of tone is required.

Nigg, Serge (1924–) French composer. He studied under Messiaen at the Paris Conservatory, but in 1946 adopted the 12-note technique under the influence of Leibowitz, with which he in turn came to disagree two years later.

Works include: the melodrama *Perséphone* (1942); symphonic movement for orchestra *Timour* (1944), *La Mort d'Arthus* for voice and orchestra; piano concerto, *Concertino* for piano, wind and percussion; *Jérôme Bosch-Symphonie* (1960); variations for piano and ten instruments; two piano concertos (1954, 1971); sonata and *Fantaisie* for piano.

Night at the Chinese Opera, A opera in three acts by Judith Weir (libretto by composer, based in part on Chi-Chun-Hsiang's *The Chao Family Orphan*), produced Cheltenham, Everyman Theatre, 8 July 1987. Chao Liu is in exile after the invasion by Kublai Khan, but after an earthquake interrupts a play which runs parallel to the course of his life, he is arrested. Although the play ends happily Chao is executed.

Nightingale, The/Soloveg opera by Stravinsky (libretto by composer and S N Mitusov, from Hans Andersen's fairy-tale), produced Paris, Opéra, 26 May 1914; revived in the form of a ballet (choreography by Leonid Massin), Paris, Opéra, 2 February 1920. Dying Emperor is revived by the sound of the nightingale.

Night on the Bare Mountain a work in various forms by Mussorgsky, more properly called *St John's Night on the Bare Mountain*, based on the incident of the witches' sabbath in Gogol's story 'St John's Eve'; composed as a symphonic poem for orchestra 1866–67; later used in a version for chorus and orchestra and called *Night on Mount Triglav* in 1872 as part of the opera *Mlada* commissioned from Mussorgsky, Borodin, Cui, and Rimsky-Korsakov, but never completed; revised version of this used as introduction to Act III of the unfinished opera *Sorotchinsty Fair*, began in 1875; this last version revised and arranged as an orchestral piece by Rimsky-Korsakov after Mussorgsky's death.

Nights in the Gardens of Spain (Falla). See ◊*Noches en los jardines de España*.

Nikisch, Arthur (1855–1922) Austro-Hungarian conductor. He conducted the first performance of Bruckner's seventh symphony in 1884, and in 1913 conducted Wagner's *Ring* at Covent Garden, London.

He studied in Vienna and played violin in the court orchestra 1874–77. He was conductor at the Leipzig Opera 1878–89. Subsequent posts included the Boston Symphony Orchestra 1889–93, Budapest Opera 1893–95, Leipzig Gewandhaus from 1895, and the Berlin Philharmonic Orchestra.

Nilsson, Bo (1937–) Swedish composer. Largely self-taught, he has belonged to the younger generation of avant-garde composers.

Works include: *Songs on the Death of Children* for soprano and small orchestra; *Moments of Time* for ten wind instruments; *Frequencies* for chamber ensemble; *A Prodigal Son* for contralto, alto flute, and chamber ensemble; *Reactions* for percussion quartet (1960); *Audiograms* for electronic generators; *Quantities* for piano *Attraktionen* for string quartet (1968), *Madonna* for mezzo and ensemble (1977); Piano Quintet (1979); *Wendepunkt* for brass and electronics (1981); *Autumn Song* for baritone and orchestra (1985); *Vagues pour Madame Curie* for soprano and orchestra (1993).

Nin (y Castellanos), Joaquín (1878–1949) Spanish pianist, musicologist, and composer. He studied at Barcelona and in Paris, where in 1906 he became piano professor at the Schola Cantorum. After short periods in Berlin and Cuba, he settled in Brussels and later in Paris again. He edited much old Spanish music and wrote three books.

Works include: the mimodrama *L'Autre*, ballet *L'Écharpe bleue*; violin pieces; piano works; songs.

Nina, o sia La pazza per amore/Nina, or the Lunatic from Love opera by Paisiello (libretto by G Carpani, with additions by G B Lorenzi, based on the French libretto by B J Marsollier), produced Naples, Caserta Palace, for the visit of Queen Maria Carolina of Sicily, 25 June 1789; first public performance Naples, Teatro Fiorentino, 1790. Nina is engaged to Lindoro but her father cancels the wedding plans when a rich suitor arrives. Lindoro fights a duel with him and is shot. Nina goes mad, but recovers her sanity when he revives.

ninth the interval a whole tone larger than an octave (major ninth) or a semitone larger (minor ninth).

Maj 9th   Min 9th

Major and minor ninths.

Ninth Symphony (Beethoven). See ◊'*Choral Symphony*'.

Nivers, Guillaume (Gabriel) (c. 1631–1714) French organist, harpsichordist, theorist, and

composer. He was a pupil of Chambonnières in Paris and organist of the church of Saint-Sulpice in 1654, also appointed organist to the king in 1678 and music master to the queen. He wrote a treatise on singing and other theoretical works.

Works include: motets and other church music.

Nixon in China opera in two acts by John Adams (libretto by Alice Goodman), produced Houston, Grand Opera, 22 October 1987. Media-conscious Dick and wife Pat are impressed by Chairman Mao. Nixon is portrayed as a superficial character, in contrast to the revolutionary Mao.

Nobilissima Visione dance legend (ballet) in six scenes by Hindemith (choreography by composer and Massine on story of St Francis), produced Drury Lane, London, 21 July 1938. Orchestral-Suite in three movements performed Venice, 13 September 1938.

Noces, Les (Stravinsky). See ◊*Wedding, The*.

Noches en los jardines de España/Nights in the Gardens of Spain symphonic impressions for piano and orchestra by Falla, begun 1909, finished 1915. First perfomed Madrid, 9 April 1916. There are three movements: 1. *En el Generalife*; 2. *Danza leJanuarya/Dance in the distance*); 3. *En los jardines de la Sierra de Córdoba*.

nocturne a reflective character piece, often for piano, introduced by John Field (1782–1837) and adopted by Chopin.

Nocturne song cycle for tenor, seven obbligato instruments, and strings by Britten (texts by Shelley, Tennyson, Coleridge, Middleton, Wordsworth, Owen, Keats, and Shakespeare), first performed Leeds, 16 October 1958, with Pears.

Nocturnes three orchestral pieces by Debussy, *Nuages*, *Fêtes*, and *Sirènes*, the last with female chorus, composed 1893–99, first performed Paris, 9 December 1900 (nos. 1 and 2); 27 October 1901 (complete).

node (from Latin *nodus*, 'knot') the point in a vibrating string at which the vibration becomes cut into segments.

Nola, Domenico da (Joan Domenico del Giovane) (c. 1510–1592) Italian composer. He was maestro di cappella of the church of the Annunciation at Naples, 1563–88. He composed motets, madrigals, and *villanelle*.

nonet composition for nine instruments, usually in several movements.

Non nobis Domine a canon for voices, probably by Byrd, often sung in England for 'grace' after public dinners. It is a riddle canon capable of being sung with the entries in various positions, also in inversion.

Nono, Luigi (1924–1990) Italian composer. He wrote attenuated pointillist works such as *Il canto sospeso/Suspended Song* 1955–56 for soloists, chorus, and orchestra, in which influences of Webern and Gabrieli are applied to issues of social conscience. After the opera *Intolleranza 1960/Intolerance 1960* his style became more richly expressionist, and his causes more overtly polemical.

Born in Venice, he abandoned law for music, and studied with Bruno Maderna and with Hermann Scherchen, who conducted his *Polifonia-monodiaritmica* at Darmstadt in 1951. His work was initially performed principally in Germany, and developed from serialism, in the manner of Schoenberg (whose daughter he married) to more politically committed works. Nono's earlier output included numerous orchestral works, but after *La fabbrica illuminata/The Illuminated Factory* 1964, he concentrated exclusively on the electronic-vocal medium.

Works include: the opera-oratorio *Intolleranza* (1961); *Variazioni canoniche* on a theme of Schoenberg's (from *Ode to Napoleon*), *Due espressioni*, and *Diario polacco '58* for orchestra; *Canti* for 13 instruments, *Incontri* for 24 instruments, *Il canto sospeso* (1956) and other choral works including *La Victoire de Guernica*, *Epitaph I for F Garcia Lorca*, *Cori di Didone*; cantata *Sul ponte di Hiroshima* for soprano and tenor and orchestra (1962); *La fabbrica illuminata* for mezzo and electronic tape; *Epitaphs II & III for F Garcia Lorca* (II for flute, strings, and percussion, III for speaker, speaking chorus, and orchestra); opera *Al gran sole carico d'amore* (1974); electronic music, including *Omaggio a Emilio Vedova*, (1960), *Sofferte onde serene* (1976); *Quando stanno morendo* for voices and ensemble (1982).

Noonday Witch, The/Polednice symphonic poem by Dvořák, op. 108; composed 1896, first performed London, 21 November 1896.

Nordgren, Pehr Henrik (1944–) Finnish composer. He studied at Helsinki and Tokyo Universities (traditional Japanese music).

Works include: the chamber opera *The Black Monk* (1981); orchestral series *Euphone I-IV* (1967–81); three violin concertos (1969, 1977, 1981), three viola concertos (1970, 1979, 1986), two symphonies (1974, 1989), two cello concertos (1980, 1983), five string quartets (1967–86), piano quintet (1978), piano trio (1983).

Nordheim, Arne (1931–) Norwegian composer. He studied in Oslo and with Vagn Holmboe in Copenhagen. He was active as a performer and composer of electronic music from 1968.

Works include: the ballets *Ariadne* (1977), *The Tempest* (1979), and *The End of Time* (1981); *Favola* musical play for TV (1965), *Colorazione* (1968), *Pace* (1970), and *Osaka-Music* (1970) for electronic instruments; *Be Not Afeared* for soprano, baritone, and ensemble (1978); *Tenebrae* for cello and orchestra (1982), *Varder* for trumpet and orchestra (1986), *Rendezvous* for strings (1987); chamber and choral music.

Norgård, Per (1932–) Danish composer. He studied with Vagn Holmboe and Nadia Boulanger, and taught at Aarhus from 1965. An early influence was Sibelius; later he turned to 'infinite' serialism, pointillism, and graphic notation.

Works include: the operas *The Labyrinth* (1967), *Gilgamesh* (1973), *Siddharta* (1983), *The Divine Tivoli* (1983); four symphonies (1954–81); *Illuminationi* for orchestra (1984); cello concerto (1985), *Helle Nacht* violin concerto (1987); *Pastorale* for strings (1988); *Spaces of Time* for piano and ensemble (1991); *Scintillation* for instruments (1993); seven string quartets (1958–93).

Norma opera by Bellini (libretto by F Romani, based on L A Soumet's tragedy), produced Milan, La Scala, 26 December 1831. Druid priestess Norma still loves Roman consul Pollione after he abandons her for another priestess, Adalgisa. Jealousy and rivalry result in the deaths of both Norma and Pollione.

North Country Sketches work for orchestra in four movements by Delius; composed 1913–14, first performed London, 10 May 1915, conductor Beecham.

Nose, The opera by Shostakovich (libretto by A Preis, A Zamyatin, G Yonin and composer, after Gogol); 1927–28, first performed Leningrad, Maly Theatre, 12 January 1930. Story concerns disappearance of nose belonging to government official; described by contemporary Russian critics as an example of bourgeois decadence. Barber Ivan discovers a nose in his morning bread; Major Kovalyov wakes up missing his nose. The nose later appears running around in human size and treating everyone with contempt, as the Police Inspector chases it. Eventually it is caught and returned to Kovalyov.

A nota cambiata as a simple passing note (1) and as a changing note group (2).

nota cambiata (Italian 'changed note') term used in two senses in the analysis of 16th-century polyphony: (1) a dissonant passing-note on the beat (in Palestrina only on the weak beats); (2) a curling figure (also called 'changing note group') in which a dissonant passing-note (not on the beat) leads to a note a third lower, which then rises one step.

notation system of signs and symbols for writing music, either for performers to read from, or to make a permanent record. Early systems of music notation were developed in China in the 3rd century BC, and by the ancient Sumerians, and later by the ancient Greeks and Romans for their music dramas. The Greeks were the first to name the notes of the ◊scale with letters of the alphabet.

A form of notation using signs called **neumes** appeared in Europe in the Middle Ages as a means of writing down ◊plainsong. These graphic signs showed the rise and fall of the notes of a ◊melody, but did not give a precise idea of ◊pitch or ◊rhythm. The system of using notes on a ◊stave or staff of horizontal lines first appeared in the 11th century, and was invented by an Italian monk, ◊Guido of Arezzo (c. 991–after 1033).

Modern music notation uses a stave of five lines, with a ◊clef to show the exact pitch of the notes on it. The position of a note on the stave represents its pitch, and the shape of the note and its 'tail' indicate its duration in time. Other signs and words can be added to the written music to show the ◊tempo, dynamics (how loudly or softly the music should be played), and how the music should be played – for example ◊legato (smoothly) or ◊staccato (each note short and separate).

the need for music notation The vast majority of music belongs to some form of oral/aural tradition, and has never been written down. It is generally passed from one performer to another by repetition and memory, and consequently, like the game 'Chinese Whispers', changes its character through the ages. The need for a more reliable system of instructing performers and recording music for posterity was felt very early in the history of music. Unfortunately, the lack of written records makes it difficult for us to know much about the music of ancient cultures, and what we do know usually comes from verbal rather than musical sources, or from examination of the instruments played.

early systems It is likely that music notation developed alongside written language, and that the ancient Sumerians and Egyptians devised symbols to accompany the system of hand signs they used – indicating the pitch and shape of the melody by a sort of 'conducting'; certainly the Chinese had a quite sophisticated system of notation as early as the 3rd century BC. These early systems consisted of either symbols to represent separate vocal syllables – a form of **solmization**; or signs and instructions for playing specific instruments – a form of ◊tablature. The use of letters of the alphabet to name notes of the scale dates back to ancient Greece and possibly earlier, and was well established by 500 BC, when letter-names were given to the ◊diatonic scale, and inflections of a semitone or even a quarter-tone could be expressed by rotation of the letter symbols. This system seems to have been developed more for the study of ◊acoustics than as an aid to performance or to make a permanent record of specific pieces of music.

neumatic notation It was not until the 7th century that a notation was developed for recording pieces of music with some degree of accuracy. As the medieval Church had a virtual monopoly on written learning, it is not surprising that it was here that modern music notation had its beginnings. The chants of plainsong had been until then an oral/aural tradition, but to the medieval mind this was not a satisfactory state of affairs; some means of writing down the plainchant melodies for performance and posterity had to be found. As this was a purely vocal tradition, the first symbols derived from written language, and resembled acute and grave accents representing the rise and fall of the melody. These signs, known as neumes, developed into a complex system in which an individual neume could represent a single note or as many as four notes in a particular sequence. The neumatic system gave a very graphic indication of the shape of a melody, but the addition of a horizontal line removed its main drawback by fixing an absolute pitch as a point of reference.

the stave Guido of Arezzo further improved the system of notating plainsong in the first half of the 11th century. As well as inventing his own version of solmization, using the syllables ut, re, mi, etc. in conjunction with a set of mnemonics related to the joints of the fingers (the 'Guidonian hand'), he also suggested the use of a stave of four horizontal lines, which would not only provide a pitch reference, but would also graphically represent relative pitch by the vertical placing of notes on its lines and spaces. He is also credited with the invention of the clef, further refining the accuracy of the system.

Guido's innovations were, however, all concerned with notating pitch, and it was not until the 13th century that any systematic reform of rhythmic notation was achieved. The first to tackle this was Franco of Cologne, who codified and rationalized the existing system, and established the relationships between different note values. A system similar to present-day rhythmic notation had evolved from this by the middle of the 15th century, but based on triple rather than duple divisions.

the modern system By about 1700 the modern system of notation, using a stave of five lines as opposed to the four used in plainsong, had become firmly established. It almost completely replaced solmization and

tablature – although some forms of solmization, such as the ◊tonic sol-fa, are still used today, especially in vocal music and as a teaching aid, and tablature has remained in use by lutenists and guitarists. Despite its drawbacks, particularly in notating non-diatonic pitches and complex rhythms, conventional modern notation is also being used outside Western art music: music of previously aural/oral traditions is being transcribed, and even classical traditions such as Chinese music now make use of Western notation.

innovations The history of music notation is one of continual evolution, and the 20th century is no exception. As composers have found new means of expression, they have developed new means of writing them down. Methods of indicating microtones, intervals less than a semitone, were found early in the century, and symbols borrowed from mathematics have been used to notate complex rhythmic relationships. Some composers, such as John ◊Cage and Karlheinz ◊Stockhausen, virtually abandoned conventional notation in favour of graphic representations or even passages of text; others, such as Pierre ◊Boulez and Luciano ◊Berio, have attempted to refine it and improve its accuracy. There have even been attempts, particularly in the first half of the century, to invent completely new systems such as Klavarscribo, but these not been enthusiastically received.

note the written symbol indicating pitch and duration, the sound of which is a tone.

note row another term for ◊tone row.

Notker Labeo (950–1022), also known as Teutonicus German monk. He lived at the monastery of St Gall, and wrote on music and other subjects, including a short treatise in Old High German on the measurement of organ pipes.

Notre-Dame opera by Franz Schmidt (libretto by composer and L Wilk, after Hugo) composed 1902–04, produced Vienna, 1 April 1914. The well-known *Intermezzo* was performed Vienna, 6 December 1903.

notturno (Italian 'night piece') eighteenth-century forerunner of the nocturne, not then a single lyrical instrumental piece, but a composition in several movements similar to the serenade or divertimento. In the 19th century it became simply the Italian equivalent of the nocturne, as for example in Mendelssohn's *Midsummer Night's Dream* music.

Novae de Infinito Laudes/New Praises of the Infinite cantata by Henze for soloists, chorus, and orchestra (text by Giordano Bruno, 1548–1600, Italian astronomer burnt at the stake by the Inquisition); composed 1962, first performed Venice, 24 April 1963, with Söderström, Meyer, Pears, and Fischer-Dieskau.

Novak, Jan (1921–1984) Czech composer. He studied at the Brno Conservatory (1940–46) and at the Prague Academy. He was influenced at first by the neoclassicism of Martinů, with whom he studied in New York, but then turned to jazz and serialism.

Works include: concerto for two pianos (1955), *Philharmonic Dances* for orchestra (1956), *Variations on a theme of Martinů* for orchestra (1959), *Dodo*, oratorio (1967), *Orpheus et Eurydice* for soprano, viola d'amore and piano (1971), *Ludi Concertantes* for 18 instruments (1981), *Symphonia bipartita* (1983).

Novák, Vitězslav (1870–1949) Czech composer. He made a career as a distinguished teacher of composition and in 1909 was appointed professor at the Prague Conservatory. After World War I, which restored his country's independence, he became professor of the 'Master School' and was its director 1919–22.

He was the son of a doctor, but lost his father early and had to support the family by teaching. While studying law at Prague University he attended the Conservatory, studying piano with Jiránek and composition with Dvořák, who persuaded him to devote himself wholly to music. His first works were published with the help of Brahms.

Works include: the operas *The Imp of Zvíkov* (1915), *A Night at Karlstein* (1916), *The Lantern* (1923), *The Grandfather's Will* (1926), *The Wood Nymph*; ballets *Signorina Gioventù* and *Nikotina*; cantatas *The Storm, The Spectre's Bride*, and choral ballads; symphony (1945), dedicated to Stalin after the liberation of Prague, symphonic poems *In the Tatra, Eternal Longing, Toman and the Wood Nymph, De profundis* (1941), overtures *The Corsair* (after Byron), *Maryša, Lady Godiva*, serenade for small orchestra; piano concerto (1895); two string quartets, two piano trios, piano quartet, piano quintet; *Sonata eroica, Manfred* (ballad after Byron), *Songs of Winter Nights, Pan, Exoticon*, six sonatinas, *Youth* (children's pieces) and other pieces for piano; song cycles *Gypsy Songs, Melancholy, In the Valley of a New Kingdom, Melancholy Songs of Love, Nocturnes, Eroticon*, and other songs; part songs.

Novelletten (German 'short stories') category title used by Schumann for his eight

piano pieces op. 21, composed 1838, also for no. 9 of the *Bunte Blätter* for piano, op. 99.

Novello, Vincent (1781–1861) English composer, organist, editor, and publisher, father of the soprano Clara Novello. He founded the music publishing firm of Novello & Company in London in 1811. He edited valuable collections of music including Masses by Haydn and Mozart, and composed church music and cantatas.

November Woods a symphonic poem by Bax, composed 1917, first performed Manchester, Hallé Orchestra, 18 November 1920.

Novotný, Jaroslav (1886–1918) Czech composer. He studied in Prague, joined the Austrian army during World War I and was a prisoner in Russia, where he wrote much in camp; he was released but was killed near the end of the war fighting on the other side with the Czech legion.

Works include: a string quartet; choruses; piano sonata; song cycles *The Eternal Wedding* and *Ballads of the Soul*.

Nowak, Leopold (1904–1991) Austrian musicologist. He wrote books on Haydn (published 1951) and Bruckner (published 1947, 1973); in 1945 he succeeded Robert ◊Haas as editor of the complete works of Bruckner.

He studied in Vienna and was professor at the University there 1932–73. He was director of the music division at the Vienna National Library 1946–69.

Nowowiejski, Feliks (1877–1946) Polish composer and conductor. He studied in Berlin, church music at Regensburg, and afterwards in France, Belgium, and Italy. In 1909 he returned to Poland, conducted the Kraków Music Society until 1914 and in 1919 became professor of organ at the Poznań Conservatory, where he conducted orchestral concerts.

Works include: the operas *Baltic Legend* (1924), *The Mountain Goblin*; opera-ballet *Leluja*; ballets *Tatra, Polish Wedding*; Masses, motets and psalms; oratorios *Quo vadis?* (1907), *Beatum scelus, Missa pro pace.*; cantata *Upper Silesian Folk Scene*; symphonic poems *Beatrix, Nina*, overture *Polish Wooing, The Prodigal Son, Jerusalem*; nine symphonies.

Noyes Fludde opera in one act by Britten (text from the Chester Miracle Play), produced Orford, 18 June 1958. Based on the biblical story of Noah's flood; setting makes much use of children's voices.

Nozze d'Ercole e d'Ebe, Le/The Nuptials of Hercules and Hebe opera by Gluck, produced Pillnitz, near Dresden, at the double wedding of Max Joseph, Elector of Bavaria, and Maria Anna, Princess of Saxony, and Frederick Christian, Prince of Saxony, and Maria Antonia Walpurgis, Princess of Bavaria, 29 June 1747.

Opera by Porpora (libretto as above), produced Venice, 18 February 1744.

Nozze di Figaro, Le/The Marriage of Figaro opera by Mozart (libretto by L da Ponte, based on Beaumarchais's comedy, *La Folle Journée, ou Le Mariage de Figaro*), produced Vienna, Burgtheater, 1 May 1786. Figaro and Susanna are to be married, but first Figaro is pursued by the elderly Marcellina (who turns out to be his mother), Susanna must evade the eager Count Almaviva, and all the characters must disentangle themselves from a web of mistaken identities.

Nozze di Teti e di Peleo, Le/The Nuptials of Thetis and Peleus opera by Cavalli (libretto by O Persiani), produced Venice, Teatro San Cassiano, probably 24 January 1639. Thetis and Peleus are to marry, but Aeolus (Peleus' father) opposes the match because he believes Jupiter has seduced Thetis. Pluto sends Discord to interrupt the lovers before the marriage proceeds.

Nuits d'été, Les/Summer Nights six songs by Berlioz (poems by T Gautier), composed 1840–41 for mezzo or tenor and piano; revised for voice and orchestra 1843 (no. 4) and 1856. 1. *Villanelle*; 2. *Le spectre de la rose*; 3. *Sur les lagunes*; 4. *Absence*; 5. *Au cimetière*; 6. *L'île inconnue*.

Nuitter, Charles (Louis Étienne) (1828–1899), actually Truinet French librettist and writer on music. A lawyer at first, he later devoted himself to the writing and translation of libretti and of books on opera. In 1865 he became archivist of the Paris Opéra.

Nunc Dimittis a musical setting of St Luke's *Song of Simeon* ('Lord, now lettest thou thy servant depart in peace'). It is sung at Roman Catholic compline and Anglican evensong, either in ◊plainsong or to a composer's polyphonic setting. It is often linked compositionally with the Anglican ◊Magnificat.

Nursery Suite orchestral suite in seven movements by Elgar. Dedicated to the then Duchess of York and her daughters Princess Elizabeth and Princess Margaret Rose; first performed (concert) London, Queen's Hall, 20 August 1931. Movements are 1. *Aubade*; 2. *The Serious Doll*; 3. *Busy-ness*; 4. *The Sad Doll*; 5. *The Waggon* (passes); 6. *The Mercy Doll*; 7. *Dreaming*; 8. *Envoi*.

Nursery, The song cycle by Mussorgsky (words by composer), composed 1868–72: 1. *With Nurse*; 2. *In the Corner*; 3. *The Cockchafer*; 4. *With the Doll*; 5. *Going to sleep*; 6. *On the Hobby-Horse*; 7. *The Cat 'Sailor'*.

Nusch-Nuschi, Das opera in one act for Burmese marionettes by Hindemith (libretto by F Blei); composed 1920, produced Stuttgart, 4 June 1921; conductor by Fritz Busch, who claimed to be shocked by satirical references to Wagner's *Tristan*. The castration of an Oriental philanderer is accompanied by a quotation from King Marke's music: '*Mir – dies?*' ('This – to me?').

nut on a stringed musical instrument, the ridge at one end of the ◊fingerboard, next to the peg box, which raises the strings from the surface of the fingerboard. On some instruments, such as the ◊ukulele, there is a movable nut, which raises the pitch of the entire instrument.

A nut is also the part of a bow which secures the horsehair at the heel and, by incorporating a screw mechanism, allows the tension of the hairs to be adjusted.

Nutcracker/Casse-Noisette ballet by Tchaikovsky (choreography by Lev Ivanovich Ivanov, based on a tale by E T A Hoffmann), produced St Petersburg, Maryinsky Theatre, 18 December 1892.

Nyman, Michael (1944–) English composer. His highly stylized music is characterized by processes of gradual modification by repetition of complex musical formulae (known as minimalism). His compositions include scores for English filmmaker Peter Greenaway and New Zealand filmmaker Jane Campion (*The Piano* 1993); a chamber opera, *The Man Who Mistook His Wife for a Hat* 1989; and three string quartets.

He studied with Alan Bush at the Royal Academy of Music in London and with Thurston Dart at King's College, London. In 1974 he published *Experimental Music – Cage and Beyond* but his music has followed more populist paths, drawing on a wide range of influences, including post-minimalism, rock and roll, Stravinsky, and a certain indebtedness to Mozart: *I'll Stake my Cremona to a Jew's Trump* 1983, and *Letters, Riddles and Writs*, TV opera for the 1991 bicentenary. He is widely known through his Peter Greenaway film scores: *The Draughtsman's Contract* 1982, *The Cook, the Thief, his Wife and her Lover* 1989, and *Prospero's Books* 1991. He formed the Michael Nyman Band for the performance of an eclectic range of pieces, for example *Piano Concerto* 1993.

Nystedt, Knut (1915–) Norwegian composer. In 1950 he founded the Norwegian Soloists Choir and conducted it 1951–90, giving many performances of modern works.

After studying at the Oslo Conservatory and with Copland in the USA, he worked as a church organist from 1938, and as a conductor with Oslo Philharmonic Orchestra from 1945.

Works include: *Christmas opera With Crown and Star* (1971); *Song of Solomon* church opera (1989); *Lucis Creator Optime* for soloists, chorus, and orchestra (1968); *Four Grieg Romances* for a cappella chorus (1992); *Sinfonia del Mare* (1983); five string quartets (1938–88).

Nystroem, Gösta (1890–1966) Swedish composer and painter. He was the son of a headmaster who taught him music and painting, which he afterwards studied at Stockholm, Copenhagen, and Paris, where d'Indy and Leonid Sabaneiev were among his masters for composition. He lived in Paris for 12 years and came under the influence of Picasso, Braque, Chirico, and other modern painters. After further studies in Italy and Spain he settled at Göteborg and in 1933 became music critic of the *Göteborgs Handelstidning*.

Works include: the ballet-pantomime *Maskerade*; incidental music to various plays includes Shakespeare's *Merchant of Venice* and *The Tempest*; four symphonies (*Sinfonia breve, Sinfonia espressiva, Sinfonia del mare, Sinfonia Shakespeariana*), symphonic poems *The Arctic Sea, The Tower of Babel*, Lyric Suite and Festival Overture for orchestra, *Concerto grosso* for string orchestra; violin concerto, viola concerto, *Sinfonia concertante* for cello and orchestra; piano suites and pieces; songs.

o abbreviation for ◊open string, marked over a note in music for a string player; or an indication that a harmonic is to be played (see ◊harmonics).

obbligato (Italian 'obligatory') in musical notation, indicating that an instrument or voice is essential and not to be omitted. However, some composers have used this term with the opposite meaning in mind: that an instrument or voice may be omitted if so desired. Generally, the older the notation, the more likely it is that obbligato retains its original meaning of an 'obliged', essential part.

Oberon, König der Elfen/Oberon, King of the Fairies opera by Wranitzky (libretto by K L Gieseke, based on Wieland's poem and F S Seyler's libretto *Hüon und Amande*), produced Vienna, Theater auf der Wieden, 7 November 1789.

Oberon, or The Elf King's Oath opera by Weber (libretto by J R Planché, based on Wieland's poem and further back on the medieval French romance *Huon de Bordeaux*), produced London, Covent Garden, 12 April 1826. Oberon, King of the Elves, and his queen, Titania, resolve to stay apart until they find a human couple who stay faithful in the face of adversity. Sir Huon and Rieza face a series of tests, restoring the elves' faith in love.

obertas, also oberek Polish folk dance performed in figures by couples following a leader. The music is in 3–4 time, not unlike that of the mazurka, but livelier in character.

Oberto, Conte di San Bonifacio opera by Verdi (libretto by A Piazza, altered by B Merelli and T Solera), produced Milan, La Scala, 17 November 1839, Verdi's first opera. Count Ricardo is to marry Cuniza, but after learning of his earlier affair with Leonora, Cuniza demands that he marry Leonora instead. Oberto, Leonora's father, is killed in a duel with Ricardo, who, stricken with guilt, leaves the country, while Leonora enters a convent.

Oberwerk German for ◊swell organ, the second manual (keyboard) of an organ.

oboe musical instrument of the woodwind family, a refined treble ◊shawm of narrow tapering bore and exposed double reed. The oboe was developed by the Hotteterre family of instrument-makers about 1700 and was incorporated in the court ensemble of Louis XIV. In C, with a normal compass of about 21/2 octaves, it has a rich tone of elegant finish. Oboe concertos have been composed by Vivaldi, Albinoni, Richard Strauss, Martinů, and others. Heinz Holliger is a modern virtuoso oboist.

Alto variants **oboe d'amore** (a minor third lower) and **oboe da caccia** (a fifth lower) feature in the work of J S Bach and other 18th-century composers, superseded by the 19th-century cor anglais in the modern orchestra. The rarely heard heckelphone is a baritone deviation.

The compass of the oboe.

oboe da caccia (Italian 'hunting oboe') an oboe tuned a fifth lower and transposing a fifth down. Its parts in early music are now generally played on the English horn, whose pitch is the same.

oboe d'amore (Italian 'love oboe') an oboe tuned a minor third lower and transposing a minor third down.

Obrecht, Jacob (c. 1450–1505) Flemish composer. One of the outstanding composers of his day, his mostly polyphonic sacred music (which in style predates that of Josquin Desprez) centred on the Mass, for which he wrote 24 compositions. He was innovative, developing borrowed material, and using a secular fixed ◊*cantus firmus* (Latin 'fixed song') in his *Missa super Maria zart*. He also wrote motets and secular works. He worked as a ◊kapellmeister (chapel master) in Utrecht, Antwerp, and Bruges. He died of the plague.

He was born at Bergen-op-Zoom and studied at Louvain University. He directed the singers at Utrecht 1476–78, Bergen-op-Zoom 1479–84, then at Cambrai, at Bruges in 1486 and 1490, and elsewhere in the Low Countries. He was obliged to resign in 1500, and after a spell at Antwerp 1501–02 went to Italy for his health. He had already spent six months at the ducal court of Ferrara in 1487–88 and returned there in 1504 as head of Ercole d'Este's choir, only to die of plague the following year.

Works include: 27 Masses, including *Fortuna desperata*, *Maria zart*, and *Sub tuum praesidium*; motets, chansons.

Obukhov, Nikolai (1892–1954) Russian composer. He was a pupil of Nikolai Tcherepnin and Steinberg at the St Petersburg Conservatory. He settled in Paris in 1918 and made further studies with Ravel and others. He experimented with a 12-note system.

Works include: mystery *Le Livre de la vie*, *Poèmes liturgiques*.

Oca del Cairo, L'/The Goose of Cario unfinished opera by Mozart (libretto by G B Varesco). Produced in a version completed with other Mozartian fragments (libretto by V Wilder), Paris, Fantaisies-Parisiennes, 6 June 1867; new version by Virgilio Mortari (libretto by L Cavicchioli), Salzburg, 22 August 1936; another by Hans Redlich, London, Sadler's Wells, 30 May 1940.

ocarina early musical instrument of the flute type with finger-holes, roughly pear-shaped, with a mouthpiece protruding like a fish's fin, and usually made of terracotta.

Occasional Oratorio oratorio by Handel (libretto from Milton's Psalms, probably completed by Morell), composed to celebrate the suppression of the Jacobite rebellion, produced London, Covent Garden, 14 February 1746.

Occasione fa il ladro, L'/Opportunity makes a Thief opera by Rossini (libretto by L Prividali), produced Venice, Teatro San Moisè, 24 November 1812.

Oceanides, The/Allottaret symphonic poem by Sibelius, op. 73; composed 1914, first performed Norfolk, Connecticut, 4 June 1914, conductor Sibelius.

Ockeghem, Johannes see Johannes ◊Okeghem.

Octandre work by Varèse for small orchestra; composed 1923, first performed New York, 13 January 1924.

octatonic scale eight-note scale in alternating tone and semitone steps thus:
One of the earliest composers to make consistent use of this scale was N ◊Rimsky-Korsakov. His pupil, I ◊Stravinsky, also used the scale, as have a number of other 20th-century composers.

An octatonic scale.

octave a span of eight notes as measured on the white notes of a piano keyboard. It corresponds to the consonance of first and second harmonics.

octet an ensemble of any eight instruments, or the music written for such a group. The most common combination of instruments is the string octet for four violins, two violas, and two cellos, as in Mendelssohn's String Octet in E♭ 1830. Stravinsky wrote an octet 1923 for a wind ensemble. A mixture of strings and winds is also possible, as in Schubert's Octet in F 1824, scored for two violins, viola, cello, double bass, clarinet, bassoon, and horn.

octo basse musical instrument, a three-stringed double bass of huge size invented in 1849 by J B Vuillaume in Paris. It was

8ve lower ____ (loco)

The opening strings of the octo basse.

capable of playing extremely low notes, but its strings were so thick and heavy that they had to be stopped by means of levers and pedals. It was very unwieldy and never became widely used.

ode composition, usually vocal, of a dedicatory character; the form of such works varies considerably, reflecting the poetry, but they may appear in several sections with alternating solos and choruses.

Work for orchestra by Stravinsky; composed 1943, first performed Boston, 8 October 1943, conductor Koussevitzky.

Ode for St Cecilia's Day setting by Handel of Dryden's poem, produced London, Theatre in Lincoln's Inn Fields, 22 November 1739.

Odes for St Cecilia's Day by Purcell; 1. *Laudate Ceciliam* (1683); 2. *Welcome to all the pleasures* (Fishburn; 1683); 3. *Hail, bright Cecilia* (Brady; 1692); 4. *Raise, raise the voice.*

Ode to Napoleon Buonaparte work by Schoenberg for string quartet, piano and reciter (text by Byron); composed 1942. Version with string orchestra performed New York, 24 November 1944, conductor Rodziński.

Ode to the West Wind work for cello and orchestra after Shelley by Henze; composed 1953, first performed Bielefeld, 30 April 1954.

Odington, Walter de (or Walter of Evesham) (fl. 1298–1316) English monk, musician, and astronomer. He entered the Benedictine monastery at Evesham and wrote a treatise *Summa de speculatione musice.*

odzmek a Slovak dance in quick 2–4 time with a more moderately paced middle section. The ninth of Dvořák's *Slavonic Dances* for piano duet is an *odzmek.*

Œdipe à Colone/Oedipus Coloneus opera by Sacchini (libretto by Nicolas François Guillard, after Sophocles), produced Versailles, at court, 4 January 1786; first Paris performance Opéra, 1 February 1787. Polynices engages Theseus to help drive his brother Eteocles from the usurped throne of Thebes, but he feels guilty about having driven his father Oedipus away in earlier years. Polynices seeks reconciliation with his father even at the price of relinquishing his claim to the throne.

Oedipus auf Kolonos incidental music by Mendelssohn for Sophocles' tragedy, op. 93, for male chorus and orchestra, produced Potsdam, 1 November 1845.

Oedipus der Tyrann musical play after Sophocles by Orff, produced Stuttgart, 11 December 1959.

Oedipus Rex stage oratorio by Stravinsky (libretto in Latin, by J Daniélou, translated from French by Jean Cocteau, after Sophocles), produced Paris, Théâtre Sarah Bernhardt, 30 May 1927. The parts are sung in costume but without action, and the words are in Latin in order not to distract the ordinary listener by verbal associations. First stage performance Vienna, Staatsoper, 23 February 1928. Oedipus unknowingly kills his father, King Laius, and marries his mother, Jocasta. When the truth is revealed to him, he blinds himself in remorse.

Oedipus Tyrannus incidental music by Mendelssohn for Sophocles' tragedy, never performed and now lost. Incidental music for ditto by Stanford, produced Cambridge, 22–26 November 1887.

Oedipus und die Sphinx unfinished opera by Varèse (text by Hofmannsthal); composed 1909–13. The manuscript is lost.

oeuvre (French 'work') in music, alternative term for ◊**opus.**

Offenbach, Jacques (1819–1880), adopted name of Jakob Levy Eberst French composer. He wrote light opera, initially for presentation at the Bouffes Parisiens. Among his works are *Orphée aux enfers/Orpheus in the Underworld* 1858, revised 1874, *La belle Hélène* 1864, and *Les contes d'Hoffmann/The Tales of Hoffmann* 1881.

Offenbach was born at Cologne, where his father was cantor at the synagogue. He was sent to Paris early in his youth, studying at the Conservatory 1833–37, perfecting himself in playing the cello, and then playing in the orchestra of the Opéra-Comique even before he left the Conservatory. In 1850 he became conductor at the Théâtre Français. In 1853 he produced his first operettas and during a quarter of a century he turned out nearly 100 light stage pieces. In 1855 he took over the management of the Théâtre Comte and renamed it the Bouffes Parisiens. This lasted until 1861, after which he had no theatre of his own until 1873, when he managed the Théâtre de la Gaîté until 1875. In 1876–77 he was in the USA, but returned to Paris, where he had some of his greatest successes. He was also popular abroad, and such works as *La belle Hélène, La vie parisienne,* and *La Périchole* helped establish musical comedy as a significant form, leading to Johann Strauss, Sullivan, and the great Broadway musicals.

His only large-scale opera, *Les contes d'Hoffmann*, occupied him for many years, but he left it not quite finished at his death, and it was revised and partly scored by Guiraud.

Works include: the opera *Les contes d'Hoffmann* (1881), 89 operettas including *Barbebleue* (1866), *Ba-ta-clan* (1855), *La belle Hélène* (1864), *Chanson de Fortunio*, *Le Docteur Ox* (after Jules Verne), *La Fille du tambour-major* (1879), *La Foire de Saint-Laurent*, *Geneviève de Brabant* (1859), *La Grande-Duchesse de Gérolstein* (1867), *L'Île de Tulipatan*, *La Jolie Parfumeuse*, *Madame Favart*, *Orphée aux enfers* (1858), *La Périchole* (1874), *Princesse de Trébizonde*, *Robinson Crusoe* (after Defoe, 1867), *Vert-Vert*, *La Vie Parisienne* (1866), *Voyage dans la lune* (after Verne), *Whittington and his Cat* (1874); ballet *Le Papillon*; incidental music for Barrière's *Le Gascon* and Sardou's *La Haine*; cello concerto. A second opera, *The Goldsmith of Toledo* (after a tale by E T A Hoffmann) is a pasticcio from various operettas, especially *Le Corsaire noir*, produced in Mannheim, 1919.

Offertory the fourth part of the Roman Catholic Mass Proper, in which the bread and wine are placed on the altar, preceding the Credo and Communion. In musical terms, a psalm in the form of a ◊chant was originally sung but composers including Palestrina and Lassus have written polyphonic works for the Offertory. The term is also used in other denominations of the Christian church.

Offrandes work by Varèse for soprano and chamber ensemble (texts by V Huidobro and J J Tablada); composed 1921, first performed New York, 23 April 1922.

Offrandes oubliées, Les/The Forgotten Offerings work for orchestra in three parts by Messiaen; composed 1930, first performed Paris, 19 February 1931.

Ogdon, John Andrew Howard (1937–1989) English pianist and composer. A contemporary of Alexander Goehr and Peter Maxwell Davies at Manchester University, he won early recognition at the Moscow Tchaikovsky Piano Competition 1962 and went on to become an ebullient champion of neglected virtuoso repertoire by Alkan, Bartók, Busoni, and Sorabji.

For a number of years unable to perform as a result of depression, he recovered to make a successful return to the concert hall shortly before his death.

Ohana, Maurice (1914–1992) English composer of Moroccan descent. He studied in Barcelona, at Rome, and at the Schola Cantorum in Paris. His music belongs to the avant-garde school of his time.

Works include: the operas *Chanson de Toile* (1969) and *La Celestine* (1987), opera for marionettes *Autodafé* (1972); ballets *Prométhée* (1956) and *Paso*; *Les Représentations de Tanit* and *Suite pour un Mimodrame* for small orchestra; guitar concerto; concertino for trumpet; piano concerto (1981); *Etudes, Choréographiques* for percussion; piano music; choral music, film music.

Oiseau de feu, L' see ◊*Firebird, The*.

Oiseaux exotiques/Exotic birds work for orchestra by Messiaen for two clarinets, xylophone, glockenspiel, percussion, and wind; composed 1955–56, first performed Paris, 10 March 1956.

Okeghem, Johannes (Jean d') (c. 1421–c. 1497), or Ockenheim, Okeghem, Hoquegan Flemish composer of church music. His works include the antiphon *Alma Redemptoris Mater* and the richly contrapuntal *Missa Prolationum/Prolation Mass*, employing complex canonic imitation in multiple parts at different levels. He was court composer to Charles VII, Louis XI, and Charles VIII of France.

He was a chorister at Antwerp Cathedral until 1444, was in the service of Charles, Duke of Bourbon at Moulins 1446–48, and in the service of the French court from about 1452, where he became the first maître de chapelle. Louis XI appointed him treasurer of Saint-Martin at Tours, where he lived during the latter part of his life, though he visited Spain in 1469. He is regarded as the most ingenious contrapuntalist of his time.

Works include: ten Masses, including *Ecce ancilla Domini*, *L'homme armé*, and *Mi-mi*; motets; French chansons.

Okeland, Robert (lived 16th century) English composer. He was a member of Eton College 1532–34, and of the Chapel Royal 1547–48. Music of his is preserved in the 'Gyffard' part-books, which date from about 1555.

Olav Trygvason unfinished opera by Grieg (libretto by Bjørnson), three scenes only, performed in concert form, Christiania, 19 October 1889; never staged in Grieg's lifetime, but produced Christiania, 8 October 1908.

Oldham, Arthur (William) (1926–) English composer. He was for a time music director at the Mercury Theatre and to the Ballet Rambert, but later devoted himself wholly to composition.

He studied composition with Herbert Howells and piano with Kathleen Long at the Royal College of Music in London; he also studied privately with Britten.

Works include: four ballets including *Bonne-Bouche* (1952), incidental music for Ronald Duncan's *This Way to the Tomb*; six anthems; orchestral music, including Sinfonietta for wind band (1974); violin and piano sonata; songs.

Olimpiade, L'/The Olympiad Olympie, libretto by Metastasio. Megacles, who loves Aristaea, is to compete in the Olympics under the name of his friend, Lycidas. He then learns that Aristaea is to be the prize for the winner. Torn between duty and love, Megacles chooses duty, but after a few twists all ends happily.

Opera by Caldara, produced Vienna, 28 August 1733; other settings by Vivaldi (Venice, 1734); Pergolesi (Rome, 1735); Galuppi (Milan, 1747); Hasse (Dresden, 1756); Traetta (Verona, 1758); Jommelli (Stuttgart, 1761); Sacchini (Padua, 1763); and Cimarosa (Vicenza, 1784).

There are at least 30 other settings of this libretto *Olimpiade* is probably the most frequently composed work by Metastasio or by any other librettist.

Olimpia vendicata/Olympia revenged opera by Alessandro Scarlatti (libretto by A Aureli), produced Naples, Palazzo Reale, 23 December 1685.

oliphant (from Old English *olifaunt* 'elephant') musical instrument, a bugle-like horn made of an elephant's tusk, often beautifully carved. It was formerly used for signalling and hunting.

Oliver, Stephen (1950–1992) English composer. He studied at Oxford electronic music with Robert Sherlaw Johnson. The best known of his many operas and theatre pieces is *Tom Jones*, after Fielding, produced Snape, Newcastle, and London 1976. Other pieces include *Perseverance* (1974), *Bad Times* (1975), *The Great McPorridge Disaster* (1976), *The Duchess of Malfi* (1971–77), *The Dreaming of the Bones* (1979), *Nicholas Nickelby* (1980), *Blondel* (1983), *Britannia Preserv'd* (1984), and *Timon of Athens* (1991). He was a popular teacher and broadcaster.

Oliveros, Pauline (1932–) US composer. Her works employ live electronics and scenic effects, often guided by meditation.

She worked at the San Francisco Tape Music Center 1961–67 and has taught electronic music at San Diego from 1967.

Works include: *To Valerie Solonis and Marilyn Monroe in recognition of their desperation* (1970); *Phantom Fathom,* mixed-media event (1972); *1,000 Acres* for string quartet (1972); *Crow Two,* ceremonial opera (1974); *The Yellow River Map,* meditation (1977); *King Kong Sings Along* for chorus (1977); *Gone with the Wind* for ensembles (1980); *The Wheel of Times* for string quartet and electronics (1982); *The New Sound Meditation* for voices (1989); *Portraits* for brass quintet (1989); *Listening for Life,* electronic (1991); *Midnight Operas,* for chorus (1992); *Nzinga, the Queen King,* music theatre (1993).

Olympians, The opera by Bliss (libretto by J B Priestley), produced London, Covent Garden, 29 September 1949. Rich Lavatte has arranged for his daughter Madeleine to marry an old nobleman, but she falls in love with young poet Hector. After the appearance of Greek gods, Lavatte is foiled and the lovers are united.

Olympie opera by Spontini (libretto by M Dieulafoy and C Brifaut, based on Voltaire's tragedy), produced Paris, Opéra, 22 December 1819.

Ombra di Don Giovanni, L'/Don Juan's Shade opera by Alfano (libretto by E Moschino), produced Milan, La Scala, 2 April 1914; revised as *Don Giovanni de Mañara,* Florence, 28 May 1941.

ondes Martenot (French 'Martenot waves') electronic musical instrument invented by Maurice Martenot (1898–1980), a French musician, teacher, and writer who first demonstrated his invention in 1928 at the Paris Opéra. A melody of considerable range and voicelike timbre is produced by sliding a contact along a conductive ribbon, the left hand controlling the tone colour.

In addition to inspiring works from Messiaen, Varèse, Jolivet, and others, the instrument has been in regular demand among composers of film and radio incidental music.

On Hearing the First Cuckoo in Spring one of two pieces for small orchestra by Delius (the other being *Summer Night on the River*), composed 1912 and 1911 respectively; first performed Leipzig Gewandhaus, 2 October 1913. The cuckoo call is heard unobtrusively on the clarinet and the main theme is a Norwegian folksong, *In Ole Dale,* previously used by Grieg, arranged for piano in *Norske Folkeviser,* op. 66 (no. 14).

Onslow, (André) George (or Georges) (Louis) (1784–1853) French composer of English descent. He settled at Clermont-

Ferrand as a country squire, held regular chamber music practices there, studied the cello and went for two years to Vienna to study composition.

He was the grandson of the first Lord Onslow. While living in London for some years as a young man, he studied piano with Nicolas Hüllmandel, Jan Dussek, and Johann Baptist Cramer. In the 1820s, wishing to write operas, he made further studies with Antonin Reicha in Paris, where he lived alternatively.

Works include: the operas *L'alcade de la Vega* (1824), *Le Colporteur* (1827), and *Le Duc de Guise* (1837); four symphonies; three string quartets, 34 string quintets, two piano sextets, piano septet, nonet for strings and wind, six piano trios; violin and piano and cello and piano sonatas; sonatas for piano duet; piano pieces.

On Wenlock Edge song cycle for tenor, piano, and string quartet by Vaughan Williams (text by A E Housman), first performed London, 15 November 1909. Version with string orchestra performed London, 24 January 1924.

op, (abbr. *opus*, Latin 'work') a prefix used for the enumeration of a composer's works. It was at first a publisher's rather than a composer's device and in the early 18th century (such as Handel) was used only for instrumental composers. Later in that century it began to become more general, being used for Haydn but not for Mozart, and from Beethoven onward it began to be used regularly, though the number of an opus is not necessarily a guide to the date of its composition.

open organ pipes whose upper end is left open and which, unlike the stopped pipes, produce notes corresponding to their full length.

open notes on wind instruments the notes produced naturally as harmonics as distinct from stopped notes produced by valves, keys or other mechanical means, or by the hand in horn playing.

open string the string of a musical instrument played without the finger touching it, allowing it to vibrate along its entire length. This is notated by an 'o' above the note. The open strings of the violin are: G3, D4, A4, and E5; of the viola: C3, G3, D4, and A4; of the cello: C2, G2, D3, and A3; and of the double bass: E1, A1, D2, and G2.

opera dramatic musical work in which singing takes the place of speech. In opera the music accompanying the action has para-mount importance, although dancing and spectacular staging may also play their parts. Opera originated in late 16th-century Florence when the musical declamation, lyrical monologues, and choruses of Classical Greek drama were reproduced in current forms.

early development One of the earliest opera composers was Jacopo Peri, whose *Euridice* influenced Claudio Monteverdi, the first great master of the operatic form. Initially solely a court entertainment, opera soon became popular, and in 1637 the first public opera house was opened in Venice. It spread to other Italian towns, to Paris (about 1645), and to Vienna and Germany, where it remained Italian at the courts but became partly German at Hamburg from about 1680.

In the later 17th century the elaborately conventional aria, designed to display the virtuosity of the singer, became predominant, overshadowing the dramatic element. Composers of this type of opera included Pier Cavalli, Pietro Antonio Cesti (1623–1669), and Alessandro Scarlatti. In France opera was developed by Jean-Baptiste Lully and Jean-Philippe Rameau, and in England by Henry Purcell, but the Italian style retained its ascendancy, as exemplified by Georg Handel.

Comic opera (opera buffa) was developed in Italy by such composers as Giovanni Battista Pergolesi (1710–1736), while in England *The Beggar's Opera* 1728 by John Gay started the vogue of the **ballad opera**, using popular tunes and spoken dialogue. **Singspiel** was the German equivalent (although its music was newly composed). A lessening of artificiality began with Christoph Willibald von Gluck, who insisted on the pre-eminence of the dramatic over the purely vocal element. Wolfgang Mozart learned much from Gluck in writing his serious operas, but excelled in Italian opera buffa. In works such as *The Magic Flute*, he laid the foundations of a purely German-language opera, using the *Singspiel* as a basis. This line was continued by Ludwig van Beethoven in *Fidelio* and by the work of Carl Weber, who introduced the Romantic style for the first time in opera.

developments into the 19th century The Italian tradition, which placed the main stress on vocal display and melodic suavity (*bel canto*), continued unbroken into the 19th century in the operas of Gioacchino Rossini, Gaetano Donizetti, and Vincenzo Bellini. It is in the Romantic operas of Weber and Giacomo Meyerbeer that the work of Richard Wagner has its roots. Dominating the operatic scene of his time, Wagner attempted to create, in his 'music-dramas', a new art form, and completely transformed the 19th-century conception of opera. In Italy, Giuseppe Verdi assimilated, in his mature work, much of the Wagnerian technique, without sacrificing the Italian virtues of vocal clarity and melody. This tradition was continued by Giacomo Puccini. In French opera in the mid-19th century, represented by such composers as Léo Delibes, Charles Gounod, Camille Saint-Saëns, and Jules Massenet, the drama was subservient to the music. Comic opera (*opéra comique*), as represented in the works of André Gréry (1741–1813) and, later, Daniel Auber, became a popular genre in Paris. More serious artistic ideals were put into practice by Hector Berlioz in *The Trojans*, but the merits of his work were largely unrecognized in his own time.

George Bizet's *Carmen* began a trend towards realism in opera; his lead was followed in Italy by Pietro Mascagni, Ruggero Leoncavallo, and Puccini. Claude Debussy's *Pelléas et Mélisande* represented a reaction against the over-emphatic emotionalism of Wagnerian opera. National operatic styles were developed in Russia by Mikhail Glinka, Nikolai Rimsky-Korsakov, Modest Mussorgsky, Alexander Borodin, and Pyotr Ilyich Tchaikovsky, and in Bohemia by Bedřich Smetana and, later, Dvořák and Janáček. Several composers of light opera emerged, including Arthur Sullivan, Franz Lehár, Jacques Offenbach, and Johann Strauss.

20th-century opera In the 20th century the Viennese school produced an outstanding opera in Alban Berg's *Wozzeck*, and the Romanticism of Wagner was revived by Richard Strauss in *Der Rosenkavalier*. Other 20th-century composers of opera include George Gershwin, Leonard Bernstein, and John Adams in the USA; Roberto Gerhard, Michael Tippett, Benjamin Britten, and Harrison Birtwistle in the UK; Arnold Schoenberg, Paul Hindemith, and Hans Henze in Germany; Luigi Dallapiccola and Goffredo Petrassi in Italy; and the Soviet composers Sergey Prokofiev and Dmitry Shostakovich. The operatic form has developed in many different directions, for example, towards oratorio in Igor Stravinsky's *Oedipus Rex* 1925, and towards cabaret and music-theatre, as represented by the works of Kurt Weill.

opera-ballet a combination of opera and ballet originating in 17th-century France and there called *opéra-ballet* from the beginning.

opéra bouffe (French 'comic opera', derived from Italian *opera buffa*) a type of French comic opera, or rather operetta, lighter in tone and sometimes flimsier in musical workmanship than an *opéra comique*

opera buffa (Italian 'comic opera') type of humorous opera with characters taken from everyday life. The form began as a musical intermezzo in the 18th century and was then adopted in Italy and France for complete operas. An example is Rossini's *The Barber of Seville*.

opéra comique (French 'comic opera') opera that includes text to be spoken, not sung; Bizet's *Carmen* is an example. Of the two Paris opera houses in the 18th and 19th centuries, the Opéra (which aimed at setting a grand style) allowed no spoken dialogue, whereas the Opéra Comique did.

Opera Factory UK opera company founded 1981 under the umbrella of the English National Opera; in 1991 it became resident at the Queen Elizabeth Hall, South Bank, London. It has an iconoclastic approach to classic operas and also performs new works. The director is David Freeman (1952–).

opera seria (Italian 'serious opera') type of opera distinct from opera buffa, or humorous opera. Common in the 17th and 18th centuries, it tended to treat classical subjects in a formal style, with most of the singing being by solo voices. Examples include many of Handel's operas based on mythological subjects.

operetta light form of opera, with music, dance, and spoken dialogue. The story line is romantic and sentimental, often employing farce and parody. Its origins lie in the 19th-century *opéra comique* and is intended to amuse. Examples of operetta are Jacques Offenbach's *Orphée aux enfers/Orpheus in the Underworld* 1858, Johann Strauss' *Die Fledermaus/The Flittermouse* 1874, and Gilbert and Sullivan's *The Pirates of Penzance* 1879 and *The Mikado* 1885.

Opernball, Der/The Ball at the Opera House operetta by Heuberger (libretto by V Léon and H von Waldberg), produced Vienna, Theater an der Wien, 5 January 1898. Mistaken identity at the ball, as Angèle and Marguerite test the fidelity of husbands Paul and Georges.

ophicleide an obsolete brass instrument of the bugle family. It was a development of the ◊serpent, patented by Halary in Paris in 1821, and was played with fingered keys and a cup-shaped mouthpiece. Although there were alto, bass, and double bass variants, only the bass model, with its compass of about three octaves, was commonly used, until superseded by the bass tuba. It was used in military bands and in the orchestral scores of composers including Berlioz, Verdi, and Wagner.

Opieński, Henryk (1870–1942) Polish musicologist, composer, and conductor. He edited Chopin's letters and wrote on him, Paderewski, and Polish music in general.

He studied piano with Paderewski, composition with d'Indy at the Schola Cantorum in Paris, and conducting and musicology with Arthur Nikisch and Hugo Riemann at Leipzig. He formed a vocal society at Lausanne in 1918 and lived in Switzerland until his death, except when he was director of the Poznań Conservatory 1920–26.

Works include: the operas *Maria* (Malczewski, 1904), and *Jacob the Lutenist* (1918); incidental music for Calderón's *El principe constante*; oratorio *The Prodigal Son*; cantata *Mickiewicz*; symphonic poems *Zymunt August i Barbara* and *Lilla Weneda*; string quartet; instrumental pieces; songs.

op. posth. abbreviation for ◊opus posthumous.

opus (Latin 'work') in music, a term, used with a figure, to indicate the numbering of a composer's works, usually in chronological order.

opus posthumous a work of which the existence became known after the composer's death.

oratorio dramatic, non-scenic musical setting of religious texts, scored for orchestra, chorus, and solo voices. Its origins lie in the *Laude spirituali* performed by St Philip Neri's Oratory in Rome in the 16th century, followed by the first definitive oratorio in the 17th century by Cavalieri. The form reached perfection in such works as J S Bach's *Christmas Oratorio*, and Handel's *Messiah*.

The term is sometimes applied to secular music drama in which there is little or no stage action, as in Stravinsky's *Oedipus Rex* 1926–27 and Messiaen's *St François d'Assise* 1975–83. In the earliest oratorios there was often an element of ritual and spatial dramatization, and Bach himself introduced audience participation with the chorales of his *St Matthew Passion*. In 1993 Jonathan Miller reintroduced simple actions to a London performance of Bach's *St John Passion* with telling effect.

Orazi ed i Curiazi, Gli/The Horatii and the Curiatii opera by Cimarosa (libretto by A S Sografi), produced Venice, Teatro La Fenice, 26 December 1796. The Horatius family of

Rome and the Curiatius family of Alba are traditional enemies, but Curiatius' betrothal to Horatia brings the families together. However, Rome and Alba go to battle and Curiatius is killed by Horatia's brother, Marcus, who then kills Horatia for not rejoicing with him.

Opera by Mercadante (libretto by S Cammarano), produced Naples, Teatro San Carlo, 10 November 1846.

orchestra group of musicians playing together on different instruments. In Western music, an orchestra is typically based on the bowed, stringed instruments of the violin family, but often contains wind, brass, and percussion sections. The size and format may vary according to the requirements of composers.

history The term was originally used in Greek theatre for the semicircular space in front of the stage, and was adopted in 17th-century France to refer first to the space in front of the stage where musicians sat, and later to the musicians themselves.

Western instruments The string section is commonly divided into two groups of violins (first and second), violas, cellos, and double basses. During the 18th century, the most common additions to the strings were pairs of horns and oboes. The woodwind section became standardized by the end of the 18th century, when it consisted of two each of flutes, oboes, clarinets, and bassoons, to which were later added piccolo, cor anglais, bass clarinet, and double bassoon. At that time, two timpani and two horns were also standard, and two trumpets were occasionally added. During the 19th century, the brass section was gradually expanded to include four horns, three trumpets, three trombones, and tuba. To the percussion section a third timpano was added, and from Turkey came the bass drum, side drum, cymbals, and triangle. One or more harps became common and, to maintain balance, the number of string instruments to a part also increased. Other instruments used in the orchestra include xylophone, celesta, glockenspiel, piano (which superseded the harpsichord in the late 18th century), and organ. In the 20th century, composers have often preferred smaller groupings of instruments, often in unconventional combinations. The orchestra used to be conducted by means of a violin bow, but by Felix Mendelssohn's time the baton was implemented.

non-Western ensembles The term may also be applied to non-Western ensembles such as the Indonesian gamelan orchestra, founded on families of percussion instruments, mainly tuned gongs and bells.

orchestration scoring of a composition for orchestra; the choice of instruments of a score expanded for orchestra (often by another hand). A work may be written for piano, and then transferred to an orchestral score.

Ordonez, Carlo d' (or Ordoñez) (1734–1786) Austrian composer and violinist, a major influence in the developing instrumental style of the years 1750–75. For most of his life he worked as a government administrator in Vienna.

Works include: two operas, over 70 symphonies, over 30 string quartets and other chamber music.

ordre old French name for the ◊suite.

Orel, Alfred (1889–1967) Austrian musicologist. A lawyer and civil servant at first, he studied music with Adler when nearly 30. He was later appointed professor at Vienna University and head of the music department of the municipal library. He wrote works on Bruckner and coedited with Robert Haas the edition of the original versions of Bruckner's works.

Oresteia trilogy of short operas by Taneiev (libretto by A A Venkstern, after Aeschylus), produced St Petersburg, 29 October 1895. Scenes depict Greek myths, *Agamemnon*, *Choephorae/The Libation Bearers*, *Eumenides/The Furies*.

Orestes opera by Weingartner (libretto by composer, after Aeschylus), produced Leipzig, 15 February 1902.
See ◊*Leben des Orest*.

Orfeide, L' cycle of operas by Malipiero (libretto by composer), produced complete, in German translation, Düsseldorf, 30 October 1925.
I. *La morte delle maschere/The Death of the Maskers*.
II. *Sette canzoni/Seven Songs*, produced in French translation, Paris, Opéra, 10 July 1920.
III. *L'Orfeo, ossia l'ottava canzone/Orpheus, or the Eighth Song*.

Orfeo (Monteverdi). See ◊*Favola d'Orfeo, La*.

Orfeo ed Euridice/Orpheus and Eurydice opera by Bertoni (libretto by R da Calzabigi, written for Gluck), produced Venice, Teatro San Benedetto, 3 January 1776.
Opera by Gluck (libretto ditto), produced Vienna, Burgtheater, 5 October 1762. (For French version see ◊*Orphée et Eurydice*.)

Orpheus descends into Hades to bring back his deceased Eurydice.

Orfeo, L'/Orpheus opera by Luigi Rossi (libretto by F Buti), produced Paris, Palais Royal, 2 March 1647.

Orff, Carl (1895–1982) German composer. An individual stylist, his work is characterized by sharp dissonances and percussion. Among his compositions are the cantata ◊*Carmina Burana* 1937 and the opera *Antigone* 1949.

He studied at Munich and became professor of composition at the Günther School there. He was also a conductor and editor of early music, notably the operas of Monteverdi. His early success with *Carmina Burana*, founded on rhythmic ostinati and appealing vocal melody, was not repeated in later works.

Works include: mainly 11 operas and musical plays, including *Carmina Burana* (settings of medieval poetry, 1937), *Die Kluge* (1943), *Catulli Carmina*, *Antigonae*, and *Oedipus der Tyrann* (both Hölderlin, after Sophocles, 1949, 1959), *Trionfo di Afrodite* (1953), *Prometheus* (1966), *De temporum fine comoedia* (1973), cantata *Des Turmes Auferstehung* (Franz Werfel); ballet *Der Feuerfarbene*; *Schulwerk* for combinations of popular instruments and similar compositions intended for use by amateurs. Incidental music for Shakespeare's *Midsummer Night's Dream*, 1939–62; first version composed to replace Mendelssohn's music, banned by the Nazis.

organ musical wind instrument of ancient origin, in which sound is produced when a depressed key opens a valve, allowing compressed air to pass through a single pipe or a series of pipes; the number of pipes in total may vary, according to the size of the instrument. Apart from its continued use in serious compositions and for church music, the organ has been adapted for light entertainment.

One note only is sounded by each pipe, but these are grouped into stops, which are ranks or scales of pipes prepared to 'speak' by a knob. These, in turn, form part of a sectional organ, one of the tonal divisions comprising the whole organ. These separate manuals are the great, swell, choir, solo, echo, and pedal organs, controlled by the player's hands and feet. By this grouping and subdivision, extremes of tone and volume are obtained.

The organ developed from the panpipes and hydraulis (water organ), and is mentioned in writings that date from the 3rd century BC. The first development of the organ was the supply of compressed air from bellows. Organs were imported to France from Byzantium in the 8th and 9th centuries, after which their manufacture in Europe began. The superseding of the old drawslides by the key system dates from the 11th–13th centuries; the first chromatic keyboard dates from 1361. Later a keyboard of pedals, played by the feet, was added to control the largest bass pipes. The number of pipes, ranging from 32 ft down to a fraction of an inch, was enormously increased, and they were made in a growing variety of shapes from different materials, and with different speaking mechanisms, each range being controlled by stops which could bring it into action or shut it off at the player's will. The number of manuals (hand keyboards) increased to three or more, which meant that a greater number of stops drawn before the performance could be controlled and varied. From the late 19th century the bellows, formerly blown by hand, were operated mechanically and devices were invented that could bring into action whole ranges of stops in various combinations. These still further increased the resources already enlarged by the couplers, by which the registration controlled by two manuals or by a manual and the pedals could be mechanically united. Expression was added by swell pedals producing crescendo and diminuendo, but beyond that the player's hands and feet have no power to vary the tone either in strength or in quality.

The electric tone-wheel organ was invented in 1934 by US engineer Laurens Hammond (1895–1973). Other types of electric organ were .developed in the 1960s. Electrically controlled organs substitute electrical impulses and relays for some of the air-pressure controls. These, such as the Hammond organs, built during the 1930s for the large cinemas of the period, include many special sound effects as well as colour displays. In electronic organs the notes are produced by electronic oscillators and are amplified at will.

organology branch of musicology which is concerned with the systematic study and classification of musical instruments, their history, design, fabrication, and taxonomy. Canon Francis Galpin's *Old English Instruments of Music* (1910) was one of the first works to attempt to deal with musical instruments systematically. The scholarly society formed in 1945 in his name – the Galpin Society – is a focus for British organologists. Its counterpart in the USA is

the American Musical Instrument Society (formed 1974).

organo pieno (or *(pro) organo pieno*, 'full organ') musical direction indicating that an organ passage is to be played with the use of the full extent of the instrument's power, or in earlier music with a substantial body of tone.

organ-point (from German *Orgelpunkt*) another term, used mainly in the USA, for ◊pedal point.

organ stop a set of organ pipes that sound together; also the knob or mechanism that operates such a set of pipes. See ◊stop.

organum a form of early medieval harmony in which voices move in parallel fourths or fifths.

Orione, o sia Diana vendicata/Orion, or Diana Avenged opera by J C Bach (libretto by G G Bottarelli), produced London, King's Theatre, 19 February 1763. J C Bach's first opera for London.

Orlandi, Santi (died 1619) Italian composer. He was maestro di cappella to Ferdinando Gonzaga at Florence and succeeded Monteverdi as maestro di cappella to the Gonzaga family at Mantua in 1612.

Works include: the opera *Gli amori di Aci e Galatea* (performed Mantua, March 1617); five books of madrigals, and other pieces.

Orlando/Roland opera by Handel (libretto by G Braccioli, based on Ariosto's *Orlando furioso*), produced London, King's Theatre, Haymarket, 27 January 1733. The knight Orlando falls in love with Angelica, but she does not return his feelings because she already loves Medoro. When Orlando discovers this he goes mad, until the magician Zoroastra (or Astolfo in the Vivaldi version) restores his reason. Orlando then blesses Angelica and Medoro's union.

Orlando Furioso opera by Vivaldi (libretto by G B Braccioli), produced Venice, Teatro Sant' Angelo, autumn 1727.

Orlando Paladino opera (*dramma eroicomico*) by Haydn (libretto by C F Badini and N Porta), produced Eszterháza, 6 December 1779. Similar to ◊*Orlando*, but here Orlando is already mad when the curtain goes up; Alcina is the sorceress who restores Orlando's senses; the additional character Rodomonte appears, who is also in love with Angelica.

Ormandy, Eugene (1899–1985) assumed name of Jenö Ormandy Blau, Hungarian-born US conductor. He was music director of the Philadelphia Orchestra 1936–80. Originally a violin virtuoso, he championed the composers Rachmaninov and Shostakovich.

Ormindo opera by Cavalli (libretto by G Faustini), produced Venice, Teatro San Cassiano, 1644. Revived in new version by Raymond Leppard, Glyndebourne, 16 June 1967. In North Africa, Ormindo has fallen in love with Erisbe, who is married to King Hariadeno (Ormindo's long-lost father). When Hariadeno learns of the couple's planned escape he captures them and is about to execute them, before relenting and allowing Erisbe to join Ormindo.

ornamentation decorative filling-in of a melody, or accentuation of a structural feature such as the end of a phrase, by rhetorical flourishes or cascades of notes, indicated by special notational signs. Examples of ornament are the turn, a form of melodic pirouette around a note, the ◊trill, the appoggiatura, an upward or downward inflection, arpeggio, and the mordent, a form of accented trill.

Throughout musical history until at least the early 19th century there are many repertories in which it was expected that the performer would add ornamental details. Shorthand signs to denote the simpler ornaments are found at least from the early 16th century (though there are traces of them much earlier in the chant repertory); but they began to be codified in elaborate systems described in detailed tables of ornaments from the 17th century and had their heyday in the first half of the 18th century. Since the early 19th century, performers have tended not to add their own improvised ornaments, relying instead on only explicitly notated embellishments written by the composer.

See also ◊acciaccatura, ◊arpeggio, ◊cadenza, ◊mordent, ◊plica, ◊shake, ◊turn, ◊tremolo, ◊vibrato.

Ornithoparcus, Andreas (c. 1490–) German music scholar. He was the author of the Latin treatise *Musicae activae micrologus* 1517, which was translated into English by John Dowland in 1609.

He studied at Tübingen University, travelled in many countries, and taught at Wittenberg University.

Orontea opera by Cesti (libretto by G A Ciognini), produced Venice, Teatro dei Apostoli, 1649; revised by G F Apolloni, produced Innsbruck, Teatro di Sala, 19 February 1656. Cesti's first opera; successfully revived in modern editions. Orontea, Queen of Egypt, falls in love with lowly painter Alidoro. There is stiff opposition to her wedding plans, but

all is resolved when it turns out Alidoro is of noble birth.

orpharion early musical instrument of the ◊cittern type. It had six or seven pairs of strings played with a plectrum.

Orphée aux enfers/Orpheus in the Underworld operetta by Offenbach (libretto by H Crémieux and L Halévy), produced Paris, Bouffes Parisiens, 21 October 1858. A spoof on the original *Orpheus*: Orpheus is delighted at the prospect of freedom when Eurydice dies, and arrives in Hades to reclaim her only because Public Opinion forces him to.

Orphée et Eurydice opera by Gluck (libretto by P L Moline, translated from Calzabigi's *Orfeo ed Euridice*, of Gluck's first setting of which it is a revised version), produced Paris, 3 August 1774. See ◊*Orfeo ed Euridice* for plot synopsis.

Orphéon French male-voice choral society similar to the German *Liedertafel*.

Orpheus ballet by Stravinsky (choreographed by George Balanchine) produced New York, 29 April 1948.

Opera by Keiser (libretto by F C Bressand), produced Brunswick (Part I: *Die sterbende Eurydice*) 1699. Hamburg (Part II: *Die verwandelte Leyer des Orpheus*), 1709.

Symphonic poem by Liszt, composed 1853–54, first performed as an introduction to Gluck's *Orfeo*, Weimar, 16 February 1854, with closing music on the same themes after the opera.

See ◊*Favola d'Orfeo, La*; ◊*Malheurs d'Orphée*; ◊*Orfeide, L'*; ◊*Orfeo*; ◊*Orfeo ed Euridice*; ◊*Orphée aux enfers*; ◊*Orpheus*; ◊*Orpheus og Euridice*; ◊*Orpheus und Eurydike*.

Orpheus ballet in two acts by Henze (scenario by Edward Bond), produced Stuttgart 17 March 1979; Suite for ballet, *Apollo triofante*, performed Gelsenkirchen, 1 September 1980; *Arias of Orpheus* for guitar, harp, harpsichord and strings performed Chicago, 25 November 1981; *Dramatic Scenes from Orpheus* for large orchestra performed in two parts: no. 2 Zurich, 6 January 1981, no. 1 Frankfurt, 12 September 1982; Concert version of the ballet performed Cologne, 4 March 1983.

Orpheus Britannicus a collection of vocal music by Purcell begun soon after Purcell's death by Henry Playford, who published a first volume in 1698 and a second in 1702; also a collection of Purcell's songs published by John Walsh in 1735.

Orpheus og Euridice opera by Naumann (libretto by C D Biehl, based on Calzabigi), produced Copenhagen, 21 January 1786. The

first grand opera on a Danish libretto. See
◊*Orfeo ed Euridice* for plot synopsis.

Orpheus und Eurydike opera by Krenek
(libretto by Oskar Kokoschka), produced
Kassel, 27 November 1926. A psychoanalyti-
cal rendering of the Greek myth.

Orr, Buxton (Daeblitz) (1924–1997) Scottish
composer and conductor. He conducted the
London Jazz Composers' Orchestra 1970–80
and the Guildhall New Music Ensemble
1975–91. In 1983 he completed Frankel's
opera *Marching Song* for a posthumous first
performance.

He studied with Benjamin Frankel 1952–55
and wrote film and theatre music until 1961.

Works include: the opera *The Wager* (1962),
A Celtic Suite for strings (1968), trombone
concerto, with brass band (1971), *Ring in the
New*, music theatre (1986), *Sinfonia Ricercante*
(1988) *Refrains VI* for chamber orchestra
(1992).

Orr, C(harles) W(ilfred) (1893–1976) English
composer. He was educated at Cheltenham
College. He suffered much from ill-health in
his youth and did not begin to study music at
the Guildhall School of Music and Drama in
London until 1917. He lived most of his life
quietly at Painswick, Gloucestershire, and
never held any official musical posts; but he
did war work in London during World War
II.

Works include: *A Cotswold Hill Tune* for
string orchestra; numerous songs, especially
settings of A E Housman, also D G Rossetti,
James Joyce.

Orr, Robin (1909–) Scottish composer. He
studied at the Royal College of Music in
London and with E J Dent at Cambridge, also
with Casella at Siena and Nadia Boulanger in
Paris. From 1938 to 1956 he was organist and
director of studies at St John's College, Cambridge. He was professor of music at Glasgow
University 1956–64, and at Cambridge 1964–
76. He was chair of the Scottish Opera 1962–
76, and director of the Welsh National Opera
1971–83.

Works include: the operas *Full Circle*
(1968), *Hermiston* (1975) and *On the Razzle*
(1988); three symphonies (1965, 1971, 1978),
Sinfonietta Helvetia (1990); divertimento for
chamber orchestra; three Latin psalms for
voice and string quartet; string quintet (1971);
sonatina for violin and piano, violin sonata,
viola sonata; piano pieces; songs.

Ortiz, Diego (c. 1510–c. 1570) Spanish
composer. He went to Naples in 1555 to
become maestro de capilla to the viceroy, the

Duke of Alva. While there, he worked with
many other Spanish musicians, including
Francisco de Salinas. He wrote an important
treatise on ornamentation in viol music, the
Trattado de Glosas, published in two editions
(Spanish and Italian) at Rome in 1553.

Works include: motets; variations for bass
viol.

**Orto, Marbrianus de (c. 1460–1529),
adopted name of Marbrianus Dujardin**
Flemish singer and composer. He changed
his name when he went to Rome, where he
was a singer in the Papal chapel 1484–94,
with Josquin Desprez. Early in the 16th
century he became chaplain and singer at
the court of Philip the Fair of Burgundy.

Works include: Masses, motets, and other
church music; chansons.

Osborne, Nigel (1948–) English composer.
He is best known for his vivid and iconoclastic stage works.

He studied at Oxford with Egon Wellesz
and Kenneth Leighton and in Poland with
Witold Rodziński. He lectured at Nottingham
University from 1978.

Works include: *Byzantine Epigrams* for
chorus (1969); *Seven Words*, cantata (1971);
Charivari for orchestra (1973); *Chansonnier* for
chamber ensemble (1975); *I am Goya* for
baritone and instruments (1977); *Concert Piece*
for cello and orchestra (1977); *In Camera* for 13
instruments (1979); *Gnostic Passion* for 36
voices (1980); Flute concerto (1980); *The Cage*
for tenor and ensemble (1981); *Sinfonia* for
orchestra (1982); *Alba* for mezzo, instruments,
and tape (1984); *Zansa* for ensemble (1985);
Pornography for mezzo and ensemble (1985),
The Electrification of the Soviet Union, opera,
(1986); *Esquisse I and II* for strings (1987–88),
violin concerto (1990), *The Sun of Venice* for
orchestra (1991); operas *Terrible Mouth* (1992)
and *Sarajevo* (1994).

oscillator an electrical generator used to
convert electricity into sound. It produces an
oscillating current that may be heard as
sound when played at a frequency between
16 Hz and 20,000 Hz and attached to an
amplifier and loudspeakers. Different types
of tone produced by an oscillator include
◊sine waves and ◊saw-toothed waves.

ossia (Italian, from *O sia*, 'or else') in
musical notation, indicating an alternative
version of a given passage. It often appears
during a technically difficult passage, providing a simpler version for less accomplished
musicians.

Ossian semimythical Gaelic bard whose works, allegedly translated by James Macpherson (1736–1796), influenced the early Romantic movement. Ossian's works were in fact by Macpherson, drawing on ancient sources. Schubert set nine Ossian songs (1815–17).

ostinato (Italian 'obstinate') in music, a persistently repeating melodic or rhythmic figure conveying an ambiguous message of dynamic action unrelated to any movement.

Ostinati play an important role in Stravinsky's *The Rite of Spring* 1913 and the *Symphony of Psalms* 1930, also in the *Carmina Burana* 1937 of Carl Orff; ostinato-like structures are also characteristic of Balinese gamelan music as transcribed by Colin McPhee. In the 1960s, tape loop recycling of fragments of melody and sound provided a starting point for the minimalism of Terry Riley, Steve Reich, Philip Glass, and John Adams.

Ostrovsky, Aleksandr Nikolaievich (1823–1886) Russian dramatist. See ◊Arensky (*Dream on the Volga*); Janáček (◊*Káta Kabanová*); ◊Serov (*Power of Evil*); Rimsky-Korsakov (◊*Snow Maiden, The*); ◊Tchaikovsky (*Snegurotchka*); N ◊Tcherepnin (*Poverty no Crime*); Tchaikovsky (◊*Voyevoda*).

Osud/Fate opera in three scenes by Janáček (libretto by composer and F Bartosova); composed 1903–04, first performed Brno Radio 18 September 1934; produced Brno, 25 October 1958. Produced London, Coliseum, 8 September 1984. Composer Živný is reunited with his former mistress Míla but she and her insane mother are killed in a fall.

Oswald von Wolkenstein see Oswald von ◊Wolkenstein.

Otello opera by Verdi (libretto by Boito, after Shakespeare), produced Milan, La Scala, 5 February 1887. Otello, driven by the evil Iago, murders his wife Desdemona in a jealous rage, and commits suicide.

Otello, ossia Il Moro di Venezia/Othello, or The Moor of Venice opera by Rossini, libretto by F B Salsa, after Shakespeare, produced Naples, Teatro Fondo, 4 December 1816.

Othello concert overture by Dvořák, op. 93, referring to Shakespeare's tragedy, composed 1892 and forming, with *Amid Nature* and *Carnival*, a cycle with thematic connections originally called *Nature, Life and Love*. See ◊*Otello*.

ottavino (Italian from ottava 'octave') musical instrument, the octave flute elsewhere called ◊piccolo (from *flauto piccolo* 'little flute').

Otto, Stephan (1603–1656) German composer. He studied at Freiberg under Christoph Demantius, and after an appointment at Augsburg became cantor at his home town in 1632 and at Schandau in 1639. Andreas Hammerschmidt was among his pupils.

Works include: *Kronen-Krönlein*, a collection of sacred vocal pieces in a mixed motet and madrigal style, for three–eight voices, setting of Luther's hymn 'Ein' feste Burg' for 19 voices.

Ottone, rè di Germania/Otho, King of Germany opera by Handel (libretto by N F Haym), produced London, King's Theatre, Haymarket, 12 January 1723. Otto defeats attempted revolt by Adalberto and is united with his promised bride, Teofane.

Our Hunting Fathers song cycle for high voice and orchestra by Britten (text by W H Auden), first performed Norwich, 25 September 1936, conductor Britten.

Ours, L'/The Bear nickname of Haydn's symphony no. 82 in C major, composed for Paris in 1786.

overblowing a technique of exciting higher harmonics in a wind instrument by increasing air pressure at the mouthpiece, causing it to sound an octave (second harmonic) or twelfth (third harmonic) higher.

The note in an ascending scale at which a player switches to overblowing is called the **break point**. For instruments of the clarinet family, which overblow at the twelfth, the break point is relatively unstable and difficult to control. Overblowing may occur in organ pipes if the air pressure is too great, but safety-valve devices can prevent this.

overspun string in musical instruments of the violin family and also those of the piano, a string that consists of a central wire around which another wire is spun. Strings manufactured in this way are thicker without losing their flexibility, and are used to produce the lower notes.

overstrung method of manufacture of modern pianos, in which the bass strings cross diagonally over the strings of higher-pitched notes, in order to secure greater length in the strings, thereby improving tone quality.

overtones tones of the harmonic series, excluding the first harmonic (fundamental), which determine the tone quality or ◊timbre of an instrument.

overture the opening piece of a concert or opera, having the dual function of settling the audience and allowing the conductor and musicians to become acquainted with the ◊acoustic of a concert auditorium. See also ◊prelude.

The use of an overture in opera began during the 17th century; the 'Italian' overture consisting of two quick movements separated by a slow one, and the 'French' of a quick movement between two in slower tempo.

ovvero (Italian 'or rather, or else') in music, an early word for *ossia*; also found in front of second, alternative titles of works.

Owen Wingrave opera in two acts by Britten (libretto by M Piper after Henry James), first performed BBC TV 16 May 1971; produced Covent Garden, London, 10 May 1973. Pacifist Owen Wingrave drops out of Spencer Coyle's military school. His family is disgusted. Fellow student Lechmere drives Owen to spend the night in a haunted room; a family prophecy comes true and Owen is found dead.

Oxford Elegy, An work by Vaughan Williams for speaker, small chorus, and orchestra (text from Matthew Arnold, *The Scholar Gipsy* and *Thyrsis*), first performed (private) Dorking, 20 November 1949; first public performance Queen's College, Oxford, 19 June 1952.

Oxford Symphony the name given to Haydn's symphony no. 92 in G major, composed 1788. It was not written for Oxford, but received its title after it was performed there in July 1791 when Haydn was given the honorary degree of MusD.

Ox Minuet/Die Ochsenmenuette a *Singspiel* by Seyfried, produced in Vienna, 1823, with music arranged from compositions by Haydn. It was based on two earlier French works, *Le Menuet de bœuf, ou Une Leçon de Haydn* (1805) and *Haydn, ou le Menuet du bœuf* (1812). The title is sometimes mistakenly thought to be the nickname of one of Haydn's minuets.

P

p abbreviation for **piano** (Italian 'softly').

Pace, Pietro (1559–1622), also called Pacius Italian composer. He was organist at Pesaro in 1597 and of the Santa Casa at Loreto, 1591–92, and again, 1611–22.

Works include: music for Ignazio Bracci's *L'ilarocosmo, ovvero Il mondo lieto* (performed Urbino, 29 April 1621); Magnificats, motets (with accompaniment), and other church music; *Arie spirituali* and madrigals with and without accompaniment.

Pacelli, Asprilio (1570–1623) Italian composer. He was choirmaster of the German College (1592–1602), and later at the Vatican basilica in Rome until 1602, when he went to the court of Sigismund III of Poland at Warsaw, succeeding Marenzio.

Works include: motets, psalms, *Sacrae cantiones*; madrigals.

Pachelbel, Johann (1653–1706) German organist and composer. Although his only well-known work today is the *Canon and Gigue* in D major for three violins and continuo, he was a leading progressive composer of keyboard and religious works, influencing J S Bach.

He studied under Heinrich Schwemmer at home and after holding brief appointments at Altdorf and Regensburg, went to Vienna about 1671–72. Between 1677 and 1695 he was organist successively at Eisenach, Erfurt, Stuttgart, and Gotha, and in 1695 was appointed organist at St Sebaldus' Church at Nuremberg. He was one of Bach's most important predecessors.

Works include: vocal music, arias, motets, sacred concertos (cantatas) and 11 Magnificat settings; 94 organ fugues on the Magnificat,

organ variations and preludes on chorales; suites for two violins, *Canon and Gigue* for three violins, *Musikalisches Ergötzen*; six sets of variations for harpsichord *Hexachordum Apollinis* (1699).

Pachelbel, Wilhelm Hieronymus (1686–1764) German organist and composer, son and pupil of Johann ◊Pachelbel. He was organist at St Sebaldus' Church, Nuremberg, from 1719. He wrote organ and harpsichord music.

Pacific 231 symphonic movement by Honegger, named after a railway engine and depicting its start and progress, not merely realistically, but, the composer claims, 'lyrically'. First performed Paris, at a Koussevitsky concert, 8 May 1924.

Pacini, Giovanni (1796–1867) Italian composer. He studied first under his father, a famous tenor, and later at Bologna and Venice. At the age of 17 he produced his first opera at Venice. He became maestro di cappella to Napoleon's widow, the Empress Marie Louise, and in 1834 settled at Viareggio, where he opened a music school, later transferred to Lucca. For this he wrote some theoretical treatises.

Works include: OPERA *Annetta e Lucindo* (1813), *La sacerdotessa d'Irminsul* (1820), *La schiava in Bagdad* (1820), *La Gioventù di Enrico V* (after Shakespeare's *Henry IV*, 1820), *L'ultimo giorno di Pompei* (not based on Bulwer-Lytton, 1825), *Gli Arabi nelle Gallie* (1827), *Saffo* (1840), *Medea* (1843), *Lorenzino de' Medici* (1845), *La regina di Cipro, Il saltimbanco, Ivanhoe* (after Scott, 1832) and over 60 others.

OTHER incidental music for Sophocles' *Oedipus Rex*; Masses, oratorios, cantata for Dante anniversary and others; six string quartets (c. 1860).

Pacius, Fredrik (1809–1891) German-born Finnish violinist and composer. He was a violinist in the court orchestra at Stockholm 1828–34, then became a music teacher at Helsinki University. He remained in the Finnish capmusic, established orchestral concerts there in 1845 and became professor of music at the university in 1860.

He studied with Louis Spohr and Moritz Hauptmann at Kassel.

Works include: the operas *Kung Karls Jakt* (1852) and *Loreley* (1887); incidental music for Topelius's *Princess of Cyprus* (1860); violin concerto; cantatas; songs including 'Suomis Saang' and 'Vaart Land', both adapted as Finnish national anthems.

Paderewski, Ignacy Jan (1860–1941) Polish pianist, composer, and politician. After his debut in Vienna in 1887, he became celebrated in Europe and the USA as an interpreter of the piano music of Chopin and as composer of the *Polish Fantasy* 1893 for piano and orchestra and the 'Polonia' Symphony 1903–09.

During World War I he helped organize the Polish army in France; in 1919 he became prime minister of the newly independent Poland, which he represented at the Peace Conference, but continuing opposition forced him to resign the same year. He resumed a musical career in 1922, was made president of the Polish National Council in Paris in 1940, and died in New York.

He studied at the Warsaw Conservatory and went on his first concert tour in 1877. After teaching 1878–81 at the Conservatory he went to Berlin for further study, finishing with Leschetizky in Vienna, and reappearing there and in Paris in 1887. He soon became established as one of the leading virtuosi of the day. In 1890 he paid his first visit to England and in 1891 to the USA. His opera *Manru* was premiered at Dresden in 1901 and performed at the New York Metropolitan Opera the following year. During World War I he collected large sums for the Polish relief fund and in 1919 became the first president of the Polish Republic. He supervised a complete edition of Chopin's music 1936–38.

Works include: the opera *Manru* (1901); symphony in B minor (1903–09); concerto in A minor (1888) and *Polish Fantasy* for piano and orchestra; violin and piano sonata; sonata in E♭ minor and many other piano works; songs.

Padlock, The opera by Dibdin (libretto by I Bickerstaffe, based on a story by Cervantes, *El celoso extremeño*), produced London, Drury Lane Theatre, 3 October 1768. Old Don Diego, hoping to marry young Leonora, locks her in the house. Young Leander, however, climbs the wall and woos her.

Padmâvatî opera-ballet by Roussel (libretto in French, by L Laloy), produced Paris, Opéra, 1 June 1923. The Sultan Aladdin encircles Chitor with his army and sues for peace, but when he sees Queen Padmâvatî and is struck by her beauty, he demands her in return for not destroying the city. King Ratan-Sen offers her, so Padmâvatî stabs him before joining him on the funeral pyre.

Padua, Bartolino da (lived 14th–15th centuries) Italian composer. He wrote madrigals and *ballate* in the Italian *ars nova* style.

Paer, Ferdinando (1771–1839) Italian composer. He was a prolific and popular composer of operas. His works, which included *Griselda* 1798, *Camilla* 1799, and *Le maître de chapelle* 1821, were performed in Italy, Austria, Germany, and France.

He was born at Parma, and studied there with Gasparo Ghiretti. At the age of 20 he became a conductor at Venice. Having married the singer Francesca Riccardi, he was invited to Vienna in 1798, where she was engaged at the court opera. There he produced *Camilla* 1799. In 1803 he went to Dresden, remaining there as an opera conductor until 1806, and producing *Leonora*, a setting of an Italian version of Gaveaux's opera on which Beethoven later based his *Fidelio*. In 1807, after accompanying Napoleon to Warsaw and Posen, he was appointed his maître de chapelle and settled in Paris.

Works include: *Circe* (1792), *Il tempo fa giustizia a tutti* (1792), *Il nuovo Figaro* (after Beaumarchais' *Mariage de Figaro*, 1794), *Il matrimonio improvviso, Idomeneo* (1794), *Eroe e Leandro* (1794), *L'intrigo amoroso, Il principe di Taranto, Camilla, o Il sotterraneo* (1799), *La sonnambula* (1800), *Achille, Leonora, o L'amore conjugale* (1804), *Sofonisba, Numa Pompilio* (1808), *Agnese di Fitz-Henry* (1809), *Didone abbandonata* (1810), *Le maître de chapelle* (1821), *La Marquise de Brinvilliers* (with Auber, Batton, Berton, Blangini, Boieldieu, Carafa, Cherubini, and Hérold, 1831) and over 20 others; oratorios *Il santo sepolcro* and *La passione*, Masses and motets; about 12 cantatas (Italian, French and German); Bacchanalian symphony for orchestra, Bridal March for the wedding of Napoleon and Joséphine.

Paganini, Niccolò (1782–1840) Italian violinist and composer. He was a concert soloist from the age of nine. A prodigious technician, he drew on folk and gypsy idioms to create the modern repertoire of virtuoso techniques.

His dissolute appearance, wild love life, and amazing powers of expression, even on a single string, fostered rumours of his being in league with the devil. His compositions include six concertos and various sonatas and variations for violin and orchestra, sonatas for violin and guitar, and guitar quartets.

Paganini's father taught him to play the guitar and violin. He afterwards studied with the theatre violinist Antonio Cervetto and the cathedral maestro di cappella Giacomo Costa. As a composer he profited by the advice of Francesco Gnecco, and in 1795 his father sent him to the violinist Alessandro Rolla at Parma. While there he also studied composition with Gasparo Ghiretti, and in 1797 made his first professional tour, winning early acclaim for his technical virtuosity and flamboyant platform personality. After that he became increasingly famous, travelled widely, beginning with Vienna and Paris 1828–1831, and in the latter year went to England for the first time. In 1834 he invited Berlioz in Paris to write a concert work for viola *Harold en Italie* was the result, but he never played it.

Works include: six violin concertos (1815–30; op. 7 with the *Rondo alla campanella*), variations (including one on 'God save the King') and concert pieces for violin and orchestra, three string quartets with a guitar part; 12 sonatas for violin and guitar; 24 *Capricci* (studies) for violin solo.

Paganini Rhapsody a work by Rachmaninov for piano and orchestra entitled *Rhapsody on a Theme by Paganini*; actually a set of variations, without opus number, composed 1934, first performed Baltimore, 7 November 1934. The theme, in A minor, from Paganini's *Capricci* for unaccompanied violin, is the same as that used by Brahms for his ◊Paganini Variations.

Paganini Studies a set of six studies for piano by Liszt, transcribed from Paganini's violin *Capricci* (except no. 3 which is another version of *La Campanella*), dedicated to Clara Schumann. There is an original version, *Études d'exécution transcendante d'après Paganini*, written in 1838, and a revised one, *Grandes Études de Paganini*, written in 1851.

Two sets of studies for piano (six each) by Schumann on themes from Paganini's violin

Capricci: op. 3, written in 1832, and op. 10, written in 1833.

Paganini Variations two sets of studies for piano in variation form by Brahms, op. 35, composed in 1866, on a theme in A minor from Paganini's violin *Capricci*.

Pagliacci/Players opera by Leoncavallo (libretto by composer), produced Milan, Teatro dal Verme, 21 May 1892. In a group of actors, Tonio reveals Nedda's lover (Silvio) to her husband Canio. During a play which reflects their real-life situation, Canio stabs his wife and then Silvio.

Paik, Nam June (1932–) Korean composer. Performance of his music involves such activities as topless cellist Charlotte Moorman using Paik's spine as a fingerboard; in *Variations on a Theme of Saint-Saëns* the pianist plays 'The Swan' while the cellist immerses herself in an oil drum.

He studied in Tokyo and with Wolfgang Fortner in Munich. After further study with Stockhausen in Cologne he moved to New York in 1964, then Los Angeles in 1970. He taught media studies at the California Institute of Arts.

In *Hommage à John Cage* 1959 two pianos are totally destroyed, while *Performable Music* 1965 has directions for the performer's forearm to be cut with a razor. Other works include *Symphony for Twenty Rooms* 1961, *Opera Sextronique* 1967, and *Young Penis Symphony* 1970. The *Earthquake Symphony* of 1971 concludes with an appropriate finale.

Paine, John Knowles (1839–1906) US organist, composer, and teacher. He studied at home and at the Hochschule für Musik in Berlin, gave organ recmusics in Germany, and returned to the USA in 1861. He became instructor of music at Harvard University in 1862, assistant professor in 1872, and full professor in 1875. In 1890 he was awarded an honorary doctorate in music by Yale University.

Works include: the opera *Azara* (produced Leipzig, 1901); incidental music for Sophocles' *Oedipus Tyrannus* and Aristophanes' *Birds*; Mass in D (1867); oratorio *St Peter* (1872); cantatas *A Song of Promise* (1888), *Phoebus arise* (William Drummond), *The Realm of Fancy* (Keats, 1882), *The Nativity* (Milton); symphony in C minor (1875) and A major (*Spring*, 1880), symphonic poems *An Island Fantasy* and *The Tempest* (after Shakespeare), overture for Shakespeare's *As You Like It*; string quartet, piano trio; violin and piano sonata; instrumental pieces.

Paisiello, Giovanni (1740–1816) Italian composer. He wrote about 100 operas, including *Il barbiere di Siviglia/Barber of Seville* 1782, which was very successful until it was displaced by Rossini's opera of the same name.

He was born at Taranto. He studied first with Durante, and later with Cotumacci and Abos at the Conservatorio Sant' Onofrio in Naples 1754–63, and there wrote his first oratorios and church music. With *Il ciarlone* 1764, however, he began his successful career as a composer of opera buffa, and over the next 20 years produced many works in Modena, Naples, and Venice. While in the service of the Russian court at St Petersburg 1776–84, he wrote his most famous opera, *Il barbiere di Siviglia* (after Beaumarchais' *Le Barbier de Séville* 1782), which held the stage until Rossini's setting of the same story in 1816. Back in Naples, he was appointed maestro di cappella and court composer to Ferdinand IV. Summoned to Paris as music director of Napoleon's household in 1802, he remained only a year before returning to his old post in Naples. Modern revivals of such operas as *Il barbiere di Siviglia, Nina,* and *Il Ré Teodoro in Venezia* reveal a composer of real charm and vivacity.

Works include: OPERA about 100, *Il ciarlone* (after Goldoni's *La pupilla,* 1764), *I Francesi brillanti, Demetrio* (1765), *Le finte Contesse* (1760), *L'idolo cinese, Socrate immaginario* (1775), *La serva padrona, Il barbiere di Siviglia* (after Beaumarchais, 1782), *Il mondo della luna* (1782), *Il Rè Teodoro in Venezia* (1784), *L'Antigono* (1785), *Nina, ossia La pazza per amore, La molinara* (1789), *Proserpine* (1803), and others; oratorios, including *La Passione di Gesù Cristo, Christus* (1783).

OTHER cantatas; Masses, two Requiems, *Miserere* and other church music; symphonies; concertos; six string quartets, 12 piano quartets; keyboard music.

Paix, Jakob (1556–after 1623) German composer. He wrote German songs and Latin church music, but his chief work was his collection of keyboard music, published in 1583, which included original compositions as well as highly ornamented arrangements of songs and motets.

He was organist at Lauingen, Swabia 1576–1601, and court organist at Neuburg an der Donau 1601–17.

Palester, Roman (1907–1989) Polish composer. He studied at Lwów and under Kazimiérz Sikorski in Warsaw. For some years he lived in Paris, later settled in War-

saw. During the 1939–45 war he was imprisoned by the Germans.

Works include: the opera *The Living Stones* (1941); ballets *Song of the Earth* (1937) and *The End of the World*; incidental and film music; Requiem (1948) and Psalm v for solo voices, chorus and orchestra; five symphonies (1935–72), symphonic suite, *Symphonic Music* (1931), *Wedding Celebration, Musique polonaise,* variations (overture) and other orchestral works, *Concertino* for saxophone, piano concerto; *Divertimento* for six instruments, three string quartets (1932–43), sonatinas for three clarinets and for violin and cello, sonata for two violins and piano.

Palestrina opera by Pfitzner (libretto by composer), produced Munich, 12 June 1917. Plot concerns the composition of Palestrina's *Missa Papae Marcelli*, which the composer undertakes only after long deliberation. In the end the Mass is performed and the Pope is greatly moved.

Palestrina, Giovanni Pierluigi da (c. 1525–1594) Italian composer. He wrote secular and sacred choral music, and is regarded as the most perfect exponent of Renaissance ◊counterpoint. Apart from motets and madrigals, he also wrote 105 masses, including *Missa Papae Marcelli*.

Paliashvili, Zakharia Petrovich (1871–1933) Georgian composer. He studied at the Moscow Conservatory under Taneiev, later taught at Tiflis, conducted the orchestra there, and made excursions into eastern Georgia to study its folk music on which his work is based.

Works include: the operas *Abessalom and Eteri* (1919), *Twilight* (1923) and *Latavra*; choral works; folksong arrangements.

palindrome a word or poem reading the same backwards as forwards. In music, a piece constructed in the same way, more or less loosely, as the prelude and postlude in Hindemith's *Ludus tonalis,* his one-act opera *Hin und zurück,* Act III of Berg's *Lulu* or Bartók's fifth string quartet. The procedure is that of *recte et retro* or *rovescio* on a larger scale.

Pallavicino, Benedetto (1551–1601) Italian composer. He was in the service of the Duke of Mantua from 1582, and succeeded Giaches de Wert as maestro di cappella there in 1596, but retired to the monastery of Camaldoli in Tuscany in 1601.

Works include: Masses, psalms, and other church music; ten volumes of madrigals.

Pallavicino, Carlo (c. 1630–1688), or Palla-vicini Italian composer. He lived at Salò, married Giulia Rossi at Padua and settled there, producing operas between 1666 and 1687 at Venice, where he also lived for a time. In 1667–73 he was at the Saxon court at Dresden; first as assistant and later as first music director. In 1674 he was back at Venice, but was recalled to Dresden in 1685 to reorganize the Italian opera.

Works include: *Demetrio* (1666), *Diocletiano* (1674), *Enea in Italia* (1675), *Vespasiano* (1678), *Nerone, Le amazoni nell' isole fortunate* (1779), *Messalina* (1679), *Bassiano, overro Il maggior impossibile* (1682), *Penelope la casta* (1685), *Massimo Puppieno, Didone delirante* (1686), *L'amazone corsara, La Gerusalemme liberata* (after Tasso, 1687), *Antiope* (finished by Strungk, 1689), and nine others; a Mass and an oratorio; arias and canzoni with instruments; string fantasies.

Palmer, Robert (1915–   ) US composer. He studied at the Eastman School of Music at Rochester, New York, where he took degrees in 1938–39, also privately with Roy Harris. In 1943 he became assistant professor of music at Cornell University, Ithaca, New York; retired 1980.

Works include: the ballet *Irish Legend* with chamber orchestra; symphony, elegy *K. 19* (1945) and concerto for orchestra; concerto for chamber orchestra (1940), piano concerto (1970); *Abraham Lincoln Walks at Midnight* (V Lindsay) for chorus and orchestra (1948); four string quartets (1939–60), two piano quartets (1947, 1974), two string trios; concerto for flute, violin, clarinet, English horn and bassoon; viola and piano sonata; sonata for two pianos; sonata and three preludes for piano.

Palmgren, Selim (1878–1951) Finnish pianist, composer, and conductor. He was professor of composition at the Eastman School of Music at Rochester, New York 1923–26 and from 1936 at the Sibelius Academy in Helsinki, where he died. His works include operas, incidental music, choral works, five piano concertos, and numerous piano pieces.

He studied at the Helsinki Conservatory, where his teachers included Martin Wegelius (1846–1906), and later with Conrad Ansorge (1862–1930) in Germany and F Busoni in Italy. On his return he became conductor of the Finnish Students' Choral Society and later of the Music Society at Turku. He also frequently appeared as a pianist. He married the singer Minna Talvik in 1930, and toured Europe and the USA with her.

Works include: the operas *Daniel Hjort* (1910) and *Peter Schlemihl* (after Chamisso); incidental music to Kyösti's *Tukhimo* (*Cinderella*); choral works; five piano concertos (II *The River;* III *Metamorphoses;* IV *April*); numerous piano pieces.

Palotta, Matteo (c. 1688–1758) Italian composer, priest, and music scholar. He studied at Naples, returned to Sicily after being ordained, but was appointed one of the court composers in Vienna in 1733. He wrote treatises on solmization and the modes and composed Masses, motets, and other church music.

Paminger, Leonhard (1495–1567) Austrian composer. He became a Lutheran and published religious pamphlets and a series of motets for the Lutheran year.

He was educated at the monastery of St Nicholas at Passau, then studied in Vienna, but returned to Passau in 1513 to become a teacher and later secretary at the monastery.

Works include: Latin motets, German hymns, psalms, and other pieces.

Pammelia the first part of a collection of canons, rounds, and catches published by Ravenscroft in 1609, the second being *Deuteromelia.*

panchromaticism extreme chromaticism, in which all twelve tones are used equally frequently. Such music might be described as 'one degree less than atonal', that is, very chromatic but still with some sense of a tonic. The term is associated particularly with Schoenberg's ultra-chromatic, but pre-serial, compositions.

pandoura (from Greek; also from Arabic *tanbur,* 'tamboura') string instrument of the lute type with a long neck and a small body, surviving in various forms only in the Balkans, Turkey, Egypt, and the East.

panpipes, or syrinx, musical wind instrument consisting of a set of unpierced pipes in cane, clay, or other material, graded by length to provide a scale of pitches when blown across their opening. Invented according to legend in ancient Greece by the god Pan, the pipes flourish in the folk-music traditions of South America, Eastern Europe, and Japan. They produce a notably pure tone with a breathy onset.

The title instrument of Mozart's opera *The Magic Flute* 1791 is a set of pitch pipes, played by the character Papageno and symbolizing innocent pastoral humanity.

pantaleon string percussion instrument of the ◊dulcimer type invented by Pantaleon

Hebenstreit in the 18th century and named after him by Louis XIV.

pantomime (from Greek 'all-imitating') properly a play in dumbshow, but in England since the 18th century a popular stage entertainment with music, deriving from the Italian *commedia dell'arte*. It is still based, even if remotely, on fairy-tales, but it has lost the Harlequinade which used to be an indispensable supplement and has become a spectacular extravaganza, often introducing songs popular at the time. Also term used in 20th centuury for mimed episode in ballet (Ravel, *Daphnis et Chloe*), or ballet as a whole (Bartók, *Miraculous Mandarin*).

pantonality alternative name for ◊atonality. The term was coined by Schoenberg, who wanted to convey a type of tonality that embraces all keys simultaneously, in preference to 'atonality', which he felt implies a negative tonality.

Panufnik, Andrzej (1914–1991) Polish-born composer and conductor. His music is based on the dramatic interplay of symbolic motifs.

He was a pupil of the Austrian composer and conductor Felix Weingartner. He also studied with Kazimierz Sikorski at the Warsaw Conservatory and received a diploma in 1936. Some of his music was destroyed in the bombardment of Warsaw. He came to Britain in 1954 and became a British citizen in 1961. He was conductor of the Birmingham Symphony Orchestra 1957–59.

Works include: the ballet *Miss Julie* (produced Stuttgart, 1970), film music; Psalm cxlv for chorus and orchestra, nine symphonies, including *Rustica* (1948), *Elegaica* (1957), *Sacra* (1963), *Sfere* (1975), *Mistica* (1977), *Votiva* (1981), no. 9, *Sinfonia di Speranza* (1986), no. 10 (1988, revised 1990), symphonic variations, symphonic studies, Tragic Overture, Heroic Overture; trumpet concerto, piano concerto (1972), bassoon concerto (1985), *Harmony* for chamber orchestra (1989); piano trio and other chamber music, five Polish folk songs for treble voices, two flutes, two clarinets, and bass clarinet; preludes, mazurkas and other works for piano, two string quartets (1976, 1980).

Pan Voyevoda opera by Rimsky-Korsakov (libretto by I F Tiumenev), produced St Petersburg, 16 October 1904. A rarely performed story of love and revenge, set in 17th-century Poland.

Paolo e Francesca opera by Mancinelli (libretto by A Colautti, after Dante), produced

Bologna, Teatro Comunale, 11 November 1907.

Paolo e Virginia opera by P C Guglielmi (libretto by G M Diodati, based on Bernardin de Saint-Pierre's novel), produced Naples, Teatro Fiorentino, 2 January 1817.

Papandopulo, Boris (1906–1991) Croatian composer and conductor. He studied at Zagreb and Vienna, and became choral and orchestral conductor at Zagreb, returning there after teaching at the Music School of Split 1935–38. He later worked as an opera conductor.

Works include: the operas *The Sun Flower* (1942), *Amphitryon* (1940), and *Rona*; ballet *Gold* (1930); oratorio for unaccompanied chorus *The Torments of Our Lord Jesus Christ* (1935), *Laudamus* for solo voices, chorus, and orchestra, *Croatian Mass* for soloists and chorus; two symphonies (1933, 1945), symphonic picture *The Overflowing*; two piano concertos; five string quartets (1927–70), and other chamber music, piano music; songs, and other pieces.

Papillons/Butterflies a set of short piano pieces by Schumann, op. 2, with a finale suggesting the end of a ball in the early morning, with a clock striking six and a quotation of the *Grossvatertanz* or *Kehraus*, which also appears in *Carnaval*, for which this smaller work might almost be a kind of preliminary sketch. There is a further connection between the two, the opening of *Papillons* being quoted in the *Florestan* piece in *Carnaval*. The first part of op. 2 was composed (before op. 1) in 1829, the end in 1831.

parable aria, especially German *Gleichnisarie* or metaphor aria, a type of mainly operatic aria cultivated in the early 18th century, especially by Zeno and Metastasio in their libretti, where certain abstract conceptions are illustrated by concrete ideas resembling them, fidelity by a rock in a stormy sea, love by cooing turtle-doves, and so on. 'As when the dove' in Handel's *Acis and Galatea* is a parable aria and 'Come scoglio/Like a rock' in Mozart's *Così fan tutte* is both verbally and musically a parody of the type. The music of a parable aria was usually illustrative of the image chosen by the librettist.

Parabosco, Girolamo (1520 or 1524–1557) Italian composer and organist. He was well known for improvisations on the organ. He published two pieces in the miscellaneous collection of instrumental music *Musica Nova* 1540.

He studied with Adrian Willaert in Venice. In 1551 he succeeded Jachet Buus as first organist at St Mark's, Venice, a post which he held until his death.

Parade ballet in one act by Satie (scenario by Cocteau), produced Paris, Théâtre de Châtelet, 18 May 1917, with Diaghilev's Ballets Russes: curtain, décor and costumes by Picasso, conductor Ansermet. Suite for piano four hands in six movements from ballet published 1917.

paradigmatic analysis see ◊semiotic analysis.

Paradise and the Peri/Das Paradies und die Peri a setting for solo voices, chorus, and orchestra of one of the poems in Thomas Moore's *Lalla Rookh*, translated into German with alterations, by Schumann, op. 50; composition first contemplated in 1841, begun February 1843; first performed Leipzig, 4 December 1843.

Paradise Lost opera, *'sacra rappresentazione'* by Penderecki (libretto by C Fry after Milton), produced Chicago, Lyric Opera, 29 November 1978.

parallel motion two or more parts in counterpoint moving up or down, in which the interval between each part does not change.

Paray, Paul (Charles) (1886–1979) French conductor and composer. He studied with Leroux and others at the Paris Conservatory and took the Prix de Rome in 1911. Returning to Paris from imprisonment during World War I, he became assistant and later successor to Chevillard, whose concerts he continued to conduct until 1933, when he succeeded Pierné as conductor of the Colonne Orchestra. In 1952 he became conductor of the Detroit Symphony Orchestra, remaining until 1963.

Works include: the oratorio *Jeanne d'Arc* (1931); ballet *Artémis troublée* (1922); Mass for the 500th anniversary of the death of Joan of Arc (revised of oratorio, 1956); symphony in C major; fantasy for piano and orchestra; string quartet; violin and piano sonata.

Pardon de Ploërmel, Le opera by Meyerbeer (libretto by J Barbier and M Carré), produced Paris, Opéra-Comique, 4 April 1859. The work is also known as *Dinorah*. Dinorah has gone mad after losing her husband Hoël during a storm on their wedding day. A year later Hoël returns, seeking a buried treasure, but does not recognize her. After saving her from drowning, Hoël realizes who she is and Dinorah recovers.

Paride ed Elena/Paris and Helen opera by Gluck (libretto by R Calzabigi), produced Vienna, Burgtheater, 3 November 1770. Paris finds Helen more beautiful than the gods and takes her back to Troy, but Athena warns that their joy will not last.

Parisina opera by Donizetti (libretto by F Romani, based on Byron's poem) produced Florence, Teatro della Pergola, 17 March 1833. Parisina, wife of Duke Azzo, falls in love with Ugo. Azzo forces her confession when she murmurs Ugo's name in her sleep, then executes Ugo, despite the revelation that Ugo is his long-lost son.

Opera by Mascagni (libretto by G d'Annunzio), produced Milan, La Scala, 15 December 1913.

Paris Symphonies a set of six symphonies by Haydn commissioned by the Concert de la Loge Olympique in Paris: no. 82 in C major (*L'Ours*), composed 1786; no. 83 in G minor (*La Poule*), 1785; no. 84 in E♭ major, 1786; no. 85 in B♭ major (*La Reine*), 1785–6; no. 86 in D major, 1786; no. 87 in A major, 1785.

'Paris' Symphony Mozart's symphony in D, K297, written in Paris for performance at the Concert Spirituel in 1778. After the first performance Mozart replaced the slow movement by another.

Paris: The Song of a Great City nocturne for orchestra by Delius; composed 1898 and dedicated to Hans Haym, who gave the first performance, Elberfeld 1902. Given by Busoni in Berlin on 15 November 1902; first British performance Liverpool, 11 January 1908, conductor Beecham.

Parker, Horatio (William) (1863–1919) US organist and composer. He held several church organist's posts in Boston and New York, and wrote choral music.

He studied at Boston and Munich, where he was a pupil of Joseph Rheinberger. In 1884 he returned to New York and became an organist and choirmaster. He also taught at the National Conservatory, directed by Dvořák. Later he became organist at Trinity Church, Boston, and in 1894 professor of music at Yale University. He visited England several times for performances of his works at music festivals and to receive an honorary doctorate from Cambridge University in 1902.

Works include: the operas *Mona* (1912) and *Fairyland* (1915); oratorios *Hora novissima* (1893), *The Legend of St Christopher* (1897), *Morven and the Grail* (1915); *The Holy Child* (1893), *The Dream of Mary* (1918) and other cantatas, choral ballads, and songs; church services; symphony in C major (1885), overtures and other orchestral works; organ concerto; string quartet in F major (1885); organ sonata; piano pieces; songs.

parlando singing in a half-speaking manner, often rapidly articulated, used in ◊recitative.

parlando, or parlante (Italian 'speaking') musical direction indicating, in instrumental music, that a passage is to be performed in a 'speaking' manner, expressively but not sustained or 'sung'; in vocal music, that the tone is to be reduced to something approximating to speech.

parody Mass see ◊Missa parodia.

Paroles tissées/Woven Words work for tenor, strings, harp, piano, and percussion by W Lutosławski (text by J F Chabrun); commissioned by Peter Pears, who gave the first performance at the Aldeburgh Festival on 20 June 1965.

Parry, (Charles) Hubert (Hastings) (1848–1918) English composer. His works include songs, motets, and the setting of Milton's 'Blest Pair of Sirens' and Blake's 'Jerusalem'.

He studied at Oxford and with George Macfarren and William Sterndale Bennett. He did not make his mark in public until his piano concerto was played by Edward Dannreuther at the Crystal Palace in 1880 and his choral scenes from Shelley's 'Prometheus Unbound' appeared at the Gloucester Festival the same year. He was awarded honorary doctorates by Cambridge University in 1883, Oxford University in 1884, and Dublin University in 1891. After examining for London University and teaching at the Royal College of Music, London, he succeeded Grove as director of the latter in 1894, remaining until his death. He was professor of music at Oxford 1900–08. He wrote several books on music, including a study of Bach and a volume of the *Oxford History of Music*.

Works include: STAGE opera *Guinevere* (1885–86); incidental music to Aristophanes' *The Birds, The Frogs* (1891), *The Clouds* (1905), and *The Acharnians* (1914).

CHORAL WITH ORCHESTRA oratorios *Job*; six motets, four *Songs of Farewell* and two other motets for chorus; scenes from Shelley's 'Prometheus Unbound' (1880), ode *Blest Pair of Sirens* (Milton, 1887), *L'Allegro ed il penseroso* (Milton), *Jerusalem* (Blake) for chorus.

ORCHESTRAL five symphonies (1878–1912), *Lady Radnor's Suite* (1894) and *An English Suite* for string orchestra (1921).

CHAMBER AND SONGS nonet for wind instruments, four piano trios; sonatas for violin and

piano and cello and piano; organ and piano music; over 100 songs including 74 in 12 books of *English Lyrics* (1885–1920).

Parsifal music drama (*Bühnenweihfestspiel*, 'sacred festival drama') by Wagner (libretto by composer), produced Bayreuth, Wagner Festival Theatre, 26 July 1882. Parsifal recovers the sacred spear from evil magician Klingsor and returns to the Kingdom of the Grail to heal the wounded Amfortas; the 'wild woman' Kundry, whom Parsifal had met earlier, is also redeemed but then dies.

Parsons, John (c. 1575–1623) English composer. He wrote a Burial Service, which Purcell used in 1685 for the funeral of Charles II.

He became parish clerk and organist at St Margaret's Church, Westminster, in 1616, and in 1621 organist and choirmaster of Westminster Abbey.

part written music designated for an individual musician or group of musicians, for example the 'soprano part', in contrast to a ◊score, which provides all the parts on each page. A part, or **voice**, can also be an independent line of a contrapuntal work, for example a fugue in four parts.

A large-scale section of a composition is also called a part, for example Part I of Elgar's *Dream of Gerontius* 1900.

Pärt, Arvo (1935–) Estonian composer. He adopted serial techniques early in his career, later shifted to aleatorism, and finally settled for minimalism and sacred music. His *Nekrolog* 1960 for orchestra was dedicated to the victims of the Holocaust.

He graduated from the Tallinn Conservatory in 1963 and settled in West Berlin in 1982.

Works include: *Stride of the World*, oratorio (1960); three symphonies (1964, 1966, 1971); *Pro et Contra* for cello and orchestra (1964); *Cantus in Memory of Britten* for strings and glockenspiel (1977); *Arbos* for seven instruments (1977); *Wenn Bach Bienen gezüchtet hätte/If Bach had been a bee-keeper*, two versions for harpsichord and ensemble (1978, 1980); *St John Passion* (1981); cello concerto (1981); concerto for violin, cello, and chamber orchestra (performed London 1981); Te Deum (1985), *Seven Magnificat Antiphons* (1988), *Magnificat* (1989), *Miserere* (1989), *Beatus Petronius* for two choruses and two organs (1990), *The Beatitudes* for chorus and organ (1990), *Berlin Mass* (1991).

Partch, Harry (1901–1974) US composer. Largely self-taught, he experimented with microtonal scales and new instrumental designs.

Works include: *Eight Hitch-hiker Inscriptions from a California Highway Railing* and *US Highball, a Musical Account of a Transcontinental Hobo Trip* for chorus and instruments (1944); *The Letter, a Depression Message from a Hobo Friend*, for voices and instruments (1944); *Oedipus*, music drama (1952); *The Bewitched*, a dance satire (1957); *Revelation in the Courthouse Park*, a music tragedy; *Water, Water*, an American ritual (1962).

Part du diable, La/The Devil's Share opera by Auber (libretto by Scribe), produced Paris, Opéra-Comique, 16 January 1843. The work is sometimes called *Carlo Broschi*, the real name of Farinelli, who is the chief character, sung by a soprano.

Partenope opera by Handel (libretto by S Stampiglia), produced London, King's Theatre, Haymarket, 24 February 1730. Couples Partenope and Armindo, and Rosmira and Arsace are united after complications of betrayal, jealousy and false identity.

Opera by Hasse (libretto by Metastasio), produced Vienna, Burgtheater, 9 September 1767.

Parthenia (Greek 'Maidenhood') punning title of a collection published 1611 of pieces for the virginals composed by William ◊Byrd, John ◊Bull, and Orlando ◊Gibbons, engraved in standard notation and aimed at a new market of domestic amateur keyboard musicians.

Parthenia inviolata a companion volume to ◊*Parthenia*, containing 20 pieces for virginals and bass viol.

Parthia a variant spelling of the German *Partie*, used by Haydn and Beethoven among others. See also ◊partita.

partials see ◊harmonics.

partita a set of classical ◊variations, or more often a ◊suite.

Partos, Ödön (1907–1977) Hungarian-Israeli composer. He studied violin with Hubay and composition with Kodály. He led various orchestras in Lucerne, Berlin, and Budapest between 1925 and 1936, and from 1938 played viola with the Israel Philharmonic Orchestra.

Works include: *Yis Kor (In Memoriam)* for viola and string orchestra (1947); *Song of Praise* for viola and orchestra (1949); symphonic fantasy *En Gev* (1952); *Phantasy on Yemeni Themes* for chorus and orchestra; *Images* for orchestra (1960); *Fuses* for viola and chamber orchestra (1970); *Arabesque* for oboe and

chamber orchestra (1975); two string quartets (1932, 1960).

part song technically, any song composed for a number of vocal parts, often used to describe ◊madrigals, but generally referring to songs of homophonic texture, that is where the melody is sung in the top voice and the other voices provide harmonic accompaniment. It is associated with 19th-century choral works by composers including Schumann, Parry, and Elgar.

part-writing in musical composition, the blending of each individual ◊voice (independent line) into a coherent whole; the successful application of ◊counterpoint to a composition.

Pasatieri, Thomas (1945–) US composer. He studied at Juilliard and with Milhaud in Aspen. He has avoided the avant garde and remained faithful to a bel canto style.

Works include: the operas *The Widow* (Aspen, 1965); *La Divina* (New York, 1966); *Padrevia* (Brooklyn, 1967); *Calvary* (Seattle, 1971); *The Trial of Mary Lincoln* (Boston, 1972); *Black Widow* (Seattle, 1972); *The Seagull* (Houston, 1974); *Signor Deluso* (Greenway, Virginia, 1974); *The Penitentes* (Aspen, 1974); *Ines de Castro* (Baltimore, 1976); *Washington Square* (Detroit, 1976); *Maria Elena* (Tuscon, 1983); *Three Sisters* (Columbus, OH, 1986).

Pasdeloup, Jules (Etienne) (1819–1887) French conductor. He founded the Société des Jeunes Artistes du Conservatoire in 1851, and the Concerts Pasdeloup in 1861, at which he produced many works previously unknown in France, including music by Wagner and Schumann. In 1868 he founded the Société des Oratories, and joined the Théâtre Lyrique the same year.

He studied at the Paris Conservatory.

Pashchenko, Andrey Filipovich (1883–1972) Russian composer. He entered the St Petersburg Conservatory in 1914, after receiving private musical instruction, and studied composition under Steinberg and Wihtol. He was active as teacher and music organizer, but devoted most of his time to composition. During World War II he remained at Leningrad throughout the siege.

Works include: the operas *The Revolt of the Eagles* (1925), *Emperor Maximilian* (1927), *The Black Cliff* (1931), *The Pompadours* (after Saltikov-Shtchedrin's story, 1939), *The Stubborn Bride* (1956), *Radda and Loyko* (after Gorki's story *Makar Tchudra*, 1957); film music; oratorios *The Liberation of Prometheus* and *Lenin, Requiem* in memory of the heroes of the great war; 15 symphonies (1915–70), *Solemn Polonaise* and *Festive Overture*, symphonic poems *The Giants* and *The Bacchantes*, scherzo *Harlequin and Columbine*, Suite in the Classical Style, *Legend* for orchestra; three pieces for a band of folk instruments; nine string quartets; songs.

Pasquali, Niccolò (c. 1718–1757) Italian violinist and composer. He wrote treatises on thorough bass and harpsichord playing.

He settled at Edinburgh about 1740, lived at Dublin 1748–51, then returned to Edinburgh, visiting London in 1752.

Works include: the opera *The Enraged Musician* (1753), Masque *The Triumph of Hibernia*; dirge in Shakespeare's *Romeo and Juliet*; oratorios *Noah* and *David*; 12 overtures for (or with) horns; sonatas for violin or two violins and bass; songs contributed to various collections.

Pasquini, Bernardo (1637–1710) Italian harpsichordist, organist, and composer. His *Accademia per musica* was performed at the Roman palace of Queen Christina of Sweden in 1687 to celebrate the accession of James II, Arcangelo Corelli leading a string orchestra of 150 players.

He studied with Loreto Vittori and Antonio Cesti. As a young man he settled in Rome and became organist of the church of Santa Maria Maggiore.

Works include: the operas *La donna ancora è fedele* (1676), *Dov' è amore e pietà* (1679), *La forza d'amore*, and 11 others; 13 sonatas and other works for harpsichord.

passacaglia Spanish dance form in three time that evolved into an instrumental form constructed over a ◊ground bass, or cyclically repeating bass line. Dramatic tension is created by the juxtaposition of a developing melody and an unchanging background.

An example is Benjamin Britten's disturbing setting of Tennyson's poem 'The Kraken' in *Nocturne* 1958.

passage a nontechnical term referring to a length of music of unfixed duration, but usually a short section, which is characterized by a single melodic or textural feature.

passage work a textural piece characterized by fast running notes that are technically difficult, and in the case of the 19th-century repertory, often 'showy'.

passaggio a term similar to ◊passage, but used in more specialized senses for modulations (that is, passing from key to key) and for florid vocal or instrumental decorations.

passamezzo (Italian, probably a corruption of *passo e mezzo*, 'pace and a half') a brisk dance of the late 16th and early 17th centuries, popular not only in Italy but throughout Europe. Its name is probably due to the fact that it was a more lively form of the pavane. It consisted basically of variations on a ground bass. The *passamezzo antico* (Shakespeare's 'passy measures pavyn') was in the minor key, the *passamezzo moderno* in the major. See ◊romanesca.

passepied old French dance in three time, less strict than a minuet, featured in classical opera and the French ◊suite.

Passereau (fl. 1533–55) French composer. His chansons, some humorous, some obscene, were published by Pierre Attaignant and others at various times between 1529 and 1572. The best known of them, 'Il est bel et bon', was arranged for organ by Girolamo Cavazzoni.

passing notes notes joining two notes a third apart, by conjunct motion; they are therefore always approached and quitted by step. They do not form part of the harmony. An unaccented passing note falls on a strong beat, creating a momentary dissonance.

Unaccented and accented passing notes.

Passione, La/The Passion name given to Haydn's symphony no. 49 in F minor, composed 1768.

Passion music the medieval recitation of the gospel story of Christ's Passion was sung, as it still is, by three singers with different vocal ranges. The singer representing the Evangelist had a medium range, Christus a low range, and the singer responsible for the other characters and the crowd (*turba*) a high range. By the 15th century the *turba* began to be entrusted to a vocal ensemble, and in the course of the 16th century the whole text was sung in a polyphonic setting. In the 17th century Lutheran composers introduced recitative, chorales and instrumental accompaniment. In the early 18th century the inclusion of arias set to non-Biblical words turned the Lutheran Passion into an oratorio, indistinguishable in form from opera. Bach's two surviving Passions belong to this new category.

Pasterwiz, Georg (1730–1803) Austrian monk, organist, and composer. He studied at Kremsmünster Abbey, where he was ordained priest in 1755, and with Johann Eberlin at Salzburg. He was choirmaster at the abbey 1767–82, but later lived chiefly in Vienna.

Works include: the opera *Samson* (1775); 14 Masses, Requiem; numerous fugues and other pieces for keyboard instruments.

pasticcio (Italian 'pie' or 'pasty') stage entertainment with music drawn from existing works by one or more composers and words written to fit the music. It was particularly popular in the 18th century.

pastoral a light-hearted English madrigal with words of a pastoral character. See ◊pastorale.

Pastoral an anthology by Bliss for mezzo, chorus, flute, drums, and strings (words by Theocritus, Poliziano, Ben Jonson, John Fletcher, and Robert Nichols), first performed London, 8 May 1929.

pastorale a type of 17th-century opera, or opera-ballet, with recitatives, airs, and choruses, often produced on festive occasions and treating pastoral subjects in a courtly and artificial manner, often allegorically. Its origin was the pastoral drama of the 16th century. In later times the term pastorale has been often used as a title for all kinds of compositions of a pastoral character.

Pastorale, La, called La Pastorale d'Issy opera by Cambert (libretto by Pierre Perrin), produced at Issy near Paris, April 1659. Long regarded as the first French opera.

'Pastoral' Sonata Beethoven's piano sonata in D major, op. 28, composed 1801 and dedicated to Joseph, Edler von Sonnenfels. The nickname was not Beethoven's own, but was invented later by the Hamburg publisher Cranz. It suits only the finale.

'Pastoral' Symphony Beethoven's sixth symphony, in F major, op. 68, composed 1807–08, first performed Vienna, 22 December 1808. The title-page bears Beethoven's own heading of *Symphonie pastorale*, and on the first violin part is the inscription, 'Pastoral-Sinfonie oder Erinnerung an das Landleben (mehr Ausdruck der Empfindung als Mahlerey/Pastoral Symphony or Recollection of Country Life [Expression of Emotion rather than Painting]'.)

Pastoral Symphony, A the third symphony by Vaughan Williams, for orchestra with a soprano voice (without words), composed 1920, first performed London, Queen's Hall, 26 January 1922, conductor Boult.

Pastor fido, Il/The Faithful Shepherd opera by Handel (libretto by G Rossi after Guarini's pastoral play), produced London, Queen's Theatre, Haymarket, 22 November 1712.

pastourelle medieval pastoral song.

Pathétique Sonata, Grande sonate pathétique Beethoven's piano sonata in C minor, op. 13, composed c. 1798 and dedicated to Prince Carl von Lichnowsky. The title (in French) is, exceptionally, Beethoven's own.

Pathétique Symphony Tchaikovsky's sixth symphony, in B minor, op. 74, composed 1893 and first performed under the composer, St Petersburg, 28 October 1893. The title 'Tragic' Symphony was suggested by the composer's brother Modest, but rejected by Tchaikovsky, who afterwards agreed to the adjective 'Pathétique'.

Patience, or Bunthorne's Bride operetta by Sullivan (libretto by W S Gilbert), produced London, Opéra-Comique, 25 April 1881. Poets Bunthorne and Grosvenor are rivals for Patience, the milkmaid.

Patiño, Carlos (died 1675) Spanish composer. He was in the service of John IV of Portugal early in the 17th century and in 1633 became choirmaster in the royal chapel at Madrid.

Works include: Masses, Benedictus for the funeral of Philip II (1599), and other church music; incidental music for plays; villancicos.

Patrie overture by Bizet (not for Sardou's play of that name), composed 1873, first performed Paris, 15 February 1874.

Patterson, Paul (1947–) English composer. He studied with Richard Rodney Bennett and at the Royal Academy of Music, London, where he became director of electronic studies in 1975.

Works include: wind quintet (1967); trumpet concerto (1969); *Concertante* (1969); *Piccola Sinfonia* (1971); horn concerto (1971); *Fiesta Sinfonica* (1972); Requiem for chorus and orchestra (1975); concerto for clarinet and strings (1976); *Cracovian Counterpoints* for 14 instruments (1977); Concerto for Orchestra (1981); *Canterbury Psalms* for chorus and orchestra (1981); *Sinfonia* for strings (1982); *Mass of the Sea* for soloists, chorus, and orchestra (1984).

patter song type of song, usually comic, the effect of which depends on a rapid, syllabic delivery of the words to quick music. Many familiar examples occur in Sullivan's operettas.

Pauke (German; plural _ital_) German name for the ◊timpani.

Paukenmesse/Kettledrum Mass the name given to Haydn's Mass in C major, composed 1796; performed Vienna, 26 December 1796. The reason for the unusually prominent timpani, especially in the _Agnus Dei_, is suggested by Haydn's own title, _Missa in tempore belli/Mass in time of war_.

Paukenschlag, Sinfonie mit dem, (Haydn). See ◊'Surprise' Symphony.

Paukenwirbel, Sinfonie mit dem, (Haydn). See ◊'Drum-Roll' Symphony.

Paul Bunyan choral operetta by Britten (libretto by W H Auden), produced Columbia University, New York, 5 May 1941; revised 1974 and given on BBC 1 February 1976: this version produced Aldeburgh, 14 June 1976.

Paulus the German title of Mendelssohn's oratorio _St Paul_.

Paulus, Stephen (Harrison) (1949–) US composer. He studied at the University of Minnesota with Dominick Argento and founded the Minnesota Composer's Forum 1973. He was composer-in-residence with the Minnesota Orchestra 1983–87, and with the Atlanta Symphony Orchestra 1987–91. He is best known for his operas, all premiered in St Louis: _The Village Singer_ (1979), _The Postman Always Rings Twice_ (1981), _The Woodlanders_ (1985), and _Harmoonia_ (1991).

Works include: _Concerto for Orchestra_ (1983), _Symphony in Three Movements_ (1985), violin concerto (1987), _Symphony for Strings_ (1989); _So Hallow'd is the Time_ for soloists, chorus and orchestra; two string quartets.

Paumann, Conrad (c. 1410–1473) German composer and organist. He travelled widely through France, Italy, Germany, and Austria as an organist and is believed to have invented a form of lute ◊tablature. His treatise, 'Fundamentum organisandi' 1452, gives examples of the ornamentation of chant, with keyboard arrangements of chants and secular melodies.

Paumann was born in Nuremberg. Blind from birth, he was educated by the Grundherr family of Nuremberg, learnt the organ and composition, and was organist at St Sebald's Church in the 1440s. In 1450 he was appointed organist to Duke Albrecht III of Bavaria at Munich, and retained the post

for the rest of his life. Few of his compositions survive, probably because he could not write them down.

Works include: a _Fundamentum organisandi_ (1452), or 'Principles of Composition', laid out in keyboard tablature, which exists in several versions; organ arrangement of monophonic and polyphonic pieces; and a German song, 'Wiplich figur'.

Paumgartner, Bernhard (1887–1971) Austrian musicologist and composer. He studied first with his parents, the critic Hans Paumgartner and the singer Rosa Paumgartner (born Papier), and afterwards with Bruno Walter. He was director of the Mozarteum at Salzburg, 1917–38, and was one of the organizers of the Salzburg festivals; his editions of Mozart's _Idomeneo_ and Cavalieri's _Rappresentazione_ were produced there 1956 and 1968. He wrote mainly on Mozart.

Works include: the operas _Das heisse Eisen_ (after Hans Sachs), _Die Höhle von Salamanca_ (after Cervantes, 1923), _Rossini in Neapel_ (1935), _Aus dem Leben eines Taugenichts_ (after Eichendorff's novel); ballet _Pagoden_; incidental music to Shakespeare's _King Lear_ and _Twelfth Night_ (on old English tunes), Goethe's _Faust_, Gozzi's _Turandot_, music for chorus and for orchestra; songs.

pause the prolongation of a note, chord or rest beyond its normal value, indicated by the fermata sign. In the 18th-century concerto it is regularly placed over the 6/4 chord which precedes the cadenza. In a _da capo_ it marks the point at which the piece ends after repetition of the first section. In the German chorale or in works based on it, it marks the end of each line and is to be ignored in performance.

Pause musical term; German 'restoration'.

Pause del silenzio/Pauses of Silence seven symphonic expressions by Malipiero, produced Rome, Augusteo, 27 January 1918.

Pauvre Matelot, Le/The Poor Sailor opera by Milhaud (libretto by Cocteau), produced Paris, Opéra-Comique, 16 December 1927. A sailor returns home to his wife, but passes himself off as a friend of her husband. He tells her that the sailor is a prisoner; when he spends the night in her house the wife kills him (still not realizing his true identity) in order to take his money and free her husband.

pavane, or pavan, a slow, stately court dance in double time, of Paduan origin, especially popular in Italy and France in the 16th and 17th centuries. Music composed for or derived from the pavane is often coupled with that composed for a ◊galliard. Composers include Dowland and Byrd, more recently Ravel, whose *Pavane pour une infante défunte/Pavane for a Dead Infanta* for piano 1899 was orchestrated 1905.

Pavane pour une infante défunte/Pavan for a dead Infant a piano piece by Ravel (1899); first performed Paris, 5 April 1902. Orchestral version 1910, first performed Paris, 25 December 1910, conductor Casella.

Pavesi, Stefano (1779–1850) Italian composer. He studied at the Conservatorio dei Turchini, Naples 1795–99, and became very popular as a composer of operas, including *La festa della rosa* 1808, *Fenella* 1831, and *Ser Marcantonio* 1810.

Payne, Anthony (1936–) English composer and critic. He studied at Durham University 1958–61, and worked as a music critic for the *Daily Telegraph* from 1965. He has written on Schoenberg and British composers.

Works include: *Phoenix Mass* for chorus and brass (1965–72); *Sonatas and Ricercars* for wind quintet (1971); Concerto for Orchestra (1975); *First Sight of her and After*, song cycle for 16 voices (texts by Hardy, 1975); *The World's Winter* for soprano and eight instruments (text by Tennyson, 1976); string quartet (1978); *Spring's Shining Wake* for chamber orchestra (1981); *Songs and Dances* for strings (1984); *Half Heard in the Stillness* for orchestra (1987); *Sea-Change* septet (1988); *Time's Arrow* for orchestra (1990); *Symphonies of Wind and Rain* for ensemble (1993).

Paz, Juan Carlos (1901–1972) Argentinian composer. He studied in Buenos Aires and was one of the founders of the Group Renovación of progressive composers in 1929. He also founded a society for the performance of new music.

Works include: incidental music for Ibsen's *Julian the Emperor*; *Canto de Navidad*, *Movimiento sinfónico*, Polytonal Variations, chamber and instrumental music.

Peacock Variations variations on a Hungarian Folk-Song, by Kodály; composed 1938–39 to celebrate the 50th anniversary of the Concertgebouw Orchestra, first performed Amsterdam, 23 November 1939, conductor Mengelberg.

Pearsall, Robert (Lucas) (1795–1856) English composer. He studied law and became a barrister in 1821, but had already composed. In 1825 he settled at Mainz and studied with Panny there, devoting himself entirely to music. Another year in England, 1829–30, was his last, except for visits; he settled in Germany for good, although he inherited a property at Willsbridge, Gloucestershire, in 1836. He sold this and bought Wartensee Castle on Lake Constance.

Works include: church music (Anglican and Roman Catholic), Requiem (1853–56); overture and chorus for Shakespeare's *Macbeth*; madrigals, part-songs.

Peasant a Rogue, The/Selma Sedlák comic opera by Dvořák (libretto by J O Veselý), produced Prague, Czech Theatre, 27 January 1878. Similar to *Le Nozze di Figaro*, a Prince wants to seduce Bětuška, who already loves Jeník; the Princess helps to stop her husband's attempted exploits by dressing up as Bětuška.

Peasant Cantata, Mer hahn en neue Oberkeet/We have a new magistracy a secular cantata by Bach for solo voices, chorus, and orchestra, composed in 1742, to words in Saxon dialect. The music is noticeably rustic and comes as near to the manner of folk song as anything Bach ever wrote.

Pêcheurs de perles, Les/The Pearl Fishers opera by Bizet (libretto by E Cormon and M Carré), produced Paris, Théâtre Lyrique, 30 September 1863. Leila, once the love of both Zurga and Nadir, returns to the men's village as a priestess of Brahma. She provokes Zurga's jealousy by seeing Nadir; Zurga orders them both to be put to death, but allows them to escape at the last moment.

ped. abbreviation used in the notation of piano music to indicate the use of the sustaining pedal. The use of the soft pedal is indicated by the words *una corda* (one string), which is abbreviated to *u.c.*) The abbreviation

A pavane in A minor by Byrd.

also occurs in organ music written on two staves, to indicate which notes or passages are to be played on the pedals.

pedal a sustained note in a polyphonic composition, generally but not invariably in the bass. It often occurs at the climax of a fugue, above which the harmony changes in order to create tension.
See also ◊pedals.

pedal board in an ◊organ, the keyboard of pedals.

Pedalflügel (German 'pedal (grand) piano') German name for the pedal ◊piano.

pedal harp the ordinary ◊harp in current use, as distinct from the chromatic harp.

pedal notes the fundamental notes of trombones and other brass wind instruments, the normal compass of which consists of the upper harmonics.

pedal piano ◊piano specially constructed with a keyboard of pedals and used mainly for organ practice at home. Very little music was written expressly for it except by Schumann.

pedal point in organ music, a bass note of indefinite length, usually at the end of a piece, establishing the final key and over which a performer improvises an elaborately decorated ◊cadence. The term also applies to piano music of a similar kind. Also a long-held bass note in orchestral music, as for example in the symphonies of Sibelius.

pedals in certain musical instruments, mechanical devices which require manipulation by the feet. Pedals may actually produce notes, as in the organ; they may be a means of obtaining certain effects of tone, as in the sustaining and soft piano pedals; or they may be used to alter the length, and thus the tuning, of strings, as in the harp.

Pedrell, Carlos (1878–1941) Uruguayan composer of Spanish descent. He studied at Montevideo, with his uncle Felipe Pedrell at Barcelona 1898–1900 and then with d'Indy and Bréville at the Schola Cantorum in Paris. In 1906 he went to Buenos Aires, where he held various official music posts and founded the Sociedad Nacional de Música in 1915. In 1921 he settled in Paris.
    Works include: the operas *Ardid de amor* (1917) and *Cuento de abril*; ballet *Alleluia* (1936); *Une Nuit de Schéhérazade* (1908), *Danza y canción de Aixa* (1910), *En el estrado de Beatriz*, *Fantasia Argentina* and *Ouverture catalane* for orchestra; choruses; songs with orchestra and with piano.

Pedrell, Felipe (1841–1922) Spanish composer and musicologist. He was the leader of the Spanish nationalist movement in composition and also became a famous scholar in the domain of old Spanish church music and folk music, much of which he edited. He was the uncle of Carlos Pedrell.
    Pedrell was almost wholly self-taught, but learnt much as a chorister at Tortosa Cathedral. He first published music in 1871 and had his first opera, *El ultimo Abencerraje*, produced at Barcelona in 1874. From that time he taught music history and aesthetics at the Madrid Conservatory, but settled at Barcelona in 1894, where he worked for the revival of old and the spread of new Spanish music. He edited the complete works of Tomás de Victoria and a collection of early Spanish church music, early stage and organ music, and other pieces.
    Among his later operas *Los Pirineos* 1902, *La Celestina* 1903, and *El Comte Arnau* 1921, are the most important; he also wrote incidental music for *King Lear*, church music, cantatas, and orchestral and chamber music. His many pupils included Falla, Granados, and Roberto Gerhard.
    Works include: the operas *El último Abencerraje* (after Chateaubriand, 1868), *Quasimodo* (on Victor Hugo's *Notre-Dame de Paris*, 1875), *Cleopatra* (1881), *Los Pirineos* (1902), *La Celestina*, *El Conde Arnau* (1904), *Visión de Randa* and four early light operas; incidental music for Shakespeare's *King Lear*; Mass, Requiem and Te Deum; symphonic poems; string quartet; piano music, songs.

Peel, John (1776–1854) English yeoman (independent farmer). He is the hero of the song 'D'ye ken John Peel', said to have been written about 1829 by his friend John Woodcock Graves to a folk tune, 'Bonnie Annie'. It is the regimental march of the Border Regiment.

Peer Gynt incidental music for Ibsen's drama by Grieg, produced Christiania, 24 February 1876. Grieg afterwards arranged two orchestral suites from it, op. 46 and op. 55.
    Opera by Egk (libretto by composer), produced Berlin 24 November 1938; admired by Hitler.

Peerson, Martin (c. 1572–1651) English organist and composer. He took a music degree at Oxford in 1613 and was soon afterwards appointed organist and choirmaster at St Paul's Cathedral in London.
    Works include: church music; airs and dialogues for voices, *Mottects or Grave Chamber Musique* for voices and instruments on

sonnets from Fulke Greville's 'Caelica' (1630); fancies and almains for viols; virginal pieces, *Private Musick* (1620); contributions to Leighton's *Teares* and Ravenscroft's psalter.

Peeters, Flor (1903–1986) Belgian organist and composer. He toured widely as a recmusicist and edited several collections of early organ music. He held teaching posts at the Lemmens Institute, Mechlin, and at the conservatories of Ghent, Tilburg, and Antwerp; he was director of the latter 1952–68.

He studied at Mechlin and with Dupré and Tournemire at Paris. In 1925 he was appointed organist of Mechlin Cathedral.

Works include: eight Masses, Te Deum; organ concerto, piano concerto, concerto for organ and piano; about 200 organ works; chamber music, piano works; songs.

Peire d'Auvergne (lived c. 1140–80) French ◊troubadour, from the Clermont region. He entered the Church but broke his vows and wandered from court to court, dying penitent. Some 25 of his poems remain. He was one of the first troubadours to write on religious subjects and was also perhaps the originator of the hermetic style known as *trobar clus.*

Peking Opera (Chinese *Ching-chu*) the most famous type of regional theatre in China, dating from 1790. A simple stage design contrasts with complex costumery, make-up, and acting. Peking Opera consists of dialogue sections and singing with orchestral accompaniment (dominated by Chinese 'fiddles' such as the *erhu* and the *pipa* plucked lute). There are well over 1,000 items in the repertory which fall into two categories: the *wen* (civilian) portraying love stories or social matters; and the *wu*, the military exploits of heroes or brigands.

Pèlerins de le Mecque (Gluck) ◊*Rencontre imprévue, La.*

Pelléas et Mélisande incidental music for Maurice Maeterlinck's play by Fauré, produced London, Prince of Wales Theatre, 21 June 1898.

Opera by Debussy (libretto Maeterlinck's play, slightly altered), produced Paris, Opéra-Comique, 30 April 1902. Married to Golaud, Mélisande falls in love with Pelléas. Golaud soon becomes jealous, and the lovers realize the futility of their situation. After their last meeting, Pelléas is killed by Golaud, and later Mélisande dies, having borne Golaud a child.

Symphonic poem after Maeterlinck by Schoenberg, op. 5, composed 1902, first performed. Vienna, 26 January 1905.

Incidental music, orchestral suite in nine movements, by Sibelius, op. 46, composed 1905, produced Helsinki, 17 March 1905.

Pellegrini, Vincenzo (died 1640) Italian cleric and composer. He was a canon at Pesaro from 1594 and maestro di cappella at Milan Cathedral 1611–31.

Works include: Masses and other church music; organ canzonets; instrumental pieces in three–four parts; secular canzonets for voices.

Penderecki, Krzysztof (1933–) Polish composer. His expressionist works, such as the *Threnody for the Victims of Hiroshima* 1961 for strings, employ cluster and percussion effects. He later turned to religious subjects and a more orthodox style, as in the *Magnificat* 1974 and the *Polish Requiem* 1980–83. His opera *The Black Mask* 1986 uncovered a new vein of surreal humour.

He studied composition with Artur Malawski and Stanisław Wiechowicz in Kraków, graduating in 1958. His music has made frequent use of aleatory techniques and microtonal clusters, belonging at one time to the avant garde; later works show an awareness of traditional values and techniques.

Works include: the operas *The Devils of Loudun* (1969), *Paradise Lost* (1978), *Die schwarze Maske* (1986), and *Ubu Rex* (1991); *St Luke Passion* for speaker, two soloists, chorus, and orchestra (1963–66); *Stabat Mater* and *Psalms of David* for chorus and orchestra (1963, 1958); *Emanations* for two string orchestras (1958); *Anaclasis* for strings and percussion (1960); *Threnody for the Victims of Hiroshima* for 52 strings (1960); *Fluorescences* for chamber ensemble (1961), *De natura sonoris* for orchestra (1966); *Dies Irae,* for soloists, chorus, and orchestra (1967); *Utrenja* for soloists, chorus, and orchestra (1969–71); two cello concertos (1972, 1982); two symphonies (1973, 1980); *Canticum canticorum* (1972); Magnificat (1974), violin concerto (1977); Te Deum (1979); Viola concerto (1983); *Polish Requiem* (1983); *Songs of Cherubim* and *Veni Creator* for chorus (1986–87), *Der Unterbrochene Gedanke* for string quartet (1988); *Passacaglia* (1988) and Adagio (1989) for orchestra; two string quartets (1960, 1968).

Penelope opera by Galuppi (libretto by P A Rolli), produced London, King's Theatre, Haymarket, 12 December 1741.
See also ◊Circe and Penelope.

Pénélope opera by Fauré (libretto by R Fauchois), produced Monte Carlo, 4 March 1913; first Paris performance, Théâtre des Champs-Elysées, 10 May 1913. Other operas on Penelope myth by Monteverdi (*Il ritorno di Ulisse*, 1641), A Scarlatti (1696), Piccinni (1785), Cimarosa (1795) and Liebermann (1954).

penillion old form of Welsh song to the harp which was improvised (often the words as well as the music) as a counterpoint or descant to the harp part. It is still cultivated, but now tends to rely on tradition rather than improvisation.

Penna, Lorenzo (1613–1693) Italian monk and composer. He wrote treatises on counterpoint and figured bass, including *Primi albori musicali* 1672, in three volumes.

He entered the Carmelite order at Bologna in 1630 and in 1672 became maestro di cappella at the Carmelite church of Parma; he was also a professor of theology.

Works include: Masses and other church music; *correnti francesi* for four instruments.

Penny for a Song opera by Richard Rodney Bennett (libretto by C Graham from John Whiting's play), produced London, Sadler's Wells, 31 October 1967. In 19th-century England, Sir Timothy Bellboys is concerned that his country is vulnerable to invasion. Comedy about the local militia that is mistaken for an for an assault force.

penny whistle small and rudimentary wind instrument, a pipe of the ◊fife or ◊recorder type, also known as a 'tin whistle'. It is played vertically and has a small range of treble notes controlled by six finger holes.

pentatone (from Greek 'five notes') another name for the ◊pentatonic scale.

pentatonic scale a scale of five notes, equivalent to the black notes of the piano and their transpositions. Found as early as 2000 BC, the pentatonic scale is common in folk music from the USA to the Celtic nations to China.

Penthesilea opera by Schoeck (libretto by composer, based on Kleist's drama), produced Dresden, 8 January 1927. Achilles falls in love with Amazon Queen Penthesilea, whom he has defeated in combat. When she recovers from her wounds she becomes deranged and kills Achilles. After coming to her senses she commits suicide.

Symphonic poem on ditto by H Wolf, composed 1883–85.

Pentland, Barbara (1912–   ) Canadian composer. She studied in Paris, at the Juilliard School, New York, and with Copland at Tanglewood. She taught at the University of British Columbia 1949–63.

Works include: four symphonies (1945–59), piano and organ concertos, five string quartets (1945–85), *Variations Concertantes* (1970), *Res Musica* for string orchestra (1975), *Disasters of the Sun* for mezzo, instruments and tape (1976), *Horizons* for piano (1985), *Ice Age* for soprano and piano (1986), *Intrade and Canzona* for recorder quartet (1988).

Pepita Jiménez opera by I Albéniz (libretto, in English, by F B Money- Coutts, based on a story by Juan Valera), produced in Spanish, Barcelona, Liceo, 5 January 1896. Rich young widow Pepita has many suitors, but she falls in love only with Don Luis. The priest warns her against this, but despite adversity the two are eventually brought together.

Pepping, Ernst (1901–1981) German composer. He studied at the Hochschule für Musik in Berlin and devoted himself chiefly to the cultivation of Protestant church music, being appointed professor at the Kirchenmusikschule at Spandau in 1947.

Works include: setting of the 90th Psalm, unaccompanied motets, Te Deum, *Spandauer Chorbuch* containing vocal pieces for two–six voices for the whole ecclesiastical year in 20 volumes, 1934–38); three symphonies (1939–44), piano concerto (1951), two organ concertos; four piano sonatas; chamber music; songs.

Pepusch, Johann Christoph (1667–1752) German composer. He settled in England about 1700 and contributed to John Gay's ballad operas *The Beggar's Opera* and *Polly*.

He was appointed to the Prussian court at the age of 14. After emigrating to Holland, he went to England about 1700, and settled in London for the rest of his life. He married Margherita de l'Epine in 1718.

Works include: recitatives and songs for a pasticcio opera *Thomyris* (1707) and probably others; incidental music for Colley Cibber's *Myrtillo* (1715); music for masques *Apollo and Daphne* (1716), *The Death of Dido* (1716), *The Union of the Sister Arts, Venus and Adonis* (1715); dramatic ode for the Peace of Utrecht; overture for *The Beggar's Opera* and arrangements for it and its sequel, *Polly*, and another ballad opera, *The Wedding* (1729); services, anthems, and Latin motets; cantatas to words by John Hughes (including *Alexis*) and others; odes, concertos, sonatas.

per arsin et thesin (Latin 'by rise and fall') imitation by contrary motion. One part goes up where the other goes down.

An example from Bach's Art of Fugue *in which the second voice enters by inversion,* per arsin et thesin.

percussion a term used in harmony for the actual incident of a discord, after its ◊preparation and before its ◊resolution.

percussion instrument musical instrument played by being struck with the hand or a beater. Percussion instruments can be divided into those that can be tuned to produce a sound of definite pitch, such as the timpani, tubular bells, glockenspiel, xylophone, and piano, and those of indefinite pitch, including the bass drum, tambourine, triangle, cymbals, and castanets.

The **timpano** is a hemispherical bowl of metal with a membrane stretched across the rim, affixed and tuned by screwtaps; **tubular bells** are suspended on a frame; the **glockenspiel** is a small keyboard of aluminium alloy keys; the **xylophone** has hardwood rather than metal bars.

The **snare drum** is a shallow double-sided drum on the underside of which gut coils or metal springs are secured by a clamp and rattle against the underside when the drum is beaten, while the **bass drum** produces the lowest sound in the orchestra; the **tambourine** has a wooden hoop with a membrane stretched across it, and has metal discs suspended in the rim; a **triangle** is formed from a suspended triangular-shaped steel bar, played by striking it with a separate bar of steel – the sound produced can be clearly perceived even when played against a full orchestra; **cymbals** are two brass dishes struck together; **castanets** are two hollow shells of wood struck together; and the **gong** is a suspended disc of metal struck with a soft hammer.

perdendosi (Italian 'losing itself') a musical direction indicating that the sound of a note or passage is to become gradually weaker until it fades away.

Perez, Davide (1711–1778) Spanish composer. He studied at the Conservatorio di Santa Maria di Loreto at Naples and produced his first opera, *La nemica amante*, in 1735. He became maestro di cappella to Prince Naselli at Palermo and in 1752 went to Lisbon, where he became attached to the royal chapel and the new opera house, which opened in 1755.

Works include: the operas *Siroe* (1740), *I travestimenti amorosi* (1740), *L'eroismo di Scipione* (1741), *Astartea* (1743), *Medea* (1744), *L'isola incantata*, *La clemenza di Tito* (1749), *Semiramide* (1750), *Alessandro nell' Indie* (1755), *Demetrio* (1766), *Demofoonte, Soimano* (1757), *Il ritorno di Ulisse in Itaca* (1774), and others, many to libretti by Metastasio; *Mattutino de' morti*, Masses and other church music; oratorio *Il martirio di San Bartolomeo*, and other pieces.

Perfect Fool, The opera by Holst (libretto by composer), produced London, Covent Garden, 14 May 1923. A mother (with help from the Wizard) tries to marry her son, the Fool, to the Princess, who falls in love with him after other suitors fail to attract her. A comic wedding.

perfect intervals intervals that do not possess alternative major and minor forms, but become augmented or diminished by being enlarged or reduced by a semitone, such as fourths, fifths and octaves, also their repetitions beyond the octave, that is 11ths and so on.

perfect pitch alternative term for ◊absolute pitch.

performance practice the study of how music was performed in the age in which it was written. A discipline associated with the ◊authenticity movement, it was first applied to music written in the ◊Baroque period and earlier, and subsequently also to that of the ◊Classical period. Recent academic interest in early recordings of the 20th century has led to the expansion of performance practice to embrace music of any period before the present day.

Pergolesi, Giovanni Battista (1710–1736) Italian composer. He wrote Masses, a *Stabat Mater* and other church music, secular cantatas, oratorios, some instrumental works, and nine operas, three of which, including *La serva padrona*, are comic intermezzi to be performed between the acts of a serious opera. His music is most often heard today through the pieces which Stravinsky selected for *Pulcinella*.

His parents were poor, and he seems to have been sent to Naples in 1725, to study at the Conservatorio dei Poveri di Gesù Cristo, under the patronage of Marchese Pianetti. His teachers there were Gaetano Greco, Leonardo Vinci, and Francesco Durante. His earliest works were sacred pieces, but he made his debut as a composer for the stage in 1731, and two years later produced the comic intermezzo *La serva padrona* (performed between the acts of his serious opera *Il prigionier superbo*), which was to be decisive in the history of opera buffa. In 1732 he became maestro di cappella to the Prince of Stigliano at Naples, for whom he wrote cantatas and chamber music, and entered the service of the Duke of Maddaloni about 1734, but returned to Naples the next year, becoming organist to the court. In February 1736 he retired on grounds of ill health to the Capuchin monastery in Pozzuoli, where he completed his last work, the *Stabat Mater*, just before his death. Much music attributed to him after his death is now known to be by other composers, but his output is nevertheless astonishing for a composer who suffered from ill-health and died of tuberculosis at the age of 26. Recent revivals of his operas reveal a resourceful and engaging composer.

Works include: the operas *Salustia* (1732), *Il prigionier superbo* (1733), *Adriano in Siria* (1734), *L'Olimpiade* (1735), *Lo frate 'nnamorato* (1732), *Flaminio* (1735); intermezzi *La serva padrona*, *Livietta e Tracollo* (1737); oratorios *La morte di S Giuseppe* (1731), *La Conversione di S Guglielmo d'Acquitania* (1731), *La morte d'Abel*, and others; Masses, *Stabat Mater* for soprano and alto soloists and strings (1736), settings of *Salve Regina* (1736), and other church music; chamber music; keyboard music, and other pieces. There are also many other works attributed to Pergolesi which are of doubtful authenticity.

Peri, Jacopo (1561–1633) Italian composer. He served the Medici family, the rulers of Florence. His experimental melodic opera *Euridice* 1600 established the opera form and influenced Monteverdi. His first opera, *Dafne* 1597, believed to be the earlieat opera, is now lost.

Peri was a pupil of Cristoforo Malvezzi, then became a canon at the church of San Lorenzo at Florence. He was attached to the Medici court from about 1588, and was later appointed their maestro di cappella and chamberlain. He became a member of the progressive artists grouped round Count Giovanni Bardi, with the composers Giulio Caccini, Jacopo Corsi, and Vincenzo Galilei, and the poet Ottavio Rinuccini. In their endeavour to revive Greek drama with the kind of music they imagined to be genuinely Greek, they stumbled on the invention of opera. They discarded counterpoint in favour of melody and expressive harmony. Peri, with Caccini, experimented in musical declamation to a suitable accompaniment, and they thus became the earliest composers of recitative. They may also be considered the world's first operatic composers.

Works include: the operas *Dafne* (1598), *Euridice* (1600), *Tetide* (composed 1608), *Adone* (composed 1611), tournament with music *La precedenza delle dame* (1625); parts of operas (with others) *La guerra d'amore* and *Flora* (with Gagliano); several ballets; *Lamento d'Iole* for soprano and instruments, madrigals, sonnets, and arias in *Songbook* of 1609.

Périchole, La operetta by Offenbach (libretto by H Meilhac and L Halévy, based on Mérimée's *Le Carrosse du Saint-Sacrement*), produced Paris, Théâtre des Variétés, 6 October 1868. The Viceroy of Peru, Don Andrès, takes on poor Périchole as chambermaid. Her lover Piguillo agrees unwittingly to marry her. Much confusion when they recognize each other, but happy ending.

périgourdine French country dance from the region of Périgord, known to musicians from at least the 18th century. Its music is in 6–8 time.

Péri, La ballet *poème dansé* by Dukas, produced Paris, Théâtre du Châtelet, 22 April 1912.

period in musical analysis, one of the basic structural units of melody, consisting of a pair of phrases, the first often ending with an 'imperfect cadence' ('half close'), the second often ending with a 'perfect cadence' ('full close').

Perle, George (1915–) US composer and theorist. His studies have centred on the Second Viennese School; books include *Twelve-tone tonality* 1977. He taught at Queens College, New York 1961–84.

His teachers included Ernst Krenek.

Works include: *Three Movements* for orchestra (1960), cello concerto (1966), *A Short Symphony* (first performance 1980); three wind quintets (1956–67), eight string quartets (1938–88); piano concerto (1990).

Perle du Brésil, LaThe Pearl of Brazil opera by Fél David (libretto by J J Gabriel and S Saint- Etienne), produced Paris, Théâtre Lyrique, 22 November 1851.

Perosi, Lorenzo (1872–1956) Italian priest and composer. He studied at Milan and Ratisbon, and among other appointments became choirmaster at St Mark's, Venice in 1894, and music director of the Sistine Chapel in Rome, 1898. In 1905 he was nominated perpetual master of the Pontifical Chapel.

Works include: 33 Masses, four Requiems, *Stabat Mater*, a Te Deum and much other church music; oratorios *The Transfiguration* (1898), *The Raising of Lazarus* (1898), *The Resurrection, Moses, Leo the Great, The Last Judgment* (1904) and *Il sogno interpretato; Florence, Rome, Venice* and *Bologna* from ten planned symphonies on the names of Italian cities; organ works.

Perotinus Magnus, now sometimes called Pérotin (c. 1160–c. 1205 or c. 1225) French composer and scholar. He was maître de chapelle of the church of the Blessed Virgin Mary (later Notre-Dame Cathedral). He is said to have revised Leoninus' *Liber organi de graduali*, and composed organa (see ◊organum) in as many as four parts. His best known organa are on the Christmas and St Stephen's Day Graduals, 1198, 1199.

perpetual canon canon in which each part begins again as soon as it is finished, the other parts being at that moment at other stages of their progress. Since even a perpetual canon must finish sooner or later, however, it is broken off at a point agreed to by the performers.

perpetuum mobile (Latin 'perpetually in motion') a piece of music in which there is a rapid and repetitive figuration of notes,

especially as part of the accompaniment. It is similar to ◊motoric rhythm.

Perrin, Pierre (c. 1620–1675) French author. He wrote libretti for operas by Robert Cambert and others.

He preceded Lully 1669–72 in holding the patent for the management of the Académie de Musique (Opéra) in Paris.

Persée/Perseus opera by Lully (libretto by Quinault), produced Paris, Opéra, 18 April 1682. Perseus and Andromeda are in love, but she must marry Phineas. Perseus proves his love in a series of tests and battles.

Perséphone melodrama for the stage or concert-room by Stravinsky (libretto by André Gide), produced Paris, Opéra, 30 April 1934. Three scenes about mythical Perse-phone, who is raped by Pluto; Stravinsky introduces the idea of self-sacrifice into the plot, so that the myth becomes similar to a Christian parable.

Persichetti, Vincent (1915–1987) US composer. His *Lincoln Address* of 1973 was scheduled for first performance at Richard Nixon's inauguration in Washington; the performance was postponed owing to an allusion to the Vietnam War.

He studied piano with Alberto Jonás (1868–1943) and Olga Samaroff (1882–1948), composition with Paul Nordoff (1909–77) and Roy Harris, and conducting with Fritz Reiner. He taught composition at the Philadelphia Conservatory 1942–48, then taught at the Juilliard School, New York .

Works include: the operas *Parable XX* (1976) and *Sibyl* (1984); nine symphonies (1942–71); ballet *King Lear*; 14 serenades for different instrumental groups; *The Hollow Men* for trumpet and string orchestra; piano concerto; two piano quintets, four string quartets (1939–72); 12 piano sonatas, six piano sonatinas; vocal music.

Perti, Giacomo (Antonio) (1661–1756) Italian composer. He studied with his uncle Lorenzo Perti, a priest at San Petronio at Bologna, and later with Petronio Franceschini. After visits to Venice and Modena in the 1680s, he became maestro di cappella at San Pietro at Bologna in 1690 and of San Petronio in 1696.

Works include: the operas *Oreste* (1685), *Marzio Coriolano, L'incoronazione di Dario* (1686), *Teodora, Il furio Camillo* (1692), *Pompeo, Nerone fatto Cesare* (1710), *Penelope la casta* (1696), *Fausta, Rodelinda* (1710), *Lucio Vero* (1717), and 17 others; Masses, including *Missa solemnis* for solo voices, chorus, and orchestra, motets, and other pieces; oratorio *Abramo* (1683), four Passion oratorios and several others.

pes (Latin 'foot') in medieval English music, the lowest part of a vocal composition in several parts, particularly one that consists of a recurrent figure, as in 'Sumer is icumen in'.

pesante (Italian 'heavy, weighty') a musical direction indicating that a passage is to be played very firmly. In the 19th century and later, often implying a slight ◊*ritenuto.*

Pescatrici, Le/The Fisher Girls opera by Bertoni (libretto by Goldoni), produced Venice, Teatro San Samuele, 26 December 1751. opera by Haydn (libretto ditto), produced Eszterháza, September 1770. Prince Lindoro must discover who the heiress of Benvento is. Both Nerina and Lesbina claim to be the princess, but their lovers Burlotto and Frisellino foil their plans. Eurilda is revealed as the true heiress.

Pescetti, Giovanni Battista (c. 1704–1766) Italian composer. He produced his first opera, *Nerone detronato*, in Venice in 1725. He lived in London 1737–45, and was for a time music director of the Covent Garden and King's theatres.

He studied with Antonio Lotti. After his return to Italy, his last opera was produced at Padua in 1761. He was appointed second organist at St Mark's, Venice, in 1762.

Works include: the operas *Gli odi delusi del sangue* (1728), *Dorinda* (1729, both with Galuppi), *Demetrio* (1732), *Diana ed Endimione* (1739), *La conquista del vello d'oro, Tamerlano* (with Cocchi, 1754) and about 20 others; oratorio *Gionata*; church music; harpsichord sonatas.

Peter and the Wolf symphonic tale for narrator and orchestra by Prokofiev (text by composer), op. 67; composed 1936, first performed Moscow, 2 May 1936.

Peter Grimes opera by Britten (libretto by M Slater, based on part of Crabbe's poem 'The Borough'), produced London, Sadler's Wells, 7 June 1945. Fisherman Peter Grimes is accused of murder when his apprentices keep dying. Only Ellen Orford has faith in him, but that is not enough to stop the villagers from hounding him until he drowns himself.

Peter Ibbetson opera by Deems Taylor (libretto by composer and C Collier, based on George du Maurier's novel), produced New York Metropolitan Opera, 7 February 1931.

Peter Schmoll und seine Nachbarn/Peter Schmoll and his Neighbours opera by Weber (libretto by J Turk, based on a novel by Carl Gottlob Cramer), produced Augsburg, March 1803.

Peterson-Berger, Wilhelm (1867–1942) Swedish composer. He wrote music criticism 1896–1930 and was stage manager of the Stockholm Opera 1908–10. He translated Wagner's *Tristan und Isolde* and was influenced by Wagner in his own stage works. His *Arnljot* 1910 is a national opera which has frequently been revived.

He studied at the Stockholm Conservatory 1886–89, and in Dresden with Hermann Kretzschmar (1848–1924).

Works include: five symphonies (1889–1933), violin concerto (1928) and 100 piano pieces, including *Frösöblomster* (1896); song collection *Svensk lyrik.*

Petite messe solennelle/Little Solemn Mass Mass setting by Rossini for soloists, chorus, two pianos, and harmonium; composed 1863, first performed Paris 14 March 1864. Arranged with full orchestra, 1867, first performed Paris, 24 February 1869.

Petites Liturgies de la Presence Divine, Trois see ◊*Trois Petites Liturgies.*

Petite Symphonie Concertante work by Frank Martin for harp, harpsichord, piano, and double string orchestra; composed 1944–45, first performed Zurich, 17 May 1946. Version with full orchestra in place of solo instruments, Symphonie Concertante, 1946.

Petits Riens, Les/The Little Nothings ballet by Mozart, K299b (choreographed by Jean Noverre), written in Paris and produced there, Opéra, 11 June 1778.

Petrarch, Francesco (1304–1374), or Petrarca Italian poet. There are three sonnets set as songs by Schubert in translation by A W Schlegel and three *Sonetti di Petrarca* in Liszt's *Années de Pèlerinage* for piano, arranged 1846 from earlier settings of the poems for voice and piano. Many settings by Italian 16th–17th-century madrigalists.

Petrassi, Goffredo (1904–) Italian composer. His music makes individual use of 12-note methods. Though mainly an instrumentalist, his big choral works, *Psalm IX* 1934, *Coro di morti* 1940, and *Noche oscura* 1950, were of prime importance.

He born at Zagarolo, near Rome, and learnt music as a child in the singing-school of the church of San Salvatore in Lauro at Rome. He only began to study music systematically at the age of 21, when he entered the Conservatorio di Santa Cecilia, winning composition and organ prizes there. He came under the influence of Casella and Hindemith, and in 1933 made his composition debut with a performance of his orchestral Partita at the Augusteo, which was later given at the International Society for Contemporary Music festival in Amsterdam. In 1939 he became professor of composition at his former school. He continued as a brilliant orchestral composer (writing seven concertos for orchestra) in the Neo-Classical idiom until the early 1950s. Eventually his style became outmoded, but in the late 1950s he renewed his prominence with a succession of smaller instrumental works in an avant-garde idiom.

Works include: the operas *Il Cordovano* (1949) and *La morte dell' aria* (1950); ballet *Il ritratto di Don Chisciotte* (after Cervantes, 1947); incidental music for A Aniante's play *Carmen*; Psalm ix for chorus and orchestra; *Il coro dei morti* and *Noche oscura* for chorus (1940); Magnificat for voice and orchestra (1940); Partita, Passacaglia, concertos, and concert overture for orchestra (1933–72); *Tre Cori* for chamber orchestra; piano concerto; *Lamento d'Arianna* (Rinuccini) for voice and chamber orchestra (1936), *Introduzione ed Allegro* for violin and 11 instruments (1933); *Sinfonia, Siciliana e Fuga* for string quartet; *Preludio, Aria e Finale* for cello and piano; toccata for piano, *Siciliana e Marcetta* for piano duet; song cycle *Colori del tempo* and other songs.

Petrić, Ivo (1931–) Slovenian composer. He studied at the Ljubljana Academy. His early music was neoclassical in inspiration; he later employed aleatory techniques and tone clusters.

Works include: three symphonies (1954, 1957, 1960), Concerto Grosso (1955), Concertante music (1962), *Dialogues Concertantes* for cello and orchestra (1972), *Three Images* for violin and orchestra (1973), *Fresque Symphonique* (1973); three wind quintets, chamber concerto (1966), *Quatuor 69* for string quartet.

Petridis, Petro (1892–1977) Greek composer. He studied at Constantinople and in Paris.

Works include: the opera *Zemfyra* (1923–25); ballet; five symphonies (1928–51), dramatic symphony *Digenis Afrikas*, Greek and Ionian Suites, Elegiac Overture, *Prelude, Aria and Fugue* for orchestra; two piano concertos, cello concerto, concerto grosso for wind instruments, violin concerto (1977); piano trio; two *Modal Suites* for piano; songs.

Petrus de Cruce (fl. c. 1290) composer, possibly from Amiens. His mensural theory is expounded in the works of Robert de

Handlo and J Hanboys. Two motets from the Montpellier manuscript can be assigned to him on the authority of the *Speculum Musicum* by Jacobus of Liège.

Petrushka ballet by Stravinsky (scenario by composer and A Benois; choreography by Fokin), produced Paris, Théâtre du Châtelet, 13 June 1911. New version in four parts with 15 movements written 1946; three dances for piano 1921, dedicated to Arthur Rubinstein; *Russian Dance, In Petrushka's's Cell, The Shrovetide Fair.*

Petrželka, Vilém (1889–1967) Czech composer. He studied with Novák in Prague and Janáček at Brno, became a conductor at Pardubice and in 1919 went to Brno as professor at the Conservatory.

Works include: the symphonic drama *Sailor Nicholas* (1928); *Hymn to the Sun* for chorus and orchestra; Symphony (1956), *Eternal Return*, two suites, Dramatic Overture for orchestra; five string quartets (1909–15), fantasy and suite for string quartet; sonata and *Intimate Hours* for violin and piano; piano pieces; songs; part songs.

Pettersson, Gustaf Allan (1911–1980) Swedish composer. He is best known for the 16 symphonies he wrote 1950–80, which were influenced by Mahler.

He was born at Stockholm and studied at Stockholm Academy. After playing viola in a local orchestra 1940–51 he studied with Honegger and René Leibowitz in Paris. In the 1960s he was crippled by rheumatoid arthritis, but was able to continue composing. The passionate intensity of Petterson's music (notably the symphonies) recalls Mahler. His undoubted compositional skill cannot, however, dispel the rather morbid effect of its unrelieved and often strident pessimism.

Works include: three concertos for string orchestra (1949–57), violin concerto (1977); *Vox humana*, 18 songs for vocal soloists, chorus, and strings (texts by Native Americans, 1974); seven sonatas for two violins (1952).

petto (Italian 'chest') musical term; hence *voce di petto*, 'chest voice'.

Pevernage, André (1543–1591) Flemish composer. After holding an appointment at Courtrai 1565–85, he moved to Antwerp about 1587 and became choirmaster at the cathedral, holding the post until his death. Apart from cultivating church music, he held weekly concerts at his house.

Works include: *Cantiones sacrae* and other church music; madrigals and five volumes of chansons; ode to St Cecilia.

pezzo (Italian, plural *pezzi*) piece of music.

Pfeifertag, Der/The Piper's Day opera by Schillings (libretto by F von Sporck), produced Schwerin, 26 November 1899.

Pfitzner, Hans (1869–1949) German composer and conductor. After the success of his opera *Palestrina* in 1917 he devoted himself mainly to composition, but wrote many essays and pamphlets attacking modern music, especially Busoni, and defending Romantic and Germanic ideals.

Pfitzner grew up in Frankfurt, where his father, a violinist, was music director of the municipal theatre. He studied piano with James Kwast (1852–1927) and composition with Iwan Knorr at the Frankfurt Conservatory. In 1893 he gave a first concert of his own works in Berlin, and after some teaching and conducting appointments he became professor at the Stern Conservatory there in 1897, and first conductor at the Theater des Westens in 1903. He also conducted the Kaim orchestra at Munich and the Opera at Strasbourg. He was a political conservative and wrote *Krakauer Begrüssung* in honour of Hans Frank, Nazi governor of Poland.

Works include: the operas *Der arme Heinrich* (1895), *Die Rose vom Liebesgarten* (1901); *Christelflein* (1906), *Palestrina* (1917), *Das Herz* (1931); incidental music to Ibsen's *Feast at Solhaug* (1890) and Kleist's *Käthchen von Heilbronn* (1905); cantatas *Von deutscher Seele* (Eichendorff, 1922), *Das dunkle Reich* (1930) and others; three symphonies, scherzo for orchestra; piano concerto (1921), violin concerto (1923), two cello concertos (1935–44); ballads and songs for voice and orchestra; four string quartets (1886–1942), piano quintet, piano trio; violin and piano sonata, cello and piano sonata, sextet (1945); 106 Lieder (1884–1931).

Phaedra dramatic cantata for mezzo and orchestra by Britten (text by R Lowell, after Racine's *Phèdre*); composed 1975, first performed Aldeburgh, 16 June 1976, with Janet Baker.

Phaéton opera by Lully (libretto by Quinault), produced Versailles, 9 January and first performed Paris, 27 April 1683. Phaéton abandons his love Théone and wants Princess Libya. He rides recklessly around the sky in a chariot until Jupiter strikes him down with a thunderbolt.

Symphonic poem by Saint-Saëns, first performed Paris, 7 December 1873.

phagotus (Italian *fagotto* 'faggot, bundle') musical instrument developed from the Serbian bagpipe by Afranio Albonese of Pavia early in the 16th century. It consisted of two pipes like those of an organ, supplied with wind from hand bellows, and with a variable pitch produced by fingering on holes.

phantasy see ◊ fantasia.

Philémon et Baucis opera by Gounod (libretto by J Barbier and M Carré, after Ovid), produced Paris, Théâtre Lyrique, 18 February 1860. Elderly Philemon and Baucis are rewarded by Jupiter: he restores their youth. But the god falls in love with Baucis, and she requests old age again to dampen his amorous enthusiasm.

Philemon und Baucis, oder Jupiters Reise auf der Erde/Philemon and Baucis, or Jupiter's journey to Earth marionette opera by Haydn (libretto by G K Pfeffel), produced Eszterháza, 2 September 1773. Jupiter restores life to Narcissa and her lover Aret, the dead son of Philemon and Baucis, after the god finds shelter in the parents' home. He transforms the hut into a temple and Philemon and Baucis into priests.

Philharmonic Society group of people organized for the advancement of music; the term is derived from Greek 'love of harmony'. The Royal Philharmonic Society was founded in London 1813 by the pianist Johann Baptist Cramer (1771–1858) for the purpose of improving musical standards by means of orchestral concerts organized on a subscription basis. Another Philharmonic Society was founded in New York 1842.

Philips, Peter (1561–1628) English organist and composer. He was famous as an organist throughout the Netherlands, and was probably the best-known English composer in northern Europe. His collections of madrigals and motets are Roman in style, with Italianate word-painting and polyphony; they were reprinted many times in Antwerp.

Philips sang in the choir of St Paul's Cathedral as a boy. He left England in 1582, probably because he was a Roman Catholic; he was received there at the English College, where he became organist. He travelled in Italy and Spain, settled at Antwerp in 1590, and became a canon at the collegiate church of Soignies. In 1585 he entered the service of Lord Thomas Paget, and spent five years travelling through Italy, Spain, and France. He settled in Brussels in 1589, and on Paget's death in 1590, moved to Antwerp. In 1593, returning from a visit to hear Jan Sweelinck play in Amsterdam, he was arrested on suspicion of being involved in a plot to assassinate Queen Elizabeth; he was released. In 1597 he entered the household of the Archduke Albert in Brussels; he was appointed organist at the royal chapel there in 1611, and remained there until the Archduke's death in 1621. He was then appointed chaplain of the church of Saint-Germain at Tirlemont and in about 1623 became canon of Béthune, but may not have resided at either place.

Some of Philips' large output of keyboard music is preserved in the Fitzwilliam Virginal Book. It belongs to the English tradition, with the most inventive pieces being based on madrigals

Works include: Masses, 106 motets published in *Paradisus sacris cantionibus* (Antwerp, 1628), hymns, *Sacrae cantiones*; madrigals; fantasies, pavans, and galliards for various instruments; organ and virginal pieces.

Phillips, Peter (1953–) English choral director. With the Tallis Scholars, he has won renown for recordings of such works as Gesualdo's *Tenebrae Responsories*, *Missa Pastores* by Clemens non Papa, Byrd's *Great Service* and three Masses, the English anthems of Tallis, and the Masses of Josquin Desprez and Palestrina.

After studying at St John's College, Oxford, he founded the Tallis Scholars in 1978. They have given many concerts in Britain, Australia (Byrd's five-part Mass at the Sydney Opera House), and the USA (from 1988). They made their London Proms debut in 1988, with Victoria's Requiem, and toured the Far East in 1991. Phillips is the author of *English Sacred Music, 1549–1649* 1991.

Philosopher, The nickname of Haydn's symphony, no. 22 in E♭ major, composed 1764 and containing, exceptionally, parts for two cors anglais.

Philtre, Le/The Love Potion opera by Auber (libretto by Scribe), produced Paris, Opéra, 20 April 1831. ◊*Elisir d'amore, L'*.

Phinot, Dominique (c. 1510–c. 1555), or Finot French composer. He was associated with the courts of Urbino and Pesaro in Italy and wrote many motets and chansons.

Phoebus and Pan (Bach). See ◊*Streit zwischen Phöbus und Pan*.

phrase one of the most basic structural units of melody, equivalent or similar in instru-

mental terms to the amount of music a singer would sing in one breath. There is no fixed length for a phrase, but many traditionally fall into four-bar units. In the 19th century some composers such as Beethoven, Chopin, Liszt, and Wagner also favoured much longer phrases. Phrases are usually indicated by ◊slur markings and are performed ◊legato (smoothly and continuously) unless otherwise directed.

Phrygian cadence a cadence which owes its name to the fact that in the Phrygian mode (E-E) the sixth degree of the scale (D) was not sharpened by *musica ficta*, since this would have resulted in an augmented sixth with the note F, and altering F to F♯ would have destroyed the character of the mode.

This cadence was so firmly established that it survived the disappearance of the modes and acquired the flavour of a kind of imperfect cadence on the dominant of A minor. Transposed into any key that was required, it was widely used in the late 17th and early 18th centuries, particularly to mark a transition from one movement to another. This transition was not always harmonically obvious; it was common practice to use it at the end of a slow middle movement in a minor key in order to lead into a final movement in a major key. In Bach's Third Brandenburg Concerto it is used by itself without any middle movement at all.

Phrygian cadence on E.

Phrygian mode the third ecclesiastical mode, represented on the piano by the scale beginning with the note E played on the white notes.

physharmonica small reed organ invented by Anton Hackel of Vienna in 1818; a forerunner of the ◊harmonium.

piacevole (Italian 'pleasing', 'agreeable') term used in musical notation; similar to ◊dolce.

Pia de'Tolomei opera by Donizetti (libretto by S Cammarano), produced Venice, Teatro Apollo, 18 February 1837. Ghino is infatuated by his sister-in-law Pia, but denounces her as unfaithful when she does not succumb. Her husband Nello imprisons her and poisons her after mistaking her brother Rodrigo for a lover. Ghino confesses, but it is too late.

pianissimo (Italian 'very soft') a musical direction rarely written out in full, but indicated by the sign **pp** or a multiplication thereof.

piano, or pianoforte (originally **fortepiano**) stringed musical instrument played by felt-covered hammers activated from a keyboard. It is therefore a form of mechanized dulcimer, a percussion instrument, unlike the earlier harpsichord, a mechanized harp in which the strings are plucked. It is capable of dynamic gradation between soft (Italian *piano*) and loud (Italian *forte*) tones, hence its name. Although its beginnings go back to Italy at the end of the 16th century, the first piano was constructed in its present form in 1704, and introduced in 1709 by Bartolommeo Cristofori, a harpsichord maker from Padua. The piano uses a clever mechanism to make the keyboard touch-sensitive. Extensively developed during the 18th century, the piano attracted admiration among many composers, although it was not until 1768 that J C Bach gave one of the first public recmusics on the instrument.

Further improvements were gradually made in the keyboard and hammer action by makers such as Broadwood, Erard, and Graf, and the invention by English makers of the iron frame, which was capable of supporting a much greater tension of strings, resulted in the production of a more powerful tone. Together with a rapid expansion of published music by Haydn, Beethoven, Schubert, and others, this led to the development of the powerfully resonant concert grand piano and the mass production of smaller upright pianos for the home.

piano, or p (Italian 'soft') term used in musical notation.

Pianola trademark for a type of ◊player piano.

piano-organ, or handle-piano mechanical instrument similar to the barrel organ in the shape of an upright piano, producing its notes in the same way by a studded cylinder, but from strings struck by hammers instead of pipes.

It was widely used by street musicians in the larger English cities in the late 19th and early 20th centuries, especially in London. It was often wrongly called 'barrel organ' and even more incorrectly 'hurdy-gurdy'.

piano quartet quartet for piano, violin, viola, and cello. The earliest examples played today

are those by Mozart (K478 and K493). The quartet of Beethoven (op. 16) and three quartets of Brahms (op. 25, op. 26, op. 60) are worthy successors.

piano quintet usually a quintet for piano and string quartet (Brahms, Schumann, and Elgar), but Schubert's 'Trout' Quintet is for piano, violin, viola, cello, and double bass.

piano score see ◊full score.

piano trio trio for piano, violin, and cello.

Piave, Francesco Maria (1810–1876) Italian librettist. He studied briefly for the priesthood and for a time earned subsistence from a publisher. A collaboration with Verdi began in 1844 with *Ernani*. Other libretti for Verdi were *I due Foscari*, *Macbeth*, *Il corsaro*, *Stiffelio*, *Rigoletto*, *La Traviata*, *Simon Boccanegra*, *Aroldo* and *La Forza del Destino*. An abandoned project, *Allan Cameron*, was taken up with Pacini and produced in Venice, 1848. In the same year Piave's libretto for Mercadante's *La schiava Saracena/The Saracen Slave-Girl* was produced in Milan. Piave did not write libretti for Ponchielli, as has been stated elsewhere.

Picander see Christian Friedrich ◊Henrici.

Piccinni, Niccolò (1728–1800) Italian composer. He wrote over 120 operas, using many of Metastasio's libretti, and was a significant figure in the development of both French and Italian opera.

He studied at the Conservatorio di Sant' Onofrio at Naples, where he was taught by Leo and Durante. He produced his first opera at Naples in 1754. It was well received and was soon followed by other operas, both comic and serious. In 1756 he married the singer Vincenza Sibilia, his pupil. In 1760 his opera *La buona figliuola*, based on Richardson's novel *Pamela*, was an enormous notation in Rome. He enjoyed some years of success there before being ousted by his former pupil Pasquale Anfossi and returning to Naples in 1773.

In 1776 he was invited to Paris, where he was at first in great difficulties, but was helped by the author Jean Marmontel, who taught him French and wrote the libretto of his first French opera, *Roland* 1778. He was pitted against Gluck by partisans who liked to have something to quarrel about, and the feud between the Gluckists and Piccinnists, in which the composers themselves took no part, reached its height when in 1781 Piccinni set the libretto of *Iphigénie en Tauride*, which had already been used by Gluck.

At the Revolution he left for Italy, visited Venice, and then returned home to Naples, where he was placed under close surveillance and lived in great poverty. In 1798 he at last succeeded in returning to Paris. After a period of comparative affluence, he again fell into poverty, was relieved by a gift from Napoleon and an inspector's post at the Conservatory, but became paralysed and finally died in distress.

His son Luigi (1766–1827) and his grandson Louis-Alexandre (1779–1850) were both composers. The former wrote operas for Paris and Stockholm, the latter ballets and melodramas for the Paris theatres.

Works include: OPERA about 120, *Le donne dispettose* (1754), *Le Gelosie, Zenobia* (1756), *Alessandro nell' Indie* (two versions), *Madama Arrighetta* (1758), *La buona figliuola, La buona figliuola maritata* (both after Richardson's *Pamela*, 1760, 1761), *Il cavaliere per amore* (1762), *Le contadine bizarre, Gli stravaganti* (1764), *L'Olimpiade* (1761), *I viaggiatori* (1775), *La pescatrice* (1766), *Le finte gemelle, Vittorina* (Goldoni), *Roland, Atys, Iphigénie en Tauride,* (1781), *Didon* (1783), *Le Faux Lord* (1783), *Pénélope, Endymion* (1784).

OTHER oratorio *Jonathan* and three others; Mass, psalms, and other church music.

Piccola musica notturna/Little night Music

work for orchestra by Dallapiccola, first performed Hanover, 7 June 1954; arranged for eight instruments, 1961.

piccolo woodwind instrument, the smallest member of the ◊flute family, for which Vivaldi composed three concertos. Used adjectivally, 'piccolo' is also an alternative term for ◊sopranino.

Piccolo Marat, Il opera by Mascagni (libretto

by G Forzano and G Targioni- Tozzetti), produced Rome, Teatro Costanzi, 2 May 1921. Story deals with the aftermath of the assassination of Marat, when Paris was scourged by revolutionary fanatics: at the end of the World War II Mascagni was in disgrace for having supported Mussolini. The Prince of Fleury joins the revolutionary movement to save his mother from the guillotine. After freeing her he escapes with his revolutionary lover Mariella.

Picco pipe woodwind instrument of the ◊recorder or ◊flageolet type which became fashionable in England on being introduced to London in 1856 by a Sardinian player named Picco.

Pichl, Wenzel (1741–1805) Bohemian violinist and composer. He was admired by Cherubini and Adalbert Gyrowetz, and Haydn performed his quartets at Eszterháza.

He studied in Prague and in 1765 became violinist and vice-director of music (under Karl Dittersdorf) to the Bishop of Grosswardein. In 1769 he moved to Vienna and thence to Milan in the service of the Archduke Ferdinand, remaining in Italy until his return to Vienna in 1796.

Works include: according to Pichl's own catalogue, 12 operas, including 4 Latin operas (1765–76), 4 opera buffe, *Der Krieg* (1776) and Italian arrangements of French operas; over 30 Masses; 89 symphonies; about 30 concertos; 172 quartets, 21 quintets, and other pieces; 148 pieces for baryton.

Pictures at an Exhibition a suite of piano

pieces by Mussorgsky, composed in 1874 in memory of the painter and architect Victor Alexandrovich Hartmann (died 1873) and illustrating pictures and designs by him shown at a memorial exhibition, organized by V V Stassov. Orchestral versions of the work have been made by Henry J Wood, Ravel, Stokowski, and Walter Goehr; brass band arrangement by Elgar Howarth. First performance of Ravel orchestration, Paris, Opéra, 19 October 1922, conductor Koussevitzky.

pieno (Italian 'full') musical direction used especially in organ music in combination, *organo pieno,* meaning either that a figured bass is to be filled with ample harmony or that the instrument is to be played with full registration.

Pierné, (Henri Constant) Gabriel (1863–1937) French composer and conductor. His numerous ballets include *Cydalise et le chèvre-pied/Cydalise and the Satyr* 1923, containing the 'Entry of the Little Fauns'. As a conductor he gave many important first performances, including Debussy's *Khamma* 1924 and *La Boîte à joujoux* 1923.

He studied at the Paris Conservatory and won the Prix de Rome in 1882. In 1890 he succeeded César Franck as organist of the church of Sainte-Clotilde, became second conductor of Edouard Colonne's orchestra in 1903 and at Colonne's death in 1910 succeeded him as chief conductor.

Works include: the operas *Les Elfes, Pandore, La coupe enchantée* (after La Fontaine, 1905), *La nuit de Noël, Vendée, La fille de Tabarin, On ne badine pas avec l'amour* (after Musset, 1910), *Fragonard, Sophie Arnould* (1927); ballets, pantomimes, and incidental music; oratorios, suites for orchestra; piano quintet, piano trio; songs.

Pierrot lunaire Schoenberg's song-cycle with chamber ensemble, op. 21, consisting of 21 poems by Albert Giraud translated into German by Otto Erich Hartleben; composed 1912, first performed Berlin, 16 October 1912. The treatment of the voice-part is one of the outstanding examples of the use of 'Speech-song' (*Sprechgesang*). The 21 poems are arranged in three sections: 1: *Mondestrunken, Colombine, Der Dandy, Eine blasse Wäscherin, Valse de Chopin, Madonna, Der Kranke Mond.* 2: *Die Nacht, Gebet an Pierrot, Raub, Rote Messe, Galgenlied, Enthauptung, Die Kreuze.* 3: *Heimweh, Gemeinheit, Parodie, Der Mondfleck, Serenade, Heimfahrt, O alter Duft.* The work was commissioned by Albertine Zehme; it was soon admired by composers as different as Puccini and Stravinsky but wider public success did not come until a performance in Berlin on 5 January 1924, with Marie Gutheil-Schoder and Gregor Piatigorsky (cello), Artur Schnabel (piano), and Fritz Stiedry (conductor).

Pierson, Henry Hugh (or Heinrich Hugo) (1815–1873), originally Pearson English-born German composer. Educated at Harrow and Cambridge, he studied music with Attwood and Corfe, and interrupted a medical course to continue music studies at Leipzig, where he met Mendelssohn, Schumann, and others. He became Reid Professor of Music at Edinburgh in 1844 in succession to Bishop, but soon resigned and returned to Germany, where he remained, married Caroline Leonhardt and changed the spelling of his name.

Works include: the operas *Der Elfensieg* (1845), *Leila* (1848) and *Contarini* (composed 1853, produced 1872), *Fenice* (1883); incidental music to Goethe's *Faust* (Part II); oratorio *Jerusalem* (1852); *Macbeth* symphony (1859), overtures to Shakespeare's *Twelfth Night, Julius Caesar* and *Romeo and Juliet* (1874), funeral march for *Hamlet* (1859); numerous songs; part songs.

Piéton, Loyset (died after 1545) French composer. He wrote Masses, motets, psalms, and chansons; his work was published in Lyon and Venice.

He has often been confused with Compère, since both are usually called only by their first names.

pietoso (**Italian from *pietà*, 'pity'**) in musical direction, pityingly, compassionately.

Pietra del paragone, La/The Touchstone opera by Rossini (libretto by I Romanelli), produced Milan, La Scala, 26 September 1812. Count Asdrubale and Marchesina Clarice meet at a party; their affections grow. Each tests the other's sincerity with the help of disguises and they are united.

piffaro (**Italian 'fife'**) small flute-like pipe, also a shepherd's pipe similar to the oboe or bagpipe. It was often played in Italian cities, especially Rome and Naples, at Christmas time, by pipers from the hills.

They seem to have played tunes like that of the second section of Bach's *Christmas Oratorio* or the 'Pastoral Symphony' in Handel's *Messiah*, which bears the word 'pifa' in the manuscript, evidently in reference to the piffaro.

Pigheaded Peasants The/Tvrdé Palice oper by Dvořák (libretto J Stolba), produced Prague, Czech Theatre, 2 October 1881. Widower Vávra and widow Říhová decide their children, Toník and Lenka, should marry, and, knowing their children to be stubborn, use reverse psychology to coax them together.

Pijper, Willem (1894–1947) Dutch composer. He was influenced by the contemporary French school on the one hand, and by Mahler on the other. Despite obvious difficulty in reconciling these influences, he became the most important Dutch composer of his generation. His works include the operatic cantata *Halewijn* 1934, music for plays by Sophocles, Euripides, and Shakespeare, three symphonies, concertos, chamber music, sonatas for various instruments, piano music, and songs.

He studied with Johan Wagenaar and was appointed professor of composition at the Amsterdam Conservatory in 1925. He was director of the Rotterdam Conservatory from 1930 until his death.

Works include: the opera *Halewijn* (1933); incidental music for Euripides' *The Cyclops* and *The Bacchantes* (1924), Sophocles' *Antigone*, and Shakespeare's *Tempest* (1930); three symphonies, six symphonic Epigrams for orchestra, piano concerto (1927), violin concerto, cello concerto; five string quartets (1914–46), two piano trios, sextet for wind and piano; violin and piano sonatas; piano music; choruses; songs.

Pilgrim's Progress, The opera by Vaughan Williams (libretto by the composer after Bunyan), produced London, Covent Garden, 26 April 1951. It incorporates most of the composer's one-act opera *The Shepherds of the Delectable Mountains* (produced London, RCM, 11 July 1922). The Pilgrim faces many trials on his way to the Celestial City.

Pilkington, Francis (c. 1570–1638) English composer. Took the BMus at Oxford in 1595 and was soon after appointed as singer at Chester Cathedral where he remained to his death, becoming a minor canon in 1612.

Works include: anthems (one in Leighton's *Teares or Lamentacions*); madrigals and pastorals for three–six voices; lute pieces; songs to the lute.

Pimmalione/Pygmalion opera by Cherubini (libretto by S Vestris), produced Paris, Tuileries, at Napoleon's private theatre, for which it was written, 30 November 1809.

Pimpinone three intermezzos by Albinoni (libretto by P Pariati), produced with the opera *Astarto* Venice, 1708. As with Pergolesi's *La serva padrona*, the intermezzo is now better known than the *opera seria* for which it was intended to provide light relief. Vespetta persuades elderly Pimpinone to employ her as a servant. She then makes him promise to marry her, after which she seeks pleasure elsewhere.

Intermezzo by Telemann, produced Hamburg, 1725.

Pincherle, Marc (1888–1974) French musicologist. He was professor at the Ecole Normale de Musique in Paris and edited successively of *Le Monde musical* and *Musique*. His works include studies of Corelli, Vivaldi, the violin, and violin music.

Pinello di Gherardi, Giovanni Battista (c. 1544–1587) Italian composer. After an appointment at Vicenza Cathedral he went to Innsbruck in the 1570s as musician to the archduke, to the Imperial chapel in Prague soon afterwards and to the Saxon court at Dresden in 1580 in succession to Scandello, but was dismissed because of differences with other musicians, and returned to Prague.

Works include: motets, German Magnificats and other church music; madrigals and *canzone napoletane*; part songs.

Pinkham, Daniel (1923–) US composer, organist, and conductor. He studied with Walter Piston at Harvard and with Nadia Boulanger in Paris. He was music director of King's Chapel, Boston from 1958.

Works include: the chamber opera *The Garden of Artemis*, arrangement of *The Beggar's Opera* (1956), four symphonies, two violin concertos, *Wedding* and *Christmas Cantatas*, Requiem and *St Mark Passion* (1965), *Daniel in the Lion's Den* (1972), *The Passion of Judas* (1976), *A Curse, a Lament and a Vision* for chorus and piano (1984), *Getting to Heaven* for

soprano and chorus (1987), concerto piccolo (1989).

piobaireachd Scots Gaelic term meaning *piping*. Its Anglicized form *pibroch* denotes a specific category of music for the Scottish Highland pipes.

pipa four-string, plucked lute with a pear-shaped soundbox, found in China and Korea. Arrived in China from Central Asia during the Northern Wei dynasty. Used as a solo or ensemble instrument in a variety of genres.

pipe small woodwind instrument popular in the 13th century. A ♭whistle flute played only with the left hand, it freed the right hand to play the traditional accompanying drum, the tabor.

'Pipe' is also a generic term used to describe the hollow cylinder or cone of woodwind and brass instruments in which air vibrates to generate sound; or one of many tubes which make up some musical instruments, as in an organ pipe or panpipes.

pipe and tabor combination of two early musical instruments: a small pipe of the recorder type, but held with one hand only while the other beats the tabor, a small drum without snares hung round the player's shoulder or waist. The instruments have been revived for folk-dancing.

piped music, or Muzak (proprietary name) music recorded to strict psychological criteria for transmission in a variety of work environments in order to improve occupier or customer morale.

Pipelare, Matthaeus (lived 15th–16th centuries) Flemish composer. He wrote Masses, motets, and secular works to French and Dutch texts. His motet *Memorare mater Christi* commemorates the seven sorrows of the Virgin Mary.

In 1498 he became master of the choristers at 's-Hertogenbosch.

Pique-Dame the German title of Tchaikovsky's opera *The Queen of Spades/Pikovaya Dama*.

Pirame et Thisbé/Pyramus and Thisbe opera by Rebel and Francœur (libretto by J L I de La Serre), produced Paris, Opéra, 17 October 1726. Pyramus and Thisbe decide to run away together. Thisbe arrives at the rendezvous first but runs away when she sees a wounded lion. Pyramus arrives and, seeing the blood, believes Thisbe has been eaten. He stabs himself; she returns to find him and does likewise.

Pirata, Il/The Pirate opera by Bellini (libretto by F Romani), produced Milan, La Scala, 27

October 1827. Ernesto has forces Imogene to marry him despite her love for Gualtiero, who in desperation turns to piracy. Gualtiero is shipwrecked near Ernesto's castle. The lovers meet, but their joy is short lived: Gualtiero kills Ernesto and is sentenced to death.

Pirates of Penzance, The, or The Slave of Duty operetta by Sullivan (libretto by W S Gilbert), produced Paignton, Bijou Theatre, 30 December 1879); pirated performance, New York, Fifth Avenue Theatre, 31 December 1879; first London performance, Opéra-Comique, 3 April 1880. Frederic, mistakenly apprenticed to some pirates, intends to turn in the outlaws when he comes of age. However, he discovers he was born on 29 February in a leap year, and is consequently not yet 21; he must remain an apprentice.

Pirro, André (1869–1943) French musicologist. He studied law and literature in Paris and at the same time picked up as much musical education as he could, attending the organ classes of Franck and Widor. In 1896 he became professor and a director of the newly-opened Schola Cantorum. In 1904 he began to lecture at the Ecole des Hautes Etudes Sociales, and in 1912 succeeded Rolland as professor of music history at the Sorbonne. His books include studies of Schütz, Buxtehude, Bach (general and organ works), the French clavecinists, Descartes and music, early German church and secular music.

Pirro e Demetrio/Pyrrhus and Demetrius opera by A Scarlatti (libretto by A Morselli), produced Naples, Teatro San Bartolommeo, probably 28 January 1694.

Pirrotta, Nino (1908–   ) Italian musicologist. He studied at the Conservatories of Palermo and Florence; librarian of the S Cecilia Conservatory, Rome, 1948–56. Professor at Harvard (1956–72) and at Rome (1972–83). His major studies have been of 14th-century Italian music, including the ars nova, and 17th-century Italian opera.

Pisendel, Johann Georg (1687–1755) German violinist and composer. He studied with Vivaldi in Venice, and wrote concertos and pieces for the violin.

He was a choirboy at the chapel of the Margrave of Ansbach, and while there studied the violin under Giuseppe Torelli and theory under Francesco Pistocchi. After studying at Leipzig University he went to Dresden to enter the service of the king of Poland there in 1712, travelled widely with the king, became concert master in 1728 on the death of Jean Baptiste Volumier, and led the opera orchestra under Johann Hasse.

Pisk, Paul A(madeus) (1893–1990) Austrian-born US musicologist and composer. He studied under Adler at Vienna University and composition with Schreker and Schoenberg. After conducting at various German theatres, he returned to Vienna, conducting and broadcasting, and became director of the music department of the Volkshochschule, but left for USA 1936 and became professor of musicology at the University of Texas. In 1963 he joined the staff of Washington University, St Louis; he retired in 1973 and moved to Los Angeles. He edited early music including Masses by Jacobus Gallus, and wrote on modern music and the Second Viennese School.

Works include: the monodrama *Schattenseite* (1931); ballet *Der grosse Regenmacher* (1927); cantata *Die neue Stadt* (1926); Requiem for baritone and orchestra; Partita for orchestra, suite for small orchestra; *Bucolic Suite* for strings and other orchestral works; string quartet and other chamber music; piano music; songs with organ.

piston on a brass musical instrument, a valve which alters the length of tubing through which air vibrates, changing the pitch. The first valve lowers the pitch a whole tone, the second a semitone, the third three semitones. Most orchestral brass instruments today employ three valves, but sometimes a fourth is added.

Piston, Walter Hamor (1894–1976) US composer and teacher. His music follows European Neo-Classical models, often favouring contrapuntal textures; his works include eight symphonies, a number of concertos, chamber music, the orchestral suite *Three New England Sketches* 1959, and the ballet *The Incredible Flutist* 1938. He wrote a number of textbooks, including *Harmony* 1941 and *Orchestration* 1955.

Piston was born at Rockland, Maine. After studying at Harvard University, and in Paris with Nadia Boulanger, he returned to the USA and taught at Harvard 1926–60. He was well regarded as a teacher; his pupils included Leonard Bernstein. Piston's music is clear and finely disciplined, and has some affinities with ◊Stravinsky's Neo-Classical work.

Works include: the ballet *The Incredible Flutist* (1938); eight symphonies (1937–65), suite, concerto, Symphonic Piece, Prelude and Fugue for orchestra; concertino for piano and chamber orchestra (1937), clarinet concertino, two violin concertos (1939, 1960); *Carnival Song* for male chorus and brass instruments; five string quartets (1933–62), piano trio, three pieces for flute, clarinet, and bassoon; violin and piano sonata, flute and piano sonata, suite for oboe and piano, partita for violin, viola, and organ.

pitch how high or low a note is. This depends on the frequency of vibration of the sound and is measured in Hertz (Hz), or cycles per second. It also means the standard to which instruments are tuned, nowadays using the A above middle C (A4 or a') with a frequency of 440Hz as a reference tone. This is often known as ◊concert pitch.

Pitch can now be measured accurately by electronic tuning devices, which are beginning to replace the traditional tuning fork, but it is still normal practice for orchestras to tune to an oboe playing a', despite the inherent inaccuracy of this practice.

Absolute pitch (also called perfect pitch) is the ability to name any note heard, or to sing any note asked for. It is usually an ability that someone is born with, and is very difficult to acquire. A person who has perfect pitch does not necessarily have any other musical ability – in fact the majority of professional musicians do not have this gift.

For any musical tone, what determines its pitch is what the ear perceives as its fundamental frequency. In stringed instruments this is dependent on the length, tension, and composition of the vibrating string, and in wind instruments on the length of the tube. Some instruments, mainly in the percussion family, are of indefinite pitch and are referred to as 'untuned' instruments. In organ terminology, ranks of pipes are classified in wavelength pitch, such as 4-foot, 8-foot, or 16-foot, according to the octave range in which they fall.

An internationally recognized standard pitch of 440Hz at a' (the A above middle C) was set in 1955 by the International Organization for Standardization, ending centuries of confusion. Before this, pitch had varied at different times and from country to country, from 410Hz to 480Hz. Generally speaking, however, the trend was a gradual rise in standard pitch, often encouraged by wind-instrument makers anxious to achieve a more brilliant sound. This meant that music in the newer pitch sometimes became too high for singers, and also necessitated the modification of many of the stringed instruments designed for the old, lower pitch. Nearly all the great stringed instruments made by Antonio Stradivari, Joseph Guarneri, and the Amati family were converted to accommodate the new pitch. At times two pitches were in use, the higher for orchestral performances and the lower 'classical' or French pitch for church and purely vocal music. This French pitch, known also as 'diapason normal', had a' at 435Hz and was fixed in Paris in 1849.

pitch-class set, pc set group of notes considered entirely from the point of view of their pitch classes; that is, independently of their tonal function, the octave in which they occur, the order in which they occur, or the number of occurrences of each pitch in the set. By convention, pitch classes are numbered from 0 to 11, with $0 = C\natural/B\sharp$, $1 = C\sharp/D\flat$ and so on. Pitch-class sets are labelled with two digits, the first indicating the number of pitches in the set, and the second the number of the set in the list of all possible sets. For example, the pitches C, E, and G (0, 4, and 7) form the set 3–11. If transpositions and inversions of sets are considered to be equivalent to one another, the 12 chromatic notes can form a total of only 234 distinct pitch-class sets. Pitch-class set analysis describes music entirely on terms of the pitch-class sets identifiable in a piece and the relationships between these sets, and is principally used in the analysis of atonal music. See Allen ◊Forte; ◊set complex; ◊subset/superset; ◊similarity relation.

Pitoni, Giuseppe Ottavio (1657–1743) Italian composer. He wrote large quantities of church music, including a 16-part *Dixit Dominus* that is still sung at St Peter's, Rome, in Holy Week. He also wrote on the history and theory of music.

He studied with Pompeo Natale from an early age, and became a chorister at the churches of S Giovanni dei Fiorentini and SS Apostoli in Rome, where he was a pupil of Foggia. After church posts in Monterotondo and Assisi he became maestro di cappella at Rieti in 1676, and from the next year to his death at the Collegio San Marco in Rome, later also at the Lateran and St Peter's.

Works include: over 250 Masses, 780 psalm settings, Magnificats, motets, Litanies, two Passions.

Pittore parigino, Il/The Parisian Painter opera by Cimarosa (libretto by G Petrosellini), produced Rome, Teatro Valle, 4 January 1781. Eurilla must marry Baron Cricca if she is to receive her inheritance, but she falls in love with Crotignac, a painter. After first choosing money, Eurilla changes her mind and decides on Crotignac.

più (Italian 'more') term used in musical notation, as in *più mosso* ('more moved', 'faster') or *più lento* ('slower').

piuttosto (Italian 'somewhat, rather') word used with musical directions where the composer wishes to make sure that an indication of tempo or expression is obeyed in moderation.

Pixérécourt, René Charles Guilbert de (1773–1844) French dramatist and librettist, biographer of Dalayrac, author of melodramas with music. See ◊*Margherita d'Anjou* (Meyerbeer).

Pixis, Johann Peter (1788–1874) German pianist and composer. He lived in Paris for several years, and acquired a reputation as a gifted pianist and piano teacher.

He studied with his father, Friedrich Wilhelm Pixis (c. 1760–c. 1810), and began to appear as a pianist with his brother Friedrich Wilhelm Pixis (1786–1842), a violinist. He settled in Munich in 1809 and in Paris in 1823, where he became a noted piano teacher. In 1845 he bought a villa at Baden-Baden and continued to train pupils there. He adopted and trained the singer Franzilla Göhringer (born 1816); she created the title role in Pacini's opera *Saffo* in 1840.

Works include: the operas *Almazinde* (1820), *Bibiana* (1829) and *Die Sprache des Herzens* (1836); piano concertos; sonatas and pieces for piano, and other pieces.

Pizzetti, Ildebrando (1880–1968) Italian composer. He is remarkable as a composer of serious, heroic, rather austere operas, for which he wrote his own libretti, except for the first, Fedra (produced 1915), which is by Gabriele d'Annunzio. He also wrote incidental music for plays, film music, choral and orchestral works, chamber music, and songs.

Pizzetti was born at Parma, the son of a piano teacher. He studied at Parma Conservatory 1895–1901. In 1908 he was appointed professor of harmony and counterpoint at the Istituto Musicale at Florence, of which he became director 1917. In 1924 he was appointed director of the Conservatory Giuseppe Verdi, Milan, and in 1936 he succeeded Respighi as professor of advanced composition at the Accademia di Santa Cecilia in Rome.

Works include: STAGE operas *Fedra* (1915), *Debora e Jaele* (1922), *Lo straniero, Fra Gherardo* (1928), *Ifigenia* (radio opera, 1950), *Assassinio nella cattedrale* (after T S Eliot, 1958); incidental music for *La Nave* and *La Pisanella* (both by d'Annunzio).

ORCHESTRAL WORKS three symphonic preludes for Sophocles' *Oedipus Rex* and *Coloneus* (1903), *Concerto dell' estate* (1928), *Rondo veneziano* (1929).

CHORUS AND ORCHESTRA *Missa di Requiem* (1922) and *De profundis* for unaccompanied chorus (1937); *Due compositioni corali* (1961); *Cantico di gloria* (1966).

CHAMBER two string quartets (1906, 1933), piano trio; sonatas for violin and piano and for cello and piano; songs, including *Due Poesie di Ungaretti*, for baritone and piano trio, three with string quartet and 21 with piano, including *I Pastori* and *Altre cinque liriche*.

pizzicato (Italian 'pinched') in music, an instruction to pluck a bowed stringed instrument (such as the violin) with the fingers.

It is heard to advantage in the *Pizzicato Polka* 1870 by Johann Strauss II and Josef Strauss and in the 'Playful Pizzicato' of Benjamin Britten's *Simple Symphony* 1933–34.

pizzicato tremolando (Italian 'pinched and trembling') musical effect first used by Elgar in the cadenza of his violin concerto, where the orchestra strings play chords by thrumming the strings both ways across with the fingers of the right hand.

plainchant, or plainsong the medieval church music still surviving in some services of the Roman Catholic Church, properly sung in unison, without harmony and with no definitely measured rhythms. Its groupings of notes have, however, a strongly rhythmic character, but it resembles the free rhythm of prose, whereas that of measured music is comparable to the rhythm of verse. The old notation on a stave of four lines, with square or diamond-shaped notes and ligatures, is still used for plainsong. It was first codified by Ambrose, bishop of Milan, and then by Pope Gregory in the 6th century. See ◊Gregorian chant.

plainte (French 'complaint') lament or memorial piece, whether vocal or instrumental.

Plamenac, Dragan (1895–1983) US musicologist of Croatian origin. He studied law at the University of Zagreb, then composition with Schreker, musicology with Adler in Vienna and with Pirro in Paris, taking his doctorate in 1925. In 1939 he went to the USA, becoming Professor of Musicology at the University of Illinois in 1955. He published a number of studies of pre-classical music and edited the works of Okeghem.

Planché, James Robinson (1796–1880) English dramatist, librettist, and critic of

French descent. He lived in London and wrote a number of libretti including *Maid Marian* for Bishop, *Oberon* for Weber, and *The Surrender of Calais*, intended for Mendelssohn and later offered to H Smart, who left it unfinished.

Planets, The suite by Holst for orchestra with organ and (in final section) female chorus. 1. *Mars, the Bringer of War*; 2. *Venus, the Bringer of Peace*; 3. *Mercury, the Winged Messenger*; 4. *Jupiter, the Bringer of Jollity*; 5. *Saturn, the Bringer of Old Age*; 6. *Uranus, the Magician*; 7. *Neptune, the Mystic*. First (private) performance, London, Queen's Hall, 29 September 1918; first public performance, London, 15 November 1920. The idea of writing music on the planets was not new: Buxtehude wrote a harpsichord suite on them; but Holst dealt with them from the astrological aspect.

Planquette, (Jean) Robert (1848–1903) French composer. He studied briefly at the Paris Conservatory and then wrote songs that were performed at café-concerts. From this he passed on to operettas, the fourth of which, *Les cloches de Corneville* 1877, was immensely successful.

Works include: the operettas *Valet de cœur*, *Le serment de Mme Grégoire*, *Paille d'avoine* (1874), *Les cloches de Corneville* (1877), *Le Chevalier Gaston* (1879), *Les Voltigeurs de la 32me* (*The Old Guard*), *La Cantinière*, *Rip van Winkle* (after Washington Irving, 1882), *Nell Gwynne* (1884), *La cremaillère*, *Surcouf* (*Paul Jones*), *Capitaine Thérèse*, *La cocarce tricolore*, *Le talisman*, *Panurge* (after Rabelais, 1895), *Mam'zelle Quat' Sous*· (1897), *Le Paradis de Mahomed* (produced 1906).

Platée/Plataea comédie-ballet by Rameau (libretto by J Autreau and A J V d'Orville), produced Versailles, at court, 31 March 1745; first Paris performance, Opéra, 4 February 1749. Jupiter decides to cure Juno's constant jealousy: he woos the ugly but vain marsh-nymph Plataea, knowing that when Juno discovers Jupiter's new lover is ugly, she will realize how groundless her jealousy is. Juno appears just in time to stop the wedding, to Plataea's rage.

Plato (c. 428 BC–c. 348 BC) Greek philosopher. He outlined a system of 'harmony', as understood by the Greeks, in *Timaeus* and discussed the nature of the modes, from their supposed moral aspect, in *The Republic*.

Platti, Giovanni (1697–1763) Italian harpsichordist and composer. He made important contributions towards the development of a modern style of keyboard music. Little is known of his life, but from 1722 he was a composer and teacher in the service of the archiepiscopal court in Würzburg.

Works include: six Masses and other church music; oratorios, cantatas, and other choral pieces; sonatas for flute, and for cello; concertos and sonatas for harpsichord and other keyboard music.

player piano mechanical piano designed to reproduce key actions recorded on a perforated paper roll. The hammers are made to touch the strings not by action of the hand on the keyboard but by air pressure. This is regulated by a roll of perforated paper running over a series of slits corresponding with the musical scale and releasing the air only where the holes momentarily pass over the slits. The mechanism is set in motion by pedals like those of a harmonium.

Dynamics were at first controlled by the action of the players' hands, more or less roughly according to their skill, but they were later reproduced mechanically exactly as played by the recording artist. Debussy, Mahler, Grainger, and Stravinsky recorded their own works on piano roll. The concert **Duo-Art** reproducing piano encoded such detailed information that audiences were unable to distinguish a live performance from a reproduced performance. However, without a player, the player piano became simply a playback device for recordings, in which role it was superseded by the gramophone. In the 1950s–70s the US composer Conlon Nancarrow realized the instrument's potential for playing pieces that no human player could encompass – with strictly controlled tempo fluctuations, or extremely large numbers of notes – and produced his *Etudes for player piano*.

In 1986 the Viennese firm Bösendorfer produced an instrument which, it is claimed, can reproduce every nuance of a performance. Optical sensors scan the keys, hammers, and pedals 800 times a second and the registered information is fed into a computer. It is stored on tape or floppy disc and can be relayed back to the piano for 'performance'.

plectrum a device for plucking a string instrument. For a guitar or lute, it may be worn on the finger, as a substitute fingernail; others are held between two fingers, for example to play the mandolin. The harpsichord employs mechanical plectra of quill or leather to pluck the strings.

Most plectra are hard, but soft felt plectra are also used to ease abrasion of the ball of the finger. A plucked sound can be simulated on a synthesizer by programming an instantaneous or rapid onset, followed by a rapid decay and longer reverberation.

plein jeu (French 'full play') French equivalent of *organo pleno* (or *pieno*).

Pleyel, Camille (1788–1855) French piano maker, publisher, and pianist. He succeeded to his father's piano-making business in 1824 and associated himself with Friedrich Kalkbrenner. He was the husband of the French pianist Marie Moke and his father was Ignaz Joseph ◊Pleyel.

He studied music with his father and Jan Dussek and published some piano pieces.

Pleyel, Ignaz Joseph (1757–1831) Austrian pianist, piano maker, and composer. After travelling widely as a conductor and Kapellmeister (court music director), and composing a large number of popular pieces, he settled in Paris as a music publisher and in 1807 opened a piano factory. His son, Camille ◊Pleyel, succeeded him in the family business.

He studied with Johann Baptist Vanhal and Haydn, and in 1777 became Kapellmeister to Count Erdödy, who gave him leave for further study in Rome. In 1783 he moved to Strasbourg as vice-Kapellmeister, succeeding Franz Xaver Richter as Kapellmeister in 1789. Three years later he visited London as conductor of a rival series of concerts to those given by Salomon and Haydn. He settled in Paris in 1795, and in 1807 founded his piano factory.

Works include: two operas, *Die Fee Urgele* (produced Eszterháza, 1776) and *Ifigenia en Aulide* (produced Naples, 1785); 29 symphonies and five *sinfonie concertanti*; concertos; 45 string quartets and much other chamber music.

plica (Latin, for *plicare*, 'to fold') an ornamental passing note indicated in medieval notation by a vertical stroke at the side of the note. Its length was determined by the length of the stroke, its pitch by the context. According to theorists, it should be sung with a kind of quavering in the throat, but its convenience as an abbreviation led to its frequent employment as a substitute for a written note.

Pli selon pli 'Portrait de Mallarmé' for soprano and orchestra in five parts by Boulez. First performed Donaueschingen, 20 October 1962.

Plummer, John (c. 1410–c. 1484) English composer. His surviving works consist of four antiphons for two and four voices, a Mass, *Omnipotens Pater*, and a Mass fragment.

He was a clerk of the Chapel Royal by 1441 and in 1444 became the first official master of its children. In about 1458 he became verger at St George's Chapel, Windsor, while continuing as a member of the Chapel Royal; he held the Windsor post until 1484.

pneuma (Greek 'breath') vocal ornament in plainsong, inserting long cadential phrases on the syllables of certain words, notably 'Alleluia'. The pneuma were also called by the Latin name of *jubili*, and they developed later into tropes and sequences. Sometimes written *neuma*, by confusion with the word for ◊neume.

Pocahontas ballet by Elliott Carter; composed 1936–39, produced New York, 24 May 1939. Pocahontas (1595–1617) was a Native American princess who befriended the early settlers in America.

poco (Italian 'little') term used in musical notation, as in *poco crescendo* ('getting a little

Various plicas (left) with literal and modern equivalents (right).

louder') or *crescendo poco a poco* ('getting louder little by little').

Poème de l'amour et de la mer/Poem of love and of the sea work for mezzo and orchestra by Chausson (text by M Bouchor), composed 1882–90, revised 1893. The work's three sections are *La fleur des eaux*, *Interlude*, and *La mort de l'amour* (closing section *Le temps de lilas*).

Poèmes pour Mi/Poems for Mi cycle of nine songs for soprano and piano by Messiaen (texts by composer), first performed Paris, 28 April 1937; orchestral version 1937, performed Paris 1946, conductor Désormière. (Mi was the composer's name for his first wife.)

Poem of Ecstasy/Poema ekstasa work for orchestra by Skriabin; composed 1905–08, first performed New York, 10 December 1908; first Russian performance St Petersburg, 1 February 1909.

Poet's Echo, The cycle of six songs for high voice and piano by Britten (texts by Pushkin), first performed Moscow, 2 December 1965, with Vishnevskaya and Rostropovich.

Pohjola's Daughter symphonic poem by Sibelius, op. 49, composed 1906 and based on an incident in the *Kalevala*; first performed St Petersburg, Siloti concerts (conducted by composer), 29 December 1906.

poi (Italian 'then') term used in musical directions where some music section is to follow another in a way not made immediately obvious by the notation; for instance, after a repeat of an earlier section, *poi la coda* or *e poi la coda*.

pointillism a form of 1950s ◊serialism in which melody and harmony are replaced by complexes of isolated tones. Pointillism was inspired by Webern and adopted by Messiaen, Boulez, Nono, Stockhausen, and Stravinsky.

Although not strictly serial, the music of Iannis Xenakis and John Cage at this time is also pointillist in texture.

pointing the distribution of the syllables of the Psalms in Anglican chant according to the verbal rhythm.

Poise, (Jean Alexandre) Ferdinand (1828–1892) French composer. He studied with Adam and others at the Paris Conservatory and in 1853 produced his first opera.

Works include: the operas *Bonsoir Voisin* (1853), *Les Charmeurs* (1855); *Polichinelle* (1856), *Le Roi Don Pèdre*, *Le Jardinier galant* (1861), *Les Absents*, *Corricolo* (1868), *Les Trois Souhaits* (1861), *La Surprise de l'amour* (after Marivaux), *L'Amour médecin* (*after Molière, 1880*), *Les Deux Billets*, *Joli Gilles*, *Carmosine* (after Musset, produced 1928); oratorio *Cécile* (1888).

Poisoned Kiss, The, or The Empress and the Necromancer opera by Vaughan Williams (libretto by Evelyn Sharp), produced Cambridge Arts Theatre, 12 May 1936. Much of the score is a satire on various musical styles. Long ago the magician Dipsacus was abandoned by one-time love Persicaria. He plans revenge: to kill her son Amaryllus with a poisoned kiss from his daughter Tormentilla. But Amaryllus has the antidote and they all live happily ever after.

polacca (Italian 'polonaise') word often more loosely used for pieces in polonaise rhythm, but not necessarily in polonaise form, in which case they are actually, as indeed they are often designated, *alla polacca*.

Polidori, John William (1795–1821) English novelist, Byron's secretary and physician. See ◊*Vampyr, Der* (Lindpaintner and Marschner).

Polifemo opera by Giovanni Bononcini (libretto by A Ariosti), produced Berlin, Lietzenburg Palace, summer 1702.

poliphant, or polyphone string instrument of the lute or cittern type but with anything from 25 to 40 strings, invented around 1600 by Daniel Farrant and played by Queen Elizabeth I.

'Polish' Symphony Tchaikovsky's third symphony, in D major, op. 29, finished August 1875 and produced Moscow, 19 November 1875. The finale is in polonaise rhythm.

Poliuto, later Martyrs and I martiri opera by Donizetti (libretto devised by A Nourrit and written by S Cammarano, based on Corneille's tragedy *Polyeucte*), finished 1838 for production at Naples, but forbidden by censor; produced in French (translation by Scribe), Paris, Opéra, 1 April 1840. In 3rd-century Armenia, Poliuto is converted to Christianity, but is captured by Callistene, the high priest of Jupiter. His wife Paolina cannot convince him to renounce his faith, and joins him in death.

polka Bohemian dance in quick duple time (2/4). Originating in the 19th century, it became popular throughout Europe. The basic step is a hop followed by three short steps. The polka spread with German immigrants to the USA, becoming a style of Texas country music. It was also used by European composers Smetana (in *The Bartered*

Bride 1866, *Bohemian Dances* 1878), Dvořák, and others.

From about 1830 it became fashionable in European society.

Pollarolo, Antonio (1676–1746) Italian composer. He was a pupil of his father, Carlo ◊Pollarolo. He became assistant maestro di cappella at St Mark's, Venice in 1723, and maestro di cappella in 1740.

Works include: the operas *Aristeo, Leucippo e Teonoe, Cosroe, I tre voti,* and ten others; church music.

Pollarolo, Carlo Francesco (1653–1723) Italian organist and composer. He was a popular composer of operas in his day, writing over 80 in all, though only about 20 have survived. He was the father of Antonio ◊Pollarolo.

He was taught by Giovanni Legrenzi at Venice, became a singer at St Mark's there in 1665, second organist in 1690, and assistant maestro di cappella in 1692. He was director of music at the Conservatorio degli Incurabili from 1696.

Works include: the operas, including *Roderico* (1686), *La forza dela virtù* (1693), *Ottone* (1694), *Faramondo, Semiramide* (1713), *Marsia deluso, Ariodante* (1716), *Le pazzie degli amanti, Gl'inganni felici, Santa Genuinda* (with Violone and A Scarlatti, 1694), most lost; 12 oratorios; organ music.

Polly ballad opera, sequel to *The Beggar's Opera* (words by John Gay), published 1729, but not allowed to be performed. Produced London, with the music arranged by Arnold, Little Haymarket Theatre, 19 June 1777. Modern version by F Austin, produced London, Kingsway Theatre, 30 December 1922. Polly Peachum and Macheath are exiled in the West Indies, where they meet plantation hands, pirates, and Indians.

polonaise Polish dance in stately 3/4 time that was common in 18th-century Europe. Chopin developed the polonaise as a pianistic form.

Polonia symphonic prelude for orchestra by Elgar, op. 76, written for a concert given for the Polish Relief Fund, London, 6 July 1915, and dedicated to Paderewski, a quotation from whose *Polish Fantasy* it contains as well as one from Chopin and the Polish National Anthem.

Polyeucte opera by Gounod (libretto by J Barbier and M Carré, based on Corneille's drama), produced Paris, Opéra, 7 October 1878.

See also ◊*Poliuto*.

polyphone alternative name for the poliphant, a musical instrument.

polyphony music combining two or more 'voices' or parts, each with an individual melody. A polyphony of widely separated groups is called **antiphony**.

It is also the ability of a synthesizer to play more than one note at a time. If the synthesizer can produce more than one type of sound – for example, a flute and a guitar – simultaneously, it is **multi-timbral**.

polyrhythm combination of different rhythmic formations.

polytonality an overlapping of multiple parts in different keys, associated in particular with Darius ◊Milhaud whose miniature *Serenade* for orchestra 1917–22 combines up to six major keys. Two keys superimposed is bitonality.

The effect is akin to multiplexing, allowing the ear to fasten on any one line at will, but the combination effect is less coherent.

Pomo d'oro, Il/The Golden Apple opera by Cesti (libretto by F Sbarra), produced Vienna, Carnival 1667, for the wedding of the Emperor Leopold I and the Infanta Margherita of Spain (reputed to be the most expensive opera production ever mounted). Discord throws a golden apple, inscribed 'to the most beautiful', to Juno, Athena and Venus. Paris judges Venus the most beautiful after she offers him Helen. Disarray amongst the goddesses until Jupiter puts and end to the bickering.

Pomone opera by Cambert (libretto by P Perrin), produced Paris, Opéra, 3 March 1671.

Pomp and Circumstance five military marches by Elgar, originally intended as a set of 6, op. 39. 1–4 composed 1901–07, 5 in 1930. The first contains, as a trio, the tune afterwards used in the *Coronation Ode* to the words 'Land of hope and glory'. The title of the set comes from *Othello*, III iii: 'pride, pomp and circumstance of glorious war'. Nos. 1 & 2 first performed Liverpool, 19 October 1901; no. 3 first performed London, 8 March 1905; no. 4 first performed London, 24 August 1907; no. 5 first performed London, 20 September 1930.

pomposo (Italian 'pompous, stately') direction used for music of a sumptuous character.

Ponce, Manuel (1882–1948) Mexican composer. He is best known for his guitar music, performed by Segovia and others.

He learnt music from his sister at first, became cathedral organist at Aguas Calientes, and at 14 composed a gavotte which was later made famous by the dancer Argentina. He entered the National Conservatory at Mexico City and in 1905 went to Europe for further study with Enrico Bossi at Bologna and Martin Krause in Berlin. In 1906 he returned home and became professor at the National Conservatory. He lived at Havana 1915–18 and at the age of 43 went to Paris to take a composition course with Dukas.

Works include: symphonic triptych *Chapultepec* (1929), *Canto y danza de los antiguos Mexicanos* (1933), *Poema elegiaco, Ferial* for orchestra (1940); piano concerto, violin concerto (1943), concerto for guitar and chamber orchestra (1941); three Tagore songs with orchestra; *Sonata en duo* for violin and viola; two Mexican Rhapsodies and many other piano works; numerous songs.

Ponchielli, Amilcare (1834–1886) Italian composer. His masterpiece, *La Gioconda*, based on Victor Hugo's Angelo, was produced at La Scala, Milan, in 1876; its inspired melody and strong dramatic characterization established him as a worthy successor to Verdi.

Ponchielli was born near Cremona. He studied at the Milan Conservatory 1843–54 and produced his first opera, based on Manzoni's famous novel *I promessi sposi*, at Cremona in 1856. In 1881 he was appointed maestro di cappella at Bergamo Cathedral.

Works include: the operas *I promessi sposi* (1856); *La Savoiarda* (1861), *Roderico* (1863), *Bertrand de Born, Il parlatore eterno* (1873), *I Lituani (Aldona)*, *Gioconda* (after Hugo's *Angelo*, 1876), *Il figliuol prodigo* (1880), *Marion Delorme* (on Hugo's play, 1885), *I Mori di Valenza*, unfinished; produced Monte Carlo, 1914; ballets *Le due gemelle* and *Clarina*; cantatas for the reception of the remains of Donizetti and Mayr at Bergamo and in memory of Garibaldi.

Poniatowski, Rotondo (1816–1873) Polish composer and tenor. He studied at the Liceo musicale at Florence and under Ceccherini. He sang at the Teatro della Pergola there and produced his first opera there in 1839, singing the title part. After the 1848 Revolution he settled in Paris, but after the Franco-Prussian war he followed Napoleon III to England, in 1871.

Works include: the operas *Giovanni da Procida* (1838), *Don Desiderio* (1840), *Ruy Blas* (after Hugo), *Bonifazio de' Geremei (I Lambertazzi*, 1843), *Malek Adel* (1846), *Esmeralda* (after Hugo's *Notre-Dame de Paris*, 1847), *La sposa d'Abido* (after Byron's *Bride of Abydos*), Pierre

de Médicis (1860), *Gelmina* (1872) and others; Mass in F major.

Ponte, Lorenzo da Italian poet and librettist, see Lorenzo ◊Da Ponte.

ponticello (Italian 'little bridge') in string instruments, the bridge over which the strings are stretched to keep clear of the body of the instrument. The direction *sul ponticello* 'on the bridge' indicates that the bow is to be drawn close to the bridge, which results in a peculiar nasal tone.

pont-neuf (French 'new bridge') satirical song of the 18th century similar to the vaudeville, sung in public mainly on the Pont-Neuf in Paris.

Poole, Geoffrey (1949–) English composer. He studied at Southampton University with Jonathan Harvey and with Goehr at Leeds. He was senior lecturer at Manchester University from 1989. He received commissions from the Hallé Orchestra and London Sinfonietta.

Works include: *Fragments* for strings (1974); *Visions* for orchestra (1975); *Crow Tyrannosaurus* for soprano and ensemble (1975); *Chamber Concerto* (1979); *Machaut-Layers* for voice and ensemble (1980); *Biggs v Stomp does it again and again* ... music theatre (1981); *The Net and Aphrodite*, symphonic poem (1982); *Cummings Choruses* (1985); *Sailing with Archangels* for wind band (1990); two string quartets (1983, 1990); *In Beauty May I Walk*, vocal duo with strings (1990); *The Magnification of the Virgin*, for female consort and 12 instruments (1992); *Blackbird*, oratorio (1993).

Poot, Marcel (1901–1988) Belgian composer. He became interested early in film, radio, and jazz music, and in 1935 founded the group known as Les Synthétistes.

He studied at the Brussels Conservatory. In 1930 he won the Rubens Prize and went to Paris to study with Dukas. On his return he held several teaching posts, including at the Brussels Conservatory, of which he became director in 1949.

Works include: the operas *Het Ingebeeld Eiland* (1925), *Het Vrouwtje van Stavoren* (1928), and *Moretus* (1944); ballets *Paris in verlegenheid* (1925) and *Pygmalion* (1951); oratorios *Le Dit du routier* and *Icaros*; six symphonies (1929–78) and other orchestral works; chamber music, and other pieces.

Pope, Alexander (1688–1744) English poet. His works inspired Handel's ◊*Acis and Galatea*, ◊*Jephtha*, and ◊*Semele*.

pop music, or popular music any contemporary music not categorizable as jazz or classical.

Characterized by strong rhythms of African origin, simple harmonic structures often repeated to strophic melodies, and the use of electrically amplified instruments, pop music generically includes the areas of rock, country and western, rhythm and blues, soul, and others. Pop became distinct from folk music with the advent of sound-recording techniques; electronic amplification and other technological innovations have played a large part in the creation of new styles. The traditional format is a song of roughly three minutes with verse, chorus, and middle eight bars.

history Before 1920 the singer Al Jolson was one of the first recording stars. ◊Ragtime was still popular. In the 1920s, in the USA Paul Whiteman and his orchestra played jazz that could be danced to, country singer Jimmie Rodgers reached a new record-buying public, and the ◊blues were burgeoning; in the UK popular singers included Al Bowlly (1899–1941), born in Mozambique. The 1930s saw crooner Bing Crosby and vocal groups such as the Andrews Sisters as alternatives to swing bands. Rhythm and blues evolved in the USA in the 1940s, whilst Frank Sinatra was a teen idol and Glenn Miller played dance music. The UK preferred such singers as Vera Lynn.

1950s In the USA in the early 1950s doo-wop group vocalizing preceded rockabilly, the earliest form of rock and roll, epitomized by the records of Elvis Presley, Little Richard, Chuck Berry, and the Everly Brothers. British pop music · remained derivative, and US records dominated the charts. At the end of the 1950s the Motown label made its first impact with hits by the Miracles and Marvelettes, and a dance craze, 'the twist', enjoyed a brief popularity.

1960s In 1962, The Beatles emerged as leaders of the new 'beat' groups and, while restoring the excitement of early rock, introduced a new element of sophistication. British rhythm and blues developed from 1963, its principal exponents being The Animals and The Rolling Stones. Bob Dylan's mature, poetic songwriting achieved commercial success, although British groups largely dominated the US charts. Psychedelic rock came to prominence on both sides of the Atlantic with groups such as The Doors, and Pink Floyd. Jimi Hendrix produced a new and exciting improvisational rhythm and blues which achieved world success, paving

the way for the later popularity of such 'heavy' rock groups as Led Zeppelin. Frank Zappa's Mothers of Invention, perhaps the most accomplished of the new groups, fused elements of jazz, symphonic, and avant-garde music. Conventional pop during this time relied on gospel-derived soul music, and Motown groups including The Supremes and The Four Tops.

1970s By the end of 1971, after the disbandment of the Beatles, and deaths of Jimi Hendrix, Janis Joplin, and Jim Morrison, it seemed that pop music was changing dramatically. The first half of the decade produced glam rock, most notably by David Bowie, heavy metal, and disco. Reggae music from Jamaica also gained wide popularity. From 1976 punk was ascendant, a harsh and aggressive style best exemplified by the Sex Pistols. The US term New Wave encompassed bands not entirely within the punk idiom (Talking Heads, Elvis Costello).

1980s Dance music developed regional US variants, most notably hip-hop in New York and house in Chicago. Live audiences grew, leading to 'stadium rock' (U2, Bruce Springsteen) and increasingly elaborate stage performances (Michael Jackson, Prince, Madonna). An interest in world music sparked new fusions.

1990s Rap, hard rock, and heavy metal predominated in the USA at the start of the decade. On the UK indie scene, guitar and dance music were increasingly merged, notably by Manchester bands including The Stone Roses and Happy Mondays. Minimalist techno dance music gained popularity; in UK clubs **jungle** crossed this with reggae. Grunge music emerged from Seattle, Washington, USA, with bands including Nirvana. The mid-1990s saw a resurgence of interest in British bands, centred around groups such as Oasis and Blur; Portishead and other English groups pioneered **trip-hop**.

Porgy and Bess classic US folk opera written 1935 by George and Ira Gershwin, based on the novel *Porgy* 1925 by DuBose Heyward, a story of the black residents of Catfish Row in Charleston, South Carolina.

Poro, rè dell' Indie/Porus, King of the Indies opera by Handel (librettist unknown, altered from Metastasio's *Alessandro nell' Indie*), produced London, King's Theatre, Haymarket, 2 February 1731. Porus faces defeat at the hands of Alexander the Great, fearing especially that he will lose his love, Cleophis, to the invader. A story of jealousy and passion before Alexander realizes the depth of feeling between Porus and Cleophis, and blesses their union.

Porpora, Nicola Antonio (1686–1768) Italian composer and singing teacher. His works are chiefly vocal pieces, and include about 50 operas, as well as cantatas and oratorios. He travelled extensively in Europe as a teacher and conductor.

Porpora was born at Naples, and studied there under Gaetano Greco and his assistants, M Giordano and O Campanile at the Conservatorio dei Poveri di Gesú Cristo, where his first opera, *Agrippina*, was produced in 1708. At first maestro di cappella to the Imperial Commandant in Naples, Prince Philip of Hesse-Darmstadt, he was appointed singing teacher at the Conservatorio di S Onofrio there in 1715, and ten years later became maestro at the Conservatorio degli Incurabili in Venice. Among his pupils were the castrati singers Farinelli and Caffarelli, and, briefly, the composer Johann Hasse. Travelling as an opera conductor, he rivalled Handel in London 1733–36 and Hasse in Dresden 1748–52. In Vienna Haydn was his pupil-valet. Porpora finally returned to Naples in 1760; he taught for a year at the Conservatorio di Sant' Onofrio, but after that fell on hard times and died in extreme poverty.

Works include: about 50 operas, *Basilio* (1713), *Berenice* (1718), *Flavio Anicio Olibrio*, *Faramondo* (1719), *Eumene*, *Amare per regnare* (1723), *Semiramide* (1724), *Semiramide riconosciuta*, *L'Imeneo* (1726), *Adelaide*, *Siface*, *Mitridate* (1730), *Annibale* (1731), *Il trionfo di Camilla*, *Arianna* (1733), *Temistocle* (1743), *Filandro*; oratorios *Il martirio di Santa Eugenia* (1721) and eight others; Masses, motets, duets on the Passion and other church music; cantatas; violin sonatas; keyboard music.

Porta, Costanzo (c. 1529–1601) Italian monk and composer. He was a pupil of Adrian Willaert at Venice. He took holy orders and became choirmaster at Osimo near Ancona 1552–64, then went to Padua to take up a similar post at the Cappella Antoniana, the church of the Minorite order to which he belonged. He left for a time to work at Ravenna 1567–74, then at Loreto 1574–80. He returned to Ravenna 1580–89.

Works include: 15 Masses, 200 motets, psalms, hymns, introits, and other church music, five books of madrigals 1555–86.

Porta, Giovanni (c. 1690–1755) Italian composer. He worked in Rome 1706–16 in the service of Cardinal Ottoboni, then at the Conservatorio della pietà in Venice. He also visited London, where his opera *Numitore* was produced in 1720. From 1736 to his death he was Kapellmeister to the court in Munich.

Works include: over 30 operas, *Arianna* (1723), *Antigono* (1724), *Ulisse* (1725), and *Semiramide* (1733); oratorios; cantatas; 19 Masses and other church music.

portamento (Italian 'carrying') in singing and on string instruments, an expressive device in which one note is 'carried' to the next by a slide, without an interruption of tone production. It is sometimes indicated by a ◊slur connecting the two notes, but is usually freely interpreted by a performer. It was used more frequently in the first half of the 20th century and earlier, when musical expression was more pronounced.

portative organ small organ with a single keyboard and one range of pipes, which can be carried, placed on a table, or suspended from the shoulder by a strap. It is often represented in medieval and Renaissance paintings.

portato (Italian 'carried') in music, a type of articulation midway between ◊staccato (detached) and ◊legato (tied). It is indicated by a ◊slur over the notes, each of which is marked by a staccato dot.

Porter, (William) Quincy (1897–1966) US composer. He studied at Yale University and School of Music with H Parker and D S Smith, later with Bloch and with d'Indy in Paris. He taught at the Cleveland Institute of Music for two periods during 1922–32, at Vassar College, Poughkeepsie, 1932–38, and at the New England Conservatory at Boston from 1938. He also played viola in various string quartets.

Works include: incidental music for Shakespeare's *Antony and Cleopatra* (1934) and T S Eliot's *Sweeney Agonistes* (1933); symphony, *Poem and Dance* for orchestra; *Ukrainian Suite* for strings (1925); *Dance in Three Time* for chamber orchestra (1937); viola concerto, harpsichord concerto (1959), concerto for two pianos; three Greek Mimes for voices, string quartet and percussion; nine string quartets (1923–58); two violin and piano sonatas, suite for viola solo.

Porter, Andrew (1928–) English music critic and scholar. He studied at Oxford University and worked for various newspapers and journals from 1949 (edited *Musical Times* 1960–67). He is noted for his research on Verdi and has prepared for performance much material for *Don Carlos* which Verdi discarded at the first production in 1867; he worked on several translations of Verdi's libretti. His translation of Wagner's *Ring* was heard at the Coliseum, London, in 1973, and his version of the *Parsifal* libretto was given there in 1986. Critic for the *Observer* from 1992; five volumes of criticism were published 1974–91.

Porter, Walter (c. 1588–1659) English composer. He became a Gentleman of the Chapel Royal in London in 1617. At some time, probably earlier, he was a pupil of the Italian composer Monteverdi. In 1639 he became choirmaster at Westminster Abbey and when the choral service was suppressed in 1644 came under the patronage of Sir Edward Spencer.

Works include: motets for two voices and instruments, psalms (George Sandys' paraphrases) for two voices and organ; madrigals and airs for voices and instruments (published 1632).

Portinaro, Francesco (c. 1520–after 1578) Italian composer. He was associated with the *Accademia degli Elevati* at Padua in 1557, and later with the d'Este family at Ferrara and Tivoli. His three books of motets and six of madrigals were published at Venice.

Portman, Richard (died c. 1655) English organist and composer. He was a pupil of Orlando Gibbons, and succeeded Thomas Day as organist of Westminster Abbey, London, in 1633. Like Walter Porter, who was choirmaster, he lost this post with the suppression of the choral service in 1644 and became a music teacher.

Works include: services, anthems; *Dialogue of the Prodigal Son* for two voices and chorus, meditation; *The Soules Life, exercising itself in the sweet fields of divine meditation*; harpsichord music, and other pieces.

Portsmouth Point concert overture by Walton, inspired by Rowlandson's drawing, first performed at the International Society for Contemporary Music (ISCM) Festival, Zurich, 22 June 1926.

Portugal, Marcus Antonio da Fonseca (called Portogallo in Italian) (1762–1830) Portuguese composer. He wrote about 50 operas, both Portuguese and Italian. He was court music director at Lisbon, followed the court when it moved to Brazil in 1810, and continued to enjoy success as a composer at Rio de Janeiro.

He was educated at the Patriarchal Seminary at Lisbon, where later he became cantor and organist, and learnt music from Joño de Sousa Carvalho. He was also a theatre conductor and in 1785 produced his first stage work. In 1792 he went to Naples and began to write Italian operas in great numbers. In 1800 he returned to Lisbon to become director of the San Carlos Theatre, where he continued to write for the stage. In 1807 the French invasion drove the court to Brazil, and he followed it in 1810, but was unable to return with it in 1821, being incapacitated by a stroke.

Works include: *Licença pastoril, A Castanheira* and 20 other Portuguese operas; *La confusione nata della somiglianza* (1793), *Demofoonte* (1794), *Lo spazzacamino principe, La donna di genio volubile* (1796), *Fernando nel Messico* (1799), *Alceste, La morte di Semiramide* (1801), *Non irritare le donne, L'oro non compra amore* (1804), *Il trionfo di Clelia* (1802), *Il diavolo a quattro, La pazza giornata* (on Beaumarchais's *La Folle Journée* [*Figaro*, 1799]) and about 25 other Italian operas; church music; cantata *La speranza*; songs.

Posaune German name for the ◊trombone, a musical instrument.

positif (French 'choir organ') French name for the third manual (keyboard) of an ◊organ.

position in harmony in music, the spacing of a chord. For example, 'root position' indicates that the ◊root of the chord is in the bass; 'open-position harmony' indicates a chord in which the notes are spread out, as opposed to 'closed-position harmony', in which every note of the harmony is filled within an octave.

position on a stringed instrument, one of a few specific areas on the ◊fingerboard where the left hand is placed in order for the player to find a set of notes. On the trombone, 'position' refers to the placement of the slide for playing different notes.

In violin positions, first position is furthest away, nearest to the ◊scroll end of the fingerboard. Second and third position are closer in, nearer to the body of the instrument.

positive organ a small chamber ◊organ.

posthorn brass instrument akin to the bugle rather than the horn, used by postillions in the 18th and early 19th centuries. It has no valves and can therefore produce only the natural harmonics, which are coarse and penetrating in tone.

The posthorn is hardly ever used in serious music, but J S Bach imitated it on the harpsichord in his Capriccio on his brother's departure, and Mozart scored parts for two in his *German Dances* K605 and in his *Posthorn Serenade* K320.

On the G string:

1st   2nd   3rd   4th

On the D string:

1st   2nd   3rd   4th

1st 2nd 3rd   4th 5th   6th   7th

Various positions on a string instrument (top and centre) and on the trombone (bottom).

Postillon de Lonjumeau, Le/The Coach-man of Lonjumeau opera by Adam (libretto by A de Leuven and L L Brunswick), produced Paris, Opéra-Comique, 13 October 1836. The coachman Chapelou abandons his bride, Madeleine, to join the Paris Opéra. Meeting her ten years later, he does not recognize her, and asks her to marry him; she reveals her identity.

postlude, or postludium the opposite of prelude or praeludium: a final piece, especially an organ piece played after service.

postmodernism a style of composition in which the composer draws on the influence of a variety of musical periods and styles. Used specifically to describe the music of certain 20th-century composers, Stravinsky was the first great postmodernist, working in neoclassical and serial styles, as well as a more traditional, yet progressive Russian style. Postmodernism began to blossom after the vogue of ◊integral serialism in the 1950s, when composers reacted against the rigid restrictions imposed by that technique (of fixing the parameters of every compositional component: pitch, rhythm, dynamics, duration, and so on). Contemporary postmodernist composers include Peter Maxwell Davies who writes in a wide range of styles, influenced by elements of music from the 16th-century masters right through to the modern techniques of the ◊twelve-tone system.

Poston, Elizabeth (1905–1987) English composer. She studied at the Royal College of Music in London and piano with Harold Samuel. In 1925 she published seven songs and in 1927 a prize work, a violin and piano sonata, was broadcast. From 1940 to 1945 she was director of music in the foreign service of the British Broadcasting Corporation (BBC).

Works include: music for radio productions; choral music, songs.

pot-pourri (French 'rotten pot') medley of preserves, identical with the Spanish *olla podrida*, the name of which is applied to selections of themes from various musical works, especially operas or operettas.

Potter (Philip), Cipriani (Hambley) (1792–1871) English pianist and composer. He had a reputation as a fine pianist. His compositions were largely instrumental.

He studied under Thomas Attwood, John Callcott, and William Crotch, and had finishing piano lessons from Joseph Woelfl 1805–10. He became an associate of the Philharmonic Society on its foundation in 1813 and a member when he reached majority, and in 1816 wrote an overture for it, also playing the piano there that year in a sextet of his own. In 1817 he went to Vienna, where he studied with Aloys Förster and met Beethoven. After visiting Germany and Italy he returned to London in 1821, became professor of piano at the Royal Academy of Music the next year and principal in succession to Crotch in 1832, but resigned in 1859. In 1855 Wagner conducted one of his symphonies with the Philharmonic Society.

Works include: cantata *Medora e Corrado*, Ode to Harmony; nine symphonies (1819–34), four overtures for orchestra; three piano concertos (1832–35), Concertante for cello and orchestra; three piano trios, sextet for piano and strings; horn and piano sonata, duo for violin and piano; two sonatas, *The*

Enigma ('Variations in the style of five eminent artists', 1825) and other music for piano; songs.

Pougin, (François Auguste) Arthur (Eugène Paroisse-) (1834–1921) French musicologist. He had little general education, but studied violin with Alard and theory with Réber at the Paris Conservatory. After working at various theatres as violinist and conductor, he began to write biographical articles on 18th-century French musicians and gradually made his way by writing for papers, contributing to dictionaries, and writing music criticism. He wrote biographies of Verdi, Campra, Meyerbeer, V Wallace, Bellini, Rossini, Auber, Adam, Méhul, and studies of French music history.

Poule, La/The Hen the nickname of a symphony by Haydn, no. 83, in G minor (no. 2 of the 'Paris' symphonies), composed 1786.

Poulenc, Francis Jean Marcel (1899–1963) French composer and pianist. A self-taught composer of witty and irreverent music, he was a member of the group of French composers known as ◊Les Six. Among his many works are the operas *Les Mamelles de Tirésias/The Breasts of Tiresias* 1947 and *Dialogues des Carmélites/Dialogues of the Carmelites* 1957, and the ballet *Les Biches/The Little Darlings* 1923.

Poulenc was born in Paris. He received a classical education, and took piano lessons from Ricardo Viñes. When he was called up for war service in 1918 he had already written one or two works under the influence of Satie, and on being demobilized he joined the group of 'Les Six' with Auric, Durey, Honegger, Milhaud, and Tailleferre, and thus came for a time under the influence of Jean Cocteau, notably with his three songs *Cocardes* 1919. A commission from Diaghilev led to the ballet score *Les Biches*, influenced by the Neo-Classical brilliance of Stravinsky but also containing Poulenc's characteristic wit, charm, and melancholy. Similar traits are found in his great series of songs 1919–60, settings of poems by Apollinaire, Ronsard, Eluard, Colette, and Vilmorin.

Works include: STAGE opera *Dialogues des Carmélites* (1957); comic opera *Les Mamelles de Tirésias* (libretto by G Apollinaire, 1947), monodrama *La voix humaine* (1959).

CHORAL Mass in G minor (1937) and cantata *Figure humaine* (P Eluard); choruses (unaccompanied), *Gloria* (1959).

ORCHESTRAL *Concert champêtre* for harpsichord and orchestra (1928), concerto in D minor for two pianos and orchestra (1932), organ concerto (1938); piano concerto (1949).

CHAMBER much music for wind instruments, including trio for oboe, bassoon, and piano (1926); also violin and piano and cello and piano sonatas (1943, 1948).

PIANO *Mouvements perpétuels* (1918), *Nocturnes* (1929–38), and other pieces.

SONGS *Tel jour, telle nuit* (1937), *Fiançailles pour rire* (1939), and other songs.

poussé (French 'pushed') upstroke of the bow in the playing of string instruments, the opposite of *tiré* ('drawn').

Pousseur, Henri (1929–) Belgian composer. His works investigate computer and aleatory techniques, influenced by Berio and Stockhausen. He was strongly influenced by post-Webernian serialism, one of his earliest works being *Quintet in Memory of Webern*. His later music makes use of open forms, where the performer has freedom to decide the order of the musical material (for example *Mobile* for two pianos and *Caractères* for piano solo).

Pousseur was born at Malmedy. He studied at Brussels Conservatory and took private composition lessons from André Souris and Pierre Boulez. In 1958 he founded a studio for electronic music in Brussels. He lectured at Darmstadt 1957–67, Cologne, and the State University of New York, Buffalo 1966–69. He was appointed professor of composition at Liège Conservatory in 1971.

Works include: the operas *Votre Faust* (1969), *Die Erprobung des Petrus Hebraïcus* (1974); *Trois Chants sacrés* for soprano and string trio; *Symphonies* for 15 solo instruments; *Modes* for string quartet; quintet to the memory of Webern (1955); *Seismographs* for magnetic tape; *Scambi* for tape (1957); *Rimes pour différentes sources sonores* for orchestra and tape (1959); *Répons* for seven musicians (1960); *Mobile* for two pianos, *Portrait de Votre Faust* for soloists, instruments, and tape (1966); *Couleurs croisées* for orchestra (1967); *L'effacement du Prince Igor* for orchestra (1971); *Système des paraboles*, seven tape studies (1972); *Schoenbergs Gegenwart* for actors, singers, and instruments (1974); *Chronique illustrée* for baritone and orchestra (1976); *Agonie* for voices and electronics (1981); *Nuits des Nuits* for orchestra (1985); *Déclarations d'Orage* for soloists, tape, and orchestra (1989); *Leçons d'enfer*, chamber opera (1991).

Powell, Mel (1923–) US composer. He played piano in dance bands, and later studied with Wagenaar, Toch, and Hindemith. He founded an electronic music studio at Yale in 1960. He was Dean of Music at the California Institute of Arts, 1969–75.

Works include: *Stanzas* for orchestra· (1957); *Filigree Setting* for string quartet (1959); *Setting* for cello and orchestra; *Immobiles* 1–5 for tape and orchestra (1967–69); string quartet (1982); *Computer Prelude* (1988); *Duplicates* concerto for two pianos and orchestra (1990).

Power, Leonel (c. 1375–1445) English composer and theorist. He wrote a treatise on the singing of descant and composed Masses, including *Alma redemptoris*, motets, and other church music.

Powers, Anthony (1953–) English composer. He studied at Oxford University, in Paris with Nadia Boulanger, and at York University with David Blake. He has taught at Dartington College of Arts and Exeter University, both in Devon.

Works include: *Souvenirs de voyage* for soprano and piano (1979), *Another Part of the Island* for ensemble (1980); opera *The Search for the Simorgh* (1981); music theatre *A Sussex Carol* (1982); *The Winter Festival*, for mezzo and nine instruments (1985); *Chamber Concerto* (1984); *Music for Strings* (1984); *Vespers* for 21 solo strings (1986); two piano sonatas (1983, 1986); string quartet (1987); *Stone, Water, Stars* for orchestra (1987); Horn concerto (1989); Cello concerto (1990); 2nd string quartet (1991).

praeludium see ◊prelude.

'Prague' Symphony Mozart's symphony in D major, K504, composed in Vienna, December 1786 and performed in Prague, 19 January 1787, during a visit for the production there of *Le nozze di Figaro*.

Pralltriller the rapid repetition of a note, with a note a degree higher in between.

Pré aux clercs, Le/The Scholars' Meadow opera by Hérold (libretto by F A E de Planard), produced Paris, Opéra-Comique, 15 December 1832. King Henry of Navarre wants Isabelle, a friend of Queen Marguerite, to marry Comminge even though she loves Mergy. Marguerite arranges for the couple's

escape and attends their wedding, then Mergy kills Comminge in a duel.

Preciosa play with music by Weber (libretto by P A Wolff, based on Cervantes's story *La Gilanella*), produced Berlin, Opera House, 15 March 1821.

precipitando (Italian 'precipitately') musical direction indicating that an *accelerando* is to be made to increase in pace very rapidly.

prelude a composition intended as the preface to further music, especially preceding a ◊fugue, forming the opening piece of a ◊suite, or setting the mood for a stage work, as in Wagner's *Lohengrin*. As used by Chopin, a prelude is a short self-contained piano work.

A prelude is often rhetorical in style, mixing fast runs and sustained chords. It thereby allows the musicians to form an aural picture of the sound quality of the auditorium. In orchestra concerts the ◊overture fulfils a similar role.

Prélude à l'Après-midi d'un faune/Prelude to 'The Afternoon of a Faun' an orchestral piece by Debussy intended as a musical introduction to Stéphane Mallarmé's poem of that name, composed 1892–94 and first performed Paris, Société Nationale, 23 December 1894.

Ballet on this work (choreographed by Vaslav Nizhinsky), produced Paris, Théâtre du Châtelet, 29 May 1912.

Préludes two sets of piano pieces, 12 in each, by Debussy, composed 1910–13. Their contents are: I. 1. *Danseuses de Delphes/Dancing Women of Delphi*; 2. *Voiles/Sails*; 3. *Le Vent dans la plaine/The wind in the plain*; 4. *Les Sons et les parfums tournent dans l'air du soir/Sounds and scents whirl in the evening air*: a quotation from Baudelaire; 5. *Les Collines d'Anacapri/The hills of Anacapri*; 6. *Des Pas sur la neige/Footprints in the snow*; 7. *Ce qu'a vu le vent d'Ouest/What the West Wind saw*; 8. *La Fille aux cheveux de lin/The Flaxen-haired Girl*: based on a Scottish song by Leconte de Lisle; 9. *La Sérénade interrompue/ The interrupted serenade*; 10. *La Cathédrale engloutie/The Submerged Cathedral*: on the old Breton tale of the sunken city of Ys); 11. *La*

The notation for pralltrillers on F and G, and the approximate notation of each.

Danse de Puck/Puck's Dance, after Shake-speare's *Midsummer Night's Dream*); 12. *Min-strels* ('music-hall artists, not troubadours'). II. 1. *Brouillards/Mists*; 2. *Feuilles mortes/Dead Leaves*; 3. *La Puerta del Vino* (a gate at Granada); 4. *Les Fées sont d'exquises dan-seuses/The Fairies are exquisite Dancers*; 5. *Bruyères/Heather*; 6. *General Lavine-eccentric* (a music-hall character); 7. *La Terrasse des audi-ences du clair de lune/The Terrace of the Moon-light Audiences*; a reference to an account of George V's Durbar in 1912; the piece contains a quotation of the folksong 'Au clair de la lune'); 8. *Ondine* (Water-spirit maiden of 19th-century story); 9. *Hommage à S Pickwick Esq.*, *PPMPC* (after Dickens; the piece quotes 'God save the King' in the bass); 10. *Canope* (a Canopic jar holding the ashes of a dead lover); 11. *Les Tierces alternées/Alternating Thirds*; 12. *Feux d'artifice/Fireworks*; quoting a few notes of the *Marchseillaise* at the end.

Préludes, Les symphonic poem by Liszt, composed 1848, revised early 1850s, first performed Weimar, 28 February 1854. The title is taken from a poem by Lamartine, with which in fact the music has no connection.

preparation term used in harmony for a chord, one note of which will create a dissonance in the chord that follows.

Percussion

Preparation   Resolution

In this example the top voice (C) is prepared for dissonance and resolution.

prepared piano piano altered in such a way as to produce a different ◊timbre or special effects. The concept was introduced by Henry Cowell; John Cage developed and popular-ized the technique, producing novel sounds by placing objects on the strings, as in his *Bacchanale* 1940.

prestissimo musical term; Italian 'extremely fast'.

presto (Italian 'quick') term used in musical notation; faster than ◊allegro. *Prestissimo* is of the greatest possible speed.

Preston, Thomas English composer. He was probably organist and master of the choris-ters, Magdalen College, Oxford, and is re-corded as having played at Windsor Chapel in 1558 and 1559. He wrote a large amount of organ music for the Latin rite, including the Proper of the Mass for Easter Day (incom-plete).

Prêtre, Georges (1924–   ) French conduc-tor. He studied at Douai and in Paris, making his debut in 1946 at the Paris Opéra-Comique; he was music director there 1956–59. He made his London debut in 1961; the New York Metropolitan Opera in 1964. He made frequent performances and recordings with Maria Callas. In 1959 he conducted the first performance of F Poulenc's *La voix humaine*.

Preussisches Märchen/Prussian Tales ballet-opera by Blacher (libretto by H von Cramer); composed 1949, produced Berlin, 23 September 1952.

Prévost (d'Exiles), Antoine François (1697–1763) French novelist. For works based on his *Manon Lescaut* see ◊Henze (*Boulevard Solitude*); Massenet (◊*Manon*); Ha-lévy, Auber, and Puccini (◊*Manon Lescaut*).

Prey, Claude (1925–   ) French composer. He wrote the chamber opera *Le coeur révélateur* 1962, after Poe's *The Tell-Tale Heart*, and is best known for the operas *Les liaisons danger-euses* 1974 and *Le rouge et le noir* 1989.

He studied with Milhaud and Messiaen at the Paris Conservatory. Other stage works include *La grand mère française* 1976, *Lunedi bleue* 1982, *Pauline* 1983, and *Sommaire Soleil* 1990.

Price, Curtis (Alexander) (1945–   ) US musicologist. He studied at Harvard 1968–74 and taught at Washington University, St Louis, 1974–81. He became professor at King's College, London, in 1988, and princi-pal of the Royal Academy of Music in 1995. Early English stage music has been at the centre of his studies; he published *Henry Purcell and the London Stage* in 1984 and edited *Dido and Aeneas* 1986. Other titles include *Italian Opera and Arson in Late 18th-Century London* 1989 and *The Early Baroque Era* (editor) 1993.

prick-song from the 15th to the 18th century 'to prick' was used to mean 'to write notes'. Hence prick-song meant written, as opposed to improvised, music.

Prigione di Edimburgo, La/Edinburgh Gaol opera by F Ricci (libretto by G Rossi, based on Scribe and Planard's *Prison d'Edimbourg* and further back on Scott's *Heart of Midlothian*), produced Trieste, 13 March 1838.

Prigioniero, Il/The Prisoner opera (prologue and one act) by Dallapiccola (libretto by composer after V de L'Isle Adam and C de Coster); composed 1944–48, first performed Turin Radio, 4 December 1949. Produced Florence, 20 May 1950. During the era of the Inquisition in Spain, the Prisoner finds hope in a comforting Gaoler. One day the cell is left open and he finds his way to freedom, only to be caught by the Grand Inquisitor.

prima donna (Italian 'first lady') strictly, the singer of the principal female role in an opera. By the 19th century the term had entered nonmusical vocabulary to describe an arrogant and histrionic person, either male or female.

prima volta (Italian 'first time') in musical notation, indicating a passage at the end of a section, before a repeat sign, to be substituted with the *seconda volta* ('second time') passage at the same point during the repeat.

primo (Italian 'first') in musical notation, word often written over the top part in piano duets, the bottom one being *secondo*; the word also appears in orchestral scores where the composer wishes to make sure that a passage is played by only the first of a pair or groups of similar instruments.

primo uomo (Italian 'first man') singer of the leading male soprano part in an opera or the leading male soprano in an opera company in the 18th century.

Prince Igor/Kniaz Igor opera by Borodin (libretto by composer, based on a skh by Stassov), composed between 1871 and 1887 and left unfinished at Borodin's death in the latter year. Completed and scored by Rimsky-Korsakov and Glazunov. Produced St Petersburg, 4 November 1890. Prince Igor and son Vladimir are taken prisoner by the Polovtsi. Khan Konchak treats his prisoners well, blessing the union of his daughter Konchakovna with Vladimir. Igor escapes and is welcomed home.

Prince of the Pagodas, The ballet by Britten (choreography by John Cranko), produced London, Covent Garden, January 1 1957.

Princesse de Navarre, La comédie-ballet by Rameau (libretto by Voltaire), produced Versailles, 23 February 1745, to celebrate the wedding of the Dauphin with Maria Teresa of Spain. Princess Constance escapes from the King of Castille and hides with Don Morillo, evading the amorous pursuit of the Duke of Foix.

Princesse jaune, La/The Yellow Princess opera by Saint-Saëns (libretto by L Gallet), produced Paris, Opéra-Comique, 12 June 1872. Kornélis loves everything Japanese. He imagines he is in Japan, but then realizes he loves his Dutch girlfriend Léna more than his fantasy.

Princess Ida, or Castle Adamant operetta by Sullivan (libretto by W S Gilbert, a parody of Tennyson's *Princess*), produced London, Savoy Theatre, 5 January 1884. Prince Hiarion's marriage to Princess Ida was arranged a long time ago, but she has since spurned all men and founded a university for women. But then she falls in love with him.

principal in an ◊organ, an open ◊diapason stop. The term is derived from the German *Prinzipal* to denote a neutral stop, in contrast with the variety of other, more colourful, diapason stops. Also, in early music, the lowest trumpet part, in which high and florid notes were not demanded. In modern terminology a principal is the leading player of any group of orchestral instruments.

principal subject the main, first theme of a piece in ◊sonata form or ◊rondo form. It is usually the first important theme to appear, doing so in the ◊tonic key.

Printemps symphonic suite for chorus and orchestra by Debussy; composed 1887, published 1904 in a reduction for piano four hands. Re-orchestrated by Henri Busser and performed Paris, Salle Gaveau, 18 April 1913.

Prinz von Homburg, Der opera by Henze (libretto by I Bachmann, after Kleist), produced Hamburg, Staatsoper, 22 May 1960. The Prince is lost in a fantasy world with his beloved Princess at its centre. As a result, he ignores battle orders and is condemned to death. Offered his freedom after Princess Natalie intervenes, he still prefers an honourable death, but the Elector shows mercy in the end.

Prise de Troie, La (Berlioz). See ◊*Troyens, Les*.

Prisoner in the Caucasus, The/Kavkasky Plennik opera by Cui (libretto by V A Krilov, based on Pushkin's poem), produced St Petersburg, 16 February 1883.

Pritchard, John (1921–1989) English conductor. He studied in Italy and went to Glyndebourne in 1947; gave three Mozart operas there in 1951; music director 1969–77. He conducted the first performances of Benjamin Britten's *Gloriana* and Michael Tippett's *Midsummer Marriage* at Covent Garden; *King Priam* with the company at Coventry, 1962. He made his US debut in

1953 with the Pittsburgh Symphony Orchestra; New York Metropolitan Opera 1971. He was music director of the London Philharmonic Orchestra 1962–66; BBC Symphony Orchestra from 1981; and principal conductor of the Cologne Opera from 1978.

Prodaná Nevěsta (Smetana). See ◊*Bartered Bride, The*.

Prod'homme, J(acques) G(abriel) (1871–1956) French musicologist. He studied in Germany and lived at Munich 1897–1900, where he founded a periodical. After his return to Paris he founded the French section of the Société Internationale de Musicologie, became its secretary and performed various other music administrative functions, succeeding Bouvert in 1931 as librarian and archivist at the Opéra, and Expert in 1934 as Conservatory librarian. He wrote several works both on Beethoven and on Berlioz, and also on Mozart, Schubert, and Wagner.

Prodigal Son, The church parable by Britten (libretto by W Plomer), produced Orford, 10 June 1968, conductor Britten. In the country, the father of two sons gives his younger son an inheritance, which is squandered during a moral decline in the city. The son repents and is reconciled with his family on his return home.

Ballet by Prokofiev (*L'Enfant prodigue*); composed 1928, first performed Paris, 21 May 1929 (Ballets Russes; scenario by B Kokno, choreography Balanchine, décor Georges Roualt; conductor Prokofiev).

See ◊*Enfant prodigue* (Debussy).

programme music instrumental music that interprets a story, depicts a scene or painting, or illustrates a literary or philosophical idea. The term was first used by Franz ◊Liszt in the 19th century, when programme music was especially popular with composers of Romantic music (see ◊Romanticism), but there had been a great deal of descriptive music before then. Examples include Antonio Vivaldi's *Four Seasons* concertos, Ludwig van Beethoven's *Eroica* and *Pastoral* symphonies, Felix Mendelssohn's *Hebrides Overture* ('Fingal's Cave'), and the ◊symphonic poems of Liszt and Richard Strauss.

narrative and descriptive music Franz Liszt coined the phrase 'programme music' in the mid-19th century, originally using it for music which is prefaced by a 'programme' and which expresses (rather than describes) a poetical idea. Nowadays, however, it is applied to any purely instrumental music based on a literary, pictorial, historical, biographical, autobiographical, or any other extra-musical subject, as opposed to ◊absolute music – music with a purely abstract meaning. The programmatic element can be as vague as simply having a decriptive title given to it by the composer to set the mood, or a much more detailed depiction of a scene or story. Often, however, it is impossible to distinguish between the depiction of a scene and the composer's reaction to it.

early programme music Musical descriptions of actions and events have existed from the earliest times. One of the first flowerings of real programme music came in Elizabethan England with composers for the ◊virginals, whose music is often overtly descriptive. Titles such as Giles Farnaby's *Dream*, and Doctor Bull's *Myself* and *Up Tails All* are typical. This tradition was continued well into the 18th century by the music of the French harpsichordists, notably François Couperin and Jean-Philippe Rameau, and German composers such as Johann Kuhnau, whose *Biblical Sonatas* are programme music in the Lisztian sense – each one is prefaced by a summary of the what the music depicts.

popular subjects One of the first popular forms was battle music, using musical sounds to depict the sounds of battle, an early example being Clement Janequin's ◊chanson *La Bataille* 1529. The tradition continued with pieces for harpsichord such as William Byrd's *The Battell*, through to the 19th century with Beethoven's *Battle Symphony* and Pyotr Tchaikovsky's *1812 Overture*. Another popular subject for musical description has been representations of nature in one form or another. Vivaldi's *Four Seasons*, Beethoven's *Pastoral Symphony*, and Claude Debussy's *La Mer* are perhaps the best-known examples.

symphonic poems In the 19th century, composers such as Hector Berlioz took Beethoven's concept of the symphony a stage further, developing the Romantic programme symphony. Despite its basically classical form and abstract tradition, the symphony provided a framework into which the Romantic composers could put all kinds of extramusical ideas. Berlioz's use of an idée fixe to depict characters in his *Harold in Italy* symphony and *Symphonie Fantastique* paved the way for the development of the ◊symphonic poem and its use of Richard Wagner's ◊leitmotif. The symphonic poem became very popular as a form in the latter half of the 19th century, and was particularly favoured by Liszt and Richard Strauss. In the 20th century programme music became for a while less popular with the rise of neoclassicism and serialism, and was even looked down upon as less 'serious' than absolute music, but its appeal to the general public has never been in doubt.

links with other arts Because programme music attempts to convey an extra-musical idea, it very often has links with other artistic disciplines, and its inspiration may come from sources such as literature or painting. Particularly during the Romantic period, music looked outside its traditional forms for inspiration – as personal expression had become the goal of the artist, the classical notion of abstract formal beauty had become outdated – and increasingly turned to the other arts. In Britain and Germany the literary tradition has been a significant source of inspiration, while in France and Italy it is more likely to be painting and sculpture.

progression logical movement of two or more chords in succession, either harmonically with all the notes moving simultaneously or polyphonically with each one being part of a continuously moving horizontal melodic line.

Prohaska, Carl (1869–1927) Austrian composer. He studied piano with d'Albert and composition with Mandyczewski and Herzogenberg, being also befriended by Brahms. He taught at the Strasbourg Conservatory 1894–95 and conducted the Warsaw Philharmonic Orchestra 1901–05. In 1908 he became professor at the Conservatory of the Vienna Philharmonic Society.

Works include: the opera *Madeleine Guimara* (1930); oratorio *Frühlingsfeier* (1913), motet *Aus dem Buch Hiob*, *Lebensmesse*, *Der Feind*, *Infanterie* and other choral works; variations on a theme from Rousseau's *Devin du village*, symphonic prelude to Anzengruber's *Das vierte Gebot*, symphonic fantasy, serenade, passacaglia and fugue for orchestra; string quartet, string quintet, piano trio; sonata and *Allegro con spirito* for violin and piano; songs, duets.

Prokofiev, Sergey Sergeyevich (1891–1953) Russian composer. His music includes operas such as *The Love for Three Oranges* 1921; ballets for Sergei Diaghilev, including *Romeo and Juliet* 1935; seven symphonies including the *Classical Symphony* 1916–17; music for film, including Eisenstein's *Alexander Nevsky* 1938; piano and violin concertos; songs and cantatas (for example, that composed for the 30th anniversary of the October Revolution); and *Peter and the Wolf* 1936 for children, to his own libretto after a Russian folk tale.

Prokofiev was essentially a classicist in his use of form, but his extensive and varied output demonstrates great lyricism, humour, and skill. His music in his earlier years was distinguished by its hard brilliance, his later works showing a mellowing and maturity of style. Born near Ekaterinoslav (now Dnepropetrovsk), he studied at St Petersburg under Rimsky-Korsakov and achieved fame as a pianist. He left Russia in 1918 and lived for some time in the USA and in Paris, but returned in 1927 and again in 1935.

Prokofiev began to compose almost before he could write, and tried his hand at an opera at the age of nine. He was sent to Glière for lessons, wrote 12 piano pieces in 1902 as well as a symphony for piano duet, and at 12 set Pushkin's play *A Feast in Time of Plague* as an opera. At the St Petersburg Conservatory, which he left in 1914, he studied piano with Anna Essipova, composition with Rimsky-Korsakov and Liadov, and conducting with Nikolai Tcherepnin. By that time he had written many works, including the first piano concerto, which won the Rubinstein prize, and he then set to work on a ballet commission for Diaghilev that became the *Scythian Suite* for orchestra.

In 1918 he left Russia, living in Britain, France, Japan, and the USA before returning to Russia. The opera *The Love for Three Oranges* was produced at Chicago in 1921, and the next year he went to live in Paris and became connected with Diaghilev's Ballets Russes/Russian Ballet, which produced several of his works. The visionary opera *The Fiery Angel* was completed in 1923 but staged until 1955. Limited opportunities in the West impelled him to return to Russia.

In 1936 he settled in Moscow; like many other Soviet composers, he was severely criticised in the Zhdanov censures, 1948, for formalism (the separation of form from content). He was induced by the Soviet government to simplify and popularize his style, a tendency which is very noticeable in such works as *Peter and the Wolf* and the quantities of film music he wrote there. However, the cantata derived from the film music for *Alexander Nevsky* is one of his most powerful scores. Two years later he began his great patriotic opera *War and Peace*, and the victory in the war against Hitler was celebrated with one of his finest scores, the exuberant and expansive 5th symphony. Ironically, after years of subjection to Stalinist oppression, he died on the same day as Stalin.

Works include: OPERA *The Love for Three Oranges* (after Gozzi, 1921), *The Fiery Angel* (1919–27, produced 1955), *War and Peace* (after Tolstoy, 1941–52, produced 1953).

BALLETS *The Buffoon* (1921), *Le pas d'acier* (1927), *L'enfant prodigue*, *Romeo and Juliet* (after Shakespeare, 1938), *Cinderella* (1945).

ORCHESTRAL includes *Classical symphony* (1921) and six other symphonies (1924–52); film music for *Lieutenant Kijé* (1934), *Ivan the Terrible*; five piano concertos (1911–32), two violin concertos (1917, 1935).

CHAMBER two string quartets (1930, 1941), sonata for two violins, sonatas in D major and F minor for violin and piano (1944, 1946).

PIANO AND SONGS nine piano sonatas, about 25 other op. nos. of piano pieces, including *Visions fugitives*; eight sets of songs (one without words, one to words by Pushkin).

CHORAL *Alexander Nevsky* (1939).

prolation system of proportional timing in Renaissance music, relating shifts in tempo to harmonic ratios, for example 1:2, 2:3, and so on.

prolongation in voice-leading analysis, the technique by which a composer 'prolongs' a single harmony over a span of time by making other chords in the passage subordinate to the one being prolonged. The prolonged harmony is said to operate at a deeper structural level than the subordinate harmonies, and may itself be a part of a larger prolongation at a still deeper level. The term may also be used of structural melodic notes rather than harmonies. See ◊structural harmony; ◊fundamental line.

promenade concert originally a concert where the audience was free to promenade (walk about) while the music was playing, now in the UK the name of any one of an annual BBC series (the 'Proms') at the Royal Albert Hall, London, at which part of the audience stands. They were originated by English conductor Henry Wood 1895.

Promessi sposi, I/The Betrothed opera by Ponchielli (libretto by E Praga based on Manzoni's novel), produced Cremona, 30 August 1856. Renzo and Lucia are to marry but the wedding is interrupted by Don Rodrigo. Having sought refuge in a convent, Lucia is kidnapped by L'Innominato; she escapes, and takes holy orders. When at last she meets Renzo again her vows are dissolved and the wedding takes place.

Prométhée/Prometheus open-air spectacle by Fauré (libretto by J Lorrain and A F Hérold, based on Aeschylus), produced Béziers, Arènes, 27 August 1900; first Paris performance Hippodrome, 5 December 1907.

Prometheus (Beethoven). See ◊*Geschöpfe des Prometheus, Die*.

Symphonic poem by Liszt, composed 1850 as an overture to the choruses from Herder's *Prometheus*, performed Weimar, 28 August 1850; revised 1855, first performed Brunswick, 18 October 1855.

Opera by Orff (libretto by composer after Aeschylus) produced Stuttgart, 24 March 1968.

Prometheus, the Poem of Fire symphonic work for piano and orchestra by Skriabin, first performed Moscow, 15 March 1911. The score contains a part for an instrument projecting coloured lights, called *Tastiera per luce*, which was however never perfected.

Prometheus Unbound setting of Shelley's poem for solo voices, chorus, and orchestra by Parry, performed Gloucester Festival, 1880.

Prometheus Variations (Beethoven). See ◊*'Eroica' Variations*.

Prophète, Le opera by Meyerbeer (libretto by Scribe), produced Paris, Opéra, 16 April 1849. John's wedding to Berthe is thwarted by Count Oberthal, when he kidnaps John's mother, Fidès. Later John is hailed as a prophet king, and Berthe, horrified, stabs herself. Imperial troops enter John's palace and he detonates himself along with the forces of order.

Prophetess, The, or *The History of Dioclesian* music by Purcell for the play adapted from Beaumont and Fletcher by Thomas Betterton, produced London, Dorset Gardens Theatre, spring 1690. Pepusch wrote new music for its revival, London, Lincoln's Inn Fields Theatre, 28 November 1724.

proportion mathematical relationship between the numbers of vibrations of different notes, which are exactly in tune with each other when the ratios between these vibrations are mathematically correct; for instance, a perfect fifth stands in the relation of 2:3 in the number of vibrations of its two notes. The term proportion was also used in early music to designate the rhythmic relationships between one time-signature and another.

Proscritto, Il/The Outlaw opera by Nicolai (libretto, originally written for Verdi, by G Rossi), produced Milan, La Scala, 13 March 1841.

prose another name, chiefly French, for the sequence (in the medieval sense of an ornamental interpolation into the music of the Mass). After the 9th century words began to be added to the sequences, and this is the reason for them being called proses, since the texts were not originally in verse.

Proserpine opera by Lully (libretto by Quinault), produced Saint-Germain, 3 February 1680; first Paris performance, 15 November 1680. Attis and Proserpina are in love, but jealous Cyane arranges for Pluto to abduct Proserpine. Attis commits suicide and Cyane confesses her plot. Mercury and Jupiter restore the couple.

Opera by Paisiello (libretto by Quinault, revised by N F Guillard), produced Paris, Opéra, 29 March 1803. Paisiello's only French opera.

Prout, Ebenezer (1835–1909) English theorist and composer. He studied piano and organ, and began to make a career as organist, piano teacher, music editor, and critic. In 1876 he became professor at the National Training-School for Music in London and three years later at the Royal Academy of Music. He wrote a number of books on harmony, counterpoint, form, and orchestration, and composed cantatas, symphonies, organ concertos, and chamber music.

Prozess, Der/The Trial opera by Einem (libretto by Blacher and H von Cramer, after Kafka), produced Salzburg, 17 August 1953. Joseph K is charged with an unspecified crime; the plot documents his feelings of helplessness and paranoia before being taken to execution.

Prunières, Henry (1886–1942) French musicologist and editor. He studied with Rolland at the Sorbonne, founded the *Revue musicale* in 1920 and was appointed editor of the complete edition of Lully's works. He wrote books on Lully, Monteverdi, Cavalli, French and Italian opera and ballet, and also a history of music (unfinished).

Pruslin, Stephen (Lawrence) (1940–   ) US pianist and librettist. He studied at Princeton until 1963; piano with Eduard Steuermann. He moved to London in 1964 and gave his debut recital at the Purcell Room in 1970. He wrote libretti for Birtwistle's *Monodrama* (1967) and *Punch and Judy* (1968). He co-founded Fires of London 1970, premiered the Maxwell Davies piano sonata and collaborated with him on music for *The Devils*. He made concert appearances with the London Sinfonietta, BBC Symphony Orchestra, and Royal Philharmonic.

'Prussian' Quartets a set of three string quartets by Mozart, composed 1789–90 and dedicated to the cello-playing King Frederick William II of Prussia. The quartets K575 in D, K589 in B♭, K590 in F are the first three of an intended set of six. All have prominent cello parts.

psalm sacred poem or song of praise. The Book of Psalms in the Old Testament is divided into five books containing 150 psalms, traditionally ascribed to David, the second king of Israel. In the Christian church they may be sung antiphonally in ◊plainsong or set by individual composers to music in a great variety of styles, from Josquin Desprez's *De profundis* to Igor Stravinsky's *Symphony of Psalms* 1930.

Psalmus Hungaricus work by Kodály for tenor, chorus, and orchestra, based on the Psalm lv, first performed Budapest, 19 November 1923.

psaltery musical instrument, triangular in shape and with strings stretched across its frame harp-wise, played with the bare fingers or with a plectrum. It became obsolete during the 17th century.

Pskovitianka/The Maid of Pskov, also known as *Ivan the Terrible* opera by Rimsky-Korsakov (libretto by composer based on a play by L A Mey), produced St Petersburg, 13 January 1873. Revived with a new prologue-opera, *Boyarina Vera Sheloga*, Moscow, 27 December 1898. Ivan the Terrible destroys Novgorod but spares nearby Pskov when he discovers his daughter Olga is there. Tucha, who has not heard of the ceasefire, leads a force against Ivan and Olga is killed in the crossfire.

Psyche opera by Locke (libretto by Shadwell), produced London, Dorset Gardens Theatre, 27 February 1675. Princess Psyche suffers the evil plots of her sisters Cidippe and Aglaura, who are jealous of her beauty. Venus, also jealous, arranges with Apollo for Psyche to marry a serpent, but Cupid saves her.

Psyché opera by Lully (libretto by T Corneille and B de Fontenelle), produced Paris, Opéra, 19 April 1678. See ◊*Psyche* for plot synopsis.

Suite by Franck for orchestra with choral interpolations, composed 1887–88, first performed Paris, Société National, 10 March 1888.

Puccini, Giacomo (Antonio Domenico Michele Secondo Maria) (1858–1924) Italian opera composer. His music shows a strong gift for melody and dramatic effect and his operas combine exotic plots with elements of *verismo* (realism). They include *Manon Lescaut* 1893, *La Bohème* 1896, *Tosca* 1900, *Madama*

Butterfly 1904, and the unfinished *Turandot* 1926.

Puccini was born in Lucca, the fifth in a line of musicians and composers. (The earlier members of the family were Giacomo Puccini (1712–1781), his son Antonio Puccini (1747–1832), his grandson Domenico Puccini (1771–1815), and his great-grandson Michele Puccini (1813–1864).) Although his father died early, Puccini was given a musical education by his uncle, and at the age of 19 was organist and choirmaster at the church of San Martino and had written a motet. In 1880 his mother managed with the aid of a grant from the queen to send him to the Milan Conservatory, where he studied composition first under Antonio Bazzini (1818–1897)and later under Amilcare Ponchielli. Here he wrote a *Capriccio sinfonico* for orchestra. Ponchielli urged him to take part in a competition for a one-act opera advertised by the music publisher Sonzogno, and he wrote *Le Villi*; but the prize was won by Mascagni's *Cavalleria rusticana*. *Le Villi*, however, was produced at Milan in 1884, and as a result Ricordi commissioned him to write a second opera, *Edgar* 1889. It failed, but Puccini had his first great success with *Manon Lescaut* at Turin in 1893; *La Bohème* was produced in the same city in 1896. His first *verismo* opera, *Tosca*, confirmed his stature: the combination of natural melody, a sure dramatic sense, and unerring aptness of orchestral colouring have made it his most enduring piece.

His successes made him immensely wealthy and he bought an estate at Torre del Lago near Lucca, where he lived with Elvira Bonturi, who had left her husband for him, but whom he was unable to marry until much later, when she became a widow. Their life together was marked by scandal in 1909 when their servant committed suicide after Elvira accused her of having a sexual relationship with Puccini. The following year *La fanciulla del West/The Golden Girl of the West* was produced at the New York Metropolitan Opera House. If this opera, and *La rondine* 1917 represent a decline in Puccini's career, his final work, *Turandot*, unites some of the elements that most fired his imagination: physical passion, cruelty, strong sentiment, and oriental flavour. In the last years of his life he suffered from cancer of the throat and died after an operation undergone at Brussels.

Puccini was the dominant figure in Italian music in his time; and his operas, which combine the sensuous melody of Verdi with

the richness of modern Impressionist harmony, are exceedingly popular.

Works include: the operas *Le Villi* (1884), *Edgar* (1889), *Manon Lescaut* (1893), *La Bohème* (1896), *Tosca* (1900), *Madama Butterfly* (1904), *La fanciulla del West* (1910), *La rondine* (1917), *Trittico*; *Il tabarro, Suor Angelica* and *Gianni Schicchi* (1918), *Turandot* (unfinished, completed by Alfano, 1926), *Scherzo sinfonico* for orchestra (later used in *La Bohème*); cantata *Juno*; two minuets for strings; a Mass and a motet: *Inno a Roma* for chorus.

Puits d'amour, Le/The Well of Love opera by Balfe (libretto by Scribe and A de Leuven), produced Paris, Opéra-Comique, 20 April 1843. Balfe's first French opera.

Pujol, Juan (c. 1573–1626) Spanish priest and composer. He was maestro de capilla at Tarragona, 1593–95, Saragossa Cathedral, 1595–1612, and Barcelona, 1612–26.

Works include: 13 Masses, 74 psalms, nine motets, nine Passions and other church music; secular songs.

Pulcinella ballet by Stravinsky with music adapted from Pergolesi and others (choreography by Massin), produced Paris, Opéra, 15 May 1920. The settings were designed by Picasso. (Orchestral Suite performed Boston, 22 December 1922.)

Pullois, Jean (c. 1420–1478) Flemish composer. His output consists mainly of songs but also includes some sacred music. He is important as one of the few named composers active during Dufay's middle years.

He was a singer in the Burgundian court chapel until 1463, then was choirmaster at Antwerp 1444–47. He sang at the papal chapel in Rome 1447–68. His single Mass cycle may really be the work of an English composer.

pulse a basic unit of rhythm and metre. See ◊beat.

Punch and Judy opera in one act by Birtwistle (libretto by S Pruslin), produced Aldeburgh, 8 June 1968, conductor Atherton. Revised version produced London, 3 March 1970. Murderous Punch stabs Judy and sets out on a quest for Pretty Polly, eventually winning her favour after hanging Jack Kh.

punta (Italian 'point') term used in musical notation, as in *a punta d'arco* ('at the point of the bow'), instructing a string player to use only the tip of the bow as opposed to the heel (the end which is held by the player's hand).

Purcell, Daniel (c. 1663–1717) English organist and composer. He finished the opera *The Indian Queen*, which his brother Henry

◊Purcell had left unfinished at his death. After a busy career writing music for plays, he became organist of St Andrew's Church, Holborn, in 1713.

He was a choirboy in the Chapel Royal and was organist at Magdalen College, Oxford 1688–95. He then went to London and added music to *The Indian Queen.*

Works include: music for *Brutus of Alba* (1696), Cibber's *Love's Last Shift* and *Love makes a Man* (1700), Durfey's *Cynthia and Endymion* (1696), Lacy's *Sawny the Scot* (based on Shakespeare's *Taming of the Shrew,* 1698), Steele's *Funeral and Tender Husband* (1705), Farquhar's *The Beaux' Stratagem* (1707), *The Inconstant* and (with Leveridge) *The Constant Couple* (1699), Vanbrugh's *The Relapse* and (with Finger) *The Pilgrim* (1701), an adaptation of Shakespeare's *Macbeth* (1704), and many others; odes for St Cecilia's Day; music for Congreve's *Judgment of Paris* (third prize in competition with Eccles, Finger, and Weldon, 1700); odes; church music; sonatas for violin and bass, and for flute and bass; sonatas for trumpet and strings; cantatas for one voice.

Purcell, Henry (c. 1659–1695) English Baroque composer. His music balances high formality with melodic expression of controlled intensity, for example, the opera *Dido and Aeneas* 1689 and music for Dryden's *King Arthur* 1691 and for *The Fairy Queen* 1692. He wrote more than 500 works, ranging from secular operas and incidental music for plays to cantatas and church music.

Born at Westminster, he became a chorister at the Chapel Royal, and subsequently was a pupil of Dr John Blow. In 1677 he was appointed composer to the Chapel Royal, and in 1679 organist at Westminster Abbey. As composer to the king, Purcell set to music odes o·· anthems.

Puritani di Scozia, I/The Puritans of Scotland opera by Bellini (libretto by C Pepoli, based on a play by J Ancelot and X B Saintine, *Têtes rondes et cavaliers,* and farther back on Scott's *Old Mortality*), produced Paris, Théâtre Italien, 25 January 1835.

Puschmann, Adam Zacharias (1532–1600) German master-singer. He was a pupil of Hans Sachs at Nuremberg 1566–60. He wrote about 200 Meisterlider (master-songs), and in 1574 published a treatise on master-singing, containing songs of his own as well as by Sachs, Behaim, and others.

Pushkin, Aleksandr Sergeevich (1790–1837) Russian poet, dramatist, and novelist. Two contrasting pieces by Pushkin are great works of literature in themselves and also form the basis of the two finest Russian compositions of the 19th century: *Eugene Onegin* and *Boris Godunov.*

Dating from 1825, *Boris Godunov* is a huge historical drama, which drew an appropriate response from Mussorgsky ·in 1869. If the wide political panorama of Pushkin's *Boris,* within the context of a gradually unfolding personal drama, suggests the influence of Shakespeare, then the presence of Byron in the verse novel *Eugene Onegin* (1828) is even more strongly felt. The figure of the sardonic outsider attracted Tchaikovsky for his opera of 1879. Here, as in other works of Pushkin, a composer was inspired by the poet's fluent naturalness of language and vivid imagery. Pushkin's huge range encompassed nationalist fairy tale, and his *Ruslan and Ludmilla* of 1820 was the inspiration for Glinka's opera of 1842. Rimsky-Korsakov was also attracted by Pushkin's fantasy, setting *The Tale of Tsar Saltan* (1831) in 1900 and *The Golden Cockerel* (1834) in 1909. Other major settings of Pushkin include Dargomizhsky's *Stone Guest* of 1872 (the poet's version of the Don Juan legend) and Tchaikovsky's *The Queen of Spades,* setting Pushkin's *Conte* of 1830 in 1890. The continued theme in his work of exile from society was personally familiar to Pushkin, and he was banished from Moscow for six years for political dissent. In 1837 he was shot dead in a duel.

Pyamour, John (1431–) English composer. He was a member of the Chapel Royal, 1420–21, and of the chapel of the Duke of Bedford in 1427. He wrote church music.

Pycard (fl. c. 1410) French composer. His music, represented in the Old Hall manuscript, is remarkable for its extensive use of canon. He served in John of Gaunt's household in the 1390s.

Pygmalion acte de ballet by Rameau (libretto by B de Savot, after A H de La Motte), produced Paris, Opéra, 27 August 1748. Sculptor Pygmalion falls in love with his statue. After it comes to life he must teach it how to move gracefully.

Pygott, Richard (c. 1485–1552) English composer. He was in Wolsey's private chapel in 1517 as Master of the Children and in 1533 became a Gentleman of the Chapel Royal. Later he was given a living allowance at Coggeshall monastery in Essex and a canonry at Tamworth, but lost some of the benefits at the dissolution of the monasteries; Henry VIII, however, and after him Edward VI, retained his services.

Works include: Masses, motets, *Salve Regina*; carols and other pieces.

Pythagoras (lived 6th century BC) Greek philosopher. He contributed to the science of music by working out by mathematics the intervals of the scale according to the number of vibrations to each note and by helping to systematize the tetrachords. Aesthetically, he developed the theory of the 'harmony of the spheres'.

Q

qin shallow, oblong, lacquered wooden box, the qin is a plucked zither of the Han Chinese. It has a curved wooden soundboard, no bridges or frets, and seven silk strings stretched along the length of the instrument and tied onto mother of pearl studs. Experts agree on its origins around the 14th and 15th centuries. It has an abundance of lore and anecdotes attached to it.

quadrille square dance for four or more couples, or the music for the dance, which alternates between two and four beats in a bar.

quadruple counterpoint counterpoint in which four parts are reversible. See also ◊triple counterpoint.

quadruplet a group of four notes to be played in the time of three. It is indicated by a ◊slur over the four notes with the number '4' written above. It usually occurs in compound time.

Quagliati, Paolo (c. 1555–1628) Italian composer. He was organist at the church of Santa Maria Maggiore in Rome from 1601. For the wedding of Carlo Gesualdo's daughter, Isabella, in 1623 he wrote a collection of instrumental pieces, entitled *La sfera armoniosa*.

Works include: the dramatic cantata *Carro di fedeltà d'amore* (1806); motets; spiritual and secular madrigals and canzonets; organ and harpsichord works.

Quantz, Johann Joachim (1697–1773) German flautist and composer. He composed 300 flute concertos, but is best remembered for writing the treatise ' Versuch einer Anweisung die Flöte traversiere zu spielen/On Playing the Transverse Flute' 1752. He improved the flute's adaptability by adding the second key and devising a sliding tuning mechanism.

As a boy he learned several instruments, and studied composition with Jan Zelenka in Vienna in 1717. The following year he was appointed oboist to the court of August II in Dresden and Warsaw, but later turned to the flute, studying under Pierre-Gabriel Buffardin (1690–1768). After travels in Italy, France, and England he returned to Dresden, becoming first flautist to the court, until in 1741 he entered the service of Frederick II of Prussia. He was the king's flute teacher and wrote for him over 500 works for flute.

Works include: about 300 concertos and about 200 other works for flute; hymns on poems by Gellert.

quartal harmony a harmonic theory, expounded by Yasser and others, which bases the harmonic system on the intervals of the fourth, instead of the third which decisively determines major or minor tonalities.

quarter tone an interval, half that of a ◊semitone. A kind of ◊microtone, it is the smallest interval commonly used in Western music by 20th-century composers such as Boulez and Stockhausen.

They were known to the Greeks and were apparently used in early plainsong but soon came to be abandoned and were not revived in Eastern music until the 20th century.

quartet ensemble of four musicians, or the music written for such a group. The most common type of quartet is the ◊string quartet.

Quartettsatz (German 'quartet movement') name given to the first movement of Schubert's unfinished string quartet in C minor, composed December 1820 (D703) and not performed until 1 March 1867, in Vienna. The work was clearly intended to be completed, for Schubert wrote 41 bars of a slow movement in A♭ major.

quasi (Latin 'as if') apparently but not actually; also used in musical notation, as in *sonata quasi fantasia* ('sonata in the manner of a fantasia').

Quatorze Juillet, Le/The Fourteenth of July play by Romain Rolland, forming part of the trilogy *Le Théâtre de la Révolution* with *Danton* and *Les Loups*, published and performed c. 1900–02, collectively published 1909. It was produced in the open air, Paris, Arènes de Lutèce, 14 July 1936, with music by Auric, Honegger, Ibert, Koechlin, Lazarus, Milhaud and Roussel.

Quattro pezzi sacri/Four Sacred Pieces four works for chorus and orchestra by Verdi: Ave Maria, Lauda alla Vergine Maria, Te Deum, and Stabat Mater, composed 1888–97. The last three pieces were performed Paris, 7 April 1898.

Quattro rusteghi, I/The Four Boors opera by Wolf-Ferrari (libretto by G Pizzolato, based on Goldoni's comedy), produced in Germany, Munich, 19 March 1906; in England as *The School for Fathers*, London, Sadler's Wells, 7 June 1946. Lunardo and Maurizio decide their children, Lucieta and Filipeto, should marry. Having forbidden the couple to meet before the wedding, the parents are foiled when Filipeto manages to meet Lucieta in disguise and they immediately fall in love.

quatuor see ◊quartet.

Quatuor pour la fin du temps/Quartet for the end of time work by Messiaen for piano, clarinet, violin, and cello; composed 1940 in a Silesian prisoner-of-war camp. First performed 15 January 1941.

quaver, US eighth note in music, a note value one-eighth the duration of a ◊semibreve. It is written as a filled black note-head with a stem and flag (tail).

Queen Mary's Funeral Music music by Purcell for the Westminster Abbey funeral in 1695 of Mary, wife of William III; sequence includes music written three years earlier for Shadwell's play *The Libertine*. Other sections

were given at Purcell's own funeral in November 1695.

Queen of Cornwall, The opera by Boughton (libretto Thomas Hardy's play, with alterations), produced Glastonbury, 21 August 1924. The subject is Tristram and Iseult.

Queen of Golconda, The/Drottningen av Golconda opera by Berwald (libretto by composer after J B C Vial and E G F de Favieres); composed 1864, first performed Stockholm, 3 April 1968. Aline, widowed Queen of Golconda, and Saint Phar meet after years of separation. Revolutionary disturbances delay only temporarily the couple's union.

Queen of Sheba see ◊*Königin von Saba, Die;* ◊*Reine de Saba, La.*

Queen of Spades, The/Pikovaya Dama opera by Tchaikovsky (libretto by M I Tchaikovsky, Tchaikovsky's brother, based on Pushkin's story), produced St Petersburg, 19 December 1890. Hermann tries to find the secret of playing cards through the old Countess. She dies but her ghost reveals the winning combination to him. After rejecting Lisa, the Countess's grand-daughter, Hermann loses everything at the gambling table when his necessary ace turns out to be the queen of spades instead.

Quentin Durward opera by Gevaert (libretto by F Cormon and M Carré, based on Scott's novel), produced Paris, Opéra-Comique, 25 March 1858.

Querflöte German name for the transverse ◊flute.

Quest, The ballet by Walton (choreography by Frederick Ashton, based on Spenser's *Faery Queen*), produced London, Sadler's Wells Ballet, 1943.

Quilter, Roger Cuthbert (1877–1953) English composer. He wrote song settings of Shakespeare and Alfred Lord Tennyson, including 'Now Sleeps the Crimson Petal' 1904, and others, as well as incidental music, such as *A Children's Overture* 1920, and chamber music.

Quilter was born at Brighton and educated at Eton. He studied music with Iwan Knorr at Frankfurt. He never held any official musical posts. His works include a light opera, incidental music for Shakespeare's *As You Like It*, and the children's fairy-play *Where the Rainbow Ends*. His songs are especially and deservedly well known. His artless melodic invention has a refined and distinctive harmonic support and outweighs limitations of manner.

Works include: the opera *Julia* (produced Covent Garden, 1936), radio opera *The Blue Boar*; incidental music for Shakespeare's *As You Like It* (1922) and the children's fairy-play *Where the Rainbow ends* (1911); *Children's Overture* on nursery tunes, serenade, *Three English Dances*, for orchestra (1910); songcycle *To Julia* (Herrick, 1906), songs to words by Shakespeare, Tennyson and others.

Quinault, Philippe (1635–1688) French poet and librettist. See ◊*Alceste* (Lully); ◊*Amadis* (Lully); ◊*Armida* (Mysliveček); ◊*Armide* (Gluck and Lully); ◊*Atys* (Lully and Piccinni); ◊*Cadmus et Hermione* (Lully); ◊*Fêtes de l'Amour* (Lully); ◊*Isis* (Lully); ◊Lully (*Églogue de Versailles*); ◊*Persée* (Lully); ◊*Phaéton* (Lully); ◊*Proserpine* (Lully and Paisiello); ◊*Roland* (Lully and Piccinni); ◊*Thésée* (Lully).

quint, or great quint in music, an ◊organ stop of 51/3 ft, transposing a fifth upwards.

quinta falsa (Latin 'false fifth') in music, another name for the tritone when it appears as a diminished fifth, not an augmented fourth.

quinte word used for the interval of the fifth. It was formerly also the name of a string instrument of the viol family, the tenor viol with five strings; also later of the viola, another French name of which was taille.

quintet ensemble of five musicians, or the music written for such a group. A common type of quintet is the piano quintet, which often consists of a ◊string quartet and piano.

quinton nineteenth-century name for a hybrid string instrument, half ◊viol and half ◊violin.

quintuplet a group of five notes to be played (usually) in the time of four. It is indicated by a ◊slur over the five notes with the number '5' written above it.

quintus (Latin 'the fifth') the fifth part in a composition for five or more voices in early music. It was so called because its range was always equal to that of one of the other parts, so that it could not be described as *cantus*, *altus*, *tenor* or *bassus*.

quire the old English spelling of choir.

quiterne French and old English name for the ◊cittern, a musical instrument.

quodlibet (Latin *quod libet*, 'as it pleases') composition made up of a medley of tunes, usually familiar songs, in polyphonic combinations. Obrecht's *Missa diversorum tenorum* is an elaborate quodlibet, introducing the melodies of *chansons* by 15th-century composers. A more familiar example is the quodlibet at the end of Bach's Goldberg Variations. The Spanish term for a quodlibet was *ensalada*.

quotations short passages in musical works taken from other music by the same composer or by another.

Examples of auto-quotations include:

Brahms, *Regenlied* in finale of G major violin sonata;

Elgar, a number of themes from earlier works in *The Music Makers*; demons' chorus from *The Dream of Gerontius* in *The Fourth of August* (as a theme for the enemy);

Mozart, 'Non più andrai' from *Figaro* in second-act finale of *Don Giovanni*;

Prokofiev, March from *The Love for Three Oranges* in ballet *Cinderella*;

Puccini, 'Mimì' theme from *La Bohème* in *Il tabarro*;

Rimsky-Korsakov, theme from *Pskovitianka* (*Ivan the Terrible*) in *The Tsar's Bride* (referring to Ivan);

Saint-Saëns, theme from *Danse macabre* in *Fossils* section of *Le Carnaval des animaux*;

Schumann, opening of *Papillons*, op. 1, in *Florestan* piece in *Carnaval*, op. 9;

Shostakovich, themes from tenth symphony and first cello concerto in eighth string quartet (1960);

Smetana, theme associated with the Vyšehrad citadel of Prague in the first symphonic poem of *Má Vlast* and referring to in the later one entitled *Vltava*;

Strauss, theme from *Guntram* in 'Childhood' section of *Tod und Verklärung*; a number of themes from earlier works in the 'Hero's Works' section of *Heldenleben* and in the dinner music in the *Bourgeois Gentilhomme* incidental music; *Ariadne auf Naxos* in *Capriccio*; transfiguration theme from *Tod und Verklärung* in *Im Abendrot* ('Last Songs');

Vaughan Williams, theme from *Hugh the Drover* in violin concerto;

Wagner, two themes from *Tristan* in *Meistersinger*, III. i; swan motive from *Lohengrin* in *Parsifal*, I; themes from *Siegfried* in *Siegfried Idyll* (some going back to a projected string quartet);

Wolf, song, 'In dem Schatten meiner Lock-en' from *Spanish Song-Book* in opera *Der Corregidor*, I.

Examples of quotations from a different composer's work include:

Bartók, Nazi march theme from Shostako-vich's seventh symphony in Concerto for Orchestra;

Beethoven's 'Song of Thanksgiving' in the third piano concerto (both composers had just recovered from illness);

Bax, theme from Wagner's *Tristan* in symphonic poem *Tintagel*; passage from Elgar's violin concerto, in G major string quartet dedicated to Elgar;

Beethoven, 'Notte e giorno faticar' from Mozart's *Don Giovanni* in Variations on a theme by Diabelli, op. 120;

Berg, themes from Wagner's *Tristan* and Zemlinsky's *Lyric Symphony* in Lyric Suite for string quartet; Bach chorale *Es ist genug* in violin concerto;

Berio, scherzo from Mahler's second symphony and other items in *Sinfonia*;

Brahms, 'Batti, batti' from Mozart's *Don Giovanni* in song *Liebe und Frühling*, op. 3 no. 2;

Bréville, 'Tarnhelm' motive from Wagner's *Ring* in *Portraits de Maîtres* for piano, indicat-ing a transformation between the pieces imitating various composers;

Britten, theme from Wagner's *Tristan* in *Albert Herring*;

Chabrier, Serenade from Mozart's *Don Giovanni* in song *Ballade des gros dindons*;

Charpentier, theme from Wagner's *Ring* in *Louise*, II;

Chopin, air from Rossini's *Gazza ladra* in Polonaise in B minor dedicated to Kolberg (1826);

Debussy, theme from Wagner's *Tristan* in *Golliwogg's Cake-Walk* (*Children's Corner*);

Elgar, theme from Mendelssohn's overture *Calm Sea and Prosperous Voyage* in 'Enigma' Variations (*Romance*); Chopin's G minor nocturne and Paderewski's *Polish Fantasy* for piano and orchestra in symphonic prelude *Polonia*;

Falla, opening motive from Beethoven's fifth symphony ('Fate knocking at the door') in ballet *The Three-cornered Hat*;

Fibich, various themes from Mozart's *Don Giovanni* in opera *Hedy* (based on Byron's *Don Juan*);

Křenek, Mendelssohn's *Spring Song* in incidental music for Goethe's *Triumph der Empfindsamkeit*;

Mahler, theme from Charpentier's *Louise* and Hunding's motive from Wagner's *Ring*

in the first movement of the ninth sym-phony; prelude to scene 3 of *Boris Godunov* in *Der Einsame im Herbst* (*Das Lied von der Erde*);

Mozart, tunes from Martín y Soler's *Una cosa rara* and Sarti's *Fra due litiganti* in second act finale of *Don Giovanni*;

Mussorgsky, Handel's 'See the conquering hero' and themes by Famitsin and from Serov's opera *Rogenda* in satirical song *The Peep-Show*; sea motive from Rimsky-Korsa-kov's *Sadko* in song *The Classicist*;

Offenbach, 'Notte e giorno faticar' from Mozart's *Don Giovanni* in *Tales of Hoffmann*, prologue; 'Che farò' from Gluck's *Orfeo* in *Orphée aux enfers*;

Rimsky-Korsakov, themes from Mozart's Requiem in opera *Mozart and Salieri*;

Saint-Saëns, themes from overture to Of-fenbach's *Orphée aux enfers* in *Tortoises* section of *Le Carnaval des animaux* (because Orpheus's lute was made of tortoise-shell), also Berlioz's *Dans des Sylphes* in *Elephants* and a phrase from Rossini's *Barber of Seville* in *Fossils* in the same work;

Schumann, theme from Beethoven's *An die ferne Geliebte* in *Carnaval*, op. 9 (written while Schumann was separated from Clara Wieck); aria from Marschner's *Der Templer und die Jüdin* in finale of *Études symphoni-ques*, op. 13;

Shostakovich, overture from Rossini's *Wil-liam Tell* and the fate motif from Wagner's *Ring*, in the 15th symphony;

Strauss, Denza's song *Funiculi, funiculá* in symphony *Aus Italien* (under the impression that it was an Italian folksong); giants' motive in Wagner's *Ring* in *Feuersnot*; Wagner's Rhinemaidens' theme in dinner music (sal-mon) of Strauss's *Bourgeois gentilhomme* (*Ar-iadne*, first version); themes by Bull, Legrenzi, Monteverdi and Peerson in *Die schweigsame Frau*; fragment from funeral march in Beetho-ven's 'Eroica' symphony in *Metamorphosen* for strings;

Stravinsky, waltz by Lanner (played on a barrel-organ) in ballet *Petrushka*; themes from Tchaikovsky's piano music and songs in ballet *The Fairy's Kiss/Le Baiser de la fée*;

Tchaikovsky, song from Grétry's *Richard, Cœur de Lion* in *The Queen of Spades*;

Vaughan Williams, opening theme from Debussy's *L'Après-midi d'un faune* in inciden-tal music for Aristophanes' *Wasps*;

Wagner, *Di tanti palpiti*, from Rossini's *Tancredi*, parodied in the tailor's episode in *Meistersinger*, III.

Walton, two themes from Rossini's *William*

Tell overture in *Façade* (*Swiss Yodelling Song*); theme from Rossini's *Tancredi* overture in *Scapino* overture.

Also numerous examples of quotations from earlier works in the music of contemporary composers Kagel, Holloway, and Stockhausen (*Beethausen, opus 1970, von Stockhoven*).

Quo vadis? opera by Nouguès (libretto by H Cain, based on Sienkiewicz's novel), produced Nice, 9 February 1909.

R

r the supertonic note in any key in tonic sol-fa notation, pronounced Ray.

Rabaud, Henri (Benjamin) (1873–1949) French composer. He wrote six operas, including *Mârouf, savetier du Caire* 1914, which was his most successful. He also wrote music for films, and was director of the Paris Conservatory 1920–41.

He studied under his father, the cellist Hippolyte Rabaud (1839–1900), and with André Gédalge and Massenet at the Paris Conservatory, where he won the Prix de Rome in 1894. After his stay in Rome he visited Vienna and travelled elsewhere, and after his return to Paris he became harmony professor at the Conservatory and conductor at the Opéra. In 1920 he succeeded Fauré as director of the Conservatory, and was in turn succeeded in that post by Claude Delvincourt in 1941.

Works include: the operas *La fille de Roland* (1904), *Le premier glaive* (1907), *Mârouf, savetier du Caire* (1914), *L'appel de la mer* (after Synge's *Riders to the Sea*, 1924), *Rolande et les mauvais garçons* (1934); incidental music for Shakespeare's *Merchant of Venice* and *Antony and Cleopatra* (1917); music for films *Joueurs d'échecs* and *Le miracle des loups*; Psalm 4 for chorus; two symphonies, symphonic poem *Andromède*, *La procession nocturne* (after Lenau's 'Faust' (1899), *Le sacrifice d'Isaac*, *La flûte de Pan*, *Divertissement grec*, *Divertissement sur des airs russes*, *Poème sur le livre de Job*, and others, for orchestra; string quartet; songs.

Rachmaninov, Sergei Vasilevich (1873–1943) Russian composer, conductor, and pianist. After the 1917 Revolution he emigrated to the USA. His music is melodious and emotional and includes operas, such as *Francesca da Rimini* 1906, three symphonies, four piano concertos, piano pieces, and songs. Among his other works are the *Prelude in C-Sharp Minor* 1892 and *Rhapsody on a Theme of Paganini* 1934 for piano and orchestra.

Rachmaninov was the son of a captain in the Imperial Guards and the descendant of a wealthy and noble family. The family fortune was gravely impaired during his childhood and his parents separated in 1882, Rachmaninov living with his mother in St Petersburg. There he took music lessons at the Conservatory in a desultory way until Siloti, who was his cousin, advised his mother to send him to Moscow to study under Nikolai Sverev. He went to the Moscow Conservatory and lived in Sverev's house for four years; later he went to live with his aunt, whose daughter, Natalia Satin, he later married. He wrote the one-act opera *Aleko* while still a student, and the piano pieces op. 3, containing the popular C♯ minor prelude, at the age of 19. In 1895 he wrote his first symphony and in 1898 was invited by the Philharmonic Society in London to appear as a pianist and to conduct his orchestral fantasy *The Rock*. In 1905–06 he became conductor of the Imperial Grand Opera at Moscow and in 1909 visited the USA for the first time, writing the third piano concerto for the occasion and playing it himself. He had by this time become one of the finest pianists of the time and he remained pre-eminent in that respect throughout his life.

He lived in Moscow again 1910–17 and conducted the Philharmonic concerts there 1911–13. During World War I he played much for charity, and at the death of Skriabin, who had been his fellow-pupil under Anton Arensky, he decided to make a tour playing that composer's works only. From that time on he became a much travelled pianist, and finding himself out of sympathy with the Revolution in Russia, he took the opportunity of a concert journey to Scandinavia in 1917 to leave his country for ever. He lived in Paris for a time and then spent most of the rest of his life in the USA, touring there each year from January to April and visiting Europe as pianist in October and November, spending some of the summer months at a small property he had acquired on Lake Lucerne in Switzerland.

Rachmaninov's reputation with the public has always been secure, although his frequently dark and emotional music has had some harsh words from the critics: the exceptionally tall Rachmaninov was summed up by the diminutive Stravinsky as 'six and-a-half feet of sheer misery'.

Works include: STAGE *Aleko* (1893), *The Miserly Knight* (1906), *Francesca da Rimini* (1906), and *Monna Vanna* (1907; performed Philadelphia, 1985); choral symphony, *The Bells* (Poe), for solo voices, chorus, and orchestra (1913); cantata *The Spring; Liturgy of St John Chrysostom* (1910) and Vesper Mass; three Russian folk songs and chorus.

ORCHESTRAL piano concertos (1890–1926) and *Rhapsody on a Theme by Paganini* for piano and orchestra (1934); three symphonies (1895, 1907, 1936), fantasy *The Rock, Caprice Bohémien* and symphonic poem *The Isle of the Dead* (after Böcklin's picture) for orchestra (1909); *Symphonic Dances* (1940).

CHAMBER AND SOLO MUSIC *Elegiac Trio* for violin, cello, and piano (1893), string quintet and piano trio (unpub); cello and piano sonata, two pieces for violin and piano and two for cello and piano; a dozen works for piano solo, including two sonatas, variations on themes by Chopin (1903) and Corelli (1931), and 57 smaller pieces (preludes, *Etudes-Tableaux*, and others); four works for two pianos; 77 songs.

Racine, Jean (1639–1699) French poet and dramatist. See ◊*Andromaque* (Grétry); ◊*Athalie* (Mendelssohn and others); ◊Boieldieu (*Athalie*); ◊*Esther* (Handel); ◊Fauré (*Cantique*); ◊*Ifigenia in Aulide* (Graun); ◊*Iphigénie en Aulide* (Gluck); ◊Lully (*Idylle sur la paix*); ◊Massenet (*Phèdre* incidental music); ◊*Mitridate, Rè di Ponto* (Mozart); ◊Moreau (*Cantiques spiritueles, Esther* and *Athalie*); ◊Roseingrave (*Phaedra and Hippolytus*); ◊Rossini (*Ermione*); ◊Saint-Saëns (*Andromaque*); ◊Vogler (*Athalie*).

rackett, also known as racket, ranket, or sausage bassoon ingenious Renaissance double-reed woodwind musical instrument incorporating a ninefold straight tube packed into a 22-cm/9-in compact cylinder. It emits a strong, rasping tone extending to F1 in double bassoon range.

Radamisto opera by Handel (libretto by N F Haym, after Tacitus), produced London, King's Theatre, Haymarket, 27 April 1720. Tyrant King Tiridate lusts after Zenobia, wife of Prince Radamisto, sending armies to conquer his rival. When Zenobia opts to die with her husband rather than yield to Tiridate, news arrives of a revolt in the tyrant's army and the married couple are saved.

Radcliffe, Philip (FitzHugh) (1905–1986) English scholar, author, and composer. He was educated at Charterhouse and King's College, Cambridge; university lecturer in music at Cambridge, 1947–72. His compositions include chamber music, part-songs and songs. Also wrote a book on Mendelssohn, and contributed chapters on the Scarlattis, Corelli and Vivaldi to *The Heritage of Music*.

Radnai, Miklós (1892–1935) Hungarian composer. He studied at Budapest and Munich, was a professor at the Budapest Conservatory 1919–25, and then director of the Opera there.

Works include: the opera *The Former Lovers;* ballet *The Infanta's Birthday* (after Wilde, 1918); Hungarian Symphony, *Mosaic* suite, five poems, *Fairy Tale, Orcan the Hero,* for orchestra; piano trio; instrumental sonatas; piano works; songs.

Raff, (Joseph) Joachim (1822–1882) Swiss composer. He is best known for such programme symphonies as *Im Walde* and *Frühlingsklänge/Voices of Spring*, suggesting Alpine imagery tinged by German Romanticism.

He studied to become a schoolmaster, but took to music and in 1843 had some works published on Mendelssohn's recommendation. He met Liszt, and at Cologne in 1846 Mendelssohn, who invited him to become his pupil at Leipzig but died before this was done. He then wrote criticism at Cologne, studied further at Stuttgart, and in 1850 settled at Weimar to be near Liszt. In 1856 he went to Wiesbaden, where he wrote incidental music for a drama by Wilhelm Genast and married his daughter Doris, an actress. In 1877 he became director of the Hoch Conservatory at Frankfurt.

Works include: the operas *König Alfred* (1851), *Dame Kobold* (on Calderón's *Dama* *duende*, 1870), and others; incidental music for Genast's *Bernhard von Weimar* and other plays; oratorio *Weltende* and other choral works; 11 symphonies, including programme symphony *An das Vaterland, Im Walde, Lenore* (on Bürger's ballad), *Gelebt, gestrebt ..., In den Alpen, Frühlingsklange, Im Sommer, Zur Herbstzeit, Der Winter* (unfinished), two suites, three overtures for orchestra; sinfonietta for wind instruments; concerto, suite, and *Ode au printemps* for piano and orchestra, two violin concertos, cello concerto; eight string quartets, string sextets, string octet, four piano trios, two piano quartets, piano quintet; five violin and piano sonatas; numerous piano works; violin pieces.

raga (Sanskrit *rāga* 'tone' or 'colour') in ◊Indian music, a scale of notes and style of ornament for music associated with a particular mood or time of day; the equivalent term in rhythm is **tala**. A choice of raga and tala forms the basis of improvised music; however, a written composition may also be based on (and called) a raga.

ragtime an American form of syncopated dance music of African-American origin and coming into fashion c. 1910, the forerunner of jazz and swing. Also title of work by Stravinsky for 11 instruments; composed 1918, first performed London, 27 April 1920, conductor Bliss.

Raimbaut de Vaqueiras (lived late 12th century) French ◊troubadour from Orange, Provence. He travelled widely with Guillaume des Baux, Prince of Orange, and the Marquis Boniface of Montferrat, and died in Thessaloníki, Greece.

Raimbaut d'Orange (died 1173) French count of Orange, Provence, and an eminent ◊troubadour. Some 40 of his poems remain (including about 30 love songs). He was an outstanding practitioner of the hermetic style known as *trobar clus*.

Raimondi, Pietro (1786–1853) Italian composer. He studied at the Conservatorio di Pietà de' Turchini at Naples and wandered all over Italy in great poverty until he succeeded in producing an opera at Genoa in 1807. He produced operas at Rome, Milan, Naples, and in Sicily until 1824, and was director of the royal theatres there until 1832, when he became professor of composition at the Palermo Conservatory. In 1852 he was appointed maestro di cappella at St Peter's in Rome in succession to Basili.

Works include: the operas *Le bizzarrie d'amore* (1807), *Il ventaglio* and 60 others including a serious and a comic one which could be performed together; 21 ballets; eight oratorios including trilogy *Giuseppe* (including *Putifar, Farao* and *Giacobbe* performable separately or simultaneously), Masses, Requiems, psalms and other church music, much of it in very numerous parts; vocal fugues, one in 64 parts and including others in four parts, four of which could be sung together in 16 parts.

Raindrop Prelude Chopin's piano prelude in Db major, op. 28 no. 15, written at Valdemosa, Majorca, in 1838 and said to have been suggested by the dripping of raindrops from the roof; hence the continuously repeated Ab = G♯, which is the dominant both of the main key and of the C♯ minor middle section.

Rainier, Priaulx (1903–1986) South African composer. She studied at Cape Town and after 1920 at the Royal Academy of Music in London; lastly with Nadia Boulanger in Paris. In 1942 she was appointed professor at the Royal Academy of Music.

Works include: *Archaic Songs* for chorus; ballet suite for orchestra (1950), *Sinfonia da camera* for strings (1947); *Incantation* for clarinet and orchestra; cello concerto (1964); *Aequora Lunae* for orchestra (1967); *Ploërmel* for winds and percussion (1973); violin concerto (1977), Concertante for oboe, clarinet, and orchestra (1981); string quartet (1939); viola and piano sonata; piano works; songs.

Raitio, Väinö (1891–1945) Finnish composer. He studied the piano with his mother, later composition with Melartin and Furuhjelm and 1916–17 with Ilyinsky in Moscow. He taught composition at Viipuri 1932–38, but settled at Helsinki and devoted himself entirely to composition.

Works include: the operas *Jephtha's Daughter* (1931), *Princess Cecilia* (1936) and three others; ballet *Waterspout* (1929); symphonies, ten symphonic poems; piano concerto, concerto for violin and cello (1936), Poem for cello and orchestra (1915); string quartet, piano quintet; violin and piano sonata; songs.

Rakastava/The Lover three songs for male chorus a capella by Sibelius, op. 14; composed 1893, first performed Helsinki, 28 April 1894. Version for male chorus and strings, 1894. Rewritten for strings, triangle and timpani, 1911: *The Lover, The Path of the Beloved, Good night*.

Rake's Progress, The opera by Stravinsky (libretto by W H Auden and C Kallman, based on Hogarth), produced Venice, 11

September 1951. Tom Rakewell inherits a fortune and leaves sweetheart Anne. Nick Shadow corrupts and ruins him, finally demanding his soul. Tom evades Nick, but loses his reason before dying.

Rakhmaninov alternative spelling for Russian composer Sergei ◊Rachmaninov.

Rakoczy Marchch a Hungarian national tune named after Prince Ferencz Rákóczy, the leader of the revolt against Austria 1703–11. The origin of the tune is unknown. The Hungarian Marchch in Berlioz's *Damnation of Faust* is an orchestral arrangement of it and Liszt's 15th Hungarian Rhapsody for piano is based on it. Liszt also made a symphonic arrangement for orchestra and himself transcribed this for piano duet.

rallentando, or rall. (Italian 'slowing down') in musical notation, indicating a gradual reduction in the speed of a passage; synonymous with *ritardando*.

Rameau, Jean-Philippe (1683–1764) French organist and composer. His *Traité de l'harmonie/Treatise on Harmony* 1722 established academic rules for harmonic progression, and his varied works include keyboard and vocal music and many operas, such as *Castor and Pollux* 1737.

Ramis de Pareja, Bartolome (c. 1440–after 1491) Spanish theorist and composer. He wrote a theoretical work in which he devised a way of tuning the ◊monochord and wrote church music.

After lecturing at Salamanca he went to Italy, living at Bologna 1480–82 and later in Rome.

Ramler, Karl Wilhelm (1725–98) German poet. His works inspired J C F ◊Bach (*Tod Jesu*); K H Graun (ditto); Kreusser (ditto); ◊Telemann (*Tod Jesu* and *Auferstehung Christi*); Veichtner (*Cephalus und Procris*); and ◊Vogler (*Ino*).

Rands, Bernard (1935–) English composer. His music uses electronic techniques and is strongly influenced by ◊Berio.

He studied at University College of North Wales, Bangor, and then in Italy with Roman Vlad and Dallapiccola. He lectured at Bangor 1961–70, and at York University 1970–76. In 1976 he moved to the USA and taught at the universities of California and Boston.

Works include: *Refractions* for 24 performers; *Actions for Six* for flute, viola, cello, harp, and two percussion players (1963), *Quartet Music* for piano quartet; *Four Compositions* for violin and piano; *Espressione IV* for two pianos; *Three Aspects* for piano; *Formants*

for harp (1965); *Agenda* for orchestra (1970); *As All Get Out* for chamber ensemble (1972); *Canti del Sole* for tenor and orchestra (won 1984 Pulitzer Prize); *Ceremonial I* and *II* for orchestra (1985–86), *Serenata 85*; *Hiraeth* for cello and orchestra (1987) *Body and Shadow* for orchestra (1988), *... in the receding mist ...* for ensemble (1988).

'Ranz des Vaches' a Swiss cowherds' song or alphorn signal by which the cattle are called in June from the valleys to the mountain pastures. There are many different tunes, varying according to the cantons or even districts. They are metrically very irregular and use only the natural notes of the alphorn. Versions are heard in the *William Tell* overture, the *Pastoral* symphony (link between last two movements), and the *Scène aux champs* in the *Symphonie fantastique*.

Rape of Lucretia, The opera by Britten (libretto by R Duncan, based on Livy, Shakespeare and Obey's *Viol de Lucrèce*), produced Glyndebourne, 12 July 1946. In ancient Rome Lucretia is reckoned to be the only chaste woman. Prince Tarquinius sets out to test this, arriving at her house and asking for a bed for the night. While Lucretia sleeps, Tarquinius appears in her bedroom and kisses her. At first Lucretia responds, believing it to be her husband, but soon she realizes the awful truth. The next morning she is overcome by shame and stabs herself.

Raphael, Günther (1903–1960) German composer. In his early 20s he succeeded in having works published, played by the Busch quartet, conducted by Wilhelm Furtwängler and others. He was professor at the Leipzig Conservatory 1926–34, resigning after the Nazis banned his music; after World War II he taught at Duisburg Conservatory 1949–53, and from 1957 at the Cologne Musikhochschule.

He studied under his father, a church organist, and later with Max Trapp and Robert Kahn at the Berlin Hochschule für Musik.

Works include: Requiem (1928), Te Deum (1930), cantata *Vater unser* (1945); 16 motets, Psalm civ and other unaccompanied sacred choral works; five symphonies (1926–53), sinfonietta, *Theme, Variations and Rondo*, divertimento, *Smetana Suite* for orchestra; two violin concertos (1921, 1960), organ concerto (1936); chamber concerto for cello with wind and strings, much other chamber music; organ and piano works.

Rapimento di Cefalo, Il/The Abduction of Cephalus opera by Caccini (libretto by G

Chiabrera), produced Florence, Palazzo Vecchio, 9 October 1600. Aurora (Dawn) seduces Cephalus, and as a result of her preoccupation, Night remains over the world. Jupiter has Cupid find Dawn and bring her back to illuminate the Earth.

Rappresentazione di anima e di corpo/ Representation of Soul and Body a dramatic allegory, words by Manni, music by Emilio de' Cavalieri, produced Rome, oratory of St Philip Neri, February 1600.

Rapsodie espagnole/Spanish Rhapsody an orchestral work by Ravel in a Spanish manner as cultivated by a typically French composer with a strong taste for and leanings towards Spanish music; composed 1907, first performed Paris, 15 March 1908.

rasch (German 'quick') term used in musical notation.

Raselius, Andreas (c. 1563–1602), born Rasel German clergyman, theorist, and composer. He wrote a treatise on the hexachord, set hymn and psalm tunes in five parts, and composed German motets.

He studied at the Lutheran University of Heidelberg, became cantor at Regensburg 1584–1600, and was then music director to the Elector Palatine at Heidelberg.

Rasumovsky Quartets Beethoven's three string quartets, op. 59 in F major, E minor and C major, composed 1806 and dedicated to the Russian ambassador to Vienna, Count (later Prince) Andrey Kiryllovich Rasumovsky (1752–1836), by whose domestic quartet, led by Schuppanizigh, they were first performed. The first two quartets contain Russian themes.

rataplan (French onomatopoeic; English 'rub-a-dub') word imitating the sound of the side-drum and used for music pieces, especially in opera, of a military-march character.

Ratcliff opera by Andreae (libretto taken from Heine's tragedy *William Ratcliff*), produced Duisburg, 25 May 1914.

Rathaus, Karol (1895–1954) Polish-born US composer. He studied with Schreker in Vienna and followed him to Berlin when Schreker became director of the Hochschule für Musik, where Rathaus taught 1925–33. In 1934 he took refuge from the Nazi regime in London and later settled in USA, becoming a US citizen in 1946.

Works include: the opera *Strange Soil* (1930); ballets *The Last Pierrot* (1927), and *Lion amoureux* (1937); incidental music to Shakespeare's *Merchant of Venice*, Gutzkow's *Uriel Acosta*, Hebbel's *Herodes und Mariamne*; choral

works; three symphonies (1921–43), overture, serenade, suites, *Four Dance Pieces*, *Kontrapunktisches Triptychon* (1934), *Jacob's Dream*, *Polonaise symphonique* for orchestra; concertino for piano and orchestra, suite for violin and orchestra, *Little Prelude* for trumpet and strings; five string quartets, two trios for violin, clarinet, and piano; film music, including *The Brothers Karamazov* (1931) and *The Dictator* (1934).

Ratswahlkantate cantata by Bach (BWV 71), *Gott ist mein König*, written for the election of the town council of Mühlhausen on 4 February 1708, and performed on that day in St Mary's Church. Bach was at the time organist of St Blasius'.

rattle noise-producing toy, a ratchet, occasionally used as a percussion instrument in the modern orchestra.

Ratto di Proserpina, Il/The Rape of Proserpine opera by Winter (libretto by L da Ponte), produced London, King's Theatre, Haymarket, 3 May 1804.

Rauchfangkehrer, Der/The Chimney-Sweep Singspiel by Salieri (libretto by L von Auenbrugger), produced Vienna, Burgtheater, 30 April 1781. Volpino, the chimney-sweep, tricks Herr von Bär and von Wölf into giving him a dowry for fiancée Lisel. Bär and Wölf become engaged to the mother and daughter of the house.

rauschpfeife medieval windcap double-reed woodwind instrument in soprano or sopranino range, of wide bore and having a powerful reedy tone. It has been revived in recent years for use in Renaissance ◊broken consorts and as a folk instrument.

Rautavaara, Einojuhani (1938–) Finnish composer. His music embraces a wide variety of idioms, including Neo-Classicism, serialism, and jazz.

He studied at the Sibelius Academy in Helsinki, at the Juilliard School in New York, and with Sessions and Copland at Tanglewood. He was professor at the Sibelius Academy 1976–90.

Works include: *The Mine* (1963), *Apollo and Marsyas* (1973), *Marjatta the Lowly Maiden* (1977), *Thomas* (1985), and *Vincent* (based on the life of Van Gogh, 1990). Other works include seven symphonies and concertos for cello, piano, and violin.

Ravel, (Joseph) Maurice (1875–1937) French composer and pianist. His work is characterized by its sensuousness, exotic harmonics, and dazzling orchestral effects. His opera *L'enfant et les sortilèges* 1924 illustrates most of the various styles which influenced him at different times. Other works include the piano pieces *Pavane pour une infante défunte/Pavane for a Dead Infanta* 1899 and *Jeux d'eau/Waterfall* 1901, and the ballets *Daphnis et Chloë* 1912 and *Boléro* 1928.

Ravel's father was of Swiss and his mother of Basque descent; they moved to Paris the year of his birth and after some preliminary teaching he entered the Conservatory 1889, studying piano with Eugene Anthiôme and later with Charles Wilfrid de Bériot (1833–1914), also theory under Emile Pessard (1843–1917) from 1891. He composed a good deal and in 1897 passed to Fauré's class for composition and to that of André Gédalge (1856–1926) for counterpoint. In 1899 he had an overture *Shéhérazade* (unconnected with the later song-cycle) and the *Pavane pour une infante défunte* in the original piano version performed by the Société Nationale. In 1905 his rejection by the Paris Conservatory of his Prix de Rome submission provoked a scandal which led to the resignation of the director. Two of his finest works, the string quartet 1903 and the piano piece *Miroirs* 1905, date from the same period. In these pieces, as in others, Ravel's indebtedness to the Impressionists as well as a concentration on minute detail may be seen. In 1908 he set a new standard of piano writing with *Gaspard de la nuit*.

During the next ten years he wrote some of his best works, but his first great public success came in 1911, when the Opéra-Comique brought out *L'heure espagnole*, and the second in 1912, when Diaghilev's Ballets Russes/Russian Ballet produced *Daphnis et Chloé*, in which Ravel displays his mastery of colourful orchestration, combining instruments in a subtle, ever-changing palette.

During World War I he served in an ambulance corps at the front, but was demobilized owing to ill-health in 1917. Although physically weakened, he produced such successful post-war works as *La valse*, depicting a Viennese ballroom at the disintegration of an era, the neoclassical *Le tombeau de Couperin*, and the childhood opera *L'enfant et les sortilèges*. He scornfully remarked of his *Boléro*, 'There's not a note of music in it', but was grateful for its popular success. His last large-scale works were the piano concerto in G and concerto for piano left hand. He made a great reputation and a comfortable living without ever holding an official musical post. In the 1920s he visited London more than once with great success and in 1928 received an honorary doctorate from Oxford University. A car accident in 1933 marked the beginning of a long illness, and he died after a brain operation.

Works include: STAGE opera *L'heure espagnole* (1911); opera-ballet *L'enfant et les sortilèges* (1925), ballet *Daphnis et Chloé* (1912), also *La valse* (composed 1919–20; first performance as ballet, 1928). Orchestral works include *Rapsodie espagnole* for orchestra (1908), *Boléro* (1928); concerto for piano and orchestra (1929–31); piano concerto for the left hand with orchestra (1930); several orchestrations of piano works.

CHAMBER string quartet (1903) *Introduction et Allegro* for harp, flute, clarinet, and string quartet, (1905), piano trio in A minor (1914); sonata for violin and cello (1922), sonata for violin and piano.

PIANO 15 piano works including five *Miroirs* (1905), *Gaspard de la nuit* (three pieces after Louis Bertrand's prose poems, 1908), suite *Le tombeau de Couperin* (1917).

SONGS 29 songs including cycles *Shéhérazade* (1903); *Chansons madécasses* for voice, flute, cello, and piano (1926); three part songs.

Ravenscroft, Thomas (c. 1582–c. 1633)

English composer. He was a chorister at St Paul's Cathedral under Edward Pearce, took a degree in music at Cambridge University in 1607 and was music master at Christ's Hospital 1618–22.

Works include: anthems, 55 of the 105 hymn-tune settings contained in his Psalter; madrigals, some of the four-part songs *The Pleasures of five usuall Recreations* in his treatise on notation *A Briefe Discourse* (1614) are by himself; some of the rounds and catches in the collections *Pammelia* (1609), *Deuteromelia* (1609), and *Melismata* (1611) are probably of his own composing.

Rawsthorne, Alan (1905–1971)

British composer. His *Theme and Variations* for two violins 1938 was followed by other tersely energetic works including *Symphonic Studies* 1939, the overture *Street Corner* 1944, *Concerto for Strings* 1950, and a vigorously inventive sonata for violin and piano, 1959.

After studying dentistry, he turned to music at the age of 20 and studied at the Royal Manchester College of Music 1926–29. He taught at Dartington Hall, Devon 1932–34; but settled in London in 1935 and married the violinist Jessie Hinchliffe. He devoted all his time to composition and produced a comparatively small number of distinctive and highly finished works. In 1938 and 1939 he had works performed at the International

Society for Contemporary Music festivals in London and Warsaw.

Works include: ORCHESTRAL three symphonies (1950, 1959, 1964), *Symphonic Studies,* overture *Street Corner* for orchestra; two piano concertos, two violin concertos (1948, 1956), concerto for clarinet and strings, cello concerto (1965).

CHAMBER AND VOCAL two string quartets (1954, 1964), Theme and Variations for string quartet (1939), quintet for piano and wind (1963); viola and piano sonata, Theme and Variations for two violins; four Bagatelles for piano; songs 'Away Delights' and 'God Lyaeus' (John Fletcher), *Three French Nursery Songs.*

Ray the name for the supertonic note in any key in tonic sol-fa, so pronounced, but in notation represented by the symbol **r**.

Raymonda ballet by Glazunov (choreography by Marius Petipa), produced St Petersburg, Maryinsky Theatre, 19 January 1898.

Raymond ou Le Secret de la Reine/Raymond, or The Queen's Secret opera by A Thomas (libretto by A de Leuven and J B Rosier), produced Paris, Opéra-Comique, 5 June 1851.

'Razor' Quartet/Rasiermesser nickname of Haydn's string quartet in F minor, op. 55, no. 2, composed 1788, so called because Haydn is said to have offered the publisher Bland his best quartet in return for a good razor.

RCA Mark II synthesizer pioneer digitally programmable analogue synthesizer developed in 1959 by Harry Olsen and Herbert Belar. It was installed in the joint Columbia-Princeton electronic studio under the direction of US composers Otto ◊Luening and Milton ◊Babbitt, its best-known advocate. It was the first integrated device for pre-programmed synthesis and mixing of electronic and concrete sound materials, employing a punched card control system.

Re the old name for the note D in solmization, still used in Latin countries, and in tonic sol-fa notation the supertonic in any key, represented by the symbol **r**, pronounced Ray.

Read, Gardner (1913–   ) US composer. He studied at the Eastman School, with Pizzetti in Italy and Copland at Tanglewood. He was professor at Boston University School for the Arts 1948–78.

Works include: the opera *Villon* (1967); four symphonies; cello concerto (1945); piano concerto (1977); piano quintet (1945), and other chamber music; organ and piano pieces.

realism a realistic style favouring simpler contemporary themes.

A realistic style of Italian opera is known as *Verismo,* in which plots draw away from elaborate traditional mythological or historical subjects.

Strictly realistic representation in music is not easily attainable. Examples are the anvils in Wagner's *Rheingold,* the sheep and wind machine in R Strauss's *Don Quixote,* and the nightingale (gramophone record of the bird's song) in Respighi's *Pini di Roma.* Imitations of bells, birds, and similar effects are very frequent, but usually the more musical they are the less they approach realism.

realization the writing out or playing at sight of the harmony from a ◊thorough-bass; may also involve the preparation for performance of uncompleted or sparsely written score, such as Friedrich Cerha's version of Act 3 of Berg's *Lulu,* or Raymond Leppard's popular and imaginative versions of Venetian opera.

In the music of the 18th century and earlier continuo lines were written in a shorthand that needs realization, often taking account of extremely refined skills cultivated in the Baroque era. Up to the end of the 18th century many works were written in the expectation that the soloists would improvise and embellish, often quite elaborately. Before about 1700 composers often do not specify the ensembles to be used, and it can be a complex business devising an ensemble appropriate to the style and techniques of the music. Beyond that, there could be a good argument for believing that an historically accurate reconstruction would be insufficient for present-day audiences; and there is a considerable history – going back to the early 19th century – of recasting earlier works to make them more acceptable to later conditions.

rebec(k) early string instrument of the violin type and of Arab origin, the ancestor of the violin family, though its shape is more like that of the mandolin, which is probably one of its descendants. It has three gut strings and is played with a bow. In France it survived until the 18th century, but only as a street instrument.

It is descended from the Arab rabab, a one- or two-stringed bowed fiddle still popular throughout the Arab world.

Rebelo, João Soares (or João Lourenço) (1609–1661) Portuguese composer. A fellow student of King John IV, who made him a nobleman on his accession in 1646.

Works include: psalms, Magnificat, Lamentations, Miserere, St Matthew Passion, Requiem, and other pieces.

Rebikov, Vladimir Ivanovich (1866–1920) Russian composer. He was the most advanced, if by no means the strongest or most important, Russian composer of his generation, using many unconventional devices (including whole-tone scales) and evolving an idiom of his own. His short piano and vocal pieces are his most characteristic work, and include a number of dramatic *melomimiki* (or *mélominiques*, small-scale works in an expressionist style).

He was born in Krasnoyarsk, Siberia, and studied at Moscow and Berlin. He later settled in southern Russia and founded music societies at Odessa and Kishinev. Some of his stage works are described as 'musico-psychological' or 'musicopsychgolographic' dramas, among them his opera *The Christmas Tree* 1903.

Works include: the operas and dramatic scenes *The Storm* (1894), *The Christmas Tree* (1903), *Thea, The Woman with the Dagger* (based on Schnitzler's play, 1911), *Alpha and Omega* (1911), *The Abyss* (after Andreiev), *Narcissus* (after Ovid's 'Metamorphoses', 1913), *Fables* (after Krilov); ballet *Snow-White*; suites for orchestra and string orchestra; numerous sets of piano pieces including *Rêveries d'automne* (1897), *Mélomimiques, Aspirer et attendre, Chansons blanches* (on the white keys).

recapitulation the section of ◊sonata form following the development section, in which the themes are presented in a manner similar or identical to the exposition, except that any material which was originally presented in the ◊dominant or any other key, appears in the ◊tonic key. A 'false' recapitulation was used at times by Beethoven and 19th-century composers either to present an additional development of musical ideas or to present temporarily the main themes in a key other than the tonic, as in the first movement of Beethoven's Sonata No. 3 1795.

reception, or reception history the study of the history of a piece of music after the date of its composition. This may take the form of studying the performance history of the work; or the reactions of audiences, both at its original performance and subsequently; or the writings of critics and scholars. The term is taken from German-speaking scholarship (where it is called *Rezeptionsgeschichte*), and treats pieces of music as historical phenomena which therefore change over time. This is in contrast to other forms of music history, which have tended to view pieces as unchanging, autonomous entities. Reception studies have become very influential in English-speaking scholarship in recent years. See Carl ◊Dahlhaus.

Re Cervo, Il/The Stag King revision made in 1962 by Henze of his 1955 opera ◊*König Hirsch*; first performed Kassel, 10 March 1963.

recherché ('searched out') French equivalent of *ricercato*, from which the ricercare is derived; Beethoven still used this old term, as meaning strict fugal writing, in his *Great Fugue* for string quartet, op. 133, which he called a fugue 'tantôt libre, tantôt recherchée'.

récit in the 17th century, a term for an accompanying solo, such as a vocal aria, an organ piece with a solo stop, and so on. Also swell organ.

recital a musical performance, usually with a miscellaneous programme, given by a single performer or by one singing or playing an instrument with a piano accompanist.

recitative in opera and oratorio, sung narration partly modelled on the rhythms and inflections of natural speech. It is usually sparingly accompanied by harpsichord or organ.

recitativo stromentato (Italian 'instrumentated recitative') another term for *recitativo accompagnato*, though a distinction was sometimes made between *recitativo accompagnato*, with a plain orchestral accompaniment, and *recitativo stromentato* with a more independent instrumental participation. See ◊recitative.

recorder any of a widespread range of woodwind instruments of the ◊whistle type which flourished in ◊consort ensembles in the Renaissance and Baroque eras, along with viol consorts, as an instrumental medium for polyphonic music. Unlike the flute, the recorder is held vertically and blown into through a mouthpiece in which the air is diverted by an obstructive block called the 'fipple' and produces a milder tone than that of the flute. A modern consort may include a sopranino in F5, soprano (descant) in C4, alto (treble) in F3, tenor in C3, bass in F2, and great bass in C2.

Early Renaissance recorders are of fairly wide bore and penetrating tone; late Renaissance and Baroque instruments are ◊fipple flutes of narrower bore and sweet to brilliant tone. The solo recorder remained a popular solo instrument into the 18th century, and the revival of popular interest in recorder playing after 1920, largely through the efforts of

Arnold ◊Dolmetsch, led to its wide adoption as a musical instrument for schools. Present-day makers have taken advantage of exotic hardwoods such as grenadilla to make instruments of brighter and stronger tone for concert soloists, and have also created hypothetical additions to existing consorts.

recte et retro (Latin 'right way and backwards') form of canon, also called, in Italian, *al rovescio*, in which a second entry brings in the tune sung or played backwards. Recte et retro is similar to ◊cancrizans.

Redemption, The English oratorio by Gounod (words compiled by the composer), produced Birmingham Festival, 1882.

Redlich, Hans (Ferdinand) (1903–1968) Austrian-born British musicologist. He studied at the Universities of Vienna, Munich, and Frankfurt. In 1925–29 he was opera conductor at Mainz, but in 1939 he took refuge in England. From 1955 to 1962 he was lecturer at Edinburgh University and in 1962 was appointed professor at Manchester University. He specialized in Monteverdi, several of whose works he edited, including the *Vespers* of 1610 and *L'Incoronazione di Poppea*, and on whom he wrote two books (1932 and 1949, English edition 1952). He also wrote on modern music including a book on Alban Berg.

redoute (French, used also in German, and derived from Italian *ridotto*) a kind of public ball, particularly in the 18th century, but carried on into the 19th in Austria and Germany where dancers gathered haphazardly from all classes of society, usually at assembly halls called *Redoutensäle* in Germany. Composers of note, especially in Vienna, often wrote dances for redoutes.

réduction an arrangement, especially from a complex to a simpler score, such as an opera 'reduced' to a vocal score or an orchestral work arranged for piano.

reed instrument any of a class of wind instruments employing a single or double flexible reed, made of cane, metal, or plastic, which vibrates under pressure within an airtight enclosure (the mouth, ◊windcap, bellows, airbag) and acts as a valve admitting pulses of pressurized air into a tubular resonator. Single-reed instruments, where the reed vibrates against the material of the instrument, include clarinets and saxophones; double-reeds, where the reeds vibrate against each other, include oboes, shawms, bagpipes, and bassoons. See also ◊free-reed instrument.

Most reed instruments incorporate finger holes to alter the pitch, and can be overblown (see ◊overblowing) to sound at the octave or twelfth. They produce complex waveforms of considerable dynamic and tonal range, and are more efficient than whistles in converting energy to sound in the tenor and bass registers.

reel a Scottish, Irish, and Scandinavian dance, either of Celtic or Scandinavian origin. It is performed with the dancers standing face to face and the music is in quick 2–4 or 4–4, occasionally 6–8, time and divided into regular eight-bar phrases. A musical characteristic of many reels is a drop into the triad of the subdominant unprepared by modulation.

Reese, Gustave (1899–1977) US musicologist. He studied at New York University and became lecturer in music there in 1927 and professor in 1955. He was associate editor of *The Music Quarterly* and its editor on the death of Carl Engel in 1944, but resigned in 1945. His work includes the books *Music in the Middle Ages* and *Music in the Renaissance*.

Reeve, William (1757–1815) English composer. He studied with Richardson, the organist at St James's Church, Westminster, and was organist at Totnes, Devon, 1781–83. After various engagements at London theatres, he joined the Covent Garden chorus, and there was asked to complete the ballet-pantomime *Oscar and Malvina* (after Ossian) left unfinished by Shield in 1791 on account of differences with the management. He then became composer at Covent Garden and in 1802 part-owner of Sadler's Wells Theatre. In one of his more popular pieces, *The Caravan* (1803), a child was rescued from a tank of water by a well-trained dog; the music of his theatre pieces failed to gain as much attention.

Works include: pieces for the stage, *The Apparition* (1794), *Merry Sherwood* (1795), *Harlequin and Oberon* (1796), *Harlequin and Quixote* (after Cervantes), *Joan of Arc* (1798), *Paul and Virginia* (with Mazzinghi, based on Saint-Pierre, 1800), *Rokeby Castle* (1813) and many others (some with Braham, Davy, Mazzinghi or Moorehead); music for Sadler's Wells pantomimes.

Refice, Licinio (1883–1954) Italian composer. His two operas combined religious sentiments with post-*verismo* Romantic expression and were promoted by the Vatican.

He became professor of church music at the Scuola Pontifica in Rome in 1910 and in 1911 conductor at the church of Santa Maria Maggiore.

Works include: the operas *Cecilia* (1934) and *Margherita da Cortona* (1938); 40 Masses, motets, Requiem, *Stabat Mater*, and other church music, two oratorios, three sacred cantatas, three choral symphonies, poems.

'Reformation' Symphony Mendelssohn's fifth symphony, op. 107, in D minor, composed 1830 for the tercentenary of the Augsburg Conference. It was not performed there owing to Roman Catholic opposition, but produced Berlin, November 1832.

refrain a recurrent strain in a song, returning with the same words at the beginning, middle or end of each verse with music which may or may not be derived from the first strain.

regal portable reed organ powered by bellows, said to have been invented about 1460 by Heinrich Traxdorff of Nuremberg in Germany, and current in Europe until the 17th century. A modern version is used in Indian popular music.

Reger, (Johann Baptist Joseph) Max(imilian) (1873–1916) German composer and pianist. He was professor at the Leipzig Conservatory from 1907. His works embody a particular blend of contrapuntal ingenuity and Romantic sentimentality, and include *Four Symphonic Poems* 1913, sonatas, Romantic character pieces, and orchestral variations and fugues on themes by Beethoven, Mozart, and other less well known composers.

Reger first learnt music from his mother and at the age of 13 he became organist at the Catholic church of Weiden in Bavaria, where his parents had moved in 1874. After three years there Heinrich Reimann was consulted about his gifts and invited him to become his pupil at Sondershausen. Reger went there in 1890 and the next year followed his master to Wiesbaden, where he soon became a teacher at the Conservatory. A period divided between hard work and dissipation led to a serious breakdown, and he lived with his parents at Weiden again 1899–1901, writing vast quantities of music, including many more pieces for organ. In 1901 he went to Munich in the hope of making his way as a composer, but posing as a progressive while being in reality a conservative, he made enemies all round and had some success only with his piano playing. The *Sinfonietta* for orchestra was a failure at its Berlin premiere, although it is now recognized as one of his most attractive works. He began to tour Germany and also visited Prague and Vienna, and gradually his work became known; he also made a reputation as a remarkable composition teacher. In 1907 he settled at

Leipzig as music director to the University and professor at the Conservatory, soon resigning the former post as uncongenial, but retaining the latter for the rest of his life. In 1911 he became conductor of the ducal orchestra at Meiningen, with which he went on tour, but this came to an end in 1914, when he went to live at Jena, travelling to Leipzig each week to carry out his duties at the Conservatory.

Reger was a master of counterpoint, integrating 19th-century chromatic developments into his works. A master of the fugue, with the ability to control tightly the form and harmonic direction of his compositions, Reger is sometimes regarded as the greatest composer for organ since J S Bach.

Works include: ORCHESTRAL variations on themes by J A Hiller (1907) and by Mozart (1914), Romantic Suite (1912), four tone-poems on pictures by Böcklin for orchestra (1913); piano concerto (1910), violin concerto (1908).

CHAMBER clarinet quintet; seven violin and piano sonatas, three clarinet and piano sonatas.

ORGAN two sonatas, two suites, Fantasy and Fugue on B.A.C.H., Variations and Fugue on original theme, Introduction, Passacaglia and Fugue, and other pieces.

PIANO AND SONGS Variations and Fugue on theme by Bach (1904) and numerous smaller works for piano, piano duets; many songs including *Schlichte Weisen*; part songs.

Regino of Prüm (c. 842–915) German Benedictine monk and music historian, canonist, and theorist. He was abbot of Prüm 892–99. He is believed to have been the first to arrange antiphons and responsories according to their mode in a *tonarius* (liturgical book containing antiphones and responsories of the Office and the Mass, arranged according to the eight psalm tones of the Gregorian chant). The first comprehensive tonary surviving after the Metz tonary of 870, the *Octo toni de musicae artis* is one of the most comprehensive plainchant sources in existence.

Regis, Jean (c. 1430–c. 1495) Flemish composer. He wrote two Masses, including one on *L'Homme armé*, songs in parts, eight motets, and other pieces.

He was choirmaster at Antwerp Cathedral and was Dufay's secretary at Cambrai in the 1440s. He went about 1451 to Soignies, and remained there.

register a set of organ pipes, controlled by one stop, used in ◊registration to produce a characteristic combination of tone and dynamics. Also, a certain vocal or instrumental range of pitches, often associated with a characteristic timbre, for example, the ◊chalumeau register of a clarinet or the ◊head voice register of a singer.

registration in organ and harpsichord playing, the selection of stops (levers affecting the tone qualities and power of the instrument) to be used, either prescribed by a composer or left to the player's taste.

Regnart, François (c. 1540–c. 1600) Flemish composer. He learnt music at Tournai Cathedral and studied at Douai University.

Works include: motets; chansons; *Poésies de Ronsard et autres* for four–five voices.

Regnart, Jacques (c. 1539–1599) Flemish composer, brother of François ◊Regnart.

He went to Vienna and Prague as a pupil to the Imperial chapel at an early age, became a tenor there in the 1560s, and in the 1570s was choirmaster and vice-Kapellmeister. In 1585–96 he was in the service of the Archduke Ferdinand at Innsbruck, but lived in Prague for the last five years of his life. His two other brothers, **Charles** and **Paschasius** contributed motets to a collection in which François and Jacques also appeared, edited by a fifth brother, **Augustin**, a canon at Lille.

Works include: 37 Masses, 195 motets; *canzone italiane* and German songs for five voices.

Reich, Steve (1936–) US composer. His Minimalist music employs simple patterns carefully superimposed and modified to highlight constantly changing melodies and rhythms; examples are *Phase Patterns* for four electronic organs 1970, *Music for Mallet Instruments, Voices, and Organ* 1973, and *Music for Percussion and Keyboards* 1984.

Reich was a pupil of Luciano Berio and Darius Milhaud. In 1966 founded the ensemble Steve Reich and Musicians, and began to study African, Balinese, and Hebrew music. He became a leading light of the Minimalist school of composers, abandoning orthodox notions of harmony and counterpoint in favour of repeated phrases which typically evolve only gradually over time. His works have had much success in Europe and the USA. His other compositions include *The Cave* 1993 and *City Life* 1994.

Works include: *Pitch Charts* for instrumental ensemble (1963); *Music for Piano and Tapes* (1964); *It's Gonna Rain* for tape (1965); *My Name Is*, with audience participation (1967); *Pulse Music* (1969); *Drumming* for eight small tuned drums, three marimbas, three glock-enspiels, two female voices and piccolo (1971); *Clapping Music* (1972); *Music for Pieces of Wood* (1973); *Music for 18 Musicians* (1975); Octet (1979); *Tehillim*, Hebrew psalms (1981); *Vermont Counterpoint* for 11 flutes (1982); *The Desert Music* for 24 amplified voices and orchestra (1984); *Sextet* (1985); *New York Counterpoint* for clarinet and tape (1985); *Impact*, dance (1985); *Three Movements* (1986) and *The Four Sections* (1987) for orchestra; *Different Trains* for string quartet and tape (1988); *The Cave*, music theatre (1989–93); *City Life* (1995).

Reicha, Antonín (1770–1836) Czech-born French theorist, teacher, and composer. After working in Bonn 1787–94, where he was friendly with Beethoven, he travelled widely in Europe, settling finally in Paris where he spent the rest of his life. He wrote much experimental music and tried many orchestral innovations but only his more conventional works were published in his lifetime. His compositions include eight operas, two symphonies, three concertos and much piano and chamber music, especially for wind quintet.

He was born in Prague, and studied at Wallerstein, Bavaria, under his uncle Joseph Reicha (1746–1795), from whose wife he learnt French. In 1785 he went to Bonn with his uncle, who became music director there and worked at the electoral court, where he got to know Beethoven. He taught music in Hamburg 1794–99, and had some success as a composer in Paris 1799–1802, but then went to Vienna, where he remained until 1808 and was patronized by the empress. He spent the rest of his life in Paris and became professor at the Conservatory in 1818, where his pupils included Berlioz, Franck, and Gounod.

He produced five books on music theory, providing a progressive course to a high compositional and aesthetic level; these were internationally successful.

Works include: the operas *Godefroid de Montfort* (1796), *Ouboualdi, ou Les Français en Egypte* (1798), *Cagliostro* (with Dourlen, 1810), *Natalie* (1816), *Sapho*; 16 symphonies, *Scènes musiciennes* for orchestra; 20 string quartets, six string quintets, Diecetto and Octet for strings and wind, 24 wind quintets, six string trios, duets for violins and for flutes; 12 violin and piano sonatas; piano sonatas and pieces.

Reichardt, Johann Friedrich (1752–1814) German composer. His output consists chiefly of vocal works, including about 1,500 songs; he was a forerunner of Schubert in song composition. His work is notable for a wide range of literary influences, including Goethe, Shakespeare, Sophocles, Schiller, Milton, and even Metastasio. He also wrote several books on music.

He studied at Königsberg University and picked up a rather haphazard musical education. He travelled widely in 1771–74 and published his experiences in *Vertraute Breife*. After working as a civil servant at Königsberg, he obtained the post of music director at the Prussian court in 1776, lived at Berlin and Potsdam, produced operas, and in 1783 founded a Concert Spirituel. He also published collections of music and wrote criticism. After the death of Frederick II he made himself disliked more and more and in 1793 he was dismissed, ostensibly for his sympathy with the French Revolution. He retired to Giebichenstein in 1794, only briefly holding a post at the court of Jérême Bonaparte at Kassel in 1808.

He married Juliane Benda (1752–1783), a singer, pianist, and composer, daughter of the composer Franz Benda, and had a daughter, Louise (1780–1826), who became a singer and also wrote songs.

Works include: the operas and plays with music *Hänschen und Gretchen* (1772), *Amors Guekkasten* (1773), *Cephalus und Procris* (1777), *Le feste galanti, Claudine von Villa Bella* (Goethe, 1789), *Erwin und Elmire* (Goethe, 1793), *L'Olimpiade* (Metastasio, 1791), *Tamerlan* (in French), *Jery und Bätely* (Goethe), *Der Taucher* (after Schiller's ballad, 1811), *Brenno, Die Geisterinsel* (after Shakespeare's *Tempest*, 1798), and about 12 others; incidental music to Shakespeare's *Macbeth* (1795), several plays by Goethe and Kotzebue's *Die Kreuzfahrer*; cantatas *Ariadne auf Naxos, Ino* (1779), *Morning Hymn* (Milton, translated by Herder) and others; instrumental works; about 1,500 songs.

Reichenau, Berno of (died 1048) German Benedictine monk and music theorist. He was first a monk at Prüm, and abbot of Reichenau from 1008. He compiled a *tonarius*, dealing with the organization of the church chants into 'tones' – eight modes of the Gregorian chant.

Reigen German musical term; 'roundelay'.

Reimann, Aribert (1936–) German composer and pianist. Many of his works are inspired by literature; his best-known work is the opera *Lear* 1978, after Shakespeare's *King Lear*.

He studied with Boris Blacher in Berlin. His early music uses serial technique, but he renounced this kind of composition in 1967, turning to literary sources for a musical starting point, including Shakespeare, Strindberg, Kafka (*Das Schloss*), Euripides (*Troades*), Günther Grass, Byron, Edgar Allan Poe, and even Sylvia Plath. He gave frequent recitals and made recordings with Dietrich Fischer-Dieskau until his retirement in 1992.

Works include: the operas *Traumspiel* (after Strindberg's *Dream Play*, 1965), *Melusine* (1971), *Gespenstersonate* (after Strindberg's *Ghost Sonata*, 1984) *Troades* (1986), and *Das Schloss* (1991); the ballet *Stoffreste*, (1957, revised as *Die Vogelscheuchen/The Scarecrows*, 1970); two piano concertos (1961, 1972), cello concerto (1959); *Totentanze* for baritone and orchestra (1960), *Hölderlin-Fragmente* for soprano and orchestra (1963); *Inane*, monologue for soprano and orchestra (1969), *Lines* for soprano and 14 instruments after Shelley (1973), *Wolkenloses Christfest/Cloudless Christmas*, Requiem for baritone, cello, and orchestra (1974), *Lear*, symphony for baritone and orchestra (1980), *Unrevealed* for baritone and string quartet (1980), *Chacun sa Chimère* for soprano, mezzo, baritone, and orchestra (1982); Trio for violin, viola, and cello (1987); *Apocalyptic Fragment* for mezzo, piano, and orchestra (1987); *I Fragmente* for orchestra (1988); Concerto for violin, cello, and orchestra (1989); *Shine and Dark* for baritone and piano (1990); nine pieces for orchestra (1994).

Reinach, Théodore (1860–1928) French archaeologist and historian. He wrote several works on Greek music and of the libretti of Maurice Emmanuel's *Salamine* (after Aeschylus' *Persae*) and Roussel's *La Naissance de la lyre*.

Re in ascolto, Un/A Listening King opera by Berio (libretto by I Calvin produced Salzburg, 7 August 1984, conductor Maazel; producer Götz Friedrich, with Theo Adam. Ageing Prospero holds auditions for a new theatre production, but is dissatisfied until he hears the female protagonist.

Reincken, Johann Adam (1623–1722), or Reinken German organist and composer. After studying with Heinrich Scheidemann 1654–57, he became his assistant at the church of St Catherine at Hamburg in 1658, and succeeded him as organist in 1663, remaining in the post until his death. Bach walked from Lüneburg as a youth and later came from Cöthen to hear him play.

Works include: chorale preludes, toccatas, fugues, and other pieces for organ; *Hortus musicus* for two violins, viola da gamba, and bass (published Hamburg, 1687); keyboard pieces.

Reinecke, Carl (Heinrich Carsten) (1824–1910) German pianist, composer, and conductor. He was conductor of the Gewandhaus concerts and professor of composition at the Leipzig Conservatory from 1860.

He settled in Leipzig in 1843. He was pianist to the Danish court 1846–48, and visited Copenhagen several times.

Works include: CHORAL fairy-tale cantatas for female voices *Schneewittchen, Dornröschen, Aschenbrödel,* and others.

ORCHESTRAL AND INSTRUMENTAL three symphonies 1870–95), overtures *Dame Kobold* (Calderón's *Dama duende*), *Aladdin, Friedensfeier, Zenobia* and other orchestral works; four piano concertos (1879–1900), concertos for violin, for cello, for flute, and for harp; five string quartets, wind octet, seven piano trios and other chamber music; three piano sonatas and many pieces, including sonatinas; songs.

Reine de Saba, La/The Queen of Sheba opera by Gounod (libretto by J Barbier and M Carré), produced Paris, Opéra, 28 February 1862. King Solomon wants to marry Balkis, Queen of Sheba, but she loves the King's architect Adoniram. They plan to elope but Adoniram is killed as they escape.

Reine (de France), La/The Queen of France nickname of Haydn's symphony No. 85 in B♭ major, composed for Paris 1785–86.

Reiner, Fritz (1888–1963) Hungarian-born US conductor. He conducted at Budapest and Dresden before emigrating to the USA in 1922. There he conducted the Pittsburgh and Chicago symphony orchestras, and continued to conduct in Europe occasionally.

He studied in Budapest and at Jura University. He held a number of conducting posts in Europe, including Budapest and Dresden, where he conducted *Parsifal* and *Die Frau ohne Schatten*, before succeeding Ysaÿe as conductor of the Cincinnati Symphony Orchestra in 1922. From 1938 to 1948 he was conductor of the Pittsburgh Symphony Orchestra, from 1948 at the New York Metropolitan Opera, and from 1953 conductor of the Chicago Symphony Orchestra. He returned to Europe from time to time as a guest conductor and in 1936 conducted *Tristan* at Covent Garden; in 1955 he conducted *Die Meistersinger* for the reopening of the Vienna Opera.

Reinthaler, Karl (Martin) (1822–1896) German composer and conductor. After some early music training he went to Berlin to study theology, but turned to music, studying under A B Marx. With a grant from Frederick William IV he then studied further in Paris

and Italy; in 1825 he joined the staff of the Cologne Conservatory and in 1858 became cathedral organist and choral conductor at Bremen. He conducted the first performance of Brahms's German Requiem, in 1868.

Works include: the operas *Edda* (1875), *Das Käthchen von Heilbronn* (after Kleist, 1881); oratorio *Jephtha* (1856), cantata *In der Wüste*; hymns and other church music; symphonies; part songs.

réjouissance (French 'enjoyment') in music, sprightly movement sometimes found as one of the accessory pieces in old suites.

relative term describing the connection between major and minor keys which bear the same ◊key signature. The relative major's ◊tonic note is three semitones higher than that of the relative minor. For example, C major is the relative major of A minor, and B minor is the relative minor of D major.

Re Lear/King Lear opera by Alberto Ghislanzoni (libretto by composer based on Shakespeare), produced Rome, Teatro Reale, 24 June 1937.

For Verdi and plot synopsis see ◊*King Lear.*

Reliquie (German, from Latin 'the relic') nickname sometimes given to Schubert's unfinished C major piano sonata begun in 1825, of which only the first and slow movements were completed. The fragmentary minuet and finale have been completed by Ludwig Stark, by Ernst Křenek, and by Willi Rehberg.

Rellstab, (Heinrich Friedrich) Ludwig (1799–1860) German critic, novelist, and poet, son of the publisher and critic Johann Karl Friedrich Rellstab (1759–1813). He studied with Ludwig Berger and Bernhard Klein, and followed his father as music critic of the *Vossische Zeitung* and edited the periodical *Iris im Gebiete der Tonkunst* 1830–42. He was imprisoned for satirizing Henriette Sontag's devotion to Rossini's operas and attacking Spontini. His books include various musical studies and several novels on musical themes. Schubert set ten of his poems to music, including *Ständchen*. See ◊*Schwanengesang.*

Remigius of Auxerre (c. 841–c. 908), also Remy of Auxerre, Remigius Autissiodorensis Benedictine monk and music theorist. He was at the monastery of St Germain in Auxerre 861–883 or 893; afterwards he worked at Rheims. At the end of his life he also taught in Paris; Odo de Cluny was amongst his pupils. Remigius's music theory takes the form of a commentary on Martianus ◊Capella, especially as concerns notation.

Renard burlesque by Stravinsky; composed 1915–16, first performed Paris, 18 May 1922. A vixen cajoles a cock out of a tree, but it is saved by the cat; during a second attempt the vixen is killed by the cat and a ram.

Rencontre imprévue, La/The Unforeseen Meeting later known as *Les Pèlerins de le Mecque/The Pilgrims to Mecca*, opera by Gluck (libretto by L H Dancourt, based on a vaudeville by Lesage and d'Orneval), produced Vienna, Burgtheater, 7 January 1764. Ali seeks his bride, the Princess Rezia, kidnapped by pirates and desired by an amorous sultan. See ◊*Incontro Improvviso, L'* (Haydn).

Re pastore, Il/The Shepherd King opera by Bonno (libretto by Metastasio), produced Vienna, Schönbrunn Palace, 13 May 1751. Shepherd Amyntas is revealed to be the heir of Sidon, but he is willing to give up the throne to marry Elisa. King Alexander of Macedonia allows him both a crown and a wedding.

Opera by Gluck (libretto ditto), produced Vienna, Burgtheater, 8 December 1756.

Opera by Mozart (libretto ditto), produced Salzburg, 23 April 1775.

repeat the restatement of a section of a composition, not written out a second time, but indicated by repeat signs.

In music of the 18th century the expositions of movements in sonata form are nearly always marked for repetition, and more rarely the working-out and recapitulation also, with or without the coda.

Repeat signs.

répétiteur (French 'coach') a musician who coaches opera singers in learning their parts, and may also run rehearsals. Many conductors of opera first began their careers as *répétiteurs*.

Répons work by Boulez for chamber orchestra and six solo instruments and computer; composed 1981, first performed Donaueschingen, 18 October 1981. Revised London, 18 June 1982.

reprise a repeat of previous material, usually following an intervening and contrasting section. In ◊sonata form the term has two meanings: usually it is synonymous with ◊recapitulation, but in early sonatas in which

a double bar precedes the development it may refer to a repeat of the ◊exposition, as in sonatas by C P E Bach. In ◊rondo form the term denotes the recurring main theme. In the ◊binary form composition of 17th-century France, the term denotes the second section, as in dance movements in the suites of Jean-Henri D'Anglebert (1635–1691).

requiem in the Roman Catholic Church, a Mass for the dead. Musical settings include those by Palestrina, Mozart, Berlioz, Verdi, Fauré, and Britten.

Requiem (Brahms). See ◊*German Requiem*.

Requiem (Verdi). See ◊*Manzoni Requiem*.

Requiem Canticles work by Stravinsky for mezzo, bass, chorus, and orchestra; composed 1965–66, first performed Princeton, 8 October 1966. Stravinsky's last major work.

Requiem for Rossini a Mass for the Dead planned by Verdi for performance in memory of Rossini's death in 1868, his suggestion being that each portion should be written by a different Italian composer of eminence. He himself composed the 'Libera me' in 1869, and the other contributors were Bazzini, Cagnoni, Coccia, Mabellini, Pedrotti, Petrella, and Ricci. Mercadante was also invited, but was unable to comply on account of blindness and infirmity. The work was never performed and the composers all withdrew their contributions. Verdi's was later used, with some alterations, for the Manzoni Requiem of 1873–74.

rescue opera a type of French opera, the libretto of which is based on plots, often taken from true happenings (the words *fait historique* sometimes appear in the subtitle), in which the hero or heroine are saved after fearful trials and tribulations. The taste for such works arose during the Revolution. The most familiar examples are Cherubini's *Les Deux Journées* and Beethoven's *Fidelio*, both with libretti by Bouilly, the latter a German translation of *Léonore* written for Gaveaux.

resin alternative name for ◊rosin.

resolution a progression from a dissonant harmony to a less dissonant or consonant harmony. For example, in an ◊appoggiatura (a form of melodic ornament), the dissonant melodic note resolves by moving a step lower, thus creating a consonant harmony. Resolving dissonance by moving a step lower is the traditional method. During the 19th century composers used other kinds of resolution more frequently than before, such as moving a step higher or sometimes incorporating a leap. Composers of the 20th century often do not resolve dissonance at all.

Respighi, Elsa (1894–1996), born Olivieri-Sangiacomo Italian singer and composer. She was a pupil of Ottorino Respighi at the Accademia di Santa Cecilia in Rome and became his wife in 1919. She finished the orchestration of his opera *Lucrezia* and wrote three of her own. She also wrote choral works, a symphonic poem, a dance suite for orchestra, songs from the *Rubáiyát of Omar Khayyám*, and many other pieces.

Respighi, Ottorino (1879–1936) Italian composer. His works include the symphonic poems *Fontane di Roma/The Fountains of Rome* 1917 and *Pini di Roma/The Pines of Rome* 1924 (incorporating the recorded song of a nightingale), operas, and chamber music. He was a student of Rimsky-Korsakov.

respond see ◊responsory.

response a type of ◊antiphony used in the churches of the Anglican communion, in which the congregation replies to the ◊plainsong chants of the priest; in Reformed churches, it refers to a short piece sung by the choir following a prayer. In this context the response often consists of a repeated 'amen'.

responsorial psalmody an ancient method of singing the psalms (borrowed from the Jews), in which a soloist is answered by a chorus.

Responsory, Latin *responsorium* chant involving the response by a choir to a verse sung by soloists, also called respond. Originally this would have taken the form of a response by the congregation to the leader or *cantor*. In the 9th century it became an elaborate musical form demanding trained soloists and choir. The Gradual, Alleluia and (for a time) the Offertory of the Mass were responsorial chants. In the Offices the most important were the *responsoria prolixa*, sung at Matins. Like those of the Mass, they became a vehicle for polyphonic settings, the polyphony being reserved for the soloists' portions of the chant. When from the mid-15th century choral polyphony became the norm the procedure was frequently, though not invariably, reversed. Late 16th-century settings, such as those by Victoria for Holy Week, assign the entire text to the polyphonic choir.

rest a silence, or the notation indicating a silence.

Resurrection (Alfano) see ◊*Risurrezione*.

Resurrection Symphony Mahler's second symphony in C minor for soprano, mezzo, chorus, and orchestra; composed 1888–94, revised 1910. The finale is a setting of Klopstock's chorale *Aufersteh'n/Resurrection*. First performed Berlin, 13 December 1895, conductor Mahler.

Retablo de Maese Pedro, El/Master Peter's Puppet Show marionette opera by Falla (libretto by composer based on a chapter from Cervantes' *Don Quixote*), produced Seville, 23 March 1923, in concert form; first stage performance Paris, 25 June 1923. With the bumbling help of Don Quixote, the knight Gayferos rescues his wife Melisendra from the Moors.

retardation a term sometimes used for a suspension which resolves upwards.

In this example the top voice (note B) undergoes retardation, resolved on note C.

Re Teodoro in Venezia, Il/Theodore at Venice opera by Paisiello (libretto by G B Casti), produced Vienna, Burgtheater, 23 August 1784. Deposed King Teodoro hides from creditors in Venice. He falls in love with Lisetta, but she is united with Sandrino and Teodoro ends up in debtors' prison.

Réti, Rudolf (1885–1957) Austrian composer, pianist, critic, and musical analyst. A champion of new music from the first, he gave the first performance of Schoenberg's op. 11 piano pieces and was one of the founders of the International Society for Contemporary Music in 1922.

He studied at Vienna Conservatory and emigrated to the USA in 1938. He wrote *The*

Breve	Semibreve	Minim	Crotchet	Quaver	Semiquaver	Demisemiquaver

The symbols for various rests. For the crotchet, modern notation favours the left-hand one of the two alternatives.

Thematic Process in Music and *Tonality, Atonality and Pantonality.*

Works include: the opera *Ivan and the Drum* (after Tolstoy), opera-ballet *David and Goliath; The Dead Mourn the Living, Three Allegories* for orchestra (1953); two piano concertos; *The Greatest of All* for chorus and orchestra; string quartet; piano pieces; songs.

retrograde term describing a process in which the order of notes is reversed. It is used as a basic technique in 20th-century ◊serialism, in addition to ◊inversion. However, it also occurs in music of the Middle Ages, as a form of musical riddle, the first known example dating from the 13th century. Haydn uses retrograde motion in the third movement of his Symphony No. 47 in G 1772, as does Beethoven in the final fugue of his piano sonata *Hammerklavier* 1818.

retrograde motion see ◊cancrizans and ◊recte et retro.

Reubke, Julius (1834–1858) German composer and pianist. The son of the organ builder Adolf Reubke (1805–75), he studied under Liszt at Weimar.

Works include: organ sonata *The 94th Psalm* (1857); sonata (1857) and pieces for piano; songs, and other pieces.

Reutter, (Johann Adam Karl) Georg (junior) (1708–1772) Austrian organist and composer. He held several posts as Kapellmeister (music director) in Vienna, both at court and at St Stephen's Cathedral.

He studied under his father Georg Reutter and with Antonio Caldara, was appointed court composer at Vienna in 1731, and in 1738 succeeded his father as chief Kapellmeister of St Stephen's Cathedral, where Haydn was his pupil as a chorister. He was second court Kapellmeister from 1747, first from 1751, he held these posts, in plurality with that at St Stephen's, to the detriment of the younger generation of composers, including Gluck and Haydn. Music at the cathedral also suffered during this period, but this was at least partly due to budget cuts at the time. He was ennobled in 1740.

Works include: about 40 operas, *Archidamia* (1727), *La forza dell' amicizia* (with Caldara, 1728), *Alessandro il Grande* (1732), *Dafne* (1734), and *Il sacrifizio in Aulide* (1735); oratorios *Abel, La Betulia liberata* (1734), *Gioas*; 81 Masses; six Requiems; 126 motets, and much other church music; symphonies; serenades; chamber music; keyboard music.

Reveil des oiseaux/Awakening of the birds works by Messiaen for piano and orchestra, first perfomed Donaueschingen, 11 October 1953, conductor Rosbaud.

Revelation and Fall work for soprano and 16 instruments by Maxwell Davies (text by Georg Trakl); composed 1965, first performed London, 26 February 1968, conductor Davies.

Rêve, Le/The Dream opera by Bruneau (libretto by L Gallet, based on Zola's novel), produced Paris, Opéra-Comique, 18 June 1891.

Revisor, Der opera in five acts by Egk (libretto by composer after Gogol's story *The Government Inspector*), produced Schwetzingen, 9 May 1957. Minor civil servant Chlestakov is mistaken for government inspector by corrupt town officials and takes advantage of the situation to woo the mayor's daughter.

Revolutionary Etude the nickname of Chopin's étude in C minor, op. 10 No. 12, for piano, written at Stuttgart in September 1831, where, on his way to Paris, he heard of the fall of Warsaw to the Russians, which marked the end of the November Uprising.

Revueltas, Silvestre (1899–1940) Mexican violinist and composer. His music has great vigour and rhythmic power. His best-known work, *Sensemaya*, is an orchestral depiction of a snake-killing ritual.

He studied at Mexico City and at St Edward's College, Austin, Texas, USA; he also studied composition with Felix Borowski at Chicago. He was appointed at Mexico City as violinist (1920–22), but continued to study the instrument under P Kochansky and Otakar Ševčik (1922–26). Later he gave recitals of modern music with Carlos Chávez as pianist, and after some theatre appointments joined the Orquesta Sinfónica at Mexico City as Chávez's assistant conductor (1929–35). He also became professor at the Conservatory there.

Works include: music for numerous films: *Cuauhnahuac, Esquinas* (1930), *Ventanas, Alcancías* (1932), *Colorines, Planos* (1934), *Caminos, Janitzio, homenaje á García Lorca, El renacuajo paseador, Sensemayá,* and other pieces for orchestra; toccata for violin and small orchestra; two string quartets (1930, 1931), *Feria* for string quartet; pieces for violin and piano; *Siete canciones* and other songs.

Reyer, Ernest (1823–1909), adopted name of Louis Etienne Rey French composer. He also worked as a music critic, becoming a champion of Wagner and the new French school. His operas *Sigurd* and *Salammbô* show inevitable indebtedness to Wagner but also reveal a Gallic charm and vitality.

He studied music at the Free School of Music at Marseille, but showed no exceptional promise. At the age of 16 he was sent to live with an uncle at Algiers. There he began to compose songs and other pieces, and in 1847 succeeded in having a Mass performed at the cathedral. In 1848 he went to Paris and studied with his aunt, the composer Louise Farrenc. He met Flaubert and Gautier, with whom he shared an interest in oriental subjects, and they provided him with subjects for his works. He became a critic in the 1850s and in 1871 succeeded Joseph d'Ortigue as music critic to the *Journal des débats*.

Works include: the operas *Maître Wolfram* (1854), *La Statue* (1861), *Erostrate*, *Sigurd* (on the Nibelung Saga, 1884), *Salammbô* (after Flaubert, 1890); ballet-pantomime *Sacountala* (after Malidasa, 1858); symphonic ode *Le Sélam* (words by Gautier), dramatic cantata *Victoire*; *L'Hymne du Rhin* for soprano, chorus, and orchestra (1865), hymn *L'Union des Arts*; *Ave Maria, Salve Regina,* and *O Salutaris*; *La Madeleine au désert* for baritone and orchestra (1874); male-voice choruses; piano pieces; songs.

Reynolds, Roger (1934–   ) US composer. His music makes use of electronics, synthesized sounds, and graphic notation. He won the 1989 Pulitzer Prize for *Whispers out of Time*.

He studied at the University of Michigan, founded avant-garde festivals there, and was director of the Center for Music Experiment at San Diego 1971–77.

Works include: the stage pieces *The Emperor of Ice Cream* (1962), *A Ritual for 23 Performers* (1971), and incidental music for *The Tempest* (1980); *Graffiti* (1964), and *Threshold* (1967) for orchestra; *Between* for chamber orchestra and electronics (1968); *Archipelago* for chamber orchestra and computer (1982); *Whispers out of Time* for string orchestra (1988); chamber and vocal music.

Rezniček, E(mil) N(ikolaus) von (1860–1945) Austrian composer and conductor. He held several conducting posts and composed light operas. His most successful work was the opera *Donna Diana* 1894.

He studied law at Graz, but at 22, when he was already married to Milka Thurn, a relation of Felix Weingartner's, he went to Leipzig to study at the Conservatory with Carl Reinecke and Salomon Jadassohn (1831–1902). He gained stage experience as a theatre conductor in various towns and finally became a military conductor at Prague, where *Donna Diana* was premiered in 1894. From 1896 to 1899 he was successively court conductor at Weimar and Mannheim. In 1906 he was appointed professor at the Klindworth-Scharwenka Conservatory in Berlin, where he founded a chamber orchestra, and later conducted the Warsaw Opera 1907–08 and the Komische Oper, Berlin 1908–11. He taught at the Hochschule für Musik in Berlin 1920–26.

Works include: the operas *Die Jungfrau von Orleans* (after Schiller, 1887), *Satanella, Emmerich Fortunat* (1889), *Donna Diana* (after Moreto, 1894), *Till Eulenspiegel* (1902), *Ritter Blaubart, Holofernes* (after Hebbel's *Judith*, 1923), *Satuala, Spiel oder Ernst* (1930), *Der Gondoliere des Dogen* (1931); incidental music for Strindberg's *Dream Play*; Mass in F major, Requiem in D minor, *Vater unser* for chorus (1919); four symphonies (including *Schlemihl* [after Chamisso], 'Tragic', and 'Ironic'), two symphonic suites, Comedy and Idyllic Overtures, fugue in C♯ minor for orchestra; serenata for strings; violin concerto (1925), Introduction and Valse-Caprice for violin and orchestra; *Ruhm und Ewigkeit* (Nietzsche) for tenor and orchestra; three string quartets (1921–32).

rf, or rfz in music, abbreviation for ◊*rinforzando*, a sudden accentuation of a short phrase.

R.H. in musical notation, abbreviation for **right hand**, directing a pianist to use the right hand. This is usually in order to facilitate a technically difficult passage, dividing the notes between both hands. It can also be notated in French or Italian as M.D. (*main droite* or *mano destra*, respectively). The opposite is L.H. ('left hand').

Rhapsodie, so-called 'Alto Rhapsody' a setting of a fragment from Goethe's *Harzreise im Winter* for contralto solo, male chorus, and orchestra by Brahms, op. 53, composed 1869, first performed Jena, 3 March 1870.

rhapsody an instrumental ◊*fantasia*, often based on folk melodies, such as Liszt's *Hungarian Rhapsodies* 1853–54.

In ancient Greece, **rhapsodes** were a class of reciters of epic poems, especially those of ◊Homer, who performed at festivals. The title means 'stitchers of songs'.

Rhapsody in Blue work for piano and orchestra by Gershwin, composed January 1924 and orchestrated by Grofé. First performed New York 12 February 1924, with Gershwin and Paul Whiteman band. Version for symphony orchestra 1942; one of the earliest orchestral works to integrate jazz elements to a large extent.

Rheinberger, Joseph (Gabriel) (1839–1901) German organist, teacher, and composer. Although successful in his lifetime in a wide variety of genres he is largely known today for his demanding organ works.

He was so precociously gifted that he was appointed organist at his local parish church at the age of seven. After some lessons at Feldkirch, he went to the Munich Conservatory 1850–54, and continued to study with F Lachner on leaving, supporting himself by teaching, and in 1859 became piano professor at the Conservatory. He also worked for a time at the Court Opera, and became a church organist and choral conductor. When the Conservatory was reorganized by Bülow in 1867, he was appointed organ and composition professor. In 1877 he became director of the court church music in succession to Franz Wüllner.

Works include: the operas *Die sieben Raben* (1869), *Der Tümers Töchterlein* (1873), and *Das Zauberwort*; incidental music for Calderón's *Mágico prodigioso*; numerous Masses, three Requiems, *Stabat Mater*, motets; cantatas and choral ballads; symphonies *Wallenstein* (after Schiller) and 'Florentine', overtures to Shakespeare's *Taming of the Shrew* and Schiller's *Demetrius*, *Academic (fugal) Overture* for orchestra; two organ concertos, piano concerto; three string quartets, two piano trios, piano quintet, piano quartet, string quintet; sonatas for violin and piano, cello and piano, horn and piano; 20 organ sonatas and many other organ works, including 22 trios, 12 *Meditations* and 24 fughettes; numerous piano works; songs, part songs; numerous piano works; songs, part songs.

Rheingold, Das/The Rhinegold (Wagner). See ◊*Ring des Nibelungen*. The dwarf Alberich steals the magic Rheingold from the Rhinemaidens and forges the all-powerful ring. Wotan, chief of the gods, steals Alberich's hoard, including the ring, in order to pay the giants Fasolt and Fafner for building the gods' palace Valhalla.

'Rhenish' Symphony the name of Schumann's third symphony, in E♭ major, op. 97, begun after a Rhine excursion in September 1850. The fourth of the five movements is said to be an impression of Cologne Cathedral. First performed Düsseldorf, 6 February 1851.

rhythm a recurring pattern of long and short values, often based on classical verse or dance, determining the character of a musical ◊movement.

Riccardo I, rè d'Inghilterra/Richard I, King of England opera by Handel (libretto by P A

Rolli), produced London, King's Theatre, Haymarket, 11 November 1727. King Richard I conquers Cyprus and marries Costanza after defeating jealous Isaac Comnenus, governor of the island.

Ricci, Federico (1809–1877) Italian composer. He studied with Bellini and Zingarelli at the Naples Conservatory. In 1835 he produced his first opera with his brother Luigi Ricci at Naples and the first of his own at Venice. After several stage successes he was music director at the Imperial theatres in St Petersburg 1853–69.

Works include: the operas *Monsieur de Chalumeaux* (1835), *La prigione d'Edimburgo* (on Scott's *Heart of Midlothian*, 1838), *Un duello sotto Richelieu* (1839), *Luigi Rolla e Michelangelo* (1841), *Corrado d'Altamura*, *Vallombra*, *Isabella de' Medici* (1845), *Estella di Murcia* (1846), *Griselda*, *I due ritratti*, *Il marito e l'amante* (1852), *Il paniere d'amore*, *Una Folie à Rome*, *Le Docteur rose* and four others in collaboration with Luigi Ricci; two Masses; cantata for the marriage of Victor Emmanuel; songs.

Ricci, Luigi (1805–1859) Italian composer, brother of Federico ◊Ricci. He studied under Zingarelli at the Naples Conservatory, where he and Bellini became sub-professors in 1819. His first opera was produced there 1823. In 1835, after a number of successful productions, he became conductor of the Opera and music director of the cathedral at Trieste. His attempt at a setting of *Le nozze di Figaro* (Milan, 1838) was a failure, and he moved with his twin-sister mistresses, Francesca and Ludmilla Stolz, to Odessa. He married Ludmilla in 1849 and wrote an opera for the sisters but was confined in an asylum in 1859, having become hopelessly insane.

Works include: the opera *L'impresario in angustie* (1823), *Il diavolo condannato* (1826), *Il Colombo*, *L'orfanella di Ginevra* (1829), *Chiara di Rosemberg Il nuovo Figaro* (1832), *Un avventura di Scaramuccia* (1834), *Gli esposti* (*Eran due ed or son tre*), *Chi dura vince*, *Chiara di Montalbano* (1835), *La Serva e l'ussaro*, *Le nozze di Figaro* (after Beaumarchais, 1838), *Il birraio di Preston* (1847), *La festa di Piedigrotta*, *Il diavolo a quattro* (1859), and 14 others including four in collaboration with Federico Ricci; church music, song-books *Mes Loisirs* and *Les Inspirations du thé*.

Operas written jointly by the two brothers: *Il colonello* (1835), *Il disertore per amore* (1836), *L'amante di richiamo* (1846) and *Crispino e la comare* (1850).

Ricciardo e Zoraide opera by Rossini (libretto by M F B di Salsa), produced Naples,

Teatro San Carlo, 3 December 1818. Zoraide, daughter of Prince Ircano, falls in love with Christian Knight Ricciardo, but the tyrant Agorante also has designs on her. The couple are captured by Agorante but are saved following a revolt.

Riccio, (Antonio) Teodoro (c. 1540–after 1599) Italian composer. After holding the post of choirmaster at a church at Brescia, he was appointed music director by the Margrave of Brandenburg-Ansbach. He settled there and followed the margrave to Königsberg in 1579, having become a Lutheran, and returned to Ansbach with his patron in 1586. Johann Eccard served under him there from 1581 and succeeded him at his death.

Works include: motets and other church music; madrigals, *Canzoni alla napoletana*; some of his canzonas are based on themes by Gabrieli.

ricercare (Italian 'researched') in music, an abstract composition, usually contrapuntal, exploring tonal and intervallic structural relationships, as in J S Bach's several examples from *The Musical Offering* 1747.

Richafort, Jean (c. 1480–c. 1547) Flemish composer, pupil of Josquin Desprez. He was choirmaster at the church of Saint-Gilles at Bruges in the 1540s. He wrote Masses, motets, chansons. Palestrina wrote a parody Mass on his four-part motet *Quem dicunt homines*.

Richard Cœur-de-Lion opera by Grétry (libretto by J M Sedaine), produced Paris, Comédie-Italienne, 21 October 1784. Beethoven wrote piano variations on the song 'Une fièvre brûlante' from it (WoO 72, 1795). Blondel, squire to King Richard, discovers that his master is held prisoner in Linz castle. He captures the castle governor Florestan and rescues Richard, reuniting him with his love Marguerita.

Richard I, Cœur de Lion (1157–1199) King of England and French trouvère. He was the son of Henry II and his mother was Eleanor of Aquitaine. She introduced the art of the Troubadours to the north of France and thus established the school of the Trouvères to which Richard belonged both as poet and as musician.

According to legend another trouvère, Blondel de Nesle, discovered his place of imprisonment in Austria in 1192, when he is said to have sung outside the castle of Dürenstein and to have been answered by Richard in song from within, a fanciful story which furnished the plot for Grétry's opera *Richard Cœur-de-Lion*.

Richardson, Ferdinand(o) (c. 1558–1618), real name Heybourne, English composer, pupil of Tallis. He was Groom of the Privy Chamber, 1587–1611. He composed virginal pieces.

Richardson, Vaughan (c. 1670–1729) English organist and composer. He was chorister in the Chapel Royal, and was appointed organist of Winchester Cathedral in 1692.

Works include: services, anthems *O Lord God of my salvation, O how amiable* and others; *Song in Praise of St Cecilia* (1700); *Entertainment for the Peace of Ryswick* (1697); songs for one–three voices with instruments.

Richter, Hans (1843–1916) Austro-Hungarian conductor. He conducted the first performance of Wagner's *Ring* at Bayreuth in 1876, and was conductor of the Hallé Orchestra, Manchester 1900–11. He gave the first performances of Brahms' second and third symphonies, Bruckner's first, third, fourth, and eighth symphonies, and Elgar's *Enigma Variations* and first symphony. By his unfailing industry over a long period, Richter set new standards for career conductors to follow.

He studied in Vienna, where he played horn at the Kärntnertortheater 1862–66. As assistant to Wagner, he conducted operas at Budapest and Vienna. He organized and played the trumpet in the private premiere of the *Siegfried Idyll* at Triebschen in 1870, and was the first to conduct Wagner's *Ring* at Bayreuth in 1876. He conducted at the Birmingham Festival 1885–1909, including the 1900 first performance of *The Dream of Gerontius*, and conducted much in London 1877–1910, notably the first *Ring* cycles in English, at Covent Garden in 1908. At Drury Lane he gave the British premieres of *Tristan* and *Die Meistersinger* 1882.

ricochet (French 'rebound') type of *staccato* in violin music, produced by letting the bow bounce on the strings, whereas in ordinary *staccato* it remains on the string and is moved in rapid jerks.

riddle canon a form of canon written in a single part with no indication where the subsequent entries of the parts are to occur, the performer being left to guess how the music fits by solving a riddle.

Riders to the Sea opera by Vaughan Williams (libretto Synge's play), produced London, RCM, 1 December 1937; first public performance Cambridge, Arts Theatre, 22 February 1938. The opera opens as the body of Maurya's drowned son Michael is identi-

fied. Later, her remaining son Bartley also
dies at sea.

Ridout, Alan (1934–) English composer.
He studied with Gordon Jacob and Herbert
Howells at the Royal College of Music; he
was professor there 1961–84.

Works include: the church operas *The Boy
from the Catacombs* (1965), *The Children's
Crusade* (1968), *Creation* (1973), *Wenceslas*
(1978) and *The White Doe* (1987); opera *The
Pardoner's Tale* (1971), *Christmas Oratorio*,
eight Cantatas, eight symphonies and 13
concertinos with strings (1975–79).

Riegger, Wallingford (1885–1961) US composer. He wrote several ballet scores in the
1930s, but later composed in an atonal idiom.

He studied in New York and Berlin, with
Percy Goetschius (1853–1943), Edgar Still-
man-Kelley, Max Bruch, and others. After
conducting in Germany, he returned to the
USA, where he held various teaching appointments.

Works include: *American Polonaise–Triple
Jazz* (1922), Rhapsody, Fantasy and Fugue
(1955), Lyric Suite, two Dance Suites, Canon
and Fugue, and other pieces for orchestra,
various works for dancers; *La Belle Dame sans
merci* (Keats) for four voices and chamber
orchestra (1924); four symphonies (1943–57);
Dichotomy and *Scherzo* for chamber orchestra;
Study in Sonority for ten violins; two string
quartets (1939, 1948), piano trio, *Divertissement* for harp, flute, and cello, three Canons
for woodwind and other chamber music;
Suite for solo flute.

**Riemann, (Karl Wilhelm Julius) Hugo
(1849–1919)** German musicologist. He studied law at Berlin and Tübingen, music at the
Leipzig Conservatory. He later became lecturer at the university there, 1878–80 and
again in 1895 until 1901, when he became
professor. Among his many publications are
a *Musiklexikon* (1882), *Handbuch der Musikgeschichte* (1904), *Opernhandbuch* (1887), works
on notation, harmony, phrasing, and history.
He edited many standard works and also
composed mainly teaching pieces for piano.

**Rienzi, der Letzte der Tribunen/Rienzi, the
Last of the Tribunes** opera in five acts by
Wagner (first called *Cola Rienzi*) (libretto by
composer based on Bulwer-Lytton's novel
and, further back, on Mary Russell Mitford's
play), produced Dresden, 20 October 1842.
Rienzi, proclaimed tribune of Rome, faces
assassination plots from the nobleman led by
Orsini and Colonna, whose son Adriano
loves Rienzi's sister Irene. After his opponents are killed Rienzi is excommunicated by

papal allies of Colonna. He is abandoned by
all except Irene, who remains loyal to the end.
As the siblings are stoned by the people,
Adriano tries to rescue Irene but all three are
killed as the burning building collapses.

Ries, Ferdinand (1784–1838) German pianist, violinist, and composer. He studied
piano with Beethoven 1802–04. He later lived
in London for several years, where he acted
as Beethoven's agent in dealings with music
publishers. Back in Germany, he was involved with F Wegeler in writing a biography
of Beethoven.

He was taught piano and violin by his
father, Franz Anton Ries (1755–1846), who
also taught Beethoven, and studied cello with
B Romberg. After a short course in composition with Peter Winter at Munich in 1801, he
went to Vienna that year, and studied piano
with Beethoven and composition with Albrechtsberger, and became pianist to Counts
Browne and Lichnowsky. Later he lived by
turns in Paris, Vienna, Kassel, Stockholm, and
St Petersburg. In 1813–24 he lived in London,
where he married an Englishwoman and
played, taught, and composed. He bought a
property at Godesberg, near Bonn, but in 1826
went to live at Frankfurt, where he returned
again after two years as a conductor at
Aachen, 1834–36. He conducted several of
the Lower Rhine Festivals.

Works include: OPERA *Die Räuberbraut*
(1828), *Liska* (*The Sorceress*, 1831), and *Eine
Nacht auf dem Libanon* (1834); oratorios *Der
Sieg des Glaubens* and *Die Könige Israels*

OTHER eight symphonies, four overtures;
eight piano concertos; 26 string quartets; eight
string quintets, three piano quartets, five
piano trios, octet, septet, and other chamber
music; 20 duets for violin and piano; ten
sonatas and many other works for piano.

Rieti, Vittorio (1898–1994) Italian-born US
composer. He studied with Frugatta at Milan
and Respighi in Rome, but destroyed all his
works written up to 1920. In 1939 he became a
US citizen.

Works include: the opera *Teresa nel bosco*
(1934); ballets *Noah's Art* (1922), *Barabau*
(1925), *Waltz Academy*, *The Sleep-walker*, *Robinson and Friday* (after Defoe, 1924) and
David's Triumph (1937); incidental music for
Pierre Corneille's *L'Illusion comique* and Gir-
audoux's *Electre*; seven symphonies (1929–
77); *Notturno* for strings; concerto for wind
instruments and orchestra, violin concerto,
harpsichord concerto, three piano concertos
(1926, 1937, 1955), two cello concertos; *Madrigal* for 12 instruments (1927), partita for

flute, oboe, string quartet and harpsichord; sonata for flute, oboe, bassoon and piano; *Second Avenue Waltzes* for two pianos, piano pieces.

Rifkin, Joshua (1944–) US musicologist, conductor, and pianist. He is known for bringing Scott ◊Joplin's piano rags to popular attention. He has researched Renaissance and Baroque music, and has given authentic performances, including a recording of the B minor Mass without full-scale chorus.

He studied at the Juilliard School in New York and at Princeton, and with Stockhausen at Darmstadt, Germany. He conducted Bach's *St Matthew Passion* at the 1994 London Promenade Concerts.

rigadoon (French *rigaudon*) a French dance, probably from the south (Provence or Languedoc), dating back to the 17th century at the latest. It is in lively common or 2–4 time and consists of three or four parts, each repeated, the third being the shortest.

rigaudon lively French country dance in two time, in four-bar phrases (like a square dance), the music for which was revived by Grieg in the *Holberg Suite* 1884.

Rigoletto opera by Verdi (libretto by F M Piave, based on Victor Hugo's play *Le Roi s'amuse*), produced Venice, Teatro la Fenice, 11 March 1851. Rigoletto's daughter Gilda is abducted by the Duke of Mantua, who has designs on her. Rigoletto rescues her, but by now she loves the Duke. Rigoletto arranges his murder, but Gilda substitutes herself instead.

Rihm, Wolfgang (1952–) German composer. He studied in Karlsruhe and with Stockhausen and Wolfgang Fortner.

Works include: the operas *Faust and Yorick* (1976), *Harlekin* (1977), *Jacob Lenz* (1979), *Die Hamletmaschine* (1986), *Oedipus* (1987), and *Die Eroberung von Mexico* (1992); three symphonies (1966–77, no. 3 to texts by Nietzsche and Rimbaud); *Ein Imaginäres Requiem* for soloists, chorus, and orchestra (1976); *Dis-kontur* and *Sub-kontur* for orchestra (1974–75); *Konzertarie* for soprano and orchestra (based on telegram sent by Ludwig II to Wagner, 1976); *Cuts and Dissolves*, concerto for 29 players (1976); *Abgesangsszene* nos. 1–5 for voice and orchestra (1979–81); *Lenz-Fragmente* and five songs for soprano and orchestra (1980); *Tutuguri*, series of seven works for various instrumental combinations inspired by Paul Claudel (1981); *Monodram* for cello and orchestra (1983), *Dies* for soloists, chorus, and orchestra (1984); *Anderer Schatten* (ditto, 1985); *Kein*

firmament, 14 players, *Fusées* for orchestra (1984); *Dämmerung* for orchestra (1985); *Dunkles Spiel* for chamber orchestra (1990), *Umfassung* for orchestra in two groups (1990); *'Mein Tod, Requiem in memoriam Jane S'*, for soprano and orchestra (1989), *Frau/Stimme* for soprano and orchestra (1989), *Départ* for chorus, narrator, and 22 players (1988); *Geheimer Block* for voice and orchestra (1989); *Engel* for two male voices and 20 instruments (1989); *Cantus firmus* for 14 players (1990); *Ricercare* for ensemble (1990); *Etude pour Séraphin*, for eight brass instruments and six percussion players (1992); eight string quartets (1968–88); *Deploration* for flute, cello, and percussion (1973); *Erscheinung*, sketch after Schubert for nine strings (1978), *Nature Morte* for 13 strings (1980); *Fremde Szene* for piano trio (1983); solo songs and music for piano and for organ.

Riisager, Knudåge (1897–1974) Danish composer. He studied political economy at Copenhagen University, but later turned to music, studying composition with Peder Gram and Otto Malling, later with Roussel and Le Flem in Paris, and finally with Hermann Grabner at Leipzig.

Works include: the opera *Susanne* (1950); ballets *Benzin* (1930), *Cocktail Party* and *Slaraffenland* (*Land of Cockaigne*, 1942); incidental music to Johannes Jensen's fairy play *Darduse*; chorus works; five symphonies (1925–50), variations *Poème mécanique*, *Jabiru T – DOXC* and overture to Holberg's *Erasmus Montanus* for orchestra; concerto for trumpet and strings; six string quartets (1918–43), sonata for flute, clarinet, violin, and cello, serenade for flute, violin, and cello; violin and piano sonata; sonata and various pieces for piano; songs.

Riley, Terry (1935–) US composer and saxophonist. He belongs to the Minimalist school of composers. His works involve repeated patterns and series, and contain freedom for improvisation. He studied at Berkeley, California, and since 1970 has been influenced by Indian music.

Works include: *Spectra* for six instruments (1959); String trio (1965); *Keyboard Studies* (1965); *Poppy Nogood and the Phantom Band* for saxophone, tape, and electronics (1968); *Rainbow in Curved Air* (1970); *Genesis '70*, ballet; *Sunrise of the Planetary Dream Collector* and *The Medicine Wheel*, both for string quartet (1981, 1983), works which reflect his interest in astrology. Five of his nine string quartets form the cycle *Salome Dances for Peace* (1988).

Rilke, Rainer Maria (1875–1926) German poet. See Conrad ◊Beck (*Lyric Cantata*); ◊Burkhard (*song cycle*); Lukas ◊Foss (*Parable of Death*); ◊Marienleben (Hindemith); Karl ◊Marx (choruses and songs); ◊Webern (songs); ◊Weill (songs with orchestra).

Rimsky-Korsakov, Nikolai Andreievich (1844–1908) Russian composer. His operas include *The Maid of Pskov* 1873, *The Snow Maiden* 1882, *Mozart and Salieri* 1898, and *The Golden Cockerel* 1907, a satirical attack on despotism that was banned until 1909. He also wrote an influential text on orchestration.

Other works include the symphonic poem *Sadko* 1867, the programme symphony *Antar* 1869, and the symphonic suite *Scheherazade* 1888. He also completed works by other composers, for example, Mussorgsky's *Boris Godunov*.

Rinaldo cantata for tenor solo, male chorus, and orchestra by Brahms, op. 50, on a ballad by Goethe, performed Vienna, 28 February 1869.

Opera by Handel (libretto by G Rossi, from a sketch based on Tasso by Aaron Hill), produced London, Queen's Theatre, Haymarket, 24 February 1711. Handel's first London opera. As knight Rinaldo prepares for victory over Saracen king Argante, the heathen temporarily avoids defeat by enlisting the help of sorceress Armida in abducting Almirena, Rinaldo's love. But Rinaldo saves her; Argante and Armida flee.

Rinaldo di Capua (c. 1705–c. 1780) Italian composer. He wrote more than 30 operas, the first of which was produced in Rome in 1737. Only fragments of his music survive.

Some of his operas appeared in Florence and Venice, and in 1752–53 the *Bouffons* in Paris performed his *La donna superba* and *La zingara*. His last opera seria was written in 1758, after which he devoted himself to comic opera. Charles Burney found him living in poor circumstances in Rome in 1770, after which nothing is known of him.

Works include: the operas *Ciro riconosciuto* (1737), *Vologeso, rè de' Parti* (1739), *Mario in Numidia* (1749), *Adriano in Siria* (1758); intermezzi *Il bravo burlato*, *La donna superba* (1738), *La zingara*, *Le donne ridicole* (1759), *I finti pazzi per amore* (1770), and others; *Cantata per la natività della Beata Vergine* (1755), and other pieces.

rinforzando, or rf or rfz (Italian 'reinforcing') in musical notation, indicating a sudden accent on a single note or short phrase or group of notes. It differs slightly from ◊sforzando, which applies to only one note per marking.

Ring des Nibelungen, Der/The Nibelung's Ring trilogy of music dramas, with a prologue, by Wagner (libretto by composer, based on the Nibelung Saga); see individual operas for plot synopses:

Das Rheingold/The Rhinegold produced Munich, Court Opera, 22 September 1869.

Die Walküre/The Valkyrie produced Munich, Court Opera, 26 June 1870.

Siegfried, produced Bayreuth, Wagner Festival Theatre, 16 June 1876.

Götterdämmerung/The Twilight of the Gods produced Bayreuth, Wagner Festival Theatre, 17 August 1876.

The whole cycle produced Bayreuth, Wagner Festival Theatre, 13–17 August 1876.

ripieno (Italian 'replenished', 'supplementary') in music of the 17th and 18th centuries, describing the full complement of players, as opposed to ◊concertante (group of instrumental soloists). It is used especially in the context of the ◊concerto grosso, designating the full orchestra, but it may be used to describe other music which exploits the textural contrast of a different number of players, as in Bach's *St Matthew Passion* 1729.

ripresa (Italian 're-taking, repetition') refrain, especially in the 14th-century Italian *ballata*.

Riquier, Guiraut (c. 1230–c. 1300) French troubadour. He was the last great exponent of the art. Of his song-tunes, 48 are extant.

Rising of the Moon, The opera by Maw (libretto by B Cross and composer), produced Glyndebourne, 19 July 1970. Cornet Beaumont, new officer of the 31st Lancers, undergoes a series of initiation tests that results in his regiment's withdrawal from Ireland and leaves admirer Cathleen without Beaumont.

rispetto a type of old Italian improvised folk poem of six to ten (usually eight) interrhyming lines, sung to popular tunes.

Ristori, Giovanni Alberto (1692–1753) Italian composer. His first opera was produced in Venice in 1713, but two years later he moved to Dresden with his father, director of an Italian theatrical company whose music director he became in 1717. Appointed director of the Polish chapel in Dresden in 1718, he became vice-Kapellmeister to the court, under Hasse, in 1750.

Works include: around 20 operas, *Calandro* (1726), *Don Chisciotte* (1727), *Le fate* (1736), *Didone* (produced Covent Garden, 1737), *Temistocle* (1738), *I lamenti di Orfeo* (1749).;

three oratorios; 15 cantatas; 15 Masses, three Requiems, motets and other church music.

Risurrezione/Resurrection opera by Alfano (libretto by C Hanau, based on Tolstoy's novel), produced Turin, Teatro Vittorio Emanuele, 30 November 1914. Katiusha and Dmitri become lovers and she becomes pregnant. He abandons her and she is sent to Siberia, convicted as a prostitute. Dmitri follows her but she rejects him, favouring another prisoner, Simouson, instead.

rit. in musical notation, abbreviation for ρritardando (Italian 'slowing'); less commonly for ρritenuto (Italian 'held back').

Rita opera in one act by Donizetti (libretto by G Vaez); composed 1841, first performed (posthumous) Paris, Opéra-Comique, 7 May 1860. Rita dominates weak husband Peppe until ex-husband Gaspar arrives and shows Peppe how to stand up to her.

ritardando, or rit. (Italian 'slowing') in musical notation, gradually getting slower; synonymous with rallentando.

ritenuto, or riten. or occasionally rit. (Italian 'held back') in musical notation, the immediate reduction of speed, as opposed to a gradual change as with ritardando and rallentando.

Rite of Spring, The ballet by Stravinsky (scenario by composer and Nikolay Roerich, choreographed by Nizhinsky), produced as *Le Sacre du printemps*, Paris, Théâtre des Champs-Élysées, 29 May 1913. The ballet caused much controversy on the first night.

ritmo di battute (Italian 'rhythm of ... beats') in music, indication that the metrical scheme of a piece or movement is to be accented in groups of as many bars as may be shown in this direction between the second and third word; used in the Scherzo of Beethoven's Ninth Symphony, where the metre changes between *ritmo di tre battute* and *ritmo di quattro battute*.

ritornello (Italian 'a little return') in music, a repeating section: in the 14th and 15th centuries, it was the refrain at the end of each madrigal verse, the music being treated separately from the previous material, often including a change of metre; in 17th-century opera and song, it was an instrumental conclusion or refrain added to the end of an aria or song; in the Classical period (1750–1820) it was used in concerto composition, denoting the return of the full orchestra (or 'tutti') after a solo passage.

Ritorno d'Ulisse in patria, Il/Ulysses' Return to his Country opera by Monteverdi (libretto by G Badoaro), produced Venice, Teatro San Cassiano, February 1641. Realizations by d'Indy (produced 1925), Dallapiccola (1942), Křenek (1959), Leppard (1972), Harnoncourt, and Henze (1985). With the help of the goddess Minerva, Ulysses finds his way back home to Penelope his wife. Dressed as a beggar, he slays her suitors. Juno and Jupiter restore his identity and Ulysses wins back Penelope.

Ritual Dances four dances for chorus and orchestra in Tippett's opera *The Midsummer Marriage: The Earth in Autumn, The Waters in Winter, The Air in Spring, Fire in Summer*. Often heard as concert work; first performed Basel, 13 February 1953 – two years before first production of opera, at Covent Garden.

Rituel in memoriam Bruno Maderna work for orchestra by Boulez, first performed London, 2 April 1975, conductor Boulez.

Roberday, François (1624–1680) French organist and composer. He held appointments as a goldsmith under Queen Anne of Austria and Queen Marie-Thérèse, and was one of Lully's teachers.

Works include: *Fugues et Caprices* for organ.

Robert le Diable/Robert the Devil opera by Meyerbeer (libretto by Scribe), produced Paris, Opéra, 21 November 1831. Bertram, the Duke Robert's father, is a demon and must repossess his son's soul by midnight. Robert is searching for his love Isabelle, and Bertram tries to lead him astray with offers of help. Alice, Robert's foster sister, saves his soul and helps reunite him with Isabelle, as Bertram returns to Hell.

Roberto Devereux, Conte d'Essex opera by Donizetti (libretto by S Cammarano, based on Jacques Ancelot's tragedy *Elisabeth d'Angleterre*), produced Naples, Teatro San Carlo, 2 October 1837. Robert Devereux wears Queen Elizabeth's ring, which guarantees him protection. But he tears it off for love of Sarah, wife of the Duke of Nottingham.

Opera by Mercadante (libretto by F Romani, based on Corneille's *Comte d'Essex*), produced Milan, La Scala, 10 March 1833.

Robertson, Alec (1892–1982) English musicologist. He studied at the Royal Academy of Music in London and became an organist and choirmaster in 1913. After serving in World War I, he lectured at LCC evening institutes and in 1920 became lecturer and later head of the Gramophone company's education department. He lived in Rome for four years to study plainsong and in 1940 joined the British Broadcasting Corporation (BBC) in charge of the music talks in the Home Service. His books include *The Interpretation of Plainchant, Art and Religion, Dvořák,* and *Requiem: Music of Mourning and Consolation.*

Robin et Marion, Le Jeu de/The Play of Robin and Marion a pastoral play with monophonic music by Adam de la Halle, written in Naples between 1283 and his death in 1286 or 1287.

Robinson, John (1682–1762) English organist and composer. He was chorister in the Chapel Royal, became organist of St Lawrence, Jewry, and St Magnus, London Bridge, and in 1727 succeeded Croft as organist of Westminster Abbey. In 1716 he married William Turner's daughter Ann (died 1741), a singer at the Italian Opera.

Works include: Double Chant in E♭ major.

Robinson Crusoé operetta by Offenbach (libretto by E Cormon and H Crémieux, based distantly on Defoe's novel), produced Paris, Opéra-Comique, 23 November 1867. Robinson meets Vendredi (Man Friday) and his friends in a farcical plot on the desert island.

Rocca, Lodovico (1895–1986) Italian composer. He was a pupil of Orefice, and appointed director of the Turin Conservatory in 1940.

Works include: the operas *La morte di Frine, La corona del rè Gaulo, Il Dibuk* (1934), *In terra di leggenda* (1933), *Monte Ivnor* (1939) and *L'uragano* (1952); symphonic poems *Contrasti, Aurora di morte, L'alba del malato* (1922), and *La foresta delle Samodive* (1921), also *La cella azzurra, Chiaroscuri* and *Interludio epico* for orchestra; chamber music.

Rochberg, George (1918–) US composer. He wrote in a serial idiom until 1964, when a family tragedy inspired a change of heart. Such works as the *Sacred Song of Reconciliation* 1970 and the *Transcendental Varieties* for strings 1975 have embraced tonality once more.

He studied composition with Georg Szell and L Manes (1899–1964) in New York, and then at the Curtis Institute, Philadelphia, with (Bartolomeo Melchiore) Rosario Scalero (1870–1954) and Menotti. In 1950 he was awarded a Fulbright Fellowship and in 1956 a Guggenheim Fellowship. He taught at the Curtis Institute 1948–54, and was professor of music at Pennsylvania University 1968–83.

Works include: the opera *The Confidence Man* (after Melville, 1982), symphonic poem *Night Music,* six symphonies (1958–87), *Time-Span* (1960), *Waltz Serenade, Sinfonia Fantasia* for orchestra; *Cantio Sacra* for chamber orchestra; seven string quartets (1952–79); *Imago Mundé* for orchestra (1975), violin concerto (1974), oboe concerto (1983); clarinet sonata; fantasia for violin and piano; two piano sonatas.

Roche, Jerome (1942–1994) English musicologist. Early Italian music was at the centre of his research and he published books on Palestrina (1971), the Italian madrigal (1972) and Lassus (1982).

He studied at Cambridge University 1959–67, and was lecturer at Durham from 1967. With his wife Elizabeth he edited the *Dictionary of Early Music, from the Troubadours to Monteverdi* (1981). He was also author of *North Italian Church Music in the Age of Monteverdi* (1984) and *The Flower of Italian Madrigals* (1988).

Rochlitz, Johann Friedrich (1769–1842) German music critic and poet. He studied under Doles at the St Thomas's School, Leipzig, later theology at the university. In 1798 he founded the *Allgemeine Musikalische Zeitung,* which he edited until 1818. He also composed, wrote libretti and poems, three of which were set by F Schubert; others were set by C M von Weber and L Spohr.

Rococo a highly florid and decorative style of the 18th century. It was first associated with the music of François Couperin and is applicable to much music until the period of Mozart, Haydn, and C P E Bach.

Rodelinda opera by Handel (libretto by A Salvi, adapted by N F Haym), produced London, King's Theatre, Haymarket, 13 February 1725. Rodelinda, wife of usurped King Bertarido, agrees to marry Grimoaldo to save her son Flavio. Bertarido returns to see Rodelinda and is captured. Unolfo rescues him, and Bertarido kills the rebel Garibaldo before assuming the role of king again.

Rodelinda, regina de' Longobardi opera by Graun (libretto by G G Bottarelli, altered from A Salvi), produced Berlin, at court, 13 December 1741. The plot is similar to that of ◊*Rodelinda.*

Rodgers, Richard Charles (1902–1979) US composer. He collaborated with librettist Lorenz Hart (1895–1943) on songs like 'Blue Moon' 1934 and musicals like *On Your Toes* 1936. With Oscar Hammerstein II, he wrote many musicals, including *Oklahoma!* 1943,

South Pacific 1949, *The King and I* 1951, and *The Sound of Music* 1959.

Rodio, Rocco (c. 1535–shortly after 1615) Italian composer. He wrote church music (including ten Masses), madrigals, and instrumental music, and a treatise, *Regole di Musica*, which was published at Naples in 1600, though it is now known only from its second and third editions (1609 and 1626), edited by his pupil Giovanni Battista Olifante.

Rodrigo opera in three acts by Handel (libretto after F Silvani's *Il duello d'Amore e di Vendetta*), produced Florence, Teatro del Cocomero, autumn 1707. Rodrigo gains the throne of Aragon by murder but eventually abdicates. Revived with recently discovered Act 3 material by Handel Opera Society, 1985.

Rodrigo, Joaquín (1901–) Spanish composer. His works are filled with Spanish folklore or ambience, as in the well-known *Concierto de Aranjuez* 1939 or the *Concierto heroico* 1943. He has always composed in a conservative, lucid Neo-Classical style that is less adventurous than Manuel de ◊Falla but nevertheless as effective and colourful.

He was born at Sagunto in Valencia. He was blind from the age of three, but persevered in studying music and in 1927 he went to Paris as a pupil of Dukas. He returned to Spain in 1933 and again, after travels in Europe, in 1936, settling in Madrid in 1939.

Works include: *Ausencias de Dulcinea* for bass, four sopranos, and orchestra; Heroic concerto and other works for orchestra; 'Aranjuez' concerto for guitar (1939), 'Summer' cóncerto for violin (1944), *Concierto en modo galante* for cello (1949), *Concierto Serenada* for harp (1954), *Fantasia para un gentil hombre* for guitar and orchestra (1954), *Concierto andaluz* for four guitars and órchestra (1967), *Concierto Pastoral*, for flute (1978), *Concierto como um divertimento* for cello (1981), *Concierto para una fiesta*, for guitar (1982). Also pieces for solo guitar, and songs.

Rodríguez de Hita, Antonio (c. 1724–1787) Spanish composer. In collaboration with the poet Ramón de la Cruz he made important contributions to Spanish opera. He was maestro de capilla of Palencia Cathedral, and from 1757 of the Convent of the Incarnation in Madrid.

Works include: the operas *Briseida* (1768), *Las segadoras de Vallecas* (1768), *Las labradoras de Murcia* (1769); hymns for four and eight voices.

Roger-Ducasse, Jean (Jules Aimable) (1873–1954) French composer. He was ap-

pointed inspector of singing in the Paris city schools in 1909, and in 1935 succeeded Paul Dukas as composition professor at the Conservatory.

He studied at the Paris Conservatory, where he was a composition pupil of Fauré.

Works include: the opera *Cantegril* (1931), mimed drama *Orphée* (1914); *Au Jardin de Marguerite* (1905) and *Ulysse et les Sirènes* for voices and orchestra; motets and secular vocal works including *Sur quelques vers de Virgile*, *Madrigal sur des vers de Molière*; *Suite française* (1909), *Le joli jeu de furet*, *Prélude d'un ballet*, *Nocturne de printemps* (1920), *Epithalame*, *Poème symphonique sur le nom de Fauré* for orchestra; *Variations plaisantes* for harp and orchestra; piano works; instrumental pieces; songs.

Rogers, Benjamin (1614–1698) English organist and composer. He held organist's posts at Windsor, Dublin, and Oxford, and wrote the *Hymnus Eucharisticus*, which is still sung at the top of the tower of Magdalen College, Oxford at 5 a.m. on 1 May each year.

He learnt music from his father, Peter Rogers, a lay-clerk at St George's Chapel, Windsor, and from the organist, Nathaniel Giles. He became himself a lay-clerk, but in 1639 went to Dublin as organist of Christ Church Cathedral. He returned to Windsor in 1641, but in 1644 the choir was disbanded and he taught music privately. He received a music degree from Cambridge University in 1658, and a doctorate from Oxford in 1669, where he had become organist and choirmaster at Magdalen College, in 1664. He was dismissed for musical and other irregularities in 1685, but was given a pension.

Works include: services and anthems, *Hymnus Eucharisticus*; instrumental pieces; organ works.

Rogers, Bernard (1893–1968) US composer. He studied at the New York Institute of Musical Art and with Bloch at Cleveland. He gained several prizes and distinctions and for a time was a music journalist. In 1938 he became professor of composition at the Eastman School of Music at Rochester, New York.

Works include: OPERA *The Marriage of Aude* (1931), *The Warrior* (1947), *The Veil* and *The Nightingale* (1940); cantatas *The Raising of Lazarus* and *The Exodus*, *Passion* with organ accompaniment.

OTHER five symphonies (1926–59), overture *The Faithful*, *Three Eastern Dances*, *Two Amer*, *Frescoes*, *Four Fairy Tales*, *The Supper at Emmaeus* (1937), *The Colours of War*, *The Dance of Salome* (1940), *The Song of the Nightingale*,

The Plains, The Sailors of Toulon, Invasion and *Characters from Hans Andersen* for orchestra; soliloquies for flute and strings and bassoon and strings, fantasy for flute, viola, and orchestra; *Pastorale* for 11 instruments, string quartet; *Music for an Industrial Film* for two pianos; songs.

Rogowski, Ludomir (Michał) (1881–1954) Polish composer. He studied at the Warsaw Conservatory and with Reimann and Nikisch at Leipzig. On his return to Poland he founded a symphony orchestra at Wilno, lived in Paris 1914–21 and withdrew to a monastery in modern-day Croatia, 1926.

Works include: the opera *Tamara* (after Lermontov, 1918) and *Prince Marco* (1930); film opera *Un Grand Chagrin de la Petite Ondine* (1920), ballets *St John's Eve* and *Fairy Tale* (1923); seven symphonies (1926–51), suites *Pictures of my Daughter, The Seasons, Les Sourires, Villafranca, Phantasmagoria* (1920), *Sporting Scene, Fantasy Pictures* for orchestra; quartet for four cellos, suites for six and nine instruments and other chamber music; instrumental pieces; piano works; choral songs with and without accompaniment.

Roi Arthus, Le/King Arthur opera by Chausson (libretto by composer); written 1886–95, under the influence of Wagner's *Tristan*, produced Brussels, Théâtre de la Monnaie, 30 November 1903. Mordred betrays Lancelot's affair with Guinevere to King Arthur. Arthur battles his knight, killing him, and Guinevere strangles herself.

Roi David, Le dramatic Psalm by Honegger (libretto by R Morax), produced Mézières, Switzerland, open-air Théâtre du Jorat, 11 June 1921.

Roi de Lahore, Le/The King of Lahore opera by Massenet (libretto by L Gallet), produced Paris, Opéra, 27 April 1877. Hindu priestess Sitâ is loved by both King and evil Scindia in exotic setting.

Roi d'Ys,ˇ Le opera by Lalo (libretto by E Blau), produced Paris, Opéra-Comique, 7 May 1888. Ys is the submerged city of Debussy's piano prelude *La Cathédrale engloutie*. Margared, daughter of the King of Ys, breaks off her engagement to Karnac when she sees childhood love Mylio. But he now loves her sister Rozenn. Margared joins forces with Kernac for revenge; she sacrifices herself as she opens the sluices, flooding the city.

Roi l'a dit, Le/The King has said it opera by Delibes (libretto by E Gondinet), produced Paris, Opéra-Comique, 24 May 1873. The Marquis di Moncontour presents young

Benoit to the King as his own son; Benoit feigns death during a duel to prevent the true identify from being revealed.

Roi malgré lui, Le/King against his Will opera by Chabrier (libretto by E de Najac and P Burani, based on a comedy by Ancelot), produced Paris, Opéra-Comique, 18 May 1887. King Henri of Poland faces a conspiracy to remove him from the throne, led by Count Laski. At Laski's ball the King attends in disguise, escaping detection. King Henri returns to the throne after the plot fails.

Roland opera by Lully (libretto by Quinault), produced Versailles, at court, 8 January 1685; first Paris performance, 8 March 1685. For plot synopsis see ◊*Orlando*.

Roland-Manuel, Alexis (1891–1966), adopted name of Roland Alexis Manuel Lévy French composer and critic. He wrote much criticism and books on Ravel and Falla.

He studied with Roussel at the Schola Cantorum in Paris, and with Ravel. In 1947 he became a professor at the Paris Conservatory.

Works include: the operas *Isabelle et Pantalon* (1920), *Le diable amoureux* (1932); ballets *Le tournoi singulier, L'écran des jeunes filles, Elvire* (on music by D Scarlatti) (1936); film music *L'ami Fritz* (after Erckmann-Chatrian) *La Bandéra* and others; oratorio *Jeanne d'Arc*; symphonic poems *Le harem du vice-roi, Tempo di ballo* (1924), suite *Pena de Francia* for orchestra; suite in the Spanish style for harpsichord, oboe, bassoon, and trumpet, string trio; part songs; songs.

roll a very rapid succession of notes on drums produced by quick alternating strokes of the two sticks.

Rolland, Romain (1866–1944) French musicologist and author. He also contributed essays on music to various periodicals and wrote plays and other literary works. His works include books on Handel and Beethoven, on early opera, *Musiciens d'autrefois, Musiciens d'aujourd'hui, Voyage musical au pays du passé*, and the ten-volume novel *Jean-Christophe* 1904–12, with a musician as hero.

He had a first-rate general education and devoted himself to music and other artistic studies. In 1901 he became president of the music section of the Ecole des Hautes Etudes Sociales and lectured on music first at the Ecole Normale Supérieure and from 1903 at the Sorbonne, Paris. From 1913 he lived in Switzerland, having retired owing to bad health. He returned to France in 1938 in order not to evade the war, was interned in a concentration camp by the Germans, and was released only when he was mortally ill.

Rolle, Johann Heinrich (1716–1785) German organist and composer. He was taught by his father, Christian Friedrich Rolle (1681–1751), and was appointed organist of St Peter's, Magdeburg, at the age of 17. After legal studies in Leipzig he entered the service of Frederick II of Prussia 1741, but returned to Magdeburg in 1746 as organist of St John's. He succeeded his father as municipal music director in 1752.

Works include: over 20 dramatic oratorios, including *David und Jonathan* (1766), *Der Tod Abels Saul* (1770); Passion oratorios; cantatas and numerous other church works; instrumental music; songs.

Roma orchestral suite by Bizet, composed 1866–68, first performed Paris, 1869.

Roman, Johan Helmich (1694–1758) Swedish composer. He was a pupil of his father, who was leader of the court orchestra in Stockholm, and entered royal service in 1711. In England from 1714, he studied with Attilo Ariosti and Johann Pepusch and was in the service of the Duke of Newcastle. Returning to Stockholm, he became vice-Kapellmeister in 1721, then Kapellmeister in 1729. He toured England, France, and Italy 1735–37, became a member of the Swedish Academy in 1740, and retired in 1745.

Works include: Mass, motets, psalms, festival cantatas; 21 symphonies, 6 overtures; concertos; over 20 violin sonatas, 12 sonatas for flute, viola da gamba and harpsichord, *Assaggio* for solo violin, and other pieces.

romance, English and French a piece or song of a 'romantic' nature, usually moderate in tempo and emotional in style. There is no prescribed form, but it is as a rule fairly short and in the character of a song. In France single-voice songs were called *romances* from about the end of the 18th century onward until recently, and the term is still in use, though the more general one now is *mélodie*.

romanesca originally the melody of a 16th-century Spanish song with a simple bass, used as a theme for variations.

A simple form of the romanesca starting on C.

Romani, Felice (1788–1865) Italian librettist and poet. His first libretti were for Simone Mayr (*Medea in Corinto*, 1813). He soon began a collaboration with Rossini and wrote *Aureliano in Palmira* and *Il Turco in Italia*. For Donizetti he wrote *L'Elisir d'amore* (1832) and *Anna Bolena* (1835). His most important work was for Bellini: *Il Pirata* (1827), *I Capuleti* (1830), *La Sonnambula*, *Norma*, (1831) and *Beatrice di Tenda* (1833). His only libretto for Verdi was *Un Giorno di Regno* (1840).

Romanticism a preoccupation with subjective emotion expressed primarily through melody, a use of folk idioms, and a cult of the musician as visionary artist and hero (virtuoso). Often linked with nationalistic feelings, the Romantic movement reached its height in the late 19th century, as in the works of Robert Schumann and Richard Wagner.

The reaction against 18th-century Classical values first appears as imagery of untamed natural forces, in the hero figure of Mozart's opera *Don Giovanni* 1787 and Haydn's *Sturm und Drang* realization of *The Creation* 1797–98. The essentially private emotional world of Franz Schubert's and Schumann's lieder (songs) was rapidly transformed into the national mythic heroism of Richard Wagner and Giuseppe Verdi, experienced in the flesh in such virtuoso figures as Niccolò Paganini and Franz Liszt. Towards the end of the 19th century, however, the heroic ideal was increasingly challenged by intimations of fallibility, as in the antihero of Mussorgsky's opera *Boris Godunov* 1874, and by the cheerful cynicism of Richard Strauss's *Till Eulenspiegel* 1894–95. In the work of Gustav Mahler and Jean Sibelius, Romanticism became expansive and elegiac, finally petering out in the fragmentary idiom of Hollywood film romance.

Romantic Symphony Bruckner's fourth symphony, in E♭. First version composed 1874, first performed Linz, 20 September 1875; version with new scherzo and revised finale performed Vienna, 20 February 1881, conductor Richter.

Romanze (German 'romance') see ◊romance (English and French).

Romberg, Andreas (Jakob) (1767–1821) German violinist and composer. He was a pupil of his father, Gerhard Heinrich Romberg (1745–1819). He appeared in string duets with his cousin Bernhard Romberg at the age of seven and at 17 played at the Concert Spirituel in Paris. In 1790 he joined the electoral orchestra at Bonn and in 1793–96 he was in Italy, Spain and Portugal with

Bernhard, whom he joined again in Paris in 1800 after visits to Vienna and Hamburg. He returned to Hamburg, where he married and remained for 15 years, after which he became court music director at Gotha.

Works include: the operas *Don Mendoce, ou Le Tuteur portugais* (with Bernhard Romberg), *Das blaue Ungeheuer* (composed 1793), *Der Rabe* (1794), *Die Ruinen zu Paluzzi* (1811), *Die Grossmut des Scipio* (1816) and others; Te Deum, Magnificat, psalms and other church music; setting of Schiller's *Lied von der Glocke* for solo voices, chorus, and orchestra, and other cantatas *The Transient and the Eternal, The Harmony of the Spheres, The Power of Song.*; six symphonies and Toy Symphony; string quartets and quintets.

Romberg, Bernhard (1767–1841) German cellist and composer, cousin of Andreas ◊Romberg. He was pupil of his father Anton Romberg; appeared at the age of seven with his cousin and in Paris at 14.

He was in the electoral orchestra at Bonn 1790–93, together with Andreas, Beethoven, Reicha, and F A Ries; then, until 1796, he was in Italy, Spain and Portugal with Andreas. After visits to Vienna and Hamburg he taught the cello at the Paris Conservatory 1801–03, and 1804–06 he was cellist in the royal orchestra in Berlin, where he was court music director 1815–19. He retired to Hamburg in 1819 after a tour in Russia. He also visited London, Paris, Vienna, St Petersburg, and Moscow.

Works include: the operas *Don Mendoce, ou le tuteur portugais* (with Andreas Romberg), *Die wiedergefundene Statue* (after Gozzi, composed 1792, *Der Schiffbruch, Alma, Ulysses und Circe* (1807), *Rittertreue*; ten cello concertos, concerto for two cellos; funeral symphony for Queen Louise of Prussia; 11 string quartets, piano quartets and other chamber music, cello pieces.

Romberg, Siegmund (1887–1951) Hungarian-born US composer. In 1909 he went to the USA as an engineer, but later began composing with great success.

He studied at the University of Bucharest and then in Vienna with Richard Heuberger.

Works include: the operettas *Blossom Time* (after music by Schubert, 1921), *The Rose of Stamboul, The Student Prince* (1924), *The Desert Song* (1926).

Romeo and Juliet fantasy overture by Tchaikovsky, based on Shakespeare's tragedy; first performed Moscow, 16 March, 1870; revised October 1870.

Ballet by Prokofiev, first performed Brno 30 December 1938.

See also ◊*Giulietta e Romeo,* ◊*Capuleti e i Montecchi, I.*

Roméo et Juliette opera by Gounod (libretto by J Barbier and M Carré, after Shakespeare), produced Paris, Théâtre Lyrique, 27 April 1867. After Shakespeare: lovers Romeo and Juliet cannot escape the feud between their families, the Montagues and the Capulets, and die for their love.

Symphony by Berlioz, op. 17, for solo voices, chorus, and orchestra, based on Shakespeare's tragedy, composed 1839, first performed Paris Conservatory, 24 November 1839.

Romeo und Julia opera by Sutermeister (libretto by composer, after Shakespeare), produced Dresden, 13 April 1940. See ◊*Roméo et Juliette* for plot synopsis.

Opera by Blacher (libretto ditto); composed 1943, produced Salzburg, 9 August 1950.

Romeo und Julia auf dem Dorfe see ◊Village Romeo and Juliet.

Romeo und Julie opera by G Benda (libretto by F W Gotter), produced Gotha, at court, 25 September 1776. The first opera to be based on Shakespeare's tragedy. See ◊*Roméo et Juliette* for plot synopsis.

Romero, Mateo (known as Maestro Capitán) (c. 1575–1647) Spanish singer, composer, and priest. He joined the Flemish section of the royal chapel at Madrid in 1594; he was a pupil of Philippe Rogier, whom he succeeded as maestro de capilla in 1598. He was ordained priest in 1609 and retired with a pension in 1633, but was sent on a musical mission to Portugal in 1638.

Works include: motets and other church music; secular songs for three and four voices, including settings of poems by Lope de Vega.

Romilda e Costanza opera by Meyerbeer (libretto by G Rossi), produced Padua, 19 July 1817.

rondeau a medieval song with a refrain. Also, by analogy, in the 17th and 18th centuries an instrumental piece in which one section recurs. See ◊rondo.

rondeña a Spanish folk song, a type of Andalusia, resembling the fandango, with words in stanzas of four lines of eight syllables.

Rondine, La/The Swallow operetta by Puccini (libretto by G Adami, translated from the German of A M Willner and H Reichert), produced Monte Carlo, 27 March 1917. Originally intended to be set to the German words for the Carl Theater in Vienna, but Italy being at war with Austria, this fell through. Prunier, a poet, convinces Magda of the power of love. She meets Ruggero, who falls in love with her; but she abandons him to return to Rambaldo, leaving him devastated.

rondo, or rondeau antique musical form in which verses alternate with a refrain. Often festive in character, it is a popular final movement of a sonata, concerto, or symphony.

root in a chord, the ◊tonic note from which the other notes are derived. For example, in a chord consisting of any spacing or arrangement of the notes C–E–G, C is always the root. A chord is considered to be in 'root position' when the root is the lowest voice or part, usually in the bass.

Root position

1st inversion   **2nd inversion**

A chord in root position on C. The second diagram shows first and second inversions. According to this theory, which takes no account of the different functions of chords, a four-note chord has three possible inversions, and so on.

Rore, Cipriano de (c. 1516–1565) Flemish composer. He spent much of his life in Italy, where he was a prolific composer of madrigals and sacred music. He wrote 125 madrigals, most of which are contained in the ten books he published 1542–46. His works made a strong impression on Monteverdi.

He studied under Adrian Willaert at Venice, where he was a singer at St Mark's, and began to publish madrigals in 1542. He left Venice about 1550 to enter the service of Duke Ercole II d'Este at Ferrara. In 1558 he visited his parents at Antwerp and the court of Margaret of Parma, governor of the Netherlands, at Brussels, into the service of whose husband, Ottavio Farnese, Duke of Parma, he passed in 1561. In 1563 he succeeded Willaert as maestro di cappella of St Mark's, Venice, but returned to Parma the following year.

Rore's parody Masses and motets follow the style of the previous generation, but it is for his madrigals that he is chiefly remembered. He set many of Petrarch's texts in his earlier madrigals; in the later ones he became more aware of sensitive treatment of the text.

Works include: five Masses, 65 motets, one Passion and other church music; 125 madrigals; instrumental fantasies and ricercari, and other pieces.

Rorem, Ned (1923–) US composer. He studied at the Curtis Institute and Juilliard School, New York. He has held academic posts at the Universities of Buffalo and Utah, and at the Curtis Institute (from 1980).

Works include: the operas *A Childhood Miracle* (1955), *The Robbers* (1958), *Miss Julie* (1965), and *Hearing* (1976); three symphonies (1950, 1956, 1958), three piano concertos (1950, 1969, 1992); *The Poet's Requiem* for soprano, chorus, and orchestra (1957); *Eagles* for orchestra (1958); Double concerto for violin, cello, and orchestra (1979); *Sunday Morning*, symphonic suite (1981); *Whitman Cantata* (1983); *An American Oratorio* (1984); *String Symphony* (1985); organ concerto (1985); violin concerto (1985); Septet: *Scenes from Childhood* (1985); *Homer* for chorus and eight instruments (1986); *Diversions*, brass quintet (1989); cor anglais concerto (1993); church music; keyboard pieces and songs; song cycles *Flight for Heaven, King Midas, Poems of Love and the Rain, War Scenes, Women's Voices,* and *After Long Silence.*

Rosa, Carl (August Nikolaus) (1842–1889), adopted name of Carl August Nikolaus Rose German violinist and conductor. He studied at the Leipzig and Paris Conservatories and became an orchestra leader at Hamburg. In 1866 he visited England and the USA, where he met and in 1867 married Euphrosyne Parape (1836–1874). They formed an opera company, which included the singers Charles Santley and Giorgio Ronconi. They went to England and carried on as the Carl Rosa Opera Company, giving many performances of English operas, and of foreign works in translation.

Rosalia the usual name for the real sequence repeating a phrase higher or lower, not within the scale of the same key, as in the tonal sequence, but by so changing the key that its steps retain exactly the same succession of whole tones and semitones. The name derives from an Italian popular song, 'Rosalia, mia cara', in which this device occurs.

A rosalia in which the first two bars are repeated a whole tone higher.

Rosamond opera by Arne (libretto by J Addison), produced London, Theatre in Lincoln's Inn Fields, 7 March 1733.

Opera by Clayton (libretto ditto), produced London, Drury Lane Theatre, 4 March 1707. Queen Eleanor, wife of King Henry, discovers his mistress Rosamond and forces her to drink a bowl of poison. When Henry repents, she reveals the liquid was not lethal, and that Rosamond has become a nun.

Rosamunde incidental music by Schubert for a play by Helmina von Chézy, *Rosamunde, Prinzessin von Cypern*, produced Vienna, Theater an der Wien, 20 December 1823. The music consists of three entr'actes, two ballet tunes, a romance for contralto, a chorus of spirits, a shepherd's melody and shepherds' chorus, and a hunting-chorus. No overture was specially written for the piece. At the first performance, that to the opera *Alfonso und Estrella* was used; later that to the melodrama *Die Zauberharfe* was published as the *Rosamunde* overture and is still played.

rose, or knot the ornamental fretwork sound hole of many flat-bellied string instruments of the lute and guitar type; also of dulcimers, harpsichords, and similar instruments, sometimes serving as the makers' trademark.

Rose et Colas opera by Monsigny (libretto by J M Sedaine), produced Paris, Comédie-Italienne, 8 March 1764.

Roseingrave (lived 17th–18th centuries) English family of musicians:

Daniel (c. 1650–1727), organist and composer. He was educated in music as a chorister in the Chapel Royal in London. From 1679 to 1698 he was successively organist of Gloucester, Winchester and Salisbury Cathedrals, and was then appointed to St Patrick's and Christ Church Cathedrals, Dublin.

Thomas (1688–1766), organist and composer, son of Daniel. He was a pupil of his father at Dublin, where he was educated at Trinity College. In 1710 he went to Italy where he met A and D Scarlatti, making great friends with the latter and travelling with him. He went to London before 1720, when he produced D Scarlatti's opera *Narcisco* with interpolations of his own. In 1725 he was appointed organist of St George's Church, Hanover Square. He retired in 1741 and moved to Dublin, living probably with his nephew William Roseingrave.

His works include the opera *Phaedra and Hippolytus* (on Edmund Smith's play based on Racine, 1753); services and anthems; organ voluntaries and fugues; suites for harpsichord and an introductory piece for his edition of Scarlatti's sonatas; 12 solos for flute and harpsichord; 12 Italian cantatas (1735).

Ralph (c. 1695–1747), composer, brother of Thomas. He studied with his father, who petitioned for him to succeed him as organist of St Patrick's Cathedral, Dublin, in 1719; but he was appointed vicar-choral and not organist till 1726. He also became organist of Christ Church Cathedral on his father's death. He wrote services and anthems.

Rosen, Charles (1927–) US pianist and musicologist. He is well known for his thoughtful interpretations of Bach, Beethoven, and modern music, including Carter, Schoenberg, and Boulez. His books include *The Classical Style* 1971, *Schoenberg* 1975, and *Sonata Forms* 1980.

He graduated from Princeton with an arts degree in 1949, and made his debut as a pianist at New York in 1951. He has taught in New York and at Berkeley, California.

Rosenkavalier, Der/The Rose Cavalier opera by Richard Strauss (libretto by Hugo von Hofmannsthal), produced Dresden, Royal Opera, 26 January 1911. Octavian, young lover of the Marschallin, bears a silver rose to Sophie, the proposed betrothed of loutish Ochs. When he meets her Octavian falls in love and conspires to end the arranged marriage, exposing Ochs as a philanderer. The Marschallin, although unhappy, gives Octavian and Sophie her blessing.

Rosenmüller, Johann (c. 1619–1684) German composer. He was a prolific and popular composer of both sacred and secular works, and was influential in introducing Italian-style music to Germany.

He studied at Leipzig University and in 1642 became assistant master at St Thomas's School there, studying music with the cantor, Tobias Michael, and acting as his deputy when Michael became infirm. He was marked out for the succession and in 1651 became organist of St Nicholas's Church; but in 1655 was imprisoned for homosexual offences with his choirboys. He escaped to Hamburg and later fled to Venice, where he settled and was influenced as a composer by the local style. There J P Krieger became his pupil. In 1674 he was recalled to Germany by an appointment to the court of Duke Anton Ulrich of Brunswick, at Wolfenbüttel.

Works include: Masses, motets, vesper psalms and Lamentations, Latin and German motets, *Kernsprüche* for three–seven voices and instruments, German motets and cantatas, hymns, hymn by Albinus 'Straf mich nicht'; *Sonata da camera* for five instruments, sonatas for two–five instruments, suites of instrumental dances.

Rose of Castille (sic), The opera by Balfe (libretto by A G Harris and E Falconer, based on a French libretto, *Le Muletier de Tolède*, by A P d'Ennery and Clairville, set by A Adam and produced 1854), produced London, Lyceum Theatre, 29 October 1857.

Rose of Persia, The, or The Story-Teller and the Slave operetta by Sullivan (libretto by B Hood), produced London, Savoy Theatre, 29 November 1899.

Rose vom Liebesgarten, Die opera by Pfitzner (libretto by J Grun); composed 1897–1900, produced Elberfeld, 9 November 1901. During the celebration of spring, Fairy queen Minneleide is abducted by the Night Sorceror. Siegnot, who loves her, is killed while rescuing her but is restored to life.

rosin resin, refined from distilled oil of turpentine. Used by makers of musical instruments and performers, it is applied to the hairs of the bow of a string instrument. By increasing the friction between bow and strings, it helps the strings to vibrate when the bow is drawn across them.

Rosina ballad opera by Shield (libretto by F Brooke, based on an episode in Thomson's *Seasons* and Favart's *Les Moissonneurs* with Duni's music, produced London, Covent Garden, 31 December 1782. Rosina is the object of both Mr Belville's and Captain Belville's attentions. After the Captain tries to abduct her, Mr Belville realizes she loves him and he proposes marriage.

Rosinda opera by Cavalli (libretto by G Faustini), produced Venice, Teatro San Apollinaire, 1651.

Roslavets, Nikolai Andreievich (1881–1944) Russian composer. He studied music at the Moscow Conservatory under Sergey Vasilenko, and developed his own 12-tone system of composition. Some of his music has been revived, including the violin concerto of 1925, but did not quite live up to its avantgarde reputation.

Works include: cantata *Heaven and Earth* (after Byron, 1912); symphony, violin concerto (1925), two symphonic poems; five string quartets (no. 3 12-tone), quintet for oboe, two violins, cello, and harp, two piano trios; five violin and piano sonatas, two cello and piano sonatas; many piano pieces; songs.

Rösler, Franz Anton (c. 1750–1792) Bohemian composer. Destined for the priesthood, he attended the Jesuit College of Olomouc, but in 1773 entered the service of the Prince of Ottingen as double bass player and later became conductor. He left for Ludwigslust in 1789 and was court music director there to his death. He wrote under the name of Francesco Antonio Rosetti.

Works include: the opera *Das Winterfest der Hirten* (1789); oratorios *Der sterbende Jesus* (1786) and *Jesus in Gethsemane*; Requiem for Mozart (1791); 34 symphonies; concertos for piano, violin, flute, oboe, clarinet and horn; chamber music, violin sonatas.

Rosmene, La, ovvero L'Infedeltà fedele/Rosmene, or Faithful Faithlessness opera by Alessandro Scarlatti (libretto by G D de Totis), produced Naples, Palazzo Reale, Carnival 1688.

Rosseter, Philip (1567 or 1568–1623) English lutenist and composer. He worked in London and was associated with Robert Jones, Philip Kingham, and Reeve in the theatre life of the capital. From 1609 he worked with Robert Keysar, managing a company of boy actors, known as the Children of Whitefriars (from 1610 the Children of the Queen's Revels). From 1615 the company performed at the Blackfriars theatre. Rosseter published a book of songs to the lute with Thomas Campion; some if not all of the words by Campion and about half of the music by Rosseter.

Works include: *A Booke of Ayres* with lute, orpheoreon, and bass viol; *Lessons for the Consort* for six instruments by various composers.

Rossi, Luigi (c. 1598–1653) Italian singer and composer. He composed in an elaborate style, and developing the innovations of Monteverdi, his *Orfeo* 1647 was lavishly produced at court; the expense provoked anti-monarchist feeling in the Parisian populace.

He was in the service of Cardinal Barberini in Rome 1641–46. In 1646 he was called to Paris at the instigation of Cardinal Mazarin and the following year produced *Orfeo*, one of the first Italian operas to be performed there.

It has been successfully revived in Bloomington and London (1988, 1990).

Works include: the operas *Il palagio d'Atlante, or Il palazzo incantato, L'Orfeo* (1647); oratorio *Giuseppe, figlio di Giacobbe,* cantatas, and other pieces.

Rossi, Michel Angelo (c. 1600–1656) Italian organist and composer. His opera *Erminia sul Giordano,* to a libretto by Giulio Rospigliosi, later Pope Clement IX, was given in Rome in 1633.

He was a pupil of Frescobaldi.

Works include: the operas *Erminia sul Giordano* (after Tasso) and *Andromeda* (1638); toccatas and *correnti* for organ or harpsichord.

Rossi, Salomone (1570–c. 1630) Italian composer. He worked at the court of Mantua 1587–1628 and enjoyed the privilege of dispensing with the wearing of the yellow badge that stigmatized the Jews in Italy.

Works include: music for Guarini's *Idropica* and oratorio *Maddalena* (both with Monteverdi and others, 1608, 1617); 28 Hebrew psalms for four–eight voices; madrigals and canzonets; instrumental works *Sinfonie e gagliarde* and *Sonate.*

Rossignol, Le (Stravinsky). See ◊*Nightingale, The.*

Rossini, Gioacchino Antonio (1792–1868) Italian composer. His first success was the opera *Tancredi* 1813. In 1816 his opera buffa *Il barbiere di Siviglia/The Barber of Seville* was produced in Rome. He was the most successful opera composer of his time, producing 20 operas in the period 1815–23. He also created (with Donizetti and Bellini) the 19th-century Italian operatic style.

After *Guillaume Tell/William Tell* 1829, Rossini gave up writing opera and his later years were spent in Bologna and Paris. Among the works of this period are the *Stabat Mater* 1842 and the piano music arranged for ballet by Respighi as *La boutique fantasque/The Fantastic Toyshop* 1919.

Rossini was born in Pesaro; his father was a horn and trumpet player, his mother an occasional singer. He learnt piano, singing, and harmony early and sang in churches and theatres; at 13 he was employed as an accompanist at the theatre; at 14, when he had already tried his hand at an opera and other works, he entered the Bologna Liceo Musicale, studying counterpoint and cello. In 1808 he won a prize with a cantata and in 1810 had his first comic opera, *La cambiale di matrimonio,* produced at Venice. From that time he went from success to success, beginning with *Tancredi* at Venice in 1813. However, *Il barbiere di Siviglia* was initially a failure when first performed in Rome in 1816. The two sides of Rossini's creative genius were now well established: the wit, effervescence, and florid vocal writing of his comic operas and the considerable dramatic power of his serious works, each in its own distinctive musical 'colour'. His huge popular following was consolidated by *Otello* 1816, *La Cenerentola* in 1817 and *Mosè in Egitto* in 1818 (later revised for Paris). *Mosè* was premiered in Naples and was one of six remarkable serious operas produced there in only five years, the others being *Armida, Ermione, La donna del lago, Maometto II,* and *Zelmira;* each of these works has only recently been revived.

His first great foreign success came during a visit to Vienna in 1822; he met Beethoven and saw his own operas achieve greater acclaim with the Viennese than any Austrian work. In the same year he married the Portuguese singer Isabella Colbran; she had already created leading roles in *Elisabetta, Otello, Mosè,* and *Armida.* At Venice in 1823 she sang the title role in Rossini's last opera written for the Italian stage, *Semiramide.* Rossini and his wife went to Paris and to London that year, remaining in England until July 1824 and being well received at court. He wrote a lament on the death of the poet Byron for eight voices.

On returning to Paris, Rossini was appointed director of the Théâtre Italien, where he produced one new work and two revised works, followed by a French comic opera, *Le Comte Ory,* and finally *Guillaume Tell* 1829 at the Opéra. The strain of composing *Guillaume Tell,* a huge summation of his life's work, brought on a prolonged period of ill-health; thereafter, although aged only 37, he gave up opera and lived alternately at Bologna and Paris. In the early 1830s he met Olympe Pélissier, a *demi-mondaine,* and entered into a liaison with her; his separation from Isabella was legalized in 1837, she died in 1845, and he married Olympe in August 1846. Serious illness afflicted him during this period, but he completed the *Stabat Mater* 1832–42. In 1839 he was commissioned to reform the Liceo Musicale at Bologna, where he had once been a pupil, and he worked there at intervals until 1848, when he left for Florence, to remain until 1855, leaving Italy for the last time for Paris that year. In his retirement he wrote many small pieces for the entertainment of his friends and in 1863 the *Petite Messe solennelle;* his musical soirées were much sought after by fashionable society and contemporary musicians.

For many years Rossini's comic operas have overshadowed his serious works, but recent productions have helped to produce a more balanced view of his output.

Works include: OPERA *Tancredi* (1813), *L'Italiana in Algeri* (1813), *Il barbiere di Siviglia* (after Beaumarchais, 1816), *Otello* (last act after Shakespeare, 1816), *La Cenerentola* (1817), *La gazza ladra* (1817), *Armida* (1818), *Mosè in Egitto* (1818), *Semiramide* (1823), *Il viaggio a Reims* (1825), *Le Comte Ory* (1828), *Guillaume Tell* (after Schiller, 1829). *Messa di Gloria* (1820), *Stabat Mater* (1842), *Petite Messe solennelle*, and some shorter sacred pieces; *Péchés de vieillesse/Sins of Old Age* small piano pieces, songs, and six string quartets.

Rota, Nino (1911–1979) Italian composer. He studied with Ildebrando Pizzetti, Alfredo Casella, and in the USA. On his return to Milan he obtained a degree with a treatise on the 16th-century Italian composer Gioseffo Zarlino and Italian Renaissance music. In 1950 he was appointed director of the Bari Conservatory.

Works include: the operas *Il principe porcaro* (after Hans Andersen, composed 1925), *Ariodante* (1942), *Il capello di paglia di Firenze/The Italian Straw Hat* 1955); oratorio *L'infanzia di San Giovanni Battista;* two Masses; three symphonies (1936–39), serenade and concerto for orchestra; *Invenzioni* for string quartet, quintet for flute, oboe, viola, cello, and harp, *Il presepio* for voice, string quartet, and piano; sonatas for violin and piano, viola and piano, and flute and harp; songs *Liriche di Tagore, Tre liriche infantili;* film music.

rote string instrument of the ◊lyre type, also called rota or rotte, and similar to the crwth. It was in use up to medieval times.

Rouget de Lisle, Claude-Joseph (1760–1836) French army officer. While in Strasbourg 1792, he composed 'La Marseillaise', the French national anthem.

round an alternative name for a ◊canon, in which voices imitate each other exactly.

rounds round dances, that is, dances performed in circles, and hence tunes intended for such dances.

Rousseau, Jean-Jacques (1712–1778) Swiss-French philosopher, author, and composer. He was a chorister at Annecy Cathedral but had little formal training in music. He went to Paris in 1741, where he presented a paper to the Académie des Sciences advocating a new system of notation (pub-

lished in 1743 as 'Dissertation sur la musique moderne') and later contributed music articles to Diderot's *Encyclopédie*, which were severely criticized by Rameau for their inaccuracy. As secretary to the French ambassador in Venice 1743–44, he became acquainted with Italian music, and during the Guerre des Bouffons sided with the Italian party, decrying French music in his controversial essay, 'Lettre sur la musique française' (1753). His most important composition, the one-act *intermède Le Devin du village*, though in French, was supposedly written in tuneful Italian style. In 1767 he published his valuable *Dictionnaire de musique*. The 'monodrama' *Pygmalion* (1770), only two pieces of which were by Rousseau, attempted to found a new form, and in its combination of spoken words and music was the ancestor of the later melodrama. Among his other writings are two essays in support of Gluck.

Works include: the operas *Iphis et Anaxerète* (1740), *La Découverte du nouveau monde* (1741), *Le Devin du village* (1752), *Daphnis et Chloé* (unfinished); opera-ballet *Les Muses galantes* (1745); monodrama *Pygmalion* (1770). c. 100 songs., published as *Consolations des misères de ma vie.*

Roussel, Albert (1869–1937) French composer. One of his most popular works is *Le festin de l'araignée/The Spider's Banquet* 1912, in which the hungry arachnid is depicted with appropriate, delicate scoring.

He was educated in Paris for the Navy, but took piano lessons at the same time. He wrote his first compositions while engaged in naval service and voyaging to the East, but resigned in 1893 to devote himself to music, studying with Eugène Gigout and d'Indy. In 1902 he became professor at the Schola Cantorum, where he had studied. In World War I he served with the Red Cross and later with the transport service, and in 1918 he retired, broken in health, to Perros-Guirec in Brittany and in 1920 to a villa near Varengeville.

His naval service in the East had a lasting impression on Roussel, colouring his finest work, the opéra-ballet *Padmâvatî* with Indian melodic patterns. Ballet and choral singing are found also in *La naissance de la lyre*, an evocation of ancient Greece. Other characteristics of Roussel's varying style appear in his third symphony, which includes polytonality and vital rhythmic patterns.

Works include: STAGE: opera *Padmâvatî* (1923); ballets *Le Festin de l'araignée* (1913), *Bacchus et Ariane* (1931).

VOCAL AND ORCHESTRAL: four symphonies, 1908–34; *Suite en Fa* (1927); sinfonietta for strings; concertino for cello and orchestra (1936).

CHAMBER AND SONGS: serenade for flute, violin, viola, cello, and harp (1925), string trio, trios for violin, clarinet, and piano and for flute, violin, and clarinet; *Joueurs de flûte* for flute and piano; Impromptu for harp; suite, sonatina, and other pieces for piano; songs.

rovescio see ◊al rovescio.

Rovetta, Giovanni (c. 1595–1668) Italian priest and composer. He learnt music as a choirboy at St Mark's, Venice and in 1623 was appointed a bass in the choir there. He was ordained priest, became vice-maestro di cappella at St Mark's in 1627, and maestro di cappella in succession to Monteverdi in 1644.

Works include: Masses, motets, psalms; operas *Ercole in Lidia* (1645) and *Argiope* (1649); madrigals.

Roxelane, La authentic name of Haydn's symphony no. 63 in C major, composed c. 1777–80, so called apparently after an old French melody used for variations in the slow movement.

Royal Academy of Music, RAM British senior music school in London, founded 1822 by John Fane, Lord Burghesh, later 11th Earl of Westmorland. It was granted a royal charter 1830. Based in Marylebone Road, it provides a full-time complete musical education.

Royal College of Music British college providing full-time complete musical education. Founded 1883, it is in Kensington, W London.

Royal College of Organists association founded in London in 1864 to promote the composition and study of organ music, and raise the standards of musicianship by issuing diplomas such as the ARCO (Associate of the Royal College of Organists).

Royal Manchester College of Music founded in 1893. First principal was Sir Charles Hallé, followed by A Brodsky (1895), J R Forbes (1929), F R Cox (1953) and J Wray (1970–72). In 1972 the RMCM merged with the Northern School of Music to form the Royal Northern College of Music (principal J Manduell).

Royal Musical Association a society formed to promote the investigation of all aspects of music. It was founded in London in 1874 as The Musical Association and became 'Royal'

in 1944. Apart from regular meetings and conferences, the Association publishes the *Proceedings of the RMA* (from 1987, *Journal of the RMA*), RMA *Research Chronicle* (founded 1961), RMA *Monographs* (founded 1985) and initiated *Musica Britannica* (1951).

Royal Northern College of Music see ◊Royal Manchester College of Music.

Royal Opera House Britain's leading opera house, sited at Covent Garden, London.
The original theatre opened 1732, was destroyed by fire 1808 and reopened 1809. It was again destroyed by fire 1856, and the third and present building dates from 1858. It has been the home of the Royal Opera and the Royal Ballet since 1946.

Royal Winter Music two sonatas on Shakespearean characters for guitar by Henze: no. 1 1975–76, first performed Berlin, 20 September 1976, with Julian Bream; no. 2 1979, first performed Brussels, 25 November 1980.

Rozkošný, Josef Richard (1833–1913) Czech pianist and composer. He studied in Prague and toured widely as a pianist. Later he had a great success as a popular opera composer.

Works include: the operas *Nicholas* (1870), *The Rapids of St John* (1871), *Cinderella* (1885), *Stoja, Zavis of Falkenstein* (1877), *Krakonos* (1889), *The Poacher, Satanella, The Black Lake* (1906); piano pieces; songs.

Rózsa, Miklós (1907–1995) Hungarian-born US composer. He studied piano and composition in Leipzig, and in 1932 settled in Paris, achieving success as a composer. In 1935 he moved to London, where he worked in the film industry and in 1940 settled in Hollywood, writing music for such films as *The Jungle Book, Spellbound* 1945, and *Ben Hur* 1959.

Works include: *Ballet Hungarica*; symphony (1930), *Scherzo, Theme, Variations and Finale* for orchestra (1933); concert overture, serenade for chamber orchestra; concerto for string orchestra; two violin concertos, viola concerto (1984); string quartet; piano quintet, trio for violin, viola, and clarinet; film music and other pieces.

Różycki, Ludomir (1883–1953) Polish conductor and composer. He studied with Noskowski at the Warsaw Conservatory and with Humperdinck in Berlin. In 1912 he became conductor at Lwów, and later lived by turns in Warsaw and Berlin.

Works include: the operas *Bolesław the Bold* (1908), *Medusa* (1911), *Eros and Psyche* (1916), *Casanova, Beatrice Cenci* (1926), *The Devil's Mill*

(1930); ballet *Pan Twardowski*; symphonic poems *Bolesław the Bold*, *Anhelli* and others, prelude *Mona Lisa Gioconda* and ballad for orchestra; piano concerto in G minor; string quartet (1916), piano quintet (1913), piano music, songs.

rubato (from Italian *tempo rubato*, 'rubbed time') in music, a pushing or dragging against the beat for expressive effect.

Rubbra, Edmund (1901–1986) English composer. He studied under the composer Gustav Holst and specialized in contrapuntal writing, as exemplified in his study *Counterpoint* 1960. His compositions include 11 symphonies, chamber music, and songs. In 1948 he became a Roman Catholic, and his later music shows the influence of Catholic mysticism.

Rubbra was born at Northampton and studied at Reading University and the Royal College of Music in London, where his teachers included Holst, R O Morris, and Vaughan Williams. He taught at Oxford University 1947–68 and at the Guildhall School of Music, London, from 1961.

Works include: STAGE AND CHORAL: *La Belle Dame sans merci* (Keats) and *The Morning Watch* (Henry Vaughan) for chorus and orchestra; Masses, motets, madrigals, and other choral works.

ORCHESTRAL: 11 symphonies (1935–79), *Improvisations on Virginal Pieces by Farnaby* (1939) for orchestra; viola concerto (1953), piano concerto (1956), *Soliloquy* for cello and small orchestra; works for voice and orchestra.

CHAMBER: four string quartets (1934–77); three sonatas and sonatina for violin and piano, cello and piano sonata; piano and organ music; songs.

Rubinstein, Anton Grigorievich (1829–1894) Russian pianist and composer. One of the great virtuosos of his day, he did not join the Russian nationalist movement of his contemporaries, The ◊Five. His music follows a more western European style, but although solidly constructed it lacks the imaginative touch of genius. His many compositions include five piano concertos and six symphonies, including the *Ocean* (no. 2); he also wrote 18 operas (of which the best known is *The Demon* 1871, performed 1875), and oratorios.

Born at Vykhvatinets, Ukraine, Rubinstein learnt the piano from his mother and from a teacher named Villoing at Moscow. He appeared in public at the age of nine and in 1840 went on tour with his teacher, who took him to Paris and placed him under Liszt for further instruction. He afterwards toured in Europe and studied composition with Dehn in Berlin 1844–46. After teaching in Vienna and Pressburg (now Bratislava) he returned to Russia in 1848, becoming chamber virtuoso to the Grand Duchess Helena Pavlovna. From 1854 he made successful tours as a concert pianist, earning a great reputation in Europe and the USA. In 1858 he was appointed imperial music director at St Petersburg, founding the Conservatory there in 1862. As a composer Rubinstein was antagonistic to the Russian nationalists; his compositions are still little known although *The Demon* was successfully revived at Wexford Festival in 1991.

Works include: OPERAS AND STAGE ORATORIOS *The Demon* (after Lermontov, 1875), *Kalashnikov* (1879), and others.

VOCAL AND ORCHESTRAL Songs and Requiem for Mignon from Goethe's *Wilhelm Meister* for solo voices, chorus, and piano; six symphonies, 1850–86: (2. *Ocean*, 4. *Dramatic*); five concertos and *Conzertstück* for piano and orchestra (1850–89).

CHAMBER piano and wind quintet, piano quintet and quartet; four sonatas, Theme and Variations and many other works for piano, including *Melody in F*, op. 3/1; songs.

Rubsamen, Walter H(oward) (1911–1973) US musicologist. He studied at Columbia University, New York, and at Munich University; he later joined the music department of his college and in 1938 became lecturer. In 1955 he became professor at the University of California at Los Angeles. His works included studies of Pierre de La Rue and of early Italian secular music.

Ruckers (lived 16th–17th centuries) family of Flemish harpsichord makers founded by ◊Hans Ruckers and continued by his sons **Iohannes** (1578–1643) and **Andreas** (1579–?), and their descendants. Their instruments were noted for their engineering precision and matchless tone, and were imitated widely. Many were commissioned for display, and featured paintings inside the lid by artists, including Brueghel and Rubens.

Ruckers, Hans (c. 1530–1598) Flemish harpsichord and virginal maker. He founded a business at Antwerp in 1584, producing instruments which provided contrast in register and tone. He was succeeded by his sons Joannes (1578–1642) and Andries (1579– c. 1645). About 100 instruments made by members of the Ruckers family survive, in both single and two-manual versions.

Rückert, Friedrich (1788–1866) German poet. His works inspired ◊Kindertotenlieder (Mahler), also five other songs by Mahler for voice and orchestra (*Ich atmet' einen linden Duft, Liebst du um Schönheit, Blicke mir nicht in die Lieder, Ich bin der Welt abhanden gekommen, Um Mitternacht,* 1901–03), 5 songs by Schubert, 18 by Schumann, 2 by Brahms.

Rückpositiv (German 'back positive') in music, a small ◊organ at the organist's back, to the front of the gallery. From the 15th to the 17th centuries, it was the second main manual (keyboard) of most organs, providing colouristic and contrasting functions.

Ruddigore* or *The Witch's Curse operetta by Sullivan (libretto by W S Gilbert), produced London, Savoy Theatre, 22 January 1887. Robin, the villainous Sir Ruthven and bad baronet of Ruddigore, is condemned by a family curse to commit a crime a day.

Ruders, Poul (1949–) Danish composer and organist. He studied at the Copenhagen Conservatory, and has had commissions from the London Sinfonietta and Ensemble Intercontemporain.

Works include: *Wind-Drumming* for wind quintet and four percussion (1979); two violin concertos (1981, 1991); two string quartets (1971, 1979); *Manhattan Abstractions* (for the New York Philharmonic Orchestra, 1982); *Thus Saw Saint Joan,* for orchestra (1984); *Break Dance* for piano and ensemble (1984); clarinet concerto (1985); *Dramaphonia* for piano and orchestra (1987); *Nightshade* for ensemble (1987); *Tycho,* opera (after the Danish astronomer who was obliged to replace his nose with a false nose made of silver, 1986); Symphony, *Himmelhoch Jauchzend-zum Tode betrubt* (1989); *The City in the Sea* for contralto and orchestra (1990), *Trapeze* (1992) and *Zenith* (1993) for orchestra; *The Bells* for soprano and chamber ensemble (1993); *Anima* cello concerto (1993).

Rudhyar, Dane (actually Daniel Chennevière) (1895–1985) French-US composer. He studied in Paris and settled in the USA in 1916, receiving a composition prize in 1920.

Works include: the ballet *Dance Poem*; symphonic poem *Surge of Fire* (1920), six 'syntonies' for orchestra (1920–59), *Cosmic Cycle* for orchestra (1981); piano music and songs.

Ruffo, Vincenzo (c. 1510–1587) Italian male soprano and composer. His sacred music shows the influence of Tridentine reforms, which insisted on verbal clarity.

He held the post of maestro di cappella at Verona Cathedral from 1554 and at Milan 1563–72. He occupied a similar post at Pistoia 1574–79, then returned to Milan.

Works include: Masses, motets, Magnificat, psalms, and other church music; madrigals.

Rugby Honegger's second symphonic movement for orchestra, following *Pacific 231* and succeeded by *Mouvement symphonique No. 3*. It is an impression of a game of rugby football. First performed Paris, Orchestre Symphonique, 19 October 1928.

ruggiero a simple bass line, first found in the 16th century, which was widely used for variations. It may originally have been a dance, though it is found also in vocal settings. See also ◊romanesca.

Ruggiero, o vero L'eroica gratitudine/ Ruggiero, or Heroic Gratitude opera by Hasse (libretto by Metastasio), produced Milan, Teatro Regio Ducal, 16 October 1771. Hasse's last opera. Rogerus, imprisoned by the Greeks after a battle, is rescued by Leone, who is now betrothed to Bradamante, Rogerus' beloved. Rogerus reluctantly accepts the situation, preferring suicide to a fight against Leone. But all resolves happily: Rogerus and Bradamante are reunited.

Ruggles, Carl (1876–1971) US composer. He was an associate, during the 1920s and 1930s, of the experimentalist composers Charles Ives, Edgard Varèse, and Henry Cowell, trying to forge a new direction in music. His instrumental forms were, however, more conservative than those of other composers, as in his best-known work *Sun-Treader* 1932

A typical ruggiero in G major.

for orchestra, which, typically, uses elements of ◊serialism but in a polyphonic texture.

Ruggles studied at Harvard University with John Knowles Paine. Afterwards he conducted the Symphony Orchestra at Winona, Minnesota, for a time. From 1917 he lived in New York, where his music was performed in concerts organized by Varèse. He also associated with Ives and was an early American exponent of atonalism.

Works include: the opera *The Sunken Bell* (composed 1912–23), *Men and Angels* (1920), *Men* (destroyed), *Angels* for four trumpets and three trombones (revised 1938), *Men and Mountains* for small orchestra (1924), *Portals* for 13 strings (1925, revised 1929, 1941 and 1953), *Sun-Treader* (1932), *Evocations* for orchestra (1971); concertino for piano and orchestra; *Vox clamans in deserto* for voice and chamber orchestra; *Polyphonic Compositions* for three pianos, *Evocations* and other works for piano.

Ruins of Athens, The incidental music by Beethoven, op. 113, for a play by Kotzebue written for the opening of the German theatre at Pest, 9 February 1812. It comprises an overture and eight numbers, including the *Turkish March*, already composed by Beethoven for his piano variations, op. 76, in 1809.

'Rule, Britannia' a patriotic song by Arne, now almost a second British national anthem, originally part of the masque *Alfred*, produced 1 August 1740, at Cliefden (now Cliveden) House near Maidenhead, the residence of Frederick, Prince of Wales.

rule of the octave an 18th-century procedure in the treatment of thorough-bass, especially in Italy (*regola dell' ottava*), providing a series of simple chords of the tonic, dominant, and subdominant for the elementary harmonization of a bass formed by a rising diatonic scale.

rumba Afro-Cuban traditional secular dance and music genre, rendered by vocals with percussion, providing complex syncopated rhythms. Characteristic quick-quick-slow dance movement and a repetitive melody accompanied by an ostinato one-bar pattern played on the maracas. Model for the mambo, cha cha cha and other Latin American ballroom dances.

Runswick, Daryl (1946–) English composer. He studied at Cambridge, and later played double bass with the London Sinfonietta, 1970–82. He was tenor singer with Electric Phoenix from 1983 and musical

director of the Green Light Theatre Company from 1990.

Works include: rock opera *Taking the Air* (1989), *Lady Lazarus* for amplified female voice (1985), *Patents: Pending* for six solo voices (1988), *Needs Must when the Devil Drives* for voices and electronics (1990), *Main-lineing*, clarinet quintet (1991). Orchestration of *Aida* for 24 players (Welsh National Opera 1983). Recordings of Berio and Cage with Electric Phoenix.

Ruslan and Ludmila opera by Glinka (libretto by V A Shirkov and C A Bakhturin, based on Pushkin's poem), produced St Petersburg, 9 December 1842. During her wedding to the knight Ruslan, Ludmilla is abducted by the evil dwarf sorceror Chernomor. Ruslan overcomes his magic and saves his bride.

Russalka/The Water-Sprite opera by Dargomizhsky (libretto by composer, from Pushkin's dramatic poem), produced St Petersburg, 16 May 1856. Natasha, abandoned by a prince, drowns herself and becomes Queen of the river nymphs who lure men into the water. Her father, the Miller, laments her loss and goes mad, throwing the Prince into the river, where he joins Natasha.

Opera by Dvořák (libretto by J Kvapil), produced Prague, Czech Theatre, 31 March 1901.

Russian bassoon musical instrument, a ◊serpent made in the shape of a bassoon.

'Russian' Quartets one of the nicknames of Haydn's six string quartets, op. 33, composed 1781 and dedicated to the Grand Duke of Russia. Also known as *Gli scherzi* or *Jungfernquartette*.

Russo, William (1928–) US composer. After study in Chicago, he worked with the Stan Kenton Orchestra 1950–54, as a trombonist and composer-arranger. He directed his own orchestra in New York 1958–61 and the London Jazz Orchestra 1962–65.

Works include: the operas *Land of Milk and Honey* and *Antigone* (both Chicago, 1967), *A Cabaret Opera* (New York 1970), *Aesop's Fables* (1971), *The Shepherds' Christmas* (1979), *Isabella's Fortune, The Pay-Off* (1984) and *Talking to the Sun* (Chicago 1989); ballets *The World of Alcina* (1954) and *The Golden Bird* (1984); two symphonies (1957–58); music for jazz bands; and rock cantatas; sonata for violin and piano (1986).

Russolo, Luigi (1885–1947) Italian composer. In 1909 he joined the Futurist movement of Marinetti and formulated a music based on noise, about which he published *L'arte dei rumori* 1916. His Futurist manifesto of 1913 expanded the orchestra to include explosions, clashes, shrieks, screams, and groans. He also invented the Russolophone, which could produce seven different noises in 12 different gradations.

Works include: *Meeting of the Automobiles and the Aeroplanes, Awakening of a City.*

Rustic Wedding/Ländliche Hochzeit symphonic poem by Goldmark, first performed Vienna, 5 March 1876. Usually described today as a symphony.

Ruy Blas opera by William Howard Glover (1819–1875) (libretto by composer, based on Victor Hugo's drama), produced London, Covent Garden Theatre, 24 October 1861. Seeking revenge against the Queen of Spain, Don Sallustio sends his servant Ruy Blas to her court disguised as a nobleman. He rises through the ranks and is exposed later by the Don as a plebeian, thus dishonouring the Queen. But Ruy Blas earns his honour by killing the vengeful villain and drinking poison.

Opera by Marchetti (libretto in Italian, by Carlo d'Ormeville, based on Hugo), produced Milan, La Scala, 3 April 1869.

Overture and chorus for Hugo's drama by Mendelssohn, op. 95 and op. 77 no. 3, composed for a production at Leipzig, 9 March 1839.

Ruyneman, Daniel (1886–1963) Dutch composer. He made many experiments with composition and instruments and invented cup-bells with a rich and long-sustained sonority, which he used in several of his works.

He was trained for commerce and was self-taught in music.

Works include: the opera *The Brothers Karamazov* (1928), psycho-symbolic play with vocal and instrumental orchestra *The Clown* (1915); scena for tenor and orchestra from Kafka's *Der Prozess/The Trial*; two symphonies, partita for strings, *Hieroglyphs* for chamber orchestra; string quartet (1946); sonata in G major and *Klaaglied van een Slaaf* for violin and piano; nine sonatas, three *Pathemologies* and sonatina for piano; two *Sacred Songs* (Tagore) and several other sets.

RV in catalogues of Vivaldi's works, refers to Peter Ryom's catalogue of his compositions.

Ryom, Peter (1937–) Danish musicologist. He catalogued Vivaldi's works in *Verzeichnis der Werke Antonio Vivaldis* 1974.

Rzewski, Frederic (Anthony) (1938–) US composer and pianist. From 1960 he worked as a pianist. In 1966 he was cofounder of an electronic music studio at Rome.

He studied at Harvard with Randall Thompson and with Dallapiccola. In the 1960s he taught at the Cologne Hochschule and was professor at the Liège Conservatory (with Henri Pousseur) from 1977. From 1984 he was visiting professor at Yale University.

Works include: *Zoologischer Garten* (1965); *Spacecraft* (1967); *Impersonation*, audiodrama (1966); *Requiem* (1968); *Symphony for Several performers* (1968); *Coming Together* for speaker and instruments (1972); *Satyrica* for jazz band (1983); *Machine* for two pianos (1984).

S

s the dominant note in any key in tonic sol-fa notation, pronounced Soh.

Saariaho, Kaija (1952–) Finnish composer. She has composed orchestral and instrumental music employing computers and electronics.

She studied at the Helsinki Conservatory 1976–81, and with Brian Ferneyhough and Klaus Huber at Freiburg.

Works include: theatre and multimedia pieces *Study for life* (1980); *Kollisionen* (1984); *Earth,* ballet (1991); *Verblendungen* for orchestra (1984), *Graal Theatre* for violin and orchestra (1994); ensemble pieces *Nymphea* (1987), *For the Moon* (1990), *Aer* (1991), *Gates* (1991); *Amers* (1992); *Nocturne* for violin (1994); vocal music *The Bride,* song cycle (1977), *No and Not,* three songs for four female voices and choir (1979), *From the Grammar of Dreams* for two sopranos (1989), *Nuits, Adieux,* for four voices and live electronics (1991); *La dame à la licorne,* sound installation, with tape (1993), *Trois rivières* for percussion quartet and electronics (1993); *Graal Theatre* for violin and orchestra (1995).

Sabbatini, Galeazzo (1597–1662) Italian composer. He was maestro di cappella at Pesaro in the 1620s and director of chamber music to the Duke of Mirandola in the 1630s. In 1628 he published a treatise on thorough bass.

Works include: Masses, motets, two books of *Sacrae faudes* (1637, 1641) and other church music; madrigals.

Sabbatini, Pietro Paolo (c. 1600–after 1657) Italian composer. He was maestro di cappella in Rome, from 1630 of the church of San Luigi de' Francesci, and professor of music from 1650, when he published a treatise on thorough bass.

Works include: psalms, spiritual songs; *villanelle* and *canzonette* for one–three voices.

Sacchini, Antonio Maria Gaspare (1730–1786) Italian composer. His operas were popular in Germany, England, and France, the most popular being *Oedipe,* which was produced at Versailles in 1786. He also composed sacred music.

He studied under Francesco Durante at the Conservatorio Santa Maria di Loreto, Naples, where his intermezzo *Fra Donato* was produced in 1756. He worked first at the Conservatory, but produced his first serious opera, *Andromaca,* in 1761, and three years later gave up teaching to devote himself to composition. After a time in Rome he went to Venice in 1769, where he became director of the Ospedaletto. He visited Germany, and in 1772 went to London, remaining there ten years and producing many operas. Settling in Paris in 1782, he had the support of Marie Antoinette, and there wrote two operas which show the influence of Gluck. But (like Gluck before him) he became unwillingly involved in rivalry with ◊Piccinni and had little success.

Works include: about 60 operas, including *Alessandro nell' Indie* (1763), *Semiramide* (1764), *Isola d'amore, Il Cidde* (after Corneille), *Armida* (1772), *Tamerlano, Perseo* (1774), *Nitetti, Montezuma* (1775), *Rosina, Dardanus, Oedipe à Colone* (1786); Masses, motets, and other church music; two symphonies; string quartets, trio sonatas and other chamber music; violin sonatas.

Sachs, Curt (1881–1959) German musicologist. His many writings extend not only over the field of musical instruments, but also over many others. He first studied history of art at Berlin University, graduating in 1904. After some years as an art critic he studied music with Kretzschmar and J Wolf, specializing in the history of musical instruments. In 1919 he became director of the Berlin Museum of Musical Instruments, and also professor at Berlin University. From 1933 to 1937 he lived in Paris, then moved to New York, where he became professor at the university. From 1953 he was professor at Columbia University, New York.

Sachs, Hans (1494–1576) German poet and composer. Working as a master shoemaker in Nürnberg, he composed 4,275 *Meisterlieder/ Mastersongs*, and figures prominently in Wagner's opera *Die Meistersinger von Nürnberg*.

Sachs-Hornbostel system system devised by the German-born musicologist, Curt ◊Sachs, and the Austrian scholar, Eric von ◊Hornbostel, which has become one of the most widely-utilised systems for classifying musical instruments. It was based on an earlier system devised by Victor Mahillon when he classified the instrument collection at the Royal Conservatory in Brussels. The Sachs-Hornbostel System uses a systematic but basic taxonomic method to classify every instrument as belonging to a particular group or 'class', according to the nature of the vibrating agent which produces sound. This system accommodates all instruments, and allows museum curators, for example, to classify and arrange musical objects without knowledge of their music, culture, or origin. The four main classes in the system are ◊aerophones, ◊idiophones, ◊membranophones, and ◊chordophones. A further main class – electrophones – was subsequently added. Each of these classes is further subdivided through a series of more detailed descriptors. Each class of instrument has a number, the numbering system being derived from the Dewey system of library classification.

sackbut musical instrument of the ◊brass family, a precursor of the trombone. It was common from the 14th century and has been revived in early music performance. Four sizes were listed by Praetorius, from alto to great bass. The sackbut has a narrow bell and its sound is dignified and mellow.

Sackman, Nicholas (1950–   ) English composer. He studied with Alexander Goehr at Leeds University. In 1990 he became a lecturer at Nottingham University.

Works include: two string quartets (1979, 1991); *Ensembles and Cadenzas*, for cello and five players (1972); *A Pair of Wings* for three sopranos and ensemble (1973); *Doubles* for two instrumental groups (1978); *And the World – A Wonder Waking*, for mezzo and eight instruments (1981); *Time-Piece*, brass quintet (1983); *Corronach* for seven players (1985); flute concerto (1989); *Hawthorn* for orchestra (premiered at the 1993 London Proms).

Sadko opera by Rimsky-Korsakov (libretto by composer and V I Bielsky), produced Moscow, 7 January 1898. The music is partly based on Rimsky-Korsakov's symphonic poem of the same name, op. 5; composed 1867, produced St Petersburg, 21 December 1867; revised 1869 and 1892. Cast adrift as a sacrifice to the sea gods, minstrel Sadko weds nymph Volkova before returning to his wife.

Sadler's Wells theatre in Islington, N London, England, built in the 17th century. Originally a music hall, it was developed by Lilian Baylis as a northern annexe to the Old Vic 1931. For many years it housed the Sadler's Wells Opera Company (relocated to the London Coliseum 1969 and known as the English National Opera Company from 1974) and the Sadler's Wells Ballet, which later became the Royal Ballet.

saeta an unaccompanied Andalusian folk-song sung during a halt in a religious procession.

Sæverud, Harald (1897–1992) Norwegian composer and conductor. He studied first at Bergen and then studied conducting under Clemens Krauss at Berlin. He returned to Bergen as a conductor and received a state pension for composition in 1933.

Works include: *Minnesota Symphony*; nine symphonies (1916–66); concertos for oboe, cello, violin, and piano; incidental music for Shakespeare's 'Rape of Lucretia' (1935) and Ibsen's *Peer Gynt*; 50 variations for chamber orchestra; three string quartets (1969, 1975, 1979), piano pieces.

Saffo/Sappho opera by Pacini (libretto by S Cammarano), produced Naples, Teatro San Carlo, 29 November 1840. Alcander (bass), angered by Sappho's song, convinces her husband Phaon that she has another lover. Phaon abandons her; she later finds him about to marry Clymene, and overturns the altar. Penitent, she leaps to her death from the Leucadian rock.

'Saga, En' symphonic poem by Sibelius, op. 9, composed 1891, first performed Helsinki, 16 February 1893, revised 1901. It depicts no particular incident, but has a distinctly narrative, ballad *'St Anne' Fugue* the fugue in E♭ major at the end of Part III of Bach's *Clavierübung*, so named in England because its subject is identical with the opening of what is probably Croft's hymn-tune *St Anne*.

'St Anthony' Variations (Brahms). See ↓'*Haydn' Variations*.

St Elizabeth (Liszt). See ↓*Legende von der heiligen Elisabeth, Die*.

Saint-Foix, (Marie Olivier) Georges (du Parc Poullain) de, Count (1874–1954) French musicologist. He wrote on various subjects, including Beethoven and Boccherini, but mainly on the classification and analysis of Mozart's works in a large five-volume work, the first two volumes in collaboration with Théodore de Wyzewa.

Saint François d'Assise opera in eight tableaux by Messiaen (libretto by composer); 1975–83, first performed Paris, Opéra, 28 November 1983. St Francis heals leper, preaches to birds and receives stigmata before his death and resurrection.

St John Passion Bach's setting of the Passion narrative as told in St John's Gospel, with interpolated texts after Brockes and chorales, for soloists, chorus, and orchestra, first performed in St Nicholas', Leipzig, on 7 April 1724; a second version was given in St Thomas's, Leipzig, on 30 March 1725.

St Ludmilla oratorio by Dvořák, op. 71 (Czech words by J Vrchlický), composed 1886 and performed 15 October at the Leeds Festival, in an English translation.

St Luke Passion work by Penderecki for narrator, soloists, choruses, and orchestra; first performed Münster, 30 March 1966, conductor Czyź.

St Matthew Passion Bach's setting of the Passion narrative as told in St Matthew's Gospel, with interpolated texts by Picander and chorales, for soloists, chorus, and orchestra, and performed in St Thomas's, Leipzig, probably on 11 April 1727 and certainly on 15 April 1729.

Sainton, Prosper (Philippe Cathérine) (1813–1890) French violinist and composer. He played at the Société des Concerts and the Opéra in Paris, then travelled widely in Europe and in 1840 became professor at the Toulouse Conservatory. He was the husband of the singer Charlotte Sainton-Dolby.

He studied violin under François Habeneck at the Paris Conservatory. In 1844 he visited London and played under Mendelssohn, returning in 1845 to settle down as a member of the Beethoven Quartet Society, orchestra leader, and teacher.

Works include: two violin concertos and other solos with orchestra; variations, romances, operatic fantasies, and other pieces for violin and piano.

St Paul oratorio by Mendelssohn, op. 36, performed Düsseldorf, Lower Rhine Festival, 22 May 1836; in England, Liverpool, 7 October 1836.

St Paul's Suite work for string orchestra in four movements by Holst. Composed for St Paul's Girls' school and performed there 1913.

Saint-Saëns, (Charles) Camille (1835–1921) French composer, pianist, and organist. Saint-Saëns was a master of technique and a prolific composer; among his many lyrical Romantic pieces are concertos, the symphonic poem *Danse macabre* 1875, the opera *Samson et Dalila* 1877, and the uncharacteristic orchestral piece *Le carnaval des animaux/The Carnival of the Animals* 1886, his most popular work.

Saint-Saëns was born in Paris. He began to compose at the age of five and played the piano well at that age. He gave a public recital in 1846 and entered the Conservatory as an organ scholar in 1848, gaining a first prize in 1851, when he entered Halévy's class for composition. He was appointed organist at the church of Saint-Merry in Paris in 1853, at the Madeleine in 1857, and piano professor at the Ecole Niedermeyer in 1861. His virtuosity at the organ was admired by Liszt, and he promoted performances of Liszt's symphonic poems. His first two symphonies were performed in 1853 and 1859, he played his second piano concerto in 1868 and founded the Société Nationale de Musique with Romain Bussine in 1871; his own symphonic poems *Le Rouet d'Omphale* and *Phaëton* date from this time. One of his most frequently performed works, the first cello concerto in A minor, was composed in 1872; it displays the composer's familiar and conservative French Romantic style together with melodic inventiveness. He played in England several times from 1871 and toured Spain and Portugal in 1880. The biblical opera *Samson et Dalila*, begun in 1868 and prohibited on the French stage on account of its subject, was conducted by Liszt at Weimar in 1877; it was allowed in Paris from 1892, the year he received an honorary doctorate from

Cambridge University. The massively proportioned 3rd symphony, with organ obbligato, dates from 1886, and his appealing 3rd violin concerto in B minor followed in 1890. Saint-Saëns recognized that its success with the public would lead to neglect of his more important compositions and banned its performance during his lifetime. In 1906 he visited the USA, and again in 1916, when he also travelled to South America.

Works include: STAGE: operas *Samson et Dalila* (1877), *Henri VIII* (1883).

ORCHESTRAL: five symphonies (1886, two unnumbered; no. 3 with organ and piano duet), symphonic poems *Le Rouet d'Omphale* (1872), *Danse macabre* (originally a song); five piano concertos (1858–96), three violin concertos (1858, 1859, 1890) and *Introduction et Rondo capriccioso* (1863), two cello concertos (1872, 1902).

CHAMBER: *Le carnaval des animaux* for chamber ensemble (1886); two piano trios, septet for piano, strings, and trumpet (1881); sonatas for oboe, clarinet, bassoon, and piano.

PIANO AND VOCAL: 24 op. nos. of piano music; seven organ works; Requiem (1878); oratorio *Le Déluge*; several cantatas; many songs.

Saite (German 'string') term used in musical notation, as in *mit einer Saite* ('with one string') instructing a pianist to use the *una corda* or ◊soft pedal.

Sala, Nicola (1713–1801) Italian composer and theorist. In 1794 he published *Regole del contrappunto prattico/Rules of Practical Counterpoint* in three volumes.

He studied with Nicola Fago and Lionardo Leo at the Conservatorio de' Turchini at Naples, and later became a master there. In 1787 he succeeded Pasquale Cafaro as principal.

Works include: the operas *Vologeso* (1737), *Zenobia* (1761), *Merope* (1769), and *Demetrio* (1762); oratorio *Giuditta*; Mass, Litany, and other church music; Prologues for the birth of kings of Naples.

Salammbô opera by Reyer (libretto by C duLocle, based on Flaubert's novel), produced Brussels, Théâtre de la Monnaie, 10 February 1890.

Unfinished opera by Mussorgsky (libretto by composer, based on Flaubert), partly composed in the 1860s. A concert performance of the available fragments was given in Milan on 10 November 1980.

The two operas have similar plots initially: Carthaginian princess Salammbô seduces Libyan warrior Mathô, to regain the sacred veil which he has stolen. After this, in Reyer's version, Salammbô commits suicide when ordered to kill Mathô, and he follows her. In Mussorgsky's version, Mathô is imprisoned and brutally killed; Salammbô is horror-stricken and dies.

Salazar, Adolfo (1890–1958) Spanish musicologist and composer. He edited the *Revista Musical Hispano-Americano* 1914–18 and was music critic to *El Sol* in Madrid 1918–36. His books include studies of modern music, Spanish music, symphonies, and ballet.

He studied with Bartolomeo Pérez Casas (1873–1956) and Manuel de Falla, also Maurice Ravel in Paris. After the Spanish Civil War he emigrated to Buenos Aires, then lived in Mexico after 1939.

Works include: symphonic poem *Don Juan en los infiernos*, *Paisajes* and *Tres preludios* for orchestra; string quartet, *Arabia* for piano quintet; violin and piano sonata; piano pieces; *Romancilla* for guitar.

Sales, Pietro Pompeo (c. 1729–1797) Italian composer. Appointed Kapellmeister to the Prince-Bishop of Augsburg in 1756, he served the Electoral Court in Koblenz in the same capacity from 1770. He also travelled in England and Italy (1776), appearing as a virtuoso gamba-player.

Works include: the operas *Le nozze di Amore e di Norizia* (1765), *L'Antigono* (1769), *Achille in Sciro*, *Il rè pastore*.; oratorios *Giefte* (1762), *Giuseppe ricognosciuto*, *La Betulia liberata*.; church music; two symphonies; concertos; arias.

Salieri, Antonio (1750–1825) Italian composer. He taught Beethoven, Schubert, Hummel, and Liszt, and was the musical rival of Mozart at the emperor's court in Vienna, where he held the position of court composer. It has been suggested, without proof, that he poisoned Mozart.

He studied with his brother Francesco Salieri, a pupil of Giuseppe Tartini. He was orphaned at 15, and his education at the school of San Marco in Venice was taken care of by the Mocenigo family. There he met Florian Gassmann, who in 1766 took him to Vienna, saw to his further education, and introduced him at court. On Gassmann's death in 1774 he became court composer and conductor of the Italian opera. He visited Italy 1778–80, where his opera *Europa riconosciuta* was produced at the opening of La Scala, Milan in 1774, and at Paris 1786–87; his *Tarare* of 1787 had sufficient dramatic strength to be ascribed initially to Gluck. From 1788, when he succeeded Giuseppe Bonno as court Kapellmeister, he lived mostly in Vienna. He was conductor of the Tonkünstler Society until 1818, and played the continuo in the first performance of Haydn's *Creation* in 1798. Recent revivals of operas such as *Les Danaides*, *La grotta di Trofonio*, and *Falstaff* show Salieri to be a more resourceful and entertaining composer than his reputation suggests.

Works include: OPERA about 40, including *Armida* (1771), *La fiera di Venezia* (1772), *La locandiera* (1773), *Europa riconosciuta* (1778), *La scuola de gelosi* (1778), *La dama pastorella*, *Der Rauchfangkehrer* (1781), *Les Danaides* (1784), *Tarare*, *Les Horaces* (the last three for Paris), *La grotta di Trofonio* (1785), *Il talismano*, *Palmira*, *regina di Persia* (1795), *Falstaff* (after Shakespeare, 1799), *Cesare in Farmacusa*, *Angiolina* (1800).

OTHER incidental music to Kotzebue's *Die Hussiten vor Naumburg*; Passion oratorio and others; seven Masses, Requiem, Litanies and other church music; cantatas including *La riconoscenza* for the 25th anniversary of the Tonkünstler-Societät (1796); three symphonies and *sinfonia concertante*; concertos; serenades; arias, duets, canons, and miscellaneous other small vocal pieces.

Salinas, Francisco de (1513–1590) Spanish organist, theorist, and folk-song investigator. In his treatise *De musica libri septem* 1579 he quotes the tunes of many Spanish folk songs.

He was the son of an official in the treasury of Charles V and became blind at the age of ten, whereupon his parents decided to let him study music. He was taken to Rome in 1538, where he met the lutenist Francesco da Milano and became a great admirer of Lassus. In 1558 he became organist to the Duke of Alba, viceroy of Naples, under Diego Ortiz. In 1561 he returned to Spain, became organist at León in 1563 and professor of music at Salamanca University, 1567. There he got to know the poet Luis de León, who wrote a poem on his organ playing.

Sallinen, Aulis (1935–   ) Finnish composer. He is best known for the strong characterization and sustained dramatic intensity of his operas.

He studied at the Sibelius Academy, Helsinki, and taught there 1963–76. He was the manager of Finnish Radio Symphony Orchestra 1960–70.

Works include: the operas *The Horseman* (1975), *The Red Line* (1978), *The King goes forth to France* (1984), and *Kullervo* (1992); ballet *Variations sur Mallarmé* (1968); six symphonies (1971–90), *Mauermusik*, for a German killed at Berlin Wall (1962), *Metamorphoses* for piano

and chamber orchestra (1964), violin concerto (1968), cello concerto (1978); *Chorali* for wind, percussion, harp, and celesta (1970), *Dies Irae* for soprano, bass, male chorus, and orchestra (1978); five string quartets (1958–82).

salmo (Italian, plural *salmi*) a psalm.

Salmon, ˙ Thomas (1648–1706) English clergyman and writer on music. He wrote on notation and temperament. His *Essay on the Advancement of Musick* 1672 involved him in a controversy with the composer Matthew Locke.

Salomé opera by Mariotte (libretto Oscar Wilde's original in French), produced Lyon, 30 October 1908. Composed earlier than R Strauss's opera, although produced later.

Salome opera by Richard Strauss (libretto H Lachmann's German translation of Oscar Wilde's play, written in French), produced Dresden, Royal Opera, 9 December 1905. Spurned by John the Baptist, Salome demands his severed head after performing a seven-veil striptease for lecherous Herod.

Ballet in two acts by Peter Maxwell Davies (choreographed by Flemming Flindt), produced Stockholm, 10 November 1978. Concert suite performed London, 6 March 1979. See ◊*Tragédie de Salomé, La.*

Salomon, Johann Peter (1745–1815) German violinist, conductor, manager, and composer. He lived in London from 1780, where he arranged concerts. He wrote four French operas and an English one, *Windsor Castle*, for the marriage of the Prince of Wales in 1795, an oratorio *Hiskias*, and violin sonatas.

He studied at Bonn and joined the electoral orchestra in 1758. After a tour in 1765 he became court musician at Rheinsberg to Prince Henry of Prussia, who, however, dissolved his orchestra about 1780, when Salomon went to Paris and thence to London, 1781, where he settled as concert violinist, quartet player, and conductor. He gave subscription concerts at the Hanover Square Rooms and invited Haydn to London in 1790 and again in 1794, later arranging for smaller forces some of the symphonies which Haydn wrote for London.

'Salomon Symphonies' the 12 symphonies written by Haydn 1791–95 for the concerts given by Johann Peter Salomon in London during Haydn's two visits to England, 1791– 92 and 1794–95. They are nos 93–104.

salsa popular music style of Cuban origin which draws on a variety of Latin American and jazz influences. Salsa rhythms are based on Afro-American dances such as the bolero

An example of a salsa rhythm.

and cha cha cha. Layered polymeters and hemiolas are common, but the distinctive feature underlying the whole structure is the two-bar clave:

saltando (Italian 'springing, bounding') in playing the violin and other string instruments, a manner of playing that makes the bow rebound from the strings.

saltarello an Italian dance, including jumps (*salti*) and in the 16th century a kind of after-dance in common time, also called by the Latin name of *proportio* and the German one of *Proporz*, the name being due to its using the same music as the first dance (Passamezzo), but with the 'proportions' (time) altered; later a Roman dance in animated 3–4 or 6–8 time, not unlike the Neapolitan tarantella, but using jerky instead of even musical figuration. In performance by dancers it gradually increased its pace towards the end. The best known saltarello is the finale of Mendelssohn's Italian symphony.

Salve Regina/Latin Hail, Queen one of four antiphons to the Virgin Mary. Earliest manuscripts source is from 11th century, probably by Adhemar of Pui. Many settings by 15th-century English composers; also set by La Rue, Josquin, Obrecht, and Okeghem. Six settings by Schubert (1812–24).

Salzburg Festival annual music festival held in the Austrian town where Mozart was born. Although the festival concentrates on the works of Mozart, other composers are also represented. It grew from the first eight Mozart festivals held between 1877 and 1910. The new theatre opened 1960 and has the largest stage in the world.

Salzman, Eric (1933–) US composer and musicologist. He studied with Beeson and Babbitt. A music critic in New York, he also founded the Quog Music Theater 1970. He edited *Music Quarterly* from 1984. He often writes for electronic forces, and calls for improvisation in his works.

Works include: *Larynx Music* (1968), *Civilization and its Discontents, opera* (1977).

Samara, Spiro (1863–1917) Greek composer. He studied at Athens, later with Delibes and others at the Paris Conservatory. The Italian publisher Sonzogno procured him his first operatic production at Milan. He subsequently produced other works at Rome,

Naples, Florence, Milan, and Genoa, with no more than ephemeral success, and the last appeared at Athens in 1914.

Works include: the operas *Flora mirabilis* (1886), *Medgé, Lionella* (1891), *La martire, La furia domata* (after Shakespeare's *Taming of the Shrew*, 1895), *Storia d'amore* (1903), *Mademoiselle de Bella-Isle, Rhea, La guerra in tempo di guerra, The Princess of Saxony* (in Greek); suite for piano duet, piano pieces; songs.

Samazeuilh, Gustave (Marie Victor Fernand) (1877–1967) French composer and critic. He was a pupil of Chausson and, after his master's death, of d'Indy and Dukas at the Schola Cantorum. His writings include studies of Rameau and Dukas, translations of Wagner's *Tristan* and Schumann's *Genoveva*, songs by Wagner and Liszt. He also made piano arrangements of modern French music.

Works include: *Etude symphonique pour 'La Nef'* (Elemire Bourges), *Nuit, Naïades au soir, Le Sommeil de Canope* for orchestra; the last also for voice and orchestra; string quartet.

samba Afro-Brazillian secular music and couple-dance form, spanning the continuum from traditional percussion and vocal-dominated street styles of the Carnival parade to the more popular renditions of the ballroom dance orchestras.

Sammartini, Giovanni Battista (c. 1700–1775) Italian composer. He was the most important Italian symphonist of his time, and contributed much towards the founding of a modern style of instrumental music.

He spent his whole life in Milan as a church musician, and from 1730 was maestro di cappella at the convent of Santa Maria Maddelena. Gluck was his pupil 1737–41, and borrowed material from Sammartini's symphonies for two of his operas.

Works include: two operas including *L'Agrippina, moglie di Tiberio* (1743); two oratorios; three Masses and other church music; over 80 symphonies; about 15 concertos; six *concerti grossi*; six string quintets, about 20 quartets, almost 200 trios, and other chamber music.

sampling a technique of computer synthesis involving the capture by microphone, conversion to digital code, storage, and subsequent manipulation of an acoustic signal.

The sample length is limited by the storage capacity of the sampling device, typically a memory chip. Keyboard transposition of a sampled sound has an effect not unlike varispeeding an analogue tape or disc.

Samson oratorio by Handel (libretto by N Hamilton, based on Milton's *Samson Agonistes*, *Hymn on the Nativity* and *At a Solemn Musick*), produced London, Covent Garden, 18 February 1743.

Samson et Dalila opera (originally oratorio) by Saint-Saëns (libretto by F Lemaire), produced Weimar, German, 2 December 1877; not performed in Paris until 31 October 1890, and at the Opéra, 23 November 1892, having been at first forbidden on account of its biblical subject. Delilah seduces Samson and betrays the secret of his strength. Later, blinded, he prays for strength and brings down the temple on himself and his Philistine enemies.

Samstag aus Licht/Saturday from Light opera by Stockhausen, second of his cycle *Licht*. The four scenes are *Lucifer's Dream*, *Kathinka's Song*, *Lucifer's Dance* and *Lucifer's Farewell*. First performed Milan, 25 May 1984.

Sánchez de Fuentes y Peláez, Eduardo (1874–1944) Cuban composer and music historian. He wrote several books on the history of Cuban folk music.

   Works include: the operas *Dolorosa* (1910), *Doreya* (1918) and three others; operettas and zarzuelas; oratorio *Novidad*; suite *Bocetos cubanos*, symphonic prelude *Temas del Patio* for orchestra; vocal *habañera Tú espera*.

Sancho Pança dans son île/Sancho Panza on his Island opera by Philidor (libretto by A H Poinsinet, based on Cervantes's *Don Quixote*), produced Paris, Comédie-Italienne, 8 July 1762.

Sancho Panza opera by Jaques-Dalcroze (libretto by R Yve-Plessis, based on Cervantes' *Don Quixote*), produced Geneva, 13 December 1897.

Sancio Panza, governatore dell' isola Barattaria/Sancho Panza, Governor of the Isle of Barataria opera by Caldara (libretto by G C Pasquini, based on Cervantes' *Don Quixote*), produced Vienna, Burgtheater, 27 January 1733.

Sancta Civitas/The Holy City oratorio by Vaughan Williams (words mainly from the Bible) for solo voices, chorus, and orchestra, first performed Oxford, 7 May 1926.

Sancta Susanna opera in one act by Hindemith (libretto by A Stramm); composed 1921, produced Frankfurt, 26 March 1922. Story concerns a sex-obsessed nun who tears the loincloth from a statue of Christ.

Sanctus the fourth chant of the Ordinary of the Roman Mass. Its text is founded on Isaiah

vi. 3 and Matthew xxi. 9, and it was incorporated into the Latin liturgy at least as early as the 6th century in Gaul. The earliest known melody is that of Mass XVIII (Vatican edition). It is basically syllabic, forms a natural continuation from the music of the Preface which precedes it, is psalmodic in structure, and its last phrase echoes the *Per omnia saecula saeculorum* formula which occurs three times during the Preface and Canon of the Mass. Later settings are more complex: a total of 231 melodies were catalogued in 1962. The Sanctus was set in polyphony from the 13th century, and became an integral part of all settings of the Ordinary of the Mass.

Sandberger, Adolf (1864–1943) German musicologist and composer. He was chief editor of the incomplete edition of Lassus and the *Denkmäler der Tonkunst in Bayern*, and his books include studies of the Bavarian court chapel under Lassus, of Cornelius. He studied in a number of European centres and in 1894 became lecturer in music at Munich University and was professor there 1900–29, being at the same time curator of the music department of the State Library.

   Works include: the operas *Ludwig der Springer* and *Der Tod des Kaisers*; symphonic poem *Viola* (on Shakespeare's *Twelfth Night*), symphonic prologue *Riccio*; chamber music; piano works; songs.

Sanderson, James (1769–c. 1841), or Saunderson English violinist and composer. He was self-taught and in 1783 obtained an engagement as violinist at the Sunderland theatre. Later he taught at Shields, became leader at the Newcastle-upon-Tyne theatre in 1787, and at Astley's Amphitheatre, London in 1788. He began to write stage pieces and in 1793 went as music director and composer to the Royal Circus (Surrey Theatre).

   Works include: stage pieces and pantomimes *Harlequin in Ireland*, *Blackbeard*, *Cora*, *Sir Francis Drake*, *The Magic Pipe*, *Hallowe'en*, and many others; instrumental interludes for Collin's *Ode to the Passions*; violin pieces; many popular songs.

Sandrin, Pierre Regnault (died after 1561) French composer. He composed only chansons, of which the majority were published by Attaingnant. Lassus based a Mass on the chanson 'Doulce memoire'.

   He was a member of the royal chapel 1543–60, during which time he also travelled to Italy.

Sanguine Fan, The ballet by Elgar, op. 81 (scenario by Ina Lowther); composed 1917, produced Chelsea, 20 March 1917, conductor Elgar; not heard again complete until recording of 1973.

Santa Cruz, Domingo (1899–1987), or Wilson Chilean composer, teacher, and critic. He studied at Santiago de Chile and Madrid. In 1918 he founded a Bach Society at Santiago and in 1932 became dean of the Fine Arts Department at the University of Chile and rector of the university from 1948 to 1951.

Works include: four symphonies (1948–69); five *Piezas brevas* for string orchestra; three string quartets; three violin and piano pieces; piano works; songs.

Sant 'Alessio, Il opera in prologue and three acts by Landi (libretto by Rospigliosi), produced Rome, Paluz Barberini, 21 February 1632. Alessio returns home from the Holy Land, resists worldly temptation and continues his life of renunciation.

Santini, Fortunato (1778–1861) Italian priest, music scholar and composer. He studied music with Jannaconi and after being ordained in 1801 began to make an immense collection of early music, scoring it from parts in various music libraries. He made friends with Felix Mendelssohn and through him introduced many works by J S Bach into Italy, as well as other German sacred music.

Works include: Requiem for eight voices, Masses and other church music.

Santoliquido, Francesco (1883–1971) Italian composer. He studied at the Liceo di Santa Cecilia in Rome, conducting his student work, *Crepuscolo sul mare*, at Nuremberg in 1909 and producing his first opera at Milan in 1910. He then went to live in Tunisia, in the small Arab village in Hammamek, where he studied the local music.

Works include: the operas *La favola di Helga* (1910), *Ferhuda* (1918), *L'ignota* and *La porta verde* (1953), mimed drama *La baiadera della maschera gialla* (1917); symphony in F major.

Sapho opera by Gounod (libretto by Emile Augier), produced Paris, Opéra, 16 April 1851. Gounod's first opera. For plot synopsis, see ◊*Saffo*.

Opera by Massenet (libretto by H Cain and A Bernède, based on Daudet's novel), produced Paris, Opéra-Comique, 27 November 1897. The heroine is not the Greek poet Sappho but artist's model Fanny Legrand who poses as Sappho. She runs away with Jean Gaussin, but he abandons her after hearing of her sordid past. Later he returns to her but she rejects him.

Sappho opera by Hugo Kaun (1863–1932) (libretto by composer, based on Grillparzer's play), produced Leipzig, 27 October 1917. See also ◊*Saffo*; ◊*Sapho*.

sarabande French 16th-century court dance, also (**saraband**) an English dance form, in moderate three time with a rhythmic emphasis on the second beat, a dance form featured in the classical music ◊suite.

Sarabande and Cortège two studies for orchestra by Busoni for his opera *Doktor Faust*; composed 1918–19, first performed Zurich, 31 March 1919.

sarangi Hindi; a bowed stringed instrument with three main playing strings and many sympathetic strings (thirty or more on a concert instrument). Used in the folk music of northwest India and Pakistan, and in the classical music of north India (Hindustani music), where it is used both as an accom-

The sarabande from Bach's English Suite, *No. 6.*

paniment to the voice (in ◊khyal and ◊thumri genres) and as a solo concert instrument.

sardana Spanish dance of Catalonia revived in the middle of the 19th century and performed to pipe and drum.

Sarema opera by Zemlinsky (libretto by composer, after R von Gottschall's play *Die Rose vom Kaukasus*), composed 1895, produced Munich, Hofoper, 10 October 1897. Zemlinsky's first opera. Circassian heroine torn between love for Russian officer and her own country.

Sargent, (Harold) Malcolm (Watts) (1895– 1967) English conductor. He was professor at the Royal College of Music from 1923, chief conductor of the BBC Symphony Orchestra 1950–57, and continued as conductor in chief of the annual Henry Wood ◊promenade concerts at the Royal Albert Hall.

He championed Vaughan Williams and Holst and conducted the first performances of Walton's oratorio *Belshazzar's Feast* 1931 and opera *Troilus and Cressida* 1954.

Šárka, Smetana, opera by Fibich (libretto by A Schulzová), produced Prague, Czech Theatre, 28 December 1897. Bohemian Šarka leads women against the oppressive Duke Přemysl and his men; but she falls in love with warrior Ctirad, eventually betraying her cause to save him. Guilty, she commits suicide.

Opera by Janáček (libretto by J Zeyer); composed 1887–88, revised 1918 and 1925, scoring completed by O Chlubna, produced Brno, 11 November 1925. UK first performance at Edinburgh, 1993 (concert).

See also ◊*Má Vlast.*

sarod Hindi; a short-necked lute used in North Indian (Hindustani) music. The sarod has four or five melody strings, which run over a polished metal fingerboard; several strings used for drone and rhythmic punctuation, and a dozen or more sympathetic strings; some have a small metal resonator attached to the upper end of the neck. A popular solo concert instrument, usually accompanied by the ◊tabla drum pair.

Sarro, Domenico (1679–1744), or Sarri Italian composer. A pupil of Durante at the Conservatorio S Onofrio in Naples, he became vice-maestro di cappella to the court in 1703. He lost his post in 1707 but returned 1725, succeeding Mancini as maestro di cappella in 1737.

Works include: around 50 operas, *Didone abbandonata* (the first setting by any composer of a libretto by Metastasio, produced Naples,

1724); four oratorios; cantatas; much church music; instrumental music.

sarrusophone any of a family of double-reed keyed brass instruments developed in 1856 by a French bandmaster named Sarrus, intended to replace oboes and bassoons in military bands. The double bass instrument is heard in Stravinsky's sacred cantata *Theni* 1958. Its tone is clear and unforced in the bass register.

Sarti, Giuseppe (1729–1802) Italian composer and conductor. As well as holding posts in Italy as an organist and music director, he spent many years in Denmark as an opera conductor. He later went to Russia, where he lived in St Petersburg and produced Russian operas for the court. His best-known works are the operas *Fra due litiganti* 1782 and *Giulio Sabino.*

He studied under Francesco Vallotti in Padua and Padre Martini in Bologna. He was organist of Faenza Cathedral 1748–51, was appointed music director of the theatre there in 1752, and produced his first opera the same year. In 1753 he went to Copenhagen as conductor of the Mingotti opera company, and two years later was appointed Kapellmeister to the Danish court. He stayed there until 1775, except for three years in Italy 1765–68. He was director of the Ospedaletto Conservatory in Venice 1775–79, and was then appointed maestro di cappella of Milan Cathedral, where Cherubini was his pupil.

In 1784 he became music director to the Russian court. He travelled to St Petersburg via Vienna, where he met Mozart, who quoted the aria 'Come un agnello' from his opera *Fra due litiganti* in the supper scene in *Don Giovanni.* He produced a number of operas in Russia, including *Oleg* on a libretto by the empress, and stayed there until 1802, founding a music school in the Ukraine and becoming director of the Conservatory in St Petersburg in 1793. He then intended to retire in Italy, but died in Berlin on the way.

Works include: the operas (libretti in Italian, Danish, French, and Russian) *Pompeo in Armenia* (1752), *Il rè pastore* (1753), *La giardiniera brillante* (1768), *Farnace, Le gelosie villane, Fra due litigani* (1782), *Medonte* (1777), *Giulio Sabino, I finti eredi, Armida e Rinaldo* (1786), *Oleg* (Russian, with Pashkevich and Canobbio); two Russian oratorios; Requiem for Louis XVI (1793); Masses, Te Deum, and other church music; keyboard music.

Sartorius, Paul (1569–1609) German organist and composer. He was organist to the

Archduke Maximilian of Austria in 1599 and lived at Nuremberg.

Works include: Masses, *Sonetti spirituali* for six voices (1601), motets, madrigals, *Neue teutsche Liedlein*.

Sarum Use the liturgy in use at Salisbury before the Reformation, differing in some respects from that of Rome and widely spread through medieval England until it was abolished in 1547, though revived from 1553–59.

Sás (Orchassal), Andrés (1900–1967) Peruvian composer of French-Belgian descent. He studied in Brussels and went to Peru in 1924 as a violin teacher at the National Academy of Music at Lima. He married the Peruvian pianist Lily Rosay and with her founded a private music school in 1929. He made extensive research into Peruvian folklore and frequently used folk tunes in his works.

Works include: *Himno al sol, Himno y danza,* and *Poema Indio* for orchestra; *Rapsodia peruana* for violin and orchestra; *Quenas* for voice, flute, and harp; *Sonatina india* for flute and piano; works for violin and piano; piano pieces; songs.

Satie, Erik (Alfred Leslie) (1866–1925) French composer. His piano pieces, such as the three *Gymnopédies* 1888, are precise and tinged with melancholy, and parody romantic expression with surreal commentary. His aesthetic of ironic simplicity, as in the *Messe des pauvres/Poor People's Mass* 1895, acted as a nationalist antidote to the perceived excesses of German Romanticism.

Mentor of the group of composers ◊Les Six, he promoted the concept of *musique d'ameublement* ('furniture music'), anticipating the impact of radio. A commission from Diaghilev led to the ballet *Parade* 1917, with instrumentation for siren, typewriter, and steamship whistle, and he invented a new style of film music for René Clair's *Entr'acte* 1924.

His father was a composer and music publisher in Paris and his mother a minor composer of piano pieces under the name of Eugénie Satie-Barnetsche. Satie spent only a year at the Paris Conservatory and later made a precarious living by playing at cafés, writing music for the Montmartre songwriter Hypsa and the music-hall singer Paulette Darty. Through his friendship with Debussy, about 1890, he came into contact with intellectual circles. He also studied at the Schola Cantorum under d'Indy and Roussel at the age of 40. He continued to publish small piano works under eccentric titles. In later years he came into touch with Jean Cocteau and established a school at Arcueil where he exercised some influence on younger composers including Poulenc, Auric, and Milhaud, leading them away from the late Romantic style influenced by German composers, especially Wagner, towards a terser, more concise and epigrammatic style.

Works include: STAGE AND CHORAL: symphonic drama *Socrate* (1920); ballets *Parade* (1917), *Relâche* (1924), and *Mercure*, 1924.

PIANO: piano pieces *Trois gymnopédies* (1888), *Trois gnossiennes* (1890), *Sonneries de la rose-croix, Trois véritables préludes flasques (pour un chien), Trois embryons desséchés* (1913), *Trois croquis et agaceries d'un gros bonhomme en bois* (1913), *Trois Chapitres tournés en tous sens* (1913), *Avant-dernières pensées,* and others; *Trois morceaux en forme de poire* (1903) for piano duet; four sets of songs.

Satyagraha opera by Philip Glass (libretto by C DeJong), based on the life of Gandhi, produced Rotterdam, 5 September 1980. Title is based on Gandhi's slogan, the two Hindi words *saty,* 'truth' and *agraha,* 'firmness'. The opera is sung in Sanskrit. Gandhi's early struggles in South Africa are balanced by portraits of Tolstoy, Tagore and Martin Luther King.

Satz (German 'setting') in music, a movement of a multimovement work (for example *erster Satz,* 'first movement'); a theme (*Hauptsatz,* 'main theme'); or a style of composition (*Freier Satz,* 'free style').

Sauguet, Henri (1901–1989) French composer and critic. He was a member of Erik Satie's circle. His works include four symphonies, songs, incidental music for plays, and the opera *La chartreuse de Parme* 1939.

After studying piano and organ at Bordeaux, he became a pupil of Joseph Canteloube at Montauban and in 1922 of Charles Koechlin in Paris. Introduced by Milhaud to Satie, he joined the latter's school at Arcueil. In 1936 he succeeded Milhaud as music critic to *Le Jour-Echo de Paris,* and his major work, the opera *La chartreuse de Parme,* followed in 1939.

Works include: the operas *La gageure imprévue* 1944 and *Les caprices de Marianne* 1954; operettas *Le plumet du colonel* 1924 and *La contrebasse* 1932; ballets *La charte, David, La nuit, Fastes,* and *Les forains;* incidental music for Molierè's *Le Sicilien,* Roger Ferdinand's *Irma,* Pierre Emmanuel's *Les lépreux,* and other plays; four symphonies including *Symphonie expiatoire* (in memory of war victims); three piano concertos; *La voyante* for soprano and chamber orchestra; two string quartets (1926, 1948); sonatina for flute and piano; sonata in D major and other works for piano; songs to poems by Tagore; film music.

Saul oratorio by Handel (libretto by C Jennens), produced London, King's Theatre, 16 January 1739.

Saul og David opera in four acts by Nielsen (libretto by E Christiansen); composed 1898–1901, produced Copenhagen, Royal Theatre, 28 November 1902, conductor Nielsen. When David defeats Goliath, Saul becomes jealous and outlaws him. David runs away with Michal, Saul's daughter. Saul commits suicide after losing a battle against the Philistines, and David becomes king.

sausage bassoon alternative name for the ◊rackett, a musical instrument.

Savile, Jeremy (lived 17th century) English composer. He contributed songs to *Select Musicall Ayres and Dialogues* in 1653. His compositions include the part-song *The Waits*, and song 'Here's a health unto His Majesty'.

Sāvitri opera by Holst (libretto by composer, based on an episode in the *Mahabharata*), produced London, Wellington Hall, 5 December 1916; first public performance London, Lyric Theatre, Hammersmith, 23 June 1921. Death comes to claim woodman Satyavān, but he is restored when his wife Sāvitri outwits the grim reaper.

Savonarola opera by Stanford (libretto by G A à Beckett), produced in Germany (translated by Ernst Frank), Hamburg, 18 April 1884.

saw-toothed wave an electronically generated tone characterized by its abrasive ◊timbre. It is named after the jagged pattern of its sound wave.

Sawyer, David (1961–) English composer. He directed premieres of works by Mauricio Kagel at the 1983 Huddersfield Festival and was piano soloist in his *Phonophonie* in London in 1987. His own works have been played by the London Sinfonietta and the BBC Symphony Orchestra (at the London Promenade Concerts in 1992) and at the Almeida Festival, London.

He studied at York University and with Kagel in Cologne.

Works include: the chamber opera *The Panic* (1992); *Etudes* for actors and ensemble (1984); *Cat's Eye* (1986), *Take Off* (1987), and *Rhetoric* (1989) for ensemble; *Songs of Love and War* for 24 voices, two harpsichords, and percussion (1990); *The Melancholy of Departure*

for piano (1990); *Byrnan Wood* for orchestra (1992); *The Memory of Water* (1993).

Sax, Adolphe (Antoine-Joseph) (1814–1894) Belgian instrument maker. He made several improvements in wind instruments and established himself in Paris in 1842. His chief inventions are the ◊saxhorn and the ◊saxophone.

He studied flute and clarinet at the Brussels Conservatory and worked in the business established in Brussels by his father Charles Joseph Sax (1791–1865), who made wind instruments and produced several inventions, especially in connection with horns and other brass instruments. Adolphe's brother **Alphonse Sax (1822–1874)** made some inventions in connection with the valves of brass instruments and established himself independently in Paris, but did not succeed.

saxhorn family of brass musical instruments played with valves, invented in 1845 by the Belgian Adolphe Sax (1814–1894). It is played with a cup mouthpiece and made in seven different pitches, covering between them a range of some five octaves: soprano in E♭, alto in B♭ (both also called flügelhorns), tenor in E♭, baritone in B♭ (both also called althorns), bass in B♭ (euphonium), bass tuba in E♭ (bombardon) and contrabass in B♭. They are rarely used in the orchestra, but are regular constituents of military and brass bands.

saxophone member of a hybrid brass instrument family of conical bore, with a single-reed woodwind mouthpiece and keyworks, invented about 1840 by Belgian instrument-maker Adolphe Sax (1814–1894). Soprano, alto, tenor, and baritone forms remain current. The soprano saxophone is usually straight; the others are characteristically curved back at the mouthpiece and have an upturned bell. Initially a concert instrument of suave tone, the saxophone was incorporated into dance bands of the 1930s and 1940s, and assumed its modern guise as an abrasive solo jazz instrument after 1945. It has a voicelike ability to bend a note.

Saxton, Robert (1953–) English composer. He studied with Elisabeth Lutyens, Robin Holloway, Robert Sherlaw Johnson, and Berio. In 1990 he was appointed head of composition at the Guildhall School of Music and Drama, London.

Works include: *La Promenade d'Automne* for soprano and ensemble (1972), *What does the song hope for?* for soprano and ensemble (1974), *Reflections on Narziss and Goldmund* for two chamber groups, harp, and piano

(1975), *Canzona* for chamber ensemble (1978), *Choruses to Apollo* for orchestra (1980), *Traumstadt* for orchestra (1980), *Processions and Dances* for 11 instruments (1981), *Piccola Musica per Luigi Dallapiccola* for chamber ensemble (1981), *Eloge* for soprano and ensemble (1981), *Ring of Eternity* for orchestra (1983), Concerto for Orchestra (1984), *Circles of Light* for chamber orchestra (1985), viola concerto (1986), *In the Beginning* for orchestra (1987), *Elijah's Violin* for orchestra (1988), concertos for violin (1989) and cello (1993), *Psalm: a Song of Ascents* for trumpet and ensemble (1992), Piano Quintet (1994), Symphony for soprano, baritone, and orchestra (1993).

saz Persian and Turkish term meaning 'musical instrument'. The term is also applied to a family of long-necked lutes found in Iran, the Caucasus, SE Europe and Asia Minor. Sazi (plural) have a pear-shaped resonator carved from a single piece of wood or fitted together from wooden staves. The neck of the saz is straight with a variable number of tied but movable gut frets.

Scacchi, Marco (c. 1602–c. 1685) Italian composer and writer on music, pupil of G F Anerio. In 1628 he was appointed director of music to the court at Warsaw. He introduced Italian opera to Warsaw, Gdańsk, and Vilna. He wrote several theoretical tracts. He returned to Italy in 1648.

Works include: the operas *Il ratto di Helena, Narciso transformato, Armida abbandonata, Enea, Le nozze d'Amore e di Psiche* and *Circe delusa;* Masses; oratorio *S Cecilia;* madrigals.

Scalabrini, Paolo (c. 1713–1806) Italian composer. He went to Copenhagen in 1747 as conductor of the Mingotti opera company, and stayed there as music director to the Danish court 1748–53 and again 1775–81, when he retired to Italy. He was among the first to write an opera to Danish words.

Works include: Danish operas *Love rewarded, or The Faithful Lovers* (1756), *The Oracle* (1776), *Love without Stockings,* and about 20 Italian operas; oratorio *Giuseppe riconosciuto;* symphonies.

Scala, La, or Teatro alla Scala the greatest Italian opera house, established in Milan 1778. Many of Italy's finest opera composers have written for La Scala, including Puccini, Verdi, and Donizetti.

scale a sequence of pitches that establishes a key, and in some respects the character of a composition. A scale is defined by its starting note and may be **major** or **minor** depending on the order of intervals. A **chromatic scale** is

Pentatonic, major, minor, and whole-tone scales on C.

the full range of 12 notes: it has no key because there is no fixed starting point.

A **whole-tone scale** is a six-note scale and is also indeterminate in key: only two are possible. A **diatonic scale** has seven notes, a **pentatonic scale** has five.

Scandello, Antonio (1517–1580) Italian composer. He became a Protestant and was music director (Kapellmeister) at the Elector of Saxony's court chapel at Dresden. Both his church music and secular songs combine Italian and German styles for the first time.

He is first heard of as a cornettist in Bergamo 1541 and was a member of the Saxon court chapel at Dresden in 1553, but he often returned to Brescia for visits, as in 1567, when he and his family took refuge there during the plague at Dresden. Among the court musicians was his brother Angelo Scandello, and also employed at the court was the Italian painter Benedetto Tola, whose daughter Agnese became Scandello's second wife in 1568. In the same year he was appointed Kapellmeister in place of Matthieu Le Maistre, whose assistant he had been for two years. He became involved in quarrels with the German court musicians and the Flemish singers because the Italians received higher pay.

Works include: Masses, motets, setting for voices of the Passion and Resurrection narrative according to St John (1561), hymn tunes for several voices and other church music; madrigals, epithalamia, *canzoni napoletane* for four voices, sacred and secular German songs for several voices and instruments; lute music.

Scapino comedy-overture by Walton; first performed Chicago, 3 April 1941, conductor Stock.

Scarlatti, (Giuseppe) Domenico (1685–1757) Italian composer. The eldest son of Alessandro ◊Scarlatti, he lived most of his life in Portugal and Spain in the service of the Queen of Spain. He wrote over 500 sonatas for harpsichord, short pieces in ◊binary form demonstrating the new freedoms of keyboard composition and inspired by Spanish musical idioms.

Scarlatti was born at Naples, and was taught by his father. In 1701 he was appointed organist and composer to the court at Naples, where his operas *L'Ottavia restituita al trono* and *Il Giustino* were produced in 1703. Sent by his father to Venice in 1705, he travelled by way of Florence, where he presented himself to Alessandro's patron, Ferdinando de' Medici. In Venice he met

Francesco Gasparini, and probably studied with him. Moving to Rome, he is said to have engaged with Handel in a contest in harpsichord and organ playing, arranged by Cardinal Ottoboni. He was maestro di cappella to Queen Maria Casimira of Poland in Rome 1709–14, and wrote seven operas for her, including *Ambleto/Hamlet*. He was at the Cappella Giulia, St Peter's, as assistant maestro from 1713, and as maestro di cappella 1714–19.

He spent some time at Palermo before going to Lisbon in the service of the Portuguese court. He made intermittent visits to Italy, and in 1729 followed the Portuguese princess Maria Barbara to Madrid on her marriage to the Spanish crown prince. It was for her that he wrote most of his harpsichord music (over 550 'exercises', now called sonatas, which exhibit an original approach to harmony and frequently demand great virtuosity). Scarlatti was the most celebrated harpsichordist of his time, and his music provided the foundation for modern piano technique.

Works include: the operas *La silvia* (1710), *Tolomeo ed Alessandro* (1711), *L'Orlando* (1711), *Tetide in Sciro, Ifigenia in Aulide* (1713), *Ifigenia in Tauride* (1713), *Amor d'un' ombra, Ambleto*; oratorios; church music; cantatas; about 600 harpsichord pieces (30 of them published in his lifetime under the title *Essercizi*), now commonly called sonatas.

Scarlatti, (Pietro) Alessandro (Gaspare) (1660–1725) Italian Baroque composer. He was maestro di capella at the court of Naples and developed the opera form. He composed more than 100 operas, including *Tigrane* 1715, as well as church music and oratorios.

Scelsi, Giacinto (1905–1988) Italian composer. Under the influence of a visit to Tibet he developed an early form of Minimalism, as in *Four pieces, each one on a single note*, for small orchestra 1961. His *Aion* for orchestra (composed 1961, first performance 1985), further evokes virtual stillness.

He studied in Geneva and Vienna and from 1936 was an early exponent of 12-note techniques.

Works include: *Pfhat* and *Konx-Om-Pax* for orchestra (1986), 11 piano suites, five string quartets.

scena (Italian 'stage, scene') subdivision of an act in a dramatic piece; a technical term for operatic solo numbers on a large scale, usually a recitative followed by one or more aria-like sections; also similar pieces designed for concert performance.

scenario the sketch or rough draft for the plot of an opera libretto or for the story of a ballet.

Scenes from Goethe's 'Faust' (Schumann). See ◊*Szenen aus Goethe's 'Faust'*.

Scènes Historiques two suites for orchestra by Sibelius: no. 1 in three movements, 1899, revised 1911; no. 2 in three movements, 1912.

Schachbrett, or Schachtbrett musical instrument, probably an early form of ◊harpsichord. It is mentioned in Cersne von Minden's *Minneregeln* of 1404. The name derives from the old Germanic word *Schacht*, meaning spring or quill (compare English 'jack').

Schadaeus, Abraham (1566–1626) German composer. His *Promptuarium musicum*, a collection of motets, was published in Strasbourg in three parts, in 1611, 1612, and 1613. A *bassus generalis* (continuo) was added by his friend Caspar Vincentius; a fourth part, dated 1617, was entirely by Vincentius.

He became *Rektor* of the *Lateinschule* (grammar school) in Speyer in 1603. Dismissed in 1611, he then held different posts in Upper Lusatia and retired in 1617 in Finsterwalde.

Schaeffer, Pierre (1910–1995) French composer, theorist, writer, and teacher. The son of two musicians, he was educated as a scientist and embarked on a career in telecommunications. In 1941 he founded 'Jeune France', an interdisciplinary arts group which became a focus in French radio for the Resistance movement. In 1948 Schaeffer's experiments in electronic media with this group led to a number of tape compositions which formed the basis of the style known as musique concrète (◊concrete music). He stopped composing in 1960, and devoted his time to a wide range of research and writings. In 1968 he was appointed associate professor at the Paris Conservatoire, where he taught electronic composition. Works are for tape alone.

Schaeffner, André (1895–1980) French musicologist. He studied at the Schola Cantorum in Paris and after 1920 became music critic to various periodicals. His books include studies of Stravinsky and of the origin of musical instruments. In 1929 he became director of the ethnomusicological section of the Musée de l'Homme in Paris.

Schafer, R Murray (1933–) Canadian composer and teacher. His works employ electronics and involve transformation and motivic distortion.

He studied in Toronto and Vienna and worked in England as a journalist.

Works include: the opera *Loving/Toi* (staged Toronto, 1978), *Minnelieder* for mezzo and wind quintet (1956), *St Jean de Brebeuf* for baritone and orchestra (1961), *Requiems for the Party Girl* for soprano and nine instruments (1966), *From the Tibetan Book of the Dead* for soprano, chorus, and ensemble (1968), *The Son of Heldenleben* (after a work by Strauss, 1968), *Sappho* for mezzo and ensemble (1970), four string quartets (1970, 1976, 1989, 1988), *In Search of Zoroaster* for male voice, chorus, and percussion (1971), *Adieu, Robert Schumann* for mezzo and orchestra (after Clara Schumann's diaries detailing her husband's madness, 1976), *Apocalypsis* for soloist, chorus, and orchestra (after St John the Divine, 1980); flute concerto (1985); series of multimedia theatre pieces, including *The Black Theatre of Hermes* (1989) and *The Crown of Ariadne* (1992).

Schäffer, Bogusław (1929–) Polish composer. He studied in Kraków with Artur Malawski and musicology in Warsaw with Zdzisław Jachimecki. For some of his works he has used graphic notation.

Works include: theatre pieces *Miniopera* (1988) and *Liebesblicke* (1989); *Scultura* for orchestra; *Monosonata* for 24 string instruments; *Topofonica* for 40 instruments; *Equivalenze sonore* for percussion instruments; concerto for harpsichord, percussion, and orchestra; *Four Movements* for piano and orchestra; *Tertium datum* for clavichord and chamber orchestra; ten symphonies (1960–79); three piano concertos (1957, 1967, 1988); two harpsichord concertos (1958, 1961); violin concerto (1963); *Kesukaan* for strings (1978); concertos for guitar (1984), organ and violin (1984), flute and harp (1986), saxophone (1986) and for violin and three oboes (1987); six string quartets (1954–73).

Schat, Peter (1935–) Dutch composer. He became well known as an experimental composer, although he later came under the influence of ◊Minimalism.

He studied in Utrecht and The Hague, and then with Mátyás Seiber and Pierre Boulez.

Works include: *Mosaics* for orchestra; *Cryptogamen* for baritone and orchestra *Signalement* for six percussion instruments and three double basses; *Improvisations and Symphonies* for wind quintet; *Labyrinth*, work for 'musical theatre' with 'happenings' (produced Amsterdam, 1966); *Houdini*, circus opera (1976); opera *Symposium* (1994) on the life of Tchaikovsky.

Schauspieldirektor, Der/The Impresario play with music by Mozart (libretto by G Stephanie, junior), produced Vienna, Schönbrunn Palace, at court, 7 February 1786; first Vienna performance, Kärntnertortheater, 18 February 1786. Rivalry between prima donnas Mme Silberklang and Mme Herz as Frank and Puf audition singers.

Scheherazade (Ravel and Rimsky-Korsakov). See ◊*Shéhérazade* and ◊*Shahrazad*.

Scheibe, Johann Adolph (1708–1776) German music theorist, critic, and composer. He edited the periodical *Der critische Musikus*, in which he attacked J S Bach.

After studying law at Leipzig University he settled in Hamburg in 1736, where he edited *Der critische Musikus* 1737–40. He was Kapellmeister to the Margrave of Brandenburg-Culmbach 1739–44, and conductor of the court opera in Copenhagen 1744–48.

Works include: one opera (*Thusnelde*, 1749); cantatas; Masses and other church music; instrumental music; songs.

Scheidt, Samuel (1587–1654) German organist and composer. His influential *Tabulatura nova* for the organ (published in 1624) was printed in score, not in the old German tablature.

He was appointed organist at St Maurice's Church, Halle, 1603. He studied under Jan Sweelinck at Amsterdam. He returned to Halle in 1609 and became court organist to the Margrave of Brandenburg, who was Protestant administrator of the archbishopric of Magdeburg, and was appointed Kapellmeister in 1619. He lost his appointment in 1625 as a result of the Thirty Years' War.

Works include: *Cantiones sacrae* for eight voices; sacred concertos for two–twelve voices with instruments; pavans and galliards for four–five voices; *Liebliche Krafft-Blümlein* for two voices and instruments; organ accompaniments for or transcriptions of 100 hymns and psalms; *Tabulatura nova* containing a great variety of organ pieces in three volumes.

Schein, Johann Hermann (1586–1630) German composer. His music is influenced by Lutheran chorales and by the latest expressive techniques of the early Italian madrigalists.

After the death of his father, a Lutheran pastor, he went to Dresden as a choirboy in the court chapel in 1599, to the grammar-school at Schulpforta in 1603, and to Leipzig University in 1607. In 1615 he was appointed Kapellmeister at the court of Weimar and in 1616 succeeded Seth Calvisius as cantor at St Thomas's School, Leipzig, remaining there until his death.

Works include: *Cantiones sacrae* for five–twelve voices; two volumes of sacred concertos for three–five voices with instruments; *Fontana d'Israel* containing biblical words set for four–five voices and instruments; *Cantional* hymn-book with about 80 tunes of his own; songs for five voices, *Venus-Kränzlein*, *Studenten-Schmaus*, and *Diletti pastorali*; instrumental dances *Banchetto musicale*; songs with instruments *Musica boscareccia*; wedding and funeral cantatas.

Schelomo Hebrew rhapsody for cello and orchestra by Bloch, based on Book of Ecclesiastes; composed 1916, first performed New York 3 May 1917, conductor Bloch.

Schenk, Johann Baptist (1753–1836) Austrian composer. A pupil of Georg Wagenseil 1774–77, he made his public debut as an opera composer in 1785. Beethoven was his pupil in 1793, and he was also a friend of Mozart and Schubert.

Works include: Singspiele, including *Die Weinlese* (1785), *Die Weihnacht auf dem Lande* (1786), *Achmet und Almanzine*, *Der Dorfbarbier* (1796), *Die Jagd*, *Der Fassbinder* (1802); Masses and other church music; cantatas *Die Huldigung* and *Der Mai*; ten symphonies; four harp concertos; five string quartets and trios; songs.

Schenker, Heinrich (1868–1935) Polish-Austrian theorist. In his literary works, including *Neue musikalische Theorien und Phantasien* and *Das Meisterwerk in der Musik*, laid down his detailed analytical methods.

He studied with Bruckner at the Vienna Conservatory and on Brahms's recommendation published some early compositions. He taught a number of pupils privately.

Scherchen, Hermann (1891–1966) German conductor. He collaborated with ◊Schoenberg 1911–12, and in 1919 founded the journal *Melos* to promote contemporary music. He moved to Switzerland 1933, and was active as a conductor and teacher. He wrote two texts, *Handbook of Conducting* and *The Nature of Music*. During the 1950s he founded a music publishing house, Ars Viva Verlag, and an electronic studio at Gravesano.

Scherchen-Hsiao, Tona (1938–) Swiss-born French composer. She studied with her father, Hermann ◊Scherchen with Henze at Salzburg, with Messiaen in Paris 1963–65, and with Ligeti in Vienna.

Works include: *Shen* for six percussion (1968); *Khouang* for orchestra (1968); *Tao*, for contralto and orchestra (1971); *Vague T'ao* for orchestra (1975); *L'Invitation au voyage* for chamber orchestra (1977); *Ziguidor*, wind quintet (1977); *Tzing* for brass quintet (1979); *L'illegitime* for orchestra and tape (1986); electronic and mixed-media pieces *Un cadre univers ouvert* (1985), *Between*, son et lumière for trombone and tape (1986), *Spaceflight* for tape (1987), and *Fuite* for low voice and ensemble (1987).

Schering, Arnold (1877–1941) German musicologist. His books include studies of the early violin concerto, the development of the oratorio and sonata, the performance of early music, early organ and chamber music and a series of attempts to prove that Beethoven's sonatas and quartets are based on Shakespeare's plays and other dramatic works.

He studied at Leipzig University, where in 1907 he became lecturer and later professor of music. From 1909 he also lectured at the Conservatory. In 1920 he became professor at Halle University and in 1928 at Berlin University.

scherzando (Italian 'playful, humorous, skittish') musical direction written by composers over passages intended to be performed in that manner. It may also be used as an adjecctive in tempo directions, such as *allegretto scherzando*.

Scherzi, Gli/The Jokes one of the nicknames of Haydn's six string quartets, op. 33, composed 1781. Also known as the *Russian* quartets or *Jungfernquartette*.

Scherz, List und Rache/Jest, Cunning and Revenge operetta by Bruch (libretto by Goethe, altered by L Bischoff), produced Cologne, 14 January 1858.
For other settings, see ◊Goethe.

scherzo (Italian 'joke') in music, a lively piece, usually in rapid triple (3/4) time; often used for the third movement of a symphony, sonata, or quartet as a substitute for the statelier ◊minuet and ◊trio.

Schicksalslied/Song of Destiny a setting by Brahms for chorus and orchestra of a poem in Hölderlin's *Hyperion*, op. 54, composed 1871; first performed Karlsruhe, 18 October 1871.

Schiedermair, Ludwig (1876–1957) German music scholar. He studied with Sandberger and Beer-Walbrunn at Munich, where he took a degree in 1901. After further studies with Riemann and Kretzschmar in Berlin, he became lecturer at Marburg and in 1914 professor of music at Bonn University. There he became director of the Beethoven Archives, and among his books are bibliographical works on Beethoven and an edition of Mozart's letters with an iconographical volume.

Schikaneder, (Johann Josef) Emanuel (1751–1812) German actor, singer, librettist, playwright, and theatre manager. He was author or part-author with Ludwig Gieseke of the libretto of Mozart's opera *The Magic Flute*, which he produced with himself as Papageno.

He settled in Vienna in 1784. He also wrote libretti for Benedict Schack, Franz Xaver Gerl, Franz Süssmayr, Joseph Woelfl, Ignaz Seyfried, Peter Winter, and others.

Schiller, (Johann Christoph) Friedrich von (1759–1805) German poet and dramatist. His works inspired numerous musical settings. Franz Schubert set 42 songs to Schiller words. See also ◊*Bride of Messina, The* (Fibich); ◊*Briganti, I* (Mercadante); ◊Bruch (*Lied von der Glocke* and *Macht des Gesanges*); ◊'Choral' Symphony (Beethoven); ◊Costa (*Don Carlos*); ◊*Don Carlos* (Verdi); ◊*Giovanna d'Arco* (Verdi); ◊*Guillaume Tell* (Rossini); ◊*Ideale* (Liszt); ◊*Luisa Miller* (Verdi); ◊*Maid of Orleans, The* (Tchaikovsky); ◊Mascagni (*Ode to Joy*); ◊*Masnadieri, I* (Verdi); ◊Seyfried (*Räuber* and *Jungfrau von Orleans*); ◊Smetana (*Wallenstein's Camp*); ◊*Turandot* (Weber); ◊Vaccai (*Giovanna d'Arco* and *Sposa di Messina*); ◊Zumsteeg (*Räuber*; *Wallensteins Lager* and *Ritter Toggenburg*).

Schillinger, Joseph (1895–1943) Russian-born US composer and theoretician. He studied at St Petersburg Conservatory with Tcherepnin (Cherepnin), among others, and then taught at Kharkov Music Academy 1918–22, and 1926–28 in Leningrad. In 1929 he settled in the USA, teaching a mathematical method of his own; among his many pupils was Gershwin. He published his system in a number of books, and also some compositions, including *March of the Orient*; *First Airphonic Suite* for theremin, orchestra, and piano; piano pieces.

Schläger (German 'beaters') in musical notation, sometimes used in scores as an abbreviation for percussion. Also in the singular, a popular song.

Schlaginstrumente (German 'beaten instruments') see ◊percussion instruments.

Schlagobers (Whipped Cream in Viennese dialect) ballet by Richard Strauss (choreography by H Kröller), produced Vienna, Opera, 9 May 1924.

Schlagzither (German 'striking-zither') musical instrument, a zither played by striking the strings with hammers, or rather, a ◊dulcimer.

Schlegel, August Wilhelm von (1767–1845) German poet, critic, and translator. He played a major role in the development of musical aesthetics of the German idealism. Seven poems by Schlegel were set as songs by Schubert. See also ◊*Fierrabras* (Schubert).

schleppen (German 'to drag') term sometimes used by German composers as a negative imperative, *nicht schleppen*, 'do not drag'.

Schlick, Arnolt (before 1460–after 1521) German organist, composer, and theorist. In 1511 he published his *Spiegel der Orgelmacher und Organisten*, a treatise on organ building and playing. The *Tabulaturen etlicher Lobgesang und Lidlein*, published at Mainz in 1512, followed; it was the first printed book of keyboard music to appear in Germany, and contained liturgical organ music, lute pieces, and songs with lute.

His early life was spent in Heidelberg, but he subsequently travelled widely: to Frankfurt in 1486, where he played the organ during the festivities for the coronation of Maximilian I; to Holland in 1490; to Strasbourg (many times); to Worms in 1495, where he met Sebastian Virdung; and subsequently to Speyer, Hagenau, and elsewhere. During these journeys he gained an enormous reputation for testing new organs. He also wrote music for the coronation of Charles V in Aachen, 1520. He was blind, probably from infancy.

Schlüssel (German 'key') in music, a ◊clef.

Schmelzer, (Johann) Heinrich (c. 1623–1680) Austrian composer. He was chamber musician at the Austrian court in Vienna from 1649, assistant conductor from 1671 and first conductor from 1679. He was the father of Andreas Schmelzer.

Works include: ballet music for about 40 operas by Giovanni Battista ◊Draghi and others; *Missa nuptialis* and other church music; instrumental sonatas including the *Sonatae unarum fidium* (1664) for violin and coninuo, the earliest of their kind; trumpet fanfares.

Schmelzer (von Ehrenruff), Andreas (Anton) (1653–1701) Austrian violinist and composer. He was in the service of the Austrian court 1671–1700.

Works include: ballet music for more than 30 of Draghi's operas.

schmetternd (German 'brassy, brazen, clanging') musical term used, like the French *cuivré*, when that kind of tone is required of brass instruments, especially horns.

Schmid(t), Bernhard the Elder (1535–1592) German composer and poet. He published a collection of music arranged for organ in two parts: the first contained motets, the second secular songs and dances, published at Strasbourg in 1577.

Schmid(t), Bernhard the Younger (1567–1625) German composer. His collection of organ arrangements, highly ornamented, was published at Strasbourg in 1607. He was the son of Bernhard ◊Schmidt the Elder.

Schmidt, Bernhard see Bernard ◊Smith.

Schmidt-Isserstedt, Hans (1900–1973) German conductor. He studied with Schreker and also at the University of Cologne, graduating in 1923. He began his career at the Wuppertal opera and then 1928–31 conducted at Rostock, 1931–33 at Darmstadt, and 1935–42 was principal conductor at the Hamburg Staatsoper. He was director of the Deutsche Oper in Berlin 1942–45 and then chief conductor of the North German Radio Symphony Orchestra. He gave performances of *Figaro* at Glyndebourne in 1958 and *Tristan* at Covent Garden, London, in 1962.

Schmieder, Wolfgang (1901–1990) German musicologist. After study at Heidelberg he was archivist at Breitkopf and Härtel in Leipzig, 1933–42; head of the music division at Frankfurt State Library, 1946–63. In 1950 he published thematic catalogue of J S Bach's music (the Bach-Werke-Verzeichnis) which provides standard numbering for the composer's works (preceded by initials BWV).

Schmitt, Florent (1870–1958) French composer. His music shows the influence of Richard Strauss and the French composers Fauré, Debussy, and Massenet. His most successful work is the ballet *La Tragédie de Salome* (revised as a symphonic poem in 1910).

He studied music at Nancy from 1887 and in 1889 was sent to the Paris Conservatory, where he was first a pupil of Dubois and Lavignac and afterwards of Massenet and Fauré for composition. He won the Prix de Rome in 1900 and wrote his first mature works during his three years in Rome. He was director of Lyon Conservatory 1922–24.

Works include: ballets *La tragédie de Salomé* (1907), *Le petit elfe Ferme-l'œil* (1924), *Reflets*, *Ourvasi* and *Oriane et le Prince d'Amour* (1938), incidental music for Shakespeare's *Antony and Cleopatra* (translated by Gide); film music for an adaptation of Flaubert's *Salammbô* (1925); Psalm 46 for soprano solo, chorus, organ, and orchestra; symphonic study *Le* *palais hanté* (after Poe), symphony (1958), *Trois Rapsodies*, *Ronde burlesque*, *Çancunik*, *Kermesse-Valse*, *Symphonie concertante* and *Suite sans esprit de suite* for orchestra; *Légende* for saxophone and orchestra (1918), *Final* for cello and orchestra; piano quintet, *Lied et Scherzo* for double wind quintet, *Andante et Scherzo for chromatic harp and string quartet*, *Suite en Rocaille* for strings, flute, and harp, *Sonatine en trio* for flute, clarinet, and harpsichord (or piano), string quartet (1949), string trio; *Sonate libre* for violin and piano; piano pieces.

Schmittbauer, Joseph Aloys (1718–1809) German composer. A pupil of Jommelli, he was Kapellmeister of Cologne Cathedral 1775–77, and at the court at Karlsruhe from 1777 to his retirement in 1804.

Works include: the operas *L'isola disabitata* (1762), *Lindor und Ismene* (1771), *Herkules auf dem Oeta* (1772), *Betrug aus Liebe*.; much church music; cantatas; symphonies; concertos; chamber music.

Schnabelflöte (German 'beak flute', from French *flûte à bec*) alternative name for the ◊recorder, a musical instrument.

Schnadahüpfeln (Austrian dialect) folk dances, often sung with words, of the *Ländler* or slow waltz type as a rule, belonging to the Tyrol or other Austrian mountain regions.

Schnebel, Dieter (1930–) German composer and theologian. He has taught religious studies from 1953. Influenced by Kagel and Stockhausen, he has produced such 'non-music' items as music for reading (*mo-no*, 1969), and for conductor only (*Nostalgie*, 1969). His orchestral pieces include *Webern-Variationen* (1972), *Wagner-Idyll* (1980), *Beethoven-Sinfonie* (1985), *Mahler-Momente* (1985) and *Sinfonie X* (1987–92).

schnell (German 'fast') term used in musical notation.

Schnittke alternative spelling for Russian composer Alfred Garriyevich ◊Shnitke.

Schobert, Johann (Jean) (c. 1720–1767) German harpsichordist and composer. Mozart arranged one of his sonata movements as the second movement of the concerto K39.

He lived in Paris, and was in the service of the Prince of Conti from about 1720, but died young, with his wife and child, as a result of fungus poisoning.

Works include: the opéra comique *Le Garde-Chasse et le braconnier*; six harpsichord concertos; six *Sinfonies* for harpsichord, violin, and two horns; piano quartets (with two

violins); piano trios; sonatas for piano and violin; sonatas for harpsichord.

Schoeck, Othmar (1886–1957) Swiss composer. Switzerland's first major composer, Schoeck cultivated a lush and lyrical post-romanticism. He excelled in vocal music of all kinds, and wrote many fine song cycles, often with chamber or orchestral accompaniment (for example *Notturno* 1933 and *Lebendig Begraben* 1947) as well as cantatas and several operas, including *Venus* 1922 and *Massimilla Doni* 1937.

He was at first undecided whether to follow his father as a painter, but at 17 went to the Zurich Conservatory to study with Friedrich Niggli (1875–1959) and others, finishing with Max Reger at the Leipzig Conservatory. He conducted choral societies at Zurich 1907–17, and remained there when appointed conductor of the St Gall symphony concerts that year. The university conferred an honorary doctorate on him in 1928. His music was successfully performed in Germany during the Nazi era.

Works include: OPERA *Venus* (after Mérimée, 1922), *Penthesilea* (after Kleist, 1927), *Massimilla Doni* (after Balzac, 1937), *Das Schloss Dürande* (after Eichendorff, 1943).

CHORAL *Der Postillon* (Lenau) for tenor solo, chorus, and orchestra (1909); *Trommelschläge* (Whitman's 'Drum Taps') for chorus and orchestra.

ORCHESTRAL Serenade for small orchestra, pastoral intermezzo *Sommernacht* (after Keller) for strings (1945), suite in A for strings; *Lebendig begraben* (Keller), song-cycle for baritone and orchestra; violin concerto, cello concerto (1947), horn concerto (1951).

CHAMBER AND SOLO VOCAL two violin and piano sonatas; song-cycle *Elegie* with chamber orchestra (1923), *Notturno* with string quartet (1933); song-cycles with piano *Wandsbecker Liederbuch* (Matthias Claudius), *Das stille Leuchten* (C F Meyer), and many others.

Schoenberg, Arnold Franz Walter (1874–1951) Austro-Hungarian composer, a US citizen from 1941. After Romantic early works such as *Verklärte Nacht/Transfigured Night* 1899 and the *Gurrelieder/Songs of Gurra* 1900–11, he experimented with ◊atonality (absence of key), producing works such as *Pierrot lunaire/Moonstruck Pierrot* 1912 for chamber ensemble and voice, before developing the ◊twelve-tone system of musical composition.

After 1918, Schoenberg wrote several Neo-Classical works for chamber ensembles. He taught at the Berlin State Academy 1925–33. The twelve-tone system was further developed by his pupils Alban ◊Berg and Anton ◊Webern. Driven from Germany by the Nazis, Schoenberg settled in the USA 1933, where he influenced music scoring for films. Later works include the opera *Moses und Aron* 1932–51.

Schöne Melusine, Die/The Fair Melusina concert overture by Mendelssohn, op. 32, composed 1833 after a performance in Berlin of K Kreutzer's opera *Melusina*, with a libretto by Grillparzer originally written for Beethoven.

Schöne Müllerin, Die/The Fair Maid of the Mill song cycle by Schubert (poems by Wilhelm Müller), composed 1823, D795. The 17 songs are 1. *Das Wandern* 2. *Wohin?* 3. *Halt; Danksagung an den Bach* 4. *Am Feierabend* 5. *Der Neugierige* 6. *Ungeduld* 7. *Morgengrüss* 8. *Des Müllers Blumen* 9. *Tränenregen* 10. *Pause; Mit dem grünen Lautenbande* 11. *Der Jäger* 12. *Eifersucht und Stolz* 13. *Die liebe Farbe* 14. *Die böse Farbe* 15. *Trockne Blumen* 16. *Der Müller und der Bach* 17. *Des Baches Wiegenlied.*

Schönzeler, Hans-Hubert (1925–) German-born English conductor and musicologist. After study at the New South Wales Conservatorium, he conducted the 20th-Century Ensemble in London, 1951–61. He led the Western Australia Symphony Orchestra at Perth from 1967. An advocate of Bruckner, he has written a book on the composer (1970) and recorded the Requiem; he gave the first performance of the original version of the 8th Symphony (1973, British Broadcasting Corporation [BBC]). Many concerts with the regional BBC orchestras. He became a UK citizen in 1947.

School for Fathers, The (Wolf-Ferrari). See ◊*Quattro rusteghi, I.*

Schoolmaster, The nickname of Haydn's symphony no. 55 in E♭ major, composed 1774.

Schöpfungsmess/Creation Mass the nickname of Haydn's Mass in B♭ major of 1801, where a theme from *The Creation* is used in the 'Qui tollis'.

Schottisch (German 'Scottish') ballroom dance fashionable in the 19th century, introduced to England 1848, not identical with the *Écossaise*. In England it is usually called by its plural, *Schottische*. The music is in 2–4 time, much like that of the polka, but played more slowly.

Schrade, Leo (1903–1964) German musicologist. He studied at several German universities and taught at Königsberg University 1929–32 and at Bonn University from 1932 to 1937, when he left Germany and settled in the

USA. He taught at Yale University 1938–58, becoming professor in 1948. From 1958 he was professor at Basel University. His studies ranged widely over medieval, Renaissance and Baroque music, and included a book on Monteverdi and editions of the works of Philippe de Vitry, Machaut, Landini, and other 14th-century composers.

Schreker, Franz (1878–1934) Austrian composer, conductor, and teacher. He conducted the first performance of Schoenberg's *Gurrelieder* in 1913. His operas were late Romantic in expression and popular in the 1920s; first performances were conducted by Otto Klemperer (at Cologne) and Bruno Walter (at Munich).

He studied under Fuchs in Vienna, and founded the Philharmonic Choir there in 1911. He taught at the Imperial Academy of Music until his appointment as director of the Academy of Music in Berlin in 1920; he was forced by the Nazis to resign in 1933.

Works include: OPERA *Flammen* (1902), *Der ferne Klang* (1912), *Die Gezeichneten* (1918), *Der Schatzgräber* (1920), *Irrelohe* (1924), *Christophorus* (1924–29; produced 1978); pantomime *Der Geburtstag der Infantin* (after Wilde, 1908; reworked as *Spanisches Fest*, 1927).

ORCHESTRAL Chamber symphony for 23 solo instruments (1917; also in version for full orchestra, as Sinfonietta), *Kleine Suite* for small orchestra (1931).

VOCAL *Zwei lyrische Gesänge* for voice and orchestra to poems by Whitman (1929); 43 Lieder to texts by Heyse, Tolstoy, and Scherenberg (1895–1916).

Schroeter, Leonhard (c. 1540–c. 1595) German composer. He succeeded Gallus Dressler as cantor of Magdeburg Cathedral in 1564.

Works include: German Te Deum for double choir (1584), *Hymni sacri* for four–five voices, *Weihnachts-Liedlein* for several voices (1587).

Schröter, Johann Samuel (c. 1752–1788) German pianist and composer. He settled in England, and succeeded J C Bach as music master to Queen Charlotte in 1782. He wrote chiefly keyboard music, including some of the earliest pieces written for the piano.

He was taught by his father, the oboist Johann Friedrich Schröter, and made his debut as a pianist in Leipzig in 1767. In 1772 he went on tour with his father and sister Corona Schröter to Holland and England, where he appeared at one of the Bach-Abel concerts.

It was his widow with whom Haydn had an autumnal affair during his first visit to

London; Haydn made copies of her letters to him.

Works include: keyboard concertos, sonatas, and other pieces; piano quintets and trios.

Schubert, Franz Peter (1797–1828) Austrian composer. His ten symphonies include the incomplete eighth in B minor (the 'Unfinished') and the 'Great' in C major. He wrote chamber and piano music, including the 'Trout Quintet', and over 600 lieder (songs) combining the Romantic expression of emotion with pure melody. They include the cycles *Die schöne Müllerin/The Beautiful Maid of the Mill* 1823 and *Die Winterreise/The Winter Journey* 1827.

Schubert was born in Vienna, the son of a schoolmaster who cultivated music in his household. He began to learn the piano and violin early and received lessons from Michael Holzer at the age of nine, learning also organ and counterpoint. He was admitted to the seminary for choristers in the Imperial Chapel 1808, played violin in the orchestra there, and sometimes conducted as deputy. At 13 he wrote a fantasy for piano duet and sketched other works, and in 1811 composed his first song. He played viola in the string quartet at home. His mother died in 1812 and his father married again in 1813, and in the same year Schubert wrote his first symphony and left the seminary, continuing studies under Salieri. At 17 he became assistant teacher in his father's school, but disliked teaching; composed the G major Mass, the second and third symphonies and several dramatic pieces. In 1814 he allegedly sold his overcoat in order to buy a ticket for the revival of Beethoven's opera *Fidelio*; his own first opera, *Des Teufels Lustschloss*, was written in the same year. Like all his stage works, it was unsuccessful, but he also composed at this time his first great song, 'Gretchen am Spinnrade'. The following year he wrote almost 150 songs. In 1816 he left the school and joined his friend Schober in rooms, gathering a circle of literary and artistic rather than musical friends round him. In 1817 he met the singer Michael Vogl, who took a great interest in his songs and succeeded in getting his play with music *Die Zwillingsbrüder/The Twin Brothers* produced in June 1820.

By this time he had written some of his finest instrumental works, including the 4th and 5th symphonies, the sonatinas for violin and piano, and the *Trout Quintet*. His reputation grew beyond his own circle, but publishers failed to recognize him until his friends had 20 songs published at their own expense

in 1821. (Most of his large-scale works were unpublished during his lifetime, however.) His mastery of various instrumental genres is demonstrated in the 'Unfinished' symphony and 'Wanderer' Fantasy for piano of 1822; the last three string quartets, in A minor, D minor, 'Death and the Maiden', and G, followed in 1824 and 1826. His 9th symphony of 1825 is one of the most carefully crafted and consistently inspired work of its kind ever written.

He lived in Vienna all his life, except for some summer excursions and two visits to Hungary as domestic musician to the Esterházy family on their country estate at Zséliz, in 1818 and 1824. He never held an official appointment and failed to stabilize his financial position, but earned enough casually to lead a modest if improvident and Bohemian existence. His industry was phenomenal. He died from typhoid, his condition having been weakened by syphilis.

Works include: OPERAS AND SINGSPIELE (some incomplete) *Der Spiegelritter* (1811–12, first performance Swiss Radio 1949), *Des Teufels Lustschloss* (1813–15; first performance Vienna, 1879), *Adrast* (1817–19, first performance Vienna, 1868), *Der vierjährige Posten* (1815, first performance Dresden, 1896), *Fernando* (1815, first performance Vienna, 1905), *Claudine von Villa Bella* (1815, first performance Vienna, 1913), *Die Freunde von Salamanka* (1815, first performance Halle, 1928), *Die Burgschaft* (1816, first performance Vienna, 1908), *Die Zwillingsbrüder* (1819, first performance Vienna, 1820), *Alfonso und Estrella* (1821–22, first performance Weimar, 1854), *Die Verschworenen* (1823, first performance Vienna, 1861), *Fierrabras* (1823, first performance Karlsruhe, 1897); also melodrama *Die Zauberharfe* (1820, first performance Vienna, 1820) and incidental music *Rosamunde, Fürstin von Zypern* (1823, first performance Vienna, 1823).

VOCAL WITH ORCHESTRA church music including five Masses, in F, G, C, A♭, and E♭ (1814–28), *Deutsche Messe* (1827), *Lazarus*, unfinished oratorio (1820), six settings of the *Salve regina* (1812–24). Works for voices, with and without accompaniment, including *Frühlingsgesang* (1822), *Gesang der Geister über den Wassern* (1817; second version with orchestra 1821), *Gondelfahrer* (1824), *Miriams Siegesgesang* (1828) and *Ständchen* (1827).

ORCHESTRAL nine symphonies: no. 1 in D (1813), no. 2 in B♭ (1815), no. 3 in D (1815), no. 4 in C minor (1816), no. 5 in B♭ (1816), no. 6 in C (1818), no. 7 in E (1821; sketches, unscored), no. 8 in B minor ('Unfinished', 1822), no. 9 in

C ('Great', 1825); two overtures in the Italian style (1817, 1819), five German Dances (1813; also in scoring by Webern), Rondo in A for violin and orchestra (1816).

CHAMBER 15 string quartets, nos. 1–7 composed 1812–14, no. 8 in B♭ (1814, D112), no. 9 in G minor (1815, D173), no. 10 in E♭ (1813, D87), no. 11 in E (1816, D353), no. 12 in C minor (*Quartettsatz*, 1820, D703), no. 13 in A minor (1824, D804), no. 14 in D minor (*Der Tod und das Mädchen/Death and the Maiden*, 1824, D810), no. 15 in G (1826, D887); Octet in F for string quartet, double bass, clarinet, bassoon, and horn (1824, D803), string quintet in C (1828, D956), piano quintet in A (*Die Forelle/The Trout*, 1819, D667), piano trios in B♭ (1827, D898) and E♭ (1827, D929); for piano and violin: sonata in A (1817, D574), three sonatinas, in D, A minor, and G minor (1816, D384, D385 and D408), *Rondo brillant* in B minor (1826, D895), Fantasia in C, based on song 'Sei mir gegrüsst' (1827, D934).

WORKS FOR PIANO including *Divertissement à la hongroise* (D818), Fantasia in F minor (D940), sonata in B♭ (D617) and sonata in C, Grand Duo (D813), all for four hands; 21 piano sonatas: nos. 1–12 composed 1815–19, some unfinished, no. 13 in A (D664), no. 14 in A minor (D784), no. 15 in C (D840), no. 16 in A minor (D845), no. 17 in D (D850), no. 18 in G (D894), no. 19 in C minor (D958), no. 20 in A (D959), no. 21 in B♭ (D960); Fantasia in C, based on the song 'Der Wanderer' (D760), eight impromptus in two sets: in C minor, E♭, G♭, and A♭ (D899), in F minor, A♭, B♭, F minor (D935), three Kalvierstücke, in E♭ minor, E♭, and C (D946), six *Moments Musicaux*, in C, A♭, F minor, C♯ minor, F minor, and A♭ (1823–28, D780); two sets of waltzes, D145 and D365.

SONGS three cycles, *Die schöne Müllerin* (1823), *Winterreise* (1827), and *Schwanengesang* (1828). Some of the best known of more than 600 Lieder are 'Abendstern' (Mayrhofer, 1824), 'Die Allmacht' (Pyrker, 1825), 'Am Bach im Frühling' (Schober, 1816, 'An den Mond' (Goethe, 1815), 'An die Entfernte' (Goethe, 1822), 'An die Musik' (Schober, 1817), 'An Schwager Kronos' (Goethe, 1816), 'An Sylvia' (Shakespeare, 1826), 'Auf dem Wasser zu singen' (Stolberg, 1823), 'Auf der Donau' (Mayrhofer, 1817), 'Auflösung' (Mayrhofer, 1824), 'Ave Maria' (Scott, translated by Storck, 1825), 'Bei dir allein' (Seidl, 1826), 'Delphine' (Schütz, 1825), 'Du bist die Ruh' (Rückert, 1823), 'Der Einsame' (Lappe, 1825), 'Erlkönig' (Goethe, 1815), 'Der Fischer' (Goethe, 1815), 'Fischerweise' (Schlechta, 1826), 'Die Forelle' (Schubart, 1817), 'Frühlingsglaube' (Uhland, 1820), 'Ganymed'

(Goethe, 1817), 'Die Götter Griechenlands' (Schiller, 1819), 'Gretchen am Spinnrade' (Goethe, 1814), 'Gruppe aus dem Tartarus' (1817), '3 Harfenspieler Lieder' (Goethe, 1816), 'Heidenröslein' (Goethe, 1815), 'Der Hirt auf dem Felsen', with clarinet obbligato (Müller, 1828), 'Horch, horch die Lerch' (Shakespeare, 1826), 'Im Frühling' (Schulze, 1826), 'Die junge Nonne' (Craigher, 1825), 'Lachen und Weinen' (Rückert, 1823), 'Liebhaber in aller Gestalten' (Goethe, 1817), 'Der Musensohn' (Goethe, 1822), 'Nacht und Träume' (Collin, 1822), 'Nur wer die Sehnsucht kennt' (Goethe, five versions), 'Prometheus' (Goethe, 1819), 'Sei mir gegrüsst' (Rückert, 1822), 'Die Sterne' (Leitner, 1828), 'Der Tod und das Mädchen' (Claudius, 1817), 'Dem Unendlichen' (Klopstock, 1815), 'Der Wanderer' (Lübeck, 1816), 'Wanderers Nachtlied' (Goethe, 1822), 'Der Zwerg' (Collin, 1822).

Schuch, Willi (1900–1986) Swiss musicologist. He studied under Courvoisier and Sandberger at Munich and Ernst Kurth at Bern, where he took a doctor's degree in 1927. He became a critic at Zurich, and from 1930 to 1944 he taught at the Zurich Conservatory. His works include studies of Schütz, Swiss folk and early music, and Schoeck. In 1976 he published the first volume in the authorized biography of Richard Strauss.

Schuhplattler Bavarian country dance with music in moderate 3–4 time similar to that of the Ländler. The dancers are men only and they strike their palms on their knees and soles.

Schulhoff, Erwin (1894–1942) Czech pianist and composer. Recent performances of his opera *Flammen/Flames* 1928 suggest a powerful assimilation of a wide range of contemporary influences, including jazz and microtonality.

He studied at the conservatories of Prague, Vienna, Leipzig, and Cologne. As a communist in Nazi-ruled Czechoslovakia, he sought refuge in Soviet citizenship, but after the 1941 invasion of Russia he was arrested, and died in a concentration camp.

Works include: the opera *Flames*; ballets *Ogelala* and *Moonstruck*; incidental music to Molière's *Bourgeois gentilhomme*; two symphonies; piano concerto; chamber music; piano works.

Schuller, Gunther (1925–) US composer and horn player. He was professor of composition at the New England Conservatory, Boston, Massachusetts 1966–77, and joint artistic director of the Berkshire Music Center

1970–85. He has written on and been influenced by jazz.

After playing horn in the Cincinnati Symphony Orchestra he joined the New York Metropolitan Orchestra 1945–59.

Works include: the operas *The Visitation*, after Kafka (1966), *The Fisherman and his Wife* (1970), and *A Question of Taste* (1989); *Seven Studies on Themes of Paul Klee* (1959), *Three Studies in Texture* for orchestra; ballet *Variants*; symphonies; concertos for cello, horn, piano; violin concerto (1976), double bassoon concerto (1978), saxophone concerto (1983), *Concerto quaternio* (1984); *Concerto festivo* for brass quintet and orchestra (1984); Concertos for bassoon (1985), Viola (1985), string quartet (1988), flute (1989) and piano three hands (1989); *Fantasia concertante* for three trombones and piano; quartet for four double basses; five pieces for five horns.

Schuloper (German 'school opera') German work of a special type of the 20th century with a didactic purpose; the same as a *Lehrstück*, but invariably intended for the stage.

Schulz, Johann Abraham Peter (1747–1800) German composer, conductor, and musicologist. He travelled widely in Europe and held musical posts in Poland, Berlin, and Copenhagen. He also wrote a number of theoretical works, including a treatise on harmony, on which he collaborated with his teacher, Johann Kirnberger.

He travelled in Austria, Italy, and France in 1768, and after holding a post in Poland returned in 1773 to Berlin, where he collaborated with Kirnberger and contributed to Johann Georg Sulzer's (1720–79) encyclopaedia *Allgemeine Theorie der schönen Künste* (1771–74). He was conductor at the French theatre in Berlin 1776–78, then was court composer to Prince Heinrich of Prussia at Rheinsberg 1780–87, then worked at the Danish court in Copenhagen until his return to Germany in 1795.

Works include: the operas (in French) *Clarisse, La Fée Urgèle* (after Voltaire, 1782), *Le barbier de Séville* (after Beaumarchais, 1786), and *Aline, reine de Golconde* (1787); (in Danish) *The Harvest Home* (1790), *The Entry* (1793), and *Peter's Wedding*; German melodrama *Minona*; incidental music for Racine's *Athalie* and other plays; *Christi Tod, Maria und Johannes* and other sacred works; chamber music, *Lieder im Volkston* and many other songs.

Schulz-Beuthen, Heinrich (1838–1915) German composer. He studied at the Leipzig Conservatory, taught at Zurich 1866–80, at

Dresden 1880–93, in Vienna 1893–95, and at the Dresden Conservatory from 1895.

Works include: the operas *Aschenbrödel* (1879; text by Mathilde Wesendonk), *Die Verschollene* and three others; Christmas play *Die Blume Wunderhold*; Requiem, six Psalms and other choral works; eight symphonies (no. 6 on Shakespeare's *King Lear*), symphonic poems on Schiller's *Wilhelm Tell*, on Böcklin's picture 'The Isle of the Dead', on Grillparzer's *Des Meeres und der Liebe Wellen* and others, two suites, two scenes from Goethe's *Faust*, serenade and other works for orchestra; piano concerto; wind octet, string quintet and trio; two sonatas and pieces for piano; numerous songs.

Schuman, William Howard (1910–) US composer and teacher. His music is melodic, if sometimes tempered by ◊polytonality, and often emphasizes ◊motoric rhythm or other intense rhythms, as in *American Festival Overture* 1939. His large-scale conception suits the orchestral medium, for which he has written nine symphonies. He has also written chamber and vocal works.

He studied at Columbia University, USA and at the Mozarteum, Salzburg. In 1936 he was appointed teacher at the Columbia University summer school and in 1938 at the Sarah Lawrence College in New York. Later he studied with Roy Harris, and had his first major success when his 3rd symphony was premiered under Stokowski in 1941. In 1945 he succeeded Carl Engel as director of music publications in the house of Schirmer in New York and Ernest Hutcheson as president of the Juilliard School of Music, New York. He was director of the Lincoln Center, New York 1961–69.

Works include: baseball opera *The Mighty Casey* (1953); ballets *Choreographic Poem, Undertone, Night Journey*; incidental music for Shakespeare's *Henry VIII*; film music for *Steeltown*; two secular cantatas for chorus and orchestra; ten symphonies (1936–76), *American Festival* and *William Billings* overtures, *Prayer in Time of War* (1943) and *Side-Show* for orchestra; symphony for string orchestra (1943); *Judith* (choreographic poem); *Newsreel* for military band; piano concerto, violin concerto (1947); four *Canonic Choruses, Pioneers, Requiescat* (without words), and other pieces for unaccompanied chorus; four string quartets (1936–50), canon and fugue for piano trio; quartettino for four bassoons; *Three-Score Set* for piano.

Schumann, Clara Josephine (1819–1896), born Wieck German pianist and composer.

She wrote a *Concerto in A Minor* for piano and orchestra 1835–36, a *Piano Trio* about 1846, and romances for piano. She married Robert ◊Schumann 1840 (her father had been his piano teacher). During his life and after his death she was devoted to popularizing his work, appearing frequently in European concert halls.

She was taught by her father, Friedrich Wieck, and made her first public appearance at the age of nine. She gave her own first concert at the Leipzig Gewandhaus on 8 November 1830. In 1837 she was in Vienna for some time. Her engagement to Schumann was violently opposed by her father, but they married after many difficulties on 12 September 1840. She appeared in public less frequently during her married life, but after Schumann's death in 1856 she was obliged to do so continuously and to teach. She went to live in Berlin with her mother, who had married the composer Woldemar Bargiel (1828–1897), but in 1863 she settled at Baden-Baden and in 1878 became chief piano professor at the Hoch Conservatory at Frankfurt.

Works include: piano concerto in A minor; piano trio in G minor; variations on a theme by Robert Schumann and about 12 other op. nos. for piano; several sets of songs.

Schumann, Robert Alexander (1810–1856)

German composer and writer. His songs and short piano pieces portray states of emotion with great economy. Among his compositions are four symphonies, a violin concerto, a piano concerto, sonatas, and song cycles, such as *Dichterliebe/Poet's Love* 1840. Mendelssohn championed many of his works.

Schumann was born at Zwickau, the son of a bookseller and publisher. He began to learn the piano from a schoolmaster and organist at the age of eight and played well by the time he was 11. He studied all the music found at his father's shop, where he also developed a literary taste. He played at school concerts and private houses, and made such progress in improvisation and composition that in 1825 Weber was approached to teach him, but could not, being busy preparing *Oberon* for London and expecting to go there. Schumann's father died in 1826, and in 1828 he was sent to Leipzig University to study law. There he met Friedrich Wieck, from whom he took piano lessons, and first met his daughter Clara. He neglected his legal studies, as he did again when in 1829 he moved to Heidelberg University, where he came under the influence of Anton Friedrich Justus Thibaut (1772–1840), legal scholar and amateur musician who, with his book *Über Reinheit der Tonkunst* (1825) made a major contribution to aesthetics and to Cecilian reforms later in the century. Back at Leipzig in 1830, Schumann lodged at Wieck's house, wrote his first published works (op. 1 and 7), and the next year went to the St Thomas cantor, Christian Weinlig, for instruction, but left him for the younger Heinrich Dorn. In 1832 he permanently injured his hand with a mechanical contrivance he had invented for finger-development and thus had to give up a pianist's career for that of a composer.

With a circle of young intellectuals (calling themselves the 'Davidsbündler') he founded the *Neue Zeitschrift für Musik* in 1834. Apart from the *Allgemeine Musikalische Zeitung* (Leipzig, 1798/9–1848), this was the most comprehensive and innovative musical journal, championing the improvement of music in Germany and promoting Romantic creativeness. He fell in love with Ernestine von Fricken in 1834, but the engagement was broken off in the following year, during which he wrote his first great keyboard work, *Carnaval*. In 1836 Wieck's daughter Clara, already a remarkable pianist, was 17 and she and Schumann fell in love. Some of his feelings were expressed in the C major Fantasy for piano, which also quotes from Beethoven's *An die ferne Geliebte/To the Distant Beloved*. Clara's father violently opposed a match and in 1839 they took legal proceedings against him; he failed to yield, but they married on 12 September 1840, the day before she came of age.

Now followed the most prolific period of Schumann's creative life: the 'Spring' symphony of 1841 seems to symbolize artistic as well as natural growth and the same fervent, vital impulse informs the song cycles *Dichterliebe* and *Liederkreis* (op. 24, op. 39), the string quartets op 41, and the Piano Quintet, all of this same period. The first, rhapsodic movement of the Piano Concerto also dates from this time (1841–42); the last two movements were added 1845. In 1843 Schumann suffered a crisis of mental exhaustion and he had a more serious breakdown after a tour in Russia with Clara in 1844, at the end of which year they settled at Dresden. Although his nervous complaint grew more marked after periods of recovery, in 1850 he accepted the conductorship at Düsseldorf, including subscription concerts, choral practices, and church music, a post for which he proved quite unfit.

In spite of his personal problems Schumann completed in 1850 the most exuberant and accomplished of all his orchestral works, the 3rd symphony in E♭, which celebrates the Rhineland, the flowing of the Rhine itself, and Cologne cathedral. The committee at Düsseldorf tactfully suggested his resignation in 1852, but with Clara's injudicious support he obstinately refused to withdraw. Signs of a mental collapse grew more and more alarming and his creative work progressively less convincing, and in February 1854 he threw himself into the Rhine. On being rescued he was sent at his own request to a private asylum at Endenich, where he died more than two years later.

Schumann's works of all genres tend towards the lyrical qualities found most obviously in his songs; although the spontaneity and melodic naturalness of his piano music and Lieder have rightly been praised, his chamber and orchestral music shows similar qualities, although on a larger scale. One of his most attractive features is the essentially private nature of his genius. The quintessential Romantic, his personal experiences, and in particular his love for Clara, found expression in his music. His inward-looking personality is reflected in the musical cryptograms of many of his works.

Works include: STAGE opera *Genoveva* (1850); incidental music to Byron's 'Manfred' (1852); 15 works for chorus and orchestra with or without solo voices, including *Requiem für Mignon* and scenes from Goethe's *Faust* (1844–53).

ORCHESTRAL four symphonies (1841, 1846, 1850, 1841 revised 1851); *Overture, Scherzo and Finale*; concertos for piano, violin, and cello (1841–45, 1853, 1850), *Concertstück* for four horns and orchestra (1849).

CHAMBER three string quartets, op. 41 nos. 1–3 (1842), three piano trios, piano quartet (1842), piano quartet, *Fantasiestücke* and *Märchenerzählungen* for piano trio (the latter with clarinet and viola).

· PIANO 36 op. nos. of piano music including *Papillons* (1831), *Davidsbündlertänze* (1837), *Carnaval* (1835), three sonatas, *Etudes symphoniques* (1837), *Kinderscenen* (1838), *Kreisleriana* (1838), *Humoreske, Nachtstücke, Faschingsschwank aus Wien* (1840), *Waldscenen*.

SONGS 35 op. nos. of songs (some containing numerous pieces), including the cycles *Frauenliebe und -leben* (1840) and *Dichterliebe* (1840), also *Liederkreis* (Heine and Eichendorff, 1840) and *Myrthen*; 14 op. nos. of part songs.

Schuricht, Carl (1880–1967) German conductor. He studied with Humperdinck and Reger. Wiesbaden 1911–44; many early performances of Debussy, Schoenberg and Stravinsky. From 1944 he was guest conductor with leading orchestras and in London was heard in the standard repertory with the London Symphony Orchestra. He toured the USA with the Vienna Philharmonic Orchestra in 1956 and in 1957 appeared with the Chicago Symphony Orchestra and the Boston Symphony Orchestra.

Schurmann, Gerard (1928–) British composer. Born in Dutch Indonesia, he went to England in 1941 and studied at the Royal College of Music; but was largely self-taught.

Works include: wind quintet (1963, revised 1976), two string quartets, flute sonatina (1968), *Variants* for orchestra (1970), *Six Studies of Francis Bacon* for orchestra (1968), piano concerto (1973), *Contrasts* for piano (1973), *The Double Heart*, cantata (1976), violin concerto (1978), *Piers Plowman* for soloists, chorus, and orchestra (1980), piano quartet (first performance Cheltenham, 1986).

Schusterfleck (German 'cobbler's patch') playful German description of a technical device, especially the rosalia, used as an easy subterfuge in composition. Beethoven called Diabelli's waltz, on which he wrote the variations op. 120, a Schusterfleck.

Schütz, Heinrich (1585–1672) German early Baroque composer. He was musical director to the Elector of Saxony from 1614. His works include *The Seven Words of Christ* about 1660, *Musicalische Exequien* 1636, and the *Deutsche Magnificat/German Magnificat* 1671. He increased the range and scope of instrumental and choral ◊polyphony and was an important precursor of J S Bach.

Schütz was born at Köstritz in Saxony. He learnt music as a choirboy in the chapel of the Landgrave of Hesse-Kassel, and studied law at Marburg University and music under Giovanni Gabrieli at Venice, 1609–12. He returned to Kassel as court organist, but left for Dresden in 1614 with an appointment as music director to the Elector Johann Georg of Saxony. He did much there to establish the fashion for Italian music and musicians, but although he had written Italian madrigals at Venice, he set his own works to German or Latin words, notably the 26 *Psalmen Davids* of 1619. In 1627 he wrote the first German opera, *Dafne*, on a translation of Rinuccini's libretto by Martin Opitz, for the marriage of the elector's daughter to the Landgrave of Hesse-Darmstadt. After the death of his wife in 1628 he again went to Italy in 1629, where he learnt about the newly established form of opera from Monteverdi. In 1633, the economic depression that followed the Thirty Years' War having disrupted the running of the Dresden court chapel, he obtained leave to go to Copenhagen, and he spent the years until 1641 there and at other courts. Returning to Dresden, he did not succeed in reorganizing the court music satisfactorily until the later 1640s. In the 1650s he became much dissatisfied with the new tendencies among the Italian court musicians and had many quarrels with Giovanni Bontempi, but did not succeed in obtaining his release, and after some improvements later on he remained at the Saxon court for the rest of his life. Schütz was the most important of Bach's German predecessors, uniting the lyric and dramatic elements of Venetian vocal style with German polyphony.

Works include: the operas *Dafne* (1627, lost) and *Orpheus und Euridice* (1638, lost); motets, *Cantiones sacrae*, psalms, *Symphoniae Sacrae* (1629, 1647, 1650) and concertos for voices and instruments (*Geistliche Concerte* (1636, 1639) and other church music; Christmas (1664), Passion, and Resurrection oratorios, *The Seven Words of Christ*; Italian madrigals; *Exequien* (funeral pieces) for six-eight voices, Elegy on the death of the electress of Saxony.

Schuyt, Cornelis (1557–1616) Flemish composer. He held a succession of organ appointments in the Netherlands. He published several books of madrigals and a book of instrumental pieces.

He travelled to Italy to study music, returning to the Netherlands in 1581.

Schwanda (Švanda) the Bagpiper see ◊*Švanda Dudák*.

Schwanenberg, Johann Gottfried (1740–1804), or Schwanenberger, German composer. After studying with Johann Hasse, he was appointed court conductor at Brunswick in 1762.

Works include: the operas *Romeo e Giulia* (1776), (after Shakespeare), *Adriano in Siria* (1762), *Solimano* (1762), *Zenobia*, and about ten others; symphonies; piano concertos; piano sonatas.

Schwanendreher, Der/The Swan-Turner concerto after German folksongs for viola and small orchestra by Hindemith; composed 1935, first performed Amsterdam, 14 November 1935, conductor Mengelberg. The title alludes to the cooking of swans by turning them on a spit.

Schwanengesang/Swan Song song cycle by Schubert, containing the last songs written by him in 1828, including seven settings of Rellstab, six of Heine (his only settings of that poet), and Seidl's *Pigeon Post/Die Taubenpost*. The idea of a cycle was not Schubert's, but that of the published, as was the title, which was invented as an allusion to Schubert's death; the inclusion of Seidl's song was also the publisher's afterthought. The songs are *Liebesbotschaft, Kriegers Ahnung, Frühlingssehnsucht, Ständchen, Aufenthalt, In der Ferne, Abschied, Der Atlas, Ihr Bild, Das Fischermädchen, Die Stadt, Am Meer, Der Doppelgänger,* and *Die Taubenpost*.

Schwarz, Boris (1906–1983) US musicologist, violinist, and conductor. He studied with Flesch and Thibaud in Berlin and Paris; after a 1920 debut he performed widely in Europe, settling in the USA in 1936. He held various academic posts in New York from 1941 and made a special study of Soviet music.

Schwarz, Rudolf (1905–1994) Austrian-born English conductor. He studied piano and violin, playing viola in the Vienna Philharmonic Orchestra. In 1923 he became an assistant conductor at the Düsseldorf Opera and from 1927 to 1933 conductor at the Karlsruhe Opera, after which he became music director of the Jewish Cultural Union in Berlin until 1941, when he was sent to Belsen concentration camp. He survived and went to Sweden in 1945 and then England, where he became conductor of Bournemouth Symphony Orchestra (1947–51), City of Birmingham Symphony Orchestra (1951–57), BBC Symphony Orchestra (1957–62), and Northern Sinfonia Orchestra (1964–73).

Schwarze Maske, Die/The Black Mask opera by Penderecki (libretto by composer after G Hauptmann), produced Salzburg, 15 August 1986. Hysterical Benigna suspects that masked party-crasher is former seducer Johnson, an escaped African-American slave.

Schweigsame Frau, Die/The Silent Woman opera by Richard Strauss (libretto by Stefan Zweig, based on Ben Jonson's *Epicoene*), produced Dresden, 24 June 1935. Henry returns home to his uncle, Sir Morosus, who hates music and noise. Henry hopes to receive an inheritance, but is instead disowned because he has joined a band of singers. He gets revenge, tricking Morosus into marriage with 'Timida', the noisy Aminta in disguise.

Schwertsik, Kurt (1935–) Austrian composer. With Friedrich Cerha he founded the ensemble *Die Reihe* in 1958, for the performance of new music. He has reacted against the contemporary avant garde.

He studied at the Vienna Academy 1949–57. In 1978 he began teaching at the Vienna Conservatory.

Works include: the operas *Der lange Weg Zur grossen Mauer* (1975) and *Das Märchen von Fanferlieschen Schönefusschen* (1982); ballets *Walzerträume* (1976) and *Macbeth* (1988); *Draculas Haus und Hofmusik*, for strings (1968); *Symphonie in MoB-Stil* (1971; association with H K Gruber); Violin concerto (1977); *Starker Tobak* for soprano and seven instruments (1983); *Verwandlungsmusik* for orchestra (1983); concerto for trombone (1988); Double bass concerto (1989).

Schwindl, Friedrich (1737–1786) Dutch or German violinist, flautist, harpsichordist, and composer. He wrote over 30 symphonies, and belonged to the Mannheim School.

He was at The Hague when Charles Burney stayed there in 1770, later at Geneva and Mulhouse, and finally at Karlsruhe as music director to the Margrave of Baden.

Works include: the operas *Das Liebesgrab* and *Die drei Pächter*; Mass in E♭; over 30 symphonies; quartets, trios.

Sciarrino, Salvatore (1947–) Italian composer. He is best known for his operas, which take an irreverent view of the conventions of the genre, filtering familiar myths through a surreal sensibility. *Amore e Psyche* (1973), *Aspern* (1978), *Vanitas* (1981), *Lohengrin 'azione invisible'* (1983), *Perseo e Andromeda* (1991).

He studied electronic music at Rome in 1969 and began teaching at the Milan Conservatory in 1974.

Works include: *Sonata da camera* for orchestra (1971), variations for cello and orchestra (1974), *Clair de Lune* for piano and orchestra (1975), *Kindertotenlied* for soprano, tenor, and chamber orchestra (1978), two string quintets (1976, 1977), violin concerto (1985), two piano trios (1975, 1986).

Scimone, Claudio (1934–) Italian conductor and musicologist. After study with Franco Ferrara, he founded the ensemble I Solisti Veneti. He has toured throughout Europe and the USA performing 18th-century repertory and modern Italian works. He was teacher of the Verona Conservatory 1967–74, and director at Padua from 1983. He has issued an edition of Rossini's works and recorded the opera *Zelmira* (1990). Other recordings include Vivaldi's *Orlando Furioso* and *La Cetra* by Marcello. He conducted *Il barbiere di Seviglia* at Caracalla, 1992.

Scipione/Scipio opera by Handel (libretto by P A Rolli, based on Zeno's *Scipione nelle Spagne*), produced London, King's Theatre, Haymarket, 12 March 1726. Roman proconsul Scipio successfully besieges New Carthage and falls in love with Berenice, a Spanish captive. But she loves Luceius, who is captured trying to rescue her. Scipio releases the couple after being impressed by the depth of Berenice's love.

Scipione Affricano opera by Cavalli (libretto by Minato), produced Venice, Teatro SS Giovanni e Paolo, 9 February 1664. Plot is similar to *Scipio*, with the addition of a sub-plot involving the efforts of King Syphax to rescue his abducted wife, Sophonisba.

scordatura (Italian 'mistuning') in music, tuning of the violin or other string instruments temporarily to other intervals than the normal perfect fifths, for the purpose of facilitating the playing of chords with certain intervals or altering the instrument's tone-quality. The music is still written as for the normal tuning (and fingering), so that the instrument becomes to that extent a transposing instrument (see ◊transposition).

There are many examples of scordatura in the violin works of Biber; also a famous passage for solo violin in Mahler's Fourth symphony.

score the orderly presentation of a musical composition in manuscript or printed form. A **full score** is a large-format conductor's score, a **short score** is condensed into fewer staves, a **piano score** is a reduction to two staves for a pianist-conductor, with remaining essentials in abbreviated form, and a **miniature** or **study score** is a full score photo-reduced to pocketbook size.

scoring see ◊orchestration.

Scotch snap the technical name for rhythmic figures inverting the order of dotted notes, the short note coming first instead of last. Its name in England, which is also Scots catch, is no doubt due to the fact that the Scotch snap is a feature in the Scottish Strathspey. It was popular in Italy in the 17th and 18th centuries and was called by German writers the 'Lombardy rhythm'.

Scott, Cyril (Meir) (1879–1970) English composer and poet. During the Edwardian era he was known as 'the English Debussy' on account of his harmonic lushness. In 1913 Alma Mahler, the composer's widow, invited him to Vienna, where he gave some performances. During World War I some of his works were produced in England and in 1925

The Scotch snap in the upper voice of a passage from Handel's Alcina.

the opera *The Alchemist* was performed, in German, at Essen.

He played the piano and began to compose as a child. He studied under Humperdinck and Knorr at the Hoch Conservatory, Frankfurt 1892–93 and 1895–98. In 1898 he settled at Liverpool as a pianist and gave some lessons, and soon after the turn of the century he began to become known as a composer in London, having some works performed and a number of songs and piano pieces published.

Later he wrote prose prolifically on subjects connected with yoga and philosophy. He wrote two autobiographies, *My Years of Indiscretion* 1924, and *Bone of Contention* 1969.

Works include: the opera *The Alchemist* (1917); ballet *The Incompetent Apothecary* (1923); *La Belle Dame sans merci* (Keats), *Nativity Hymn* (Milton), *Let us now praise famous men* for chorus and orchestra (1935); two symphonies, piano concerto, violin concerto; three string quartets; piano music, songs.

Scott, Marion M(argaret) (1877–1953) English musicologist. She studied at the Royal College of Music in London, 1896–1904, with which she afterwards remained associated as secretary of the Royal College of Music Union and editor of the *Royal College of Music Magazine*. She wrote criticism for various periodicals and many articles, notably on Haydn, in whose work she specialized. She also contributed a volume on Beethoven to the Master Musicians Series (1934).

Scott, Walter (1771–1832) Scottish poet and novelist. Celtic romance, a popular subject in the 19th century, was celebrated by Scott in his narrative poems, which were successful in translation throughout Europe. Turning later to the novel, often based on English history, he met with similar success. On a visit to Paris in 1826 Scott attended a pastiche of his *Ivanhoe* (1820) with music by Rossini; more faithful versions of the story were composed by Marschner (*Der Templer und die Jüdin*, 1829) and Sullivan (1891). The first major Italian

setting of Scott was Rossini's *La donna del lago* (1819) based on the poem of 1810, *The Lady of the Lake*. This was followed by Donizetti's *Elisabetta al castelio di Kenilworth* (1829) and the most successful setting of Scott, *Lucia di Lammermoor* (1835) based on *The Bride of Lammermoor* (1819). Notable French music derived from Scott includes the *Waverley* and *Rob Roy* overtures of Berlioz (1828, 1832) and Bizet's unjustly neglected opera *La Jolie fille de Perth* (1867), after Scott's *The Fair Maid of Perth*, 1828.

Settings *The Bride of Lammermoor*: **Adam** (*Le Caleb de Walter Scott*, 1827), **Carafa** (*Le nozze di Lammermoor*, 1829), **Donizetti** (*Lucia di Lammermoor*, 1835).

The Fair Maid of Perth: **Bizet** (*La Jolie Fille de Perth*, 1867).

The Heart of Midlothian: **Bishop** (1819), **Carafa** (*La Prison d'Edimbourg*, 1833), **F. Ricci** (*La prigione d'Edimburgo*, 1838).

Ivanhoe: **Marschner** (*Der Templer und die Jüdin*, 1829), **Nicolai** (*Il Templario*, 1840), **Pacini** (1832), **Sullivan** (1891).

Kenilworth: **Auber** (*Leicester*, 1823), **Donizetti** (*Elizabetta al castello di Kenilworth*, 1829).

The Lady of the Lake: **Bishop** (*The Knight of Snowdoun*, 1811), **Rossini** (*La donna del lago*, 1819).

Rob Roy: **Flotow** (1836).

The Italian: **Adam** (*Richard en Palestine*, 1844), **Balfe** (1874), **Bishop** (1826), **Pacini** (*Il Talismano, La terza crociata in Palestina*, 1829).

Also: overtures by **Berlioz**, *Rob Roy* (1832) and *Waverley* (1828), and eight songs by **Schubert** in German translation.

Scottish Fantasy work for violin and orchestra in four movements by Bruch, based on Scottish folksongs. Composed 1879–80 and dedicated to Sarasate, who gave the first performance in Hamburg, 1880.

'Scottish' Symphony Mendelssohn's third symphony, op. 56, in A minor and major, begun in Italy in 1831 and finished in Berlin, 20 January 1842; first performed Leipzig, Gewandhaus, 3 March 1842.

Scriabin alternative transcription of ◊Skriabin, Russian composer.

Scribe, Eugène (1791–1861) French playwright and librettist. He supplied many of the libretti for the most successful French operas of the 19th century, in particular the Parisian grand operas of Meyerbeer.

See ◊*Adriana Lecouvreur* (Cilea); ◊*Africaine, L'* (Meyerbeer); ◊*Ali Baba, ou Les Quarante Voleurs* (Cherubini); ◊*Ballo in maschera, Un* (Verdi); ◊*Chalet, Le* (Adam); ◊*Cheval de bronze, Le* (Auber); ◊*Comte Ory, Le* (Rossini); ◊*Dame blanche, La* (Boieldieu); ◊*Diamants de la Couronne, Les* (Auber); ◊*Domino noir* (Auber); ◊*Dom Sébastien, Roi de Portugal* (Donizetti); ◊*Elisir d'amore, L'* (ditto); ◊*Etoile du Nord, L'* (Meyerbeer); ◊*Favorite, La* (Donizetti); ◊*Fra Diavolo, ou L'Hôtellerie de Terracine* (Auber); ◊*Gustave III, ou Le Bal masqué* (ditto); ◊*Huguenots, Les* (Meyerbeer); ◊*Juive, La* (Halévy); ◊*Leicester, ou Le Château de Kenilworth* (Auber); ◊*Lortzing* (*Yelva*) (Auber); ◊*Maçon, Le* (Auber); ◊*Manon Lescaut* (Auber); ◊*Martyrs, Les* (Donizetti); ◊*Muette de Portici, La* (Auber); ◊*Philtre, Le* (Auber); ◊*Prophète, Le* (Meyerbeer); ◊*Robert le Diable* (Meyerbeer); A ◊*Schmitt* (*Trilby*); Giacomo Setaccioli (*Adrienne Lecouvreur*); ◊*Shebalin* (*Glass of Water*); ◊*Vêpres siciliennes, Les* (Verdi).

scroll the decorative, curved part of an instrument of the violin family, situated at the end of the fingerboard, away from the body of the instrument.

Sculthorpe, Peter (1929–) Australian composer. He studied at Melbourne University Conservatory and at Oxford University. In 1963 he became a lecturer at Sydney University.

Works include: the opera *Rites of Passage* (1971–73) and theatre music *Tatea* (1988); *Sun Music I* for orchestra; *Irkanda IV* for strings and percussion; *Sun Music II* for chorus and percussion (1969); *Mangrove* for orchestra (1979); piano concerto (1983); two sonatas for strings (1983, 1988); twelve string quartets (1947–88), string trio, piano trio; sonata for viola and percussion; piano sonatina.

Scylla et Glaucus opera by Leclair (libretto by d'Albaret), produced Paris, Opéra, 4 October 1746; revived London (concert) 1979. In pursuit of the nymph Scylla, Glaucus asks Circe for help but the jealous sorceress turns Scylla into the rock which accompanies the whirlpool Charybdis.

'Sea Drift' setting of a poem by Walt Whitman for baritone solo, chorus, and orchestra by Delius, composed 1903; in German, Essen Music Festival, 24 May 1906; in English, Sheffield Festival, 7 October 1908.

Sea Interludes (Britten). See ◊*Four Sea Interludes*.

Seal Woman, The opera by Bantock (libretto by Marjorie Kennedy Fraser), produced Birmingham, Repertory Theatre, 27 September 1924. A Celtic folk opera containing many traditional Hebridean tunes.

Sea Pictures song cycle for contralto and orchestra by Elgar, op. 37: 1. *Sea Slumber Song* (Roden Noel); 2. *In Haven* (Alice Elgar); 3. *Sabbath Morning at Sea* (Elizabeth Barrett Browning); 4. *Where Corals lie* (Richard Garnett); 5. *The Swimmer* (A L Gordon); first performed Norwich Festival, 5 October 1899, with Clara Butt.

Searle, Humphrey (1915–1982) English composer and writer on music. After studying with the serialist composer Anton Webern, he later employed 12-note methods extensively in his own music. He was a professor at the Royal College of Music 1965–77.

He was educated at Winchester College and Oxford University, and studied music with John Ireland at the Royal College of Music in London and in Vienna under Webern. In 1938 he joined the BBC, then served in the army 1940–46, and in 1947 became honorary secretary to the International Society for Contemporary Music.

Works include: the operas *The Diary of a Madman* (after Gogol, 1958), *The Photo of the Colonel* (after Ionesco, 1964), *Hamlet* (Shakespeare, 1968); ballets *The Great Peacock*, *Dualities*; *Gold Coast Customs* and *The Shadow of Cain* (Edith Sitwell) and *The Riverrun* (James Joyce) for speakers, chorus, and orchestra; *Jerusalem* for speaker, tenor, chorus, and orchestra (1970); five symphonies (1953–64), two suites and *Highland Reel* for orchestra; two nocturnes and two suites for chamber orchestra; piano concerto; *Intermezzo* for chamber ensemble, quintet for horn and strings; quartet for violin, viola, clarinet, and bassoon; sonata, *Vigil* and *Ballad* for piano; two Housman songs.

Seasons, The ballet by Glazunov (choreography by Petipa), produced St Petersburg, Maryinsky Theatre, 20 February 1900.

Oratorio (*Die Jahreszeiten*) by Haydn (German words by Gottfried van Swieten, based on Thomson's poem), composed 1798–1801; produced Vienna, Schwarzenberg Palace, 24 April 1801.

Sea Symphony, A the first symphony by Vaughan Williams, for solo voices, chorus, and orchestra (words by Walt Whitman), performed Leeds Festival, 12 October 1910.

Sebastiani, Claudius (died 1565) German music theorist. He held organist's posts at Fribourg and Metz, but is famous particularly for his treatise *Bellum Musicale*, published at Strasbourg in 1563.

Sebastiani, Johann (1622–1683) German composer. He went to Königsberg about 1650, where he became cantor in 1661 and was music director at the electoral church 1663–79. He wrote a Passion for voices and strings, with chorales included in a Passion setting for the first time.

He probably studied in Italy.

Works include: a Passion for voices and strings; sacred concertos for voices and instruments and other church music; wedding and funeral cantatas; sacred and secular songs *Parnass-Blumen*.

sec (French 'dry') term used by some French composers, especially Debussy, where a note or chord is to be struck and released again abruptly without any richness of tone.

secco (Italian 'dry') an abbreviation for recitativo secco, a 19th-century musical term for a type of recitative accompanied by a keyboard instrument, played from figured bass.

Sechter, Simon (1788–1867) Bohemian-Austrian theorist, organist, and composer. When the Italian musician Domenico Dragonetti was in Vienna in 1809, Sechter wrote piano accompaniments for his double bass concertos. In 1825 he succeeded Vořišek as court organist, and in 1850 became a professor at the Conservatory.

He settled in Vienna in 1804 and continued his studies there. In 1812 he became a teacher of piano and singing at the Institute for the Blind. He wrote several theoretical works.

Works include: the opera *Ali Hitsch-Hatsch* (1844); Masses, Requiem, and other church music; oratorios and cantatas; choruses from Schiller's *Braut von Messina*; chorale preludes, fugues, and other pieces for organ; variations, fugues, and other works for piano.

second an interval of two diatonic notes. A second is an 'imperfect interval' (having 'major' and 'minor' variants). A major second consists of two semitones (for example, C–D). A minor second consists of one semitone (C–D♭).

secondo (Italian 'second') the part of the second player in a piano duet, that of the first being called primo. Also as an adjective, applied to the second player of a pair or a group, as in *clarinetto secondo*.

second subject see ◊sonata.

Second Viennese School name given to a group of composers (namely Schoenberg, Berg, and Webern), working in Vienna during the first years of the 20th century, who developed the ◊atonality in its early stages and discovered the ◊twelve-tone system.

Secret, The/Tajemstvi opera by Smetana (libretto by E Krásnohorská), produced Prague, Czech Theatre, 18 September 1878. Kalina and Róza are finally united when Kalina discovers a secret passage leading to his beloved's house. In a subplot, Blaženka and Vít make public their secret love.

Sedaine, Michel Jean (1719–1797) French playwright and librettist. See ◊Aucassin et Nicolette (Grétry); ◊Grétry (Raoul Barbe-bleue); ◊Guillaume Tell (Grétry); J A Hiller ◊Jagd, Die; ◊Richard Cœur-de-Lion (Grétry).

Seeger, Charles (Louis) (1886–1979) US conductor, teacher, and composer. After conducting at the Cologne Opera in 1910, he was professor of music at California University 1912–19, and from 1958 he was engaged in research there. He wrote books on theory and ethnomusicology.

He studied at Harvard University.

Works include: masques *Derdra* and *The Queen's Masque*; overture *Shadowy Waters* for orchestra; chamber music; violin and piano sonata; numerous songs.

Segerstam, Leif (1944–) Finnish conductor and composer. He was principal conductor of the Austrian Radio Orchestra 1975–82, of the Finnish Radio Symphony Orchestra 1977–87, and of the Danish Radio Symphony Orchestra from 1989.

He studied at the Sibelius Academy, Helsinki, and the Juilliard School, New York. He was conductor of the Finnish National Opera, then Stockholm Royal Opera 1965–72, and the Deutsche Oper, Berlin 1971–73. He

Major, minor, and augmented seconds.

made his Salzburg Festival debut in 1971 with *Die Entführung*.

Works include: Divertimento for strings (1963), *Concerto Serioso* for violin and orchestra (1967), two piano concertos (1978, 1981), 16 symphonies (1977–90), six cello concertos, eight violin concertos, many works for orchestra under the title *Orchestral Diary Sheets*; *Song of Experience* after Blake and Auden for soprano and orchestra (1971); 26 string quartets (1962–82), two piano trios (1976–77), three string trios (1977–78), 22 Episodes for various instrumental combinations (1978–81).

Segni, Giulio (Giulio da Modena) (1498–1561) Italian composer. He composed three *ricercari à 4* (published in *Musica Nova* in 1540) and other instrumental works.

After a short period as organist of St Mark's, Venice, 1530–33, he entered the service of Pope Clement VII.

Segreto di Susanna, Il/Susanna's Secret opera by Wolf-Ferrari (libretto by E Golisciani), produced Munich, Court Opera, in German translation by Max Kalbeck, 4 December 1909. Susanna is a secret smoker and her jealous husband Count Gil suspects she has been harbouring a lover because of her mysterious disappearances (to the tobacconist's).

segue (Italian 'follows') an indication, like *attacca*, that a piece, number or section is to be played or sung immediately after another one. In manuscripts the word is sometimes used instead of *VS* (*volti subito*) where a blank space is left at the bottom of a page to avoid turning over during the performance of what follows on the next.

seguidilla Spanish dance dating back to at least the 16th century and first heard of in La Mancha, though possibly of earlier Moorish origin. The original form was the seguidilla manchega, but when the dance spread over Spain others developed: the seguidilla bolero, slow and stately, and the seguidilla gitana, slow and sentimental. The seguidilla is usually played on guitars, often with castanet accompaniment and sometimes with violin or flute. Frequently popular verses are sung to the seguidilla consisting of *coplas*, 'couplets' of four lines followed by *estribillos* 'refrains' of three lines.

Seiber, Mátyás (1905–1960) Hungarian-born British composer, conductor, and cellist. Influences in his music range from Bartók and Schoenberg to jazz. He is best known for

his cantata *Ulysses* 1947, based on a chapter from James Joyce's novel.

He was born in Budapest, and studied with Kodály at the Budapest Academy of Music 1919–24. After travelling abroad, including North and South America; he taught 1928–33 in the newly established jazz class at the Hoch Conservatory in Frankfurt. He also played cello in a string quartet there and conducted a theatre orchestra and a workers' chorus. In 1935 he settled in London as a choral conductor and film composer, and joined the teaching staff at Morley College.

Works include: the opera *Eva plays with Dolls* (1934); two operettas; incidental music for plays; film and radio music; *Missa brevis* for unaccompanied chorus); cantata *Ulysses* (Joyce, 1947); two Besardo Suites (from 16th-century lute tablatures), *Transylvanian Rhapsody* for orchestra; *Pastorale and concertante* for violin and strings (1944), *Notturno* for horn and strings; concertino for clarinet and strings; four Greek songs for voice and strings; three string quartets (1924, 1935, 1951), wind sextet, quintet for clarinet and strings, duo for violin and cello; fantasy for cello and piano, violin pieces; piano works; songs, choruses, folk-song arrangements.

Seidl, Anton (1850–1898) Hungarian-born German conductor. He conducted the first US performances of Wagner's operas *Tristan*, *Die Meistersinger*, and *The Ring* and the first performance of Dvořák's 'New World' symphony (1893).

He studied at the Leipzig Conservatory from 1870 and two years later went to Bayreuth as Wagner's assistant. After a period as conductor at the Leipzig Opera, 1879–82, he toured and conducted German opera at the Metropolitan Opera House in New York from 1885 to his death.

Selle, Thomas (1599–1663) German composer. He held various rector's and cantor's posts at Heide, Wesselburen, and Itzehoe, and finally at the Johanneum in Hamburg from 1641. His large output includes sacred and secular music.

Works include: Passion music including St John Passion (1641), the first Passion to include instrumental interludes; motets, sacred concertos; madrigals; sacred and secular songs.

Semele opera-oratorio by Handel (libretto by Congreve with anonymous alterations), performed London, Covent Garden, 10 February 1744. Congreve's libretto was originally intended for an opera. Revived Covent Garden 1982. After Semele aspires to immortality, jealous Juno tricks her into being consumed by the fire of her lover Jupiter.

semibreve, US whole note in music, a note value four times the duration of a ♩crotchet. It is written as an empty white note-head without a stem. Once the shortest-value note of medieval notation, it is now one of the longest commonly used.

semichorus group of singers detached from a chorus for the purpose of obtaining antiphonal effects or changes of tone colour. It does not often literally consist of half the voices, but is more usually a much smaller contingent.

semicroma Italian term for semiquaver.

semiotic analysis method of analysing music according to theories of meaning drawn from linguistics. In practice, the musical work is divided up ('segmented') into units which are then grouped into similar classes or paradigms; the relationships between these paradigms within and outside the work in question are then explored. There is no single technique of semiotic analysis; the method is distinguished by the desire to treat music as a structured, communicative form, and by the attempt to define the nature of musical meaning and relate it to meaning in other art forms.

semiquaver, US 16th note in music, a note value 1/16th the duration of a ♩semibreve. It is written as a filled black note-head with a stem and two flags (tails).

Semiramide/Semiramis opera by Rossini (libretto by Giacomo Rossi, based on Voltaire's tragedy), produced Venice, Teatro La Fenice, 3 February 1823. Queen of Babylon, Semiramide, murders her husband but dies at the hand of Arsace, her long-lost and unrecognized son.

Semiramide riconosciuta/Semiramis Recognized opera by Gluck (libretto by Metastasio), produced Vienna, Burgtheater, 14 May 1748. Also settings by Vinci (Rome, 1729) and Hasse (Venice, 1744). Semiramide rules Assyria disguised as a man, and eventually marries her former lover Scitalce after complications involving princess Tamiri and her suitors.

semiseria (Italian 'half-serious') in music, term used for a hybrid between *opera seria* and *opera buffa*.

semitone, or half tone or half step the smallest interval normally used in traditional Western music.

The octave is divided into 12 semitones.

semplice (Italian 'simple') in musical notation, a term indicating unaffected expression, without extremes.

Senallié, Jean Baptiste (1687–1730), or Senaillé French violinist and composer. He was a member of the French king Louis XIV's string orchestra, known as the '24 Violons du Roi'. He spent some time in Italy, and was one of the first composers to combine the French and Italian styles in his violin sonatas.

He studied under his father, Jean Senallié, who was a member of the royal orchestra, and with his father's colleague there, Queversin; later, probably, with Corelli's pupil Jean-Jacques-Baptiste Anet, and with Tomaso Vitali at Modena, where he was appointed to the ducal court. Later studied with Giovanni Antonio Piani (1678–c. 1757). He returned to Paris in 1720 and received an appointment at court under the regent, the Duke of Orleans, later confirmed under Louis XV.

Works include: about 50 sonatas for unaccompanied violin; violin sonatas with bass; pieces for violin and harpsichord.

Senfl, Ludwig (c. 1486–c. 1542) Swiss composer. He made imaginative arrangements of traditional German melodies, ranging from chordal harmonization to canons, and is regarded as the most important German-speaking composer of motets and songs during the Reformation.

He studied under Henricus Isaac in Vienna and sang 1496–1513 in the *Hofkapelle* of Maximilian I in Vienna, Augsburg, and Constance. He worked with Isaac in copying a large amount of music which was later published as part of Isaac's *Choralis constantinus* 1550–55, a task Senfl completed around 1520. In 1513 he succeeded Isaac as Kapellmeister to Emperor Maximilian I, holding the post until the emperor's death in 1519. In 1520 he went to Augsburg and in 1523 to Munich, where he settled as first musician at the ducal court of Wilhelm of Bavaria. In 1530 he was in correspondence with the religious reformer Martin Luther.

Works include: seven Masses, Magnificats, motets and other church music; odes by Horace for voices; about 250 German songs.

Senilov, Vladimir Alekseievich (1875–1918) Russian composer. He initially studied law, but went to Leipzig for musical studies under Riemann. He later worked under Glazunov and Rimsky-Korsakov at the St Petersburg Conservatory.

Works include: the operas *Vassily Buslaiev* and *Hippolytus* (after Euripides), music action *George the Bold*; symphony in D major, overture *In Autumn,* symphonic poems *The Wild Geese* (after Maupassant), *The Mtsyrs* (after Lermontov), *Pan, The Scythians* and *Variations on a Chant of the Old Believers* for orchestra; *Chole forsaken* for voice and orchestra; cantata *John of Damascus;* three string quartets; poems for cello and piano, scherzo for flute and piano.

sensible (French noun, or *note sensible*) in musical notation, leading note.

senza (Italian 'without') term used in musical notation, as in *senza tempo* ('without tempo'), meaning playing in a free tempo, or *senza sordino* ('without mute'), meaning, on a bowed string instrument, playing without the mute or, on a piano, using the ◊sustaining pedal, to release the dampers.

septet an ensemble of seven musicians, or the music written for such a group. For example, Beethoven's Septet in E 1823 is scored for violin, viola, cello, double bass, horn, clarinet, and bassoon.

Sept Haï-kaï̄ work by O Messiaen for piano, 13 wind instruments, xylophone, marimba, four percussion instruments, and eight violins; composed 1962, first performed Paris, 30 October 1963.

septimole or septuplet a group of seven notes to be fitted into a beat or other time-unit in which its number is irregular.

sequence a device allowing key ◊modulation favoured by early keyboard composers in which a phrase is repeated sequentially, each time transposing to a different key.

Serafin, Tullio (1878–1968) Italian conductor. He is chiefly remembered for his performances of Italian Romantic operas, especially those of Donizetti and Bellini, but also conducted the first performances of several new works by US composers at the Metropolitan Opera House, New York.

He studied at the Milan Conservatory and made his debut at Ferrara in 1900. In 1909 he became conductor at La Scala, Milan, and gave the Italian premieres of *Der Rosenkavalier* and *Oberon.* He conducted *La Bohème, Carmen,* and *La Gioconda* at Covent Garden in 1907, returning in 1931 for *Falstaff, Fedra, La forza del destino,* and *La Traviata.* From 1924 he was one of the chief conductors at the New York Metropolitan Opera, where he conducted the first performances of operas by Deems Taylor, Louis Gruenberg, and Howard Hanson with the US first performances of *Turandot* and *Simon Boccanegra.* He returned to Italy in 1935, where he worked mostly in Milan and Rome, conducting operas by Pizzetti, Alfano, Berg, and Britten. He also appeared in Paris and London, conducting *Lucia* at Covent Garden in 1959.

Serafino, Giorgio (lived 18th century) Italian violin maker who worked in Venice.

Serafino, Santo (lived 17th–18th centuries) Italian violin maker, uncle of Giorgio ◊Serafino. He worked in Udine around 1678–98, and then in Venice until around 1735.

serenade musical piece for chamber orchestra or wind instruments in several movements, originally intended for informal evening entertainment, such as Mozart's *Eine kleine Nachtmusik/A Little Night Music.*

Serenade work for violin, percussion, and strings by L Bernstein, after Plato's *Symposium,* first performed Venice, 12 September 1954, with Isaac Stern.

Serenade for Tenor, Horn, and Strings song cycle by Britten (texts by Cotton, Tennyson, Blake, Jonson, and Keats, all on the theme of night), first performed London, 15 October 1943, with Dennis Brain and Peter Pears.

Serenaden, Die cantata by Hindemith for soprano, oboe, viola, and cello (texts by A Licht, J L W Gleim, L Tieck, J von Eichendorff, J W Meinhold, and S A Mahlmann), first performed Winterthur, 15 April 1925.

Serenade to Music work by Vaughan Williams for 16 solo voices and orchestra (text from *The Merchant of Venice*); composed 1938 for the jubilee of Henry Wood and conducted by him London, 5 October 1938. Version for orchestra performed London 10 February 1940, conductor Wood.

serenata actually the Italian word for serenade, but used in English with a specific meaning for 18th-century works, often of an occasional or congratulatory type, either produced on the stage as small topical and allegorical operas or at concerts (and even then sometimes in costume) in the manner of a secular cantata.

seria (Italian 'serious') see ◊opera seria.

An example of a sequence from Handel's Acis and Galatea.

serialism a later form of the ◊twelve-tone system of composition.

It usually refers to post-1950 compositions in which further aspects such as dynamics, durations, and attacks are brought under serial control. These other series may consist of fewer than 12 degrees while some pitch series can go higher.

series the numerical expression of note orders of a ◊tone row, related to a starting ◊pitch of 1. The US composer Milton ◊Babbitt introduced a convention of numbering a series as intervals from zero (unison with the starting note) to a maximum of 11 half-steps or semitones.

Serly, Tibor (1901–1978) Hungarian-born US composer. He worked as a violinist and conductor in the USA. He completed the last bars of Bartók's 3rd piano concerto and in 1945 made a version of Bartók's viola concerto from the surviving sketches.

After being taken to the USA as a child in 1905 and becoming a citizen in 1911, he returned to Budapest 1922–24 to study with Bartók and Kodály. On his return to the USA he played the violin with the Philadelphia Orchestra 1928–35. He played with the National Broadcasting Company Symphony Orchestra under Toscanini and befriended Bartók when he arrived in New York as a refugee.

Sermisy, Claudin de (c. 1490–1562), usually known as Claudin French composer. He was master of the choristers at the French royal chapel, and wrote about 110 sacred works, including motets, Masses, and a Passion. His reputation, however, both during his lifetime and since, has rested on his chansons, of which about 175 survive. They have attractive melodies and are simpler and more homophonic and syllabic in style than those of his contemporaries. Many of them were arranged by other composers for a variety of vocal and instrumental forces.

He was attached to the Sainte-Chapelle in Paris 1508–14, and in 1515 became a singer in the royal chapel just before Louis XII's death, and in the same year his choir competed with the Papal choir before Leo X; he later succeeded Antoine de Longueval as master of the choristers. In 1520, with François I, he met the English king Henry VIII at the Field of the Cloth of Gold. A similar meeting followed in 1532 at Boulogne; and on both occasions the French and English choirs sang together.In 1533 he was made a canon of the Sainte-Chapelle, with a living and a substantial salary attached to it; but his duties there

were light and he remained in the royal chapel, with which, under François I, he visited Bologna.

Works include: 11 Masses, motets; about 175 chansons for several voices.

Serocki, Kazimierz (1922–1981) Polish composer. He appeared in Europe as a pianist 1950–52, but later devoted himself to composition in a modernist idiom, including aleatory devices.

He studied at Łódź and later with Nadia Boulanger 1947–48.

Works include: two symphonies (1952, 1953; second for soprano, baritone, chorus, and orchestra), *Triptych* for orchestra; piano concerto, trombone concerto; choral music; *Episodes* for strings and three percussion groups, *Segmenti* for chamber ensemble and percussion (1960); *Symphonic Frescoes* (1963); *Dramatic Story* for orchestra (1971); *Ad Libitum*, five pieces for orchestra (1976); *Pianophonie* for piano and electronics (1978); chamber music.

Serov, Aleksandr Nikolaievich (1820–1871) Russian composer and critic. He greatly admired Wagner, and disliked the Russian nationalist composers. Among his own compositions, the operas *Judith* 1863, and *Rogneda* 1865 were highly successful, and had a pronounced effect on later composers.

He studied law, but found time to cultivate music, which eventually, after a career as a civil servant, he took up professionally. He studied cello and theory from around 1840 and began an opera on Shakespeare's *Merry Wives of Windsor* in 1843, but was reduced to taking a correspondence course of musical instruction when transferred to Simferopol. He became a music critic and in 1858, when he returned from a visit to Germany as an ardent admirer of Wagner, he began to attack the Russian nationalist school of composers, but found a powerful opponent in Vladimir Stasov. He was over 40 when he began his first opera. When he died from heart disease, he had just begun a fourth opera, based on Gogol's *Christmas Eve Revels*.

He married the composer Valentina Semionovna Bergman (1846–1927), who wrote some operas of her own, including *Uriel Acosta* (based on Gutzkow's play).

Works include: the operas *Judith* (1863), *Rogneda* (1865), *The Power of Evil* (after Ostrovsky's play; orchestration finished by Soloviev, 1871); incidental music to Nikolai Pavlovich Zhandr's tragedy *Nero*; *Stabat Mater* and *Ave Maria*; *Gopak, Dance of the*

Zaporogue Cossacks, and other orchestral works.

serpent keyed tubular brass or wooden musical instrument of the cornett family, played with a cup mouthpiece, originating in the 16th century, probably in France. It has a distinctive S-shape (resembling a serpent, hence its name) and became popular as a church and military band instrument. It was superseded in the 19th century by the ◊ophicleide and tuba, but has seen a revival in the 20th century as a result of the ◊authenticity movement.

Serse/Xerxes opera by Handel (libretto by N Minato, altered), produced London, King's Theatre, Haymarket, 15 April 1738. It contains the famous so-called *Largo*, 'Ombra mai fù'. The original libretto was that for Cavalli's *Xerse* (1654). King Xerxes of Persia falls in love with Romilda, who is in love with Arsamene. After complications, the lovers are allowed to marry when Amastre, who was earlier jilted by Xerxes, arrives to reclaim him.

See also ◊*Xerse*.

Serva padrona, La/The Maid as Mistress intermezzo by Paisiello (libretto by G A Federico), produced St Petersburg, Hermitage, at court, 10 September 1781. Serpina tricks her master Uberto into marriage, when she threatens to run away with a soldier, in fact servant Vespone in disguise.

Intermezzo by Pergolesi (libretto ditto), produced Naples, Teatro San Bartolommeo, between the acts of Pergolesi's serious opera *Il prigionier superbo*, 28 August 1733.

service term implying the setting of those parts of the services of the Anglican Church which lend themselves to musical treatment, that is, the Morning Prayer, Evening Prayer (Magnificat and Nunc dimittis) and Communion.

Servilia opera in five acts by Rimsky-Korsakov (libretto by composer, based on a play by L A Mey), produced St Petersburg, 14 October 1902. Daughter of Neronian senator converts to Christianity and provides an example for many noble Romans.

sesquialtera in musical notation, short for *pars sesquialtera*, 'a quantity 1 1/2 times as much'; in mensural notation the proportion 3:2. See also ◊proportion.

Sessions, Roger Huntington (1896–1985) US composer. His international Modernist style secured a US platform for serious German influences, including Hindemith and Schoenberg, and offered an alternative

to the lightweight, fashionable Modernism of Milhaud and Paris. An able symphonist, his works include *The Black Maskers* (incidental music) 1923, eight symphonies, and *Concerto for Orchestra* 1971.

Born in Brooklyn, New York, he attended Harvard and Yale Universities, then studied under Ernest Bloch. In 1917–21 he taught at Smith College, Northampton, Massachusetts, and was head of the theoretical department of the Cleveland Institute of Music 1921–25. He lived in Italy and Germany 1925–33. He became a leading teacher of composition, serving on the faculties of Boston University, Princeton University 1935–44 and 1953–65, the University of California at Berkeley, and the Juilliard School, New York 1965–85.

Works include: ORCHESTRAL AND CHAMBER: nine symphonies (1927–80), three dirges for orchestra; violin concerto (1940), piano concerto, concerto for orchestra (1981); two string quartets (1935, 1951), piano trio; sonata and three chorale preludes for organ; two sonatas and pieces for piano; songs to words by James Joyce and others.

set old English name for the suite. Also a series, normally of pitches but also of rhythms or other musical parameters, used in the composition of a piece. See also ◊serialism.

set complex in pitch-class set analysis, a group of sets related to each other by being subsets or supersets of a single 'nexus set'.

Sette canzoni/Seven Songs opera by Malipiero (libretto by composer), produced, in French version by Henry Prunières, Paris, Opéra, 10 July 1920. Part II of the operatic cycle *L'Orfeide*; a series of contrasting moral and emotional principles, drawn from the composer's own life.

Settle, Elkanah (1648–1724) English poet and dramatist. See J ◊Clarke (*World in the Moon*, with D Purcell); ◊*Fairy Queen* (Purcell); Gottfried ◊Finger (*Virgin Prophetess*).

seventh an ◊interval of seven diatonic notes. A seventh is an 'imperfect interval' (having 'major' and 'minor' variants). A major seventh consists of eleven semitones (for example, C–B♮). A minor seventh consists of ten semitones (C–B♭).

'Seven, They are Seven' Akkadian Incantation for tenor, chorus, and orchestra by Prokofiev, op. 30 (text by K Balmont), composed 1917–18, first performed Paris, 29 May 1924, conductor Koussevitzky.

Seven Words of the Saviour on the Cross, The, or *The Seven Last Words* orchestral

Major, minor, and diminished sevenths.

work by Haydn consisting of seven slow movements, commissioned by Cádiz Cathedral in 1785 as musical meditations for a three-hour service on Good Friday. Later arranged by Haydn for string quartet (op. 51, 1787) and as a choral work (1796). Oratorio by Schütz (*The Seven Words of Christ*) (words from the four Gospels plus two verses of a chorale), composed 1645.

Séverac, (Joseph Marie) Déodat de (1873–1921) French composer. He studied at the Toulouse Conservatory and with Magnard and d'Indy at the Schola Cantorum, Paris. He returned to the south of France and devoted himself entirely to composition, neither his health nor his taste permitting him to hold any official position.

Works include: the opera *Le Cœur du moulin* (1909); ballet *La Fête des vendanges*; incidental music for Sicard's *Héliogabale* and for Verhaeren's *Hélène de Sparte*; *Ave, verum corpus* and other church music; *Chant de vacances* for chorus; string quintet; 19 songs to poems by Ronsard, Verlaine, Maeterlinck ,and Poe.

sevillana/Spanish Andalusian folk-song type similar to the seguidilla and originally confined to Seville.

sextet an ensemble of six musicians, or music written for such a group. Brahms wrote several string sextets.

sextolet group of six notes, or double triplet, when used in a composition or movement whose time-unit is normally divisible into two, four, or eight note-values.

sextuplet a group of six notes of equal length, played (usually) in the time of four. It is indicated by a ◊slur over the six notes with the number '6' written above.

sextus in old vocal music, the sixth part in a composition for six or more voices, always equal in compass to one of the voices in a four-part composition: soprano, alto, tenor, or bass.

Seyfried, Ignaz Xaver von (1776–1841) Austrian composer, teacher, and conductor. He conducted and composed music for Schikaneder's theatre at Vienna 1797–1828, and in 1806 he conducted the first revival of Beethoven's opera *Fidelio* there. As a compo-

ser he was known for the quantity, rather than the quality, of his output.

Originally intended for a legal career, he turned to music, and studied piano with Mozart and Kozeluch, and composition with Albrechtsberger and Winter. From 1797 to 1828 he was conductor and composer to Schikaneder's theatre (from 1801 known as the Theater an der Wien). After his retirement he composed almost exclusively church music. He also edited Albrechtsberger's theoretical works and in 1832 published an account of Beethoven's studies in figured bass, counterpoint, and composition.

Works include: over 100 operas and *Singspiele*, including *Der Löwenbrunnen*, *Der Wundermann am Rheinfall* (1799), *Die Ochsenmenuette* (pasticcio arranged from Haydn's works, 1823), *Ahasverus* (arranged from piano works of Mozart); biblical dramas; incidental music to Schiller's *Die Räuber* and *Die Jungfrau von Orleans*, and others; about 20 Masses, Requiem, motets, and other church music; *Libera me* for Beethoven's funeral.

Sf. in musical notation, abbreviation for *sforzando*.

sfogato (Italian 'airy') in musical direction, an indication of a delicate and ethereal performance of certain passages; composers, such as Chopin sometimes used this. Also an adjective, especially *soprano sfogato*, 'light soprano'.

sforzando, or sforzato; sf or sfz (Italian 'forcing') in musical notation, a sudden accent placed on a single note or chord. Its loudness depends on the surrounding dynamics. For example, if the dynamic marking prior to 'sforzando' is 'piano' (soft), then it is not accented as loudly as if the prior marking were 'forte' (loud).

Sfz. in musical notation, abbreviation for *sforzando*.

Shahrazad/Sheherazade symphonic suite by Rimsky-Korsakov on the subject of the story-teller in the *Arabian Nights* and of some of the tales, op. 35, finished summer 1888 and produced St Petersburg, 3 November 1888. Ballet based on it (choreographed by Mikhail Fokin, settings by Leon Bakst), produced Paris, Opéra, 4 June 1910. See ◊*Shéhérazade*.

shake an alternative name for ◊trill, in which two adjacent notes rapidly alternate.

Shakespeare, William (1564–1616) English poet and dramatist. Among works based on his plays are:

Antony and Cleopatra: ◊Barber (opera, 1966); R ◊Kreutzer (ballet, *Amours d'Antoine et de Cléopâtre*, 1808); ◊Malipiero (opera, 1938); ◊Prokofiev (Symphonic Suite, *Egyptian Nights*, 1934).

As You Like It: ◊Veracini (opera, *Rosalinda*, 1744).

Comedy of Errors: ◊Storace (opera, *Gli equivoci*, 1786).

Coriolanus: Ján Cikker (opera, 1974).

Cymbeline: ◊Schubert (*Hark, hark, the lark*, 1826); ◊Zemlinsky (incidental music, 1914).

Hamlet: ◊Berlioz (*La Mort d'Ophélie* and *Marche funèbre* from *Tristia*, 1848); ◊Blacher (ballet, 1950); ◊Bridge (*There is a willow* for orchestra, 1928); Faccio (opera, 1865); ◊Liszt (symphonic poem, 1858); ◊Mercadante (opera, 1822); ◊Searle (opera, 1967); ◊Shostakovich (incidental music, 1931, and suite, 1932); ◊Szokolay (opera, 1969); ◊Tchaikovsky (Fantasy overture, 1888); Ambrose ◊Thomas (opera, 1868); ◊Walton (film music, 1947).

Henry IV, parts 1 and 2: ◊Elgar (*Falstaff*, symphonic study, 1913); ◊Holst (opera, *At the Boar's Head*, 1925); ◊Mercadante (opera, *La gioventù di Enrico V*, 1834); ◊Pacini (opera, ditto, 1820).

Henry V: ◊Vaughan Williams (*Thanksgiving for Victory*, 1945); ◊Walton (film music, 1944).

Julius Caesar: ◊Klebe (opera, *Die Ermordrung Cäsars*, 1959); ◊Malipiero (opera, 1936); ◊Schumann (overture, 1851).

King Lear: ◊Berlioz (overture, 1831); Frazzi (opera, *Re Lear*, 1939); ◊Ghislanzoni (opera, ditto, 1937); ◊Reimann (opera, *Lear*, 1978); ◊Shostakovich (incidental music, 1940).

Love's Labours Lost: ◊Nabokov (opera, 1973).

Macbeth: ◊Bloch (opera, 1910); ◊Collingwood (opera, 1934); ◊Strauss (tone poem, 1890); ◊Verdi (opera, 1847).

Measure for Measure: ◊Wagner (opera, *Das Liebesverbot*, 1836).

Merchant of Venice: ◊Castelnuovo-Tedesco (opera, *Il mercante di Venezia*, 1961); ◊J B Foerster (opera, *Jessika*, 1905); ◊Vaughan Williams (*Serenade to Music*, 1938).

Merry Wives of Windsor: Adolphe ◊Adam (opera, *Falstaff*, 1856); ◊Balfe (opera, ditto, 1838); ◊Dittersdorf (opera, *Die lustigen Weiber von Windsor und der dicke Hans*, 1796); ◊Nicolai (opera, *Die lustigen Weiber von Windsor*, 1849); ◊Salieri (opera, *Falstaff osia le tre burle*, 1799); ◊Vaughan Williams (opera, *Sir John in Love*, 1929); ◊Verdi (opera, *Falstaff*, 1893).

Midsummer Night's Dream: ◊Britten (opera, 1960); ◊Mendelssohn (incidental music, 1842; overture written 1826); ◊Orff (incidental

Various shakes and their approximate realizations.

music, 1939; commissioned under the Nazi régime to replace Mendelssohn's music); ◊Purcell (*The Fairy Queen*, 1692); Elie Siegmeister (opera, *Night of the Moonspell*, 1976).

Much Ado About Nothing: ◊Berlioz (opera, *Béatrice et Bénédict*, 1862); ◊Stanford (opera, 1901).

Othello: ◊Blacher (ballet, *Der Mohr von Venedig*, 1955); ◊Dvořák (overture, 1892); ◊Rossini (opera – last act only after Shakespeare – 1816); ◊Verdi (opera, 1887).

Richard III: ◊Smetana (symphonic poem, 1856); ◊Walton (film music, 1954).

Romeo and Juliet: ◊Bellini (opera, *I Capuleti e i Montecchi*, based on Shakespeare's sources, 1830); ◊Berlioz (dramatic symphony, 1839); ◊Blacher (scenic oratorio, 1947; revised as opera, 1950); ◊Gounod (opera, 1867); ◊Malipiero (opera, 1950); ◊Prokofiev (ballet, 1938); ◊Sutermeister (opera, 1940); ◊Tchaikovsky (Fantasy overture, 1869, revised 1870 and 1880); ◊Vaccai (opera, 1825); ◊Zandonai (opera, 1922); ◊Zingarelli (opera, 1796).

Taming of the Shrew: ◊Götz (opera, *Der Widerspänstigen Zähmung*, 1874); ◊Wolf-Ferrari (opera, *Sly*, 1927).

Tempest: ◊Arne (incidental music, 1740); ◊Eaton (opera, 1985); Jacques ◊Halévy (opera, *La Tempestà*, 1850); ◊Martin (opera, *Der Sturm*, 1956); ◊Sibelius (incidental music, 1924); ◊Sutermeister (opera, *Die Zauberinsel*, 1942); ◊Tchaikovsky (Symphonic fantasy, 1873); John ◊Weldon (incidental music, 1712; formerly attributed to Purcell), ◊Winter (opera, *Der Sturm*, 1798); ◊Zumsteeg (opera, *Die Geisterinsel*, 1798).

Timon of Athens: Antonio ◊Draghi (1634–1700) (opera, *Timone misantropo*, 1696); *Oliver* (opera, 1991).

Troilus and Cressida: ◊Zillig (opera, 1951).

Twelfth Night: ◊Smetana (opera, *Viola*, 1874–84, unfinished; produced 1924).

Two Gentlemen of Verona: ◊Schubert (*An Sylvia*, 1826).

Winter's Tale: Max ◊Bruch (opera, *Hermione*, 1872), Karoly ◊Goldmark (opera, *Ein Wintermärchen*, 1908).

shakuhachi end-blown, notched bamboo flute of Japan. The modern version, originating from around the 15th century, has four finger-holes and one thumb-hole. It is used for meditative solos, in ensembles, folksong, and in modern works by composers worldwide. The shakuhachi is manufactured in a graduated series of sizes a semitone apart; the size used depends on the genre, the other performers/instruments (if any) and the personal preference of the player.

Shankar, Ravi (1920–) Indian composer and musician. A virtuoso of the ◊sitar, he has been influential in popularizing Indian music in the West. He has composed two concertos for sitar and orchestra 1971 and 1981, and film music, including scores for Satyajit Ray's *Pather Panchali* 1955 and Richard Attenborough's *Gandhi* 1982, and founded music schools in Bombay and Los Angeles.

He worked first with a group of musicians and dancers led by his brother, Uday Shankar (1900–77). He founded the National Orchestra of All-India Radio and was founder-director of the Kinnara School of Music at Bombay in 1962. Other compositions include the opera-ballet *Ghanashyam/A Broken Branch*, premiered by the City of Birmingham Touring Opera in 1989.

Shapero, Harold (Samuel) (1920–) US composer and pianist. His music includes elements of jazz and serialism.

He studied with Nicolas Slonimsky at Boston 1936–38 and with Krenek and Piston at Harvard. He was appointed professor of music at Brandeis University in 1952 and founded an electronic music studio there.

Works include: *Symphony for Classical Orchestra* (1947); *On Green Mountain* for jazz ensemble (1957; version for orchestra 1981); *Studies* for piano and synthesizer (1969); *Hebrew Cantata* (1954); piano music and songs.

Shaporin, Yuri Aleksandrovich (1887– 1966) Russian composer. Educated at St Petersburg, where he graduated in law at the university. In 1913 he entered the Conservatory there, studying under Sokolov, Steinberg, and N Tcherepnin. On leaving he became interested in stage music and founded the Great Dramatic Theatre with Gorky and Blok. In 1937 he moved to Moscow.

Works include: the opera *The Decembrists* (libretto by A N Tolstoy, 1953); incidental music for Shakespeare's *King Lear* and *Comedy of Errors*, Schiller's *Robbers*, Molière's *Tartuffe*, Pushkin's *Boris Godunov*, Beaumarchais' *Marriage of Figaro*, Turgenev's *The Nest of Gentlefolk* (*Liza*), Labiche's *The Playian Straw Hat*; film music including *General Suvarov*; symphonic cantata *On the Kulikov Field* (1939); symphony in E minor, suite *The Flea* for orchestra, two suites for piano; song cycles to words by Pushkin and Tiutchev, and other songs.

sharp sounding higher in pitch than the indicated note value, or than expected. A sharp sign (♯) in front of a written note indicates that it is to be raised by a semitone. It is cancelled by a natural sign (♮).

Sharp, Cecil (James) (1859–1924) English collector and compiler of folk songs and dances. He visited the USA 1916–18 to collect songs in the Appalachian mountains, where many English songs were still preserved in their early form by descendants of 17th-century emigrants. His work ensured that the English folk-music revival became established throughout the English-speaking world.

He led a movement to record a threatened folk-song tradition for posterity, publishing *English Folk Song* (1907; two volumes).

He was educated at Uppingham and Clare College, Cambridge. After living in Australia 1889–92, he returned to London and in 1896 became principal of the Hampstead Conservatory. In 1899 he began to collect folk songs and dances; later he joined the Folk Song Society and in 1911 founded the English Folk-Dance Society.

shawm member of a family of double-reed conical bore musical instruments of piercing tone. The Renaissance shawm emerged around 1200 as a consort instrument, the reed enclosed by a ◊windcap. It was a forerunner of the ◊oboe.

Shchedrin, Rodion (1932–) Russian composer. He studied at the Moscow Conservatory with Shaporin, graduating in 1955.

Works include: the opera *Not for Love Alone* (1961), *Dead Souls* (1976), *Lolita* (1994); ballets *The Little Hump-backed Horse* (1955), *Carmen Suite* (1968), and *Anna Karenina* (1972); two symphonies (1958, 1964); Musical Offering for organ and ensemble (1982); three piano concertos; oratorio *Poetoria* for poet, woman's voice, chorus, and orchestra (1968); cantata *Lenin Lives* (1972), piano quintet, two string quartets, 24 Preludes and Fugue for piano (1963–70); songs.

Shebalin, Vissarion Yakovlevich (1902–1963) Russian composer. He was director of the Moscow Conservatory 1942–58, but was sacked after being denounced by Stalinists, as a formalist (along with other leading contemporary composers in the USSR).

He was the son of a teacher, and received his first musical training at the Omsk School of Music. In 1923 he entered the Moscow Conservatory as a pupil of Miaskovsky and stayed there as a professor in 1928, as well as teaching at the Gnessin School of Music.

Works include: the operas *The Taming of the Shrew* (1957), *Sun over the Steppes* (1958), comic opera *The Embassy Bridegroom* (1942);

incidental music for Schiller's *Die Räuber* and *Mary Stuart*, Pushkin's *Mozart and Salieri* and *The Stone Guest* (Don Juan), Lermontov's *Masquerade*, Scribe's *A Glass of Water*, and others; film music; symphonic cantata *Lenin* for solo voices, chorus, and orchestra; five symphonies (1925–62), two suites and two overtures for orchestra; violin concerto, concertinos for violin and strings and for harp and small orchestra; nine string quartets (1923–63), string trio; sonatina for violin and viola, suite for solo violin; two piano sonatas and three sonatinas; songs (including settings of works by Pushkin and Heine), popular choruses and war songs.

Sheherazade (Rimsky-Korsakov). See ◊*Shahrazad*.

Shéhérazade song cycle with orchestra by Ravel (poems by Tristan Klingsor), composed 1903 on the basis of an unpublished overture of the same name of 1898. There are three songs: *Asie*, *La Flûte enchantée* and *L'indifférent*. First performed Paris, 17 May 1904.

Shekhter, Boris Semionovich (1900–1961) Russian composer, a pupil of Miaskovsky at the Moscow Conservatory. He made a close study of Turkmen folk music, and based some of his works on it.

Works include: the operas *The Year 1905* (with Davidenko, 1935) and *The Son of the People*; suite *Turkmenia* for orchestra, five symphonies (1929–51, including symphony *Dithyramb* for the 20th anniversary of the Russian revolution; piano concerto; song cycles.

Shepherds of the Delectable Mountains, The opera by Vaughan Williams (libretto by composer, based on Bunyan's *Pilgrim's Progress*), produced London, RCM, 11 July 1922. Pilgrim on way to Celestial City is summoned by heavenly messenger and is duly anointed by three Shepherds, who assist his journey on the River of Death. See ◊*Pilgrim's Progress, The*.

shepherd's pipe rustic wind instrument similar to the oboe, the French ◊musette, played with a double reed, like the chanter of a bagpipe, but usually used separately.

Sheppard, John (c. 1515–c. 1563) English composer. In 1542 he became organist and choirmaster at Magdalen College, Oxford, and later was in Queen Mary's Chapel Royal.

He learnt music as a choirboy at St Paul's Cathedral in London under Thomas Mulliner.

Works include: Masses *The Western Wynde*, *The French Masse*, *Be not afraide*, and *Playn Song Mass for a Mene*, 21 Office responds, 18 hymns, motets, two Te Deums, two Magnificats, anthems, and other choral pieces.

Shield, William (1748–1829) English violinist and composer. He embarked on a career as a violinist, but from 1778 produced his own works with great success at London theatres. His most popular piece was the opera *Rosina* 1782.

Orphaned at the age of nine, he was apprenticed to a shipbuilder, but studied music with Charles Avison in Newcastle-upon-Tyne, where he also appeared as a solo violinist and led the subscription concerts from 1763. After engagements in Scarborough and Stockton-on-Tees he went to London as second violin of the Opera orchestra in 1772, becoming principal viola the following year. After the success of his first opera, *The Flitch of Bacon* 1778, he was appointed composer to Covent Garden Theatre 1778–91 and again 1792–1807. In 1791 he met Haydn in London, and visited France and Italy. Two treatises, on harmony and thorough-bass, were published 1800 and 1817, in which year he was appointed Master of the King's Musick.

Works include: over 50 works for the stage, including *The Flitch of Bacon* (1778), *Rosina* (1782), *Robin Hood* (1784), *Richard Cœur de Lion* (1786), *The Marriage of Figaro* (after Beaumarchais, 1797), *Aladdin*, *The Woodman* (1791), *The Travellers in Switzerland* (1794), *Netley Abbey*, *The Italian Villagers*; string quartets and trios; violin duets; songs.

Shifrin, Seymour J (1926–1979) US composer. His music is known for its chromatic intensity.

He studied with Otto Luening and William Schuman, and taught at Brandeis University, Massachusetts, from 1966.

Works include: Chamber Symphony (1953), three pieces for orchestra (1958), *Five Last Songs* (1979); five string quartets (1949–72), piano trio (1974), *A Renaissance Garland* (1975), *The Nick of Time* for ensemble (1978).

Shnitke, Alfred Garriyevich (1934–), or Schnittke Russian composer. He has experimented with ◊integral serialism and unusual instrumental textures, which are characteristically rich with a prominent use of strings, often using quotations and parodies. Among his many works are ... *pianissimo* ... 1969 for orchestra, *Sinfonia* 1972, the oratorio *Nagasaki* 1958, and *Minnesang/Lovesong* 1981 for 48 voices.

He studied in Vienna and at the Moscow Conservatory; and taught at the latter 1961–72. His music often plays on the dichotomy between reality and illusion. For example, his cadenza of the Beethoven violin concerto strikes a sensitive balance between an orderly traditional formula and atonal disintegration. He has adopted the term 'polystylism', to describe music which is many-layered and highly allusive.

The operas *Historia von Dr Johann Fausten* and *Gesualdo* were premiered at Hamburg and Vienna respectively in 1995.

Works include: the operas *Life with an Idiot* (1992), *Historia von Dr Johann Fausten* (1995), and *Gesualdo* (1995); eight symphonies: no. 1 (1969–72), no. 2 *St Florian* for small chorus and orchestra (1979), no. 3 (1981), no. 4 for SATB soloists and chamber orchestra (1984), no. 5 (*Concerto Grosso*, no. 4 (1988), no. 6 (1992), no. 7 (1993), no. 8 (1994); four violin concertos (1957–82), piano concerto (1960), concerto for piano and strings, five concerti grossi (1977, 1982, 1985, 1988, 1991), two cello concertos (1986, 1990), (*Ein Sommernachtstraum* for orchestra (1985), *Epilogue, Peer Gynt* for orchestra and tape (1987), Trio-Sonata (orchestration of string trio, 1987); two oratorios, *Nagasaki* (1958) and *Songs of War and Peace* (1959); *Der gelbe Klang* for nine instruments, tape, chorus, and light projection, after Kandinsky; *Requiem* (1975), *Minnesang* (Lovesong) for 48 voices a cappella (1981), *Seid nüchtern und wachet* ... based on the Faust legend of 1587, for chorus (1983); two violin sonatas (1963, 1968), three string quartets (1966, 1981, 1984); cello sonata (1978), *Moz-art* for two violins; *Stille Musik* for violin and cello (1979), Septet for flute, two clarinets, and string quartet (1982), string trio (1985), piano quartet (1988); *Moz-art à la Mozart* for eight flutes and harpsichord (1990).

short octave the bottom octave on an old keyboard instrument, where the notes governed by the extreme bottom keys are sometimes not tuned to the ordinary scale, but to a selection of lower notes more likely to be frequently required.

An example of the possible appearance and tuning of a short octave.

short score see ◊score.

Shostakovich, Dmitri Dmitrievich (1906–1975) Russian composer. His music is tonal, expressive, and sometimes highly dramatic; it was not always to official Soviet taste. He wrote 15 symphonies, chamber and film music, ballets, and operas, the latter including *Lady Macbeth of the Mtsensk District* 1934, which was suppressed as 'too divorced from the proletariat', but revived as *Katerina Izmaylova* 1963. His symphonies are among the greatest of the 20th century.

His son Maxim (1938–), a conductor, defected to the West after his father's death.

Shostakovich was born in St Petersburg. He entered the conservatory there in 1919 and studied with Leonid Vladimirovich Nikolaiev (1878–1942), Maximilian Steinberg, and Alexander Glazunov; he left in 1925, having already written a great many works. The first symphony, which dates from that year, was performed in 1926 and subsequently throughout Europe, quickly establishing his reputation internationally. He came into conflict with Soviet authority in 1930, when his opera, *The Nose*, based on a story by Gogol, was denounced as bourgeois and decadent. The next, *Lady Macbeth of the Mtsensk District*, produced in 1934, was even more violently attacked in 1936 and had to be withdrawn; his fourth symphony was also withdrawn. It has been claimed that Stalin himself dictated the *Pravda* article entitled 'Chaos instead of Music', in which the composer was denounced for 'petty-bourgeois sensationalism': Stalin had been seated very near the orchestra at a performance of the opera, and had caught the full blast of the brass as they depicted the violent love-making of Sergei and Katerina. Already of a nervous disposition, Shostakovich was shattered by official denunciation. His popular 5th symphony, labelled by a party hack (not the composer himself) as 'A Soviet artist's practical creative reply to just criticism' helped to restore him in official favour, although the deliberately empty bombast of the finale may betray the composer's true feelings. Similar subterfuge is found in the first movement of the 7th Symphony, arising from the siege of Leningrad: the banal march theme suggests Stalinist oppression as much as it does invading Nazis.

In his later years he largely suited his manner to the government's requirements, which in turn became somewhat modified, and established himself as the leading composer of the day, gaining the Stalin Prize with his piano quintet in 1941. With other leading composers he was again denounced in 1948 and did not resume significant composition

until 1953, when he wrote his mighty 10th symphony in which the recently deceased Stalin is depicted in a sarcastic scherzo.

Works include: STAGE AND FILM operas *The Nose* and *Lady Macbeth of the Mtsensk District*; incidental music to several plays including Shakespeare's *Hamlet*, *King Lear*, and *Othello*; music to about 14 films.

ORCHESTRAL 15 symphonies, including no. 1 in F minor (1925), no. 5 in D minor (1937; subtitled *A Soviet Artist's Practical Creative Reply to Just Criticism*), no. 6 in B minor (1939), no. 7 in C (*Leningrad*, 1941), no. 8 in C minor (1943), no. 10 in E minor (1953), no. 13 in B♭ minor (*Babi Yar*, with bass, bass chorus, and orchestra, 1962), no. 14 for soprano, bass, strings, and percussion (1969), no. 15 in A (1971); two piano concertos (1933, 1957), two violin concertos (1948, 1967), two cello concertos (1959, 1966).

CHAMBER 15 string quartets (1938–74); two piano trios (1923, 1944), piano quintet (1940), sonatas for cello (1934), violin (1968), viola (1975), all with piano.

VOCAL AND PIANO Songs to texts by Pushkin, Shakespeare, Lermontov, Blok, Michelangelo, and Dostoevsky; 24 Preludes and Fugues for piano (1951).

Shudi, Burkat (Burkhardt Tschudi) (1702–1773) Swiss-born English harpsichord maker. He settled in London as a cabinet maker in 1718, joined the harpsichord maker Tabel and set up on his own account in the 1730s. See John ◊Broadwood.

Sibelius, Jean Julius Christian (1865–1957) Finnish composer. His works include nationalistic symphonic poems such as *En saga* 1893 and *Finlandia* 1900, a violin concerto 1904, and seven symphonies. In 1940 he abruptly ceased composing and spent the rest of his life as a recluse. Restoration of many works to their original state has helped to dispel his conservative image and reveal unexpectedly radical features.

Sibelius was the son of a surgeon; he had a classical education, and entered Helsinki University intending to pursue a career in law. He learned piano and violin as a child and tried composing long before he had any instruction. While studying law he managed to take a special course under Martin Wegelius at the Conservatory, and in 1885 gave up law altogether to attend the Conservatory. He left in 1889 and had a string quartet and a suite for string orchestra performed in public. With a government grant he went to study counterpoint with Albert Becker in Berlin and later orchestration with Robert Fuchs in

Vienna, where he also consulted Carl Goldmark. When he returned home he became a passionate nationalist, studying the 'Kalevala' and other Finnish literature for subjects for his works, the first being *Kullervo*, performed at Helsinki in 1892. Sibelius had a great success with the work, capturing a popular feeling of protest against foreign, particularly Russian, oppression. Further nationalist sentiments were aroused by the tone-poem *Finlandia* 1899, which became an unofficial national anthem. An annual grant was voted to Sibelius by the Finnish government in 1897 and increased in 1926, and he was thus enabled to devote himself entirely to composition without having to fill any official or administrative post.

The 1st symphony, influenced by Tchaikovsky, was premiered in 1899. The 2nd symphony followed in 1902 and is a wholly individual work, building massive paragraphs of sound from short phrases, and moving inevitably towards a triumphant finale. Sibelius gradually made his way abroad, but not in every country. Much of his work was published in Germany, but was not widely performed there. In Britain he became much better known after the performance of the 4th symphony at the Birmingham Festival in 1912; composed the previous year, it seems to exemplify the view expressed by Sibelius to Mahler in 1907 that a symphony's justification is the 'profound logic creating a connection between all the motifs'. The heavily revised 5th Symphony of 1915–19 further develops this ideal.

Sibelius conducted the first performance of *The Oceanides* at Norfolk, Connecticut, USA, in 1914, when Yale University conferred a doctor's degree on him. During the Russian Revolution and after World War I there was much unrest in Finland, and Sibelius's country home at Järvenpää was invaded. He spent most of his life there quietly, however, devoted wholly to composition. The 7th symphony of 1924 is a summation of the composer's career, beyond which it was difficult to develop. The conventional four movements are linked thematically into a single unit, creating an awe-inspiring structure as each idea unfolds and develops over a huge span.

Works include: STAGE opera, *The Maiden in the Tower/Jungfrun i Tornet*, 1896); incidental music to Adolf Paul's *King Christian* (1898), Arvid Järnefelt's *Kuolema* (including *Valse triste*, 1903), Maeterlinck's *Pelléas et Mélisande* (1905), Hjalmar Procopé's *Belshazzar's Feast* (1906), Strindberg's *Svanevit*, Paul Knudsen's

Scaramouche, Hofmannsthal's version of *Everyman*, Shakespeare's *Tempest*.

ORCHESTRAL seven symphonies, no. 1 in E minor (1899), no. 2 in D (1902), no. 3 in C (1904–7), no. 4 in A minor (1911), no. 5 in E♭ (1915), no. 6 in D minor (1923), no. 7 in C (1924; *Kullervo*, with solo voices and chorus (1892), symphonic poem *En Saga* (1892), *Rakastava* for strings and timpani, Four Legends (*Lemminkäinen and the Maidens of Saari*, *The Swan of Tuonela/Lemminkäinen in Tuonela*, *Lemminkäinen's Return* (1895), tone-poem *Finlandia* (1899), violin concerto (1903), symphonic fantasy *Pohjola's Daughter* (1906), tone-poem *Night-Ride and Sunrise* (1907), tone-poem *The Bard* (1913); symphonic poems *The Oceanides* (1914) and *Tapiola* (1926), a number of smaller orchestral pieces;

CHAMBER String quartet *Voces intimae* (1909), sonatina and many smaller pieces for violin and piano; *Malinconia* (1901) and two *Serious Pieces* for cello and piano; 18 op. nos. of piano works including sonata in F major, *Pensées lyriques* (1914), *Kyllikki*, three sonatinas; two organ pieces.

VOCAL *Luonnotar* for soprano and orchestra (1910–13); 85 songs.

Siberia opera by Giordano (libretto by L Illica), produced Milan, La Scala, 19 December 1903; revised 1921, produced Milan, 5 December 1927. Vassili is exiled to Siberia for wounding rival Prince Alexis in a duel and is joined there by Stephana; they are both killed trying to escape.

siciliano a dance of the 17th and 18th centuries which originated in Sicily, Italy. In a relaxed compound time (6/8 or 12/8), it is closely associated with the ◊pastorale. It appears as a slow movement in Baroque sonatas, for example in those by Bach, Handel, and Corelli.

Sicilian Vespers (Verdi). See ◊*Vêpres siciliennes, Les*.

sicilienne French term for siciliana, or siciliano.

side drum percussion instrument, see ◊snare drum.

Sieben Todsünden der Kleinbürger, Die/ The Seven Deadly Sins of the Petit-Bourgeois ballet with songs by Weill (libretto by Brecht), produced Paris, 7 June 1933; choreographed by Balanchine.

Siège de Corinthe (Rossini). See ◊*Maometto Secondo*.

Siege of Rhodes, The opera by Locke, H Lawes, H Cooke, Coleman and Hudson (libretto by W Davenant), produced London,

Rutland House, September 1656. The first English opera. The music is now lost.

Siegfried (Wagner) also ◊*Ring des Nibelungen*; first performed 16 August 1876. Siegfried, having been brought up by the dwarf Mime, slays the dragon Fafner and acquires the ring. He confronts the god Wotan, shattering his spear; the end of the gods is near. Although fearless in the face of battle, Siegfried awakens Brünnhilde and is frightened by the prospect of love, before being overcome by its power.

Siegfried Idyll a symphonic piece for small orchestra by Wagner, composed at Triebschen on the Lake of Lucerne in November 1870 and performed on Cosima Wagner's birthday, 25 December, on the staircase of the villa. It was therefore at first entitled *Triebschener Idyll* and called 'Treppenmusik' in the family circle. The thematic material is taken from *Siegfried*, except the German cradle song 'Schlaf, Kindlein, schlaf', but some of it, even though included in *Siegfried*, dates back to a string quartet of 1864. The musicians had to rehearse in secret, to maintain the element of surprise for Cosima; Hans Richter (six years later to premiere the *Ring* at Bayreuth) practised his trumpet part from a rowing boat in the middle of Lake Lucerne.

Siegl, Otto (1896–1978) Austrian composer, conductor, and violinist. After working as an orchestra violinist in Austria, he went to Germany, where he began teaching and became professor of composition at Cologne Conservatory.

He studied violin with the Austrian composer Egon Kornauth (1891–1959) and composition with Roderich Mojsisovics-Mojsvár (1877–1953) in Vienna. He joined the Vienna Symphony Orchestra as a violinist, worked at the Graz Opera, and then went to Germany. There he became music director at Paderborn, at the same time conducting and teaching at Bielefeld and Essen. In 1933 he became composition professor at the Cologne Conservatory, returning to Vienna in 1948.

Works include: fairy opera *Der Wassermann*; music for two puppet plays; oratorios *Das Grosse Halleluja* (Claudius), *Eines Menschen Lied* (1931), *Klingendes Jahr* (1933), *Trostkantate, Mutter Deutschland*; *Missa Mysterium Magnum*; *Verliebte alle Reime* for chorus; three symphonies, sinfonietta, *Lyrische Tanzmusik, Festliche Ouvertüre, Pastoralouvertüre* (1939), *Concerto grosso antico* (1936), *Galante Abendmusik, Festmusik und Trauermusik* for orchestra; piano concerto (1963), violin concerto, concerto for string quartet and string orchestra; five string quartets; songs.

signature see ◊key signature; ◊time signature.

Signor Bruschino, Il, ossia Il figlio per azzardo/Mr Bruschino, or The Son by Accident opera by Rossini (libretto by G M Foppa), produced Venice, Teatro San Moisè, January 1813. Sofia must marry Bruschino's son, but her lover Florville, disguised as the proposed groom, wins her hand.

Sigtenhorst Meyer, Bernhard van den (1888–1953) Dutch musicologist and composer. He edited works by Sweelinck and also wrote books on him. He studied with Zweers, D de Lange and others and later in Paris, afterwards travelling to Java and the Far East. He returned to Amsterdam, but moved to The Hague, where he lived for many years.

Works include: incidental music to Tagore's play *The King's Letter*; oratorio *The Temptation of Buddha, Stabat Mater, Hymn to the Sun* (St Francis of Assisi); two string quartets; songs.

Sigurd opera by Reyer (libretto by C du Locle and A Blau, based on the Nibelung Saga), produced Brussels, Théâtre de la Monnaie, 7 January 1884. Similar to the plot of *Götterdämmerung*. Sigurd rescues Brunehild under the influence of Hilda's love potion and gives her to King Gunther. However, evil Hagen convinces Gunther that Sigurd and Brunehild are lovers, and Gunther then kills Sigurd. Brunehild throws herself on his funeral pyre.

Siklós, Albert (1878–1942) Hungarian cellist, musicologist, and composer. He studied at the Hungarian Music School in Budapest and appeared as cellist in 1891, as lecturer in 1895, and began to compose seriously in 1896, when he finished a cello concerto, a symphony, and an opera. He held distinguished teaching posts in Budapest and was appointed professor 1913.

Works include: three operas, two ballets, choral, and a vast number of orchestral works, concertos, chamber and much piano music; also ten books of songs.

Sikorski, Kazimierz (1895–1985) Polish composer. In 1936 he was one of the founders of the Society for the Publication of Polish Music. He studied at the Chopin High School in Warsaw and later in Paris. In 1927 he became professor at the Warsaw Conservatory.

His son **Tomasz** (1939–) is a pianist and composer who has written instrumental music in various advanced idioms; he is noted as an early Polish minimalist.

Works include: Psalm 7 for chorus and orchestra; four symphonies (1918–71) and symphonic poem for orchestra; three string quartets, string sextet; songs; part-songs.

Silbermann (lived 17th–18th centuries) German family of organ builders and harpsichord makers:

Andreas Silbermann (1678–1734), son of the carpenter Michael Silbermann. He worked with Casparini in Görlitz 1797–c. 99. He settled in Strasbourg in 1721 and built the cathedral organ there 1713–16.

Gottfried (1683–1753), the brother of Andreas. At first apprenticed to a bookbinder, he joined his brother in Strasbourg in 1702, staying there till 1710. He then settled in Freiberg, where he built the cathedral organ (1711–14), and died while at work on a new organ for the Dresden court. This organ, for the Katholische Hofkirch in Dresden, was largely destroyed by the British Royal Air Force in 1945. He also built harpsichords and clavichords (one of them commemorated by a piece by C P E Bach entitled 'Farewell to my Silbermann Clavichord'), and was the first German to make pianos, including a grand which may have been used by J S Bach.

Johann Andreas (1712–1783), the son of Andreas. He built 54 organs, including two at Strasbourg and another at Arlesheim Cathedral.

Johann Daniel (1717–1766), the son of Andreas. He worked with his uncle, Gottfried, whose organ at Dresden he finished.

Johann Heinrich (1727–99), the son of Andreas. He .made harpsichords and pianos, some with pedal boards.

Silbersee, Der opera by Weill (libretto by G Kaiser), produced Leipzig, Erfurt and Magdeburg, 18 February 1933. Wounded by Olim, Severin joins him in a house by Silver Lake; when they enter suicide pact the water freezes over and they escape across the surface to a new life.

Silcher, Friedrich (1789–1860) German composer and conductor. He became a schoolmaster, but in 1815 went to Stuttgart as a conductor and in 1817 to the University of Tübingen in the same capacity. Some of his songs have become folk songs in Germany.

Works include: two hymn-books (three and four voices), collections of songs, some arranged, some composed by himself, including *Aennchen von Tharau, Loreley* (Heine), *Morgen muss ich fort, Zu Strassburg auf der Schanz.*

Silent Woman (R Strauss). See ◊*Schweigsame Frau, Die.*

Siloti, Alexander (Ilyich) (1863–1945) Russian pianist and conductor. He studied at the Moscow Conservatory under Pyotr Tchaikovsky, Nikolai Rubinstein, and others, later with Franz Liszt. He first appeared at Moscow in 1880 and later travelled widely. He left Russia 1919 and lived in the USA at the end of his life. From 1925 to 1942 he taught at the Juilliard School in New York.

Silvana opera by Weber (libretto by F K Hiemer, altered from Steinsberg's *Waldmädchen*), produced Frankfurt, 16 September 1810. Weber's second version of *Das Waldmädchen* of 1800. Struck dumb after being kidnapped, Silvana eventually revives when discovered in the forest by Count Rudolf.

similarity relation in pitch-class set analysis, a method of comparing sets containing the same number of pitches, according to the intervals between the consitituent pitches. Maximally similar sets will share many subsets and supersets; maximally dissimilar sets will share no subsets.

simile (Italian 'similar') in musical notation, directing the musician to continue performing a previously notated indication. For example, if the first few bars of a piece are marked ◊staccato (detached) a composer may simply write *simile* rather than continue to mark individual staccato dots.

Simon Boccanegra opera by Verdi (libretto by F M Piave, based on a Spanish drama by A G Gutiérrez), produced Venice, Teatro La Fenice, 12 March 1857; revised version, with the libretto altered by Boito, produced Milan, La Scala, 24 March 1881. Doge of Venice Boccanegra discovers long-lost illegitimate daughter, Amelia. She loves his enemy, Gabriele Adorno, and he and Boccanegra are reconciled. Finally Boccanegra dies, poisoned by his jealous courtier, Paolo.

simple intervals any intervals not larger than an octave, those exceeding that width being called compound interval.

simple time a metre in which each beat divides into two units. For example, 4/4 consists of four beats, each of two quavers.

Simpson, Christopher (c. 1605–1669) English viola da gamba player, theorist, and composer. He was employed as a private tutor to the family of Sir Robert Bolles, and wrote many works for solo viol and for viol consorts. His instruction book for the viola da gamba, *The Division-Violist* 1659, was highly successful.

He joined the royalist army under the Duke of Newcastle in 1643 and endured much hardship, but later came under the patronage of Sir Robert Bolles, at whose residences at Scampton and in London he lived in comfort, teaching the children of the family and taking charge of the domestic music-making. He bought a house and farm at Pickering, Yorkshire, but died at one of Sir John Bolles's houses. He wrote another treatise, *The Principles of Practicle Musick* and annotations to Campion's *Art of Descant*.

Works include: *Months and Seasons* for a treble and two bass viols, fancies and consorts for viols, suite in three parts for viols, divisions (variations) and pieces for viola da gamba.

Simpson, Robert (Wilfred Levick) (1921–) English composer and music critic. He was active in the BBC and has written on music, especially that of Bruckner, Nielsen, and Sibelius. His own music displays tonal stability and an emphasis on organic unity, influenced by Beethoven and Bruckner.

He studied privately with Howells and took a degree in music at Durham University in 1952.

Works include: 11 symphonies (1951–90), *Nielsen Variations* (1986), concertos for violin (1959), piano (1967), flute (1989) and cello (*Variations and Fugue on a theme of Bach* for strings (1991); fantasia for strings; 15 string quartets (1952–91); piano music.

Sinding, Christian August (1856–1941) Norwegian composer. His works include songs and four symphonies, but he is chiefly remembered for the popular piano piece *Frühlingsrauschen/Rustle of Spring* 1896. His brothers Otto (1842–1909) and Stephan (1846–1922) were a painter and sculptor respectively.

He studied at Oslo and later, with the Norwegian Government's support, went to Germany, continuing his studies at Liepzig, Berlin, and Munich, where he spent many years of his life. For a time he was professor of composition at Rochester, New York.

Works include: the opera *The Holy Mountain* (1912); four symphonies and *Rondo infinito* for orchestra, piano concerto in D♭ major, three violin concertos (1898, 1901, 1917); string quartet (1904), piano quintet, piano trio; sonatas and suite for violin and piano; variations for two pianos; suite, studies, and numerous pieces for piano, including the well-known *Frühlingsrauschen/Rustle of Spring*; songs.

sine wave an electronically-generated tone considered to be 'pure' because of its lack of ◊overtones.

sinfonia a symphony. In the early 18th century the sinfonia was simply an instrumental piece in an opera or other vocal work, especially the overture; it is in fact out of the overture that the symphony developed.

Also, the title of work by Berio (1968) which uses collage techniques: the scherzo of Mahler's second symphony is quoted.

'Sinfonia Antartica' symphony by Vaughan Williams (his seventh) for soprano, women's chorus and orchestra; composed 1949–52 and based on his music for the film *Scott of the Antarctic*, 1947–48; first performed Manchester, 14 January 1953, conductor Barbirolli.

sinfonia concertante work in symphonic form with one or more solo instruments, similar to a concerto. Familiar examples are Mozart's K364 for violin, viola, and orchestra of 1779 and Haydn's Op. 84 in B♭ for violin, cello, oboe, and bassoon (1792).

Sinfonia da Requiem work for orchestra in three movements by Britten; commissioned to celebrate the 2,600th anniversary of the Imperial Japanese dynasty. The work was rejected for its allusions to the Catholic liturgy and the first performance was in conducted by Barbirolli in New York on 29 March 1941; eight months before Pearl Harbor.

Sinfonia domestica (R Strauss). See ◊*Symphonia domestica*.

'Sinfonia Espansiva' symphony no. 3 (with wordless soprano and baritone voices) by Nielsen, op. 27; composed 1910–11, first performed Copenhagen, 30 April 1912, conductor Nielsen. Not performed in public in the UK until London, 7 May 1962, conductor B Fairfax.

Sinfonia Semplice sub-title of Nielsen's sixth and last symphony; composed 1924–25, first performed Copenhagen, 11 December 1925, conductor Nielsen.

sinfonietta orchestral work that is of a shorter, lighter nature than a ◊symphony, for example Janáček's *Sinfonietta* 1926. It is also the name for a small-scale orchestra specializing in such works, for example the London Sinfonietta.

Singakademie (German 'singing-academy', 'vocal academy') name of certain choral societies in Germany and Austria.

Singspiel (German 'sung play') term originally applied to all opera, later confined to opera with spoken dialogue. Mozart provided the greatest examples with *Die Entführung aus dem Serail/The Abduction from the Seraglio* 1782 and *Die Zauberflöte/The Magic Flute* 1791. During the 19th and 20th centuries *Singspiel* came to imply a comic or light opera of contemporary manners or ordinary life.

Sinigaglia, Leone (1868–1944) Italian composer. He studied at the Turin Conservatory and with Eusebius Mandyczewski in Vienna. He returned to Turin and settled down to composition and folk-song collecting.

Works include: suite *Piemonte*, overture to Goldoni's *Le baruffe chiozzote, Danze piemontesi* for orchestra (1903); concerto, *Rapsodia piemontese* and romance for violin and orchestra; string quartet in D major, concert study and variations on a theme by Brahms for string quartet; sonatas for cello and violin, folk songs.

sino (Italian 'until') in music, a word used in such directions as that indicating a repeat *sin' al fine* (until the end) or *sin' al segno* ... (to the sign ...). It is abbreviated to *sin'* when followed by a vowel.

Sirius work by Stockhausen for soprano, baritone, and ensemble, dedicated to American pioneers and astronauts. First performed Washington, DC, 18 July 1976.

Sir John in Love opera by Vaughan Williams (libretto selected by composer from Shakespeare's *Merry Wives of Windsor*), produced London, RCM, 21 March 1929.

Siroe, rè di Persia/Siroes, King of Persia libretto by Metastasio.

Opera by Handel, produced London, King's Theatre, Haymarket, 17 February 1728. Also settings by Vinci (Venice, 1726), Hasse (Bologna, 1733) and Pérez (Naples, 1740). Passed over by·his father Cosroe for succession to throne, Siroe is accused of treachery but survives the plots of Laodice and brother Medarse to gain crown.

sistrum ancient percussion instrument, probably originating in Egypt, played like a rattle. It has a metal frame fitted to a handle and metal bars or loops are loosely hung on the frame and made to strike against it by shaking the instrument.

sitar Hindi, from Persian *seh tar*, 'three strings'; a long-necked lute used mainly in North Indian (Hindustani) music. Modern sitars have 6 or 7 playing strings (several of which are used mainly for drone and rhythmic punctuation) and 12 or more sympathetic strings; some have a small gourd resonator attached to the upper end of the neck. The best known solo concert instrument in the tradition, where it is usually accompanied by the ◊tabla drum pair, the sitar is also well known outside India.

Sitsky, Larry (1934–   ) Australian composer of Russian descent. He studied at the New South Wales Conservatorium 1951–55, and with Egon Petri, former pupil of Busoni, in San Francisco. He was active as a pianist in the music of Busoni and other major moderns; head of keyboard studies at the Canberra School of Music 1966–78, and of composition from 1981.

Works include: the operas *Fall of the House of Usher* (1965); *Lenz* (1972) and *Golem* (composed 1980, premiered 1993); three violin concertos (1971–87), concertos for clarinet (1981), trombone (1982), guitar (1984) and piano (1991); three string quartets (no. 3 1993) and piano pieces with accompanying electronic effects.

Six, Les group of French 20th-century composers; see ◊Les Six.

sixth an ◊interval of six diatonic notes. A sixth is an 'imperfect interval' (having 'major'

Major, minor, and augmented sixths; major and minor 6–3 and 6–4 chords.

and 'minor' variants). A major sixth consists of nine semitones (for example, C–A). A minor sixth consists of eight semitones (C–A♭).

Sjögren, (Johan Gustaf) Emil (1853–1918)

Swedish composer. In 1891 he became organist at St John's Church, Stockholm, but devoted most of his time to teaching and composition.

He studied at the Stockholm Conservatory and later in Berlin; he also came under the influence of the Danish composer Peter Lange-Müller (1850–1926) during six months' stay at Meran.

Works include: five violin and piano sonatas; organ works; two piano sonatas, *Erotikon*, *Novellettes*, and numerous other works for piano; songs.

Skalkottas, Nicos (1904–1949)

Greek composer. Until 1938 his compositions were influenced by the 12-note method of Schoenberg. Skalkottas was Greece's first composer of international stature; only after his death did his vast output begin to be performed.

He was intended for a career as a concert violinist and studied at the Athens Conservatory and with Economidis. Later he spent 12 years in Germany, where he studied composition with Schoenberg, Weill, and Jarnach. In 1933 he returned to Greece and spent the remainder of his life as an obscure orchestral player, composing in his spare time.

Works include: two ballets *The Maid and Death* (1938) and *The Sea* (1949), 36 Greek Dances (1931–6), *Sinfonietta*, overture *The Return of Ulysses* and two suites for orchestra; concerto and symphony for wind instruments, three piano concertos (1931, 1938, 1939), violin concerto (1938), cello concerto (1938), concerto for violin and viola (1940), concerto for two violins; four string quartets (1928–40), Octet for woodwind quartet and string quartet (1931), four sonatinas for violin and piano (1929–35).

Skilton, Charles Sanford (1868–1941)

US composer. He studied at Yale University and in Germany. In 1903 he was appointed Professor of Music at Kansas University and there made a study of native American tunes.

Works include: the operas *Kalopin* (composed 1927), *The Sun Bride* (1930), *The Day of Gayomair* (composed 1936); incidental music for Sophocles' *Electra* and Barrie's *Mary Rose*; oratorio *The Guardian Angel* and cantatas; *Primeval Suite* and other suites and overtures for orchestra; *Two Indian Dances* for string quartet; violin and piano sonata; organ and piano works.

skočná Czech dance in quick 2–4 time in which three-bar phrases are a feature. The 5th, 7th, and 11th of Dvořák's *Slavonic Dances* for piano duet are *skočnás*.

Skriabin, Aleksandr Nikolaievich (1872–1915), or Scriabin

Russian composer and pianist. His visionary tone poems such as *Prometheus* 1911, and symphonies such as *Divine Poem* 1903, employed unusual scales and harmonies.

Škroup, František Jan (1801–1862)

Bohemian composer. A song he wrote for the play *Shoemakers' Fair* 1834 later became the Czech national anthem. He also composed the first Czech opera and compiled a six-volume anthology of Czech patriotic songs 1834–44.

He studied law, but was from 1827 second and in 1837–57 first conductor at the National Theatre in Prague; from 1860 he conducted at the Opera of Rotterdam.

Works include: the operas *Drátenik (The Tinker*, 1826), *The Marriage of Libuša* (1835), *Oldřich and Božena* (1828), *Drahomira* (1848) and some other Czech and German operas; incidental music to Tyl's *Fidlovačka*; three string quartets and other chamber music; songs.

Skyscrapers ballet by Carpenter (choreography by Heinrich Kröller), produced Monte Carlo, Russian Ballet, 1925; first US performance New York Metropolitan Opera 19 February 1926.

Sleeping Beauty, The/Spyashchaya krasavitsa ballet by Tchaikovsky (choreography by Petipa), produced St Petersburg, Maryinsky Theatre, 15 January 1890; new version, with additional orchestration by Stravinsky and additions to the choreography by Bronislava Nizhinska, London, Alhambra Theatre, 2 November 1921.

slentando the Italian phrase meaning 'gradually decreasing in pace'.

slide in playing string instruments, the technique of passing from one note to another by moving the finger along the string instead of lifting it to make way for another finger. Also, the movable part of the tube of the trombone by which the positions, and therefore the notes, are altered, as well as mechanisms on other wind instruments by which the pitch can be adjusted by a change in the length of the tube.

slit drum not a true drum but a 'percussion tube' made by cutting, burning, or gouging a slit in the wall of a hollowed-out piece of wood (such as a tree trunk). Used for musical or signalling purposes in cultures from Oceania to Africa.

Slonimsky, Nicolas (originally Nikolai) (1894–1995) Russian musical author, conductor, and composer. He is best known for editing major reference works such as *Baker's Biographical Dictionary of Musicians*. As a conductor he gave early performances of works by Varèse, Ruggles, Cowell, and Ives.

He studied at the St Petersburg Conservatory and in 1923 settled in the USA, becoming a US citizen in 1931. He compiled a survey, *Music since 1900* (1937, revised 1971; supplements 1986 and 1995); edited *Baker's Biographical Dictionary of Musicians*, editions 5, 6, 7, and 8 (1958, 1978, 1985, 1992; editions 7 and 8 with Dennis McIntire).

The opera *Mary Stuart* by his nephew, Sergei Slonimsky (1932–), was produced at the 1986 Edinburgh Festival.

Works include: *Fragment from Orestes* (Euripides) for orchestra (in quarter-tones); *Studies in Black and White* for piano.

slur in musical notation, a curved line written above or below a group of notes, indicating that all the associated notes are to be played or sung ◊legato (smoothly). If staccato dots appear beneath the slur, then this indicates ◊portato, a form of detached articulation. A slur connecting two notes of the same pitch is called a ◊tie.

Sly, Christopher Sly opera by Wolf-Ferrari (libretto by G Forzano, based on the prologue of Shakespeare's *Taming of the Shrew*), produced Milan, La Scala, 29 December 1927. Sly suffers a practical joke: he is made to believe he is an aristocrat suffering from amnesia rather than a poor poet. Dolly, mistress of the Duke of Westmoreland, falls for him, but she cannot save him from a lowly death in the dungeon.

Smalley, Roger (1943–) English composer and pianist. He is an important and uncompromising exponent of the ideas of his former teacher, Stockhausen, and of the avant-garde stance in general. Of his own works, several, including the Missa Brevis 1967, are based on 16th-century models by William Blitheman. He was active with the electronic group Intermodulation 1969–76; aleatory are effects also present in his music.

He studied at the Royal College of Music with Peter Fricker 1961–65; study with Stockhausen in Cologne 1965–66 was a formative influence. He began teaching at the University of Western Australia in 1976.

Works include: septet for soprano and ensemble (text by cummings, 1963), *Gloria tibi Trinitas* for orchestra (1965), *Missa Parodia* for ensemble (1967), *The Song of the Highest Tower* for soprano, baritone, chorus, and orchestra (texts by Blake and Rimbaud, 1968), *Pulses* for five × four players (1969), *Beat Music* for four electronic instruments and orchestra (1971), *Zeitebenen* for four players and tape (1973), *William Derrincourt* for baritone, chorus, and ensemble (1977), string quartet (1979), *Konzertstück* for violin and orchestra (1980), Symphony in one movement (1981), *The Narrow Road to the Deep North*, music theatre (1983), piano concerto (1985), *Ceremony I* for percussion quartet (1987), *Strung Out* for 13 solo strings (1988).

Smareglia, Antonio (1854–1929) Italian composer. He produced the first of his ten operas at Milan in 1879, but never had any real success, in spite of the good quality of his work. He was able to continue composing due to the support of his patron, the industrialist Carlo Sai and the conductor Arturo Toscanini.

He was sent to Vienna to study engineering, but on hearing works by the great masters there he left for Milan in 1872 and studied composition under Franco Faccio at the Conservatory. In 1900 he went blind.

Works include: the operas *Preziosa* (1879), *Bianca da Cervia* (1882), *Rè Nala* (1887), *Der Vasall von Szigeth* (1889), *Cornelius Schutt* (1893), *Nozze istriane*, *La Falena* (1897), *Oceàna* (1903), *L'Abisso*; symphonic poem *Leonore*, songs.

Smetana, Bedřich (1824–1884) Bohemian composer. He established a Czech nationalist style in, for example, the operas *Prodaná Nevěsta/The Bartered Bride* 1866 and *Dalibor* 1868, and the symphonic suite *Má Vlast/My Country* 1875–80. He conducted at the National Theatre of Prague 1866–74.

Smetana was the son of a brewer. He played piano and violin at a very early age and was soon able to play in the family's string quartet. He was educated in Germany and all his life, in spite of his musical nationalism, spoke and wrote Czech like a foreigner. He was sent to school first in Prague and then at Pilsen. His father opposed a musical career, but eventually allowed him to study music in Prague, though with a very small allowance. In 1844 he obtained the post of music master in Count Thun's family, which helped to support him until 1847. In 1848 he took part in the revolution against

Austria, married the pianist Kateřina Kolaŕ-ová, established a school of music for which Liszt supplied funds, and was recommended by Liszt to the Leipzig publisher Kistner.

In 1856 he went to Göteborg in Sweden, where at first he taught but later became conductor of the new Philharmonic Society and gave piano and chamber music recitals. He returned to Prague in 1859 because the northern climate did not suit his wife, who died at Dresden on the way back. He married Bettina Ferdinandová in 1860 and returned to Sweden in the autumn, but finally returned to Prague in the spring of 1861. After a long tour in Germany, Holland, and Sweden to raise money, he settled in the Czech capital in 1863 and opened another school of music, this time with distinctly national tendencies, and became conductor of the Hlahol choral society. His work was now becoming thoroughly Czech in character, and he began to produce Czech operas in the national theatre established in 1864, of which he became conductor in 1866.

The nationalist opera *The Brandenburgers in Bohemia* was a success in January 1866, although *The Bartered Bride*, with which he was to be most closely identified, was a failure in May. In 1872 he began composing his great cycle of symphonic poems, *Má Vlast/ My Country* which is often performed in the Czech Republic at times of national celebration. In 1874 he suddenly became totally deaf, as the result of a syphilitic infection, but still composed operas as well as the string quartet *From my Life*, with its strong autobiographical theme, depicting his love for his wife and children (all of whom had died by 1859) and at the beginning of the last movement the onset of his deafness, portrayed by a piercing high note on the violin. In 1881 he had his last major success, when his great patriotic festival opera *Libuše*, was premiered in Prague. In 1883 he became insane and in May 1884 was taken to an asylum, where he died.

Works include: OPERA *The Bartered Bride* (1866), *Dalibor* (1868), *Libuše* (1881), *Two Widows* (1874).

ORCHESTRAL cycle of symphonic poems *My Country* containing *Vyšehrad, Vltava, Šárka, In the Bohemian Woods and Fields, Tábor, Blaník* (1872–79).

CHAMBER AND PIANO piano trio in G minor (1855), two string quartets (1876, 1883; first *From my Life*); 8 op. nos. of piano works and many miscellaneous piano pieces including *Wedding Scenes, Scenes from Macbeth,* and Czech dances.

Smirnov, Dmitri (1948–) Russian composer. His music draws on eclectic stylistic sources and is often concerned with refinement of instrumental texture. It includes settings of poems by Blake, Pushkin, Coleridge, and Alexander Blok.

He studied with Edison Denisov at the Moscow Conservatory 1967–72. After the collapse of Communism he emigrated to the West, and with his wife Elena Firsova was joint composer-in-residence at Keele University, UK, from 1992.

Works include: three string quartets (1973, 1985, 1993), two violin sonatas (1969, 1979), piano quintet (1993); operas *Triel* (1983) and *The Lamentations of Thel* (1986); Symphony no. 1 (*The Seasons*) (1980), two piano concertos (1971, 1978), concerto for violin and 13 strings (1990), cello concerto (1992), *Mozart-Variations* for orchestra (1987); *Jacob's Ladder* for 16 players (1990; premiered under Rozhdestvensky in London, 1991).

Smit, Leo (1921–) US composer. He was pianist with Balanchine's American Ballet Company 1936–37; he taught at the University College of Los Angeles 1957–63 and was director of the Monday Evening concerts there.

He studied at the Curtis Institute, Philadelphia 1930–32, and studied composition with Nicolas Nabokov.

Works include: the operas *The Alchemy of Love* (1969; libretto by astronomer Fred Hoyle) and *Magic Water* (1978); three symphonies (1956, 1965, 1981); piano concerto (1968); *Symphony of Dances and Songs* (1981); sonata for solo cello (1982); string quartet (1984).

Smith, Bernard (Bernhard Schmidt) (1629– 1708), or Father Smith German organ builder. He settled in England in 1660. His first English organ was at the Chapel Royal in London. He was appointed organist at St Margaret's Church, Westminster, after building the organ there. He also built organs at Durham Cathedral and St Paul's Cathedral, London.

Smith, Carleton Sprague (1905–) US critic, musicologist, and flautist. He studied at Harvard University and in Vienna. After a year as critic to the *Boston Transcript*, he became chief librarian of the music section of the New York Public Library and lecturer in history of music at Columbia University. In 1938 he became president of the American Musicological Society.

Smith, John Christopher (1712–1795) German-born English organist and composer. He acted as Handel's amanuensis during the composer's blindness. Between 1759 and 1768 he conducted annual performances of *Messiah* at the Foundling Hospital in London where he was organist. He was the son of Johann Christoph Schmidt of Ansbach, who went to London as Handel's treasurer and copyist.

He studied with Handel, and later with Johann Pepusch and Thomas Roseingrave. In 1746–48 he travelled on the Continent and in 1754 became organist of the Foundling Hospital..

Works include: the operas *Teraminta*, *Ulysses* (1733), *Issipile* (1743), *Ciro riconosciuto* (1745), *Dario* (1746), *The Fairies* (from Shakespeare's *Midsummer Night's Dream*, 1755), *The Tempest* (after Shakespeare, 1756); *Rosalinda* (1740), *The Enchanter, or Love and Magic* (Garrick, 1760); oratorios *David's Lamentation over Saul and Jonathan* (1738), *Paradise Lost* (after Milton, 1758), *Rebecca, Judith* (1758), *Jehoshaphat* (1764), *The Redemption* (1774); Burial Service; instrumental works.

Smith, John Stafford (1750–1836) English music scholar and composer. He was one of the first people to undertake the study of early music, and in 1812 published his *Musica Antiqua*, which includes pieces from the 12th century onwards. The tune of his song 'Anacreon in Heaven' was later adopted as the US national anthem, 'The Star-spangled Banner'.

He studied under his father, Martin Smith, who was organist at Gloucester Cathedral. Later he went to London, where he was a chorister in the Chapel Royal and studied under William Boyce and James Nares. He became a Gentleman of the Chapel Royal in 1784, organist of Gloucester Cathedral in 1790, and in 1802 succeeded Arnold as organist of the Chapel Royal. He succeeded Ayrton as Master of the Children in 1805. He assisted Hawkins in his *History of Music*.

Works include: anthems, glees, catches, canons, madrigals, part songs; songs including 'Anacreon in Heaven' (now 'The Star-spangled Banner').

Smith, Robert (c. 1648–1675) English composer. He was a chorister at the Chapel Royal in London under Cooke; became Musician in Ordinary to the King on the death of Humfrey in 1674.

Works include: incidental music for numerous plays (some with Staggins and others); music for strings; harpsichord pieces; songs, duets.

Smith Brindle, Reginald (1917–   ) English composer, teacher, and writer on music. His

music is influenced by Berio and Stockhausen, and employs electronic techniques. His writings include *Serial Composition* 1966 and *The New Music* 1975.

He studied in Italy with Ildebrando Pizzetti and Dallapiccola and worked for Italian radio (RAI) 1956–61. He was professor at the University of Surrey 1970–85.

Works include: the chamber opera *Antigone* (1969), Symphony (1954), *Variations on theme of Dallapiccola* for orchestra (1955), *Extremum carmen* for voices and orchestra (1956), *String quartet Music* (1958), *Creation Epic* for orchestra (1964), *Worlds without End* for speaker, voices, orchestra, and tapes (1973), *The Walls of Jericho* for tuba and tape (1974), *Guitar Cosmos* (1976), *Journey towards Infinity* for orchestra (1987).

Smithers, Don (Le Roy) (1933–   ) US music historian and trumpeter. He studied at Columbia University, New York, and Oxford). He has taught at Syracuse University, New York, 1966–75, and at the Hague, Netherlands. He was active as trumpeter and cornet player in various early music groups, including the New York Pro Musica, the Leonhardt Consort, Concentus Musicus Wien, and the Early Music Consort of London. His books include *The Music and History of the Baroque Trumpet Before 1721* 1973.

smorzando (Italian 'dying') in musical notation, getting gradually softer, dying away. It can also imply some ritardando (slowing down).

Smyth, Ethel Mary (1858–1944) English composer. Her works include *Mass in D* 1893 and operas *The Wreckers* 1906 and *The Boatswain's Mate* 1916. In 1911 she was imprisoned as an advocate of women's suffrage.

She studied at the Leipzig Conservatory and then privately there with Heinrich von Herzogenberg. She had some works performed there and after her return to England one or two appeared in London, including the Mass in 1893. She was encouraged by the conductor Hermann Levi (who had premiered Wagner's *Parsifal* in 1882) to write an opera. *Fantasio* was performed at Weimar in 1898 and was taken up three years later by Felix Mottl in Karlsruhe. *Der Wald/The Forest* was premiered at the Royal Opera Berlin in 1902 and was performed at Covent Garden three months later; the following year it became the first opera by a woman to be shown at the New York Metropolitan Opera. *The Wreckers* was completed in 1904 and premiered at Leipzig in 1906; its 1909 performance in London under Thomas Beecham almost caused the conductor to alter his unflattering opinion of women composers.

Smyth lived much abroad, but in 1910 received an honorary doctorate from Durham University and about that time joined actively in the movement for women's suffrage. In 1911 when jailed at Holloway she led her fellow suffragettes in her song 'March of the Women', conducting them with a Government-issue toothbrush. She continued to be fierce in the promotion of her music and in 1916 her most successful opera *The Boatswain's Mate* was premiered in London. After the war she turned increasingly to writing, producing ten entertaining volumes of memoirs, including the autobiographical *Female Pipings in Eden* 1933 and *What Happened Next* 1940. In her later years she lived at Woking in Surrey and, regarding herself as neglected on account of her sex, composed less and less. During her last years she suffered much from deafness and distorted hearing.

Works include: the operas *Fantasio*, after Musset (Weimar, 1898), *The Forest* (Berlin, 1902), *The Wreckers* (Leipzig, 1906), *The Boatswain's Mate* (after W W Jacobs, 1916), *Fête galante* (1923), *Entente cordiale* (1925); Mass in D major; *The Prison*, for solo voices, chorus, and orchestra; overture to Shakespeare's *Antony and Cleopatra*, serenade for orchestra (1890); concerto for violin, horn, and orchestra; three Anacreontic Odes for voice and orchestra; string quintet, string quartet; sonatas, songs.

Smythe, William (c. 1550–c. 1600) English composer. He was a minor canon and later master of the choristers (1594–98) at Durham Cathedral. He wrote a number of works for the Anglican church, not to be confused with those by his later namesake, 'William Smith of Durham'.

snare in some types of drum, especially the snare drum, a string of gut, wire, or plastic, stretched over one of the heads. Snares add brilliance to a drum's tone by vibrating against the skin as the drum is struck. If that effect is not required, the snares can be temporarily slackened.

snare drum, or side drum double-headed drum used in military bands and in orchestras, with skins at both upper and lower ends of the instrument. A snare of catgut string or wire is stretched over the lower skin, to produce a rattling sound when the upper skin is struck by a pair of hard wooden drumsticks. Single strokes on the side drum are ineffective: it is usually made to produce

small patterns of repeated notes or more or less prolonged rolls. Its tone is bright and hard, without definite pitch. It can be muted by relaxing the tension of the snare. There is a famous orchestral snare-drum solo in Carl Nielsen's Fifth symphony.

Snow Maiden, The, Snegurotchka, opera by Rimsky-Korsakov (libretto by composer, based on a play by A N Ostrovsky), produced St Petersburg, 10 February 1882. The Snow Maiden lives amongst humans but cannot love. She falls for Mizgir and, granted the ability to love by Spring, melts in the sunlight.

Socrate, Socrates, symphonic drama by Satie (libretto taken from Victor Cousin's French translation of Plato's *Dialogues*), produced Paris, 14 February 1920, and performed Prague, festival of the International Society for Contemporary Music (ISCM), May 1925. Philosophical musings end in suicide.

Söderman, (Johan) August (1832–1876) Swedish composer. He learnt music from his father, a theatre conductor, and at 18 went to Finland as director of music to a Swedish company of musicians; in 1856 he produced his first operetta at Helsinki. After a period of study at Leipzig he was appointed chorus master at the Royal Opera at Stockholm 1860 and second conductor 1862.

Works include: the operetta *The Devil's First Lesson* (1856) and others; incidental music to Schiller's *Maid of Orleans*, Topelius's *Regina* and other plays; Mass for solo voices, chorus and orchestra; *Swedish Wedding* for female voices, cantatas and part-songs; vocal settings of Bellman's rhapsodies; *Circassian Dance* and concert overture for orchestra; sacred songs and hymns with organ; ballads and songs for voice and piano.

Sofonisba, La opera by Caldara (libretto by Francesco Silvani), produced Venice, Teatro S Giovanni Crisostomo, December 1708. Siface, King of Numidia, is captured by the Romans. Wife Sophonisba joins him, but commits suicide rather than face the humiliation of her chains.

Opera by Gluck (libretto ditto, with airs from different libretti by Metastasio), produced Milan, Teatro Regio Ducal, 18 January 1744.

soft pedal, or una corda pedal on the piano, the left pedal, which reduces volume. On a grand piano this is achieved by moving the position of the hammers so that fewer strings per note are struck. On an upright piano the hammers are moved closer to the strings.

soggetto Italian 'subject', in the musical sense, especially the subject of a fugue.

soggetto cavato (Italian 'extracted subject') in the 15th century and afterwards, a vocal theme sung to a melody formed from the vowels of a sentence converted by the composer into musical notes of the hexachord: a = fa or la, e = re, i = mi, o = do, u = ut.

Sogno di Scipione, Il/Scipio's Dream dramatic serenade by Mozart (libretto by Metastasio), produced Salzburg, at the installation of the new archbishop, Hieronymus von Colloredo, 1 May 1772. Faced with two goddesses in a dream, Scipio chooses Constancy rather than Fortune.

Soh the name for the dominant note in any key in tonic sol-fa, so pronounced, but in notation represented by the letter s.

Sohal, Naresh (1939–) Indian composer. He first came to attention with his *Asht Prahar* 1965, performed by the London Philharmonic Orchestra in 1970; *The Wanderer* for baritone, chorus, and orchestra was performed at the 1982 London Promenade Concerts, and *From Gitanjali* by the New York Philharmonic Orchestra under Zubin Mehta in 1985.

He studied with Jeremy Dale Roberts and Alexander Goehr in England.

Works include: *Indra-Dhanush* for orchestra (1973), *Inscape* for chorus, flute, and percussion (1979), two brass quintets (1983, 1984), *Undulation* for cello (1984) and *Tandova Nritya* for orchestra (1984).

Sol the old name for the note G (see ◊solmization), still used in Latin countries, and in tonic sol-fa notation the dominant note in any key represented by the symbol **s**, pronounced Soh.

Soldaten, Die/The Soldiers opera in four acts by Bernd Alois Zimmermann (libretto by composer, after the play by Jakob Lenz, 1776); composed 1958–60, revised 1963–64, first performed Cologne, 15 February 1965, conductor Gielen. Vocal Symphony for five soloists and orchestra derived from the opera in 1958; use is made of ballet, mime, *sprechstimme*, electronics, and film. The composer committed suicide in 1970, two years before the first British performance, in Edinburgh. The moral degradation of Marie: she is at first engaged to Stolzius and then seduced by Baron Desportes and Major Mary. Stolzius poisons himself and Deziortes; Marie becomes a beggar.

Soleil des eaux, Le/The Sun of the Waters music by Boulez for a radio play by René Char, 1948; revised as cantata for soprano, tenor, baritone, and chamber orchestra; first performed Paris, 18 July 1950; revised with addition of chorus and performed Darmstadt, 9 September 1958; further revised for soprano and chorus and given in Berlin 1965.

Soler, Antonio (1729–1783) Spanish organist and composer. He wrote much church music as well as organ concerti and incidental music for plays; but his most celebrated works are probably his many harpsichord sonatas, distinguished successors to those of Domenico Scarlatti, with whom he probably studied 1752–57.

A chorister at Montserrat, he was maestro de capilla at Lérida Cathedral and entered the Escorial monastery in 1752, becoming organist and choirmaster there the following year. His treatise *Llave de la Modulación* was published in 1762.

Works include: incidental music for plays by Calderón and others; nine Masses, motets and other church music; 132 villancicos; quintets for organ and strings; organ concertos; 120 harpsichord sonatas.

Solerti, Angelo (1865–1907) Italian musicologist. He wrote several works on the origins of dramatic music in the early 17th century

sol-fa short for **tonic sol-fa**, a method of teaching music, usually singing, systematized by John Curwen (1816–1880). The notes of a scale are named by syllables (doh, ray, me, fah, soh, lah, te, with the ◊key indicated) to simplify singing by sight.

solfège (Italian *solfeggio*) an elementary method of teaching sight-reading and of ear-training, practised mainly in France and Italy. The names of the notes ('do, re, mi', and so on) are pronounced while the notes are sung unaccompanied and the intervals have thus to be learnt by ear.

soli a group of solo performers as distinct from the whole vocal or orchestral body employed in a work.

solmization (from Latin *solmisatio*) the designation of the musical scales by means of syllables. The notes of the Greek tetrachords were already designated by syllables, but Guido d'Arezzo in the 11th century replaced them by the hexachords and used the Latin syllables Ut, Re, Mi, Fa, Sol, La for their six notes, Si being added later for the seventh and Ut being replaced by Do in Italy and elsewhere, though still largely retained in France. These syllables, as in modern tonic sol-fa with movable Doh, were not immutably fixed to C, D, E, F, G, A, but could be transferred by mutation to other degrees of the scale, so long as the semitone always occurred between Mi and Fa. The so-called 'natural hexachord' beginning on C could thus be changed to the 'hard hexachord' beginning on G, in which case mi-fa corresponded with B–C, or to the 'soft hexachord' beginning on F (see ◊hexachord). The syllables were derived from a hymn of the year 770 for the festival of St John the Baptist, the lines of the plainsong of which began on the successive notes of the hexachord: UT queant laxis; REsonare fibris; MIra gestorum; FAmuli tuorum; SOLve polluti; LAbii reatum; Sancte Ioannes. The seventh syllable, Si, was derived from the initial letters of the last line.

solo (Italian 'alone') in musical notation, a piece or passage written for one performer. Sometimes this implies an accompaniment provided by another player or players; for instance, Bach's solo cello sonatas are written for unaccompanied cello, but his solo violin concertos are written for a single violinist with orchestral accompaniment.

Solomon oratorio by Handel (libretto probably by Newburgh Hamilton), performed London, Covent Garden, 17 March 1749.

solo organ the fourth manual (keyboard) of an organ, characterized by pipes and stops of distinctive tone quality, (resembling individual instruments). Typically, one hand plays a 'solo' on this manual, while the other provides a softer accompaniment on another manual.

Soloviev, Nikolai Feopemptovich (1846–1916) Russian composer and music critic. In 1875 his opera *Vakula the Smith* lost to Tchiakovsky's entry in a competition, but some members of the jury apparently preferred Soloviev's work. He was highly critical of Tchiakovsky as well as the nationalist composers Vladimir Stasov and César Cui.

He began by studying medicine, but turned to music and entered the St Petersburg Conservatory, where his teachers included Nikolai Zaremba (1821–1879). He became a professor there himself in 1874. In 1871 the

dying Alexander ◊Serov charged him with the orchestration of his opera *The Power of Evil*. He was also a critic and collector of folk songs.

Works include: the operas *Cordelia* (after Sardou's *La Haine*, 1885), *Vakula the Smith* (on Gogol's *Christmas Eve*, 1875), and *The Cottage of Kolomua*; cantata for the bicentenary of Peter the Great; symphonic poem *Russians and Mongols* and Fantasy on a Folksong for orchestra; piano pieces; songs.

Solti, Georg (1912–1997) Hungarian-born British conductor. He was music director at the Royal Opera House, Covent Garden, London, 1961–71, and director of the Chicago Symphony Orchestra (1969–91). He was also principal conductor of the London Philharmonic Orchestra 1979–83. KBE 1971. He made more than 250 recordings, including 45 operas, throughout his recording career, and was honoured with 32 Grammy awards – more than any other artist.

Sombrero de tres picos, El/The Three-cornered Hat ballet by Falla (scenario by Martínez Sierra, based on Alarcón's story; choreographed by Massin), produced London, Alhambra Theatre, 22 July 1919. The setting and costumes were designed by Picasso.

Somervell, Arthur (1863–1937) English composer and educationist. His songs, especially settings of lyrics from Tennyson's 'Maud', Housman's 'A Shropshire Lad', and Browning's 'James Lee's Wife', are his best-known works. He also composed two Masses, choral works, including a setting of Wordsworth's 'Intimations of Immortality', and a symphony, and edited *Songs of the Four Nations* and other folk songs.

He was educated at Uppingham School and King's College, Cambridge, where he studied composition with Stanford. He later went to Kiel and Berlin, to the Royal College of Music in London in 1885, and to Hubert Parry as a private pupil in 1887. In 1894 he

Solmization of the gamut, with different possible readings according to the particular hexachord.

became professor at the Royal College of Music, and in 1901 an inspector of music in schools, this led to an appointment as official inspector of music to the Board of Education, which he resigned in 1928.

Works include: Masses in C minor (1891) and D minor (the latter for male voices, 1907), anthem 'Let all the world', oratorio *The Passion of Christ*, cantatas *A Song of Praise*, *The Power of Sound*, *The Forsaken Merman* (Matthew Arnold), *Ode to the Sea* and others; symphony in D minor, *Thalassa* (1912), concerto in G minor and *Concertstück* for violin and orchestra; clarinet quintet; violin and piano sonata; Variations on an Original Theme for two pianos; violin pieces; piano pieces; song cycles *Maud* (Tennyson), *A Shropshire Lad* (A E Housman, 1904).

Somfai, László (1934–) Hungarian musicologist. He studied at the Franz Liszt Academy, Budapest, and was appointed professor of musicology there in 1980. He published several works on Haydn: as opera director (1960), his life on contemporary pictures (1966) and on the piano sonatas (1979). He also conducted research on the lives and works of Liszt, Stravinsky, Webern, and Bartók.

Sommeils ˙ (French, plural of *sommeil*, 'sleep') quiet airs in old French operas, supposed to induce sleep.

Son and Stranger (Mendelssohn). See ◊*Heimkehr aus der Fremde*.

sonata (Italian 'sounded') in music, an essay in instrumental composition for a solo player or a small ensemble and consisting of a single movement or series of movements. The name signifies that the work is not beholden to a text or existing dance form, but is self-sufficient.

sonata da camera (Italian 'chamber sonata') instrumental work of the late 17th and early 18th centuries of the suite or partita type in several movements, mainly in dance forms, but always for more than one instrument, most usually two violins with continuo for bass viol or cello with a keyboard instrument, generally harpsichord. Unlike the sonata da chiesa, the sonata da camera usually had a quick first movement.

sonata da chiesa (Italian 'church sonata') an instrument work of the late 17th and early 18th centuries frequently, though not invariably, in four movements (slow introduction, fugal *allegro*, slow *cantabile* movement and quick finale), written for more than one instrument, most usually two violins with

continuo for bass viol or cello with a keyboard instrument, which if played in church must have been generally the organ.

sonata form rules determining the structure of a ◊sonata first movement, typically divided into exposition, development, and recapitulation sections. It introduced the new possibility of open and continuous development to an 18th-century music previously limited to closed dance routines. It provides the framework for first movements in general, including symphonies, concertos, and string quartets.

sonata quasi una fantasia (Italian 'sonata, as it were a fantasy') term invented by Beethoven for some of his sonatas in which he began to modify the form freely, the two works of op. 27 for piano being the first of the kind.

sonatina a small-scale ◊sonata. Although usually light and relatively easy to play, some 20th-century composers such as Ravel and Darius Milhaud have written technically demanding works of this kind. Formally, sonatinas often differ from sonatas in having a reduced development (central) section.

Sondheim, Stephen (Joshua) (1930–) US composer and lyricist. He wrote the lyrics for Bernstein's *West Side Story* 1957 and Styne's *Gypsy* 1959. Later he wrote both words and music for such shows as *A Funny Thing Happened on the Way to the Forum* 1962, *Sunday in the Park with George* 1984, and *Into the Woods* 1987.

He studied at Williams College, Massachusetts, and with Milton Babbitt. Other shows for which he wrote words and music include *A Little Night Music* (1972), *Pacific Overtures* (1976), *Sweeney Todd* (1979), *Assassins* (1990), and *Passion* (1994).

song a setting of words to music for one or more singers, with or without instrumental accompaniment. Song may be sacred, for example a psalm, motet, or cantata, or secular, for example a folk song or ballad. In verse song, the text changes in mood while the music remains the same; in ◊lied and other forms of art song, the music changes in response to the emotional development of the text.

song cycle sequence of songs related in mood and sung as a group, used by romantic composers such as Schubert, Schumann, and Wolf.

Songe d'une nuit d'été, Le/The Dream of a Midsummer Night opera by A Thomas (libretto by J B Rosier and A de Leuven, not based on Shakespeare's play), produced Paris, Opéra-Comique, 20 April 1850. Shakespeare, Queen Elizabeth and Falstaff appear in it as characters.

song form alternative name for ◊ABA form.

'Song of Destiny' (Brahms). See ◊'Schicksalslied'.

'Song of the Earth' (Mahler). See ◊'Lied von der Erde, Das'.

Song of the High Hills, The work by Delius for wordless chorus and orchestra; composed 1911, first performed London, 26 February 1920, conductor Albert Coates.

Song of Triumph (Brahms) see ◊Triumphlied.

Songs and Dances of Death song cycle by Mussorgsky (poems by A A Golenishtchev-Kutuzov), composed 1875–77: 1. The Peasant's Lullaby; 2. Serenade; 3. Trepak; 4. The Field Marshal. Orchestrated by Shostakovich, 1962.

Songs of Farewell work by Delius for chorus and orchestra (text by Walt Whitman); composed 1930, first performed London, 21 March 1932, conductor Sargent.

Songs of Sunset work by Delius for mezzo, baritone, chorus, and orchestra (text by Ernest Dowson); composed 1906–08, first performed London, 16 June 1911, conductor Beecham.

Songs of Travel nine songs for voice and piano by Vaughan Williams (texts by Robert Louis Stevenson), first performance of nos. 1–8 London, 2 December 1904, with Hamilton Harty at the piano; first complete performance BBC, 21 May 1960.

Songs without Words (Mendelssohn). See ◊Lieder ohne Worte.

Sonnambula, La/The Sleepwalker opera by Bellini (libretto by F Romani), produced Milan, Teatro Carcano, 6 March 1831. Amina is found at night in the bedroom of Count Rodolfo, to the dismay of her betrothed Elvino; he is only placated when Amina's sonambulistic tendencies are revealed.

sonore (French **'sonorous'**) in music, an indication that a passage is to be played or sung with full tone. The Italian term is sonoro.

Sophocles (497 or 495 BC–405 BC) Greek dramatist. His powerful tragedies inspired ◊Antigonae (Orff); ◊Antigone (incidental music, Mendelssohn; operas, Honegger, Zingarelli); Granville ◊Bantock (Electra); ◊Elektra (R Strauss); George ◊Enescu (Oe(lig)dipe); Anselm Hüttenbrenner (Odipus auf Kolonos); ◊Oedipus auf Kolonos (Mendelssohn); ◊Oedipus Rex (Stravinsky); ◊Oedipus der Tyrann (Orff); ◊Oedipus und die Sphinx (Varèse); Ildebrando

◊Pizzetti (Trachiniae, Oedipus Rex and Coloneus); Camille ◊Saint-Saëns (Antigone); Niccolò ◊Zingarelli (Edipo a Colono).

sopra (Italian **'above'**) word used in piano music to indicate in passages for crossed hands whether the right is to go above the left or vice versa. See also ◊come sopra.

sopranino term in music describing an instrument of higher range than ◊soprano. An alternative term is **piccolo**.

soprano the highest range of the female voice, stretching from around D4 to A6. Some operatic roles require the extended upper range of a ◊coloratura soprano, reaching to around F6, for example Kiri Te Kanawa. Some instruments use the prefix soprano for those models which sound in the compass of the soprano voice.

The soprano range has approximately the compass shown, but is often extended further in florid operatic arias requiring dexterity.

soprano clef in musical notation, the C ◊clef in which middle C (C4) is represented by the lowest line of a five-line stave.

The soprano clef.

Sor, (Joseph) Fernando (Macari) (1778–1839) Spanish guitarist and composer. He was educated at the Escolanía at Montserrat, produced his first opera at the age of 19, then went to Paris and in about 1815 went to London, where he played and taught the guitar, returning to Paris in 1823. He wrote an important guitar tutor which was published in 1830.

Works include: the opera Telemaco nell' isola di Calipso (1797); eight ballets, including Cendrillon (1822), successful in London, Paris, and Moscow; over 60 guitar pieces and studies.

Sorabji, Kaikhosru Shapurji (1892–1988), adopted name of Leon Dudley English Parsee pianist and composer. His piano works are in a complex, late Romantic style and test the endurance of performers and audiences: Opus clavicembalistium lasts for almost three hours and concludes with a passacaglia of 81 variations.

He lived in England all his life. Except for the piano, he was mainly self-taught, but was fortunate in being able to give all his time to musical studies. He performed his own piano works in London, Paris, and Vienna, and also wrote criticism, including a book, *Around Music*. Sorabji premiered the *Opus clavicembalistium* at Glasgow in 1930 but forbade further performances of all his music 1936–76. The pianist Yonty Solomon premiered the 3rd Sonata, and *Opus* was performed at Chicago in 1983.

Works include: two symphonies for orchestra, piano, organ, and chorus (1922, 1951); *Chaleur and Opusculum* for orchestra; eight piano concertos (1915–22), symphonic variations for piano and orchestra; two symphonies for organ; two piano quintets (1920, 1953); five sonatas, *Opus clavicembalisticum*, *Fantasia Hispanica*, three toccatas, symphony, variations on *Dies irae* for piano; *Trois Poèmes* (Verlaine and Baudelaire), *Fêtes galantes* (Verlaine) for voice and piano.

Sorcerer's Apprentice, The (Dukas). See ◊*Apprenti sorcier*.

Sorcerer, The operetta by Sullivan (libretto by W S Gilbert), produced London, Opera Comique, 17 November 1877. Plot similar to Donizetti's *L'elisir d'amore*, with characters Alexis and Aline, sorcerer John Wellington Wells, and parents Sir Marmaduke and Lady Sangazure.

Sordello (c. 1200–1270) Italian ◊troubadour. He came under the protection first of Guillaume de Blacatz, and afterwards of Charles d'Anjou, and wrote in Provençal. He is credited with about 30 love songs, and his lament on the death of Blacatz is notable.

sordino (Italian 'mute') a ◊mute, usually of a violin, viola, or cello. In printed music the phrase *con sord.* means 'with the mute in place' (on the bridge), while *senza sord.* means 'take the mute off'.

sordune Renaissance ◊windcap double-reed musical instrument in tenor or bass register, of folded-back conical bore, an ancestor of the bassoon.

Soriano, Francesco (c. 1549–1621) Italian composer. After a first appointment he went to the court of Mantua 1583–86, and then became maestro di cappella in Rome, by turns at Santa Maria Maggiore, St John Lateran, St Peter's in 1603, and the Cappella Giulia 1603–20.

He was a choirboy at the church of St John Lateran in Rome and studied with various masters including G B Nanini and Palestrina.

Works include: Masses, an arrangement of Palestrina's *Missa Papae Marcelli* for eight voices, motets, psalms, Magnificat, a Passion, and other church music; madrigals.

Sorochintsy Fair/Sorochinskaya Yarmarka unfinished opera by Mussorgsky (libretto by composer, based on Gogol's *Evenings on a Farm near Dakanka*), composition begun 1875; revised by Liadov for concert performance, 1904; performed in original form, St Petersburg, Comedia Theatre, 30 December 1911; a version by Sakhnovsky produced Moscow, Free Theatre, 3 November 1913; version by Cui with music of his own added produced St Petersburg, Musical Drama Theatre, 26 October 1917; version by N Tcherepnin produced Monte Carlo, 17 March 1923 (in French); another version made by Shebalin in 1931 was produced Leningrad, Little Opera Theatre, 21 December 1931. Parasya meets lover Gritzke at the Fair but her mother objects to their marriage.

sortita (Italian from *sortire*, 'to come out') the aria sung by a principal character in an 18th-century opera at his of her first entry on the stage.

Sosarme, rè di Media/Sosarmes, King of the Medes opera by Handel (libretto based on Matteo Noris's *Alfonso primo*), produced London, King's Theatre, Haymarket, 15 February 1732. Haliate besieges the city controlled by his rebellious son Argone; Melo is announced as Haliate's successor instead of Argone. Sosarme reconciles the rival claimants to throne and weds Elmira.

sostenuto (Italian 'sustained') term used in musical notation, similar to ◊legato ('tied'). It can also imply a slower speed than the overall tempo marking, similar to ◊ritenuto.

sostenuto pedal the middle pedal on a grand piano with three pedals (many have only two). When depressed while certain keys are held down, it prevents the dampers of those particular keys from returning to the string until the pedal is released. It allows the hands to play other notes while still sustaining the sound of a previous set of notes.

sotto voce (Italian 'under the voice') in musical notation, indicating very soft playing or singing.

soubrette (French from Provençal *soubret*, 'coy') in opera, a stock part given to a singer with a light soprano voice. The typical soubrette character is a servant, a young confidante, or a girl connected with the sub-plot.

Examples include Despina in Mozart's *Così fan tutte* and Aennchen in Weber's *Der Freischütz*. Occasionally the soubrette may assume a principal part, for example, Serpina in Pergolesi's *La Serva padrona*, Susanna in Mozart's *Figaro*.

soundboard in many musical instruments, including the organ, piano, dulcimer, and cimbalom, a resonant wooden part which vibrates with the notes, amplifying the sound.

soundbox, or resonator in a musical instrument, an enclosed space in which the vibrations of a string or strings are captured and naturally amplified (that is, without electronic amplification). On a member of the string family, it forms the body of the instrument. On a string keyboard instrument the ◊soundboard forms one surface of the soundbox.

sound-holes the holes in the tables of string instruments, also in the soundboards of harpsichords. In instruments of the violin family they take the shape of f holes or something approximating to them; in keyboard instruments and flat-bellied string instruments such as the guitar, they are usually shaped like a 'rose'.

soundpost in a string musical instrument, a piece of wood inside the body of the instrument which connects the front and back surfaces of the ◊soundbox. It supports the weight of the bridge and helps to distribute vibrations throughout the instrument.

sourdine (French from *sourd* 'deaf') in music, a mute (◊sordino); also an instrument of the bassoon type, common in the late 16th and early 17th centuries and made in five sizes. It derived its name from the fact that its tone was muffled.

It was known as *Sordun* in Germany and *sordone* in Italy.

Sousa, John Philip (1854–1932) US bandmaster and composer of marches. He wrote 'The Stars and Stripes Forever' 1897.

After some years' experience as an orchestra violinist he became master of the US Marine Corps Band in 1880; he became known as a brilliant bandmaster. He went on to form the Sousa Band in 1892 and toured internationally with this group until his death. In addition to about 140 stirring marches, including 'The Washington Post' 1889, 'El capitan' 1895, and 'Imperial Edward', he composed operettas, symphonic poems, suites, waltzes, and songs.

Works include: songs 'The Stars and Stripes Forever' (1897), 'The Washington Post' (1889), 'Hands Across the Sea' (1899); operettas *The Queen of Hearts* (1885), *El capitan* (1895).

sousaphone large bass ◊tuba designed to wrap round the player in a circle and having a forward-facing bell. The form was suggested by US bandmaster John Sousa. Today sousaphones are largely fabricated in light-weight fibreglass.

sousedská Bohemian country dance in slow triple time. The 3rd, 4th, and 16th of Dvořák's *Slavonic Dances* for piano duet are sousedskás.

Souster, Tim(othy) Andrew James (1943–1994) English composer. He was co-founder with Roger ◊Smalley of the group Intermodulation, to explore electronic and aleatory techniques.

He studied at Oxford and Darmstadt and was assistant to Stockhausen in Cologne 1971–73. He worked at King's College, Cambridge, and Keele University.

Works include: *Songs of the Seasons* for soprano and viola (1965), *Poem in Depression* for soprano and ensemble (1965), *Metropolitan Games* for piano duet (1967), *Titus Groan Music* for wind quintet, tape, and electronics (1969), *Chinese Whispers* for percussion and synthesizers (1970), *Waste Land Music*, for saxophone, piano, and organ (1970), *Triple Music* for three orchestras (1970), *Song of an Average City* for small orchestra and tape (1974), *Afghan Amplitudes* for keyboards and synthesizers (1976), *Arcane Artefact*, trio (1977), *Driftwood Cortège*, tape (1978), *Sonata* for cello and ensemble (1979), *Equalisation*, brass quintet (1980), *The Transistor Radio of St Narcissus* (1983), *Curtain of Light* for percussion (1984), *Hambledon Hill*, for amplified string quartet (1985), trumpet concerto (1986).

souter liedekens (Dutch 'little psalter songs') metrical psalms sung in Holland to popular tunes, translated and provided with appropriate melodies by (probably) Willem van Zuylen van Nyevelt. The first complete collection, printed by Symon Cock at Antwerp in 1540, contained 159 texts: Psalm 119 was in four sections, and the Te Deum and five canticles were included. Clemens non Papa later arranged the whole collection for three voices, published in Antwerp as the fourth–seventh of Susato's *Musyck Boexken* (little music books) in 1556–57. Ten settings are by Susato himself, perhaps because of Clemens's premature death. The eighth–eleventh books contained another complete setting, the work of Gerhard Mes.

Sowerby, Leo (1895–1968) US composer and pianist. He served as a bandmaster in Europe during World War I and in 1922 won the American Prix de Rome. He was organist of St James's Episcopal Cathedral in Chicago 1927–62.

He studied at the American Conservatory of Chicago, where he later taught. He appeared as a pianist in the USA, England, Italy, and Austria.

Works include: oratorio *Christ Reborn*, cantata *Great is the Lord* and Te Deum for mixed chorus and organ; five symphonies (1921, 1928, 1940, 1947, 1964), suite *From the Northland*, overture *Comes Autumn Time*, *Irish Washerwoman*, *Money Musk*, *Set of Four*, symphonic poem *Prairie*, *Theme in Yellow* for orchestra; sinfonietta for strings; rhapsody for chamber orchestra; *Sinconata* for jazz orchestra; two piano concertos (1912, 1932), organ concerto, two cello concertos (1917, 1934), violin concerto, ballad *King Estmere* for two pianos and orchestra, *Medieval Poem* for organ and orchestra; two string quartets (1924, 1935), wind quintet, serenade for string quartet; sonata and suite for violin and piano; symphony, sonata and suite for organ; *Florida Suite* and other piano works; songs.

space-time notation a form of ◊graph notation pioneered by Earle ◊Brown in which notes are individually lengthened to give a precise visualization of relative durations. It involves the performer 'reading time' instead of counting beats, and is useful where musical time is measured chronometrically, as in Stockhausen's instrumental score for the electronic composition *Kontakte/Contacts* 1959–60.

It originates with piano-roll music, which is cut from an original paper roll representing pitches and durations by pencilled lines (see ◊player piano).

Spagna, la fifteenth-century *basse danse* tune originating in Castile.

Spanisches Liederbuch/Spanish Song Book H Wolf's settings of Spanish poems in German translation by Emanuel Geibel and Paul Heyse, composed October 1889–April 1890. There are ten sacred and 34 secular poems in his set.

Spanish Lady, The unfinished opera by Elgar (libretto by B Jackson, based on Ben Jonson's play *The Devil is an Ass*). Begun 1932–33; only a number of skhes are left; arrangements by Percy Young published 1955–56. A performing version of the skhes was made by Dr Young and premiered at Cambridge (University Opera) 24 November, 1994.

špasírka Czech dance in alternating slow and quick 4–8 time. The 13th of Dvořák's *Slavonic Dances* for piano duet is a špasírka.

Spataro, Giovanni (c. 1458–1541) Italian composer and theorist. He was involved in a protracted controversy with the theorist Franchino Gafori, against whom two of his printed treatises are directed. He composed a number of sacred works; six motets and one *laude* are extant.

He was a pupil of Ramos de Pareia and corresponded with Pietro Aron; he was maestro di cappella at San Petronio, Bologna from 1512.

speaker keys extra keys fitted to reed wind instruments, to facilitate the production of harmonic notes. Two on the oboe produce octaves (also known as octave keys) and one on the clarinet produces 12ths.

speaking-length that portion of an ◊organ pipe in which the air vibrates to produce the note.

species the various types of counterpoint taught in academic contrapuntal instruction.

specification a detailed list of the pipes, stops, keyboards, and mechanisms of an organ given to the builder or used to describe the instrument.

Spectre's Bride, The, actually *The Wedding-Shift* dramatic cantata by Dvořák, op. 69 (Czech words by K J Erben), composed 1884, performed in England, Birmingham Festival, August 1885.

speech-song see ◊Sprechgesang.

Speziale, Lo/The Apothecary opera by Haydn (libretto by Goldoni), produced Eszterháza, autumn 1768. Elderly apothecary Sempronio has designs on Griletta but she weds young Mengone, his assistant.

spianato in musical direction; Italian 'smoothed, level'.

spiccato (Italian 'articulated') musical direction indicating a special kind of bowing on instruments of the violin family, possible only in rapid passages of notes of equal duration, which are played with the middle of the bow and a loose wrist, allowing the bow to rebound off the strings after each note.

Spiegel von Arkadien, Der/The Mirror of Arcadia opera by Süssmayr (libretto by Schikaneder), produced Vienna, Theater auf der Wieden, 14 November 1794. Noble pair Ballamo and Philanie, with comic duo (the viper-catchers Metallio and Giganie) in *Zauberflöte* sequel. See also ◊magic opera.

Spieloper (German 'play-opera') type of light German opera of the 19th century, the subject of which is a comedy and the musical numbers of which are interspersed with dialogue.

Spielwerk und die Prinzessin, Das/The Musical Box and the Princess opera by Schreker (libretto by composer); 1909–12, produced Frankfurt and Vienna, 15 March 1913; revised in one act as a mystery play, *Das Spielwerk*, and produced Munich, 30 October 1920, conductor Walter. Sound from Meister Florian's musical box intoxicates Princess but she is redeemed by a flute-playing wayfarer.

Spies, Claudio (1925–) Chilean-born US composer. He moved to the USA in 1942 and studied at the New England Conservatory and with Fine and Piston at Harvard. He was appointed Professor of Music at Princeton in 1970. He has written extensively on Stravinsky and conducted the first performance of an early version of *The Wedding*.

Works include: *Music for a Ballet* for orchestra (1955), *Il Cantico del frate Sole* for baritone and orchestra (1958), *Tempi* for 14 instruments (1962), seven *Enzensberglieder* for baritone and ensemble (1972).

spinet seventeenth-century domestic keyboard instrument. It has a laterally tapered case with a single manual (keyboard) of up to a three-and-a-half octave range, having a plucking action and single strings. It was the precursor of the ◊harpsichord.

Spinner, Leopold (1906–1980) Polish-born Austrian composer. He settled in England in 1938. His works are influenced by Webern, with whom he studied 1935–38.

Works include: symphony (1934), Passacaglia for chamber orchestra (1936), Concerto for Orchestra (1957); two string quartets (1941, 1952), piano trio (1950), sonatina for cello and piano (1973).

Spirit of England, The three cantatas for soprano solo, chorus, and orchestra by Elgar, op. 80, *The Fourth of August*, *To Women*, and *For the Fallen* (poems by Laurence Binyon); composed 1916–17; nos 1 and 2 performed London, 7 May 1916; complete performance London, 24 November 1917.

spiritoso (Italian 'spirited') musical direction indicating that a composition, movement or passage is to be performed briskly and energetically.

spiritual an African-American song of the southern states of the USA, with religious words and folksong tunes. It is one of the chief influences from which jazz and swing have sprung. It has influenced many serious US composers as well as some European ones; Tippett's oratorio *A Child of our Time* (1939–41) uses spirituals.

Spitta, (Julius August) Philipp (1841–1894) German musicologist. He studied at Göttingen University and in 1875 became professor of music history at Berlin University. He also taught the subject at the Hochschule für Musik, of which he became director in 1882. He was joint editor with Adler and Chrysander of the *Vierteljahrsschrift für Musikwissenschaft*, and edited the complete works of Schütz and the organ works of Buxtehude. His chief literary work is his book on Bach in two volumes (1873–80).

Spofforth, Reginald (1768 or 1770–1827) English composer. He was a pupil of his uncle Thomas Spofforth, organist of Southwell Minster, and of B Cooke in London, where he settled. He gained several of the Glee Club's prizes.

Works include: farce with music *The Witch of the Wood, or The Nutting Girls* (1796), additions to Salomon's *Windsor Castle* (1795); many glees, including 'Hail, smiling morn'.

Spohr, Ludwig (Louis) (1784–1859) German violinist, composer, and conductor. He travelled throughout Europe as a soloist and leader of orchestras, playing with the London Philharmonic Society 1820. His music reflects his career as a violinist, including 15 violin concertos, chamber music, and 9 symphonies. He was one of the first conductors to use a ◊baton. Spohr's music was widely performed during the 19th century, and he was particular popular in Victorian England. Today he is known largely through the 8th violin concerto and a few tuneful chamber works.

He first learnt music from his parents, who were both musical, although his father was a physician. They lived at Seesen in his childhood, and he was afterwards taught by two amateurs, but was sent to school and for further studies at Brunswick. He played a violin concerto of his own at a school concert and at 14 went to Hamburg trying to gain a hearing. He failed, but on his return petitioned the duke for assistance and was sent to Franz Eck for lessons. They went to Russia in 1802, where he met Muzio Clementi and John Field. He performed and composed a great deal at that time, returned to Brunswick in 1803, heard Pierre Rode there and entered the ducal orchestra. In 1804 he visited Berlin and played there with the 13-year-old Meyerbeer.

In 1805 he became leader in the Duke of Gotha's orchestra and married the harpist Dorette Scheidler, with whom he toured widely. After producing his third opera at Hamburg in 1811, he visited Vienna in 1812, becoming leader at the Theater an der Wien and staying there until 1815.

In 1813 and 1814 he wrote two of his most popular pieces, the nonet and octet; after producing *Faust* in Prague, he travelled in Italy 1816–17 and then became conductor at the Frankfurt opera 1817–19. In 1820 he visited London and Paris for the first time, meeting Cherubini, Rodolphe Kreutzer, and Giovanni Battista Viotti.

After a visit to Dresden he became court music director at Kassel on 1 January 1822, having been recommended for the post by Weber, who had declined it. He remained there for the rest of his life, but continued to travel. In 1831 he finished writing his *Violin School*, in 1834 his wife died, and in 1836 he married the pianist Marianne Pfeiffer. In 1839 he revisited England for the performance of *Cavalry* at the Norwich Festival, and was commissioned to write an English oratorio, *The Fall of Babylon*, for the next festival in 1842, in which year he conducted Wagner's *Flying Dutchman* at Kassel. He was not allowed leave to go to England for the oratorio, but went during his summer vacation in 1843, when he appeared before Queen Victoria and Prince Albert and toured England and Wales. During the 1848 revolutions he showed liberal leanings and so annoyed the elector that he was refused leave of absence, and having taken his vacation without leave, he became involved in a long lawsuit, which he lost after four years. In 1852 he adapted *Faust* without recitatives for a production in Italian in London and in 1853 he produced Wagner's *Tannhäuser* at Kassel. He was pensioned off against his will in 1857.

Works include: STAGE operas *Faust* (1816, revised 1852), *Zemire und Azor* (1819), *Jessonda* (1823).

ORCHESTRAL nine symphonies (4. *Die Weihe der Töne*, 1832, 6. Historic Symphony, 1839, 9. *The Seasons*, 1850), five overtures (including one on Shakespeare's *Macbeth*); 15 violin concertos (8. *In modo d'una scena cantante*, 1816); four clarinet concertos (1812–28).

CHAMBER 33 string quartets (1807–57), eight string quintets, octet for strings and wind (1814), nonet for ditto (1813); sonatas for violin and harp; harp pieces.

Spontini, Gaspare (Luigi Pacifico) (1774–1851) Italian composer and conductor. He

produced several operas in Italy, but had little success until 1807, when he produced *La vestale* in Paris. In 1820 he went to Berlin as music director to Frederick William III; his greatest success in this post was the opera *Agnes von Hohenstaufen* 1837. He was hindered throughout his career, however, by his difficult and quarrelsome personality, which led to his dismissal on more than one occasion.

His family intended him for the priesthood, but he ran away to Monte San Vito, where an uncle allowed him to study music. When he had advanced sufficiently, he returned home and was allowed to study at the Conservatorio de' Turchini at Naples from 1791, where his teachers included Nicola Sala and Giacomo Tritto. In 1796 he produced his first opera in Rome, having run away from the Conservatory, but he was readmitted at the intercession of Niccolò Piccinni, from whom he learnt much. He now produced one opera after another, and in 1798 went to Palermo with the Neapolitan court, which took refuge there and appointed him music director in the place of Domenico Cimarosa, who refused to leave Naples.

In 1803 he left for Paris, where he taught singing and tried his hand at French comic opera, but made his first real success with the serious opera *La vestale* in 1807. He was appointed composer to the Empress Joséphine and in 1810 became director of the Italian opera at the Théâtre de l'Impératrice, giving the first local performance of *Don Giovanni*. In 1812 he was dismissed, but the Bourbon restoration in 1814 reinstated him. He soon sold his post to the soprano Angelica Catalani, however.

In 1820 he was summoned to the court of Frederick William III in Berlin as general music director to the Prussian court. He was not on good terms with the intendant, Count Brühl, though he succeeded in introducing excellent reforms at the court opera; but his success was obscured in 1821 by that of Weber's *Freischütz*, which aroused an appetite for German opera, as distinct from foreign opera set to German words. In 1822–23 he visited Dresden, where he met Weber; he also visited Vienna and Paris. In 1838 he spent the summer in England to study English history and local colour for an opera about the poet Milton, differing from an earlier one, which was never finished. On the king's death in 1840 his position became more and more difficult; this was partly his own fault, for he quarrelled with the new intendant, Count Redern, and became involved in a law-suit, and after much trouble and threatened imprisonment he left Berlin in July 1842. He went to live in Paris, and visited Dresden in 1844 to conduct a performance of *La vestale* rehearsed for him by Wagner. In 1848 he became deaf and returned to his birthplace, founding a music school at Jesi.

In recent years Spontini's operas have enjoyed a limited revival, with performances in Europe of *Fernand Cortez*, *Agnes von Hohenstaufen*, and *Olympie*.

Works include: the operas *I puntigli delle donne* (1796), *Adelina Senese* (1798), *L'eroismo ridicolo*, *Il finto pittore*, *La finta filosofa*, *La fuga in maschera*, and eight other Italian operas, *La petite maison* (1804), *Julie, ou Le pot de fleurs* (1805), *Milton* (in French), *La vestale* (1807), *Fernand Cortez* (1809), *Olympie* (French, revised in German as *Olympia*, 1819), *Pélage, ou Le roi de la paix*, (1814), *Nurmahal* (German, after Moore's 'Lalla Rockh', 1821), *Alcidor*, *Agnes von Hohenstaufen* (1837), *Les dieux rivaux* (with Berton, R Kreutzer, and Persuis); festival play with music on Moore's 'Lalla Rookh' (original version of the opera); ballet for Salieri's *Les Danaïdes*; *Domine salvum fac* and other church music; cantata *L'eccelsa gara* for the victory of Austerlitz, coronation cantata for Nicholas I of Russia; vocal duets and trios; songs with piano or harp; *Sensations douces*.

Sporer, Thomas (c. 1490–1534) German composer. He wrote songs with accompaniment, which were rare at that time, but were cultivated by Henricus Isaac, Paul Hofhaimer, Ludwig Senfl, and others besides Sporer.

Sprechgesang (German 'speech-song') in music, a type of vocal technique, a hybrid of pure song and speech. It consists of recitation on approximate pitches, notated usually by cross-shaped symbols instead of usual notes. Although the pitches are approximate, the rhythm tends to be notated by traditional means. It was first introduced in Engelbert ◊Humperdinck's melodrama *Königskinder* 1910. Schoenberg used it in several works, including *Pierrot lunaire* 1912, as did Berg in his operas *Wozzeck* 1920 and *Lulu* 1935.

'Spring' Sonata the familiar nickname given to Beethoven's violin and piano sonata in F major, op. 24, composed 1801.

'Spring' Symphony Schumann's original name for his first symphony, in B♭ major, op. 38, finished February 1841 and first performed at Leipzig by Mendelssohn, 31 March 1841. Also the title of a choral work by Britten, first performed Amsterdam, 9 July 1949.

sprung rhythm term invented by Gerard Manley Hopkins for displacements of metrical stresses in poetry, not new to his verse, but exploited by him consciously and with great persistence and variety; and transferred to musical terminology by Michael Tippett in the prefatory notes to his second string quartet, where sprung rhythm is used with a deliberation similar to Hopkins's in the finale.

Squire, W(illiam) Barclay (1855–1927) English musicologist. He published catalogues for the British Museum and the Royal College of Music, edited Purcell's harpsichord music and other works, and with Fuller-Maitland the *Fitzwilliam Virginal Book*.

He was educated at Frankfurt and Pembroke College, Cambridge. In 1885 he took charge of the department of printed music in the British Museum. He was also a critic and the author of the libretto of Standford's opera *The Veiled Prophet*, honorary secretary of the Purcell Society, and one of the honorary secretaries of the International Musical Society.

'Stabat Mater' a medieval Latin sacred poem, probably by Jacopone da Todi, not originally liturgical, but increasingly used for devotional purposes until it was admitted as a Sequence to the Roman missal in 1727.

Stabile, Annibale (c. 1535–1595) Italian composer. He was a pupil of Palestrina in Rome, where he became maestro di cappella at the Lateran. From 1579 to 1590 he held a similar post at the Collegio Germanico there, and in 1591 at the church of Santa Maria Maggiore.

Works include: motets, Litanies and other church music; madrigals.

staccato (Italian 'detached') in music, a term used to describe a continuous passage in which every note is separately articulated rather than phrased continuously (legato 'joined'). Staccato gives an upbeat feel to a passage, for example the opening of the scherzo to Beethoven's 'Pastoral' *Symphony No 6* 1807–08.

Staden, Johann (1581–1634) German organist and composer. He was in the service of the Margrave of Kulmbach and Bayreuth 1603–16, after which he became organist of St Lorenz's Church at Nuremberg and soon afterwards of St Sebald's Church.

Works include: motets for voices alone, motets with instrumental thorough-bass, sacred concertos for voices and instruments; *Hauss-Music* for voices and instruments with

German words (1623–28); sacred and secular songs with continuo for organ or lute; secular songs for four–five voices; instrumental pavans, galliards, canzoni.

Stadler, Maximilian (1748–1833) Austrian priest, organist, and composer. He completed some of the unfinished works of his friend Mozart, and his defence of the authenticity of Mozart's Requiem was published at Vienna in 1825.

He studied under Johann Albrechtsberger, and entered the Benedictine monastery of Melk in 1766. He was ordained in 1772, became a prior there in 1784, was appointed abbot of Lilienfeld in 1786, and of Kremsmünster in 1789. In 1796 he settled in Vienna, and after working as a parish priest 1803–15 returned there to devote himself entirely to music.

Works include: Masses, two Requiems, Te Deum, three Magnificat settings, and other church music; oratorio *Die Befreyung von Jerusalem* (1811); music for Collin's tragedy *Polyxena* (1811); cantatas, including *Frühlingsfeyer* (Klopstock, 1813); organ sonatas and fugues; piano music.

Staempfli, Edward (1908–) Swiss composer. He studied medicine initially, but gave it up for music, which he studied with Jarnach at Cologne and with Dukas in Paris.

Works include: ballets *Das Märchen von den zwei Flöten* and *Le Pendu* (1942); cantata *Filles de Sion* for solo voices, chorus and orchestra; three symphonies (1938, 1942, 1945), four *Sinfonie concertanti* and other orchestral works; four piano concertos (1932–63), two violin concertos, concerto for two pianos and strings; music for 11 instruments, concerto for piano and eight instruments, six string quartets (1926–62), quintet for wind, quartet for flute, and strings, piano trio, string trio and other chamber music; piano pieces; songs.

staff alternative name for ◊stave.

staff notation the ordinary musical notation, so called to distinguish it from the notation used for tonic sol-fa.

Staggins, Nicholas (1645–1700) English composer. Charles II appointed him Master of the King's Band in 1674. He advanced to the post of Master of the King's Musick, and was succeeded in it after his death by John Eccles.

He took a degree in music at Cambridge University in 1682, and became professor of music there in 1684.

Works include: the masque *Calisto, or The Chaste Nimph* (Crowne); incidental music for Etheredge's *The Man of Mode*, Lee's *Gloriana*, Dryden's *Conquest of Granada* and *Marriage à la Mode*, and Shadwell's *Epsom Wells* (last two with Robert Smith); odes for the birthday of William III; songs.

stagione (Italian 'season') musical term is used especially for an opera season.

Stahlspiel (German 'steel-play') percussion instrument with tuned steel plates or bars which are played with hammers. It is known in English military bands as a lyra, being made for them in the shape of a lyre. The modern glockenspiel, being also made of steel bars, and no longer of actual bells, is now to all intents and purposes the same instrument.

Stainer, Jacob (1621–1683) Austrian violin maker. He learnt his craft at Innsbruck and, probably, with either one of the Amati family in Cremona or with Vimercati in Venice. He began to work on his own account at Absam around 1640. He died insane, after being accused of Lutheran tendencies.

Stainer, John (1840–1901) English organist and composer. He became organist of St Paul's Cathedral, London in 1872. His religious choral works are *The Crucifixion* 1887, an oratorio, and *The Daughter of Jairus* 1878, a cantata.

He became a choirboy at St Paul's Cathedral at the age of seven and before long was able to deputize at the organ. After working under various masters and receiving an organist's appointment in the City of London, Frederick Ouseley appointed him organist of St Michael's College, Tenbury, in 1856. In 1860 he went to Oxford as an undergraduate at St Edmund Hall and organist to Magdalen College, then succeeded George Elvey (1816–1893) as organist to the University; in 1865 he took a degree in music. In 1872 he returned to London as organist at St Paul's Cathedral. In 1888, having resigned from St Paul's through failing eyesight, he was knighted and in 1889 became professor of music at Oxford. He wrote on music in the Bible, and edited *Early Bodleian Music, Dufay and his Contemporaries*, and other books.

Works include: the oratorios *Gideon* (1865) and *The Crucifixion* (1887); *Sevenfold Amen*, services and anthems; cantatas *The Daughter of Jairus* (1878) and *St Mary Magdalen* (1887).

Stamitz (lived 18th–early 19th centuries) Bohemian family of musicians:
Johann Wenzel Anton (1717–1757), violinist and composer. He entered the service of the

Electoral court at Mannheim in 1741, became principal violinist in 1743 and later music director. Under him the orchestra became the most famous in Europe, called by Charles Burney 'an army of generals'. He was the founder and most important member of the Mannheim school of symphonists, which had a profound influence on Mozart's instrumental style.

His works include 74 symphonies (58 extant); concertos for violin, harpsichord, flute, oboe, clarinet; trio sonatas and other chamber music, violin sonatas.

Carl (1745–1801), violinist and composer, son and pupil of Johann. He entered the Mannheim orchestra as second violin in 1762, then went to Strasbourg (1770), Paris, and London, appearing as a virtuoso on the violin and viola d'amore. He continued to travel widely, visiting Prague in 1787 and Russia in 1790, until in 1794 he settled in Jena as music director to the university.

His works include the operas *Der verliebte Vormund* (1787) and *Dardanus* (1800); c. 80 symphonies and *sinfonies concertantes*; concertos; chamber music.

Johann Anton (1750–before 1809), violinist and composer, son and pupil of Johann. In 1770 he went with his brother Carl to Paris, where he settled as violinist in the court orchestra. Kreutzer was his pupil. He wrote 12 symphonies, concertos for violin, viola, flute, and oboe, as well as chamber music.

Ständchen a German serenade.

Standford, Patric (actually John Patric Standford Gledhill) (1939–) English composer and teacher. He studied with Rubbra at Guildhall School of Music and Drama and Witold Lutosławski at Dartington. He was professor of composition at the Guildhall School of Music and Drama, London, 1967–80; director of music at Bretton Hall College, University of Leeds, 1980–93.

Works include: the opera *Villon* (1972–84); five symphonies: no. 1 for orchestra (1972), no. 2 *Christus-Requiem* for soloists, chorus, and orchestra (1972), no. 3 *Towards Paradise* for chorus and orchestra (1973), no. 4 *Taikyoku* for two pianos and six percussion (1976), no. 5 for orchestra (1984); cello concerto (1974), violin concerto (1975), piano concerto (1979), *Rage* for orchestra (1993); Mass for brass and chorus (1980), *Mass of our Lady St Rochas* (1988), *A Messiah Reborn* for soloist, chorus, and orchestra (1992); three string quartets (1964, 1973, 1992).

Standfuss, J C (died c. 1759) German violinist and composer. At one time a member of G H Koch's opera troupe in Leipzig, he was the first to produce a German *Singspiel*, in adapting Charles Coffey's (d. 1745) *The Devil to Pay* as *Der Teufel ist los* 1752. Coffey's sequel *The Merry Cobbler* was similarly arranged as *Der lustige Schuster* in 1759. His third *Singspiel* was *Der stolze Bauer Jochem Tróbs* 1759.

Stanford, Charles Villiers (1852–1924) Irish composer and teacher. He was a leading figure in the 19th-century renaissance of British music. His many works include operas such as *Shamus O'Brien* 1896, seven symphonies, chamber music, and church music. Among his pupils were Vaughan Williams, Gustav Holst, and Frank Bridge.

In 1870 he became choral scholar at Queens' College, Cambridge, and in 1873 organist of Trinity College, where he took classical honours the next year; he was also conductor of the Cambridge University Musical Society. He studied with Reinecke at Leipzig 1874–76 and with Kiel in Berlin, and in 1876 Tennyson suggested him as composer of incidental music for his *Queen Mary*. He received a doctorate from Oxford in 1883 and in 1888 from Cambridge, where he had succeeded Macfarren as professor of music in 1887. He was also conductor of the Bach Choir in London and professor of composition at the Royal College of Music, where he conducted the orchestral and opera classes.

Works include: the opera *Shamus O'Brien* (after Le Fanu).

ORCHESTRAL seven symphonies (1876–1911); five Irish Rhapsodies (1901–14), cello concerto (1919), clarinet concerto.

CHAMBER two sonatas for cello and piano, clarinet and piano sonata, some smaller instrumental pieces with piano; piano works including sonata, three *Dante Rhapsodies*; 11 organ works including five sonatas; oratorios *The Three Holy Children*, *Eden* (1891); cantatas *Stabat Mater*, Magnificat: *The Revenge*, *Songs of the Fleet*, *Songs of the Sea*; two psalms, six services, three anthems; 20 op. nos. of songs.

Stanley, John (1713–1786) English composer and organist. His works, which include organ ◊voluntaries (solos) and concertos for strings, influenced Handel. He succeeded William Boyce as ◊Master of the King's Musick 1779.

He was blind from the age of two, but became a pupil of Maurice Greene and later held various organist's appointments in London. In 1759 he joined John Christopher Smith to continue Handel's oratorio concerts, and when Smith retired in 1774, he continued with the younger Thomas Linley.

Works include: the opera *Teraminta*; dramatic cantata *The Choice of Hercules*; music for Lloyd's *Arcadia, or The Shepherd's Wedding* (1761) and *Tears and Triumphs of Parnassus* and Southerne's *Oroonoko* (1759); oratorios *Jephtha* (1752), *Zimri* (1760), and *The Fall of Egypt* (1774); 12 cantatas to words by John Hawkins; six concertos for strings; solos for flute or violin; cantatas and songs for voice and instruments.

Stappen, Crispinus van (c. 1470–1532) Flemish composer. He wrote sacred and secular works, including a *strambotto* in praise of the town of Padua.

He became a singer at the Sainte-Chapelle, Paris, in 1492, and shortly afterwards, until 1507, at the Papal Chapel in Rome. In 1524–25 he was maestro di cappella at the Casa Santa, Loreto. He held a canonry at Cambrai from 1504.

Starer, Robert (1924–) Austrian-born US composer. He studied in Vienna, then moved to Jerusalem at the Anschluss. He moved to the USA in 1947, studying at Juilliard; he has taught at Brooklyn College from 1963.

Works include: the operas *The Intruder* (1956), *Pantagleize* (1973), *The Last Lover* (1975) and *Apollonia* (1979); ballets *The Dybbuk* (1960), *Samson Agonistes* (1961), *Phaedra* (1962), *The Lady of the House of Sleep* (1968), *Holy Jungle* (1974); three symphonies (1950–69); three piano concertos (1947, 1953, 1972), concertos for viola (1959), violin and cello (1968), violin (1981) and cello (1988); *Voice at Brooklyn* (in seven parts) for soloists, chorus, and orchestra (1980–84); string quartet (1947), two piano sonatas; cantatas on biblical subjects.

Starlight Express, The incidental music by Elgar for a play by V Pearn, after Algernon Blackwood's *A Prisoner from Fairyland*; composed 1915. Suite in nine movements, with soprano and bass soloists, performed Kingsway Theatre, London, 29 December 1915; very popular as escapist entertainment during the worst days of World War I, but forgotten until recent recording.

Starzer, Josef (1726–1787) Austrian composer and violinist. Violinist at the French theatre in Vienna from 1752, he was court composer and leader of the orchestra in St Petersburg 1758–70. Back in Vienna he wrote music for Noverre's ballets, and was active in the Tonkünstler-Society, for whose concerts he re-orchestrated Handel's *Judas Maccabeus*

in 1779. From 1783 increasing corpulence enforced his retirement.

Works include: Singspiele *Die drei Pächter* and *Die Wildschützen*; ballets *Roger et Bradamante* (1771), *Adèle de Ponthieu* (1773), *Gli Orazi ed i Curiazi* (all with Noverre) and many others; oratorio *La Passione di Gesù Cristo*; symphonies, divertimenti. for orchestra; violin concerto; chamber music.

Stassov, Vladimir Vassilevich (1824–1906) Russian scholar and art critic. He was the first champion of the Russian nationalist school of composers, writing on Cui, Glinka, Borodin, and Mussorgsky and coining the phrase 'Moguchaya Kuchka' ('Mighty Handful').

Educated at the School of Jurisprudence, he joined the Imperial Public Library in 1845. He studied in Italy from 1851 to 1854, after which he returned to the Library and in 1872 became director of the department of fine arts there.

Statkowski, Roman (1860–1925) Polish composer. He studied with Zeleński at Warsaw and with Soloviev at St Petersburg. On the death of Noskowski in 1909 he was appointed professor of composition at the Warsaw Conservatory.

Works include: the operas *Philaenis* (1904) and *Maria* (after Malczewski, 1906); fantasy, polonaise and other works for orchestra; five string quartets (1896–1929); violin and piano pieces; *Krakowiak* and other works for piano; songs.

stave, or staff the five-line grid, reading from left to right, on which music is notated. The pitch range of stave notation is indicated by a ♭clef.

Steffani, Agostino (1654–1728) Italian diplomat and composer. While he was engaged as music director at Hanover and Düsseldorf, he was sent on various diplomatic missions in Germany, Belgium, and Italy. His most important musical works are about 70 chamber duets – pieces for two singers and continuo; Handel was influenced by them. He also wrote several operas, of which the best known is *Tassilone* 1709.

Learnt music as a choirboy at Padua and was taken to Munich, where he studied music under Johann Kerl at the expense of the Elector Ferdinand Maria. After further studies in Rome 1673–74, he returned to Munich and became court organist in 1675. Having also studied mathematics, philosophy, and theology, he was ordained in 1680. He was made director of the court chamber music, but in 1688 the younger Bernabei was appointed general music director on the death of his father, and Steffani, disappointed in his hopes of obtaining the post, left Munich. After a visit to Venice he went to the court of Hanover, where the post of music director was offered him, and there he also filled other posts, including diplomatic ones. The philosopher Leibniz, who was also at the court, sent him on a diplomatic mission to various German courts in 1696; in 1698 he was ambassador to Brussels, and on the death of the Elector Ernest Augustus transferred his services to the Elector Palatine at Düsseldorf. In 1706 he was made a nominal bishop. In 1708–09 he was on a diplomatic mission in Italy, where he met Handel, who went into service at the Hanoverian court at his suggestion. His best known opera, *Tassilone*, dates from this time; it unites the Italian and German musical influences which were paramount in Steffani's life. In 1722–25 he lived at Padua and in 1727 he was elected honorary president of the London Academy of Vocal Music. In 1727 he went to Italy for the last time. He died at Frankfurt during a diplomatic visit.

Works include: the operas *Marco Aurelio* (1680), *Solone* (1685), *Servio Tullio, Alarico il Baltha* (1687), *Niobe* (1688), *Enrico Leone, La lotta d'Hercole con Achelao* (1689), *La superbia d'Alessandro* (1690), *Orlando generoso* (1691), *Le rivali concordi, La libertà contenta* (1693), *I trionfi del fato* (1695), *Baccanali, Briseide, Arminio, Enea,* and *Tassilone* (1709); music for a tournament *Audacia e rispetto;* motets, vesper psalms for eight voices, *Stabat Mater* for six voices, strings, and organ (1727), *Confitebor* for three voices and strings and other church music; madrigals; vocal chamber duets with bass; chamber sonatas for two violins, viola, and bass.

Steibelt, Daniel (1765–1823) German composer and pianist. His setting of *Romeo and Juliet* was his most successful work after an initial rejection. It was admired by Berlioz, who may have been influenced by it in his own dramatic symphony.

He learnt much about keyboard instruments in his childhood, being the son of a harpsichord and piano maker, and studied music with Johann Kirnberger. After serving in the army, he made his first appearance as a pianist and composer in Paris during the late 1780s. At the end of 1796 he visited London, where he remained until 1799 and married an Englishwoman. He visited Hamburg, Dresden, Prague, Berlin, and Vienna, where he met Beethoven, and in 1800 again settled in Paris, but spent as much of his time in London. In 1808 he left for the court at St

Petersburg, where he became director of the French Opera on the departure of Boieldieu in 1810.

Works include: the operas *Roméo et Juliette* (after Shakespeare, 1793), *La princesse de Babylone, Cendrillon* (1810), *Sargines,* and *Le jugement de Midas* (unfinished); ballets *Le retour de Zéphyr* (1802), *Le jugement du berger Paris* (1804), *La belle laitière, La fête de l'empereur* (1809); intermezzo *La fête de Mars* for the victory at Austerlitz; incidental music; eight piano concertos (1796–1820); 50 studies and numerous pieces and transcriptions for piano.

Stein (lived 18th–19th centuries) German family of piano makers:

Johann Andreas (1728–1792), organ builder and piano maker. He learnt his craft from his father, Johann Georg Stein (1697–1754), worked with J A Silbermann in Strasbourg, and settled in Augsburg in 1751. Mozart preferred his pianos above all others.

Maria Anna (Nanette) (1769–1833), pianist and piano maker, daughter of Johann. She played to Mozart as a child during his visit to Augsburg in 1777, and on her father's death in 1792 carried on the business with her brother, Matthäus, but married Andreas Streicher in 1794 and moved with him to Vienna, where they established a new firm, jointly with Matthäus. Later she and her husband became friends of Beethoven.

Matthäus Andreas (1776–1842), piano maker, son of Johann. He accompanied his sister and her husband to Vienna in 1793 and joined their firm, but established himself independently in 1802.

Andreas Friedrich (1784–1809), pianist and composer, son of Johann. He went to Vienna as a child with his sister and brother, and studied piano playing and also composition with Albrechtsberger. He appeared in public frequently, especially with Mozart's concertos.

His works include three operettas; pantomime *Die Fee Radiante;* violin concerto; piano trio; piano sonata; songs.

Karl Andreas (1797–1863), composer and piano maker, son of Matthäus. He was a pupil of Förster. He first devoted himself to composition, but later mainly to his father's factory, to which he succeeded. He wrote a comic opera *Die goldene Gans,* two overtures, and two piano concertos.

Stein, Erwin (1885–1958) Austrian musicologist. He was a pupil of Arnold Schoenberg. After conducting at various places, he joined the Universal Edition in Vienna, but settled in

London after the Anschluss. He wrote much on Schoenberg.

Steinberg, Maksimilian Osseievich (1883–1946) Russian composer. Stravinsky's *Fireworks* was given its first performance at his wedding in 1908.

He studied at St Petersburg University and Conservatory. He was the pupil (and later son-in-law) of Rimsky-Korsakov, and also studied with Liadov and Glazunov. He became professor at the Leningrad Conservatory.

Works include: ballets *Midas* (after Ovid) and *Till Eulenspiegel*; incidental music; oratorio *Heaven and Earth* (after Byron); four symphonies (1907, 1909, 1929, 1933), dramatic fantasy on Ibsen's *Brand*, overture to Maeterlinck's *La Princesse Maleine* and other orchestral works; violin concerto (1946); two string quartets; songs including two Tagore cycles, folk-song arrangements.

Steiner, Max(imilian Raoul Walter) (1888–1971) Austrian-born US film composer. With Erich Korngold, he brought the style of Gustav Mahler and Richard Strauss to Hollywood movie scores. He pioneered the use of the ◊click-track for feature films to guarantee absolute coordination of music and film action. His richly sentimental scores include *King Kong* 1934, *Gone With the Wind* 1939, and *Casablanca* 1942.

Steinitz, (Charles) Paul (Joseph) (1909–1988) English organist and conductor. He studied at the Royal College of Music, London, and was church organist in Ashford 1933–42. Founded South London Bach Society 1947 (later known as London Bach Society). With the Steinitz Bach Players (founded 1969) he gave annual performances in London of the *St Matthew Passion*. Professor, Royal Academy of Music, from 1945.

Steinway and Sons company of piano manufacturers founded in New York 1853 by German-born Heinrich Engelhard Steinweg (later Henry Steinway) (1797–1871), who emigrated from Brunswick, Germany, with his five sons. Branches of the firm were later established in London, Hamburg, and Berlin.. Steinway transformed the 19th-century piano into the modern instrument, introducing 'overstringing' (where the bass strings pass at an angle above some of the higher-pitched strings, thereby enriching the tone quality), larger metal frames that allowed the inclusion of strings of higher tension and better tone quality, and various improvements in the ◊action. Since Russian pianist and composer Anton Rubinstein represented the company

in the 1870s, most concert artists have preferred the brilliant tone and superior control of Steinway instruments.

stem in musical notation, the stroke attached to the heads of all notes of smaller value than a semibreve.

Stenhammar, (Karl) Wilhelm (Eugen) (1871–1927) Swedish composer, conductor, and pianist. He became conductor of the royal orchestra at Stockholm and also conductor at Göteborg.

He studied with his father, the composer Per Ulrik Stenhammar (1829–75), and later with Emil Sjögren and others; he also studied in Berlin.

Works include: OPERA *Tirfing* (1898); incidental music to plays including Strindberg's *Ett römspel*, Tagore's *Chitra*; cantata *Sangen*.

ORCHESTRAL AND CHAMBER two symphonies (1903, 1915), serenade in F major for orchestra; two piano concertos (1893–1907); six string quartets (1894–1909); violin and piano sonata; four sonatas and fantasy for piano; part songs including *Sverige*; songs.

'Stenka Razin' symphonic poem by Glazunov, op. 13, composed 1884, first performed St Petersburg, 1885. It contains the tune of the Volga boatmen's song *Ey ukhnem*.

stentando (Italian 'toiling, labouring') musical direction indicating a dragging delivery of a passage.

Steptoe, Roger (1953–   ) English composer, pianist, and teacher. He studied at the Royal Academy of Music 1974–77 and was administrator of the International Composer Festivals there 1986–93. He made his debut as a pianist at the Wigmore Hall in 1982.

Works include: the opera *The King of Macedon* (1979); symphony (1988), *Sinfonia Concertante* for string trio and strings (1981), concertos for oboe (1982), tuba (1983), clarinet (1989), organ (1990), and cello (1991); *Winter's Cold Embraces Dye*, for soloists, chorus, and orchestra (1985), *Life's Unquiet Dream* for baritone, chorus, and chamber orchestra (1992); two string quartets (1976, 1985) and other chamber music; choral music and pieces for brass.

Sterndale Bennett see William Sterndale ◊Bennett.

Sternklang/Starsound 'park music' for five electronic groups by Stockhausen. First performed Berlin, 5 June 1971.

stesso tempo, lo (Italian, more frequently l'istesso tempo, 'the same pace') musical direction given where a change is indicated in the time-signature, but the composer wishes the music to continue at the same pace or beat.

Stevens, Bernard (1916–1983) English composer. In 1948 he was appointed professor of composition at the Royal College of Music.

He studied at Cambridge with E J Dent and C B Rootham and at the Royal College of Music in London with R O Morris. He won the Leverhulme Scholarship and Parry Prize for composition. He served in the army 1940–46.

Works include: film music; cantata *The Harvest of Peace* (1952) and other choral works; symphony, *Symphony of Liberation* (1946) and Fugal Overture for orchestra, *Ricercar* and *Sinfonietta* for strings, overture *East and West* for wind band; violin concerto (1946), cello concerto (1952); string quartet, piano trio, theme and variations for string quartet (1949), *Fantasia* for two violins and piano; violin and piano sonata; piano music; songs.

Stevens, Denis (William) (1922–) English musicologist and conductor. He studied at Oxford 1940–42 and 1946–49, and after playing in orchestras was a member of the British Broadcasting Corporation (BBC) music department in London 1950–54. He has edited the Mulliner Book in *Musica Britannica* and Monteverdi's *Vespers* and *Orfeo*, and published books on Tomkins and Tudor church music. He was a professor at Columbia University, New York, 1964–74. He conducted Monteverdi at Salzburg and the London Proms (both 1967); published editions of the *Vespers* (1961, revised 1993) and *Orfeo* (1967). He was cofounder of the Ambrosian Singers.

Stevens, Halsey (1908–1989) US composer, teacher, and writer on music. He studied at Syracuse University and with Bloch at Berkeley, 1944. He was chair of the music department at University of California at Los Angeles, 1948–76. He is best known for his *Life and Music of Béla Bartók* (1953, revised 1964); he also wrote three symphonies (1945–46), three string quartets, three piano sonatas (1933–48), *The Ballad of William Sycamore* for chorus and orchestra (1955), and *Te Deum* for chorus, brass septet, and organ (1967).

Stevens, John (Edgar) (1921–) English literary historian and musicologist. He was lecturer in English at Cambridge University in 1952, and professor of Medieval and Renaissance English there in 1978. In addition to his important editions of early English music he is particularly regarded for his books *Music and Poetry in the Early Tudor Court* (1961) and *Words and Music in the Middle Ages* (1986).

Stevenson, Robert M(urrell) (1916–) US musicologist. He studied at Juilliard, Yale, Harvard, and Oxford (with Jack Westrup). He was professor at University of California (Los Angeles) from 1949, and faculty research lecturer from 1981. His chief areas of study have been Latin American colonial music and Spanish music; his books include *La Musica en las Catedrales de España durante el siglo do oro* (1992). He has wriiten many articles for *The New Grove's Dictionary of Music and Musicians* (1980).

Stevenson, Ronald (1928–) English composer, pianist, and writer on music. He has made a special study of Busoni: his first piano concerto, *Triptych* 1960, is based on themes from Busoni's *Doktor Faust*.

He studied at the Royal Manchester College of Music and in Italy, and has taught at Edinburgh University.

Works include: *Passacaglia on DSCH*, an 80-minute work for piano (first performance Cape Town, 1963), and *Peter Grimes Fantasia* for piano (1971). Piano concerto no. 2 (*The Continents*, 1972), *Ben Dorain*, choral symphony (1973), violin concerto (The Gypsy, 1973), *Corroboree for Grainger* for piano and wind ensemble (1987), *St Mary's May Songs* for soprano and strings (1988).

sticcado-pastrole musical instrument, a glass ◊dulcimer popular in England in the 18th century.

Stierhorn (German 'bull horn') primitive wind instrument, made of a bull's or a cow's horn, sounding a single note of rough quality. Wagner used it for the watchman in *Die Meistersinger von Nürnberg*.

Stiffelio opera by Verdi (libretto by F M Piave), produced Trieste, 16 November 1850. Revised as *Aroldo* (1856–57). Priest Stiffelio forgives adulterous wife Lina after her father Stankar has killed her lover, Raffaele.

stile rappresentativo (Italian 'representative style') term used by Italian musicians of the new monodic school in the early years of the 17th century to describe the new vocal style of declamatory, recitative-like dramatic music, which tried to imitate human speech as closely as possible and thus endeavoured to 'represent' dramatic action in a naturalistic way.

Still, William Grant (1895–1978) US composer. His music employs American elements, blues melodies, and American folk songs.

He was educated at Wilberforce University and studied music at Oberlin Conservatory; later he studied with George Chadwick at Boston and with Edgard Varèse. *The Afro-American Symphony* of 1930 was the first by a black American composer to be performed by a major orchestra and the opera *Troubled Island* 1949 was the first premiere given by the newly-formed City Center Opera Company of New York.

Works include: the operas *Blue Steel* (1934), *Troubled Island* (1949), *A Bayou Legend* (1941, first performance 1974), *Highway no. 1* (1942–63), *Costaso* (1949, first performance 1992), and *Minette Fontaine* (1958, first performance 1985); ballets *La Guiablesse* (1927) and *Sahdji* (1930), *Lenox Avenue* for radio announcer, chorus, and orchestra (1937); five symphonies, including *Afro-American Symphony* (no. 1, 1930), *Africa, Poem, Phantom Chapel* for strings and other orchestral works; *Kaintuck* for piano and orchestra (1935); *From the Black Belt* and *Log Cabin Ballads* for chamber orchestra.

Stimme (German 'voice and part') in music, the human voice, or any part, vocal or instrumental, in a composition, especially a polyphonic one; also the copy of an orchestral, vocal, or chamber music part used for performance.

Stimmführung German musical term, meaning 'part-writing'.

Stimmung/Mood work by Stockhausen for six amplified voices. First performed Paris, 9 December 1968.

sting an old musical term describing the effect of vibrato in lute playing.

Stobaeus, Johann (1580–1646) German composer and bass. While attending the university at Königsberg, he studied music with Johann Eccard, and after holding various minor appointments there became Kapellmeister to the Elector of Brandenburg in 1626.

Works include: *Cantiones sacrae* for five–ten voices (published 1624), *Magnificats* for five–six voices, five-part settings of hymn-tunes; Prussian Festival Songs for five–eight voices (with Eccard; two volumes, published 1624 and 1644); sacred and secular occasional compositions.

stochastic term used to describe a compositional procedure based on probability theory, where the work's inner details are left to chance (a random sequence of notes), the main outline having been fixed by the composer. Iannis Xenakis introduced this

technique to 20th-century composition, relying on computers to generate specific notes, having written a program determining the overall parameters.

stock-and-horn early Scottish musical instrument, similar to the pibgorn, made of wood or bone fitted with a cow horn. It is played like the chanter of a bagpipe, with a single reed.

It is a different instrument from the stockhorn, which is a forester's horn.

Stockhausen, Karlheinz (1928–) German composer of avant-garde music. He has continued to explore new musical sounds and compositional techniques since the 1950s. His major works include *Gesang der Jünglinge* 1956, *Kontakte* 1960 (electronic music), and *Sirius* 1977.

Since 1977 all his works have been part of *LICHT*, a cycle of seven musical ceremonies intended for performance on the evenings of a week. He has completed *Donnerstag* 1980, *Samstag* 1984, *Montag* 1988, and *Dienstag* 1992. Earlier works include *Klavierstücke I–XIV* 1952–85, *Momente* 1961–64, and *Mikrophonie I* 1964.

He studied at the Cologne Musikhochschule and in Paris with Messiaen and Milhaud. He also learned from the example of Webern, whose tightly controlled brand of serialism inspired Stockhausen's brief venture into 'integral' serialism (in which all elements of sound – such as pitch, duration, and dynamics – are controlled according to pre-determined formulae). Webern's orchestrational technique also influenced Stockhausen's 'group' compositions of the 1950s. From 1953 he worked intensively at German Radio's studio for electronic music at Cologne, influencing contemporaries such as Berio and Boulez and younger composers such as Tim Souster and Brian Ferneyhough. He is one of the most enterprising of the composers creating electronic music, but has also written music for traditional media.

Stockhausen's creative process begins with the premise that all elements of composition can be vigorously controlled, with the progress of a work determined by pre-set acoustic and scientific formulae. In spite of this performers are often allowed a multitude of choices in terms of how they 'read' a score and deploy the equipment at their disposal (the influence of John Cage is evident here). He has lectured in the USA and Britain, building up a specialist audience for his music.

Works include: *Kreuzspiel,* for oboe, clarinet, piano, and three percussion (1951), *Formel* for 29 instruments (1951), *Punkte* for orchestra (1952), *Kontra-Punkte* for ensemble (1952), *Klavierstücke I–XI* (1952–56), *Zeitmasze* for wind quintet (1956), *Gruppen* for three orchestras (1957), *Gesang der Jünglinge* for voice and tapes (1956), *Zyklus* for percussion (1959), *Carré* for four choruses and four orchestras (1960), *Refrain* for ensemble (1959), *Kontakte* for piano, percussion, and four-track tape (1960), *Momente* for soprano, four choruses, and ensemble (1961–64), *Mikrophonie I and II* for electronics (1964–65), *Mixtur* for five orchestras, sine wave generators, and four ring modulators (1964–67), *Stop* for instrumental ensemble (1969–73), *Telemusik* for four-track tape (1966), *Hymnen* for four-track tape (1967), *Stimmung* for voices and ensemble (1968), *Kurzwellen* (*Short Waves*) for electronics and four short-wave radios (1968); *Aus den sieben Tagen,* 15 pieces for various instrumental groups (1968), *Spiral* for soloist and short-wave receiver (1969), *Mantra* for two pianos, woodblock, and two ring modulators (1970), *Sternklang,* park music for five groups (1971), *Trans* for orchestra and tape (1971), '*Am Himmel wandre ich ...*' for soprano and baritone (1972), *Intervall* for piano duo (1972), *Inori* for one/two soloists and orchestra (1974), *Atmen gibt das Leben* for chorus (1974), *Herbstmusik* for four players (1974), *Musik im Bauch/Music in the Belly,* for six percussion, 1975), *Sirius* for soprano, baritone, and ensemble (1977), *Jubiläum* for orchestra (1977).

Operas in *Licht* cycle: *Donnerstag* (1981), *Samstag* (1984), *Montag* (1988), *Dienstag* (1992); scenes from *Licht* have been given as concert pieces: no. 1 *Der Jahreslauf* for dancers and orchestra (1977), no. 2 *Michaels Reise um die Erde* for trumpet and ensemble (1978), no. 3 *Michaels Jugend* for soprano, tenor, brass instruments, piano, dancers, and tape (1979), no. 4 *Michaels Heimkehr* for soloists, chorus, and orchestra (1979); also *Lucifer's Dream* from *Samstag* (1983).

Beethausen, opus 1970, von Stockhoven was compiled for the Beethoven bicentenary and includes fragments of music in quotation and a reading of the Heiligenstadt Testament (developed from *Kurzwellen*).

Stodart (lived 18th–19th centuries) firm of English harpsichord and piano makers. It was founded about 1776 by Robert Stodart, carried on by his son William Stodart, whose employee William Allen invented the metal frame for the piano, and later by his grandson Malcolm Stodart.

Stokem, Johannes (also Stokhem) (c. 1440–c. 1500) Flemish composer. A few sacred and secular works by him survive, including four chansons printed in Ottaviano Petrucci's *Odhecaton A* 1501.

He was probably born and spent his early life near Liège. He was in the service of Beatrice of Hungary in the early 1480s and a singer in the Papal Choir 1487–89. He was a friend of Johannes Tinctoris, who sent him portions of his 12th treatise (all that survives) with a letter.

Stoker, Richard (1938–) English composer. He studied in Huddersfield and at the Royal Academy of Music with Lennox Berkeley; professor 1963–87.

Works include: the operas *Johnson Preserv'd* (1967) and *Thérèse Raquin* (after Zola, 1975), *Petite Suite* (1962) and *Little Symphony* (1969) for orchestra; three string quartets (1960–69), Wind quintet (1963), violin sonata (1964), Sextet (1965), piano trio (1965), Oboe quartet (1970).

Stokowski, Leopold Antoni Stanisław (1882–1977) US conductor. An outstanding innovator, he promoted contemporary music with enthusiasm, was an ardent popularist, and introduced changes in orchestral seating. He cooperated with Bell Telephone Laboratories in early stereophonic recording experiments in the mid-1930s. He was also a major collaborator with Walt Disney in the programming and development of 'Fantasound' optical surround-sound recording technology for the animated film *Fantasia* 1940.

He was born in London, the son of a Polish father and an Irish mother. He studied at the Royal College of Music and took a degree in music at Oxford University. In 1900 he became organist at St James's Church, Piccadilly, London, and later studied in Paris and Munich. From 1905 to 1908 he was an organist in New York , and in 1908 a conductor in London; in 1909 he became conductor of the Cincinnati Symphony Orchestra. As conductor of the Philadelphia Symphony Orchestra he introduced much modern music: he gave the 1926 first performance of *Amériques,* by Varèse, and in 1931 conducted the US premiere of Berg's *Wozzeck*; he also gave the first US performances of Mahler's eighth symphony, *The Rite of Spring,* and the *Gurrelieder*. He was a champion of Rakhmaninov, and led the first performances of the 3rd symphony, 4th piano concerto, and *Rhapsody on a Theme of Paganini*. From 1942 to

1944 he conducted the National Broadcasting Company's Symphony Orchestra with Toscanini, giving the 1944 first performance of Schoenberg's piano concerto: the NBC terminated his contract after the concert. In 1945 he became music director of the Hollywood Bowl and 1949–50 of the New York Philharmonic Orchestra, taking over the Houston Symphony Orchestra in 1955. In 1962 he formed the American Symphony Orchestra in New York , and in 1965 they gave the first performance of Ives' fourth symphony. In 1940 he won wider fame when he appeared in the cartoon film *Fantasia*.

Stollen (German 'props') songs of the German Minnesinger and Meistersinger usually had stanzas divided into three sections: two stollen of equal length often sung to the same and always to very similar music (called *Aufgesang;* fore-song) followed by an *Abgesang* (after-song) forming a concluding section of unspecified length and with different music. The whole song was called a *Bar*.

Stoltzer, Thomas (c. 1486–1526) German composer. He became Kapellmeister to King Louis of Bohemia and Hungary at Buda, but left after the battle of Mohács in 1526 and took up a post in the service of Duke Albert of Prussia at Königsberg. He drowned in the river Taja.

Works include: Latin motets and psalms, Latin hymns for four–five voices, Psalm 37 in Luther's German translation for three–seven voices in motet form and four others; German sacred and secular songs.

Stolz, Robert (Elisabeth) (1880–1975) Austrian composer and conductor. His early career was as a pianist; he was conductor at the Theater an der Wien from 1907. The first of about 60 operettas and musicals was *Die lustigen Weiber von Wien* (produced Munich, 1909). He worked in Berlin in the 1920s, writing for early film musicals. He moved to Hollywood in 1940 and after returning to Vienna in 1946 wrote music for ice revues. He conducted while in his 90s.

Works include: *Der Favorit* (1916), *Der Tans ins Glück* (1921), *Mädi* (1923), *Wenn die kleinen Veilchen blühen* (1932), *Venus in Seide* (1932), *Der verlorene Walzer* (1933), *Frühling in Prater* (1949), *Trauminsel* (1962); c. 100 film scores, many individual songs, waltzes, and a funeral march for Hitler, written in anticipation of his death.

Stölzel, Gottfried Heinrich (1690–1749) German composer. He studied at Leipzig University, taught in Breslau 1710–12, and visited Italy 1713–14, meeting Gasparini, Vivaldi,

and others. He lived in Prague, Bayreuth, and Gera, and from 1719 was Kapellmeister to the court at Gotha.

Works include: 22 operas, *Narcissus* (1711), *Orion* (1712), *Venus und Adonis* (1714).; 14 oratorios; Masses, motets; Passions; *concerti grossi*; trio sonatas.

Stone Flower, The/Kamenny Tsvetok ballet in three acts by Prokofiev (scenario by L Lavrovsky and M Mendelson-Prokofieva after a story by P Bazhov); composed 1948–53, produced Moscow, Bolshoi, 12 February 1954.

Stone Guest, The/Kamenny Gost opera by Dargomizhsky (libretto Pushkin's drama, set unaltered), not performed in the composer's lifetime; produced St Petersburg, 28 February 1872. Don Juan dallies with Laura and Donna Anna on way to Hell.

Stone to Thorn, From work by Peter Maxwell Davies for mezzo and ensemble, first performed Oxford, 30 June 1971, conductor Davies.

stop a knob which controls a ◊register on an organ or a manual (keyboard) on some harpsichords, enabling the player to alter the instrument's tone quality in various ways. See also ◊registration.

stopped notes on string instruments, notes produced by shortening the vibrating length of the string with a finger (stopping); on wind instruments, the notes not produced naturally as harmonics, but by valves, keys or other mechanical means, or sometimes by the hand in horn playing.

stopping an action affecting ◊pitch: on a string instrument, the shortening of the vibrating length of the string (raising pitch), by pressing the finger onto the string, bringing the string into contact with the fingerboard; on a horn (especially a valveless natural horn), the alteration of pitch and timbre by blocking the bell to varying degrees, with the hand; in an organ, the blocking of one end of a pipe, lowering pitch by one octave.

Storace, Stephen (1762–1796) English composer. He wrote operas in Italian and English, including his Mozart-influenced Shakespearean opera *Gli equivoci* 1786, and his most successful English opera *The Pirates* 1792.

He studied at the Conservatorio di Sant' Onofrio in Naples, and in about 1784 went to Vienna, where he produced two operas and became friendly with Mozart. In 1787 he returned to London with his sister, the soprano Ann Storace, and became composer to Sheridan's company at the Drury Lane Theatre. *Gli equivoci* has been successfully revived in London in 1974 and at Wexford in 1992.

Works include: the operas *Gli sposi malcontenti* (1785), *Gli equivoci* (after Shakespeare's *Comedy of Errors*, 1786), *La cameriera astuta* (1788), *The Haunted Tower, No Song, No Supper* (1790), *The Siege of Belgrade* (1791), *The Pirates, Dido: Queen of Carthage* (1792), *The Cherokee* (1794), *The Iron Chest* (Colman), *Mahmoud, or The Prince of Persia* (unfinished, completed by Michael Kelly and Ann Storace, produced 1796) and others; ballet *Venus and Adonis*.

Story of a Real Man, The/Povest' o nastoyashchem cheloveke opera in four acts by Prokofiev (libretto by composer and M Mendelson-Prokofieva); composed 1947–48. Prokofiev sought to gain official favour with story of heroic legless Soviet aviator, but after private performance in Leningrad, 3 December 1948, it was not staged until 8 October 1960, at the Bolshoi, Moscow.

Stradella see ◊*Alessandro Stradella*.

Stradella, Alessandro (1644–1682) Italian composer, singer, and violinist. He taught singing in Venice, and wrote operas and oratorios for Rome, Modena, and Genoa. He had numerous love affairs, the last of which led to his assassination.

As he was of noble birth, he was probably educated privately in music. He never held any official posts, and most of what is known of his career seems to be based on legend rather than fact, notably in Friedrich Flotow's opera *Alessandro Stradella* 1844, in which a composer avoids being murdered by a pair of bandits by singing to them of kindness and mercy.

Works include: the operas *La forza dell' amor paterno* (1678), *Doriclea, Il trespolo tutore balordo* (1679), *Il Floridoro*; motets and other church music; oratorio *San Giovanni Battista* (1675) and others; sacred and secular cantatas; serenade *Qual prodigio che io miri* and others; madrigals; concerto for strings.

Stradivari, Antonio (c. 1644–1737), Latin form Stradivarius Italian stringed instrument maker, generally considered the greatest of all violin makers. He produced more than 1,100 instruments from his family workshops, over 600 of which survive; they have achieved the status (and sale-room prices) of works of art.

He was born at Cremona, served an apprenticeship there with Niccolò ◊Amati, and founded a workshop at there in the

1660s. He continually modified the design of his instruments, achieving by 1690 the 'Long Strad'. His finest instruments, including cellos and violas, were produced in the first two decades of the 18th century. The secret of his skill is said to be in the varnish but is probably a combination of fine proportioning and ageing.

His sons Francesco Stradivari (1671–1743) and Omobono Stradivari (1679–1742) carried on the business.

Straeten, Edmond van der (1826–1895) Belgian musicologist. He studied law at Alost and Ghent, but on returning home cultivated music history. He became secretary to Fétis for the purpose of studying with him and contributed to his Dictionary. He also acted as critic and wrote books on Flemish music, including *La Musique aux Pays-bas* in eight volumes. He also composed incidental music and a Te Deum.

strambotto a form of verse used by the composers of *frottole* in the 15th-16th centuries. It had eight lines (*ottava rima*), the first six rhyming alternately and the last two consecutively. In the *strambotto siciliano* all eight lines rhyme alternately.

Straniera, La/The Stranger opera by Bellini (libretto by F Romani), produced Milan, La Scala, 14 February 1829. Arturo, betrothed to Isoletta, becomes infatuated with the veiled stranger, Agnese disguised as Alaide. Arturo seems to kill Agnesi's brother Vableburgo, believing him to be a lover; in fact he is only wounded. When it is revealed that Agnese is the Queen of France, Arturo kills himself.

strascinando Italian musical term; 'dragging, slurring'.

strathspey a Scottish folk dance in quick common time, similar to the reel, but with dotted rhythms. The name derives from the strath (valley) of Spey and is first heard of in 1780, though dances of the kind are much older.

Straube, (Montgomery Rufus) Karl (Siegfried) (1873–1950) German organist and conductor. He travelled all over Europe with the choir of St Thomas's, Leipzig. He published many editions of organ and choral music of the past.

He was the son of a German father and an English mother. He studied with his father, an organist and harmonium maker, and with Heinrich Reimann. He was appointed organist of Wesel Cathedral in 1897 and of St Thomas's, Leipzig, in 1902. There he became conductor of the Bach Society in 1903, professor of organ at the Conservatory in 1907, and cantor of St Thomas's in 1918. Leipzig University awarded him an honorary doctorate in 1923.

Straus, Oskar (1870–1954) Austrian composer and conductor. A pupil of Max Bruch, he was chief conductor and composer at the Überbrettl cabaret, becoming a master of light satirical stage pieces. His first major success came in 1907 and 1908, with the operettas *Ein Walzertraum/A Waltz Dream* and *Der tapfere Soldat/The Chocolate Soldier*.

He studied with Hermann Grädener (1844–1929) and Max Bruch in Berlin and became a theatre conductor at various towns, including Bratislava, where he premiered his first operetta, *Der Weise von Cordoba*, in 1895. After *Ein Walzertraum* and *Der tapfere Soldat* he settled in Berlin and in 1927 in Vienna and subsequently in Paris. In 1940 he emigrated to the USA, returning to Europe in 1948.

Works include: the operas *Die Waise von Cordova* and *Das Tal der Liebe* (1909), operettas *Ein Walzertraum/A Waltz Dream*, 1907), *Der tapfere Soldat/The Chocolate Soldier*, after Shaw's *Arms and the Man*, 1908), *Love and Laughter* (1913), *The Last Waltz, Riquette*, and others; overture to Grillparzer's *Der Traum ein Leben*, serenade for string orchestra.

Strauss (lived 19th–early 20th centuries) Austrian family of musicians:
Johann (Baptist) (1804–1849), composer, conductor and violinist. His parents were innkeepers and apprenticed him to a bookbinder, but he learnt the violin and viola and was eventually allowed to study with Seyfried. He played viola in private string quartets, at 15 managed to join Pamer's orchestra at the Sperl, a place of entertainment, music, and dancing, then Lanner's band, in which he became deputy conductor. In 1825 he and Lanner parted and he began a rival band, for which he wrote dances, especially waltzes, which had by that time become fashionable. He was invited to return to the Sperl, which had enlarged the orchestra, and in 1833 began travelling abroad with a visit to Pest. By 1837 he had been to Germany, Holland, Belgium, France, and the UK. He added the quadrille to the music of the Viennese ballrooms, having picked it up in Paris, and made a great hit with the *Radetzky Marsch*. He toured again and was then made conductor of the court balls.

His work includes: 150 waltzes (*Täuberl, Kettenbrücken, Donaulieder Walzer*), 35 quadrilles, 28 galops, 19 marches, 14 polkas.

Johann (1825–1899), composer, conductor, and violinist, son of Johann Baptist. He was not allowed to follow his father's profession, but learnt the violin and studied secretly with Drechsler and others. In 1844 he appeared as conductor at Dommayer's hall in the Heitzing suburb, and his father capitulated. After his father's death he amalgamated his orchestra with his own, toured in Austria, Poland, and Germany and in 1855–65 visited St Petersburg. In 1863 he became conductor of the court balls, and directed them until 1872. The previous year his first operetta had been produced at the Theater am der Wien and in 1874 he had his most enduring stage success with *Die Fledermaus*. His greatest popularity was achieved with such waltzes as *Tales from the Vienna Woods* (1868), *The Blue Danube* (1867), *Wiener Blut* (1870), *Roses from the South* (1880), *Frühlingsstimmen* (1883) and the *Emperor Waltz* (1885).

His work includes the operettas *Indigo und die vierzig Räuber* (1871), *Der Karneval in Rom* (1873), *Die Fledermaus* (1874), *Cagliostro in Wien* (1875), *Prinz Methusalem, Blindekuh, Das Spitzentuch der Königin* (1880), *Der lustige Krieg* (1881), *Eine Nacht in Venedig, Der Zigeunerbaron* (1885), *Simplizius* (1887), *Ritter Pázmán, Fürstin Ninetta* (1893), *Jabuka, Waldmeister* (1895), *Die Göttin der Vernunft* (1897); ballet *Aschenbrödel; Traumbilder* for orchestra; polkas, galops, and other dances.
Josef (1827–1870), composer and conductor, son of Johann Baptist. He became an architect at his father's wish, but secretly studied music and during his father's illness conducted his band with success. He then formed his own band and wrote 283 dances for it. He died after a visit to Warsaw, where he injured his hand in a fall on the platform at his last concert.
Eduard (1835–1916), composer and conductor, son of Johann Baptist. He studied harp and composition and appeared as a conductor in 1862. After 1865 he took his brother Johann's place at the summer concerts in St Petersburg and in 1870 became conductor of the court balls. He toured much, appearing at the Inventions Exhibition in London in 1885. His works include over 300 dances.

Strauss, Richard (Georg) (1864–1949) German composer and conductor. He followed the German Romantic tradition but had a strongly personal style, characterized by his bold, colourful orchestration. He first wrote tone poems such as *Don Juan* 1889, *Till Eulenspiegel's Merry Pranks* 1895, and *Also sprach Zarathustra/Thus Spake Zarathustra* 1896.

He then moved on to opera with *Salome* 1905 and *Elektra* 1909, both of which have elements of polytonality. He reverted to a more traditional style with *Der Rosenkavalier/The Knight of the Rose* 1909–10.

His father, Franz Strauss (1822–1905), was horn player at the Court Opera in Munich. Strauss began to compose at the age of six and at ten wrote his first two published works, the *Festival March* and the serenade for wind instruments. In 1880 he finished a symphony in D minor and the next year his A major string quartet was performed in public. He entered Munich University in 1882, but left in 1883 and went to Berlin for a short period of study, but became assistant conductor to Hans von Bülow at Meiningen very soon after. A member of the orchestra, Alexander Ritter, turned his classical leanings into admiration for Berlioz, Wagner, and Liszt. In 1885 Bülow resigned and Strauss became first conductor at Meiningen; his first truly characteristic piece, the first horn concerto, had been premiered under Bülow in March. In spring 1886 he visited Italy and afterwards wrote the symphony *Aus Italien*, produced at Munich in spring 1887, when he became sub-conductor at the Opera there. *Macbeth*, his first symphonic poem, was composed that year. In 1889 he became assistant conductor to Lassen at the Weimar Court Opera and gained his first major success with the tone poem *Don Juan*; the famous exuberant opening of the work seems to announce the young composer in all his confidence and technical assurance. In 1891 Cosima Wagner invited him to conduct *Tannhäuser* at Bayreuth.

Under Wagner's influence he wrote his first opera, *Guntram*, most of it during a tour in the Mediterranean undertaken to counteract ill health. It was produced at Weimar in May 1894. The heroine was sung by Pauline de Ahna, whom he married in June, and he was that year appointed conductor of the Berlin Philharmonic Orchestra in succession to Bülow. Although *Guntram* was not a success, in the next five years he composed some of his most popular and enduring tone poems, each one superbly orchestrated and with its own distinctive character: *Till Eulenspiegel, Also sprach Zarathustra, Don Quixote*, and *Ein Heldenleben*. In 1905 his opera *Salome* was premiered at Dresden; in Vienna, London, and New York it was to have trouble with the censors for its lurid treatment of a Biblical subject. Strauss further collaborated with librettist Hugo von Hofmannstahl in a setting of Sophocles' *Elektra*, in which he was

considered wild and dissonant. More general favour was found with *Der Rosenkavalier* 1911, a comedy set in 18th-century Vienna, with anachronistic waltzes. Strauss had been conductor of the Berlin Royal Opera from 1898 but resigned in 1918 and the following year his masterpiece, *Die Frau ohne Schatten*, was produced in Vienna; the rich allusiveness and symphonic amplitude of the score was a fitting farewell to a world which had all but disappeared in World War I.

Strauss had bought a country house at Garmisch in the Bavarian highlands, and all his later works were written there. After Hofmannsthal's death in 1929 Strauss, who had already written a libretto of his own for the autobiographical *Intermezzo*, produced 1924 at Dresden, worked with Stefan Zweig on *Die schweigsame Frau* (based on Ben Jonson's *Epicoene*). It was produced at Dresden in 1935 but was quickly withdrawn on a trumped-up excuse because Zweig, as a Jew, had to be boycotted by the Nazi party. Strauss thereupon resigned his appointment as president of the Reichs-Musikkammer and was himself under a cloud for a time, but had long been too important a figure in German musical life to be ignored. He wrote music for the 1936 Berlin Olympic Games and composed four further operas during the Nazi regime. The best known of these is *Capriccio*, although some of Strauss's most attractive music is in the trilogy of operas based on Greek mythology. The *Four Last Songs* were premiered posthumously.

Works include: OPERA *Salome* (1905), *Elektra*, *Der Rosenkavalier* (1911), *Ariadne auf Naxos* (1912), *Die Frau ohne Schatten* (1919), *Arabella* (1933), *Die schweigsame Frau* (1935), *Capriccio* (1942).

ORCHESTRAL *Don Juan* (1889), *Tod und Verklärung* (1890), *Till Eulenspiegels lustige Streiche* (1895), *Ein Heldenleben* (1899), *Eine Alpensinfonie* (1915); two horn concertos (1885, 1942), oboe concerto (1945); *Metamorphosen* for 23 solo string instruments (1946).

VOCAL *Vier letzte Lieder/Four Last Songs* for soprano and orchestra (1948); 26 op. nos. of songs (about 150).

stravaganza (Italian 'extravagance') musical term sometimes used for a composition of a freakish nature.

Stravinsky, Igor Fyodorovich (1882–1971) Russian composer, later of French (1934) and US (1945) nationality. He studied under ◊Rimsky-Korsakov and wrote the music for the Diaghilev ballets *The Firebird* 1910, *Petrushka* 1911, and *The Rite of Spring* 1913 (controversial at the time for their unorthodox rhythms and harmonies). His works also include symphonies, concertos (for violin and piano), chamber music, and operas; for example, *The Rake's Progress* 1951 and *The Flood* 1962.

Along with Schoenberg, Stravinsky was the most important composer of the early 20th century, who determined more than any others the course of music for the following 50 years. His versatile work ranges from his Neo-Classical work to the choral-orchestral *Symphony of Psalms* 1930. He later made use of serial techniques in such works as the *Canticum Sacrum* 1955 and the ballet *Agon* 1953–57.

Stravinsky was born near St Petersburg, where his father, Fyodor Stravinsky, was the leading bass at the Imperial Opera. His creative output can be divided into three distinct phases, beginning with Russian nationalism and continuing through Neo-Classicism to twelve-note technique. In 1903 he met Rimsky-Korsakov at Heidelberg and played him his early compositions, but did not become his pupil until 1907, by which time he had finished a piano sonata, begun a symphony, and married his second cousin, Nadezhda Sulima, in 1906. In 1908 he had the symphony performed and wrote the orchestral piece *Fireworks* for the marriage of Nadia Rimsky-Korsakov and Maximilian Steinberg, and a *Funeral Chant* on Rimsky-Korsakov's death. The performance of the *Fantastic Scherzo* in 1909 attracted the attention of the impresario Diaghilev, who commissioned Stravinsky to write *The Firebird* for the Ballets Russes. It was produced in Paris in 1910, and Stravinsky began to be known in western Europe. *Petrushka* followed in 1911 and *The Rite of Spring* in 1913; both were produced in Paris, where the latter provoked a riot of protest and fanatical partisanship. In spite of the public protest at its premiere, *The Rite of Spring* was soon successfully performed all over Europe, Russia, and the USA, establishing Stravinsky, with Schoenberg, as the leading avant-garde composer of his time.

In 1914 he settled on Lake Geneva, Switzerland, and in Paris the same year Diaghilev produced the fairy-tale opera-ballet *The Nightingale*. From 1914 he became as well known in London as in Paris, and in 1925 made his first tour of the USA. In the interwar years many of his works were written in the spirit of Neo-Classicism, beginning most clearly with the ballet *Pulcinella* 1920, based on pieces attributed to Pergolesi, and continuing with the concerto for piano with wind

instruments 1925. *Oedipus Rex*, an opera-oratorio after Sophocles, was premiered 1927, followed by the classically-inspired ballet *Apollon Musagète* 1928, the ballet *The Fairy's Kiss* (after Tchaikovsky), *Capriccio* for piano and orchestra, and the *Symphony of Psalms*, premiered in 1930 under Ernest Ansermet.

In 1937 Stravinsky's ballet *Jeu de Cartes* was produced by Balanchine at the New York Metropolitan Opera. He settled in Hollywood in 1939, and the following year he conducted the Chicago Symphony Orchestra in his symphony in C. The powerful *Symphony in Three Movements* was premiered by the New York Philharmonic Orchestra 1946 and in 1948 Balanchine staged the ballet *Orpheus*. A meeting with W H Auden led to the summation of Stravinsky's Neo-Classical music, the Hogarth-inspired opera *The Rake's Progress*, premiered at Venice in 1951. Stravinsky had meanwhile met the conductor Robert Craft and under his influence turned towards the serial music of the Second Viennese School. This marks the beginning of the composer's third great period. Interestingly, Stravinsky began fully to explore this kind of music only after its chief proponent, Arnold Schoenberg, had died. Although the two men lived only a short distance away from each other in Los Angeles, they never met, exisitng in their own entirely separate musical and social circles. The ballet *Agon* and the religious vocal works *Canticum Sacrum* (1955) and *Threni* combine rigorous methods with Stravinsky's familiar creative generosity. Later music was increasingly sparse, however. His *Requiem Canticles* of 1966 was performed at his funeral in Venice, a city which he regarded as his spiritual home.

He published *Chronicles of my Life* 1936, and (with Robert Craft) *Conversations with Igor Stravinsky* 1959 and *Memories and Commentaries* 1960.

Works include: STAGE *The Firebird* (ballet, 1910), *Petrushka* (ballet, 1911), *The Rite of Spring* (ballet, 1913), *The Soldier's Tale* (dance scene, 1918), *Pulcinella* (ballet with song, 1920), *Les Noces/The Wedding* (Russian choreographic scenes; composed 1914–17 and 1921–23, first performance 1923), *Oedipus Rex* (opera-oratorio, 1927), *Apollon Musagète* (ballet, 1928), *Perséphone* (melodrama, 1934), *Orpheus* (ballet, 1948), *The Rake's Progress* (opera, 1951), *Agon* (ballet, 1957), *The Flood* (musical play, 1962).

CHORAL *Symphony of Psalms* (1930), *Mass*, with double wind quintet (1944–48), *Canticum Sacrum* (1955), *Requiem Canticles* (1966).

ORCHESTRAL *Symphonies of Wind Instruments* (1920), Concerto for piano and wind (1924), *Capriccio* for piano and orchestra (1929), Violin concerto in D (1931), Concerto, *Dumbarton Oaks* (1938), *Symphony in C* (1940), *Danses concertantes* (1942), *Symphony in three movements* (1945), *Ebony concerto* for clarinet and jazz band (1945), Concerto in D for strings (1946).

CHAMBER AND INSTRUMENTAL three Pieces for string quartet (1914), Octet (1923), *Duo Concertant* for violin and piano (1932), Septet (1952).

Street Scene opera in two acts by Kurt Weill (libretto by Elmer Rice), produced Philadelphia, Shubert Theatre, 16 December 1946. Also produced New York 1947 and London 1987 (Camden Festival). Slice of New York tenement life, as Anne Maurrant is murdered by her jealous husband Frank, and Sam Kaplan fails to make out with Anne's daughter Rose.

Streicher German family of piano makers. The Streicher company was founded at Vienna in 1802 by Maria Anna (Nanette) Streicher (daughter of the piano maker Johann Stein). She married in 1794 Johann Andreas Streicher (1761–1833), who was a music teacher in Vienna and founded a piano manufacture there after 1794.

Their son Johann Baptist Streicher (1796–1871) succeeded his parents in business, and from him it descended to his son Emil.

Streicher, or Streichinstrumente, (German 'strings') German term for string instruments.

Streicher, Theodor (1874–1940) Austrian composer, the great-grandson of Johann and Maria ◊Streicher. He studied in Vienna, Dresden, and Bayreuth.

Works include: *Mignons Exequien* (after Goethe's *Wilhelm Meister*) for chorus, children's chorus, and orchestra (1907), *Die Schlacht bei Murten* for chorus and orchestra; *Kleiner Vogel Kolibri* for chamber orchestra; *Um Inez weinten* for soprano and orchestra; *Die Monologe des Faust* (after Goethe) for string sextet (1912); many songs, including 36 settings from *Des Knaben Wunderhorn*.

Streichzither (German 'stroke-zither') musical instrument, a variety of ◊zither played with a violin bow instead of being plucked with the fingers or with a plectrum.

Streit zwischen Phöbus und Pan, Der/The Dispute between Phoebus and Pan secular cantata by Bach, written in 1731 and satirizing

Johann Adolf Scheibe, editor of *Der critische Musikus*, in the part of Midas.

strepitoso (Italian 'noisy') musical direction suggesting a forceful and spirited performance, but more often used in the sense of a climax growing in force and speed.

stretta (Italian 'pressure, tightening, squeezing') a passage, usually at the end of a composition, especially an operatic finale, in which the tempo is accelerated either gradually or by sections and so makes a climax.

stretto (Italian 'drawn together') in musical notation, in a ◊fugue, the imitative entry of the subject in different voices, so that each voice begins before the previous statement of the subject has finished. The result is an intensification, appropriate to the close of a fugue; alternatively, indicating the acceleration or intensification of a passage, such as the end of the last movement of Beethoven's Fifth Symphony.

stretto maestrale (Italian 'masterly stretto') stretto in which the fugal subject not only appears in close, overlapping entries, but is carried through from beginning to end at each entry.

strict counterpoint the traditional name for counterpoint written according to the rules of the species.

Striggio, Alessandro (c. 1535–1592) Italian composer. He was a nobleman from Mantua, and travelled abroad in a diplomatic capacity, visiting England in 1567. He was celebrated as a composer of madrigals and as a virtuoso player of the lira da gamba and viol. His son, Alessandro ◊Striggio, was a friend of Monteverdi.

Striggio was in the service of Cosimo de' Medici at Florence 1560–74, collaborating with other composers on contributions to the local *intermedi* (see ◊intermezzo) for great festivities. His music was admired in Italy and abroad, and in 1568 his 40-part motet, *Ecce beatam lucem*, was performed at the marriage of Duke Albrecht IV of Bavaria. He subsequently visited several European courts, including that of Ferrara in 1584. He returned to Mantua later that year, to the court of Duke Guglielmo Gonzaga. He published seven books of madrigals 1558–97.

Works include: Masses, motet in 40 parts for voices and instruments; madrigal comedy *Il cicalamento delle donne al bucato* (1567); intermezzi for performance between the acts of plays; madrigals; various works for voices and instruments in many parts.

Striggio, Alessandro (1573–1630) Italian librettist. He wrote the text of Monteverdi's *Orfeo* and *Tirsi e Clori*. Like his father, Alessandro Striggio, he also served the Gonzaga family at Mantua.

He was secretary to the Duke of Mantua and a string player at court until 1628.

stringendo (Italian 'tightening') in musical notation, indicating an increase in the tension of a passage by intensifying the tempo, in a manner similar to ◊accelerando ('quickening').

string instrument musical instrument that produces a sound when a stretched string is made to vibrate. Today the strings are made of gut, metal, and Pearlon (a plastic). Types of string instruments include: **bowed**, the violin family and viol family; **plucked**, the guitar, ukulele, lute, sitar, harp, banjo, and lyre; **plucked mechanically**, the harpsichord; **struck mechanically**, the piano and clavichord; and **hammered**, the dulcimer.

string quartet ◊chamber music ensemble consisting of first and second violins, viola, and cello. The 18th-century successor to the domestic viol consort, the string quartet with its stronger and more rustic tone formed the basis of the symphony orchestra. Important composers for the string quartet include Haydn (more than 80 string quartets), Mozart (27), Schubert (20), Beethoven (17), Dvořák (8), Bartók (6), and Shostakovich (15).

String-quartet music evolved from the decorative but essentially vocal style of viol music into a vigorously instrumental style exploiting the instruments' full expressive potential. The older hierarchy of solo and accompanying voices also changed to a concertante style offering solo opportunities for each player, a trend accelerated by the adoption of shriller metal strings in the 19th century.

string quintet ◊chamber music ensemble consisting of two violins, a viola, and two cellos. Boccherini wrote many works for the string quintet; the same form was adopted by Schubert for the greatest of his chamber works (1828). Two violins, two violas, and a cello were favoured by Mozart – in four of his finest instrumental pieces – and by Beethoven, Brahms, and Nielsen. Dvořák's string quintet op. 77 uses a double bass instead of second viola.

strings the cords, usually of gut (as in the violin family and harps) or wire (as in the lute, violin, and guitar families, and pianos), by means of which the notes are produced on

such instruments. The term 'strings' is also used to designate string instruments collectively, especially those of the violin family in the orchestra.

string sextet ◊chamber music ensemble consisting of two violins, two violas, and two cellos. Pieces written for string sextet include Dvořák's op. 48, Brahms's op. 18 and op. 36, and Schoenberg's *Verklärte Nacht/Transfigured Night*, 1899). The prologue to Strauss's *Capriccio* (1940–41) is a string sextet.

string trio the conventional combination of violin, viola, and cello. It is found in one of Mozart's finest works, the Divertimento K563. Haydn and Boccherini had earlier used the combination in occasional works. Beethoven emulated Mozart's example in his trio op. 3, and his set of three trios op. 9. After comparative neglect during the Romantic period, notable trios of the 20th century include those of Roussel, Hindemith, Dohnányi, Schoenberg, and Webern.

Strohfiedel (German 'straw fiddle') sixteenth-century percussion instrument similar to the ◊xylophone.

stromentato (Italian 'instrumented, orchestrated, scored') word associated mainly with recitative (*recitativo stromentato*), where it implies a more or less independent orchestral accompaniment.

Strong, G(eorge) Templeton (1856–1948) US composer. He studied at the Leipzig Conservatory, became a member of the Liszt circle, and was in close touch with MacDowell while living at Wiesbaden 1886–89. After teaching at Boston in 1891–92, he settled in Switzerland on the Lake of Geneva, living first at Vevey and later in Geneva.

Works include: *Knights and Dryads* for solo voices, chorus, and orchestra; two cantatas for solo voices, male chorus and orchestra; three symphonies: *Sintram* (after Fouqué, 1888), *In the Mountains* (1886) and *By the Sea*, symphonic poem *Undine* (after Fouqué); two *American Skhes* for violin and orchestra; trio for two violins and viola *A Village Music-Director* and other chamber music.

strophic bass instrumental bass part used without change throughout a series of verses of a song or chorus the upper parts of which vary at each occurrence; or a similar device in instrumental music.

strophic song structurally, the simplest form of song, in which each verse of a poem is set to the same music.

Strozzi, Barbara (1619–c. 1664) Italian singer and composer. She composed madrigals, cantatas, sacred songs with continuo, duets, ariettas, and other pieces. She studied with Francesco Cavalli, and sang in several of his operas.

She was the adopted daughter of the poet Giulio Strozzi, and sang at the Accademia degli Unisoni, which he established in 1637.

structural cadence See ◊structural harmony.

structural harmony, or structural cadence, structural progression in voice-leading analysis, a structural harmony is one which operates at a deeper structural level than the surface or foreground of the music. Voice-leading analysis identifies and distinguishes between structural and non-structural harmonies in order to describe the harmonic structure of the piece. The terms **structural cadence** and **structural progression** are used to describe the harmonic features at the background level of the piece; the structural cadence is that which closes the fundamental line.

structural level, foreground, middleground, background voice-leading analysis distinguishes between three levels of harmonic structure in music. The foreground level consists of the harmonic progressions in the piece itself, ignoring only very local features such as ornamentation of the melodic line or figuration of accompanimental texture. The middleground is identified by reducing the foreground to the harmonies which are prolonged over spans of time, ignoring subordinate harmonies such as chromatic chords. Finally, the background is the deepest level of harmonic structure, consisting of the simple contrapuntal harmony which underlies the whole piece. It is at the background level that the ◊fundamental line and ◊fundamental structure can be identified.

structural progression See structural harmony.

Strungk, Nikolaus Adam (1640–1700) German composer, violinist, and organist. After working as music director at Hanover, Hamburg, and Dresden, he went to Leipzig, where he produced operas. His most successful operas were two of those produced at Hamburg, *Esther* 1680 and *Semiramis* 1681.

He studied under his father, Delphin Strungk, for whom he deputized at the organ at Brunswick from the age of 12. While at Helmstedt University he learnt the violin at Lübeck during vacations. In 1660 he joined the court orchestra at Wolfenbüttel, then at Celle, and in 1665 went to the court of Hanover. After a period at Hamburg from

1678, two visits to Vienna, and one to Italy, he returned to Hanover 1682–86, but in 1688 took up a position at Dresden as chamber organist and second Kapellmeister to the Saxon court in succession to Christian Ritter, and in 1692 succeeded Christoph Bernhard (1628–1692) as first Kapellmeister. In 1693 he opened an opera house at Leipzig, where he produced his later stage works and where his daughters Philippine and Elisabeth sang.

Works include: the operas *Der glückseligsteigende Sejanus, Der unglücklichfallende Sejanus* (1678), *Esther, Doris* (1680), *Semiramis* (1681), *Nero, Agrippina* (1699), and others, completion of Pallavicini's *L'Antiope*; oratorio *Die Auferstehung Jesu* (1688); *ricercare* on the death of his mother; sonatas and chaconnes for violin or viola da gamba; sonatas for two violins and viola and for six strings; airs and dances for recorders.

Strunk, (William) Oliver (1901–1980) US musicologist. He was among the most influential musicological teachers of his generation, but his most important publications concerned Byzantine chant. His *Source Readings in Music History* 1950 remains a classic.

He studied at Cornell University and in Berlin, worked at the Library of Congress from 1928, and taught at Princeton University 1937–66.

Stuckenschmidt, Hans Heinz (1901–1988) German musicologist. He studied piano, violin, and composition in Berlin, and also analysis with A Schoenberg. He held many posts as music critic and from 1948 taught at the Technical University in Berlin; Professor Emeritus 1967. He is an especially well-known writer on 20th-century music, including Schoenberg and the Viennese School; he published biographies of Schoenberg in 1951 and 1978.

study an instrumental piece, usually for a single instrument, written mainly for the purpose of technical exercise and display, but not necessarily devoid of expression and high artistic quality. The French word *étude* is more often used for it.

stump string instrument of the ◊cittern type invented around 1600 by Daniel Farrant. The manuscript of the only surviving piece written for it, 'To the Stump by F P', is in Christ Church, Oxford. From it have been inferred various details such as length of strings, number of courses, and compass.

Stumpf, Carl (1848–1936) German music scientist and psychologist. He studied at Göttingen University and held professorships at Würzburg, Prague, Halle, Munich, and Berlin from 1893. He collaborated with Hornbostel in editing the *Beiträge zur Akustik und Musikwissenschaft* and wrote much on the psychological aspects of acoustic phenomena.

Sturgeon, Nicholas (c. 1390–1454) English composer. He contributed to the Old Hall Manuscript during the second phase of its existence, when it was in use at the Chapel Royal. Five known works by him survive.

He was a scholar of Winchester College as a child. In 1442, after serving as a clerk of the Chapel Royal, he became a canon of Windsor and precentor of St Paul's Cathedral.

Sturm, Der/The Tempest operas based on Shakespeare's play with this title by Peter Winter (Munich, 1798) and Frank Martin (Vienna, 17 June 1956): work for chorus and orchestra by Haydn (not based on Shakespeare) composed 1798 and performed at his concerts in London.

Also commonly used as title to Beethoven's piano sonata Op. 31 no. 2 in D minor.

Sturton, Edmund (lived 15th–16th centuries) English composer. He wrote an *Ave Maria* and *Gaude virgo mater*; the latter is in the Eton Choirbook.

St Victor, Adam of, French monk. In about 1130 he joined the abbey of St Victor near Paris. He wrote sequences composed in pairs of metrically regular three-line stanzas, and was the first important exponent of this type. He apparently composed the melodies of his sequences.

subdiapente (from Latin and Greek 'a fifth lower') musical term used especially for canons at the fifth. See ◊diapente.

subdiatessaron (from Latin and Greek 'a fourth lower') see ◊diapente.

subdominant the fourth note (or degree) of the ◊diatonic scale, for example, F in the C major scale. The chord of the subdominant is a ◊triad built upon the subdominant note.

subito (Italian 'sudden') term used in musical notation, as in *subito piano* ('suddenly soft'), a direction to play softly immediately, without any gradual dynamic change (unlike decrescendo).

subject a principal melody of a work, similar to a ◊theme. The term is used specifically to describe the main musical ideas of a sonata-form movement, as in first and second subjects. It is also used to describe the opening melody of a ◊fugue, which appears in imitation in all the voices. A fugue has only one subject, except in double and triple fugues.

submediant the sixth note (or degree) of the ◊diatonic scale, for example A in the C major scale. The chord of the submediant is a ◊triad built upon the submediant note.

Subotnick, Morton (1933–) US composer. His works often employ synthesizers. In 1969 he was appointed director of electronic music at the California Institute of Arts, Los Angeles.

He studied at Mills College, California, with Darius Milhaud. He is married to Joan ◊La Barbara.

Works include: *Concert,* for wind quintet and electronics; *Music for 12 Elevators; Silver Apples of the Moon* (1967); *Before the Butterfly* for orchestra (1975); *The Double Life of Amphibians,* music drama; *Angels* for string quartet and electronics (first performance 1984); *The Key to Songs* for chamber orchestra and synthesizer (1985), *In Two Worlds* saxophone concerto (1988), *And the Butterflies Began to Sing* (1988), *All my Hummingbirds have Alibis,* for flute, cello, midi piano, mallets, and computer (1991; available on CD Rom); incidental music for plays by Brecht and Beckett.

subsemitonium (Latin 'under-semitone') in music, the old name for the leading-note, especially when used in the modes by sharpening the seventh of the scale.

subset/superset in pitch-class set analysis, a method of relating sets containing different numbers of pitches. One set is a subset of another, larger set if its pitches can be contained within the second set. For example, the set 3–2 (pitches 0, 1, 3) is a subset of set 4–3 (pitches 0, 1, 3, 4); and also, if transposed up two semitones, of set 4–10 (0, 2, 3, 5). The larger set is called a superset of the smaller. See ◊set complex; ◊similarity relation.

subtonium (Latin 'under-(whole) tone') in music, the old name for the seventh degree of the modes, except the Lydian (and later the Ionian), so called because it was a whole tone below the final, though it was often sharpened in performance according to the principle of *musica ficta*.

Suchoň, Eugen (1908–1993) Slovakian composer. His earlier music reflects the style of the Czechoslovakian nationalist composers, while his later works are influenced by ◊serialism.

He studied at Bratislava Conservatory 1927–31, and then in Prague with Vitězslav Novák 1931–33. He taught at the Bratislava

Academy of Music 1933–41 and was professor at the State Conservatory 1941–47. From 1947 to 1953 he was professor at the Slovak University and from 1953 at the Pedagogic High School in Bratislava.

Works include: the operas *The Whirlpool* (1949) and *Svätopluk* (1960); serenades for strings, for wind quintet (1932–33); choral music; piano quartet, piano pieces.

suite in Baroque music, a set of contrasting instrumental pieces based on dance forms, known by their French names as allemande, bourrée, courante, gavotte, gigue, minuet, musette, passepied, rigaudon, sarabande, and so on. The term refers in more recent usage to a concert arrangement of set pieces from an extended ballet or stage composition, such as Tchaikovsky's *Nutcracker Suite* 1891–92. Stravinsky's suite from *The Soldier's Tale* 1920 incorporates a tango, waltz, and ragtime.

suivez (French 'follow') musical direction used in two senses: (1) to indicate that one movement of a composition is to follow the preceding one immediately (equivalent to Italian *attacca*); (2) to indicate that accompanying parts are to follow a vocal or other solo part moving independently of the prescribed rhythm or tempo (equivalent to Italian *colla parte*).

Suk, Josef (1874–1935) Czech composer, violinist, and viola player. He studied in Prague with Dvořák, whose daughter he married in 1898. His earlier works are in the style of Dvořák; later he developed a more modern style of his own. Much of his music was influenced by personal experiences, especially the death of his wife in 1905 (including the piano pieces *About Mother* written for his infant son) and that of Dvořák in 1904. The *Asrael* symphony 1906 in particular refers to these two deaths.

In 1892 he formed the Bohemian String Quartet with Karel Hofmann, Oscar Nedbal, and Otto Berger, playing second violin. He began to compose early and in 1922 became professor of composition at the Prague Conservatory, of which he was director 1924–26. His work includes symphonies (*Asrael* 1906), chamber music, choral works, piano pieces, and incidental music for three plays.

Works include: Mass in B♭ major; incidental music for Julius Zeyer's *Radúz and Mahulena* (1898); *Epilogue* for baritone solo, women's chorus, and orchestra; symphony in E major (1899) and *Asrael* (1906), symphonic poems *Prague*, *A Summer Tale*, and *Maturity*; Dramatic Overture and overture to Shakespeare's *Winter's Tale* (1894), *A Tale* and *Under*

the Appletrees for orchestra; serenade (1892) and meditation on a chorale for string orchestra; fantasy for violin and orchestra (1902); two string quartets (1896, 1911), piano quartet, piano trio, elegy for violin and cello with string quartet, harmonium, and harp; *Ballade and Serenade* for cello and piano; sets of piano pieces; part songs.

Sullivan, Arthur Seymour (1842–1900) English composer. He wrote operettas in collaboration with William Gilbert, including *HMS Pinafore* 1878, *The Pirates of Penzance* 1879, and *The Mikado* 1885. Their partnership broke down 1896. Sullivan also composed serious instrumental, choral, and operatic works – for example, the opera *Ivanhoe* 1890 – which he valued more highly than the operettas.

Other Gilbert and Sullivan operettas include *Patience* (which ridiculed the Aesthetic Movement) 1881, *The Yeomen of the Guard* 1888, and *The Gondoliers* 1889.

sul ponticello (Italian 'on the bridge') direction in music for bowed string instruments to play a passage very near (not actually on) the bridge to produce a peculiar nasal and rustling sound.

sul tasto musical direction indicating that a passage of string music is to be played with the bow over the finger-board.

'Sumer is icumen in'/*Summer has come** an English song in parts, dating from around 1270 and known as the Reading Rota (round). It is a canon for four voices and there are two additional bass voices adding a pes or ground-bass, also in canon. In the manuscript the tune is also provided with Latin words, beginning *Perspice, Christicola*, but the accompanying voices (or pes) merely have 'Sing cuccu nu' in both versions, though the music they sing is actually part of an Easter antiphon.

Sunless song cycle by Mussorgsky (words by A A Golenishchev-Kutuzov), composed 1874: 1. *Between four walls*; 2. *Thou didst not know me in the crowd*; 3. *The idle, noisy day is ended*; 4. *Boredom*; 5. *Elegy*; 6. *On the River*.

'Sun' Quartets the nickname of the six string quartets op. 20 by Haydn, composed 1772.

Suor Angelica (Puccini) see ◊*Trittico*.

supertonic the second degree of the major or minor scale, so called because it stands above the tonic.

Suppé, Franz von (1819–1895), adopted name of Francesco Ezechiele Ermenegildo Suppe Demelli Austrian composer and conductor of Belgian descent. His *Das Pensionat* 1860 was the first successful Viennese operetta in response to the French model. His later works are largely known today outside German-speaking countries through their tuneful overtures.

He showed a talent for composition early, producing a Mass and a comic opera *Der Apfel* at Zara in 1834; but he was sent to Padua University by his father to study medicine. On his father's death, however, he settled in Vienna with his mother. He studied there with Ignaz Xaver von Seyfried and conducted at various Viennese and provincial theatres, including the Josephstadt, Wieden, and Leopoldstadt Theatres in Vienna from 1841 until his death.

Works include: the operettas *Das Mädchen vom Lande* (1847), *Das Pensionat* (1860), *Paragraph 3, Zehn Mädchen und kein Mann* (1862), *Pique Dame/Die Kartenschlägerin*, (1862) *Flotte Bursche* (with an overture on students' songs, 1863), *Die schöne Galatee* (1865), *Leichte Kavallerie/Light Cavalry* 1866), *Fatinitza*, *Boccaccio* (1879), *Donna Juanita* (1880), *Die Afrikareise*, and several others; farces; ballets; incidental music to Elmar's *Dichter und Bauer/Poet and Peasant* (1846), Shakespeare's *Midsummer Night's Dream*, Schiller's *Wallensteins Lager*, and others (more than 200 stage works); Mass, Requiem (*L'estremo giudizia*, 1855; first British performance 1984, BBC).

surbahar Indian bass lute, a relative of the ◊sitar.

'Surprise' Symphony Haydn's symphony no. 94 in G major, composed for London in 1791, so called after the sudden loud interruption after 16 quiet bars at the beginning of the slow movement. Known in Germany as 'Symphonie mit dem Paukenschlag/Symphony with the Drum-beat'.

Survivor from Warsaw, A work by Schoenberg for narrator, men's chorus, and orchestra, op. 46 (text by composer), first performed Albuquerque, 4 November 1948.

Surzyński, Józef (1851–1919) Polish priest and composer. He studied at Regensburg and Leipzig, later taking holy orders in Rome. In 1882 he became director of the cathedral choir at Poznań and in 1894 provost at Kościan. He edited the *Monumenta Musices Sacrae in Polonia* and *Musica Ecclesiastica*.

Works include: numerous Masses, hymns and other church music, *Polish Songs of the Catholic Church*.

Susa, Conrad (1935–) US composer. He studied at Juilliard and from 1988 has taught

at the San Francisco Conservatory of Music. He was dramaturg of the Eugene O'Neill Center in Conneticut from 1986. He has composed a symphony, *A Sonnet Voyage* (1963), and choral works including *Dawn Greeting* (1986) and *Earth Song* (1988) but is best known for his operas: *Transformations* (Minnesota, 1973) is a re-telling of Grimm's *Fairy Tales* and has been widely performed. *Black River: A Wisconsin Idyll* (1975) tells of rural angst in 19th-century America, and *The Love of Don Perlimplin* (1984) draws on 18th-century musical sources.

Susanna oratorio by Handel (libretto anonymous), performed London, Covent Garden, 10 February 1749.

Susanna's Secret (Wolf-Ferrari). See ◊*Segreto di Susanna, Il.*

Susato, Tielman (c. 1500–between 1561 and 1564) Flemish composer, publisher, and editor. He was the outstanding Dutch music publisher of his time. His 11 *Musyck Boexken*, 'little music books', of 1551 contained Dutch songs, dance music, and the *Souter Liedekens* of the composers Clemens non Papa and Gerhard Mes.

He worked in Antwerp from 1529, established his business 1543, and in 1547 built his own premises 'At the Sign of the Crumhorn'. He also published volumes of Masses, motets, and chansons by the leading composers of his day; many of these include works by himself.

suspension a progression of chords in which one note of a chord is tied over to the next chord, while the other voices move to a new harmony, thereby causing ◊dissonance with the tied note. The dissonance is traditionally resolved by the tied note moving a step lower, to a note consonant with the local harmony.

In this example the top voice (note C) is suspended before resolution on note B.

Susskind, Walter (1913–1980) English conductor and pianist of Czech origin. He studied composition with Josef Suk and Alois Hába, conducting with Georg Szell, and making his debut at the German Opera House in Prague in 1932. From 1942 to 1945 he conducted with the Carl Rosa Opera Company and then at Sadler's Wells in 1946. From 1946 to 1952 he was also conductor of the Scottish National Orchestra, and from 1954 to 1956 he conducted in Australia, becoming conductor of the Toronto Symphony Orchestra 1956–65. In 1968 he took over the St Louis Symphony Orchestra and conducted it until 1975, when he became principal guest conductor with the Cincinnati Symphony Orchestra. In England he was heard as a piano soloist, and in 1977 gave the first performance in Britain of Alexander von Zemlinsky's Lyric Symphony.

Süssmayr, Franz (Xaver) (1766–1803) Austrian composer. He assisted Mozart with the opera La clemenza di Tito (probably the recitatives) and completed his unfinished Requiem. In 1792 he became conductor of the Kärntnertortheater.

He was educated at the monastery of Kremsmünster and was a pupil of Salieri and Mozart in Vienna. His completion of Mozart's Requiem has been reviled in recent years by scholars but it remains the most satisfactory solution to a remaining musical problem.

Works include: the operas Moses (1792), L'incanto superato (1793), Der Spiegel von Arkadien (1794), Il Turco in Italia (1794), Idris und Zenide (1795), Die edle Rache, Die Freiwilligen, Der Wildfang (after Kotzebue), Der Marktschreier (1799), Soliman II (after Favart, 1799), Gulnare (1800), Phasma, and others; two ballets; Masses and other church music; cantatas Der Retter in Gelfahr (1796) and Der Kampf für den Frieden (1800); clarinet concerto; serenades for flute, viola, and horn and for violin, guitar, and English horn; instrumental pieces.

sustaining pedal, or damper pedal or loud pedal on a piano, the pedal on the right which, when depressed, lifts all the dampers. This allows the notes to continue vibrating after the fingers release the keys. In addition to prolonging the notes played by the fingers, it also enriches the tone quality by allowing other strings to vibrate by means of ◊sympathetic resonance. Used sparingly in 18th-century music, in the 19th century the sustaining pedal was used increasingly to create impressionistic effects.

Sutermeister, Heinrich (1910–1995) Swiss composer. He wrote in a consistently conservative idiom, and is best known as a composer of operas.

He studied philology at Paris and Basel, where he entered the Conservatory, later

studying with Courvoisier and Pfitzner at Munich. In 1934 he settled at Bern, at first as operatic coach at the municipal theatre. In 1963 he was appointed professor of composition at the Hochschule für Musik in Hanover.

Works include: the operas Romeo und Julia (1940) and Die Zauberinsel (The Tempest, 1942) (both based on Shakespeare), Niobe, Raskolnikov (on Dostoevsky's Crime and Punishment, 1948), Madame Bovary (after Flaubert, 1967), Das Flaschenteufel (TV, 1971), Le roi Bérenger (1985), radio opera Die schwarze Spinne (after Jeremias Gotthelf, 1936; produced 1949); ballet Das Dorfunter dem Gletscher; Christmas radio play Die drei Geister (after Dickens); incidental, film, and radio music; chamber oratorio Jorinde und Jorindel (after Mörike); Baroque Songs for tenor, women's chorus, and instruments, songs for chorus; Cantata 1944 for contralto, small chorus, and piano; Requiem (1952) and seven other cantatas; Sieben Liebesbriefe for tenor and orchestra; divertimento for string orchestra; three piano concertos (1943, 1953, 1962), two cello concertos; three string quartets, string trio and other chamber music; piano and organ pieces; songs.

Sutton, John (lived 15th century) English composer. He was a fellow of Magdalen College, Oxford in 1476, and of Eton from 1477 to about 1479. His Salve regina for seven voices is in the Eton Choirbook.

Švanda Dudák/Shvanda the Bagpiper opera by Weinberger (libretto by Miloš Kareš), produced Prague, Czech Theatre, 27 April 1927. Shvanda beguiles Queen Ice Heart with his piping, but finding him already married she orders his execution, and he has to be saved by Babinsky.

Svendsen, Johan (Severin) (1840–1911) Norwegian composer, violinist, and conductor. After a career as a virtuoso violinist, he took up composing. He was a friend of Grieg, who admired his orchestrational technique. His style, though Romantic, shows elements of Norwegian folk music. He wrote two symphonies and other orchestral works, as well as chamber and vocal works. He was the greatest Scandinavian conductor of his period.

He learnt music from his father, a bandmaster, and at first adopted that profession himself. But, playing several instruments, he joined the orchestra at the Christiania theatre, began extensive travels in Sweden and Germany in 1861, and studied at the Leipzig Conservatory 1863–67. After travelling in Scandinavia and Scotland in 1867, he settled in Paris in 1868. In 1870–71 he was in Germany again, mainly at Leipzig and Weimar, and taught and conducted at Christiania 1872–77. After visits to Munich, Rome, London, and Paris, he was court conductor at Copenhagen 1883–1908.

Works include: incidental music to Coppée's *Le Passant* (1869), two symphonies, overture to Bjønson's *Sigurd Slembe, Carnaval à Paris, Carnaval des artistes norvégiens*, four Norwegian Rhapsodies, legend *Zorahayda*, overture to Shakespeare's *Romeo and Juliet*, and other pieces for orchestra; violin concerto (1870) and romance, cello concerto (1870); string quartet (1865), string quintet, string octet; Marriage Cantata; songs.

Swan Lake/Lebedinoye ozero ballet by Tchaikovsky (choreography by Marius Petipa and L I Ivanov), produced Moscow, Bolshoi Theatre, 4 March 1877.

Swan of Tuonela, The symphonic legend by Sibelius, op. 22, one of four on subjects from the *Kalevala*; composed 1893–95, first performed Helsinki, 1895.

Swan Song (Schubert) see ◊*Schwanengesang*.

Swayne, Giles (1946–) English composer. He studied with Messiaen. In the early 1980s he visited the Gambia and Senegal to study the music of the Jola people.

He studied at Cambridge University and the Royal Academy of Music, and with Messiaen from 1976. He has worked as an opera répétiteur and has taught at Bryanston School, Dorset and St Paul's Girls' School, London.

Works include: two string quartets (1971, 1977), *The Good Morrow*, for mezzo and piano (to texts by Donne, 1971), *Synthesis* for two pianos (1974), *Orlando's Music* for orchestra (1974), *Pentecost-Music* for orchestra (1977), string quartets nos. 1 and 2 (1971, 1977), *Cry* for 28 amplified solo voices, in which the creation of the world is depicted (1979), *A World Within*, ballet with tape, on the life of the Brontës (1978), *Count-Down* for 16-part chorus and two percussion (1981), *Song for Hadi* for drums and instruments (1983), symphony for small orchestra (1984), opera *Le nozze di Cherubino* (1984), *Missa Tiburtina* (1985), *Into the Light* for seven players (1986), *Tonos* for five players (1987), *Songlines* for flute and guitar (1987), *Harmonies of Hell*, melodrama (1988), *The Song of Leviathan* for chamber orchestra (1988), *A Memory of Sky*, brass quintet (1989), *Circle of Silence*, for six voices (1991), *The Song of the Tortoise*, children's drama (1992), *The Owl and the Pussycat*,

for narrator and seven instruments (1993), string quartet no. 3 (1993).

Sweelinck, Jan Pieterszoon (1562–1621) Dutch composer, organist, harpsichordist, and teacher. He was the first composer to write an independent part for the pedal keyboard (pedalboard) in organ works, a technique which reached its peak in J S Bach's organ compositions. He taught many of the next generation's organists of the German school.

He studied under his father, Pieter Sweelinck, who became organist at the Old Church at Amsterdam in 1566. His father died in 1573 and he succeeded to his post between 1577 and 1580, holding it to his death. His music was influenced by the English virginalists and the Venetian organists. The poet Joost van den Vondel (1587–1679) wrote an epitaph on his death.

Works include: four books of psalms of four–eight voices, including three books of *Psalms of David* (1604–14), *Cantiones sacrae* for several voices; organ fantasias, toccatas and chorale variations; harpsichord pieces; chansons for five voices, *Rimes françoises et italiennes*.

swell device on the harpsichord and organ for the artificial production of crescendo and diminuendo, which these instruments are incapable of producing by touch. It takes various forms, the most successful being a contrivance in the form of a slatted blind (hence the name Venetian swell), which, opening and shutting by means of a pedal, increased or reduced the volume of tone.

swell organ the second manual (keyboard) of an organ, characterized by a 'swell' mechanism which can vary the volume given by any combination of stops. The swell organ sometimes has the greatest number of stops and pipes, ranging from a wide variety of flues to a selection of reeds.

Sygar, John (lived 15th century) English composer. He was a singer and chaplain at King's College, Cambridge 1499–1501 and 1508–15, and contributed a Magnificat (now incomplete) to the Eton Choirbook.

Sylphides, Les ballet with music adapted from Chopin (choreography by Fokin), produced Paris, Théâtre du Châtelet, 2 June 1909.

Sylvia, ou La Nymphe de Diane ballet by Delibes (scenario by Jules Barbier and Baron de Reinach, choreography by Louis Mérante), produced Paris, Opéra, 14 June 1876.

sympathetic resonance the physical phenomenon whereby a vibrating string can induce another, initially unmoving, string to vibrate also, without any physical contact. Only strings which are related to others within the harmonic series are subject to sympathetic resonance. For example, a string will cause another, an octave higher, to vibrate by sympathetic resonance because the latter is the first ◊overtone of the former.

sympathetic string a string on a musical instrument which is not plucked, bowed, or hit by a hammer, but sounded by means of ◊sympathetic resonance. Instruments employing sympathetic strings in order to enrich the timbre include the Hardanger fiddle, viola d'amore, and certain pianos.

symphonia symphony, especially in the earlier sense of any piece of music in which instruments play together in consort; also an early instrument, possibly a kind of bagpipe and, in a later sense, a clavichord. See ◊sinfonia (the Italian term).

Symphonia domestica/Domestic Symphony a symphony by Richard Strauss, op. 53, composed 1903, first performed New York, 31 March 1904. Like *Heldenleben* the work is autobiographical, but describes the composer's private life, including love-making and bathing the baby, while the earlier work showed him as a public figure.

Symphonic Metamorphosis, or Themes by Carl Maria von Weber work for orchestra by Hindemith; composed 1940–43, first performed New York, 20 January 1944, conductor Rodziński. The four movements use material from Weber's piano music and the incidental music for a Stuttgart production of Gozzi's *Turandot* in Schiller's translation, 1809.

symphonic poem a term originated by Franz Liszt for his 13 one-movement orchestral works that interpret a story from literature or history, also used by many other composers. Richard Strauss preferred the term 'tone poem'.

symphonic study a term invented by Elgar for his *Falstaff*, probably because it is intended to be as much an outline of Falstaff's character as a description of the events surrounding him. Schumann's *Etudes Symphoniques* (Symphonic Studies) of 1835 consists of a theme and variations for piano solo.

symphonie concertante see ◊sinfonia concertante.

'Symphonie fantastique' symphony by Berlioz, op. 14, composed 1830, revised in Italy and first performed Paris, 5 December 1830, and with its sequel, *Lélio*, Paris, 9 December

1832. Berlioz gave it a programme arising out of his disappointed love for Harriet Smithson and representing the crazy dreams of a poet crossed in love who has taken poison. The five movements are: 1. *Rêveries-passions*; 2. *Un bal*; 3. *Scène aux champs*; 4. *Marche au supplice*; 5. *Songe d'une nuit de Sabbat*.

'Symphonie funèbre et triomphale' symphony by Berlioz, op. 15, for military band, strings, and chorus, composed 1840 by order of the French government and performed at the tenth anniversary of the 1830 Revolution, Paris, 28 July 1840.

Symphonie liturgique Honegger's third symphony, composed 1945–46 and dedicated to Charles Munch, who gave the first performance in Zurich on 17 August 1946.

Symphonies of Wind Instruments work by Stravinsky, dedicated to the memory of Debussy; composed 1920, revised 1945–47, first performed London, 10 June 1921, conductor Koussevitzky.

symphony abstract musical composition for orchestra, traditionally in four separate but closely related movements. It developed from the smaller ◊sonata form, the Italian ◊overture, and the ◊concerto grosso.

Haydn established the mature form of the symphony, written in slow, minuet, and allegro movements. Mozart and Beethoven (who replaced the ◊minuet with the ◊scherzo) expanded the form, which has since been modified and dramatized as quasi programme music by Brahms, Tchaikovsky, Bruckner, Dvořák, Mahler, Sibelius, Vaughan Williams, Walter Piston, Prokofiev, Carl Nielsen, Shostakovich, Stravinsky, and Aaron Copland.

Symphony in Three Movements work for orchestra by Stravinsky; composed 1942–45, first performed New York, 24 January 1946. The outer movements were inspired by Stravinsky's experiences of the war, as viewed from the USA. The central slow movement derives from music for a planned film on St Bernadette.

Symphony of a Thousand name sometimes given to Mahler's eighth symphony, in E♭, composed 1906–07. Forces required include eight vocal soloists, double chorus, boys' chorus, and orchestra with 20 woodwind, 17 brass instruments, celesta, piano, harmonium, and mandolin. The first movement is a setting on the hymn *Veni creator spiritus* and the second the closing scene from Goethe's *Faust*. The first performance, in Munich on 12 September 1910, was conducted by Mahler and was the greatest public success of his career. First US performance Philadelphia, 2 March 1916, conductor Stokowski. Not performed in the UK until 15 April 1930 (London, conductor Wood).

Symphony of Psalms work by Stravinsky for mixed chorus and orchestra; written 1930, to celebrate the 50th anniversary of the Boston Symphony Orchestra, but the first performance was in Brussels on 13 December 1930, conductor Ansermet.

synaesthesia theory which relates musical sound to the perception of colour. Some composers have specified colour displays to be performed as part of a musical work (for instance, A Skriabin's *Prometheus*, 1913). The composer Olivier ◊Messiaen used a synaesthetic description of modes and harmonies to organise the structure of certain of his works.

syncopation the deliberate upsetting of rhythm by shifting the accent to a beat that is normally unaccented.

synthesis technique of generating sound by artificial means, either by using electronic devices such as oscillators and filters, or by using a computer. See ◊acousmatic music; ◊Fourier transform.

synthesizer musical device for the simulation of vocal or instrumental ◊timbre by mechanical or electro-acoustic means.

history The pipe organ was the first major synthesizer, allowing the mixture of timbres at the unison or harmonic intervals. Modern electrical synthesizers date from 1904 and the Telharmonium of US inventor Thaddeus Cahill, incorporating the tone wheel, a programmable oscillator subsequently incorporated in the ◊Hammond organ.

Later synthesizers include the analogue ◊trautonium, ◊ondes Martenot, ◊RCA Mark II synthesizer, ◊Moog (the first electronic synthesizer), ARP, and ◊Synthi 100; and digital Fairlight, Synclavier, Roland, Oberheim, and Yamaha keyboards, and the ◊IRCAM 4X series synthesizer.

types of synthesizer In **preset synthesizers**, the sound of various instruments is produced by a built-in computer-type memory, which triggers all the control settings required to produce the sound of a particular

instrument. For example, the 'sawtooth' sound wave produced by a violin is artificially produced by an electrical tone generator, or oscillator, and then fed into an electrical filter set to have the resonances characteristic of a violin body.

In **programmable synthesizers** any number of new instrumental or other sounds may be produced at the will of the performer.

Speech synthesizers can break down speech into 128 basic elements (allophones), which are then combined into words and sentences, as in the voices of electronic teaching aids.

Synthi 100 computer-controlled analogue synthesizer developed 1972–75 by Peter Zinovieff (1934–   ) from his successful EMS briefcase synthesizer. It incorporates a sequencer which allows the continuous recycling of a series of values applicable to pitch, dynamics, or structural parameters.

Compositions using the Synthi 100 include Henze's *Tristan* 1973 for piano, orchestra, and tape music and Stockhausen's *Sirius* 1975–77 for soloists and tape music.

Syrian chant the earliest of the independent branches of Christian chant. Its language was the Eastern Aramaic dialect, also called Syriac. In addition to the cantillation of the lessons and the singing of psalms, common to all liturgies, a repertory of hymns emerged, anticipating in some cases the forms of Byzantine chant. The *memrâ* was a poetical homily, sung to a recitative formula. The *madrâshâ* was a strophic hymn sung by a soloist, with a refrain sung by the choir (*cf.* Byzantine *kontakion*). The *sogîthâ* was a poem of dramatic character. Lesser forms, inserted between the verses of psalms, are comparable to the *troparion* and *sticheron* of the Byzantine liturgy. The outstanding poet was St Ephraem (306–73). Apart from some indecipherable cantillation formulae the music of the early Syrian church has not survived; and it is impossible to say how closely what is sung today resembles it.

syrinx alternative name for the ◊panpipe, a musical instrument.

system the number of staves required for the scoring of a composition, such as two for a piano work, one + two for a song, four for a

Syncopation in a passage from Handel's Water Music. *The second notes of bars 2–5 are syncopated.*

quartet, and so on, up to any number needed for an orchestral full score. Such a system is connected on the left-hand side of the page by various kinds of braces or brackets; an open space between these shows that the next system begins lower down on the same page.

Szabelski, Bolesław (1896–1979) Polish composer. He studied with Szymanowski and Statkowski at the Warsaw Conservatory, and from 1945 taught composition and organ at the Katowice Conservatory. He embraced the ideals of the Polish avant garde from the late 1950s.

Works include: five symphonies (1926–68), sinfonietta, *Concerto grosso* for orchestra; concertino and concerto for piano and orchestra; two string quartets; Magnificat for soprano, chorus and orchestra; piano and organ music.

Szałowski, Antoni (1907–1973) Polish composer. He studied with his father, a violin professor at the Warsaw Conservatory, also piano with two masters and composition with Sikorski; later with Nadia Boulanger in Paris, where he settled and produced works in which local French influences predominated.

Works include: symphonies, symphonic variations; capriccio and overture for string orchestra; piano concerto (1930); three songs with orchestra; four string quartets (1928–56); trio for oboe, clarinet and bassoon; suite for violin and piano, sonatina for clarinet and piano; violin and piano pieces; partita for solo cello; sonata, two sonatinas and other works for piano.

Szamotulczyk, Wacław (c. 1524–1560), Wacław z Szamotuł Polish composer. He wrote much *a cappella* church music, some of which was published by printers Johann Berg 'Montanus' (d 1563) and his partner Ulrich Neuber (d 1571) of Nuremberg.

He studied at Poznań and at Kraków University, and in 1547 became composer to the king. From 1555 he was Kapellmeister to Prince Michał Radziwiłł.

Szeligowski, Tadeusz (1896–1963) Polish composer. He studied at Lwów and Kraków, later with Nadia Boulanger in Paris. He taught at Poznań, Lublin, Wilno, and Warsaw. He made special studies of folksong and early church music and was also influenced in his compositions by French neoclassicism.

Works include: incidental music for plays, Maeterlinck's *Blue Bird*; two psalms for solo voices, chorus, and orchestra; concerto, *Phantaisie rapsodique*, suite *St Casimir Fair* for orchestra; clarinet concerto, piano concerto; two string quartets (1929, 1934); *Lithuanian*

Song for violin and piano; *Children's Album* for piano; *Green Songs*, *Flower Allegories* and other songs.

Szell, Georg (1897–1970) Hungarian-born US conductor and pianist. He conducted at the Berlin Staatsoper 1924–30. In 1939 he settled in the USA, and conducted the Cleveland Philharmonic Orchestra from 1946 until his death. Bartók and Janáček were among the few modern composers in his programmes.

A child prodigy, he studied with Richard Robert (1861–1924) in Vienna, playing a work of his own with the Vienna Symphony Orchestra at the age of 11. He studied composition with Josef Foerster, Eusebius Mandyczewski, and Max Reger, and then, through the influence of Richard Strauss, he obtained a conducting post in Strasbourg, which he held 1917–18, having already made his debut in Berlin in 1914. After further posts in Prague, Darmstadt, and Düsseldorf he was first conductor at the Berlin Staatsoper 1924–30, also teaching at the Berlin Hochschule für Musik 1927–30. From 1930 to 1936 he again conducted in Prague, and took over the Scottish National Orchestra 1937–39. He then went to the USA, where he was guest conductor with the National Braodcasting Company Symphony Orchestra 1941–42, and conductor at the New York Metropolitan Opera. His performances of Wagner's works were much admired. From 1942 to 1945, and from 1943 to 1956, he was a frequent guest conductor with the New York Philharmonic Orchestra. In 1946 he became permanent conductor of the Cleveland Philharmonic Orchestra. He conducted *Der Rosenkavalier* at Salzburg in 1949, returning for the first performances of Liebermann's *Penelope* in 1954 and Egk's *Irische Legend* in 1955. Szell was one of the last of a generation of composers who dominated orchestras with iron discipline and sarcastic humour.

Szenen aus Goethes 'Faust' a setting of a number of scenes from Goethe's drama for solo voices, chorus, and orchestra by Schumann; composition begun with a setting of the final chorus, August 1844, resumed 1849, completed without the overture, 1850, overture added 1853.

Szokolay, Sándor (1931–) Hungarian composer. He has been influenced by Hungarian national music and by Stravinsky and Orff.

He studied at the Budapest Academy and taught there from 1966.

Works include: a violin concerto (1957), *Urban and the Devil*, ballet (1958), piano concerto (1958), *Fiery March*, oratorio (1958), *The Ballad of Horror*, ballet (1960), *Ishtar's Descent into Hell*, oratorio (1960), *Blood Wedding*, opera after Lorca (1964), *Déploration*, Requiem for Poulenc for piano, chorus, and chamber orchestra (1964), trumpet concerto (1968), *Hamlet*, opera (1968), *Apocalypse*, oratorio after Dürer (1971), *Samson*, opera (1974), *Deluded Peter*, radio opera (1978), Passion-opera *Ecce Homo* (1987).

Szymanowski, Karol Maciej (1882–1937)
Polish composer. He wrote piano music, violin concertos, four symphonies, a *Stabat Mater* 1926, and the opera *Król Roger/King Roger* 1918–24, in richly glamorous idiom drawing on national folklore and French impressionist style. He was director of the Warsaw Conservatory from 1926.

He learnt music privately as a child and composed a set of piano preludes, op. 1, in 1900. In 1903 he entered the Warsaw Conservatory, studying with Zygmunt Noskowski (1846–1909). At the Lwów Chopin Festival in 1905 he won a first prize with a C minor piano sonata. He lived in Berlin for a time from 1906 and worked on behalf of Polish music. He was initially influenced by Debussy and Richard Strauss, but also created his own lyrical late-Romantic vision, particularly in the 3rd symphony *Song of the Night*, the violin concerto, the *Stabat Mater*, and the opera *King Roger*. His more abstract works such as his piano sonatas and mazurkas embrace more modern techniques within traditional forms, and his masques seem almost improvisatory.

As an aristocrat he lost his property in World War I and was imprisoned in Russia, but escaped to Warsaw, where in 1926 he became professor of composition and director of the State Conservatory. His last years were marred by tuberculosis and he died in a sanatorium in Switzerland. He is regarded as the founder of 20th-century Polish music and the most distinguished Polish composer after Chopin.

Works include: STAGE opera *King Roger* (1926); ballet *Harnasie* (1935).

ORCHESTRAL four symphonies, including no. 3 for tenor or soprano, male chorus, and orchestra (*Song of the Night*, 1916), *Sinfonia concertante* for piano and orchestra (1932); two violin concertos (1916, 1933); *Hafiz Love Songs* for voice and orchestra; *Stabat Mater* (1926).

CHAMBER two string quartets (1917, 1927); *Masques*, *Métopes*, Mazurkas, and many other works for piano; many songs including cycles *Songs of the Infatuated Muezzin* (J Iwaszkiewicz), *Słopiewnie* (Julian Tuwim), settings of poems by Kasprowicz.

T

t the leading note in tonic sol-fa notation, pronounced Te.

Tabarro, Il (Puccini) see ◊*Trittico*.

tabla Hindi; a pair of drums used in North Indian (Hindustani) music both for accompaniment (to vocal, instrumental, and dance performance) and as a solo instrument. One drum (usually played with the right hand) is made of wood, shaped as a truncated cone, and tuned to the *Sa* (system tonic); the other (left-hand) is kettle-shaped, made of metal or clay, lower in pitch but not precisely tuned. The player produces different tones by striking the drum heads in a variety of ways with the fingers; the various strokes are known by mnemonic syllables called *bols*.

tablature an old form of notation indicating finger positions on a graph representing the fingerboard and strings, and therefore specific only to the instrument to which it applies, for example, the lute, guitar, or ukelele.

Prior to 1700, tablature protected the status of court lutenists, as the notation could not be interpreted by other instruments, but with the introduction of a universal standard ◊notation, for example in the *Parthenia* 1611, a collection of pieces for virginals by Byrd, Bull, and Gibbons, the way was open for amateur ◊keyboard instrumentalists to perform music at a level of virtuosity of the professional lutenist.

table (French) in music, the belly of a string instrument; also the sounding board of the harp. In harp-playing, *près de la table* is an instruction to play near the sounding board, producing a metallic sound.

Tableau parlant, Le/The Speaking Picture opera by Grétry (libretto by L Anseaume), produced Paris, Comédie-Italienne, 20 September 1769. Isabelle's tutor Cassandre has designs on her after her lover Léandre has been missing for two years, but he returns in time to marry her.

table entertainment eighteenth-century English entertainment, only partly musical in character, given by a single performer sitting at a table and telling stories and jokes, giving displays of mimicry, singing songs, and so on. The first table entertainments on record are those of George Alexander Steevens at Dublin in 1752. Dibdin began a series in London in 1789 and continued for 20 years, introducing most of his songs in this way.

tabor small drum with a high, narrow body and small drum-heads, originally made of animal skin, sounding an indefinite pitch and struck with drumsticks. Historically, it was rarely used alone, but accompanied a pipe of a fife or recorder type, similar to the modern tin whistle. It is occasionally used in the modern orchestra to produce a dry, dull, percussive sound, and has been revived for folk-dancing.

Tabor (Smetana). See ◊*Má Vlast*.

Tabulatur (German 'tablature') musical term; in one sense the German word differs from the English, meaning also the table of rules for the instruction and guidance of the mastersingers.

tacet (Latin 'be silent') in written music, a score indication signifying that during a complete movement, or a specific section of a movement, an instrument is not required to play and therefore that no counting of bars will be necessary.

Tacitus, Cornelius (c. 55–120) Roman historian. See ◊*Incoronazione di Poppea, L'* (Monteverdi) and ◊*Radamisto* (Handel).

Tafelmusik (German 'table music') music for voices or instruments performed around a table, often as relaxation after a meal. A group or society of singers is called a *Liedertafel*.

Tag des Gerichts, Der/The Day of Judgement oratorio by Telemann (text by C W Alers), composed 1762.

Tageszeiten, Die/The Times of the Day song cycle for male chorus and orchestra by Richard Strauss (text by Eichendorff); composed 1927, first performed Vienna, 21 July 1928. The movements are 'Der Morgen', 'Mittagsruh', 'Der Abend', and 'Die Nacht'. Cantata by Telemann.

Tageweisen (German 'day tunes') songs formerly used in Germany to announce the break of day from church towers or by nightwatchmen in the streets. They were often folksongs and some have passed into currency as hymns for the Lutheran church.

Taglia, Pietro (lived 16th century) Italian composer. He was active at Milan, and wrote three books of madrigals which were published in 1555, 1557, and 1564.

Tailer, John (died 1569), also Taylor English composer. From 1561 to 1569 he was master of the choristers at Westminster Abbey. A *Christus resurgens* (Christ Church, Oxford, manuscripts 948–8) may be by him, or by Thomas Taylor, who obtained the BMus at Oxford in 1531.

taille (French 'cut, edge') the tenor part in a vocal and instrumental ensemble, applied particularly in the 17th and 18th centuries to the viola and the *oboe da caccia*.

Tailleferre, Germaine (1892–1983) French composer. She was the only woman member of the group known as ◊Les Six. Her works, though never attaining the popularity of her colleagues', include the opera *Il était un petit navire* 1951, the ballet *Le marchand d'oiseaux* 1923, and several instrumental works.

She studied in Paris and joined Les Six, first appearing as a composer in public in 1920. She lived in the USA 1942–46.

Works include: the opera *Il était un petit navire* (1951); ballet *Le marchand d'oiseaux* (1923); *Pastorale* for small orchestra; piano concerto (1919) and ballade for piano and orchestra; string quartet (1918); two violin

and piano sonatas (1921, 1951); *Jeux de plein air* for two pianos (1918); songs.

tail pin, or end pin in music, an adjustable metal rod protruding from the bottom of a cello or double bass, used to stabilize the instrument on the floor at a height comfortable to the player.

Takemitsu, Toru (1930–1996) Japanese composer. He was mainly self-taught and was initially influenced by Schoenberg, Messiaen, and *musique concrète*. Like other composers of his generation (such as Ligeti), he is interested in the treatment of texture. His use of the electronic medium is well exemplified in *Relief statique* 1955. He also wrote the music for over 100 films, including *Kwaidan* 1964 and *The Rising Sun* 1993.

He was born in Tokyo, and grew up in China. His family later returned to Japan and he served in the Japanese army in World War II. In 1951 he co-founded an experimental laboratory in Tokyo to examine oriental music and the best in Western techniques.

Works include: *Requiem* for strings (1957), *Music of Trees* for orchestra (1961), *Textures* for piano and orchestra (1964), *The Dorian Horizon* for 17 strings (1966), *November Steps* for biwa, shakuhachi, and orchestra (1967), *Asterism* for piano and orchestra (1968), *Corona* for 22 strings (1971), *Cassiopea* for percussion and orchestra (1971), *Gemeaux* for oboe, trombone, and two orchestras (1972), *Bouquet of Songs* for marimba and orchestra (1975), *A Flock Descends into the Pentagonal Garden* for orchestra (1977), *Dream Time* for orchestra (1981; ballet version 1983), *Rain Coming* for chamber orchestra (1982), *To the Edge of Dream* for guitar and orchestra (1983), *Star Isle* for orchestra (1984); *Orion and Pleiades* for cello and orchestra (1984), *Riverrun* for piano and orchestra (1984); *I hear the water dreaming* for flute and orchestra (1987); *Tree Line* for chamber orchestra (1988); *A String Around Autumn* for viola and orchestra (1989); *Visions* for orchestra (1990); *My Way of Life* for baritone, chorus, and orchestra (1990); *From me flows what you call time* for five percussion and orchestra (1990); chamber music including string quartet *A Way Alone* (1981), series of works for instruments with title *Stanza*, *Entre-temps* for oboe and string quartet (1986); *All in Twilight* for guitar (1987); *Itinerant* for flute (1989); works for tape alone.

Takt (German 'time') term used in musical notation, as in *im Takt* ('in time'). It can also mean 'beat' or 'bar'.

Tal, Josef (1910–) Polish-born Israeli composer. He studied in Berlin with Tiessen and

Trapp, settling in Palestine in 1934. In 1937 he became professor of composition and piano at the Jerusalem Conservatory and in 1950 lecturer at the Hebrew University there, also being director of the Conservatory 1948–55.

Works include: the operas *Saul at Ein Dor* (1957), *Amnon and Tamar* (1961), *Ashmedai* (1971), *Massada 967* (1973), *Die Versuchung* (1976), *Der Turm* (1987), *Der Garten* (1988), and *Josef* (1993); *The Death of Moses*, requiem oratorio for soloists, chorus, and tape (1967); two symphonies; *Exodus*, choreographed poem for orchestra; *Visions* for string orchestra; six piano concertos (1944–70), viola concerto; symphonic cantata *A Mother Rejoices*; sonatas for violin, oboe; piano pieces; songs; electronic music.

tala a term used to describe the cyclically repeated patterns which form the rhythmic basis of much Indian music, especially as played by a percussion instrument.

Talbot, Michael (Owen) (1943–) English musicologist. He studied at Cambridge and the Royal College of Music, and was appointed professor of music at Liverpool University in 1986. An authority on Venetian music of the 18th century, he published studies of A Vivaldi (in the Master Musicians series) and T Albinoni (*The Venetian Composer and his World*, 1994).

talea (Latin 'a cutting') name given to the repeated rhythmic pattern used in isorhythmic motets. See also ◊isorhythmic.

Tales of Hoffmann (Offenbach). See ◊*Contes d'Hoffmann, Les*.

Talismano, II unfinished opera by Balfe, completed by Macfarren (libretto *The Knight of the Leopard*, based on Scott's *Talisman*, by A Matthison; Italian translation by G Zaffira), produced London, Her Majesty's Theatre, 11 June 1874.

talking drum hourglass pressure drum with great tonal flexibility found in many parts of Africa. Used for signalling and for conveying certain features of an unvocalized text. Incorporated into a variety of West African popular musics.

Tallis, Thomas (c. 1505–1585) English composer. He was a master of ◊counterpoint. His works include *Tallis's Canon* ('Glory to thee my God this night') 1567, the antiphonal *Spem in alium non habui* (about 1573) for 40 voices in various groupings, and a collection of 34 motets, *Cantiones sacrae*, 1575 (of which 16 are by Tallis and 18 by Byrd).

Tallis was organist at the Benedictine Priory, Dover, in 1532, and held a post at Waltham Abbey before its dissolution in 1540. He became a Gentleman of the Chapel Royal about 1543. He was one of the earliest composers to write for the Anglican liturgy (1547–53) but some of his most ornate music, including the Mass *Puer natus est nobis* dates from the brief Catholic reign of Mary Tudor (1553–58). In 1557 Queen Mary granted him, jointly with Richard Bowyer, Master of the Children in the Chapel Royal, a lease of the manor of Minster, Thanet, and at her death he passed into the service of Elizabeth I, who in 1575 granted him, jointly with Byrd, a patent for the sole right to print music and music paper in English; but two years later, not finding this immediately profitable, they petitioned for an annual grant, which was sanctioned. The two masters were then joint organists at the Chapel Royal. A tune written for Archbishop Parker's Psalter of 1567 was used by Vaughan Williams in his celebrated *Fantasia*. Tallis has become best known for the elaborate and ingenious 40-part motet *Spem in alium non habui*. In his last years he and his wife Joan, whom he had married about 1552, lived at their own house at Greenwich.

Works include: Three Masses, including *Puer natus est nobis* (1554), two Latin Magnificats, two sets of Lamentations for voices, about 40 Latin motets, and other pieces, including *Spem in alium* in 40 parts; services; psalms, Litanies, about 30 anthems and other English church music; secular vocal pieces; two In Nomines for strings; organ and virginal pieces.

talon, French, in music, the heel (or nut) of the bow of a string instrument.

Tamara symphonic poem by Balakirev, based on a poem by Lermontov (sometimes called *Thamar* in English), begun 1866, finished 1882; first performed St Petersburg, Free School of Music, 1882. Ballet on this work (choreographed by M Fokine, setting by L Bakst), produced Paris, Théâtre du Châtelet, 20 May 1912.

tambourin (French 'tabor') musical instrument. The *tambourin du Béarn* was a zither with strings sounding only tonic and dominant and struck by a stick. Hence tambourin was used to mean a dance with a drone bass.

tambourine musical percussion instrument of ancient origin, almost unchanged since Roman times, consisting of a shallow frame drum with a single skin and loosely set jingles in the rim which add their noise when the drum skin is struck or rubbed, or sound separately when the instrument is shaken.

tambura Indian plucked drone instrument which has four strings tuned by a movable bridge, providing an accompaniment for such instruments as the ◊sitar. The South Indian version, the *mayuri*, can also be played with a bow.

tamburo (Italian 'drum') term used in musical scores, with various adjectival qualifications, for any kind of drum except the kettledrums, which are called ◊timpani in Italian.

Tamerlano/Tamburlane opera by Handel (libretto by A Piovene, adapted by N F Haym), produced London, King's Theatre, Haymarket, 31 October 1724. Tamerlano offers his betrothed, Irene, to ally Andronicus in return for his beloved Asteria, daughter of the captured emperor Bajazet. After feigning cooperation Asteria refuses and is imprisoned; her father takes poison before the original relationships are restored.

Taming of the Shrew, The see ◊Sly; ◊Widerspänstigen Zähmung, Der.

tampur three-stringed Caucasian musical instrument of the lute type, but played with a bow.

tam-tam musical instrument, a large gong originating in China. It has been used in Western music since the 19th century by composers including Puccini, Stravinsky, and Stockhausen.

Tancrède tragédie-lyrique by Campra (libretto by A Danchet after Tasso), produced Paris, Opéra, 7 November 1702. Revived Aix-en-Provence, 1986. Saracen Clorinde saves her crusader lover Tancrèdi from death, but must return to her people. Later Tancrèdi despairs when he kills her in battle, believing that she was the Saracen leader Argante.

Tancredi/Tancred opera by Rossini (libretto by G Rossi, based on Tasso's *Gerusalemme liberata* and Voltaire's tragedy *Tancrède*), produced Venice, Teatro La Fenice, 6 February 1813. Rossini's first serious opera. Revived Wexford, 1986. Amenaide, daughter of Argirio, refuses to marry her family's enemy, Orbazzano; she is later accused of aiding the Saracens when her letter to lover Tancredi is found. He champions her, kills Orbazzano, and leads the Syracusans against the Saracens.

Taneiev, Aleksandr Sergeievich (1850–1918) Russian composer. Entered state service after studies at St Petersburg University, but also studied music there and at Dresden, and came under the influence of the Balakirev circle.

Works include: the operas *Cupid's Revenge* (1899) and *The Snowstorm*; three symphonies (1890, 1903, 1908), symphonic poem *Alesha Popovich*, overture to Shakespeare's *Hamlet*, two suites for orchestra; three string quartets; pieces for violin and piano and for piano; songs, part songs.

Taneiev, Sergey Ivanovich (1856–1915) Russian composer and pianist, nephew of Aleksandr Taneiev. He studied composition with Tchaikovsky in Moscow, and after touring as a pianist became director of the Moscow Conservatory in 1885. His works include the operatic trilogy *The Oresteia* 1895, cantatas and unaccompanied choral works, four symphonies, six string quartets and other chamber music, and about 50 songs.

He studied at the Moscow Conservatory, intending at first to become a pianist, but also studying composition with Tchaikovsky. In 1875 he gave the Moscow first performance of Tchaikovsky's 1st Piano Concerto, and completed the original, vocal version of *Romeo and Juliet*. In 1876 he toured Russia, in 1877–78 visited Paris, and after playing in the Baltic Provinces became professor of orchestration at the Moscow Conservatory. In 1881 he succeeded his former teacher Nikolai Rubinstein as chief professor of piano and in 1885 succeeded Nikolai Albertovich Gubert (Hubert; 1840–1888) as director. He was succeeded by Vassily Safonov in 1889 and concentrated on teaching counterpoint and fugue. He achieved a major success with his last work, the cantata *At the Reading of a Psalm* 1915.

Works include: the operatic trilogy *Oresteia* (based on Aeschylus, 1895); cantata *John of Damascus* for solo voices, chorus, and orchestra (1884); four symphonies, Overture on Russian Themes for orchestra; concert suite for violin and orchestra; 11 string quartets, two string trios, piano trio; prelude and fugue for two pianos; about 40 songs to words by Tiutchev and others; part songs.

tañer (Spanish 'to touch') sixteenth-century lute prelude with which the strings were 'touched', or tried; equivalent to a toccata.

tangents in the ◊clavichord, the screwdriver-shaped pins that strike the wire strings. The strings continue to sound while the tangents touch them, and their tone can thus approximate a violin's ◊vibrato by altering the pressure of the finger on the depressed key.

tango dance for couples, developed in Argentina during the early 20th century, or the music for it. The dance consists of two long steps followed by two short steps then one long step, using stylized body positions. The music is in moderately slow duple time (2/4) and employs syncopated rhythms. Similar to the ◊habanera, from which it evolved, the tango consists of two balanced sections, the second usually in the ◊dominant key or the ◊relative minor of the first section. William Walton uses a tango in his suite *Façade* 1923.

Tannhäuser und der Sängerkrieg auf der Wartburg/Tannhäuser and the Singers' Contest at the Wartburg opera by Wagner (libretto by composer), produced Dresden, 19 October 1845; revised for Paris, with bacchanale in first act, and produced at the Opéra, 13 March 1861. Torn between conflicting demands of carnal Venus and virginal Elisabeth, Tannhäuser expires before absolution arrives from Rome.

Tansman, Alexandre (1897–1986) Polish-born French composer. He studied at home and then at Warsaw, and in 1919 took two prizes for composition. He settled in Paris, but travelled extensively as pianist and conductor. He married the French pianist Colette Cras.

Works include: OPERA *La nuit Kurde* (1927), *La toison d'or* (1938); ballets *Sextuor* (1924) and *La grande ville* (1932); seven symphonies (1925–44), *Sinfonietta* (1925), *Etudes symphoniques*, *Rapsodie polonaise*, and suites for orchestra; two concertos (1925–26) and concertino for piano and orchestra; concertos for viola, violin, and cello (1936, 1937, 1963), and for clarinet (1958).

CHAMBER eight string quartets (1917–56), *Danse de la sorcière* for five wind instruments and piano; *Sonata quasi una fantasia* for violin and piano; flute sonata (1925); five sonatas and other piano works; songs, including 'Stèle in memoriam Igor Stravinsky' (1972).

tape music music composed from tape-recorded material and reproducible only with the aid of audio equipment. It may include acoustic, ◊concrete, or synthesized elements. Tape music can be edited to create juxtaposition effects, composed direct to tape by layer-on-layer addition, and electronically treated and balanced.

Tapiola symphonic poem by Sibelius, op. 112, composed in 1926 for the Symphonic Society in New York. The title is the old mythological name of Finland, derived from the forest god Tapio, who appears in the *Kalevala*. First performed New York, 26 December 1926.

Tapissier, Johannes (c. 1370–1410), adopted name of Jean de Noyers French composer. Two Mass movements and an isorhythmic motet by him survive, though records indicate that he was a prominent and prolific composer.

Though at the Burgundian court from 1391 to the end of his life, he seems to have been active mainly in Paris.

Tappert, Wilhelm (1830–1907) German music scholar. He studied with Dehn and Kullak in Berlin and after eight years as teacher and critic at Glogau (Głogów in modern-day Poland), settled in Berlin in 1866. There he taught at Tausig's piano school and wrote numerous musico-literary works, including a *Wagner-Lexikon* (a collection of anti-Wagner reviews) and other works on Wagner, studies of notation, old lute music, and the settings of Goethe's *Erlkönig* (54). He also wrote piano pieces, including 50 studies for the left hand, and songs.

taqsim, or Turkish taksim, Greek taxim in Arab, Turkish, and Greek music an improvisation in one or more melodic modes, in free-rhythmic style. The performer improvises passages in which he realises structurally important degrees of a chosen melodic mode, in an order peculiar to that mode. See: ◊maqam.

tarantella southern Italian dance in very fast compound time (6/8); also a piece of music composed for, or in the rhythm of, this dance. It is commonly believed to be named after the tarantula spider which was (incorrectly) thought to cause tarantism (hysterical ailment), at one time epidemic in the S Italian town of Taranto, and whose cure was thought to involve wild dancing. The dance became popular during the 19th century, several composers writing tarantellas employing a ◊perpetuum mobile in order to generate intense energy. Examples include those by Chopin, Liszt, and Weber.

Tarare opera by Salieri (libretto by Beaumarchais), produced Paris, Opéra, 8 June 1787. It became known later under the title of *Axur, re d'Ormus* (Italian version by Da Ponte, produced Vienna, Burgtheater, 8 January 1788). Captain Tarare rescues abducted wife Astasie from King Atar and stages successful rebellion.

Taras Bulba rhapsody for orchestra by Janáček, after Gogol; composed 1915–18, first performed Brno, 9 October 1924, conductor F Neumann. The three movements are 'Death of Andrea', 'Death of Ostap', and 'Capture and Death of Taras Bulba'.

tardando (Italian 'delaying') musical direction indicating that a passage is to be played in a lingering manner.

Tarr, Edward H(ankins) (1936–) US trumpeter and musicologist. He studied in Boston, Chicago, and Basel (with Schrade). He founded the Edward Tarr Brass Ensemble (1967) for performances of Renaissance and Baroque music, and edited the complete trumpet works of Torelli. He also plays works by Kagel, Berio and Stockhausen (*Michaels Reise um die Erde*).

Tartini, Giuseppe (1692–1770) Italian composer and violinist. In 1728 he founded a school of violin playing in Padua. A leading exponent of violin technique, he composed numerous sonatas and concertos for strings, including the *Devil's Trill* sonata, about 1714.

Taruskin, Richard (Filler) (1945–) US musicologist. He has published *Opera and Drama in Russia* 1981 and wrote the articles on Russian composers and operas in *Opera Grove*, four volumes, 1992. He also writes for the *New York Times* and is a critic of the early music movement.

He took a PhD at Columbia University in 1975 and taught there 1973–87. In 1987 he was appointed professor at Berkeley.

Tasso, Torquato (1544–1595) Italian poet. His works inspired ◊*Armida* and ◊*Armide* (11 operas on *Gerusalemme liberata*), (*Aminta*); F ◊*Caccini*, (*Rinaldo innamorato*); ◊*Combattimento di Tancredi e Clorinda* (Monteverdi); ◊madrigal comedy (*Aminta*); ◊Pizzetti (*Aminta*); Vincenzo Righini (*Gerusalemme liberata*); ◊*Rinaldo* (Handel); M A ◊Rossi (*Erminia sul Giordano*); ◊*Tancrède* (Campra); ◊*Tancredi* (Rossini); ◊*Torquato Tasso* (Donizetti).

Tasso, lamento e trionfo/Tasso's Lament and Triumph symphonic poem by Liszt, based on a poem by Byron; composed 1849. First performed Weimar, 28 August 1849, as an overture to Goethe's drama *Torquato Tasso*; revised 1850–51 with a new middle section and performed Weimar, 19 April 1854.

tastar (Italian, from *tastare*, 'to touch') a 16th-century lute prelude with which the strings were 'touched', or tried; equivalent to a toccata.

tastiera per luce (Italian 'keyboard for light') instrument that appears in the score of Skriabin's *Prometheus*, designed to throw differently coloured lights. It was never perfected for practical use.

tasto Italian musical term meaning 'key' (of keyboard instruments); also fingerboard (of string instruments).

tasto solo (Italian 'key alone') musical direction indicating that in a composition with a thorough-bass the bass notes are for the moment to be played alone on the keyboard instrument used, without any harmony above them.

Tate, Phyllis Margaret Duncan (1911–1987) English composer. Her works include *Concerto for Saxophone and Strings* 1944, the opera *The Lodger* 1960, based on the story of Jack the Ripper, and *Serenade to Christmas* for soprano, chorus, and orchestra 1972. Her works were generally small scale, and carefully crafted.

She studied composition with Harry Farjeon at the Royal Academy of Music in London 1928–32. Several of her works were performed when she was still a student, and in 1933 her cello concerto was her first work heard at a public concert.

Works include: the operas *The Lodger* (1960), *Dark Pilgrimage* (1963), and *Twice in a Blue Moon* (1968); operetta *The Policeman's Serenade* (A P Herbert); *Secular Requiem* for chorus and orchestra (1967); *Serenade to Christmas* for mezzo, chorus, and orchestra (1972), *All the World's a Stage* for chorus and orchestra (1977); symphony and suite for orchestra, *Valse lointaine* and prelude, interlude, and postlude for chamber orchestra (1941); cello and saxophone concertos (1933, 1944), *Panorama* for string orchestra (1977); *Divertimento* for string quartet, sonata for clarinet and cello (1947), *Nocturne* (S Keyes) for four voices, string quintet, celesta, and bass clarinet; *London Waits* for two pianos; *Songs of Sundry Natures* on Elizabethan poems for voice and piano, songs to words by Blake, W H Davies, Hardy, Hood, Tennyson, and others, *The Phoenix and the Turtle* for tenor and instrumental ensemble.

Tavener, John Kenneth (1944–) English composer. He has written austere vocal works including the dramatic cantata *The Whale* 1968 and the opera *Thérèse* 1979. *The Protecting Veil*, composed 1987 for cello and strings alone, became a best-selling classical recording.

Tavener studied at the Royal Academy of Music with Lennox Berkeley and David Lumsdaine. He is a member of the Greek Orthodox Church, and draws on Eastern European idioms and Orthodox Christian traditions; he described his chamber opera

Mary of Egypt 1991, premiered at Aldeburgh Music Festival in 1992, as 'a moving icon'.

Works include: three *Holy Sonnets* for baritone and orchestra (texts by Donne, 1962), piano concerto (1963), *The Cappemakers*, dramatic cantata (1965), *Cain and Abel*, dramatic cantata (1965), *Little Concerto* (1965), *The Whale*, cantata (1966), *Grandma's Footsteps* for ensemble (1968), *Introit for the Feast of St John Damascene* for soloists, chorus, and orchestra (1968), *Concerto for Orchestra* (1968), *In alium* for soprano, orchestra, and tape (1968), *Celtic Requiem* (1969), *Ultimos Ritos* for soloists, speakers, chorus, and orchestra (1969–72), *Coplas* for soloist, chorus, and tape (1970), *Ma fin est mon commencement* for tenor, chorus, brass, and percussion (1972), *Little Requiem for Father Malachy Lynch* (1972), *Requiem for Father Malachy* (1973); *Thérèse*, opera (1973–76; produced 1979), *Kyklike kinesis* for soprano, chorus, cello, and orchestra (1977), *Palintropos* for piano and orchestra (1977), *Liturgy of St John Chrysostom* for unaccompanied chorus (1978), *Akhmatova: rekviem* (1980), *Sappho: Lyrical Fragments* for two sopranos and strings (1980), *Risen!* for chorus, piano, organ, and orchestra (1980), *Funeral Ikos* for chorus (1981), *Trisagion* for brass quintet (1981), *Ikon of Light* for chorus and string trio (1984), *Eis Thanaton*, dramatic cantata (1987); *The Protecting Veil* for cello and strings (1987), *Akathist of Thanksgiving* (1987), *Ikon of St Seraphini* (1988), *Resurrection* for soloists, actors, chorus, and orchestra (1989), *The Repentant Thief*, for clarinet and ensemble (1990), *Mary of Egypt*, music theatre (1991), *We Shall See Him as he is* for soloists, chorus, and ensemble (1992), *Eternal Memory* for cello and ensemble (1992), *Hymns of Paradise* for bass, chorus, and strings (1993), *The Apocalypse* for soloists, chorus, and orchestra (1994).

Taverner opera by Maxwell Davies (libretto by composer); composed 1962–70, produced London, Covent Garden, 12 July 1972. Plot is based on now discredited story that John Taverner was an agent of Thomas Cromwell dedicated to the persecution of the Catholic Church.

Taverner, John (c. 1495–1545) English organist and composer. He wrote masses and motets in polyphonic style, showing great contrapuntal skill, but as a Protestant renounced his art. He was imprisoned 1528 for heresy, and, as an agent of Thomas Cromwell, assisted in the dissolution of the monasteries.

Taylor, (Joseph) Deems (1885–1966) US composer and critic. He became music critic to the *New York World* in 1921, but from 1925 devoted himself to composition.

He studied at the Ethical Culture School and the University in New York , and received piano lessons, but was self-taught in other musical subjects.

Works include: the operas *The King's Henchman* (1927), *Peter Ibbetson* (after G du Maurier, 1931), and *Ramuntcho* (after Loti, 1942); incidental music for T Wilder's *Lucrece* and for other plays; symphonic poems *The Siren Song* and *Jurgen* (after J B Cabell), suites *Through the Looking-Glass* (after L Carroll) and *Circus Day* (1925), *Lucrece* suite for string quartet; choral works.

Tchaikovsky, Pyotr Il'yich (1840–1893) Russian composer. His strong sense of melody, personal expression, and brilliant orchestration are clear throughout his many Romantic works, which include six symphonies, three piano concertos, a violin concerto, operas (including *Eugene Onegin* 1879), ballets (including *The Nutcracker* 1891–92), orchestral fantasies (including *Romeo and Juliet* 1870), and chamber and vocal music.

Professor of harmony at Moscow 1865, he later met Balakirev, becoming involved with the nationalist movement in music. He successfully united western European influences with native Russian fervour and emotion, and was the first Russian composer to establish a reputation with Western audiences.

Tchaikovsky's father, an inspector of mines, allowed him to have music lessons from the age of four, and at six he played well. The family moved to St Petersburg in 1848; he received more systematic teaching there and in 1850 was sent to the School of Jurisprudence, which he left in 1859 to become a clerk in the Ministry of Justice. He approached music as an amateur, but in 1862 entered the newly opened Conservatory, having already studied with Nikolai Zaremba, and had lessons in orchestration from Anton Rubinstein. Nikolai Rubinstein, having opened a similar Conservatory at Moscow, engaged him as professor of harmony in 1865, and there he began to compose seriously and professionally. In 1868 he met Balakirev and his circle of nationalist composers in St Petersburg, but remained aloof. In the same year his first symphony *Winter Daydreams* was successfully performed in Moscow; it remains in some ways the freshest and most spontaneous music in this form. His first opera *The Voyevoda* was premiered at the Bolshoi Theatre in 1869 and *Romeo and Juliet* in 1870.

The second symphony, a distinctly nationalist work, was performed 1873, and the B♭ minor piano concerto, though at first rejected by Nikolai Rubinstein, was given at Boston by Hans von Bülow in 1875 and given its first Moscow performance later that year by Alexander Taneiev. In 1876 he began a correspondence with Nadezhda von Meck, the widow of a wealthy engineer. She greatly admired his work and made him an allowance to free him from financial anxiety, but never met him face to face. His first important opera *Vakula the Smith* was premiered 1876 and the following year the first of his great ballets, *Swan Lake*, was premiered at the Bolshoi. The hero's name (Siegfried) is probably derived from Wagner's *Ring*, which Tchaikovsky had just seen at Bayreuth. Also in 1877 he married Antonina Milyukova; but he was an undeclared homosexual and left her less than a month after the wedding, on the verge of mental collapse. After some months in Switzerland and Italy, he resigned the post at the Moscow Conservatory and lived in the country, wholly devoted to composition. The first of his universally popular symphonies, the 4th in F minor, was premiered in 1878; its insistent 'Fate' motive heralds a trilogy of works in which the tension between life affirmation and self-annhilation, is dominant. *Eugene Onegin* 1879 mirrors some of the recent circumstances of Tchaikovsky's own life; Tatiana writes an optimistic love letter to the reluctant Onegin just as Antonina had done to Tchaikovsky. His most brilliant and least introverted orchestral work, the Violin Concerto in D, was given at Vienna in 1881 and seven years later he composed the most powerful and fully integrated of the symphonies, the 5th in E minor.

In 1888 he made a first international tour as conductor of his own works, which became known in many countries, and the following year he completed the finest of his three ballets, *The Sleeping Beauty*. In 1890 he had a misunderstanding with Mme von Meck which brought their friendship by correspondence to an end; but he was by that time quite able to earn his own living.

He visited the USA in 1892 and London in the summer of 1893, when a doctorate was conferred on him by Cambridge University. On his return to Russia he completed the sixth symphony ('Pathétique'), which was first performed at St Petersburg in October.

Nine days later Tchaikovsky was dead; the cause of death is usually given as cholera, although it has recently been suggested that he took poison at the decree of a secret court of honour instituted to avert a scandal following allegations of a liaison between him and an aristocrat's nephew.

Works include: STAGE the operas *Eugene Onegin* (1879), *Maid of Orleans* (1881), *The Queen of Spades* (1890); ballets *Swan Lake* (1877), *The Sleeping Beauty* (1890), and *The Nutcracker* (1892).

ORCHESTRAL seven symphonies: no. 1 in G minor (*Winter Daydreams*, 1866, revised 1874), no. 2 in C minor (*Little Russian*, 1872, revised 1880), no. 3 in D (*Polish*, 1875), no. 4 in F minor (1878), no. 5 in E minor (1888), no. 6 in B minor (*Pathétique*, 1893), no. 7 in E♭ (unfinished, 1892); *Manfred* symphony, after Byron (1885); fantasy-overture *Romeo and Juliet* (1869), *Capriccio italien* (1880), Serenade for string orchestra (1880), overture *The Year 1812* (1880); three piano concertos, including no. 1 in B♭ minor (1875), violin concerto (1878), *Variations on a Rococo Theme* for cello and orchestra (1876).

CHAMBER string sextet *Souvenir de Florence* (1887), three string quartets (1871, 1874, 1876), piano trio (1882); 17 op. nos. of piano compositions including *The Seasons*; 13 op. nos. of songs (nearly 100).

Tcherepnin, Alexander (Nikolaievich) (1899–1977), also Cherepnin Russian-born US composer. He wrote ballets and orchestral and chamber pieces in a neoclassical style.

He was born at St Petersburg and studied under his father, Nikolai ◊Tcherepnin and Nikolai Aleksandrovich Sokolov (1859–1922), learning the piano from Annette Nikolaevna Essipova (1850–1914). He appeared as a boy pianist and began to publish his works, but in 1921 settled in Paris with his father, studying composition with André Gédalge and piano with Isidore Philipp at the Conservatory. He taught in Paris 1925–38, and from 1949 at De Paul University in Chicago. He settled in the USA in 1950.

Works include: OPERA *01–01* (after Andreiev, 1928) and *Die Hochzeit der Sobeide* (after Hofmannsthal, 1933); ballets including *The Frescoes of Ajanta* (1923) and (with Honegger and Harsányi) *Shota Roustaveli*; incidental music for Wilde's *Salome*, Rolland's *L'esprit triomphant*, and Hauptmann's *Hannele*; cantata *Le jeu de la nativité*.

OTHER four symphonies (1927–58), three pieces for chamber orchestra, six piano concertos (1923–72), *Rapsodie géorgienne* for cello and piano, *Concerto da camera* for flute, violin, and small orchestra; two string quartets (1922, 1926), piano trio; violin and piano sonata, three cello and piano sonatas; sonata, studies and pieces for piano.

Tcherepnin, Nikolai (Nikolaievich) (1873–1945), also Cherepnin Russian composer and conductor. He studied with Rimsky-Korsakov and wrote ballets for Diaghilev, including *Armida's Pavilion* 1908. In 1921 he settled in Paris. He was the father of Alexander ◊Tcherepnin.

He gave up a legal career at the age of 22 and studied at the St Petersburg Conservatory with Rimsky-Korsakov and others. Having appeared as a pianist, in 1901 he became conductor of the Belaiev Symphony Concerts (established in 1885 by music publisher Mitrofan Petrovich Belaiev, 1836–1904), and then began conducting operas at the Maryinsky Theatre. In 1908 he joined Diaghilev and conducted Russian opera and ballet in Paris and elsewhere, remaining with the Ballets Russes until 1914, when he returned to Petrograd, to become director of the Conservatory at Tiflis in 1918.

Works include: OPERA *Vanka the Chancellor* (after Sologub, 1935), and *Poverty no Crime* (after Ostrovsky); ballets *Armida's Pavilion* (1908), *Narcissus* (1911), *A Russian Fairy-Tale*, *The Romance of a Mummy* (after Gautier), *The Masque of the Red Death* (after Poe, 1916), *The Tale of the Princess Ulyba*, *Dionysius*.

OTHER Symphony, sinfonietta, symphonic poems *Narcissus and Echo* and *The Enchanted Kingdom*, witches' caves from *Macbeth*, suite *The Enchanted Garden* (1904), overture to Rostand's *La princesse lointaine* (1903), six pieces on Pushkin's 'The Golden Fish' for orchestra; piano concerto in C♯ minor (1907), lyric poem for violin and orchestra; string quartet in A minor; piano pieces on Benois' picture-book *The Russian Alphabet* and other piano works; songs.

Te the name for the leading-note in any key in tonic sol-fa, so pronounced, but in notation represented by the symbol **t**.

tedesca, or tedesco (Italian 'German') musical term; *alla tedesca* means 'in the German manner', but more particularly indicates a piece or movement in rather slow waltz time, in the character of the *Deutscher* or *Ländler*.

Te Deum hymn based on the text *Te Deum laudamus* (Latin 'We praise Thee, O God'), originating possibly in the writings of St Ambrose or Bishop Nicetius of Remesiana. In the Roman Catholic liturgy it is sung at ◊matins on feast days and on Sundays. In addition to its ◊plainsong variant, composers including Palestrina, Handel, and Berlioz have set the Te Deum.

Te Deum laudamus/We praise thee, O God Latin hymn or psalm in 'rhythmical prose', possibly by Nicetas of Remesiana (c. 400). It is in three sections: a hymn to the Trinity, a hymn to Christ, and a series of prayers. The first part is set to a psalmodic formula ending on G, and the second to a similar formula ending on E, but concluding with a more extended melody in the same mode to the words 'Aeterna fac'. The third part makes further use of these last two melodies.

The Te Deum was set in polyphony during the Middle Ages, especially in England, for voices or organ in alternation with the plainsong. It became a normal part of the Anglican 'Morning Service' and it has also been set in English for occasions of rejoicing (for example, by Handel and Walton). The Latin text has often been set with orchestral accompaniment by composers such as Haydn, Berlioz, Bruckner, and Kodály.

Telemaco, Il, ossia L'isola di Circe/Telemachus, or Circe's Island opera by Gluck (libretto by M Coltellini), produced Vienna, Burgtheater, 30 January 1765. Sorceress Circe loves prisoner Ulysses on her enchanted island. His son Telemachus, also shipwrecked, falls in love with Asteria, Circe's maid (later revealed to be his intended wife). They escape while Circe swears revenge.

Telemann, Georg Philipp (1681–1767) German Baroque composer, organist, and conductor. He was the best-known German composer of his time with a contemporary reputation much greater than J S Bach's. His prolific output of concertos for both new and old instruments, including violin, viola da gamba, recorder, flute, oboe, trumpet, horn, and bassoon, represents a methodical and fastidious investigation into the tonal resonances and structure of the new Baroque orchestra, research which was noted by Bach. Other works include 25 operas, numerous sacred cantatas, and instrumental fantasias.

Telemann was born at Magdeburg and educated there and at Hildesheim. He went on to read law at Leipzig University, and seems to have been largely self-taught in music. In Leipzig he founded a student *Collegium musicum* and was appointed organist of the New Church (St Matthew's) in 1704, but the same year moved to Sorau as Kapellmeister to Count Promnitz. In the service of the court at Eisenach 1708–12

(Kapellmeister from 1709) he made the acquaintance of J S Bach in nearby Weimar. He then worked in Frankfurt until his appointment in 1721 as Cantor of the Johanneum (Johanneum Lateinschule, established in the 16th century) and municipal music director in Hamburg, where he stayed for the rest of his life. In 1722 he declined the post of Cantor of St Thomas's, Leipzig, and Bach was appointed. He travelled a good deal, several times visiting Berlin, and in 1737 made a successful visit to Paris. He is famed for his huge output, although some of his instrumental music can sound routine and written to order. His most attractive music is often in his vocal works, notably the operas, oratorios, and cantatas.

Works include: about 45 operas (few survive complete), including *Der geduldige Socrates* (1721), *Der neumodische Liebhaber Damon* (1724), *Miriways* (1728), *Pimpinone* (1725), *Emma und Eginhard* (1728); oratorios, including *Die Tageszeiten*, *Die Auferstehung und Himmelfahrt Christi* (1760), *Der Tag des Gerichts* (1762); Passion oratorios (Brockes and Ramler); 46 liturgical Passions; 12 sets of cantatas for the church's year; motets, psalms; large quantities of instrumental music, including a collection called *Musique de table* (Hamburg, 1733); concertos, orchestral suites, trio sonatas, and other chamber music; keyboard music.

Temistocle/Themistocles opera by Porpora (libretto by A Zeno), produced Vienna, 1 October 1718.

Opera by J C Bach (libretto M Verazi, after Metastasio) produced Mannheim, Hoftheater, 5 November 1772. Driven away by the people of Athens, Themistocles seeks refuge in the land of his enemy, Xerxes, King of Persia. Themistocles finds his daughter Aspacia there suffering the advances of Xerxes. When Aspacia would choose suicide rather than marriage to him and when Themistocles would do likewise rather than renounce Greece, Xerxes is impressed by their virtue and makes a happy ending.

temperament a system of tuning ('tempering') the ◊pitches of a ◊mode or ◊scale whereby ◊intervals are lessened or enlarged, away from the 'natural'. In folk music this is done to preserve its emotional or ritual meaning; in Western music to allow a measure of freedom in changing key. J S Bach composed *The Well-Tempered Clavier*, a sequence of 48 preludes and fugues in every key of the ◊chromatic scale, to demonstrate the superior versatility of tempered tuning.

Temperley, Nicholas (1932–) English-born US musicologist. He studied at Cambridge 1954–59 and was assistant lecturer there 1961–66; he became professor at the University of Illinois in 1972, and chairman of the musicology division in 1992. He has published editions of Loder's *Raymond and Agnes* (produced Cambridge 1966) and the *Symphonie Fantastique* in the New Berlioz edition, 1972. He edited collections of *English Songs, 1800–60* (1979), *The Music of the English Parish Church* (two volumes, 1979), and *London Pianoforte School* (20 volumes 1984–87). His completion of Mozart's *L'oca del Cairo* was produced in Illinois in 1991.

Tempestà, La opera by Halévy (libretto by Scribe, originally written in French for Mendelssohn, based on Shakespeare's *Tempest* and translated into Italian), produced London, Her Majesty's Theatre, 8 June 1850.

Tempest, The incidental music by Sibelius, op. 109, composed for production of Shakespeare's play at the Theatre Royal, Copenhagen, 1926.

Opera by Fibich (libretto by J Vrchlický, based on Shakespeare), produced Prague, Czech Theatre, 1 March 1895.

Prospero, Miranda and Ferdinand shipwrecked on an island with Ariel and Caliban. Symphonic fantasy by Tchaikovsky, after Shakespeare, suggested by Stassov, begun August 1873, first performed Moscow, 19 December 1873.

Tempest, The, or The Enchanted Island opera adapted from Shakespeare by T Shadwell, with music by Locke, Humfrey, Reggio, James Hart, G B Draghi, and Banister, produced London, Dorset Gardens Theatre, 30 April 1674.

Opera adapted from Shakespeare by Shadwell, with music by Weldon, formerly attributed to H Purcell, composed c. 1712.

Templario, Il/The Templar opera by Nicolai (libretto by G M Marini, based on Scott's *Ivanhoe*), produced Turin, Teatro Regio, 11 February 1840.

Templer und die Jüdin, Die/The Templar and the Jewess opera by Marschner (libretto by W A Wohlbrück, based on Scott's *Ivanhoe*), produced Leipzig, 22 December 1829. Saxon Rowena and Jewish Rebecca compete for the attention of knight Ivanhoe. Ivanhoe champions Rebecca after she is accused of witchcraft.

tempo (Italian 'time') in music, the speed at which a piece should be played. One way of indicating the tempo of a piece of music is to give a ◊metronome marking, which states the number of beats per minute; for example, 'crotchet = 60' means that there should be 60 crotchet beats to the minute. Modern electronic metronomes measure tempo very accurately, but performers often change or even ignore metronome markings, playing at a tempo that suits their interpretation of the music.

Before the invention of an accurate metronome, tempo was indicated by Italian words such as 'allegro' (lively), 'presto' (quick), or 'lento' slow. Many composers still use these Italian terms, or similar words in their own language, to describe the speed of a piece of music rather than give a precise metronome marking.

Although tempo in music can be measured as accurately as the other parameters such as ◊pitch, ◊dynamics, and even ◊timbre, precise indications of tempo are seldom adhered to in performance. Music written before the development of precise chronometers could give no more than a vague idea of speed, often notated in a confusing and ambiguous manner. The system of ◊time signatures developed during the Renaissance used symbols which, as well as indicating the number of beats per bar, had some implications of speed, but this was superseded in the 17th century by verbal indications of tempo. These – by convention in Italian but often in the native language of the composer – gave only a vague idea of speed, but had the advantage of indicating mood: for example 'allegro' not only conveys the idea of quickness, but also brightness, and 'largo' means broad and expansive, but also implies slowness. The expressive qualities of these verbal tempo indications have ensured their continued use to the present day, where they are often used in conjunction with precise metronome markings.

With the appearance of Johann ◊Maëlzel's metronome, a means of describing precise tempo became possible, in terms of the frequency of the underlying beat of the music, expressed as the number of beats per minute. The indication 'crotchet = 120', for example, specifies both the frequency of the beat and the unit (in this case, crotchet). It is now theoretically possible, using electronic metronomes, to indicate and perform music to a very high degree of accuracy, but it is seldom desirable to do so: many subjective factors may influence the choice of tempo at any one time, and a truly musical interpretation often relies on changes in the underlying tempo throughout a piece, such as 'acceler-

ando' (getting faster), 'ritardando' (getting slower), or 'rubato' (with a beat that is not strictly regular).

tempo giusto (Italian 'strict time') in music, strict time (also the right speed).

tempo ordinario (Italian 'common time, ordinary pace') in music, either moderate speed or four beats in a bar (as opposed to *Alla breve*, where there are two beats in a bar).

tempo primo (Italian 'first time'; 'first tempo') musical term; after a change of tempo the direction *tempo primo* means that the pace first indicated is to be resumed.

Tender Land, The opera by Copland (libretto by H Everett), produced New York, 1 April 1954, conductor Schippers. Orchestral suite 1956. High-school graduate Laurie comes of age when young Martin fails to show up after agreeing to elope with her.

Tenducci, Giusto Ferdinando (1735–1790) Italian castrato soprano and composer. He made his debut in Naples, then went to London in 1758, remaining there, apart from visits to Ireland (1765–68) and Scotland (1768–69), until 1791, when he returned to Italy. Popular in England as a singer of Handel, he was also heard in his own adaptation of Gluck's *Orfeo*. He published a treatise on singing, composed songs and harpsichord sonatas, and compiled song collections.

tenor the highest range of adult male singing voice when not using ◊falsetto, approximately C3–A5. It is the preferred voice for operatic heroic roles. Exponents are Luciano Pavarotti and Placido Domingo.

The word is derived from the Latin *teneo* 'I hold', because it 'held' the plainsong theme in early polyphony.

The approximate range of the tenor voice.

tenor clef the C ◊clef in which middle C (C4) is represented by the second highest line of the five-line ◊stave. It was used by musicians and singers until the 18th century, but is now used mainly by instruments which read bass clef, except in their higher registers, such as the cello and bassoon.

The tenor clef.

tenor cor brass military-band instrument invented around 1860 to provide a better substitute for the horn than had been found in the saxhorn. It is in the circular form of a horn, though half the length, and has valves. It is made in F, with an extra slide to change it to E♭.

tenor drum drum with skin stretched over either end, similar in shape to the side drum and bass drum, but of intermediate size. It produces a duller sound than that of the side drum, having no snares, but gives out clearer notes, though of indefinite pitch, than the bass drum.

tenore robusto (Italian 'robust tenor') one of the categories of operatic singing voices: a tenor capable of sustaining parts of a heroic type; equivalent to the German *Heldentenor*.

tenor horn valved brass wind instrument of the ◊saxhorn type, made in various tunings and compasses.

tenoroon early musical instrument of the ◊bassoon type, but smaller and tuned higher than the bassoon.

tenor tuba another name for the ◊euphonium, a musical instrument.

tenor violin early name for the ◊viola. A small cello, tuned a fifth or a fourth above the normal cello, was sometimes known as a tenor violin.

tenson troubadour, trouvère, or Minnesinger song, the words of which took the form of a dispute.

tenuto (Italian 'held') in musical notation, instruction to hold a note for its full value. In music since the late 18th century, it often also implies that the note should be held beyond its notated value, causing an expressive effect, similar to an ◊agogic accent.

ternary vocal or instrumental piece in three distinct sections, the third of which is a repetition of the first, is said to be in ternary form. The middle section is usually a contrast, sometimes based on similar but more often on different thematic material, but always relevant in style if not in mood. In vocal music *da capo* arias and in instrumental music minuets or scherzos with trios are outstanding examples of ternary form.

ternary form a three-part form of which the outer parts form a near-symmetrical pair separated by a contrasting middle section. An example is the ◊minuet and trio; 18th-century ◊sonata form is a sophisticated ternary form with an extended middle (development) section. Ternary form can be

recognized in popular music by the 'middle-8' or eight-bar middle section preceding the verse and chorus reprise.

Terradellas, Domingo Miguel Bernabe (1713–1751) Spanish composer. He produced his first opera in 1739 in Rome, where he was maestro di cappella at the Spanish church 1743–45. He visited London 1746–47, producing three operas there and in Paris, then returned to Rome.

He studied 1732–38 with Francesco Durante at the Conservatorio dei Poveri di Gesù at Naples, where he composed two oratorios.

Works include: the operas *Astarto* (1739), *Gli intrighi delle cantarine, Cerere, Merope* (1743), *Artaserse, Semiramide riconosciuta, Mitridate* (1746), *Bellerofonte* (1747), *Imeneo in Atene, Didone, Sesostri, rè d'Egitto*; oratorios, *Giuseppe riconosciuto* (1736), and *Ermenegildo martire*; Masses, motets, and other church music.

Terrasse, Claude (Antoine) (1867–1923) French composer and organist. He studied at the Lyon Conservatory, then at Louis Niedermeyer's school in Paris, and afterwards privately with Eugène Gigout. After living obscurely as an organist at Auteuil and a piano teacher at Arcachon, he began to compose and settled in Paris in 1895 as organist of the Trinité.

Works include: the opera *Pantagruel* (after Rabelais), operettas *La fiancée du scaphandrier, Choncette, Le Sire de Vergy* (1903), *Monsieur de la Palisse* (1904), *L'ingénu libertin, Le coq d'Inde, Le mariage de Télémaque* (1910), *Les transatlantiques* (1911), *La petite femme de Loth* (T Bernard), *Les travaux d'Hercule* (1901), *Cartouche* (1912), *Le cochon qui sommeille, Faust en ménage, Le manoir enchanté*, and several others; incidental music for various comedies; music for T Gautier's and T de Banville's *Matinées poétiques*; *Trio bouffe* for strings, *Sérénade bouffe* for piano and strings; songs.

Terry, Charles Sanford (1864–1936) English music historian. He was appointed professor of history at Aberdeen University in 1903. He did valuable work for music by writing an authoritative biography of J S Bach (1928) as well as numerous detailed studies of various aspects of his work, and a biography of J C Bach (1929, revised 1967 by H C R Landon).

terzet (Italian *terzetto*) musical composition for three voices or for instruments in three parts.

Teseo/Theseus opera by Handel (libretto by N F Haym), produced London, Queen's Theatre, Haymarket, 10 January 1713. Teseo, prince of Athens, marries Algilea in spite of interference from the enchantress Medea.

Tessier, Charles (fl. c. 1600) French lutenist and composer. He was a *musicien de la chambre du roy* (court composer) to Henri IV and visited England for some time in the 1590s, dedicating a book of chansons to Lady Penelope Rich (the poet Philip Sidney's 'Stella').

Works include: chansons for four–five voices (1597), *Airs et villanelles* for three–five voices (1604), setting of the eighth song in Sidney's *Astrophel and Stella*.

tessitura (Italian 'texture') in music, term indicating the average register of a part (high, middle, low) within the total range of the voice or instrument concerned. It is used specifically to refer to the voice and brass instruments before the invention of valves, when players often specialized in high or low tessituras.

Testament de la Tante Caroline, Le opéra-bouffe by Roussel (libretto by Nino), produced Olomouc, 14 November 1936. Aunt Caroline leaves fortune to first of three nieces to produce a male child; spinster niece obliges.

testudo (Latin 'tortoise') Latin name for the Greek ◊lyre, a musical instrument which was often made of tortoiseshell. The name was transferred to the lute in 16th-century Latin.

tetrachord (from Greek 'having four strings') scale of four notes embracing the interval of a perfect fourth; a basis for melodic construction in ancient Greek music theory and 20th-century serial technique.

Teufels Lustschloss, Des/The Devil's Pleasure Palace opera by Schubert (libretto by A von Kotzebue), composed 1814 but not performed until 1879. Knight Oswald, wife Luitgarde, and squire Robert endure series of trials at haunted castle of Luitgarde's uncle.

Teutsche see ◊*Deutsche Tänze*.

texture the vertical density of a musical composition. While the nature of the texture is often one of the main distinguishing features of a work, particularly in 20th-century music, variety of texture is an important component of a work's progression and life in virtually all music.

Thaïs opera by Massenet (libretto by L Gallet, based on the novel by A France), produced Paris, Opéra, 16 March 1894. It contains the popular *Méditation* as an orchestral interlude. Young monk Athanaël persuades courtesan Thaïs to enter a convent but falls in love with her before she dies.

Thalberg, Sigismond (Fortuné François) (1812–1871) Austrian pianist and composer. He travelled widely on concert tours, playing mostly his own compositions. By the 1850s he was pursuing an international career, rivalled only by Liszt as a virtuoso performer.

When he was ten, his father sent him to school in Vienna, where he later studied piano with Hummel and theory with Sechter. He soon played at private parties, appeared at Prince Metternich's house in 1826, and in 1830 made his first tour, in Germany, having by this time begun to publish his compositions. In 1835 he made further studies with Johann Pixis and Friedrich Kalkbrenner in Paris, and in 1836 first appeared in London.

Works include: the operas *Florinda* (1851) and *Cristina di Suezia* (1855); piano concerto; piano sonata, studies, nocturnes, romances, and numerous other pieces for piano, operatic fantasies on works by Rossini, Weber, and Verdi, and other transcriptions for piano; over 50 German songs.

thalumeau short, thickset double-reed wind instrument, ancestor of the ◊clarinet. It is also the term used to describe the dark lowest register of clarinet tone.

Thamos, König in Aegypten/Thamos, King of Egypt incidental music by Mozart (K345) to T P von Gebler's play, composed 1779 (two choruses already 1773), not produced in Mozart's lifetime except in an adaptation to another play, Plümicke's *Lanassa*.

Theile, Johann (1646–1724) German composer. He learnt music as a youth at Magdeburg and Halle, and later studied at Leipzig University, where he took part in the students' performances as singer and viola da gamba player. He then became a pupil of Schütz at Weissenfels, and taught music at Stettin and Lübeck. He was Kapellmeister to the Duke of Holstein at Gottorp 1673–75, but fled to Hamburg during the Danish invasion. In 1676 he competed unsuccessfully for the post of cantor at St Thomas's Church, Leipzig. He was the first composer to contribute to the repertory of the newly opened opera at Hamburg in 1678. In 1685 he succeeded Rosenmüller as music director at Wolfenbüttel and in 1689 he was appointed to a similar post at Merseburg. In his last years he lived in retirement at his birthplace.

Works include: the operas *Adam und Eva* (1678; lost) and *Orontes* (1678; seven arias extant); ten Masses, seven Psalms; Passion according to St Matthew, church cantatas.

Theinred of Dover (lived 12th century) English music theorist. His treatise, a study of intervals and proportions, is known only from an early 15th-century copy in the Bodleian Library, Oxford. It includes a diagram of the different forms of alphabetical notation, and a section on the measurement of organ pipes. He was a monk at Dover Priory.

theme a basic melody or musical figure, which often occurs with variations.

Theodora oratorio by Handel (libretto by T Morell), produced London, Covent Garden, 16 March 1750.

Theodorakis, Mikis (1925–) Greek composer. He was imprisoned 1967–70 for attempting to overthrow the military regime of Greece.

theorbo musical instrument, a bass ◊lute or archlute developed around 1500 and incorporating dual sets of strings, a set of freely vibrating bass strings for plucking with the thumb in addition to five to seven courses over a fretted fingerboard. It survived to form part of the Italian Baroque orchestra about 1700.

theremin early electronic musical instrument invented by Leon ◊Theremin in 1922. It is played by the player's hand moving in a magnetic field around a metal loop and rod. It uses ◊beat frequency generation between two high frequency oscillators, one signal of which is fixed, while the other depends on the position of the player's hand in the vicinity of an aerial. Its monophonic sound is voicelike in the soprano register, and trombonelike at a lower pitch. Since the player makes no contact with the instrument, it is difficult to obtain a steady pitch, hence the instrument's wavering quality. Because any position of the hand generates a pitch, the theremin is incapable of detaching notes, so that all intervals are linked together by a wailing ◊portamento, like that of a siren.

Theremin subsequently invented another instrument shaped like a cello on which notes could be produced detached from each other by means of a cello fingerboard.

Edgard ◊Varèse incorporated two theremins in *Ecuatorial* 1932–33; it has also featured in film scores such as Bernard ◊Herrmann's music for the science-fiction film *The Day the Earth Stood Still* 1951. A transistorized theremin is heard in the Beach Boys' hit 'Good Vibrations' 1966.

Theremin, Leon (1896–1993) Russian inventor of the ◊theremin 1922, a monophonic synthesizer, and of other valve-amplified instruments in the 1930s. Following commercial and public success in the USA and Hollywood, he returned to Russia 1938 to imprisonment and obscurity. After 1945 he continued acoustic research in Moscow and reappeared at a Stockholm electronic music symposium 1990.

inventions The theremin was played without being touched by converting the operator's arm movements into musical tones. The instrument could produce a wide range of sounds and was mainly used to make eerie sound effects for films. Theremin also invented an electronic dance platform, called the terpsitone, in which a dancer's movements were converted into musical tones. Other inventions included a stringless electronic cello, the first syncopated rhythm machine, a colour television system, and a security system which was installed at Sing Sing and Alcatraz prisons in the USA.

life Theremin was educated as a physicist and musician. In 1922 he demonstrated his theremin to the Soviet revolutionary leader Lenin and was sent on a tour which included sell-out concerts in Berlin, Paris, London, and New York. He established a studio in New York, where he lived 1927–38. He was then ordered to return to the USSR and sent to a Siberian labour camp during the Great Purge carried out by the Soviet leader Stalin against real and imagined enemies. During World War II Theremin worked in a military laboratory, producing a radio-controlled aircraft, tracking systems for ships and submarines, and television systems which are still in use. He also invented a miniature listening device, or 'bug', for the KGB. For this he received the Stalin Prize, First Class, and was allowed to live in Moscow, where he became professor of acoustics at the Moscow Conservatory of Music. He was sacked and his laboratory closed when a chance encounter with a reporter from the *New York Times* resulted in a newspaper article which revealed his earlier imprisonment. He continued his acoustics research, and work aimed at reversing the ageing process, until he died.

Thérèse opera by Massenet (libretto by J Claretie), produced Monte Carlo, 7 February 1907. Torn between her husband André and former love Armand, Thérèse decides to run away with Armand until André is captured by revolutionaries. She decides to join him at the guillotine.

Opera by John Tavener (libretto by G McLarnon); composed 1973–76, produced Covent Garden, 1 October 1979, conductor

Downes. Poet Rimbaud guides spiritual growth of St Thérèse of Lisieux, as she experiences various 20th-century horrors.

Theresienmesse/Theresa Mass Haydn's Mass in B♭ no. 12, composed 1799. Despite its name, it seems to have no connection with Maria Theresa, wife of the Emperor Franz II.

Thésée/Theseus opera by Lully (libretto by Quinault), produced at Saint-Germain, 12 January 1675; first Paris performance, April 1675. Jealous Medea tries to prevent union of Theseus and Aegle. She fails when King Aegeus recognizes Theseus as his long-lost son.

thesis (Greek 'lowering') in musical analysis, a term borrowed from Greek poetry, denoting a stressed beat (◊downbeat), usually in comparison with or reference to an arsis, or unstressed beat (◊upbeat). In German usage, 'arsis' and 'thesis' have opposite meanings to the original Greek and English words.

Thespis, or The Gods Grown Old operetta by Sullivan (libretto by W S Gilbert), produced London, Gaiety Theatre, 26 December 1871. Sullivan's first work written in association with Gilbert.

Thétis et Pélée/Thetis and Peleus opera by Colasse (libretto by B de Fontenelle), produced Paris, Opéra, 11 January 1689.

Thibaut IV (1201–1253) French King of Navarre and Count of Champagne and Brie. He was a trouvère (see ◊troubadour), and wrote a large quantity of poetry and music in a variety of styles. More than 45 of his songs survive.

third an ◊interval of three diatonic notes.

A third is an 'imperfect interval' (having 'major' and 'minor' variants). A major third consists of four semitones (for example, C–E). A minor third consists of three semitones (C–E♭).

Thomas, (Charles Louis) Ambroise (1811–1896) French composer. His operas were written to please contemporary bourgeois Parisian taste; his most successful works *Mignon* 1866, and *Hamlet* 1868 were written in emulation of Gounod. He also wrote numerous cantatas, part songs, and choral pieces.

He learnt music from his father as a child and in 1828 entered the Paris Conservatory, where he won the Prix de Rome in 1832. He also studied piano privately with Friedrich Kalkbrenner and composition with Lesueur. Soon after his return from Rome he began to win operatic successes in Paris. In 1852 he became professor at the Conservatory and in 1871 succeeded Auber as director.

Works include: the operas *La double échelle* (1837), *Le perruquier de la Régence* (1838), *Le panier fleuri* (1839), *Carline* (1840), *Le Comte de Carmagnola, Le guerillero* (1842), *Angélique et Médor* (1843), *Mina, Le Caïd, Le songe d'une nuit d'été* (not Shakespeare, 1850), *Raymond* (1851), *La Tonelli, La cour de Célimène* (1855), *Psyché* (1857), *Le carnaval de Venise, Le roman d'Elvire* (1860), *Mignon* (after Goethe's *Wilhelm Meister*, 1866), *Gille et Gillotin, Hamlet* (after Shakespeare, 1868), *Françoise de Rimini* (after Dante, 1882); ballets *La Gipsy* (1839), *Betty* and *La tempête* (1889); *Messe solennelle* (1857), *Messe de Requiem*, motets; cantata *Hermann et Ketty*, cantatas for the unveiling of a Lesueur statue and for the Boieldieu centenary; fantasy for piano and orchestra; string quartet, string quintet, piano trio; piano pieces; songs, including six Italian songs, part songs.

Thomas, Arthur Goring (1850–1892) English composer. His music reflects the comfortable, undemanding French style of his time, and includes the operas *Esmeralda* 1883, based on Victor Hugo's *Notre-Dame de Paris*, and *Nadeshda* 1885.

He was educated for the civil service, but later studied music with Emile Durand in Paris and with Sullivan and Prout at the Royal Academy of Music in London. Later he studied orchestration with Max Bruch in Berlin. He began to work on an opera to a libretto by his brother, *Don Braggadocio*, and although he did not finish it, he persevered and eventually received a commission from the Carl Rosa Opera Company. He became insane in 1891.

Works include: the operas *The Light of the Harem* (after Thomas Moore), *Esmeralda* (after Hugo's *Notre-Dame de Paris*, 1883), *Nadeshda* (1885), and *The Golden Web*; anthem *Out of the Deep* for soprano, chorus, and orchestra; cantatas *The Sun Worshippers* and *The Swan*

Major, minor, and diminished thirds.

and the Skylark; *Suite de Ballet* for orchestra; songs, duets.

Thomas and Sally, or The Sailor's Return opera by Arne (libretto by I Bickerstaffe), produced London, Covent Garden, 28 November 1760. Thomas returns from sea in time to scupper Squire's attempts to woo Sally.

Thomé, Francis (actually Joseph François Luc) (1850–1909) French composer. He studied at the Paris Conservatory, then became a private teacher of music.

Works include: the operas *Martin et Frontin* (1877), *Le Caprice de la reine* (1892), operettas *Vieil Air, jeune chanson* (1894), *Le Château de Koenigsberg* (1896), *Le Chaperon rouge* (1900); ballets including *Endymion et Phœbé*, *La Bulle d'amour* (1898), *La Folie parisienne* (1900); incidental music to plays, including Shakespeare's *Romeo and Juliet*, and mystery *l'Enfant Jésus*; *Hymne à la nuit* for chorus; *Simple Aveu* for piano with many arrangements.

Thompson, Randall (1899–1984) US composer. He is chiefly remembered for his choral music and symphonies. He was professor of music at University of California in 1937, director of the Curtis Institute at Philadelphia in 1939, and professor at Harvard University from 1948.

He studied at Harvard University, where his teachers included Bloch. He lived in Rome 1922–25, was assistant professor of music at Wellesley College, and was later appointed to study musical conditions at the US colleges.

Works include: the opera *Solomon and Balkis* (after Kipling's *Just So Stories*, 1942); incidental music for Labiche's *The Italian Straw Hat*; three symphonies (1930–49), *Pierrot and Cothurnus* (1923) and *The Piper at the Gates of Dawn* (1924), for orchestra; *Jazz Poem* for piano and orchestra (1928); *Passion according to St Luke*, cantata *The Testament of Freedom*, *Odes of Horace* for unaccompanied chorus, *Rosemary* for women's chorus, *Americana* for mixed chorus and piano; two string quartets (1941, 1967), *The Wind in the Willows* for string quartet; sonata and suite for piano; songs.

Thomson, Virgil (1896–1989) US composer and critic. His music is notable for a refined absence of expression, his criticism for trenchant matter-of-factness, both at odds with the prevailing US musical culture. He is best known for his opera *Four Saints in Three Acts* 1927–33 to a libretto by Gertrude Stein, and the film scores *The Plow That Broke the Plains* 1936 and *Louisiana Story* 1948.

After studying in France with Nadia ◊Boulanger 1921–22 he was organist at King's Chapel in Boston 1923–24, and returned to Paris 1925–40, mixing with Gertrude Stein and her circle. From 1940 he was music critic to several papers and periodicals in the USA, becoming known for his perceptive views. The most important influences on his music were Satie and the Neo-Classical Stravinsky.

Works include: the operas *Four Saints in Three Acts* (1934), *The Mother of us all* (1947) (libretti by G Stein), *Byron* (1972); ballet *The Filling-Station*; incidental music for Euripides' *Medea*, Shakespeare's *Hamlet*, and other plays, film music; two symphonies, suite *The Plough that Broke the Plains* (1936), two *Sentimental Tangoes*, *Portraits*, *Symphony on a Hymn-Tune* (1948), *Sonata da Chiesa* for orchestra; *Oraison funèbre* (Bossuet) for tenor and orchestra; 2 *Missae breves*, three Psalms for women's voices, *Capital Capitals* (G Stein) for men's chorus and piano; two string quartets (1922, 1932), 5 *Portraits* for four clarinets; *Stabat Mater* for soprano and string quartet, *Five Phrases from the Song of Solomon* for soprano and percussion; 50 *Portraits* for violin and piano, sonata for violin and piano; piano music, songs.

Thorne, John (died 1573) English organist, composer, and poet. He was appointed organist of York Minster in 1542, and worked there in various capacities until two years before his death.

A motet, *Stella coeli*, was copied by John Baldwin, and another, *Exsultabant sancti*, survives in organ score. A four-part in nomine also survives, and there are three poems by him in the same manuscript as Redford's 'Play of Wit and Science' in the British Library and in the 'Paradyse of Daintie Devices' 1576.

thorough bass an alternative term for ◊continuo. 'Thorough' in this case is derived from the old spelling for 'through', meaning the technique is carried out continuously throughout a piece.

Thrane, Waldemar (1790–1828) Norwegian composer. He studied Norwegian folk music and wrote the first Norwegian opera, *Fjeldeventyret/The Mountain Adventure* in 1825, though it was not staged until 1850.

He learnt music at home, his parents being keen amateurs at whose house many musicians met.

Works include: the opera *Fjeldeventyret/The Mountain Adventure* (1825); overtures for orchestra; choral works, and other pieces.

Er kommt, er kommt derBraut -gam kommt! Ihr Toch -ter

Zi - ons, kommt her - aus sein Aus - gang ei - let aus der Ho - he in

eu - er Mut - ter Haus

Bach, *Cantata 140*

The figured bass symbols from Bach's Cantata 140 (a) and a possible realization (b).

Three-Cornered Hat see ◊*Sombrero de tres picos, El* and ◊*Corregidor, Der*.

Three Places in New England work for orchestra by Ives, also known as *Orchestral Set no. 1*; composed 1903–14, first performed New York, 10 January 1931, conductor Slonimsky. The three movements are: 1. 'The 'St Gaudens' in Boston Common: Colonel Shaw and his Colored Regiment'; 2. 'Putnam's Camp, Redding, Connecticut'; 3. 'The Housatonic at Stockbridge'.

Threni, id est Lamentationes Jeremiae Prophetae work by Stravinsky for soprano, mezzo, two tenors, two basses, chorus, and orchestra; composed 1957–58, first performed Venice, 23 September 1958, conductor Stravinsky. See also ◊*Lamentations*.

Threnody for the Victims of Hiroshima work by K Penderecki for 52 solo strings; composed 1959–60; first performed Warsaw, 31 May 1961.

Thuille, Ludwig (1861–1907) Austrian composer. He learnt music from his father, an amateur, on whose death he was sent as a choirboy to the monastery of Kremsmünster. At the age of 15 he began to study with Joseph Pembaur in Innsbruck, and in 1879 he went to the Music School at Munich, where Rheinberger was among his masters. In 1883 he became professor at the Munich school, and there was influenced by Richard Strauss and Alexander Ritter, who wrote the libretto for his first opera, the two later ones being by Otto Julius Bierbaum. Apart from teaching and composition, he also conducted the male-voice choir Liederhort.

Works include: the operas *Theuerdank* (1897), *Lobetanz* (1898) and *Gugeline* (1901); *Romantic Overture* (originally for *Theuerdank*) for orchestra; *Weihnaht im Walde* for male chorus, *Traumsommernacht* and *Rosenlied* for female chorus; piano quintet, sextet for wind and piano; cello and piano sonata; piano pieces; songs.

thump Old English musical term, meaning the plucking of strings (*pizzicato*); also a piece employing *pizzicato*.

thumri Hindi; vocal genre of North Indian (Hindustani) music. A text setting (usually in two sections, *sthayi* and *antara*) is used as the basis of extended improvisations intended to draw out the expressive potential of the (normally romantic) text. Traditionally associated with female courtesan entertainers, it can now be heard sung by singers (of both sexes) specialising in other "light-' or 'semi-classical' genres or in ◊*khyal*.

Thus spake Zarathustra (Richard Strauss). See ◊*Also sprach Zarathustra.*

tie in musical notation, a ◊slur or curved line connecting two notes of the same pitch (or a group of such notes in a chord), usually over a bar line. It indicates that the second note is not to be reiterated, but played continuously as one long note.

Tiefland/The Lowland opera by d'Albert (libretto by R Lothar, based on a Catalan play, *Terra baixa*, by A Guimerá), produced Prague, German Theatre, 15 November 1903. Sebastiano marries off his mistress Marta to simple shepherd Pedro, who does not realize that he has been dishonoured by marrying her. Later, Pedro learns the truth and strangles Sebastiano when he again stakes a claim on Marta.

tiento a 16th-century type of organ piece similar to the ◊ricercare.

tierce an early musical term for the interval of the third, major or minor. It survives, however, as the technical term for one of the tones of a church bell, a minor third above the note of the bell.

tierce de Picardie (French 'Picardy third') in music, the major third introduced into the final chord of a composition in a minor key. The major third corresponds to a natural harmonic, the ◊tierce, but the minor third does not; it was therefore for a long time considered if not an actual dissonance, at any rate not a finally satisfactory ingredient in a concluding chord, for which reason the tierce

de Picardie was often substituted. The origin of the name is not known.

Tigers, The opera by Havergal Brian (libretto by composer); 1916–19, orchestrated 1928–29. The score was lost, but rediscovered in 1977 and given by the BBC on 3 May 1983. Comical adventures of World War I Home Guard.

Tigrane, Il/Tigranes opera by Gluck (libretto by F Silvani, altered by Goldoni), produced Crema, 26 September 1743. Also operas by A Scarlatti (Naples, 1715) and Hasse (Naples, 1729). As a child Tigranes was kidnapped by the Emperor Cyrus from his mother Thonyris. Later he is torn between love for his betrothed, Meroe, and duty. Eventually, all is resolved when Tigranes' true identity is revealed.

Till Eulenspiegels lustige Streiche/Till Eulenspiegel's Merry Pranks symphonic poem by Richard Strauss, op. 28, based on the old Low German folk tale, composed 1894–95, first performed Cologne, 5 November 1895.

timbre (French 'tone') in music, the tone colour, or quality of tone, of a particular sound. Different instruments playing a note at the same ◊pitch have different sound qualities, and it is the timbre that enables the listener to distinguish the sound of, for example, a trumpet from that of a violin. The tone quality of a sound depends on several things, including its waveform, the strength of its ◊harmonics, and its attack and decay – the 'shape' of the sound. The study of the elements of sound quality is part of the science of ◊acoustics.

sound production The characteristic tone quality of any instrument or voice is dependent on a number of factors: the various means of producing sound – for example vibrating strings or reeds; their methods of excitation – such as plucking, bowing, or blowing; and means of amplification – either mechanical, such as a soundboard, or electrical. These differences have their effect on the waveform, the mixture of ◊harmonics, and the envelope shape of the sound.

analysis of waveform By means of an oscilloscope, sounds can be represented visually, and an accurate analysis made of certain of their component parts. Most immediately apparent from these visual representations is the complexity of seemingly simple sounds: picking out the characeristics that distinguish one instrumental colour from another is not easy. Many complex waveforms can be seen as mixtures of pure tones, and in musical sounds as mixtures of harmonics in particular. The two principal parameters of sound – frequency and amplitude – are used in the analysis of timbre to describe the presence and relative strength of the harmonics that make up the sound in its 'steady state', that is, when playing a sustained note. Instruments such as the recorder and flute have tones that are comparatively 'pure', with only a few weak harmonics above the fundamental tone; whereas the double reed instruments such as the bassoon and oboe have complex tones, rich in higher harmonics.

sound shapes Analysis of a sound in its steady state alone, however, does not completely define its timbre. Equally important is the overall shape of the sound – its starting transient (attack) and envelope shape (the steady state and subsequent decay), which can be studied with the aid of spectrum analysers such as sonagraphs, or real-time analysers. The first attempts at electronic synthesis of musical sounds concentrated on producing precise copies of waveforms, but they sounded quite unlike the tones they were trying to mimic, because they did not replicate anything other than the steady-state waveform. Experiments have shown that recordings of an instrument playing a sustained note, minus its initial attack, are very difficult to identify. Variations of amplitude during the course of a note and the speed with which they occur have a major effect on timbre. A sound may start very quietly and comparatively slowly reach the volume of its sustained tone, as with the flute; or it may begin almost immediately at maximum volume and quickly die away, as does the plucked string of a harpsichord. These changes in amplitude also affect the waveform during the note, as the harmonics may increase or decrease in volume at different rates – thus a note may have a noticeably different timbre at different stages of its production, and even a perceived difference of pitch. There may also be slight variations in frequency in some notes, particularly when some form of ◊vibrato forms an integral part of the timbre.

time an alternative word for ◊metre or ◊tempo.

time signature in musical notation, a numerical sign placed after the ◊clef and ◊key signature indicating the metre of the music. Consisting usually of two numbers, the upper number represents the number of beats in a bar, the lower number the type of beat, expressed as a fraction of a unit (◊semibreve).

Hence 3/4 is three crotchet beats to the bar and 6/8 is two beats each of three quavers; alla breve represents 2/2, or two ◊minim beats to a bar; C (common time) represents 4/4, four crotchet beats to a bar.

timpan, or timpe (from Latin *tympanum*) musical instrument, a kind of psaltery used in the British Isles in medieval times. It had wire strings stretched on a frame, which were plucked by the fingers or a plectrum, later struck with a rod.

timpani, or kettledrums tuned drums derived from medieval nakers (from Arabic *naqqara*), with a single head of skin stretched over a cauldron-shaped hemisphere. They produce notes of definite pitch which can be altered by turning screws at the rim of the 'kettle', thus tightening or relaxing the skin. A mechanical device now widely used enables the player to increase or relax the tension by means of a pedal. A variety of sticks covered with different materials can be used to produce a harder or softer impact.

Originally used in pairs tuned to the tonic and dominant key, their numbers were increased and mechanisms introduced during the 19th century to allow pitch changes during a performance. A normal symphony orchestra will have up to five timpani, ranging in pitch from about B1 to G3.

Tinctoris, Johannes (c. 1435–c. 1511) Franco-Flemish music theorist and composer. He wrote a number of important theoretical works and composed Masses, motets, and chansons. His dictionary of musical terms, *Terminorum musicae diffinitorium* 1495, was the first of its kind and defines 299 musical terms.

He was born at Nivelles, and studied both law and theology. He was ordained, and became a canon of Poperinghe. He may have been a singer at Cambrai in 1460, under Guillaume Dufay, and in 1463 was choirmaster at Orleans Cathedral. He went to Italy and from about 1472 was in the service of Ferdinand of Aragon, the King of Naples, maintaining connections with the court there for at least the next 15 years. He founded a school of music and was in the papal chapel at Rome 1484–1500.

Tinctoris is remembered as one of the most important music theorists of his day; he wrote 12 treatises, two of which were printed. His other writings deal with composition, improvisation, the aesthetics of music, its role in education and religion. His writings provide an insight on Renaissance music.

tin whistle, or penny whistle musical instrument, a small and rudimentary pipe of the ◊fife or ◊recorder type, played vertically and having a small range of high notes controlled by six finger holes.

Tippett, Michael Kemp (1905–1998) English composer. With Britten, he became the foremost English composer of his generation. His works include the operas The Midsummer Marriage 1952, The Knot Garden 1970, and New Year 1989; four symphonies; Songs for Ariel 1962; and choral music including The Mask of Time 1982.

Tippett was born in London. He studied with Charles Wood and R O Morris at the Royal College of Music. He became conductor of educational organizations under the London County Council and music director at Morley College, a post formerly held by Gustav Holst. During the war he was a conscientious objector and was imprisoned for refusing to help the war effort by working on the land. His oratorio A Child of our Time 1941 was written in response to the persecution of the Jews during the Nazi era. His first major success was with the Concerto for Double String Orchestra 1939; it was followed by the Fantasia Concertante on a theme of Corelli 1953. Tippett's early lyrical exuberance reached its zenith in the opera The Midsummer Marriage and the associated piano concerto 1953–55. A sparer sound was achieved with the opera King Priam 1962 and second piano sonata, although by the time of The Knot Garden some reconciliation between his two earlier styles was achieved. In this context, his most significant later works are the Triple Concerto, the oratorio The Mask of Time, and the fifth string quartet. The Rose Lake for orchestra 1994 was announced as his last major work.

Tippett was very deliberate and highly self-critical, so that his works appeared in slow succession, but always showed closely concentrated craftsmanship and great originality. Amidst many contemporaries whose music could be described as static, one gains above all from Tippett's music a sense of movement.

Works include: OPERA five, including The Midsummer Marriage (1955), King Priam (1962), The Knot Garden (1970).

CHORAL oratorios A Child of our Time for soloists, chorus, and orchestra (1939–41), The Vision of St Augustine for baritone, chorus, and orchestra (1963–65) and The Mask of Time for soloists, chorus, and orchestra (1981–84).

ORCHESTRAL four symphonies (1944, 1957, 1972, 1976), concerto for double string orchestra (1939), concerto for orchestra, Fantasia concertante on a theme by Corelli (1953); piano

concerto (1953–55), concerto for string trio and orchestra (1979).

CHAMBER AND SOLO VOCAL five string quartets (1935, 1943, 1946, 1979, 1991); four piano sonatas (1938, 1962, 1973, 1979); cantata Boyhood's End for tenor and piano (from W H Hudson's Far Away and Long Ago, 1943).

tirade (French 'pulling' or 'dragging') in music, an ornamental scale passage between two notes of a melody or two chords.

tirana Spanish dance of Andalusia in 6–8 time, usually danced to guitar music and accompanied by words in four-lined coplas.

tiré (French 'drawn') in the playing of string instruments, the downstroke of the bow; the opposite of poussé, 'pushed'.

Tishchenko, Boris (1939–) Russian composer. He studied with Dmitri Shostakovich at the Leningrad Conservatory 1962–65, and taught there from 1965; he was appointed professor in 1986.

Works include: the operas The Stolen Sun (1968), ballets The Twelve (1963), Fly-bee (1968), and The Eclipse (1974; six symphonies (1961–68), piano concerto (1962), two cello concertos, two violin concertos, five string quartets (1957–84), nine piano sonatas (1957–92); Akhmatova Requiem (1966); Garden of Music, cantata (1987); film music.

Tito Manlio opera by Vivaldi (libretto by M Noris), produced Mantua, Teatro Arciducale, carnival 1720. Titus Manlius, the Roman Consul, must condemn his son Manlius to death for disobeying orders; but later the two are reconciled.

Tito Vespasiano, ovvero La clemenza di Tito/Titus Vespasian, or The Clemency of Titus opera by Caldara (libretto by Metastasio, partly based on Corneille's Cinna), produced Vienna, 1734.

Opera by Hasse (libretto ditto), produced Pesaro, Teatro Pubblico, 24 September 1735.

toccata a display piece for keyboard instruments, such as the organ. The word 'toccata' refers to the finger technique being emphasized.

Toch, Ernst (1887–1964) Austrian-born US composer and pianist. After an early modernist phase most of his music was Neo-Classical in spirit. He is remembered chiefly for his chamber music, symphonies, and film scores

He studied medicine and philosophy at first and was self-taught in music, but in 1909 was awarded the Frankfurt Mozart prize and studied there under Willy Rehberg, being appointed piano professor at the Mannheim

Hochschule für Musik in 1913. He served in World War I, and settled in Berlin in 1929, but emigrated in 1932, going first to the USA, then to London, and settling permanently in the USA in 1934. After teaching in New York for two years he moved to Hollywood as a film composer and teacher.

Works include: the operas *Wegwende* (1925), *Die Prinzessin auf der Erbse* (1927), *Egon und Emilie* (1928), *Der Fächer* (1930); incidental music for Euripides' *Bacchantes*, Shakespeare's *As You Like It*, Zweig's *Die Heilige aus USA*, and other plays; music for radio play *The Garden of Jade* and others; film music for *Catherine the Great*, *The Private Life of Don Juan*, and others.

Passover Service (1938); cantata *Das Wasser* (1930); *Der Tierkreis* for unaccompanied chorus; seven symphonies (1949–64), *Bunte Suite*, *Kleine Theater Suite*, *Big Ben*, *Pinocchio* overture (after Collodi's story) for orchestra; *Spiel* for wind band; concerto (1926) and symphony for piano and orchestra; *Poems to Martha* for baritone and strings; 13 string quartets (1902–53), piano quintet, string trio, divertimento for violin and viola; two violin and piano sonatas; sonata, 50 studies and about 12 op. nos. of piano pieces.

Tod und das Mädchen, Der/Death and the Maiden song, D531, by Schubert on words by M Claudius, composed 1817.

The latter part was adapted as a theme for variations in the second movement of his D minor quartet (1824, D810), which is for that reason commonly known by the same name.

Tod und Verklärung/Death and Transfiguration symphonic poem by Richard Strauss, op. 24, composed 1888–89, first performed Eisenach, 21 June 1890.

Tolomeo, Rè di Egitto/Ptolemy, King of Egypt opera by Handel (libretto by N F Haym), produced London, King's Theatre, Haymarket, 30 April 1728. Cleopatra favours younger son Alessandro for succession and exiles Tolomeo to Cyprus, where is is joined by his wife Seleuce; Tolomeo is eventually crowned King of Egypt.

Tomášek, Václav Jan Křtitel Wenzel Johann (1774–1850), or Tomaschek Bohemian composer, organist, and pianist. He wrote songs, piano and chamber music, three symphonies, church music, and three operas. His early symphonies followed Classical models, while his keyboard works pioneer the type of short lyric piano pieces of the Romantic era. His 13 volumes in this genre were popular all over Europe and directly influenced Schubert. His memoirs provide much information about the musical life of his time.

His father having been reduced to poverty, he was educated at the expense of two elder brothers. He became a choirboy at the monastery of Jihlava, but left in 1790 to study law and philosophy in Prague. He also studied the great theoretical treatises on music, and any music he could obtain, and established a reputation as a teacher and composer before the end of the century. Count Bucquoi von Longueval offered him a well-paid post in his household, to which he remained attached even after his marriage to Wilhelmine Ebert in 1823. He often visited Vienna, where he met Beethoven in 1814, and he played his settings of Goethe's poems to the poet at Eger. He published his autobiography in instalments 1845–50.

Works include: the opera *Seraphine* (1811) and two not produced; three Masses, including Coronation Mass (1836), two Requiems and other church music; vocal scenes from Goethe's *Faust* and Schiller's *Wallenstein*, *Maria Stuart*, and *Die Braut von Messina*; three symphonies (1801, 1805, 1807), two piano concertos (1805–06); three string quartets (1792–93), piano trio; five piano sonatas, *Elegie auf eine Rose* (after Hölty), seven sets of *Eclogues* and two of *Dithyrambs* and many other works for piano; numerous songs to words by Goethe, Schiller, and others.

Tomasi, Henri (1901–1971) French composer and conductor. He studied at the Paris Conservatory and in 1927 won the Prix de Rome. On his return from Rome in 1930 he became conductor of the national Radio-Paris. He conducted the Monte Carlo Opera 1946–50. His music has typical French qualities of wit, sophistication, and virtuosic orchestration.

Works include: the operas *Don Juan de Mañara* (1956) and *Sampiero Corso* (1956); ballets *La Grisi* (1935), *La Rosière du village* (1936), and *Les Santons* (1938); symphony, *Scènes municipales* (1933), *Chants laotiens* (1934), *Petite Suite médiévale*, *Deux Danses cambodgiennes*, *Danses brésiliennes* for orchestra; capriccio for violin and orchestra; flute concerto (1947), trumpet concerto (1949), viola concerto, saxophone concerto (1951), horn concerto (1955); *Ajax* and *Chants de Cyrnos* for chorus and orchestra.

tombeau (French 'tomb[stone]') commemorative composition, especially in 17th-century French music.

Tombeau de Couperin, Le/Couperin's Tomb a suite for piano by Ravel in the form of a suite such as Couperin might have written, but resembling his music in spirit rather than in style, Ravel's idiom being as modern here as in any of his works. It was written 1914–17 and consists of six movements: *Prélude, Fugue, Forlane, Menuet, Rigaudon* and *Toccata*. Ravel orchestrated it in 1919, without the fugue and toccata; first performance of that version, Paris, 8 November 1920.

Tom Jones opera by Philidor (libretto by A A H Poinsinet, based on Fielding's novel), produced Paris, Comédie-Italienne, 27 February 1765.

Tommasini, Vincenzo (1878–1950) Italian composer. He travelled much before 1910 and then settled down to compose; his best-known piece is his ballet after Scarlatti, *The Good-Humoured Ladies*.

He studied at the Liceo di Santa Cecilia in Rome and became an associate of the Accademia di Santa Cecilia.

Works include: the operas *Medea* (1906) and *Uguale Fortuna* (1913); ballet *The Good-humoured Ladies* (on music by D Scarlatti, 1917); *Il Carnevale di Venezia* for orchestra (1929), violin concerto (1932); choral works on Dante, Petrarch, and others; overture to Calderón's *Life is a Dream, Poema erotico,* prelude to Baudelaire's 'Hymne à la beauté', suite, *Chiari di luna, Il beato regno, Paesaggi toscani* for orchestra; three string quartets; violin and piano sonata.

Ton (German 'tone, sound') in its early sense, word used by the German Minnesinger for the words and melody of their songs, and by the Meistersinger for the melody alone. The latter used all kinds of adjectives to differentiate the numerous tunes. Specimens of such names appear in Wagner's *Meistersinger*, where a *Ton* is also called a *Weis* (*Weise*, 'tune').

tonada a type of Castilian ballad at least as old as the 16th century.

tonadilla (Spanish, from 'tonada') stage interlude for a few singers, introduced in the 18th century.

tonale, also tonarium medieval theoretical work dealing with the arrangement of chants according to their mode, and especially of the antiphons and the choice of psalm-tone to go with them. The earliest known is by Regino of Prüm (c. 900).

tonality a sense of key orientation in relation to form, for example the step pattern of a dance as expressed by corresponding changes of direction from a tonic or 'home' key to a related key. Most popular and folk music worldwide recognizes an underlying tonality or reference pitch against which the movement of a melody can be clearly heard. The opposite of tonality is atonality.

Tondichtung German tone-poem, symphonic poem.

tone the quality of sound – for instance, different strings of a violin may be able to sound the same note (pitch) given certain fingerings, but each string has a different tone. A tone can also be a ◊plainsong melody; it is also the US term (or **wholetone**) for a note, an interval consisting of two semitones, for example the interval of C–D.

tone colour, or timbre in music, the term used for the sound of an instrument or voice as regards the peculiar quality produced by it; also for combinations of such sounds.

tone poem an alternative name for ◊symphonic poem.

tone row, or note row in music, alternative term for **series**.

tonguing on a woodwind or brass instrument, the technique used to separate and articulate notes. The flow of wind is interrupted by subtle movements of the tongue, as if pronouncing the letter 't'. In fast passages **double tonguing** ('t-k') or **triple tonguing** ('t-t-k') is possible on certain instruments, especially the flute and brass instruments. **Flutter tonguing**, introduced by Richard Strauss for a trilling effect, consists of an extended rolled 'r'.

tonic the key note of a scale (for example, the note C in the scale of C major), or the 'home key' in a composition (for example, the chord of C major in a composition in the same key).

tonic sol-fa a system of musical notation without staves and notes, invented by John Curwen in the middle of the 19th century on a basis of the principles of solmization and solfeggio, and once widely used in the UK and the dominions by choral singers, for whom it simplifies the sight-reading of music. Tonic sol-fa notation is based on the old syllabic system of Do (Ut), Re, Mi, and so on, and takes the following from: **d, r, m, f, s, l, t,** the names of the notes being Doh, Ray, Me, Fah, Soh, Lah, Te. The substitution of 'Te' for the old 'Si' was made to avoid the duplication of the letter 's' in the abbreviations. The range of voices being limited, upper and lower octaves can be sufficiently indicated by a simple stroke placed behind the letters in a higher or lower position, thus: **d**- represents the note an octave above **d**, which in turn is an octave above **d'**. Accidentals are indicated by the addition of a letter 'a' (ra, ma, etc., or exceptionally 'u' for du) for flats and 'e' (de, re, etc., or exceptionally 'y' for my) for sharps. But accidentals appear comparatively rarely now that the system of the 'movable Doh' has been adopted. This is a system of transposition according to which everything is except, for some very short incidental modulations, sung from a notation that looks as though the music were always in C major or A minor.

The actual key is indicated at the beginning of a piece, so that singers know at once, for example, if the composition is in A major, that their **d** is to be read as A, their **r** as B, and so on. If the piece modulates to another key, a change is indicated, so that, for instance, **d** may become temporarily any other note of the scale; but in major keys it will always remain the tonic, in whatever key the music moves, **s** always the dominant, **f** always the sub-dominant, while in minor keys **l** will be the tonic, **m** the dominant, **r** the sub-dominant. (A special syllable, 'ba', is used for the sharp sixth in the melodic minor scale.) Time divisions are indicated by short bar lines, and there are subdivisions between these. The way in which the notes fill these spaces determines their time-values, though there are special signs for dotted notes, triplets, and others. A blank space means a rest, whereas dashes after a note mean that it is to be held beyond the space it occupies over one or more of the following time-divisions.

The merits of tonic sol-fa have always been subject to controversy, no doubt because there is much to be said on either side. Its great defect is that it is insufficient for any general study of music as an art and that it is apt to keep choral singers from expanding their musical experience. Its advantages to instrumental players, even where it might be applicable, as in the case of non-harmonic instruments, are very slight, since it is not so much easier to learn than staff notation, nor so flexible in picturing the composer's intentions. For choral singers it has not only the merit of simplicity, but the greater one of teaching them a sense of relative pitch as well as removing all difficulties connected with transposition.

tonos (Spanish) short vocal pieces for several voices sung at the opening of plays in 17th-century Spain.

Tonreihe see ◊tone-row.

tonus lascivus (Latin 'playful, frolicsome, wanton tone') medieval name for what later became the Ionian mode and the major scale, not recognized as a church mode at the time, but often used for secular songs by minstrels and not unknown in plainsong melodies.

tonus peregrinus (Latin 'foreign tone') plainsong chant which, unlike the eight regular psalm tones, had two reciting notes, one in the first half of the chant and another in the second. For this reason it was described as 'foreign' and was reserved for the psalm 'In exitu Israel/When Israel came out of Egypt'. So far as its tonality is concerned it is in Mode I with flattened B. The melody was also sung in the Lutheran church: Bach uses it in his *Magnificat* and also in the cantata *Meine Seel' erhebt den Herren* (a setting of the German Magnificat).

Toovey, Andrew (1962–) English composer. He studied with Jonathan Harvey, and with Morton Feldman at Dartington. He was director of Ixion from 1987, giving performances of music by Xenakis, Cage, and Ferneyhough.

Works include: *Winter Solstice* for voice and seven players; *Untitled String Quartet* (1985); *Ate* for chamber ensemble (1986); *Shining* for violin and cello (1987); *String Quartet Music* (1987); *Shimmer Bright* for string trio (1988); *Black Light* for chamber ensemble (1989); music theatre pieces *The Spurt of Blood* (1990), *Ubu* (1992) and *The Juniper Tree* (1993); *Mozart* for strings (1991); piano music *Artaud* (1986), *Out Jumps Jack Death* (1989), *Down there by the Sea* (1989) and *Embrace* (two pianos, 1990).

Torelli, Giuseppe (1658–1709) Italian composer and violinist. With Arcangelo Corelli he was one of the most important composers in the history of the early concerto.

He played in the orchestra of San Petronio at Bologna 1686–96, then went to Vienna, and was Konzertmeister at the court of the Margrave of Brandenburg 1697–99. He returned to Bologna in 1701.

In   ex - i - tu Is - ra - el de Ae - gy - pto   do - mus Ja - cob de po - pu - lo bar - ba - ro

The two bars of the example are centred on different notes, illustrating the essential quality of tonus peregrinus.

Works include: *Concerti grossi* (op. 8, 1709); violin concertos; *sinfonie* (concertos) for trumpet and orchestra.

Torke, Michael (1961–) US composer. His music is highly eclectic, with some popular modern idioms.

He studied at the Eastman School in New York and with Jacob Druckman at Yale University 1984–85.

Works include: the opera *The Directions* (1986) and ballet *Black and White* (1988); *Ceremony of Innocence* (1983) and *The Yellow Pages* (1984), both for flute and ensemble; *Vanada* (1984), *Bright Blue Music* (1985), *Ecstatic Orange* (1986), and *Green* (1986), all for orchestra; *Adjustable Wrench* for chamber ensemble (1987); *Purple* for orchestra (1987); *Copper* for brass quintet and orchestra (1987); *Rust* for piano and winds (1989); *Mass* for baritone, chorus, and ensemble (1990); *Bronze* for orchestra (1990); piano concerto (1991); *Chalk* for string quartet (1992); *Run* for orchestra (1992); *Four Proverbs* for female voice and ensemble (1993).

tornada, Spanish, refrain which is a feature of many old Catalan songs.

Torquato Tasso opera by Donizetti (libretto by J Ferretti), produced Rome, Teatro Valle, 9 September 1833. Poet Tasso is in love with Eleonore but her brother, Duke Alfonso, sends him to an asylum for seven years; on his return Eleonore has died and Tasso must seek refuge in his poetry.

Tortelier, Yan Pascal (1947–) French conductor, son of Paul Tortelier. He studied with Nadia Boulanger at the Paris Conservatoire. He made his debut in 1962, as violinist in the London performance of the Brahms Double Concerto, with his father. He studied conducting with Franco Ferrara and was associate with the Orchestre du Capitole, Toulouse, 1974–83. He led the RPO in a London concert in 1978 and the Seattle SO in 1985. He was principal of the Ulster Orchestra 1988–92, BBC Philharmonic from 1992. Orchestration of the Ravel Piano Trio performed 1993. He led the London first performance of Hindemith's opera *Sancta Susanna* in 1995.

Torvaldo e Dorliska opera by Rossini (libretto by C Sterbini), produced Rome, Teatro Valle, 26 December 1815. Defeated Torvaldo returns in disguise to castle of Duke of Ordow to rescue Dorliska, but both are imprisoned until the Duke's servants rescue them.

Tosca, La opera by Puccini (libretto by G Giacosa and L Illica, based on Sardou's drama), produced Rome, Teatro Costanzi, 14 January 1900. Tosca commits suicide when she unsuccessfully bargains with lecherous Baron Scarpia for the life of her lover Cavaradossi, who is executed for treason and harbouring the convict Angelotti.

Toscanini, Arturo (1867–1957) Italian conductor. He made his mark in opera as three-times musical director of La Scala, Milan, 1898–1903, 1906–08, and 1921–29, and subsequently as conductor 1937–54 of the NBC Symphony Orchestra which was established for him by NBC (National Broadcasting Company) Radio. His wide-ranging repertoire included Debussy and Respighi, and he imparted an Italianate simplicity to Mozart and Beethoven when exaggerated solemnity was the trend in Germany.

Tosi, Pier Francesco (c. 1653–1732) Italian castrato, teacher, and composer, son of Giuseppe Tosi (fl. 1677–93). He learnt music from his father and travelled much until 1682, when he settled as singing-master in London. From 1705 to 1711 he was composer at the Imperial court in Vienna. After a further visit to London he finally returned to Italy and was ordained in 1730. He published a book on florid singing (1723), and wrote an oratorio, and cantatas for voice and harpsichord.

Tosti, (Francesco) Paolo (1846–1916) Italian singing teacher and composer. In 1880 he settled in London as singing teacher to the royal family. His songs were highly popular in his day, and include 'At Vespers', 'Forever', and 'Goodbye'.

He studied at Naples under Saverio Mercadante and others from 1858 and was appointed a student-teacher, remaining until 1869. During a long illness at home he wrote his first songs. He then went to Rome, where Sgambati helped him to give a concert and Princess Margherita of Savoy (afterwards queen of Italy) appointed him her singing-master. In 1875 he first visited London, returning each year until 1880, where he remained and taught singing to the royal family.

Works include: Italian, English, and French songs, including 'Non m'ama più', 'Lamento d'amore', 'Aprile', 'Vorrei morire', 'Forever', 'Goodbye', 'Mother', 'At Vespers', 'That Day', 'Mattinata', 'Serenata'; 'Canti popolari abruzzesi' for vocal duet.

Tost Quartets 12 string quartets written by Haydn 1788–90 for the Viennese merchant and violinist Johannes Tost: op. 54 nos. 1–3, op. 55 nos. 1–3, op. 64 nos. 1–6; Tost also commissioned works from Mozart, including the D major string quintet K593.

Toten Augen, Die/The Dead Eyes opera by d'Albert (libretto originally French by M Henry, German translation by H H Ewers), produced Dresden, 5 March 1916. Blind Myrtocle is granted her sight by Jesus but when she looks upon ugliness of her husband Arcesius decides she would rather remain blind, by staring at the sun.

Tote Stadt, Die/The Dead City opera by Korngold (libretto by P Schott, based on G Rodenbach's play *Bruges-la-morte*), produced Hamburg and Cologne, 4 December 1920. Paul exorcizes memory of dead wife Marie when he meets Mariette, who bears a striking resemblance to her. But he strangles his new lover when she insults his faith.

'To the Memory of an Angel'/Dem Andenken eines Engels Berg's dedication for his violin concerto, composed 1935 in memory of Manon Gropius, the daughter of Walter Gropius and Mahler's widow, Alma. The work begins with a musical portrait of Manon and ends with an adagio based on the Bach chorale *Es ist genug*. First performed Barcelona, 19 April 1936, with Louis Krasner, conductor Scherchen. First London performance 1 May 1936, conductor Webern.

touch in piano playing, the way of approaching the keys to produce the tone required. The main factor in the player's touch which affects the quality of tone is weight, because of the mechanical action which mediates between the player's hand and the hammers and strings. However, different 'touches' can subtly but directly influence the player's attack and release of each key, thereby causing minute variations of articulation and dynamics which the conscious mind alone would be challenged to achieve. It is these infinitesimal inequalities and inaccuracies which account for subtleties of touch, especially noticeable in passages whose texture invites contrast between several notes played together.

As a verb, up until the early 17th century, touch meant simply to 'sound' an instrument, exactly as *toccare* does in Italian; as a noun ('touch' or 'touche') it was equivalent to ◊toccata.

Tournai Mass an early 14th-century polyphonic setting of the Ordinary of the Mass, including *Ite missa est*. It is not the work of a single composer, nor is it necessarily from Tournai, where the manuscript now is, but may have been written at least in part in southern France.

Tournemire, Charles (Arnould) (1870–1939) French composer and organist. Much of his work is on religious themes, including *L'orgue mystique* 1932, which consists of an organ Mass for each Sunday of the Church year. In 1898 he succeeded Franck as organist at the church of Sainte-Clotilde. Later he became professor of chamber music at the Paris Conservatory and travelled much as an organ recitalist in Europe.

He studied under Widor at the Paris Conservatory and later with d'Indy.

Works include: the operas *Les dieux sont morts* (1924) and *Nittetis* (1905–07); *Le sang de la sirène* for solo voices, chorus, and orchestra; eight symphonies; piano quartet, piano trio, and other chamber music; *Pièces symphoniques, Triple Choral, L'orgue mystique* (1932), *Petites fleurs musicales*, and other organ works; piano pieces; songs.

Tourte, François (Xavier) (1747–1835) French bowmaker. He made great improvements in the violin bow, especially after 1775. From around 1786 his bows set the pattern for the type of bow used today.

He learnt his craft from his father and set up in business with his elder brother, known in literature as Tourte *L'aîné*, probably named Xavier, but they quarrelled and afterwards worked separately.

Tovey, Donald (Francis) (1875–1940) English music scholar, pianist, and composer. His music is classical in form and style; as a pianist he was for some time in the front rank with his interpretations of Bach, Beethoven, and Brahms. He was Reid professor of music at Edinburgh University from 1914, and conducted the Reid orchestral concerts there. He wrote several books, including six volumes of *Essays in Musical Analysis*, which were notes for performances by the Reid Orchestra.

From childhood his knowledge of the musical classics, his memory, and his contrapuntal skill were prodigious. At 13 he was a pupil of Parry. In 1894, after giving a concert with Joseph Joachim at Windsor, he went to Balliol College, Oxford, where he studied classics. He distinguished himself there by brilliant scholarship and by taking a leading part in the university's musical life. He gave piano recitals at St James's Hall in London 1900–01, and in Berlin and Vienna 1901–02. In 1914 he was appointed Reid professor of music at Edinburgh University, a post he held until his death. His *Essays and Lectures on Music* were edited by H Foss in 1950.

Works include: the opera *The Bride of Dionysus* (1929); incidental music for Maeterlinck's *Aglavaine et Sélysette*; symphony in D major; suite for wind band; piano concerto (1903), cello concerto (1935); two string quartets; conjectural completion of Bach's *Art of Fugue* (1931).

Tower, Joan (1938–) US composer. Her music has moved from serial influences to a more impressionistic style.

She studied at Columbia University with Otto Luening and founded the Da Capo Chamber Players in 1969. She taught at Bard College, New York from 1972, returning in 1988.

Works include: percussion quartet (1963); *Breakfast Rhythms* for clarinet and five instruments (1975); *Amazon II* and *Sequoia* for orchestra (1979, 1981); *Petroushskates* for ensemble (1980); *Amazon III* for chamber orchestra (1983); *Music* for cello and orchestra (1984); Piano concerto (1985); clarinet and flute concertos (1988, 1989); Concerto for Orchestra (1991); violin concerto (1992); *Stepping Stones: A Ballet*, for orchestra (1993).

Toy Symphony piece by Leopold Mozart (formerly attributed to Haydn) with parts for toy instruments (cuckoo, quail, nightingale). Similar works have been written by Mendelssohn, A Romberg, and others, most recently Malcolm Arnold.

Traci Amanti, I/The Amorous Turks opera by Cimarosa (libretto by G Palomba), produced Naples, Teatro Nuovo, 19 June 1793.

tract chant with penitential words, sung after the Gradual in the Mass in Lent (in place of the Alleluia). Tracts are the only surviving examples in the regular chants of the Mass of 'direct psalmody', sung without antiphon or respond. They occur only in modes two and eight, and it is possible that those of mode two were originally Graduals. Their structure is that of a highly elaborated psalm-tone. The number of verses ranges from two to 14.

Traetta, Tommaso (Michele Francesco Saverio) (1727–1779) Italian composer. He was much influenced by recent innovations of French opera, in particular the *tragédies lyriques* of Rameau, but also continued the Metastasian tradition of opera seria. The early comic opera *Buovo d'Antona* 1758 and later serious works have been successfully revived in recent years.

He studied with Nicola Porpora and Francesco Durante at the Conservatorio di Santa Maria di Loreto in Naples 1738–48, he first worked as a composer of church music,

but after the success of *Farnace* in 1751 soon established himself as an opera composer. He was maestro di cappella and singing teacher at the court of the Infante Felipe of Spain in Parma 1758–65, then director of the Conservatorio dell' Ospedaletto in Venice 1765–68, then went to St Petersburg as music director at the court of Catherine II of Russia. He returned to Italy in 1775, visited London in 1777, and finally lived in Venice.

Works include: over 40 operas, including *Farnace* (1751), *Didone abbandonata* (1757), *Ippolito ed Aricia* (1759), *I Tindaridi* (1760), *Le serve rivali* (1766), *Amore in trappola*, *Antigona* (1772), *Merope* (1776), *Germondo* (1776), *Il cavaliere errante*; oratorio *Rex Salomone*; Passion; *Stabat Mater* and other church music; divertimenti for four orchestras *Le Quattro stagioni e il dodici mesi dell'anno*; sinfonie, and other pieces.

Tragédie de Salomé, La ballet by Florent Schmitt (choreography by Guerra), produced Paris, Théâtre des Arts, 9 November 1907.

tragédie lyrique a 17th–18th-century term for French opera of a serious character, for example Rameau's *Les Boréades* (1764).

Tragic Overture/Tragische Ouvertüre overture by Brahms, op. 81, composed 1880 as a companion-piece to the *Academic Festival Overture*, written as an acknowledgment of the honorary degree of doctor of philosophy conferred on him by Breslau University (Wrocław in modern-day Poland) in 1879. First performed Vienna, 26 December 1880.

'Tragic' Symphony Schubert's fourth symphony, in C minor, composed 1816, first public performance Leipzig, 19 November 1849. The title was added to the score by the composer.

Tragoedia work for wind quintet, harp and string quartet by Birtwistle, composed 1965.

tranquillo (Italian 'quiet, calm, tranquil') musical term; the adverb, more rarely used as a direction, is *tranquillamente*.

Trans work by K Stockhausen for string orchestra, wind, and percussion with tape and light projection. First performed Donaueschingen, 16 October 1971.

transcription the arrangement by a composer of a piece by another composer for a different combination of instruments. Liszt and Rachmaninov were famous for their transcriptions for piano, the playing of which required virtuosic skill.

Transfiguration de Notre Seigneur Jésus-Christ, La work in 14 movements for soloists, chorus, and orchestra by Messiaen (texts from the Bible, the Missal and St Thomas Aquinas); composed 1965–69, first performed Lisbon, 7 June 1969, conductor Baudo.

transition a passage connecting two sections of a piece. For example, in a sonata-form movement a transition often connects the first and second subjects (principal melodies). The **retransition** is the transition connecting the development and the recapitulation. Transition is also an alternative name for ◊modulation, especially if the change of keys is abrupt.

transposing instrument musical instrument that does not play at the pitch of their notation, but automatically at a higher or lower pitch. The English horn, clarinet, horn, and trumpet are transposing instruments; the flute, oboe, bassoon, and trombone are not. In brass bands, all the instruments except the bass trombone are transposing instruments.

transposing keyboards contrivances of various sorts to shift the manuals of keyboard instruments so that the music played becomes automatically higher or lower, saving the players from learning to transpose at sight. Such keyboards appeared on some organs as early as the 16th century and later on Ruckers harpsichords. Several inventions of the kind were made for the piano late in the 18th century and throughout the 19th century.

transposition performance in a different key from that indicated in the printed music, or the appearance of a theme or motif in an alternative key. A ◊transposing instrument is one that is normally written for in one key

and played in another, for example an instrument in B♭ such as a clarinet sounds a tone lower, one in D sounds a tone higher, while a basset horn or French horn in F sounds a fifth lower than written (all written music is considered as being 'in C').

A passage of music in which a phrase is repeatedly transposed is a sequence.

transverse flute the modern ◊flute held horizontally, as distinct from the flutes of the recorder type, which are held vertically.

Trapp, Max (1887–1971) German composer. He studied composition with Juon and piano with Dohnányi at the Berlin Hochschule für Musik, became piano professor there in 1920 and professor of advanced composition in 1924. He also taught at Dortmund. The first performance of his second *Concerto for Orchestra* (1935) was conducted by Furtwängler.

Works include: marionette play *Der letzte König von Orplid* (after Mörike); incidental music to Shakespeare's *Timon of Athens*; seven symphonies, two concertos, two divertimenti, symphonic suite, *Notturno* for orchestra; piano concerto, violin concerto (1926), cello concerto (1937); two string quartets, piano quintet, three piano quartets; variations for two pianos; sonatina for piano.

traquenard (French 'trap, snare also racking-pace' of horses) seventeenth-century dance, the dotted rhythm of which refers to the second sense of the word.

Trauermarsch a German funeral march.

Trauermusik work for viola and strings in four movements by Hindemith; composed 21

This passage from Bach's St John Passion is transposed from E major to F major.

January 1936 in response to the death of George V and performed the next day in London with Hindemith as soloist, conductor Boult.

Trauer-Ode/Funeral Ode Bach's cantata no. 198, written on the death of the Electress Christiane Eberhardine of Saxony and performed at the memorial ceremony at Leipzig, 17 October 1727.

Trauer-Sinfonie/Mourning Symphony the nickname of a symphony by Haydn, no. 44, in E minor, composed c. 1771.

Trauerwalzer/Mourning Waltz the title given by the publisher to Schubert's waltz for piano, op. 9 no. 2, in 1821, a piece later wrongly attributed to Beethoven. Schubert, who wrote it in 1816, disapproved of the title. The attribution to Beethoven occurred in 1826, when Schott of Mainz brought out a *Sehnsuchtswalzer* (also called *Le Désir*) under his name, although it was a compound of Schubert's piece and Himmel's *Favoritwalzer*.

Traumgörge, Der/Dreaming George opera by Zemlinsky (libretto by L Feld); composed 1904–06 and accepted for production at the Vienna Hofoper by Mahler. Not performed until 11 October 1980, at Nuremberg. Idealist Görge abandons fiancée Grete and takes up with Gertraud, through whom his dreams are eventually realized.

trautonium polyphonic keyboard synthesizer invented in 1928 by German acoustician Friedrich Trautwein (1888–1956) and subsequently developed by Oskar Sala as the *Mixtur-trautonium*. A Neo-Classical *Concerto for Trautonium and Strings* was composed by Hindemith in 1931, and Richard Strauss included the instrument in his *Japanese Festival Music* 1940.

The instrument remained popular with Hollywood composers until the 1950s.

traversa (Italian 'transverse') abbreviation sometimes used in old musical scores for the *flauto traverso*, the modern ◊flute played sideways, as distinct from flutes of the recorder type, which are held vertically.

traversière (French 'transverse') French name for the transverse ◊flute, a musical instrument.

Traviata, La/The Lady Gone Astray opera by Verdi (libretto by F M Piave, based on the younger Dumas' *La Dame aux camélias*), produced Venice, Teatro La Fenice, 6 March 1853. Consumptive courtesan persuaded by Alfredo's father to renounce love for the sake of his family's honour. She has an affair with Baron Douphol before Alfredo learns the

truth about her actions; the lovers are reconciled before she dies.

Travis, Roy (1922–) US composer. He studied at Juilliard and Columbia University (1947–51) and with Milhaud at the Paris Conservatoire. He taught first in New York, then at UCLA (professor from 1968).

Works include: the operas *The Passion of Oedipus* (1968) and *The Black Bacchantes* (1982); string quartet (1958); *Duo Concertante* for violin and piano (1967); *Barma*, septet (1968), *Collage* for orchestra (1968); Piano concerto (1969); electronic music pieces (studio at University of California at Los Angeles, from 1969).

treble the highest register of a boy's singing voice (approximately equivalent in range to the ◊soprano voice of a woman), about F4–C6, or the highest-pitched member of a family of instruments, for example the treble viol. The term is also used to refer to the right hand of a piano piece.

The term is derived from the Latin *triplum*, the top part of early three-part motets.

treble clef G ◊clef in which the G above middle C (G4) is represented by the second-lowest line of a five-line stave. Most instruments with a range above middle C use treble clef, including the violin, clarinet, trumpet, and piano (right hand).

The treble clef (a), and the treble clef transposed an octave lower (b).

treble viol musical instrument, the smallest of the normal members of the ◊viol family.

Open strings of the treble viol.

tre corde (Italian 'three strings') direction in piano music indicating that after the use of the left pedal (*una corda*) normal playing is to be resumed.

tremolando (Italian 'trembling') musical direction sometimes used instead of the conventional notation for string tremolo, or for a passage to be sung in a tremulous voice.

tremolo a rapidly pulsating tremor on one note, created by rapid movement of the bow on a stringed instrument, or shake of the voice. A buzzing tremolo produced by brass instruments is called *flatterzunge* ('fluttertongue').

The effect is exploited to picturesque effect in Rimsky-Korsakov's 'Flight of the Bumble-Bee' interlude from the opera *The Legend of Tsar Saltan* 1900.

The notation of a tremolo on a single note, and between two notes.

tremulant on the ◊organ, a mechanical device operated by a draw stop, for producing ◊vibrato.

trenchmore English country dance 'longways for as many as will', known in the 16th and 17th centuries and introduced into the court and noble houses as a kind of democratic dance in which masters and servants could take part together, temporarily relaxing strict class distinctions.

Trento, Vittorio (1761–1833) Italian composer. He was a pupil of Bertoni. In the last decade of the 18th century he visited London as conductor at the King's Theatre and in 1806 became impresario at Amsterdam, going to Lisbon in the same capacity soon after. After a further visit to London he returned to Venice before his death.

Works include: the operas *La finta ammalata*, *Quanti casi in un giorno* (1801), *Teresa vedova*, *Ifigenia in Aulide*, *Climene* (1812) and c. 35 others; ballet *Mastino della Scala* and more than 50 others; oratorios *The Deluge*, *The Maccabees* and others.

trepak Russian dance of Cossack origin in animated 2–4 time.

triad a chord of three notes consisting of a ◊root, ◊third, and ◊fifth. There are four types of triad: major (for example C–E–G), minor (C–E♭–G), augmented (C–E–G♯), and diminished (C–E♭–G♭).

trial French term for a special type of operatic tenor voice of a high, thin, rather nasal quality suited to comic parts. The name is derived from the singer Antoine Trial.

Trial by Jury one-act opera by Sullivan (libretto by W S Gilbert), produced London, Royalty Theatre, 25 March 1875. When Angelina takes Edwin to court for breach of promise, the judge proposes to her himself.

triangle small percussion instrument consisting of a thin metal bar bent into the shape of a triangle. Hit by a metal rod, it produces a tinkling tone of high, indefinite pitch. Compositions which call for a prominent triangle part include Liszt's Piano Concerto in E♭ 1849 (revised 1853, 1856) and the third movement of Brahms' Fourth Symphony 1885.

trihoris old French dance of Lower Brittany, allied to the branle; also called trihory, triori, or triory.

trill a rapid oscillation between adjacent notes, also called a **shake**, exploited both for impressionistic effect, as in the opening bars of Bartók's *Piano Concerto No 3* 1945, or to create dramatic tension and ambiguity, as at end of a solo ◊cadenza in a concerto.

Trillo del diavolo, Il/The Devil's Trill Tartini's violin sonata written at Assisi c. 1745 and said to have been inspired by a dream in which he bargained with the devil for his soul in return for musical inspiration, the devil playing the violin to him. He related that on waking he immediately wrote down what he had heard, but that the music as written fell far short of the dream devil's performance. The work is in four movements, written for violin and continuo; the famous trill is in the finale. An opera on the story of the sonata was written by Falchi.

Trinity College of Music a school of music in London incorporated in 1875.

trio an ensemble of three instruments, also an interlude between repeats of a ◊minuet or ◊scherzo, for a trio of players.

Trionfi del fato, I, ovvero Le glorie d'Enea/ The Triumphs of Fate, or The Glories of Aeneas opera by Steffani (libretto by O Mauro), produced Hanover, Court Opera, December 1695.

Major, minor, augmented, and diminished triads.

Trionfo dell' onore, Il/The Triumph of Honour opera by A Scarlatti (libretto by F A Tullio), produced Naples, Teatro dei Fiorentini, autumn 1718. Honour wins out as Flaminio is united with Cornelia and Riccardo with Leonora.

Trionfo di Afrodite/Aphrodite's Triumph concerto scenico by Orff, second of three works called collectively *Trionfi* (text by composer, after Catullus, Sappho, and Euripides), produced Milan, La Scala, 14 February 1953, conductor Karajan. Songs and games in honour of bridal couple.

Trionfo di Clelia, Il/Clelia's Triumph opera by Gluck (libretto by Metastasio), produced Bologna, Teatro Comunale, 14 May 1763. Also settings by Hasse (Vienna, 1762) and Jommelli (Lisbon, 1774). Roman noblewoman Clelia is captured by Etruscan king but saves her city with her courage and nobility.

Opera by Jommelli (libretto ditto), produced Lisbon, Teatro d'Ajuda, 6 June 1774.

Trionfo di Dori, Il/The Triumph of Doris collection of Italian madrigals published by Gardano of Venice in 1592. It contains 29 six-part madrigals on various poems all ending with the line 'Viva la bella Dori', which suggested the similar uniform final line in the English collection modelled on this, *The Triumphes of Oriana*. The composers, all represented by one piece each, include Anerio, Asola, Baccusi, Croce, G Gabrieli, Gastoldi, Marenzio, Palestrina, Striggio, and Vecchi.

trio sonata the most important genre of Baroque chamber music, usually written for two violins (or viols) and cello (or bass viol), with a keyboard continuo. At the end of the 17th century it developed into the *sonata da chiesa* and the *sonata da camera* (see ◊sonata). Notable examples include those by Couperin, Handel, Vivaldi, Corelli, and Purcell.

tripla old term for triple time in old mensurable music, but also the figure three shown in the time-signature and later, when the device of the triplet came into use, the figure '3' set over a group of notes. Also a dance in quick triple time.

triple concerto a concerto with three solo parts, for example Beethoven's concerto for violin, cello, piano, and orchestra, or Tippett's concerto for string trio and orchestra.

triple counterpoint counterpoint in which three parts are reversible, each being capable of appearing at the top, in the middle or at the bottom.

triplet a group of three notes of equal length, played in the time of two. It is indicated by a slur over the three notes with the number '3' written above.

Example of a triplet (bar 2).

triple time a metre in which the bar may be divided into three beats, as in 3/4 and 9/8.

triplum (Latin 'the third') the highest of the original three voices in the motet, and thus the origin of the English word treble.

Tristan work by Henze for piano, tape, and orchestra; composed 1973, first perfomed London, 20 October 1974, conductor C Davis.

Tristan chord see ◊augmented sixth chords.

Tristan und Isolde music-drama by Wagner (libretto by composer, based on the Tristram and Iseult legend), produced Munich, Court Opera, 10 June 1865. Tristan and Isolde fall under spell of a love potion during a journey prior to her marriage with King Mark of Cornwall; Mark's servant Melot mortally wounds Tristan and Isolde sings the famous Liebestod over his corpse.

tritone the interval of the diminished fifth, exactly half the octave, and considered in the Middle Ages to be the moral antithesis of the octave's perfect consonance, or 'diabolus in musica' (devil in music). Its prominence during the late 19th and early 20th centuries helped to undermine the remaining foundations of ◊tonality, as in Debussy's *Prélude à l'après-midi d'un faune* 1894.

The alternative term 'mi contra fa' refers to B in the dominant key of G (do-re-*mi*) in relation to F in the tonic key of C (do-re-mi-*fa*).

Tritonius, Petrus (c. 1465–c. 1525), Latinized name of Peter Treybenreif Austrian composer and scholar. He wrote music for Horatian odes for four voices, and in 1524 published a hymnbook containing the text of about 130 hymns and blank staves for the music to be written on.

He studied at Vienna and Ingolstadt Universities and later became a teacher of Latin and music at the cathedral school of Brixen. He later studied at Padua University, and while in Italy he met the Viennese professor Conradus Celtis, who invited him to settle at Vienna. Once there, he joined Celtis's literary and humanist society and wrote a setting of Horatian odes, which were published in 1507.

Ludwig Senfl later took the tenor parts of these as *canti firmi* for his own settings, and Paul Hofhaimer imitated Tritonius's settings. On the death of Celtis in 1508 Tritonius returned to the Tyrol and became director of the Latin school at Bozen; in 1513 he was in Halle, and in 1521 he retired to Schwaz am Inn.

Works include: hymns in four parts; odes by Horace and other Latin poems set in four parts, and other pieces.

Trittico/Triptych cycle of three one-act operas by Puccini, produced New York Metropolitan Opera, 14 December 1918:
Il Tabarro/The Cloak (libretto by G Adami, based on D Gold's *Houppelande*). Michele kills wife Giorgetta's lover and hides the body under a cloak.
Suor Angelica/Sister Angelica (libretto by G Forzano). As convent dweller Angelica is told of death of her illegitimate son she takes poison and is granted a vision of the Virgin with her child.
Gianni Schicchi (libretto by ditto, based on the story of a rogue who is mentioned in Dante's *Divina commedia*). Gianni Schicchi assumes the identity of the rich, recently-deceased Bicose Donati and dictates a will favourable to himself.

Tritto, Giacomo (1733–1824) Italian composer. A pupil of Cafaro at the Conservatorio dei Turchini in Naples, he later taught there and in 1806 became co-director (with Paisiello and Fenarolo). From around 1760 he wrote over 50 operas. He also wrote treatises on thorough-bass and counterpoint.

Works include: the operas *La fedeltà in amore* (1764), *Il convitato di pietra* (on the Don Giovanni story), *Arminio, La canterina, Gli Americani* (1802), and *Marco Albinio* (1810); Masses and other church music.

Triumphes of Oriana, The an English collection of madrigals written in honour of Queen Elizabeth I, edited by Morley and published 1601. It was modelled on the Italian collection of *Il Trionfo di Dori* of 1592 and contains a similar series of different poems all ending with the same line, 'Long live fair Oriana'. There are 25 pieces by 23 English composers: Bennet, Carlton, Cavendish, Cobbold, Este, Farmer, E Gibbons (2), Hilton, Holmes, Hunt, E Johnson, R Jones, Kirby, Lisley, Marson, Milton, Morley (2), Mundy, Nicolson, Norcome, T Tomkins, Weelkes, and Wilbye. A madrigal by Bateson intended for the collection arrived too late and was included in his own *First Set of English Madrigals* (1604).

Triumphlied/Song of Triumph a setting by Brahms of words from the Revelation of St John for eight-part chorus, orchestra, and organ *ad lib*, op. 55, composed in spring 1871 to celebrate the German victory in the Franco-Prussian war; first perfomed Karlsruhe, 5 June 1872.

Triumph of Neptune, The ballet by Lord Berners (scenario by S Sitwell, choreographed by Balanchine), produced London, Lyceum Theatre, 3 December 1926. The settings were based on B Pollock's 'penny plain, two-pence coloured' toy theatre designs.

Triumph of Peace, The masque by James Shirley with music by W Lawes and Simon Ive, produced at the Banqueting House in Whitehall, 3 February (Candlemas) 1634.

Troades opera by Reimann (libretto based on Werfel's version of Euripides' *The Trojan Women*), produced Munich, 7 July 1986.

Troilus and Cressida opera in three acts by Walton (libretto by C Hassall, after Chaucer), produced Covent Garden, 3 December 1954. Revived with Cressida's role altered to mezzo (Janet Baker), London, Covent Garden, 12 November 1976. Trojan Troilus follows Cressida when she accompanies her father Calchas to the Greek camp; although they love each other, she agrees to marry Diomede after she believes Troilus has abandoned her. But all is revealed before Calchas stabs Troilus in a fight and Cressida commits suicide.

Trois Petites Liturgies de la Présence Divine/Three Little Liturgies of the Divine Presence work by Messiaen for 18 sopranos, piano, ondes Martenot, celesta, vibraphone, three percussion, and strings (text by composer), first performed Paris, 21 April 1945, conductor Désormière.

tromba da tirarsi (Italian 'trumpet to draw itself [out]') the slide trumpet, a musical instrument of the ◊trumpet type. It was used in Germany in the 18th century and had the advantage before the invention of valves of being capable of producing more notes than the fundamental harmonics by the temporary changes in the length of the tube, as in the trombone. It never attained a wide currency.

Trombetti, Ascanio (1544–1590) Italian composer. He wrote four books of madrigals 1573–87. From the 1560s he was in the service of the Signoria of Bologna, where he played the cornett. From 1583 he was maestro di cappella at the church of S Giovanni at Monte.

Works include: motets in 5–12 parts for voices and instruments; madrigals for four–five voices, *napolitane* for three voices.

Tromboncino, Bartolomeo (c. 1470–after 1534) Italian composer. He was famous as a composer of frottole – songs for several singers or for one singer and instruments – he wrote over 170. He enjoyed brief fame for having murdered his adulterous wife in 1499 and was in the service of Lucrezia Borgia at Ferrara 1502–08.

He was at the ducal court of Mantua 1487–95, then at Venice, Vicenza, Casale, at Mantua again 1501–13, and then at Ferrara.

Works include: lamentations, one motet and 17 *laude*; over 170 frottole for four voices.

trombone brass wind instrument of mainly cylindrical bore, incorporating a movable slide which allows a continuous glissando (slide) in pitch over a span of half an octave. The longer the tube length, the lower the note. All the notes of the chromatic scale are therefore available by placing the slide in any of seven basic positions, and blowing a harmonic series of notes built upon each basic note. A descendant of the Renaissance ◊sackbut, the Baroque trombone has a shallow cup mouthpiece and modestly flared bell giving a firm, noble tone, to which the modern wide bell adds a brassy sheen. The tenor and bass trombones are staple instruments of the orchestra and brass band, also of Dixieland and jazz bands, either separately or as a

8ve lower

The compass of the alto, tenor, and bass trombones; the compass of the tenor-bass trombone; 'pedal' notes on the trombone.

tenor-bass hybrid. The hybrid has a switch which lowers the pitch a fourth from B♭ to F.

Trommelbass (German 'drum bass') musical technical term for the notes of a bass part divided up into groups of repeated even quavers, a device used especially in the 18th century to give a kind of artificial animation to music.

Trompeter von Säckingen, Der/The Trumpeter of Säckingen opera by Nessler (libretto by R Bunge, based on Scheffel's poem), produced Leipzig, 4 May 1884. Trumpeter Werner loves Maria but her parents prefer Damian, who turns out to be a coward and a simpleton. After being banished, Werner returns to save the Baron from an uprising and is allowed to marry Maria. Very popular in its day and often conducted by Mahler.

tronco (Italian 'truncated, cut off, interrupted') musical direction indicating that a note or chord is to cease abruptly.

trope an interpolation into liturgical chants dating from the 8th or 9th centuries, probably of Byzantine origin. Tropes were at first vocalized as purely musical ornamentations or sung on syllables of certain words, especially 'Alleluia', but later they became so important that special words were newly written for them. Sometimes new words came first and demanded new music; thus the sequence, which began merely as a special kind of trope, developed into a poetical form with musical setting.

Tropen (German 'tropes') musical term used by Josef Hauer for his own version of the system of twelve-note music. He divided the possible combinations of the 12 notes of the chromatic scale, which run into hundreds of millions, into 44 main groups, and these are what he called *Tropen*, and he further divided each row of 12 notes into two halves of six, which form two fundamental chords, whatever the order in which each six may appear. The *Tropen* for him were equivalent to keys in the diatonic system, and a change from one *Trope* to another is equivalent to modulation.

troppo (Italian 'too much') word often used in the negative in musical directions; *non troppo*, 'not too much'; or *ma non troppo*, 'but not too much'.

troubadour (French, from Provençal *trobador* [? from Latin *tropus*]) poet-musician of Provence and southern France in the 12th–13th centuries. The troubadours originated a type of lyric poetry devoted to themes of courtly love and the idealization of women and to glorifying the chivalric ideals of the period. Little is known of their music, which was passed down orally.

The **trouvères** were a similar class of poet-musicians active during the same period in northern France and England.

Among the troubadours were Bertran de Born (1140–c. 1215), who was mentioned by Dante; Arnaut Daniel; and Bernard de Ventadour. The troubadour tradition had a parallel in the German Minnesingers.

The troubadours' poems were usually *poésies courtoises* (courtly poems, mainly love-songs, but also satires and other styles), while *chansons à personnages* (narrative songs) belonged chiefly to the trouvères. Troubadours wrote their own poems and probably composed the tunes as well; approximately 2,500 troubadour songs have survived, and the melodies of about 280 of these are known. About 2,000 of the trouvères' poems have survived, and most of these have music. The melodies were written down in a notation which showed only the pitch of the notes. The rhythm was either committed to memory or else determined by the poetic metre, a question that has never been solved beyond controversy. It is believed that the songs were accompanied on instruments of the harp or lute type, either by the troubadours and trouvères themselves or by attendants, for many troubadours were not poor wandering musicians but nobles whose audiences were at courts and noble houses.

'Trout' Quintet a quintet in A major for violin, viola, cello, double bass and piano, D667, by Schubert, composed summer 1819 during an excursion to Upper Austria; so called because the fourth of the five movements is a set of variations on his song *The Trout/Die Forelle*, D550, (1817).

trouvère (French, from old French *trovere* or *troveur*) a poet-musician of northern France in the 12th and 13th centuries. The trouvères cultivated an art similar to that of the ◊troubadours in southern France. The art was encouraged in the north by Eleanor of Aquitaine, who married Louis VII in 1137; about 1,700 melodies have been preserved. The poems include *chansons à personnages* (narrative songs), *poésies courtoises* (courtly poems, mainly love-songs) and crusaders' songs. The notation and manner of performance of the songs was similar to that of the troubadours.

Trovatore, Il/The Troubadour or The Minstrel opera by Verdi (libretto by S Cammarano, based on a Spanish play, *El trovador*, by A G Gutiérrez), produced Rome, Teatro Apollo, 19 February 1853. Manrico and Count Luna are rivals for the love of Leonora; when Luna is unsuccessful he orders Manrico's execution. Leonora offers her body to the Count in exchange for Manrico's life, but she takes poison before he is freed and Manrico is subsequently killed. It is revealed that he is the Count's brother.

Trowell, Brian (1931–) English musicologist. He studied at Cambridge with Thurston Dart and was lecturer at Birmingham University 1957–62. He was director of opera at the Guildhall School of Music and Drama, London, 1963–67, and reader then professor at King's College from 1970. Professor of music at Oxford University 1988–97; edited music by Dunstable (joint editor, complete works); published *The Early Renaissance* (1963), translations and articles on opera; also *Elgar's Use of Literature*.

Troyens, Les/The Trojans opera by Berlioz in two parts (libretto by composer, after Virgil):
La Prise de Troie/The Taking of Troy, produced Karlsruhe (in German), 6 December 1890; Cassandra's warnings are ignored as the departing Greeks leave their wooden horse; warned by the ghost of Hector, Aeneas escapes the massacre of the Trojans.
Les Troyens à Carthage, produced Paris, Théâtre-Lyrique, 4 November 1863, and later at Karlsruhe (in German), 7 December 1890 (the first performance of the complete work). Aeneas and Dido, Queen of Carthage, fall in love but he must depart for Italy to found Rome, and as he leaves Dido mounts her funeral pyre. The first performance of the complete work in French was at Brussels, 26 and 27 December 1906; first performed in French complete on one night, Covent Garden, 17 September 1969, conductor C Davis.

trumpet member of an ancient family of lip-reed instruments existing worldwide in a variety of forms and materials, and forming part of the brass section in a modern orchestra. Its distinguishing features are a generally cylindrical bore and straight or coiled shape, producing a penetrating tone of stable pitch for signalling and ceremonial use. Valve trumpets were introduced around 1820, giving access to the full range of chromatic pitches.

Today's orchestral trumpet is valued for its clearly focused, brilliant tone, and variants of the normal C4 trumpet in current use include the soprano in D, piccolo (clarino) trumpet in C5, and bass trumpet in C3, an addition suggested by Wagner. In brass bands the B♭ soprano instrument is normally used. The trumpet is a traditional solo jazz instrument, and players demonstrate particular skill in high harmonics.

The written compass and actual notes of the B flat trumpet; the actual compass of the trumpet in D.

trumpet marine early string instrument with a single string and thus allied to the monochord, played with a bow. It was used mainly for popular music-making, especially in Germany, but also in convents, as its German name *Nonnengeige*, 'nun's fiddle' indicates. The instrument produced harmonics very easily and, like the old trumpet, often restricted itself to them, its normally produced notes being very poor and coarse in quality.

It was also called *Trummscheit*, 'trumpet wood' or *Brummscheit*, 'humming wood', and the Italian and English names connecting it with a trumpet were doubtless due to its penetrating tone. The provenance of the adjective 'marine' is unknown.

trumpet voluntary in the late 17th century, a piece, not for trumpet, but an organ voluntary the tune of which was played on the trumpet stop. The example still familiar is that by J Clarke, long wrongly attributed to Purcell, popularized by Henry Wood's orchestral arrangement. This is in fact *The Prince of Denmark's March*, which Clarke published in 1700 as a harpsichord piece, but which also occurs in a suite for wind instruments by Clarke.

Tsar and Carpenter (Lortzing). See ◊*Zar und Zimmermann, oder Die zwei Peter.*

Tsar Saltan (Rimsky-Korsakov). See ◊*Legend of Tsar Saltan, The.*

Tsar's Bride, The/Tsarskaya Nevesta opera by Rimsky-Korsakov (libretto by I F Tumenev, based on a play by L A Mey), produced Moscow, Imperial Opera, 3 November 1899. Marfa is chosen by Ivan the Terrible as his bride, but she loves Lykov and is poisoned by a jealous rival; Lykov is beheaded for the crime as Marfa expires.

tuba member of a family of valved lip-reed brass instruments of conical bore and deep, mellow tone, introduced around 1830 as bass members of the orchestra brass section and the brass band. The tuba is surprisingly agile and delicate for its size and pitch, qualities exploited by Berlioz, Ravel, and Vaughan Williams.

Different shapes of tuba exist, including oval, upright with forward-facing bell, and the circular or helicon sousaphone which wraps around the player. The Wagner tuba is a horn variant. 'Tuba' is also the name of an ancient Roman military trumpet.

The orchestral tuba is normally in F (nontransposing) with four valves and this compass.

Tubin, Eduard (1905–1982) Estonian-born Swedish composer. He studied at the Tartu Academy 1924–30 and conducted in Estonia 1931–44, before settling in Sweden.

Works include: the operas *Barbara of Tisenhusen* (1969) and *The Priest from Reigi* (1971); ten symphonies (1934–73), two violin concertos (1942, 1945), balalaika concerto (1964); *Requiem for Fallen Soldiers* (1979); two violin sonatas (1936, 1949).

tubular bells percussion instrument (approximate range C2–F3), consisting of 18 tuned metal tubes of different lengths, which hang in a frame. They are struck at the top end with a rawhide mallet, and the resonance can be muted with a foot-operated damper. They produce bell effects, used both in orchestral works and opera music.

Tucker, Norman (1910–1978) English administrator and translator. He studied at Oxford and the Royal College of Music. He was joint director at Sadler's Wells, London, 1947–54; sole director 1954–66. He translated the UK first performances of Janáček's *Káta Kabanová* and *Cunning Little Vixen* (1951, 1961); also translated *Simon Boccanegra* for its UK first performance (1948), and Verdi's

Don Carlos. He encouraged the careers of such conductors as Charles Mackerras and Colin Davis.

Tucker, William (died 1679) English composer. He was Gentleman of the Chapel Royal in London, and minor canon and precentor of Westminster Abbey from 1660. He wrote services and anthems.

Tuder, John (fl. 1466–96) English composer. He wrote responsories, lamentations, and the hymn *Gloria, laus*, all of which are included in the Pepys manuscript of about 1465 at Magdalene College, Cambridge. There is a carol by him in the Fayrfax Book of about 1500.

Tunder, Franz (1614–1667) German composer and organist. As organist of St Mary's, Lübeck, he greatly improved the church music and also instituted the *Abendmusiken/ Evening Music* concerts, which soon became famous beyond the town, and were further developed by Dietrich Buxtehude.

In 1632 he was appointed court organist at Gottorf and in 1641 organist of St Mary's Church at Lübeck, where he preceded Buxtehude, who had to marry his daughter in order to secure the post.

Works include: church cantatas, sacred arias with strings and organ; chorale variations for organ.

tune colloquial word for melody. 'In tune' denotes accurate intonation, 'out of tune' the opposite. 'To tune' is to adjust the intonation of an instrument.

tuning the adjusting of ◊pitch in instruments to the correct intonation, in order to avoid dissonance. For example, orchestral instruments tune to ◊concert pitch (A4). Keyboard instruments are more difficult to adjust, often requiring a professional tuner.

tuning fork a device for providing a reference pitch, invented in England 1711. It is made from hardened metal and consists of parallel bars about 10 cm/3–4 in long joined at one end and terminating in a blunt point. When the fork is struck and the point placed on a wooden surface, a pure tone is heard.

There are tuning forks for each musical pitch. A is known as 'concert pitch', since the instruments of the orchestra are tuned to A above middle C.

Turandot incidental music for Schiller's Germany version of Gozzi's play by Weber, op. 37, composed 1809 and including the *Overtura cinese/Chinese Overture*, composed on a Chinese theme, 1805.

Opera by Busoni (German libretto by composer, based on Gozzi's play), produced Zurich, 11 May 1917, together with another short opera *Arlecchino*. The music of *Turandot* was elaborated from incidental music for M Reinhardt's production of K Vollmöller's version of Gozzi's play, produced Berlin, Deutsches Theater, 27 October 1911.

Opera by Puccini (Italian libretto by G Adami and R Simoni, based on Gozzi's play), left unfinished by Puccini and completed by Alfano; produced Milan, La Scala, 25 May 1926. Calaf saves his head by answering three riddles of cold-hearted Turandot, and eventually wins her love.

Turangalîla-symphonie work for orchestra in ten movements by Messiaen, with prominent parts for piano solo and the ondes Martenot. Commissioned by Koussevitzky and composed 1946–48; first performed Boston, 2 December 1949, conductor Bernstein. The middle of a triptych of works inspired by the Tristan legend; the others are *Harawi* for soprano and piano (1945) and *Cinq Rechants* for unaccompanied chorus. ('Turangalîla' is a compound Sanskrit word: *turanga*, 'time', *lîla*, 'divine action'.)

turca (Italian 'Turkish') word used in the combination *alla turca* (in the Turkish manner) by Mozart for the finale of the A major piano sonata, K331, and by Beethoven for the *Marcia alla turca* in *The Ruins of Athens*, which is the theme of the piano variations, op. 76.

Turco in Italia, Il/The Turk in Italy opera by Rossini (libretto by F Romani), produced Milan, La Scala, 14 August 1814. Turkish Prince Selim arrives in Naples and after much confusion is reconciled with his former love, Zaida.

Turina, Joaquín (1882–1949) Spanish composer. He devoted much time to teaching as well as composition and wrote a small treatise expounding his aims in teaching music, *Enciclopedia abreviada de música* 1917. His most successful works are those which employ local Spanish colours, such as *La procesion del Rocio* 1913 and *Danzas fantásticas* 1920.

He studied at Seville and Madrid, and later with Vincent.d'Indy at the Schola Cantorum in Paris. He adopted conventional European forms more consistently than his contemporaries Albéniz, Granados, and Falla.

Works include: the operas *Margot* (1914) and *Jardin de oriente* (1923) (libretti by G Martínez Sierra); incidental music for Moreto's *La adúltera penitente* (1917), Martínez Sierra's *Navidad* (1916), and other plays; *La* *procesión del Rocio* (1913), *Danzas fantásticas*, *Sinfonía sevillana* (1920), *Ritmos*, and other works for orchestra; string quartet (1911), piano quintet (1907), *Escena andaluza* for viola, piano, and string quartet; *Poema de una Sanluquena* for violin and piano; suites *Rincones sevillanos* and *Sevilla* and other works for piano; songs.

Turini, Francesco (c. 1589–1656) Italian composer. His father Gregorio Turini was cornett player and composer to the Emperor Rudolph II in Prague, but died early, whereupon the emperor sent Turini to Venice and Rome to study music and later made him his chamber organist. He left Prague in 1624 to become cathedral organist at Brescia.

Works include: Masses and motets; madrigals, canons.

Türk, Daniel Gottlob (1750–1813) German theorist and composer. He settled at Halle in 1776 and became a central figure in the musical life of the town. He was famous as a teacher, and wrote treatises on organ and clavier playing, thorough-bass, and temperament.

He studied under his father and under Gottfried Homilius at Dresden. Later he went to Leipzig University, where he became a pupil and friend of Johann Hiller, who procured him appointments as violinist at the Opera and the orchestral concerts. In 1776 he became organist at St Ulrich's Church at Halle, in 1779 music director of the university, and in 1787 organist at the church of Our Lady.

Works include: the opera *Pyramus und Thisbe* (1784); cantata *Die Hirten bei der Krippe zu Bethlehem* (1782); piano sonatas and pieces.

turn ornament in musical notation. Composers have more recently applied the turn to denote an ornament which starts on the principal note.

Turnage, Mark-Anthony (1960–) English composer. His music admits a wide range of influences, including popular elements. His major success has been with *Greek*, performed at Munich and Edinburgh in 1988.

He studied at the Royal College of Music with Oliver Knussen 1974–78, and with Henze and Schuller at Tanglewood. He was composer-in-association with the City of Birmingham Symphony Orchestra 1989–93; and was featured composer at the 1986 Bath Festival and 1987 Glasgow Musica Viva.

Works include: *Night Dances* (1982) and *Kind of Blue* (1982) for orchestra; *Let us Sleep Now* for chamber orchestra (1979–82); *After Dark* for wind quintet and string quintet (1983); *Lament for a Hanging Man* for soprano and ensemble (1983); *Ekaya* for orchestra (1984); *On all Fours* for ensemble (1985); *One Hand in Brooklyn Heights*, for 16 mixed voices, *Release* for eight players (1987); *Greek*, opera (1988); *Three Screaming Popes* for orchestra (1989); *Kai* for cello and ensemble (1990); *Momentum* for orchestra (1991); *Are you sure?* for string quartet (1991); *Leaving* for soloists, chorus, and ensemble (1991); *Set To* for brass ensemble (1992); *Drowned Out* for orchestra (1993); *Your Rockaby* saxophone concerto (1993); *Blood on the Floor* for ensemble (1994).

Turner, William (1651–1740) English tenor and composer. Most of his works were church music, but he also wrote songs and music for plays.

He was a chorister at Christ Church, Oxford, and later in the Chapel Royal in London, where he joined John Blow and Pelham Humfrey in composing the so-called 'club anthem'. He later became a singer successively at Lincoln Cathedral, St Paul's Cathedral, and Westminster Abbey. He received a doctorate in music from Cambridge University in 1696. His youngest daughter, Ann Turner (died 1741), was a singer, and

Various turns and their possible executions.

married the organist and composer John Robinson in 1716.

Works include: services, anthems (one for Queen Anne's coronation); masque *Presumptuous Love*; songs for Durfey's *A Fond Husband* (1677) and *Madam Fickle* (1676), Shadwell's *The Libertine* (1675), Settle's *Pastor fido* (1676), and other plays; catches, songs.

Turn of the Screw, The opera in a prologue and two acts by Britten (libretto by M Piper, after Henry James), produced Venice, 14 September 1954, and in London, 6 October 1954). The Governess arrives at her new post to find children Flora and Miles in the power of two malevolent ghosts Quint and Jessil. Eventually the evil spirits are banished but Miles dies in the process.

Tusch (German 'fanfare') word probably derived from French *touche* and is thus related to the English tucket or tuck.

tut device used in playing the ◊lute: the damping of a note by a finger not used for stopping.

tutti (Italian 'all') in instrumental works, especially concertos, term used to indicate passages in which the orchestra plays, as opposed to the soloist.

Tveitt, (Nils) Geirr (1908–1981) Norwegian composer and pianist. After studying in Vienna and Paris he toured Europe as a pianist. In his compositions he made effective use of Norwegian folk melodies.

Works include: the operas *Dragaredokko, Roald Amundsen*, and *Jeppe* (1964); three ballets; six piano concertos (1930–60), concerto for string quartet and orchestra (1933), violin concerto (1939), two harp concertos, two concertos for hardanger fiddle four symphonies; two string quartets; 29 piano sonatas.

twelve-tone system, or twelve-note system method of musical composition invented by Arnold ◊Schoenberg about 1921 in which all 12 notes of the ◊chromatic scale are arranged in a particular order of the composer's choice, without repeating any of the notes. Such an arrangement is called a 'series' or 'tone row'. The initial series may be transposed, divided, and otherwise mutated to provide a complete resource for all melodic and harmonic material in a work.

Twilight of the Gods, The (Wagner). See ◊*Ring des Nibelungen.*

Two Widows/Dvě Vdovy opera by Smetana (libretto by E Züngel, based on a French comedy by P J F Mallefille), produced Prague, Czech Theatre, 27 March 1874. Anežka falls for landowner Ladislav, but as a widow feels she must instead mourn her dead husband. Widow Karolina feigns a seduction of Ladislav and Anežka finally admits her love.

Tye, Christopher (c. 1505–c. 1572) English composer and poet. His music shows considerable acquaintance with contemporary continental composers, for example, the Mass for six voices *Euge bone*. He wrote a good deal of verse in his later years.

He became a lay clerk at King's College, Cambridge in 1537. In 1543 he was appointed choirmaster at Ely Cathedral; he received a doctorate in music from Cambridge University in 1545, and from Oxford in 1548. In 1561 he resigned his post at Ely and was succeeded by Robert White. Having been ordained, he accepted the living at Doddington-cum-Marche in the Isle of Ely, and for some time later held two other livings in the neighbourhood; but he had to resign them because of carelessness in the matter of payments due.

Works include: Masses (including *Euge bone* and *Western Wind*), motets, services, anthems, *The Actes of the Apostles* in English

A passage from Schoenberg's 'Waltz' (5 Piano Pieces op.23); the numbers represent the particular sequence of notes in the note-row.

metrical versions set for four voices (1533, dedicated to Edward VI); In Nomines for instruments.

tyrolienne (French 'Tyrolese') country dance similar to the *Ländler* or slow waltz, supposed to be native of the mountain regions of the Tyrol, but really an artificial growth introduced into ballets and operas and loosely based on melodic figurations imitating various forms of yodel. Tyroliennes also became fashionable in the form of piano pieces and songs.

Tyrrell, John (1942–) English musicologist. He studied at Cape Town and Oxford Universities. He was lecturer at Nottingham University 1976, reader in opera studies 1989, and was on the editorial staff of *New Grove* (1980) and *Opera Grove* (1992) dictionaries, with articles on Janáček and his operas. He published *Káta Kabanová* (1982), *Czech Opera* (1988), *Janáček's Operas: A Documentary Account* (1992) and *Intimate Letters: Janáček's Correspondence with Kamila Stösslova* (1994).

Tyrwhitt, Gerald see Lord ◊Berners.

tzigane, or *tsigane* a gypsy or musician of the bohemian world of Paris. The title of a rhapsody for violin and piano by Ravel composed 1924; first performed London, 26 April 1924, with Jelly d'Aranyi.

U

UC in piano music, an abbreviation for *una corda* 'one string', indicating the use of the damping pedal.

Uccellini, Marco (c. 1603–1680) Italian composer and violinist. He was master of instrumental music at the ducal court of Modena 1641–62 and maestro di cappella at Modena Cathedral 1647–65. He was then appointed maestro di cappella at the Farnese Court at Parma.

Works include: the opera *Gli eventi di Filandro ed Edessa* (1675); ballets *La nave d'Enea* (1673) and *Giove di Elide fulminato* (1677); psalms and litanies for voices and instruments; *Composizioni armoniche* and *Sinfonici concerti* for violin and other instruments, *Sinfonie boscareocie* and sonatas for violin and bass.

ud short-necked and fretless lute of the Arab world (from Morocco to Iraq), the direct ancestor of the European lute, whose name derives from al 'ud ('the lute'). The five course ud is the most common and popular form among performers and the instrument is used in a great variety of art, folk, and popular musics. See: ◊maqam, ◊taqsim.

Ugarte, Floro M(anuel) (1884–1975) Argentine composer. He studied with Fourdrain in Paris and became a private music teacher on his return in 1913 and professor at the National Conservatory at Buenos Aires, 1924. He also became music director of the Teatro Colón, resigning in 1943.

Works include: the opera *Saika* (1918) and others; symphonic poems and suites for orchestra; instrumental pieces.

Ugolini, Vincenzo (c. 1580–1638) Italian composer. He was a pupil of Bernardino Nassini. He was maestro di cappella at the church of Santa Maria Maggiore in Rome, 1603–09. He then retired after a severe illness, but in 1610 became maestro di cappella at Benevento Cathedral and returned in 1616 to Rome, where after some other appointments he became Soriano's successor in the Julian Chapel in 1620 and maestro di cappella of San Luigi dei Francesi in 1631, a post he had held 1616–20.

Works include: Masses, motets, psalms and other church music, madrigals.

Ugolino of Orvieto (c. 1380–1457) Italian composer and theorist. His *Declaratio musicae discipline* 1435 is mainly a practical handbook for the performing musician of his day.

Uhland, Johann Ludwig (1787–1862) German poet. See ◊*Black Knight* (Elgar); ◊Humperdinck (*Glück von Edenhall*); ◊Schoeck (songs); ◊Schumann (*Glück von Edenhall*); R ◊Strauss (*Schloss am Meer*).

Uhlig, Theodor (1822–1853) German violinist, composer, and author of theoretical works. He was a pupil of Schneider at Dessau, entered the royal orchestra at Dresden in 1841, and became a close friend of Richard Wagner there. He published articles in Wagner's praise and had an extensive correspondence with him.

ukulele musical instrument, a small four-stringed Hawaiian guitar, of Portuguese origin. It is easy to play; music for ukulele is written in a form of ◊tablature showing finger positions on a chart of the fingerboard.

Ulisse opera by Dallapiccola (libretto by composer, after Homer); composed 1959–68, produced Berlin, Deutsche Oper, 29

September 1968, conductor Maazel. British Broadcasting Corporation (BBC) studio performance, 20 September 1969. Ulysses meets Princess Nausicaa and recounts his story. He then spends a year with the enchantress Circe before visiting the Sirens and Hades on the way home to his wife Penelope.

Ullmann, Viktor (1898–1944) Austro-Hungarian composer. He was imprisoned in Theresienstadt concentration camp, where he wrote a one-act opera, *Der Kaiser von Atlantis* 1943, about a tyrannical monarch who outlaws death; it was first performed at Amsterdam in 1975. In October 1944 he was transferred to Auschwitz, where he died.

He studied with Schoenberg in Vienna, and was later a theatre conductor at Aussig and a music teacher in Prague.

Works include: the operas *Peer Gynt* (after Ibsen), *Der Sturz des Antichrist*, and *Der Kaiser von Atlantis* (1943); variations and double fugue on a theme by Schoenberg for orchestra; octet, two string quartets.

Ultimo giorno di Pompei, L'/The Last Day of Pompeii opera by Pacini (libretto by Tottola, not founded on Bulwer- Lytton's novel, which was not then published), produced Naples, Teatro San Carlo, 19 November 1825. Rejected by Ottavia, wife of Sallustio, Diomede attempts to revenge himself on her, but all are engulfed by Vesuvius.

Ultimos Ritos/Last Rites oratorio by Tavener for soloists, five speakers, chorus, and orchestra; composed 1972, first performed Haarlem, 22 June 1974.

Ulysses opera by Keiser (libretto by F M Lersner), produced (in German) Copenhagen, at court, November 1722.

Cantata by Seiber for tenor, chorus, and orchestra (text by composer, after Joyce); 1946–47, first performed London, 27 May 1949.

See also ◊*Circe and Penelope*.

Umlauf, Ignaz (1746–1796) Austrian composer. He was appointed director of Joseph II's new national *Singspiel* theatre in 1778, the inaugural work being his *Die Bergknappen*.

He became a viola player in the orchestra of the court opera in 1772, and on the foundation of the national *Singspiel* theatre by Joseph II in 1778 became its director. From 1789 he was Salieri's deputy as Kapellmeister of the court chapel. He also took part with Mozart in the performance of Handel's oratorios organized by Gottfried van Swieten. He was the father of Michael ◊Umlauf.

Works include: *Singspiele Die Insel der Liebe* (1722), *Die Bergknappen* (1778), *Die Apotheke, Die schöne Schusterin oder die pucegefarbenen Schuhe* (1779), *Das Irrlicht* (1782), *Welches ist die beste Nation?*, *Die glücklichen Jäger* (1786), *Die Ringe der Liebe* (sequel to Grétry's *Zémire et Azor*); incidental music for *Der Oberamtmann und die Soldaten* (after Calderón); church music.

Umlauf, Michael (1781–1842) Austrian composer and conductor. He was director of music at the court theatres in Vienna. On and after the revival of *Fidelio* in 1814 he assisted Beethoven, who was then too deaf to hear the orchestra, to conduct some of his major works.

He studied under his father, Ignaz ◊Umlauf, then became a violinist at the Opera and was conductor of the two court theatres 1810–25 and again from 1840.

Works include: the opera *Das Wirtshaus in Granada* (1812), play with music *Der Grenadier* (1812); 12 ballets; church music; piano sonatas.

una corda (Italian 'one string') in piano music, a direction used to indicate the use of the damping pedal, which so shifts the hammers that they touch only one or two strings for each note, instead of two or more.

Una cosa rara, o sia Bellezza ed onestà/A Rare Thing, or Beauty and Honesty opera by Martin y Soler (libretto by L da Ponte, based on a story by L V de Guevara), produced Vienna, Burgtheater, 17 November 1786. Mozart quotes an air from it in the finale of the second act of *Don Giovanni*. Lilla remains faithful to Lubino in spite of attentions from Don Lisergo, Prince Giovanni and Corrado.

Unanswered Question the first of Two Contemplations for orchestra by Charles Ives (no. 2 *Central Park in the Dark*). First performed New York 11 May 1946 (composed 1906).

Undine opera by E T A Hoffmann (libretto by the composer), produced Berlin, Schauspielhaus, 3 August 1816. Water nymph Undine can gain a soul by marrying a mortal. She meets and falls in love with the knight Huldbrand, but when he changes allegiance to Berthalda, Undine kisses him, drowning him.

Opera by Lortzing (libretto by composer, based on Fouqué), produced Magdeburg, 21 April 1845. Similar to Hoffmann's version, but Huldebrand is called Hugo von Ringstetten.

Ballet in three acts by Henze (choreographed by Ashton); composed 1956–57, produced London, Covent Garden, 27 October 1958, conductor Henze, with Fonteyn. *Wedding Music* from the ballet arranged for wind orchestra 1957; two orchestral suites 1958; *Undine, Trois pas des Tritons* for orchestra, performed Rome, 10 January 1959, conductor Celibidache.

unequal temperament a system of tuning, especially on old keyboard instruments, in which some of the accidentals were treated as sharps according to just intonation and some as flats (for instance, F♯, not G♭; B♭, not A♯). An attempt was thus made to make some of the more frequently used keys come nearer to just intonation than is possible in the tempered scale of the modern piano, but the result was also that the more extreme sharp and flat keys were out of tune. This is one of the chief reasons why these keys were rarely used by early composers.

unequal voices composition for several voices which do not lie within the same compass is said to be for unequal voices.

'Unfinished' Symphony Schubert's *'Unfinished' Symphony*, in B minor, written October/November 1822, was planned as a four-movement work, though only the first two movements, and a sketch of the scherzo, survive. Some authorities, however, believe that the finale was used a year later as the basis of the B minor Entr'acte in *Rosamunde*. After the Styrian Music Society, through Josef and Anselm Hüttenbrenner, had awarded Schubert their Diploma of Honour in 1823, he promised to send in return 'one of my symphonies at the earliest opportunity'. Later he handed to Josef the score of the two completed movements. Anselm Hüttenbrenner made an arrangement of the work for piano duet in 1853, but made no attempt to get it performed. Johann Herbeck, who gave the first performance in Vienna in December 1865, coaxed the score out of Anselm with a promise to perform one of the latter's own works. Schubert was the first composer to associate a tragic tone and intense personal feeling with B minor in a substantial symphonic work; in this the 'Unfinished' looks forward to late Romantic works such as Tchaikovsky's *'Pathetique' Symphony* and Dvořák's *Cello Concerto*. In the original *Gesamtausgabe* it is called no. 8, but is more often referred to simply as the 'Unfinished'.

unfolding in voice-leading analysis, an interval is unfolded if two notes are presented consecutively in the same voice in the music,

but can be considered at a deeper structural level to occur simultaneously (that is, to be separate voices within a single harmony). Very often, the interval between the two notes is filled in by passing notes or an arpeggiation.

Unger, (Gustav) Hermann (1886–1958) German composer. He studied in Munich and later with Reger at Meiningen. He taught for more than 30 years in Cologne, and wrote books on Reger and Bruckner, and a treatise on harmony (1946).

Works include: the operas *Richmondis* (1928) and *De Zauberhandschuh*; incidental music for Shakespeare's *Tempest*, Kleist's *Penthesilea*, Hofmannsthal's *Der Tor und der Tod*, Hauptmann's *Hannele*, Unruh's *Heinrich aus Andernach* and many other plays; *Der Gott und die Bajadere* (Goethe) and *Old German Songs* for chorus and orchestra; two symphonies; chamber music; songs.

unison term used to describe music in which all musicians play or sing the same notes without harmony. Strictly, unison implies that all musicians sound the same pitch in the same octave, but it is also used for same pitch doubled at the octave.

un poco (Italian 'a little') qualifying musical direction used where any indication of tempo or expression is to be applied in moderation. Often used in the abbreviation form *poco*.

Unterbrochene Opferfest, Das/The Interrupted Sacrificial Feast opera by Winter (libretto by F X Huber), produced Vienna, Kärntnertortheater, 14 June 1796. During Inca sacrifice Elvira and Villacumar unsuccessfully attempt to make Murneg, lover of Myrha, the victim.

upbeat, or anacrusis, arsis in music, at the beginning of certain pieces, one or several notes preceding the first full bar of music; also, the last or the weak beat of a bar, analogous to the upstroke of a conductor's hand. The opposite is downbeat.

up bow in the playing of string instruments, the motion of the bow in the direction from the point to the heel.

Uribe Holguín, Guillermo (1880–1971) Colombian composer. In 1910 he became director of the National Conservatory at Bogotá, where he founded and conducted symphonic concerts.

He studied at home and with Vincent d'Indy at the Schola Cantorum in Paris.

Works include: Requiem; 11 symphonies (1916–59), 3 *Danzas, Carnavelesca, Marche funèbre, Marche de fête, Suite tipica*, all for orchestra; concert and *Villanesca* for piano and orchestra, two violin concertos; ten string quartets, piano quartet, two piano quintets; five violin and piano sonatas, two cello and piano sonatas; piano pieces, including 300 folk dances; songs.

Urio, Francesco Antonio (c. 1632–1719 or later) Italian priest and composer. A Franciscan monk, he was maestro di cappella at the church of SS Apostoli in Rome in 1690, seven years later at the Frari church in Venice, and finally from 1715 at S Francesco in Milan.

Works include: Te Deum (once attributed to Handel, who borrowed from it for his *Dettingen Te Deum, Saul, Israel in Egypt*, and *L'Allegro*); oratorios; motets and psalms for voices and instruments.

Urtext (German 'original text') an edition of music which tries to capture the original intentions of the composer, minimizing editorial interpretation as much as possible. *Urtext* editions are usually based upon the composer's sketches and manuscripts, as well as original and early editions of the works.

Usper, Francesco (before 1570–1641), adopted name of Francesco Sponga Italian priest, organist, and composer. In 1614 he became organist at the church of San Salvatore at Venice, in 1621 he deputized for Giovanni Battista Grillo (d 1622) as organist at St Mark's, and in 1627 he became principal of the school of St John the Evangelist.

Works include: Masses, motets, psalms, for voices with instruments, vesper psalms for four–eight voices and bass, some for double choir; *La battaglia* for voices and instruments, madrigals; *ricercari* and *arie francesi* in four parts.

Ussachevsky, Vladimir (Aleksei) (1911–1990) US composer of Russian parentage. He moved to the USA in 1930 and studied with Hanson at the Eastman School. He was professor at Columbia University, New York, 1964–80, and collaborated with Luening in pioneering the development of electronic music.

Works include: (some with Luening) *Sonic Contours* for tape (1952), *Incantation* for tape (1953), *Rhapsodic Variations* for orchestra and tape (1954), *Creation Prologue* for four chorus and tape (1961), *Missa brevis* for soprano, chorus and brass (1972), *Celebration* for string orchestra and electronic valve instruments (1980).

Ustvolskaya, Galina (1919–   ) Russian composer. Employing the minimum of means, her music has drawn from serialism and from local Russian traditions; but ultimately her style is completely independent: Dmitri Shostakovich commented that he felt under her influence and not the reverse.

Ustvolskaya studied 1939–50 at the Leningrad Conservatory with Shostakovich, and was defended by him when she was criticized by Stalinist authorities.

Works include: five symphonies: no. 1 for two descant voices and orchestra (1955), no. 2 'True and Eternal Bliss' for boy speaker and orchestra (1979), no. 3 'Jesus, Messiah, Save Us' with boy speaker (1983), no. 4 'Prayer' with trumpet, tam-tam, and piano (1987), no. 5 'Amen' with male speaker (1990); Trio for clarinet, violin, and piano (1949); Octet (1950); *Composition I-III* (1970–75); six piano sonatas (1947–88).

Ut the old name for the note C, still used in France, but elsewhere replaced by Do. For its origin, see ◊solmization.

Utendal, Alexander (c. 1535–1581) Flemish composer. He learnt music as a choirboy in the Archduke Ferdinand's chapel in Prague, and in 1566 became a singer in his chapel at Innsbruck. In c. 1572 he became second Kapellmeister. On the death of Scandello at Dresden in 1580 he was offered the post of Kapellmeister to the Saxon court, but declined it.

Works include: three Masses, motets, *Sacrae cantiones*; secular French and German songs.

Uthal opera by Méhul (libretto by J M B B de Saint-Victor, based on Ossian), produced Paris, Opéra-Comique, 17 May 1806. The work is scored without violins. Malvina's husband Uthal deposes her father Larmor as tribal chief: she is torn between love for them both. Larmor's troops defeat Uthal and Malvina joins him in exile before being pardoned.

Utrecht Te Deum and Jubilate work by Handel, composed for the celebration of the Peace of Utrecht and performed London, St Paul's Cathedral, 7 July 1713.

Utrenja/Morning Service work in two parts by Penderecki, for soloists, choruses, and orchestra: 1. *The Entombment of Christ* (first performed Altenberg Cathedral, 8 April 1970); 2. *Resurrection of Christ* (first performed Münster Cathedral, 28 May 1971).

V

Vaccai, Nicola (1790–1848) Italian composer. Of his 17 operas, only two were successful: *Zadig ed Astartea* and *Giulietta e Romeo*, both 1825. He taught singing and was director of the Milan Conservatory 1838–44. In 1832 he published a well-known singing tutor, *Metodo pratico di cento italiano per camera*.

Vaccai went to school at Pesaro, then studied law in Rome, but at the age of 17 or 18 gave it up for music and studied counterpoint with Giuseppe Jannaconi (also known as Giannacconi or Jannacconi; c. 1740–1816). In 1811 he studied with Giovanni Paisiello at Naples and in 1815 produced his first opera there. He then lived at Venice for seven years, produced two operas there, afterwards taught singing at Trieste and Vienna, in 1824 produced two operas at Parma and Turin and in 1825 had his greatest success, at Milan, with *Giulietta e Romeo*, after Shakespeare. In 1829–31 he lived in Paris and afterwards briefly in London, which he visited again 1833–34. In 1838 he succeeded Francesco Basili as director of the Milan Conservatory, retiring to Pesaro in 1844.

Works include: the operas *I solitari di Scozia* (1815), *Pietro il grande* (1824), *La pastorella feudataria*, *Giulietta e Romeo* (1825), *Marco Visconti* (1838), *Giovanna Grey* (1836), *Virginia*, *Giovanna d'Arco* (1827), *La sposa di Messina* (both after Schiller), and others; church music; cantata on the death of Malibran and others; *Ariette per camera* for voice and piano.

Vaet, Jacobus (1529–1567) Flemish composer. He was choirmaster to Maximilian, King of Bohemia, in the 1560s and succeeded Jachet Buus as chief music director in Vienna in 1564, when his patron became the Emperor Maximilian II.

Works include: Masses, motets, Magnificats, Te Deum for eight voices and other church music; chansons.

vagans (Latin 'wandering, vagrant') name sometimes given in five-part 15th- and 16th-century polyphonic music to the fifth part, which duplicates in range one of the basic four voices: treble, alto, tenor, and bass. The voice required within one quintus part-book, though usually a second tenor, may vary from piece to piece; whence *vagans*.

vagrant chord a term coined by A Schoenberg (as *vagierender Akkord*) to describe chromatic chords which confuse or lead away from any definite key-centre.

Vaisseau-fantôme, Le/The Phantom Vessel opera by Dietsch (libretto by B H Révoil and P H Foucher, founded on Wagner's scenario for *Der fliegende Holländer*, intended for an opera of his own to be produced at the Opéra, which however accepted the libretto only and had it set by Dietsch), produced Paris, Opéra, 9 November 1842.

Vakula the Smith/Vakula Kuznets opera by Tchaikovsky (libretto by Y P Polonsky, based on Gogol's *Christmas Eve*), produced St Petersburg, 6 December 1876; revised version entitled *Cherevichki/The Little Boots*, produced Moscow, 31 January 1887. It is also known as *Oxana's Caprices*. At Oxana's request Vakula flies on the back of the Devil to St Petersburg, to claim from the Tsaritsa a pair of high-heeled leather boots.

Valen, (Olav) Fartein (1887–1952) Norwegian composer. He studied languages at Oslo

University, but later entered the Conservatory, finishing his studies with Max Reger at the Hochschule für Musik in Berlin. In 1925–35 he worked in the music department of the library of Oslo University, but then received a government grant for composition.

Works include: three sets of motets and other choral works; five symphonies (1937–51), *Sonetto di Michelangelo*, *To Hope* (after Keats), *Pastorale*, *Epithalamion*, *Le cimetière marin* (after P Valéry), *La isla en las calmas*, *Ode to Solitude* for orchestra; piano concerto, violin concerto (1940); six works for soprano and orchestra; two string quartets (1928–31), piano trio, serenade for five wind instruments; violin and piano sonata; two sonatas, variations and other works for piano; organ music; songs.

Valentini, Giuseppe (c. 1680–after 1759) Italian composer. He was in the service of the Grand Duke of Tuscany at Florence from about 1735. His most characteristic music is in his florid violin sonatas.

Works include: the opera *La costanza in amore* (1715); oratorios *Absalone* (1705) and *S Alessio* (1733); Concerti grossi; symphony, *Bizarrie*, 12 fantasies, *Idee per camera* and 12 sonatas for three string instruments and bass; chamber sonatas and *Alletamenti* for violin, cello, and bass.

Valentini, Pier Francesco (c. 1570–1654) Italian composer. He was a pupil of Giovanni Maria Nanino in Rome. He was best known for music involving elaborate counterpoint, for example his canon for 96 voices.

Works include: the operas (*favole*) *La mitra* (1620) and *La transformazione di Dafne* (1623); motets, litanies, and other church music; *Canzonetti spirituali* and *Musiche spirituali* for the Nativity; madrigals and canons; *canzoni* and arias for one–two voices.

Valkyrie, The/Die Walküre (Wagner). See ◊*Ring des Nibelungen*.

Vallotti, Francesco Antonio (1697–1780) Italian composer and theorist. He became third organist at the basilica of Sant' Antonio at Padua in 1722 and maestro di cappella in 1730. He wrote a learned treatise, 'Della scienza teorica e pratica della moderna musica'.

Works include: motets, Requiem for Tartini and other church music.

Valls, Francisco (1665–1747) Spanish composer. He was controversial in his day for his use of dissonance in church music, as in the Mass *Scala aretina*, for which he is best known today.

After posts at Mataró and Gerona Valls moved to Barcelona in 1696; he was maestro de capilla at the cathedral there from 1709. He retired in 1740 to write a treatise called *Mapa armónico*, in which he defended the use of dissonance in sacred music as employed by Spanish composers against the more orthodox views of Alessandro Scarlatti.

Works include: Masses *Scala aretina* for 11 voices and orchestra (1702), *Regalis* (for the King of Portugal), 1740), ten others; 22 responsories, 16 Magnificats, 12 psalms, two Misereres, about 35 motets, about 120 *villancicos*.

valse French spelling of ◊waltz.

Valse, La choreographic poem for orchestra by Ravel, finished 1920; first performed Paris, 12 December 1920. It imitates or parodies the style of J Strauss's waltzes and has several times served for ballets, as its description shows that it was intended to do.

Valses nobles et sentimentales a set of waltzes by Ravel, composed 1911 and afterwards scored for orchestra. The title is derived from Schubert, who published two sets: *Valses nobles*, D969, and *Valses sentimentales*, D779. Ravel's work was turned into a ballet, *Adélaïde, ou Le Langage des fleurs*, produced Paris, 22 April 1912.

valve in brass wind instruments, a mechanism for diverting the air flow through an extension loop, to vary the length and thus the pitch of the instrument. Most valve instruments are of the piston type, but older French horns have rotary valves operated by levers.

Vampyr, Der/The Vampire opera by Lindpaintner (libretto by C M Heigel, based on J W Polidori's story, published in 1819 and thought to be by Byron, and more directly on a French melodrama by C Nodier, P F A Carmouche and A de Jouffroy), produced Stuttgart, 21 September 1828.

Opera by Marschner (libretto by W A Wohlbrück, based on the sources above), produced Leipzig, 29 March 1828. To postpone Satan's claim on his soul, the newly created vampire Lord Ruthven must sacrifice three girls; Janthe and Emmy fall victim but Malvina escapes the fangs.

Vanessa opera by Barber (libretto by Menotti), produced New York Metropolitan Opera, 15 January 1958. Vanessa marries Anatol, son of her former lover by the same name, in spite of the fact that her niece Erika is pregnant by him.

Vanhal, Johann Baptist (1739–1813) Bohemian composer. He wrote about 100 symphonies and 100 quartets; his works were performed by Mozart and Haydn.

Vanhal went to Vienna in 1760 and studied there with Karl Dittersdorf; he travelled in Italy 1769–71, and lived on the estate of Count Erdödy in Hungary 1772–80. Back in Vienna, he supported himself as a freelance composer.

Works include: two operas (*Demofoonte* and *Il trionfo di Clelia*, both lost); over 50 Masses and much other church music; about 70 symphonies; about 100 string quartets; many caprices and programmatic works for keyboard.

Varèse, Edgard Victor Achille Charles (1883–1965) French composer. He left Paris for New York 1916 where he co-founded the New Symphony Orchestra in 1919 with the French-born US harpist Carlos Salzédo (1885–1961) to promote modern and pre-classical music. Renouncing the values of tonality, he discovered new resources of musical expression in the percussion sonorities of *Ionisation* 1929–31, the swooping sound of two ◊theremins in *Hyperprism* 1933–34, and the combination of taped and live instrumental sounds in *Déserts* 1950–54.

variation a form based on constant repetition of a simple theme, each new version being elaborated or treated in a different manner. The theme is easily recognizable; it may be a popular tune or – as a gesture of respect – the work of a fellow composer; for example, Brahms' *Variations on a Theme by Haydn* 1873, based on a theme known as the *St Antony Chorale*, although it may also be an original composition. The principle of variations has been adopted in larger-scale and orchestral works by modern composers, for example Elgar's *Enigma Variations* 1899.

Variations on a Theme by Haydn (Brahms). See ◊'Haydn' Variations.

Variations on a Theme of Frank Bridge work for string orchestra by Britten, composed 1937 for the Boyd Neel Orchestra, performed Salzburg, 27 August 1937. The theme is from Bridge's Idyll no. 2 for string quartet.

Varvoglis, Mario (1885–1967) Greek composer. He studied painting at first, then music in Paris with Leroux and Caussade from 1904 and d'Indy from 1913, having his first successes there. He returned to Greece 1922, became professor at the Athens Conservatory, and in 1924 at the Hellenic Conserva-

tory, of which he became director with Evangelatos, 1947.

Works include: the one-act opera *The Afternoon of Love* (1935, produced 1944); classical Greek plays; *Pastoral Suite* (1912), *Meditation* and incidental music to prelude, chorale and fugue on BACH for strings; chamber music; piano works; songs.

Vásquez, Juan see Juan ◊Vázquez.

Vaterländischer Künstlerverein **(German 'Patriotic Artists' Association')** title of Part II of the variations commissioned by Cappi and Diabelli of Vienna to be written by Beethoven and others on a waltz by Diabelli. Beethoven eventually wrote 33 variations instead of one, and they were published separately as Part I in 1824, Part II following with contributions by Czerny, Hummel, Kalkbrenner, C Kreutzer, Liszt (aged 11), Moscheles, Franz Xaver Mozart, the Archduke Rudolph, Schubert, Sechter, and c. 40 others.

vaudeville (French) term with various meanings and of uncertain origin. Le Roy, in his *Airs de Cour* of 1571, says that such songs were formerly called *voix de ville*, 'town voices'; but the form *vau de Vire* is also known, and may have referred to the valley of Vire in Normandy, the home of Olivier Basselin (c. 1400–50), a composer of such songs. In 18th-century France, vaudevilles were at first satirical songs, then songs with words set to popular tunes used in comedies with music (*comédies mêlées de vaudevilles*), as in the English ballad opera (songs specially composed being called *ariettes*). In time vaudevilles in France became songs sung at the end of spoken stage pieces, taken up verse-by-verse by all the characters and sometimes by the chorus, and this device was sometimes introduced into opera in France and elsewhere, as for example at the end of Rousseau's *Devin du village* and Mozart's *Entführung aus dem Serail*. The next step from this was to call a whole light music stage entertainment a vaudeville.

Vaughan Williams, Ralph (1872–1958) English composer. His style was tonal and often evocative of the English countryside through the use of folk themes. Among his works are the orchestral *Fantasia on a Theme by Thomas Tallis* 1910; the opera *Sir John in Love* 1929, featuring the Elizabethan song 'Greensleeves'; and nine symphonies 1909–57.

Vaughan Williams was born at Down Ampney, Gloucestershire, the son of a clergyman. He was educated at Charterhouse School 1887–90, and Trinity College, Cambridge 1892–95, the intervening years being devoted to study at the Royal College of Music in London, where he returned for another year after Cambridge. He learnt the piano and organ but was from the first determined to be a composer. On leaving the Royal College of Music in 1896 he became organist at South Lambeth Church in London and saved enough money to gain further experience by study abroad, first at the Akademie der Künste in Berlin, under Bruch, and in 1909 with Ravel, who was younger than him, in Paris. In 1901 he completed a doctorate at Cambridge.

In 1904 he joined the Folk-Song Society (established in 1898) and began to take an active share in the recovery and study of old country tunes, collecting some in Norfolk. (When the society amalgamated with the English Folk Dance Society to form the English Folk Dance and Song Society in 1932, Vaughan Williams became its president.) His first public success was with *Toward the Unknown Region* at the Leeds Festival 1907 and this was followed 1909 by his first great and charactistic compositions, the *Wasps* overture, song cycle *On Wenlock Edge*, and *A Sea Symphony* (the first to employ a chorus throughout). From 1906 he was editor of the *English Hymnal*, and this resulted in one of his best-loved works, the *Fantasia on a theme of Thomas Tallis* for strings, 1910. (The sense of religious wonder evoked by this music was later enhanced in such Biblically-inspired works as the masque *Job* and the opera *The Pilgrim's Progress*).

In World War I he first served as a private in Macedonia and France, but later rose to officer's rank. After the war he was appointed professor of composition at the Royal College of Music. The English pastoral tradition was revived in his 3rd symphony, 1921, and the complementary, visionary source of his inspiration was renewed in such sacred works as the Mass in G minor, *Sancta Civitas*, and *Benedicite*. His two best-known symphonies, nos. 4 and 5, were composed between 1934 and 1943; the angularity and fierce accents of the earlier work lead to the repose and serenity of its companion. The last four symphonies continue the composer's spiritual quest, already begun in *The Pilgrim's Progress*. Although Vaughan Williams' compositions are usually classified broadly as pastoral, making use of folk melodies, or at least the lyrical and often model aspects of such melodies, he was conscious of contem-

porary musical developments and often involved a greater degree of dissonance in his later works.

Works include: OPERA *The Pilgrim's Progress* (after Bunyan, begun 1925, premiered 1951); masque *Job* (on Blake's illustrations, 1931); incidental music for Aristophanes' *Wasps* (1909), film music including *Scott of the Antarctic* (1948).

CHORAL Mass in G minor, Anglican services; (with orchestra) *Toward the Unknown Region* (Whitman), *A Sea Symphony* (no. 1) (Whitman, 1903–09), *Five Mystical Songs* (Herbert, 1911), *Flos Campi* (Song of Solomon, 1925), *Five Tudor Portraits* (Skelton, 1935), *Serenade to Music* for 16 solo voices and orchestra (from Shakespeare's *Merchant of Venice*, 1938).

ORCHESTRAL *In the Fen Country, Fantasia on a Theme by Thomas Tallis* (strings, 1910), *A London Symphony* (no. 2, 1912–13), *A Pastoral Symphony* (no. 3, 1921), symphonies nos. 4–9 (1937, 1943, 1947, 1952, 1955, 1957), *Five Variants of 'Dives and Lazarus'* (strings and harps, 1939); *The Lark Ascending* (after Meredith) for violin and orchestra (1914), concerto for oboe and strings (1944), tuba concerto (1954).

CHAMBER AND SONGS *On Wenlock Edge* (Housman) for tenor, string quartet, and piano (1909); many songs including *Songs of Travel* (Stevenson, 1901–04); ten Blake songs for high voice and oboe; folk-song arrangements.

Vautor, Thomas (fl. 1600–20) English composer. He was educated at Lincoln College, Oxford, where he took the BMus in 1616. He was for many years in the service of Sir George Villiers, father of the later Duke of Buckingham, at Brooksby, and later of his widow at Goadby. He published one book of madrigals (1619–20).

Vázquez, Juan (c. 1510–c. 1560) Spanish composer. He was maestro di cappella at Badajoz Cathedral 1545–50, and was later in the service of Don Antonio de Zuñiga. He was an important exponent of the Spanish song form known as the *villancico*, and also wrote church music.

Vecchi, Lorenzo (1564–1628) Italian composer. He was a pupil at San Petronio at Bologna, where he became maestro di cappella in 1605. He wrote Masses, Requiem and other church music.

Vecchi, Orazio (Tiberio) (1550–1605) Italian composer. Although he was a priest and wrote sacred music, it is for his canzonettes and madrigals that he is remembered. He was celebrated as a composer of entertainments;

his madrigal-comedy *L'Amfiparnaso* 1597 is an important forerunner of comic opera.

Vecchi was born in Modena. He was maestro di cappella at Salò Cathedral from 1581, at Modena from 1584, and at Reggio Emilia in 1586, then became a canon at Correggio and an archdeacon in 1591. Wishing to devote himself to music, he returned to Modena as maestro di cappella in 1593, and then became maestro di cappella at the d'Este court in 1598. He became famous, being summoned to the court of the Emperor Rudolph II at one time and invited to compose music for the king of Poland. In 1604 his pupil Geminiano Capi-Lupi intrigued successfully against him and supplanted him in his post.

L'Amfiparnaso comprises 14 madrigals for five voices, with a dramatic plot set to a *commedia dell'arte* text. The characters' parts are not acted, but are sung by concerted voices in the madrigal style.

Works include: madrigal comedy *L'Amfiparnaso* (1597); Masses, motets, Lamentations, and other church music; madrigals, canzonets.

Vecchi, Orfeo (c. 1550–1604) Italian composer. He was maestro di cappella of the church of Santa Maria della Scala at Milan from c. 1590.

Works include: Masses, motets, psalms, Magnificats, *Cantiones sacrae* and other church music; madrigals.

Veilchen, Das/The Violet song by Mozart, K476: his only setting of a poem by Goethe, composed 8 June 1785.

Vejvanovský, Pavel Josef (c. 1655–1693) Moravian composer and trumpeter. Many of his Masses, offertories, and motets feature technically fluent parts for trumpets, trombones, and cornets.

He studied at Opava and from 1661 and worked at Kroměříž, where he composed and played the trumpet at the court. Much of his music shows the influence of Heinrich Schmelzer and other composers at the court of Emperor Leopold I in Vienna.

Velluti, Giovanni Battista (1780–1861) Italian soprano castrato (one of the last). Made his first stage appearance at Forlì in 1800, and then appeared in Naples, Milan, and Venice in operas by Guglielmi, Cimarosa, and Mayr. In 1812 he visited Vienna. He created Arsace in Rossini's *Aureliano in Palmira* (Milan, 1813) and Armando in Meyerbeer's *Il crociato in Egitto* (Venice, 1824), and sang the latter role on his first visit to London (1825).

veloce (Italian 'quick, swift, rapid, fluent') musical direction that does not so much indicate increased speed, though it may include that meaning, as smoothness of rapid figuration.

Vendredis, Les a set of pieces for string quartet by Artsibushev, Blumenfeld, Borodin, Glazunov, Kopylov, Liadov, M d'Osten-Sacken, Rimsky-Korsakov, Sokolov, and Wihtol, written for Friday chamber-music reunions in St Petersburg.

Venegas de Henestrosa, Luis (c. 1510–c. 1557 or later) Spanish composer. He published a book of variations and transcriptions in a special tablature suitable for keyboard instruments, harp, vihuela, or guitar (*Libro de cifra nueva*, 1557). The notation was later used by Antonio de Cabezón (1510–66) and Francisco Correa de Arauxo (1576–1654).

Venite music based on the text of Psalm 95, *Venite, exultemus Domino* (Latin 'O come let us sing unto the Lord'). It is sung at Anglican ◊matins, either in ◊plainsong or to a composed setting. It is used as a prelude to the psalms.

Ventadorn, Bernart de French troubadour. 45 of his poems and 19 of his melodies have been preserved.

Vento, Mattia (1735–1776) Italian composer. He produced operas in Rome and Venice, and settled in London in 1763, staging six Italian operas and several pasticcios there.

Works include: the operas *La finta semplice* (1759), *La Egiziana* (1763), *Leucippo* (1764), *Demofoonte, Sofonisba* (1766), *La conquista del vello d'orco* (1767), *Artaserse* (1771), *Il bacio* (1776), *La Vestale*; cantata *Threnodia augustilia* (Goldsmith) on the death of George III's mother; trio sonatas; violin sonatas; keyboard music; songs.

Venus and Adonis masque by Blow (librettist unknown), produced London, at court, *c* 1682; Chelsea, Josiah Priest's boarding school for young gentlewomen, 17 April 1684. Venus persuades Adonis to join the hunt but he returns mortally wounded, gored by a boar.

Vénus et Adonis opera by Desmarets (libretto by J B Rousseau), produced Paris, Opéra, 17 March 1697.

Vêpres siciliennes, Les/The Sicilian Vespers opera by Verdi (libretto by Scribe and C Duveyrier), produced Paris, Opéra, 13 June 1855. Verdi's first French opera, the only other set to French words being *Don Carlos*. Produced in Italy, as *Giovanna di Guzman*, Milan, La Scala, 4 February 1856, but later called *I vespri siciliani* there. Sicilians Procida, Hélène and Henri engage in a plot to assassinate Montfort, the French Governor of the island. But when Henri learns that Montfort is his father he prevents the murder and Procida and Hélène are arrested, later being released when Henri reluctantly accepts Montfort as his parent. At Henri's and Hélène's wedding the Sicilians rise and kill Montfort.

Veracini, Francesco Maria (1690–1768) Italian composer and violinist. He travelled widely in Europe, and had operas produced in London. He wrote concertos and about 60 sonatas for violin; his instrumental music was influenced by Arcangelo Corelli and Vivaldi.

Veracini studied with his uncle, Antonio Veracini and later with Giovanni Maria Casini and Francesco Gasparini in Rome, possibly also with Corelli. He began touring as a virtuoso in 1711, and visited England in 1714. Returning via Germany to Italy, he demonstrated his superiority over Giuseppe Tartini (two years his junior) in a contest in Venice in 1716. The following year he entered the service of the Elector of Saxony in Dresden, but left for Prague in 1723, then returned to Italy. In 1735 he went again to London, where he produced his first opera, *Adriano in Siria*, followed by several others 1735–44, but as a violinist was overshadowed by Francesco Geminiani. He probably lived in Pisa around 1750–55, then retired to Florence.

Works include: the operas *Adriano in Siria* (1753), *La clemenza di Tito* (1737), *Partenio* (1738), *Rosalinda* (after Shakespeare's *As You Like It*, 1744), eight oratorios (music lost); cantatas include *Nice e Tirsi* (1741) and *Parla al ritratto della amata*; violin sonatas; concertos; treatise *Il Erionfo della pratica musicale*.

Vera costanza, La/True Constancy opera by Anfossi (libretto by F Puttini), produced Rome, Teatro delle Dame, 2 January 1776.

Opera by Haydn (libretto ditto, altered by P Travaglia), produced Eszterháza, 25 April 1779. Secretly married to wayward Count Enrico, fisher maid Rosina faces Baroness Irene, who has arrived to arrange a marriage between Rosina and Villoto. Enrico and Rosina are reconciled when he meets their son; the Baroness marries Ernesto.

Vera Sheloga (Rimsky-Korsakov).

See ◊*Pskovitianka*.

verbunkos eighteenth-century Hungarian recruiting dance for soldiers, who performed it in full uniform with swords and spurs. Like the later csárdás, to which it is related, it contained a slow (*lassú*) and quick (*friss*) section. Liszt's Hungarian Rhapsodies make use of the dance.

Verdelot, Philippe (c. 1470–c. 1552) French composer. His sacred music includes two Masses, about 57 motets, and a Magnificat, and was popular throughout Europe, but he was admired chiefly for his nine volumes of madrigals. He was one of the first composers to write madrigals (he was writing them as early as the 1520s), and influenced other madrigalists.

Verdelot was born in northern France. He went to Italy, probably at an early age, and was maestro at the baptistry in Florence 1523–25 and at Florence Cathedral 1523–27.

His motets were parodied by other composers, including Roland de Lassus and Palestrina.

Works include: two Masses, about 57 motets; about 100 madrigals, three chansons.

Verdi, Giuseppe Fortunino Francesco (1813–1901) Italian opera composer of the Romantic period. He took his native operatic style to new heights of dramatic expression. In 1842 he wrote the opera *Nabucco*, followed by *Ernani* 1844 and *Rigoletto* 1851. Other works include *Il trovatore* and *La traviata* both 1853, *Aïda* 1871, and the masterpieces of his old age, *Otello* 1887 and *Falstaff* 1893. His *Requiem* 1874 commemorates the poet and novelist Alessandro Manzoni.

His music is essentially Italian in character, and owes nothing to Wagnerian influences, although in his late works (*Otello* and *Falstaff*) he developed a more continuous, orchestrally dominated texture and dramatic structure. During the mid-1800s, Verdi became a symbol of Italy's fight for independence from Austria, frequently finding himself in conflict with the Austrian authorities, who felt that his operas encouraged Italian nationalism.

Verdi was born at Roncole, near Busseto, the son of an innkeeper and grocer. From the age of only three he was taught by the local organist, in whose place he was appointed at nine. At 11 he was sent to Busseto and went to school there, walking home twice a week to carry out the organist's duties. Barezzi, a friend of Verdi's father at Busseto, took him into his house in 1826, and he learnt much from the cathedral organist Provesi. He had an overture for Rossini's *Il barbiere di Siviglia* performed 1828, and the next year he wrote a symphony and deputized for Provesi. In 1831 he was sent to Milan with a scholarship and some financial help from Barezzi, but was rejected by the Conservatory as over entrance age. Instead, he studied with Vincenzo Lavigna, the maestro al cembalo at La Scala. When Provesi died in 1833, Verdi tried for the post of cathedral organist, and when it was given to an inferior musician the Philharmonic Society made him an allowance. In 1836 he married Barezzi's daughter, Margherita, with whom he had two children, but both mother and children died between 1837 and 1840. Meanwhile he had composed his first opera, *Oberto*, produced at La Scala in 1839.

A second (comic) opera, *Un giorno di regno* 1840, was a failure, his wife having died during its composition; but *Nabucco*, produced at La Scala in 1842, had a great success; the chorus of the Hebrew slaves was later to provide a rallying cry for the disaffected Italian people in their quest for freedom. In the cast of *Nabucco* was the soprano Giuseppina Strepponi, who lived with Verdi from 1848 and in 1859 became his second wife. He now went from strength to strength as an operatic composer, and his fame spread beyond Milan: *Ernani* was produced at Venice in 1844, *I due Foscari* in Rome 1844, *Alzira* at Naples 1845, and *Macbeth* at Florence 1847. Meanwhile *Ernani* had gone to Paris in 1846 and London commissioned *I masnadieri*, which was produced there 1847.

From 1848 most of Verdi's life was spent at his estate of Sant' Agata near Busseto. *Luisa Miller* 1849 and *Stiffelio* 1850, were the last of his 'galley' operas, in which vigorous drama and strongly expressed emotion are accompanied by some basic orchestration. *Rigoletto*, the first of his great masterpieces, was premiered at Venice in 1851; together with *Il trovatore* and *La traviata* 1853, it marks Verdi's emergence as a supreme melodist. At the same time he shows new refinement of characterization and a radically improved awareness of orchestral timbre. The first version of *Simon Boccanegra* was performed in 1857 and two years later *Un ballo in maschera* was premiered in Rome – it was one of several operas which ran into trouble with the censors. Verdi's support for Italian independence from Austrian rule was sometimes detected in his work.

An opera on Shakespeare's *King Lear*, at which he worked intermittently, was never completed; otherwise all his plans materialized once they had taken definite shape. France, Russia, and Egypt offered him special commissions and his fame spread all over the world. In 1862 he represented Italy at the International Exhibition in London, and

wrote a *Hymn of the Nations*, and in the same year *La forza del destino* was produced at St Petersburg. The potentially sensitive subject of *Don Carlos*, dealing with Spanish oppression of the Netherlands, was performed in Paris in 1867; it is Verdi's most sombre, powerful, and richly varied opera.

Aida was performed at Cairo in 1871 and the Requiem followed three years later; it was described by the conductor Hans von Bülow as an opera in ecclesiastical garb, and is melodically the most consistently inspired of all Verdi's works. In 1868 he had suggested a Requiem for Rossini, to be written by various Italian composers, but the plan came to nothing. He used his contribution in 1873 for a Requiem commemorating the writer, Manzoni. *Otello* was produced at La Scala in 1887, and with its musical and dramatic unity marked Verdi's greatest public success. After a six-year break from composition, *Falstaff* was given at the same theatre in 1893, when Verdi was in his 80th year; though the unique subtlety of this work was at first lost on its audiences. Giuseppina died in 1897 and Verdi was himself growing very weak, but still wrote some sacred pieces for chorus and orchestra 1895–97.

Verdi is the artistic successor of Donizetti and Bellini, but shows a far greater wealth of passionate feeling, musicianly craftsmanship, and power of enlightening pathos or tragedy by a simple and suggestive spirituality. His musical development was as varied as that of Beethoven; his lyricism was always constant, but his last works show also a rare spirituality, a refinement and religious consciousness, which place him among the foremost composers in the field of sacred, as well as of operatic, music.

Works include: OPERA *Oberto, Conte di San Bonifacio* (1839), *Un giorno di regno* (1840), *Nabucco* (1842), *I Lombardi alla prima crociata* (1843), *Ernani* (1844), *I due Foscari* (1844), *Giovanna d'Arco* (1845), *Alzira* (1845), *Attila* (1845–46), *Macbeth* (1847), *I masnadieri* (1846–47), *Jérusalem* (French revised version of *I Lombardi*, 1847), *Il corsaro* (1848), *La battaglia di Legnano* (1849), *Luisa Miller* (1849), *Stiffelio* (1850), *Rigoletto* (1851), *Il trovatore* (1853), *La traviata* (1853), *Les Vêpres siciliennes* (1855), *Simon Boccanegra* (1857, revised 1881), *Aroldo* (revision of *Stiffelio*, 1857), *Un ballo in maschera* (1859), *La forza del destino* (1862), *Don Carlos* (1867, revised 1884), *Aida* (1871), *Otello* (1887), *Falstaff* (1893).

CHORAL *Inno delle nazioni*, Requiem (1874), *Pater noster, Ave Maria, Stabat Mater, Lauda alla Vergine Maria*, Te Deum (1896); *Ave Maria* for soprano and strings; 16 songs; one part song; string quartet (1871).

Verdonck, Cornelis (1563–1625) Flemish singer and composer. He was in the service of Cornelius Pruenen, treasurer and later sheriff of Antwerp, until 1598, then on the death of his patron he served two of his nephews. He was singer at the royal chapel in Madrid 1584–98.

Works include: Magnificat, *Ave gratia plena*, four motets; 21 chansons, 42 madrigals.

Veress, Sándor (1907–1992) Hungarian pianist and composer. He began collecting folk songs in 1929, and settled at Budapest as a teacher of piano and composition and assistant to Bartók at the Scientific Academy of Folk Music.

Veress learnt the piano from his mother and later entered the Budapest Conservatory. He also studied with Bartók and Kodály. In 1929 he studied at the Ethnological Museum and began collecting folk songs.

Works include: the ballet *The Miraculous Pipe* (1937, produced Rome 1941); two symphonies (1940, 1953) and divertimento for orchestra; violin concerto (1939); *Hommage à Paul Klee* for orchestra (1952); clarinet concerto (19882); flute concerto (1989); Concerto for two trombones (1989). Cantata and folk song arranged for unaccompanied chorus; two string quartets (1931, 1937), string trio, trio for oboe, clarinet, and bassoon; violin and piano sonata, cello and piano sonata; two piano sonatas.

Veretti, Antonio (1900–1978) Italian composer. He studied at Bologna and took a diploma, also a newspaper prize in 1927 for the opera *Il medico volante* (after Molière). In 1943 he became director of the Conservatorio della Gioventù Italiana in Rome and in 1950 of the Pesaro Conservatory.

Works include: the opera *Il favorito del re* (1932); ballets *Il galante tiratore* and *Una favola di Andersen* (1934); film music; oratorio *Il figliuol prodigo* (1942), *Sinfonia sacra* for men's chorus and orchestra; *Sinfonia musiciana* (1929), *Sinfonia epica* (1938) and *Ouverture della Campanella* for orchestra.

verismo term in music referring to opera of 'extravagant realism', particularly Italian late Romantic opera of Leoncavallo, Puccini, and others.

Verklärte Nacht/Transfigured Night string sextet by Schoenberg, op. 4, composed September 1899, first performed Vienna, 18 March 1902. Arranged for string orchestra c. 1917, revised 1942; given as ballet, *The Pillar of Fire*, at the New York Metropolitan Opera on 8 April 1942. It was inspired by a poem in R Dehmel's *Weib und die Welt*.

Véronique operetta by Messager (libretto by A Vanloo and G Duval), produced Paris, Bouffes Parisiens, 10 December 1898. Hélène, disguised as shopgirl Véronique, meets the man she has arranged to marry, the Viscount Florestan. He falls in love with 'Véronique' and is shocked to meet her as Hélène at the altar, but nevertheless a happy ending.

Verschworenen, Die, oder Der häusliche Krieg/The Conspirators, or Domestic Warfare operetta by Schubert (libretto by I F Casteli, based on Aristophanes' *Lysistrata*), never performed in Schubert's lifetime; produced Frankfurt, 29 August 1861. Crusaders' wives attempt to convert their husbands to peace by withdrawing sexual favours.

verse anthem see ◊anthem.

verset, French, *versetto* Italian in music, a short organ piece, often but not necessarily fugal and frequently incorporating or containing some reference to a given plainsong tune. The name is derived from the former practice in the Roman Catholic service of replacing every other sung verse of psalms, etc. by interludes on the organ to relieve the supposed monotony of plainsong.

Versunkene Glocke, Die opera by Zöllner (libretto by composer, based on G Hauptmann's play), produced Berlin, Theater des Westens, 8 July 1899.
See also ◊*Campana Sommersa, La*.

vertical an adjective applied to the combination of simultaneous sounds, as seen on the page, in contrast to the horizontal appearance of notes in succession.

Vesalii Icones/Images of Vesalius theatre piece by Maxwell Davies for dancer, solo cello, and instrumental ensemble; composed 1969, first performed London, 9 December 1969. The 14 movements are based on anatomical drawings in a treatise (1543) by the physician Andreas Vesalius depicting Christ's Passion and Resurrection.

vespers the seventh of the eight canonical hours in the Catholic church; the seventh Roman Catholic office (or non-Eucharistic service) of the day. It is also used by the Anglican Church to refer to ◊evensong. Claudio Monteverdi and W A Mozart composed notable settings for this service.

The phrase **Sicilian Vespers** refers to the massacre of the French rulers in Sicily 1282, signalled by vesper bells on Easter Monday.

Vespri siciliani, I (Verdi). See ◊*Vêpres siciliennes, Les.*

Vestale, La opera by Mercadante (libretto, in Italian, by S Cammarano), produced Naples, Teatro San Carlo, 10 March 1840.

Opera by Spontini (libretto, in French, by V J E de Jouy, based on Winckelmann's *Monumenti antichi inediti*), produced Paris, Opéra, 16 January 1807. Holy fire of vestal virgins becomes extinguished as Julia attempts to elope with former betrothed Lycinius; as she is led to execution lightning rekindles the flame and she is spared.

Viadana, Lodovico (c. 1560–1627), real name Grossi da Viadana Italian composer. He was a prolific composer, writing mostly vocal church music. His works include 100 *Concerti ecclesiastici* 1602, for one–four voices with organ continuo.

Viadana studied with Costanzo Porta and before 1590 was appointed maestro di cappella at Mantua Cathedral. In 1596 he joined the Franciscan order, in 1609 became maestro di cappella at Concordia, and in 1612 at Fano Cathedral. In 1615 he went to live at Piacenza, whence he retired to the Franciscan monastery at Gualtieri.

Works include: Masses, psalms, and other church music; 100 *Concerti ecclesiastici* for one–four voices with organ continuo (1602); madrigals, canzonets.

Viaggio a Reims, Il, ossia L'albergo del giglio d'oro/The Journey to Rheims, or the Golden Lily Inn opera by Rossini (libretto by G L Balochi), produced Paris, Théâtre-Italien, 19 June 1825. The opera failed but the music was largely re-used in *Le Comte Ory* (1828). Assorted national types including Lord Sidney, Don Profondo and Belfiore are delayed at the inn of Madame Cortese on way to coronation at Rheims.

vibraphone electrophonic percussion instrument resembling a ◊xylophone but with metal keys. Electrically driven discs spin within resonating tubes under each key to add a tremulant effect that can be controlled in length with a foot pedal.

vibrato a rapid fluctuation of pitch for dynamic and expressive effect. It is distinct from a tremolo, which is a fluctuation in intensity of the same note.

Vicentino, Nicola (1511–c. 1576) Italian composer and theorist. He sought to revive the Greek modes in his madrigals, and invented an instrument he called the archicembalo, which could play various microtones.

Vicentino studied with Adrian Willaert at Venice, then entered the service of Ippolito d'Este, cardinal of Ferrara, with whom he went to live in Rome. His treatise *L'antica musica ridotta alla moderna prattica* 1555 involved him in a controversy with Vicente Lusitano in which he was defeated. He returned to Ferrara with his patron and became his maestro di cappella. He wrote madrigals and motets.

Victoria, Tomás Luis de (1548–1611) Spanish composer. He was the greatest Spanish composer of the Renaissance. He wrote only sacred music, including 20 Masses, 52 motets, and many other liturgical pieces, and is noted for his expressive settings of the Mass (for example, *Ave regina caelorum*) and other Latin texts.

Victoria sang as a boy at the cathedral of his native Ávila. In 1565 he received a grant from Philip II and went to Rome, where he became a priest and singer at the German College. From 1569 he was employed at the Roman church of Sta Maria di Monserrato; from 1571 he taught music at the German College, ans was choirmaster there from 1573 to about 1577. He was a chaplain at San Girolamo della Carità 1578–85. From 1587 to 1603 he was chaplain to the dowager empress María, Philip II's sister and the widow of Maximilian II, at the convent of the Descalzas Reales in Madrid, where the empress lived and her daughter, the Infanta Margaret, became a nun. On the death of the empress in 1603 he wrote an *Officium defunctorum* (Requiem Mass) for six voices.

Victoria is as great a master of polyphony in the Spanish school as his contemporaries Palestrina, Lassus, and Byrd were in the Italian, Flemish, and English.

Works include: 20 Masses (including two Requiems), 18 Magnificats, one *Nunc dimittis*, nine Lamentations, 25 responsories, 13 antiphons, eight polychoral psalms, 52 motets, 36 hymns, one Litany, two Passions, three Sequences.

Victory opera by R R Bennett (libretto by B Cross, after Conrad), produced Covent Garden, 13 April 1970. Reclusive Heyst is tempted into a fuller life by chorus girl Lena.

Vida breve, La/Life is Short opera by Falla (libretto in Spanish, by C F Shaw), produced Nice, in French, translated by P Milliet, 1 April 1913. Gypsy Salud hopes to marry Paco but is jilted for Carmela. Salud confronts Paco at the wedding and falls dead.

Vidal, Peire (fl. c. 1175–c. 1210) French troubadour. About 50 of his poems are preserved, 12 with music.

vielle organisée (French 'organed'; 'not organized'; 'hurdy-gurdy'; Italian *lira organizata*) musical instrument, a ◊hurdy-gurdy (*vielle*) into which are incorporated one or two sets (stops) or organ pipes. These can be made to sound separately or together, or shut off at will.

Haydn wrote five concertos for two of these instruments.

Vienna State Opera the greatest Austrian opera house and company, originally known as the Vienna Court Opera. There have been various theatres associated with the company, from the Theater bei der Hofburg 1748 to the most recent theatre, rebuilt 1955. The company reached its height in the 1890s when Mahler was conductor.

Vie parisienne, La/Life in Paris operetta by Offenbach (libretto by H Meilhac and L Halévy), produced Paris, Théâtre du Palais-Royal, 31 October 1866. Bobinet and Gardefeu trick Swedish aristocrats on tour in Paris, posing as guests in the Grand Hôtel. Gardefeu pursues the Baroness while her husband is too preoccupied with other women to notice.

Vier ernste Gesänge/Four Serious Songs settings by Brahms for baritone and piano of words from the Bible, op. 121, composed May 1896. The corresponding passages in English are 'One thing befalleth', 'So I returned', 'O death, how bitter is thy sting', 'Though I speak with the tongues of men and of angels'.

Vierjährige Posten, Der/The Four Years' Sentry comic opera by Schubert (libretto by T Körner), composed 1815, but never performed in Schubert's lifetime. Produced Dresden, Opera, 23 September 1896. Abandoned French soldier is in trouble for desertion with returning army, after four-year dalliance with village girl.

Vier letzte Lieder (R Strauss). See ◊*Four Last Songs*.

Vierne, Louis (1870–1937) French organist and composer. He studied with Franck and Widor at the Paris Conservatory. He became assistant organist to Widor and succeeded him as organist at the church of Saint-Sulpice and later became organist at Notre-Dame, where he died at the console.

Works include: *Messe solennelle* for chorus and two organs; symphonies; string quartets; sonatas for violin and piano and cello and piano; six symphonies (1899–1930) 24 *Pièces* *en style libre*, 24 *Pièces de fantaisie*, and other works for organ.

Vieuxtemps, Henry (1820–1881) Belgian violinist and composer. He was admired for his virtuosity in playing his own works and those of other composers. He is remembered for his seven violin concertos and several short pieces for violin. He taught at the St Petersburg and Brussels Conservatories.

He learnt the violin at home and at the age of six was able to play a concerto by Rode. At seven he was taken on tour by his father; Charles Bériot heard him and offered to teach him at Brussels. In 1828 he performed in Paris, and in 1833 he went on tour in Germany and Austria, remaining in Vienna to study counterpoint with Simon Sechter. In 1834 he first visited London, where he met Paganini, and the following year he studied composition with Antonin Reicha in Paris. He afterwards travelled long and extensively in Europe and in 1844 went to the USA. In 1845 he married the Viennese pianist Josephine Eder. In 1846–52 he was violin professor at the St Petersburg Conservatory. In 1871–73 he taught at the Brussels Conservatory; he suffered a stroke in 1873, and finally resigned in 1879.

Works include: seven violin concertos, *Fantaisie-Caprice, Ballade et Polonaise*, and other pieces for violin and orchestra; violin and piano sonata; cadenzas for Beethoven's violin concerto.

vihuela Spanish plucked-string instrument, approximately guitar-shaped but strung like a lute with six paired courses and normally ten frets. The name, used for any stringed instrument with a flat back, appears in the 13th century, and as early as the 14th century there is a distinction between the *vihuela de arco* (bowed vihuela) and the *vihuela de peñola* (plectrum vihuela) which, with the development of finger-plucking, became the *vihuela de mano*. It seems likely that the *vihuela de arco* evolved into the viol at the end of the 15th century.

Its repertory appears mainly in seven printed anthologies of the 16th century, starting with Luis Milan's *El maestro* (1536), Luis de Narváez's *Delphin de música* (1538) and Alonso Mudarra's *Tres libros* (1546). Some pieces in these volumes appear also in French lute collections, and there is little technical difference between lute and vihuela music except that the vihuela, with its small body and long neck, was able to be played in higher positions than the lute, as exploited particularly in the collections of Valderrábano (1547) and Fuenllana (1554).

Vilar, José Teodor (1836–1905) Spanish composer and conductor. Returning to Barcelona from his studies in Paris in 1863, he became conductor at one of the minor theatres in Barcelona, and later at the principal theatre. He also did much teaching.

He studied with the cathedral organist Ramón Vilanova (1801–1870) at Barcelona and in 1859 went to Paris to study piano with Henri Herz and composition with François Bazin (1816–1878) and Jacques Halévy.

Works include: the zarzuelas *La romería de Recaseéns* (1867), *L'ultim rey de Magnolia* (1868), *Los pescadores de San Pol* (1869), *Una prometensa* (1870), *La rambla de las flores* (1870), *Pot més que pinta* (1870), *La lluna en un cove*, *L'esca del pecat* (1871), *La torre del amore* (1871).

Village Romeo and Juliet an opera in prologue and three acts by Delius (libretto by composer, after Keller's *Leute von Seldwyla*), produced Berlin, Komische Oper, 21 February 1907. Sali and Vreli are encouraged by the Dark Fiddler to leave their warring fathers and wander through Paradise Garden to liebestod on river.

Villa-Lobos, Heitor (1887–1959) Brazilian composer and conductor. He absorbed Russian and French influences in the 1920s to create Neo-Baroque works in Brazilian style, using native colours and rhythms. His gift for melody is displayed in the 'Chôros' (serenades) series 1920–29 for various ensembles, and the series of nine *Bachianas Brasileiras* 1930–45, treated in the manner of Bach. His other works include guitar and piano solos, chamber music, choral works, film scores, operas, and 12 symphonies.

After studying the cello for a while, Villa-Lobos became a pianist and for some time toured as a concert artist. In 1912 he began to explore his country's folk music and in 1915 gave the first concert devoted to his own works at Rio de Janeiro. A government grant enabled him to live in Paris for a few years from 1923, but on his return he did much useful work as a conductor and music educationist, being appointed director of music education for the schools in the capital in 1930. In 1929 he published a book on Brazilian folk music, *Alma de Brasil*.

Works include: the operas *Izath* (1914, concert performance 1940), *Yerma* (1956, produced 1971); musical comedy *Magdalena* (1948); ballet *Uirapuru*; oratorio *Vidapura*; 14 works entitled *Chôros* cast in a new form and consisting of four for orchestra, one for piano and orchestra, one for two pianos and orchestra, two for chorus and orchestra, and six for various combinations and solo instruments (1920–28); orchestral works including symphonic poem *Amazonas*, *Bachianas Brasileiras* (nine suites in the spirit of Bach, 1930–44), 12 symphonies (1916–57); five piano concertos, two cello concertos, harp concerto; nonet for wind, harp, percussion, and chorus, quintet for wind instruments (1923); 17 string quartets (1915–58), three piano trios (1911–18); four sonata-fantasies for violin and piano (1912–23); a very large number of piano works; songs.

villancico a type of verse with a refrain and a complex rhyme-scheme; also the music to which such poems were set, at first tunes without harmony, later pieces similar to madrigals; sometimes a composition for solo voices, strings, and organ to sacred words, especially connected with the Nativity.

villanella (Italian 'country girl') Italian part-song of the middle 16th to the earlier 17th centuries, set to rustic words and light in character.

Villanella rapita, La/The Ravished Country Girl opera by Bianchi (libretto by G Bertati, based on J M Favart's *Le Caprice amoureux*), produced Venice, Teatro San Moisè, autumn 1783. Mozart wrote an additional quartet and a trio for the Vienna performance, 25 November 1785. Mandina is abducted by the Count before her wedding to Pippo. Her father Biaggio and her betrothed rescue her after questioning her allegiance, and welcome her back to the village.

villanelle in French music a *villanelle* is not the equivalent of the Italian *villanella* and the Spanish *villancico*, but a vocal setting of a poem in *villanelle* form, which consists of stanzas of three lines, the first and third lines of the opening stanza being repeated alternately as the third line of the succeeding stanzas. Best known example is first song of Berlioz' cycle *Les Nuits d'été*.

Villi, Le/The Witches opera by Puccini (libretto by F Fontana), produced Milan, Teatro dal Verme, 31 May 1884. Roberto abandons his betrothed, Anna, who dies of grief. When he later returns Anna's ghost haunts him with other ghosts of jilted girls, dancing with him until he dies.

vina Indian plucked string instrument in a variety of forms, including the ◊sitar, combining features of a ◊zither and ◊lute and consisting of a fretted or unfretted fingerboard overlaying dual resonant chambers. It has ◊sympathetic strings, giving a shimmering tone.

Vinaccesi, Benedetto (c. 1670–c. 1719) Italian composer. He was maestro di cappella to Prince Ferdinand Gonzaga di Castiglione in 1687, and was appointed second organist at St Mark's, Venice in 1704.

Works include: two operas (lost); four oratorios (only *Susanna* (1694) extant); motets and other church music; six *Suonate da camera* and 12 *Sonate da chiesa* for two violins and continuo.

Vincentius, Caspar (c. 1580–1624) Flemish composer and organist. He provided a *bassus generalis* to the three volumes of Abraham Schadaeus's *Promptuarium musicum*, and in 1617 added a fourth volume of his own. He also wrote a continuo part for Lassus' *Magnum opus musicum*.

Vincentius was a choirboy at the Imperial chapel in Vienna 1595–97. While serving as town organist at Speyer, about 1602–15, he met Schadaeus. He later held appointments at Worms and, from 1618 until his death, at Würzburg.

Vinci, Leonardo (c. 1690–1730) Italian composer. He wrote chiefly for the stage, and composed 11 comedies before progressing to opere serie, of which he wrote more than 20. His most successful opera was his last, *Artaserse* 1730.

Vinci studied with Gaetano Greco at the Conservatorio dei Poveri di Gesù Cristo in Naples. From 1919 he established himself as a composer of Neapolitan dialect *commedie musicali*, and produced his first opera seria in 1722. Appointed as acting maestro di cappella at court in 1725, he was from 1728 also maestro at his old Conservatory, where his pupils included the composer Pergolesi.

Works include: commedie musicali: *Lo cecato fauzo* (1719, lost), *Le zite 'n galera* (1722); opere serie: *Silla dittatore* (1723), *L'Astianatte* (1725), *Siroe* (1726), *La caduta dei Decemviri* (1727), *Artaserse* (1730), and 19 others; six cantatas; chamber music.

Vingt regards sur l'Enfant Jésus work for piano in 20 sections by Messiaen; composed 1944, first perfomed Paris, 26 March 1945, by Yvonne Loriod.

viol member of a Renaissance family of bowed six-stringed musical instruments with flat backs, fretted fingerboards, and narrow shoulders that flourished particularly in England about 1540–1700, before their role was taken by the violins. Normally perform-

ing as an ensemble or consort, their repertoire is a development of ◊madrigal style with idiomatic decoration.

The three principal instruments, treble, tenor, and bass, are played upright, resting on the leg (da gamba), and produce a transparent, harmonious sound. The smaller instruments are rested on the knee, not held under the chin. Tuning is largely in fourths, like a guitar. The double bass viol or **violone**, used in Baroque orchestras as bass-line support to the harpsichord or organ, became the model for the present-day ◊double bass.

viola bowed, stringed musical instrument, the alto member of the ◊violin family. Its four strings are tuned C3, G3, D4, and A5. With its dark, vibrant tone, it is often used for music of reflective character, as in Stravinsky's *Elegy* 1944 or Britten's *Lachrymae* 1950. Its principal function is harmonic in string quartets and orchestras. Concertos have been written for the viola by composers such as Telemann, Berlioz, Walton, Hindemith, and Bartók.

Viola unfinished opera by Smetana (libretto by E Krasnohorská, on Shakespeare's *Twelfth Night*), begun 1883.

The open strings of the viola.

viola alta (Italian 'high viola') musical instrument, an exceptionally large ◊viola designed by Hermann Ritter and made by Hörlein of Würzburg in the 1870s for use in the orchestra at the Wagner festivals at Bayreuth. In 1898 a fifth string was added, tuned to the E of the highest violin string.

viola bastarda (Italian 'bastard viol') Italian name for the lyra viol, called *bastarda* because it was midway in size between the tenor viol and the bass viol.

viola da braccio (Italian 'arm viol') the generic name for members of the ◊violin family in the 16th and early 17th centuries, since the smaller instruments were played on the arm and not, as was the case with the viola da gamba family, on or between the legs. Since the cello was the bass of the family it was known, illogically, as *bassa viola da braccio*. The treble instrument came to be known exclusively by the diminutive *violino*, and *viola da braccio* was reserved for the alto or tenor, shortened to *viola* in Italy and corrupted into *Bratsche* in Germany.

Treble

Tenor or

Bass

The open strings of the treble, tenor, and bass viols.

viola da gamba (Italian 'leg viol') the generic name for the members of the ◊viol family, all of which, small or large, are played on or between the legs. Unlike the violin family they have flat backs, sloping shoulders, six strings, and frets. The smaller instruments of the family gradually went out of use in the course of the 17th century, but the bass was retained as a solo instrument and for ◊continuo playing. Hence in the 18th century viola da gamba normally means the bass viol. Examples of its use are J S Bach's three sonatas with harpsichord and the obbligatos in the *St Matthew Passion*. All the members of the family have been successfully revived in modern times.

viola d'amore (Italian 'love viol') musical instrument, a member of the ◊viol family, though without frets and not *da gamba* ('on the leg') but played under the chin. More substantial than the modern viola, it has seven bowed strings as well as seven ◊sympathetic strings. It was most popular during the Baroque period, but was used occasionally by 19th-century composers, including Giacomo Meyerbeer and Berlioz. It has been revived in the context of the 20th-century ◊authenticity movement.

In the 17th century, viola d'amore referred to a violin with wire strings.

viola da spalla (Italian 'shoulder viola') musical instrument, a portable ◊cello used mainly by wandering musicians in the 17th and 18th centuries, held by a shoulder strap. Also an alternative name for the cello.

viola di bordone (Italian 'drone viol') alternative name for the ◊baryton, a musical instrument.

viola pomposa bowed string instrument of the ◊violin family, very rarely used. It seems to have had five strings, the lower four tuned

as on the viola and the fifth tuned to the E of the violin.

violet the English name sometimes given to the viola d'amore, a musical instrument.

violetta marina (Italian 'little marine viol') special type of viol, allied to the ◊viola d'amore, like which it has ◊sympathetic strings.

violetta piccola (Italian 'small little viol') early name for the treble ◊viol and the ◊violin.

violin bowed, four-stringed musical instrument, the smallest and highest pitched (treble) of the violin family.

The strings are tuned in fifths (G3, D4, A5, and E5).

evolution Developed gradually during the 16th century from a variety of fiddle types, the violin was perfected in Italy by a group of makers including Nicolò Amati, Antonio Stradivari, and Guarneri del Gesù working in Cremona around 1670–1710. Designed without frets and with a complex body curvature to radiate sound, its voicelike tone and extended range established a new humanistic aesthetic of solo instrumental expression and, together with the viola and cello, laid the foundation of the modern orchestra.

Today's violin has not changed in form since that time, but in the late 18th century aspects of the design were modified to

The open strings of the violin.

produce a bigger sound and greater projection for the concert hall and to allow for evolving virtuoso expression. These include a lengthened fingerboard, an angled neck, and larger-sized basebar and soundpost.

repertoire The repertoire for solo violin exceeds that for most other instruments. Composers include Vivaldi, Tartini, J S Bach, Mozart, Beethoven, Brahms, Mendelssohn, Paganini, Elgar, Berg, Bartók, and Carter.

violin family family of bowed stringed instruments developed in 17th-century Italy, which eventually superseded the viols and formed the basis of the modern orchestra. There are four instruments: violin, viola, cello (or violoncello), and the double bass which is descended from the bass viol (or violone).

violino piccolo (Italian 'little violin') small string instrument of the ◊violin family with four strings. It stands a fourth or a minor third above the violin in pitch.

Violins of St Jacques, The opera by Williamson (libretto by W Chappell), produced London, Sadler's Wells, 29 November 1966.

violoncello full name of the ◊cello, tenor member of the ◊violin family.

The open strings of the violoncello.

violoncello piccolo musical instrument, a small ◊cello on which the playing of high passages was easier than on the normal cello. A familiar example of its use is the obbligato in J S Bach's aria 'Mein gläubiges Herze/My heart ever faithful' in the cantata no. 68, *Also hat Gott die Welt geliebt/God so loved the world*.

The open strings of the violino piccolo.

violon d'amour (French 'love violin') musical instrument, the member of the modern string family corresponding to the viola d'amore of the viol family, used in the 18th century, but now obsolete. It had five strings and six ◊sympathetic strings, not touched by

The open strings of the violon d'amour.

the bow but vibrating with those actually played.

violone musical instrument, the double bass of the ◊viol family, similar to the bass viol but larger, with six strings similarly tuned an octave lower. The name was also applied to the double bass of the violin family.

violotta modern string instrument of the ◊violin family, invented by Alfred Stelzner (died 1906) of Dresden. It has four strings tuned so as to stand in pitch between the viola and the cello.

The open strings of the violotta.

Viotti, Giovanni Battista (1755–1824) Italian violinist and composer. He was the most important violinist of his day, encompassing both the earlier Italian tradition of Corelli and the beginnings of the 19th-century French Romantic school. He is best known for his 29 violin concertos. After a successful stay in Paris 1782–92, where he was violinist to Marie Antoinette and founded an opera house, he settled in London, where he became manager of the King's Theatre in 1797.

After studying with Gaetano Pugnani, Viotti joined the court orchestra at Turin in 1775, but obtained leave of absence in 1780 to go on tour with Pugnani. He visited Switzerland, Dresden, Berlin, Warsaw, and St Petersburg, and in 1782 arrived in Paris, where he stayed for ten years. He played at the Concert spirituel, was solo violinist to Marie Antoinette at Versailles 1784–86, conducted some concerts of the Loge Olympique (for which Haydn wrote his 'Paris' symphonies), and from 1788 was involved in the foundation of a new opera company at the Théâtre de Monsieur. In 1792 he went to London, where he played in Salomon's concerts and became acting manager and leader of the orchestra at the King's Theatre opera, but was forced to leave England for political reasons in 1798, and lived near Hamburg, writing an autobiographical sketch. Returning to London in 1801, he withdrew almost completely from music and entered the wine trade, but twice visited Paris (in 1802 and 1814) and in 1819 became director of the Opéra there, finally returning to London in 1823.

Works include: 29 violin concertos (c. 1782–c. 1805); two *Symphonies concertantes* for two violins and orchestra; 15 string quartets (c. 1783–1817); 21 string trios for two violins and cello; violin duos, sonatas, and other pieces; six piano sonatas.

Virdung, Sebastian (c. 1465–c. 1511) German cleric and writer on music. He studied at Heidelberg University. He sang, and then was Kapellmeister at the Palatine court chapel in Heidelberg, and in 1507 became succentor at Konstanz Cathedral. In 1511 he published at Basel his book on musical instruments, *Musica getutscht und ausgezogen*, dedicated to the Bishop of Strasbourg.

virelai (French, from *virer*, 'to turn', and *lai*, 'a song') type of medieval French song with a refrain before and after each verse.

virginal plucked stringed keyboard instrument of the 16th and 17th centuries, often called 'virginals' or 'a pair of virginals' in England, where the term was applied to any quilled keyboard instrument well into the 17th century. The virginal is rectangular or polygonal in shape and is distinguished from the ◊harpsichord and ◊spinet by its strings being set at right angles to the keys, rather than parallel with them.

The most likely explanation of the name is that the instrument was often played by girls. There are several manuscript collections of virginal music by English composers, including *The Fitzwilliam Virginal Book, My Ladye Nevells Booke, Will Forster's Book, Benjamin Cosyn's Book* and *Elizabeth Rogers's Book*.

Vision of St Augustine, The work by Tippett for baritone, chorus, and orchestra (text in Latin); composed 1963–65, first performed London, 19 January 1966, with Fischer-Dieskau.

Visions de l'Amen suite by Messiaen in seven movements for two pianos; composed 1943, first perfomed Paris, 10 May 1943, by Loriod and Messiaen.

Visions Fugitives 20 pieces for piano by Prokofiev; composed 1915–17, first perfomed Petrograd, 15 April 1918, by composer. Orchestral version by Rudolf Barschai.

Vitali, Giovanni Battista (1632–1692) Italian viol player and composer. In 1673 he became maestro di cappella of the Santissimo Rosario, and in 1674 he went to Modena as vice-maestro of the ducal chapel. His oratorio on the execution of the English Duke of Monmouth was produced there in 1686, the year after Monmouth's execution.

Vitali was a pupil of Maurizio Cazzati, maestro di cappella of San Petronio at Bologna, where Vitali himself was a string player and singer from 1658.

Works include: psalms for two–five voices and instruments; oratorios *Il Giono* and *L'ambitione debellata overo La Caduta di Monmouth*; ten cantatas; numerous dances for several instruments; sonatas for two violins and continuo and others for various instrumental combinations.

Vitali, Tomaso (Antonio) (1663–1745) Italian violinist and composer. He was best known for his instrumental music; notably trio sonatas and a celebrated chaconne for violin and keyboard (which has recently come into doubt regarding Vitali's authorship of it).

Vitali was taught by his father, Giovanni Battista ◊Vitali, and was later a member of the court chapel at Modena under him. He taught the violin to distinguished pupils, including Evaristo Dall' Abaco and Jean Baptiste Senallié.

Works include: sonatas for two violins and continuo.

Vitava (Smetana). See ◊*Má Vlast*.

Vitry, Philippe de (1291–1361) French composer, poet, and theorist. One of the masters of ◊ars nova, his works are characterized by contrapuntal intricacy. He wrote four treatises on ars nova and some of his motets survive today.

vivace (Italian 'lively') term used in musical notation, as in *allegro vivace* ('fast and lively').

Vivaldi, Antonio Lucio (1678–1741) Italian Baroque composer, violinist, and conductor. One of the most prolific composers of his day, he was particularly influential through his concertos, several of which were transcribed by J S Bach. He wrote 23 symphonies; 75 sonatas; over 400 concertos, including *The Four Seasons* 1725 for violin and orchestra; over 40 operas; and much sacred music. His work was largely neglected until the 1930s.

Vivaldi was born at Venice. He was taught by his father Giovanni Battista Vivaldi, a violinist at St Mark's, and possibly also by the composer Giovanni Legrenzi. He entered the church in 1693 and was ordained priest in 1703 (being commonly known as *il prete rosso*, 'the red [-haired] priest'), but soon afterwards was given dispensations from priestly duties; he nevertheless later came into conflict with Church authorities for keeping a mistress. He was associated 1703–40 with a girls' orphanage, the Conservatorio dell' Ospedale della Pietà in Venice, for which he wrote oratorios and instrumental music, even sending manuscripts by post during his frequent absences.

His first opera, *Ottone in Villa* was produced in Vicenza in 1713, and was followed by many others in Venice, Florence, Munich, Parma, and Milan. He was in Mantua 1720–23 as *maestro di cappella da camera* to the Margrave Philip of Hesse-Darmstadt, wrote *The Four Seasons* about 1725, and toured Europe 1729–33, but of his extensive travels throughout his career little is known. He returned to Venice in 1739, but his popularity was declining, and two years later he died in poverty in Vienna.

Vivaldi's real importance lies in some 450 concertos for various solo instruments and combinations of instruments, the majority of the violin family, but also woodwind and rare instruments such as the piccolo, viola d'amore, and mandolin; he also wrote 73 sonatas for one and two violins and for cello. In recent years his vocal music has become increasingly admired, in particular the oratorio *Juditha Triumphans*, the settings of the Gloria, and the Serenatas.

Works include: OPERA about 21 extant, including *Tito Manlio* (1720), *Ercole* (1723), *Orlando furioso* (1727); Latin oratorio *Juditha* and others.

SACRED VOCAL including Gloria (two settings), *Salve regina* (3), *Stabat mater*.

INSTRUMENTAL over 230 violin concertos (including *The Four Seasons*, nos. 1–4 of *Il cimento dell'armonia e dell'inventione*, op. 8), about 120 solo concertos (for bassoon, cello, oboe, flute, oboe d'amore, recorder, and mandolin), over 40 double concertos (about 24 for violins, three for two oboes), over 30 ensemble concertos (instruments included clarinets, horns, theorbos, and timpani), nearly 60 string orchestra concertos (without soloists) and over 20 concertos for solo ensemble (without string ripieno; about 90 solo and trio sonatas.

vivo Italian term meaning 'lively, animated', the same as *vivace*, but more rarely used.

Vlad, Roman (1919–) Romanian-born Italian composer. He studied at the Cernauṭi Conservatory but in 1938 settled in Rome, where he finished studies under Casella. He is the author of books on Dallapiccola and Stravinsky.

Works include: the radio opera *Il dottore di vetro* (1959), ballets *La strada sul caffè* (1945) and *La dama delle camelie* (after Dumas); film music; *De profundis* for soprano, chorus, and orchestra; *Divertimento* for 11 instruments; *Studi dodecafonici* for piano.

Vladigerov, Pancho (1899–1978) Bulgarian composer. He studied with Juon and Georg

Schumann in Berlin and at the Sofia Conservatory.

Works include: the opera *Tsar Kaloyan* (1936); incidental music for Strindberg's *A Dream Play*; Bulgarian Rhapsody *Vardar*; two violin concertos (1921, 1968); piano concerto; piano trio; violin and piano sonata; piano pieces; songs.

vocalise a concert work for voice without words, sung on one or more vowels, usually 'ah', which is sustainable over the widest range and allows an open tone. Examples include Rachmaninov's *Vocalise for Soprano and Orchestra* 1912, revised 1915, and Villa-Lobos' *Bachianas Brasileiras No 5* 1938–45.

Electric instruments such as the ◊theremin and ◊ondes Martenot are employed in the manner of a vocalise, with the added advantages of amplification and extended range.

voce (Italian 'voice') term used in musical notation, as in *colla voce* ('with the voice'), directing an accompanist to follow carefully a singer's changes of tempo.

Vogel, (Johannes) Emil (Eduard Bernhard) (1859–1908) German music scholar. He studied at Berlin University and privately. In 1883 he went to Italy as assistant to F X Haberl on his Palestrina edition. From 1893 to 1901 he was librarian of the Musikbibliothek Peters and editor of the Peters *Jahrbuch*.

Vogel, Vladimir Rudolfovich (1896–1984) Swiss composer of German and Russian descent. He studied in Russia, and later with Tiessen and Busoni in Berlin; he settled in Switzerland in 1933. From the time of his violin concerto (1937) he wrote serial music, striving to maintain clarity in his writing and to emphasize the less dissonant aspects of his 12-note rows.

Works include: cantatas *Wagadu's Untergang* for solo voices, chorus, speaking chorus and five saxophones (1930); *Thyl Claes* (after *Till Eulenspiegel*, 1938–45); *Sinfonia fugata*, four studies; *Devise, Tripartita* for orchestra; violin concerto (1937), cello concerto (1955); *Komposition* and *Etude Toccata* for piano.

Vogelhändler, Der/The Bird Dealer operetta by Zeller (libretto by M West and L Held), produced Vienna, Theater an der Wien, 10 January 1891. When village postmistress Christel attempts to secure a job for birdseller boyfriend Adam, a case of mistaken identify causes complications eventually resolved with the couple's reconciliation.

Vogelweide, Walther von der (c. 1170–c. 1230) German poet, minnesinger, and composer. He was in service at the court of Duke Leopold V in Vienna, then led a wandering life in Germany and after 1220 probably lived at an estate given to him at Würzburg. Only a few of his tunes have survived. He appears as a character in Wagner's *Tannhäuser*.

He was a pupil of Reinmar von Hagenau in Austria.

Vogler, Georg Joseph (known as Abbé Vogler) (1749–1814) German composer, teacher, and theorist. He studied in Italy and became music director to the courts of Mannheim, Munich, Stockholm, and Darmstadt. He was a notable teacher; his pupils included Weber, Meyerbeer, and Crusell, and he wrote a number of theoretical works.

Vogler was the son of an instrument maker and violinist. He studied theology at Würzburg and Bamberg Universities, went to Mannheim in 1771, becoming court chaplain the following year, and in 1773 received a scholarship from the Elector to go to Italy. He studied with Padre Martini in Bologna and Palotti in Padua, and in 1775 returned to Mannheim as vice-Kapellmeister. Mozart met him there in 1778 and disliked him. When the electoral court moved to Munich in 1778 Vogler at first remained in Mannheim, but later followed, becoming Kapellmeister in 1784. He was Kapellmeister to the Swedish court in Stockholm 1786–99, but was able to travel extensively, going as far afield as North Africa and Greece. After leaving Stockholm he lived successively in Copenhagen, Berlin, Prague, Vienna, and Munich, until in 1807 he was appointed Kapellmeister to the Grand Duke of Hesse-Darmstadt. His opera *Gustav Adolph och Ebba Brahe* has been revived at Drottningholm.

Works include: *Singspiele: Albert III von Bayern* (1781), *Erwin und Elmire* (1781, Goethe); operas *La Kermesse* (1783), *Castore e Polluce* (1787), *Gustav Adolph och Ebba Brahe* (1788), *Samori* (1804), and others; operetta *Der Kaufmann von Smyrna* (1771); ballet *Jäger-Ballet* (1772); incidental music to Shakespeare's *Hamlet* (1779); choruses for Racine's *Athalie* and Skjöldebrand's *Hermann von Unna*; Masses, seven Requiems, motets, psalms, and other church music; cantata *Ino* (Ramler); symphonies; several piano variations for piano and orchestra; piano trios and much other chamber music; piano and violin sonatas; piano sonatas and variations; six sonatas for two pianos.

voice the human singing voice. Sound is produced by forcing air from the lungs through the larynx and making the vocal cords vibrate. The ◊pitch of the sound can be altered by tightening or loosening the muscles of the larynx, and the sound is amplified and modified by the mouth and nasal cavities.

The term 'voice' is also used to refer to the separate parts of a piece of music – even when they are played rather than sung. It is especially used when talking about the separate lines in ◊counterpoint, such as a ◊fugue in four voices.

There are several categories of singing voice, which depend on how high or low the performer normally sings. Female singers are usually classified as either ◊soprano (the highest voice) or ◊contralto (often shortened to 'alto', the lowest female voice), but sometimes also as ◊mezzo-soprano (a medium-high voice). Boys whose voices have not yet broken sing in the same range as the female voices, but are referred to as ◊trebles and altos, rather than sopranos and contraltos. The main categories of men's voices are ◊tenor (the higher male voice) and ◊bass (the lowest), with ◊baritone between the two, and ◊countertenor above the tenor range. Some men can use ◊falsetto, a sort of false high voice, to sing in the countertenor, alto, and even soprano ranges.

acoustics of the voice The human voice produces sound in the manner of a ◊free-reed instrument, driven by air in the lungs pressurized by contraction of the diaphragm. The sound source is a set of vocal folds, flanges of tissue in the larynx, which act as a flexible valve controlling the escape of air as a series of pulses, creating a sound rich in ◊harmonics. The pitch of this sound can be varied by tension or relaxation of the larynx. The ◊timbre of the voice is created by the resonances of the mouth and nasal cavities, and can be varied by changing the shape of the mouth and throat to produce the different vowel and consonant sounds.

vocal registers Until comparatively recently, theorists divided the voice into different registers, known as the ◊chest voice, throat voice, and ◊head voice, based on what was believed to be the physiological source of voice production; the terms are now used more as a description of tonal quality. These are the equivalent of the low, medium, and high parts of a singer's range, felt rather than produced in those parts of the body. The term 'head voice' was probably used in early music to describe falsetto. Modern vocal registers are categorized primarily by the vocal range and gender of the singer.

voices in counterpoint Western art music has its roots in medieval church music, which was a purely vocal form. As ◊polyphony developed in the late Middle Ages, each line of music was referred to as a 'voice', a practice that persisted even when describing the parts of an instrumental piece. The term refers not only to the separate instruments or singers in an ensemble, but also to the component lines of a contrapuntal work. So, for example, a fugue in four voices may be written for four separate instruments (or singers), but is just as likely to be for a keyboard instrument such as the organ or harpsichord.

voice-leading generally in harmony, the method by which the composer creates continuity within each strand of a harmonic texture; so that in instrumental music, each note of a chord is regarded as part of a separate 'voice', which must lead logically to the next note in that voice within the next chord. Now used more specifically to describe analytical techniques which reduce the harmonic structure of music to its contrapuntal outlines, identifying the principles of voice-leading underlying even the most outwardly complex passages. Voice-leading analysis was originally developed to describe tonal works, especially those of the Austro-German tradition from Bach to Brahms; however, its principles have in recent years also been widely applied to pre-tonal, post-tonal and non-Germanic repertoires. See Heinrich ◊Schenker.

Voice of Ariadne, The opera by Thea Musgrave (libretto by A Elguera, after Henry James's *The Last of the Valerii*); composed 1972–73, first performed Aldeburgh, 11 June 1974. Count Valerio becomes obsessed with an excavated statue of Ariadne, neglecting his wife, until Countess merges her voice with that of the goddess.

Voices work by Henze for mezzo, tenor, and instrumental ensemble (22 settings based on texts by Ho Chi Minh (*Prison Song*), E Fried, Brecht, M Enzensberger and others); composed 1973, first performed London, 4 January 1974.

voices the parts in a polyphonic composition, even those for instruments.

voice-to-MIDI converter microphone which sends human vocal input to a synthesizer. This system of singing to run a synthesizer does not work well unless the singer has perfect pitch, so it is not commonly used.

voicing in the construction of an ◊organ, the production of particular qualities of tone by mechanical means, and more particularly the control of the tone of a whole range of pipes governed by a single stop in such a way that the tone-colour is exactly the same throughout.

Also, regulating the mechanism of a piano so that its response to the player is even across the range: the response to the player's touch may be made quite 'heavy' and resistant, or 'light' like a hair-trigger. Also, in piano playing, the emphasis of one voice over another simultaneously played note, usually in order to create a singing effect.

voix céleste (French 'heavenly voice') in an ◊organ, an 8-ft stop with two pipes to each note, one tuned slightly sharper than the other, so that they produce a quivering effect.

Voix Humaine, La/The Human Voice tragédie lyrique (monodrama) by Poulenc (libretto by Cocteau), produced Paris, Opéra-Comique, 6 February 1959. Jilted woman in fruitless telephone conversation with her lover strangles herself with the flex.

Volans, Kevin (1949–) South African composer. His music combines avant-garde techniques with native African idioms. The opera *The Man Who Strides the Wind* was performed at the 1993 Almeida Festival, London.

He studied with Kagel and Stockhausen at Cologne. He was composer-in-residence at Princeton University in 1992.

Works include: *Chevron* (1989) and *One Hundred Frames* (1991) for orchestra; *White Man Sleeps* for two harpsichords, viola da gamba, and percussion (1982), four string quartets: no. 1 *White Man Sleeps* (1986), no. 2 *Hunting: Gathering* (1987), no. 3 *The Songlines* (1988); no. 4 *The Ramanujan Notebook* (1990); *She Who Sleeps with a small blanket* for percussion (1986); *Kneel my Dance* for two pianos (1985, six pianos, 1992); *Cicada* for two pianos (1994); electronic music.

Volkmann, (Friedrich) Robert (1815–1883) German composer. He spent much of his life teaching music in Budapest, where he became professor of composition at the Hungarian National Music Academy in 1875. As a composer he was influenced by Schumann and Mendelssohn.

Volkmann was taught music by his father, who was a schoolmaster and cantor, and another local musician taught him to play string instruments. In 1836 he went to Leipzig for further study, and was a private music tutor in Prague 1839–41. He lived and taught at Budapest 1841–54 and Vienna 1854–75, then returned to Budapest as professor of composition at the National Music Academy.

Works include: incidental music for Shakespeare's *Richard III*; two Masses for male voices; two symphonies, three serenades, Festival Overture for orchestra; *Concertstück* for piano and orchestra; cello concerto, six string quartets, two piano trios and other chamber music; two sonatinas for violin and piano, violin and piano pieces, cello and piano pieces; sonata and about 20 other op. nos. for piano; several piano duet works; nine op. nos. of songs.

Volkonsky, Andrei Mikhailovich (1933–) Russian composer. He is a modernist among Russian composers, using a form of the 12-note system. Discouraged from composing by the Soviet authorities, he emigrated to Israel in 1973.

Volkonsky studied piano with Dinu Lipatti and composition with Nadia Boulanger in Paris, and in 1948 went to Moscow to study with Yuri Shaporin.

Works include: cantata *The Image of the World* (1953); *The Laments of Shchaza* for soprano and chamber orchestra; concerto for orchestra (1954); piano quintet (1954); viola sonata.

Volkslied (German 'folksong') popular German song. Although Germany possesses a treasury of old folksongs, many of which became hymns for the Lutheran church, the term *Volkslied* no longer exclusively or even principally designates them: what Germans now mean by *Volkslied* is a type of popular song, such as Silcher's *Loreley*, the composers of which are known (which is not the case with genuine folksongs), and which have passed into general currency.

volkstümlich (German adj. from *Volkstum*, 'folk matters, folklore') word used in Germany to describe popular music that has become or is likely to become part of the nation's musical heritage, without actually belonging to traditional folk music.

Volo di Notte/Night Flight opera in one act by Dallapiccola (libretto by the composer, after St-Exupéry), produced Florence, 18 May 1940. Airfield director Rivière is a pioneer in promoting night flights during the 1930s, but his stubborn insistence is partially responsible for the death of Simona Fabien's pilot husband, whose plane runs out of fuel.

volta (Italian 'time, turn, jump') word used in such musical directions as *prima volta* ('first time'), *seconda volta* ('second time'), *ancora una*

volta ('once again'). It is also the name of an old dance including a characteristic jump. See also ◊lavolta.

voluntary a generic term for a quasi-improvisatory composition of the 16th century, but more specifically a piece for solo organ played at the beginning or end of a church service. As the name suggests, the organ voluntary is often free in style, and may be improvised. During the 16th century voluntaries were usually short contrapuntal pieces, without a ◊cantus firmus ('fixed melody'). In the 17th and 18th centuries they developed a more secular style, incorporating elements of the suite, sonata, toccata, and even the operatic aria. Composers of voluntaries include Purcell, John Blow, and Samuel Wesley.

Vom Fischer un syner Fru/The Fisherman and his Wife dramatic cantata by Schoeck (libretto by composer, after P O Runge, after Grimm); composed 1928–30, produced Dresden, Staatsoper, 3 October 1930, conductor Busch. Fisherman catches turbot which turns out to be a prince under a spell; fisher wife expects series of wishes to be fulfilled.

Von deutscher Seele romantic cantata by Pfitzner for soloists, chorus, and orchestra (text after Eichendorff); composed 1921, first performed Berlin, 27 January 1922.

Von Heute auf Morgen/From Today until Tomorrow opera in one act by Schoenberg (libretto by 'Max Blonda', the composer's wife Gertrud), produced Frankfurt, 1 February 1930. Husband and wife quarrel over supposed lovers and are then reconciled, in 12-tone conversation piece.

von Karajan, Herbert Austrian conductor. See ◊Karajan, Herbert von.

Voříšek, Jan Václav (1791–1825) Bohemian composer and organist. He became pianist and conductor to the Philharmonic Society at Vienna in 1818 and court organist in 1823. He was an important contemporary and admirer of Beethoven and was a successful composer in a wide variety of genres.

He was taught by his father, who was a schoolmaster, and later by Václav Jan Tomášek (1774–1850). He went to Vienna in 1813 and when Johann Nepomuk Hummel (1778–1837) left Vienna for Stuttgart in 1816, he recommended Voříšek as piano teacher to all his pupils.

Works include: church music, including Mass (1824); symphony; duet for cello and piano; divertissement for two pianos; piano works.

Voyevoda opera by Tchaikovsky (libretto by composer and A N Ostrovsky, based on a play by the latter), produced Moscow, 11 February 1869. Elderly Voyevoda (provincial governor) attempts to wed sister of his betrothed but is thwarted by a replacement governor.

Vos, Laurent de (1533–1580), or Voz Flemish composer. He worked at Antwerp Cathedral and was appointed music director and choirmaster at Cambrai Cathedral by the archbishop Louis de Berlaymont. When the latter's place was usurped by Baron d'Inchy, Voz composed a motet compiled from words from the Psalms in such a way as to attack Inchy, who had Voz hanged without trial. He was the brother of the painter Martin de Vos.

Works include: motets, chansons.

Vrchlický, Jaroslav (1853–1912) Czech poet and playwright. Works based on his writings include Dvořák, opera *Armida*, oratorio *St Ludmilla*; Fibich, operatic trilogy *Hippodamia* and melodramas *Haakon* and *Queen Emma*; J B Forster, melodramas *The Three Riders* and *The Legend of St Julia*; Janáček, choral work *Amarus*; Novák, opera *A Night at Karlstein*.

Vrieslander, Otto (1880–1950) German musicologist and composer. He studied at the Cologne Conservatory, settled at Munich in 1906, and went to live at Locarno in Switzerland in 1920. As a musicologist he was a pupil of Schenker, whose unfinished *Harmonielehre* he completed. He also wrote on C P E Bach and edited some of his works.

Works include: songs from *Des Knaben Wunderhorn*, on Giraud's 'Pierrot lunaire'

(1904) and to words by Goethe, Keller, and Theodor Storm.

VS (Italian *volti subito*, 'turn at once') in musical notation, term often written at the foot of a right-hand page in manuscript music as an indication that a quick turn is necessary in order to be ready for what follows on the next page.

Vučković, Vojislav (1910–1942) Yugoslav composer, musicologist, and conductor. He studied in Prague and became professor and conductor at Belgrade. He was murdered by the Nazi police.

Works include: several choral compositions; two symphonies, three symphonic poems; string quartet; two songs for soprano and wind instruments.

Vuillaume, Jean-Baptiste (1798–1875) French violin and cello maker. Established independently in Paris, 1828.

Vulpius, Melchior (c. 1570–1615) German composer and writer on music. He became cantor at Weimar in 1602 and remained there until his death. He harmonized many hymn tunes by other composers and wrote a treatise, *Musicae compendium* 1608.

Works include: *Sacrae cantiones* for five–eight voices, canticles, hymns for four–five voices, and other sacred music; *St Matthew Passion* (1613).

vuota (Italian 'void, empty') musical direction to string players to play a note or notes on an open string. Also the equivalent of GP, 'general pause'.

Vyšehrad (Smetana). See ◊*Má Vlast*.

Wächterlieder (German 'watchmen's songs') songs formerly used in Germany by night watchmen in the streets to announce the hours and by fire-watchers on church towers to proclaim festival days, . They were often folksongs and some have passed into currency as hymns for the Lutheran Church.

Wacław z Szamotuł see Wacław ◊Szamotulczyk.

Wadsworth, Stephen (1953–) US stage director, librettist, and translator. He directed operas by Monteverdi with Skylight Opera, Milwaukee, from 1982. He wrote libretto for Bernstein's *A Quiet Place* (1983) and directed it in Milan and Vienna. Productions for Seattle Opera include *Jenůfa* and Gluck's *Orphée*; *Fidelio* and *Clemenza di Tito* for Scottish Opera, 1991. San Francisco 1990, *Die Entführung*. Covent Garden debut 1992, *Alcina*; also translated operas by Handel.

Waffenschmied (von Worms), Der/The Armourer (of Worms) opera by Lortzing (libretto by composer, based on F J W Ziegler's comedy *Liebhaber und Nebenbuhler in einer Person*), produced Vienna, Theater an der Wien, 31 May 1846. Weigl's opera *Il rivale di se stesso/His own Rival*, production Milan 1808, was based on the same play. Marie, daughter of armourer Stadinger, is wooed by Count Liebenau in his own person and, successfully, as an apprentice smith, Conrad. Marie's father Hans Stadinger opposes the match but eventually gives in.

Wagenaar, Bernard (1894–1971) Dutch-born US composer. He studied with his father, Johan Wagenaar, and at the Utrecht Conservatory and learnt the violin and keyboard instruments. In 1921 he settled in New York, joined the New York Philharmonic Orchestra and from 1927 taught at the Juilliard Graduate School there.

Works include: the chamber opera *Pieces of Eight* (1944); four symphonies (1926–46), sinfonietta, divertimento, *Feuilleton*. for orchestra; violin concerto, triple concerto for flute, harp, and cello (1935); three string quartets (1932–60), concertino for eight instruments; violin and piano sonata, sonatina for cello; three Chinese songs for voice, flute, harp, and piano; piano sonata; Eclogue for organ; including settings of Edna St Vincent Millay.

Wagenaar, Johan (1862–1941) Dutch composer. He wrote operas and orchestral pieces, and was noted for his orchestration. He taught at the conservatories of Utrecht and The Hague. He was the father of US composer Bernard Wagenaar.

He studied with Rijk (Richard) Hol (1825–1904) and with Heinrich von Herzogenberg in Berlin. He succeeded Hol as organist at Utrecht Cathedral in 1888 and became director of the conservatory there in 1904, also conductor of a choral society. In 1919 he became director of the Royal Conservatory at The Hague, retiring in 1937 in favour of Sem Dresden.

Works include: the operas *The Doge of Venice* (1901), *El Cid* (after Corneille, 1916), and *Jupiter amans* (1925); overtures to Shakespeare's *Taming of the Shrew*, Goldoni's *Philosophical Princess*, Kleist's *Amphitryon*, and Rostand's *Cyrano de Bergerac* (1905), overture *Saul and David* (1906), funeral march and waltz suite for orchestra; fantasy on Dutch folk songs for male chorus and orchestra, female choruses with piano; violin and piano pieces; piano pieces; songs.

Wagenseil, Georg Christoph (1715–1777)
Austrian composer. He was also organist to the dowager Empress Elisabeth Christine 1741–50, and was appointed music master to the Empress Maria Theresa and her daughters. Mozart at the age of six played at court a concerto by Wagenseil, who turned pages for him.

He studied in Vienna with Johann Fux and others and in 1735 was recommended for a court scholarship, becoming court composer in 1739.

Works include: the operas *Ariodante* (1745), *Le cacciatrici amanti* (1755), and about ten others (six to libretti by Metastasio); oratorios *La rendenzione* and *Gioas, rè di Giuda* (both 1735); nearly 20 Masses, Requiem, motets, and other church music; symphonies; keyboard concertos; divertimenti for solo keyboard.

Wagenseil, Johann Christoph (1633–1708)
German historian and librarian. He wrote a treatise on the art of the Meistersinger, published in 1697, which served Richard Wagner as a source for *Die Meistersinger*.

Wagner, (Wilhelm) Richard (1813–1883)
German opera composer. He revolutionized the 19th-century conception of opera, envisaging it as a wholly new art form in which musical, poetic, and scenic elements should be unified through such devices as the ◊leitmotif. His operas include *Tannhäuser* 1845, *Lohengrin* 1848, and *Tristan und Isolde* 1865. In 1872 he founded the Festival Theatre in Bayreuth; his masterpiece *Der Ring des Nibelungen/The Ring of the Nibelung*, a sequence of four operas, was first performed there 1876. His last work, *Parsifal*, was produced 1882.

Wagner's early career was as director of the Magdeburg Theatre, where he unsuccessfully produced his first opera *Das Liebesverbot/ Forbidden Love* 1836. He lived in Paris 1839–42 and conducted the Dresden Opera House 1842–48. He fled Germany to escape arrest for his part in the 1848 revolution, but in 1861 he was allowed to return. He won the favour of Ludwig II of Bavaria 1864 and was thus able to set up the Festival Theatre in Bayreuth. The Bayreuth tradition was continued by his wife Cosima (1837–1930; Liszt's daughter, whom he married after her divorce from Hans von ◊Bülow); by his son **Siegfried Wagner** (1869–1930), a composer of operas such as *Der Bärenhäuter*; and by later descendants.

Wagner's father was a clerk to the Leipzig city police; he died six months after Wagner's birth, and Wagner's mother moved to Dresden and married the actor and painter Ludwig Geyer in 1815, who in turn died in 1821. Wagner learnt the piano but tried to read vocal scores of operas instead of practising and also acquired knowledge of opera from two elder sisters who were both stage singers. He wrote poems and a tragedy at the age of about 13, and at 14 went to school at Leipzig, where the family had returned. There he heard Beethoven's works and tried to imitate them in compositions of his own. In 1830 Heinrich Dorn conducted Wagner's overture *Columbus* in the theatre, but it was received with scorn as a very crude work. He then studied harmony and counterpoint with Christian Weinlig at St Thomas's School and entered the university in 1831. At 19 he began an opera, *Die Hochzeit*, but on the advice of his sister abandoned it for *Die Feen*. The libretti of these two works, as in his later works, he wrote himself. *Die Feen* remained unperformed until 1888 although it contains many premonitions of the composer's talent.

He became chorus master at the theatre of Würzburg in 1833 and conductor of a summer theatre at Lauchstädt, the company of which was at Magdeburg in winter, where he went with it. Minna Planer (1809–66) was there as an actress, and he married her in November 1836, at Königsberg, where she had a new engagement. The Magdeburg company had been dissolved soon after a disastrous production of Wagner's third opera, *Das Liebesverbot*, in March 1836. The opera was much influenced by Bellini and Donizetti and has been successfully revived in heavily cut versions. The Königsberg theatre also went into liquidation just after Wagner had been appointed conductor, but in the summer of 1837 he became conductor at Riga. In January 1839 his post was given to Dorn and he decided to go to Paris by sea. A very stormy voyage took Wagner and his wife as far as the coast of Norway and then to England, and they did not reach Paris until September. Until April 1842 their time in Paris was spent in wretched poverty, but Wagner, in such time as he could spare from hack work, had managed to finish both *Rienzi* and *Der fliegende Holländer*, the former of which had been accepted by Dresden and was produced there in October 1842. *Rienzi* finds Wagner attempting the contemporary grand opera of Meyerbeer, a composer he affected to despise. The opera was Wagner's first major success with the public and was followed by *Der fliegende Holländer* two months later. Although less immediately popular it reveals for the first time Wagner's individual voice as a composer; the evocation of stormy seas and the sense of impending doom are particularly effective. The opera was premiered in January 1843, and Wagner was appointed second conductor at the court opera a month later. *Tannhäuser* was finished April 1845 and produced in October. The lifelong theme of the conflict between sacred and profane love is most powerfully projected in this opera. The spiritual side of the issue was portrayed in *Lohengrin*, composed 1845–48.

When the French Revolution of 1848 spread its influence across Europe, Wagner showed sympathy with liberal ideas, and after the revolt at Dresden failed in May 1849 he had to flee when a warrant for his arrest was issued, should he be found in Saxony. He went to Switzerland, where he worked in Zurich on the libretti and music for the *Ring des Nibelungen* cycle. The text had been written by 1853 and Wagner began composing the prologue *Das Rheingold* in the same year. The music of the first scene, set at the bottom of the river Rhine, shows the composer's genius for creating convincing sound worlds. Composition of the *Ring* was interrupted at Act II of *Siegfried* by work on *Tristan und Isolde*, written under the influence of Mathilde Wesendonck, the wife of a friend and benefactor with whom he fell more and more deeply in love. In 1858 Minna confronted Wagner and Mathilde; the latter decided to stay with her husband, and Wagner went to Venice and later to Lucerne, where *Tristan* was finished in August 1859. In 1860 a revised version of *Tannhäuser*, with a ballet, was commissioned by the Paris Opéra, and Wagner complied so far as his artistic conscience would let him, which was not enough for the patrons, who saw to it that after the production in March 1861 the work should fail disastrously. Wagner next went to Vienna, where he heard *Lohengrin* for the first time, though it had been produced by Liszt at Weimar in 1850.

In 1862 he settled at Biebrich, a village on the Rhine opposite Mainz, to work on *Die Meistersinger*, but he was in Vienna again by the end of the year, and stayed there until March 1864, when he was pursued by his creditors and threatened with imprisonment. At the critical moment he was invited by Ludwig II of Bavaria to join his court at Munich as friend and artistic adviser, and he ensured that Hans von Bülow was appointed

conductor. Bülow's wife, Cosima and Wagner soon fell deeply in love. This created a scandal which was fully exploited by his enemies, the courtiers and officials who feared his influence on the youthful and idealistic king, and soon after the production of *Tristan* in June 1865, Wagner was obliged to go into exile once more. *Tristan* was an immensely influential work, and an enduringly great piece of music in its own right. Wagner extended chromaticism and modulatory devices to new heights in this opera in order to portray the love of his protagonists, a love that transcends all human passion by its awareness of mortality: the belief that fulfilment can be found only in death. *Tristan's* antithesis is found in *Die Meistersinger von Nürnberg*, a partly autobiographical comedy in which a romantic hero and a profound poet combine to confound their pedant enemies. While composing *Meistersinger*, Wagner moved to Tribschen on Lake Lucerne in Switzerland, where Cosima joined him in March 1866. Bülow divorced her in 1870 and she married Wagner, whose first wife had died in January 1866.

After the production of *Die Meistersinger* on 21 June 1868 at Munich, Wagner quietly continued work on the *Ring* cycle, dropped so many years before, and planned a festival theatre to be erected by subscription at Bayreuth in Bavaria. The family took a house there in 1874; rehearsals began the following year, and the four works were produced 13–17 August 1876. (*Das Rheingold* and *Die Walküre* had already been given in Munich, against Wagner's wishes, 1869–70.) Although Wagner was dissatisfied with some aspects of the Bayreuth *Ring*, his genius as a composer and dramatist was triumphantly vindicated. The immensely complex musical and moral strands of the *Ring* are brought together in the final opera, *Götterdämmerung*; drama on a cosmic scale is matched by a constantly allusive orchestral accompaniment through the use of leitmotifs. Wagner's creative testament came with *Parsifal* in which his concept of the *Gesamtkunstwerk* ('complete art work'), was further refined. By the time of his death in 1883 Wagner's influence had already spread throughout the musical world and far beyond; his belief in music drama as a synthesis of all the arts represents the culmination of his Romantic philosophy.

Works include: OPERA *Die Hochzeit* (unfinished), *Die Feen* (composed 1833; produced 1888), *Das Liebesverbot* (1836), *Rienzi* (1842), *Der fliegende Holländer* (1843), *Tannhäuser* (1845), *Lohengrin* (1850), *Tristan und Isolde*

(1865), *Die Meistersinger von Nürnberg* (1868), *Der Ring des Nibelungen*, comprising *Das Rheingold* (1869), *Die Walküre* (1870), *Siegfried* (1876) and *Götterdämmerung* (1876), *Parsifal* (1882).

ORCHESTRAL symphonies, nine concert overtures (two unpublished), including *Eine Faust Ouvertüre* (after Goethe), three marches for orchestra, *Siegfried Idyll* for small orchestra (1870); several choral works.

SONGS seven from Goethe's *Faust*, five poems by Mathilde Wesendonck (1857–58) and six settings of French poems.

Wagner, Siegfried (Helferich Richard) (1869–1930) German composer and conductor. He was the son of Richard ◊Wagner. Although intended to become an architect, he studied music with Engelbert Humperdinck and Julius Kniese (1848–1905), and gained much experience by assisting at the Wagner festival performances at Bayreuth, some of which he conducted after 1896. When his mother, Cosima, became too old to manage the affairs of the theatre, he took its direction in hand in 1909.

Works include: the operas *Der Bärenhäuter* (1899), *Herzog Wildfang* (1901), *Der Kobold* (1904), *Bruder Lustig* (1905), *Sternengebot* (1908), *Banadietrich* (1910), *An allem ist Hütchen schuld* (1917), *Schwarzschwanenreich* (1918), *Sonnenflammen* (1918), *Der Schmied von Marienburg* (1923), *Der Friedensengel* (1926), *Der Heidenkönig* (1933), and two others not performed or published; symphonic poem *Sehnsucht*; violin concerto, flute concerto.

Wagner tuba brass wind instrument devised by Wagner for his opera cycle *Der Ring des Nibelungen/The Nibelung's Ring*. The two tenor tubas are not unlike the euphonium, but have funnel-shaped mouthpieces.

The compass of tenor and bass Wagner tubas.

Waisenhaus, Das/The Orphanage opera by Weigl (libretto by G F Treitschke), produced Vienna, Kärntnertortheater, 4 October 1808.

waits originally the keepers of town gates, in the 15th–16th centuries, salaried bands employed to play at various functions, afterwards amateur singers and players performing outside the houses of the wealthier citizens for rewards in money and refreshment at Christmas.

Waldhorn (German 'forest horn') German name for the ◊horn without valves, producing only the natural harmonics, like the Italian *corno da caccia.*

Brahms's Horn Trio op. 40 was written for the waldhorn.

Waldmädchen, Das/The Woodland Maid opera by Weber (libretto by C F von Steinsberg), produced Freiberg, Saxony, 23 November 1800. Early version of *Silvana*; only two fragments survive.

'Waldstein' Sonata Beethoven's piano sonata in C major, op. 53, composed 1804, so called (not by Beethoven) because it is dedicated to Ferdinand Waldstein.

Waldteufel (1837–1915), adopted name of (Charles) Emile Lévy French composer and pianist. He joined a piano factory and was later appointed pianist to the Empress Eugénie. He had great success as a composer of waltzes.

He studied at the Paris Conservatory.

Works include: many hundreds of waltzes and other dances, including a waltz on Chabrier's *España.*

Walküre, Die/The Valkyrie (Wagner). See ◊*Ring des Nibelungen.*

The saga continues as siblings Sieglinde and Siegmund meet and fall in love. Brünnhilde disobeys Wotan by attempting to allow Siegmund to escape death; she helps Sieglinde to escape to bear her child, the future Siegfried. Wotan punishes Brünnhilde by sending her to sleep, surrounded by a ring of fire.

Wallace, (William) Vincent (1812–1865) Irish composer. He established himself internationally as a pianist and violinist on tours that included Europe, Australia, and North and South America. He used the musical influences from the places he visited in his own compositions, such as the highly successful opera *Maritana* 1845, with its Spanish and gypsy elements.

He studied with his father, a bandmaster and bassoon player who moved to Dublin, where Wallace played the organ and violin in public as a boy. In 1831 he married Isabella Kelly, but they separated in 1835 (in New York in 1850 he met the pianist Hélène Stoepel, with whom he lived and had two sons). In 1834 he appeared at Dublin with a violin concerto of his own. He was in Australia and elsewhere abroad 1835–45, then went to London and was induced to compose *Maritana*. After a successful operatic career, including a visit to South America in 1849 and 14 years in Germany, a commission from the Paris Opéra (which he was unable to finish owing to failing eyesight), and another visit to South and North America 1850–53, his health broke down and he was ordered to the Pyrenees.

Works include: the operas *Maritana* (1845), *Matilda of Hungary* (1847), *Lurline* (1860), *The Maid of Zurich* (unpublished), *The Ambler Witch* (1861), *Love's Triumph* (1862), *The Desert Flower* (1863), *Estrella* (unfinished), operettas *Gulnare* and *Olga*; cantata *Maypole*; violin concerto; piano music.

Wallace, William (1860–1940) Scottish music author and composer. He was educated at Edinburgh and Glasgow Universities and in Vienna as an eye specialist, he began to practise in 1888, but gave up his profession for music except during World War I. In 1889 he entered the Royal Academy of Music in London for a brief course in composition, and later he became successively secretary and trustee of the Philharmonic Society. His books include *The Threshold of Music* (1908), *The Musical Faculty* (1914), *Richard Wagner as He Lived* (1925) and *Liszt, Wagner and the Princess* (1927).

Works include: the opera *Brassolis*; symphony *Koheleth* for chorus and orchestra; symphony *The Creation*, symphonic poems *The Passing of Beatrice* (after Dante's *Paradiso*, 1892), *Anvil or Hammer* (after Goethe's *Koptisches Lied*), *Sister Helen* (after D G Rossetti), *To the New Country, Wallace, AD 1305–1905*, *Villon*, suite *The Lady from the Sea* (after Ibsen), symphonic prelude to Aeschylus' *Eumenides*; cantatas, chamber music, and songs.

Wallenstein three symphonic poems by d'Indy, op. 12, after Schiller's dramatic trilogy, composed 1873–79: 1. *Le Camp de Wallenstein*; 2. *Max et Thécla* (first called *Piccolomini*); 3. *La Mort de Wallenstein*. First complete performance Paris, 26 February 1888.

Wally, La opera by Catalani (libretto by L Illica, based on W von Hillern's novel *Die Geyer-Wally*), produced Milan, La Scala, 20 January 1892. Wally is intended for Gellner but she loves Hagenbach, and after complications and reconciliation, they die together in an avalanche. Championed by Toscanini, who named his daughter Wally.

Walpurga, Maria Antonia (1724–1780), or Walpurgis German composer. She was a member of the Arcadian Academy in Rome under the name of Ermelinda Talèa Pastorella Arcada (pseudonym ETPA). She was the daughter of the Elector of Bavaria (afterwards Emperor Charles VII). She studied with Giovanni Ferrandini, Nicola Porpora, and Johann Hasse; she married Frederick Christian, electoral prince of Saxony.

Works include: the operas *Il trionfo della fedeltà* (with additional music by Hasse, 1754) and *Talestri, regina della Amazoni* (1760).

Walsh, John (1665 or 1666–1736) English music publisher and instrument maker. He founded his publishing house in London about 1690, and in 1692 became instrument maker to King William III. He published much of Handel's music.

Walter, Bruno (1876–1962), actually Bruno Walter Schlesinger German conductor and pianist. He excelled in the works of Mozart and of Romantic composers, especially Mahler, of whose *Lied von der Erde* and ninth symphony he gave the first performances in 1911 and 1912. As a pianist he accompanied many of the famous singers of his time, including Lotte Lehmann and Kathleen Ferrier, and also appeared as soloist in Mozart's concertos. He published a study of Mahler, an autobiography (*Theme and Variations*), and three volumes of essays.

Walter studied at Stern Conservatory in Berlin and made his first appearance as a conductor at Cologne in 1894. After appointments as an opera conductor at Hamburg (under Mahler), Breslau, Pressburg, Riga, Berlin, and Vienna (1901–12) he was director of the Munich Opera 1913–22. He conducted the first performances of Pfitzner's *Palestrina* 1917 and Schreker's *Das Spielwerk* 1920. He was director of the Städtische Oper, Berlin 1925–33, and of the Gewandhaus concerts in Leipzig 1929–33, in succession to Furtwängler. He first appeared in England in 1909 and was the regular conductor of the German seasons at Covent Garden 1924–31 (productions included *Figaro* and *Rosenkavalier*). He was also active during this period as conductor at the Salzburg festival. He was compelled to leave Germany in 1933 and was artistic director of the Vienna Opera 1936–38. After the Anschluss he emigrated to France in 1938 and to the USA in 1939, where he lived until his death. From 1941 he conducted frequently at the New York Metropolitan Opera House (debut with *Fidelio*; also *Don Giovanni* in first season). From 1946 he returned to Europe as a guest conductor, he appeared at the 1947 Edinburgh Festival.

Waltershausen, Hermann Wolfgang (Sartorius) Freiherr von (1882–1954) German composer and music author. He studied at Strasbourg, lost his right arm and foot in an accident, but learnt to play the piano and conduct with the left hand. He further studied at Munich from 1901 and attended Sandberger's lectures at the university. He founded a music school in 1917, and in 1920 became professor at the Munich State Academy of Music, being appointed director in 1922. His books include works on musical style, opera, and R Strauss.

Works include: the operas *Else Klapperzehen* (1909), *Oberst Chabert* (after Balzac, 1912), *Richardis* (1915), *Die Rauensteiner Hochzeit* (1919), *Die Gräfin von Tolosa* (composed 1938); *Apocalyptic SymphoNA, Hero und Leander*, Partita on three Hymn-tunes, comedy overture, *Passions- und Auferstehungsmusik* for orchestra; *Krippenmusik* for harpsichord and chamber orchestra; piano works; songs.

Walther, Johann Gottfried (1684–1748) German composer, organist, and lexicographer. He studied under Johann Bernhard Bach (1676–1749) at Erfurt, where in 1702 he became organist at St Thomas's Church. In 1707 he was appointed town organist at Weimar, where he was in close touch with Johann Sebastian Bach, to whom he was related. He published a *Musicalisches Lexicon* in 1732.

Works include: much organ music, including preludes and fugues and chorale variations; concertos by other composers arranged for solo harpsichord.

Walton, William Turner (1902–1983) English composer. Among his works are *Façade* 1923, a series of instrumental pieces designed to be played in conjunction with the recitation of surrealist poems by Edith Sitwell; the oratorio *Belshazzar's Feast* 1931; and *Variations on a Theme by Hindemith* 1963.

Walton showed great talent as a child and was sent to Christ Church Cathedral, Oxford, as a chorister, later becoming an undergraduate at Christ Church. He had some composition lessons from the organist Hugh Allen (1869–1946), but after the age of 16 was self-taught, though he later received advice from Busoni and others. In 1923 he appeared for the first time at the International Society for Contemporary Music festival, at Salzburg, where his spiky first string quartet was performed. He settled in London and was in close touch with the literary Sitwell family:

Edith, Osbert, and Sacheverell; their association led to *Façade*, for reciter and ensemble, whose 1923 premiere provoked an uproar. Hindemith was the soloist in Walton's first widely successful work, the viola concerto of 1929, and two years later the aggressively mannered cantata *Belshazzar's Feast* was premiered at Leeds.

In 1934 his symphony in B♭ minor was performed in London before it was completed (the finale was added the next year). In 1938 he went to the USA to confer with the violinist Jascha Heifetz about the solo part of the violin concerto, which is dedicated to him. As in the viola concerto and the First Symphony, the best of contemporary continental influences, including Stravinsky, Poulenc, and Prokofiev can be discerned here. A more ruminant, quasi-Romantic strain is evident in the post-war works, beginning with the opera for Covent Garden *Troilus and Cressida* (1948–54) and continuing with the cello concerto for Piatigorsky.

Works include: DRAMATIC operas *Troilus and Cressida* (after Chaucer, 1954, revised 1976) and *The Bear* (after Chekhov, 1967); film music for *As You Like It, Henry V* and *Hamlet* (Shakespeare), *The First of the Few* (including *Spitfire* prelude and fugue).

VOCAL *Façade* for reciter and instrumental ensemble; (E Sitwell, 1922). Cantata *Belshazzar's Feast* (Bible, arranged by O Sitwell, 1931); *A Song for the Lord Mayor's Table* for soprano and orchestra or piano (1962).

ORCHESTRAL overtures *Portsmouth Point* (on Rowlandson's drawing) and *Scapino*, two symphonies (1931–35 and 1960), Coronation Marches *Crown Imperial* and *Orb and Sceptre* (1937 and 1953), viola concerto (1929), violin concerto (1939), cello concerto (1956), *Variations on a theme of Hindemith* (1963), *Improvisations on an Impromptu of Benjamin Britten* (1969), Sonata for Strings (from string quartet of 1947, 1971).

waltz ballroom dance in moderate triple time (3/4) that developed in Germany and Austria during the late 18th century from the Austrian *Ländler* (traditional peasants' country dance). Associated particularly with Vienna and the ◊Strauss family, the waltz has remained popular up to the present day and has inspired composers including Chopin, Brahms, and Ravel.

Waltz Dream (Strauss) see ◊*Walzertraum*.

Walzertraum, Ein/A Waltz Dream operetta by Oscar Straus (libretto by F Dörmann and L Jacobson), produced Vienna, Karl Theatre, 2 March 1907. Newly married Lieutenant Niki abandons wife Helene to go to a ball on his wedding night. There he falls in love with Franzi, who teaches Helene how to win back Niki's heart.

Wand, Günter (1912–) German conductor and composer. After study in Cologne he held posts at Wuppertal and Detmold. He conducted at the Cologne Opera 1939–44 and was musical director there 1945–48. He was responsible for the Gürzenich concerts, Cologne, 1946–74, giving frequent performances of Ligeti, Varèse, and Schoenberg. London debut 1951 (with the London Symphony Orchestra at Covent Garden). He conducted the Bern Symphony Orchestra from 1974 and has been principal conductor of the Nord-Deutsche Rundfunk Symphony Orchestra (Hamburg) 1982–91.

'Wanderer' Fantasy Schubert's fantasy in C major for piano, D760, composed November 1822. It is so called because it contains material from his song 'The Wanderer', written 1816.

Wand of Youth, The two orchestral suites by Elgar, opp. 1a and b, which are based on music he wrote for a play in his childhood, 1869. Revised and scored in the present form in 1907; first performed London, 14 December 1907, conductor Wood.

Wannenmacher, Johannes (c. 1485–1551) Swiss priest and composer. He wrote vocal pieces, of which 26 survive.

Wannenmacher was appointed cantor of the collegiate foundation of St Vincent at Bern in 1510, but left in 1514 after a dispute and went to Germany as canon and cantor at Freiburg, Baden. After a brief return to Switzerland in 1519, when he went to Sion (Valais), he went back to Freiburg, but having come under the influence of the Swiss religious reformer Zwingli, he embraced Protestantism in 1530, was tortured and banished, returned to Bern and, finding no employment there, became town clerk at Interlaken.

Works include: Psalm cxxxvii for three–six voices, motets; German sacred and secular songs.

War and Peace/Voyna i mir opera by Prokofiev (libretto by M Mendelson, based on Tolstoy's novel), performed in concert, Moscow, 17 October 1944; produced Leningrad, 12 June 1946 (first eight of 13 scenes only). Revised 1941–52, in 11 scenes, and produced Florence, 26 May 1953, conductor Rodzinski. First seven scenes concern Peace, with the love of Andrei and Natasha, and the last six War, with Napoleon's capture of Moscow.

Ward, John (1571–1638) English composer. He wrote madrigals and church music. He was in the service of Sir Henry Fanshawe, Remembrancer of the Exchequer, at Ware Park, Hertfordshire, and in London.

Works include: services and 22 verse anthems; madrigals; fantasies for viols.

Warlock, Peter (1894–1930), pen name of Philip Arnold Heseltine English composer. His style was influenced by the music of the Elizabethan age and by that of Delius. His works include the orchestral suite *Capriol* 1926 based on 16th-century dances, and the song cycle *The Curlew* 1920–22. His works of musical theory and criticism were published under his real name.

Warlock was educated at Eton, and was later influenced by Delius and van Dieren. He founded the *Sackbut*, a combative music paper, wrote numerous articles, edited early English music, especially of the lutenist school, and published books on the English ayre, Delius, and (with Cecil Gray) Gesualdo. His music reflects the extreme mood swings of his personality; he died by suicide.

Works include: *Three Dirges by Webster* (1925) and other choral works; *An Old Song* and *Serenade* for string orchestra; *The Curlew* for tenor, flute, English horn, and string quartet (1921), *Corpus Christi* and *Sorrow's Lullaby* (Beddoes) for soprano, baritone, and string quartet; *Capriol* suite for full or string orchestra on dances from Arbeau's *Orchésographie* (1926); over 100 songs, many on Elizabethan and Jacobean poems.

Warrack, Guy (Douglas Hamilton) (1900–1986) Scottish composer and conductor. He studied at Oxford and with Boult and Vaughan Williams at the Royal College of Music; taught there 1925–35. He made his debut as conductor in London, in 1925, and conducted the British Broadcasting Corporation (BBC) Scottish Orchestra 1936–45, the Sadler's Wells Ballet 1948–51. He wrote music for various documentary films, including the official film of the 1953 coronation.

War Requiem choral work by Britten, op. 66 (text of the Requiem Mass, together with poems by W Owen), first performed Coventry Cathedral, 30 May 1962.

Wasps, The incidental music for Aristophanes' comedy by Vaughan Williams, first performed Cambridge, in Greek, by undergraduates, 26 November 1909; orchestral suite performed London, 23 July 1912.

Water Music a set of instrumental pieces by
Handel, first performed London, 1715, on a
boat following the royal barge on the Thames.
The music is said to have reconciled George I
to Handel after the latter's desertion from the
court of Hanover, but the story is doubtful.

Watkins, Michael Blake (1948–) English
composer. He studied with Elisabeth Lutyens
and Richard Rodney Bennett 1966–75.

Works include: *Double Concerto* for oboe,
guitar, and orchestra (1973); *Youth's Dream*
and *Time's Truth* for tenor, trumpet, harp, and
strings (1973); Concertante for 11 players
(1973); horn concerto (1974); violin concerto
(1977); *The Spirit of the Universe* for soprano
and ensemble (1978); string quartet (1979);
Sinfonietta (1982); concertos for trumpet
(1988) and cello (1992); oboe quartet (1984).

Watson, Thomas (c. 1557–1592) English
scholar and amateur musician. He published
in 1590 *The First Sett of Italian Madrigalls
Englished*, the successor of Nicholas Yonge's
Musica Transalpina 1588, and with it the
foundation of the native English school of
madrigalists.

Waverley overture by Berlioz, op. 1b, inspired
by Walter Scott, first performed Paris, 26 May
1828.

Webber, Andrew Lloyd English composer of
musicals: see ◊Lloyd Webber.

Weber, (Jacob) Gottfried (1779–1839) German composer and theorist. He pursued a
lawyer's profession at Mannheim (1804),
Mainz (1812), and Darmstadt (1818). In 1810
his family provided refuge for their name-
sakes, Carl Maria von Weber and his father,
after the former's banishment from Stuttgart,
and they formed a music and cultural society.
Weber wrote a number of theoretical books.

Works include: three Masses and other
church music; instrumental sonatas and
pieces; songs with piano and guitar.

Weber, Bernhard Christian (1712–1758)
German organist and composer. It was long
claimed that he anticipated Bach by writing a
set of preludes and fugues for keyboard in all
the keys, entitled *Das wohltemperierte Clavier*,
but he was actually an imitator, the work,
wrongly dated 1689 (23 years before his
birth), being in fact written in 1743. He was
appointed organist at Tennstedt in 1732.

**Weber, Carl Maria Friedrich Ernst von
(1786–1826)** German composer. He established the Romantic school of opera with *Der
Freischütz/The Marksman* 1821 and *Euryanthe*
1823. He was Kapellmeister (chief conductor)
at Breslau 1804–06, Prague 1813–16, and

Dresden in 1816. He died during a visit to
London, where he produced his opera *Oberon*
1826, written for the Covent Garden Theatre.

Weber was taken about the country in his
childhood and received little education, but
his father, anxious to make a prodigy of him,
taught him all the music he knew. When at
last they settled at Salzburg, the ten-year-old
Weber became a pupil of Michael Haydn.
After his mother's death in 1798 he was taken
to Vienna and Munich. There he studied
under Giovanni Valesi and Johann Kalcher,
and at 13 was a good enough pianist to
appear at concerts. By 1800 he had written a
good deal of juvenile music and learned
lithography with the Austrian engraver Se-
nefelder; but the wandering life was resumed
and he continued his studies with the aid of
theoretical books.

At Augsburg in 1803 he succeeded in
having his opera *Peter Schmoll und seine
Nachbarn* produced. In Vienna again 1803–
04, he studied for a time with Georg Vogler,
who recommended him for a conductorship
at Breslau, where he went in the autumn of
1804. In 1806 he became domestic musician to
Duke Eugen of Württemberg, who, on being
obliged to dismiss his musicians, recommended Weber as private secretary to his
younger brother Ludwig. Weber settled at
Stuttgart in 1807, but led a rather dissolute life
there and incurred the displeasure of the
king, his patron's elder brother. In 1810 he
was banished from the kingdom on a
trumped-up charge and went to Mannheim
and later to Darmstadt, where he resumed his
studies with Vogler more seriously. His
brilliant works for clarinet and orchestra
(two concertos and a concertina) date from
1811; the clarinet quintet followed four years
later.

After much travelling he secured the
conductorship at the German theatre in
Prague in 1813. In 1816 he was appointed
conductor of the Dresden court opera, where
he did much to establish German opera in the
face of the strong opposition of Morlacchi and
other Italians. In 1817 he married the opera
singer Caroline Brandt, who was still at
Prague, and took her to Dresden after a
concert tour. In 1821 his most famous opera,
Der Freischütz, was produced in Berlin; it was
immediately recognized throughout Germany as helping to establish a truly national
style. *Euryanthe* followed in Vienna in 1823,
and marked a major development with the
way in which spoken dialogue, traditional in
German opera, was replaced by continuously
composed music. In 1824 Covent Garden

commissioned an English opera from him, and he took English lessons to make a success of *Oberon*. He suffered badly from a severe disease of the throat and felt unfit to visit London, but in order to keep his family from want he took the risk in February 1826, visiting Paris on the way. He arrived in London in March, conducted works of his own at a Philharmonic concert, and produced *Oberon* in April. Although ill with tuberculosis, he still conducted the succeeding performances and appeared at several concerts. Utterly worn out early in June, he made preparations for a hasty return home but died during the night at the house of his host, George Smart.

In spite of his early death Weber created a body of work which forms an important foundation of 19th-century German Romanticism. Wagner and Mahler were particularly indebted to him.

Works include: STAGE operas *Der Freischütz* (1821), *Euryanthe* (1823), *Oberon* (1826).

ORCHESTRAL two symphonies (1807); 22 works for solo instruments and orchestra, including two piano concertos (1810–12), *Concertstück* for piano and orchestra (1821), concertino for clarinet and orchestra (1811), two concertos for clarinet and one for bassoon (all 1811).

INSTRUMENTAL quintet for clarinet, two violins, viola and cello (1815), trio for flute, cello, and piano (1819); 27 piano works including four sonatas (1812–22), *Aufforderung zum Tanz/Invitation to the Dance*.

Webern, Anton (Friedrich Wilhelm von) (1883–1945) Austrian composer. He wrote spare, enigmatic miniatures combining a pastoral poetic with severe structural rigour. A Renaissance musical scholar, he became a pupil of Arnold ◊Schoenberg, whose twelve-tone system he reinterpreted as abstract design in works such as the *Concerto for Nine Instruments* 1931–34 and the *Second Cantata* 1941–43. His constructivist aesthetic influenced the postwar generation of advanced composers.

Webern studied musicology with Guido Adler and took a doctorate at Vienna University in 1906. He studied compoition with Schoenberg. His first major work was the Passacaglia for orchestra, written with an awareness of the example of Brahms; it was followed by the Five Movements for string quartet, which exhibit some of Weber's later epigrammatic style. Song settings of Schoenberg's favourite poet, Stefan George, are Webern's first excursions into atonality. He

conducted for a time at German provincial theatres and in Prague. After World War I he settled near Vienna and devoted himself to teaching and composition, though he still conducted, especially the modern performances of the Verein für Musikalische Privataufführungen and the workers' symphony concerts. He adopted Schoenberg's 12-note method of composition in the *Three Traditional Rhymes* of 1925. In succeeding works, such as the string trio, the symphony op. 21, and the concerto op. 24, Webern adopted ever more rigidly controlled methods; he was also influenced there by the Renaissance composer Heinrich Isaac.

His death was the result of a misunderstanding (he was shot by a US soldier). Although almost entirely unrecognized during his lifetime, Webern's music has proved very influential since his death: it introduced new concepts of sound, rhythm, and quasi-mathematical organization. It is almost as much through his work as through Schoenberg's that the 12-tone system came to find so wide an acceptance; Webern's serial technique was stricter than Schoenberg's and Berg's, and later composers have capitalized on its rigour in their development of integral serialism (in which rhythm, dynamics, and even timbre are serialized). Among composers who have been particularly influenced by Webern are Stravinsky (from the early 1950s), Stockhausen, and Boulez.

Works include: ORCHESTRAL Six Pieces op. 6 (1909, revised 1928), Five Pieces op. 10 (1911–13, first performance 1926), Five Movements arranged for string orchestra from Five Movements for string quartet (1928–29), symphony op. 21 (1928), Variations op. 30 (1940).

VOCAL *Entflieht auf leichten Kähnen* for unaccompanied chorus op. 2 (1908, first performance 1927), two songs for chorus and ensemble op. 19 (texts by Goethe, 1926), *Das Augenlicht* for chorus and orchestra op. 26 (1935), Cantata no. 1 for soprano, chorus, and orchestra (1938–9), Cantata no. 2 for soprano, bass, chorus, and orchestra (1941–3, first performance 1950); two sets of five songs for voice and piano opp. 3 and 4 (texts by George, 1909), two songs for voice and ensemble op. 8 (texts by Rilke, 1910), four songs for voice and piano op. 12 (1915–17), four songs for voice and orchestra op. 13 (1914–18), six songs for voice and instruments (texts by Trakl, 1919–21), *Five Sacred Songs* for voice and instruments op. 15 (1917–22), five canons on Latin texts for voice, clarinet, and bass clarinet op. 16 (1923–24, first performance New York , 1951), *Three Traditional Rhymes* for voice and instruments op. 17 (1925, first performance New York , 1952), three songs for voice, clarinet, and guitar op. 18 (1925, first performance Los Angeles, 1954), three songs for voice and piano op. 23 (1934), three songs for voice and piano op. 25 (1934).

INSTRUMENTAL Five Movements for string quartet op. 5 (1909), six Bagatelles for string quartet op. 9 (1911–13), *Three Little Pieces* for cello and piano op. 11 (1914), string trio op. 20 (1927), concerto for nine instruments op. 24 (1934), string quartet op. 28 (1938), variations for piano op. 27 (1936).

We Come to the River opera ('actions for music') by Henze (libretto by E Bond); composed 1974–76, produced London, Covent Garden, 12 July 1976. After a battle, the General sentences the Deserter to be shot; he later finds the condemned man's wife trying to survive amongst the corpses. Realizing the misery he has caused, the General refuses orders and is sent to a mental asylum where the inmates imagine a river carries them to freedom.

Wedding, The ballet by Stravinsky (choreographed by B Nizhinska), produced Paris, Théâtre Lyrique, 13 June 1923. The work is scored for chorus (Russian words), four pianos, and percussion. It is more generally known as *Les Noces*.

Wedekind, Frank (1864–1918) German dramatist. See ◊Ettinger (*Frühlingserwachen*); ◊Lulu (Berg).

'Wedge' Fugue Bach's E minor organ fugue, BWV 548.ii, so called because of the progressively widening intervals of its subject.

Weelkes, Thomas (c. 1576–1623) English composer. He wrote ten Anglican services and around 40 anthems, including 'When David heard'. He was also one of the most significant madrigalists of his time, contributing *As Vesta was from Latmos Hill descending* to the *Triumphs of Oriana* 1601.

Weelkes was in the service of George Phillpot at Compton near Winchester in his early years and then that of Edward Darcye, Groom of the Privy Chamber. In 1598 he was appointed organist at Winchester College, in 1601 he became organist and choirmaster at

Chichester Cathedral, and in 1602 was awarded a degree in music at Oxford University. His career at Chichester was turbulent: he received repeated reprimands for unruliness, drunkenness, and neglect of duty, and was dismissed in 1617. He later resumed the post, but died during a visit to London.

Weelkes published almost 100 madrigals, often for four, five, and six voices; they demonstrate his intricate style, fine counterpoint, and brilliant imagery.

Works include: services and numerous anthems; three books of madrigals, *Ayeres or Phantasticke Spirites* for three voices (1608), two vocal pieces contributed to Leighton's *Teares or Lamentacions*; three In Nomines for four–five viols and other pieces for five viols.

Weerbeke, Gaspar van (c. 1445–c. 1517) Flemish composer and singer. Of his works, about eight Masses, 28 motets, and several other liturgical works survive. Five of his Masses were published by the Venetian printer and publisher Ottaviano Petrucci.

Weerbeke took holy orders at Tournai and went to Italy in the 1470s, becoming maestro di cappella at Milan Cathedral and a singer in the service of the Sforza family at the ducal court. He was in Rome as a singer at the papal chapel 1481–89, but in 1488 produced music for allegorical plays given at the marriage of Galeazzo Sforza, Duke of Milan, to Isabella of Aragon. He returned to the Sforza court in 1489. From 1495 he spent two years as a singer in the court choir of Philip Handsome, Archduke of Austria and Duke of Burgundy. He returned to Rome in 1500, where he again sang in the papal choir. He is last heard of as a canon at St Maria ad Gradus in Mainz.

Works include: eight Masses, 28 motets, *Stabat Mater*, and other church music. He studied under the *maîtrise* at Oudenaarde and with Johannes Okeghem. He visited his home town in 1490 and was received with honours. Weerbeke worked with Josquin Desprez at the Sforza court.

Weigl, Karl (1881–1949) Austrian composer. He studied musicology at Vienna University, worked as assistant conductor under Mahler at the Vienna Opera, became a teacher at the New Vienna Conservatory in 1918 and later

The subject of Bach's 'Wedge' Fugue, BWV 548.ii.

lecturer at the university. He settled in the USA in 1938, becoming an American citizen in 1943 and teaching successively at Hartford, Brooklyn and Boston.

Works include: cantata *Weltfeier* for solo voices, chorus, orchestra and organ; six symphonies (1908–47); various concertos; eight string quartets (1903–49); cello and piano sonata; songs with piano and with chamber accompaniment.

Weihe des Hauses, Die/The Consecration of the House overture by Beethoven, op. 124, written in 1822 for the opening of the Josefstadt Theatre in Vienna, and performed there 3 October.

Weill, Kurt Julian (1900–1950) German composer; a US citizen from 1943. He wrote chamber and orchestral music and collaborated with Bertolt ◊Brecht on operas such as *Die Dreigroschenoper/The Threepenny Opera* 1928 and *Aufstieg und Fall der Stadt Mahagonny/The Rise and Fall of the City of Mahagonny* 1929, both of which attacked social corruption (*Mahagonny*, which satirized US frontier values, caused a riot at its premiere in Leipzig). He tried to evolve a new form of ◊music theatre, using subjects with a contemporary relevance and the simplest musical means. In 1933 he left Germany, and from 1935 was in the USA, where he wrote a number of successful scores for Broadway, among them the antiwar musical *Johnny Johnson* 1936, *Knickerbocker Holiday* 1938 (including the often covered 'September Song'), and *Street Scene* 1947, based on an Elmer Rice play set in the Depression.

His musical *Love Life* 1948, with lyrics by Alan Jay Lerner, describes a typical US couple over a period of 150 years of US history, and expresses Weill's mixture of fascination and repulsion towards the 'American Dream'.

Weill was born in Dessau, where his father was a cantor. He studied locally at first, and later with Humperdinck in Berlin. At the age of 19 he was appointed conductor at a small opera house, but after a year of conducting he decided to return to Berlin to study composition under Busoni. He had his first stage success at the age of 26 when his first opera, *Der Protagonist*, was produced at Dresden. Also at 26, he married the singer Lotte Lenya, who performed many of his songs. His collaboration with Brecht on a modern version of Gay's *Beggar's Opera/Die Dreigroschenoper* 1928 was a huge success, but in 1933 the Nazi regime condemned his works as both Jewish and decadent, and he left Germany. Official opinion also disapproved of Weill's

effective use of jazz in his stage works, and there was further suspicion of the sharp social satire in *Die Dreigroschenoper*. He visited London in 1935 for the production of *A Kingdom for a Cow*, an English version of an earlier operetta, but went the same year to settle in the USA. Among the US writers who collaborated with Weill on musicals for Broadway were Ogden Nash and Maxwell Anderson. In 1949 he wrote *Lost in the Stars*, a musical tragedy based on Alan Paton's novel *Cry, the Beloved Country*, and he was planning a folk opera based on Mark Twain's *Huckleberry Finn* when he died suddenly of a heart attack.

Works include: STAGE (several on libretti by Brecht) *Der Protagonist* (1926), *Der Silbersee* (1933), *Der Zar lässt sich photographieren* (libretto by G Kaiser), *Royal Palace* (1927), *Die Dreigroschenoper* (1928), *Happy End* (1929), *Aufstieg und Fall der Stadt Mahagonny* (1929), *Der Jasager* (1930), *Die Bürgschaft, A Kingdom for a Cow* (1935), *Johnny Johnson* (1936), *Knickerbocker Holiday* (1938), *The Firebrand of Florence* (1945), *Down in the Valley* (1948), *Street Scene* (1947), *Love Life* (1948), *Lost in the Stars* (1949); ballet *Die sieben Todsünden* (*Anna Anna*, 1933) .

CHORAL WITH ORCHESTRA Biblical music drama *The Eternal Road*; cantatas *Der neue Orpheus* and *Der Lindberghflug* (1929).

ORCHESTRAL two symphonies (1921, 1933), *Fantasia, Passacaglia und Hymnus, Divertimento* and *Quodlibet* for orchestra; concerto for violin and wind band (1924).

OTHER two string quartets (1919, 1923); works for voices and chamber orchestra, songs (Rilke) with orchestra.

Weinberger, Jaromír (1896–1967) Czech composer. He was professor of composition at the Conservatory of Ithaca, New York 1922–26; he later returned to Europe to conduct and teach. His best-known work, the folk-opera *Schvanda the Bagpiper* was premiered at Prague in 1927. His four later operas did not repeat its success, but the orchestral variations on 'Under the Spreading Chestnut Tree' 1939 made a momentary hit.

Weinberger studied with Hoffmeister and Kricka in Prague and with Reger in Germany. He settled in the USA in 1938.

Works include: the operas *Shvanda the Bagpiper* (1927), *The Beloved Voice* (1931), *The Outcasts of Poker Flat* (after Bret Harte, 1932), and *Wallenstein* (after Schiller); pantomime *The Abduction of Eveline*; incidental music for Shakespeare's and other plays; variations on the English song, 'Under the Spreading

Weisgall, Hugo (David)

Chestnut Tree' for piano and orchestra (1939), *Lincoln Symphony*, *Czech Rhapsody* for orchestra; works for organ, piano, violin.

Wein, Der/The Wine concert aria by Berg (text by Baudelaire, in German translation by S George); composed 1929, first performed Königsberg, 4 June 1930, conductor Scherchen.

Weiner, Leó (1885–1960) Hungarian composer. He studied at the National Academy of Music in Budapest, where he became a professor in 1908.

Works include: ballet on and incidental music for Vörösmarty's *Csongor and Tünde* (1916); three divertimentos (1934–49), scherzo, serenade, and humoresque *Carnival* for orchestra; *Pastoral, Fantasy and Fugue* for strings; two violin concertos; three string quartets (1906–38), string trio; two violin and piano sonatas; piano works.

Weingartner, (Paul) Felix (1863–1942) Austrian conductor and composer. He was noted as a conductor of the Classical repertoire, and especially of the works of Schubert and Beethoven. He wrote seven symphonies and several operas. His writings include books on conducting and on Beethoven's symphonies.

Weingartner studied at Graz, at the Leipzig Conservatory, and under Liszt at Weimar, where he produced his first opera in 1884. He became conductor at Königsberg, Gdansk, Hamburg, and Mannheim before 1891, when he was appointed conductor of the Court Opera in Berlin and conductor of the symphony concerts. In 1898 he left for Munich to become conductor of the Kaim orchestra and in 1908 succeeded Mahler as chief conductor at the Vienna Hofoper. He resigned in 1911 but conducted Vienna Philharmonic Orchestra concerts until 1927 and continued to conduct throughout Europe and the USA, notably in the symphonies of Beethoven. At Covent Garden he conducted Wagner's *Tannhäuser* and *Parsifal* in 1939. The last years of his life he spent, still actively, in Switzerland, especially at Basel.

Works include: the operas *Sakuntala* (after Kalidasa, 1884), *Malawika* (1886), *Genesius*, *Orestes* trilogy (after Aeschylus, 1902), *Kain und Abel* (1914), *Dame Kobold* (after Calderón), *Die Dorfschule, Meister Andrea, Der Apostat*; incidental music for Shakespeare's *Tempest* and Goethe's *Faust*; seven symphonies (1899–1937), symphonic poem *King Lear* (after Shakespeare); three string quartets; songs.

Weinlig, Christian Theodor (1780–1842) German theorist and composer. He was a pupil of his uncle, Christian Ehregott Weinlig

(1743–1813), cantor of the Kreuzschule at Dresden. He succeeded Schicht as cantor of St Thomas's School at Leipzig in 1823. Clara Schumann and Richard Wagner were his pupils for a short time. He wrote a treatise on fugue. His compositions include an oratorio, two German Magnificats and church cantatas.

Weir, Judith (1954–) Scottish composer. She studied with John Tavener and worked with computer music at the Massachusetts Institute of Technology in 1973. Later she studied with Robin Holloway at Cambridge. Her most successful compositions are the opera *A Night at The Chinese Opera* 1987, and *The Art of Touching the Keyboard* 1983, for piano.

Works include: the operas *The Black Spider* (1985), *A Night at The Chinese Opera* (1987), *The Vanishing Bridegroom* (1990), and *Blond Eckbert* (1994); orchestral pieces *Wunderhorn* (1979), *The Ride Over Lake Constance* (1984), *Variations on 'Summer is icumen in'* (1987), *Music Untangled* (1992), *Heroic Strokes of the Bow* (1992); *Heaven Ablaze in his Breast* for chorus, two pianos, and eight dancers (1989); re-compositions of Mozart's *Il sogno di Scipione* (1991) and Monteverdi's *Il Combattimento di Tancredi e Clorinda* (1992); music for ensemble, chamber music; songs and keyboard pieces.

Weis, Flemming (1898–1981) Danish composer. A member of a musical family, he began to compose as a child. In 1916 he entered the Copenhagen Conservatory and in 1920 finished studies at Leipzig. He was active on behalf of contemporary music and also as a music critic.

Works include: *The Promised Land* for chorus and orchestra; two symphonies (1942, 1948), symphonic overture and *In temporis vernalis* for orchestra; *Introduction grave* for piano and strings, four string quartets (1922–77) and other chamber music; sonatas for various instruments, suite and sonatina for piano; songs.

Weisgall, Hugo (David) (1912–) Czech-born US composer. His family settled in the USA in 1920. He studied at the Peabody Conservatory, Baltimore, and later with Sessions in New York and R Scalero at the Curtis Institute in Philadelphia. He taught at the Juilliard School 1957–68. His music admits a wide range of influences (including neo-classical and serial) and his operas have been particularly successful.

Works include: the operas *Night* (1932), *Lillith* (1934), *The Tenor* (1952), *Six Characters in Search of an Author* (after Pirandello, 1959),

Athaliah (1964), *Nine Rivers from Jordan* (1968), *The 100 Nights* (1976), *The Gardens of Adonis* (1992, composed 1959), *Esther* (1994); ballets *Quest, One Thing is Certain, Outpost*; overture in F major for orchestra; choral music; songs.

Weismann, Julius (1879–1950) German composer. He gained Nazi favour by accepting a commission to compose music for *A Midsummer Night's Dream* which was intended to replace Mendelssohn's; his *Die pfiffige Magd* 1939 was performed throughout Germany during the war years.

Weismann studied at Munich, then with Heinrich von Herzogenberg in Berlin, and again at Munich with Ludwig Thuille.

Works include: the operas *Schwanenweiss* (1923), *Traumspiel* (1925), *Gespenstersonate* (all after Strindberg), *Leonce und Lena* (G Büchner, 1924), *Landsknechte, Regina del Lago* (1928), *Die pfiffige Magd* (after Holberg, 1939); three symphonies, three pieces for orchestra, three sinfoniettas; four violin concertos, three piano concertos, cello concerto; 11 string quartets (1905–47), three piano trios (1908–21) sonata for violin solo, five violin sonatas, two cello sonatas, variations for oboe and piano; choral works; variations for two pianos; seven op. nos. of piano pieces; 15 op. nos. of songs.

Weiss, Adolph (1891–1971) US composer of German parentage. He studied piano, violin, and bassoon, and at the age of 16 played first bassoon with the Russian Symphony Orchestra of New York and then in the New York Philharmonic Orchestra under Mahler. He then studied composition at Columbia University with C Rybner and later with Schoenberg in Vienna. Later worked with various California orchestras.

Works include: *I Segreti* (1923) and *American Life* (1928) for orchestra; *The Libation Bearers*, choreographed cantata for soloists, chorus, and orchestra; theme and variations for orchestra; trumpet concerto; three string quartets (1925–32); music for wind instruments; songs; piano music.

Weiss, Sylvius Leopold (1686–1750) German lutenist and composer. He was a both a virtuoso player and a prolific composer, writing nearly 600 pieces of music for solo lute, including over 70 partitas. He also wrote sonatas and concertos for combinations of instruments including the lute.

Weiss was in the service of the Polish Prince Alexander Sobieski, with whom he went to Rome about 1708, later at the courts of Hesse-Kassel, Düsseldorf, and from 1718 at Dresden, where he worked with Lotti, Hasse, Porpora, Hebenstreit, Pisendel, and others; he

was sent to Vienna with a visiting Saxon orchestra that year. In 1723 he played in Prague with Quantz and H Graun in Fux's coronation opera *Costanza e fortezza*.

welcome-odes, or welcome-songs cantatas by Purcell for the return to London of Charles II and James II on various occasions. One, of 1682, is addressed to James as Duke of York, before his accession.

Weldon, George (1906–1963) English conductor. He studied at the Royal College of Music with Sargent, and conducted various provincial orchestras, in 1943 becoming conductor of the City of Birmingham Symphony Orchestra (CBSO), a post he held until 1951; he was later assistant conductor of the Hallé Orchestra under Barbirolli.

Weldon, John (1676–1736) English organist and composer. He held various organist's posts in Oxford and London, and in 1700 won first prize for his setting of Congreve's masque *The Judgement of Paris* against John Eccles, Gottfried Finger, and Daniel Purcell.

Weldon was educated at Eton, where he studied music under the college organist John Walton; he later became a pupil of Purcell in London. In 1694 he was appointed organist of New College, Oxford. In 1701 he became a Gentleman of the Chapel Royal and in 1708 organist there on the death of John Blow; he also became organist of St Bride's and in 1714 of St Martin-in-the-Fields.

Works include: masque *The Judgment of Paris* (1701); music for *The Tempest* (about 1712), songs for Cibber's *She would and she would not* and other plays; anthems; songs.

Wellesz, Egon Joseph (1885–1974) Austrian-born British composer and musicologist. He taught at Vienna University 1913–38, specializing in the history of Byzantine, Renaissance, and modern music. He moved to England 1938 and lectured at Oxford from 1943. His compositions include operas such as *Alkestis* 1924; symphonies, notably the Fifth 1957; ballet music; and a series of string quartets.

Wellesz studied with Schoenberg and Bruno Walter in Vienna, and also musicology with Guido Adler at the university there, receiving a doctorate in 1908. In 1913 he became a lecturer in music history in Vienna and was professor 1930–38.

He edited and wrote books on Byzantine music, and published works on Schoenberg, Cavalli and the Venetian opera, and the modern orchestra. In 1932 he received an honorary doctorate from Oxford University and in 1938 he settled there, becoming a lecturer in 1943 and Reader 1948–56. He was a member of the editorial board of the *New Oxford History of Music* and editor of volume I and one of the editions of *Monumenta Musicae Byzantinae*. His books include *A History of Byzantine Music* and *Eastern Elements in Western Chant*.

Works include: OPERA *Alkestis* (Hofmannsthal, 1924) and *Die Bacchantinnen* (after Euripides, 1931), *Incognita* (on Congreve's story, 1951).

VOCAL AND ORCHESTRA nine symphonies (1945–71), symphonic suite *Prosperos Beschwörungen* (after Shakespeare's *Tempest*, 1938), violin concerto; three Masses.

CHAMBER AND INSTRUMENTAL *The Leaden Echo and the Golden Echo* (G M Hopkins) for soprano, clarinet, viola, cello and piano (1944); nine string quartets (1911–66); octet; solo sonatas for violin, cello, oboe, clarinet; piano pieces; songs.

Well-tempered Clavier see ◊*Wohltemperierte Clavier, Das*.

Werckmeister, Andreas (1645–1706) German organist and theorist. He was organist at Hasselfelde, Quedlinburg and Halberstadt in succession. He wrote theoretical works, especially on keyboard tuning.

Werfel, Franz (1890–1945) Austrian novelist and playwright. He studied at Prague and Leipzig University His works include a novel on Giuseppe Verdi and translations of Verdi's operas, such as *Forza del destino* (1925), *Simon Boccanegra* (1929), and *Don Carlos*. See ◊Grosz (*Spiegelmensch*); ◊*Maximilien* (Milhaud); ◊Orff (*Turmes Auferstehung*); ◊*Troades* (Reimann); ◊*Zwingburg* (Krenek).

Werle, Lars Johann (1926–) Swedish composer. He studied at Uppsala University with Bäck. Teacher at the National School of Music in Stockholm. He is best known for his technically varied output of operas: *Dream about Thérèse* (1964), *The Journey* (1969), *Tintomara* (1973), *A Midsummer Night's Dream* (1985), *Lionardo* (1988), *The Painting: An Afternoon at the Prado* (1990), double-bill *Hercules* and *Väntarna* (1995).

Werner, Gregor Joseph (1693–1766) Austrian composer. He was appointed music director to the Esterházy family in 1728; Haydn became his assistant there in 1761and succeeded him five years later. Shortly before his death Werner reported to Prince Nikolaus von Esterházy on Haydn's alleged laziness and ineptitude.

Works include: over 20 Masses, three Requiems and other church music; 18 orator-

ios; symphony; string quartet, six introductions and fugues for string quartet (published by Haydn); sonatas and other pieces for two violins and bass.

Werrecore, Matthias Hermann (died c. 1574) Flemish composer. In 1522 he succeeded Franchino Gafori as maestro di cappella of Milan Cathedral.

Works include: motets for five voices, four-part song on the battles of Bicocca and Pavia, in which Francesco Sforza gained the mastery of Milan.

Wert, Giaches de (1535–1596) Flemish composer. He was music director at the ducal court of Mantua from the early 1560s until 1595. He was a prolific composer, and wrote over 150 sacred vocal pieces, but his most celebrated compositions are his madrigals. He publiushed 16 books of madrigals and other secular works, and had a great influence on his successors, especially Monteverdi.

Wert was sent to Italy as a choirboy when a small child, to sing at the court of the marchese della Padulla at Avellino near Naples. At age nine he entered the service of Count Alfonso Gonzaga as a member of the choir of the Novellara at Reggio. He began to publish madrigals towards the end of the 1550s and about 1560 went into service at the ducal court of Mantua under Gugliel-mo Gonzaga. He was also attached to the church of Santa Barbara, where he succeeded Giovanni Contina as maestro di cappella in 1565. In 1566 he accompanied the Duke to Augsburg and there declined an offer from the Emperor Maximilian II. In 1567 he visited Venice with the court and later Ferrara under Alfonso (II) d'Este. About that time he suffered much from the intrigues of the Italian musicians, who disliked him as a foreigner, and in 1570 one of them, Agostino Bonvicino, was dismissed for a love-affair with Wert's wife. In 1580 he and his family were given the freedom of the city of Mantua in perpetuity.

His madrigals often had high-quality texts, and were declamatory in style and with the three upper voices frequently emphasized; they were written for virtuoso court singers, particularly the *concerto delle donne* or 'singing ladies' of Ferrara.

Works include: motets, 11 books of madrigals for five voices (1558–95), one for four voices, canzonets, villanelle.

Werther opera by Massenet (libretto by E Blau, P Milliet and G Hartmann, based on Goethe's novel), produced in German, Vienna, Opera, 16 February 1892, conductor Jahn;

first Paris performance, Opéra-Comique, 16 January 1893. Charlotte promised her dead mother that she would marry Albert, but Werther falls in love with her. Unable to reconcile himself to the situation, Werther shoots himself, dying in her arms.

Wesendonck Lieder five songs for voice and piano by Wagner (texts by Mathilde Wesendonck (1828–1902), with whom the composer was in love); composed Zurich, 1857–58. Usually heard in orchestral arrangement by Felix Mottl. Titles are 1. *Der Engel*; 2. *Stehe still*; 3. *Im Treibhaus*; 4. *Schmerzen*; 5. *Träume*. Nos. 3 and 5 were studies for *Tristan*, also written under the influence of Mathilde Wesendonck.

Wesley, Charles (1757–1834) English organist and composer. He was a pupil of Kelway and Boyce in London and later organist at various churches and chapels. He also appeared in public as harpsichordist.

Works include: incidental music for Mason's *Caractacus*; concerto grosso; six organ or harpsichord concertos; six string quartets (1776); anthems, hymns, harpsichord pieces; songs.

Wesley, Samuel (1766–1837) English organist, composer, and conductor. He was brother of Charles Wesley, and nephew of John Wesley (the founder of Methodism). Like his brother he showed precocious musical gifts at a very early age. At the age of six he was taught by the organist of the church of St James, in Barton, Bristol; at age eight he finished the oratorio *Ruth*, and soon after appeared at the organ as a prodigy. He did much to spread a knowledge of Bach in England, and edited some of his works. He conducted the Birmingham Festival in 1811, lectured at the Royal Institution, and gave frequent organ recitals.

Works include: the oratorios *Ruth* (1744) and *The Death of Abel* (1799); four masses, numerous Latin and English anthems, including *In exitu Israel, Exultate Deo, Dixit Dominus, All go unto one place, Behold how good, Hear, O thou shepherd* (some with organ), Morning and Evening Service in F major and other church music; *Ode on St Cecilia's Day*; four symphonies (1784–1802), and five overtures; organ and violin concertos; two string quartets and other chamber music; opera fugues, voluntaries; numerous piano works' glees, songs, and duets.

Wesley, Samuel Sebastian (1810–1876) English organist and composer, illegitimate son of Samuel Wesley. He was a pupil of his father and choirboy in the Chapel Royal from 1820. In 1826 he became organist of Hereford Cathedral, and in 1835 (when he married) of Exeter Cathedral; he was organist of Leeds Parish Church 1842–1849, of Winchester Cathedral 1849–1865, and then, until his death, of Gloucester Cathedral. He was awarded a doctorate in music at Oxford in 1839, and became organ professor at the Royal Academy of Music in London in 1850. He continued his father's promotion of Bach's music and conducted the St Mathew Passion at Gloucester (Three Choirs Festival) in 1871.

Works include: five services, 24 anthems, two settings of *By the waters of Babylon* with soprano and with contralto solo, chants and hymn tunes; organ works; *Ode to Labour* and *The Praise of Music* for chorus; three glees; nine songs (two with cello *ad lib*); piano pieces.

Westrup, Jack (Allan) (1904–1975) English musicologist, critic, composer, and conductor. He was educated at Dulwich College and Balliol College, Oxford, where as an undergraduate he edited Monteverdi's *Orfeo* and *Incoronazione di Poppea* for performance by the Oxford University Opera Club. He taught classics at Dulwich College 1928–34, and was an assistant music critic on the *Daily Telegraph* 1934–40. From 1941 to 1944 he was lecturer in music at King's College, Newcastle-upon-Tyne, 1944–46 professor of music at Birmingham University and 1947–71 professor at Oxford. He conducted *Idomeneo* and *Les Troyens*, the first performance of E Wellesz's *Incognita* and the first UK performance of *Hans Heiling* and *L'Enfant et les sortilèges*. He was chairman of the editorial board of the *New Oxford History of Music* and editor of the sixth volume thereof. Editor of *Music and Letters* from 1959. Other literary work includes a book on Purcell and the fourth and fifth editions of the *Everyman Dictionary of Music* (1962 and 1971).

Works include: motet *When Israel came out of Egypt* for unaccompanied double chorus; part-song *Weathers*; passacaglia for orchestra; three Shakespeare songs.

Wheatstone, Charles (1802–1875) English physicist and inventor. With William Cooke, he patented a railway telegraph 1837, and, developing an idea of Samuel Christie (1784–1865), devised the **Wheatstone bridge**, an electrical network for measuring resistance. He also invented the concertina.

In 1834 Wheatstone made the first determination of the velocity of electricity along a wire. He also improved on early versions of the dynamo so that current was generated continuously.

Wheatstone was born in Gloucester and joined the family business making musical instruments. His work in acoustics led to his appointment as professor of experimental physics at King's College, London, 1834, a position he retained for the rest of his life.

In 1827 Wheatstone invented a device called the kaleidophone, which visually demonstrated the vibration of sounding surfaces by causing an illuminated spot to vibrate and produce curves by the persistence of vision. He went on to investigate the transmission of sound in instruments and discovered modes of vibration in air columns 1832 and vibrating plates 1833.

Wheatstone showed in 1835 that spectra produced by spark discharges from metal electrodes have different lines and colours formed by different electrodes. He predicted correctly that with development, spectroscopy would become a technique for the analysis of elements.

In 1860, he demonstrated how the visual combination of two similar pictures in a stereoscope gives an illusion of three dimensions.

When Lilacs Last in the Dooryard Bloom'd
US Requiem for mezzo, baritone, chorus, and orchestra by Hindemith (text by W Whitman); first performed New York, 14 May 1946, conductor Robert Shaw. Written in memory of Roosevelt and US war dead.

Whettham, Graham (Dudley) (1927–)
English composer. Largely self-taught, he writes in a fairly conservative style: more honoured abroad then in his own country, he has published his works himself from 1970.

Works include: the opera *The Chef who Wanted to Rule the World* (1969), ballet *The Masque of the Red Death* (after Poe, 1968); concertos for oboe, clarinet, and violin; four symphonies, *Sinfonietta stravagante* (1964), Sinfonia concertante (1966); *Hymnos* for strings (1978); *An English Suite* for orchestra (1984), Ballade for violin and orchestra (1988), two oboe quartets (1960, 1973), three string quartets (1967, 1978, 1980), horn trio (1976), concerto for ten wind (1979); choral music, including *A Mass for Canterbury* (1986), songs; music for brass band and for organ.

whistle any of a class of wind instruments including recorders, flutes, organ pipes, and panpipes, that uses a rigid edge as an aerofoil to split the air flow, giving a characteristic 'chuff' onset to the tone. Among the most ancient and widespread of musical instru-

ments, whistles produce a relatively pure tone and simple waveform.

Most whistles relying on human breath are soprano or higher in pitch range; those of lower pitch such as organ pipes are usually powered by bellows. Some whistles are of single pitch, others have finger holes to vary the pitch and may be overblown to sound an octave or twelfth higher.

Whitbroke, William (fl. 1520–50) English cleric and composer. He was educated at Cardinal College (later Christ Church), Oxford, where he was ordained in 1529. In 1531 he was appointed sub-dean at St Paul's Cathedral in London and soon afterwards also vicar of All Saints' Church at Stanton, Suffolk, where he may have retired on leaving St Paul's in 1535.

Works include: Mass for four voices, Magnificat, and other church music.

White, Robert (c. 1538–1574), also known as Whyte English composer. He was choirmaster at Ely, Chester, and Westminster Abbey, and wrote church music including psalm motets, anthems, and Lamentations.

White was probably the son of a London organ builder, also named Robert White, and took a degree in music at Cambridge University in 1560. In 1561 he succeeded Tye as choirmaster at Ely Cathedral. He married Tye's daughter Ellen in 1565 and left Ely in 1566 (he was succeeded by John Farrant) to become choirmaster of Chester Cathedral until about 1570, when he went to London to take up a similar post at Westminster Abbey. Along with nearly all his family, he succumbed to the plague of 1574.

Works include: 19 Latin motets; English anthems; In Nomines for viols; hexachord fantasia for keyboard.

whithorn, or May-horn early English musical instrument of the ◊oboe type, made of willow bark with a double reed of material from the same tree. It was formerly used in Oxfordshire for the Whit-Monday hunt.

Whitman, Walt(er) (1819–1892) US poet. See ◊Brian (*For Valour*); ◊Carpenter (*Sea Drift*); ◊Carter (*Warble for Lilac Time*); ◊Coleridge-Taylor (*Sea Drift*); ◊Converse (*Mystic Trumpeter* and *Night and Day*); R ◊Harris (suite); ◊Harty (*Mystic Trumpeter*); ◊Henze (chamber cantata); ◊Holst (*Ode to Death*); ◊Loeffler (*Beat! Beat! Drums!*); ◊'Morning Heroes' (Bliss); ◊*Mystic Trumpeter* (Holst); ◊Schoeck (*Trommelschläge*); ◊*Sea Drift* (Delius); ◊*Sea Symphony* (Vaughan Williams); ◊Sessions (*Turn, O Libertad*); ◊Vaughan Williams (*Toward the*

Unknown Region); ◊When Lilacs Last in the Dooryard Bloom'd (Hindemith).

Who is Silvia? song by Schubert from Shakespeare's *Two Gentlemen of Verona*, translated by E von Bauernfeld as *An Silvia* and composed 1826.

whole tone an interval consisting of two semitones, for example the interval of C–D.

whole-tone scale a scale consisting of six whole tones per octave. There are only two possible variants: the scale including the notes C–D–E–F♯–G♯–A sharp, and the scale including the notes D♭–E♭–F–G–A–B. In Western music the whole-tone scale became popular with impressionist composers, including Debussy.

The two possible whole-tone scales.

Whyte, Robert see Robert ◊White.

Whythorne, Thomas (1528–1596) English composer. He travelled in Italy and elsewhere in Europe, and published his first book of music, *Songes* for several voices, in 1571 and his second, a book of duets, in 1590; the second volume contains the earlier printed English instrumental music. His autobiography, written around 1576, was published in 1961.

Works include: psalms and secular songs for two–five voices or solo voice with instruments.

Widerspänstigen Zähmung, Der/The Taming of the Shrew opera by Götz (libretto by J V Widmann, after Shakespeare), produced Mannheim, 11 October 1874. Before Lucentio and Bianca can wed, Petruchio must tame Katherine.

Widor, Charles-Marie (-Jean-Albert) (1844–1937) French composer and organist. He created the solo organ symphony, which in effect treats the instrument itself as an orchestra of variously coloured pipes and ◊stops. He wrote ten such symphonies; the famous *Toccata* c. 1880 is the finale of his Fifth Symphony. He also wrote songs, concertos, ballets, and operas.

Widor was born at Lyon and studied under his father, who was an organist there. Later he studied with Lemmens and Fétis in Brussels. In 1870 he became organist of the church of Saint-Sulpice in Paris, and in 1890 succeeded Franck as organ professor at the Paris Conservatory. He succeeded Dubois as professor of composition in 1896.

Works include: the operas *Maître Ambros* (1886), *Les pêcheurs de Saint-Jean* (1905), *Nerto* (after Mistral); ballet *La Korrigane*; pantomime *Jeanne d'Arc*; incidental music to *Conte d'Avril* (adaptation of Shakespeare's *Twelfth Night*) and Coppée's *Les Jacobites*; Mass for double chorus and two organs, Psalm cxii for chorus, orchestra, and organ; two symphonies (1870, 1886), symphonic poem *Une nuit de Valpurgis*; symphony for organ and orchestra, two concertos for piano (1876 and 1906) and one for cello (1882); piano quintet, piano trio; violin and piano sonata, suite for flute and piano; six duets for piano and organ; ten symphonies (1876–1900) and pieces for organ; piano works; songs.

Wieck, Clara see Clara ◊Schumann.

Wiegenlied (German 'cradle song') title often given by German composers to vocal lullabies or to instrumental pieces in their manner.

Wieniawski, Henryk (1835–1880) Polish violinist and composer. He travelled widely, studying in Paris, then settling in St Petersburg, and later teaching in Brussels. He was a celebrated violinist and composed spirited Romantic pieces for the violin, notably his second violin concerto in D minor.

Wieniawski was sent to the Paris Conservatory at the age of eight, and in 1846 made his first tour, in Poland and Russia. From 1850 he travelled with his brother Józef and in 1860 was appointed solo violinist to the Tsar, living in St Petersburg most of his time until 1872, when he toured the USA with Anton Rubinstein. In 1875 he succeeded Henry Vieuxtemps as first violin professor at the Brussels Conservatory. Towards the end of his life he travelled again, in spite of serious ill-health which caused his sudden death in Russia.

Works include: two violin concertos (1853, 1862); *Souvenir de Moscou, Le carnaval russe, Légende* and numerous other pieces, fantasies and studies for violin.

Wihtol, Joseph (1863–1948) Latvian composer. He studied with Rimsky-Korsakov and others at the St Petersburg Conservatory; in 1886 he returned to Latvia and took an important share in its musical independence as a separate nation, becoming director of the National Opera at Riga and director of the Latvian Conservatory.

Works include: music for fairy play *King Brussubard*; symphonies, symphonic poem *The Feast of Ligo*, Latvian overture *Spriditis*, dramatic overture for orchestra; fantasy on Latvian folksongs for cello and orchestra.

Wilby, Philip (1949–) English composer. He studied at Oxford University and with Herbert Howells. He was appointed lecturer at Leeds University in 1972.

Works include: *Voyaging*, symphony (1991); *Laudibus in Sanctis* for wind band (1993); *Trinity Service* for chorus and organ (1992); chamber and keyboard music. Mozart reconstructions include concerto for violin and piano K315f and concerto for string trio and orchestra K320e.

Wilbye, John (1574–1638) English composer. He was not only one of the first English composers to write madrigals, but also one of the finest. Among his most characteristic works are the popular madrigals 'Draw on Sweet Night' and 'Sweet honey sucking bees', both 1609.

Wilbye was born at Diss, Norfolk, where his father was a tanner and landowner. Wilbye was patronized by the Cornwallis family at Brome Hall near Diss. In about 1595 he went into the service of their son-in-law, Sir Thomas Kytson, at Hengrave Hall near Bury St Edmunds, and was frequently in London with the family. After the death of his patron he remained in the service of Kytson's widow, Lady Elizabeth Kytson, who died in 1628, whereupon he went to Colchester to join the household of her daughter, Lady Rivers. He never married and was well-to-do, having been granted the lease of a sheep-farm by Kyston and gradually acquiring property at Diss, Bury St Edmunds, and elsewhere.

Wilbye was influenced by Morley and Ferrabosco. He published two books of madrigals (1598 and 1609), the second of which is generally regarded as one of the greatest English madrigal collections. It contains 'Draw on sweet Night', which uses major and minor tonalities to depict deep melancholy.

Works include: two sacred vocal pieces contributed to Leighton's *Teares or Lamentacions*; two books of 64 madrigals (1598, 1609), madrigal 'The Lady Oriana' contributed to *The Triumphes of Oriana*; five sacred works; three fantasies for viols (incomplete), lute lessons (lost).

Wildschütz, Der, oder Die Stimme der Natur/The Poacher, or The Voice of Nature opera by Lortzing (libretto by composer, based on a play by Kotzebue), produced Leipzig, 31 December 1842. Schoolmaster Baculus shoots a buck on the estate of Count of Eberbach and his betrothed, young Grhen, offers to intercede for him. But knowing his philandering reputation, the Count's sister (Baroness Freimann) impersonates Grhen instead. After disguise and confusion, a happy ending.

Wilkinson, Robert (c. 1450–c. 1515) English composer. He composed two settings of *Salve Regina* for five and nine voices, a *Credo in Deum/Jesus autem* for 13 voices in canon, and four incomplete works. All are in the Eton Choirbook.

Wilkinson, Thomas (fl. 1579–96) English composer. He may have been a singer at King's College, Cambridge, and he contributed three anthems to Myriell's *Tristitiae remedium* in 1616.

Works include: services, 12 verse anthems, three pavans for viols.

Willaert, Adrian (c. 1490–1562) Flemish composer. One of the most prolific and influential musicians of the mid-16th century, he was one of the earliest composers of madrigals, though his most important works are his motets. He also had a great influence on church music, broadening its character and achieving effect by a wide use of chromatic scales.

Willaert was trained in law but studied music with Jean Mouton in Paris. In 1515 he became a singer in the household of Cardinal Ippolito d'Este his extensive travels with the cardinal included visits to Rome, Ferrara, and Esztergom, and a two-year stay in Hungary. On the cardinal's death in 1520 Willaert transferred to the service of Duke Alfonso I d'Este. In 1527 he became maestro di cappella at St Mark's, Venice, where his pupils included Cipriano de Rore, Nicola Vicentino, Andrea Gabrieli, Gioseffe Zarlino, and Costanzo Porta. He revisited Flanders in 1542 and 1556–57.

Willaert's works include a large quantity of church music, as well as many madrigals, chansons, villanelles, and some instrumental pieces. *Salmi spezzati* 1550 contains music for double choirs and set a tradition for polychoral music in St Mark's. His most important work is the collection of motets and madrigals, *Musica nova*, published in 1559, though probably written much earlier.

Works include: Masses, hymns, psalms, motets, madrigals, chansons, and instrumental ensemble pieces.

William Ratcliff opera by Cui (libretto by A N Pleshtcheiev, based on Heine's drama), produced St Petersburg, 26 February 1869. Betty's jealous husband MacGregor kills her lover Edward Ratcliffe; Betty dies soon afterwards. Edward's son William is haunted by their ghosts until multiple deaths appease the ghosts.

See also ◊*Guglielmo Ratcliff*.

Williams, Grace (Mary) (1906–1977) Welsh composer. She was educated at Cardiff University, where she took a degre in music in 1926; she also studied with Vaughan Williams at the Royal College of Music 1926–30 and with Egon Wellesz in Vienna 1930–31.

Works include: the opera *The Parlour* (1961); *Hymn of Praise* (*Gogonedawg Arglwydd*, from the 12th-century Black Book of Carmarthen) for chorus and orchestra (1939); Welsh overture *Hen Walia*, legend *Rhiannon*, *Fantasy on Welsh Nursery Rhymes*, symphonic impressions *Owen Glendower* (after Shakespeare's *Henry IV*), *Penillion* (1955); violin concerto (1950); two psalms for soprano and orchestra, *The Song of Mary* (Magnificat) for soprano and orchestra; *Sinfonia concertante* for piano and orchestra (1941); elegy and *Sea Sketches* for string orchestra; songs to words by Herrick, Byron, Belloc, D H Lawrence, and others; arrangements of Welsh folk songs.

Williamson, Malcolm (Benjamin Graham Christopher) (1931–) Australian composer, pianist, and organist. He settled in Britain in 1953. His works include operas such as *Our Man in Havana* 1963, symphonies, and chamber music.

Williamson studied with Eugene Goossens at the Sydney Conservatory and with Elisabeth Lutyens in London, where he later became an organist. His music draws on a wide range of influences, moving from an awareness of the avant garde to a more popular style, and includes several operas, a ballet *The Display*, two symphonies, concertos, church music, and dramatic works for children. He was appointed Master of the Queen's Musick in 1975.

Works include: the operas *English Eccentrics* (1964), *Our Man in Havana* (1966), *The Violins of St Jacques* (1966), *Lucky Peter's Journey* (1969); concerto for organ and orchestra, four piano concertos (1957–94), violin concerto (1965), seven symphonies (1957–84); *Santiago de Espada*, overture for orchestra; *Mass of Christ the King*, for soloists, chorus, and orchestra (1975–78); *Mass of St Etheldreda* (1990), *A Year of Birds* for soprano and orchestra (1995); chamber music; piano and organ works.

Wilm, (Peter) Nikolai von (1834–1911) Latvian composer. He studied at the Leipzig Conservatory. In 1857 he became second conductor at the Riga municipal theatre and in 1860 went to St Petersburg as professor at the Nikolai Institute. He lived at Dresden 1875–78 and then at Wiesbaden.

Works include: motets; string quartet, string sextet; two sonatas and two suites for violin and piano, sonata for cello and piano; numerous piano pieces; songs; part songs.

Wilson, John (1595–1674) English lutenist, singer, and composer. He was a musician at the court of Charles I, and wrote many songs, including songs for plays. During the Commonwealth he lived in Oxfordshire and was professor of music at Oxford University, returning to London after the Restoration.

Wilson contributed, possibly with Coperario and Lanier, to *The Maske of Flowers*, performed at Whitehall in 1614. He became one of the king's musicians in 1635 and moved to Oxford with the court during the Civil War. In 1645 he took a doctorate in music there, and soon afterwards was in private service in Oxfordshire. He was professor of music at Oxford University 1656–61, then returned to London to be at or near the restored court and succeeded Henry Lawes as a Gentleman of the Chapel Royal in 1662.

Works include: music for Brome's *The Northern Lass* (1629), songs for *The Maske of Flowers*; anthem *Hearken, O God*; *Psalterium Carolinum* for three voices and continuo; elegy on the death of William Lawes; *Cheerful Ayres* for three voices; airs and dialogues with lute; songs including Shakespeare's 'Take, O take those lips away' and 'Lawn as white as driven snow'; catches.

Wilson, Thomas (Brendan) (1927–) US-born Scottish composer. He studied at Glasgow University and lectured there from 1927. His works have employed serial technique and include the operas *The Charcoal Burners* (1968) and *Confessions of a Justified Sinner* (1976).

Works include: four symphonies (1956, 1965, 1982, 1988), *Touchstone*, 'portrait for orchestra' (1967), concerto for orchestra (1967), piano concerto (1984), chamber concerto (1986), viola concerto (1987), chamber symphony (1990), violin concerto (1993); four string quartets, piano trio (1966), cello sonata (1973); three Masses, Te Deum and other church music; piano sonata and sonatina.

windcap a cylindrical cover protecting the double reed of a woodwind instrument, such as the crumhorn or shawm. It prevents the player's lips from making direct contact with the reeds and forms a secure airtight container, ensuring consistency of air pressure and tone. In omitting the windcap, Baroque instruments introduced a new aesthetic of controlled variability of tone for expressive effect.

wind machine, or aeoliphone stage device for creating sound effects. It is a barrel covered with silk, the friction of which on being turned produces a sound like a whistling wind.

It used by Richard Strauss in *Don Quixote*, by Ravel in *Daphnis et Chloé*, by Vaughan Williams in *Sinfonia antartica* and by Tippett in his fourth symphony.

Winter, Peter (von) (1754–1825) German composer. He wrote over 40 works for the stage, including *Das Labyrinth* 1798, a sequel to Mozart's *Magic Flute*. His later works are mainly church music.

Winter played as a boy in the court orchestra at Mannheim, where he was a pupil of Georg Vogler and met Mozart in 1778. He moved with the court to Munich, but went to Vienna 1780–81 and studied with Salieri. On his return to Munich he produced the first of his many operas, *Helena und Paris*, and became vice-Kapellmeister to the court in 1787 and Kapellmeister in 1798, but was periodically absent on tour.

Works include: the operas *Helena und Paris* (1782), *Der Bettelstudent* (1785), *I fratelli rivali* (1793), *Das unterbrochene Opferfest* (1796), *Das Labyrinth* (sequel to Mozart's *Magic Flute*, 1798), *Maria von Montelban* (1800), *Tamerlan* (1802), *La grotta di Calipso* (1803), *Il trionfo dell' amor fraterno*, *Il ratto di Proserpina* (1804), *Zaira*, *Colmal* (1809), *Maometto II* (1817), *Scherz, List und Rache* and *Jery und Bätely* (both libretti by Goethe), and about 20 others; ballets *Heinrich IV* (1779), *Inez de Castro*, *La mort d'Hector* and six others; Masses and other church music; oratorios *Der Sterbende Jesus*, *La Betulia liberata*, and others; cantata *Timoteo, o Gli effetti della musica* and others; three symphonies, *Schlachtsymphonie* and overtures; concerted pieces for various instruments; songs, part songs.

Winter Journey (Schubert). See ◊*Winterreise*.

Wintermärchen, Ein/A Winter's Tale opera by Goldmark (libretto by A M Willner, after Shakespeare), produced Vienna, Opera, 2 January 1908.

Winterreise/The Winter Journey song cycle by Schubert (poems by Wilhelm Müller), composed, Part i, February 1827; Part ii,

October 1827. The 24 songs are 1. *Gute Nacht*; 2. *Die Wetterfahne*; 3. *Gefrorne Tränen*; 4. *Erstarrung*; 5. *Der Lindenbaum*; 6. *Wasserflut*; 7. *Auf dem Flusse*; 8. *Rückblick*; 9. *Irrlicht*; 10. *Rast*; 11. *Frühlingstraum*; 12. *Einsamkeit*; 13. *Die Post*; 14. *Der greise Kopf*; 15. *Die Krähe*; 16. *Letzte Hoffnung*; 17. *Im Dorfe*; 18. *Der stürmische Morgen*; 19. *Täuschung*; 20. *Der Wegweiser*; 21. *Das Wirtshaus*; 22. *Mut*; 23. *Die Nebensonnen*; 24. *Der Leiermann*.

'Winter Wind' Study the nickname sometimes given to Chopin's piano Study in A minor, op. 25 no. 11.

Winter Words song cycle to poems by Thomas Hardy for high voice and piano by Britten; first performed Harewood House, Leeds, 8 October 1953, by Peter Pears. The titles of the songs are 1. 'At Day-close in November'; 2. 'Midnight on the Great Western'; 3. 'Wagtail and Baby'; 4. 'The Little Old Table'; 5. 'The Choirmaster's Burial'; 6. 'Proud Songsters'; 7. 'At the Railway Station'; 8. 'Before Life and After'.

Wipo, (or Wigbert) (c. 995–c. 1050) German poet and priest, who ended his life as a hermit. He is the alleged author (and perhaps adaptor of the music) of the sequence *Victimae paschali*.

Wirén, Dag (Ivar) (1905–1986) Swedish composer and critic. He studied at the Stockholm Conservatory; in 1932 he received a stage grant and continued his studies with Leonid Sabaneiev in Paris. On his return he became a music critic at Stockholm.

Works include: five symphonies (1932–64), sinfonietta; serenade for strings; cello concerto, violin concerto, piano concerto; five string quartets (1930–70), two piano trios, two sonatinas for cello and piano; piano pieces; songs.

Wise, Michael (c. 1647–1687) English organist and composer. He held various organist's and choirmaster's positions in London, Windsor, and Salisbury, and wrote church music, especially anthems with fine parts for treble voices.

Wise was a choirboy at the Chapel Royal in London in 1660. In 1663 he became a lay-clerk at St George's Chapel, Windsor, and in 1668 organist and choirmaster of Salisbury Cathedral. He was appointed a Gentleman of the Chapel Royal in 1676, but retained his post at Salisbury until 1685. At the time of the coronation of James II he was suspended from the Chapel Royal, probably because of characteristically difficult conduct. In 1687 he became almoner and choirmaster at St Paul's

Cathedral in London, but continued to visit Salisbury, where his wife had remained. After a dispute with her at night he left the house and was killed in a quarrel with a watchman.

Works include: services and anthems (including *The Ways of Zion Mourn*); songs and catches.

Wishart, Peter (1921–1984) English composer. He studied with Nadia Boulanger and at Birmingham University; lecturer there 1950–59. King's College, London, 1972–77, professor Reading University 1977–84. His music was influenced by Stravinsky and Orff.

Works include: the operas *Two in the Bush* (1956), *The Captive* (1960), *The Clandestine Marriage* (1971) and *Clytemnestra* (1973); ballets *Beowulf* and *Persephone* (1957); two symphonies (1953, 1973), two violin concertos (1951, 1968), concerto for orchestra (1957); Te Deum (1952) and much other choral music; string quartet (1954); organ sonata.

Wohltemperierte Clavier, Das/The Well-tempered Clavier two sets of preludes and fugues by Bach for keyboard (not exclusively clavichord, as has sometimes been inferred from a misunderstanding of the title), finished in 1722 and 1744 respectively. Each set consists of a cycle of 24 preludes and fugues in all the major and minor keys in ascending order. The two books together are commonly known in England as 'The 48'. See also ◊Weber (Bernhard Christian) .

wolf a technical term for a jarring sound produced between certain intervals on keyboard instruments tuned in meantone ◊temperament or on string instruments by defective vibration on a certain note or notes.

Wolf, Hugo (Filipp Jakob) (1860–1903) Austrian composer. His more than 250 lieder (songs) included the *Mörike-Lieder/Mörike Songs* 1888 and the two-volume *Italienisches Liederbuch/Italian Songbook* 1892, 1896.

Wolf brought a new concentration and tragic eloquence to the art of lieder, seeking to enhance the dramatic and emotional potential of the poetry he set by establishing an equal partnership between singer and pianist. Among his other works are the opera *Der Corregidor/The Magistrate* 1895 and orchestral works, such as *Italian Serenade* 1892.

His father, a leather merchant, encouraged his early gifts by teaching him piano and violin. He entered the Vienna Conservatory in 1875, but left it the following year, preferring to pick up his own instruction where he could. From 1877, his father having incurred great financial losses, he was obliged to earn his own living by teaching. He often

lived in great poverty, but was befriended by various musical families; the conductors Franz Schalk and Felix Mottl took a professional interest in him. In 1881 he was engaged as second conductor at Salzburg under Carl Muck, but was found to be temperamentally so unfitted for the post that the engagement was terminated within three months. He was music critic for the Vienna *Salonblatt* 1884–87, but here again he offended many people by his irascibility and intolerance (which saw no fault in Wagner and no good in Brahms). Meanwhile his masterful song settings of Mörike and Eicherdorff won him wide recognition. However, he had contracted syphilis, and in 1897 became insane. He was sent to a sanatorium. Discharged as cured in 1898, he had a relapse after becoming involved in a quarrel with Mahler at the Vienna Opera, and was taken to an asylum in a hopeless condition at the end of the year, remaining there until his death.

Works include: the operas *Der Corregidor* (1896) and *Manuel Venegas* (unfinished); incidental music to Ibsen's *The Feast at Solhaug* (1891); 48 early songs, 53 songs to words by Mörike (1888); 20 to words by Eichendorff (1880–88), 51 to words by Goethe (1888–89), *Italienisches Liederbuch* (46 songs, 1892, 1896), *Spanisches Liederbuch* (44 songs, 1889–90), 31 songs to words by various poets, including six by G Keller and three sonnets by Michelangelo (1897); symphonic poem *Penthesilea* (after Kleist, 1883); *Italian Serenade* for string quartet in D minor (1880); *Christnacht* for solo voices, chorus, and orchestra, *Elfenlied* from Shakespeare's *Midsummer Night's Dream* for soprano, chorus, and orchestra (1890), *Der Feuerreiter* and *Dem Vaterland* for chorus and orchestra; six part songs.

Wolf, Johannes (1869–1947) German musicologist. He studied with Spitta in Berlin and took a doctor's degree at Leipzig in 1893. In 1908 he became professor of music at Berlin University and in 1915 librarian of the music section of the Prussian State Library, where he succeeded Altmann as director in 1928. He specialized in and wrote on early music, treatises, and notations.

Wolff, Christian (1934–) French-born US composer. His music makes use of a strictly mathematical basis, particularly with regard to rhythms and rests, while also including chance elements.

Wolff went to the USA in 1941. He studied with Cage, and also studied classical languages at Harvard University, obtaining a doctorate, and becoming a lecturer there in classics in 1962.

Works include: *Nine* for nine instruments (1951), *For six or seven players*, *Summer* for string quartet, *In Between Pieces* for three players, *For five or ten Players* (1962), *For one, two or three people*, septet for any instruments (1964), *For Pianist*, *For Piano I, II*, *Duo for Pianists I and II*, *Duet I* for piano (four hands), *Duet II* for horn and piano, *You Blew It* for chorus (1971).

Wolf-Ferrari, Ermanno (1876–1948) Italian composer. His operas include *Il segreto di Susanna/Susanna's Secret* 1909 and the realistic tragedy *I gioielli di Madonna/The Jewels of the Madonna* 1911.

He was sent to Rome to study art by his German father, who was a painter. However, he turned to music and studied with Joseph Rheinberger at Munich. In 1899 he sent his oratorio to Venice and succeeded in having it performed, and in 1900 he brought out his first opera, after which his stage successes were frequently repeated. Many of his operas were first produced in Germany, including several that sought to evoke the spirit of 18th-century Venetian comedy. In 1902–12 he was director of the Liceo Benedetto Marcello at Venice.

Works include: the operas *Cenerentola* (1900), *Le donne curiose* (1903), *I quattro rusteghi* (1906), *Il segreto di Susanna* (1909), *I gioielli della Madonna* (1911), *Amor medico* (after Molière, 1913), *Gli amanti sposi* (1925), *Das Himmelskleid* (1927), *Sly* (after Shakespeare's *Taming of the Shrew*, 1927), *La vedova scaltra* (1931), *Il campiello* (1936), *La dama boba* (after Lope de Vega, 1939), *Gli dei a Tebe* (1943); cantatas *La Sulamita* and *La vita nuova* (after Dante, 1903); violin concerto, chamber symphony for strings, woodwind, piano, and horn (1901); piano quintet, piano trio, two violin and piano sonatas; organ pieces; cello pieces; *Rispetti* for soprano and piano.

Wolfram von Eschenbach (c. 1170–c. 1220) German Minnesinger. He took part in a singing contest at Wartburg in 1207. Seven lyric poems by him survive, without music, though two tunes are ascribed to him. He wrote an epic, *Parzival*, which was the principal source for Wagner's *Parsifal*. He appears as a character in Wagner's earlier opera, *Tannhäuser*.

Wolkenstein, Oswald von (c. 1377–1445) Austrian Minnesinger and politician. He travelled much, reputedly even as far as Asia and Africa. From 1415 he was in the service of King (later Emperor) Sigismund and was sent to Spain and Portugal on diplomatic missions. In 1421–27 he involved himself in much strife and was twice imprisoned in his endeavour to extend his land by encroaching on that of his neighbours. Although he sang of courtly love, he enjoyed a long adulterous affair.

Works include: songs on themes such as love, spring, and travel, for one–three voices (to his own words).

Wolpe, Stefan (1902–1972) US composer. He studied with Paul Juon and Schreker in Franz Berlin and in 1933–34 with Webern, then went to Palestine and in 1938 settled in the USA.

Works include: the operas *Schöne Geschichten* and *Zeus und Elida*; ballet *The Man from Midian* (1942); symphonies, symphony for 21 instruments (1956), Passacaglia and two Fugues for orchestra; cantatas *The Passion of Man, On the Education of Man, About Sport* (1932), *Unnamed Lands, Israel and his Land*; chamber music.

Wolzogen, Ernst von (1855–1934) German writer. He studied at the Universities of Strasbourg and Leipzig. With O J Bierbaum and F Wedekind he established the satirical cabaret *Das Überbrettl* in Berlin in 1901, for which A von Zemlinsky, O Straus and A Schoenberg provided some of the music. The cabaret lasted two successful years, before finally closing. He was the author of the libretto of R Strauss's *Feuersnot*.

Woman's Love and Life (Schumann). See ◊*Frauenliebe und -leben*.

Wood, Charles (1886–1926) Irish music scholar, teacher, and composer. He taught at the Royal College of Music in London from 1883 and at Cambridge University from 1897. As a composer he is remembered for his church music.

Wood learnt music from the organist of Armagh Cathedral, where his father was a lay vicar, and studied at the Royal College of Music in London 1883–87, becoming professor there in 1888. He conducted the University Music Society at Cambridge 1888–94, and took a doctorate in music there in 1894. In 1897 he became music lecturer to the University and in 1924 succeeded Stanford as professor of music.

Works include: the opera *The Pickwick Papers* (after Dickens, 1922); incidental music to Euripides' *Ion* and *Iphigenia in Tauris*; *Ode to the West Wind* (1890) and *The Song of the Tempest* for solo voices, chorus, and orchestra; *Ode on Music* (Swinburne, 1894), *Ode on Time* (Milton, 1898), *Dirge for Two Veterans*

(Whitman), *Ballad of Dundee* for chorus and orchestra; *Passion according to St Mark*; eight string quartets.

Wood, Haydn (1882–1959) British composer. A violinist, he wrote a violin concerto among other works, and is known for his songs, which include 'Roses of Picardy', associated with World War I.

Having appeared as a child prodigy, Wood studied violin with Enrique Fernández Arbós (1863–1939) and composition with Charles Villiers Stanford at the Royal College of Music in London; he also studied violin with César Thomson in Brussels.

Works include: cantata *Lochinvar* (from Scott's 'Marmion'); rhapsodies, overtures, picturesque suites, variations, and other works for orchestra; concertos for violin and for piano; fantasy string quartet; instrumental pieces; over 200 songs.

Wood, Henry Joseph (1869–1944) English conductor. From 1895 until his death, he conducted the London Promenade Concerts, now named after him. He promoted a national interest in music and encouraged many young composers. As a composer he is remembered for the *Fantasia on British Sea Songs* 1905, which ends each Promenade season.

Wood was a talented child, especially as an organist, and gave recitals and held church appointments as a boy. He studied at the Royal Academy of Music and in 1889 had his first experience as a conductor, and toured as an opera conductor for the next few years; he conducted the British premiere of *Eugene Onegin* in 1892. In 1895 he was engaged by Robert Newman to take charge of the Promenade Concerts at the newly built Queen's Hall, and he remained in charge of them for 50 years, until the end of his life, celebrating their half-centenary just before his death. He began modestly with popular programmes, but soon included many of the latest foreign and English novelties as they appeared; gave the first performance of Schoenberg's *Five Orchestral Pieces* in 1912 and first British performances of Mahler's first, fourth, seventh, and eighth symphonies. He conducted further performances of music by Bartók, Strauss, Sibelius, and Skriabin. He also conducted many music festivals and gave the first performances of works by Delius and Vaughan Williams (*Serenade to Music*, 1938). In 1898 he married the Russian soprano Olga Urussov (who died in 1909) and in 1911 Muriel Greatorex.

Wood, Hugh (1932–) English composer. He studied composition with A Milner, I Hamilton, and Seiber. He taught at Morley College 1959–62, at Liverpool University 1971–73, and at Cambridge University from 1976.

Works include: *Scenes from Comus* for soprano, tenor, and orchestra (1965); cello concerto (1969), chamber concerto (1971), violin concerto (1972), symphony (1982), piano concerto (1991); four string quartets (1959–93), quintet for clarinet, horn, and piano trio (1967), piano trio (1984), horn trio (1989); songs to texts by Logue, Hughes, Muir, and Neruda.

wood chimes musical instrument of the Tay people of central Vietnam (Nguyen) and now common throughout Vietnam. It consists of differing lengths of hanging bamboo that are struck with a stick.

Wooden Prince, The/A fából faragott kir- ályfi ballet in one act by Bartók (scenario by Bela Balazs); composed 1914–16, produced Budapest, 12 May 1917, conductor Tango. Orchestral suite (1931) performed Budapest, 23 November 1931, conductor Ernö Dohná- nyi.

Woodson, Thomas (lived 16th–17th cen- turies) English composer. In 1581 he became a member of the Chapel Royal, his place being taken by William West in 1605. He composed 40 canonic settings of the plain- song *Miserere* for keyboard, only 20 of which survive.

woodwind musical instrument from which sound is produced by blowing into a tube, causing the air within to vibrate. Woodwind instruments include those, like the flute, originally made of wood but now more commonly of metal. The saxophone, made of metal, is an honorary woodwind instru- ment because it is related to the clarinet. The oboe, bassoon, flute, and clarinet make up the normal woodwind section of an orchestra.

Woodwind instruments fall into two cate- gories: **reed instruments**, in which air passes via an aperture controlled by a vibrating flexible reed or pair of reeds; and those **without a reed** where air is simply blown into or across a tube. In both cases, different notes are obtained by changing the length of the tube by covering holes along it.

Reed instruments include the clarinet, oboe, cor anglais, saxophone, and bassoon. In the recorder, flute, and piccolo, the func- tion of a reed is achieved by design of the mouthpiece.

There is an enormous variety of woodwind instruments throughout the world.

Wooldridge, H(arry) E(llis) (1845–1917) English painter and music scholar. He was Slade Professor of Fine Arts at Oxford 1895–1904, but made a special study of medieval music. His chief works were the first two volumes of the *Oxford History of Music*.

Woolrich, John (1954–   ) English composer. He has taught at Durham, the Guildhall School of Music in London, Dartington, and Reading. *The Ghost in the Machine* for orchestra was performed at the 1990 Promenade Concerts, London.

He studied with Edward Cowie at Lancaster.

Works include: *The Barber's Timepiece* (1986), and *The Theatre Represents a Garden: Night* for orchestra (1991); *It is Midnight, Dr Schweitzer* for strings (1992); *Quick Steps*, wind octet (1990); *The Death of King Renaud*, string quintet (1992); ensemble pieces and songs.

Wordsworth, William B(rocklesby) (1908–1988) English composer. He did not begin to study music seriously until he was 20, and in 1935 became a pupil of Donald Tovey. During World War II he took to farming, but after that devoted himself entirely to composition. He was a direct descendant of the poet's brother.

Works include: the oratorio *Dies Domini* (1944); *The Houseless Dead* (D H Lawrence) for baritone chorus and orchestra, *Hymn of Dedication* (Chesterton) for chorus and orchestra; eight symphonies (1944–86), theme and variations, *Three Pastoral Sketches* for orchestra, *Sinfonia* and *Canzone and Ballade* for strings; piano concerto, cello concerto; six string quartets (1941–64); string trio; two sonatas for violin and piano, two sonatas for cello and piano; sonata and suite for piano; three hymn-tune preludes for organ; *Four Sacred Sonnets* (Donne, 1944) and other songs; rounds for several voices.

Worgan, John (1724–1790) English organist and composer. He became famous as an organ recitalist and was organist at Vauxhall Gardens.

Worgan was a pupil of Thomas Roseingrave. In about 1749 he was appointed organist of the church of St Andrew Undershaft and succeeded his brother James Worgan (c. 1715–1753), as organist of Vauxhall Gardens about 1751. He remained attached to Vauxhall Gardens as a composer until 1761, and again 1770–74. He was awarded a doctorate in music in 1775.

Works include: the oratorios *The Chief of Maon, Hannah* (1764), *Manasseh* (1766) and *Gioas* (unfinished); anthem for a victory, psalm-tunes; serenata *The Royal Voyage*, dirge in memory of Frederick, Prince of Wales; ode on the rebellion of 1745; organ pieces; harpsichord lessons; glees; songs.

working-out, or development the second section of a movement in sonata form, following the exposition, where thematic material is subjected to various developments, and the harmony undergoes more adventurous modulation than in the exposition or recapitulation, generally avoiding the tonic key before its reappearance in the recapitulation. The usual procedure is to develop the first or second subjects or both, but the procedure is by no means fixed and new matter may be introduced at will.

Worldes Blis work for orchestra by Peter Maxwell Davies, first performed London, 28 August 1968; although not well received by older members of the Promenade audience, the work established Davies with the younger set as a leading composer.

Woytowicz, Bolesław (1899–1980) Polish pianist and composer. He began by studying mathematics and philosophy at Kiev University and law at Warsaw University, but turned to the piano, which he studied at the Chopin High School at Warsaw, where he later became a teacher. He next took to composition, studying first with Felicjan Szopski (1865–1939) and Witold Maliszewski (1873–1939), and in 1930 with Nadia Boulanger in Paris.

Works include: concertino, concert suite, *Poème funèbre* on the death of Piłsudski, three symphonies (1926–63), variations in the form of a symphony for orchestra; piano concerto; two string quartets, trio for flute, clarinet, and bassoon, *Cradle Song* for soprano, clarinet, bassoon, and harp (1931); variations and other works for piano.

Wozzeck opera by A Berg (libretto by composer, from G Büchner's drama of 1836), produced Berlin, Opera, 14 December 1925. Jealous soldier Wozzeck knifes mistress Marie after she is seduced by the Drum Major and he is taunted by the Captain and Doctor. Insane, he drowns himself.

Opera by M Gurlitt (libretto ditto), produced Bremen, 22 April 1926.

Wranitzky, Paul (1756–1808) Moravian violinist and composer. In the 1780s he was in the service of Count Esterházy (not to be confused with Prince Esterházy, Haydn's employer) and in about 1790 became leader of the court opera orchestra in Vienna. He was the brother of Anton Wranitzky.

He studied with J M Kraus and Haydn in Vienna.

Works include: the operas and *Singspiele*, including *Oberon, König der Elfen* (1789), *Das Fest der Lazzaroni* (1794), *Der Schreiner* (1799); ballet divertissements *Das Waldmädchen* (1796), *Die Weinlese* (1794), *Zemire und Azore*, *Das Urteil von Paris* (1801); 51 symphonies; about 100 string quartets and quintets; piano quartets; violin sonatas and large numbers of other instrumental works; over 200 canons; vocal duets and trios; church music.

wrest the old English term for a tuning-key, from the verb meaning to twist or wrench. The tuning-pins of the piano are still called wrest-pins and the board into which they are inserted is the wrest-plank.

Wuorinen, Charles (1938–) US composer, conductor, and pianist. His early works are tonal but he was later influenced by Varèse, Babbitt, and serial technique.

He studied at Columbia University, and taught there 1964–71.

Works include: the masque *The Politics of Harmony* (1967), 'baroque burlesque' *The Whore of Babylon* (1975); three symphonies (1958–59), four chamber concertos (1957–59), *Evolutio transcripta* for orchestra (1961), two piano concertos (1966, 1974), *Contrafactum* for orchestra (1969), concerto for amplified violin and orchestra (1971), *Percussion Symphony* (1976), *Bamboula Squared* for orchestra (1983), Concerto for saxophone quartet and orchestra (1993), *The Mission of Virgil* for orchestra (1993); *Dr Faustus Lights the Light* for narrator and instruments (1957), octet (1962), string trio (1968), chamber concerto (1970), wind quintet (1977), horn trio (1981), three string quartets (1971, 1979, 1987), Saxophone quartet (1992); *Symphonia sacra* for vocal soloists and instrumental ensemble (1961), *The Prayer of Jonah* for voices and string quintet (1962), *The Celestial Sphere*, sacred oratorio for chorus and orchestra (1979); electronic music.

Wurlitzer trademark for a large pipe ◊organ that was often installed in the huge cinemas of the 1930s (Compton was another make). Such organs were equipped with percussive and other special effects, and had many keyboards, pedals, and stops. A musician would play before the start of the film or between films.

In the early 1960s the US manufacturer Wurlitzer introduced an electric piano in which vibrating metal reeds produced the note or signal sent to the amplifier.

Wyk, Arnold van (1916–1983) South African composer. He began to learn the piano at the age of 12 and, after working in an insurance office at Cape Town, entered Stellenbosch University in 1936. In 1937 he was commissioned to write music for the centenary of the Voortrekkers and in 1938 he went to live in London, having gained the Performing Right Society's scholarship. He studied composition with Theodore Holland and piano with Harold Craxton at the Royal Academy of Music, joined the British Broadcasting Corporation (BBC) for a short time, and later devoted himself to composition.

Works include: two symphonies (1944, 1952), suite for small orchestra on African tunes *Southern Cross* (1943); *Saudade* for violin and orchestra; string quartets, five elegies for string quartet (1941); three improvisations on a Dutch folksong for piano duet.

Wylde, John (fl. c. 1425–50) English music theorist, precentor of Waltham Abbey, near London. He wrote a summary of Guido d'Arezzo's theoretical work, entitled *Musica Gwydonis monachi*. This stands at the head of a collection compiled by him (British Library, Lansdowne MS 763) which later belonged to Tallis, whose signature it bears.

Wynne, David (1900–1983) Welsh composer. He worked as a coalminer during adolescence and studied at University College, Cardiff, from 1925. He was active in the promotion of Welsh music.

Works include: the operas *Jack and Jill* (1975) and *Night and Cold Peace* (1979); five symphonies (1952–80), two rhapsody concertos, *Octade* for orchestra (1978); five string quartets (1944–80); sextet for piano and orchestra (1977); song cycles and choral music.

Wyzewa, Théodore de (1862–1917), originally Wyzewski French musicologist of Polish parentage. He lived in France from 1869. In 1884 he founded the *Revue Wagnérienne* with Edouard Dujardin and in 1901 the Société Mozart with Boschot. He became a political and literary journalist, but his chief work is his study of Mozart, of which he completed two volumes in collaboration with Georges de Saint-Foix. He was a friend of Renoir and Mallarmé.

Xenakis, Iannis (1922–) Romanian-born Greek composer. He studied music in Paris 1947–51 while practising as an engineering draughtsman for French architect Le Corbusier. Compositions such as *Metastasis/After Change* 1953–54 for 61 players apply stochastic principles (for example, describing particle motion in fluids) to the composition of densely textured effects in which change is perceived globally. Later works, including a setting of the *Oresteia* 1965–66 for choir and ensemble, draw on Greek mythology.

Xenakis was born at Braila, Romania. He studied music with Honegger, Milhaud, and Messiaen, and evolved a method of stochastic composition using the mathematics of chance and probability and also employing computers. His ideas have exercised considerable influence on other composers. He published *Formalized Music: Thought and Mathematics in Composition* 1972.

Works include: THEATRE MUSIC *Oresteia* (1966) and *The Bacchae* (1993); *Metastasis* for orchestra (1954), *Pithoprakta* for string orchestra (1956), *Achorripsis* for 21 instruments (1957), *Syrmos* for 18 strings (1959); *Akrata* for 16 wind (1965), *Polytope* for small orchestra (1967), *Synaphai* for piano and orchestra (1969), *Noomena* for orchestra (1975), *Palimpsest* for piano and ensemble (1982), *Keqrops* for piano and orchestra (1986), *Tracées* for orchestra (1987), *Tuorakemsu* for orchestra (1990).

ELECTRONIC COMPOSITIONS *Diamorphosis* (1958), *Orient-Occident* (1960).

OTHER *Morsima-Amorsima* (1) for four players (1956–62), (2) for ten players (1962); ballets *Kraanerg* for orchestra and tape (1969) and *Antikhton* (1971); *Oresteia* for chorus and chamber ensemble (1966), *Chants des Soleils* (1983), *Idmen A* for chorus and percussion quartet (1985), *Idmen B* for chorus and percussion sextet (1986), *Knephas* for unaccompanied chorus (1990); chamber works *Atrées* (1962), *Anaktoria* (1969), *Auroura* (1971), *Phlegra* (1975), *Retours-Windungen* (1976), *Tetras* for string quartet (1983), *Thallein* for 14 players (1984), *Jalons* for 15 players (1986), *Akea* piano quartet (1986), *Waarg* for 13 players (1988), *Okho* for 3 players (1989), *Epicycle* for cello and 12 players (1989), *Dox-Orkh* for violin and 89 players (1991); *Akanthos* for soprano and ensemble (1977).

Xerse/Xerxes opera by Cavalli (libretto by N Minato), produced Venice, Teatro dei SS Giovanni e Paolo, 12 January 1654.
See also ◊*Serse*.

xylophone musical ◊percussion instrument of African and Indonesian origin, consisting of a series of hardwood bars of varying lengths, each with its own distinct pitch, arranged in sequence over a resonator or resonators, and played with hard sticks. It first appeared as an orchestral instrument in Saint-Saëns's *Danse macabre* 1874, illustrating dancing skeletons.

xylorimba percussion instrument, a small ◊marimba made in the USA.

Y

Yansons, Arvid (1914–1984), or Jansons Latvian conductor. Debut Riga Opera, 1944. He conducted the Leningrad Philharmonic Orchestra from 1952, and chief guest conductor Hallé Orchestra from 1964. His son is Marriss Jansons.

Yan Tan Tethera opera by Harrison Birtwistle; (text by T Harrison). Written 1983–84 for television, first performed London, 5 August 1986. Shepherd Alan arouses jealousies of Caleb Raven, who causes wife Hannah and twins to be imprisoned; they are released after seven years.

Year 1812, The festival overture by Tchaikovsky, op. 49, written for the commemoration of the 70th anniversary of Napoleon's retreat from Moscow and first performed during the Moscow Arts and Industrial Exhibition, 20 August 1882, at the consecration of the Cathedral of the Redeemer in the Kremlin.

Yellow Cake Review, The work by Maxwell Davies for singers and piano (text by composer), which describes threat to Orkneys posed by uranium mining, first performed Kirkwall, Orkney, 21 June 1980.

Yeoman of the Guard, The, or The Merryman and his Maid operetta by Sullivan (libretto by W S Gilbert), produced London, Savoy Theatre, 3 October 1888.

yodel an elaborate form of song in Switzerland, Tyrol, and Styria, usually sung by men in falsetto, with rapid changes to chest voice, very free in rhythm and metre and using as a rule the restricted scale of the natural harmonics of instruments like the alphorn. The yodel is thus very probably derived or copied from the *ranz des vaches*.

Yorkshire Feast Song, The an ode or cantata by Purcell, 'Of old when heroes', for two altos, tenor, two basses, five-part chorus, recorders, oboes, trumpets, and strings, words by Thomas Durfey, written in 1690 for the annual reunion of Yorkshiremen in London, intended to be held that year on 14 February but postponed to 27 March owing to parliamentary elections.

Young, La Monte (1935–) US composer. He studied at the University of California, Los Angeles 1956–57 and at Berkeley 1957–60. In 1959 he also studied with Stockhausen, and then lectured for a time on guerrilla warfare at the New York School for Social Research.

Works include: *The Tortoise Droning Selected Pitches from the Holy Numbers for the Two Black Tigers, the Green Tiger and the Hermit* (1964); *The Tortoise Recalling the Drone of the Holy Numbers as they were Revealed in the Dreams of the Whirlwind and the Obsidian Gong, Illuminated by the Sawmill, the Green Sawtooth Ocelot and the High-Tension Line Stepdown Transformer* (both works staged with voice, gong, and strings, 1964); *Orchestral Dreams* (1984); Piano music including the six-hour *Well-Timed Piano* from 1964).

Young Apollo work by Britten for piano, string quartet, and string orchestra (1939, first performed Toronto, 27 August 1939; withdrawn until 1979).

Yradier, Sebastian (1809–1865) Spanish composer. He was in Paris for a time as singing-master to the Empress Eugénie and later lived in Cuba for some years. He wrote popular Spanish songs, including 'La Paloma' and the melody which formed the basis of the habañera in Bizet's *Carmen*.

Ysaÿe, Eugène-Auguste (1858–1931) Belgian violinist, conductor, and composer. One of the greatest and most individual virtuosos of his day, he toured as a soloist and conductor throughout Europe and America. Although he never studied composition formally, he mastered writing in a Romantic style.

He studied with his father, Nicolas Ysaÿe, then at the Liège Conservatory, and later with Henryk Wieniawski and Henry Vieuxtemps. Having already appeared in public in 1865, he played at Pauline Lucca's concerts at Cologne and Aachen, where he met Ferdinand Hiller and Joseph Joachim, and later, at Frankfurt, he came into touch with Joachim Raff and Clara Schumann. He was based in Paris 1883–86, becoming close to Debussy, Fauré, and Saint-Saëns. In 1886 he formed the Ysaÿe Quartet, and premiered Debussy's quartet in 1893. He was violin professor at the Brussels Conservatory 1886–98, and founded and conducted orchestral concerts in the Belgian capital. He toured extensively, first visiting England in 1889 and the USA in 1894, playing the Beethoven Concerto with the New York Philharmonic Orchestra. Admired everywhere for his skill and musicianship, he often performed the Franck Sonata dedicated to him and the Elgar Concerto. He conducted the Cincinnati Symphony Orchestra 1918–22.

Works include: the opera *Piére li Houîeu* (in Walloon dialect, 1931); eight violin concertos;

Poème élégiaque, mazurkas and other pieces for violin and piano.

Yun, Isang (1917–1995) Korean-born German composer. He studied in Korea and Japan, and with Blacher and Rufer in Berlin. An espousal of serial techniques led to withdrawal of works written before 1959. In 1967 he was kidnapped from West Berlin by South Korean agents and charged with sedition; after release taught at Hochschule für Musik, Berlin, 1970–85.

Works include: STAGE operas *Der Traum des Liu-Tung* (1965), *Die Witwe des Schmetterlings* (1967), *Geisterliebe* (1971), *Sim Tjong* (1972).

ORCHESTRA *Colloides sonores* for string orchestra (1961), *Dimensionen* for orchestra (1971).

CONCERTOS cello (1976), flute (1977).

SYMPHONIES no 1 (1983), no 2 (1984), no 3 (1985), no 4 'Singing in the Dark' (1986), no 5 for baritone and orchestra (1987).

CHORAL WITH ORCHESTRA *Om Mani padame hum*, cycle for soprano, baritone, chorus, and orchestra (1964), *Der weise Mann*, for baritone, chorus, and small orchestra (1977).

CHAMBER four string quartets, piano trio (1975), *Pièce concertante* for chamber ensemble (1977), flute quartet (1988).

Yvain, Maurice (Pierre Paul) (1891–1965) French composer. His studies at the Paris Conservatory were interrupted by army service during World War I. Resuming his studies after the war, he devoted his whole attention to the composition of operettas, the first of which, *Ta bouche*, was an immediate success in 1922. It was followed by many others, as well as a ballet, *Vent* 1937.

Z

Zacara (fl. c. 1400), or Zacharie either of two composers active in Italy during the late 14th and early 15th centuries: the works of **Antonio Zacara** of Teramo (fl. 1391–c. 1420) are found in manuscripts from many parts of Europe and were evidently very influential; they include Mass movements and Italian and French songs. **Nicola Zacharie** of Brindisi (fl. 1420–1434) was a singer in the papal chapel 1420–24 and again in 1434; he also sang in Florence. His works include perhaps only one Italian song, motets, and one Mass movement.

Zacconi, Lodovico (1555–1627) Italian priest and music theorist. He wrote a four-volume treatise on figured chant, *Prattica di musica* 1592–1622.

Zacconi went to live at Venice, joined the monastic order of St Augustine, and was maestro di cappella at its church. In 1593, at the invitation of the Archduke Charles, he went to Vienna, where he became court music director and remained until 1619, when he returned to Venice.

Zach, Jan (1699–1773) Bohemian organist and composer. He worked as a violinist and organist in Prague, where he came under the influence of Cernohorský. He later left for Germany, and in 1745 was appointed Kapellmeister to the Electoral court in Mainz. He was dismissed c. 1757, and spent the rest of his life travelling, without permanent employment.

Works include: 33 Masses, three Requiems; *Stabat Mater* and other church music; symphonies and partitas for orchestra; chamber music; organ music.

Zadok the Priest first of four anthems composed 1727 by Handel for coronation of George II; given at all subsequent coronations.

Zaide unfinished opera by Mozart (libretto in German, by J A Schachtner), begun 1779, first produced Frankfurt, 27 January 1886. Sultan Soliman's favourite Zaide escapes with prisoner Gomatz but they are recaptured.

Zaïs ballet *héroïque* in a prologue and four acts by Rameau (libretto by L de Cahusac), produced Paris, Opéra, 29 February 1748. Spirit Zaïs sacrifices magic powers for love of shepherdess Zélide but they are restored by spirit-ruler Oromases.

Zampa, ou La Fiancée de marbre/*Zampa, or The Marble Betrothed* opera by Hérold (libretto by A H J Mélesville), produced Paris, Opéra-Comique, 3 May 1831. The wedding of Camille and Alphonse is interrupted by the pirate Zampa, the older brother of Alphonse. Before Zampa can force Camille to marry him the statue of his former bride Alice kills him.

Zandonai, Riccardo (1883–1944) Italian composer. His greatest success was with the verismo opera *Francesca da Rimini* 1914, which is still performed in Europe and at the New York Metropolitan Opera House.

Zandonai studied at Roveredo and later at the Liceo Musicale of Pesaro, where Mascagni was director. He left in 1902 and at Milan met the librettist Arrigo Boito, who introduced him to the publisher Giulio Ricordi, by whom his first opera was commissioned.

Works include: the operas *Il grillo sul focolare* (after Dickens' *Cricket on the Hearth*, 1908), *Conchita* (after Louÿs's *La Femme et le pantin*, 1911), *Melenis* (1912), *La via della* *finestra, Francesca da Rimini* (on d'Annunzio's play, 1914), *Giulietta e Romeo* (after Shakespeare, 1922), *I cavalieri di Ekebù* (after Selma Lagerlöf, 1925), *Giuliano* (1928), *La farsa amorosa* (1933), *Una partitia;* film music for *Princess Tarakanova;* Requiem (1915), *Pater noster* for chorus, organ, and orchestra; *Ballata eroica, Fra gli alberghi delle Dolomiti, Quadri di Segantini* (1931), *Rapsodia trentina,* overture *Colombina* for orchestra; *Concerto romantico* for violin and orchestra (1919); serenade and *Concerto andaluso* for cello and orchestra; string quartet; songs.

Zarathustra (R Strauss). See ◊*Also sprach Zarathustra.*

Zar lässt sich photographieren, Der/The Tsar has his photograph taken opera in one act by Weill (libretto by Kaiser), produced Leipzig, 18 February 1928. Amorous Tsar flirts at Parisian photo studio with would-be assassin.

Zarlino, Gioseffo (1517–1590) Italian music theorist and composer. He wrote two large treatises, the three-volume *Istitutioni armoniche* 1558 and *Dimostrationi armoniche* 1571. He was attacked for these by Vincenzo Galilei, whereupon he issued another volume, *Sopplimenti musicali* 1588; a fourth, nonmusical volume, was added to the complete edition later. In his theories he discussed modes and intervals, and also looked back to classical models, seeking to summarise and develop the musical theory of the Greeks.

Born in Chioggia, Zarlino was educated by Franciscan monks, and joined the order in 1521. In 1536 he was a singer at Chioggia Cathedral. He studied theology and received minor orders in 1539 (when he became organist at the cathedral), but was learned also in philosophy, sciences, and languages. He settled in Venice in 1541, became a fellow-student with Cipriano de Rore under Adrian Willaert, and in 1565 became first maestro di cappella at St Mark's. In 1583 he was offered the bishopric of Chioggia, but declined it, preferring to remain at St Mark's.

Zarlino wrote motets and madrigals, but was chiefly a theorist. *Le istitutioni harmoniche* caused Willaert's methods of contrapuntal writing to become models of the style.

Works include: Mass for the foundation of the church of Santa Maria della Salute and other church music; pageant for the victory of Lepanto.

Zar und Zimmermann, oder Die zwei Peter/ Tsar and Carpenter, or the Two Peters opera by Lortzing (libretto by composer, based on a French play by A H J Mélesville,

J T Merle and E Cantiran de Boirie), produced Leipzig, 22 December 1837. Under disguise in a foreign shipyard, Tsar Peter the Great is confused with deserter Peter Ivanov, whom he befriends.

See also ◊*Borgomastro di Saardam.*

zarzuela (from La Zarzuela, royal country house where it was first developed) Spanish musical theatre form combining song, dance, and speech. It originated as an amusement for royalty in the 17th century and found an early exponent in the playwright Calderón. Often satirical, zarzuela gained renewed popularity in the 20th century with the works of Frederico Moreno Tórroba (1891–1982).

His *La Chulapona,* staged at the 1989 Edinburgh Festival was claimed to be the first zarzuela to be seen in Britain.

Zauberflöte, Die opera by Mozart (libretto by E Schikaneder, with the aid of K L Giesecke), produced Vienna, Theater auf der Wieden, 30 September 1791. Winter's opera *Das Labyrinth* is a sequel to it. There is also an unfinished libretto by Goethe intended for a sequel. Prince Tamino and Pamina undergo trials of their love while birdcatcher Pagageno finds a mate.

Zauberharfe, Die/The Magic Harp magic play with music by Schubert (libretto by G E von Hofmann), produced Vienna, Theater an der Wien, 19 August 1820).

Zauberoper see ◊magic opera.

Zauberzither, Die, oder Caspar der Fagottist/The Magic Zither, or Jasper the Bassoonist *Singspiel* by Wenzel Müller, produced Vienna, Leopoldstadt Theatre, 8 June 1791. The plot shows close resemblances to that of Schikaneder's libretto for Mozart's *Zauberflöte,* which may have been borrowed from it or based on the same source.

Zazà opera in four acts by Leoncavallo (libretto by composer, after play by Simon and Berton). Produced Milan, Teatro Lirica, 10 November 1900. Music hall singer Zazà returns to Cascart after learning that her current lover Milio Dufresne is a married man.

Zdravitsa/Hail to Stalin cantata for chorus and orchestra on folk texts by Prokofiev, op. 85; composed 1939, first performed Moscow, 21 December 1939; first British performance British Broadcasting Corporation (BBC), 21 December 1944, conductor Boult: the performance had been scheduled for a Prom concert in August 1944 but was cancelled owing to the threat of bombardment.

Zedda, Alberto (1928–) Italian conductor and musicologist. He studied with Giulini in Milan and made his debut 1956. He conducted at the Deutsche Oper Berlin 1961–63 and New York City Opera from 1963, and led revivals of Rossini's *Ermione* and *Maometto II* in Europe and the USA. Zedda made his Covent Garden debut in 1975. He was co-editor with Philip Gossett of the Rossini complete edition, and artistic director of La Scala from 1992.

Zeitmasze work by K Stockhausen for flute, oboe, horn, clarinet, and bassoon; composed 1955–56, first performed Paris, 15 December 1956, conductor P Boulez.

Zelenka, Jan Dismas (1679–1745) Bohemian composer. He wrote lightweight orchestral works, trio sonatas, and solemn religious works including Magnificats in D 1725 and C 1727. He worked at the court of Dresden and became director of church music in 1735. His compositions were rediscovered in the 1970s. He is best known today for his bold and adventurous instrumental music, including *Hippocondrie* 1723.

Zelenka studied at Prague, was double bass player in the court band at Dresden from 1710, and in 1716 went to Vienna to study under Johann Fux. After this he went to Italy but returned to Dresden to collaborate with Heinichen, whom he succeeded as director of church music in 1735.

Works include: Latin *Melodrama de Sancto Wenceslao* (1723); oratorios *I penitenti al sepolcro* (1736), *Il serpente di bronzo* (1730), and *Gesù al Calvario* (1735); 20 Masses, motets, psalms, and other church music; Latin cantatas.

Zeleński, Władysław (1837–1921) Polish teacher and composer. He studied at Prague University, also music (with Krejci) there and later in Paris. He became professor at the Warsaw Conservatory 1872 and director of the Kraków Conservatory 1881.

Works include: the operas *Konrad Wallenrod* (1885), *Goplana* (1896), *Janek* (1900), *Balladyna* and *An Old Story* (1907); Masses and motets; cantatas; two symphonies (1871, 1912), *Woodland Echoes*, concert overture *In the Tatra* and other orchestral works; piano concerto; four string quartets, piano quartet, variations for string quartet, sextet for strings and piano, piano trio; violin and piano sonata; piano pieces.

Zeller, Carl (Johann Adam) (1842–1898) Austrian composer. He made his career in the civil service but was continuously active as a composer.

He was a chorister in the Imperial chapel in Vienna and studied law at the university. He also had counterpoint lessons from Simon Sechter.

Works include: the operettas *Der Vogelhändler* (1891), *Der Obersteiger* (1894), *Der Vagabund* (1886), and many others.

Zelmira opera by Rossini (libretto by A L Tottola, based on a French tragedy by P L B de Belloy), produced Naples, Teatro San Carlo, 16 February 1822. Zelmira is rescued by returning husband, Ilo, Prince of Troy, after usurper Antenore and Leucippo accuse her of killing her father Polidoro, whom in fact she has kept safe from treacherous Antenore.

Zelter, Carl Friedrich (1758–1832) German conductor, teacher, and composer. He taught at the Berlin Sinakademie from 1800, where he did much to revive interest in J S Bach's music, and founded the Royal Institute of Church Music in 1822. He was a personal friend of Goethe, many of whose poems he set. He wrote principally songs, also church music, cantatas, and instrumental music.

Having completed his training as a master mason Zelter joined his father's firm, and abandoned the trade completely only in 1815, but meanwhile was active as a musician. He studied with Schultz and Fasch, and succeeded the latter as conductor of the Berlin Singakademie in 1800. In 1809 he founded the Berliner Liedertafel, in the same year became professor at the academy, and in 1822 founded the Royal Institute of Church Music. Among his pupils were Nicolai, Loewe, Meyerbeer, and Mendelssohn, whose plans to revive Bach's *St Matthew Passion* in 1829 he at first opposed but later approved. He rejected Schubert's Lieder

Zémire et Azore opera by Grétry (libretto by Marmontel), produced Fontainbleau, at court, 9 November 1771; first Paris performance, Théâtre Italien, 16 December 1771. Prince Azor has been transformed into an ugly beast until he is loved by a woman. Zémire offers herself as a sacrifice to him to save her father Sandor. Of course she eventually falls in love and Azor is restored.

Zemire und Azor opera by Spohr (libretto by J J Ihlee, based on that by Marmontel) produced Frankfurt, 4 April 1819. The familiar song 'Rose, softly blooming' is in this work. For plot synopsis, ◊*Zémire et Azore.*

Zemlinsky, Alexander von (1871–1942) Austrian composer and conductor. He gave the first performance of Schoenberg's monodrama *Erwartung* in 1924. He taught Schoenberg and married his sister, but his personal ties with Schoenberg scarcely influenced his own music; he started composing in a Classical style and later was drawn to the progressive, late-Romantic style of Mahler, Strauss, and even Schreker.

Zemlinsky studied at the Vienna Conservatory. He became conductor at the Vienna Volksoper in 1906 and at the Hofoper in 1908. Later he went to Prague, where he conducted the German Opera and the 1924 first performance of Schoenberg's *Erwartung*. He was one of the conductors at the Berlin State Opera and at the Kroll Opera 1927–31, where he gave the first Berlin performance of *Erwartung*. He returned to Vienna in 1933 and later emigrated to the USA.

Works include: the operas *Sarema* (1897), *Es war einmal* (1900), *Kleider machen Leute* (G Keller, 1908, produced 1922), *Eine florentinische Tragödie, Der Zwerg* (both after O Wilde, 1917, 1922), *Der Kreidekreis* (after Klabund, 1933), *Der Traumgörge* (1906, produced 1980), *Der König Kandaules* (c. 1935, produced 1996); ballet *Das gläserne Herz* (after Hofmannsthal, 1903), incidental music for *Cymbeline* (1914); two symphonies (1892, 1897), suite for orchestra (1894), *Die Seejungfrau* for orchestra (1903), sinfonietta (1934), *Lyric Symphony* for soprano, baritone, and orchestra (1923), *Symphonische Gesänge* for voice and orchestra (1926); string quintet (1895), trio for clarinet, cello, and piano (1895), four string quartets (1895–1936); Lieder to texts by Heine and Eichendorff.

Zender, Hans (1936–) German conductor and composer. He worked at opera houses in Freiburg, Bonn, and Kiel, and was music director of Hamburg Opera 1984–87 (principal conductor from 1977). In 1987 he became conductor of the Netherlands Radio Chamber Orchestra.

Zender studied at Frankfurt and Freiburg, and in Rome under Bernd Alois Zimmermann, whose works he has frequently conducted. He conducted *Parsifal* at Bayreuth in 1975 and *Fidelio* at Brussels Opera in 1989.

Works include: the opera *Stephen Climax* (1986), piano concerto (1956), *Zeitströme* for orchestra (1974), cantata *Der Mann von La Mancha* for voices and Moog synthesizer (1969), *Continuum and Fragments* for chorus, *Cantos I–V* for voices and instruments; electronic works.

Zeno, Apostolo (1668–1750) Italian poet and librettist. For operas on his libretti see ◊*Ambleto* (Gasparini and D Scarlatti); ◊*Fara-*

mondo (Handel); ◊*Ifigenia in Aulide* (Caldara); ◊*Lucio Papiro* (ditto and Hasse); ◊*Merope* (Gasparini, Jommelli and Terradellas); ◊*Scipione* (Handel); ◊*Temistocle* (Porpora and J C Bach).

Ziani, Marc' Antonio (1653–1715) Italian composer. He was maestro di cappella at the church of Santa Barbara and conductor at the theatre at Mantua, 1686. He went to Vienna, where he became vice-music director 1700 and first music director 1711.

Works include: the operas *Alessandro magno in Sidone* (1679), *Damira placata* (1680), *Meleagro* (1706), *Chilonida* (1709) and 41 others; Masses, motets and other church music; oratorios, cantatas.

Ziani, Pietro Andrea (1620–1684) Italian composer, uncle of Marc' Antonio ◊Ziani. He was organist at Venice, then at Santa Maria Maggiore, Bergamo, visited Vienna and Dresden in 1660–67, and became organist at St Mark's, Venice, in succession to Cavalli in 1669. He went to Naples on failing to be appointed maestro di cappella in 1676, becoming a teacher at the Conservatorio di Sant' Onofrio and in 1680 royal maestro di cappella.

Works include: the operas *Le fortune di Rodope e di Damira* (1657), *L'Antigona delusa da Alceste* (1660) and 21 others; Masses, psalms, oratorios; instrumental sonatas; organ pieces.

Zich, Otakar (1879–1934) Czech composer. He was at first a secondary schoolmaster, but took a degree at the University of Brno and was appointed professor of aesthetics there. He also collected folk songs.

Works include: the operas *The Painter's Whim* (1910), *The Sin* (1922) and *Les Précieuses ridicules* (after Molière, 1926); *The Ill-Fated Marriage* and *Polka Rides* for chorus and orchestra; songs.

Zieleński, Mikołaj (1550–1615) Polish organist and composer. He composed offertories and communions for the service of the whole year. He was in the service of Archbishop of Gniezno 1608–15 and studied with Andrea Gabrieli in Italy.

Zigeunerbaron, Der/The Gypsy Baron operetta by J Strauss, junior (libretto by I Schnitzer, based on another by M Jókai founded on his own story *Saffi*), produced Vienna, Theater an der Wien, 24 October 1885. After returning from exile Sándor Barinkay finds family lands occupied by gypsies but falls for Sáffi, gypsy princess in disguise.

Zillig, Winfried (1905–1963) German composer and conductor. He studied with Schoenberg in Vienna and from 1927 to 1928 was assistant to Kleiber at the Berlin Staatsoper. From 1928 to 1947 he conducted various German theatres, becoming director of music at the radio station, first in Frankfurt and then in Hamburg. He also made a performing version of Schoenberg's unfinished oratorio *Die Jakobsleiter* (performed Vienna, 1961).

Works include: the operas *Die Windesbraut* (1941), *Troilus und Cressida* (1951), *Das Opfer*, TV opera *Bauernpassion* (1955), radio opera *Die Verlobung von St Domingo* (1956); violin and cello concertos; four serenades for various instrumental groups; choral music; songs.

Zimmerman, Franklin B(ershir) (1923–) US musicologist. He studied in California and at Oxford, where his teachers included Egon Wellesz and Jack Westrup. He has taught at New York, Dartmouth, and the universities of Kentucky and Pennsylvania. He is best known for his research on Baroque music and H Purcell. His Purcell thematic catalogue (1963) gives the definitive numbering for the composer's works.

Zimmermann, Bernd Alois (1918–1970) German composer. He is widely known for his expressionist opera *Die Soldaten*, which employs film, electronics, mime, and other avant-garde effects.

Zimmerman studied music in Cologne with Heinrich Lemacher (1891–1966) and Philipp Jarnach. He also studied linguistics and philosophy at the Universities of Bonn, Cologne, and Berlin. He taught at Cologne University 1950–52 and at the Hochschule für Musik in Cologne from 1958. He committed suicide.

Works include: the opera *Die Soldaten* (1965); ballets *Kontraste* (1953) and *Alagoana* (1955); cantata *Lob der Torheit* (1948); symphonies; concertos for violin, oboe, and cello; concerto for string orchestra (1948): *Photoptosis*, prelude for orchestra (1968), *Stille und Umkehr*, sketches for orchestra (1970); *Die Soldaten*, vocal symphony from opera (1959); *Requiem for a Young Poet* (1969).

Zimmermann, Udo (1943–) German composer. He founded the Studio for New Music at Dresden in 1974, and has worked in experimental music there. In 1970 he was appointed composer and producer at the Dresden Opera; in 1976 he became director of the Studio Neue Musik concerts at Dres-

den; and in 1990 became intendant of the Leipzig Opera.

Works include: the operas *Die Weisse Rose* (1967), *Die zweite Entscheidung* (1970), *Levins Mühle* (1973), *Der Schuh und die fliegende Prinzessin* (1975), *Die Wundersame Schustersfrau* (1982); *Music for Strings* (1967), *Sieh, meine Augen* for chamber orchestra (1970), *Mutazioni* for orchestra (1972); *Der Mensch*, cantata for soprano and 13 instruments (1969), *Psalm der Nacht* for chorus, percussion, and organ (1973), *Pax questousa* for five soloists, three choruses, and orchestra (1980); *Choreographieren nach Edgar Degas* for 21 instruments (1974).

Zingara, La/The Gypsy Girl intermezzo by Rinaldo di Gapua, produced Académie Royale de Musique, 19 June 1753. Assisted by brother Tagliaborsi, gypsy Nisa tricks rich miser Calcante into marrying her.

Zingarelli, Niccolò Antonio (1752–1837) Italian composer. He wrote 37 operas, chiefly on serious and mythological themes; the best-known of these is *Giulietta e Romeo* 1796. In 1793 he was appointed to the first of several church posts, and after 1804 devoted himself to writing large quantities of church music.

Zingarelli studied at the Conservatorio S Maria di Loreto in Naples, where his intermezzo *I quattro pazzi* was produced in 1768. In 1772 he left the Conservatory and at first worked as an organist, but with *Montezuma*, produced at Naples in 1781, he began his career as an opera composer. From 1785 to 1803 he produced works in all the main Italian cities and also in Paris. He was appointed maestro di cappella at the cathedral in Milan in 1793, at Loreto in 1794, and in 1804 succeeded Pietro Alessandro Guglielmi at St Peter's, Rome; from about this time he devoted himself chiefly to church music. He became director of the Real Collegio di Musica in Naples in 1813, and maestro di cappella of the cathedral there in 1816. Bellini and Mercadante were among his pupils.

Works include: 37 operas, including *Montezuma* (1781), *Armida* (1786), *Antigono, Ifigenia in Aulide* (1787), *Antigone* (1790), *Il mercato di Monfregoso* (1792), *Artaserse, Quinto Fabio, Gli Orazi e Curazi, Giulietta e Romeo* (after Shakespeare, 1796), *Andromeda, La morte di Mitridate* (1797), *I veri amici* (1798), *Il ratto delle Sabine* (1799), *Edipo a Colono* (after Sophocles, 1802), *Berenice, regina d'Armenia*; oratorios *La Passione* (1787), *Gerusalemme distrutta* (1812), *La medificazione di Gerusalemme*, and others; many cantatas; 23 Masses, Requiems, and other church music, including 55 Magnificats;

canon for eight voices; *partimenti* and *solfeggi* for vocal exercise.

zingaresa, or zingarese words used to describe music in, or supposed to be in, a gypsy manner; the finale of Brahms's violin concerto. The adjective is used in the form of *alla zingarese*.

Zingari, Gli/The Gypsies opera by Leoncavallo (libretto by E Cavacchioli and G Emanuel, after Pushkin), produced London, Hippodrome, 16 September 1912.

Zipoli, Domenico (1688–1726) Italian composer. He studied with Alessandro Scarlatti in Naples and Bernardo Pasquini in Rome, where he became organist of the Jesuit church in 1715. He entered the Jesuit Order and in 1717 went to South America as a missionary.

Works include: three oratorios (music lost); church music; keyboard music (two volumes of *Sonate d'intavolatura* published 1716).

zither member of a family of musical instruments consisting of one or more strings stretched over a resonating frame or soundbox. The modern concert zither has up to 45 strings of which five, passing over frets, are plucked with a plectrum for melody, and the remainder are plucked with the fingers for harmonic accompaniment.

Simple stick and board zithers are widespread in Africa; in India the ◊vina represents a developed form of stick zither, while in Indonesia and the Far East versions of the **long zither** prevail. Tuning is by movable bridges and the long zither is played with a plectrum, producing an intense tone of sharp attack.

Zopfstil (German 'pigtail style') derogatory term sometimes applied to the formal courtly style of the later 18th century.

zoppa (Italian 'limp') a strong accent on a second note off the beat or a long note following a short one, as in the ◊Scotch snap. The motion of a musical piece in such a rhythm is called *alla zoppa*.

Zoraida di Granata opera seria by Donizetti (libretto by B Merelli after F Gonzales), produced Rome, Teatro Argentina, 28 January 1822. Almuzir murders king and hopes to marry his daughter Zoraide but is defeated in combat by Knight Abenamet.

Zoroastre opera by Rameau (libretto by L de Cahusac) produced Paris Opéra, 5 December 1749. Following the death of the Bactrian King, High Priest Abramane seizes power, enlisting the help of Princess Erinice. Zoroastre is banished and his beloved Amélite is dragged away to be tormented by demons.

Later, Zoroastre returns to free his people, defeating the evil powers of Abramane and marrying Amélite.

Zumsteeg, Johann Rudolf (1760–1802) German composer. His extended ballads were especially influential, some later being used as models by Schubert.

Zumsteeg was a fellow-pupil and friend of the playwright Schiller at the Karlschule in Stuttgart. In 1781 he entered the service of the Stuttgart court as a cellist, becoming *Konzertmeister* in 1792.

Works include: the operas *Das Tartarische Gesetz* (1780), *Le delizie campestri, o Ippolito e Atricia* (1782), *Armida* (1785), *Die Geisterinsel* (after *The Tempest*, 1798), *Das Pfauenfest* and others; melodrama *Tamira*; incidental music to *Hamlet* (1785), *Macbeth*, Schiller's *Die Räuber*, and other plays; cantatas; Masses and other church music; ten cello concertos (1777–92), songs and ballads *Lenore* (Bürger), *Colma* (Ossian), *Die Büssende, Ritter Toggenburg* (Schiller), *Die Entführung*.

Zusammenschlag (German 'hit together') see ◊acciaccatura or ◊mordent.

Zweig, Stefan (1881–1942) Austrian novelist and dramatist. See ◊*Schweigsame Frau, Die* (R Strauss); ◊Toch (*Heilige aus USA*).

He collaborated with Strauss from 1932; *Die schweigsame Frau* was produced at Dresden (1935) but soon proscribed because of Zweig's Jewish ancestry. Zweig intended to write the libretto for Strauss's *Friedenstag*, suggested to him by Joseph Gregor; but because the Nazi régime made Zweig's appearance on any German stage impossible after 1935, this was afterwards undertaken by Gregor himself.

Zwerg, Der/The Dwarf opera in one act by Zemlinsky (libretto by G C Klaren, after Wilde's *The Birthday of the Infanta*); 1920–21, first performed Cologne, 28 May 1922, conductor Klemperer. At Edinburgh and at Covent Garden the work has been given in a production by the Hamburg Opera, under the new title *The Birthday of the Infanta*, with new libretto by A Dresen. The Spanish Infanta is given the Dwarf as a birthday present. She toys with him as he declares his love for her. When the Dwarf sees his reflection in a mirror he is horrified by his ugliness and dies of a broken heart.

Zwilich, Ellen Taaffe (1939–) US composer. Her music is basically tonal in idiom, sometimes recalling minimalist or late Romantic precedents. Her *Symposium* for orchestra was conducted by Boulez in 1974, and her 1st symphony won the 1983 Pulitzer Prize.

Zwilich studied at Florida State University and with Ivan Galamian in New York. She played violin in the American Symphony Orchestra under Stokowski and studied further at the Juilliard School in New York, and with Sessions and Carter.

Works include: *Symbolom* for orchestra (1988), Symphony no. 2 'Cello' (1985) and no. 3 (1992, commissioned by the New York Philharmonic Orchestra), concertos for trombone (1988), flute (1990), oboe (1990), bassoon (1992), horn (1993), and trumpet (1994); choral and solo vocal music, chamber pieces including Double Quartet for strings (1984) and Quintet for clarinet and strings (1990).

Zwillingsbrüder, Die/The Twin Brothers play with music by Schubert (libretto by G E von Hofmann), produced Vienna, Kärntnertortheater, 14 June 1820. The betrothal of Anton and Lieschen is complicated by prior claim of Franz Spiers and reappearance of his missing twin brother Friedrich.

Zwingburg scenic cantata by Krenek (libretto by F Werfel), composed 1922, first performed Berlin, Staatsoper, 21 October 1924; Krenek's first work for the stage. Tyrannical overlord is overthrown in coup but new masters establish the same regime.

Zwischenspiel German 'interlude'.

Zyklus work for percussion by K Stockhausen, involving random choice and improvisation; first performed Darmstadt, 25 August 1959.

Zywny, Wojciech (1756–1842) Polish piano teacher and composer. He studied with Jan Kuchar and worked at the Polish court of Stanisław August during the 1780s. Later moved to Warsaw and was Frédérick Chopin's piano teacher 1816–22. Works include piano pieces, overtures, and songs.

Illustrations

Key signatures. Both the major and minor keys are shown in this diagram. The white note represents the major key and the black note the minor.

analytical name	scale degree	note in key of C	abbreviation of harmony chord	basic chord in the key of C
tonic	1	C	I	CEG
supertonic	2	D	ii	DFA
mediant	3	E	iii	EGB
subdominant	4	F	IV	FAC
dominant	5	G	V	GBD
submediant	6	A	vi	ACE
leading note	7	B	(vii)	(BDF)

Note names and harmonies. The terms 'tonic . . . leading note' may describe either a single note or a chord. The diagram lists both scale degrees and chord abbreviations applicable to any key, in addition to providing the specific cases of C major. The roman numerals are upper-case if the associated harmony is major and lower-case if minor. The leading note is rarely harmonized and therefore appears in parentheses.

name		note	rest
semibreve	(whole note)	o	▬
Minim	(half note)	♩	▬
crotchet	(quarter note)	♩	♩ or ♩
quaver	(eighth note)	♪	♪
semiquaver	(16th note)	♬	♬
demisemiquaver	(32nd note)	♬	♬
hemidemisemi-quaver	(64th note)	♬	♬

Notes and rests.

Pitch-naming system. Pitches are specified using the system A0 to C8. For example, concert-tuning pitch is A4, in which 'A' is the name of the ntoe and '4' describes the particular register (in this case the fourth octave from the bottom note of the keyboard).

simple time			number of beats to each bar	compound time		
note-value of each beat				note-value of each note		
𝅗𝅥	♩	♪		𝅗𝅥.	♩.	♪.
²⁄₂ or ¢	²⁄₄	²⁄₈	2	⁶⁄₄	⁶⁄₈	⁶⁄₁₆
³⁄₂	³⁄₄	³⁄₈	3	⁹⁄₄	⁹⁄₈	⁹⁄₁₆
⁴⁄₂	⁴⁄₄ or C	⁴⁄₈	4	¹²⁄₄	¹²⁄₈	¹²⁄₁₆

Time signatures.

Chronology

Guillaume de Machaut born (–1377)	c. 1300	
	1360	*Messe de Nostre Dame* (Machaut)
	1364	Mass for the Coronation of Charles V of France (Machaut)
	1365	*Voir-dit* (Machaut)
Guillaume de Machaut dies (77)	1377	
Guillaume Dufay born (–1474)	1400	
	1436	*Nuper rosarum flores* (Dufay)
Josquin des Prés born (–1521)	1440	
Guillaume Dufay dies (c. 74)	1474	
	1502	First book of masses (Josquin des Prés)
Thomas Tallis born (–1585)	1505	
	1512	Second book of masses (Josquin des Prés)
	1516	Third book of masses (Josquin des Prés)
Josquin des Prés dies (c. 81)	1521	
Giovanni Pierluigi Palestrina born (–1594)	c. 1525	
Orlande de Lassus born (–1594)	1532	
William Byrd born (–1623)	1543	
	1554	First book of Masses (Palestrina) pub. *Puer natus est nobis* (Tallis)
	1555	*Missa Papae Marcelli* (Palestrina)
Claudio Monteverdi born (–1643)	1567	
	1573	*Spem in Alium* (Tallis)
	1575	*Cantiones sacrae* (Byrd & Tallis) pub.
	1580	*Laudi spirituali* (Palestrina)
Thomas Tallis dies (c. 80)	1585	
	1589	*Songes of Sundrie Natures* (Byrd) *Cantiones sacrae*, Book 1 (Byrd)
	1591	*Cantiones sacrae*, Book 2 (Byrd)
Orlando di Lassus dies (c. 64) Giovanni Pierluigi Palestrina dies (c. 69)	1594	
	1607	*Gradualia* (Byrd)
	1611	*Parthenia, or the Maidenhead of the First Music that was Ever Printed for Virginals* (Gibbons, Byrd & Bull)
William Byrd dies (c. 80)	1623	
	1624	*Il combattimento di Tancredi e Clorinda* (Monteverdi) fp
Jean-Baptiste Lully born (–1687)	1632	

	1642	*L'Incoronazione di Poppea* (Monteverdi) fp
Claudio Monteverdi dies (c. 76)	1643	
Henry Purcell born (–1695)	c. 1659	
	1663	*Le Mariage forcé* (Lully)
	1669	*Monsieur de Pourceaugnac* (Lully) fp
	1670	*Le Bourgeois Gentilhomme* (Lully) fp
	1673	*Cadmus and Hermione* (Lully)
	1674	*Alceste* (Lully) fp
Antonio Vivaldi born (–1741)	1678	*Psyché* (Lully) fp
	1681	*Le Triomphe de l'Amour* (Lully) fp
Jean Philippe Rameau born (–1764)	1683	*Phaëton* (Lully) fp
George Frideric Handel born (–1759)	1685	
Johann Sebastian Bach born (–1750)		
Domenico Scarlatti born (–1757)		
	1686	*Armide and Renaud* (Lully) fp
Jean-Baptiste Lully dies (54)	1687	
	1689	*Dido and Aeneas* (Purcell) fp
	1692	*The Fairy Queen* (Purcell)
		Ode for Saint Cecilia's Day (Purcell)
Henry Purcell dies (36)	1695	*Elegy on the Death of Queen Mary* (Purcell)
		The Indian Queen (Purcell) fp
	1708	*Gloria in D* (Vivaldi)
	1711	*Rinaldo* (Handel) fp
	1712	*Harmonic Inspiration* (Vivaldi) pub.
Christoph Willibald von Gluck born (–1787)	1714	
	1717	*Water Music* (Handel)
	1720	Partita in D minor for solo violin (Bach)
	1721	*The Brandenburg Concertos* (Bach)
	1722	*French Suites* (Bach)
		The Well-tempered Klavier (Bach)
	1723	*St John Passion* (Bach)
	1725	*The Four Seasons* (Vivaldi) pub.
		Easter Oratorio (Bach)
	1729	*St Matthew Passion* (Bach)
	1731	*German Suites* (Bach)
Franz Joseph Haydn born (–1809)	1732	*Acis and Galatea* (Handel) fp
	1733	*Hippolyte et Aricie* (Rameau) fp
	1734	*Christmas Oratorio* (Bach)
	1735	*Italian Concerto* (Bach)
		Les Indes Galantes (Rameau) fp
	1737	*Castor et Pollux* (Rameau) fp
	1739	*Dardanus* (Rameau) fp
		Israel in Egypt (Handel) fp
Antonio Vivaldi dies (63)	1741	
	1742	*Goldberg Variations* (Bach)
		Messiah (Handel) fp
	1744	*Semele* (Handel) fp
	1747	*The Musical Offering* (Bach)
		Judas Maccabaeus (Handel) fp
	1748	Mass in B minor (Bach)

	1749	*Die Kunst der Fuge* (Bach)
		Zoroastre (Rameau) fp
		Music for the Royal Fireworks (Handel)
Johann Sebastian Bach dies (65)	1750	
	1752	*Jeptha* (Handel)
Wolfgang Amadeus Mozart born	1756	
(–1791)		
Domenico Scarlatti dies (71)	1757	
George Frideric Handel dies (74)	1759	
	1761	Minuet and Trio in G for solo piano (K 1) (Mozart)
	1762	*Orfeo ed Eridice* (Gluck) fp
	1763	*Abaris* (Rameau) fp
Jean Philippe Rameau dies (81)	1764	Symphonies No 21, No 22, the *Philosopher*, and No 23 (Haydn)
	1765	Symphony No 5 (K 22) (Mozart)
	1768	*Missa brevis* in G (K 49) (Mozart)
	1769	Mass in C (K 66), the *Pater Domenicus* (Mozart)
		Symphony No 48, *Maria Theresa* (Haydn)
Ludwig van Beethoven born (–1827)	1770	*Mitridate, Rè di Ponto* (Mozart) fp
	1771	*Grosse Orgelmesse* (Haydn)
	1772	String Quartets No 2 (K 155) and No 3 (K 156) (Mozart)
		Symphony No 45, the *Farewell* (Haydn)
	1773	*Exultate, jubilate* (K 165) (Mozart)
	1774	*Iphigénie en Aulide* (Gluck)
	1777	Piano Concerto No 9 (K 271) (Mozart)
	1778	Symphony No 31 (K 297), the *Paris* (Mozart)
		Flute Concertos No 1 (K 313) and No 2 (K 314) (Mozart)
		Symphony No 53, the *Imperial (Haydn)*
	1779	Mass in C (No 16) (K 317), the *Coronation* (Mozart)
		Iphigenia en Tauride (Gluck) fp
	1781	String Quartets Nos 3742, the *Russian* (or *Maiden*) Quartets (Haydn)
		Idomeneo (Mozart)
	1782	Symphony No 35 (K 385), the *Haffner* (Mozart)
	1783	Symphony No 36 (K 425), the *Linz (Mozart)*
	1785	String Quartets Nos 14 to 19, the *Haydn Quartets*
		Piano Concertos No 20 (K466), No 21 (K467), and No 22 (K482) (Mozart)
		The Seven Last Words of Our Saviour on the Cross (Haydn)

Carl Maria von Weber born (–1826)

Christoph Willibald von Gluck dies
(73)

Wolfgang Amadeus Mozart dies (35)
Giacomo Meyerbeer born (–1864)

Gioacchino Rossini born (–1868)

Franz Schubert born (–1828)
Gaetano Donizetti born (–1848)

Vincenzo Bellini born (–1835)

Hector Berlioz born (–1869)

1786 *Le Nozze di Figaro* (Mozart) fp
Symphony No 38 (K 504), the *Prague*
(Mozart)
String Quartet No 20 (K 499), the
Hoffmeister (Mozart)

1787 *Don Giovanni* (Mozart) fp
String Quintet No 3 (K 515) (Mozart)

1788 Symphonies No 39 (K 543), No 40 (K
550), and No 41 (K 551), the *Jupiter*
(Mozart)

1789 Piano Sonatas Nos 16 (K 570) and 17
(K 576) (Mozart)
Symphony No 92, the *Oxford* (Haydn)

1790 *Così fan tutte* (Mozart) fp
String Quartets, Nos 21 to 23, the
King of Prussia Quartets (Mozart)

1791 *Die Zauberflöte* (Mozart) fp
Clarinet Concerto in A major (K 622)
(Mozart)
Requiem Mass (K 626) (unfinished)
(Mozart)

1792

1794 Symphony No 100, the *Military* and
No 101, the *Clock* (Haydn)

1795 Symphony No 103, the *Drum Roll*
and No 104, the *London* (Haydn)

1797

1798 *The Creation* (Haydn)

1799 *Pathétique* Piano Sonata No 8 (op. 13)
(Beethoven)

1801 Mass No 13 in B flat, *The Creation
Mass* (Haydn)
The Seasons (Haydn)
Moonlight Sonata (op. 27 No 2)
(Beethoven)

1802 *7 Bagatelles*, op. 33 (Beethoven)

1803 *Kreutzer Sonata* in A major (op. 47)
(Beethoven)
String Quartet No 83 (op. 103)
(Haydn)

1804 *Eroica* Symphony No 3 (op. 55)
(Beethoven)
Waldstein Piano Sonata No 21 (op. 53)
(Beethoven)

1805 *Fidelio* (Beethoven) fp
Appassionata Piano Sonata No 23 (op.
57) (Beethoven)

1806 Violin Concerto in D (op. 61)
(Beethoven)
Piano Concerto No 4 in G (op. 58)
(Beethoven)

		Rasumovsky Quartets (op. 59) (Beethoven)
	1807	Mass in C major (op. 86) (Beethoven)
	1808	Symphony No 5 in C minor (op. 67) (Beethoven)
		Pastoral Symphony No 6 in F (op. 68) (Beethoven)
		Cello Sonata in A major (op. 69) (Beethoven)
Franz Joseph Haydn dies (77)	1809	*Emperor* Piano Concerto No 5 in E flat (op. 73) (Beethoven)
Felix-Bartholdy Mendelssohn born (–1847)		String Quartet No 10, the *Harp Quartet* (op. 74) (Beethoven)
Frédéric Chopin born (–1849)	1810	*Egmont* (op. 84) (Beethoven)
Robert Schumann born (–1856)		
Franz Liszt born (–1886)	1811	*Archduke* Piano Trio in B flat (op. 97) (Beethoven)
	1812	Symphony No 7 in A (op. 92) (Beethoven)
		Symphony No 8 in F (op. 93) (Beethoven)
Richard Wagner born (–1883)	1813	*Tancredi* (Rossini) fp
Giuseppe Fortunio Francesco Verdi born (–1901)		
	1816	*The Barber of Seville* (Rossini) fp
	1817	*The Thieving Magpie* (Rossini) fp
Charles François Gounod born (–1893)	1818	*Hammerklavier* Piano Sonata No 29 (op. 106) (Beethoven)
		Moses in Egypt (Rossini) fp
	1821	Der Freischütz (Weber) fp
César (-Auguste) Franck born (–1890)	1822	*Missa Solemnis* (op. 123) (Beethoven)
	1823	*Choral* Symphony in D minor (No 9) (op. 125) (Beethoven)
		Variations on a Waltz by Diabelli (op. 120) (Beethoven)
		Euryanthe (Weber) fp
Bedrich Smetana born (–1884)	1824	
Josef Anton Bruckner born (–1896)		
	1825	String Quartets No 12 (op. 130) and No 15 (op. 132) (Beethoven)
Carl Maria von Weber dies (39)	1826	String Quartets No 13 (op. 130) No 14 (op. 131) and No 16 (op. 135) (Beethoven)
		Elvida (Donizetti) fp
		Oberon (Weber) fp
		A Midsummer Night's Dream (Mendelssohn)
Ludwig van Beethoven dies (56)	1827	*Il pirata* (Bellini) fp
Franz Schubert dies (31)	1828	*Count Ory* (Rossini) fp
		Impromptus (Schubert)
	1829	*William Tell* (Rossini) fp
	1830	*Symphonie fantastique* (Berlioz)
		Abegg Variations (op. 1) (Schumann)
	1831	*La sonnambula* (Bellini) fp
		Norma (Bellini) fp

		Robert le Diable (Meyerbeer) fp
	1832	*L'Elisir d'amore* (Donizetti) fp
Johannes Brahms born (–1897)	1833	Symphony No 4 (op. 90) the *Italian*
Alexander Porfiryevich Borodin born		(Mendelssohn)
(–1887)		
	1834	*Harold en Italie* (Berlioz)
Vincenzo Bellini dies (33)	1835	*Lucia di Lammermoor* (Donizetti) fp
(Charles-) Camille Saint-Saëns born		
(–1921)		
	1836	*Les Huguenots* (Meyerbeer) fp
Mily Alexeyevich Balakirev born	1837	*Requiem*, op. 5 (Berlioz)
(–1910)		
Georges (Alexandre César Léopold)	1838	*Benvenuto Cellini* (Berlioz) fp
Bizet born (–1875)		*Kinderszenen* (op. 15) (Schumann)
Modest Petrovich Mussorgsky born	1839	*Roméo et Juliette* (Berlioz)
(–1881)		
Pyotr Il'yich Tchaikovsky born	1840	*La Fille du régiment* (Donizetti) fp
(–1893)		*Liederkreise* (Schumann)
		Dichterliebe (op. 48) (Schumann)
		Frauenliebe und Leben (op. 42)
		(Schumann)
Anton Dvořák born (–1904)	1841	Symphony No 1 (op. 38), the *Fruling*
		(Schumann)
Jules Massenet born (–1912)	1842	Symphony No 3 (op. 56), the *Scottish*
Arthur Seymour Sullivan born		(Mendelssohn)
(–1900)		*Stabat Mater* (Rossini)
		Nabucco (Verdi)
Edvard Grieg born (–1907)	1843	*Don Pasquale* (Donizetti) fp
		Die fliegende Holläder (Wagner)
Nikolai Andreievich Rimsky-	1844	
Korsakov born (–1908)		
Gabriel (Urbain) Fauré born (–1924)	1845	*Tannhäuser* (Wagner)
	1846	*The Damnation of Faust*, op. 24
		(Berlioz)
		Elijah (op. 70) (Mendelssohn) fp
		Sonetti del Petrarca (Liszt)
		Symphony No 2 (op. 61) (Schumann)
Felix-Bartholdy Mendelssohn dies	1847	
(38)		
(Charles) Hubert (Hastings) Parry	1848	*Les Préludes* (Liszt)
born (–1918)		
Gaetano Donizetti dies (50)		
Frédéric Chopin dies (39)	1849	*Le Prophete* (Meyerbeer) fp
		Totentanz (Liszt) revised
		Manfred (Schumann)
	1850	*Te Deum*, op. 22 (Berlioz)
		Symphony No 3 (op. 97), the *Rhenish*
		(Schumann)
		Lohengrin (Wagner) fp
	1851	Symphony No 4 (op. 120)
		(Schumann)
		Rigoletto (Verdi)
Charles Villiers Stanford born (–1924)	1852	
	1853	*Il Trovatore* (Verdi) fp
		La Traviata (Verdi) fp

Leoš Janáček born (–1928)

Robert Schumann dies (46)
Edward Elgar born (–1934)
Giacomo Puccini born (–1924)

Gustav Mahler born (–1911)

Claude Debussy born (–1918)
Frederick Delius born (–1934)

Giacomo Meyerbeer dies (73)
Richard Strauss born (–1949)
Carl Nielsen born (–1931)
Jean Sibelius born (–1957)
Ferruccio Busoni born (–1924)
Erik Satie born (–1926)
Enrique Granados born (–1916)

Gioacchino Rossini dies (76)

Hector Berlioz dies (65)

Ralph Vaughan Williams born
  (–1958)

Sergey Vasilevich Rachmaninov born
  (–1943)
Arnold Schoenberg born (–1951)
Gustav Holst born (–1934)
Charles Ives born (–1954)
Maurice Ravel born (–1937)
Georges (Alexandre César Léopold)
  Bizet dies (36)
Manuel de Falla born (–1946)

1854	*L'Enfance du Christ* (op. 25) (Berlioz)
1855	*Sicilian Vespers* (Verdi) fp
1856	*Dante Symphony* (Liszt)
1857	
1858	*Les Troyens* (Berlioz)
	Piano Concerto No 1, op. 15 (Brahms)
1859	*A Masked Ball* (Verdi) fp
1860	
1861	*Mephisto Waltz No 1* (Liszt)
1862	*Béatrice et Bénédict* (Berlioz) fp
	Die Legende von der heilige Elisabeth (Liszt)
1863	*Les Pêcheurs de perles* (Bizet) fp
1864	
1865	*Rákóczy March* (Liszt)
	Tristan and Isolde (Wagner) fp
1866	*The Bartered Bride* (Smetana)
1867	Symphony No 1 (Borodin)
	Roméo et Juliette (Gounod) fp
	Night on a Bare Mountain (Mussorgsky)
	Don Carlos (Verdi) fp
1868	Piano Concerto (op. 16) (Grieg)
	Ein deutsche Requiem (Brahms)
	Die Meistersinger von Nürnberg (Wagner)
1869	*Die Walküre* (Wagner) fp
	Romeo and Juliet (Tchaikovsky)
1871	*Jeux d'Enfants* (piano) (Bizet)
	Aida (Verdi) fp
1872	*L'Arlésienne* (Bizet)
	Symphony No 2 (Bruckner)
	Boris Godunov (Mussorgsky) fp
1873	Symphony No 3 (Bruckner)
1874	*Pictures at an Exhibition* (Mussorgsky)
	Requiem (Verdi)
1875	*Carmen* (Bizet) fp
	Danse macabre (Saint-Saëns)
1876	*Les Eolides/The Breezes* (Franck)
	Symphony No 2 (Borodin)
	Symphony No 1 (Brahms)
	Symphony No 5 (Bruckner)
	Götterdammerung (Wagner) fp
	Siegfried (Wagner) fp
1877	*Swan Lake* (Tchaikovsky) fp
	Samson and Delilah (Saint-Saëns)
	Stabat Mater (Dvořák)
1878	Violin Concerto No 1, op. 77 (Brahms)
	HMS Pinafore (Sullivan) fp

Symphony No 4 (op. 36)
(Tchaikovsky)
Violin Concerto (Tchaikovsky)
1879 *Les Béatitudes/The Beatitudes* (Franck)
Violin Sonata No 1, op. 78 (Brahms)
Má Vlast (Smetana)
The Pirates of Penzance (Sullivan) fp
Eugene Onegin (Tchaikovsky) fp
1880 *In the Steppes of Central Asia* (Borodin)
Symphony No 6 (Dvořák)
Serenade for Strings (op. 48)
(Tchaikovsky)

Modest Petrovich Mussorgsky dies   1881 Piano Concerto No 2, op. 83 (Brahms)
(42)   *Academic Festival Overture*, op. 80
Béla Bartók born (–1945)   (Brahms)
                                           Tragic Overture, op. 81 (Brahms)
Zoltán Kodály born (–1967)   1882 *Le Chasseur maudit* (Franck)
Karol Szymanowski born (–1937)   *The Snow Maiden* (Rimsky-Korsakov)
Igor Stravinsky born (–1971)   fp
                                           Parsifal (Wagner) fp
Richard Wagner dies (69)   1883 Symphony No 3 (Brahms)
Anton Webern born (–1945)   *Mephisto Waltz No 3* (Liszt)
                                           Symphony No 7 (Bruckner)
Bedrich Smetana dies (59)   1884 *Canterbury Pilgrims* (Stanford) fp
                                           Symphony No 1 (Mahler)
                                           Te Deum (Bruckner)
Alban Berg born (–1935)   1885 Symphonic Variations (Franck)
                                           Symphony No 4 (Brahms)
                                           Symphony No 7 (Dvořák)
                                           Mephisto Waltz No 4 (Liszt)
                                           20 Hungarian Rhapsodies (Liszt)
                                           The Mikado (Sullivan)
Franz Liszt dies (74)   1886 *Carnival of the Animals* (Saint-Saëns)
                                           Aus Italien (R Strauss)
Alexander Porfiryevich Borodin dies   1887 Symphony No 8 (Bruckner)
(53)   *Ruddigore* (Sullivan) fp
                                           Concerto for Violin and Cello (op.
                                            102) (Brahms)
                                     1888 *Judith* (Parry)
                                           Trois gymnopédies (Satie)
                                           Symphony in D minor (Franck)
                                           Scheherazade (Rimsky-Korsakov)
                                           Symphony No 5 (op. 64)
                                            (Tchaikovsky)
                                           Yeoman of the Guard (Sullivan)
                                     1889 *The Gondoliers* (Sullivan)
César (-Auguste) Franck dies (67)   1890 *Prince Igor* (Borodin) fp
Bohuslav Martinu born (–1959)   *Requiem* (Fauré)
                                           The Queen of Spades (Tchaikovsky) fp
                                           The Sleeping Beauty (Tchaikovsky) fp
                                           Tod und Verklärung (R Strauss)

Sergey Sergeyevich Prokofiev born (–1953)	1891	
Darius Milhaud born (–1974)	1892	*Job* (Parry)
		Nutcracker (Tchaikovsky) fp
Charles François Gounod dies (75)	1893	Symphony No 9, *From the New World*
Pyotr Il'yich Tchaikovsky dies (53)		(Dvořák)
		String Quartet in F major (op. 96),
		American (Dvořák)
		Karelia Suite (Sibelius)
		Fallstaff (Verdi) fp
		Symphony No 6, the *Pathetique* (op.
		74) (Tchaikovsky)
	1894	*Lady Radnor's Suite* (Parry)
		Symphony No 2, the *Resurrection*
		(Mahler)
		Symphony No 9 (Bruckner)
Paul Hindemith born (–1963)	1895	*Till Eulenspiegel* (R Strauss)
Josef Anton Bruckner dies (72)	1896	*Vier ernste Gesänge* (op. 121) (Brahms)
		La Bohème (Puccini) fp
		Also sprach Zarathustra (Strauss)
Johannes Brahms dies (63)	1897	
George Gershwin born (–1937)	1898	
Francis Poulenc born (–1963)	1899	*The Tsar's Bride* (Rimsky-Korsakov) fp
		Des Knaben Wunderhorn (Mahler)
		Enigma Variations (Elgar)
Aaron Copland born (–1990)	1900	Symphony No 4 (Mahler)
Arthur Seymour Sullivan dies (58)		*The Dream of Gerontius* (Elgar)
		Tosca (Puccini) fp
		Finlandia (Sibelius)
Giuseppe Fortunio Francesco Verdi dies (87)	1901	*Cockaigne* (Elgar)
		Rusalka (Dvořák) fp
		Piano Concerto No 2 (Rachmaninov)
William Walton born (–1983)	1902	Symphony No 5 (Mahler)
		Pelléas et Mélisande (Debussy) fp
		Symphony No 2 (Sibelius)
	1903	*Trois Morceaux en forme de poire* (Satie)
		Symphonia Domestica (R Strauss)
Anton Dvořák dies (62)	1904	Symphony No 6 (Mahler)
		Kindertotenlieder (Mahler)
		L'Ille joyeuse/The Island of Joy
		(Debussy)
		Jenufa (Janáček) fp
		Madame Butterfly (Puccini)
		Symphony No 3, *The Camp Meeting*
		(Ives)
Michael Tippett born (–1998)	1905	*La Mer/The Sea* (Debussy)
		Introduction and Allegro for Strings
		(Elgar)
		Symphony No 7 (Mahler)
		Salome (Strauss)
		String Quartet (Webern)

Dmitri Shostakovitch born (–1975)

Edvard Grieg dies (64)

Nikolai Andreievich Rimsky-
Korsakov dies (64)
Olivier Messiaen born (–1992)

Mily Alexeyevich Balakirev dies (73)

Gustav Mahler dies (50)

Jules Massenet dies (70)

Witold Lutosławski born (–1994)
Benjamin Britten born (–1976)

1906   *Central Park in the Dark in the Good
Old Summertime* (Ives)
Maskarade (C A Nielsen) fp
1907   Symphony No 8 (Mahler)
Symphony No 3 (Sibelius)
1908   Symphony No 1 (Elgar)
The Unanswered Question (Ives)

1909   *Das Lied von der Erde* (Mahler)
Symphony No 3 (Rachmaninov)
Piano Concerto No 3 (Rachmaninov)
Erwartung (Schoenberg)
Elektra (Strauss)
On Wenlock Edge (Vaughan Williams)
1910   *Fantasia contrappuntistica* (Busoni)
Préludes I (Debussy)
Symphonies No 9 & 10 (Mahler)
La fanciulla del West (Puccini)
Litany of Saint John Chrysostom
(Rachmaninov)
Pavane pour une infante défunte (Ravel)
The Firebird (Stravinsky)
Fantasia on a Theme of Thomas Tallis
(Vaughan Williams)
1911   Symphony No 3, *The Camp Meeting*
(Ives)
Symphony No 3, *Expansive Symphony*
(C A Nielsen)
Ma Mere l'Oye (Ravel)
Gurrelieder (Schoenberg)
Symphony No 4 (Sibelius)
Der Rosenkavalier (Strauss)
Petrushka (Stravinsky)
On Hearing the First Cuckoo in Spring
(Delius)
1912   *Images* (Debussy)
Daphnis et Chloé (Ravel) fp
Valses nobles et sentimentales (Ravel)
Pierrot Lunaire (Schoenberg)
14 Songs (op. 34) (Rachmaninov)
Ariadne auf Naxos (R Strauss)
1913   *Altenberglieder / Altenberg Songs* (Berg)
fp
Indianische Fantasie (Busoni)
The Rite of Spring (Stravinsky)
Préludes II (Debussy)
St Paul's Suite (Holst)
New England Holidays (Ives)
The Bells (Rachmaninov)
1914   *3 Pieces for Orchestra*, op. 6 (Berg)
1915   *Indianische Tagebuch II* (Busoni)
Symphony No 5 (Sibelius)
An Alpine Symphony (R Strauss)

Enrique Granados dies (48)

Claude Debussy dies (55)
Leonard Bernstein born (–1990)
(Charles) Hubert (Hastings) Parry
    dies (70)

(Charles-) Camille Saint-Saëns dies
    (86)

György Ligeti born
Charles Villiers Stanford dies (71)
Ferruccio Busoni dies (58)
Gabriel (Urbain) Fauré dies (79)
Giacomo Puccini dies (66)
Pierre Boulez born
Luciano Berio born
Erik Satie dies (59)

Leoš Janáček dies (74)
Karlheinz Stockhausen born

Carl Nielsen dies (66)

1916   *Jerusalem* (Parry)
        Nights in the Gardens of Spain (de
            Falla)
        The Planets (Holst)
        Symphony No 4, *The Inextinguishable*
            (Nielsen)
1917   *Parade* (Satie) fp
        Arlecchino (Busoni) fp
        Violin Sonata (Debussy)
1918   *Duke Bluebeard's Castle* (Bartók) fp
        Taras Bulba (Janáček)
        Il trittico (Puccini)

1919   *The Three-Cornered Hat* (de Falla)
        Le Tombeau de Couperin (Ravel)
        Die Frau ohne Schatten (R Strauss)
1920   *Le Tombeau de Claude Debussy* (Ravel)
        La Valse (Ravel)
1921   *Káta Kabanova* (Janáček) fp
        Love for Three Oranges (Prokofiev) fp
        Faust (Walton)
        Symphony No 1, the *Classical*
            (Prokofiev)
1923   *Psalmus Hungaricus* (Kodály)
1924   *Rhapsody in Blue* (Gershwin)
        The Cunning Little Vixen (Janáček) fp

1925   *Wozzeck* (Berg) fp
        Piano Concerto (Gershwin)

1926   *The Miraculous Mandarin* (Bartók) fp
        Lyric Suite (Berg)
        Król Roger (Szymanowski)
        Glagolitic Mass (Janáček)
        The Makropoulos Case (Janáček) fp
        Háry János (Kodály) fp
        Turandot (Puccini)
1927   *Oedipus Rex* (Stravinsky)
1928   String Quartet No 4 (Bartók)
        Symphony, op. 21 for chamber
            orchestra (Webern)
        An American in Paris (Gershwin)
        Boléro (Ravel)
1930   *From the House of the Dead* (Janáček)
        Piano Concerto for the Left Hand
            (Ravel)
        Symphony of Psalms (Stravinsky)
1931   Piano Concerto No 2 (Bartók)
        Harnasie (Szymanowski)
        Piano Concerto in G (Ravel)
        Belshazzar's Feast (Walton)

	1932	*Sinfonietta* (Britten)
Krysztof Penderecki born	1933	*Hungarian Sketches* (Bartók)
		A Simple Symphony, op. 2 (Britten)
Edward Elgar dies (76)	1934	String Quartet No 5 (Bartók)
Gustav Holst dies (59)		*Matthis der Maler* (Hindemith)
Frederick Delius dies (71)		*Rhapsody on a Theme of Paganini*
Peter Maxwell Davies born		(Rachmaninov)
Alban Berg dies (50)	1935	Violin Concerto (Berg)
		Porgy and Bess (Gershwin) fp
		Die schweigsame Frau (R Strauss)
		Symphony No 1 (Walton)
	1936	*Music for Strings, Percussion, and Celeste* (Bartók)
		Divertimento for Strings (Bartók)
		Poemes pour Mi (Messiaen)
		Donanobis pacem (Vaughan Williams)
George Gershwin dies (38)	1937	*Lulu* (Berg) fp
Maurice Ravel dies (62)		*Variations on a Theme by Frank Bridge* (Britten)
Karol Szymanowski dies (54)		
	1938	Violin Concerto No 2 (Bartók)
		String Quartet, op. 28 (Webern)
		Piano Concerto, op. 13 (Britten)
		Mathis de Maler (Hindemith) fp
		Romeo and Juliet (Prokofiev)
	1939	*Billy the Kid* (Copland) fp
		String Quartet No 6 (Bartók)
		Violin Concerto (Walton)
	1940	*Sinfonia da Requiem* (op. 20) (Britten)
	1941	*Quartet for the End of Time* (Messiaen)
		A Child of Our Time (Tippett)
	1942	*Rodeo* (Copland)
		Fanfare for the Common Man (Copland)
		Hymn to St Cecilia (Britten)
Sergey Vasilevich Rachmaninov dies (69)	1943	*Serenade* (Britten)
	1944	*Concerto for Orchestra* (Bartók)
		Symphony No. 1, *Jeremiah* (Bernstein)
		On the Town (Bernstein) fp
		Appalachian Spring (Copland)
		Vingt Regards sur l'Enfant Jésus (Messiaen)
		Symphony No 5 (Prokofiev)
Anton Webern dies (61)	1945	Piano Concerto No 3 (Bartók)
Béla Bartók dies (64)		*Peter Grimes* (Britten) fp
		Violin Sonata No 1 (Prokofiev)
Manuel de Falla dies (69)	1946	*Young Person's Guide to the Orchestra* (Britten)
	1947	*Albert Herring* (Britten) fp
	1948	*Calligrammes* (Poulenc)
		Four Last Songs (Strauss)

A Survivor from Warsaw (Schoenberg) fp		Richard Strauss dies (85)
	1949	Symphony No 2, *The Age of Anxiety* (Bernstein) fp
		Turangalila Symphony (Messiaen) fp
Arnold Schoenberg dies (76)	1951	*Billy Budd* (Britten) fp
		The Rake's Progress (Stravinsky)
Sergey Sergeyevich Prokofiev dies (61)	1953	*Gloriana* (Britten) fp
		Fantasia Concertante on a Theme by Corelli (Tippett)
Charles Ives dies (79)	1954	*Serenade* (Bernstein)
		The Turn of the Screw (Britten)
		Concerto for Orchestra (Messiaen)
		Troilus and Cressida (Walton) fp
	1955	*Le Marteau sans maître* (Boulez)
	1956	*Candide* (Bernstein) fp
Jean Sibelius dies (91)	1957	*West Side Story* (Bernstein) fp
		The Prince of the Pagodas (Britten) fp
		Moses and Aaron (Schoenberg) fp
		Les Dialogues des Carmélites (Poulenc)
Ralph Vaughan Williams dies (85)	1958	*Threni* (Stravinsky)
Bohuslav Martinu dies (68)	1959	
	1960	*Circles* (Berio)
		A Midsummer Night's Dream (Britten) fp
		Kontakte (Stockhausen)
		Symphony No 2 (Walton)
	1961	*Atmosphères* (Ligeti)
		Gry weneckie/Venetian Games (Lutoslawski)
		Magnificat and Nunc Dimiitis (Tippett)
		War Requiem (Britten)
	1962	*Poème Symphonique/Symphonic Poem* (Ligeti)
		Pli selon pli/Fold upon Fold (Boulez)
		King Priam (Walton) fp
Francis Poulenc dies (64)	1963	Symphony No 3, *Kaddish* (Bernstein)
Paul Hindemith dies (68)		Cello Symphony (Britten)
	1965	*Chichester Psalms* (Bernstein)
		Paroles tissées/Woven Words (Lutoslawski)
	1966	*St Luke Passion* (Penderecki)
Zoltán Kodály dies (84)	1967	*Antechrist* (P Davies)
		Symphony No 2 (Lutosławski)
		Hymnen (Stockhausen)
	1969	*Eight Songs for a Mad King* (Davies)
		La Transfiguration de Notre Seigneur Jésus-Christ (Messiaen)
		The Devils of Loudon (Penderecki) fp
Igor Stravinsky dies (88)	1971	*Trans* (Stockhausen)
	1972	*Recital I (for Cathy)* (Berio)
		Symphony No 3 (Tippett)
		Taverner (P Davies) fp

	1973 *Clocks and Clouds* (Ligeti)
	Death in Venice (Britten) fp
Darius Milhaud dies (81)	1974 *San Francisco Polyphony* (Ligeti)
Dmitri Shostakovitch dies (68)	1975 *Rituel in memoriam Bruno Maderna*
	(Boulez)
Benjamin Britten dies (63)	1976 *Coro* (Berio)
	1978 *Paradise Lost* (Penderecki)
	Le Grand Macabre (Ligeti)
	1980 *The Lighthouse* (P Davies) fp
	Notations (Boulez)
	1981 *Répons* (Boulez)
	Donnerstag aus Licht (Stockhousen)
	1982 *The Mask of Time* (Tippett)
William Walton dies (80)	1983 *Into the Labyrinth* (P Davies)
	Symphony No 3 (Lutosławski)
	1984 *Polish Requiem* (Penderecki) fp
	Un Re in ascolto (Berio) fp
	1986 *Die schwarze Maske* (Penderecki) fp
	1988 Concerto for Piano and Orchestra
	(Ligeti)
	1989 *New Year* (Tippett) fp
Aaron Copland dies (90)	1990 Concerto for Violin and Orchestra
Leonard Bernstein dies (72)	(Ligeti)
Olivier Messiaen dies (83)	1992
	1993 *Strathclyde Concerto* No 8 (Davies)
Witold Lutosławski dies (81)	1994 Symphony No 5 (Davies)
	1996 *Outis* (Berio) fp
Michael Tippett dies (93)	1998